TYPES OF DRAMA

Plays and Essays

Second Edition

SYLVAN BARNET
Tufts University

MORTON BERMAN
Boston University

WILLIAM BURTO
University of Lowell

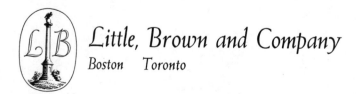

Little, Brown and Company
Boston   Toronto

PREFACE

In this version of *Types of Drama* we have added Aristophanes' *Lysistrata*, Shakespeare's *A Midsummer Night's Dream*, Pirandello's *Six Characters in Search of an Author*, and Peter Shaffer's *Equus*. We have also added an essay by Peter Arnott, "The Script and the Stage," which gives the reader an idea of how a director turns a script into a performance, and an essay of our own, "Writing About Drama," which — with the other editorial apparatus — will, we hope, help students to write essays in their courses.

The PLAYS, arranged chronologically within the categories of tragedy, comedy, and tragicomedy, cover a range of years and types, but in no case were they chosen only to represent a period or a type. All were chosen because of their dramatic value. Those not written in English are represented in the best modern translations. The COMMENTARIES are relatively short. They are not attempts to explicate the plays, but they do contain some useful and relevant points, which will also be useful with other plays. For example, the commentary on *A Midsummer Night's Dream* includes comments on two traditions of comedy, "critical" comedy and "romantic" comedy, but most of this material is relevant to other plays in the book. Similarly, the discussion of pathos in the commentary on *Death of a Salesman* goes beyond the play in question. At the beginning of the book is a general introduction to basic concepts and critical terminology, but it may be best to postpone reading it until the students have carefully read at least a few plays. The ESSAYS are not analyses of particular plays, though of course they do include some specific discussions; they are fairly general, and therefore any of the essays on tragedy, for example, can be profitably read in conjunction with any of the tragedies. The GLOSSARY, drawn in part from the more detailed glossary in our *Aspects of Drama*, is a dictionary of two hundred basic critical and historical terms that are likely to come up in an introductory course. Some of these terms are discussed at length in the commentaries, but they are given again in the glossary itself; no one has to read the commentaries, unless he wants to know the dates of the plays.

Our ideas about drama have been shaped by many playwrights and many critics. Doubtless we are not aware of all of the influences upon us, but we know we are much indebted to Gerald Else, Northrop Frye, Helen Gardner, Richmond Lattimore, Konrad Lorenz, Maynard Mack, D. H. Monro, Reinhold Niebuhr, and L. J. Potts. If other critics find they have contributed to this book, we hope that they will be as charitable as lovers in a comedy, and will accept our apologies and our thanks.

We have been fortunate in getting permission to print important modern plays and distinguished modern translations of older plays, and we are grateful to the authors, translators, and publishers who have cooperated. Many teachers have given advice that helped us prepare this new edition: Joy Berkley, Patricia Bianco, Victor Bobb, Thomas Cotner, Wallace Coyle, Dr. Margaret Esmonde, Julius Feazell, Robert Griffin, Mary Loubris Jones, Marjorie Kirrie, Helene Koon, Zelma Kubik, Leona Lakehomer, Timothy Materer, Arnie Preussner, John Reiss, Emma Rieth, Dr. Dolores Sarafinski, Kenneth Seid, J. D. Shout, John Stork, Simone Turbeville, and Robert Vales.

We are especially indebted to Helen Willard and Jeanne Newlin of the Harvard Theatre Collection, Athan Anagostopoulos, Arthur Friedman, and Seymour Simches for assistance in finding photographs. Oscar Brockett and Harry Ritchie generously answered queries, and Marcia Stubbs provided many helpful suggestions. Our thanks also go to Charles Christensen, Jane Aaron, Martha Clasquin, Margaret Zusky, David Giele, Ellen Silver, and Lynn Lloyd of Little, Brown, who never let us get away with anything.

S.B.
M.B.
W.B.

TABLE OF CONTENTS

THE NATURE OF DRAMA 1

1. **Tragedy and Comedy** 3

    Imitation of an Action. Happenings and Happenings. Unity. The
    Tragic Hero. Hamartia. Hybris. Peripeteia. Anagnorisis. Tragic Joy.
    Comic Assertion. Comic Joy. Comic Isolation. Detachment and
    Engagement. Tragic Fate and Comic Fortune in Plots. Comic
    Beginnings and Endings. Self-Knowledge.

2. **Tragicomedy** 14

    Tragicomedy Before 1900. Detachment and Engagement Again. Theater
    of the Absurd. Diminution of Man. Dissolution of Character and Plot.
    The Tragedy of Comedy.

THE LANGUAGE OF DRAMA 21

Setting. Costume. Gestures. Sound Effects. Dialogue. Plot and
Structure. Character. Theme.

THE EMPEROR JONES Eugene O'Neill 29

TRAGEDY 45

OEDIPUS THE KING Sophocles 47
Translated into English Verse by H. D. F. Kitto

Commentary 69

THE TRAGEDY OF KING LEAR William Shakespeare 73
Edited by Russell Fraser

Commentary 135

HEDDA GABLER Henrik Ibsen 139
Translated by Otto Reinert

Commentary 178

DEATH OF A SALESMAN Arthur Miller 183

Commentary 230

DUTCHMAN LeRoi Jones (Imamu Amiri Baraka) 235

Commentary 245

EQUUS Peter Shaffer 251

Commentary 295

The Poetics Aristotle 300
Translated by L. J. Potts

Tragedy and the Common Man Arthur Miller 306

COMEDY 309

LYSISTRATA Aristophanes 311
Translated by Dudley Fitts

Commentary 335

A MIDSUMMER NIGHT'S DREAM
William Shakespeare 341
Edited by Wolfgang Clemen

Commentary 374

THE MISANTHROPE Molière 379
English Version by Richard Wilbur

Commentary 406

MAJOR BARBARA   Bernard Shaw   411
Commentary   457

The Comic Rhythm   Susanne K. Langer   460
The Rise and Fall of the Custard Pie   Richard Boston   464

TRAGICOMEDY 469

THE CHERRY ORCHARD   Anton Chekhov   471
Translated by Stark Young

Commentary   497

SIX CHARACTERS
IN SEARCH OF AN AUTHOR   Luigi Pirandello   503
English Version by Edward Storer

Commentary   530

THE GOOD WOMAN OF SETZUAN
Bertolt Brecht   535
Translated by Eric Bentley

Commentary   573

WILD STRAWBERRIES   Ingmar Bergman   579
Translated by Lars Malmström and David Kushner

Commentary   608

THE GAP   Eugène Ionesco   613
Translated by Rosette Lamont

Commentary   617

THE EFFECT OF GAMMA RAYS ON
MAN-IN-THE-MOON MARIGOLDS   Paul Zindel   621

Commentary   640

Comedy, Tragedy, and Tragicomedy Cyrus Hoy 642
Comedy and Tragedy Transposed
Ellen Douglass Leyburn 649

THE SCRIPT AND THE STAGE Peter Arnott 655

The Author. The Actors. The Director. The Designers. The Mechanics of Production.

WRITING ABOUT DRAMA 669

Why Write? Analysis. A Sample Analysis. Writing a Comparison. Communicating Judgments. Asking Questions to Get Answers. Review: How to Write an Effective Essay. Remarks About Manuscript Form.

A GLOSSARY OF DRAMATIC TERMS 687

THE NATURE OF DRAMA

1. Tragedy and Comedy

Whimsical assertions that all men are Platonists or Aristotelians, or liberals or conservatives ("Nature wisely does contrive / That every boy and every gal / That's born into the world alive / Is either a little Liberal / Or else a little Conservative") reveal a tendency to divide things into two. Two is about right: peace and war, man and woman, day and night, life and death. There may be middle cases; there is the cold war, and Edmund Burke suggested that no man can point to the precise moment that divides day from night — but Burke also suggested that everyone can make the useful distinction between day and night. The distinction between comedy and tragedy may not always be easy to make, but until the twentieth century it was usually clear enough. *Hamlet,* which in Horatio's words is concerned with "woe or wonder," is a tragedy; *A Midsummer Night's Dream,* which in Puck's words is concerned with things that pleasingly "befall preposterously," is a comedy. The best plays of our century, however, are another thing, and discussion of these plays — somewhat desperately called tragicomedy — will be postponed until the end of this introduction.

What befalls — preposterous or not — is the *action of the play.* The gestures on the stage are, of course, "actions," but they are not the action of the play in the sense of Aristotle's use of *praxis* or "action" in *The Poetics,* a fragmentary treatise of the fourth century B.C. that remains the starting point for most discussions of drama. For Aristotle, drama is the imitation (i.e., representation, re-presentation, re-creation) by impersonators, of an action. In tragedy the action is serious and important, something that matters, done by people who count (e.g., King Oedipus' discovery that he has killed his father and married his mother); in comedy (for Aristotle), the action is done by unimportant laughable people who make mistakes that do not cause us pain. Commonly the tragic action is a man's perception of a great mistake he has made; he suffers intensely and perhaps dies, having exhausted all the possibilities of his life. The comic action often is the exposure of folly and the renewal rather than the exhaustion of human nature. Crabby parents, for example, find that they cannot keep young lovers apart, and so they join in the marriage festivities. Byron jocosely put the matter thus:

> All tragedies are finished by a death,
> All comedies are ended by a marriage.

All tragedies and all comedies do not in fact end thus, but the idea is right; tragedy has the solemnity, seriousness, and finality we often associate with death,* and comedy has the joy and fertility and suggestion of a new life we

IMITATION OF AN ACTION

---

* Shakespeare's tragedies all end with the death of the tragic hero, but a good many Greek tragedies do not. In *Oedipus the King* the hero remains alive, but he is blind and banished and seems to have exhausted the possibilities of his life. Some other Greek tragedies have what can reasonably be called a happy ending, i.e., some sort of joyful reconciliation. For ex-

often associate with marriage. This concept of *an action* (i.e., an underlying motif, not merely gestures) in tragedy and in comedy makes clear that comedy is not a mere matter of jokes or funny bits of business. It also makes clear what the Greek comic playwright Menander meant when he told a friend that he had composed a play, and now had only to write the dialogue: he had worked out the happenings that would embody the action, and there remained only the slighter task of providing the spirited words. The same idea is implicit in Ibsen's comment that the drafts of his plays differed "very much from each other in characterization, not in action." The action or happening dramatized in a tragedy or a comedy may be conceived of as a single course or train of events manifested on the stage by a diversity of activities. Think of such expressions as "the closing of the frontier," or "the revival of learning"; each might be said to denote an action, though such action is seen only in its innumerable manifestations. The *Iliad* announces its action in the first line: "Sing, goddess, of the wrath of Achilles." The "action" is not, of course, always explicitly announced in a literary work. Among Ibsen's preliminary notes as he worked toward *Hedda Gabler* we find such entries as "They [i.e., women] all have a leaning towards sensuality, but are afraid of the scandal," "Men and women don't belong to the same century," and "The play is to be about 'the insuperable' — the longing and striving to defy convention, to defy what people accept (including Hedda)." Clearly, Ibsen was trying to get hold of his central point and then develop a plot that would reveal it.

HAPPENINGS
AND
HAPPENINGS

A tragic playwright takes some happening, from history (for example, the assassination of Julius Caesar), or from fiction (Shakespeare derived *Othello* from an Italian short story), or from his own imagination, and he makes or shapes or arranges episodes that clarify the action. He makes (in common terminology) a *plot* that embodies the action or spiritual content. (Even when the playwright draws on history, he makes his own plot because he selects and rearranges the available historical facts.) A glance at a very different kind of drama, recently popular, helps to clarify the distinction between a plot that embodies an action or a happening, and mere unconnected activities, happenings, events. In the early 1960's there was a good deal of interest in "Events" or "Happenings" (the latter term was derived from a performance in 1959 of something called *18 Happenings in 6 Parts*), performances in which activities were not connected so as to form a coherent plot that manifested an underlying action. Sample: a girl alternately washes her feet, puts tape over her mouth, dances with a board, sprays paint from a can onto a wall, and finally disrobes. Such a performance may display wit, agility, and other virtues and skills, but it is not a play in the traditional sense, despite its playfulness. Neither would a re-enactment of everything that Julius Caesar did during his last

---

ample, in Sophocles' *Philoctetes*, the weapon which has been taken from the sick Philoctetes is returned to him, and Heracles, a messenger from Zeus, announces that Philoctetes will be healed. But these tragedies with happy endings, like those with unhappy endings, deal with "important" people, and they are about "serious" things. If there is finally joy, it is a solemn joy.

days or hours be a play with an action, for drama is not so much concerned with what in fact *happened* as with some sort of typical and coherent or unified thing that *happens*, a significant action. Sometimes, of course, history provides substantial material for drama, but even Shakespeare's *Julius Caesar* takes frequent liberties with the facts as Shakespeare knew them, and Shakespeare's source, the biographer Plutarch, doubtless had already assimilated the facts to a literary form. At most we can say that history provided Shakespeare with a man whose life lent itself well to an established literary form. Not every life does lend itself thus. We are told that Aeschylus, the earliest tragic playwright who has left us any complete plays, was killed when an eagle mistook his bald head for a rock and dropped a turtle on it to break the shell. Aeschylus' death was a great loss, but it did not have the unified significant action required of tragedy. By chance an eagle that had captured a turtle was near to Aeschylus, and Aeschylus by chance (or rather by his chemistry) was bald. There is no relation between these two circumstances; Aeschylus' death (allegedly) happened this way, and we can account for it, but the event has no intelligible unity. (A sentence from Vladimir Nabokov's *Pale Fire* comes to mind: if one is contemplating suicide, "jumping from a high bridge is not recommended even if you cannot swim, for wind and water abound in weird contingencies, and tragedy ought not to culminate in a record dive or a policeman's promotion.") In tragedy things cohere. The hero normally does some deed and suffers as a consequence. Actions have consequences in the moral world no less than in the materialistic world of the laboratory. The tragic playwright's solemn presentation of "the remorseless working of things," Alfred North Whitehead pointed out (in his *Science and the Modern World*, 1925), is "the vision possessed by science," and it cannot be accidental that the two great periods of tragic drama, fifth-century B.C. Athens and England around 1600, are periods of scientific inquiry.

UNITY

This emphasis on causality means that the episodes are related, connected, and not merely contiguous. Generally the formula is to show the tragic hero moving toward committing some deed that will cause great unintended suffering, committing it, and then, by seeing the consequences, learning the true nature of his deed. The plot, that is, involves a credible character whose doings are related to his nature. For Aristotle, in the best sort of tragedy the tragic hero is an important person, almost pre-eminently virtuous, who makes some sort of great mistake that entails great suffering. Calamity does not descend upon him from above, does not happen *to* him, nor does he consciously will a destructive act; he merely makes a great mistake. The mistake is Aristotle's *hamartia*, sometimes translated as "error," sometimes as "flaw." Probably Aristotle did not mean by hamartia a trait, such as rashness or ambition, which the translation "flaw" implies, but simply meant an action based on a mental error, a sort of false step. Oedipus, erroneously thinking that Polybus and Meropê are his parents, flees from them when he hears that he will kill his father and sleep with his mother. His action is commendable, but it happens to be a great mistake because it brings him to his real parents. Nevertheless, despite the

THE TRAGIC HERO

HAMARTIA

scholarly elucidations of Aristotle, we can sometimes feel that the erring action proceeds from a particular kind of character, that a person with different traits would not have acted in the same way. The Oedipus that we see in the play, for example, is a self-assured quick-tempered man — almost a rash man, we might say — who might well have neglected to check the facts before he fled from Corinth. There are at least times, even when reading *Oedipus the King*, when one feels with George Meredith (1828–1909) that

> in tragic life, God wot,
> No villain need be! Passions spin the plot:
> We are betrayed by what is false within.

HYBRIS From this it is only a short step to identifying hamartia with a flaw, and the flaw most often attributed to the tragic hero is *hybris*, a word that for the Greeks meant something like "bullying," "abuse of power," but in dramatic criticism usually is translated as "overweening pride." The tragic hero forgets that (in Montaigne's words) "on the loftiest throne in the world we are still sitting only on our own rear," and he believes his actions are infallible. King Lear, for example, banishes his daughter Cordelia with "Better thou / Hadst not been born than not t' have pleased me better." Macbeth, told that he will be king of Scotland, chooses to make the prophecy come true by murdering his guest, King Duncan; Brutus decides that Rome can be saved from tyranny only by killing Caesar, and he deludes himself into thinking he is not murdering Caesar but sacrificing Caesar for the welfare of Rome.

PERIPETEIA We have talked of hamartia and hybris in tragedy; two more Greek words, *peripeteia* and *anagnorisis*, also common in discussions of tragedy, ought to be mentioned. A peripeteia (sometimes anglicized to "peripety" or translated as "reversal") occurs when the action takes a course not intended by the doer. Aristotle gives two examples: (1) the Messenger comes to cheer up Oedipus by freeing him from fears but the message heightens Oedipus' fears; (2) Danaus (in a lost play) prosecutes a man but is himself killed. The second example, by the way, reminds one of *The Merchant of Venice*, in which Shylock, calling upon the law, in effect demands Antonio's death and finds that his own life may be lawfully taken. A few other examples may be useful: Oedipus fled from Corinth to avoid contact with his parents, but his flight brought him to them; Macbeth kills Duncan to gain the crown but his deed brings him fearful nights instead of joyful days; Lear, seeking a peaceful old age, puts himself in the hands of two daughters who maltreat him, and banishes the one daughter who later will comfort him. The Bible — especially the Old Testament — is filled with such peripeties or ironic actions. For example, the Philistines brought Samson before them to entertain them, and he performed his most spectacular feat by destroying his audience. But the archetypal tragic story is that of Adam and Eve: aiming to be like gods, they lost their immortality and the earthly paradise, and brought death to themselves.

ANAGNORISIS The other Greek word, anagnorisis, translated as "recognition" or "discovery" or "disclosure," seems to have meant for Aristotle a clearing up of some misunderstanding, for example, the proper identification of someone or the

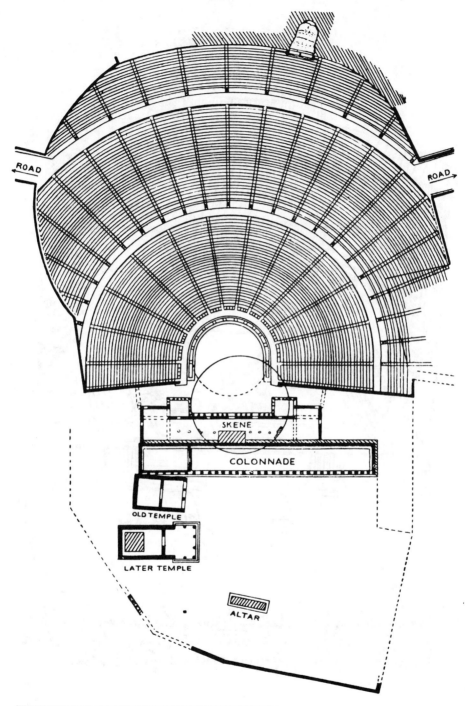

A drawing of "The Lycurgos Theatre of Dionysus at Athens" from *Greek Theatre and Its Drama* by R. C. Flickinger, p. 64. Reprinted by permission of The University of Chicago Press.

Johannes de Witt, a Continental visitor to London, made a drawing of the Swan Theatre in about the year 1596. The original drawing is lost; this is Arend van Buchel's copy of it.

revelation of some previously unknown fact. But later critics have given it a richer meaning and used it to describe the hero's perception of his true nature or his true plight. In the narrow sense, it is an anagnorisis or "recognition" when King Lear learns that Regan and Goneril are ungrateful and cruel. In the wider sense, the anagnorisis is in his speech in III.ɪᴠ when he confesses his former ignorance and neglect:

> Poor naked wretches, wheresoe'er you are,
> That bide the pelting of this pitiless storm,
> How shall your houseless heads and unfed sides,
> Your looped and windowed raggedness, defend you
> From seasons such as these? O, I have ta'en
> Too little care of this! Take physic, pomp;
> Expose thyself to feel what wretches feel,
> That thou mayst shake the superflux to them,
> And show the heavens more just.

Similarly Hamlet's "There is special providence in the fall of a sparrow," and Othello's "one that loved not wisely, but too well," may be called recognition scenes. Here is Macbeth's recognition that his purpose has been frustrated, that his deed has been ironic:

> My way of life
> Is fall'n into the scar, the yellow leaf,
> And that which should accompany old age,
> As honor, love, obedience, troops of friends,
> I must not look to have.

"Troops of friends" abound in comedy. Where tragedy is primarily the dramatization of the single life that ripens and then can only rot, that reaches its fullest and then is destroyed, comedy is primarily the dramatization of the renewing of the self and of social relationships. The tragic figure is isolated from society, partly by his different nature, and partly by his tragic act; comedy suggests that selfhood is found not in assertion of individuality, but in joining in the fun, in becoming part of the flow of common humanity. Where tragedy suggests an incompatibility between the energy or surge of life and the laws of life or the norms of society, comedy suggests that norms are valid and necessary. The tragic hero does what he feels compelled to do; he asserts himself, and is intensely aware that he is a special person and not a member of the crowd. But that his mistake always reveals that he is hybristic is not at all certain. The Greek tragic hero is commonly set against a chorus of ordinary mortals who caution him, wring their hands, and lament his boldness, but these ordinary mortals are always aware that if they are law-abiding men, they are also less fully men than the hero. That they obey society's laws is not due to superior virtue, to the triumph of reason over will, to self-discipline; rather, their obedience is due to a lower vision, or to timidity, and indeed sometimes to a fear of what resides in their own breasts. The tragic hero is, of course, in one way inferior to those about him; his mistake costs him great suffering, and he is thus immobilized as the others are not. But his greatness remains indisputable; the anguish that at times paralyzes Hamlet also makes him greater

THE SOCIAL WORLD OF COMEDY

TRAGIC ISOLATION

than, say, Horatio and Laertes. In fact the tragic hero is circumscribed, certainly after the deed, when he is necessarily subject to the consequences (Brutus kills Caesar and finds that he brings to Rome a turmoil that makes him flee from Rome, and ultimately makes him take his own life); even before doing the tragic deed the hero is circumscribed because his action proceeds from something, either from his personality or his circumstances. Still, his action seems to him to be freely his, and indeed we feel that it is an action that a lesser man could not perform. Which is almost a way of saying that it can be argued that a tragic hero may err not so much from weakness as from strength. Why can Iago so easily deceive Othello? Not because Othello is an unthinking savage, or an unsophisticated foreigner, but because (as Iago admits) Othello is of a "loving noble nature," and, again,

TRAGIC
VIRTUE

> The Moor is of *a free and open nature*
> *That thinks men honest* that but seem to be so;
> And will as tenderly be led by th' nose
> As asses are.

Why can Claudius see to it that Laertes murders Hamlet during a fencing match? Not because Hamlet is a poor fencer, or a coward, but because Hamlet,

> *Most generous, and free from all contriving,*
> Will not peruse the foils.

This is not to say that the tragic hero is faultless, or that he is quite happy with himself and with his action; but he does experience a kind of exultation even in his perception that disaster is upon him. If he grieves over his deed, we sense a glory in his grief, for he finds, like Captain Ahab, that in his topmost grief lies his topmost greatness. At last he sees everything and knows that nothing more can be experienced. He has lived his life to its limits. Othello puts it thus:

TRAGIC JOY

> Here is my journey's end, here is my butt,
> And very seamark of my utmost sail.

(In a comedy Shakespeare tells us that "journeys end in lovers meeting," that is, the end is a new beginning.) In "Under Ben Bulben" William Butler Yeats (1865–1939) suggests the sense of completeness that the tragic hero experiences when, under the influence of a great passion, he exhausts his nature and seems to be not a man among men but a partner (rather than a subject) of fate:

> Know that when all words are said
> And a man is fighting mad,
> Something drops from eyes long blind,
> He completes his partial mind,
> For an instant stands at ease,
> Laughs aloud, his heart at peace.
> Even the wisest man grows tense
> With some sort of violence
> Before he can accomplish fate,
> Know his work or choose his mate.

Elsewhere Yeats put his distinction between the tragic hero and the world he is up against thus: "Some Frenchman* has said that farce is the struggle against a ridiculous object, comedy against a movable object, tragedy against an immovable; and because the will, or energy, is greatest in tragedy, tragedy is the more noble; but I add that 'will or energy is eternal delight,' and when its limit is reached it may become a pure, aimless joy, though the man, the shade, still mourns his lost object." And one more passage by Yeats, this one from a play, again calling attention to the revelation of life — joyful to behold — apparent when an impassioned man expresses his fullest nature:

> I would have all know that when all falls
> In ruin, poetry calls out in joy,
> Being the scattering hand, the bursting pod,
> The victim's joy among the holy flame,
> God's laughter at the shattering of the world.

All this is to say splendidly that we sometimes feel admiration for the passionate man, for the man determined to do and to be, and we sense his superiority (as he himself senses it) to the law-abiding men who surround him, perhaps no more so than when his nobility undoes him, i.e., when we see the incompatibility between passionate self-assertion and the laws of life.

But there are contexts and times when we find passionate self-assertion funny (there are contexts and times, too, when we find it vicious, but that is another matter). Much depends on what is being asserted, and what or who COMIC the antagonist is. Recall Brunetière's opinion, or rather Yeats' version of it, ASSERTION that tragedy dramatizes a struggle against an immovable object, comedy a struggle against a movable one. King Lear against his tigerish daughters is a tragic figure, but a pedant against a dull schoolboy may be a comic one. The lament of the tragic hero is proportionate to the event, but the effort extended by the comic figure is absurdly disproportionate. Furthermore, as Henri Bergson (1859–1941) pointed out, the comic figure usually is a sort of mechanism, repeating his actions and catch phrases with clocklike regularity in contexts where they are inappropriate. He quotes Latin on every occasion, or he never travels without his pills, or he always wants to know how much something costs, or he is forever spying on his wife. Bergson, who suggested that the comic is "the mechanical encrusted on the living," illustrated his point by telling of the customs officers who bravely rescue the crew of a sinking vessel, and then ask, the moment the shore is reached, "Have you anything to declare?" The mechanical question, inappropriate in the situation, reveals that the officers value trivial regulations as much as they value life itself. In *The Circus* Charlie Chaplin is dusting things off; he comes upon the magician's bowl of goldfish, takes the fish out and wipes them, and then returns them to the bowl. Real life, too, affords examples of this sort of comic behavior. Emerson mentions that the biologist Camper, who had spent six months studying hairless water mammals, said he almost began to see people as narwhales, por-

---

* Yeats is rather freely summarizing Ferdinand Brunetière's *La Loi du théâtre*. A translation of Brunetière's treatise is available in *European Theories of the Drama*, ed. Barrett H. Clark.

poises, and marsouins. This is whimsy, of course, but Emerson goes on to tell of a visit to a dying friend. On his way to the friend, Emerson met the physician, who had just left the patient. The physician, Emerson says, "accosted me in great spirits, with joy sparkling in his eyes. 'And how is my friend, the reverend Doctor?' I inquired. 'O, I saw him this morning; it is the most correct apoplexy I have ever seen: face and hands livid, breathing stertorous, all the symptoms perfect.' And he rubbed his hands with delight."

COMIC JOY   Emerson's doctor, valuing symptoms rather than life, nicely fulfills Bergson's formula. And in his high spirits — ludicrously out of place in the context — he inadvertently illustrates another aspect of comedy, its prevailing high spirits. The comic world is a world of delight in variety; even its hardships are not lasting. In *As You Like It* when Rosalind, daughter of a banished duke, complains of the frustrations of life, "O, how full of briers is this working-day world," Celia gives the right reply: "They are but burrs, cousin, thrown upon thee in holiday foolery." (But if Celia were to give this answer too often she would become laughable herself.) The comic world seems to be presided over by a genial tolerant deity who enjoys the variety that crosses the stage. The sketchbooks of the Japanese artist Hokusai (1760–1849) wonderfully reveal this comic delight in humanity. There are pages of fat men, pages of thin men (no less engagingly drawn), pages of men making funny faces, and there is a delightful drawing of a man holding a magnifying glass in front of his face so that his nose seems enormous. The comic playwright gives us something of this range of types and grotesques, and he gives us also variety in language (e.g., puns, inverted clichés, malapropisms) and variety in episodes (much hiding behind screens, dressing in disguise). The character, then, who insists on being himself, who mechanically holds to a formula of language or of behavior, is laughably out of place in the world of varied people who live and let

COMIC
ISOLATION
live. What comedy does not tolerate is intolerance; it regularly suggests that the intolerant — for example the pedant and the ascetic — are fools and probably hypocrites. Here is the self-righteous Alceste, in Molière's *The Misanthrope*:

> Some men I hate for being rogues: the others
> I hate because they treat the rogues like brothers,
> And, lacking a virtuous scorn for what is vile,
> Receive the villain with a complaisant smile.
> Notice how tolerant people choose to be
> Toward that bold rascal who's at law with me.

Philinte genially replies, "Let's have an end of rantings and of railings, / And show some leniency toward human failings. / This world requires a pliant rectitude; / Too stern a virtue makes one stiff and rude." Here is the puritanical Malvolio in *Twelfth Night*, trying to quiet down some tipsy but genial revelers:

> My masters, are you mad? Or what are you? Have you no wit, manners nor honesty, but to gabble like tinkers at this time of night? Do ye make an alehouse of my lady's house? . . . Is there not respect of place, persons, nor time in you?

He is aptly answered: "Art any more than a steward? Dost thou think, because thou art virtuous, there shall be no more cakes and ale?" This suspicion of a "virtue" that is opposed to cakes and ale runs through the history of comedy. In Shakespeare's *Love's Labor's Lost*, the young noblemen who vow to devote themselves to study, and to forgo the company of women, are laughed at until they accept their bodies and admit interest in those of the ladies. The celebration of the human body, or at least the good-natured acceptance of it which is present in comedy is well-put by the General in Anouilh's *The Waltz of the Toreadors*. (The life-buoy he refers to is "the ideal.")

> You're in the ocean, splashing about, doing your damndest not to drown, in spite of whirlpools and cross currents. The main thing is to do the regulation breast-stroke and if you're not a clod, never to let the life-buoy out of sight. No one expects any more than that out of you. Now if you relieve yourself in the water now and then, that's your affair. The sea is big, and if the top half of your body still looks as though it's doing the breast-stroke, nobody will say a word.

One way of distinguishing between comedy and tragedy is summarized in Horace Walpole's aphorism, "This world is a comedy to those that think, a tragedy to those that feel." Life seen thoughtfully, with considerable detachment, viewed from above, as it were, is an amusing pageant, and the comic writer gives us something of this view. With Puck we look at the antics in the forest, smile tolerantly, and say with a godlike perspective, "Lord, what fools these mortals be!" But in tragedy we are to a greater degree engaged; the tragic dramatist manages to make us in large measure identify ourselves with the hero, feel his plight as if it were our own, and value his feelings as he values them, so that with Othello we may say "The pity of it."* Yeats noticed this when he said that "character is continuously present in comedy alone," and that "tragedy must always be a drowning and breaking of the dykes that separate man from man. . . . It is upon these dykes comedy keeps house." And Yeats again: "Nor when the tragic reverie is at its height do we say, 'How well that man is realised, I should know him were I to meet him in the street,' for it is always ourselves that we see upon the [tragic] stage."

DETACHMENT AND ENGAGEMENT

One consequence of this distinction between tragedy and comedy, between looking-at and feeling-with, is that the comic plot is usually more intricate than the tragic plot, and less plausible. The comic plot continues to trip up its characters, bringing them into numerous situations that allow them to display their folly over and again. The complex comic plot is often arbitrary, full of the workings of Fortune or Chance, and we delight at each new unexpected or unlikely happening. In tragedy, Fate (sometimes in the form that "character is destiny") or Necessity rules, there is the consistency and inevitability, the "remorseless working of things," that has already been mentioned. If Macbeth were struck dead by a falling roof tile while he dozed in the palace

TRAGIC FATE AND COMIC FORTUNE IN PLOTS

---

* Bergson's theory that a human being — an organism — is comical when it behaves mechanically requires, as Bergson said, a modification: feelings must be suppressed. A crippled man is not comic despite his mechanical limp, because we feel for him. Comedy requires, Bergson said, an "anesthesia of the heart."

after a good meal, instead of dying on Macduff's sword, or if Brutus were to die by slipping in his bath, instead of dying on the very sword with which he killed Caesar, we would have arbitrary happenings that violate the spirit of everything that precedes. But the unexpected letters and the long-lost relatives that often turn up at the close of a comedy are thoroughly in the spirit of the comic vision, which devalues not only rigidly consistent character but rigidity of every sort, even of plot. Tragedy usually follows a straight course, comedy a delightfully twisted one.

The rigid behavior of some of comedy's laughably serious characters (e.g., misers, jealous husbands, stern fathers) is paralleled in the rigid circumstances that often are sketched at the beginning of a comedy. In *As You Like It*, the rightful duke has been banished by his usurping brother, and (a sort of parallel) an attractive young nobleman has been confined "rustically at home" by *his* brother. Gilbert and Sullivan, to draw on familiar material, afford plenty of examples of comedy's fondness for a cantankerous beginning: *The Mikado* opens with a chorus of Japanese noblemen whose code of etiquette makes them appear to be "worked by strings"; they live in a town where a law ordered that "all who flirted, leered or winked / Should forthwith be beheaded." (Comedy often begins with a society dominated by some harsh law.) Although this law has been suspended, another harsh decree is in effect: the pretty Yum-Yum is betrothed to her old guardian, Ko-Ko. We learn, too, that her appropriate wooer, Nanki-Poo, is a prince who has had to disguise himself as a humble wandering minstrel to escape his father's decree that he marry Katisha, an old and ugly lady of the court. After various doings in a comedy, a new — presumably natural, prosperous, fertile, and free — society is formed, usually centered around lovers who are going to be married. Yum-Yum and Nanki-Poo finally contrive to get married, evading Katisha and Ko-Ko, who make the best of things by marrying each other. The whole business is satisfactorily explained to the Mikado, who affably accepts, and ruffled tempers are soothed:

> The threatened cloud has passed away,
> And brightly shines the dawning day;
> What though the night may come too soon,
> We've years and years of afternoon!
>
> Then let the throng
> Our joy advance,
> With laughing song
> And merry dance,
> With joyous shout and ringing cheer,
> Inaugurate our new career!

The first four lines are sung by the young lovers, the remaining six are sung by "All," the new, or renewed, society, free from unnatural law. *H.M.S. Pinafore* begins with lovers who cannot marry because of disparity in rank, but ends with appropriate shifts in rank so that there can be "three loving pairs on the same day united."

In comedy there is often not only an improbable turn in events but an improbable (but agreeable) change in character — or at least in rank; trouble-some persons become enlightened, find their own better nature, and join in the fun, commonly a marriage-feast. Finding one's own nature is common in tragedy, too, but there self-knowledge is co-terminous with death or some death-like condition, such as blindness. *Oedipus the King* ends with a note of finality, even though Oedipus is alive at the end; the fact that twenty-five years later Sophocles decided to write a play showing Oedipus' apotheosis does not allow us to see the earlier play as less than complete. The chorus in *Oedipus the King* has the last word:

SELF-
KNOWLEDGE

> This man was Oedipus.
> That mighty King, who knew the riddle's mystery,
> Whom all the city envied, Fortune's favorite.
> Behold, in the event, the storm of his calamities,
> And, being mortal, think on that last day of death,
> Which all must see, and speak of no man's happiness
> Till, without sorrow, he hath passed the goal of life.

Or consider the irreparable loss at the end of Shakespeare's tragedies: "This was the noblest Roman of them all"; "We that are young / Shall never see so much, nor live so long"; "The rest is silence." But comedy ends with a new beginning, a newly formed society, usually a wedding party; the tragic figure commonly awakens to the fact that he has made a big mistake and his life is over, but the comic figure commonly awakens to his better nature. He usually sheds his aberration and is restored to himself and to a renewed society. In *As You Like It*, for example, Oliver is for much of the play a "most unnatu-ral brother," but he is at last converted by his brother's natural goodness and he gains a lovely wife. Alceste's refusal to change, at the end of *The Misan-thrope*, helps to push that comedy toward the borderline between comedy and tragedy. Oedipus learns that his parents were not those whom he had sup-posed, and he learns that even the mighty Oedipus can be humbled. Othello comes to see himself as a man "that loved not wisely but too well," and, hav-ing reached his journey's end, he executes justice upon himself by killing him-self. That is, at the end of the play he finds himself, but this finding of the self separates him forever from those around him, whereas the comic figure who finds himself usually does so by putting aside in some measure his individuality and by submitting himself to a partner or to the group.

Thomas Hardy, whose view of life was bleak (it has been said that in Hardy fornication always produces offspring), said:

> Tragedy is true guise,
> Comedy lies.

But the visions of comedy and tragedy are equally true and do not conflict; rather, they are different visions and represent different psychological states. And they are equally useful. The tragic vision may have more prestige, but it is no small thing to make men laugh, to call attention amusingly to the follies and joys of life, and to help develop the sense of humor — and humility — that may be indispensable to survival in a world continually threatened by aggressive ideals that demand uncritical acceptance. Infants smile easily, and children laugh often, but growing up is often attended by a frightening seriousness. True, hostile laughter, the scarcely veiled aggressiveness that manifests itself in derision, remains an adult possession, but the laughter evoked by the best comedy is good-natured while it is critical, and it is in part directed at ourselves. We look at bumbling humanity and we recall Puck's words, "Lord, what fools these mortals be." This is not to say that the comic vision is cynical; rather, it attributes to folly what less generous visions attribute to ill-will or to hopeless corruption, and when it laughs it forgives. Analyses of laughter are sometimes funny but more often they are tedious; still, they at least pay the comic spirit the compliment of recognizing it as worthy of man's best efforts.

2. Tragicomedy

TRAGICOMEDY BEFORE 1900

The word "tragicomedy" is much newer than the words "tragedy" and "comedy"; it first appears about 186 B.C., when Plautus spoke of *tragicocomoedia* in his *Amphitryon*, a Roman comedy in which gods assume mortal shapes in order to dupe a husband and seduce his wife. Mercury, in a joking prologue to the play, explains the author's dilemma:

> I'll make it a mixture, a tragicomedy. It wouldn't be right for me to make
> it all a comedy since kings and gods appear. Well, then, since there's a
> slave part too, I'll do as I said and make it a tragicomedy.

But the play is a traditional comedy, unalloyed with the solemnity, terror, and pity of tragedy. It shows laughable activities that finally turn out all right. It should be mentioned again, however, that although tragedy and comedy were clearly separated in the ancient world, not all ancient tragedies ended with death, or even ended unhappily. Aeschylus' trilogy, *The Oresteia*, ends with reconciliation and solemn joy (but it has been bought at the price of great suffering), and Sophocles' *Philoctetes* and Euripides' *Iphigeneia at Taurus* end with catastrophes averted. They were tragic for the Greeks because momentous issues were treated seriously, though we might say that the plots have a comic structure because they end happily. In the Renaissance there was much fussing over the meanings of tragedy, comedy, and tragicomedy, but most theoreticians inclined to the view that tragedy dealt with noble figures engaged in serious actions, was written in a lofty style, and ended unhappily; comedy dealt with humbler figures engaged in trivial actions, was written in relatively common diction, and ended happily. Tragicomedy, whether defined as some mixture (e.g., high people in trivial actions) or as a play in which, to quote Sir Philip Sidney, the writer "thrust in the clown by head and shoulders to play a part in majestical matters," was for the most part scorned by academic critics as a mongrel. It was merely additive, bits of comedy added to a tragedy. At best the advocates for tragicomedy could argue that a play without the terror of tragedy and the absurdity of comedy can cover a good deal of life and can please a good many tastes. But this sort of play, unlike modern tragicomedy, is not so much a union of tragedy and comedy as an exclusion of both, lacking, for example, the awe we associate with tragedy and the fun we associate with comedy.

In the twentieth century the word and the form have become thoroughly respectable; indeed, it is now evident that most of the best plays of our century are best described not as tragedies or as comedies but as tragicomedies — distinctive fusions (not mere aggregations) of tragedy and comedy. For a start we can take William Hazlitt's statement that "man is the only animal that laughs and weeps; for he is the only animal that is struck with the difference between what things are, and what they ought to be." This implication that the subjects of tragedy and of comedy are one rather than two has recently been amplified by Cyrus Hoy, who suggests that a single principle underlies tragedy and comedy (pp. 642–648): man has an ideal of human conduct, but circumstances and his own limitations make his belief that he can fulfill this ideal illusory. Still man persists, appearing "nobly enduring, stubbornly unyielding . . . foolishly blind," or (as in most tragicomedy) some indissoluble combination of these. Most of the best playwrights of the twentieth century have adopted the more complicated mixed view. Comedy had customarily invoked a considerable degree of detachment; in Bergson's formula (1900), already quoted, comedy requires an anesthesia of the spectator's heart as he watches folly on the stage. Tragedy, on the other hand, customarily invoked a considerable degree of involvement or sympathy; in Walpole's formula, also already quoted, "The world is a comedy to those that think, a tragedy to those that feel." But tragicomedy shows us comic characters for whom we feel deep sympathy. Pirandello in his essay *Umorismo* (1908) gives an interesting example of the phenomenon. Suppose, he says, we see an elderly woman with dyed hair and much too much make-up. We find her funny; but if we realize that she is trying to hold the attention of her husband, our sympathy is aroused. Our sense of her absurdity is not totally dissipated, but we feel for her and so our laughter is combined with pity. There are moments like this in earlier comedies, the most famous probably is Shylock's "Hath not a Jew eyes . . .? It you poison us do we not die?" in which we suddenly see Shylock not unsympathetically from the outside, as a funny-looking man with odd dietary habits but sympathetically as a man who shares our feelings. Despite such a moment, *The Merchant of Venice* is clearly a comedy, a festive play with a happy ending, and on the whole Shylock is a figure for unsympathetic laughter.

DETACHMENT AND ENGAGEMENT AGAIN

Changes in our ethical conceptions, however, have caused us to see him with increased sympathy, just as we now see madness, or the sufferings of animals, with greater sympathy than our ancestors did. Our attitudes since, say,

16 THE NATURE OF DRAMA

the middle of the eighteenth century have shifted a good deal, giving us a new sense of the nature of man, and we ought briefly to look at this new sense and its background.

First, a disclaimer. There are still many different attitudes and many kinds of plays. But the theater that is vital today is not the Broadway musical, the earnest problem-play, or the well-made drawing-room comedy (though these

THEATER OF THE ABSURD

continue to be written) but a fairly unified body of drama called the absurd, whose major writers are Beckett, Genet, and Ionesco. Their theme is man's anguish, but their techniques are those of comedy: improbable situations and unheroic characters who say funny things. These writers differ, of course, and differ from play to play, but they are all preoccupied with the loneliness of man in a world without the certainties afforded by God or by optimistic rationalism. This loneliness is heightened by a sense of impotence derived partly from an awareness of man's inability to communicate in a society that has made language meaningless, and partly from an awareness of the precariousness of man's existence in an atomic age. Behind this vision are some two hundred years of thinking that have conspired to make it difficult to think of any man as a hero who confronts a mysterious cosmic order. Man, Ionesco says in *Notes and Counter Notes*, is "cut off from his religious and metaphysical roots."* One of the milestones in Western man's journey toward contemporary nihilism is the bourgeois drama of the middle of the eighteenth century, which sought to show the dignity of the common man but which, negatively put, undermined the concept of a tragic *hero*. Instead of showing a heroic yet universal man, it showed man in relation to his society, thus paving the way for Arthur Miller's Willy Loman, who apparently would have been okay, as we all would be, if our economic system allowed for early retirement. Miller's play makes no claim for Willy's grandeur or for the glory of life; it claims only that he is an ordinary man at the end of his rope in a deficient society and that he is entitled to a fair deal.

DIMINUTION OF MAN

Other landmarks on the road to man's awareness of his littleness are, like bourgeois drama, developments in thinking that were thought by their builders to be landmarks on the road to man's progressive conquest of fear. Among these we can name Darwin's *The Origin of Species* (1859), which, in the popular phrase, seemed to record man's progress "up from apes," but which, more closely read, reduced man to the product of "accidental variations" and left God out of the picture, substituting for a cosmic order a barbaric struggle for existence. (In the second edition, 1860, Darwin spoke of life as "breathed by the creator," but the creator was not Darwin's concern and he later abandoned all religious beliefs. Probably he retained his belief that the process of "natural selection works solely by and for the good of each being," but by 1889 his disciple Huxley saw it differently. Huxley said he knew of no study "so

* From *Notes and Counter Notes: Writings on the Theatre* by Eugène Ionesco, p. 257. Translated from the French by Donald Watson. Copyright © 1964 by Grove Press, Inc. Reprinted by permission of the publisher, Grove Press, Inc.

unutterably saddening as that of the evolution of humanity.") Karl Marx, studying the evolution of societies at about the same time, was attributing man's sense of alienation to economic forces, thereby implying that man had no identity he could properly call his own. Moreover, Marxist thinking, like Darwinian thinking, suggested that a man could not do anything of really great importance, nor could he be blamed for his misfortunes. (Economic determinism need not lead to pessimism. Brecht, in *The Good Woman of Setzuan*, seizes joyfully on this development in thinking; since man's personality is not really his, it can be changed for the better under Communism.) At the end of the nineteenth century, and in the early twentieth century, Freud, also seeking to free man from tyranny, turned to the forces within man's mind. Ironically, the effort to chart man's unconscious drives and anarchic impulses in order to help man to know himself induced a profound distrust of the self: we can scarcely be confident of our behavior, for we know that apparently heroic behavior has unconscious unheroic motives rooted in the experiences of infancy. Tragic heroes are men with complexes, and religious codes are only wishful thinking.

The result of such developments in thought seems to be that, a "tragic sense" in the twentieth century commonly means a despairing or deeply uncertain view, something very different from what it meant in Greece and in Elizabethan England. This uncertainty, is not merely about the cosmos but even about character or identity. In 1888, in the Preface to *Miss Julie*, Strindberg called attention to the new sense of the instability of character:

DISSOLUTION OF CHARACTER AND PLOT

> I have made the people in my play fairly "characterless." The middle-class conception of a fixed character was transferred to the stage, where the middle class has always ruled. A character there came to mean an actor who was always one and the same, always drunk, always comic or always melancholy, and who needed to be characterized only by some physical defect such as a club foot, a wooden leg, or a red nose, or by the repetition of some such phrase such as, "That's capital," or "Barkis is willin'."
> ... Since the persons in my play are modern characters, living in a transitional era more hurried and hysterical than the previous one at least, I have depicted them as more unstable, as torn and divided, a mixture of the old and the new.

In 1902, in his preface to *A Dream Play*, he is more explicit: "Anything may happen, anything seems possible and probable.... The characters split, double, multiply, vanish, solidify, blur, clarify." Strindberg's view of the fluidity of character — the characterlessness of character, one might say — has continued and is apparent in O'Neill's *The Emperor Jones*, in almost all of Pirandello's work, in the underground film, and in much of the Theater of the Absurd. Ionesco, in *Fragments of a Journal*, says "I often find it quite impossible to hold an opinion about a fact, a thing or a person. Since it's all a matter of interpretation, one has to choose a particular interpretation."* (One thinks too

---

* From *Fragments of a Journal* by Eugène Ionesco, p. 131. Translated by Jean Stewart. Copyright © by Faber and Faber Ltd. Reprinted by permission of the publishers, Grove Press, Inc., and Faber and Faber Ltd.

of Dr. Borg in Bergman's *Wild Strawberries* who in effect withdrew from society because a man cannot really know his fellows.) In *Notes and Counter Notes* Ionesco said, "chance formed us," and that we would be different if we had different experiences; characteristically a few years later he said that he was no longer sure that he believed in chance.

Along with the sense of characterlessness, or at least of the mystery of character, there developed in the drama (and in the underground film and the novel) a sense of plotlessness, or fundamental untruthfulness of the traditional plot that moved by cause and effect. "Plots," Ionesco has said in *Conversations*, "are never interesting," and again he has said that a play should be able to stop at any point; it ends only because "the audience has to go home to bed. . . . It's true for real life. Why should it be different for art?"* Ionesco has treated his own plots very casually, allowing directors to make "all the cuts needed" and suggesting that endings other than those he wrote are possibilities. After all, in a meaningless world one can hardly take a dramatic plot seriously. In Ionesco's *Victims of Duty* a character defends a new kind of irrational, anti-Aristotelian drama: "The theater of my dreams would be irrationalist. . . . The contemporary theater doesn't reflect the cultural tone of our period, it's not in harmony with the general drift of the other manifestations of the modern spirit. . . . We'll get rid of the principle of identity and unity of character. . . . Personality doesn't exist." A policeman-psychologist (a materialist who demands law and order) offers an old-fashioned view: "I don't believe in the absurd, everything hangs together, everything can be comprehended . . . thanks to the achievements of human thought and science," but he is murdered by the anti-Aristotelian.†

Not surprisingly, Brecht, also an anti-Aristotelian, invites us at the end of *The Good Woman of Setzuan* to work out our own ending; he has shown us a piece of life, but he doesn't give it the joyous conclusion of a comedy or the finality of a tragedy. He leaves it open, and invites us to think of a better ending. Similarly, Beckett's *Waiting for Godot* ends — as the first act ended — without anything ending:

> VLADIMIR: Well? Shall we go?
> ESTRAGON: Yes, let's go.
>
> *They do not move.*
> *Curtain.*‡

To bring an action to a completion, as drama traditionally did, is to imply an orderly world of cause and effect, of beginnings and endings, but for the dram-

---

* From *Conversations with Eugène Ionesco* by Claude Bonnefoy, p. 82. Translated by Jan Dawson. Holt, Rinehart and Winston, 1970. Reprinted by permission of the publisher.

† From *Three Plays* by Eugène Ionesco, pp. 157–159. Translated by Donald Watson. Copyright © 1958 by John Calder (Publishers) Limited. Reprinted by permission of the publisher, Grove Press, Inc.

‡ Translated from the French by the author. Copyright © 1954 by Grove Press. Reprinted by permission of the publisher, Grove Press, Inc.

atists of the absurd, there is no such pattern. At best it is *Hamlet* as Tom Stoppard's Rosencrantz and Guildenstern see it: they are supposed to do a job they don't understand, and instead of a pattern or "order" they encounter only "Incidents! Incidents! Dear God, is it too much to expect a little sustained action?" Well, yes; it is too much to expect.

There can be no tragedy, because, as Ionesco explains in *Notes*, tragedy admits the existence of fate or destiny, which is to say it admits the existence of objective (however incomprehensible) laws ruling the universe, whereas the new comic perception of incongruity is that existence itself is absurd because there is no objective law. The new comic vision is far darker than the old tragic vision; it has nothing in it of what Yeats called "tragic joy." But what is our reaction to this joyless comedy? Let Ionesco, whose plays sometimes include meaningless babble, have the last word:

THE TRAGEDY OF COMEDY

> The fact of being astonishes us, in a world that now seems all illusion and pretense, in which all human behavior tells of absurdity and all history of absolute futility; all reality and all language appear to lose their articulation, to disintegrate and collapse, so what possible reaction is there left, when everything has ceased to matter, but laugh at it all.*

* From *Notes and Counter Notes: Writings on the Theatre* by Eugène Ionesco, p. 163. Translated from the French by Donald Watson. Copyright © 1964 by Grove Press, Inc. Reprinted by permission of the publisher, Grove Press, Inc.

THE LANGUAGE OF DRAMA

Although a play usually tells a story, "the medium of drama," as Ezra Pound shrewdly observed, "is not words, but persons moving about on a stage using words." Take Eugene O'Neill's *The Emperor Jones* as an example. The gist of the story is this: Jones, a black fugitive from a chaingang, has turned up on an island in the West Indies and established himself as Emperor. By his own admission he has tyrannized over his subjects, and he was able to get away with it because they believed that he could be killed only by a silver bullet. (This is the *antecedent action*; we learn it during the play, but it reports what happened before the play begins.) At the beginning of the play, hearing that a rebellion is in progress Jones confidently sets out to leave the island; he becomes increasingly terrified, and at the end of the play he is shot with a silver bullet.

This is moderately interesting, and not totally different from some historical episodes: President Guillaume Sam of Haiti boasted he would kill himself with a silver bullet, but he was hacked to pieces by his oppressed subjects in 1915, only five years before O'Neill wrote *The Emperor Jones*; and a century earlier, Henri Christophe, a slave who had become the merciless ruler of part of Haiti, shot himself when confronted with an insurrection. O'Neill knew these bits of history, and used them to shape *The Emperor Jones*, but even if he had not changed some facts, a play about Sam or Christophe inevitably would — if it were any good — be very different from an encyclopedia entry on them because, as Pound says, a play is made not out of words but out of "persons moving about on a stage using words."

Let's begin with the stage and its setting. When the curtain goes up on a   SETTING performance of *The Emperor Jones*, the audience sees "the audience chamber in the palace of the Emperor." It is furnished solely with "one huge chair . . . painted a dazzling eye-smiting scarlet," a cushion that serves as a footstool, and two scarlet mats that go "from the foot of the throne to the two entrances." This stage, at least in the context of what follows, "says" a lot. It conveys Jones's dominance, for he alone can sit in the room, and it conveys something of his bloody career, for if the scarlet throne on which Jones sits at first suggests royalty, it also in retrospect suggests the blood that surrounds his career. Whether or not O'Neill was conscious of the fact when he was writing the play, the huge scarlet chair, which at the start is boldly emblematic of Jones both as Emperor and as murderer, is a notable contrast to the "little reddish-purple hole under his left breast" when his corpse is brought onstage at the end of the play. The imperial murderer has diminished to this.

The play uses only two other sets, and these are almost one: the edge of the Great Forest, and within the Great Forest. The Forest, again, in the context of the action, says something. O'Neill tells us, in his first description of it, that it gives an impression of "relentless immobility" and of "brooding, implacable silence." Fleeing through the forest Jones becomes terrified, and we see that the dark forest is, in part at least, the jungle of man's mind, the world of inarticulate, elemental passions that seethe beneath the fragile surface of reason. Its darkness, a strong contrast to the brightly illuminated throne room where Jones was the confident master, provides us with an example of the way in which a dramatist uses lighting — or, rather, darkness — symbolically. Not every dramatist uses his stage sets quite so obviously, but the subway setting of LeRoi Jones's *Dutchman* is, in Jones's words, "the flying underbelly of the city," and even a "realistic" play like *The Cherry Orchard* juxtaposes the orchard (the dying, aristocratic way of life) with telephone poles and a town (the new, industrial way of life). In *Death of a Salesman*, Willy Loman's "fragile-seeming home" is surrounded by "a solid vault of apartment houses," Miller thereby conveying the vulnerability of the individual. A bare stage, too (much used in contemporary drama), by virtue of its barrenness says something about man's isolation or alienation. Although one frequently hears that the Elizabethan stage was bare and that Shakespeare's plays are most effective on a bare stage, in fact the Elizabethan stage was an elaborate piece of architecture, suggestive of a completely ordered universe, and when appropriate the stage was decorated with banners. But it could be bleak when bleakness was required. At the end of the second act of *King Lear* Gloucester tells us what we are to imagine: "Alack, the night comes on, and the high winds / Do sorely ruffle. For many miles about / There's scarce a bush." Again, this locale says something about the impoverished people who move in it.

In returning to *The Emperor Jones*, and to Ezra Pound's comment on the nature of drama, let us continue for a moment to talk about the ways in which COSTUME drama even without dialogue says something. Costumes tell us a good deal, on the stage as in life. They do not necessarily tell the truth about their wearers, but they tell us what the wearers want us to believe. If, on the street, we see someone who is wearing workman's clothes, we conclude that he may be a workman — or that for some reason (say, political or sexual) he wants us to think that he is a workman; in any case the clothes make a statement, conscious or not. Jones at the outset is certainly making a conscious statement through his clothes, a uniform whose blue coat is "sprayed with brass buttons, heavy gold chevrons on his shoulders, gold braid on the collar, cuffs, etc. His pants are bright red." The clothes say, quite as explicitly as Jones says to Smithers, "Ain't I de Emperor?" When he begins his flight from the palace at the end of the first scene, he goes out with imperial dignity, in full uniform and with a Panama hat on his head. By the third scene, "he has lost his Panama hat. His face is scratched, his brilliant uniform shows several large rents." In the fourth scene, "his uniform is ragged and torn," in the fifth he discards his worn-out shoes, in the sixth "his pants have been so torn away that what is left of them is no better than a breech cloth." This stripping away of Jones's clothing is clearly also a stripping away both of his external power and of his control over himself. At the start he was "self-reliant" and coolly calculating, but now he is a primitive bundle of inarticulate terrors. O'Neill did not, of course, invent the use of costumes as dramatic language; it goes back to the beginnings of drama, and one has only to think of Hamlet's "inky cloak" or of Lear tearing off his clothing, or of the fresh clothing in which Lear is garbed after his madness, to see how eloquently costumes can speak. To this can be added the matter of disguises — for example Edgar's disguise in *King Lear* and Rosalind's in *As You Like It* — which are removed near the ends of the plays, when the truth is finally revealed and the characters can again be fully themselves. In short, the removal of disguises *says* something.

Gestures too are part of the language of drama. When in the first scene GESTURES Jones knows that his role as Emperor is over, he leaves the palace — but by the front door. Somewhat needlessly he explains the gesture to Smithers, the cowardly white man: "Does you think I'd slink out de back door like a common nigger? I'se Emperor yit, ain't I? And de Emperor Jones leaves de way he comes." And in this scene, when Smithers sees Jones's hand go to his revolver, Smithers is in no doubt about the meaning of the gesture. One last example: against Jones's terrified flight, O'Neill in the final scene juxtaposes his foe Lem, who "imperturbably" squats to await Jones's inevitable death.

Although dialogue is the most conspicuous way of telling a story in plays that are also literature, first we should notice another sort of sound in *The Emperor Jones*, nonverbal sounds. The most obvious is the tom-tom, which SOUND "starts at a rate exactly corresponding to the normal pulse beat — seventy-two EFFECTS to the minute — and continues at a gradually accelerating rate from this point uninterruptedly to the very end of the play." Though this stage direction is O'Neill's, it is not quite accurate, for in the last scene another stage direction tells us that at the moment that Jones is shot "the beating of the tom-tom abruptly ceases." The tom-tom is a powerful way of working on the audience's emotions, but it is more than a gimmick, for its acceleration clearly corresponds to Jones's increasing fears that make his heart beat faster and faster, and it stops beating when a bullet causes his heart to stop beating. Other less conspicuous but no less meaningful sound effects are the moaning wind (not merely a realistic effect, but a sound related to Jones's state of mind), the "low mocking laughter like a rustling of leaves" in the second scene, the pistol shots at the ends of scenes 2, 3, 4, 5, and 7 when he seeks unsuccessfully to dispel his fears by relying on technology, and finally the shots of the rifles that bring him down. Simply to widen the canvas, we can add an example from Shakespeare: the sound of the storm in *King Lear* is a reflection of Lear's disordered kingdom, disordered family, and disordered mind. Similarly, the "scream" of the subway in LeRoi Jones's *Dutchman*, the sound of the axes cutting down the trees in *The Cherry Orchard*, and the flute ("telling of grass and trees and the horizon") in *Death of a Salesman* are not merely realism.

Dialogue is the most persistent and significant sound in a play. A good DIALOGUE playwright gives us not a transcript of our chaotic fragmentary sentences but language that continually reveals character and furthers plot. In the first line of *The Emperor Jones*, when Smithers grabs a black woman and says, "Easy! None o' that, me birdie. You can't wriggle out now. I got me 'ooks on yer," O'Neill reveals a good deal about Smithers: his Cockney birth, his inclination toward violence, and his contempt for blacks. And now that Jones's hours as Emperor are numbered, Smithers, though essentially a coward, is impudent and even openly angry with Jones, who recognizes the change in tone and imperiously warns, "Talk polite, white man!" Smithers, understanding the pressure in Jones's words, lapses into a cringing "No 'arm meant, old top." Within a few minutes O'Neill has let us see and hear exactly what sort of man Smithers is. The language is fully dramatic: (1) it can be spoken effectively by an actor, though the dialect is a bit tiresome in print; and (2) it seems to proceed not from O'Neill the author but from the specific characters. Notice, too, that the *amount* of dialogue is meaningful. After the first scene, the play is almost a monologue spoken by Jones, but he becomes increasingly inarticulate, so that the confident talkative Emperor of the first scene is pretty much reduced by the seventh scene to repeating a few clichés, "Oh, Lawd pertect dis sinner," "Mercy, Lawd, Mercy." What he is unable to say is as much a part of the play's meaning as what he does say.

This diminution in speech as Jones becomes increasingly terrified, and as "civilization" (e.g., the confidence and cunning by which he deceived his subjects) is peeled from him along with his uniform, works along with the play's structure, the arrangement of scenes. Three scenes of increasing terror to Jones take place in the Great Forest: First, "little formless fears," then the memory of the murder of Jeff, and then the memory of the murder of the prison guard. The next three scenes are more terrifying, and they are from sources deeper than Jones's own experience. They are racial memories of a slave auction in Amer-

PLOT AND STRUCTURE

ica, of a slave ship, and, earliest of all, of an African ceremony in which Jones is to be the sacrificial victim. We have moved backward to the very beginnings of man's experience. As the play moves forward, stripping Jones of all flimsy accretions, reducing the once proud emperor to a whimpering motionless creature face down on the ground, we learn that Jones's flight through the forest has brought him back to the very point at which he entered the forest. Smithers sees in this only the meaningless fact that Jones ran in a circle, but we can perhaps see in it a further suggestion: Jones's life had run its course; at birth he came inarticulate and naked from the dark, and at death he returns inarticulate and naked to the dark. Possibly, too, we can say that there is a sort of circularity implied in the fact that he lived by robbing his subjects of their money, and he died by money, for the natives shoot him with a silver bullet made by melting coins. No one wants to reduce the play to a neat moral, but surely in dramatic form it sets forth, among other things, the idea that there are mysterious connections in life, that if the pattern is obscure, there nevertheless is a pattern, and here the pattern suggests something like "Those who live by silver die by silver." (For further comments on this sort of tragic pattern, see the discussions of peripeteia on page 6 and of irony in the glossary, page 699.)

Finally, what sort of man *is* Jones? The best answer is that he is what the play says he is, and it says this through scenery, gestures, sound effects, dialogue, contrasting characters, arrangement of scenes, etc., in short, through ev-

CHARACTER

erything in the play. Still, we can hazard a few rough comments. First, notice that O'Neill makes him a very specific black man, not simply a type. Among the stock dramatic types available to O'Neill in 1920, the chief were the Tom (faithful colored retainer), the Buffoon (clownish lazy servant), the Bull (villain who wants to rape white women), and the Tragic Mulatto (hovering between two races). Almost all depictions of blacks on the American stage of the time fall into these classifications. O'Neill, in a remarkable step forward in the history of American drama, and therefore in the history of American thought, used none of these stereotypes. (In *The Emperor Jones* the lazy man is not the black, who diligently learned the language of the islanders and who for two years has worked hard and efficiently at his job of robbing his subjects; the lazy man is the white man, Smithers, who in ten years has not bothered to learn the language.) Today, more than fifty years after O'Neill wrote the play, inevitably we are disturbed by some racist implications in the play, but O'Neill was far ahead of most whites of his time in presenting a black whose face showed "an underlying strength of will, a hardy, self-reliant confidence," and whose eyes showed "a keen, cunning intelligence." If these words put us in mind of any type, it is, paradoxically, the rugged white individualist who was so worshipped in the nineteenth and early twentieth centuries. O'Neill gives us not a stereotyped black man (and none of the stereotypes was flattering), but a fresh conception, a black who has the virtues and faults of white society, of America as it was and is, and perhaps of mankind. (The very name "Jones" suggests Everyman — though "Brutus" adds to it both a sense of high Roman dignity and a sense of grotesque incongruity.) Jones is quite explicit about his code: his aim is to get rich in the great white man's way, by hard work and by cunning immorality on a grand scale.

> You heah what I tells you, Smithers. Dere's little stealin' like you does, and dere's big stealin' like I does. For de little stealin' dey gits you in jail soon or late. For de big stealin' dey makes you Emperor and puts you in de Hall o' Fame when you croaks. (*Reminiscently.*) If dey's one thing I learns in ten years on de Pullman ca's listenin' to de white quality talk, it's dat same fact. And when I gits a chance to use it I winds up Emperor in two years.

Smithers is no less unscrupulous or cruel than Jones is, but he simply does not have Jones's courage, perseverance, intelligence, and vision. In short, O'Neill gives us a fresh, fully realized picture of believable human beings and we should not be deceived by the funny spelling into thinking that Jones is the conventional black man of the stage up to O'Neill's time.

What does it add up to? Something has already been said about the theme or underlying idea or meaning of the play. Some critics, arguing that the concept of theme is meaningless, hold that any play gives us only an extremely detailed history of some imaginary people. But surely this view is desperate. We *can* say that we see in *The Emperor Jones* something of the savagery of our so-called civilization, and, on the other hand, something of the grandeur that may transfigure pride. (As O'Neill says in a stage direction, Jones "has a way of carrying it off," and at the end of the play Smithers grants that Jones died "in the 'eighth o' style.") To the reply that these are mere truisms, we can counter: Yes, but the truisms are presented in such a way that they take on life and become a part of us rather than remain things of which we say, "I've heard it said, and I guess it's so." And surely we are in no danger of equating the play with the theme that we sense underlies it. We never believe that our statement of the theme is really the equivalent of the play itself. The play, we recognize, presents the theme with such detail that our statement of the theme is only a wedge that helps us to enter the play so that we may more fully (in Henry James's word) "appropriate" it.

THEME

THE EMPEROR JONES

Eugene O'Neill

Eugene O'Neill (1888–1953), the son of an actor, was born in a hotel room near Broadway and spent his early years traveling with his parents throughout the United States. He entered Princeton University in 1906 but left before the end of the first year. In 1909 he traveled to Honduras looking for gold, contracted malaria, and returned to the United States in 1910. After touring briefly with his father's company, he shipped to Buenos Aires, jumped ship there, did odd jobs, shipped to South Africa, and returned to the United States in 1911. The following year he learned that he had tuberculosis. In a sanatorium he began seriously reading plays, and in 1916 he joined the Provincetown Players, who put on some of his one-act plays. *The Emperor Jones* (1920), produced by the Provincetown Players in New York, was his first major play. In time he was awarded four Pulitzer Prizes (one, posthumous, was for *A Long Day's Journey into Night*, written in 1940, but not produced until 1955), and a Nobel Prize.

CHARACTERS

BRUTUS JONES, *Emperor*
HENRY SMITHERS, *A Cockney Trader*
AN OLD NATIVE WOMAN
LEM, *A Native Chief*
SOLDIERS, *Adherents of Lem*
THE LITTLE FORMLESS FEARS
JEFF

THE NEGRO CONVICTS
THE PRISON GUARD
THE PLANTERS
THE AUCTIONEER
THE SLAVES
THE CONGO WITCH-DOCTOR
THE CROCODILE GOD

The action of the play takes place on an island in the West Indies as yet not self-determined by white Marines. The form of native government is, for the time being, an empire.

Paul Chevalier as Smithers and Habib Benglia as Jones in a 1949 production of *The Emperor Jones* in Paris. (Photograph: Bernand.)

SCENE I

Scene — The audience chamber in the palace of the Emperor — a spacious, high-ceilinged room with bare, white-washed walls. The floor is of white tiles. In the rear, to the left of center, a wide archway giving out on a portico with white pillars. The palace is evidently situated on high ground for beyond the portico nothing can be seen but a vista of distant hills, their summits crowned with thick groves of palm trees. In the right wall, center, a smaller arched doorway leading to the living quarters of the palace. The room is bare of furniture with the exception of one huge chair made of uncut wood which stands at center, its back to rear. This is very apparently the Emperor's throne. It is painted a dazzling, eye-smiting scarlet. There is a brilliant orange cushion on the seat and another smaller one is placed on the floor to serve as a footstool. Strips of matting, dyed scarlet, lead from the foot of the throne to the two entrances.

It is late afternoon but the sunlight still blazes yellowly beyond the portico and there is an oppressive burden of exhausting heat in the air.

As the curtain rises, a native Negro woman sneaks in cautiously from the entrance on the right. She is very old, dressed in cheap calico, bare-footed, a red bandana handkerchief covering all but a few stray wisps of white hair. A bundle bound in colored cloth is carried

over her shoulder on the end of a stick. She hesitates beside the doorway, peering back as if in extreme dread of being discovered. Then she begins to glide noiselessly, a step at a time, toward the doorway in the rear. At this moment, SMITHERS *appears beneath the portico.*

SMITHERS *is a tall, stoop-shouldered man about forty. His bald head, perched on a long neck with an enormous Adam's apple, looks like an egg. The tropics have tanned his naturally pasty face with its small, sharp features to a sickly yellow, and native rum has painted his pointed nose to a startling red. His little, washy-blue eyes are red-rimmed and dart about him like a ferret's. His expression is one of unscrupulous meanness, cowardly and dangerous. He is dressed in a worn riding suit of dirty white drill, puttees, spurs, and wears a white cork helmet. A cartridge belt with an automatic revolver is around his waist. He carries a riding whip in his hand. He sees the woman and stops to watch her suspiciously. Then, making up his mind, he steps quickly on tiptoe into the room. The woman, looking back over her shoulder continually, does not see him until it is too late. When she does* SMITHERS *springs forward and grabs her firmly by the shoulder. She struggles to get away, fiercely but silently.*

SMITHERS (*tightening his grasp — roughly*): Easy! None o' that, me birdie. You can't wriggle out now. I got me 'ooks on yer.

WOMAN (*seeing the uselessness of struggling, gives way to frantic terror, and sinks to the ground, embracing his knees supplicatingly*): No tell him! No tell him, Mister!

SMITHERS (*with great curiosity*): Tell 'im? (*Then scornfully.*) Oh, you mean 'is bloomin' Majesty. What's the gaime, any 'ow? What are you sneakin' away for? Been stealin' a bit, I s'pose. (*He taps her bundle with his riding whip significantly.*)

WOMAN (*shaking her head vehemently*): No, me no steal.

SMITHERS: Bloody liar! But tell me what's up. There's somethin' funny goin' on. I smelled it in the air first thing I got up this mornin'.

You blacks are up to some devilment. This palace of 'is is like a bleedin' tomb. Where's all the 'ands?

(*The woman keeps sullenly silent.* SMITHERS *raises his whip threateningly.*)

Ow, yer won't, won't yer? I'll show yer what's what.

WOMAN (*coweringly*): I tell, Mister. You no hit. They go — all go. (*She makes a sweeping gesture toward the hills in the distance.*)

SMITHERS: Run away — to the 'ills?

WOMAN: Yes, Mister. Him Emperor — Great Father. (*She touches her forehead to the floor with a quick mechanical jerk.*) Him sleep after eat. Then they go — all go. Me old woman. Me left only. Now me go too.

SMITHERS (*his astonishment giving way to an immense, mean satisfaction*): Ow! So that's the ticket! Well, I know bloody well wot's in the air — when they runs orf to the 'ills. The tom-tom 'll be thumping out there bloomin' soon. (*With extreme vindictiveness.*) And I'm bloody glad of it, for one! Serve 'im right! Puttin' on airs, the stinkin' nigger! 'Is Majesty! Gawd blimey! I only 'opes I'm there when they takes 'im out to shoot 'im. (*Suddenly.*) 'E's still 'ere all right, ain't 'e?

WOMAN: Yes. Him sleep.

SMITHERS: 'E's bound to find out soon as 'e wakes up. 'E's cunnin' enough to know when 'is time's come.

(*He goes to the doorway on right and whistles shrilly with his fingers in his mouth. The old woman springs to her feet and runs out of the doorway, rear.* SMITHERS *goes after her, reaching for his revolver.*)

Stop or I'll shoot! (*Then stopping — indifferently.*) Pop orf then, if yer like, yer black cow. (*He stands in the doorway, looking after her.*)

(JONES *enters from the right. He is a tall, powerfully-built, full-blooded Negro of middle age. His features are typically negroid, yet there is something decidedly distinctive about his face — an underlying strength of will, a hardy, self-reliant confidence in himself that inspires respect. His eyes are alive with a keen, cunning intelligence. In manner he is shrewd, suspicious, evasive. He wears a light blue uniform coat, sprayed with brass buttons, heavy gold chevrons on his shoulders, gold braid on the collar, cuffs, etc. His pants are bright red with a light blue stripe down the side. Patent-leather laced boots with brass spurs, and a belt with a long-barreled, pearl-handled revolver in a holster complete his make up. Yet there is something not altogether ridiculous about his grandeur. He has a way of carrying it off.*)

JONES (*not seeing anyone — greatly irritated and blinking sleepily — shouts*): Who dare whistle dat way in my palace? Who dare wake up de Emperor? I'll git de hide fravled off some o' you niggers sho'!

SMITHERS (*showing himself — in a manner half-afraid and half-defiant*): It was me whistled to yer. (*As* JONES *frowns angrily.*) I got news for yer.

JONES (*putting on his suavest manner, which fails to cover up his contempt for the white man*): Oh, it's you, Mister Smithers. (*He sits down on his throne with easy dignity.*) What news you got to tell me?

SMITHERS (*coming close to enjoy his discomfiture*): Don't yer notice nothin' funny today?

JONES (*coldly*): Funny? No. I ain't perceived nothin' of de kind!

SMITHERS: Then yer ain't so foxy as I thought yer was. Where's all your court? (*Sarcastically.*) The Generals and the Cabinet Ministers and all?

JONES (*imperturbably*): Where dey mostly runs de minute I closes my eyes — drinkin' rum and talkin' big down in de town. (*Sarcastically.*) How come you don't know dat? Ain't you sousin' with 'em most every day?

SMITHERS (*stung but pretending indifference — with a wink*): That's part of the day's work. I got ter — ain't I — in my business?

JONES (*contemptuously*): Yo' business!

SMITHERS (*imprudently enraged*): Gawd blimey, you was glad enough for me ter take yer in on it when you landed here first. You didn' 'ave no 'igh and mighty airs in them days!

JONES (*his hand going to his revolver like a flash — menacingly*): Talk polite, white man! Talk polite, you heah me! I'm boss heah now, is you fergettin'? (*The Cockney seems about to challenge this last statement with the facts but something in the other's eyes holds and cows him.*)

SMITHERS (*in a cowardly whine*): No 'arm meant, old top.

JONES (*condescendingly*): I accepts yo' apology. (*Lets his hand fall from his revolver.*) No use'n you rakin' up ole times. What I was den is one thing. What I is now's another. You didn't let me in on yo' crooked work out o' no kind feelin's dat time. I done de dirty work fo' you — and most o' de brain work, too, fo' dat matter — and I was wu'th money to you, dat's de reason.

SMITHERS: Well, blimey, I give yer a start, didn't I — when no one else would. I wasn't afraid to 'ire yer like the rest was — 'count of the story about your breakin' jail back in the States.

JONES: No, you didn't have no s'cuse to look down on me fo' dat. You been in jail you'self more'n once.

SMITHERS (furiously): It's a lie! (Then trying to pass it off by an attempt at scorn.) Garn! Who told yer that fairy tale?

JONES: Dey's some tings I ain't got to be tole. I kin see 'em in folk's eyes. (Then after a pause — meditatively.) Yes, you sho' give me a start. And it didn't take long from dat time to git dese fool, woods' niggers right where I wanted dem. (With pride.) From stowaway to Emperor in two years! Dat's goin' some!

SMITHERS (with curiosity): And I bet you got yer pile o'money 'id safe some place.

JONES (with satisfaction): I sho' has! And it's in a foreign bank where no pusson don't ever git it out but me no matter what come. You didn't s'pose I was holdin' down dis Emperor job for de glory in it, did you? Sho'! De fuss and glory part of it, dat's only to turn de heads o' de low-flung, bush niggers dat's here. Dey wants de big circus show for deir money. I gives it to 'em an' I gits de money. (With a grin.) De long green, dat's me every time! (Then rebukingly.) But you ain't got no kick agin me, Smithers. I'se paid you back all you done for me many times. Ain't I pertected you and winked at all de crooked tradin' you been doin' right out in de broad day? Sho' I has — and me makin' laws to stop it at de same time! (He chuckles.)

SMITHERS (grinning): But, meanin' no 'arm, you been grabbin' right and left yourself, ain't yer? Look at the taxes you've put on 'em! Blimey! You've squeezed 'em dry!

JONES (chuckling): No, dey ain't all dry yet. I'se still heah, ain't I?

SMITHERS (smiling at his secret thought): They're dry right now, you'll find out. (Changing the subject abruptly.) And as for me breakin' laws, you've broke 'em all yerself just as fast as yer made 'em.

JONES: Ain't I de Emperor? De laws don't go for him. (Judicially.) You heah what I tells

you, Smithers. Dere's little stealin' like you does, and dere's big stealin' like I does. For de little stealin' dey gits you in jail soon or late. For de big stealin' dey makes you Emperor and puts you in de Hall o' Fame when you croaks. (Reminiscently.) If dey's one thing I learns in ten years on de Pullman ca's listenin' to de white quality talk, it's dat same fact. And when I gits a chance to use it I winds up Emperor in two years.

SMITHERS (unable to repress the genuine admiration of the small fry for the large): Yes, yer turned the bleedin' trick, all right. Blimey, I never seen a bloke 'as 'ad the bloomin' luck you 'as.

JONES (severely): Luck? What you mean — luck?

SMITHERS: I suppose you'll say as that swank about the silver bullet ain't luck — and that was what first got the fool blacks on yer side the time of the revolution, wasn't it?

JONES (with a laugh): Oh, dat silver bullet! Sho' was luck! But I makes dat luck, you heah? I loads de dice! Yessuh! When dat murderin' nigger ole Lem hired to kill me takes aim ten feet away and his gun misses fire and I shoots him dead, what you heah me say?

SMITHERS: You said yer'd got a charm so's no lead bullet'd kill yer. You was so strong only a silver bullet could kill yer, you told 'em. Blimey, wasn't that swank for yer — and plain, fat-'eaded luck?

JONES (proudly): I got brains and I uses 'em quick. Dat ain't luck.

SMITHERS: Yer know they wasn't 'ardly liable to get no silver bullets. And it was luck 'e didn't 'it you that time.

JONES (laughing): And dere all dem fool, bush niggers was kneelin' down and bumpin' deir heads on de ground like I was a miracle out o' de Bible. Oh Lawd, from dat time on I has dem all eatin' out of my hand. I cracks de whip and dey jumps through.

SMITHERS (with a sniff): Yankee bluff done it.

JONES: Ain't a man's talkin' big what makes him big — long as he makes folks believe it? Sho', I talks large when I ain't got nothin' to back it up, but I ain't talkin' wild just de same. I knows I kin fool 'em — I knows it — and dat's backin' enough fo' my game. And ain't I got to learn deir lingo and teach some of dem English befo' I kin talk to 'em? Ain't dat wuk? You ain't never learned ary word er it, Smithers, in de ten years you been heah, dough yo' knows it's money in yo' pocket tradin' wid 'em if you does. But you'se too shiftless to take de trouble.

SMITHERS (*flushing*): Never mind about me. What's this I've 'eard about yer really 'avin' a silver bullet moulded for yourself?

JONES: It's playin' out my bluff. I has de silver bullet moulded and I tells 'em when de time comes I kills myself wid it. I tells 'em dat's 'cause I'm de on'y man in de world big enuff to git me. No use'n deir tryin'. And dey falls down and bumps deir heads. (*He laughs.*) I does dat so's I kin take a walk in peace widout no jealous nigger gunnin' at me from behind de trees.

SMITHERS (*astonished*): Then you 'ad it made — 'onest?

JONES: Sho' did. Heah she be. (*He takes out his revolver, breaks it, and takes the silver bullet out of one chamber.*) Five lead an' dis silver baby at de last. Don't she shine pretty? (*He holds it in his hand, looking at it admiringly, as if strangely fascinated.*)

SMITHERS: Let me see. (*Reaches out his hand for it.*)

JONES (*harshly*): Keep yo' hands whar dey b'long, white man. (*He replaces it in the chamber and puts the revolver back on his hip.*)

SMITHERS (*snarling*): Gawd blimey! Think I'm a bleedin' thief, you would.

JONES: No, 'tain't dat. I knows you'se scared to steal from me. On'y I ain't 'lowin' nary body to touch dis baby. She's my rabbit's foot.

SMITHERS (*sneering*): A bloomin' charm, wot? (*Venomously.*) Well, you'll need all the bloody charms you 'as before long, s' 'elp me!

JONES (*judicially*): Oh, I'se good for six months yit 'fore dey gits sick o' my game. Den, when I sees trouble comin', I makes my getaway.

SMITHERS: Ho! You got it all planned, ain't yer?

JONES: I ain't no fool. I knows dis Emperor's time is sho't. Dat why I make hay when de sun shine. Was you thinkin' I'se aimin' to hold down dis job for life? No, suh! What good is gittin' money if you stays back in dis raggedy country? I wants action when I spends. And when I sees dese niggers gittin' up deir nerve to tu'n me out, and I'se got all de money in sight, I resigns on de spot and beats it quick.

SMITHERS: Where to?

JONES: None o' yo' business.

SMITHERS: Not back to the bloody States, I'll lay my oath.

JONES (*suspiciously*): Why don't I? (*Then with an easy laugh.*) You mean 'count of dat story 'bout me breakin' from jail back dere? Dat's all talk.

SMITHERS (*skeptically*): Ho, yes!

JONES (*sharply*): You ain't 'sinuatin' I'se a liar, is you?

SMITHERS (*hastily*): No, Gawd strike me! I was only thinkin' o' the bloody lies you told the blacks 'ere about killin' white men in the States.

JONES (*angered*): How come dey're lies?

SMITHERS: You'd 'ave been in jail if you 'ad, wouldn't yer then? (*With venom.*) And from what I've 'eard, it ain't 'ealthy for a black to kill a white man in the States. They burns 'em in oil, don't they?

JONES (*with cool deadliness*): You mean lynchin' 'd scare me? Well, I tells you, Smithers, maybe I does kill one white man back dere. Maybe I does. And maybe I kills another right heah 'fore long if he don't look out.

SMITHERS (*trying to force a laugh*): I was on'y spoofin' yer. Can't yer take a joke? And you was just sayin' you'd never been in jail.

JONES (*in the same tone — slightly boastful*): Maybe I goes to jail dere for gettin' in an argument wid razors ovah a crap game. Maybe I gits twenty years when dat colored man die. Maybe I gits in 'nother argument wid de prison guard was overseer ovah us when we're wukin' de roads. Maybe he hits me wid a whip and I splits his head wid a shovel and runs away and files de chain off my leg and gits away safe. Maybe I does all dat an' maybe I don't. It's a story I tells you so's you knows I'se de kind of man dat if you evah repeats one word of it, I ends yo' stealin' on dis yearth mighty damn quick!

SMITHERS (*terrified*): Think I'd peach on yer? Not me! Ain't I always been yer friend?

JONES (*suddenly relaxing*): Sho' you has — and you better be.

SMITHERS (*recovering his composure — and with it his malice*): And just to show yer I'm yer friend, I'll tell yer that bit o' news I was goin' to.

JONES: Go ahead! Shoot de piece. Must be bad news from de happy way you look.

SMITHERS (*warningly*): Maybe it's gettin' time for you to resign — with that bloomin' silver bullet, wot? (*He finishes with a mocking grin.*)

JONES (*puzzled*): What's dat you say? Talk plain.

SMITHERS: Ain't noticed any of the guards or servants about the place today, I 'aven't.

JONES (*carelessly*): Dey're all out in de garden sleepin' under de trees. When I sleeps, dey sneaks a sleep, too, and I pretends I never suspicions it. All I got to do is to ring de bell and dey come flyin', makin' a bluff dey was wukin' all de time.

SMITHERS (*in the same mocking tone*): Ring the bell now an' you'll bloody well see what I means.

JONES (*startled to alertness, but preserving the same careless tone*): Sho' I rings. (*He reaches below the throne and pulls out a big, common dinner bell which is painted the same vivid scarlet as the throne. He rings this vigorously — then stops to listen. Then he goes to both doors, rings again, and looks out.*)

SMITHERS (*watching him with malicious satisfaction, after a pause — mockingly*): The bloody ship is sinkin' an' the bleedin' rats 'as slung their 'ooks.

JONES (*in a sudden fit of anger flings the bell clattering into a corner*): Low-flung, woods' niggers! (*Then catching* SMITHERS' *eye on him, he controls himself and suddenly bursts into a low chuckling laugh.*) Reckon I overplays my hand dis once! A man can't take de pot on a bob-tailed flush all de time. Was I sayin' I'd sit in six months mo'? Well, I'se changed my mind den. I cashes in and resigns de job of Emperor right dis minute.

SMITHERS (*with real admiration*): Blimey, but you're a cool bird, and no mistake.

JONES: No use'n fussin'. When I knows de game's up I kisses it good-bye widout no long waits. Dey've all run off to de hills, ain't dey?

SMITHERS: Yes — every bleedin' man jack of 'em.

JONES: Den de revolution is at de post. And de Emperor better git his feet smokin' up de trail. (*He starts for the door in rear.*)

SMITHERS: Goin' out to look for your 'orse? Yer won't find any. They steals the 'orses first thing. Mine was gone when I went for 'im this mornin'. That's wot first give me a suspicion of wot was up.

JONES (*alarmed for a second, scratches his head, then philosophically*): Well, den I hoofs it. Feet, do yo' duty! (*He pulls out a gold watch and looks at it.*) Three-thuty. Sundown's at six-thuty or dereabouts. (*Puts his watch back — with cool confidence.*) I got plenty o' time to make it easy.

SMITHERS: Don't be so bloomin' sure of it. They'll be after you 'ot and 'eavy. Ole Lem is at the bottom o' this business an' 'e 'ates you like 'ell. 'E'd rather do for you than eat 'is dinner, 'e would!

JONES (*scornfully*): Dat fool no-count nigger! Does you think I'se scared o' him? I stands him on his thick head more'n once befo' dis, and I does it again if he come in my way . . . (*Fiercely.*) And dis time I leave him a dead nigger fo' sho'!

SMITHERS: You'll 'ave to cut through the big forest — an' these blacks 'ere can sniff and follow a trail in the dark like 'ounds. You'd 'ave to 'ustle to get through that forest in twelve hours even if you knew all the bloomin' trails like a native.

JONES (*with indignant scorn*): Look-a-heah, white man! Does you think I'se a natural bo'n fool? Give me credit fo' havin' some sense, fo' Lawd's sake! Don't you s'pose I'se looked ahead and made sho' of all de chances? I'se gone out in dat big forest, pretendin' to hunt, so many times dat I knows it high an' low like a book. I could go through on dem trails wid my eyes shut. (*With great contempt.*) Think dese ign'rent bush niggers dat ain't got brains enuff to know deir own names even can catch Brutus Jones? Huh, I s'pects not! Not on yo' life! Why, man, de white men went after me wid bloodhounds where I come from an' I jes' laughs at 'em. It's a shame to fool dese black trash around heah, dey're so easy. You watch me, man! I'll make dem look sick, I will. I'll be 'cross de plain to de edge of de forest by time dark comes. Once in de woods in de night, dey got a swell chance o' findin' dis baby! Dawn tomorrow I'll be out at de oder side and on de coast whar dat French gunboat is stayin'. She picks me up, take me to Martinique when she go dar, and dere I is safe wid a mighty big bankroll in my jeans. It's easy as rollin' off a log.

SMITHERS (*maliciously*): But s'posin' somethin' 'appens wrong an' they do nab yer?

JONES (*decisively*): Dey don't — dat's de answer.

SMITHERS: But, just for argyment's sake — what'd you do?

JONES (*frowning*): I'se got five lead bullets in dis gun good enuff fo' common bush niggers — and after dat I got de silver bullet left to cheat 'em out o' gittin' me.

SMITHERS (*jeeringly*): Ho, I was fergettin' that silver bullet. You'll bump yourself orf in style, won't yer? Blimey!

JONES (*gloomily*): You kin bet yo' whole roll on one thing, white man. Dis baby plays out his string to de end and when he quits, he quits wid a bang de way he ought. Silver bullet ain't none too good for him when he go, dat's a fac'! (*Then shaking off his nervousness — with a confident laugh.*) Sho'! What is I talkin' about? Ain't come to dat yit and I never will — not wid trash niggers like dese yer. (*Boastfully.*) Silver bullet bring me luck anyway. I kin outguess, outrun, outfight, an' outplay de whole lot o' dem all ovah de board any time o' de day er night! You watch me!

(*From the distant hills comes the faint, steady thump of a tom-tom, low and vibrating. It starts at a rate exactly corresponding to normal pulse beat — 72 to the minute — and continues at a gradually accelerating rate from this point uninterruptedly to the very end of the play.*

JONES starts at the sound. A strange look of apprehension creeps into his face for a moment as he listens. Then he asks, with an attempt to regain his most casual manner.)

What's dat drum beatin' fo'?

SMITHERS (*with a mean grin*): For you. That means the bleedin' ceremony 'as started. I've 'eard it before and I knows.

JONES: Cer'mony? What cer'mony?

SMITHERS: The blacks is 'oldin' a bloody meetin', 'avin' a war dance, gettin' their courage worked up b'fore they starts after you.

JONES: Let dem! Dey'll sho' need it!

SMITHERS: And they're there 'oldin' their 'eathen religious service — makin' no end of devil spells and charms to 'elp 'em against your silver bullet. (*He guffaws loudly.*) Blimey, but they're balmy as 'ell!

JONES (*a tiny bit awed and shaken in spite of himself*): Huh! Takes more'n dat to scare dis chicken!

SMITHERS (*scenting the other's feeling — maliciously*): Ternight when it's pitch black in the forest, they'll 'ave their pet devils and ghosts 'oundin' after you. You'll find yer bloody 'air 'll be standin' on end before termorrow mornin'. (*Seriously.*) It's a bleedin' queer place, that stinkin' forest, even in daylight. Yer don't know what might 'appen in there, it's that rotten still. Always sends the cold shivers down my back minute I gets in it.

JONES (*with a contemptuous sniff*): I an't no chicken-liver like you is. Trees an' me, we'se

friends, and dar's a full moon comin' bring me light. And let dem po' niggers make all de fool spells dey'se a min' to. Does yo' s'pect I'se silly enuff to b'lieve in ghosts an' ha'nts an' all dat ole woman's talk? G'long, white man! You ain't talkin' to me. (*With a chuckle.*) Doesn't you know dey's got to do wid a man was member in good standin' o' de Baptist Church? Sho' I was dat when I was porter on de Pullmans, befo' I gits into my little trouble. Let dem try deir heathen tricks. De Baptist Church done pertect me and land dem all in hell. (*Then with more confident satisfaction.*) And I'se got little silver bullet o' my own, don't forgit.

SMITHERS: Ho! You 'aven't give much 'eed to your Baptist Church since you been down 'ere. I've 'eard myself you 'ad turned yer coat an' was takin' up with their blarsted witch-doctors, or whatever the 'ell yer calls the swine.

JONES (*vehemently*): I pretends to! Sho' I pretends! Dat's part o' my game from de fust. If I finds out dem niggers believes dat black is white, den I yells it out louder 'n deir loudest. It don't git me nothin' to do missionary work for de Baptist Church. I'se after de coin, an' I lays my Jesus on de shelf for de time bein'. (*Stops abruptly to look at his watch — alertly.*) But I ain't got de time to waste no more fool talk wid you. I'se gwine away from heah dis secon'. (*He reaches in under the throne and pulls out an expensive Panama hat with a bright multi-colored band and sets it jauntily on his head.*) So long, white man! (*With a grin.*) See you in jail sometime, maybe!

SMITHERS: Not me, you won't. Well, I wouldn't be in yer bloody boots for no bloomin' money, but 'ere's wishin' yer luck just the same.

JONES (*contemptuously*): Yo're de frightenedest man evah I see! I tells you I'se safe's 'f I was in New York City. It takes dem niggers from now to dark to git up de nerve to start somethin'. By dat time, I'se got a head start dey never kotch up wid.

SMITHERS (*maliciously*): Give my regards to any ghosts yer meets up with.

JONES (*grinning*): If dat ghost got money, I'll tell him never ha'nt you less'n he wants to lose it.

SMITHERS (*flattered*): Garn! (*Then curiously.*) Ain't yer takin' no luggage with yer?

JONES: I travels light when I wants to move fast. And I got tinned grub buried on de edge o' de forest. (*Boastfully.*) Now say dat I don't look ahead an' use my brains! (*With a wide, liberal gesture.*) I will all dat's left in de palace to you — and you better grab all you kin sneak away wid befo' dey gits here.

SMITHERS (*gratefully*): Righto — and thanks ter yer. (*As* JONES *walks toward the door in rear — cautioningly.*) Say! Look 'ere, you ain't goin 'out that way, are yer?

JONES: Does you think I'd slink out de back door like a common nigger? I'se Emperor yit, ain't I? And de Emperor Jones leaves de way he comes, and dat black trash don't dare stop him — not yit, leastways. (*He stops for a moment in the doorway, listening to the far-off but insistent beat of the tom-tom.*) Listen to dat roll-call, will you? Must be mighty big drum carry dat far. (*Then with a laugh.*) Well, if dey ain't no whole brass band to see me off, I sho' got de drum part of it. So long, white man. (*He puts his hands in his pockets and with studied carelessness, whistling a tune, he saunters out of the doorway and off to the left.*)

SMITHERS (*looks after him with a puzzled admiration*): 'E's got 'is bloomin' nerve with 'im, s'elp me! (*Then angrily.*) Ho — the bleedin' nigger — puttin' on 'is bloody airs! I 'opes they nabs 'im an' gives 'im what's what! (*Then putting business before the pleasure of this thought, looking around him with cupidity.*) A bloke ought to find a 'ole lot in this palace that'd go for a bit of cash. Let's take a look, 'Arry, me lad. (*He starts for the doorway on right as*

THE CURTAIN FALLS

SCENE II

Scene — Nightfall. The end of the plain where the Great Forest begins. The foreground is sandy, level ground dotted by a few stones and clumps of stunted bushes covering close against the earth to escape the buffeting of the trade wind. In the rear the forest is a wall of darkness dividing the world. Only when the eye becomes accustomed to the gloom can the outlines of separate trunks of the nearest trees be made out, enormous pillars of deeper blackness. A somber monotone of wind lost in the leaves moans in the air. Yet this sound serves but to intensify the impression of the forest's relentless immo-bility, to form a background throwing into relief its brooding, implacable silence.

JONES *enters from the left, walking rapidly. He stops as he nears the edge of the forest, looks around him quickly, peering into the dark as if searching for some familiar landmark. Then, apparently, satisfied that he is where he ought to be, he throws himself on the ground, dog-tired.*

Well, heah I is. In de nick o' time, too! Little mo' an' it'd be blacker'n de ace of spades heahabouts. (*He pulls a bandana handkerchief from his hip pocket and mops off his perspiring face.*) Sho'! Gimme air! I'se tuckered out sho' nuff. Dat soft Emperor job ain't no trainin' fo' a long hike ovah dat plain in de brilin' sun. (*Then with a chuckle.*) Cheah up, nigger, de worst is yet to come. (*He lifts his head and stares at the forest. His chuckle peters out abruptly. In a tone of awe.*) My goodness, look at dem woods, will you? Dat no-count Smithers said dey'd be black an' he sho' called de turn. (*Turning away from them quickly and looking down at his feet, he snatches at a chance to change the subject — solicitously.*) Feet, you is holdin' up yo' end fine an' I sutinly hopes you ain't blisterin' none. It's time you git a rest. (*He takes off his shoes, his eyes studiously avoiding the forest. He feels of the soles of his feet gingerly.*) You is still in de pink — on'y a little mite feverish. Cool yo'selfs. Remember you done got a long journey yit befo' you. (*He sits in a weary attitude, listening to the rhythmic beating of the tom-tom. He grumbles in a loud tone to cover up a growing uneasiness.*) Bush niggers! Wonder dey wouldn' get sick o' beatin' dat drum. Sound louder, seem like. I wonder if dey's startin' after me? (*He scrambles to his feet, looking back across the plain.*) Couldn't see dem now, nohow, if dey was hundred feet away. (*Then shaking himself like a wet dog to get rid of these depressing thoughts.*) Sho', dey's miles an' miles behind. What you gittin' fidgety about? (*But he sits down and begins to lace up his shoes in great haste, all the time muttering reassuringly.*) You know what? Yo' belly is empty, dat's what's de matter wid you. Come time to eat! Wid nothin' but wind on yo' stumach, o' course you feels jiggedy. Well, we eats right heah an' now soon's I gits dese pesky shoes laced up! (*He finishes lacing up his shoes.*) Dere! Now le's see. (*Gets on his hands and knees and searches the* ground around him with his eyes.) White stone, white stone, where is you? (*He sees the first white stone and crawls to it — with satisfaction.*) Heah you is! I knowed dis was de right place. Box of grub, come to me. (*He turns over the stone and feels in under it — in a tone of dismay.*) Ain't heah! Gorry, is I in de right place or isn't I? Dere's 'nother stone. Guess dat's it. (*He scrambles to the next stone and turns it over.*) Ain't heah, neither! Grub, whar is you? Ain't heah. Gorry, has I got to go hungry into dem woods — all de night? (*While he is talking he scrambles from one stone to another, turning them over in frantic haste. Finally, he jumps to his feet excitedly.*) Is I lost de place? Must have! But how dat happen when I was followin' de trail across de plain in broad daylight? (*Almost plaintively.*) I'se hungry, I is! I gotta git my feed. Whar's my strength gonna come from if I doesn't? Gorry, I gotta find dat grub high an' low somehow! Why it come dark so quick like dat? Can't see nothin'. (*He scratches a match on his trousers and peers about him. The rate of the beat of the far-off tom-tom increases perceptibly as he does so. He mutters in a bewildered voice.*) How come all dese white stones come heah when I only remembers one? (*Suddenly, with a frightened gasp, he flings the match on the ground and stamps on it.*) Nigger, is you gone crazy mad? Is you lightin' matches to show dem whar you is? Fo' Lawd's sake, use yo' haid. Gorry, I'se got to be careful! (*He stares at the plain behind him apprehensively, his hand on his revolver.*) But how come all dese white stones? And whar's dat tin box o' grub I had all wrapped up in oil cloth?

(*While his back is turned,* THE LITTLE FORMLESS FEARS *creep out from the deeper blackness of the forest. They are black, shapeless, only their glittering little eyes can be seen. If they have any describable form at all it is that of a grubworm about the size of a creeping child. They move noiselessly, but with deliberate, painful effort, striving to raise themselves on end, failing and sinking prone again.* JONES *turns about to face the forest. He stares up at the tops of the trees, seeking vainly to discover his whereabouts by their conformation.*)

Can't tell nothin' from dem trees! Gorry, nothin' 'round heah look like I evah seed it

befo'. I'se done lost de place sho' 'nuff! (*With mournful foreboding.*) It's mighty queer! It's mighty queer! (*With sudden forced defiance — in an angry tone.*) Woods, is you tryin' to put somethin' ovah on me?

(*From the formless creatures on the ground in front of him comes a tiny gale of low mocking laughter like a rustling of leaves. They squirm upward toward him in twisted attitudes.* JONES *looks down, leaps backward with a yell of terror, yanking out his revolver as he does so — in a quavering voice.*)

What's dat? Who's dar? What is you? Git away from me befo' I shoots you up! You don't? . . .

(*He fires. There is a flash, a loud report, then silence broken only by the far-off, quickened throb of the tom-tom. The formless creatures have scurried back into the forest.* JONES *remains fixed in his position, listening intently. The sound of the shot, the reassuring feel of the revolver in his hand, have somewhat restored his shaken nerve. He addresses himself with renewed confidence.*)

Dey're gone. Dat shot fix 'em. Dey was only little animals — little wild pigs, I reckon. Dey've maybe rooted out yo' grub an' eat it. Sho', you fool nigger, what you think dey is — ha'nts? (*Excitedly.*) Gorry, you give de game away when you fire dat shot. Dem niggers heah dat fo' su'tin! Time you beat it in de woods widout no long waits. (*He starts for the forest — hesitates before the plunge — then urging himself in with manful resolution.*) Git in, nigger! What you skeered at? Ain't nothin' dere but de trees! Git in! (*He plunges boldly into the forest.*)

SCENE III

Scene — Nine o'clock. In the forest. The moon has just risen. Its beams, drifting through the canopy of leaves, make a barely perceptible, suffused, eerie glow. A dense low wall of underbrush and creepers is in the nearer foreground, fencing in a small triangular clearing. Beyond this is the massed blackness of the forest like an encompassing barrier. A path is dimly discerned leading down to the clearing from left, rear, and winding away from it again toward the right. As the scene opens nothing can be distinctly made out. Except for the beating of the tom-tom, which is a trifle louder and quicker than in the previous scene, there is silence, broken every few seconds by a queer, clicking sound. Then gradually the figure of the Negro, JEFF, can be discerned crouching on his haunches at the rear of the triangle. He is middle-aged, thin, brown in color, is dressed in a Pullman porter's uniform, cap, etc. He is throwing a pair of dice on the ground before him, picking them up, shaking them, casting them out with the regular, rigid, mechanical movements of an automaton. The heavy, plodding footsteps of someone approaching along the trail from the left are heard and JONES' *voice, pitched in a slightly higher key and strained in a cheering effort to overcome its own tremors.*

De moon's rizen. Does you heah dat, nigger? You gits more light from dis out. No mo' buttin' yo' fool head agin' de trunks an' scratchin' de hide off yo' legs in de bushes. Now you sees whar yo'se gwine. So cheer up! From now on you has a snap. (*He steps just to the rear of the triangular clearing and mops off his face on his sleeve. He has lost his Panama hat. His face is scratched, his brilliant uniform shows several large rents.*) What time's it gittin' to be, I wonder? I dassent light no match to find out. Phoo'. It's wa'm an' dat's a fac'! (*Wearily.*) How long I been makin' tracks in dese woods? Must be hours an' hours. Seems like fo'evah! Yit can't be, when de moon's jes' riz. Dis am a long night fo' yo', yo' Majesty! (*With a mournful chuckle.*) Majesty! Der ain't much majesty 'bout dis baby now. (*With attempted cheerfulness.*) Never min'. It's all part o' de game. Dis night come to an end like everything else. And when you gits dar safe and has dat bankroll in yo' hands you laughs at all dis. (*He starts to whistle but checks himself abruptly.*) What yo' whistlin' for, you po' dope! Want all de worl' to heah you? (*He stops talking to listen.*) Heah dat ole drum! Sho' gits nearer from de sound. Dey're packin' it along wid 'em. Time fo' me to move. (*He takes a step forward, then stops — worriedly.*) What's dat odder queer clickety sound I heah? Dere it is! Sound close! Sound like — sound like — Fo' God sake, sound like some nigger was shootin' crap! (*Frightenedly.*) I better beat it quick when I gits dem

notions. (*He walks quickly into the clear space — then stands transfixed as he sees* JEFF — *in a terrified gasp.*) Who dar? Who dat? Is dat you, Jeff? (*Starting toward the other, forgetful for a moment of his surroundings and really believing it is a living man that he sees — in a tone of happy relief.*) Jeff! I'se sho' mighty glad to see you! Dey tol' me you done died from dat razor cut I gives you. (*Stopping suddenly, bewilderedly.*) But how you come to be heah, nigger? (*He stares fascinatedly at the other who continues his mechanical play with the dice.* JONES' *eyes begin to roll wildly. He stutters.*) Ain't you gwine — look up — can't you speak to me? Is you— is you — a ha'nt? (*He jerks out his revolver in a frenzy of terrified rage.*) Nigger, I kills you dead once. Has I got to kill you again? You take it den. (*He fires. When the smoke clears away* JEFF *has disappeared.* JONES *stands trembling — then with a certain reassurance.*) He's gone, anyway. Ha'nt or no ha'nt, dat shot fix him. (*The beat of the far-off tom-tom is perceptibly louder and more rapid.* JONES *becomes conscious of it — with a start, looking back over his shoulder.*) Dey's gittin' near! Dey's comin' fast! And heah I is shootin' shots to let 'em know jes' whar I is. Oh, Gorry, I'se got to run. (*Forgetting the path he plunges wildly into the underbrush in the rear and disappears in the shadow.*)

SCENE IV

Scene — Eleven o'clock. In the forest. A wide dirt road runs diagonally from right, front, to left, rear. Rising sheer on both sides the forest walls it in. The moon is now up. Under its light the road glimmers ghastly and unreal. It is as if the forest had stood aside momentarily to let the road pass through and accomplish its veiled purpose. This done, the forest will fold in upon itself again and the road will be no more. JONES *stumbles in from the forest on the right. His uniform is ragged and torn. He looks about him with numbed surprise when he sees the road, his eyes blinking in the bright moonlight. He flops down exhaustedly and pants heavily for a while. Then with sudden anger.*

I'm meltin' wid heat! Runnin' an' runnin' an' runnin'! Damn dis heah coat! Like a straitjacket! (*He tears off his coat and flings it away from him, revealing himself stripped to the waist.*) Dere! Dat's better! Now I kin breathe! (*Looking down at his feet, the spurs catch his eye.*) And to hell wid dese high-fangled spurs. Dey're what's been a-trippin' me up an' breakin' my neck. (*He unstraps them and flings them away disgustedly.*) Dere! I gits rid o' dem frippety Emperor trappin's an' I travels lighter. Lawd! I'se tired! (*After a pause, listening to the insistent beat of the tom-tom in the distance.*) I must 'a put some distance between myself an' dem — runnin' like dat — and yit — dat damn drum sound jes' de same — nearer, even. Well, I guess I a'most holds my lead anyhow. Dey won't never catch up. (*With a sigh.*) If on'y my fool legs stands up. Oh, I'se sorry I evah went in for dis. Dat Emperor job is sho' hard to shake. (*He looks around him suspiciously.*) How'd dis road evah git heah? Good level road, too. I never remembers seein' it befo'. (*Shaking his head apprehensively.*) Dese woods is sho' full o' de queerest things at night. (*With a sudden terror.*) Lawd God, don't let me see no more o' dem ha'nts! Dey gits my goat! (*Then trying to talk himself into confidence.*) Ha'nts! You fool nigger, dey ain't no such things! Don't de Baptist parson tell you dat many time? Is you civilized, or is you like dese ign'rent black niggers heah? Sho'! Dat was all in yo' own head. Wasn't nothin' dere. Wasn't no Jeff! Know what? You jus' get seein' dem things 'cause yo' belly's empty and you's sick wid hunger inside. Hunger 'fects yo' head and yo' eyes. Any fool know dat. (*Then pleading fervently.*) But bless God, I don't come across no more o' dem, whatever dey is! (*Then cautiously.*) Rest! Don't talk! Rest! You needs it. Den you gits on yo' way again. (*Looking at the moon.*) Night's half gone a'most. You hits de coast in de mawning! Den you'se all safe.

(*From the right forward a small gang of Negroes enter. They are dressed in striped convict suits, their heads are shaven, one leg drags limpingly, shackled to a heavy ball and chain. Some carry picks, the others shovels. They are followed by a white man dressed in the uniform of a prison guard. A Winchester rifle is slung across his shoulders and he carries a heavy whip. At a signal from the* GUARD *they stop on the road opposite where* JONES *is sitting.* JONES, *who has been staring up at the sky, unmindful of their noiseless approach, suddenly looks down and sees*

them. *His eyes pop out, he tries to get to his feet and fly, but sinks back, too numbed by fright to move. His voice catches in a choking prayer.*)

Lawd Jesus!

(*The* PRISON GUARD *cracks his whip — noiselessly — and at that signal all the convicts start to work on the road. They swing their picks, they shovel, but not a sound comes from their labor. Their movements, like those of* JEFF *in the preceding scene, are those of automatons — rigid, slow, and mechanical. The* PRISON GUARD *points sternly at* JONES *with his whip, motions him to take his place among the other shovelers.* JONES *gets to his feet in a hypnotized stupor. He mumbles subserviently.*)

Yes, suh! Yes, suh! I'se comin'.

(*As he shuffles, dragging one foot, over to his place, he curses under his breath with rage and hatred.*)

God damn yo' soul, I gits even wid you yit, sometime.

(*As if there were a shovel in his hands he goes through weary, mechanical gestures of digging up dirt, and throwing it to the roadside. Suddenly the* GUARD *approaches him angrily, threateningly. He raises his whip and lashes* JONES *viciously across the shoulders with it.* JONES *winces with pain and cowers abjectly. The* GUARD *turns his back on him and walks away contemptuously. Instantly* JONES *straightens up. With arms upraised as if his shovel were a club in his hands he springs murderously at the unsuspecting* GUARD. *In the act of crashing down his shovel on the white man's skull,* JONES *suddenly becomes aware that his hands are empty. He cries despairingly.*)

Whar's my shovel? Gimme my shovel till I splits his damn head! (*Appealing to his fellow convicts.*) Gimme a shovel, one o' you, fo' God's sake!

(*They stand fixed in motionless attitudes, their eyes on the ground. The* GUARD *seems to wait expectantly, his back turned to the attacker.* JONES *bellows with baffled, terrified rage, tugging frantically at his revolver.*)

I kills you, you white debil, if it's de last thing I evah does! Ghost or debil, I kill you again!

(He frees the revolver and fires point blank at the GUARD'S *back. Instantly the walls of the forest close in from both sides, the road and the figures of the convict gang are blotted out in an enshrouding darkness. The only sounds are a crashing in the underbrush as* JONES *leaps away in mad flight and the throbbing of the tom-tom, still far distant, but increased in volume of sound and rapidity of beat.)*

SCENE V

Scene — One o'clock. A large circular clearing, enclosed by the serried ranks of gigantic trunks of tall trees whose tops are lost to view. In the center is a big dead stump worn by time into a curious resemblance to an auction block. The moon floods the clearing with a clear light. JONES *forces his way in through the forest on the left. He looks wildly about the clearing with hunted, fearful glances. His pants are in tatters, his shoes cut and misshapen, flapping about his feet. He slinks cautiously to the stump in the center and sits down in a tense position, ready for instant flight. Then he holds his head in his hands and rocks back and forth, moaning to himself miserably.*

Oh Lawd, Lawd! Oh Lawd, Lawd! *(Suddenly he throws himself on his knees and raises his clasped hands to the sky — in a voice of agonized pleading.)* Lawd Jesus, heah my prayer! I'se a po' sinner, a po' sinner! I knows I done wrong, I knows it! When I cotches Jeff cheatin' wid loaded dice my anger overcomes me and I kills him dead! Lawd, I done wrong! When dat guard hits me wid de whip, my anger overcomes me, and I kills him dead. Lawd, I done wrong! And down heah whar dese fool bush niggers raises me up to the seat o' de mighty, I steals all I could grab. Lawd, I done wrong! I knows it! I'se sorry! Forgive me, Lawd! Forgive dis po' sinner! *(Then beseeching terrifiedly.)* And keep dem away, Lawd! Keep dem away from me! And stop dat drum soundin' in my ears! Dat begin to sound ha'nted, too. *(He gets to his feet, evidently slightly reassured by his prayer — with attempted confidence.)* De Lawd'll preserve me from dem ha'nts after dis. *(Sits down on the stump again.)* I ain't skeered

o' real men. Let dem come. But dem odders . . . *(He shudders — then looks down at his feet, working his toes inside the shoes — with a groan.)* Oh, my po' feet! Dem shoes ain't no use no more 'ceptin' to hurt. I'se better off widout dem. *(He unlaces them and pulls them off — holds the wrecks of the shoes in his hands and regards them mournfully.)* You was real, A-one patin' leather, too. Look at you now. Emperor, you'se gittin' mighty low!

(He sits dejectedly and remains with bowed shoulders, staring down at the shoes in his hands as if reluctant to throw them away. While his attention is thus occupied, a crowd of figures silently enter the clearing from all sides. All are dressed in Southern costumes of the period of the fifties of the last century. There are middle-aged men who are evidently well-to-do planters. There is one spruce, authoritative individual — the AUCTIONEER. *There is a crowd of curious spectators, chiefly young belles and dandies who have come to the slave-market for diversion. All exchange courtly greetings in dumb show and chat silently together. There is something stiff, rigid, unreal, marionettish about their movements. They group themselves about the stump. Finally a batch of slaves are led in from the left by an attendant — three men of different ages, two women, one with a baby in her arms, nursing. They are placed to the left of the stump, beside* JONES.*

The white planters look them over appraisingly as if they were cattle, and exchange judgments on each. The dandies point with their fingers and make witty remarks. The belles titter bewitchingly. All this in silence save for the ominous throb of the tom-tom. The* AUCTIONEER *holds up his hand, taking his place at the stump. The group strain forward attentively. He touches* JONES *on the shoulder peremptorily, motioning for him to stand on the stump — the auction block.*

JONES *looks up, sees the figures on all sides, looks wildly for some opening to escape, sees none, screams and leaps madly to the top of the stump to get as far away from them as possible. He stands there, cowering, paralyzed with horror. The* AUCTIONEER *begins his silent spiel. He points to* JONES, *appeals to the planters to see for themselves. Here is a good field hand, sound in wind and limb as they can see. Very strong still in spite of his being middle-aged. Look at that back. Look at those shoulders. Look at the muscles in his arms and his sturdy legs. Capable of any amount of hard labor. Moreover, of a good disposition, intelligent and tractable. Will any gentleman start the bidding? The* PLANTERS *raise their fingers, make their bids. They are apparently all eager to possess* JONES. *The bidding is lively, the crowd interested. While this has been going on,* JONES *has been seized by the courage of desperation. He dares to look down and around him. Over his face abject terror gives way to mystification, to gradual realization — stutteringly.)*

What you all doin', white folks? What's all dis? What you all lookin' at me fo'? What you doin' wid me, anyhow? (*Suddenly convulsed with raging hatred and fear.*) Is dis a auction? Is you sellin' me like dey uster befo' de war? (*Jerking out his revolver just as the* AUCTIONEER *knocks him down to one of the planters — glaring from him to the purchaser.*) And you sells me? And *you* buys me? I shows you I'se a free nigger, damn yo' souls!

(*He fires at the* AUCTIONEER *and at the* PLANTER *with such rapidity that the two shots are almost simultaneous. As if this were a signal the walls of the forest fold in. Only blackness remains and silence broken by* JONES *as he rushes off, crying with fear — and by the quickened, ever louder beat of the tom-tom.*)

SCENE VI

Scene — Three o'clock. A cleared space in the forest. The limbs of the trees meet over it forming a low ceiling about five feet from the ground. The interlocked ropes of creepers reaching upward to entwine the tree trunks give an arched appearance to the sides. The space thus enclosed is like the dark, noisome hold of some ancient vessel. The moonlight is almost completely shut out and only a vague, wan light filters through. There is the noise of someone approaching from the left, stumbling and crawling through the undergrowth. JONES' *voice is heard between chattering moans.*

Oh, Lawd, what I gwine do now? Ain't got no bullet left on'y de silver one. If mo' o' dem ha'nts come after me, how I gwine skeer dem away? Oh, Lawd, on'y de silver one left — an' I gotta save dat fo' luck. If I shoots dat one I'm a goner sho'! Lawd, it's black heah! Whar's de moon? Oh, Lawd, don't dis night evah come to an end? (*By the sounds, he is feeling his way cautiously forward.*) Dere! Dis feels like a clear space. I gotta lie down an' rest. I don't care if dem niggers does cotch me. I gotta rest.

(*He is well forward now where his figure can be dimly made out. His pants have been so torn away that what is left of them is no better than a breech cloth. He flings himself full length, face downward on the ground, panting with exhaustion. Gradually it seems to grow lighter in the enclosed space and two rows of seated figures can be seen behind* JONES. *They are sitting in crumpled, despairing attitudes, hunched, facing one another with their backs touching the forest walls as if they were shackled to them. All are Negroes, naked save for loin cloths. At first they are silent and motionless. Then they begin to sway slowly forward toward each other and back again in unison, as if they were laxly letting themselves follow the long roll of a ship at sea. At the same time, a low, melancholy murmur rises among them, increasing gradually by rhythmic degrees which seem to be directed and controlled by the throb of the tom-tom in the distance, to a long, tremulous wail of despair that reaches a certain pitch, unbearably acute, then falls by slow gradations of tone into silence and is taken up again.* JONES *starts, looks up, sees the figures, and throws himself down again to shut out the sight. A shudder of terror shakes his whole body as the wail rises up about him again. But the next time, his voice, as if under some uncanny compulsion, starts with the others. As their chorus lifts he rises to a sitting posture similar to the others, swaying back and forth. His voice reaches the highest pitch of sorrow, of desolation. The light fades out, the other voices cease, and only darkness is left.* JONES *can be heard scrambling to his feet and running off, his voice sinking down the scale and receding as he moves farther and farther away in the forest. The tom-tom beats louder, quicker, with a more insistent, triumphant pulsation.*)

SCENE VII

Scene — Five o'clock. The foot of a gigantic tree by the edge of a great river. A rough structure of boulders, like an altar, is by the tree. The raised river bank is in the nearer background. Beyond this the surface of the river spreads out, brilliant and unruffled in the moonlight, blotted out and merged into a veil of bluish mist in the distance. JONES' voice is heard from the left rising and falling in the long, despairing wail of the chained slaves, to the rhythmic beat of the tom-tom. As his voice sinks into silence, he enters the open space. The expression of his face is fixed and stony, his eyes have an obsessed glare, he moves with a strange deliberation like a sleep-walker or one in a trance. He looks around at the tree, the rough stone altar, the moonlit surface of the river beyond, and passes his hand over his head with a vague gesture of puzzled bewilderment. Then, as if in obedi-ence to some obscure impulse, he sinks into a kneeling, devotional posture before the altar. Then he seems to come to himself partly, to have an uncertain realization of what he is doing, for he straightens up and stares about him horrifiedly — in an incoherent mumble.

What — what is I doin'? What is — dis place? Seems like — seems like I know dat tree — an' dem stones — an' de river. I remember — seems like I been heah befo'. (*Tremblingly.*) Oh, Gorry, I'se skeered in dis place! I'se skeered! Oh, Lawd, pertect dis sinner!

(*Crawling away from the altar, he cowers close to the ground, his face hidden, his shoulders heaving with sobs of hysterical fright. From behind the trunk of the tree, as if he had sprung out of it, the figure of the* CONGO WITCH-DOCTOR *appears. He is wiz-ened and old, naked except for the fur of some small animal tied about his waist, its bushy tail hanging down in front. His body is stained all over a bright red. Antelope horns are on each side of his head, branching up-ward. In one hand he carries a bone rattle, in the other a charm stick with a bunch of white cockatoo feathers tied to the end. A great number of glass beads and bone orna-ments are about his neck, ears, wrists, and an-kles. He struts noiselessly with a queer prancing step to a position in the clear ground between* JONES *and the altar. Then with a preliminary, summoning stamp of his foot on the earth, he begins to dance and to chant. As if in response to his summons the beating of the tom-tom grows to a fierce, ex-ultant boom whose throbs seem to fill the air with vibrating rhythm.* JONES *looks up, starts to spring to his feet, reaches a half-kneeling, half-squatting position and remains rigidly fixed there, paralyzed with awed fascination by this new apparition. The* WITCH-DOCTOR *sways, stamping with his foot, his bone rattle clicking the time. His voice rises and falls in a weird, monotonous croon, without articu-late word divisions. Gradually his dance be-comes clearly one of a narrative in panto-mime, his croon is an incantation, a charm to allay the fierceness of some implacable deity demanding sacrifice. He flees, he is pursued by devils, he hides, he flees again. Ever wilder and wilder becomes his flight, nearer and nearer draws the pursuing evil, more and more the spirit of terror gains possession of him. His croon, rising to intensity, is punc-tuated by shrill cries.* JONES *has become com-pletely hypnotized. His voice joins in the in-cantation, in the cries, he beats time with his hands and sways his body to and fro from the waist. The whole spirit and meaning of the dance has entered into him, has become his spirit. Finally the theme of the pantomime halts on a howl of despair, and is taken up again in a note of savage hope. There is a sal-vation. The forces of evil demand sacrifice. They must be appeased. The* WITCH-DOCTOR *points with his wand to the sacred tree, to the river beyond, to the altar, and finally to* JONES *with a ferocious command.* JONES *seems to sense the meaning of this. It is he who must offer himself for sacrifice. He beats his forehead abjectly to the ground, moaning hysterically.*)

Mercy, Oh Lawd! Mercy! Mercy on dis po' sin-ner.

(*The* WITCH-DOCTOR *springs to the river bank. He stretches out his arms and calls to some god within its depths. Then he starts backward slowly, his arms remaining out. A huge head of a crocodile appears over the bank and its eyes, glittering greenly, fasten upon* JONES. *He stares into them fascinat-edly. The* WITCH-DOCTOR *prances up to him, touches him with his wand, motions with*

hideous command toward the waiting mon-
ster. JONES *squirms on his belly nearer and*
nearer, moaning continually.)

Mercy, Lawd! Mercy!

(*The crocodile heaves more of his enormous*
bulk onto the land. JONES *squirms toward*
him. The WITCH-DOCTOR'S *voice shrills out*
in furious exultation, the tom-tom beats
madly. JONES *cries out in a fierce, exhausted*
spasm of anguished pleading.)

Lawd, save me! Lawd Jesus, heah my prayer!

(*Immediately, in answer to his prayer, comes*
the thought of the one bullet left him. He
snatches at his hip, shouting defiantly.)

De silver bullet! You don't git me yit!

(*He fires at the green eyes in front of him.*
The head of the crocodile sinks back behind
the river bank, the WITCH-DOCTOR *springs*
behind the sacred tree and disappears. JONES
lies with his face to the ground, his arms
outstretched, whimpering with fear as the
throb of the tom-tom fills the silence about
him with a somber pulsation, a baffled but re-
vengeful power.)

SCENE VIII

Scene — Dawn. Same as Scene II, the divid-
ing line of forest and plain. The nearest tree
trunks are dimly revealed but the forest be-
hind them is still a mass of glooming shad-
ows. The tom-tom seems on the very spot, so
loud and continuously vibrating are its beats.
LEM *enters from the left, followed by a small*
squad of his soldiers, and by the Cockney
trader, SMITHERS. LEM *is a heavy-set, ape-*
faced old savage of the extreme African type,
dressed only in a loin cloth. A revolver and
cartridge belt are about his waist. His soldiers
are in different degrees of rag-concealed
nakedness. All wear broad palm-leaf hats.
Each one carries a rifle. SMITHERS *is the*
same as in Scene I. One of the soldiers, evi-
dently a tracker, is peering about keenly on
the ground. He grunts and points to the spot
where JONES *entered the forest.* LEM *and*
SMITHERS *come to look.*

SMITHERS (*after a glance, turns away in dis-*
gust): That's where 'e went in right enough.

Much good it'll do yer. 'E's miles orf by this an'
safe to the Coast, damn 'is 'ide! I tole yer yer'd
lose 'im, didn't I? — wastin' the 'ole bloomin'
night beatin' yer bloody drum and castin' yer
silly spells! Gawd blimey, wot a pack!

LEM (*gutturally*): We cotch him. You see.
(*He makes a motion to his soldiers who squat*
down on their haunches in a semicircle.)

SMITHERS (*exasperatedly*): Well, ain't yer
goin' in an' 'unt 'im in the woods? What the
'ell's the good of waitin'?

LEM (*imperturbably — squatting down him-*
self): We cotch him.

SMITHERS (*turning away from him con-*
temptuously): Aw! Garn! 'E's a better man
than the lot o' you put together. I 'ates the
sight o' 'im but I'll say that for 'im.

(*A sound of snapping twigs comes from the*
forest. The soldiers jump to their feet, cock-
ing their rifles alertly. LEM *remains sitting*
with an imperturbable expression, but listen-
ing intently. The sound from the woods is re-
peated. LEM *makes a quick signal with his*
hand. His followers creep quickly but noise-
lessly into the forest, scattering so that each
enters at a different spot.)

SMITHERS (*in the silence that follows — in a*
contemptuous whisper): You ain't thinkin'
that would be 'im, I 'ope?

LEM (*calmly*): We cotch him.

SMITHERS: Blarsted fat 'eads! (*Then after*
a second's thought — wonderingly.) Still an'
all, it might 'appen. If 'e lost 'is bloody way in
these stinkin' woods 'e'd likely turn in a circle
without 'is knowin' it. They all does.

LEM (*peremptorily*): Sssh!

(*The reports of several rifles sound from the*
forest, followed a second later by savage, ex-
ultant yells. The beating of the tom-tom
abruptly ceases. LEM *looks up at the white*
man with a grin of satisfaction.)

We cotch him. Him dead.

SMITHERS (*with a snarl*): 'Ow d'yer know
it's 'im an' 'ow d'yer know 'e's dead?

LEM: My mens dey got 'um silver bullets.
Dey kill him shore.

SMITHERS (*astonished*): They got silver bullets?

LEM: Lead bullet no kill him. He got um
strong charm. I cook um money, make um silver bullet, make um strong charm, too.

SMITHERS (*light breaking upon him*): So
that's wot you was up to all night, wot? You

was scared to put after 'im till you'd moulded silver bullets, eh?

LEM (*simply stating a fact*): Yes. Him got strong charm. Lead no good.

SMITHERS (*slapping his thigh and guffawing*): Haw-haw! If yer don't beat all 'ell! (*Then recovering himself — scornfully.*) I'll bet yer it ain't 'im they shot at all, yer bleedin' looney!

LEM (*calmly*): Dey come bring him now.

(*The soldiers come out of the forest, carrying* JONES' *limp body. There is a little reddish-purple hole under his left breast. He is dead. They carry him to* LEM, *who examines his body with great satisfaction.* SMITHERS *leans over his shoulder — in a tone of frightened awe.*)

Well, they did for yer right enough, Jonsey, me lad! Dead as a 'erring! (*Mockingly.*) Where's yer 'igh an' mighty airs now, yer bloomin' Majesty? (*Then with a grin.*) Silver bullets! Gawd blimey, but yer died in the 'eighth o' style, any'ow!

(LEM *makes a motion to the soldiers to carry the body out left.* SMITHERS *speaks to him sneeringly.*)

SMITHERS: And I s'pose you think it's yer bleedin' charms and yer silly beatin' the drum that made 'im run in a circle when 'e'd lost 'imself, don't yer?

(*But* LEM *makes no reply, does not seem to hear the question, walks out left after his men.* SMITHERS *looks after him with contemptuous scorn.*)

Stupid as 'ogs, the lot of 'em! Blarsted niggers!

CURTAIN FALLS

TRAGEDY

OEDIPUS THE KING

Sophocles

Translated into English verse by H. D. F. Kitto

Sophocles (c. 495 B.C.–406 B.C.), the son of a wealthy Athenian, is one of the three Greek tragic writers whose work survives. (The other two are Aeschylus and Euripides.) Of Sophocles' more than one hundred and twenty plays, we have seven. The exact date that *Oedipus the King* was written is not known, but 430 B.C. is a reasonable guess. Some twenty-five years later, when he was almost ninety, Sophocles wrote *Oedipus at Colonus*, dramatizing Oedipus' last deeds.

DRAMATIS PERSONAE

OEDIPUS, *King of Thebes*
PRIEST OF ZEUS
CREON, *brother of Iocasta*
TEIRESIAS, *a Seer*
IOCASTA, *Queen of Thebes*
A CORINTHIAN SHEPHERD
A THEBAN SHEPHERD
A MESSENGER
CHORUS *of Theban citizens*
PRIESTS, ATTENDANTS, *etc.*

Scene: Thebes, before the royal palace.

Giant puppets of Iocasta and Oedipus, made by Remo Buffano, for a Philadelphia production of *Oedipus the King*, designed in 1931 by Robert Edmund Jones. (Photograph: Will Rapport. Harvard Theatre Collection.)

48   SOPHOCLES

OEDIPUS:

My children, latest brood of ancient Cadmus,
What purpose brings you here, a multitude
Bearing the boughs that mark the suppliant?
Why is our air so full of frankincense,
So full of hymns and prayers and lamenta-
5   tions?
This, children, was no matter to entrust
To others: therefore I myself am come
Whose fame is known to all — I, Oedipus.
— You, Sir, are pointed out by length of years
10   To be the spokesman: tell me, what is in
Your hearts? What fear? What sorrow? Count
      on all
That I can do, for I am not so hard
As not to pity such a supplication.

PRIEST:

Great King of Thebes, and sovereign Oedipus,
15   Look on us, who now stand before the altars —
Some young, still weak of wing; some bowed
      with age —
The priests, as I, of Zeus; and these, the best
Of our young men; and in the market-place,
And by Athena's temples and the shrine
20   Of fiery divination, there is kneeling,
Each with his suppliant branch, the rest of
      Thebes.
The city, as you see yourself, is now
Storm-tossed, and can no longer raise its head
Above the waves and angry surge of death.
25   The fruitful blossoms of the land are barren,
The herds upon our pastures, and our wives
In childbirth, barren. Last, and worst of all,
The withering god of fever swoops on us
To empty Cadmus' city and enrich
30   Dark Hades with our groans and lamentations.
No god we count you, that we bring our
      prayers,
I and these children, to your palace-door,
But wise above all other men to read
Life's riddles, and the hidden ways of Heaven;
35   For it was you who came and set us free
From the blood-tribute that the cruel Sphinx
Had laid upon our city; without our aid
Or our instruction, but, as we believe,
With god as ally, you gave us back our life.
40   So now, most dear, most mighty Oedipus,
We all entreat you on our bended knees,

From *Three Tragedies* by Sophocles, translated by
H. D. F. Kitto. © 1962 by Oxford University Press.
Reprinted by permission.

Come to our rescue, whether from the gods
Or from some man you can find means to
      save.
For I have noted, *that* man's counsel is
Of best effect, who has been tried in action.   45
Come, noble Oedipus! Come, save our city.
Be well advised; for that past service given
This city calls you Savior; of your kingship
Let not the record be that first we rose
From ruin, then to ruin fell again.   50
No, save our city, let it stand secure.
You brought us gladness and deliverance
Before; now do no less. You rule this land;
Better to rule it full of living men
Than rule a desert; citadel or ship   55
Without its company of men is nothing.

OEDIPUS:

My children, what you long for, that I know
Indeed, and pity you. I know how cruelly
You suffer; yet, though sick, not one of you
Suffers a sickness half as great as mine.   60
Yours is a single pain; each man of you
Feels but his own. My heart is heavy with
The city's pain, my own, and yours together.
You come to me not as to one asleep
And needing to be wakened; many a tear   65
I have been shedding, every path of thought
Have I been pacing; and what remedy,
What single hope my anxious thought has
      found
That I have tried. Creon, Menoeceus' son,
My own wife's brother, I have sent to Delphi   70
To ask in Phoebus' house what act of mine,
What word of mine, may bring deliverance.
Now, as I count the days, it troubles me
What he is doing; his absence is prolonged
Beyond the proper time. But when he comes   75
Then write me down a villain, if I do
Not each particular that the god discloses.

PRIEST:

You give us hope. — And here is more, for
      they
Are signaling that Creon has returned.

OEDIPUS:

O Lord Apollo, even as Creon smiles,   80
Smile now on us, and let it be deliverance!

PRIEST:

The news is good; or he would not be wearing
That ample wreath of richly-berried laurel.

OEDIPUS:

We soon shall know; my voice will reach so
      far:

85 Creon my lord, my kinsman, what response
Do you bring with you from the god of
Delphi?

[*Enter* CREON.]

CREON:
Good news! Our sufferings, if they are guided
right,
Can even yet turn to a happy issue.
OEDIPUS:
This only leaves my fear and confidence
90 In equal balance: what did Phoebus say?
CREON:
Is it your wish to hear it now, in public,
Or in the palace? I am at your service.
OEDIPUS:
Let them all hear! Their sufferings distress
Me more than if my own life were at stake.
CREON:
95 Then I will tell you what Apollo said —
And it was very clear. There is pollution
Here in our midst, long-standing. This must
we
Expel, nor let it grow past remedy.
OEDIPUS:
What has defiled us? and how are we to purge
it?
CREON:
100 By banishing or killing one who murdered,
And so called down this pestilence upon us.
OEDIPUS:
Who is the man whose death the god de-
nounces?
CREON:
Before the city passed into your care,
My lord, we had a king called Laius.
OEDIPUS:
105 So I have often heard. — I never saw him.
CREON:
His death, Apollo clearly charges us,
We must avenge upon his murderers.
OEDIPUS:
Where are they now? And where shall we
disclose
The unseen traces of that ancient crime?
CREON:
The god said, Here. — A man who hunts with
110 care
May often find what other men will miss.
OEDIPUS:
Where was he murdered? In the palace here?
Or in the country? Or was he abroad?
CREON:
He made a journey to consult the god,
115 He said — and never came back home again.

OEDIPUS:
But was there no report? no fellow traveler
Whose knowledge might have helped you in
your search?
CREON:
All died, except one terror-stricken man,
And he could tell us nothing — next to nothing.
OEDIPUS:
And what was that? One thing might lead to
much,   120
If only we could find one ray of light.
CREON:
He said they met with brigands — not with
one,
But a whole company; they killed Laius.
OEDIPUS:
A brigand would not *dare* — unless perhaps
Conspirators in Thebes had bribed the man.   125
CREON:
There *was* conjecture; but disaster came
And we were leaderless, without our king.
OEDIPUS:
Disaster? With a king cut down like that
You did not seek the cause? Where was the
hindrance?
CREON:
The Sphinx. *Her* riddle pressed us harder still; 130
For Laius — out of sight was out of mind.
OEDIPUS:
I will begin again; *I'll* find the truth.
The dead man's cause has found a true
defender
In Phoebus, and in you. And I will join you
In seeking vengeance on behalf of Thebes   135
And Phoebus too; indeed, I must: if I
Remove this taint, it is not for a stranger,
But for myself: the man who murdered him
Might make the same attempt on me; and so,
Avenging him, I shall protect myself. —   140
Now you, my sons, without delay, arise,
Take up your suppliant branches. — Someone,
go
And call the people here, for I will do
What can be done; and either, by the grace
Of God we shall be saved — or we shall fall.   145
PRIEST:
My children, we will go; the King has prom-
ised
All that we came to ask. — O Phoebus, thou
Hast given us an answer: give us too
Protection! grant remission of the plague!
[*Exeunt* CREON, PRIESTS, *etc.*
OEDIPUS *remains.*]

[*Enter the* CHORUS *representing the citizens
of Thebes.*]

STROPHE 1

CHORUS:
Sweet is the voice of the god, that
[*mainly dactyls:* $\frac{4}{4}$][1]   sounds in the
Golden shrine of Delphi.
What message has it sent to Thebes? My
      trembling
Heart is torn with anguish.
5   Thou god of Healing, Phoebus Apollo,
How do I fear! What hast thou in mind
To bring upon us now? what is to be fulfilled
From days of old?
Tell me this, O Voice divine,
10 Thou child of golden Hope.

ANTISTROPHE 1

First on the Daughter of Zeus I call for
Help, divine Athene;
And Artemis, whose throne is all the earth,
      whose
Shrine is in our city;
5   Apollo too, who shoots from afar:
Trinity of Powers, come to our defence!
If ever in the past, when ruin threatened us,
You stayed its course
And turned aside the flood of Death,
10 O then, protect us now!

STROPHE 2

[*agitated:* $\frac{3}{8}$] Past counting are the woes we
      suffer;
Affliction bears on all the city, and
Nowhere is any defence against destruction.

[1] Taking a hint from the French translators for the
Budé series I have here and there added to the lyrical
portions a quasi-musical indication of tempo or mood,
on no authority except that of common sense. These
may at least serve to remind the reader, if he needs
reminding, that the lyrics were not recited; they were
a fusion of intense poetry, music, and dancing. Of the
music we know nothing; of the dance we can at least
infer that its range extended from grave processional
movements to the expression of great excitement,
whether of joy or despair. [Kitto.]

The holy soil can bring no increase,
Our women suffer and cry in childbirth   5
But do not bring forth living children.
The souls of those who perish, one by one,
Unceasingly, swift as raging fire,
Rise and take their flight to the dark realms of
      the dead.

ANTISTROPHE 2

Past counting, those of us who perish:
They lie upon the ground, unpitied,
Unburied, infecting the air with deadly pollu-
      tion.
Young wives, and grey-haired mothers with
      them,
From every quarter approach the altars   5
And cry aloud in supplication.
The prayer for healing, the loud wail of
      lament,
Together are heard in dissonance:
O thou golden Daughter of Zeus, grant thy
      aid!

STROPHE 3

[*mainly iambic:* $\frac{3}{8}$] The fierce god of War has
      laid aside
His spear; but yet his terrible cry
Rings in our ears; he spreads death and
      destruction.
Ye gods, drive him back to his distant home!
   For what the light of day has spared,   5
   That the darkness of night destroys.
   Zeus our father! All power is thine:
The lightning-flash is thine: hurl upon him
Thy thunderbolt, and quell this god of War!

ANTISTROPHE 3

We pray, Lord Apollo: draw thy bow
In our defense. Thy quiver is full of
Arrows unerring: shoot! slay the destroyer!
And thou, radiant Artemis, lend thy aid!
   Thou whose hair is bound in gold,   5
Bacchus, lord of the sacred dance,
   Theban Bacchus! Come, show thyself!
Display thy blazing torch; drive from our
      midst

The savage god, abhorred by other gods!
OEDIPUS:
Would you have answer to these prayers?
10   Then hear
My words; give heed; your help may bring
Deliverance, and the end of all our troubles.
Here do I stand before you all, a stranger
Both to the deed and to the story. — What
15   Could I have done alone, without a clue?
But I was yet a foreigner; it was later
That I became a Theban among Thebans.
So now do I proclaim to all the city:
If any Theban knows by what man's hand
20   He perished, Laius, son of Labdacus,
Him I command to tell me all he can;
And if he is afraid, let him annul
Himself the charge he fears; no punishment
Shall fall on him, save only to depart
Unharmed from Thebes. Further, if any
25   knows
The slayer to be a stranger from abroad,
Let him speak out; I will reward him, and
Besides, he will have all my gratitude.
But if you still keep silent, if any man
30   Fearing for self or friend shall disobey me,
This will I do — and listen to my words:
Whoever he may be, I do forbid
All in this realm, of which I am the King
And high authority, to shelter in their houses
35   Or speak to him, or let him be their partner
In prayers or sacrifices to the gods, or give
Him lustral water; I command you all
To drive him from your doors; for he it is
That brings this plague upon us, as the god
40   Of Delphi has but now declared to me. —
So stern an ally do I make myself
Both of the god and of our murdered king. —
And for the man that slew him, whether he
Slew him alone, or with a band of helpers,
45   I lay this curse upon him, that the wretch
In wretchedness and misery may live.
And more: if with my knowledge he be found
To share my hearth and home, then upon me
Descend that doom that I invoke on him.
50   This charge I lay upon you, to observe
All my commands: to aid myself, the god,
And this our land, so spurned of Heaven, so
    ravaged.
For such a taint we should not leave un-
    purged —
The death of such a man, and he your king —
55   Even if Heaven had not commanded us,
But we should search it out. Now, since 'tis I
That wear the crown that he had worn before
    me,

And have his Queen to wife, and common
    children
Were born to us, but that his own did perish,
And sudden death has carried him away —   60
Because of this, I will defend his cause
As if it were my father's; nothing I
Will leave undone to find the man who killed
The son of Labdacus, and offspring of
Polydorus, Cadmus, and of old Agênor.   65
On those that disobey, this is my curse:
May never field of theirs give increase, nor
Their wives have children; may our present
    plagues,
And worse, be ever theirs, for their destruction.
But for the others, all with whom my words   70
Find favour, this I pray: Justice and all
The gods be ever at your side to help you.
CHORUS-LEADER:
Your curse constrains me; therefore will I
    speak.
I did not kill him, neither can I tell
Who did. It is for Phoebus, since he laid   75
The task upon us, to declare the man.
OEDIPUS:
True; but to force the gods against their will —
That is a thing beyond all human power.
CHORUS-LEADER:
All I could say is but a second best.
OEDIPUS:
Though it were third best, do not hold it back.   80
CHORUS-LEADER:
I know of none that reads Apollo's mind
So surely as the lord Teiresias;
Consulting him you best might learn the truth.
OEDIPUS:
Not even this have I neglected: Creon
Advised me, and already I have sent   85
Two messengers. — Strange he has not come.
CHORUS-LEADER:
There's nothing else but old and idle gossip.
OEDIPUS:
And what was that? I clutch at any straw.
CHORUS-LEADER:
They said that he was killed by travelers.
OEDIPUS:
So I have heard; but no one knows a witness.   90
CHORUS-LEADER:
But if he is not proof against *all* fear
He'll not keep silent when he hears your curse.
OEDIPUS:
And will they fear a curse, who dared to kill?
CHORUS-LEADER:
Here is the one to find him, for at last
They bring the prophet here. He is inspired,   95
The only man whose heart is filled with truth.

[*Enter* TEIRESIAS, *led by a boy.*]

OEDIPUS:
Teiresias, by your art you read the signs
And secrets of the earth and of the sky;
Therefore you know, although you cannot see,
100   The plague that is besetting us; from this
No other man but you, my lord, can save us.
Phoebus has said — you may have heard already —
In answer to our question, that this plague
Will never cease unless we can discover
105   What men they were who murdered Laius,
And punish them with death or banishment.
Therefore give freely all that you have learned
From birds or other form of divination;
Save us; save me, the city, and yourself,
110   From the pollution that his bloodshed causes.
No finer task, than to give all one has
In helping others; we are in your hands.
TEIRESIAS:
Ah! what a burden knowledge is, when knowledge
Can be of no avail! I knew this well,
115   And yet forgot, or I should not have come.
OEDIPUS:
Why, what is this? Why are you so despondent?
TEIRESIAS:
Let me go home! It will be best for you,
And best for me, if you will let me go.
OEDIPUS:
But to withhold your knowledge! This is wrong,
120   Disloyal to the city of your birth.
TEIRESIAS:
I know that what you say will lead you on
To ruin; therefore, lest the same befall me too . . .
OEDIPUS:
No, by the gods! Say all you know, for we
Go down upon our knees, your suppliants.
TEIRESIAS:
125   Because *you* do *not* know! I never shall
Reveal my burden — I will not say *yours.*
OEDIPUS:
You know, and will not tell us? Do you wish
To ruin Thebes and to destroy us all?
TEIRESIAS:
My pain, and yours, will not be caused by me.
Why these vain questions? — for I will not
130   speak.
OEDIPUS:
You villain! — for you would provoke a stone

To anger: you'll not speak, but show yourself
So hard of heart and so inflexible?
TEIRESIAS:
You heap the blame on me; but what is yours
You do not know — therefore *I* am the villain!   135
OEDIPUS:
And who would not be angry, finding that
You treat our people with such cold disdain?
TEIRESIAS:
The truth will come to light, without *my* help.
OEDIPUS:
If it is bound to come, you ought to speak it.
TEIRESIAS:
I'll say no more, and you, if so you choose,   140
May rage and bluster on without restraint.
OEDIPUS:
Restraint? Then I'll show none! I'll tell you all
That I can see in you: I do believe
This crime was planned and carried out by you,
All but the killing; and were you not blind   145
I'd say your hand alone had done the murder.
TEIRESIAS:
So? Then I tell you this: submit yourself
To that decree that you have made; from now
Address no word to these men nor to me:
You are the man whose crimes pollute our city.   150
OEDIPUS:
What, does your impudence extend thus far?
And do you hope that it will go scot-free?
TEIRESIAS:
It will. I have a champion — the truth.
OEDIPUS:
Who taught you that? For it was not your art.
TEIRESIAS:
No; you! You made me speak, against my will.   155
OEDIPUS:
Speak what? Say it again, and say it clearly.
TEIRESIAS:
Was I not clear? Or are you tempting me?
OEDIPUS:
Not clear enough for me. Say it again.
TEIRESIAS:
You are yourself the murderer you seek.
OEDIPUS:
You'll not affront me twice and go unpunished!   160
TEIRESIAS:
Then shall I give you still more cause for rage?
OEDIPUS:
Say what you will; you'll say it to no purpose.
TEIRESIAS:
I know, *you* do not know, the hideous life

Of shame you lead with those most near to
    you.

OEDIPUS:

165 You'll pay most dearly for this insolence!

TEIRESIAS:

No, not if Truth is strong, and can prevail.

OEDIPUS:

It is — except in you; for you are blind
In eyes and ears and brains and everything.

TEIRESIAS:

You'll not forget these insults that you throw
170 At me, when all men throw the same at you.

OEDIPUS:

You live in darkness; you can do no harm
To me or any man who has his eyes.

TEIRESIAS:

No; I am not to bring you down, because
Apollo is enough; he'll see to it.

OEDIPUS:

175 Creon, or you? Which of you made this plot?

TEIRESIAS:

Creon's no enemy of yours; you are your own.

OEDIPUS:

O Wealth! O Royalty! whose commanding art
Outstrips all other arts in life's contentions!
How great a store of envy lies upon you,
180 If for this scepter, that the city gave
Freely to me, unasked — if now my friend,
The trusty Creon, burns to drive me hence
And steal it from me! So he has suborned
This crafty schemer here, this mountebank,
185 Whose purse alone has eyes, whose art is
    blind. —
Come, prophet, show your title! When the
    Sphinx
Chanted her music here, why did not *you*
Speak out and save the city? Yet such a
    question
Was one for augury, not for mother wit.
You were no prophet then; your birds, your
190   voice
From Heaven, were dumb. But I, who came
    by chance,
I, knowing nothing, put the Sphinx to flight,
Thanks to my wit — no thanks to divination!
And now you try to drive me out; you hope
195 When Creon's king to bask in Creon's favor.
You'll expiate the curse? Ay, and repent it,
Both you and your accomplice. But that you
Seem old, I'd teach you what you gain by
    treason!

CHORUS-LEADER:

My lord, he spoke in anger; so I think,
200 Did you. What help in angry speeches? Come,

This is the task, how we can best discharge
The duty that the god has laid on us.

TEIRESIAS:

King though you are, I claim the privilege
Of equal answer. No, I have the right;
I am no slave of yours— I serve Apollo,   205
And therefore am not listed *Creon's* man.
Listen — since you have taunted me with
    blindness!
You have your sight, and yet you cannot see
Where, nor with whom, you live, nor in what
    horror.
Your parents — do you know them? or that you   210
Are enemy to your kin, alive or dead?
And that a father's and a mother's curse
Shall join to drive you headlong out of Thebes
And change the light that now you see to
    darkness?
Your cries of agony, where will they not reach? 215
Where on Cithaeron will they not re-echo?
Where you have learned what meant the
    marriage-song
Which bore you to an evil haven here
After so fair a voyage? And you are blind
To other horrors, which shall make you one   220
With your own children. Therefore, heap your
    scorn
On Creon and on me, for no man living
Will meet a doom more terrible than yours.

OEDIPUS:

What? Am I to suffer words like this from
    him?
Ruin, damnation seize you! Off at once   225
Out of our sight! Go! Get you whence you
    came!

TEIRESIAS:

Had you not called me, I should not be here.

OEDIPUS:

And had I known that you would talk such
    folly,
I'd not have called you to a house of mine.

TEIRESIAS:

To you I seem a fool, but to your parents,   230
To those who did beget you, I was wise.

OEDIPUS:

Stop! Who were they? Who *were* my parents?
    Tell me!

TEIRESIAS:

This day will show your birth and your destruc-
    tion.

OEDIPUS:

You are too fond of dark obscurities.

TEIRESIAS:

But do you not excel in reading riddles?   235

OEDIPUS:
I scorn your taunts; my skill has brought me
    glory.
TEIRESIAS:
And this success brought you to ruin too.
OEDIPUS:
I am content, if so I saved this city.
TEIRESIAS:
Then I will leave you. Come, boy, take my
    hand.
OEDIPUS:
240 Yes, let him take it. You are nothing but
Vexation here. Begone, and give me peace!
TEIRESIAS:
When I have had my say. No frown of yours
Shall frighten *me*; you cannot injure me.
Here is my message: that man whom you seek
245 With threats and proclamations for the death
Of Laius, he is living here; he's thought
To be a foreigner, but shall be found
Theban by birth — and little joy will this
Bring *him*; when, with his eyesight turned to
    blindness,
250 His wealth to beggary, on foreign soil
With staff in hand he'll tap his way along,
His children with him; and he will be known
Himself to be their father and their brother,
The husband of the mother who gave him
    birth,
255 Supplanter of his father, and his slayer.
— There! Go, and think on this; and if you
    find
That I'm deceived, say then — and not be-
    fore —
That I am ignorant in divination.
    [*Exeunt severally* TEIRESIAS *and* OEDIPUS.]

STROPHE 1

CHORUS:
The voice of god rang out in the holy cavern,
Denouncing one who has killed a King — the
    crime of crimes.
    Who is the man? Let him begone in
    Headlong flight, swift as a horse!
5 [*anapaests*] For the terrible god, like a warrior
    armed,
Stands ready to strike with a lightning-flash:
    The Furies who punish crime, and never
    fail,
    Are hot in their pursuit.

ANTISTROPHE 1

The snow is white on the cliffs of high
    Parnassus.
It has flashed a message: Let every Theban
    join the hunt!
    Lurking in caves among the mountains,
    Deep in the woods — where is the man?
[*anapaests*] In wearisome flight, unresting,
    alone,   5
An outlaw, he shuns Apollo's shrine;
    But ever the living menace of the god
    Hovers around his head.

STROPHE 2

[*choriambics*] Strange, disturbing, what the
    wise
Prophet has said. What can he mean?
Neither can I believe, nor can I disbelieve;
I do not know what to say.
I look here, and there; nothing can I find —   5
No strife, either now or in the past,
Between the kings of Thebes and Corinth.
A hand unknown struck down the King;
Though I would learn who it was dealt the
    blow,
That *he* is guilty whom all revere —   10
How can I believe this with no proof?

ANTISTROPHE 2

Zeus, Apollo — they have knowledge;
They understand the ways of life.
Prophets are men, like me; that they can
    understand
More than is revealed to me —
Of that, I can find nowhere certain proof,   5
Though one man is wise, another foolish.
Until the charge is manifest
I will not credit his accusers.
I saw myself how the Sphinx challenged him:
He proved his wisdom; he saved our city;   10
Therefore how can I now condemn him?

[*Enter* CREON]

CREON:
They tell me, Sirs, that Oedipus the King
Has made against me such an accusation

That I will not endure. For if he thinks
15 That in this present trouble I have done
Or said a single thing to do him harm,
Then let me die, and not drag out my days
With such a name as that. For it is not
One injury this accusation does me;
20 It touches my whole life, if you, my friends,
And all the city are to call me traitor.
   CHORUS-LEADER:
The accusation may perhaps have come
From heat of temper, not from sober judg-
   ment.
   CREON:
What was it made him think contrivances
25 Of mine suborned the seer to tell his lies?
   CHORUS-LEADER:
Those were his words; I do not know his
   reasons.
   CREON:
Was he in earnest, master of himself,
When he attacked me with this accusation?
   CHORUS-LEADER:
I do not closely scan what kings are doing. —
30 But here he comes in person from the palace.

[*Enter* OEDIPUS.]

   OEDIPUS:
What, *you*? You dare come here? How can
   you find
The impudence to show yourself before
My house, when you are clearly proven
To have sought my life and tried to steal my
   crown?
35 Why, do you think me then a coward, or
A fool, that you should try to lay this plot?
Or that I should not see what you were
   scheming,
And so fall unresisting, blindly, to you?
But you were mad, so to attempt the throne,
40 Poor and unaided; this is not encompassed
Without the strong support of friends and
   money!
   CREON:
This you must do: now you have had your say
Hear my reply; then yourself shall judge.
   OEDIPUS:
A ready tongue! But I am bad at listening —
To you. For I have found how much you hate
45   me.
   CREON:
One thing: first listen to what I have to say.
   OEDIPUS:
One thing: do not pretend you're not a villain.

   CREON:
If you believe it is a thing worth having,
Insensate stubbornness, then you are wrong.
   OEDIPUS:
If you believe that one can harm a kinsman   50
Without retaliation, you are wrong.
   CREON:
With this I have no quarrel; but explain
What injury you say that I have done you.
   OEDIPUS:
Did you advise, or did you not, that I
Should send a man for that most reverend
   prophet?   55
   CREON:
I did, and I am still of that advice.
   OEDIPUS:
How long a time is it since Laius . . .
   CREON:
Since Laius did *what*? How can I say?
   OEDIPUS:
Was seen no more, but met a violent death?
   CREON:
It would be many years now past and gone.   60
   OEDIPUS:
And had this prophet learned his art already?
   CREON:
Yes, his repute was great — as it is now.
   OEDIPUS:
Did he make any mention then of me?
   CREON:
He never spoke of you within my hearing.
   OEDIPUS:
Touching the murder: did you make no
   search?   65
   CREON:
No search? Of course we did; but we found
   nothing.
   OEDIPUS:
And why did this wise prophet not speak *then*?
   CREON:
Who knows? Where I know nothing I say
   nothing.
   OEDIPUS:
This much you know — and you'll do well to
   answer:
   CREON:
What is it? If I know, I'll tell you freely.   70
   OEDIPUS:
That if he had not joined with you, he'd not
Have said that I was Laius' murderer.
   CREON:
If he said this, I did not know. — But I
May rightly question you, as you have me.

56 SOPHOCLES

OEDIPUS:
Ask what you will. You'll never prove *I* killed
75　him.
CREON:
Why then: are you not married to my sister?
OEDIPUS:
I am indeed; it cannot be denied.
CREON:
You share with her the sovereignty of Thebes?
OEDIPUS:
She need but ask, and anything is hers.
CREON:
80　And am I not myself conjoined with you?
OEDIPUS:
You are; not rebel therefore, but a traitor!
CREON:
Not so, if you will reason with yourself,
As I with you. This first: would any man,
To gain no increase of authority, ·
Choose kingship, with its fears and sleepless
85　nights?
Not I. What I desire, what every man
Desires, if he has wisdom, is to take
The substance, not the show, of royalty.
For now, through you, I have both power and
ease,
90　But were I king, I'd be oppressed with cares.
Not so: while I have ample sovereignty
And rule in peace, why should I want the
crown?
I am not yet so mad as to give up
All that which brings me honor and advantage.
95　Now, every man greets me, and I greet him;
Those who have need of you make much of
me,
Since I can make or mar them. Why should I
Surrender this to load myself with that?
A man of sense was never yet a traitor;
100　I have no taste for that, nor could I force
Myself to aid another's treachery.
　　But you can test me: go to Delphi; ask
If I reported rightly what was said.
And further: if you find that I had dealings
105　With that diviner, you may take and kill me
Not with your single vote, but yours and mine,
But not on bare suspicion, unsupported.
How wrong it is, to use a random judgment
And think the false man true, the true man
false!
110　To spurn a loyal friend, that is no better
Than to destroy the life to which we cling.
This you will learn in time, for Time alone
Reveals the upright man; a single day
Suffices to unmask the treacherous.

CHORUS-LEADER:
My lord, he speaks with caution, to avoid　115
Grave error. Hasty judgment is not sure.
OEDIPUS:
But when an enemy is quick to plot
And strike, I must be quick in answer too.
If I am slow, and wait, then I shall find
That he has gained his end, and I am lost.　120
CREON:
What do you wish? To drive me into exile?
OEDIPUS:
No, more than exile: I will have your life.[2]
CREON:
<When will it cease, this monstrous rage of
yours?>
OEDIPUS:
When your example shows what comes of
envy.
CREON:
Must you be stubborn? Cannot you believe
me?　125
OEDIPUS:
<You speak to me as if I were a fool!>
CREON:
Because I know you're wrong.
OEDIPUS:　　　　　　Right, for myself!
CREON:
It is not right for me!
OEDIPUS:　　　　　But you're a traitor.
CREON:
What if your charge is false?
OEDIPUS:　　　　　I have to govern.
CREON:
Not govern badly!

[2] The next two verses, as they stand in the mss., are
impossible. Editors are agreed on this, though no
single remedy has found general acceptance. The mss.
attribute v. 624 [Oedipus' next speech] to Creon, and
v. 625 [Creon's next speech] to Oedipus. I can make
no real sense of this: the only φθόνος, "envy," that is
in question is the envy of his royal power that
Oedipus is attributing to Creon; and the words
ὑπείξων, "yield," "not to be stubborn," and πιστεύσων,
"believe," must surely be used by Creon of Oedipus,
not by Oedipus of Creon. Since a translator who
hopes to be acted must give the actors something to
say, preferably good sense, and cannot fob them off
with a row of dots, I have reconstructed the passage
by guesswork, putting my guesses within brackets. I
have assumed that two verses were lost, one after v.
623 and one after v. 625, and that the wrong attribu-
tion of vv. 624 and 625 followed almost inevitably.
[Kitto.]

130 OEDIPUS: Listen to him, Thebes!
CREON:
You're not the city! I am Theban too.
CHORUS-LEADER:
My lords, no more! Here comes the Queen, and not
Too soon, to join you. With her help, you must
Compose the bitter strife that now divides you.

[*Enter* IOCASTA.]

IOCASTA:
135 You frantic men! What has aroused this wild
Dispute? Have you no shame, when such a plague
Afflicts us, to indulge in private quarrels?
Creon, go home, I pray. You, Oedipus,
Come in; do not make much of what is nothing.
CREON:
140 My sister: Oedipus, your husband here,
Has thought it right to punish me with one
Of two most awful dooms: exile, or death.
OEDIPUS:
I have: I have convicted him, Iocasta,
Of plotting secretly against my life.
CREON:
145 If I am guilty in a single point
Of such a crime, then may I die accursed.
IOCASTA:
O, by the gods, believe him, Oedipus!
Respect the oath that he has sworn, and have
Regard for me, and for these citizens.

[*In what follows, the parts given to the chorus are sung, the rest, presumably, spoken. The rhythm of the music and dance is either dochmiac, 5-time, or a combination of 3- and 5-time.*]

STROPHE

CHORUS:
My lord, I pray, give consent.
Yield to us; ponder well.
OEDIPUS:
What is it you would have me yield?
CHORUS:
Respect a man ripe in years,
5 Bound by this mighty oath he has sworn.
OEDIPUS:
Your wish is clear?

CHORUS: It is.
OEDIPUS: Then tell it me.
CHORUS:
Not to repel, and drive out of our midst a friend,
Scorning a solemn curse, for uncertain cause.
OEDIPUS:
I tell you this: your prayer will mean for me
My banishment from Thebes, or else my death. 10
CHORUS:
No, no! by the Sun, the chief of gods,
Ruin and desolation and all evil come upon me
If I harbor thoughts such as these!
No; our land racked with plague breaks my heart.
Do not now deal a new wound on Thebes to crown the old! 15
OEDIPUS:
Then let him be, though I must die twice over,
Or be dishonored, spurned and driven out.
It's your entreaty, and not his, that moves
My pity; he shall have my lasting hatred.
CREON:
You yield ungenerously; but when your wrath 20
Has cooled, how it will prick you! Natures such
As yours give most vexation to themselves.
OEDIPUS:
O, let me be! Get from my sight.
CREON: I go,
Misjudged by you — but these will judge me better [*indicating* CHORUS].

[*Exit* CREON.]

ANTISTROPHE

CHORUS:
My lady, why now delay?
Let the King go in with you.
IOCASTA:
When you have told me what has passed.
CHORUS:
Suspicion came. — Random words, undeserved,
Will provoke men to wrath. 5
IOCASTA:
It was from both?
CHORUS: It was.
IOCASTA: And what was said?

CHORUS:
It is enough for me, more than enough, when I
Think of our ills, that this should rest where it
    lies.
OEDIPUS:
You and your wise advice, blunting my wrath,
10 Frustrated me — and it has come to this!
CHORUS:
This, O my King, I said, and say again:
    I should be mad, distraught,
    I should be a fool, and worse,
    If I sought to drive you away.
15   Thebes was near sinking; you brought her safe
Through the storm. Now again we pray that
    you may save us.
IOCASTA:
In Heaven's name, my lord, I too must know
What was the reason for this blazing anger.
OEDIPUS:
There's none to whom I more defer; and so,
20 I'll tell you: Creon and his vile plot against me.
IOCASTA:
What has he done, that you are so incensed?
OEDIPUS:
He says that I am Laius' murderer.
IOCASTA:
From his own knowledge? Or has someone
    told him?
OEDIPUS:
No; that suspicion should not fall upon
25 Himself, he used a tool — a crafty prophet.
IOCASTA:
Why, have no fear of *that*. Listen to me,
And you will learn that the prophetic art
Touches our human fortunes not at all.
I soon can give you proof. — An oracle
30 Once came to Laius — from the god himself
I do not say, but from his ministers:
His fate it was, that should he have a son
By me, that son would take his father's life.
But he was killed — or so they said — by
    strangers,
35 By brigands, at a place where three ways meet.
As for the child, it was not three days old
When Laius fastened both its feet together
And had it cast over a precipice.
Therefore Apollo failed; for neither did
40 His son kill Laius, nor did Laius meet
The awful end he feared, killed by his son.
    So much for what prophetic voices uttered.
Have no regard for them. The god will bring
To light himself whatever thing he chooses.
OEDIPUS:
45 Iocasta, terror seizes me, and shakes
My very soul, at one thing you have said.

IOCASTA:
Why so? What have I said to frighten you?
OEDIPUS:
I think I heard you say that Laius
Was murdered at a place where three ways
    meet?
IOCASTA:
So it was said — indeed, they say it still.   50
OEDIPUS:
Where is the place where this encounter
    happened?
IOCASTA:
They call the country Phokis, and a road
From Delphi joins a road from Daulia.
OEDIPUS:
Since that was done, how many years have
    passed?
IOCASTA:
It was proclaimed in Thebes a little time   55
Before the city offered you the crown.
OEDIPUS:
O Zeus, what fate hast thou ordained for me?
IOCASTA:
What is the fear that so oppresses you?
OEDIPUS:
One moment yet: tell me of Laius.
What age was he? and what was his appear-
    ance?   60
IOCASTA:
A tall man, and his hair was touched with
    white;
In figure he was not unlike yourself.
OEDIPUS:
O God! Did I, then, in my ignorance,
Proclaim that awful curse against myself?
IOCASTA:
What are you saying? How you frighten me!   65
OEDIPUS:
I greatly fear that prophet was not blind.
But yet one question; that will show me more.
IOCASTA:
For all my fear, I'll tell you what I can.
OEDIPUS:
Was he alone, or did he have with him
A royal bodyguard of men-at-arms?   70
IOCASTA:
The company in all were five; the King
Rode in a carriage, and there was a Herald.
OEDIPUS:
Ah God! How clear the picture is! . . . But who,
Iocasta, brought report of this to Thebes?
IOCASTA:
A slave, the only man that was not killed.   75
OEDIPUS:
And is he round about the palace now?

IOCASTA:

No, he is not. When he returned, and saw
You ruling in the place of the dead King,
He begged me, on his bended knees, to send him
80 Into the hills as shepherd, out of sight,
As far as could be from the city here.
I sent him, for he was a loyal slave;
He well deserved this favor — and much more.

OEDIPUS:

Could he be brought back here — at once — to see me?

IOCASTA:

85 He could; but why do you desire his coming?

OEDIPUS:

I fear I have already said, Iocasta,
More than enough; and therefore I will see him.

IOCASTA:

Then he shall come. But, as your wife, I ask you,
What is the terror that possesses you?

OEDIPUS:

And you shall know it, since my fears have
90 grown
So great; for who is more to me than you,
That I should speak to *him* at such a moment?
My father, then, was Polybus of Corinth;
My mother, Meropè. My station there
95 Was high as any man's — until a thing
Befell me that was strange indeed, though not
Deserving of the thought I gave to it.
A man said at a banquet — he was full
Of wine — that I was not my father's son.
100 It angered me; but I restrained myself
That day. The next I went and questioned both
My parents. They were much incensed with him
Who had let fall the insult. So, from them,
I had assurance. Yet the slander spread
105 And always chafed me. Therefore secretly,
My mother and my father unaware,
I went to Delphi. Phoebus would return
No answer to my question, but declared
A thing most horrible: he foretold that I
110 Should mate with my own mother, and beget
A brood that men would shudder to behold,
And that I was to be the murderer
Of my own father.   Therefore, back to Corinth
I never went — the stars alone have told me
115 Where Corinth lies — that I might never see
Cruel fulfillment of that oracle.
So journeying, I came to that same spot

Where, as you say, this King was killed. And now,
This is the truth, Iocasta: when I reached
The place where three ways meet, I met a
herald,   120
And in a carriage drawn by colts was such
A man as you describe. By violence
The herald and the older man attempted
To push me off the road, I, in my rage,
Struck at the driver, who was hustling me.   125
The old man, when he saw me level with him,
Taking a double-goad, aimed at my head
A murderous blow. He paid for that, full
measure.
Swiftly I hit him with my staff; he rolled
Out of his carriage, flat upon his back.   130
I killed them all. — But if, between this
stranger
And Laius there was any bond of kinship,
Who could be in more desperate plight than I?
Who more accursèd in the eyes of Heaven?
For neither citizen nor stranger may   135
Receive me in his house, nor speak to me,
But he must bar the door. And it was none
But I invoked this curse on my own head!
And I pollute the bed of him I slew
With my own hands! Say, am I vile? Am I   140
Not all impure? Seeing I must be exiled,
And even in my exile must not go
And see my parents, nor set foot upon
My native land; or, if I do, I must
Marry my mother, and kill Polybus   145
My father, who engendered me and reared me.
If one should say it was a cruel god
Brought this upon me, would he not speak
right?
No, no, you holy powers above! Let me
Not see that day! but rather let me pass   150
Beyond the sight of men, before I see
The stain of such pollution come upon me!

CHORUS-LEADER:

My lord, this frightens me. But you must
hope,
Until we hear the tale from him that saw it.

OEDIPUS:

That is the only hope that's left to me;   155
We must await the coming of the shepherd.

IOCASTA:

What do you hope from him, when he is
here?

OEDIPUS:

I'll tell you: if his story shall be found
The same as yours, then I am free of guilt.

IOCASTA:

But what have *I* said of especial note?   160

OEDIPUS:
You said that he reported it was brigands
Who killed the King. If he still speaks of
   "men,"
It was not I; a single man, and "men,"
Are not the same. But if he says it was
165 A traveler journeying alone, why then,
The burden of the guilt must fall on me.

IOCASTA:
But that *is* what he said, I do assure you!
He cannot take it back again! Not I
Alone, but the whole city heard him say it!
170 But even if he should revoke the tale
He told before, not even so, my lord,
Will he establish that the King was slain
According to the prophecy. For that was clear:
His son, and mine, should slay him. — He,
   poor thing,
175 Was killed himself, and never killed his father.
Therefore, so far as divination goes,
Or prophecy, I'll take no notice of it.

OEDIPUS:
And that is wise. — But send a man to bring
The shepherd; I would not have that ne-
   glected.

IOCASTA:
180 I'll send at once. — But come with me; for I
Would not do anything that could displease
   you.

[*Exeunt* OEDIPUS *and* IOCASTA.]

STROPHE 1

CHORUS:
I pray that I may pass my life
[*in a steady rhythm*] In reverent holiness of
   word and deed.
For there are laws enthroned above;
Heaven created them,
5 Olympus was their father,
And mortal men had no part in their birth;
Nor ever shall their power pass from sight
In dull forgetfulness;
A god moves in them; he grows not old.

ANTISTROPHE 1

Pride makes the tyrant — pride of wealth
And power, too great for wisdom and restraint;
For Pride will climb the topmost height;
Then is the man cast down
5 To uttermost destruction.

There he finds no escape, no resource.
But high contention for the city's good
May the gods preserve.
For me — may the gods be my defense!

STROPHE 2

If there is one who walks in pride
Of word or deed, and has no fear of Justice,
No reverence for holy shrines —
May utter ruin fall on him!
So may his ill-starred pride be given its reward. 5
Those who seek dishonorable advantage
And lay violent hands on holy things
And do not shun impiety —
Who among these will secure himself from the
   wrath of God?
If deeds like these are honored, 10
Why should I join in the sacred dance?

ANTISTROPHE 2

No longer shall Apollo's shrine,
The holy center of the Earth, receive my
   worship;
No, nor his seat at Abae, nor
The temple of Olympian Zeus,
If what the god foretold does not come to
   pass. 5
Mighty Zeus — if so I should address Thee —
O great Ruler of all things, look on this!
Now are thy oracles falling into contempt, and
   men
Deny Apollo's power.
Worship of the gods is passing away. 10

[*Enter* IOCASTA, *attended by a girl carrying a
wreath and incense.*]

IOCASTA:
My lords of Thebes, I have bethought myself
To approach the altars of the gods, and lay
These wreaths on them, and burn this frankin-
   cense.
For every kind of terror has laid hold
On Oedipus; his judgment is distracted. 15
He will not read the future by the past
But yields himself to any who speaks fear.
Since then no words of mine suffice to calm
   him
I turn to Thee Apollo — Thou art nearest —
Thy suppliant, with these votive offerings. 20
Grant us deliverance and peace, for now

Fear is on all, when we see Oedipus,
The helmsman of the ship, so terrified.

[*A reverent silence, while* IOCASTA *lays the
wreath at the altar and sets fire to the
incense. The wreath will remain and the
incense smoke during the rest of the play.*]
[*Enter a* SHEPHERD *from Corinth.*]

CORINTHIAN:
Might I inquire of you where I may find
25 The royal palace of King Oedipus?
Or, better, where himself is to be found?

CHORUS-LEADER:
There is the palace; himself, Sir, is within,
But here his wife and mother of his children.

CORINTHIAN:
Ever may happiness attend on her,
30 And hers, the wedded wife of such a man.

IOCASTA:
May you enjoy the same; your gentle words
Deserve no less. — Now, Sir, declare your purpose;
With what request, what message have you
come?

CORINTHIAN:
With good news for your husband and his
house.

IOCASTA:
What news is this? And who has sent you
35 here?

CORINTHIAN:
I come from Corinth, and the news I bring
Will give you joy, though joy be crossed with
grief.

IOCASTA:
What is this, with its two-fold influence?

CORINTHIAN:
The common talk in Corinth is that they
40 Will call on Oedipus to be their king.

IOCASTA:
What? Does old Polybus no longer reign?

CORINTHIAN:
Not now, for Death has laid him in his grave.

IOCASTA:
Go quickly to your master, girl; give him
The news. — You oracles, where are you now?
45 This is the man whom Oedipus so long
Has shunned, fearing to kill him; now he's
dead,
And killed by Fortune, not by Oedipus.

[*Enter* OEDIPUS, *very nervous.*]

OEDIPUS:
My dear Iocasta, tell me, my dear wife,

Why have you sent to fetch me from the
palace?

IOCASTA:
Listen to *him*, and as you hear, reflect   50
What has become of all those oracles.

OEDIPUS:
Who is this man? — What has he to tell me?

IOCASTA:
He is from Corinth, and he brings you news
About your father. Polybus is dead.

OEDIPUS:
What say you, sir? Tell me the news yourself.   55

CORINTHIAN:
If you would have me first report on this,
I tell you; death has carried him away.

OEDIPUS:
By treachery? Or did sickness come to him?

CORINTHIAN:
A small mischance will lay an old man low.

OEDIPUS:
Poor Polybus! He died, then, of a sickness?   60

CORINTHIAN:
That, and the measure of his many years.

OEDIPUS:
Ah me! Why then, Iocasta, should a man
Regard the Pythian house of oracles,
Or screaming birds, on whose authority
I was to slay my father? But he is dead;   65
The earth has covered him; and here am I,
My sword undrawn — unless perchance *my* loss
Has killed him; so might I be called his slayer.
But for those oracles about my father,
Those he has taken with him to the grave   70
Wherein he lies, and they are come to nothing.

IOCASTA:
Did I not say long since it would be so?

OEDIPUS:
You did; but I was led astray by fear.

IOCASTA:
So none of this deserves another thought.

OEDIPUS:
Yet how can I not fear my mother's bed?   75

IOCASTA:
Why should we fear, seeing that man is ruled
By chance, and there is room for no clear
forethought?
No; live at random, live as best one can.
So do not fear this marriage with your mother;
Many a man has suffered this before —   80
But only in his dreams. Whoever thinks
The least of this, he lives most comfortably.

OEDIPUS:
Your every word I do accept, if she

That bore me did not live; but as she does —

85 Despite your wisdom, how can I but tremble?

IOCASTA:

Yet there is comfort in your father's death.

OEDIPUS:

Great comfort, but still fear of her who lives.

CORINTHIAN:

And who is this who makes you so afraid?

OEDIPUS:

Meropê, my man, the wife of Polybus.

CORINTHIAN:

90 And what in *her* gives cause of fear in *you*?

OEDIPUS:

There was an awful warning from the gods.

CORINTHIAN:

Can it be told, or must it be kept secret?

OEDIPUS:

No secret. Once Apollo said that I

Was doomed to lie with my own mother, and

95 Defile my own hands with my father's blood.

Wherefore has Corinth been, these many years,

My home no more. My fortunes have been
    fair. —

But it is good to see a parent's face.

CORINTHIAN:

It was for fear of *this* you fled the city?

OEDIPUS:

100 This, and the shedding of my father's blood.

CORINTHIAN:

Why then, my lord, since I am come in
    friendship,

I'll rid you here and now of that misgiving.

OEDIPUS:

Be sure, your recompense would be in keeping.

CORINTHIAN:

It was the chief cause of my coming here

That your return might bring me some advan-
105   tage.

OEDIPUS:

Back to my parents I will never go.

CORINTHIAN:

My son, it is clear, you know not what you
    do. . . .

OEDIPUS:

Not know? What is this? Tell me what you
    mean.

CORINTHIAN:

If for this reason you avoid your home.

OEDIPUS:

110 Fearing Apollo's oracle may come true.

CORINTHIAN:

And you incur pollution from your parents?

OEDIPUS:

That is the thought that makes me live in
    terror.

CORINTHIAN:

I tell you then, this fear of yours is idle.

OEDIPUS:

How? Am I not their child, and they my
    parents?

CORINTHIAN:

Because there's none of Polybus in you. 115

OEDIPUS:

How can you say so? Was he not my father?

CORINTHIAN:

I am your father just as much as he!

OEDIPUS:

A stranger equal to the father? How?

CORINTHIAN:

Neither did he beget you, nor did I.

OEDIPUS:

Then for what reason did he call me son? 120

CORINTHIAN:

He had you as a gift — from my own hands.

OEDIPUS:

And showed such love to me? Me, not his
    own?

CORINTHIAN:

Yes, his own childlessness so worked on him.

OEDIPUS:

You, when you gave me: had you bought, or
    found me?

CORINTHIAN:

I found you in the woods upon Cithaeron. 125

OEDIPUS:

Why were you traveling in that neighborhood?

CORINTHIAN:

I tended flocks of sheep upon the mountain.

OEDIPUS:

You were a shepherd, then, wandering for hire?

CORINTHIAN:

I was, my son; but that day, your preserver.

OEDIPUS:

How so? What ailed me when you took me
    up? 130

CORINTHIAN:

For that, your ankles might give evidence.

OEDIPUS:

Alas! why speak of this, my life-long trouble?

CORINTHIAN:

I loosed the fetters clamped upon your feet.

OEDIPUS:

A pretty gift to carry from the cradle!

CORINTHIAN:

It was for this they named you Oedipus. 135

OEDIPUS:

Who did, my father or my mother? Tell me.

CORINTHIAN:

I cannot; he knows more, from whom I had
    you.

OEDIPUS:
It was another, not yourself, that found me?
CORINTHIAN:
Yes, you were given me by another shepherd.
OEDIPUS:
Who? Do you know him? Can you name the
140   man?
CORINTHIAN:
They said that he belonged to Laius.
OEDIPUS:
What — him who once was ruler here in
  Thebes?
CORINTHIAN:
Yes, he it was for whom this man was
  shepherd.
OEDIPUS:
And is he still alive, that I can see him?
CORINTHIAN [turning to the CHORUS]:
145 You that are native here would know that best.
OEDIPUS:
Has any man of you now present here
Acquaintance with this shepherd, him he
  speaks of?
Has any seen him, here, or in the fields?
Speak; on this moment hangs discovery.
CHORUS-LEADER:
150 It is, I think, the man that you have sent for,
The slave now in the country. But who should
  know
The truth of this more than Iocasta here?
OEDIPUS:
The man he speaks of: do you think, Iocasta,
He is the one I have already summoned?
IOCASTA:
155 What matters who he is? Pay no regard. —
The tale is idle; it is best forgotten.
OEDIPUS:
It cannot be that I should have this clue
And then not find the secret of my birth.
IOCASTA:
In God's name stop, if you have any thought
160 For your own life! My ruin is enough.
OEDIPUS:
Be not dismayed; nothing can prove you base.
Not though I find my mother thrice a slave.
IOCASTA:
O, I beseech you, do not! Seek no more!
OEDIPUS:
You cannot move me. I will know the truth.
IOCASTA:
165 I know that what I say is for the best.
OEDIPUS:
This "best" of yours! I have no patience with it.
IOCASTA:
O may you never learn what man you are!

OEDIPUS:
Go, someone, bring the herdsman here to me,
And leave her to enjoy her pride of birth.
IOCASTA:
O man of doom! For by no other name   170
Can I address you now or evermore.
              [Exit IOCASTA.]
CHORUS-LEADER:
The Queen has fled, my lord, as if before
Some driving storm of grief. I fear that from
Her silence may break forth some great disas-
  ter.
OEDIPUS:
Break forth what will! My birth, however
  humble,   175
I am resolved to find. But she, perhaps,
Is proud, as women will be; is ashamed
Of my low birth. But I do rate myself
The child of Fortune, giver of all good,
And I shall not be put to shame, for I   180
Am born of Her; the Years who are my
  kinsmen
Distinguished my estate, now high, now low;
So born, I could not make me someone else
And not do all to find my parentage.

STROPHE 1

CHORUS:
If I have power of prophecy,
[animated rhythm] If I have judgment wise
  and sure, Cithaeron
(I swear by Olympus),
Thou shalt be honored when the moon
Next is full, as mother and foster-nurse   5
And birth-place of Oedipus, with festival and
  dancing,
For thou hast given great blessings to our
  King.
To Thee, Apollo, now we raise our cry:
O grant our prayer find favor in thy sight!

ANTISTROPHE

Who is thy mother, O my son?
Is she an ageless nymph among the mountains,
That bore thee to Pan?
Or did Apollo father thee?
For dear to him are the pastures in the hills.   5
Or Hermes, who ruleth from the summit of
  Kyllene?

Or Dionysus on the mountain-tops,
Did he receive thee from thy mother's arms,
A nymph who follows him on Helicon?

OEDIPUS:

10 If I, who never yet have met the man,
May risk conjecture, I think I see the herds-
    man
Whom we have long been seeking. In his age
He well accords; and more, I recognize
Those who are with him as of my own
    household.
15 But as for knowing, you will have advantage
Of me, if you have seen the man before.

CHORUS-LEADER:

'Tis he, for certain — one of Laius' men,
One of the shepherds whom he trusted most.

[*Enter the* THEBAN SHEPHERD.]

OEDIPUS:

You first I ask, you who have come from
    Corinth:
Is that the man you mean?

20 CORINTHIAN: That very man.

OEDIPUS:

Come here, my man; look at me; answer me
My questions. Were you ever Laius' man?

THEBAN:

I was; his slave — born in the house, not
    bought.

OEDIPUS:

What was your charge, or what your way of
    life?

THEBAN:

25 Tending the sheep, the most part of my life.

OEDIPUS:

And to what regions did you most resort?

THEBAN:

Now it was Cithaeron, now the country round.

OEDIPUS:

And was this man of your acquaintance there?

THEBAN:

In what employment? Which is the man you
    mean?

OEDIPUS:

30 Him yonder. Had you any dealings with him?

THEBAN:

Not such that I can quickly call to mind.

CORINTHIAN:

No wonder, Sir, but though he has forgotten
I can remind him. I am very sure,
He knows the time when, round about Cithae-
    ron,
35 He with a double flock, and I with one,
We spent together three whole summer sea-
    sons,

From spring until the rising of Arcturus.
Then, with the coming on of winter, I
Drove my flocks home, he his, to Laius' folds.
Is this the truth? or am I telling lies?   40

THEBAN:

It is true, although it happened long ago.

CORINTHIAN:

Then tell me: do you recollect a baby
You gave me once to bring up for my own?

THEBAN:

Why this? Why are you asking me this
    question?

CORINTHIAN:

My friend, *here* is the man who was that baby!   45

THEBAN:

O, devil take you! Cannot you keep silent?

OEDIPUS:

Here, Sir! This man needs no reproof from you.
Your tongue needs chastisement much more
    than his.

THEBAN:

O best of masters, how am I offending?

OEDIPUS:

Not telling of the child of whom he speaks.   50

THEBAN:

He? He knows nothing. He is wasting time.

OEDIPUS [*threatening*]:

If you'll not speak from pleasure, speak from
    pain.

THEBAN:

No, no, I pray! Not torture an old man!

OEDIPUS:

Here, someone quickly! Twist this fellow's
    arms!

THEBAN:

Why, wretched man? What would you know
    besides?   55

OEDIPUS:

That child: you gave it him, the one he speaks
    of?

THEBAN:

I did. Ah God, would I have died instead!

OEDIPUS:

And die you shall, unless you speak the truth.

THEBAN:

And if I do, then death is still more certain.

OEDIPUS:

This man, I think, is trying to delay me.   60

THEBAN:

Not I! I said I gave the child — just now.

OEDIPUS:

And got it — where? Your own? or someone
    else's?

THEBAN:

No, not my own. Someone had given it me.

OEDIPUS:
Who? Which of these our citizens? From what house?
THEBAN:
65 No, I implore you, master! Do not ask!
OEDIPUS:
You die if I must question you again.
THEBAN:
Then, 'twas a child of one in Laius' house.
OEDIPUS:
You mean a slave? Or someone of his kin?
THEBAN:
God! I am on the verge of saying it.
OEDIPUS:
70 And I of hearing it, but hear I must.
THEBAN:
His own, or so they said. But she within
Could tell you best — your wife — the truth of it.
OEDIPUS:
What, did she give you it?
THEBAN: She did, my lord.
OEDIPUS:
With what intention?
THEBAN: That I should destroy it.
OEDIPUS:
Her own? — How could she?
75 THEBAN: Frightened by oracles.
OEDIPUS:
What oracles?
THEBAN: That it would kill its parents.
OEDIPUS:
Why did you let it go to this man here?
THEBAN:
I pitied it, my lord. I thought to send
The child abroad, whence this man came. And he
80 Saved it, for utter doom. For if you are
The man he says, then you were born for ruin.
OEDIPUS:
Ah God! Ah God! This is the truth, at last!
O Sun, let me behold thee this once more,
I who am proved accursed in my conception,
85 And in my marriage, and in him I slew.
[*Exeunt severally* OEDIPUS, CORINTHIAN, THEBAN.]

STROPHE 1

CHORUS:
Alas! you generations of men!
[*glyconics*] Even while you live you are next to nothing!
Has any man won for himself

More than the shadow of happiness,
A shadow that swiftly fades away?   5
Oedipus, now as I look on you,
See your ruin, how can I say that
Mortal man can be happy?

ANTISTROPHE 1

For who won greater prosperity?
Sovereignty and wealth beyond all desiring?
The crooked-clawed, riddling Sphinx,
Maiden and bird, you overcame;
You stood like a tower of strength to Thebes.   5
So you received our crown, received the
Highest honors that we could give —
King in our mighty city.

STROPHE 2

Who more wretched, more afflicted now,
With cruel misery, with fell disaster,
Your life in dust and ashes?
    O noble Oedipus!
    How could it be? to come again   5
A bridegroom of her who gave you birth!
How could such a monstrous thing
Endure so long, unknown?

ANTISTROPHE 2

Time sees all, and Time, in your despite,
Disclosed and punished your unnatural marriage —
A child, and then a husband.
    O son of Laius,
    Would I had never looked on you!   5
I mourn you as one who mourns the dead.
First you gave me back my life,
And now, that life is death.

[*Enter, from the palace, a* MESSENGER.]

MESSENGER:
My Lords, most honored citizens of Thebes,
What deeds am I to tell of, you to see!   10
What heavy grief to bear, if still remains
Your native loyalty to our line of kings.
For not the Ister, no, nor Phasis' flood.
Could purify this house, such things it hides,
Such others will it soon display to all,   15

Evils self-sought. Of all our sufferings
Those hurt the most that we ourselves inflict.
CHORUS-LEADER:
Sorrow enough — too much — in what was known
Already. What new sorrow do you bring?
MESSENGER:
20 Quickest for me to say and you to hear:
It is the Queen, Iocasta — she is dead.
CHORUS-LEADER:
Iocasta, dead? But how? What was the cause?
MESSENGER:
By her own hand. Of what has passed, the worst
Cannot be yours: that was, to see it.
25 But you shall hear, so far as memory serves,
The cruel story. — In her agony
She ran across the courtyard, snatching at
Her hair with both her hands. She made her way
Straight to her chamber; she barred fast the doors
30 And called on Laius, these long years dead,
Remembering their by-gone procreation.
"Through this did you meet death yourself, and leave
To me, the mother, child-bearing accursed
To my own child." She cried aloud upon
35 The bed where she had borne a double brood,
Husband from husband, children from a child.
And thereupon she died, I know not how;
For, groaning, Oedipus burst in, and we,
For watching him, saw not *her* agony
And how it ended. He, ranging through the
40 palace,
Came up to each man calling for a sword,
Calling for her whom he had called his wife,
Asking where was she who had borne them all,
Himself and his own children. So he raved.
45 And then some deity showed him the way,
For it was none of us that stood around;
He cried aloud, as if to someone who
Was leading him; he leapt upon the doors,
Burst from their sockets the yielding bars, and fell
50 Into the room; and there, hanged by the neck,
We saw his wife, held in a swinging cord.
He, when he saw it, groaned in misery
And loosed her body from the rope. When now
She lay upon the ground, awful to see
Was that which followed: from her dress he tore
55 The golden brooches that she had been wearing,

Raised them, and with their points struck his own eyes,
Crying aloud that they should never see
What he had suffered and what he had done,
But in the dark henceforth they should behold 60
Those whom they ought not; nor should recognize
Those whom he longed to see. To such refrain
He smote his eyeballs with the pins, not once,
Nor twice; and as he smote them, blood ran down
His face, not dripping slowly, but there fell 65
Showers of black rain and blood-red hail together.
Not on his head alone, but on them both,
Husband and wife, this common storm has broken.
Their ancient happiness of early days
Was happiness indeed; but now, today, 70
Death, ruin, lamentation, shame — of all
The ills there are, not one is wanting here.
CHORUS-LEADER:
Now is there intermission in his agony?
MESSENGER:
He shouts for someone to unbar the gates,
And to display to Thebes the parricide, 75
His mother's — no, I cannot speak the words;
For, by the doom he uttered, he will cast
Himself beyond our borders, not remain
To be a curse at home. But he needs strength,
And one to guide him; for these wounds are greater 80
Than he can bear — as you shall see; for look!
They draw the bolts. A sight you will behold
To move the pity even of an enemy.

[*The doors open.* OEDIPUS *slowly advances.*]

CHORUS:
O horrible, dreadful sight. More dreadful far

[*These verses sung or chanted in a slow march-time.*]

Than any I have yet seen. What cruel frenzy 85
Came over you? What spirit with superhuman leap
Came to assist your grim destiny?
Ah, most unhappy man!
But no! I cannot bear even to look at you,
Though there is much that I would ask and see and hear. 90
But I shudder at the very sight of you.
OEDIPUS [*sings in the dochmiac rhythm*]:
Alas! alas! and woe for my misery!
Where are my steps taking me?

My random voice is lost in the air.
95 O God! how hast thou crushed me!
CHORUS-LEADER [*spoken*]:
Too terribly for us to hear or see.
OEDIPUS [*sings*]:
O cloud of darkness abominable,
My enemy unspeakable,
In cruel onset insuperable.
100 Alas! alas! Assailed at once by pain
Of pin-points and of memory of crimes.
CHORUS-LEADER:
In such tormenting pains you well may cry
A double grief and feel a double woe.
OEDIPUS [*sings*]:
Ah, my friend!
105 Still at my side? Still steadfast?
Still can you endure me?
Still care for me, a blind man?
[*Speaks.*] For it is you, my friend; I know 'tis you;
Though all is darkness, yet I know your voice.
CHORUS-LEADER:
110 O, to destroy your sight! How could you bring
Yourself to do it? What god incited you?
OEDIPUS [*sings*]:
It was Apollo, friends, Apollo.
He decreed that I should suffer what I suffer;
But the hand that struck, alas! was my own,
115 And not another's.
For why should I have sight.
When sight of nothing could give me pleasure?
CHORUS:
It was even as you say.
OEDIPUS:
What have I left, my friends, to see,
120 To cherish, whom to speak with, or
To listen to, with joy?
Lead me away at once, far from Thebes;
Lead me away, my friends!
I have destroyed; I am accursed, and, what is more,
125 Hateful to Heaven, as no other.
CHORUS-LEADER [*speaks*]:
Unhappy your intention, and unhappy
Your fate. O would that I had never known you!
OEDIPUS [*sings*]:
Curses on him, whoever he was,
Who took the savage fetters from my feet,
130 Snatched me from death, and saved me.
No thanks I owe him,
For had I died that day
Less ruin had I brought on me and mine.

CHORUS:
That wish is my wish too.
OEDIPUS:
I had not then come and slain my father.   135
Nor then would men have called me
Husband of her that bore me.
Now am I God's enemy, child of the guilty,
And she that bore me has borne too my children;
And if there is evil surpassing evil,   140
That has come to Oedipus.
CHORUS-LEADER:
How can I say that you have counseled well?
Far better to be dead than to be blind.
OEDIPUS:
That what is done was not done for the best
Seek not to teach me: counsel me no more.   145
I know not how I could have gone to Hades
And with these eyes have looked upon my father
Or on my mother; such things have I done
To them, death is no worthy punishment.
Or could I look for pleasure in the sight   150
Of my own children, born as they were born?
Never! No pleasure there, for eyes of mine,
Nor in this city, nor its battlements
Nor sacred images. From these — ah, miserable! —
I, the most nobly born of any Theban   155
Am banned for ever by my own decree
That the defiler should be driven forth,
The man accursed of Heaven and Laius' house.
Was I to find such taint in me, and then
With level eyes to look *them* in the face?   160
Nay more: if for my ears I could have built
Some dam to stay the flood of sound, that I
Might lose both sight and hearing, and seal up
My wretched body — that I would have done.
How good to dwell beyond the reach of pain!   165
   Cithaeron! Why did you accept me? Why
Did you not take and kill me? Never then
Should I have come to dwell among the Thebans.
   O Polybus! Corinth! and that ancient home
I thought my father's — what a thing you nurtured!   170
How fair, how foul beneath! For I am found
Foul in myself and in my parentage.
   O you three ways, that in a hidden glen
Do meet: you narrow branching roads within
The forest — you, through my own hands, did drink   175
My father's blood, that was my own. — Ah! do you

Remember what you saw me do? And what
I did again in Thebes? You marriages!
You did beget me: then, having begotten,
180 Bore the same crop again, and brought to light
Commingled blood of fathers, brothers, sons,
Brides, mothers, wives; all that there can be
Among the human kind most horrible!
    But that which it is foul to do, it is
185 Not fair to speak of. Quick as you can, I beg,
Banish me, hide me, slay me! Throw me forth
Into the sea, where I may sink from view.
I pray you, deign to touch one so afflicted,
And do not fear: there is no man alive
190 Can bear this load of evil but myself.

    CHORUS-LEADER:
To listen to your prayers, Creon is here,
For act or guidance opportune; for he,
In your defection, is our champion.

    [*Enter* CREON.]

    OEDIPUS:
Alas! alas! How can I speak to him?
195 What word of credit find? In all my commerce
With him aforetime I am proven false.
    CREON:
No exultation, Oedipus, and no reproach
Of injuries inflicted brings me here;
But if the face of men moves not your shame,
200 Then reverence show to that all-nurturing fire,
The holy Sun, that he be not polluted
By such accursèd sight, which neither Earth
Nor rain from Heaven nor sunlight can en-
    dure.
    Take him within, and quickly: it is right
205 His kinsmen only should behold and hear
Evils that chiefly on his kinsmen fall.
    OEDIPUS:
In Heaven's name — since you cheat my expec-
    tation,
So noble towards my baseness — grant me this:
It is for you I ask it, not myself.
    CREON:
210 What is this supplication that you make?
    OEDIPUS:
Drive me at once beyond your bounds, where I
Shall be alone, and no one speak to me.
    CREON:
I would have done it; but I first desired
To ask the God what he would have me do.
    OEDIPUS:
215 No, his command was given in full, to slay
Me, the polluter and the parricide.
    CREON:
Those were his words; but in our present need
It would be wise to ask what we should do.

    OEDIPUS:
You will inquire for such a wretch as I?
    CREON:
I will; for now you may believe the god.   220
    OEDIPUS:
Yes; and on you I lay this charge and duty:
Give burial, as you will, to her who lies
Within — for she is yours, and this is proper;
And, while I live, let not my father's city
Endure to have me as a citizen.   225
My home must be the mountains — on Cithae-
    ron,
Which, while they lived, my parents chose to
    be
My tomb: they wished to slay me; now they
    shall.
For this I know: sickness can never kill me,
Nor any other evil; I was not saved   230
That day from death, except for some strange
    doom.
My fate must take the course it will. — Now,
    for my sons,
Be not concerned for them: they can, being
    men,
Fend for themselves, wherever they may be:
But my unhappy daughters, my two girls,   235
Whose chairs were always set beside my own
At table — they who shared in every dish
That was prepared for me — oh Creon! these
Do I commend to you. And grant me this:
To take them in my arms, and weep for them.   240
My lord! most noble Creon! could I now
But hold them in my arms, then I should
    think
I had them as I had when I could see them.
Ah! what is this?
Ah Heaven! do I not hear my dear ones,
    sobbing?   245
Has Creon, in his pity, sent to me
My darling children? Has he? Is it true?
    CREON:
It is; they have been always your delight;
So, knowing this, I had them brought to you.
    OEDIPUS:
Then Heaven reward you, and for this kind
    service   250
Protect you better than it protected me!
    Where are you, children? Where? O come
    to me!
Come, let me clasp you with a brother's arms,
These hands, which helped your father's eyes,
    once bright,
To look upon you as they see you now —   255
Your father who, not seeing, nor inquiring,
Gave you for mother her who bore himself.

See you I cannot; but I weep for you,
For the unhappiness that must be yours,
260 And for the bitter life that you must lead.
What gathering of the citizens, what festivals,
Will you have part in? Your high celebrations
Will be to go back home, and sit in tears.
And when the time for marriage comes, what man
265 Will stake upon the ruin and the shame
That *I* am to my parents and to you?
Nothing is wanting there: your father slew
His father, married her who gave him birth,
And then, from that same source whence he himself
270 Had sprung, got you. — With these things they will taunt you;
And who will take you then in marriage? — Nobody;
But you must waste, unwedded and unfruitful.
Ah, Creon! Since they have no parent now
But you — for both of us who gave them life
275 Have perished — suffer them not to be cast out
Homeless and beggars; for they are your kin.
Have pity on them, for they are so young,
So desolate, except for you alone.
Say "Yes," good Creon! Let your hand confirm it.
280 And now, my children, for my exhortation
You are too young; but you can pray that I
May live henceforward — where I should; and you
More happily than the father who begot you.

CREON:
Now make an end of tears, and go within.

OEDIPUS:
285 Then I must go — against my will.

CREON:
There is a time for everything.

OEDIPUS:
You know what I would have you do?

CREON:
If you will tell me, I shall know.

OEDIPUS:
Send me away, away from Thebes.

CREON:
The God, not I, must grant you this.   290

OEDIPUS:
The gods hate no man more than me!

CREON:
Then what you ask they soon will give.

OEDIPUS:
You promise this?

CREON: Ah no! When I
Am ignorant, I do not speak.

OEDIPUS:
Then lead me in; I say no more.   295

CREON:
Release the children then, and come.

OEDIPUS:
What? Take these children from me? No!

CREON:
Seek not to have your way in all things:
Where you had your way before,
Your mastery broke before the end.   300

[*There was no doubt a short concluding utterance from the* CHORUS. *What stands in the mss. appears to be spurious.*][3]

[3] Few other scholars share Professor Kitto's suspicion that the concluding lines in the manuscript are spurious. The passage is translated thus by J. T. Sheppard:

CHORUS:
Look, ye who dwell in Thebes. This man was Oedipus.
That mighty King, who knew the riddle's mystery,
Whom all the city envied, Fortune's favorite.
Behold, in the event, the storm of his calamities,
And, being mortal, think on that last day of death,
Which all must see, and speak of no man's happiness
Till, without sorrow, he hath passed the goal of life.
[Eds.]

Classroom discussions of *Oedipus the King,* like discussions in books, are often mostly devoted to the problem of fate and free will. Students (who ought to be filled with youthful confidence in the freedom of the will) generally argue that Oedipus is fated; instructors (who ought to be old enough to know that the inexplicable and unwilled often comes about) generally argue that Oedipus is free and of his own accord performed the actions that fulfilled the prophecy. Prophecy or prediction or foreknowledge, instructors patiently explain, is not the same as foreordination. The physician who says that the newborn babe will never develop mentally beyond the age of six is predicting, but he is not ordaining or willing. So, the argument usually runs, the oracle who predicted that Oedipus would kill his father and marry his mother was not *causing* Oedipus to do these things but was simply, in his deep knowledge, announcing what a man like Oedipus would do. But that may be too sophisticated a reading, and a reading that derives from the much later European view of man as a creature who can shape his destiny. It is hard for us — especially if the tragedy we know best is Shakespeare's — to recognize the possibility of another sort of tragic drama which does not relate the individual's suffering to his own actions but which postulates some sort of Necessity that works within him.

Whatever the merits of these views, the spectators or readers undeniably know, when they set out to see or read the play, that Oedipus must end wretchedly. The story is known to us, fixed in Sophocles' text, and Oedipus cannot extricate himself from it. Something along these lines was suggested in the middle of the fourth century B.C. when a Greek comic dramatist complained that the comic writer's task was harder than the tragic writer's: "Tragedy has the best of it since the stories are known beforehand to the spectators even before anyone speaks; so the poet only has to remind them. For if I merely say the name Oedipus, they all know the rest — his father Laius, mother Iocasta, daughters, who his sons are, what will happen to him, what he did." In fact, it should be mentioned, the tragic writer's task was not quite so easy. First of all, we have Aristotle's statement that "even the known legends are known to only a few," and, second, we have evidence that the tragic writer could vary the details. In Homer's *Iliad* we read that Oedipus continued to rule even after his dreadful history was known, but Sophocles exiles him. And a fragment of Euripides indicates that Euripides' Oedipus was blinded by Laius' followers, but Sophocles' Oedipus blinds himself. These are details, but they are rather important ones. Probably the ancient Greeks knew the legends in a rough sort of way, as most of us know the Bible or some nuggets of Roman history. Robert Frost and Archibald MacLeish have both drawn from the Book of Job, but their works are enormously different. A writer who uses Job can scarcely omit Job's great suffering, and he can assume that his audience will know that Job had a wife and some comforters, but he is free to go on from there. Similarly, Brutus must stab Julius Caesar, but that leaves lots of room for other material in a play about Caesar. Shakespeare, by the way, could even assume that the audience that saw his *Julius Caesar* would accept a different version of the facts in his *Antony and Cleopatra*. In *Julius Caesar*, Brutus kills himself, but in *Antony and Cleopatra* Antony says (and presumably he is speaking the truth — the truth, that is, for *that* play) that Brutus died at Antony's hands.

Still, the main outline of Oedipus' life must have been fixed, and for us even the details are forever fixed in Sophocles' version. (We know that the Greeks wrote a dozen plays about Oedipus' discovery of his terrible actions, but only Sophocles' survives.) This means that as we read or watch it, each speech has for us a meaning somewhat different from the meaning it has for the speaker and the audience on the stage. Oedipus says he will hunt out the polluted man; we know, as he and the Thebans do not, that *he* is the hunted as well as the hunter. Oedipus says the killer of King Laius may well try to strike at him; we know that Oedipus will find himself out and will strike out his own eyes. A messenger from Corinth tries to allay Oedipus' fears, but he sets them going. What we are talking about, of course, is tragic irony, or Sophoclean irony, in which words and deeds have a larger meaning for the spectator than for the dramatis personae. And surely it is in part because Sophocles so persistently uses this device of giving speeches a second, awesome significance that we feel the plot is a masterpiece of construction in which Oedipus is caught. If ever a man had confidence in his will, it was Oedipus, but if ever a man moved toward a predicted point, it was Oedipus. He had solved the riddle of the sphinx (by himself, without the aid of birds, he somewhat hybristically boasts), but he did not yet know himself. That knowledge was to come later, when he commendably pursued the quest for Laius' slayer and inevitably found himself. The thing is as inevitable as the history described in the sphinx's riddle, which in J. T. Sheppard's version goes thus:

> A thing there is whose voice is one;
> Whose feet are four and two and three.
> So mutable a thing is none
> That moves in earth or sky or sea.
> When on most feet this thing doth go,
> Its strength is weakest and its pace most slow.

This is the history of man, willy-nilly. In Sophocles' time men grew from crawling infancy, through erect manhood, to bent old age supported by a stick, and so they do in our time, as the child's rhyme still claims:

> Walks on four feet,
> On two feet, on three,
> The more feet it walks on,
> The weaker it be.

There was scarcely an infant weaker than the maimed Oedipus; there was scarcely a man stronger than King Oedipus at his height; and there was scarcely a man more in need of a staff than the blind exile. However free each of his actions — and we can only feel that the man whom we see on the stage is acting freely when he abuses Teiresias and Creon — Oedipus was by fate a man, and thus the largest pattern of his life could be predicted easily enough.

THE TRAGEDY OF KING LEAR

William Shakespeare

Edited by Russell Fraser

William Shakespeare (1564–1616) was born in Stratford, England, of middle-class parents. Nothing of interest is known about his early years, but by 1590 he was acting and writing plays in London. He early worked in all three Elizabethan dramatic genres — tragedy, comedy, and history. *Romeo and Juliet*, for example, was written about 1595, the year of *Richard II*, and in the following year he wrote *A Midsummer Night's Dream*. *Julius Caesar* (1599) probably preceded *As You Like It* by one year, and *Hamlet* probably followed *As You Like It* by less than a year. Among the plays that followed *King Lear* (1605–1606) were *Macbeth* (1605–1606) and several "romances" — plays that have happy endings but that seem more meditative and closer to tragedy than such comedies as *A Midsummer Night's Dream*, *As You Like It*, and *Twelfth Night*.

[*DRAMATIS PERSONAE*

LEAR, *King of Britain*
KING OF FRANCE
DUKE OF BURGUNDY
DUKE OF CORNWALL, *husband to Regan*
DUKE OF ALBANY, *husband to Goneril*
EARL OF KENT
EARL OF GLOUCESTER
EDGAR, *son to Gloucester*
EDMUND, *bastard son to Gloucester*
CURAN, *a courtier*
OSWALD, *steward to Goneril*
OLD MAN, *tenant to Gloucester*

DOCTOR
LEAR'S FOOL
A CAPTAIN *subordinate to Edmund*
GENTLEMEN *attending on Cordelia*
A HERALD
SERVANTS *to Cornwall*
GONERIL ⎫
REGAN ⎬ *daughters to Lear*
CORDELIA ⎭
KNIGHTS *attending on Lear*, OFFICERS,
    MESSENGERS, SOLDIERS, ATTENDANTS

Scene: Britain]

Charles Laughton as King Lear and Ian Holm as the Fool in the Shakespeare Memorial Theatre production directed by Glen Byam Shaw at Stratford-upon-Avon, England, 1959. (Photograph: Angus McBean. Harvard Theatre Collection.)

ACT I

SCENE I. [*King* LEAR'*s palace.*]

Enter KENT, GLOUCESTER, *and* EDMUND.

KENT: I thought the king had more affected°¹ the Duke of Albany° than Cornwall.

GLOUCESTER: It did always seem so to us; but now, in the division of the kingdom, it

5 appears not which of the dukes he values most, for equalities are so weighed that curiosity in neither can make choice of either's moiety.°

KENT: Is not this your son, my lord?

GLOUCESTER: His breeding,° sir, hath been at

10 my charge. I have so often blushed to acknowledge him that now I am brazed° to't.

KENT: I cannot conceive° you.

GLOUCESTER: Sir, this young fellow's mother could; whereupon she grew round-wombed,

15 and had indeed, sir, a son for her cradle ere she had a husband for her bed. Do you smell a fault?

KENT: I cannot wish the fault undone, the issue° of it being so proper.°

20 GLOUCESTER: But I have a son, sir, by order of law, some year elder than this, who yet is no dearer in my account:° though this knave° came something saucily° to the world before he was sent for, yet was his mother fair, there was

25 good sport at his making, and the whoreson° must be acknowledged. Do you know this noble gentleman, Edmund?

From *King Lear* by William Shakespeare, edited by Russell Fraser. Copyright © Russell Fraser 1963. Copyright © 1963 Sylvan Barnet. Reprinted by arrangement with The New American Library, Inc., New York, N.Y.
¹The degree sign (°) indicates a footnote, which is keyed to the text by the line number. Text references are printed in **boldface** type; the annotation follows in lightface type. The notes are Russell Fraser's. [Eds.]
I.1.2 **affected** loved   2 **Albany** Albanacte, whose domain extended "from the river Humber to the point of Caithness" (Holinshed)   6–7 **equalities . . . moiety** shares are so balanced against one another that careful examination by neither can make him wish the other's portion   9 **breeding** upbringing   11 **brazed** made brazen, hardened   12 **conceive** understand (pun follows)   19 **issue** result (child)   19 **proper** handsome   22 **account** estimation; **knave** fellow (without disapproval)   23 **saucily** (1) insolently (2) lasciviously   25 **whoreson** fellow (literally, son of a whore)

EDMUND: No, my lord.

GLOUCESTER: My Lord of Kent. Remember him hereafter as my honorable friend.   30

EDMUND: My services to your lordship.

KENT: I must love you, and sue° to know you better.

EDMUND: Sir, I shall study deserving.

GLOUCESTER: He hath been out° nine years,   35 and away he shall again. The king is coming.

(*Sound a sennet.° Enter one bearing a coronet,° then King* LEAR, *then the Dukes of* CORNWALL *and* ALBANY, *next* GONERIL, REGAN, CORDELIA, *and* ATTENDANTS.)

LEAR:
Attend the lords of France and Burgundy, Gloucester.

GLOUCESTER:
I shall, my lord.   (*Exit,* [*with* EDMUND].)

LEAR:
Meantime we shall express our darker purpose.°
Give me the map there. Know that we have   40 divided
In three our kingdom; and 'tis our fast° intent
To shake all cares and business from our age,
Conferring them on younger strengths, while we
Unburthened crawl toward death. Our son of Cornwall,   45
And you our no less loving son of Albany,
We have this hour a constant will to publish°
Our daughters' several° dowers, that future strife
May be prevented° now. The princes, France and Burgundy,
Great rivals in our youngest daughter's love,
Long in our court have made their amorous   50 sojourn,
And here are to be answered. Tell me, my daughters
(Since now we will divest us both of rule,

32 **sue** entreat   35 **out** away, abroad   36 s.d. **sennet** set of notes played on a trumpet, signaling the entrance or departure of a procession; **coronet** small crown, intended for Cordelia   39 **darker purpose** hidden intention   41 **fast** fixed   46 **constant . . . publish** fixed intention to proclaim   47 **several** separate   48 **prevented** forestalled

Interest° of territory, cares of state),
Which of you shall we say doth love us most,
55 That we our largest bounty may extend
Where nature doth with merit challenge.°
    Goneril,
Our eldest-born, speak first.
    GONERIL:
Sir, I love you more than word can wield° the
    matter;
Dearer than eyesight, space,° and liberty;
Beyond what can be valued, rich or rare;
No less than life, with grace, health, beauty,
    honor;
As much as child e'er loved, or father found;
A love that makes breath° poor, and speech
    unable:°
Beyond all manner of so much° I love you.
    CORDELIA [aside]:
What shall Cordelia speak? Love, and be
5   silent.
    LEAR:
Of all these 'bounds, even from this line to
    this,
With shadowy forests, and with champains
    riched,°
With plenteous rivers, and wide-skirted
    meads,°
We make thee lady. To thine and Albany's
    issues°
Be this perpetual.° What says our second
'0   daughter,
Our dearest Regan, wife of Cornwall? Speak.
    REGAN:
I am made of that self mettle° as my sister,
And prize me at her worth.° In my true heart
I find she names my very deed of love;°
75 Only she comes too short, that° I profess
Myself an enemy to all other joys
Which the most precious square of sense
    professes,°
And find I am alone felicitate°
In your dear highness' love.

CORDELIA [aside]:   Then poor Cordelia!
And yet not so, since I am sure my love's   80
More ponderous° than my tongue.
    LEAR:
To thee and thine hereditary ever
Remain this ample third of our fair kingdom,
No less in space, validity,° and pleasure
Than that conferred on Goneril. Now, our joy,   85
Although our last and least;° to whose young
    love
The vines of France and milk° of Burgundy
Strive to be interest;° what can you say to draw
A third more opulent than your sisters? Speak.
    CORDELIA:
Nothing, my lord.   90
    LEAR: Nothing?
    CORDELIA: Nothing.
    LEAR:
Nothing will come of nothing. Speak again.
    CORDELIA:
Unhappy that I am, I cannot heave
My heart into my mouth. I love your majesty   95
According to my bond,° no more nor less.
    LEAR:
How, how, Cordelia? Mend your speech a
    little,
Lest you may mar your fortunes.
    CORDELIA: Good my lord,
You have begot me, bred me, loved me. I
Return those duties back as are right fit,°   100
Obey you, love you, and most honor you.
Why have my sisters husbands, if they say
They love you all? Haply,° when I shall wed,
That lord whose hand must take my plight°
    shall carry
Half my love with him, half my care and duty.   105
Sure I shall never marry like my sisters,
To love my father all.
    LEAR:
But goes thy heart with this?
    CORDELIA: Ay, my good lord.
    LEAR:
So young, and so untender?
    CORDELIA:
So young, my lord, and true.   110
    LEAR:
Let it be so, thy truth then be thy dower!

---

53 **Interest** legal right   56 **nature . . . challenge** natural affection contends with desert for (or lays claim to) bounty   58 **wield** handle   59 **space** scope   63 **breath** language; **unable** impotent   64 **Beyond . . . much** beyond all these comparisons   67 **champains riched** enriched plains   68 **wide-skirted meads** extensive grasslands   69 **issues** descendants   70 **perpetual** in perpetuity   72 **self mettle** same material or temperament   73 **prize . . . worth** value me the same (imperative)   74 **my . . . love** what my love really is (a legalism)   75 **that** in that   77 **Which . . . professes** which the choicest estimate of sense avows   78 **felicitate** made happy

81 **ponderous** weighty   84 **validity** value   86 **least** youngest, smallest   87 **milk** i.e., pastures   88 **interest** closely connected, as interested parties   96 **bond** filial obligation   100 **Return . . . fit** i.e., am correspondingly dutiful   103 **Haply** perhaps   104 **plight** troth plight

For, by the sacred radiance of the sun,
The mysteries of Hecate° and the night,
By all the operation of the orbs°
115 From whom we do exist and cease to be,
Here I disclaim all my paternal care,
Propinquity and property of blood,°
And as a stranger to my heart and me
Hold thee from this for ever. The barbarous
   Scythian,°
120 Or he that makes his generation messes°
To gorge his appetite, shall to my bosom
Be as well neighbored, pitied, and relieved,
As thou my sometime° daughter.
     KENT: Good my liege —
     LEAR:
Peace, Kent!
125 Come not between the dragon° and his wrath.
I loved her most, and thought to set my rest°
On her kind nursery.° Hence and avoid my
   sight!
So be my grave my peace, as here I give
Her father's heart from her! Call France. Who
   stirs?
130 Call Burgundy. Cornwall and Albany,
With my two daughters' dowers digest° the
   third;
Let pride, which she calls plainness, marry
   her.°
I do invest you jointly with my power,
Preeminence, and all the large effects
That troop with majesty.° Ourself,° by monthly
135 course,
With reservation° of an hundred knights,
By you to be sustained, shall our abode
Make with you by due turn. Only we shall
   retain
The name, and all th' addition° to a king. The
   sway,

113 **mysteries of Hecate** secret rites of Hecate (goddess of the infernal world, and of witchcraft)   114 **operation . . . orbs** astrological influence   117 **Propinquity . . . blood** relationship and common blood   119 **Scythian** type of the savage   120 **makes . . . messes** eats his own offspring   123 **sometime** former   125 **dragon** (1) heraldic device of Britain (2) emblem of ferocity   126 **set my rest** (1) stake my all (a term from the card game of primero) (2) find my rest   127 **nursery** care, nursing   131 **digest** absorb   132 **Let . . . her** Let her pride be her dowry and gain her a husband   134–135 **effects . . . majesty** accompaniments that go with kingship   135 **Ourself** the royal "we"   136 **reservation** the action of reserving a privilege (a legalism)   139 **addition** titles and honors

Revènue, execution of the rest,   140
Belovèd sons, be yours; which to confirm,
This coronet° part between you.
     KENT: Royal Lear,
Whom I have ever honored as my king,
Loved as my father, as my master followed,
As my great patron thought on in my
   prayers —   145
     LEAR:
The bow is bent and drawn; make from the
   shaft.°
     KENT:
Let it fall° rather, though the fork° invade
The region of my heart. Be Kent unmannerly
When Lear is mad. What wouldst thou do,
   old man?
Thinkst thou that duty shall have dread to
   speak   150
When power to flattery bows? To plainness
   honor's bound
When majesty falls to folly. Reserve thy state,°
And in thy best consideration° check
This hideous rashness. Answer my life my
   judgment,°
Thy youngest daughter does not love thee
   least,   155
Nor are those empty-hearted whose low sounds
Reverb° no hollowness.°
     LEAR: Kent, on thy life, no more!
     KENT:
My life I never held but as a pawn°
To wage° against thine enemies; nor fear to
   lose it,
Thy safety being motive.°
     LEAR: Out of my sight! 160
     KENT:
See better, Lear, and let me still° remain
The true blank° of thine eye.
     LEAR:
Now by Apollo —
     KENT: Now by Apollo, king,
Thou swear'st thy gods in vain.

142 **coronet** the crown that was to have been Cordelia's   146 **make . . . shaft** avoid the arrow   147 **fall** strike; **fork** forked head of the arrow   152 **Reserve thy state** retain your kingly authority   153 **best consideration** most careful reflection   154 **Answer . . . judgment** I will stake my life on my opinion   157 **Reverb** reverberate; **hollowness** (1) emptiness (2) insincerity   158 **pawn** stake in a wager   159 **wage** (1) wager (2) carry on war   160 **motive** moving cause   161 **still** always   162 **blank** the white spot in the center of the target (at which Lear should aim)

LEAR: O vassal! Miscreant!°

[*Laying his hand on his sword.*]

165 ALBANY, CORNWALL: Dear sir, forbear!
KENT:
Kill thy physician, and the fee bestow
Upon the foul disease. Revoke thy gift,
Or, whilst I can vent clamor° from my throat,
I'll tell thee thou dost evil.
LEAR: Hear me, recreant!°
170 On thine allegiance,° hear me!
That thou hast sought to make us break our
      vows,
Which we durst never yet, and with strained°
      pride
To come betwixt our sentence° and our power,
Which nor our nature nor our place can bear,
175 Our potency made good,° take thy reward.
Five days we do allot thee for provision°
To shield thee from diseases° of the world,
And on the sixth to turn thy hated back
Upon our kingdom. If, on the tenth day
      following,
Thy banished trunk° be found in our
180   dominions,
The moment is thy death. Away! By Jupiter,
This shall not be revoked.
KENT:
Fare thee well, king. Sith° thus thou wilt
      appear,
Freedom lives hence, and banishment is here.

[*To* CORDELIA.]

185 The gods to their dear shelter take thee, maid,
That justly think'st, and hast most rightly said.

[*To* REGAN *and* GONERIL.]

And your large speeches may your deeds
      approve,°
That good effects° may spring from words of
      love.
Thus Kent, O princes, bids you all adieu;
190 He'll shape his old course° in a country new.
                                        (*Exit.*)

(*Flourish.*° *Enter* GLOUCESTER, *with* FRANCE
and BURGUNDY; ATTENDANTS.)

GLOUCESTER:
Here's France and Burgundy, my noble lord.
LEAR:
My Lord of Burgundy,
We first address toward you, who with this
      king
Hath rivaled for our daughter. What in the
      least
Will you require in present° dower with her,   195
Or cease your quest of love?
BURGUNDY: Most royal majesty,
I crave no more than hath your highness
      offered,
Nor will you tender° less.
LEAR: Right noble Burgundy,
When she was dear° to us, we did hold her so;
But now her price is fallen. Sir, there she
      stands.   200
If aught within that little seeming substance,°
Or all of it, with our displeasure pieced,°
And nothing more, may fitly like° your grace,
She's there, and she is yours.
BURGUNDY: I know no answer.
LEAR:
Will you, with those infirmities she owes,°   205
Unfriended, new adopted to our hate,
Dow'red with our curse, and strangered° with
      our oath,
Take her, or leave her?
BURGUNDY: Pardon me, royal sir.
Election makes not up° on such conditions.
LEAR:
Then leave her, sir; for, by the pow'r that
      made me,   210
I tell you all her wealth. [*To* FRANCE.] For
      you, great king,
I would not from your love make such a stray
To° match you where I hate; therefore
      beseech° you
T' avert your liking a more worthier way°

190 s.d. **Flourish** trumpet fanfare   195 **present** immediate   198 **tender** offer   199 **dear** (1) beloved (2) valued at a high price   201 **little seeming substance** person who is (1) inconsiderable (2) outspoken   202 **pieced** added to it   203 **fitly like** please by its fitness   205 **owes** possesses   207 **strangered** made a stranger   209 **Election ... up** no one can choose   212–213 **make ... To** stray so far as to   213 **beseech** I beseech   214 **avert ... way** turn your affections from her and bestow them on a better person

164 **vassal! Miscreant!** base wretch! Misbeliever   168 **vent clamor** utter a cry   169 **recreant** traitor   170 **On thine allegiance** to forswear, which is to commit high treason   172 **strained** forced (and so excessive)   173 **sentence** judgment, decree   175 **Our ... good** my royal authority being now asserted   176 **for provision** for making preparation   177 **diseases** troubles   180 **trunk** body   183 **Sith** since   187 **approve** prove true   188 **effects** results   190 **shape ... course** pursue his customary way

215 Than on a wretch whom nature is ashamed
Almost t' acknowledge hers.
    FRANCE: This is most strange,
That she whom even but now was your best object,°
The argument° of your praise, balm of your age,
The best, the dearest, should in this trice of time
220 Commit a thing so monstrous to dismantle°
So many folds of favor. Sure her offense
Must be of such unnatural degree
That monsters it,° or your fore-vouched° affection
Fall into taint;° which to believe of her
225 Must be a faith that reason without miracle
Should never plant in me.°
    CORDELIA: I yet beseech your majesty,
If for° I want that glib and oily art
To speak and purpose not,° since what I well intend
I'll do't before I speak, that you make known
230 It is no vicious blot, murder, or foulness,
No unchaste action or dishonored step,
That hath deprived me of your grace and favor;
But even for want of that for which I am richer,
A still-soliciting° eye, and such a tongue
235 That I am glad I have not, though not to have it
Hath lost° me in your liking.
    LEAR: Better thou
Hadst not been born than not t' have pleased me better.
    FRANCE:
Is it but this? A tardiness in nature°
Which often leaves the history unspoke°
240 That it intends to do. My Lord of Burgundy,
What say you° to the lady? Love's not love

When it is mingled with regards° that stands
Aloof from th' entire point.° Will you have her?
She is herself a dowry.
    BURGUNDY: Royal king,
Give but that portion which yourself proposed, 245
And here I take Cordelia by the hand,
Duchess of Burgundy.
    LEAR:
Nothing. I have sworn. I am firm.
    BURGUNDY:
I am sorry then you have so lost a father
That you must lose a husband.
    CORDELIA: Peace be with Burgundy. 250
Since that respects of fortune° are his love,
I shall not be his wife.
    FRANCE:
Fairest Cordelia, that art most rich being poor,
Most choice forsaken, and most loved despised,
Thee and thy virtues here I seize upon. 255
Be it lawful I take up what's cast away.
Gods, gods! 'Tis strange that from their cold'st neglect
My love should kindle to inflamed respect.°
Thy dow'rless daughter, king, thrown to my chance,°
Is queen of us, of ours, and our fair France. 260
Not all the dukes of wat'rish° Burgundy
Can buy this unprized precious° maid of me.
Bid them farewell, Cordelia, though unkind.
Thou losest here,° a better where° to find.
    LEAR:
Thou hast her, France; let her be thine, for we 265
Have no such daughter, nor shall ever see
That face of hers again. Therefore be gone,
Without our grace, our love, our benison.°
Come, noble Burgundy.
    (*Flourish. Exeunt* [LEAR, BURGUNDY,
        CORNWALL, ALBANY, GLOUCESTER,
           and ATTENDANTS].)
    FRANCE:
Bid farewell to your sisters. 270
    CORDELIA:
The jewels of our father,° with washed° eyes

217 **your best object** the one you loved most 218 **argument** subject 220 **dismantle** strip off 223 **That monsters it** as makes it monstrous, unnatural; **fore-vouched** previously sworn 224 **Fall into taint** must be taken as having been unjustified all along; i.e., Cordelia was unworthy of your love from the first 225–226 **reason . . . me** my reason would have to be supported by a miracle to make me believe 227 **for** because 228 **purpose not** not mean to do what I promise 234 **still-soliciting** always begging 236 **lost** ruined 238 **tardiness in nature** natural reticence 239 **leaves . . . unspoke** does not announce the action 241 **What say you** i.e., will you have

242 **regards** considerations (the dowry) 242–243 **stands . . . point** have nothing to do with the essential question (love) 251 **respects of fortune** mercenary considerations 258 **inflamed respect** more ardent affection 259 **chance** lot 261 **wat'rish** (1) with many rivers (2) weak, diluted 262 **unprized precious** unappreciated by others, and yet precious 264 **here** in this place; **where** other place 268 **benison** blessing 271 **The jewels . . . father** you creatures prized by our father; **washed** (1) weeping (2) clearsighted

Cordelia leaves you. I know you what you are,
And, like a sister,° am most loath to call
Your faults as they are named.° Love well our
  father.
275 To your professèd° bosoms I commit him.
But yet, alas, stood I within his grace,
I would prefer° him to a better place.
So farewell to you both.
  REGAN:
Prescribe not us our duty.
  GONERIL: Let your study
Be to content your lord, who hath received
280   you
At Fortune's alms.° You have obedience
  scanted,°
And well are worth the want that you have
  wanted.°
  CORDELIA:
Time shall unfold what plighted° cunning
  hides,
Who covers faults, at last shame them de-
  rides.°
Well may you prosper.
285   FRANCE: Come, my fair Cordelia.
                  (Exit FRANCE and CORDELIA.)
  GONERIL: Sister, it is not little I have to say
of what most nearly appertains to us both. I
think our father will hence tonight.
  REGAN: That's most certain, and with you;
290 next month with us.
  GONERIL: You see how full of changes his
age is. The observation we have made of it
hath not been little. He always loved our sister
most, and with what poor judgment he hath
295 now cast her off appears too grossly.°
  REGAN: 'Tis the infirmity of his age; yet he
hath ever but slenderly known himself.
  GONERIL: The best and soundest of his time°
hath been but rash; then must we look from
300 his age to receive not alone the imperfections

of long-ingrafted° condition,° but therewithal°
the unruly waywardness that infirm and choleric years bring with them.
  REGAN: Such unconstant starts° are we like
to have from him as this of Kent's banish-   305
ment.
  GONERIL: There is further compliment° of
leave-taking between France and him. Pray
you, let's hit° together; if our father carry
authority with such disposition as he bears,°   310
this last surrender° of his will but offend° us.
  REGAN: We shall further think of it.
  GONERIL: We must do something, and i' th'
heat.°

                  (Exeunt.)

          SCENE II. [The Earl of GLOUCESTER's
                       castle.]

  Enter EDMUND [with a letter].

  EDMUND:
Thou, Nature,° art my goddess; to thy law
My services are bound. Wherefore should I
Stand in the plague of custom,° and permit
The curiosity° of nations to deprive me,
For that° I am some twelve or fourteen moon-
  shines°   5
Lag of° a brother? Why bastard? Wherefore
  base?
When my dimensions are as well compact,°
My mind as generous,° and my shape as true,
As honest° madam's issue? Why brand they us
With base? With baseness? Bastardy? Base?
  Base?   10
Who, in the lusty stealth of nature, take
More composition° and fierce° quality
Than doth, within a dull, stale, tired bed,
Go to th' creating a whole tribe of fops°

301 **long-ingrafted** implanted for a long time; **condi-tion** disposition; **therewithal** with them   304 **uncon-stant starts** impulsive whims   307 **compliment** formal courtesy   309 **hit** agree   309–310 **carry . . . bears** continues, and in such frame of mind, to wield the sovereign power   311 **last surrender** recent abdi-cation; **offend** vex   313–314 **i' th' heat** while the iron is hot
I.II.1 **Nature** Edmund's conception of Nature ac-cords with our description of a bastard as a natural child   3 **Stand . . . custom** respect hateful conven-tion   4 **curiosity** nice distinctions   5 **For that** be-cause; **moonshines** months   6 **Lag of** short of being (in age)   7 **compact** framed   8 **generous** gallant   9 **honest** chaste   12 **composition** completeness; **fierce** energetic   14 **fops** fools

273 **like a sister** because I am a sister, i.e., loyal, affectionate   274 **as . . . named** by their right and ugly names   275 **professèd** pretending to love   277 **prefer** recommend   281 **At Fortune's alms** as a charitable bequest from Fortune (and so, by exten-sion, as one beggared or cast down by Fortune); **scanted** stinted   282 **worth . . . wanted** deserve to be denied, even as you have denied   283 **plighted** pleated, enfolded   284 **Who . . . derides** Those who hide their evil are finally exposed and shamed ("He that hideth his sins, shall not prosper")   295 **grossly** obviously   298 **of his time** period of his life up to now

---

15 Got° 'tween asleep and wake? Well then,
Legitimate Edgar, I must have your land.
Our father's love is to the bastard Edmund
As to th' legitimate. Fine word, "legitimate."
Well, my legitimate, if this letter speed,°
20 And my invention° thrive, Edmund the base
Shall top th' legitimate. I grow, I prosper.
Now, gods, stand up for bastards.

(*Enter* GLOUCESTER.)

GLOUCESTER:
Kent banished thus? and France in choler parted?
And the king gone tonight? prescribed° his pow'r?
25 Confined to exhibition?° All this done
Upon the gad?° Edmund, how now? What news?
EDMUND:
So please your lordship, none.
GLOUCESTER:
Why so earnestly seek you to put up° that letter?
EDMUND:
I know no news, my lord.
GLOUCESTER:
30 What paper were you reading?
EDMUND: Nothing, my lord.
GLOUCESTER: No? What needed then that terrible dispatch° of it into your pocket? The quality of nothing hath not such need to hide
35 itself. Let's see. Come, if it be nothing, I shall not need spectacles.
EDMUND: I beseech you, sir, pardon me. It is a letter from my brother that I have not all o'er-read; and for so much as I have perused, I
40 find it not fit for your o'erlooking.°
GLOUCESTER: Give me the letter, sir.
EDMUND: I shall offend, either to detain or give it. The contents, as in part I understand them, are to blame.°
45 GLOUCESTER: Let's see, let's see.
EDMUND: I hope, for my brother's justification, he wrote this but as an essay or taste° of my virtue.
GLOUCESTER (*reads*): "This policy and rev-

erence° of age makes the world bitter to the
50 best of our times;° keeps our fortunes from us till our oldness cannot relish° them. I begin to find an idle and fond° bondage in the oppression of aged tyranny, who sways, not as it hath power, but as it is suffered.° Come to me, that
55 of this I may speak more. If our father would sleep till I waked him, you should enjoy half his revenue° for ever, and live the beloved of your brother,
                                              Edgar."
60 Hum! Conspiracy? "Sleep till I waked him, you should enjoy half his revenue." My son Edgar! Had he a hand to write this? A heart and brain to breed it in? When came you to this? Who brought it?
65 EDMUND: It was not brought me, my lord; there's the cunning of it. I found it thrown in at the casement of my closet.°
GLOUCESTER: You know the character° to be your brother's?
70 EDMUND: If the matter were good, my lord, I durst swear it were his; but in respect of that,° I would fain° think it were not.
GLOUCESTER: It is his.
EDMUND: It is his hand, my lord; but I hope
75 his heart is not in the contents.
GLOUCESTER: Has he never before sounded° you in this business?
EDMUND: Never, my lord. But I have heard him oft maintain it to be fit that, sons at
80 perfect° age, and fathers declined, the father should be as ward to the son, and the son manage his revenue.
GLOUCESTER: O villain, villain! His very opinion in the letter. Abhorred villain, unnatu-
85 ral, detested,° brutish villain; worse than brutish! Go, sirrah,° seek him. I'll apprehend him. Abominable villain! Where is he?
EDMUND: I do not well know, my lord. If it shall please you to suspend your indignation
90 against my brother till you can derive from him better testimony of his intent, you should

49–50 **policy and reverence** policy of reverencing (hendiadys) 51 **best . . . times** best years of our lives (i.e., our youth) 52 **relish** enjoy 53 **idle and fond** foolish 54–55 **who . . . suffered** which rules, not from its own strength, but from our allowance 58 **revenue** income 68 **casement . . . closet** window of my room 69 **character** handwriting 72–73 **in . . . that** in view of what it is 73 **fain** prefer to 77 **sounded** sounded you out 81 **perfect** mature 86 **detested** detestable 87 **sirrah** sir (familiar form of address)

15 **Got** begot 19 **speed** prosper 20 **invention** plan 24 **prescribed** limited 25 **exhibition** an allowance or pension 26 **Upon the gad** on the spur of the moment (as if pricked by a gad or goad) 28 **put up** put away, conceal 33 **terrible dispatch** hasty putting away 40 **o'erlooking** inspection 44 **to blame** blameworthy 47 **essay or taste** test

run a certain course;° where, if you violently
proceed against him, mistaking his purpose, it
would make a great gap° in your own honor
and shake in pieces the heart of his obedience.
I dare pawn down° my life for him that he
hath writ this to feel° my affection to your
honor, and to no other pretense of danger.°

GLOUCESTER: Think you so?

EDMUND: If your honor judge it meet,° I will
place you where you shall hear us confer of
this, and by an auricular assurance° have your
satisfaction, and that without any further delay
than this very evening.

GLOUCESTER: He cannot be such a monster.

EDMUND: Nor is not, sure.

GLOUCESTER: To his father, that so tenderly
and entirely loves him. Heaven and earth!
Edmund, seek him out; wind me into him,° I
pray you; frame° the business after your own
wisdom. I would unstate myself to be in a due
resolution.°

EDMUND: I will seek him, sir, presently;°
convey° the business as I shall find means, and
acquaint you withal.°

GLOUCESTER: These late° eclipses in the sun
and moon portend no good to us. Though the
wisdom of nature° can reason° it thus and thus,
yet nature finds itself scourged by the sequent
effects.° Love cools, friendship falls off,° brothers divide. In cities, mutinies;° in countries,
discord; in palaces, treason; and the bond
cracked 'twixt son and father. This villain of
mine comes under the prediction,° there's son
against father; the king falls from bias of
nature,° there's father against child. We have
seen the best of our time.° Machinations,

hollowness,° treachery, and all ruinous disorders follow us disquietly° to our graves. Find
out this villain, Edmund; it shall lose thee
nothing.° Do it carefully. And the noble and
true-hearted Kent banished; his offense, honesty. 'Tis strange.   (*Exit.*)

EDMUND: This is the excellent foppery° of
the world, that when we are sick in fortune,
often the surfeits of our own behavior,° we
make guilty of our disasters the sun, the moon,
and stars; as if we were villains on° necessity;
fools by heavenly compulsion; knaves, thieves,
and treachers by spherical predominance;°
drunkards, liars, and adulterers by an enforced
obedience of planetary influence;° and all that
we are evil in, by a divine thrusting on.° An
admirable evasion of whoremaster° man, to lay
his goatish° disposition on the charge of a star.
My father compounded° with my mother
under the Dragon's Tail,° and my nativity° was
under Ursa Major,° so that it follows I am
rough and lecherous. Fut!° I should have been
that° I am, had the maidenliest star in the
firmament twinkled on my bastardizing.
Edgar —

(*Enter* EDGAR.)

and pat he comes, like the catastrophe° of the
old comedy. My cue is villainous melancholy,
with a sigh like Tom o' Bedlam.° — O, these
eclipses do portend these divisions. Fa, sol, la,
mi.°

EDGAR: How now, brother Edmund; what
serious contemplation are you in?

EDMUND: I am thinking, brother, of a pre-

129 **hollowness** insincerity   130 **disquietly** unquietly
131–132 **it ... nothing** you will not lose by it   135
foppery folly   137 **often ... behavior** often caused
by our own excesses   139 **on** of   141 **treachers ...
predominance** traitors because of the ascendancy of a
particular star at our birth   142–143 **by ... influence** because we had to submit to the influence of
our star   144 **divine thrusting on** supernatural
compulsion   145 **whoremaster** lecherous   146 **goat-
ish** lascivious   147 **compounded** (1) made terms (2)
formed (a child)   148 **Dragon's Tail** the constel-
lation Draco; **nativity** birthday   149 **Ursa Major**
the Great Bear   150 **Fut** 'S foot (an impatient
oath)   151 **that** what   154 **catastrophe** conclusion   155–156 **My ... Bedlam** I must be doleful, like
a lunatic beggar out of Bethlehem (Bedlam) Hospital, the London madhouse   157–158 **Fa, sol, la, mi**
Edmund's humming of the musical notes is perhaps
prompted by his use of the word *division*, which
describes a musical variation

93 **run ... course** proceed safely, know where you are
going   95 **gap** breach   97 **pawn down** stake   98
feel test   99 **pretense of danger** dangerous purpose
101 **meet** fit   103 **auricular assurance** proof heard
with your own ears   110 **wind ... him** insinuate
yourself into his confidence for me   111 **frame** manage   112–113 **unstate ... resolution** forfeit my earl-
dom to know the truth   114 **presently** at once   115
convey manage   116 **withal** with it   117 **late**
recent   119 **wisdom of nature** scientific learning;
reason explain   120–121 **yet ... effects** nonetheless
our world is punished with subsequent disasters   121
falls off revolts   122 **mutinies** riots   124–125 **This
... prediction** my son's villainous behavior is included in these portents, and bears them out   126–
127 **bias of nature** natural inclination (the metaphor
is from the game of bowls)   128 **best ... time** our
best days

diction I read this other day, what should
follow these eclipses.

EDGAR: Do you busy yourself with that?

165 EDMUND: I promise you, the effects he
writes of succeed° unhappily: as of unnatural-
ness° between the child and the parent, death,
dearth, dissolutions of ancient amities,° divisions in state, menaces and maledictions
170 against king and nobles, needless diffidences,°
banishment of friends, dissipation of cohorts,°
nuptial breaches, and I know not what.

EDGAR: How long have you been a sectary
astronomical?°

175 EDMUND: Come, come, when saw you my
father last?

EDGAR: Why, the night gone by.

EDMUND: Spake you with him?

EDGAR: Ay, two hours together.

180 EDMUND: Parted you in good terms? Found
you no displeasure in him by word nor countenance?°

EDGAR: None at all.

EDMUND: Bethink yourself wherein you may
185 have offended him; and at my entreaty forbear
his presence° until some little time hath quali-
fied° the heat of his displeasure, which at this
instant so rageth in him that with the mischief
of your person it would scarcely allay.°

190 EDGAR: Some villain hath done me wrong.

EDMUND: That's my fear, brother. I pray you
have a continent forbearance° till the speed of
his rage goes slower; and, as I say, retire with
me to my lodging, from whence I will fitly°
195 bring you to hear my lord speak. Pray ye, go;
there's my key. If you do stir abroad, go
armed.

EDGAR: Armed, brother?

EDMUND: Brother, I advise you to the best.
200 Go armed. I am no honest man if there be any
good meaning toward you. I have told you
what I have seen and heard; but faintly,
nothing like the image and horror° of it. Pray
you, away.

EDGAR: Shall I hear from you anon?°   205

EDMUND: I do serve you in this business.
                          (Exit EDGAR.)

A credulous father, and a brother noble,
Whose nature is so far from doing harms
That he suspects none; on whose foolish
     honesty
My practices° ride easy. I see the business.   210
Let me, if not by birth, have lands by wit.
All with me's meet° that I can fashion fit.°
                                      (Exit.)

SCENE III. [The Duke of ALBANY's palace.]

Enter GONERIL, and [OSWALD, her] steward.

GONERIL: Did my father strike my gentleman for chiding of his Fool?°

OSWALD: Ay, madam.

GONERIL:
By day and night he wrongs me. Every hour
He flashes into one gross crime° or other   5
That sets us all at odds. I'll not endure it.
His knights grow riotous,° and himself up-
     braids us
On every trifle. When he returns from hunt-
     ing,
I will not speak with him. Say I am sick.
If you come slack of former services,°   10
You shall do well; the fault of it I'll answer.°

[Horns within.]

OSWALD: He's coming, madam; I hear him.

GONERIL:
Put on what weary negligence you please,
You and your fellows. I'd have it come to
     question.°
If he distaste° it, let him to my sister,   15
Whose mind and mine I know in that are one,
Not to be overruled. Idle° old man,
That still would manage those authorities
That he hath given away. Now, by my life,
Old fools are babes again, and must be used   20
With checks as flatteries, when they are seen
     abused.°
Remember what I have said.

166 **succeed** follow   166–167 **unnaturalness** unkindness   168 **amities** friendships   170 **diffidences** dis-
trusts   171 **dissipation of cohorts** falling away of
supporters   173–174 **sectary astronomical** believer in
astrology   181–182 **countenance** expression   185–
186 **forbear his presence** keep away from him   186–
187 **qualified** lessened   188–189 **with . . . allay** even
an injury to you would not appease his anger   192
have . . . forbearance be restrained and keep yourself
withdrawn   194 **fitly** at a fit time   203 **image and
horror** true horrible picture

205 **anon** in a little while   210 **practices** plots   212
meet proper; **fashion fit** shape to my purpose
I.III.2 **Fool** court jester   5 **crime** offense   7 **riotous**
dissolute   10 **come . . . services** are less serviceable
to him than formerly   11 **answer** answer for   14
come to question be discussed openly   15 **distaste**
dislike   17 **Idle** foolish   21 **With . . . abused** with
restraints as well as soothing words when they are mis-
guided

OSWALD: Well, madam.

GONERIL:

And let his knights have colder looks among
    you.
What grows of it, no matter; advise your
    fellows so.
I would breed from hence occasions, and I
25   shall,
That I may speak.° I'll write straight° to my
    sister
To hold my course. Go, prepare for dinner.
                                        (*Exeunt.*)

SCENE IV. [*A hall in the same.*]

Enter KENT [*disguised*].

KENT:

If but as well I other accents borrow
That can my speech defuse,° my good intent
May carry through itself to that full issue°
For which I razed my likeness.° Now, banished
    Kent,
If thou canst serve where thou dost stand
5   condemned,
So may it come,° thy master whom thou lov'st
Shall find thee full of labors.

(*Horns within.° Enter* LEAR, [KNIGHTS,] *and*
    ATTENDANTS.)

LEAR: Let me not stay° a jot for dinner; go,
get it ready. [*Exit an* ATTENDANT.] How now,
10 what art thou?

KENT: A man, sir.

LEAR: What dost thou profess?° What
wouldst thou with us?

KENT: I do profess° to be no less than I
15 seem, to serve him truly that will put me in
trust, to love him that is honest, to converse
with him that is wise and says little, to fear
judgment,° to fight when I cannot choose, and
to eat no fish.°

25 LEAR: What art thou?

KENT: A very honest-hearted fellow and as
poor as the king.

LEAR: If thou be'st as poor for a subject as
he's for a king, thou art poor enough. What
wouldst thou?   25

KENT: Service.

LEAR: Who wouldst thou serve?

KENT: You.

LEAR: Dost thou know me, fellow?

KENT: No, sir, but you have that in your   30
countenance° which I would fain° call master.

LEAR: What's that?

KENT: Authority.

LEAR: What services canst thou do?

KENT: I can keep honest counsel,° ride, run,   35
mar a curious tale in telling it,° and deliver a
plain message bluntly. That which ordinary
men are fit for, I am qualified in, and the best
of me is diligence.

LEAR: How old art thou?   40

KENT: Not so young, sir, to love a woman
for singing, nor so old to dote on her for
anything. I have years on my back forty-eight.

LEAR: Follow me; thou shalt serve me. If I
like thee no worse after dinner, I will not part   45
from thee yet. Dinner, ho, dinner! Where's
my knave?° my Fool? Go you and call my Fool
hither.   [*Exit an* ATTENDANT.]

(*Enter* OSWALD.)

You, you, sirrah, where's my daughter?
OSWALD: So please you —   (*Exit.*)   50
LEAR: What says the fellow there? Call the
clotpoll° back. [*Exit a* KNIGHT.] Where's my
Fool? Ho, I think the world's asleep.

[*Reenter* KNIGHT.]

How now? Where's that mongrel?
KNIGHT: He says, my lord, your daughter is   55
not well.
LEAR: Why came not the slave back to me
when I called him?
KNIGHT: Sir, he answered me in the round-
est° manner, he would not.   60
LEAR: He would not?
KNIGHT: My lord, I know not what the
matter is; but to my judgment your highness is
not entertained° with that ceremonious affection as you were wont. There's a great abate-   65
ment of kindness appears as well in the general

25–26 **breed ... speak** find in this opportunities for
speaking out   26 **straight** at once
I.iv.2 **defuse** disguise   3 **full issue** perfect result   4
razed my likeness shaved off, disguised my natural
appearance   6 **So ... come** so may it fall out   7 s.d.
within offstage   8 **stay** wait   12 **What ... profess**
What do you do?   14 **profess** claim   18 **judgment**
by a heavenly or earthly judge   19 **eat no fish** i.e., (1)
I am no Catholic, but a loyal Protestant (2) I am no
weakling (3) I use no prostitutes

31 **countenance** bearing; **fain** like to   35 **honest
counsel** honorable secrets   36 **mar ... it** i.e., I
cannot speak like an affected courtier ("curious" =
elaborate, as against plain)   47 **knave** boy   52 **clot-
poll** clodpoll, blockhead   59–60 **roundest** rudest
64 **entertained** treated

dependants° as in the duke himself also and your daughter.

LEAR: Ha? Say'st thou so?

70 KNIGHT: I beseech you pardon me, my lord, if I be mistaken; for my duty cannot be silent when I think your highness wronged.

LEAR: Thou but rememb'rest° me of mine own conception.° I have perceived a most faint
75 neglect° of late, which I have rather blamed as mine own jealous curiosity° than as a very pretense° and purpose of unkindness. I will look further into't. But where's my Fool? I have not seen him this two days.

80 KNIGHT: Since my young lady's going into France, sir, the Fool hath much pined away.

LEAR: No more of that; I have noted it well. Go you and tell my daughter I would speak with her. Go you, call hither my Fool.

[Exit an ATTENDANT.]

(Enter OSWALD.)

85 O, you, sir, you! Come you hither, sir. Who am I, sir?

OSWALD: My lady's father.

LEAR: "My lady's father"? My lord's knave, you whoreson dog, you slave, you cur!

90 OSWALD: I am none of these, my lord; I beseech your pardon.

LEAR: Do you bandy° looks with me, you rascal?

[Striking him.]

OSWALD: I'll not be strucken,° my lord.

95 KENT: Nor tripped neither, you base football° player.

[Tripping up his heels.]

LEAR: I thank thee, fellow. Thou serv'st me, and I'll love thee.

KENT: Come, sir, arise, away. I'll teach you
100 differences.° Away, away. If you will measure your lubber's° length again, tarry; but away. Go to!° Have you wisdom?° So.°

[Pushes OSWALD out.]

LEAR: Now, my friendly knave, I thank thee. There's earnest° of thy service. [Giving KENT money.]

(Enter FOOL.)

FOOL: Let me hire him too. Here's my   105 coxcomb.°

[Offering KENT his cap.]

LEAR: How now, my pretty knave? How dost thou?

FOOL: Sirrah, you were best° take my cox-comb.   110

KENT: Why, Fool?

FOOL: Why? For taking one's part that's out of favor. Nay, an° thou canst not smile as the wind sits,° thou'lt catch cold shortly. There, take my coxcomb. Why, this fellow has ban-   115 ished° two on's daughters, and did the third a blessing against his will. If thou follow him, thou must needs wear my coxcomb. — How now, nuncle?° Would I had two coxcombs and two daughters.   120

LEAR: Why, my boy?

FOOL: If I gave them all my living,° I'd keep my coxcombs myself. There's mine; beg another of thy daughters.

LEAR: Take heed, sirrah — the whip.   125

FOOL: Truth's a dog must to kennel; he must be whipped out, when Lady the Brach° may stand by th' fire and stink.

LEAR: A pestilent gall° to me.

FOOL: Sirrah, I'll teach thee a speech.   130

LEAR: Do.

FOOL: Mark it, nuncle.

Have more than thou showest,
Speak less than thou knowest,
Lend less than thou owest,°
Ride more than thou goest,°   135
Learn more than thou trowest,°
Set less than thou throwest;°
Leave thy drink and thy whore,
And keep in-a-door,   140

---

67 **dependants** servants   73 **rememb'rest** remindest   74 **conception** idea   74–75 **faint neglect** i.e., "weary negligence" (I.iii.13)   76 **mine . . . curiosity** suspicious concern for my own dignity   76–77 **very pretense** actual intention   92 **bandy** exchange insolently (metaphor from tennis)   94 **strucken** struck   95–96 **football** a low game played by idle boys, to the scandal of sensible men   100 **differences** of rank   101 **lubber's** lout's   102 **Go to** expression of derisive incredulity; **Have you wisdom** i.e., Do you know what's good for you?; **So** good

104 **earnest** money for services rendered   106 **coxcomb** professional fool's cap, shaped like a coxcomb   109 **you were best** you had better   113 **an if**   113–114 **smile . . . sits** ingratiate yourself with those in power   115–116 **banished** alienated (by making them independent)   119 **nuncle** contraction of "mine uncle"   122 **living** property   127 **Brach** bitch   129 **gall** sore   135 **owest** ownest   136 **goest** walkest   137 **trowest** knowest   138 **Set . . . throwest** bet less than you play for (get odds from your opponent)

And thou shalt have more
Than two tens to a score.°

KENT: This is nothing, Fool.

145 FOOL: Then 'tis like the breath of an unfee'd° lawyer — you gave me nothing for't. Can you make no use of nothing, nuncle?

LEAR: Why, no, boy. Nothing can be made out of nothing.

150 FOOL [to KENT]: Prithee tell him, so much the rent of his land comes to; he will not believe a fool.

LEAR: A bitter° fool.

FOOL: Dost thou know the difference, my boy, between a bitter fool and a sweet one?

155 LEAR: No, lad; teach me.

FOOL:

That lord that counseled thee
To give away thy land,
Come place him here by me,
Do thou for him stand.
160 The sweet and bitter fool
Will presently appear;
The one in motley° here,
The other found out° there.°

LEAR: Dost thou call me fool, boy?

165 FOOL: All thy other titles thou hast given away; that thou wast born with.

KENT: This is not altogether fool, my lord.

FOOL: No, faith; lords and great men will not let me.° If I had a monopoly° out, they 170 would have part on't. And ladies too, they will not let me have all the fool to myself; they'll be snatching. Nuncle, give me an egg, and I'll give thee two crowns.

LEAR: What two crowns shall they be?

175 FOOL: Why, after I have cut the egg i' th' middle and eat up the meat, the two crowns of the egg. When thou clovest thy crown i' th' middle and gav'st away both parts, thou bor'st thine ass on thy back o'er the dirt.° Thou hadst 180 little wit in thy bald crown when thou gav'st

thy golden one away. If I speak like myself° in this, let him be whipped° that first finds it so. [Singing.]

Fools had ne'er less grace in a year,
For wise men are grown foppish,
And know not how their wits to wear,   185
Their manners are so apish.°

LEAR: When were you wont to be so full of songs, sirrah?

FOOL: I have used° it, nuncle, e'er since thou mad'st thy daughters thy mothers; for 190 when thou gav'st them the rod, and put'st down thine own breeches, [Singing.]

Then they for sudden joy did weep,
And I for sorrow sung,
That such a king should play bo-peep°   195
And go the fools among.

Prithee, nuncle, keep a schoolmaster that can teach thy Fool to lie. I would fain learn to lie.

LEAR: And° you lie, sirrah, we'll have you whipped.   200

FOOL: I marvel what kin thou and thy daughters are. They'll have me whipped for speaking true; thou'lt have me whipped for lying; and sometimes I am whipped for holding my peace. I had rather be any kind o'   205 thing than a fool, and yet I would not be thee, nuncle: thou hast pared thy wit o' both sides and left nothing i' th' middle. Here comes one o' the parings.

(Enter GONERIL.)

LEAR: How now, daughter? What makes   210 that frontlet° on? Methinks you are too much of late i' th' frown.

FOOL: Thou wast a pretty fellow when thou hadst no need to care for her frowning. Now thou art an O without a figure.° I am better   215 than thou art now: I am a fool, thou art nothing. [To GONERIL.] Yes, forsooth, I will

141–142 have . . . score i.e., come away with more than you had (two tens, or twenty shillings, make a score, or one pound)   145 unfee'd unpaid for   152 bitter satirical   162 motley the drab costume of the professional jester   163 found out revealed; there the Fool points at Lear, as a fool in the grain   169 let me i.e., let me have all the folly to myself; monopoly James I gave great scandal by granting to his "snatching" courtiers royal patents to deal exclusively in some commodity   178–179 bor'st . . . dirt like the foolish and unnatural countryman in Aesop's fable

181 like myself like a fool   182 let . . . whipped i.e., let the man be whipped for a fool who thinks my true saying to be foolish   183–186 Fools . . . apish i.e., fools were never in less favor than now, and the reason is that wise men, turning foolish, and not knowing how to use their intelligence, imitate the professional fools and so make them unnecessary   189 used practiced   195 play bo-peep (1) act like a child (2) blind himself   199 And if   211 frontlet frown (literally, ornamental band)   215 figure digit, to give value to the cipher (Lear is a nought)

hold my tongue. So your face bids me, though you say nothing. Mum, mum,

220   He that keeps nor crust nor crum,°
         Weary of all, shall want° some.

[*Pointing to* LEAR.]

That's a shealed peascod.°

GONERIL:
Not only, sir, this your all-licensed° Fool,
But other° of your insolent retinue
225 Do hourly carp and quarrel, breaking forth
In rank° and not-to-be-endurèd riots. Sir,
I had thought by making this well known unto
      you
To have found a safe° redress, but now grow
      fearful,
By what yourself too late° have spoke and
      done,
230 That you protect this course, and put it on
By your allowance;° which if you should, the
      fault
Would not 'scape censure, nor the redresses
      sleep,°
Which, in the tender of° a wholesome weal,°
Might in their working do you that offense,
235 Which else were shame, that then necessity
Will call discreet proceeding.°
   FOOL: For you know, nuncle,

   The hedge-sparrow fed the cuckoo° so long
   That it had it head bit off by it° young.

240 So out went the candle, and we were left
darkling.°
   LEAR: Are you our daughter?
   GONERIL:
Come, sir,
I would you would make use of your good
      wisdom
Whereof I know you are fraught° and put
245   away

These dispositions° which of late transport you
From what you rightly are.
   FOOL: May not an ass know when the cart
draws the horse? Whoop, Jug,° I love thee!
   LEAR:
Does any here know me? This is not Lear.   250
Does Lear walk thus? Speak thus? Where are
      his eyes?
Either his notion° weakens, or his discernings°
Are lethargied° — Ha! Waking? 'Tis not so.
Who is it that can tell me who I am?
   FOOL: Lear's shadow.   255
   LEAR: I would learn that; for, by the marks
of sovereignty,° knowledge, and reason, I
should be false° persuaded I had daughters.
   FOOL: Which° they will make an obedient
father.   260
   LEAR: Your name, fair gentlewoman?
   GONERIL:
This admiration,° sir, is much o' th' savor°
Of other your° new pranks. I do beseech you
To understand my purposes aright.
As you are old and reverend, should be wise.   265
Here do you keep a hundred knights and
      squires,
Men so disordered, so deboshed,° and bold,
That this our court, infected with their man-
      ners,
Shows° like a riotous inn. Epicurism° and lust
Makes it more like a tavern or a brothel   270
Than a graced° palace. The shame itself doth
      speak
For instant remedy. Be then desired°
By her, that else will take the thing she begs,
A little to disquantity your train,°
And the remainders° that shall still depend,°   275
To be such men as may besort° your age,
Which know themselves, and you.
   LEAR: Darkness and devils!
Saddle my horses; call my train together.

220 **crum** soft bread inside the loaf   221 **want** lack
222 **shealed peascod** empty pea pod   223 **all-
licensed** privileged to take any liberties   224 **other**
others   226 **rank** gross   228 **safe** sure   229 **too late**
lately   230–231 **put . . . allowance** promote it by
your approval   232 **redresses sleep** correction fail to
follow   233 **tender of** desire for; **weal** state   234–
236 **Might . . . proceeding** as I apply it, the correction might humiliate you; but the need to take action
cancels what would otherwise be unfilial conduct in
me   238 **cuckoo** which lays its eggs in the nests of
other birds   239 **it** its   241 **darkling** in the dark
245 **fraught** endowed

246 **dispositions** moods   249 **Jug** Joan (a quotation
from a popular song?)   252 **notion** understanding;
discernings faculties   253 **lethargied** paralyzed
256–257 **marks of sovereignty** i.e., tokens that Lear
is king, and hence father to his daughters   258
false falsely   259 **Which** whom (Lear)   262 **admiration** (affected) wonderment; **is . . . savor** smacks
much   263 **other your** others of your   267 **deboshed**
debauched   269 **Shows** appears; **Epicurism** riotous
living   271 **graced** dignified   272 **desired** re-
quested   274 **disquantity your train** reduce the number of your dependents   275 **remainders** those who
remain; **depend** attend on you   276 **besort** befit

Degenerate° bastard, I'll not trouble thee:
280 Yet have I left a daughter.

GONERIL:
You strike my people, and your disordered rabble
Make servants of their betters.

(*Enter* ALBANY.)

LEAR:
Woe, that too late repents. O, sir, are you come?
Is it your will? Speak, sir. Prepare my horses.
285 Ingratitude! thou marble-hearted fiend,
More hideous when thou show'st thee in a child
Than the sea-monster.
            ALBANY: Pray, sir, be patient.
            LEAR:
Detested kite,° thou liest.
My train are men of choice and rarest parts,°
290 That all particulars of duty know,
And, in the most exact regard,° support
The worships° of their name. O most small fault,
How ugly didst thou in Cordelia show!
Which, like an engine,° wrenched my frame of nature
From the fixed place;° drew from my heart all
295   love,
And added to the gall.° O Lear, Lear, Lear!
Beat at this gate that let thy folly in

[*Striking his head.*]

And thy dear judgment out. Go, go, my people.
            ALBANY:
My lord, I am guiltless, as I am ignorant
Of what hath moved you.
300   LEAR: It may be so, my lord.
Hear, Nature, hear; dear goddess, hear:
Suspend thy purpose if thou didst intend
To make this creature fruitful.
Into her womb convey sterility,
305 Dry up in her the organs of increase,°
And from her derogate° body never spring
A babe to honor her. If she must teem,°

Create her child of spleen,° that it may live
And be a thwart disnatured° torment to her.
Let it stamp wrinkles in her brow of youth,   310
With cadent° tears fret° channels in her cheeks,
Turn all her mother's pains and benefits°
To laughter and contempt, that she may feel
How sharper than a serpent's tooth it is
To have a thankless child. Away, away!   315
                                        (*Exit.*)
            ALBANY:
Now, gods that we adore, whereof comes this?
            GONERIL:
Never afflict yourself to know the cause,
But let his disposition° have that scope
As° dotage gives it.

(*Enter* LEAR.)

            LEAR:
What, fifty of my followers at a clap?°   320
Within a fortnight?
            ALBANY: What's the matter, sir?
            LEAR:
I'll tell thee. [*To* GONERIL.] Life and death, I am ashamed
That thou hast power to shake my manhood° thus!
That these hot tears, which break from me perforce,°
Should make thee worth them. Blasts and fogs upon thee!   325
Th' untented woundings° of a father's curse
Pierce every sense about thee! Old fond° eyes,
Beweep° this cause again, I'll pluck ye out
And cast you, with the waters that you loose,°
To temper° clay. Yea, is it come to this?   330
Ha! Let it be so. I have another daughter,
Who I am sure is kind and comfortable.°
When she shall hear this of thee, with her nails
She'll flay thy wolvish visage. Thou shalt find

---

279 **Degenerate** unnatural 288 **kite** scavenging bird of prey 289 **parts** accomplishments 291 **exact regard** strict attention to detail 292 **worships** honor 294 **engine** destructive contrivance 294–295 **wrenched . . . place** i.e., disorders my natural self 296 **gall** bitterness 305 **increase** childbearing 306 **derogate** degraded 307 **teem** conceive

308 **spleen** ill humor 309 **thwart disnatured** perverse unnatural 311 **cadent** falling; **fret** wear 312 **benefits** the mother's beneficent care of her child 318 **disposition** mood 319 **As** that 320 **at a clap** at one stroke 323 **shake my manhood** i.e., with tears 324 **perforce** involuntarily, against my will 326 **untented woundings** wounds too deep to be probed with a tent (a roll of lint) 327 **fond** foolish 328 **Beweep** if you weep over 329 **loose** (1) let loose (2) lose, as of no avail 330 **temper** mix with and soften 332 **comfortable** ready to comfort

That I'll resume the shape° which thou dost
335   think
I have cast off for ever.

(*Exit* [LEAR, *with* KENT
and ATTENDANTS].)

GONERIL: Do you mark that?

ALBANY:
I cannot be so partial, Goneril,
To the great love I bear you° —

GONERIL:
Pray you, content. What, Oswald, ho!

[*To the* FOOL].

You, sir, more knave than fool, after your
340   master!

FOOL: Nuncle Lear, nuncle Lear, tarry. Take
the Fool° with thee.

    A fox, when one has caught her,
    And such a daughter,
345   Should sure to the slaughter,
    If my cap would buy a halter.°
    So the Fool follows after.°   (*Exit.*)

GONERIL:
This man hath had good counsel. A hundred
  knights!
'Tis politic° and safe to let him keep
At point° a hundred knights: yes, that on every
350   dream,
Each buzz,° each fancy, each complaint, dis-
  like,
He may enguard° his dotage with their pow'rs
And hold our lives in mercy.° Oswald, I say!

ALBANY:
Well, you may fear too far.

GONERIL: Safer than trust too far.
355 Let me still take away the harms I fear,
Not fear still to be taken.° I know his heart.
What he hath uttered I have writ my sister.
If she sustain him and his hundred knights,
When I have showed th' unfitness —

(*Enter* OSWALD.)

    How now, Oswald?
360 What, have you writ that letter to my sister?
OSWALD: Ay, madam.

GONERIL:
Take you some company,° and away to horse.
Inform her full of my particular° fear,
And thereto add such reasons of your own
As may compact° it more. Get you gone,   365
And hasten your return. [*Exit* OSWALD.] No,
  no, my lord,
This milky gentleness and course° of yours,
Though I condemn not,° yet under pardon,
You are much more attasked° for want of
  wisdom
Than praised for harmful mildness.°   370

ALBANY:
How far your eyes may pierce I cannot tell;
Striving to better, oft we mar what's well.

GONERIL: Nay then —

ALBANY: Well, well, th' event.°   (*Exeunt.*)

SCENE V. [*Court before the same.*]

Enter LEAR, KENT, *and* FOOL.

LEAR: Go you before to Gloucester with
these letters. Acquaint my daughter no further
with anything you know than comes from her
demand out of the letter.° If your diligence be
not speedy, I shall be there afore you.   5

KENT: I will not sleep, my lord, till I have
delivered your letter.   (*Exit.*)

FOOL: If a man's brains were in's heels,
were't° not in danger of kibes?°

LEAR: Ay, boy.   10

FOOL: Then I prithee be merry. Thy wit
shall not go slipshod.°

LEAR: Ha, ha, ha.

FOOL: Shalt° see thy other daughter will use
thee kindly;° for though she's as like this as a   15
crab's° like an apple, yet I can tell what I can
tell.

LEAR: Why, what canst thou tell, my boy?

FOOL: She will taste as like this as a crab

---

362 **company** escort   363 **particular** own   365 **compact** strengthen   367 **milky . . . course** mild and gentle way (hendiadys)   368 **condemn not** condemn it not   369 **attasked** taken to task, blamed   370 **harmful mildness** dangerous indulgence   374 **th' event** i.e., we'll see what happens
I.v.3–4 **than . . . letter** than her reading of the letter brings her to ask   9 **were't** i.e., the brains; **kibes** chilblains   11–12 **Thy . . . slipshod** Your brains shall not go in slippers (because you have no brains to be protected from chilblains)   14 **Shalt** thou shalt   15 **kindly** (1) affectionately (2) after her kind or nature   16 **crab** crab apple

335 **shape** i.e., kingly role   337–338 **I cannot . . . you** i.e., even though my love inclines me to you, I must protest   342 **Fool** (1) the Fool himself (2) the epithet or character of "fool"   346–347 **halter, after** pronounced "hauter," "auter"   349 **politic** good policy   350 **At point** armed   351 **buzz** rumor   352 **enguard** protect   353 **in mercy** at his mercy   356 **Not . . . taken** rather than remain fearful of being overtaken by them

20 does to a crab. Thou canst tell why one's nose stands i' th' middle on's° face?

LEAR: No.

FOOL: Why, to keep one's eyes of° either side's nose, that what a man cannot smell out,
25 he may spy into.

LEAR: I did her wrong.

FOOL: Canst tell how an oyster makes his shell?

LEAR: No.

30 FOOL: Nor I neither; but I can tell why a snail has a house.

LEAR: Why?

FOOL: Why, to put's head in; not to give it away to his daughters, and leave his horns°
35 without a case.

LEAR: I will forget my nature.° So kind a father! Be my horses ready?

FOOL: Thy asses are gone about 'em. The reason why the seven stars° are no moe° than
40 seven is a pretty° reason.

LEAR: Because they are not eight.

FOOL: Yes indeed. Thou wouldst make a good fool.

LEAR: To take't again perforce!° Monster
45 ingratitude!

FOOL: If thou wert my fool, nuncle, I'd have thee beaten for being old before thy time.

LEAR: How's that?

FOOL: Thou shouldst not have been old till
50 thou hadst been wise.

LEAR:

O, let me not be mad, not mad, sweet heaven! Keep me in temper;° I would not be mad!

[*Enter* GENTLEMAN.]

How now, are the horses ready?

GENTLEMAN: Ready, my lord.

55 LEAR: Come, boy.

FOOL:

She that's a maid now, and laughs at my departure,
Shall not be a maid long, unless things be cut shorter.°

(*Exeunt.*)

---

21 **on's** of his   23 **of** on   34 **horns** (1) snail's horns (2) cuckold's horns   36 **nature** paternal instincts 39 **seven stars** the Pleiades; **moe** more   40 **pretty** apt   44 **To...perforce** (1) of Goneril, who has forcibly taken away Lear's privileges; or (2) of Lear, who meditates a forcible resumption of authority 52 **in temper** sane   56–57 **She...shorter** The maid who laughs, missing the tragic implications of this quarrel, will not have sense enough to preserve her virginity ("things" = penises)

ACT II

SCENE I. [*The Earl of* GLOUCESTER's *castle.*]

Enter EDMUND *and* CURAN, *severally.*°

EDMUND: Save° thee, Curan.

CURAN: And you, sir. I have been with your father, and given him notice that the Duke of Cornwall and Regan his duchess will be here with him this night.   5

EDMUND: How comes that?

CURAN: Nay, I know not. You have heard of the news abroad? I mean the whispered ones, for they are yet but ear-kissing arguments.°

EDMUND: Not I. Pray you, what are they?   10

CURAN: Have you heard of no likely° wars toward,° 'twixt the Dukes of Cornwall and Albany?

EDMUND: Not a word.

CURAN: You may do, then, in time. Fare you   15
well, sir.   (*Exit.*)

EDMUND:

The duke be here tonight? The better!° best!
This weaves itself perforce° into my business.
My father hath set guard to take my brother,
And I have one thing of a queasy question°   20
Which I must act. Briefness° and Fortune, work!
Brother, a word; descend. Brother, I say!

(*Enter* EDGAR.)

My father watches. O sir, fly this place.
Intelligence° is given where you are hid.
You have now the good advantage of the night.   25
Have you not spoken 'gainst the Duke of Cornwall?
He's coming hither, now i' th' night, i' th' haste,°
And Regan with him. Have you nothing said

II.i.s.d. **severally** separately (from different entrances onstage)   1 **Save** God save   9 **ear-kissing arguments** subjects whispered in the ear   11 **likely** probable   12 **toward** impending   17 **The better** So much the better   18 **perforce** necessarily   20 **of... question** that requires delicate handling (to be "queasy" is to be on the point of vomiting)   21 **Briefness** speed   24 **Intelligence** information   27 **i' th' haste** in great haste

Upon his party° 'gainst the Duke of Albany?
Advise yourself.°
30   EDGAR: I am sure on't,° not a word.
EDMUND:
I hear my father coming. Pardon me:
In cunning° I must draw my sword upon you.
Draw, seem to defend yourself; now quit you°
    well.
Yield! Come before my father! Light ho,
    here!
35 Fly, brother. Torches, torches! — So farewell.
                                    (*Exit* EDGAR.)
Some blood drawn on me would beget opin-
    ion°

[*Wounds his arm.*]

Of my more fierce endeavor. I have seen
    drunkards
Do more than this in sport. Father, father!
Stop, stop! No help?

(*Enter* GLOUCESTER, *and* SERVANTS *with
torches.*)

GLOUCESTER:
40 Now, Edmund, where's the villain?
EDMUND:
Here stood he in the dark, his sharp sword
    out,
Mumbling of wicked charms, conjuring the
    moon
To stand auspicious mistress.
    GLOUCESTER: But where is he?
EDMUND:
Look, sir, I bleed.
45   GLOUCESTER: Where is the villain, Edmund?
EDMUND:
Fled this way, sir, when by no means he
    could —
GLOUCESTER:
Pursue him, ho! Go after. [*Exeunt some*
SERVANTS.] By no means what?
EDMUND:
Persuade me to the murder of your lordship;
But that I told him the revenging gods
50 'Gainst parricides did all the thunder bend;°
Spoke with how manifold and strong a bond
The child was bound to th' father. Sir, in fine,°
Seeing how loathly opposite° I stood

To his unnatural purpose, in fell° motion°
With his preparèd sword he charges home   55
My unprovided° body, latched° mine arm;
But when he saw my best alarumed° spirits
Bold in the quarrel's right,° roused to th'
    encounter,
Or whether gasted° by the noise I made,
Full suddenly he fled.
    GLOUCESTER: Let him fly far.   60
Not in this land shall he remain uncaught;
And found — dispatch.° The noble duke my
    master,
My worthy arch° and patron, comes tonight.
By his authority I will proclaim it,
That he which finds him shall deserve our
    thanks,   65
Bringing the murderous coward to the stake.
He that conceals him, death.°
    EDMUND:
When I dissuaded him from his intent,
And found him pight° to do it, with curst°
    speech
I threatened to discover° him. He replied,   70
"Thou unpossessing° bastard, dost thou think,
If I would stand against thee, would the
    reposal°
Of any trust, virtue, or worth in thee
Make thy words faithed?° No. What I should
    deny —
As this I would, ay, though thou didst produce 75
My very character° — I'd turn it all
To thy suggestion,° plot, and damnèd prac-
    tice.°
And thou must make a dullard of the world,°
If they not thought° the profits of my death
Were very pregnant° and potential spirits°   80
To make thee seek it."
    GLOUCESTER: O strange and fastened° villain!
Would he deny his letter, said he? I never got°
    him.

54 **fell** deadly; **motion** thrust (a term from fencing)   56 **unprovided** unprotected; **latched** wounded
(lanced)   57 **best alarumed** wholly aroused   58
Bold . . . right confident in the rightness of my cause
59 **gasted** struck aghast   62 **dispatch** i.e., he will
be killed   63 **arch** chief   67 **death** the same ellipti-
cal form that characterizes "dispatch," line 62   69
pight determined; **curst** angry   70 **discover** expose
71 **unpossessing** beggarly (landless)   72 **reposal**
placing   74 **faithed** believed   76 **character** handwriting   77 **suggestion** instigation; **practice** device
78 **make . . . world** think everyone stupid   79 **not
thought** did not think   80 **pregnant** teeming with
incitement; **potential spirits** powerful evil spirits   81
fastened hardened   82 **got** begot

29 **Upon his party** censuring his enmity   30 **Advise yourself** Reflect; **on't** of it   32 **In cunning** as a
pretense   33 **quit you** acquaint yourself   36 **beget
opinion** create the impression   50 **bend** aim   52 **in
fine** finally   53 **loathly opposite** bitterly opposed

(*Tucket° within.*)

Hark, the duke's trumpets. I know not why he
    comes.
All ports° I'll bar; the villain shall not 'scape;
The duke must grant me that. Besides, his
    picture
85 I will send far and near, that all the kingdom
May have due note of him; and of my land,
Loyal and natural° boy, I'll work the means
To make thee capable.°

(*Enter* CORNWALL, REGAN, *and* ATTEN-
DANTS.)

CORNWALL:
How now, my noble friend! Since I came
90   hither,
Which I can call but now, I have heard
    strange news.
REGAN:
If it be true, all vengeance comes too short
Which can pursue th' offender. How dost, my
    lord?
GLOUCESTER:
O madam, my old heart is cracked, it's
    cracked.
REGAN:
95 What, did my father's godson seek your life?
He whom my father named, your Edgar?
GLOUCESTER:
O lady, lady, shame would have it hid.
REGAN:
Was he not companion with the riotous
    knights
That tended upon my father?
GLOUCESTER:
100 I know not, madam. 'Tis too bad, too bad.
EDMUND:
Yes, madam, he was of that consort.°
REGAN:
No marvel then, though he were ill affected.°
'Tis they have put° him on the old man's
    death,
To have th' expense and waste° of his reve-
    nues.
105 I have this present evening from my sister
Been well informed of them, and with such
    cautions

That, if they come to sojourn at my house,
I'll not be there.
    CORNWALL: Nor I, assure thee, Regan.
Edmund, I hear that you have shown your
    father
A childlike° office.
    EDMUND: It was my duty, sir.   110
GLOUCESTER:
He did bewray his practice,° and received
This hurt you see, striving to apprehend him.
    CORNWALL:
Is he pursued?
    GLOUCESTER:
                    Ay, my good lord.
    CORNWALL:
If he be taken, he shall never more
Be feared of doing° harm. Make your own
    purpose,   115
How in my strength you please.° For you,
    Edmund,
Whose virtue and obedience° doth this instant
So much commend itself, you shall be ours.
Natures of such deep trust we shall much
    need;
You we first seize on.
    EDMUND: I shall serve you, sir,   120
Truly, however else.
    GLOUCESTER: For him I thank your grace.
    CORNWALL:
You know not why we came to visit you?
    REGAN:
Thus out of season, threading dark-eyed night.
Occasions, noble Gloucester, of some prize,°
Wherein we must have use of your advice.   125
Our father he hath writ, so hath our sister,
Of differences,° which° I best thought it fit
To answer from° our home. The several mes-
    sengers
From hence attend dispatch.° Our good old
    friend,
Lay comforts to your bosom,° and bestow   130
Your needful° counsel to our businesses,
Which craves the instant use.°

82 s.d. **Tucket** Cornwall's special trumpet call   84
ports exits, of whatever sort   88 **natural** (1) kind
(filial) (2) illegitimate   89 **capable** able to inherit
101 **consort** company   102 **ill affected** disposed to
evil   103 **put** set   104 **expense and waste** squander-
ing

110 **childlike** filial   111 **bewray his practice** disclose his plot   115 **of doing** because he might do
115–116 **Make . . . please** Use my power freely, in
carrying out your plans for his capture   117 **virtue
and obedience** virtuous obedience   124 **prize** importance   127 **differences** quarrels; **which** referring
not to "differences," but to the letter Lear has written
128 **from** away from   129 **attend dispatch** are
waiting to be sent off   130 **Lay . . . bosom** console
yourself (about Edgar's supposed treason)   131
needful needed   132 **craves . . . use** demands immediate transaction

GLOUCESTER: I serve you, madam.
Your graces are right welcome.
                              (*Exeunt. Flourish.*)

SCENE II. [*Before* GLOUCESTER's *castle.*]

Enter KENT *and* OSWALD, *severally.*

OSWALD: Good dawning° to thee, friend. Art
of this house?°
    KENT: Ay.
    OSWALD: Where may we set our horses?
5   KENT: I' th' mire.
    OSWALD: Prithee, if thou lov'st me, tell me.
    KENT: I love thee not.
    OSWALD: Why then, I care not for thee.
    KENT: If I had thee in Lipsbury Pinfold,° I
10 would make thee care for me.
    OSWALD: Why dost thou use me thus? I
know thee not.
    KENT: Fellow, I know thee.
    OSWALD: What dost thou know me for?
15   KENT: A knave, a rascal, an eater of broken
meats;° a base, proud, shallow, beggarly, three-
suited,° hundred-pound,° filthy worsted-stock-
ing° knave; a lily-livered, action-taking,° whoreson, glass-gazing,° superserviceable,° finical°
20 rogue; one-trunk-inheriting° slave; one that
wouldst be a bawd in way of good service,° and
art nothing but the composition° of a knave,
beggar, coward, pander, and the son and heir
of a mongrel bitch; one whom I will beat into
25 clamorous whining if thou deniest the least
syllable of thy addition.°
    OSWALD: Why, what a monstrous fellow art
thou, thus to rail on one that is neither known
of thee nor knows thee!
30   KENT: What a brazen-faced varlet art thou

to deny thou knowest me! Is it two days since
I tripped up thy heels and beat thee before the
king? [*Drawing his sword.*] Draw, you rogue,
for though it be night, yet the moon shines.
I'll make a sop o' th' moonshine° of you. You   35
whoreson cullionly barbermonger,° draw!
    OSWALD: Away, I have nothing to do with
thee.
    KENT: Draw, you rascal. You come with
letters against the king, and take Vanity the   40
puppet's° part against the royalty of her father.
Draw, you rogue, or I'll so carbonado° your
shanks. Draw, you rascal. Come your ways!°
    OSWALD: Help, ho! Murder! Help!
    KENT: Strike, you slave! Stand, rogue!   45
Stand, you neat° slave! Strike!

[*Beating him.*]

    OSWALD: Help, ho! Murder, murder!

(*Enter* EDMUND, *with his rapier drawn,*
CORNWALL, REGAN, GLOUCESTER, SERVANTS.)

    EDMUND: How now? What's the matter?
Part!
    KENT: With you,° goodman boy,° if you   50
please! Come, I'll flesh° ye, come on, young
master.
    GLOUCESTER: Weapons? Arms? What's the
matter here?
    CORNWALL: Keep peace, upon your lives. He   55
dies that strikes again. What is the matter?
    REGAN: The messengers from our sister and
the king.
    CORNWALL: What is your difference?° Speak.
    OSWALD: I am scarce in breath, my lord.   60
    KENT: No marvel, you have so bestirred°
your valor. You cowardly rascal, nature dis-
claims in thee.° A tailor made thee.°

II.II.1 **dawning** dawn is impending, but not yet arrived   1–2 **Art ... house** Do you live here?   9 **Lipsbury Pinfold** a pound or pen in which strayed animals
are enclosed ("Lipsbury" may denote a particular
place, or may be slang for "between my teeth")   15–
16 **broken meats** scraps of food   16–17 **three-suited**
the wardrobe permitted to a servant or "knave"   17
hundred-pound the extent of Oswald's wealth, and
thus a sneer at his aspiring to gentility   17–18
worsted-stocking worn by servants   18 **action-taking**
one who refuses a fight and goes to law instead   19
glass-gazing conceited   19 **superserviceable** syco-
phantic, serving without principle; **finical** overfastid-
ious   20 **one-trunk-inheriting** possessing only a
trunkful of goods   21 **bawd ... service** pimp, to
please his master   22 **composition** compound   26
addition titles

35 **sop ... moonshine** i.e., Oswald will admit the
moonlight, and so sop it up, through the open wounds
Kent is preparing to give him   36 **cullionly barbermonger** base patron of hairdressers (effeminate man)
40–41 **Vanity the puppet's** Goneril, here identified
with one of the personified characters in the morality
plays, which were sometimes put on as puppet shows
42 **carbonado** cut across, like a piece of meat before
cooking   43 **Come your ways** Get along!   46 **neat**
(1) foppish (2) unmixed, as in "neat wine"   50
With you i.e., the quarrel is with you; **goodman boy**
young man (peasants are "goodmen"; "boy" is a
term of contempt)   51 **flesh** introduce to blood
(term from hunting)   59 **difference** quarrel   61
bestirred exercised   62–63 **nature ... thee** nature
renounces any part in you   63 **A tailor made thee**
from the proverb "The tailor makes the man"

CORNWALL: Thou art a strange fellow. A
65 tailor make a man?

KENT: A tailor, sir. A stonecutter or a
painter could not have made him so ill, though
they had been but two years o' th' trade.

CORNWALL:
Speak yet, how grew your quarrel?

70 OSWALD: This ancient ruffian, sir, whose life
I have spared at suit of° his gray beard —

KENT: Thou whoreson zed,° thou unnecessary letter! My lord, if you will give me leave,
I will tread this unbolted° villain into mortar
75 and daub the wall of a jakes° with him. Spare
my gray beard, you wagtail!°

CORNWALL: Peace, sirrah!
You beastly° knave, know you no reverence?

KENT:
Yes, sir, but anger hath a privilege.

CORNWALL:
80 Why art thou angry?

KENT:
That such a slave as this should wear a sword,
Who wears no honesty. Such smiling rogues as
these,
Like rats, oft bite the holy cords° atwain
Which are too intrince° t' unloose; smooth°
every passion
85 That in the natures of their lords rebel,
Being oil to fire, snow to the colder moods;
Renege,° affirm, and turn their halcyon beaks°
With every gale and vary° of their masters,
Knowing naught, like dogs, but following.
90 A plague upon your epileptic° visage!
Smile you° my speeches, as I were a fool?
Goose, if I had you upon Sarum Plain,°
I'd drive ye cackling home to Camelot.°

CORNWALL:
What, art thou mad, old fellow?

GLOUCESTER:
How fell you out? Say that.   95

KENT:
No contraries° hold more antipathy
Than I and such a knave.

CORNWALL:
Why dost thou call him knave? What is his
fault?

KENT:
His countenance likes° me not.

CORNWALL:
No more perchance does mine, nor his, nor
hers.   100

KENT:
Sir, 'tis my occupation to be plain:
I have seen better faces in my time
Than stands on any shoulder that I see
Before me at this instant.

CORNWALL: This is some fellow
Who, having been praised for bluntness, doth
affect   105
A saucy roughness, and constrains the garb
Quite from his nature.° He cannot flatter, he;
An honest mind and plain, he must speak
truth.
And° they will take it, so; if not, he's plain.
These kind of knaves I know, which in this
plainness   110
Harbor more craft and more corrupter ends
Than twenty silly-ducking observants°
That stretch their duties nicely.°

KENT:
Sir, in good faith, in sincere verity,
Under th' allowance° of your great aspect,°   115
Whose influence,° like the wreath of radiant
fire
On flick'ring Phoebus' front° —

CORNWALL: What mean'st by this?

KENT: To go out of my dialect,° which you
discommend so much. I know, sir, I am no
flatterer. He° that beguiled you in a plain   120

71 **at suit of** out of pity for 72 **zed** the letter Z,
generally omitted in contemporary dictionaries 74
unbolted unsifted, i.e., altogether a villain 75 **jakes**
privy 76 **wagtail** a bird that bobs its tail up and
down, and thus suggests obsequiousness 78 **beastly**
irrational 83 **holy cords** sacred bonds of affection
(as between husbands and wives, parents and children) 84 **intrince** entangled, intricate; **smooth** appease 87 **Renege** deny; **halcyon beaks** the halcyon
or kingfisher serves here as a type of the opportunist
because, when hung up by the tail or neck, it was
supposed to turn with the wind, like a weathervane
88 **gale and vary** varying gale (hendiadys) 90 **epi-
leptic** distorted by grinning 91 **Smile you** do you
smile at 92 **Sarum Plain** Salisbury Plain 93 **Camelot** the residence of King Arthur (presumably a particular point, now lost, is intended here)

96 **contraries** opposites 99 **likes** pleases 106–107
constrains ... nature forces the manner of can-
did speech to be a cloak, not for candor but for
craft 109 **And if** 112 **silly-ducking observants**
ridiculously obsequious attendants 113 **nicely** punctiliously 115 **allowance** approval; **aspect** (1) appearance (2) position of the heavenly bodies 116
influence astrological power 117 **Phoebus' front**
forehead of the sun 118 **dialect** customary manner
of speaking 120 **He** i.e., the sort of candid-crafty
man Cornwall has been describing

accent was a plain knave, which, for my part, I
will not be, though I should win your displea-
sure to entreat me to't.°
    CORNWALL:
What was th' offense you gave him?
    OSWALD:
125 I never gave him any.
It pleased the king his master very late°
To strike at me, upon his misconstruction;°
When he, compact,° and flattering his displea-
    sure,
Tripped me behind; being down, insulted,
    railed,
130 And put upon him such a deal of man°
That worthied him,° got praises of the king
For him attempting who was self-subdued;°
And, in the fleshment° of this dread exploit,
Drew on me here again.
    KENT: None of these rogues and cowards
But Ajax is their fool.°
135   CORNWALL: Fetch forth the stocks!
You stubborn° ancient knave, you reverent°
    braggart,
We'll teach you.
    KENT: Sir, I am too old to learn.
Call not your stocks for me, I serve the king,
On whose employment I was sent to you.
You shall do small respect, show too bold
140   malice
Against the grace and person° of my master,
Stocking his messenger.
    CORNWALL:
Fetch forth the stocks. As I have life and
    honor,
There shall he sit till noon.
    REGAN:
Till noon? Till night, my lord, and all night
145   too.

122–123 **though ... to't** even if I were to succeed in
bringing your graceless person ("displeasure" personified, and in lieu of the expected form, "your grace")
to beg me to be a plain knave   126 **very late** recently   127 **misconstruction** misunderstanding   128
compact in league with the king   130 **put ... man**
pretended such manly behavior   131 **worthied him**
made him seem heroic   132 **For ... self-subdued**
for attacking a man (Oswald) who offered no resistance   133 **fleshment** the bloodthirstiness excited
by his first success or "fleshing"   134–135 **None ...
fool** i.e., cowardly rogues like Oswald always impose
on fools like Cornwall (who is likened to Ajax: [1]
the braggart Greek-warrior [2] a jakes or privy)   136
stubborn rude; **reverent** old   141 **grace and person**
i.e., Lear as sovereign and in his personal character

    KENT:
Why, madam, if I were your father's dog,
You should not use me so.
    REGAN: Sir, being his knave, I will.
    CORNWALL:
This is a fellow of the selfsame color°
Our sister speaks of. Come, bring away° the
    stocks.

(*Stocks brought out.*)

    GLOUCESTER:
Let me beseech your grace not to do so.   150
His fault is much, and the good king his
    master
Will check° him for't. Your purposed° low
    correction
Is such as basest and contemnèd'st° wretches
For pilf'rings and most common trespasses
Are punished with.   155
The king his master needs must take it ill
That he, so slightly valued in° his messenger,
Should have him thus restrained.
    CORNWALL: I'll answer° that.
    REGAN:
My sister may receive it much more worse,
To have her gentleman abused, assaulted,   160
For following her affairs. Put in his legs.

[KENT *is put in the stocks.*]

Come, my good lord, away!
    [*Exeunt all but* GLOUCESTER *and* KENT.]
    GLOUCESTER:
I am sorry for thee, friend. 'Tis the duke's
    pleasure,
Whose disposition° all the world well knows
Will not be rubbed° nor stopped. I'll entreat
    for thee.   165
    KENT:
Pray do not, sir. I have watched° and traveled
    hard.
Some time I shall sleep out, the rest I'll whistle.
A good man's fortune may grow out at heels.°
Give° you good morrow.
    GLOUCESTER:
The duke's to blame in this. 'Twill be ill
    taken.°   (*Exit.*) 170

---

148 **color** kind   149 **away** out   152 **check** correct;
purposed intended   153 **contemnèd'st** most despised
157 **slightly valued in** little honored in the person of
158 **answer** answer for   164 **disposition** inclination
165 **rubbed** diverted (metaphor from the game of
bowls)   166 **watched** gone without sleep   168 **A
... heels** Even a good man may have bad fortune
169 **Give** God give   170 **taken** received

KENT:
Good king, that must approve° the common
    saw,°
Thou out of heaven's benediction com'st
To the warm sun.°
Approach, thou beacon to this under globe,°
175 That by thy comfortable° beams I may
Peruse this letter. Nothing almost sees miracles
But misery.° I know 'tis from Cordelia,
Who hath most fortunately been informed
Of my obscurèd° course. And shall find time
180 From this enormous state, seeking to give
Losses their remedies.° All weary and o'er-
    watched,
Take vantage,° heavy eyes, not to behold
This shameful lodging. Fortune, good night;
Smile once more, turn thy wheel.°

    (*Sleeps.*)

[SCENE III. *A wood.*]

Enter EDGAR.

EDGAR:
I heard myself proclaimed,
And by the happy° hollow of a tree
Escaped the hunt. No port is free, no place
That guard and most unusual vigilance
Does not attend my taking.° Whiles I may
5 'scape,
I will preserve myself; and am bethought°
To take the basest and most poorest shape
That ever penury, in contempt of man,
Brought near to beast;° my face I'll grime with
    filth,
10 Blanket° my loins, elf° all my hairs in knots,
And with presented° nakedness outface°

The winds and persecutions of the sky.
The country gives me proof° and precedent
Of Bedlam° beggars, who, with roaring voices,
Strike° in their numbed and mortified° bare
    arms   15
Pins, wooden pricks,° nails, sprigs of rosemary;
And with this horrible object° from low° farms,
Poor pelting° villages, sheepcotes, and mills,
Sometimes with lunatic bans,° sometime with
    prayers,
Enforce their charity. Poor Turlygod, Poor
    Tom,°   20
That's something yet: Edgar I nothing am.°
                      (*Exit.*)

[SCENE IV. *Before* GLOUCESTER's *castle.* KENT
           in the stocks.]

Enter LEAR, FOOL, *and* GENTLEMAN.

LEAR:
'Tis strange that they should so depart from
    home,
And not send back my messenger.
   GENTLEMAN: As I learned,
The night before there was no purpose° in
    them
Of this remove.°
   KENT: Hail to thee, noble master.
LEAR: Ha!   5
Mak'st thou this shame thy pastime?°
   KENT: No, my lord.
   FOOL: Ha, ha, he wears cruel° garters. Horses
are tied by the heads, dogs and bears by th'
neck, monkeys by th' loins, and men by th'
legs. When a man's overlusty at legs,° then   10
he wears wooden netherstocks.°
LEAR:
What's he that hath so much thy place
    mistook
To set thee here?
   KENT: It is both he and she,
Your son and daughter.

---

171 **approve** confirm; **saw** proverb   172–173 **Thou
. . . sun** i.e., Lear goes from better to worse, from
heaven's blessing or shelter to lack of shelter   174
beacon . . . globe i.e., the sun, whose rising Kent anticipates   175 **comfortable** comforting   176–177
Nothing . . . misery i.e., True perception belongs only
to the wretched   179 **obscurèd** disguised   179–181
shall . . . remedies a possible reading: Cordelia, away
from this monstrous state of things, will find occasion
to right the wrongs we suffer   182 **vantage** advantage
(of sleep)   184 **turn thy wheel** i.e., so that Kent,
who is at the bottom, may climb upward
II.III.2 **happy** lucky   5 **attend my taking** watch to
capture me   6 **am bethought** have decided   8–9
penury . . . beast poverty, to show how contemptible
man is, reduced to the level of a beast   10 **Blanket**
cover only with a blanket; **elf** tangle (into "elflocks,"
supposed to be caused by elves)   11 **presented** the
show of; **outface** brave

13 **proof** example   14 **Bedlam** see I.II.155–156   15
Strike stick; **mortified** not alive to pain   16 **pricks**
skewers   17 **object** spectacle; **low** humble   18 **pelting** paltry   19 **bans** curses   20 **Poor . . . Tom** Edgar
recites the names a Bedlam beggar gives himself   21
That's . . . am There's a chance for me in that I am
no longer known for myself
II.IV.3 **purpose** intention   4 **remove** removal   6
Mak'st . . . pastime Are you doing this to amuse yourself?   7 **cruel** (1) painful (2) "crewel," a worsted yarn
used in garters   10 **overlusty at legs** (1) a vagabond
(2) sexually promiscuous (?)   11 **netherstocks** stockings (as opposed to knee breeches, or upperstocks)

LEAR: No. 15
KENT: Yes.
LEAR: No, I say.
KENT: I say yea.
LEAR: No, no, they would not.
KENT: Yes, they have. 20
LEAR:
By Jupiter, I swear no!
KENT:
By Juno, I swear ay!
LEAR: They durst not do't;
They could not, would not do't. 'Tis worse
     than murder
To do upon respect° such violent outrage.
Resolve° me with all modest° haste which way 25
Thou mightst deserve or they impose this
     usage,
Coming from us.
KENT: My lord, when at their home
I did commend° your highness' letters to them,
Ere I was risen from the place that showed
My duty kneeling, came there a reeking post,° 30
Stewed° in his haste, half breathless, panting
     forth
From Goneril his mistress salutations,
Delivered letters, spite of intermission,°
Which presently° they read; on° whose con-
     tents
They summoned up their meiny,° straight took
     horse, 35
Commanded me to follow and attend
The leisure of their answer, gave me cold
     looks,
And meeting here the other messenger,
Whose welcome I perceived had poisoned
     mine,
Being the very fellow which of late 40
Displayed° so saucily against your highness,
Having more man than wit° about me, drew;
He raised° the house, with loud and coward
     cries.
Your son and daughter found this trespass
     worth°
The shame which here it suffers. 45

24 upon respect (1) on the respect due to the king
(2) deliberately   25 Resolve inform; modest becoming   28 commend deliver   30 reeking post sweating
messenger   31 stewed steaming   33 spite of intermission in spite of the interrupting of my business
34 presently at once; on on the strength of   35
meiny retinue   41 Displayed showed off   42 more
... wit more manhood than sense   43 raised aroused
44 worth deserving

FOOL: Winter's not gone yet, if the wild
geese fly that way.°
     Fathers that wear rags
        Do make their children blind,°
     But fathers that bear bags° 50
        Shall see their children kind.
     Fortune, that arrant whore,
        Ne'er turns the key° to th' poor.
But for all this, thou shalt have as many
dolors° for thy daughters as thou canst tell° in 55
a year.
LEAR:
O, how this mother swells up toward my
     heart!
Hysterica passio,° down, thou climbing sorrow,
Thy element's° below. Where is this daughter?
KENT:
With the earl, sir, here within.
LEAR: Follow me not; 60
Stay here.   (Exit.)
GENTLEMAN:
Made you no more offense but what you speak
of?
KENT: None.
How chance° the king comes with so small a
     number?
FOOL: And° thou hadst been set i' th' stocks 65
for that question, thou'dst well deserved it.
KENT: Why, Fool?
FOOL: We'll set thee to school to an ant, to
teach thee there's no laboring i' th' winter.° All
that follow their noses are led by their eyes but 70
blind men, and there's not a nose among
twenty but can smell him that's stinking.° Let
go thy hold when a great wheel runs down a
hill, lest it break thy neck with following. But

46–47 Winter's ... way More trouble is to come,
since Cornwall and Regan act so ("geese" is used
contemptuously, as in Kent's quarrel with Oswald,
II.ii.92–93)   49 blind i.e., indifferent   50 bags
moneybags   53 turns the key i.e., opens the door   55
dolors (1) sorrows (2) dollars (English name for Spanish and German coins); tell (1) about (2) count   57–
58 mother ... Hysterica passio hysteria, causing suffocation or choking   59 element proper place   64
How chance how does it happen that   65 And if
68–69 We'll ... winter in the popular fable the ant,
unlike the improvident grasshopper, anticipates the
winter when none can labor by laying up provisions in
the summer; Lear, trusting foolishly to summer days,
finds himself unprovided for, and unable to provide,
now that "winter" has come   69–72 All ... stinking
i.e., all can smell out the decay of Lear's fortunes

75 the great one that goes upward, let him draw
thee after. When a wise man gives thee better
counsel, give me mine again. I would have
none but knaves follow it since a fool gives it.

That sir, which serves and seeks for gain,
80   And follows but for form,°
Will pack,° when it begins to rain,
     And leave thee in the storm.
But I will tarry; the Fool will stay,
     And let the wise man fly.
85 The knave turns Fool that runs away,
     The Fool no knave,° perdy.°

KENT: Where learned you this, Fool?
FOOL: Not i' th' stocks, fool.

(*Enter* LEAR *and* GLOUCESTER.)

LEAR:
Deny° to speak with me? They are sick, they
     are weary,
90 They have traveled all the night? Mere fetches,°
The images° of revolt and flying off!°
Fetch me a better answer.
          GLOUCESTER: My dear lord,
You know the fiery quality° of the duke,
How unremovable and fixed he is
In his own course.
95   LEAR: Vengeance, plague, death, confusion!
Fiery? What quality? Why, Gloucester,
     Gloucester,
I'd speak with the Duke of Cornwall and his
     wife.
GLOUCESTER:
Well, my good lord, I have informed them so.
     LEAR:
Informed them? Dost thou understand me,
     man?
GLOUCESTER:
100 Ay, my good lord.
     LEAR:
The king would speak with Cornwall. The
     dear father
Would with his daughter speak, commands —
     tends° — service.

80 **form** show   81 **pack** be off   85–86 **The . . .
knave** i.e., the faithless man is the true fool, for wisdom requires fidelity; Lear's Fool, who remains faithful, is at least no knave   86 **perdy** by God (French
par Dieu)   89 **Deny** refuse   90 **fetches** subterfuges,
acts of tacking (nautical metaphor)   91 **images** exact likenesses; **flying off** desertion   93 **quality** temperament   102 **tends** attends (i.e., awaits); with,
possibly, an ironic second meaning, "tenders," or
"offers"

Are they informed of this? My breath and
     blood!
Fiery? The fiery duke, tell the hot duke that —
No, but not yet. May be he is not well.   105
Infirmity doth still neglect all office
Whereto our health is bound.° We are not
     ourselves
When nature, being oppressed, commands the
     mind
To suffer with the body. I'll forbear;
And am fallen out° with my more headier will°   110
To take the indisposed and sickly fit
For the sound man. [*Looking on* KENT.] Death
     on my state!° Wherefore
Should he sit here? This act persuades me
That this remotion° of the duke and her
Is practice° only. Give me my servant forth.°   115
Go tell the duke and's wife I'd speak with them!
Now, presently!° Bid them come forth and
     hear me,
Or at their chamber door I'll beat the drum
Till it cry sleep to death.°
     GLOUCESTER:
I would have all well betwixt you.   (*Exit.*)   120
     LEAR:
O me, my heart, my rising heart! But down!
     FOOL: Cry to it, nuncle, as the cockney° did
to the eels when she put 'em i' th' paste° alive.
She knapped° 'em o' th' coxcombs° with a
stick and cried, "Down, wantons,° down!"   125
'Twas her brother that, in pure kindness to his
horse, buttered his hay.°

(*Enter* CORNWALL, REGAN, GLOUCESTER, SER-
VANTS.)

LEAR:
Good morrow to you both.
     CORNWALL: Hail to your grace.

(KENT *here set at liberty.*)

107 **Whereto . . . bound** duties which we are required
to perform, when in health   110 **fallen out** angry;
headier will headlong inclination   112 **state** royal
condition   114 **remotion** (1) removal (2) remaining
aloof   115 **practice** pretense; **forth** i.e., out of the
stocks   117 **presently** at once   119 **cry . . . death**
follow sleep, like a cry or pack of hounds, until it kills
it   122 **cockney** Londoner (ignorant city dweller)
123 **paste** pastry pie   124 **knapped** rapped; **coxcombs** heads   125 **wantons** i.e., playful things (with
a sexual implication)   127 **buttered his hay** i.e., the
city dweller does from ignorance what the dishonest
ostler does from craft: greases the hay the traveler has
paid for, so that the horse will not eat

REGAN:
I am glad to see your highness.
LEAR:
130 Regan, I think you are. I know what reason
I have to think so. If thou shouldst not be glad,
I would divorce me from thy mother's tomb,
Sepulchring an adultress.° [*To* KENT.] O, are you free?
Some other time for that. Beloved Regan,
135 Thy sister's naught.° O Regan, she hath tied
Sharp-toothed unkindness, like a vulture, here.

[*Points to his heart.*]

I can scarce speak to thee. Thou'lt not believe
With how depraved a quality° — O Regan!
REGAN:
I pray you, sir, take patience. I have hope
140 You less know how to value her desert
Than she to scant her duty.°
LEAR: Say? how is that?
REGAN:
I cannot think my sister in the least
Would fail her obligation. If, sir, perchance
She have restrained the riots of your followers,
'Tis on such ground, and to such wholesome
145 end,
As clears her from all blame.
LEAR:
My curses on her!
REGAN: O, sir, you are old,
Nature in you stands on the very verge
Of his confine.° You should be ruled, and led
150 By some discretion that discerns your state
Better than you yourself.° Therefore I pray you
That to our sister you do make return,
Say you have wronged her.
LEAR: Ask her forgiveness?
Do you but mark how this becomes the house:°
155 "Dear daughter, I confess that I am old.

[*Kneeling.*]

Age is unnecessary. On my knees I beg
That you'll vouchsafe me raiment, bed, and food."
REGAN:
Good sir, no more. These are unsightly tricks.
Return you to my sister.
LEAR [*rising*]:   Never, Regan.
She hath abated° me of half my train,   160
Looked black upon me, struck me with her tongue,
Most serpentlike, upon the very heart.
All the stored vengeances of heaven fall
On her ingrateful top!° Strike her young bones,°
You taking° airs, with lameness.
CORNWALL: Fie, sir, fie!   165
LEAR:
You nimble lightnings, dart your blinding flames
Into her scornful eyes! Infect her beauty,
You fen-sucked° fogs, drawn by the pow'rful sun,
To fall and blister° her pride.
REGAN: O the blest gods!
So will you wish on me when the rash mood is on.   170
LEAR:
No, Regan, thou shalt never have my curse.
Thy tender-hefted° nature shall not give
Thee o'er to harshness. Her eyes are fierce, but thine
Do comfort, and not burn. 'Tis not in thee
To grudge my pleasures, to cut off my train,   175
To bandy° hasty words, to scant my sizes,°
And, in conclusion, to oppose the bolt°
Against my coming in. Thou better know'st
The offices of nature, bond of childhood,°
Effects° of courtesy, dues of gratitude.   180
Thy half o' th' kingdom hast thou not forgot,
Wherein I thee endowed.
REGAN: Good sir, to th' purpose.°

(*Tucket within.*)

132–133 **divorce . . . adultress** i.e., repudiate your dead mother as having conceived you by another man   135 **naught** wicked   138 **quality** nature   139–141 **I have . . . duty** despite the double negative, the passage means, "I believe that you fail to give Goneril her due, rather than that she fails to fulfill her duty"   148–149 **Nature . . . confine** i.e., you are nearing the end of your life   150–151 **some . . . yourself** some discreet person who understands your condition more than you do   154 **becomes the house** suits my royal and paternal position

160 **abated** curtailed   164 **top** head; **young bones** the reference may be to unborn children, rather than to Goneril herself   165 **taking** infecting   168 **fen-sucked** drawn up from swamps by the sun   169 **fall and blister** fall upon and raise blisters   172 **tender-hefted** gently framed   176 **bandy** volley (metaphor from tennis); **scant my sizes** reduce my allowances   177 **oppose the bolt** bar the door   179 **offices . . . childhood** natural duties, a child's duty to its parent   180 **Effects** manifestations   182 **to th' purpose** come to the point

LEAR:
Who put my man i' th' stocks?
CORNWALL: What trumpet's that?
REGAN:
I know't — my sister's. This approves° her
    letter,
That she would soon be here.

    (*Enter* OSWALD.)

185   Is your lady come?
LEAR:
This is a slave, whose easy borrowed° pride
Dwells in the fickle grace° of her he follows.
Out, varlet,° from my sight.
CORNWALL: What means your grace?
LEAR:
Who stocked my servant? Regan, I have good
    hope
Thou didst not know on't.

    (*Enter* GONERIL.)

190   Who comes here? O heavens!
If you do love old men, if your sweet sway
Allow° obedience, if you yourselves are old,
Make it° your cause. Send down, and take my
    part.

    [*To* GONERIL.]

195 Art not ashamed to look upon this beard?
O Regan, will you take her by the hand?
GONERIL:
Why not by th' hand, sir? How have I
    offended?
All's not offense that indiscretion finds°
And dotage terms so.
LEAR: O sides,° you are too tough!
Will you yet hold? How came my man i' th'
    stocks?
CORNWALL:
200 I set him there, sir; but his own disorders°
Deserved much less advancement.°
LEAR: You? Did you?
REGAN:
I pray you, father, being weak, seem so.°
If till the expiration of your month
You will return and sojourn with my sister,

Dismissing half your train, come then to me. 205
I am now from home, and out of that
    provision
Which shall be needful for your entertain-
    ment.°
LEAR:
Return to her, and fifty men dismissed?
No, rather I abjure all roofs, and choose
To wage° against the enmity o' th' air,   210
To be a comrade with the wolf and owl,
Necessity's sharp pinch.° Return with her?
Why, the hot-blooded° France, that dowerless
    took
Our youngest born, I could as well be brought
To knee° his throne, and, squirelike,° pension
    beg   215
To keep base life afoot. Return with her?
Persuade me rather to be slave and sumpter°
To this detested groom. [*Pointing at* OSWALD.]
GONERIL: At your choice, sir.
LEAR:
I prithee, daughter, do not make me mad.
I will not trouble thee, my child; farewell.   220
We'll no more meet, no more see one another.
But yet thou art my flesh, my blood, my
    daughter,
Or rather a disease that's in my flesh,
Which I must needs call mine. Thou art a
    boil,
A plague-sore, or embossèd carbuncle°   225
In my corrupted blood. But I'll not chide thee.
Let shame come when it will, I do not call it.
I do not bid the Thunder-bearer° shoot,
Nor tell tales of thee to high-judging° Jove.
Mend when thou canst, be better at thy
    leisure,   230
I can be patient, I can stay with Regan,
I and my hundred knights.
REGAN: Not altogether so.
I looked not for you yet, nor am provided
For your fit welcome. Give ear, sir, to my
    sister,
For those that mingle reason with your pas-
    sion°   235

---

184 **approves** confirms   186 **easy borrowed** (1) facile and taken from another (2) acquired without anything to back it up (like money borrowed without security)   187 **grace** favor   188 **varlet** base fellow 192 **Allow** approve of   193 **it** my cause   197 **finds** judges   198 **sides** breast   200 **disorders** misconduct 201 **advancement** promotion   202 **seem so** act weak

207 **entertainment** maintenance   210 **wage** fight 212 **Necessity's sharp pinch** a summing up of the hard choice he has just announced   213 **hot-blooded** passionate   215 **knee** kneel before; **squirelike** like a retainer   217 **sumpter** pack horse   225 **embossèd carbuncle** swollen boil   228 **Thunder-bearer** Jupiter 229 **high-judging** (1) supreme (2) judging from heaven   235 **mingle . . . passion** i.e., consider your turbulent behavior coolly and reasonably

Must be content to think you old, and so —
But she knows what she does.
LEAR: Is this well spoken?
REGAN:
I dare avouch° it, sir. What, fifty followers?
Is it not well? What should you need of
    more?
Yea, or so many, sith that° both charge° and
240   danger
Speak 'gainst so great a number? How in one
    house
Should many people, under two commands,
Hold° amity? 'Tis hard, almost impossible.
GONERIL:
Why might not you, my lord, receive atten-
    dance
From those that she calls servants, or from
245   mine?
REGAN:
Why not, my lord? If then they chanced to
    slack° ye,
We could control them. If you will come to
    me
(For now I spy a danger), I entreat you
To bring but five-and-twenty. To no more
250 Will I give place or notice.°
LEAR:
I gave you all.
REGAN: And in good time you gave it.
LEAR:
Made you my guardians, my depositaries,°
But kept a reservation° to be followed
With such a number. What, must I come to
    you
255 With five-and-twenty? Regan, said you so?
REGAN:
And speak't again, my lord. No more with
    me.
LEAR:
Those wicked creatures yet do look well-
    favored°
When others are more wicked; not being the
    worst
Stands in some rank of praise.° [To GONERIL.]
    I'll go with thee.

Thy fifty yet doth double five-and-twenty,   260
And thou art twice her love.°
GONERIL: Hear me, my lord.
What need you five-and-twenty? ten? or five?
To follow° in a house where twice so many
Have a command to tend you?
REGAN: What need one?
LEAR:
O reason° not the need! Our basest beggars   265
Are in the poorest thing superfluous.°
Allow not nature more than nature needs,°
Man's life is cheap as beast's. Thou art a lady:
If only to go warm were gorgeous,
Why, nature needs not what thou gorgeous
    wear'st,   270
Which scarcely keeps thee warm.° But, for true
    need —
You heavens, give me that patience, patience I
    need.
You see me here, you gods, a poor old man,
As full of grief as age, wretched in both.
If it be you that stirs these daughters' hearts   275
Against their father, fool° me not so much
To bear° it tamely; touch me with noble
    anger,
And let not women's weapons, water drops,
Stain my man's cheeks. No, you unnatural
    hags!
I will have such revenges on you both   280
That all the world shall — I will do such
    things —
What they are, yet I know not; but they shall
    be
The terrors of the earth. You think I'll weep.
No, I'll not weep.

(*Storm and tempest.*)

I have full cause of weeping, but this heart   285
Shall break into a hundred thousand flaws°
Or ere° I'll weep. O Fool, I shall go mad!
                    (*Exeunt* LEAR, GLOUCESTER,
                            KENT, and FOOL.)

238 **avouch** swear by   240 **sith that** since; **charge** expense   243 **Hold** preserve   246 **slack** neglect   250
notice recognition   252 **depositaries** trustees   253
reservation condition   257 **well-favored** handsome
258–259 **not . . . praise** i.e., that Goneril is not so bad
as Regan is one thing in her favor

261 **her love** i.e., as loving as she   263 **follow** attend
on you   265 **reason** scrutinize   266 **Are . . . superfluous** have some trifle not absolutely necessary   267
needs i.e., to sustain life   269–271 **If . . . warm** If to
satisfy the need for warmth were to be gorgeous, you
would not need the clothing you wear, which is worn
more for beauty than warmth   276 **fool** humiliate
277 **To bear** as to make me bear   286 **flaws** (1)
pieces (2) cracks (3) gusts of passion   287 **Or ere**
before

CORNWALL:
Let us withdraw, 'twill be a storm.
REGAN:
This house is little; the old man and's people
290 Cannot be well bestowed.°
GONERIL:
'Tis his own blame; hath° put himself from
rest°
And must needs taste his folly.
REGAN:
For his particular,° I'll receive him gladly,
But not one follower.
GONERIL: So am I purposed.°
295 Where is my Lord of Gloucester?
CORNWALL:
Followed the old man forth.

(*Enter* GLOUCESTER.)

He is returned.
GLOUCESTER:
The king is in high rage.
CORNWALL: Whither is he going?
GLOUCESTER:
He calls to horse, but will I know not whither.
CORNWALL:
'Tis best to give him way, he leads himself.°
GONERIL:
300 My lord, entreat him by no means to stay.
GLOUCESTER:
Alack, the night comes on, and the high winds
Do sorely ruffle.° For many miles about
There's scarce a bush.
REGAN: O, sir, to willful men
The injuries that they themselves procure
Must be their schoolmasters. Shut up your
305   doors.
He is attended with a desperate train,
And what they may incense° him to, being apt
To have his ear abused,° wisdom bids fear.
CORNWALL:
Shut up your doors, my lord; 'tis a wild night.
My Regan counsels well. Come out o' th'
310   storm.
(*Exeunt.*)

---

290 **bestowed** lodged   291 **hath** he hath; **rest** (1)
place of residence (2) repose of mind   293 **his particular** himself personally   294 **purposed** determined
299 **give . . . himself** let him go; he insists on his own
way   302 **ruffle** rage   307 **incense** incite   307–308
being . . . abused he being inclined to harken to bad
counsel

ACT III

SCENE I. [*A heath.*]

Storm still.° Enter KENT *and a* GENTLEMAN
severally.

KENT:
Who's there besides foul weather?
GENTLEMAN:
One minded like the weather most unquietly.°
KENT:
I know you. Where's the king?
GENTLEMAN:
Contending with the fretful elements;
Bids the wind blow the earth into the sea,   5
Or swell the curlèd waters 'bove the main,°
That things might change° or cease; tears his
white hair,
Which the impetuous blasts, with eyeless°
rage,
Catch in their fury, and make nothing of;
Strives in his little world of man° to outscorn 10
The to-and-fro-conflicting wind and rain.
This night, wherein the cub-drawn° bear would
couch,°
The lion, and the belly-pinchèd° wolf
Keep their fur dry, unbonneted° he runs,
And bids what will take all.°
KENT: But who is with him? 15
GENTLEMAN:
None but the Fool, who labors to outjest
His heart-struck injuries.
KENT: Sir, I do know you,
And dare upon the warrant of my note°
Commend a dear thing° to you. There is
division,

III.i.s.d. **still** continually   2 **minded . . . unquietly**
disturbed in mind, like the weather   6 **main** land
7 **change** (1) be destroyed (2) be exchanged (i.e.,
turned upside down) (3) change for the better
8 **eyeless** (1) blind (2) invisible   10 **little . . . man**
the microcosm, as opposed to the universe or macrocosm, which it copies in little   12 **cub-drawn** sucked
dry by her cubs, and so ravenously hungry; **couch**
take shelter in its lair   13 **belly-pinched** starved
14 **unbonneted** hatless   15 **take all** like the reckless
gambler, staking all he has left   18 **warrant . . . note**
strength of what I have taken note (of you)   19
Commend . . . thing entrust important business

20 Although as yet the face of it is covered
   With mutual cunning, 'twixt Albany and
     Cornwall;
   Who have — as who have not, that° their great
     stars
   Throned° and set high? — servants, who seem
     no less,°
   Which are to France the spies and specula-
     tions
25 Intelligent° of our state. What hath been seen,
   Either in snuffs and packings° of the dukes,
   Or the hard rein which both of them hath
     borne°
   Against the old kind king, or something
     deeper,
   Whereof, perchance, these are but furnish-
     ings° —
   But, true it is, from France there comes a
30   power°
   Into this scattered° kingdom, who already,
   Wise in our negligence, have secret feet
   In some of our best ports, and are at point°
   To show their open banner. Now to you:
35 If on my credit you dare build° so far
   To° make your speed to Dover, you shall find
   Some that will thank you, making° just° report
   Of how unnatural and bemadding° sorrow
   The king hath cause to plain.°
40 I am a gentleman of blood and breeding,°
   And from some knowledge and assurance° offer
   This office° to you.
        GENTLEMAN:
   I will talk further with you.
        KENT: No, do not.
   For confirmation that I am much more
45 Than my out-wall,° open this purse and take
   What it contains. If you shall see Cordelia,
   As fear not but you shall, show her this ring,
   And she will tell you who that fellow° is

That yet you do not know. Fie on this storm!
I will go seek the king.   50
     GENTLEMAN:
Give me your hand. Have you no more to say?
     KENT:
Few words, but, to effect,° more than all yet:
That when we have found the king — in which
  your pain°
That way, I'll this — he that first lights on
  him,
Holla the other.   (Exeunt [severally].)   55

SCENE II. [Another part of the heath.]

Storm still. Enter LEAR and FOOL.

LEAR:
Blow, winds, and crack your cheeks. Rage,
  blow!
You cataracts and hurricanoes,° spout
Till you have drenched our steeples, drowned
  the cocks.°
You sulph'rous and thought-executing° fires,
Vaunt-couriers° of oak-cleaving thunderbolts,   5
Singe my white head. And thou, all-shaking
  thunder,
Strike flat the thick rotundity° o' th' world,
Crack Nature's molds,° all germains spill° at
  once,
That makes ingrateful° man.
     FOOL: O nuncle, court holy-water° in a dry   10
house is better than this rain water out o'
door. Good nuncle, in; ask thy daughters
blessing. Here's a night pities neither wise man
nor fools.
     LEAR:
Rumble thy bellyful. Spit, fire. Spout, rain!   15
Nor rain, wind, thunder, fire are my daughters.
I tax° not you, you elements, with unkindness.
I never gave you kingdom, called you children,
You owe me no subscription.° Then let fall

---

22 **that** whom   22–23 **stars Throned** destinies have
throned   23 **seem no less** seem to be so   24–25
speculations Intelligent giving intelligence   26
snuffs and packings quarrels and plots   27 **hard ...
borne** close and cruel control they have exercised
29 **furnishings** excuses   30 **power** army   31 **scattered** disunited   33 **at point** ready   35 **If ... build**
if you can trust me, proceed   36 **To** as to   37
making for making; **just** accurate   38 **bemadding**
maddening   39 **plain** complain of   40 **blood and
breeding** noble family   41 **knowledge and assurance** sure and trustworthy information   42 **office**
service (i.e., the trip to Dover)   45 **out-wall** superficial appearance   48 **fellow** companion

52 **to effect** in their importance   53 **pain** labor
III.II.2 **hurricanoes** waterspouts   3 **cocks** weather-
cocks   4 **thought-executing** (1) doing execution as
quick as thought (2) executing or carrying out the
thought of him who hurls the lightning   5 **Vaunt-
couriers** heralds, scouts who range before the main
body of the army   7 **rotundity** i.e., not only the
sphere of the globe, but the roundness of gestation
(Delius)   8 **Nature's molds** the molds or forms in
which men are made; **all germains spill** destroy the
basic seeds of life   9 **ingrateful** ungrateful   10
court holy-water flattery   17 **tax** accuse   19 **subscription** allegiance, submission

Your horrible pleasure.° Here I stand your
20   slave,
A poor, infirm, weak, and despised old man.
But yet I call you servile ministers,°
That will with two pernicious daughters join
Your high-engendered battles° 'gainst a head
25 So old and white as this. O, ho! 'tis foul.
    FOOL: He that has a house to put's head in
has a good headpiece.°

        The codpiece° that will house
            Before the head as any,
30   The head and he° shall louse:
            So beggars marry many.°
        The man that makes his toe
            What he his heart should make
35   Shall of a corn cry woe,
            And turn his sleep to wake.°

For there was never yet fair woman but she
made mouths in a glass.°

    (*Enter* KENT.)

    LEAR:
No, I will be the pattern of all patience,
I will say nothing.
40 KENT: Who's there?
    FOOL: Marry,° here's grace and a codpiece;
that's a wise man and a fool.°
    KENT:
Alas, sir, are you here? Things that love night
Love not such nights as these. The wrathful
        skies
45 Gallow° the very wanderers of the dark
And make them keep° their caves. Since I was
        man,

Such sheets of fire, such bursts of horrid°
        thunder,
Such groans of roaring wind and rain, I never
Remember to have heard. Man's nature cannot
        carry°
Th' affliction nor the fear.
    LEAR: Let the great gods   50
That keep this dreadful pudder° o'er our heads
Find out their enemies now.° Tremble, thou
        wretch,
That hast within thee undivulgèd crimes
Unwhipped of justice. Hide thee, thou bloody
        hand,
Thou perjured;° and thou simular° of virtue   55
That art incestuous. Caitiff,° to pieces shake,
That under covert and convenient seeming°
Has practiced on° man's life. Close° pent-up
        guilts,
Rive° your concealing continents° and cry
These dreadful summoners grace.° I am a man   60
More sinned against than sinning.
    KENT: Alack, bareheaded?
Gracious my lord,° hard by here is a hovel;
Some friendship will it lend you 'gainst the
        tempest.
Repose you there, while I to this hard house
(More harder than the stones whereof 'tis
        raised,   65
Which even but now, demanding after° you,
Denied me to come in) return, and force
Their scanted° courtesy.
    LEAR: My wits begin to turn.
Come on, my boy. How dost, my boy? Art cold?
I am cold myself. Where is this straw, my
        fellow?   70
The art° of our necessities is strange,
That can make vile things precious. Come,
        your hovel.
Poor Fool and knave, I have one part in my
        heart
That's sorry yet for thee.

20 **pleasure** will   22 **ministers** agents   24 **high-engendered battles** armies formed in the heavens   27 **headpiece** (1) helmet (2) brain   28 **codpiece** penis (literally, padding worn at the crotch of a man's hose) 30 **he** it   31 **many** i.e., lice   28–31 **The . . . many** The man who gratifies his sexual appetites before he has a roof over his head will end up a lousy beggar 32–35 **The . . . wake** The man who, ignoring the fit order of things, elevates what is base above what is noble, will suffer for it as Lear has, in banishing Cordelia and enriching her sisters   37 **made . . . glass** posed before a mirror (irrelevant nonsense, except that it calls to mind the general theme of vanity and folly)   41 **Marry** a mild oath, from "By the Virgin Mary"   41–42 **here's . . . fool** Kent's question is answered: the king ("grace") is here, and the Fool— who customarily wears an exaggerated codpiece; but which is left ambiguous, since Lear has previously been called a codpiece   45 **Gallow** frighten   46 **keep** remain inside

47 **horrid** horrible   49 **carry** endure   51 **pudder** turmoil   52 **Find . . . now** i.e., discover sinners by the terror they reveal   55 **perjured** perjurer; **simular** counterfeiter   56 **Caitiff** wretch   57 **seeming** hypocrisy   58 **practiced on** plotted against; **Close** hidden   59 **Rive** split open; **continents** containers   59– 60 **cry . . . grace** beg mercy from the vengeful gods (here figured as officers who summoned a man charged with immorality before the ecclesiastical court)   62 **Gracious my lord** my gracious lord   66 **demanding after** asking for   68 **scanted** stinted   71 **art** magic powers of the alchemists, who sought to transmute base metals into precious

FOOL [*Singing.*]

75 He that has and a little tiny wit,
   With heigh-ho, the wind and the rain,
   Must make content with his fortunes fit,°
   Though the rain it raineth every day.

LEAR: True, my good boy. Come, bring us
80 to this hovel.   (*Exit, [with* KENT].)
FOOL: This is a brave° night to cool a
courtesan. I'll speak a prophecy ere I go:

   When priests are more in word than matter;
   When brewers mar their malt with water;
85 When nobles are their tailors' tutors,
   No heretics burned, but wenches' suitors;°
   When every case in law is right,
   No squire in debt nor no poor knight;
   When slanders do not live in tongues;
90 Nor cutpurses come not to throngs;
   When usurers tell their gold i' th' field,°
   And bawds and whores do churches build,°
   Then shall the realm of Albion°
   Come to great confusion.
95 Then comes the time, who lives to see't,
   That going shall be used with feet.°

This prophecy Merlin° shall make, for I live
before his time.   (*Exit.*)

SCENE III. [GLOUCESTER's *castle*.]

Enter GLOUCESTER *and* EDMUND.

GLOUCESTER: Alack, alack, Edmund, I like
not this unnatural dealing. When I desired
their leave that I might pity° him, they took
from me the use of mine own house, charged
5 me on pain of perpetual displeasure neither to

77 **Must . . . fit** must be satisfied with a fortune as tiny
as his wit   81 **brave** fine   83–86 **When . . . suitors**
the first four prophecies are fulfilled already, and
hence "confusion" has come to England: the priest
does not suit his action to his words; the brewer
adulterates his beer; the nobleman is subservient to
his tailor (i.e., cares only for fashion); religious heretics escape, and only those burn (i.e., suffer) who are
afflicted with venereal disease   91 **tell . . . field** count
their money in the open   87–92 **When . . . build** the
last six prophecies, as they are Utopian, are meant
ironically; they will never be fulfilled   93 **Albion**
England   96 **going . . . feet** people will walk on their
feet   97 **Merlin** King Arthur's great magician who,
according to Holinshed's *Chronicles*, lived later than
Lear
III.III.3 **pity** show pity to

speak of him, entreat for him, or any way
sustain° him.
EDMUND: Most savage and unnatural.
GLOUCESTER: Go to; say you nothing. There
is division° between the dukes, and a worse° 10
matter than that. I have received a letter this
night — 'tis dangerous to be spoken° — I have
locked the letter in my closet.° These injuries
the king now bears will be revenged home;°
there is part of a power° already footed;° we 15
must incline to° the king. I will look° him and
privily° relieve him. Go you and maintain talk
with the duke, that my charity be not of° him
perceived. If he ask for me, I am ill and gone
to bed. If I die for it, as no less is threatened 20
me, the king my old master must be relieved.
There is strange things toward,° Edmund;
pray you be careful.   (*Exit.*)
EDMUND:
This courtesy forbid° thee shall the duke
Instantly know, and of that letter too.   25
This seems a fair deserving,° and must draw
   me
That which my father loses — no less than all.
The younger rises when the old doth fall.
                                   (*Exit.*)

SCENE IV. [*The heath. Before a hovel.*]

Enter LEAR, KENT, *and* FOOL.

KENT:
Here is the place, my lord. Good my lord,
   enter.
The tyranny of the open night's too rough
For nature to endure.

(*Storm still.*)

LEAR: Let me alone.
KENT:
Good my lord, enter here.
LEAR: Wilt break my heart?°
KENT:
I had rather break mine own. Good my lord,
   enter.   5

7 **sustain** care for   10 **division** falling out; **worse**
more serious (i.e., the French invasion)   12 **spoken**
spoken of   13 **closet** room   14 **home** to the utmost
15 **power** army; **footed** landed   16 **incline to** take
the side of; **look** search for   17 **privily** secretly   18
of by   22 **toward** impending   24 **courtesy forbid**
kindness forbidden (i.e., to Lear)   26 **fair deserving**
an action deserving reward
III.IV.4 **break my heart** i.e., by shutting out the
storm which distracts me from thinking

LEAR:
Thou think'st 'tis much that this contentious
  storm
Invades us to the skin: so 'tis to thee;
But where the greater malady is fixed,°
The lesser is scarce felt. Thou'dst shun a bear;
10 But if thy flight lay toward the roaring sea,
Thou'dst meet the bear i' th' mouth.° When
  the mind's free,°
The body's delicate. The tempest in my mind
Doth from my senses take all feeling else,
Save what beats there. Filial ingratitude,
15 Is it not as° this mouth should tear this hand
For lifting food to't? But I will punish home.°
No, I will weep no more. In such a night
To shut me out! Pour on, I will endure.
In such a night as this! O Regan, Goneril,
Your old kind father, whose frank° heart gave
20   all —
O, that way madness lies; let me shun that.
No more of that.
    KENT: Good my lord, enter here.
    LEAR:
Prithee go in thyself; seek thine own ease.
This tempest will not give me leave to ponder
25 On things would hurt me more, but I'll go in.

[*To the* FOOL.]

In, boy; go first. You houseless poverty° —
Nay, get thee in. I'll pray, and then I'll sleep.
                              (*Exit* [FOOL].)
Poor naked wretches, wheresoe'er you are,
That bide° the pelting of this pitiless storm,
30 How shall your houseless heads and unfed sides,
Your looped and windowed° raggedness, de-
  fend you
From seasons such as these? O, I have ta'en
Too little care of this! Take physic, pomp;°
Expose thyself to feel what wretches feel,
35 That thou mayst shake the superflux° to them,
And show the heavens more just.
    EDGAR [*within*]: Fathom and half, fathom
and half!° Poor Tom!

(*Enter* FOOL.)

FOOL: Come not in here, nuncle, here's a
spirit. Help me, help me!   40
    KENT:
Give me thy hand. Who's there?
    FOOL: A spirit, a spirit. He says his name's
Poor Tom.
    KENT:
What art thou that dost grumble there i' th'
  straw?
Come forth.   45

(*Enter* EDGAR [*disguised as a madman*].)

EDGAR: Away! the foul fiend follows me.
Through the sharp hawthorn blows the cold
wind.° Humh! Go to thy cold bed, and warm
thee.°
    LEAR: Didst thou give all to thy daughters? 50
And art thou come to this?
    EDGAR: Who gives anything to Poor Tom?
Whom the foul fiend hath led through fire
and through flame, through ford and whirl-
pool, o'er bog and quagmire; that hath laid   55
knives under his pillow and halters in his pew,°
set ratsbane° by his porridge,° made him proud
of heart, to ride on a bay trotting horse over
four-inched bridges,° to course° his own
shadow for° a traitor. Bless thy five wits,°   60
Tom's a-cold. O, do, de, do, de, do, de. Bless
thee from whirlwinds, star-blasting,° and taking.° Do Poor Tom some charity, whom the
foul fiend vexes. There could I have him
now — and there — and there again — and   65
there.

(*Storm still.*)

    LEAR:
What, has his daughters brought him to this
  pass?°
Couldst thou save nothing? Wouldst thou give
  'em all?

8 **fixed** lodged (in the mind)   11 **i' th' mouth** in the
teeth; **free** i.e., from care   15 **as** as if   16 **home** to
the utmost   20 **frank** liberal (magnanimous)   26
houseless poverty the unsheltered poor, abstracted
29 **bide** endure   31 **looped and windowed** full of
holes   33 **Take physic, pomp** Take medicine to cure
yourselves, you great men   35 **superflux** superfluity
37–38 **Fathom and half** Edgar, because of the down-
pour, pretends to take soundings   47–48 **Through . . . wind** a line from the ballad of
"The Friar of Orders Gray"   48–49 **Go . . . thee** a
reminiscence of *The Taming of the Shrew*, Induction,
line 10, which itself is an echo of a line in Thomas
Kyd's *The Spanish Tragedy*   56–57 **knives . . . halters
. . . ratsbane** the fiend tempts Poor Tom to suicide
56 **pew** gallery or balcony outside a window   57 **porridge** broth   58–59 **ride . . . bridges** i.e., risk his life
59 **course** chase   60 **for** as; **five wits** common wit,
imagination, fantasy, estimation, memory   62 **star-
blasting** the evil caused by malignant stars   62–63
taking pernicious influences   67 **pass** wretched condition

FOOL: Nay, he reserved a blanket,° else we
70 had been all shamed.

LEAR:
Now all the plagues that in the pendulous° air
Hang fated o'er° men's faults light on thy
    daughters!

KENT:
He hath no daughters, sir.

LEAR:
Death, traitor; nothing could have subdued°
    nature
75 To such a lowness but his unkind daughters.
Is it the fashion that discarded fathers
Should have thus little mercy on° their flesh?
Judicious punishment — 'twas this flesh begot
Those pelican° daughters.

80 EDGAR: Pillicock sat on Pillicock Hill.° Alow,
alow, loo, loo!°

FOOL: This cold night will turn us all to
fools and madmen.

EDGAR: Take heed o' th' foul fiend; obey thy
85 parents; keep thy word's justice;° swear not;
commit not° with man's sworn spouse; set not
thy sweet heart on proud array. Tom's a-cold.

LEAR: What hast thou been?

EDGAR: A servingman, proud in heart and
90 mind; that curled my hair, wore gloves in my
cap;° served the lust of my mistress' heart, and
did the act of darkness with her; swore as
many oaths as I spake words, and broke them
in the sweet face of heaven. One that slept in
95 the contriving of lust, and waked to do it.
Wine loved I deeply, dice dearly; and in
woman out-paramoured the Turk.° False of
heart, light of ear,° bloody of hand; hog in
sloth, fox in stealth, wolf in greediness, dog in
100 madness, lion in prey.° Let not the creaking° of
shoes nor the rustling of silks betray thy poor
heart to woman. Keep thy foot out of brothels,
thy hand out of plackets,° thy pen from

lenders' books,° and defy the foul fiend. Still
through the hawthorn blows the cold wind; 105
says suum, mun, nonny.° Dolphin° my boy,
boy, sessa!° let him trot by.

(*Storm still.*)

LEAR: Thou wert better in a grave than to
answer° with thy uncovered body this extrem-
ity° of the skies. Is man no more than this? 110
Consider him well. Thou ow'st° the worm no
silk, the beast no hide, the sheep no wool, the
cat° no perfume. Ha! here's three on's° are
sophisticated.° Thou art the thing itself; unac-
commodated° man is no more but such a poor, 115
bare, forked° animal as thou art. Off, off, you
lendings!° Come, unbutton here.

[*Tearing off his clothes.*]

FOOL: Prithee, nuncle, be contented, 'tis a
naughty° night to swim in. Now a little fire in
a wild° field were like an old lecher's heart — a 120
small spark, all the rest on's° body, cold. Look,
here comes a walking fire.

(*Enter* GLOUCESTER *with a torch.*)

EDGAR: This is the foul fiend Flibbertigibbet.° He begins at curfew,° and walks till the
first cock.° He gives the web and the pin,° 125
squints° the eye, and makes the harelip; mil-
dews the white° wheat, and hurts the poor
creature of earth.

Swithold footed thrice the old;°
He met the nightmare,° and her nine fold;° 130
    Bid her alight°
    And her troth plight,°
And aroint° thee, witch, aroint thee!

---

69 **blanket** i.e., to cover his nakedness 71 **pendu-
lous** overhanging 72 **fated o'er** destined to punish
74 **subdued** reduced 77 **on** i.e., shown to 79
pelican supposed to feed on its parent's blood 80
Pillicock . . . Hill probably quoted from a nursery
rhyme, and suggested by "pelican"; "pillicock" is a
term of endearment and the phallus 80–81 **Alow
. . . loo** a hunting call, or the refrain of the song (?)
85 **keep . . . justice** i.e., do not break thy word 86
commit not i.e., adultery 90–91 **gloves . . . cap** i.e.,
as a pledge from his mistress 97 **out-paramoured
the Turk** had more concubines than the sultan 98
light of ear ready to hear flattery and slander 100
prey preying; **creaking** deliberately cultivated, as
fashionable 103 **plackets** opening in skirts

103–104 **pen . . . books** i.e., do not enter your name
in the moneylender's account book 106 **suum, mun,
nonny** the noise of the wind 106 **Dolphin** the
French dauphin (identified by the English with the
devil; Poor Tom is presumably quoting from a ballad)
107 **sessa** an interjection: "Go on!" 109 **answer**
confront, bear the brunt of 109–110 **extremity** extreme severity 111 **ow'st** have taken from 113 **cat**
civet cat, whose glands yield perfume; **on's** of us
114 **sophisticated** adulterated, made artificial 114–
115 **unaccommodated** uncivilized 116 **forked** i.e.,
two-legged 117 **lendings** borrowed garments 119
naughty wicked 120 **wild** barren 121 **on's** of his
123–124 **Flibbertigibbet** a figure from Elizabethan
demonology 124 **curfew** 9 P.M. 125 **first cock**
midnight; **web . . . pin** cataract 126 **squints** crosses
127 **white** ripening 129 **Swithold . . . old** Withold
(an Anglo-Saxon saint who subdued demons)
walked three times across the open country 130
nightmare demon; **fold** offspring 131 **alight** i.e.,
from the horse she had possessed 132 **her troth
plight** pledge her word 133 **aroint** be gone

KENT:
How fares your grace?

135 LEAR: What's he?

KENT:
Who's there? What is't you seek?

GLOUCESTER:
What are you there? Your names?

EDGAR: Poor Tom, that eats the swimming
frog, the toad, the todpole, the wall-newt and
140 the water;° that in the fury of his heart, when
the foul fiend rages, eats cow-dung for sallets,°
swallows the old rat and the ditch-dog,° drinks
the green mantle° of the standing° pool; who is
whipped from tithing° to tithing, and stocked,
145 punished, and imprisoned; who hath had three
suits to his back, six shirts to his body,

  Horse to ride, and weapon to wear,
  But mice and rats, and such small deer,°
  Have been Tom's food for seven long year.°

150 Beware my follower!° Peace, Smulkin,° peace,
thou fiend!

GLOUCESTER:
What, hath your grace no better company?

EDGAR:
The Prince of Darkness is a gentleman.
Modo° he's called, and Mahu.°

GLOUCESTER:
155 Our flesh and blood, my lord, is grown so vile
That it doth hate what gets° it.

EDGAR: Poor Tom's a-cold.

GLOUCESTER:
Go in with me. My duty cannot suffer°
T' obey in all your daughters' hard commands.
160 Though their injunction be to bar my doors
And let this tyrannous night take hold upon
  you,
Yet have I ventured to come seek you out
And bring you where both fire and food is
  ready.

LEAR:
First let me talk with this philosopher.
165 What is the cause of thunder?

KENT:
Good my lord, take his offer; go into th'
  house.

LEAR:
I'll talk a word with this same learnèd The-
  ban.°
What is your study?°

EDGAR:
How to prevent° the fiend, and to kill vermin.

LEAR:
Let me ask you one word in private.   170

KENT:
Importune him once more to go, my lord.
His wits begin t' unsettle.

GLOUCESTER: Canst thou blame him?

(Storm still.)

His daughters seek his death. Ah, that good
  Kent,
He said it would be thus, poor banished
  man!
Thou say'st the king grows mad — I'll tell thee,
  friend,   175
I am almost mad myself. I had a son,
Now outlawed from my blood;° he sought my
  life
But lately, very late.° I loved him, friend,
No father his son dearer. True to tell thee,
The grief hath crazed my wits. What a night's
  this!   180
I do beseech your grace —

LEAR: O, cry you mercy,° sir.
Noble philosopher, your company.

EDGAR: Tom's a-cold.

GLOUCESTER:
In, fellow, there, into th' hovel; keep thee
  warm.

LEAR:
Come, let's in all.

KENT: This way, my lord.

LEAR: With him!   185
I will keep still with my philosopher.

KENT:
Good my lord, soothe° him; let him take the
  fellow.

GLOUCESTER:
Take him you on.°

KENT:
Sirrah, come on; go along with us.

LEAR:
Come, good Athenian.°   190

139–140 **todpole . . . water** tadpole, wall lizard, water
newt 141 **sallets** salads 142 **ditch-dog** dead dog in
a ditch 143 **mantle** scum; **standing** stagnant 144
tithing a district comprising ten families 148–149
But . . . year adapted from a popular romance, "Bevis
of Hampton" 148 **deer** game 150 **follower** familiar 150–154 **Smulkin . . . Modo . . . Mahu** Elizabethan devils, from Samuel Harsnett's *Declaration*
of 1603 156 **gets** begets 158 **suffer** permit me

167 **Theban** i.e., Greek philosopher 168 **study**
particular scientific study 169 **prevent** balk 177
outlawed . . . blood disowned and tainted, like a
carbuncle in the corrupted blood 178 **late** recently
181 **cry you mercy** I beg your pardon 187 **soothe**
humor 188 **you on** with you 190 **Athenian** i.e.,
philosopher (like "Theban")

GLOUCESTER:

No words, no words! Hush.

EDGAR:

Child Rowland to the dark tower came;°
His word was still,° "Fie, foh, and fum,
I smell the blood of a British man."°

(Exeunt.)

SCENE V. [GLOUCESTER's castle.]

Enter CORNWALL *and* EDMUND.

CORNWALL: I will have my revenge ere I
depart his house.

EDMUND: How, my lord, I may be censured,°
that nature thus gives way to loyalty, some-
5 thing fears° me to think of.

CORNWALL: I now perceive it was not altogether your brother's evil disposition made him
seek his death; but a provoking merit, set
a-work by a reprovable badness in himself.°

10 EDMUND: How malicious is my fortune that
I must repent to be just! This is the letter
which he spoke of, which approves° him an
intelligent party° to the advantages° of France.
O heavens, that his treason were not! or not I
15 the detector!

CORNWALL: Go with me to the duchess.

EDMUND: If the matter of this paper be
certain, you have mighty business in hand.

CORNWALL: True or false, it hath made thee
20 Earl of Gloucester. Seek out where thy father
is, that he may be ready for our apprehension.°

EDMUND [aside]: If I find him comforting°
the king, it will stuff his suspicion more
fully. — I will persever° in my course of loyalty,
25 though the conflict be sore between that and
my blood.°

CORNWALL: I will lay trust upon° thee, and
thou shalt find a dearer father in my love.

(Exeunt.)

---

192 **Child . . . came** from a lost ballad (?); "child" =
a candidate for knighthood; "Rowland" was Charle-
magne's nephew, the hero of *The Song of Roland*
193 **His . . . still** his motto was always   193–194 **Fie
. . . man** a deliberately absurd linking of the chivalric
hero with the nursery tale of Jack the Giant-Killer
III.v.3 **censured** judged   4–5 **something fears** somewhat frightens   8–9 **a provoking . . . himself** a stimu-
lating goodness in Edgar, brought into play by a
blamable badness in Gloucester   12 **approves** proves
13 **intelligent party** (1) spy (2) well-informed person; **to the advantages** on behalf of   21 **apprehension** arrest   22 **comforting** supporting (a legalism)
24 **persever** persevere   26 **blood** natural feelings
27 **lay trust upon** (1) trust (2) advance

SCENE VI. [A *chamber in a farmhouse adjoining the castle.*]

Enter KENT *and* GLOUCESTER.

GLOUCESTER: Here is better than the open
air; take it thankfully. I will piece out the
comfort with what addition I can. I will not
be long from you.

KENT: All the power of his wits have given   5
way to his impatience.° The gods reward your
kindness.   (*Exit* [GLOUCESTER].)

(*Enter* LEAR, EDGAR, *and* FOOL.)

EDGAR: Fraterretto° calls me, and tells me
Nero° is an angler in the lake of darkness.
Pray, innocent,° and beware the foul fiend.   10

FOOL: Prithee, nuncle, tell me whether a
madman be a gentleman or a yeoman.°

LEAR:

A king, a king.

FOOL: No, he's a yeoman that has a gentleman to his son; for he's a mad yeoman that   15
sees his son a gentleman before him.

LEAR:

To have a thousand with red burning spits
Come hizzing° in upon 'em —

EDGAR: The foul fiend bites my back.

FOOL: He's mad that trusts in the tameness   20
of a wolf, a horse's health, a boy's love, or a
whore's oath.

LEAR:

It shall be done; I will arraign° them straight.°

[*To* EDGAR.]

Come, sit thou here, most learned justice.°

[*To the* FOOL.]

Thou, sapient° sir, sit here. Now, you she-
foxes —   25

EDGAR: Look, where he° stands and glares.
Want'st thou eyes at trial, madam?°
Come o'er the bourn,° Bessy, to me.

III.vi.6 **impatience** raging   8 **Fraterretto** Elizabethan
devil, from Harsnett's *Declaration*   9 **Nero** who is
mentioned by Harsnett, and whose angling is reported
by Chaucer in "The Monk's Tale"   10 **innocent** fool
12 **yeoman** farmer (just below a gentleman in rank;
the Fool asks what class of man has most indulged
his children, and thus been driven mad)   18 **hizzing**
hissing   23 **arraign** bring to trial; **straight** straightaway   24 **justice** justicer, judge   25 **sapient** wise
26 **he** i.e., a fiend   27 **Want'st . . . madam** (to
Goneril) i.e., Do you want eyes to look at you during
your trial? The fiend serves that purpose   28 **bourn**
brook (Edgar quotes from a popular ballad)

FOOL:
Her boat hath a leak,
30   And she must not speak
Why she dares not come over to thee.°
EDGAR: The foul fiend haunts Poor Tom in
the voice of a nightingale.° Hoppedance° cries
in Tom's belly for two white herring.° Croak°
35   not, black angel; I have no food for thee.
KENT:
How do you, sir? Stand you not so amazed.°
Will you lie down and rest upon the cushions?
LEAR:
I'll see their trial first. Bring in their evidence.°

[*To* EDGAR.]

Thou, robèd man of justice, take thy place.

[*To the* FOOL.]

40   And thou, his yokefellow of equity,°
Bench° by his side. [*To* KENT.] You are o' th'
commission;°
Sit you too.
EDGAR: Let us deal justly.

Sleepest or wakest thou, jolly shepherd?
45   Thy sheep be in the corn;°
And for one blast of thy minikin° mouth
Thy sheep shall take no harm.°

Purr, the cat is gray.°
LEAR: Arraign her first. 'Tis Goneril, I here
50   take my oath before this honorable assembly,
she kicked the poor king her father.
FOOL: Come hither, mistress. Is your name
Goneril?
LEAR: She cannot deny it.
55   FOOL: Cry you mercy, I took you for a joint
stool.°

LEAR:
And here's another, whose warped looks pro-
claim
What store° her heart is made on. Stop her
there!
Arms, arms, sword, fire! Corruption in the
place!°
False justicer, why hast thou let her 'scape?   60
EDGAR: Bless thy five wits!
KENT:
O pity! Sir, where is the patience now
That you so oft have boasted to retain?
EDGAR [*aside*]:
My tears begin to take his part so much
They mar my counterfeiting.°   65
LEAR:
The little dogs and all,
Tray, Blanch, and Sweetheart — see, they bark
at me.
EDGAR: Tom will throw his head at them.
Avaunt, you curs.

Be thy mouth or black or° white,   70
Tooth that poisons if it bite;
Mastiff, greyhound, mongrel grim,
Hound or spaniel, brach° or lym,°
Or bobtail tike, or trundle-tail° —
Tom will make him weep and wail;   75
For, with throwing° thus my head,
Dogs leaped the hatch,° and all are fled.

Do, de, de, de. Sessa!° Come, march to wakes°
and fairs and market towns. Poor Tom, thy
horn° is dry.   80
LEAR: Then let them anatomize Regan. See
what breeds about her heart.° Is there any
cause in nature that make° these hard hearts?
[*To* EDGAR.] You, sir, I entertain° for one of
my hundred;° only I do not like the fashion of 85

29–31 **Her . . . thee** the Fool parodies the ballad   33
nightingale i.e., the Fool's singing; **Hoppedance** Ho-
berdidance (another devil from Harsnett's *Declaration*)   34 **white herring** unsmoked (as against the
black and sulfurous devil?); **Croak** rumble (because
his belly is empty)   36 **amazed** astonished   38 **evidence** the evidence of witnesses against them   40
yokefellow of equity partner in justice   41 **Bench** sit
on the bench; **commission** those commissioned as
king's justices   44–47 **Sleepest . . . harm** probably
quoted or adapted from an Elizabethan song   45
corn wheat   46 **minikin** shrill   48 **gray** devils were
thought to assume the shape of a gray cat   55–56
Cry . . . stool proverbial and deliberately impudent
apology for overlooking a person; a joint stool was a
low stool made by a joiner, perhaps here a stage property to represent Goneril and, in line 57, Regan; "joint
stool" can also suggest the judicial bench; hence
Goneril may be identified by the Fool, ironically,
with those in power, who judge

58 **store** stuff   59 **Corruption . . . place** bribery in the
court   65 **counterfeiting** i.e., feigned madness   70
or . . . or either . . . or   73 **brach** bitch; **lym** blood-
hound (from the liam or leash with which he was led)
74 **bobtail . . . trundle-tail** short-tailed or long-tailed
cur   76 **throwing** jerking (as a hound lifts its head
from the ground, the scent having been lost)   77
leaped the hatch leaped over the lower half of a
divided door (i.e., left in a hurry)   78 **Sessa** Be off!;
wakes feasts attending the dedication of a church   80
horn horn bottle which the Bedlam used in begging a
drink (Edgar is suggesting that he is unable to play
his role any longer)   81–82 **Then . . . heart** i.e., If
the Bedlam's horn is dry, let Regan, whose heart has
become as hard as horn, be dissected   83 **make** sub-
junctive   84 **entertain** engage   85 **hundred** i.e.,
Lear's hundred knights

your garments. You will say they are Persian;°
but let them be changed.

KENT:
Now, good my lord, lie here and rest awhile.

LEAR:
Make no noise, make no noise; draw the
    curtains.°
90 So, so. We'll go to supper i' th' morning.

FOOL: And I'll go to bed at noon.°

(*Enter* GLOUCESTER.)

GLOUCESTER:
Come hither, friend. Where is the king my
    master?

KENT:
Here, sir, but trouble him not; his wits are
    gone.

GLOUCESTER:
Good friend, I prithee take him in thy arms.
95 I have o'erheard a plot of death upon him.
There is a litter ready; lay him in't
And drive toward Dover, friend, where thou
    shalt meet
Both welcome and protection. Take up thy
    master.
If thou shouldst dally half an hour, his life,
100 With thine and all that offer to defend him,
Stand in assurèd loss. Take up, take up,
And follow me, that will to some provision°
Give thee quick conduct.°

KENT: Oppressèd nature sleeps.
This rest might yet have balmed thy broken
    sinews,°
105 Which, if convenience° will not allow,
Stand in hard cure.° [*To the* FOOL.] Come,
    help to bear thy master.
Thou must not stay behind.

GLOUCESTER: Come, come, away!
(*Exeunt* [*all but* EDGAR].)

EDGAR:
When we our betters see bearing our woes,
We scarcely think our miseries our foes.°
110 Who alone suffers suffers most i' th' mind,
Leaving free° things and happy shows° behind;
But then the mind much sufferance° doth
    o'erskip

When grief hath mates, and bearing fellow-
    ship.°
How light and portable° my pain seems now,
When that which makes me bend makes the
    king bow.   115
He childed as I fathered. Tom, away.
Mark the high noises,° and thyself bewray°
When false opinion, whose wrong thoughts°
    defile thee,
In thy just proof repeals and reconciles thee.°
What will hap more° tonight, safe 'scape the
    king!   120
Lurk,° lurk.   [*Exit.*]

SCENE VII. [GLOUCESTER'*s castle.*]

Enter CORNWALL, REGAN, GONERIL, EDMUND,
and SERVANTS.

CORNWALL [*to* GONERIL]: Post speedily to
my lord your husband; show him this letter.
The army of France is landed. [*To* SERVANTS.]
Seek out the traitor Gloucester.
                    [*Exeunt some of the* SERVANTS.]
REGAN: Hang him instantly.   5
GONERIL: Pluck out his eyes.
CORNWALL: Leave him to my displeasure.
Edmund, keep you our sister company. The
revenges we are bound° to take upon your
traitorous father are not fit for your beholding. 10
Advise the duke where you are going, to a
most festinate° preparation. We are bound to
the like. Our posts° shall be swift and intelli-
gent° betwixt us. Farewell, dear sister; farewell,
my Lord of Gloucester.°   15

(*Enter* OSWALD.)

How now? Where's the king?
OSWALD:
My Lord of Gloucester hath conveyed him
    hence.
Some five or six and thirty of his knights,
Hot questrists° after him, met him at gate;

86 **Persian** gorgeous (ironically of Edgar's rags)   89
curtains Lear imagines himself in bed   91 **And . . .
noon** the Fool's last words   102 **provision** maintenance   103 **conduct** direction   104 **balmed . . . sin-
ews** soothed thy racked nerves   105 **convenience**
fortunate occasion   106 **Stand . . . cure** will be hard
to cure   109 **our foes** enemies peculiar to ourselves
111 **free** carefree, **shows** scenes   112 **sufferance**
suffering

113 **bearing fellowship** suffering has company   114
portable able to be supported or endured   117 **Mark
. . . noises** observe the rumors of strife among those in
power; **bewray** reveal   118 **wrong thoughts** misconceptions   119 **In . . . thee** on the manifesting of your
innocence recalls you from outlawry and restores
amity between you and your father   120 **What . . .
more** whatever else happens   121 **Lurk** hide
III.vii.9 **bound** (1) forced (2) purposing to   12
festinate speedy   13 **posts** messengers   13–14 **intelligent** full of information   15 **Lord of Gloucester**
Edmund, now elevated to the title   19 **questrists**
searchers

20 Who, with some other of the lords depen-
      dants,°
Are gone with him toward Dover, where they
      boast
To have well-armèd friends.
      CORNWALL: Get horses for your mistress.
                              [*Exit* OSWALD.]
      GONERIL:
Farewell, sweet lord, and sister.
      CORNWALL:
Edmund, farewell.
                    [*Exeunt* GONERIL *and* EDMUND.]
                    Go seek the traitor Gloucester,
25 Pinion him like a thief, bring him before us.
                    [*Exeunt other* SERVANTS.]
Though well we may not pass upon° his life
Without the form of justice, yet our power
Shall do a court'sy to° our wrath, which men
May blame, but not control.

      (*Enter* GLOUCESTER, *brought in by two or
      three.*)

                    Who's there, the traitor?
      REGAN:
30 Ingrateful fox, 'tis he.
      CORNWALL:
Bind fast his corky° arms.
      GLOUCESTER:
What means your graces? Good my friends,
      consider
You are my guests. Do me no foul play,
      friends.
      CORNWALL:
Bind him, I say. [SERVANTS *bind him.*]
      REGAN: Hard, hard! O filthy traitor.
      GLOUCESTER:
35 Unmerciful lady as you are, I'm none.
      CORNWALL:
To this chair bind him. Villain, thou shalt
      find —

      [REGAN *plucks his beard.*°]

      GLOUCESTER:
By the kind gods, 'tis most ignobly done
To pluck me by the beard.
      REGAN:
So white, and such a traitor?
      GLOUCESTER: Naughty° lady,

These hairs which thou dost ravish from my
      chin   40
Will quicken° and accuse thee. I am your
      host.
With robber's hands my hospitable favors°
You should not ruffle° thus. What will you do?
      CORNWALL:
Come, sir, what letters had you late° from
      France?
      REGAN:
Be simple-answered,° for we know the truth.   45
      CORNWALL:
And what confederacy have you with the
      traitors
Late footed in the kingdom?
      REGAN:
To whose hands you have sent the lunatic
      king:
Speak.
      GLOUCESTER:
I have a letter guessingly° set down,   50
Which came from one that's of a neutral
      heart,
And not from one opposed.
      CORNWALL: Cunning.
      REGAN: And false.
      CORNWALL:
Where hast thou sent the king?
      GLOUCESTER:
To Dover.
      REGAN:
Wherefore to Dover? Wast thou not charged
      at peril° —   55
      CORNWALL:
Wherefore to Dover? Let him answer that.
      GLOUCESTER:
I am tied to th' stake, and I must stand the
      course.°
      REGAN:
Wherefore to Dover?
      GLOUCESTER:
Because I would not see thy cruel nails
Pluck out his poor old eyes; nor thy fierce
      sister   60
In his anointed° flesh rash° boarish fangs.

20 **lords dependants** attendant lords (members of
Lear's retinue)   26 **pass upon** pass judgment on   28
do . . . to indulge   31 **corky** sapless (because old)
36 s.d. **plucks his beard** a deadly insult   39 **Naughty**
wicked   41 **quicken** come to life   42 **hospitable favors** face
of your host   43 **ruffle** tear at violently   44 **late** recently   45 **simple-answered** straight forward in answering   50 **guessingly** without certain knowledge
55 **charged at peril** ordered under penalty   57
course coursing (in which a relay of dogs baits a bull
or bear tied in the pit)   61 **anointed** holy (because
king); **rash** strike with the tusk, like a boar

The sea, with such a storm as his bare head
In hell-black night endured, would have
   buoyed° up
And quenched the stellèd° fires.
Yet, poor old heart, he holp° the heavens to
65   rain.
If wolves had at thy gate howled that dearn°
   time,
Thou shouldst have said, "Good porter, turn
   the key."°
All cruels else subscribe.° But I shall see
The wingèd° vengeance overtake such children.
   CORNWALL:
70 See't shalt thou never. Fellows, hold the chair.
Upon these eyes of thine I'll set my foot.
   GLOUCESTER:
He that will think° to live till he be old,
Give me some help. — O cruel! O you gods!
   REGAN:
One side will mock° another. Th' other too.
   CORNWALL:
If you see vengeance —
75   FIRST SERVANT: Hold your hand, my lord!
I have served you ever since I was a child;
But better service have I never done you
Than now to bid you hold.
   REGAN: How now, you dog?
   FIRST SERVANT:
If you did wear a beard upon your chin,
I'd shake it° on this quarrel. What do you
80   mean!°
   CORNWALL: My villain!°

(Draw and fight.)

   FIRST SERVANT:
Nay, then, come on, and take the chance of
   anger.
   REGAN:
Give me thy sword. A peasant stand up thus?

(She takes a sword and runs at him behind,
kills him.)

---

63 **buoyed** risen   64 **stellèd** (1) fixed (as opposed to
the planets or wandering stars) (2) starry   65 **holp**
helped   66 **dearn** dread   67 **turn the key** i.e., un-
lock the gate   68 **All . . . subscribe** All cruel creatures but man are compassionate   69 **wingèd** (1)
heavenly (2) swift   72 **will think** expects   74 **mock**
make ridiculous (because of the contrast)   80 **shake
it** an insult comparable to Regan's plucking of
Gloucester's beard; **What . . . mean** i.e., What terrible thing are you doing?   81 **villain** serf (with a suggestion of the modern meaning)

   FIRST SERVANT:
O, I am slain! my lord, you have one eye left
To see some mischief° on him. O!   85
   CORNWALL:
Lest it see more, prevent it. Out, vile jelly.
Where is thy luster now?
   GLOUCESTER:
All dark and comfortless. Where's my son
   Edmund?
Edmund, enkindle all the sparks of nature°
To quit° this horrid act.
   REGAN: Out, treacherous villain,   90
Thou call'st on him that hates thee. It was he
That made the overture° of thy treasons to us;
Who is too good to pity thee.
   GLOUCESTER:
O my follies! Then Edgar was abused.°
Kind gods, forgive me that, and prosper him.   95
   REGAN:
Go thrust him out at gates, and let him smell
His way to Dover.
                (Exit [one], with GLOUCESTER.)
                How is't, my lord? How look you?°
   CORNWALL:
I have received a hurt. Follow me, lady.
Turn out that eyeless villain. Throw this slave
Upon the dunghill. Regan, I bleed apace.   100
Untimely comes this hurt. Give me your arm.
                             (Exeunt.)
   SECOND SERVANT:
I'll never care what wickedness I do,
If this man come to good.
   THIRD SERVANT: If she live long,
And in the end meet the old course of death,°
Women will all turn monsters.   105
   SECOND SERVANT:
Let's follow the old carl, and get the Bedlam
To lead him where he would. His roguish
   madness
Allows itself to anything.°
   THIRD SERVANT:
Go thou. I'll fetch some flax and whites of
   eggs
To apply to his bleeding face. Now heaven
   help him.
                      [Exeunt severally.]

---

85 **mischief** injury   89 **enkindle . . . nature** fan your
natural feeling into flame   90 **quit** requite   92 **over-
ture** disclosure   93 **abused** wronged   97 **How look
you** How are you?   104 **meet . . . death** die the customary death of old age   107–108 **His . . . anything**
his lack of all self-control leaves him open to any
suggestion

ACT IV

Scene i. [*The heath*.]

Enter EDGAR.

EDGAR:
Yet better thus, and known to be contemned,°
Than still contemned and flattered. To be
    worst,
The lowest and most dejected° thing of for-
    tune,
Stands still in esperance,° lives not in fear:
5 The lamentable change is from the best,
The worst returns to laughter.° Welcome then,
Thou unsubstantial air that I embrace!
The wretch that thou hast blown unto the
    worst
Owes° nothing to thy blasts.

(*Enter* GLOUCESTER, *led by an* OLD MAN.)

                                But who comes here?
My father, poorly led?° World, world, O
10   world!
But that thy strange mutations make us hate
    thee,
Life would not yield to age.°
    OLD MAN: O, my good lord,
I have been your tenant, and your father's
    tenant,
These fourscore years.
    GLOUCESTER:
15 Away, get thee away; good friend, be gone:
Thy comforts° can do me no good at all;
Thee they may hurt.°
    OLD MAN: You cannot see your way.
    GLOUCESTER:
I have no way and therefore want° no eyes;
I stumbled when I saw. Full oft 'tis seen,
20 Our means secure us, and our mere defects
Prove our commodities.° Oh, dear son Edgar,

The food° of thy abusèd° father's wrath!
Might I but live to see thee in° my touch,
I'd say I had eyes again!
    OLD MAN: How now! Who's there?
    EDGAR [*aside*]:
O gods! Who is't can say, "I am at the worst"? 25
I am worse than e'er I was.
    OLD MAN: 'Tis poor mad Tom.
    EDGAR [*aside*]:
And worse I may be yet: the worst is not
So long as we can say, "This is the worst."°
    OLD MAN:
Fellow, where goest?
    GLOUCESTER: Is it a beggar-man?
    OLD MAN:
Madman and beggar too.   30
    GLOUCESTER:
He has some reason,° else he could not beg.
I' th' last night's storm I such a fellow saw,
Which made me think a man a worm. My son
Came then into my mind, and yet my mind
Was then scarce friends with him. I have
    heard more since.   35
As flies to wanton° boys, are we to th' gods,
They kill us for their sport.
    EDGAR [*aside*]:   How should this be?°
Bad is the trade that must play fool to sorrow,
Ang'ring° itself and others. Bless thee, master!
    GLOUCESTER:
Is that the naked fellow?
    OLD MAN: Ay, my lord.   40
    GLOUCESTER:
Then, prithee, get thee gone: if for my sake
Thou wilt o'ertake us hence a mile or twain
I' th' way toward Dover, do it for ancient°
    love,
And bring some covering for this naked soul,
Which I'll entreat to lead me.
    OLD MAN: Alack, sir, he is mad. 45
    GLOUCESTER:
'Tis the time's plague,° when madmen lead the
    blind.

IV.i.1 **known . . . contemned** conscious of being
despised   3 **dejected** abased   4 **esperance** hope   6
returns to laughter changes for the better   9 **Owes**
is in debt for   10 **poorly led** (1) led like a poor man,
with only one attendant (2) led by a poor man
11–12 **But . . . age** We should not agree to grow old
and hence die, except for the hateful mutability of
life   16 **comforts** ministrations   17 **hurt** injure   18
want require   20–21 **Our . . . commodities** Our resources make us overconfident, while our afflictions
make for our advantage

22 **food** i.e., the object on which Gloucester's anger
fed; **abusèd** deceived   23 **in** i.e., with, by means of
27–28 **the . . . worst** so long as a man continues to
suffer (i.e., is still alive), even greater suffering may
await him   31 **reason** faculty of reasoning   36 **wanton** (1) playful (2) reckless   37 **How . . . be** i.e.,
How can this horror be?   39 **Ang'ring** offending   43
ancient (1) the love the Old Man feels, by virtue of
his long tenancy (2) the love that formerly obtained
between master and man   46 **time's plague** characteristic disorder of this time

Do as I bid thee, or rather do thy pleasure;°
Above the rest,° be gone.
  OLD MAN:
I'll bring him the best 'parel° that I have,
50 Come on't what will.   (*Exit.*)
  GLOUCESTER:
Sirrah, naked fellow —
  EDGAR:
Poor Tom's a-cold. [*Aside.*] I cannot daub it°
  further.
  GLOUCESTER:
Come hither, fellow.
  EDGAR [*aside*]:
And yet I must. — Bless thy sweet eyes, they
  bleed.
  GLOUCESTER:
55 Know'st thou the way to Dover?
  EDGAR:
Both stile and gate, horse-way and footpath.
Poor Tom hath been scared out of his good
  wits.
Bless thee, good man's son, from the foul
  fiend!
Five fiends have been in Poor Tom at once; of
60 lust, as Obidicut;° Hobbididence, prince of
dumbness;° Mahu, of stealing; Modo, of mur-
der; Flibbertigibbet, of mopping and mowing;°
who since possesses chambermaids and wait-
ing-women. So, bless thee, master!
  GLOUCESTER:
Here, take this purse, thou whom the heavens'
65 plagues
Have humbled to all strokes:° that I am
  wretched
Makes thee the happier. Heavens, deal so still!
Let the superfluous° and lust-dieted° man,
That slaves° your ordinance,° that will not see
Because he does not feel, feel your pow'r
70 quickly;
So distribution should undo excess,°

47 **thy pleasure** as you like it 48 **the rest** all 49 **'parel** apparel 52 **daub it** lay it on (figure from plastering mortar) 60 **Obidicut** Hoberdicut, a devil (like the four that follow, from Harsnett's *Declaration*) 61 **dumbness** muteness (like the crimes and afflictions in the next lines, the result of diabolic possession) 62 **mopping and mowing** grimacing and making faces 66 **humbled . . . strokes** brought so low as to bear anything humbly 68 **superfluous** possessed of superfluities; **lust-dieted** whose lust is gratified (like Gloucester's) 69 **slaves** (1) tramples, spurns like a slave (2) tears, rends (Old English *slaefan*) (?); **ordinance** law 71 **So . . . excess** Then the man with too much wealth would distribute it among those with too little

And each man have enough. Dost thou know
  Dover?
  EDGAR: Ay, master.
  GLOUCESTER:
There is a cliff whose high and bending° head
Looks fearfully° in the confinèd deep:°   75
Bring me but to the very brim of it,
And I'll repair the misery thou dost bear
With something rich about me: from that
  place
I shall no leading need.
  EDGAR: Give me thy arm:
Poor Tom shall lead thee.   (*Exeunt.*) 80

SCENE II. [*Before the Duke of* ALBANY's
palace.]

Enter GONERIL *and* EDMUND.

  GONERIL:
Welcome, my lord: I marvel our mild husband
Not met° us on the way.

(*Enter* OSWALD.)

              Now, where's your master?
  OSWALD:
Madam, within; but never man so changed.
I told him of the army that was landed:
He smiled at it. I told him you were coming; 5
His answer was, "The worse." Of Gloucester's
  treachery,
And of the loyal service of his son
When I informed him, then he called me sot,°
And told me I had turned the wrong side out:
What most he should dislike seems pleasant to
  him;   10
What like,° offensive.
  GONERIL [*to* EDMUND]:
Then shall you go no further.
It is the cowish° terror of his spirit,
That dares not undertake:° he'll not feel
  wrongs,
Which tie him to an answer.° Our wishes on
  the way 15
May prove effects.° Back, Edmund, to my
  brother;

74 **bending** overhanging 75 **fearfully** occasioning fear; **confinèd deep** the sea, hemmed in below
IV.II.2 **Not met** did not meet 8 **sot** fool 11 **What like** what he should like 13 **cowish** cowardly 14 **undertake** venture 15 **tie . . . answer** oblige him to retaliate 15–16 **Our . . . effects** Our desires (that you might be my husband), as we journeyed here, may be fulfilled

Hasten his musters° and conduct his pow'rs.°
I must change names° at home and give the
    distaff°
Into my husband's hands. This trusty servant
Shall pass between us: ere long you are like to
20 hear,
If you dare venture in your own behalf,
A mistress's° command. Wear this; spare
    speech;

[*Giving a favor.*]

Decline your head.° This kiss, if it durst speak,
Would stretch thy spirits up into the air:
25 Conceive,° and fare thee well.
        EDMUND:
Yours in the ranks of death.
        GONERIL: My most dear Gloucester!
                                (*Exit* [EDMUND].)
O, the difference of man and man!
To thee a woman's services are due:
My fool usurps my body.°
        OSWALD: Madam, here comes my lord.
                                (*Exit.*)

(*Enter* ALBANY.)

        GONERIL:
I have been worth the whistle.°
30   ALBANY: O Goneril!
You are not worth the dust which the rude
    wind
Blows in your face. I fear your disposition:°
That nature which contemns° its origin
Cannot be bordered certain in itself;°
35 She that herself will sliver and disbranch°
From her material sap,° perforce must wither
And come to deadly use.°

        GONERIL:
No more; the text° is foolish.
        ALBANY:
Wisdom and goodness to the vile seem vile:
Filths savor but themselves.° What have you
    done?   40
Tigers, not daughters, what have you per-
    formed?
A father, and a gracious agèd man,
Whose reverence even the head-lugged bear°
    would lick,
Most barbarous, most degenerate, have you
    madded.°
Could my good brother suffer you to do it?   45
A man, a prince, by him so benefited!
If that the heavens do not their visible spirits°
Send quickly down to tame these vile offenses,
It will come,
Humanity must perforce prey on itself,   50
Like monsters of the deep.
        GONERIL: Milk-livered° man!
That bear'st a cheek for blows, a head for
    wrongs;
Who hast not in thy brows an eye discerning
Thine honor from thy suffering;° that not
    know'st
Fools do those villains pity who are punished 55
Ere they have done their mischief.° Where's
    thy drum?
France spreads his banners in our noiseless°
    land,
With plumèd helm° thy state begins to threat,°
Whilst thou, a moral° fool, sits still and cries,
"Alack, why does he so?"
        ALBANY: See thyself, devil!   60
Proper° deformity seems not in the fiend
So horrid as in woman.

---

17 **musters** collecting of troops; **conduct his pow'rs** lead his army   18 **change names** i.e., exchange the name of "mistress" for that of "master"; **distaff** spinning stick (wifely symbol)   22 **mistress's** lover's (and also, Albany having been disposed of, lady's or wife's)   23 **Decline your head** i.e., that Goneril may kiss him   25 **Conceive** understand (with a sexual implication, that includes "stretch thy spirits," line 24; and "death," line 26: "to die," meaning "to experience sexual intercourse")   29 **My . . . body** My husband wrongfully enjoys me   30 **I . . . whistle** i.e., Once you valued me (the proverb is implied, "It is a poor dog that is not worth the whistling")   32 **disposition** nature   33 **contemns** despises   34 **bordered . . . itself** kept within its normal bounds   35 **sliver and disbranch** cut off   36 **material sap** essential and lifegiving sustenance   37 **come . . . use** i.e., be as a dead branch for the burning

38 **text** i.e., on which your sermon is based   40 **Filths . . . themselves** the filthy relish only the taste of filth   43 **head-lugged bear** bear-baited by the dogs, and hence enraged   44 **madded** made mad   47 **visible spirits** avenging spirits in material form   51 **Milk-livered** lily-livered (hence cowardly, the liver being regarded as the seat of courage)   53–54 **discerning . . . suffering** able to distinguish between insults that ought to be resented and ordinary pain that is to be borne   55–56 **Fools . . . mischief** Only fools are sorry for criminals whose intended criminality is prevented by punishment   57 **noiseless** i.e., the drum, signifying preparation for war, is silent   58 **helm** helmet; **thy . . . threat** France begins to threaten Albany's realm   59 **moral** moralizing; but also with the implication that morality and folly are one   61 **Proper** (1) natural (to a fiend) (2) fair-appearing

GONERIL: O vain fool!
ALBANY:
Thou changèd and self-covered° thing, for shame,
Be-monster not thy feature.° Were't my fit-ness°
65 To let these hands obey my blood,°
They are apt enough to dislocate and tear
Thy flesh and bones: howe'er° thou art a fiend,
A woman's shape doth shield thee.
GONERIL:
Marry, your manhood mew° —

(*Enter a* MESSENGER.)

70 ALBANY: What news?
MESSENGER:
O, my good lord, the Duke of Cornwall's dead,
Slain by his servant, going to° put out
The other eye of Gloucester.
ALBANY: Gloucester's eyes!
MESSENGER:
A servant that he bred,° thrilled with remorse,°
75 Opposed against the act, bending his sword
To his great master, who thereat enraged
Flew on him, and amongst them felled° him dead,
But not without that harmful stroke which since
Hath plucked him after.°
ALBANY: This shows you are above,
80 You justicers,° that these our nether° crimes
So speedily can venge.° But, O poor Gloucester!
Lost he his other eye?
MESSENGER: Both, both, my lord.
This letter, madam, craves° a speedy answer;
'Tis from your sister.
GONERIL [*aside*]:   One way I like this well;
85 But being widow, and my Gloucester with her,

63 **changèd and self-covered** i.e., transformed, by the contorting of her woman's face, on which appears the fiendish behavior she has allowed herself (Goneril has disguised nature by wickedness)   64 **Be-monster . . . feature** do not change your appearance into a fiend's; **my fitness** appropriate for me   65 **blood** passion   67 **howe'er** but even if   69 **your manhood mew** (1) coop up or confine (pretended) manhood (2) molt or shed it, if that is what is supposed to "shield" me from you   72 **going to** as he was about to   74 **bred** reared; **thrilled with remorse** pierced by compassion   77 **amongst them felled** others assisting, they felled   79 **plucked him after** i.e., brought Cornwall to death with his servant   80 **justicers** judges; **nether** committed below (on earth)   81 **venge** avenge   83 **craves** demands

May all the building in my fancy pluck
Upon my hateful life.° Another way,°
The news is not so tart.° — I'll read, and answer.   (*Exit.*)
ALBANY:
Where was his son when they did take his eyes?
MESSENGER:
Come with my lady hither.
ALBANY: He is not here.   90
MESSENGER:
No, my good lord; I met him back° again.
ALBANY:
Knows he the wickedness?
MESSENGER:
Ay, my good lord; 'twas he informed against him,
And quit the house on purpose, that their punishment
Might have the freer course.
ALBANY: Gloucester, I live   95
To thank thee for the love thou showed'st the king,
And to revenge thine eyes. Come hither, friend:
Tell me what more thou know'st.   (*Exeunt.*)

[SCENE III. *The French camp near Dover.*]

Enter KENT *and a* GENTLEMAN.

KENT: Why the King of France is so suddenly gone back, know you no reason?
GENTLEMAN: Something he left imperfect in the state,° which since his coming forth is thought of, which imports° to the kingdom so   5
much fear and danger that his personal return was most required and necessary.
KENT:
Who hath he left behind him general?
GENTLEMAN: The Marshal of France, Monsieur La Far.   10
KENT: Did your letters pierce° the queen to any demonstration of grief?
GENTLEMAN:
Ay, sir; she took them, read them in my presence,

86–87 **May . . . life** These things (line 85) may send my future hopes, my castles in air, crashing down upon the hateful (married) life I lead now   87 **Another way** looked at another way   88 **tart** sour   91 **back** going back
IV.iii.3–4 **imperfect . . . state** unsettled in his own kingdom   5 **imports** portends   11 **pierce** impel

And now and then an ample tear trilled° down
15 Her delicate cheek: it seemed she was a queen
Over her passion, who most rebel-like
Sought to be king o'er her.
KENT: O, then it moved her.
GENTLEMAN:
Not to a rage: patience and sorrow strove
Who should express her goodliest.° You have
     seen
Sunshine and rain at once: her smiles and
20   tears
Were like a better way:° those happy smilets°
That played on her ripe lip seemed not to
     know
What guests were in her eyes, which parted
     thence
As pearls from diamonds dropped. In brief,
25 Sorrow would be a rarity most belovèd,
If all could so become it.°
KENT: Made she no verbal question?
GENTLEMAN:
Faith, once or twice she heaved° the name of
     "father"
Pantingly forth, as if it pressed her heart;
Cried, "Sisters! Sisters! Shame of ladies!
     Sisters!
Kent! Father! Sisters! What, i' th' storm? i'
30   th' night?
Let pity not be believed!"° There she shook
The holy water from her heavenly eyes,
And clamor moistened:° then away she started
To deal with grief alone.
KENT: It is the stars,
35 The stars above us, govern our conditions;°
Else one self mate and make could not beget
Such different issues.° You spoke not with her
     since?
GENTLEMAN: No.
KENT:
Was this before the king returned?
GENTLEMAN: No, since.

KENT:
Well, sir, the poor distressèd Lear's i' th' town;   40
Who sometime in his better tune° remembers
What we are come about, and by no means
Will yield to see his daughter.
GENTLEMAN: Why, good sir?
KENT:
A sovereign° shame so elbows° him: his own
     unkindness
That stripped her from his benediction, turned
     her   45
To foreign casualties,° gave her dear rights
To his dog-hearted daughters: these things
     sting
His mind so venomously that burning shame
Detains him from Cordelia.
GENTLEMAN: Alack, poor gentleman!
KENT:
Of Albany's and Cornwall's powers you heard
     not?   50
GENTLEMAN:
'Tis so;° they are afoot.
KENT:
Well, sir, I'll bring you to our master Lear,
And leave you to attend him: some dear cause°
Will in concealment wrap me up awhile;
When I am known aright, you shall not grieve   55
Lending me this acquaintance. I pray you, go
Along with me.   [Exeunt.]

[SCENE IV. *The same. A tent.*]

Enter, with drum and colors, CORDELIA,
DOCTOR, *and* SOLDIERS.

CORDELIA:
Alack, 'tis he: why, he was met even now
As mad as the vexed sea; singing aloud;
Crowned with rank femiter and furrow-weeds,
With hardocks, hemlock, nettles, cuckoo-
     flow'rs,
Darnel,° and all the idle weeds that grow   5

---

14 **trilled** trickled 19 **Who ... goodliest** which
should give her the most becoming expression 21
Were ... way i.e., improved on that spectacle; **smilets**
little smiles 25–26 **Sorrow ... it** sorrow would be a
coveted jewel if it became others as it does her 27
heaved expressed with difficulty 31 **Let ... be-**
lieved Let it not be believed for pity 33 **clamor**
moistened moistened clamor, i.e., mixed (and perhaps assuaged) her outcries with tears 35 **govern**
our conditions determine what we are 36–37 **Else**
... issues otherwise the same husband and wife could
not produce such different children

41 **better tune** composed, less jangled intervals 44
sovereign overpowering; **elbows** jogs his elbow (i.e.,
reminds him) 46 **casualties** chances 51 **'Tis so**
i.e., I have heard of them 53 **dear cause** important
reason
IV.iv.3–5 **femiter ... Darnel:** *femiter* fumitory,
whose leaves and juice are bitter; *furrow-weeds* weeds
that grow in the furrow, or plowed land; *hardocks*
hoar or white docks (?), burdocks, harlocks; *hemlock*
a poison; *nettles* plants that sting and burn; *cuckoo*
flow'rs identified with a plant employed to remedy
diseases of the brain; *Darnel* tares, noisome weeds

In our sustaining corn.° A century° send forth;
Search every acre in the high-grown field,
And bring him to our eye. [*Exit an* OFFICER.]
    What can man's wisdom°
In the restoring his bereavèd° sense?
10 He that helps him take all my outward° worth.
    DOCTOR:
There is means, madam:
Our foster-nurse° of nature is repose,
The which he lacks: that to provoke° in him,
Are many simples operative,° whose power
Will close the eye of anguish.
15   CORDELIA: All blest secrets,
All you unpublished virtues° of the earth,
Spring with my tears! be aidant and remedi-
    ate°
In the good man's distress! Seek, seek for him,
Lest his ungoverned rage dissolve the life
That wants the means to lead it.°
    (*Enter* MESSENGER.)
20   MESSENGER: News, madam;
The British pow'rs are marching hitherward.
    CORDELIA:
'Tis known before. Our preparation stands
In expectation of them. O dear father,
It is thy business that I go about;
25 Therefore° great France
My mourning and importuned° tears hath
    pitied.
No blown° ambition doth our arms incite,
But love, dear love, and our aged father's
    right:
Soon may I hear and see him!   (*Exeunt.*)

      [SCENE V. GLOUCESTER'S *castle.*]

   Enter REGAN *and* OSWALD.

    REGAN:
But are my brother's pow'rs set forth?
    OSWALD: Ay, madam.
Himself in person there?
    OSWALD: Madam, with much ado:°
Your sister is the better soldier.

    REGAN:
Lord Edmund spake not with your lord at
    home?
    OSWALD:
No, madam.   5
    REGAN:
What might import° my sister's letter to him?
    OSWALD:
I know not, lady.
    REGAN:
Faith, he is posted° hence on serious matter.
It was great ignorance,° Gloucester's eyes being
    out,
To let him live. Where he arrives he moves   10
All hearts against us: Edmund, I think, is
    gone,
In pity of his misery, to dispatch
His nighted° life; moreover, to descry
The strength o' th' enemy.
    OSWALD:
I must needs after him, madam, with my
    letter.   15
    REGAN:
Our troops set forth tomorrow: stay with us;
The ways are dangerous.
    OSWALD: I may not, madam:
My lady charged my duty° in this business.
    REGAN:
Why should she write to Edmund? Might not
    you
Transport her purposes° by word? Belike,°   20
Some things I know not what. I'll love thee
    much,
Let me unseal the letter.
    OSWALD: Madam, I had rather —
    REGAN:
I know your lady does not love her husband;
I am sure of that: and at her late° being here
She gave strange eliads° and most speaking looks 25
To noble Edmund. I know you are of her
    bosom.°
    OSWALD: I, madam?
    REGAN:
I speak in understanding: y' are; I know't:
Therefore I do advise you, take this note:°

6 **sustaining corn** life-maintaining wheat; **century**
sentry (?); troop of a hundred soldiers 8 **What . . .
wisdom** what can science accomplish 9 **bereavèd**
impaired 10 **outward** material 12 **foster-nurse**
fostering nurse 13 **provoke** induce 14 **simples
operative** efficacious medicinal herbs 16 **unpublished virtues** i.e., secret remedial herbs 17 **reme-
diate** remedial 20 **wants . . . it** i.e., lacks the reason
to control the rage 25 **Therefore** because of that
26 **importuned** importunate 27 **blown** puffed up
IV.v.2 **ado** bother and persuasion

6 **import** purport, carry as its message 8 **is posted**
has ridden speedily 9 **ignorance** folly 13 **nighted**
(1) darkened, because blinded (2) benighted 18
charged my duty ordered me as a solemn duty 20
Transport her purposes convey her intentions; **Belike**
probably 24 **late** recently 25 **eliads** amorous looks
26 **of her bosom** in her confidence 29 **take this note**
take note of this

30 My lord is dead; Edmund and I have talked;
And more convenient° is he for my hand
Than for your lady's: you may gather more.°
If you do find him, pray you, give him this;°
And when your mistress hears thus much from you,
35 I pray, desire her call° her wisdom to her.
So, fare you well.
If you do chance to hear of that blind traitor,
Preferment° falls on him that cuts him off.

OSWALD:
Would I could meet him, madam! I should show
What party I do follow.
40 REGAN: Fare thee well. (*Exeunt.*)

[SCENE VI. *Fields near Dover.*]

Enter GLOUCESTER *and* EDGAR.

GLOUCESTER:
When shall I come to th' top of that same hill?

EDGAR:
You do climb up it now. Look, how we labor.

GLOUCESTER:
Methinks the ground is even.

EDGAR: Horrible steep.
Hark, do you hear the sea?

GLOUCESTER: No, truly.

EDGAR:
5 Why then your other senses grow imperfect
By your eyes' anguish.°

GLOUCESTER: So may it be indeed.
Methinks thy voice is altered, and thou speak'st
In better phrase and matter than thou didst.

EDGAR:
Y' are much deceived: in nothing am I changed
But in my garments.

10 GLOUCESTER: Methinks y' are better spoken.

EDGAR:
Come on, sir; here's the place: stand still. How fearful
And dizzy 'tis to cast one's eyes so low!
The crows and choughs° that wing the midway air°
Show scarce so gross° as beetles. Half way down

31 **convenient** fitting   32 **gather more** surmise more
yourself   33 **this** this advice   35 **call** recall   38
Preferment promotion
IV.vi.6 **anguish** pain   13 **choughs** a kind of crow;
midway air i.e., halfway down the cliff   14 **gross**
large

Hangs one that gathers sampire,° dreadful trade!
15
Methinks he seems no bigger than his head.
The fishermen that walk upon the beach
Appear like mice; and yond tall anchoring° bark
Diminished to her cock;° her cock, a buoy
Almost too small for sight. The murmuring surge
20
That on th' unnumb'red idle pebble° chafes
Cannot be heard so high. I'll look no more,
Lest my brain turn and the deficient sight
Topple° down headlong.

GLOUCESTER: Set me where you stand.

EDGAR:
Give me your hand: you are now within a foot   25
Of th' extreme verge: for all beneath the moon
Would I not leap upright.°

GLOUCESTER: Let go my hand.
Here, friend, 's another purse; in it a jewel
Well worth a poor man's taking. Fairies° and gods
Prosper it with thee! Go thou further off;   30
Bid me farewell, and let me hear thee going.

EDGAR:
Now fare ye well, good sir.

GLOUCESTER: With all my heart.

EDGAR [*aside*]:
Why I do trifle thus with his despair
Is done to cure it.°

GLOUCESTER: O you mighty gods!

(*He kneels.*)

This world I do renounce, and in your sights   35
Shake patiently my great affliction off:
If I could bear it longer and not fall
To quarrel with° your great opposeless° wills,
My snuff° and loathèd part of nature should
Burn itself out. If Edgar live, O bless him!   40
Now, fellow, fare thee well. (*He falls.*)

EDGAR: Gone, sir, farewell.

15 **sampire** samphire, an aromatic herb associated
with Dover Cliffs   18 **anchoring** anchored   19 **cock**
cockboat, a small boat usually towed behind the ship
21 **unnumb'red idle pebble** innumerable pebbles,
moved to and fro by the waves to no purpose   23–
24 **the . . . Topple** my failing sight topple me   27
upright i.e., even up in the air, to say nothing of
forward, over the cliff   29 **Fairies** who are supposed
to guard and multiply hidden treasure   33–34 **Why
. . . it** I play on his despair in order to cure it   37–38
fall . . . with rebel against   38 **opposeless** not to be,
and not capable of being, opposed   39 **snuff** the
guttering (and stinking) wick of a burnt-out candle

And yet I know not how° conceit° may rob
The treasury of life, when life itself
Yields to° the theft. Had he been where he
     thought,
45 By this had thought been past. Alive or dead?
Ho, you sir! friend! Hear you, sir! speak!
Thus might he pass° indeed: yet he revives.
What are you, sir?
     GLOUCESTER: Away, and let me die.
     EDGAR:
Hadst thou been aught but gossamer, feathers,
     air,
50 So many fathom down precipitating,°
Thou'dst shivered like an egg: but thou dost
     breathe;
Hast heavy substance; bleed'st not; speak'st; art
     sound.
Ten masts at each° make not the altitude
Which thou hast perpendicularly fell:
55 Thy life's° a miracle. Speak yet again.
     GLOUCESTER:
But have I fall'n, or no?
     EDGAR:
From the dread summit of this chalky bourn.°
Look up a-height;° the shrill-gorged° lark so far
Cannot be seen or heard: do but look up.
     GLOUCESTER:
60 Alack, I have no eyes.
Is wretchedness deprived that benefit,
To end itself by death? 'Twas yet some
     comfort,
When misery could beguile° the tyrant's rage
And frustrate his proud will.
     EDGAR: Give me your arm.
Up, so. How is't? Feel you° your legs? You
65   stand.
     GLOUCESTER:
Too well, too well.
     EDGAR: This is above all strangeness.
Upon the crown o' th' cliff, what thing was
     that
Which parted from you?
     GLOUCESTER: A poor unfortunate beggar.
     EDGAR:
As I stood here below, methought his eyes
Were two full moons; he had a thousand
70   noses,

Horns whelked° and waved like the enridgèd°
     sea:
It was some fiend; therefore, thou happy
     father,°
Think that the clearest° gods, who make them
     honors
Of men's impossibilities,° have preserved thee.
     GLOUCESTER:
I do remember now: henceforth I'll bear   75
Affliction till it do cry out itself,
"Enough, enough," and die. That thing you
     speak of,
I took it for a man; often 'twould say,
"The fiend, the fiend" — he led me to that
     place.
     EDGAR:
Bear free° and patient thoughts.

     (*Enter* LEAR [*fantastically dressed with wild
     flowers*].)

                              But who comes here?   80
The safer° sense will ne'er accommodate°
His master thus.
     LEAR: No, they cannot touch me for
coining;° I am the king himself.
     EDGAR:
O thou side-piercing sight!   85
     LEAR: Nature's above art in that respect.°
There's your press-money.° That fellow handles
his bow like a crow-keeper;° draw me a
clothier's yard.° Look, look, a mouse! Peace,
peace; this piece of toasted cheese will do't.   90
There's my gauntlet;° I'll prove it on° a giant.

42 **how** but what; **conceit** imagination   44 **Yields to** allows   47 **pass** die   50 **precipitating** falling   53 **at each** one on top of the other   55 **life's** survival   57 **bourn** boundary   58 **a-height** on high; **gorged** throated, voiced   63 **beguile** cheat (i.e., by suicide)   65 **Feel you** have you any feeling in

71 **whelked** twisted; **enridgèd** i.e., furrowed into waves   72 **happy father** fortunate old man   73 **clearest** purest   73–74 **who...impossibilities** who cause themselves to be honored and revered by performing miracles of which men are incapable   80 **free** i.e., emancipated from grief and despair, which fetter the soul   81 **safer** sounder, saner; **accommodate** dress, adorn   83–84 **touch...coining** arrest me for minting coins (the king's prerogative)   86 **Nature's...respect** i.e., a born king is superior to legal (and hence artificial) inhibition; there is also a glance here at the popular Renaissance debate concerning the relative importance of nature (inspiration) and art (training)   87 **press-money** paid to conscripted soldiers   88 **crow-keeper** a farmer scaring away crows   89 **clothier's yard** the standard English arrow was a cloth-yard long; here the injunction is to draw the arrow back, like a powerful archer, a full yard to the ear   91 **gauntlet** armored glove, thrown down as a challenge; **prove it on** maintain my challenge even against

Bring up the brown bills.° O, well flown,°
bird! i' th' clout, i' th' clout:° hewgh!° Give
the word.°

95   EDGAR: Sweet marjoram.°

LEAR: Pass.

GLOUCESTER:
I know that voice.

LEAR: Ha! Goneril, with a white beard!
They flattered me like a dog,° and told me I
100 had white hairs in my beard ere the black ones
were there.° To say "ay" and "no" to
everything that I said! "Ay" and "no" too was
no good divinity.° When the rain came to wet
me once and the wind to make me chatter;
105 when the thunder would not peace at my
bidding; there I found 'em, there I smelt 'em
out. Go to, they are not men o' their words:
they told me I was everything; 'tis a lie, I am
not ague-proof.°

GLOUCESTER:
110 The trick° of that voice I do well remember:
Is't not the king?

LEAR: Ay, every inch a king.
When I do stare, see how the subject quakes.
I pardon that man's life. What was thy cause?°
Adultery?
115 Thou shalt not die: die for adultery! No:
The wren goes to't, and the small gilded fly
Does lecher° in my sight.
Let copulation thrive; for Gloucester's bastárd
son
Was kinder to his father than my daughters
120 Got° 'tween the lawful sheets.
To't, luxury,° pell-mell! for I lack soldiers.°
Behold yond simp'ring dame,

Whose face between her forks presages snow,°
That minces° virtue and does shake the head
To hear of pleasure's name.°   125
The fitchew,° nor the soilèd° horse, goes to't
With a more riotous appetite.
Down from the waist they are Centaurs,°
Though women all above:
But to the girdle° do the gods inherit,°   130
Beneath is all the fiend's.
There's hell, there's darkness, there is the
sulphurous pit, burning, scalding, stench,
consumption; fie, fie, fie! pah, pah! Give me
an ounce of civet;° good apothecary, sweeten   135
my imagination: there's money for thee.

GLOUCESTER:
O, let me kiss that hand!

LEAR:
Let me wipe it first; it smells of mortality.°

GLOUCESTER:
O ruined piece of nature! This great world
Shall so wear out to nought.° Dost thou know
   me?   140

LEAR: I remember thine eyes well enough.
Dost thou squiny° at me? No, do thy worst,
blind Cupid;° I'll not love. Read thou this
challenge;° mark but the penning of it.

GLOUCESTER:
Were all thy letters suns, I could not see.   145

EDGAR:
I would not take° this from report: it is,
And my heart breaks at it.

LEAR: Read.

GLOUCESTER:
What, with the case° of eyes?

LEAR: O, ho, are you there with me?° No   150
eyes in your head, nor no money in your
purse? Your eyes are in a heavy case,° your

---

92 **brown bills** halberds varnished to prevent rust
(here the reference is to the soldiers who carry them);
well flown falconer's cry; and perhaps a reference to
the flight of the arrow   93 **clout** the target shot at;
hewgh imitating the whizzing of the arrow (?)   94
word password   95 **Sweet marjoram** herb, used as a
remedy for brain disease   99 **like a dog** as a dog
flatters   99–101 **I . . . there** I was wise before I had
even grown a beard   103 **no good divinity** bad the-
ology, because contrary to the biblical saying (II
Corinthians 1:18), "Our word toward you was not
yea and nay"; see also James 5:12, "But let your yea
be yea, and your nay, nay; lest ye fall into condemnation"; and Matthew 5:36–37   109 **ague-proof** secure against fever   110 **trick** intonation   113 **cause**
offense   117 **lecher** copulate   120 **Got** begot   121
luxury lechery; **for . . . soldiers** i.e., (1) whom copulation will supply (?) (2) and am therefore power-
less (?)

123 **Whose . . . snow** whose cold demeanor seems
to promise chaste behavior ("forks" = legs)   124
minces squeamishly pretends to   125 **pleasure's
name** the very name of sexual pleasure   126 **fitchew**
polecat (and slang for prostitute); **soiled** put to pas-
ture, and hence wanton with feeding   128 **Centaurs**
lustful creatures, half man and half horse   130 **girdle**
waist; **inherit** possess   135 **civet** perfume   138 **mortality** (1) death (2) existence   139–140 **This . . .
nought** i.e., The universe (macrocosm) will decay to
nothing in the same way as the little world of man
(microcosm)   142 **squiny** squint, look sideways, like
a prostitute   143 **blind Cupid** the sign hung before a
brothel   144 **challenge** a reminiscence of lines 90–
91   146 **take** believe   149 **case** empty sockets   150
are . . . me is that what you tell me   152 **heavy case**
sad plight (pun on line 149)

purse in a light,° yet you see how this world goes.

GLOUCESTER:

155 I see it feelingly.°

LEAR: What, art mad? A man may see how this world goes with no eyes. Look with thine ears: see how yond justice rails upon yond simple° thief. Hark, in thine ear: change
160 places, and, handy-dandy,° which is the justice, which is the thief? Thou hast seen a farmer's dog bark at a beggar?

GLOUCESTER: Ay, sir.

LEAR: And the creature run from the cur?
165 There thou mightst behold the great image of authority:° a dog's obeyed in office.°
Thou rascal beadle,° hold thy bloody hand!
Why dost thou lash that whore? Strip thy own back;
Thou hotly lusts to use her in that kind°
For which thou whip'st her. The usurer hangs
170 the cozener.°
Through tattered clothes small vices do appear;
Robes and furred gowns° hide all. Plate sin with gold,
And the strong lance of justice hurtless° breaks;
Arm it in rags, a pygmy's straw does pierce it.
None does offend, none, I say, none; I'll able° 'em:
175 Take that° of me, my friend, who have the power
To seal th' accuser's lips. Get thee glass eyes,°
And, like a scurvy politician,° seem
To see the things thou dost not. Now, now, now, now.
180 Pull off my boots: harder, harder: so.

EDGAR:
O, matter and impertinency° mixed!
Reason in madness!

LEAR:
If thou wilt weep my fortunes, take my eyes.
I know thee well enough; thy name is Gloucester:
Thou must be patient; we came crying hither: 185
Thou know'st, the first time that we smell the air
We wawl and cry. I will preach to thee: mark.

GLOUCESTER:
Alack, alack the day!

LEAR:
When we are born, we cry that we are come
To this great stage of fools. This'° a good block.° 190
It were a delicate° stratagem, to shoe
A troop of horse with felt: I'll put't in proof;°
And when I have stol'n upon these son-in-laws,
Then, kill, kill, kill, kill, kill, kill!

(*Enter a* GENTLEMAN, [*with* ATTENDANTS].)

GENTLEMAN:
O, here he is: lay hand upon him. Sir, 195
Your most dear daughter —

LEAR:
No rescue? What, a prisoner? I am even
The natural fool° of fortune. Use me well;
You shall have ransom. Let me have surgeons;
I am cut° to th' brains.

GENTLEMAN: You shall have anything. 200

LEAR:
No seconds?° all myself?
Why, this would make a man a man of salt,°

---

153 **light** i.e., empty   155 **feelingly** (1) by touch (2) by feeling pain (3) with emotion   159 **simple** common, of low estate   160 **handy-dandy** i.e., choose, guess (after the children's game — "Handy-dandy, prickly prandy" — of choosing the correct hand)   165–166 **image of authority** symbol revealing the true meaning of authority   166 **a dog's . . . office** i.e., whoever has power is obeyed   167 **beadle** parish constable   169 **kind** i.e., sexual act   170 **The usurer . . . cozener** i.e., The powerful money-lender, in his role as judge, puts to death the petty cheat   172 **Robes . . . gowns** worn by a judge   173 **hurtless** i.e., without hurting the sinner   175 **able** vouch for   176 **that** the immunity just conferred (line 175)   177 **glass eyes** spectacles   178 **scurvy politician** vile politic man

181 **matter and impertinency** sense and nonsense   190 **This** this is; **block** various meanings have been suggested, for example, the stump of a tree, on which Lear is supposed to climb; a mounting-block, which suggests "horse" (line 192); a hat (which Lear or another must be made to wear), from the block on which a felt hat is molded, and which would suggest a "felt" (line 192); the proposal here is that "block" be taken to denote the quintain, whose function is to bear blows, "a mere lifeless block" (*As You Like It*, I.II.247), an object shaped like a man and used for tilting practice; see also *Much Ado About Nothing*, II.I.231–32, "She misused me past the endurance of a block!" and, in the same passage, the associated reference, "I stood like a man at a mark [target]" (lines 237–38)   191 **delicate** subtle   192 **put't in proof** test it   198 **natural fool** born sport (with pun on "natural" = imbecile)   200 **cut** wounded   201 **seconds** supporters   202 **man of salt** i.e., all (salt) tears

To use his eyes for garden water-pots,
Ay, and laying autumn's dust.
    GENTLEMAN:
205 Good sir —
    LEAR:
I will die bravely,° like a smug° bridegroom.°
    What!
I will be jovial: come, come; I am a king;
Masters, know you that?
    GENTLEMAN:
You are a royal one, and we obey you.
210   LEAR: Then there's life in't.° Come, and you
get it, you shall get it by running. Sa, sa, sa,
sa.°
        (Exit [running; ATTENDANTS follow].)
    GENTLEMAN:
A sight most pitiful in the meanest wretch,
Past speaking of in a king! Thou hast one
    daughter
215 Who redeems Nature from the general curse
Which twain have brought her to.°
    EDGAR:
Hail, gentle° sir.
    GENTLEMAN:
            Sir, speed° you: what's your will?
    EDGAR:
Do you hear aught, sir, of a battle toward?°
    GENTLEMAN:
Most sure and vulgar:° every one hears that,
Which can distinguish sound.
220   EDGAR: But, by your favor,
How near's the other army?
    GENTLEMAN:
Near and on speedy foot; the main descry
Stands on the hourly thought.°
    EDGAR: I thank you, sir: that's all.
    GENTLEMAN:
Though that the queen on special cause is
    here,
Her army is moved on.
225   EDGAR: I thank you, sir.
            (Exit [GENTLEMAN].)

    GLOUCESTER:
You ever-gentle gods, take my breath from me;
Let not my worser spirit° tempt me again
To die before you please.
    EDGAR: Well pray you, father.
    GLOUCESTER:
Now, good sir, what are you?
    EDGAR:
A most poor man, made tame° to fortune's
    blows;   230
Who, by the art of known and feeling
    sorrows,°
Am pregnant° to good pity. Give me your
    hand,
I'll lead you to some biding.°
    GLOUCESTER: Hearty thanks;
The bounty and the benison° of heaven
To boot, and boot.°

    (Enter OSWALD.)

    OSWALD:
            A proclaimed prize!° Most happy!° 235
That eyeless head of thine was first framed°
    flesh
To raise my fortunes. Thou old unhappy
    traitor,
Briefly thyself remember:° the sword is out
That must destroy thee.
    GLOUCESTER: Now let thy friendly° hand
Put strength enough to't. [EDGAR interposes.]
    OSWALD: Wherefore, bold peasant, 240
Dar'st thou support a published° traitor?
    Hence!
Lest that th' infection of his fortune take
Like hold on thee. Let go his arm.
    EDGAR:
Chill° not let go, zir, without vurther 'casion.°
    OSWALD:
Let go, slave, or thou diest!   245
    EDGAR: Good gentleman, go your gait,° and

---

206 **bravely** (1) smartly attired (2) courageously;
smug spick and span; **bridegroom** whose "brave"
sexual feats are picked up in the pun on "die" 210
there's life in't there's still hope 211–212 **Sa . . .
sa** hunting and rallying cry; also an interjection of
defiance 215–216 **general . . . to** (1) universal condemnation which Goneril and Regan have made for
(2) damnation incurred by the original sin of Adam
and Eve 217 **gentle** noble; **speed** God speed 218
toward impending 219 **vulgar** common knowledge
222–223 **the main . . . thought** we expect to see the
main body of the army any hour

227 **worser spirit** bad angel, evil side of my nature 230 **tame** submissive 231 **art . . . sorrows**
instruction of sorrows painfully experienced 232
pregnant disposed 233 **biding** place of refuge
234 **benison** blessing 235 **To . . . boot** also, and in
the highest degree; **proclaimed prize** i.e., one with a
price on his head; **happy** fortunate (for Oswald)
236 **framed** created 238 **thyself remember** i.e.,
pray, think of your sins 239 **friendly** i.e., because
it offers the death Gloucester covets 241 **published**
proclaimed 244 **Chill** I will (Edgar speaks in rustic
dialect); **vurther 'casion** further occasion 246 **gait**
way

let poor volk° pass. And chud ha' bin
zwaggered° out of my life, 'twould not ha' bin
zo long as 'tis by a vortnight. Nay, come not
250 near th' old man; keep out, che vor' ye,° or
I'se° try whether your costard° or my ballow°
be the harder: chill be plain with you.

OSWALD: Out, dunghill!

(*They fight.*)

EDGAR: Chill pick your teeth,° zir: come; no
255 matter vor your foins.°

[OSWALD *falls.*]

OSWALD:
Slave, thou hast slain me. Villain, take my
    purse:
If ever thou wilt thrive, bury my body,
And give the letters which thou find'st about°
    me
To Edmund Earl of Gloucester; seek him out
260 Upon the English party.° O, untimely death!
Death!   (*He dies.*)
EDGAR:
I know thee well. A serviceable° villain,
As duteous° to the vices of thy mistress
As badness would desire.
    GLOUCESTER: What, is he dead?
    EDGAR:
265 Sit you down, father; rest you.
Let's see these pockets: the letters that he
    speaks of
May be my friends. He's dead; I am only sorry
He had no other deathsman.° Let us see:
Leave,° gentle wax;° and, manners, blame us
    not:
To know our enemies' minds, we rip their
270   hearts;
Their papers° is more lawful.

(*Reads the letter.*)

"Let our reciprocal vows be remembered. You
have many opportunities to cut him off: if
your will want not,° time and place will be

fruitfully offered. There is nothing done, if he   275
return the conqueror: then am I the prisoner,
and his bed my jail; from the loathed warmth
whereof deliver me, and supply the place for
your labor.
    "Your—wife, so I would° say—affectionate   280
servant, and for you her own for venture,°
                              Goneril."
O indistinguished space of woman's will!°
A plot upon her virtuous husband's life;
And the exchange° my brother! Here in the
    sands   285
Thee I'll rake up,° the post unsanctified°
Of murderous lechers; and in the mature°
    time,
With this ungracious paper° strike° the sight
Of the death-practiced° duke: for him 'tis well
That of thy death and business I can tell.   290
    GLOUCESTER:
The king is mad: how stiff° is my vile sense,°
That I stand up, and have ingenious° feeling
Of my huge sorrows! Better I were distract:°
So should my thoughts be severed from my
    griefs,
And woes by wrong imaginations° lose   295
The knowledge of themselves.
                              (*Drum afar off.*)
    EDGAR: Give me your hand:
Far off, methinks, I hear the beaten drum.
Come, father, I'll bestow° you with a friend.
                              (*Exeunt.*)

SCENE VII. [*A tent in the French camp.*]

Enter CORDELIA, KENT, DOCTOR, *and* GENTLE-
MAN.

CORDELIA:
O thou good Kent, how shall I live and work,
To match thy goodness? My life will be too
    short,
And every measure fail me.

247 **volk** folk   247–248 **And . . . zwaggered** if I
could have been swaggered   250 **che vor' ye** I warrant you   251 **I'se** I shall; **costard** head (literally,
"apple");   **ballow** cudgel   254 **Chill . . . teeth** I will
knock your teeth out   255 **foins** thrusts   258 **about**
upon   260 **party** side   262 **serviceable** ready to be
used   263 **duteous** obedient   268 **deathsman** exe-
cutioner   269 **Leave** by your leave; **wax** with which
the letter is sealed   271 **Their papers** i.e., to rip their
papers   273–274 **if . . . not** if your desire (and lust)
be not lacking

280 **would** would like to   281 **and . . . venture** i.e.,
and one who holds you her own for venturing (Edmund had earlier been promised union by Goneril,
"If you dare venture in your own behalf," IV.ii.21)
283 **indistinguished . . . will** unlimited range of woman's lust   285 **exchange** substitute   286 **rake up**
cover up, bury; **post unsanctified** unholy messenger
287 **mature** ripe   288 **ungracious paper** wicked letter; **strike** blast   289 **death-practiced** whose death
is plotted   291 **stiff** unbending; **vile sense** hateful
capacity for feeling   292 **ingenious** conscious   293
distract distracted, mad   295 **wrong imaginations**
delusions   298 **bestow** lodge

KENT:
To be acknowledged, madam, is o'erpaid.
5 All my reports go° with the modest truth,
Nor more nor clipped,° but so.
　　　CORDELIA:　　　　　　　Be better suited:°
These weeds° are memories° of those worser
　　　hours:
I prithee, put them off.
　　　KENT:　　　　　　　Pardon, dear madam;
Yet to be known shortens my made intent:°
10 My boon I make it,° that you know me not
Till time and I think meet.°
　　　CORDELIA:
Then be't so, my good lord. [*To the* DOCTOR.]
　　　How does the king?
　　　DOCTOR:
Madam, sleeps still.
　　　CORDELIA:
O you kind gods!
15 Cure this great breach in his abusèd° nature.
Th' untuned and jarring senses, O, wind up°
Of this child-changèd° father.
　　　DOCTOR:　　　　　　So please your majesty
That we may wake the king: he hath slept
　　　long.
　　　CORDELIA:
Be governed by your knowledge, and proceed
20 I' th' sway of° your own will. Is he arrayed?

(*Enter* LEAR *in a chair carried by*
SERVANTS.)

GENTLEMAN:
Ay, madam; in the heaviness of sleep
We put fresh garments on him.
　　　DOCTOR:
Be by good madam, when we do awake
　　　him;
I doubt not of his temperance.°
　　　CORDELIA:　　　　　　Very well.
　　　DOCTOR:
Please you, draw near. Louder the music
25　　　there!
　　　CORDELIA:
O my dear father, restoration hang
Thy medicine on my lips, and let this kiss

Repair those violent harms that my two sisters
Have in thy reverence° made.
　　　KENT:　　　　　　　Kind and dear princess.
　　　CORDELIA:
Had you not been their father, these white
　　　flakes°　　　　　　　　　　　　　　　　30
Did challenge° pity of them. Was this a face
To be opposed against the warring winds?
To stand against the deep dread-bolted°
　　　thunder?
In the most terrible and nimble stroke
Of quick, cross° lightning to watch — poor
　　　perdu!° —　　　　　　　　　　　　　　　35
With this thin helm?° Mine enemy's dog,
Though he had bit me, should have stood that
　　　night
Against my fire; and wast thou fain,° poor
　　　father,
To hovel thee with swine and rogues° forlorn,
In short° and musty straw?° Alack, alack!　　40
'Tis wonder that thy life and wits at once
Had not concluded all.° He wakes; speak to
　　　him.
　　　DOCTOR:
Madam, do you; 'tis fittest.
　　　CORDELIA:
How does my royal lord? How fares your
　　　majesty?
　　　LEAR:
You do me wrong to take me out o' th' grave:　45
Thou art a soul in bliss; but I am bound
Upon a wheel of fire,° that mine own tears
Do scald like molten lead.
　　　CORDELIA:　　　　　　Sir, do you know me?
　　　LEAR:
You are a spirit, I know. Where did you die?
　　　CORDELIA:
Still, still, far wide.°　　　　　　　　　　50

IV.vii.5 **go** conform　6 **clipped** curtailed; **suited** attired　7 **weeds** clothes; **memories** reminders　9 **Yet . . . intent** to reveal myself just yet interferes with the plan I have made　10 **My . . . it** I ask this reward　11 **meet** fitting　15 **abusèd** disturbed　16 **wind up** tune　17 **child-changèd** changed, deranged (and also, reduced to a child) by the cruelty of his children　20 **I' . . . of** according to　24 **temperance** sanity

29 **reverence** revered person　30 **flakes** hairs (in long strands)　31 **challenge** claim　33 **deep dread-bolted** deep-voiced and furnished with the dreadful thunderbolt　35 **cross** zigzag; **perdu** (1) sentry in a forlorn position (2) lost one　36 **helm** helmet (his scanty hair)　38 **fain** pleased　39 **rogues** vagabonds　40 **short** when straw is freshly cut, it is long, and suitable for bedding, given its flexibility and crispness; as it is used, it becomes musty, shreds into pieces, is "short"; in contemporary Maine usage, "short manure" refers to dung mixed with straw that has been broken up, "long manure" to dung mixed with coarse new straw　42 **concluded all** come to a complete end　47 **wheel of fire** torment associated by the Middle Ages with hell, where Lear thinks he is　50 **wide** i.e., of the mark (of sanity)

DOCTOR:
He's scarce awake: let him alone awhile.

LEAR:
Where have I been? Where am I? Fair
  daylight?
I am mightily abused.° I should ev'n die with
  pity,
To see another thus. I know not what to say.
55 I will not swear these are my hands: let's see;
I feel this pin prick. Would I were assured
Of my condition.
    CORDELIA: O, look upon me, sir,
And hold your hand in benediction o'er me.
You must not kneel.
    LEAR: Pray, do not mock me:
60 I am a very foolish fond° old man,
Fourscore and upward, not an hour more nor
  less;
And, to deal plainly,
I fear I am not in my perfect mind.
Methinks I should know you and know this
  man,
65 Yet I am doubtful; for I am mainly° ignorant
What place this is, and all the skill I have
Remembers not these garments, nor I know
  not
Where I did lodge last night. Do not laugh at
  me,
For, as I am a man, I think this lady
To be my child Cordelia.
70   CORDELIA: And so I am, I am.
    LEAR:
Be your tears wet? Yes, faith. I pray, weep not.
If you have poison for me, I will drink it.
I know you do not love me; for your sisters
Have, as I do remember, done me wrong.
You have some cause, they have not.
75   CORDELIA: No cause, no cause.
    LEAR:
Am I in France?
    KENT: In your own kingdom, sir.
    LEAR:
Do not abuse° me.
    DOCTOR:
Be comforted, good madam: the great rage,°
You see, is killed in him: and yet it is danger
80 To make him even o'er° the time he has lost.
Desire him to go in; trouble him no more
Till further settling.°

53 **abused** deluded   60 **fond** in dotage   65 **mainly**
entirely   77 **abuse** deceive   78 **rage** frenzy   80
even o'er smooth over by filling in; and hence, "recollect"   82 **settling** calming

CORDELIA:
Will't please your highness walk?°
    LEAR: You must bear with me.
Pray you now, forget and forgive. I am old and
  foolish.
              (*Exeunt. Mane[n]t*° KENT
                    and GENTLEMAN.)
GENTLEMAN: Holds it true, sir, that the   85
Duke of Cornwall was so slain?
KENT: Most certain, sir.
GENTLEMAN: Who is conductor of his
people?
KENT: As 'tis said, the bastard son of   90
Gloucester.
GENTLEMAN: They say Edgar, his banished
son, is with the Earl of Kent in Germany.
KENT: Report is changeable.° 'Tis time to   95
look about; the powers° of the kingdom
approach apace.
GENTLEMAN: The arbitrement° is like to be
bloody. Fare you well, sir.   [*Exit.*]
    KENT:
My point and period will be throughly
  wrought,°
Or well or ill, as this day's battle's fought.   100
                       (*Exit.*)

ACT V

SCENE I. [*The British camp near Dover.*]

Enter, with drum and colors, EDMUND,
REGAN, GENTLEMEN, *and* SOLDIERS.

EDMUND:
Know° of the duke if his last purpose hold,°
Or whether since he is advised° by aught
To change the course: he's full of alteration
And self-reproving: bring his constant plea-
  sure.°
        [*To a* GENTLEMAN, *who goes out.*]
    REGAN:
Our sister's man is certainly miscarried.°   5

83 **walk** perhaps in the sense of "withdraw"   84 s.d.
Mane[n]t remain   95 **Report is changeable** rumors
are unreliable   96 **powers** armies   98 **arbitrement**
deciding encounter   99 **My . . . wrought** the aim and
end, the close of my life, will be completely worked
out
V.i.1 **Know** learn; **last purpose hold** most recent
intention (to fight) be maintained   2 **advised** induced   4 **constant pleasure** fixed (final) decision
5 **miscarried** come to grief

EDMUND:
'Tis to be doubted,° madam.
REGAN: Now, sweet lord,
You know the goodness I intend upon you:
Tell me, but truly, but then speak the truth,
Do you not love my sister?
EDMUND: In honored° love.
REGAN:
10 But have you never found my brother's way
To the forfended° place?
EDMUND: That thought abuses° you.
REGAN:
I am doubtful that you have been conjunct
And bosomed with her, as far as we call hers.°
EDMUND:
No, by mine honor, madam.
REGAN:
15 I shall never endure her: dear my lord,
Be not familiar with her.
EDMUND: Fear° me not. —
She and the duke her husband!

(Enter, with drum and colors, ALBANY,
GONERIL, [and] SOLDIERS.)

GONERIL [aside]:
I had rather lose the battle than that sister
Should loosen° him and me.
ALBANY:
20 Our very loving sister, well be-met.°
Sir, this I heard, the king is come to his
    daughter,
With others whom the rigor of our state°
Forced to cry out. Where I could not be
    honest,°
I never yet was valiant: for this business,
25 It touches us, as° France invades our land,
Not bolds the king, with others, whom, I fear,
Most just and heavy causes make oppose.°
EDMUND:
Sir, you speak nobly.
REGAN: Why is this reasoned?°
GONERIL:
Combine together 'gainst the enemy;

For these domestic and particular broils°   30
Are not the question° here.
ALBANY: Let's then determine
With th' ancient of war° on our proceeding.
EDMUND:
I shall attend you presently at your tent.
REGAN:
Sister, you'll go with us?°
GONERIL: No.   35
REGAN:
'Tis most convenient;° pray you, go with us.
GONERIL [aside]:
O, ho, I know the riddle.° — I will go.
                    (Exeunt both the ARMIES.)

(Enter EDGAR [disguised].)

EDGAR:
If e'er your grace had speech with man so
    poor,
Hear me one word.
ALBANY [to those going out]:
             I'll overtake you. [To EDGAR.] Speak.
    (Exeunt [all but ALBANY and EDGAR].)
EDGAR:
Before you fight the battle, ope this letter.   40
If you have victory, let the trumpet sound
For° him that brought it: wretched though I
    seem,
I can produce a champion that will prove°
What is avouchèd° there. If you miscarry,
Your business of° the world hath so an end,   45
And machination° ceases. Fortune love you.
ALBANY:
Stay till I have read the letter.
EDGAR: I was forbid it.
When time shall serve, let but the herald cry,
And I'll appear again.
ALBANY:
Why, fare thee well: I will o'erlook° thy paper. 50
                                 (Exit [EDGAR].)

(Enter EDMUND.)

EDMUND:
The enemy's in view: draw up your powers.
Here is the guess° of their true strength and
    forces

6 **doubted** feared 9 **honored** honorable 11 **for-
fended** forbidden; **abuses** (1) deceives (2) demeans,
is unworthy of 12–13 **I . . . hers** I fear that you have
united with her intimately, in the fullest possible way
16 **Fear** distrust 19 **loosen** separate 20 **be-met**
met 22 **rigor . . . state** tyranny of our government
23 **honest** honorable 25 **touches us, as** concerns me,
only in that 26–27 **Not . . . oppose** and not in that
France emboldens the king and others, who have
been led, by real and serious grievances, to take up
arms against us 28 **reasoned** argued

30 **particular broils** private quarrels 31 **question**
issue 32 **th' ancient of war** experienced comman-
ders 34 **us** me (rather than Edmund) 36 **convenient** fitting, desirable 37 **riddle** real reason (for
Regan's curious request) 41–42 **sound For** summon 43 **prove** i.e., by trial of combat 44 **avouchèd**
maintained 45 **of** in 46 **machination** plotting 50
o'erlook read over 52 **guess** estimate

By diligent discovery;° but your haste
Is now urged on you.
    ALBANY: We will greet° the time. (*Exit.*)
    EDMUND:
55 To both these sisters have I sworn my love;
Each jealous° of the other, as the stung
Are of the adder. Which of them shall I take?
Both? One? Or neither? Neither can be
    enjoyed,
If both remain alive: to take the widow
60 Exasperates, makes mad her sister Goneril;
And hardly° shall I carry out my side,°
Her husband being alive. Now then, we'll use
His countenance° for the battle; which being
    done,
Let her who would be rid of him devise
65 His speedy taking off. As for the mercy
Which he intends to Lear and to Cordelia,
The battle done, and they within our power,
Shall never see his pardon; for my state
Stands on me to defend, not to debate.°
                         (*Exit.*)

       SCENE II. [*A field between the two camps.*]

    *Alarum° within. Enter, with drum and
colors,* LEAR, CORDELIA, *and* SOLDIERS, *over
the stage; and exeunt.
    Enter* EDGAR *and* GLOUCESTER.

    EDGAR:
Here, father,° take the shadow of this tree
For your good host; pray that the right may
    thrive.
If ever I return to you again,
I'll bring you comfort.
    GLOUCESTER: Grace go with you, sir.
                     (*Exit* [EDGAR].)

    (*Alarum and retreat° within.* [*Re*]*enter*
    EDGAR.)

    EDGAR:
5 Away, old man; give me thy hand; away!

King Lear hath lost, he and his daughter ta'en:°
Give me thy hand; come on.
    GLOUCESTER:
No further, sir; a man may rot even here.
    EDGAR:
What, in ill thoughts again? Men must endure
Their going hence, even as their coming
    hither: 10
Ripeness° is all. Come on.
    GLOUCESTER: And that's true too.
                         (*Exeunt.*)

    SCENE III. [*The British camp near Dover.*]

    Enter, in conquest, with drum and colors,
    EDMUND; LEAR *and* CORDELIA, *as prisoners;*
    SOLDIERS, CAPTAIN.

    EDMUND:
Some officers take them away: good guard,°
Until their greater pleasures° first be known
That are to censure° them.
    CORDELIA: We are not the first
Who with best meaning° have incurred the
    worst.
For thee, oppressèd king, I am cast down;   5
Myself could else out-frown false Fortune's
    frown.
Shall we not see these daughters and these
    sisters?
    LEAR:
No, no, no, no! Come, let's away to prison:
We two alone will sing like birds i' th' cage:
When thou dost ask me blessing, I'll kneel
    down   10
And ask of thee forgiveness: so we'll live,
And pray, and sing, and tell old tales, and
    laugh
At gilded butterflies,° and hear poor rogues
Talk of court news; and we'll talk with them
    too,
Who loses and who wins, who's in, who's out;   15
And take upon's the mystery of things,
As if we were God's spies:° and we'll wear
    out,°

---

53 **By diligent discovery** obtained by careful reconnoitering 54 **greet** i.e., meet the demands of 56 **jealous** suspicious 61 **hardly** with difficulty; **carry ... side** (1) satisfy my ambition (2) fulfill my bargain (with Goneril) 63 **countenance** authority 68–69 **for ... debate** my position requires me to act, not to reason about right and wrong
V.II.s.d. **Alarum** a trumpet call to battle 1 **father** i.e., venerable old man (Edgar has not yet revealed his identity) 4 s.d. **retreat** signaled by a trumpet

6 **ta'en** captured 11 **Ripeness** maturity, as of fruit that is ready to fall
V.III.1 **good guard** let them be well guarded 2 **their greater pleasures** the will of those in command, the great ones 3 **censure** pass judgment on 4 **meaning** intentions 13 **gilded butterflies** i.e., gorgeously attired courtiers, fluttering after nothing 16–17 **take ... spies** profess to read the riddle of existence, as if endowed with divine omniscience 17 **wear out** outlast

In a walled prison, packs and sects of great
 ones
That ebb and flow by th' moon.°
  EDMUND: Take them away.
  LEAR:
20 Upon such sacrifices, my Cordelia,
The gods themselves throw incense.° Have I
 caught thee?
He that parts us shall bring a brand from heaven,
And fire us hence like foxes.° Wipe thine eyes;
The good years° shall devour them,° flesh and
 fell,°
Ere they shall make us weep. We'll see 'em
25 starved first.
Come. [*Exeunt* LEAR *and* CORDELIA, *guarded.*]
  EDMUND:
Come hither, captain; hark.
Take thou this note: go follow them to prison:
One step I have advanced thee; if thou dost
30 As this instructs thee, thou dost make thy way
To noble fortunes: know thou this, that men
Are as the time is:° to be tender-minded
Does not become a sword:° thy great em-
 ployment
Will not bear question;° either say thou'lt do't,
Or thrive by other means.
35   CAPTAIN: I'll do't, my lord.
  EDMUND:
About it; and write happy° when th' hast done.
Mark; I say, instantly, and carry it so°
As I have set it down.
  CAPTAIN:
I cannot draw a cart, nor eat dried oats;
40 If it be man's work, I'll do't. (*Exit* CAPTAIN.)

(*Flourish. Enter* ALBANY, GONERIL, REGAN
[*another* CAPTAIN, *and*] SOLDIERS.)

  ALBANY:
Sir, you have showed today your valiant strain,°
And fortune led you well: you have the
 captives
Who were the opposites of° this day's strife:
I do require them of you, so to use them
As we shall find their merits° and our safety 45
May equally determine.
  EDMUND: Sir, I thought it fit
To send the old and miserable king
To some retention and appointed guard;°
Whose° age had charms in it, whose title
 more,
To pluck the common bosom on his side,° 50
And turn our impressed lances in our eyes°
Which do command them. With him I sent
 the queen:
My reason all the same; and they are ready
Tomorrow, or at further space,° t'appear
Where you shall hold your session.° At this
 time 55
We sweat and bleed: the friend hath lost his
 friend;
And the best quarrels, in the heat, are cursed
By those that feel their sharpness.°
The question of Cordelia and her father
Requires a fitter place.
  ALBANY: Sir, by your patience, 60
I hold you but a subject of° this war,
Not as a brother.
  REGAN: That's as we list to grace° him.
Methinks our pleasure might have been de-
 manded,
Ere you had spoke so far. He led our powers,
Bore the commission of my place and person; 65
The which immediacy may well stand up
And call itself your brother.°
  GONERIL: Not so hot:

18–19 **packs . . . moon** intriguing and partisan cliques
of those in high station, whose fortunes change every
month 20–21 **Upon . . . incense** i.e., the gods approve our renunciation of the world 22–23 **He . . .
foxes** No human agency can separate us, but only
divine interposition, as of a heavenly torch parting us
like foxes that are driven from their place of refuge
by fire and smoke 24 **good years** plague and pestilence ("undefined malefic power or agency," *Oxford
English Dictionary*); **them** the enemies of Lear and
Cordelia; **fell** skin 32 **as . . . is** i.e., absolutely determined by the exigencies of the moment 33 **become a sword** befit a soldier 34 **bear question**
admit of discussion 36 **write happy** style yourself
fortunate 37 **carry it so** manage the affair in exactly that manner (as if Cordelia had taken her own
life)

41 **strain** (1) stock (2) character 43 **opposites of**
opponents in 45 **merits** deserts 48 **retention . . .
guard** confinement under duly appointed guard 49
Whose i.e., Lear's 50 **pluck . . . side** win the sympathy of the people to himself 51 **turn . . . eyes** turn
our conscripted lancers against us 54 **further space**
a later time 55 **session** trial 57–58 **best . . . sharpness** worthiest causes may be judged badly by those
who have been affected painfully by them, and whose
passion has not yet cooled 61 **subject of** subordinate
in 62 **list to grace** wish to honor 65–67 **Bore . . .
brother** was authorized, as my deputy, to take command; his present status, as my immediate representative, entitles him to be considered your equal

In his own grace he doth exalt himself
More than in your addition.°
    REGAN: In my rights,
70 By me invested, he compeers° the best.
    GONERIL:
That were the most,° if he should husband
    you.°
    REGAN:
Jesters do oft prove prophets.
    GONERIL: Holla, holla!
That eye that told you so looked but a-squint.°
    REGAN:
Lady, I am not well; else I should answer
75 From a full-flowing stomach.° General,
Take thou my soldiers, prisoners, patrimony;°
Dispose of them, of me; the walls is thine:°
Witness the world, that I create thee here
My lord, and master.
    GONERIL: Mean you to enjoy him?
    ALBANY:
80 The let-alone° lies not in your good will.
    EDMUND:
Nor in thine, lord.
    ALBANY: Half-blooded° fellow, yes.
    REGAN [to EDMUND]:
Let the drum strike, and prove my title thine.°
    ALBANY:
Stay yet; hear reason. Edmund, I arrest thee
On capital treason; and in thy attaint°
This gilded serpent [pointing to GONERIL]. For
85   your claim, fair sister,
I bar it in the interest of my wife.
'Tis she is subcontracted° to this lord,
And I, her husband, contradict your banes.°
If you will marry, make your loves° to me;
My lady is bespoke.°
90   GONERIL: An interlude!°

69 **your addition** honors you have bestowed on him
70 **compeers** equals   71 **most** most complete invest-
ing in your rights; **husband you** become your husband   73 **a-squint** cross-eyed   75 **From . . . stomach**
angrily   76 **patrimony** inheritance   77 **walls is
thine** i.e., Regan's person, which Edmund has
stormed and won   80 **let-alone** power to prevent
81 **Half-blooded** bastard, and so only half noble   82
prove . . . thine prove by combat your entitlement to
my rights   84 **in thy attaint** as a sharer in the treason
for which you are impeached   87 **subcontracted**
pledged by a contract which is called into question
by the existence of a previous contract (Goneril's
marriage)   88 **contradict your banes** forbid your
announced intention to marry (by citing the pre-
contract)   89 **loves** love-suits   90 **bespoke** already
pledged; **interlude** play

    ALBANY:
Thou art armed, Gloucester: let the trumpet
    sound:
If none appear to prove upon thy person
Thy heinous, manifest, and many treasons,
There is my pledge° [throwing down a glove]:
    I'll make° it on thy heart,
Ere I taste bread, thou art in nothing less   95
Than I have here proclaimed thee.
    REGAN: Sick, O, sick!
    GONERIL [aside]:
If not, I'll ne'er trust medicine.°
    EDMUND [throwing down a glove]:
There's my exchange:° what in the world he is
That names me traitor, villainlike he lies:°
Call by the trumpet:° he that dares approach,   100
On him, on you — who not? — I will maintain
My truth and honor firmly.
    ALBANY:
A herald, ho!
    EDMUND: A herald, ho, a herald!
    ALBANY:
Trust to thy single virtue;° for thy soldiers,
All levied in my name, have in my name   105
Took their discharge.
    REGAN: My sickness grows upon me.
    ALBANY:
She is not well; convey her to my tent.
                 [Exit REGAN, led.]

(Enter a HERALD.)

Come hither, herald. Let the trumpet sound —
And read out this.
    CAPTAIN: Sound, trumpet!   110

(A trumpet sounds.)

    HERALD (reads): "If any man of quality or
degree° within the lists° of the army will
maintain upon Edmund, supposed Earl of
Gloucester, that he is a manifold traitor, let
him appear by the third sound of the trumpet: 115
he is bold in his defense."
    EDMUND: Sound!

(First trumpet.)

    HERALD: Again!

(Second trumpet.)

94 **pledge** gage; **make** prove   97 **medicine** poison
98 **exchange** technical term, denoting the glove Edmund throws down   99 **villainlike he lies** the lie
direct, a challenge to mortal combat   100 **trumpet**
trumpeter   104 **single virtue** unaided valor   111–
112 **quality or degree** rank or position   112 **lists**
rolls

HERALD: Again!

(*Third trumpet.*

   Trumpet answers within. Enter EDGAR, *at the third sound, armed, a trumpet before him.*°)

ALBANY:
120 Ask him his purposes, why he appears
Upon this call o' th' trumpet.
  HERALD: What are you?
Your name, your quality,° and why you answer
This present summons?
  EDGAR: Know, my name is lost;
By treason's tooth bare-gnawn and canker-
  bit:°
125 Yet am I noble as the adversary
I come to cope.°
  ALBANY: Which is that adversary?
EDGAR:
What's he that speaks for Edmund, Earl of
  Gloucester?
EDMUND:
Himself: what say'st thou to him?
  EDGAR: Draw thy sword,
That if my speech offend a noble heart,
130 Thy arm do thee justice: here is mine.
Behold it is my privilege,
The privilege of mine honors,
My oath, and my profession.° I protest,
Maugre° thy strength, place, youth, and emi-
  nence,
135 Despite thy victor sword and fire-new° fortune,
Thy valor and thy heart,° thou art a traitor,
False to thy gods, thy brother, and thy father,
Conspirant° 'gainst this high illustrious prince,
And from th' extremest upward° of thy head
140 To the descent and dust below thy foot,°
A most toad-spotted traitor.° Say thou "No,"
This sword, this arm and my best spirits are
  bent°

To prove upon thy heart, whereto I speak,°
Thou liest.
  EDMUND:
       In wisdom° I should ask thy name,
But since thy outside looks so fair and warlike,   145
And that thy tongue some say° of breeding
  breathes,
What safe and nicely° I might well delay°
By rule of knighthood, I disdain and spurn:
Back do I toss these treasons° to thy head;
With the hell-hated° lie o'erwhelm thy heart;   150
Which for they yet glance by and scarcely
  bruise,
This sword of mine shall give them instant
  way,
Where they shall rest for ever.° Trumpets,
  speak!

(*Alarums.* [*They*] *fight.* [EDMUND *falls.*])

ALBANY:
Save° him, save him!
  GONERIL: This is practice,° Gloucester:
By th' law of war thou wast not bound to
  answer   155
An unknown opposite;° thou art not vanquished,
But cozened and beguiled.
  ALBANY: Shut your mouth, dame,
Or with this paper shall I stop it. Hold, sir;°
Thou° worse than any name, read thine own
  evil.
No tearing, lady; I perceive you know it.   160
  GONERIL:
Say, if I do, the laws are mine, not thine:
Who can arraign me for't?
  ALBANY: Most monstrous! O!
Know'st thou this paper?
  GONERIL: Ask me not what I know.
                           (*Exit.*)
  ALBANY:
Go after her; she's desperate; govern° her.

---

119 s.d. **trumpet before him** trumpeter preceding him   122 **quality** rank   124 **canker-bit** eaten by the caterpillar   126 **cope** encounter   131–133 **it . . . profession** my knighthood entitles me to challenge you, and to have my challenge accepted   134 **Maugre** despite   135 **fire-new** fresh from the forge or mint   136 **heart** courage   138 **Conspirant** conspiring, a conspirator   139 **extremest upward** the very top   140 **the . . . foot** your lowest part (sole) and the dust beneath it   141 **toad-spotted traitor** spotted with treason (and hence venomous, as the toad is allegedly marked with spots that exude venom)   142 **bent** directed

143 **whereto I speak** Edgar speaks from the heart, and speaks to the heart of Edmund   144 **wisdom** prudence (since he is not obliged to fight with one of lesser rank)   146 **say** assay (i.e., touch, sign)   147 **safe and nicely** cautiously and punctiliously; **delay** i.e., avoid   149 **treasons** accusations of treason   150 **hell-hated** hated like hell   151–153 **Which . . . ever** which accusations of treason, since as yet they do no harm, even though I have hurled them back, I now thrust upon you still more forcibly, with my sword, so that they may remain with you permanently   154 **Save** spare; **practice** trickery   156 **opposite** opponent   158 **Hold, sir** to Edmund: "Just a moment!"   159 **Thou** probably Goneril   164 **govern** control

EDMUND:
What you have charged me with, that have I
165   done;
And more, much more; the time will bring it
    out.
'Tis past, and so am I. But what art thou
That hast this fortune on° me? If thou'rt
    noble,
I do forgive thee.
          EDGAR: Let's exchange charity.°
170 I am no less in blood° than thou art, Edmund;
If more,° the more th' hast wronged me.
My name is Edgar, and thy father's son.
The gods are just, and of our pleasant° vices
Make instruments to plague us:
175 The dark and vicious place° where thee he got°
Cost him his eyes.
          EDMUND: Th' hast spoken right, 'tis true;
The wheel is come full circle; I am here.°
          ALBANY:
Methought thy very gait did prophesy°
A royal nobleness: I must embrace thee:
180 Let sorrow split my heart, if ever I
Did hate thee or thy father!
          EDGAR: Worthy° prince, I know't.
          ALBANY:
Where have you hid yourself?
How have you known the miseries of your
    father?
          EDGAR:
By nursing them, my lord. List a brief tale;
And when 'tis told, O, that my heart would
185   burst!
The bloody proclamation to escape°
That followed me so near — O, our lives'
    sweetness,
That we the pain of death would hourly die
Rather than die at once!° — taught me to shift
190 Into a madman's rags, t' assume a semblance
That very dogs disdained: and in this habit°

168 **fortune on** victory over   169 **charity** forgiveness
and love   170 **blood** lineage   171 **If more** if I am
more noble (since legitimate)   173 **of our pleasant**
out of our pleasurable   175 **place** i.e., the adulterous
bed; **got** begot   177 **wheel . . . here** i.e., Fortune's
wheel, on which Edmund ascended, has now, in its
downward turning, deposited him at the bottom,
whence he began   178 **gait did prophesy** carriage
did promise   181 **Worthy** honorable   186 **to escape** (my wish) to escape the sentence of death
187–189 **O . . . once** How sweet is life, that we
choose to suffer death every hour rather than make
an end at once   191 **habit** attire

Met I my father with his bleeding rings,°
Their precious stones new lost; became his
    guide,
Led him, begged for him, saved him from
    despair;
Never — O fault! — revealed myself unto him,   195
Until some half-hour past, when I was armed,
Not sure, though hoping, of this good success,
I asked his blessing, and from first to last
Told him our pilgrimage.° But his flawed°
    heart —
Alack, too weak the conflict to support —   200
'Twixt two extremes of passion, joy and grief,
Burst smilingly.
          EDMUND:
                    This speech of yours hath moved me,
And shall perchance do good: but speak you
    on;
You look as you had something more to say.
          ALBANY:
If there be more, more woeful, hold it in;   205
For I am almost ready to dissolve,°
Hearing of this.
          EDGAR: This would have seemed a period°
To such as love not sorrow; but another,
To amplify too much, would make much
    more,
And top extremity.°   210
Whilst I was big in clamor,° came there in a
    man,
Who, having seen me in my worst estate,°
Shunned my abhorred° society; but then,
    finding
Who 'twas that so endured, with his strong
    arms
He fastened on my neck, and bellowed out   215
As he'd burst heaven; threw him on my father;
Told the most piteous tale of Lear and him
That ever ear received: which in recounting
His grief grew puissant,° and the strings of life
Began to crack: twice then the trumpets
    sounded,   220
And there I left him tranced.°
          ALBANY: But who was this?

192 **rings** sockets   199 **our pilgrimage** of our (purga-
torial) journey; **flawed** cracked   206 **dissolve** i.e.,
into tears   207 **period** limit   208–210 **but . . . extremity** just one woe more, described too fully, would
go beyond the extreme limit   211 **big in clamor**
loud in lamentation   212 **estate** condition   213
abhorred abhorrent   219 **puissant** overmastering
221 **tranced** insensible

EDGAR:
Kent, sir, the banished Kent; who in disguise
Followed his enemy° king, and did him service
Improper for a slave.

(*Enter a* GENTLEMAN, *with a bloody knife.*)

GENTLEMAN:
Help, help, O, help!
EDGAR: What kind of help?
225   ALBANY: Speak, man.
EDGAR:
What means this bloody knife?
GENTLEMAN: 'Tis hot, it smokes;°
It came even from the heart of — O, she's
    dead!
ALBANY:
Who dead? Speak, man.
GENTLEMAN:
Your lady, sir, your lady: and her sister
230   By her is poisoned; she confesses it.
EDMUND:
I was contracted° to them both: all three
Now marry° in an instant.
EDGAR: Here comes Kent.
ALBANY:
Produce the bodies, be they alive or dead.
                                    [*Exit* GENTLEMAN.]
This judgment of the heavens, that makes us
    tremble,
Touches us not with pity.

(*Enter* KENT.)

235   O, is this he?
The time will not allow the compliment°
Which very manners° urges.
KENT: I am come
To bid my king and master aye° good night:
Is he not here?
ALBANY: Great thing of° us forgot!
Speak, Edmund, where's the king? and where's
    Cordelia?
240   See'st thou this object,° Kent?

(*The bodies of Goneril and Regan are
brought in.*)

KENT:
Alack, why thus?

EDMUND: Yet° Edmund was beloved:
The one the other poisoned for my sake,
And after slew herself.
ALBANY:
Even so. Cover their faces.   245
EDMUND:
I pant for life:° some good I mean to do,
Despite of mine own nature. Quickly send,
Be brief in it, to th' castle; for my writ°
Is on the life of Lear and on Cordelia:
Nay, send in time.
ALBANY: Run, run, O, run!   250
EDGAR:
To who, my lord? Who has the office?° Send
Thy token of reprieve.°
EDMUND:
Well thought on: take my sword,
Give it the captain.
EDGAR: Haste thee, for thy life.
                                    [*Exit* MESSENGER.]
EDMUND:
He hath commission from thy wife and me   255
To hang Cordelia in the prison, and
To lay the blame upon her own despair,
That she fordid° herself.
ALBANY:
The gods defend her! Bear him hence awhile.
                                    [EDMUND *is borne off.*]

(*Enter* LEAR, *with* CORDELIA *in his arms,*
[GENTLEMAN, *and others following*].)

LEAR:
Howl, howl, howl, howl! O, you are men of
    stones: 260
Had I your tongues and eyes, I'd use them so
That heaven's vault should crack. She's gone
    for ever.
I know when one is dead and when one lives;
She's dead as earth. Lend me a looking-glass;
If that her breath will mist or stain the stone,°   265
Why, then she lives.
KENT: Is this the promised end?°
EDGAR:
Or image° of that horror?
ALBANY: Fall and cease.°

223 **enemy** hostile   226 **smokes** steams   231 **contracted** betrothed   232 **marry** i.e., unite in death
236 **compliment** ceremony   237 **very manners** ordinary civility   238 **aye** forever   239 **thing of** matter
by   241 **object** sight (the bodies of Goneril and
Regan)

242 **Yet** in spite of all   246 **pant for life** gasp for
breath   248 **writ** command (ordering the execution)
251 **office** commission   252 **token of reprieve** sign
that they are reprieved   258 **fordid** destroyed   265
stone i.e., the surface of the crystal looking-glass
266 **promised end** doomsday   267 **image** exact likeness; **Fall and cease** i.e., Let the heavens fall, and
all things finish

LEAR:
This feather stirs; she lives. If it be so,
It is a chance which does redeem° all sorrows
That ever I have felt.

270 **KENT:**   O my good master.

LEAR:
Prithee, away.

EDGAR: 'Tis noble Kent, your friend.

LEAR:
A plague upon you, murderers, traitors all!
I might have saved her; now she's gone for
ever.
Cordelia, Cordelia, stay a little. Ha,
What is't thou say'st? Her voice was ever
275 soft,
Gentle and low, an excellent thing in woman.
I killed the slave that was a-hanging thee.

GENTLEMAN:
'Tis true, my lords, he did.

LEAR: Did I not, fellow?
I have seen the day, with my good biting
falchion°
280 I would have made them skip: I am old now,
And these same crosses° spoil me.° Who are
you?
Mine eyes are not o' th' best: I'll tell you
straight.°

KENT:
If Fortune brag of two° she loved and hated,
One of them we behold.

LEAR:
This is a dull sight.° Are you not Kent?

285 **KENT:**   The same,
Your servant Kent. Where is your servant
Caius?°

LEAR:
He's a good fellow, I can tell you that;
He'll strike, and quickly too: he's dead and
rotten.

KENT:
No, my good lord; I am the very man.

LEAR:
290 I'll see that straight.°

KENT:
That from your first of difference and decay°
Have followed your sad steps.

LEAR: You are welcome hither.

KENT:
Nor no man else:° all's cheerless, dark and
deadly.
Your eldest daughters have fordone° themselves,
And desperately° are dead.

LEAR: Ay, so I think. 295

ALBANY:
He knows not what he says, and vain is it
That we present us to him.

EDGAR: Very bootless.°

(*Enter a* MESSENGER.)

MESSENGER:
Edmund is dead, my lord.

ALBANY: That's but a trifle here.
You lords and noble friends, know our intent.
What comfort to this great decay may come° 300
Shall be applied. For us, we° will resign,
During the life of this old majesty,
To him our absolute power: [*to* EDGAR *and*
KENT] you, to your rights;
With boot,° and such addition° as your honors
Have more than merited. All friends shall taste 305
The wages of their virtue, and all foes
The cup of their deservings. O, see, see!

LEAR:
And my poor fool° is hanged: no, no, no life?
Why should a dog, a horse, a rat, have life,
And thou no breath at all? Thou'lt come no
more, 310
Never, never, never, never, never.
Pray you, undo this button.° Thank you, sir.
Do you see this? Look on her. Look, her
lips,
Look there, look there. (*He dies.*)

EDGAR: He faints. My lord, my lord!

KENT:
Break, heart; I prithee, break.

---

269 **redeem** make good   279 **falchion** small curved sword   281 **crosses** troubles; **spoil me** i.e., my prowess as a swordsman   282 **tell you straight** recognize you straightaway   283 **two** i.e., Lear, and some hypothetical second, who is also a prime example of Fortune's inconstancy ("loved and hated")   285 **dull sight** (1) melancholy spectacle (2) faulty eyesight (Lear's own, clouded by weeping)   286 **Caius** Kent's name, in disguise   290 **see that straight** attend to that in a moment

291 **your ... decay** beginning of your decline in fortune   293 **Nor ... else** no, I am not welcome, nor is anyone else   294 **fordone** destroyed   295 **desperately** in despair   297 **bootless** fruitless   300 **What ... come** whatever aid may present itself to this great ruined man   301 **us, we** the royal "we"   304 **boot** good measure; **addition** additional titles and rights   308 **fool** Cordelia ("fool" being a term of endearment; but it is perfectly possible to take the word as referring also to the Fool)   312 **undo this button** i.e., to ease the suffocation Lear feels

315 EDGAR: Look up, my lord!
KENT:
Vex not his ghost:° O, let him pass! He hates
    him
That would upon the rack° of this tough world
Stretch him out longer.°
    EDGAR: He is gone indeed.
    KENT:
The wonder is he hath endured so long:
320 He but usurped° his life.

316 **Vex . . . ghost** do not trouble his departing spirit
317 **rack** instrument of torture, stretching the victim's
joints to dislocation   318 **longer** (1) in time (2) in
bodily length   320 **usurped** possessed beyond the
allotted term

ALBANY:
Bear them from hence. Our present business
Is general woe. [*To* KENT *and* EDGAR.] Friends
    of my soul, you twain,
Rule in this realm and the gored state sustain.
    KENT:
I have a journey, sir, shortly to go;
My master calls me, I must not say no.   325
    EDGAR:
The weight of this sad time we must obey,°
Speak what we feel, not what we ought to say.
The oldest hath borne most: we that are
    young
Shall never see so much, nor live so long.
            (*Exeunt, with a dead march.*)

326 **obey** submit to

The best way to understand Shakespeare's tragic vision is, of course, to see
and read the tragedies very intelligently, but some help may be gained from a
brief consideration of two speeches in *Hamlet*. In the final scene, when Fortinbras and others enter the stage looking for Claudius, they find to their amazement the corpses of Claudius, Gertrude, Laertes, and Hamlet. Horatio, Hamlet's friend, endeavors to bring the visitors up to date:

> What is it you would see?
> If aught of woe or wonder, cease your search.

Fortinbras and his associates are indeed struck with woe and wonder:

> FORTINBRAS: O proud Death,
> What feast is toward in thine eternal cell
> That thou so many princes at a shot
> So bloodily hast struck?
> AMBASSADOR: The sight is dismal.

Horatio seeks to explain: the visitors will hear

> Of carnal, bloody, and unnatural acts,
> Of accidental judgments, casual slaughters,
> Of deaths put on by cunning and forced cause,
> And, in this upshot, purposes mistook
> Fall'n on th'inventors' heads.

The spectators of the play itself have indeed seen "unnatural acts," "deaths put
on by cunning," etc., and presumably these spectators have experienced the
"woe" and "wonder" that the new arrivals will experience as Horatio sets forth
the details.

Let us now look at a second passage from *Hamlet*. The speaker is the despicable Rosencrantz, and there is some flattery of King Claudius in his speech,
but the gist of his argument about the death of a king rings true, makes sense:

> The cess of majesty
> Dies not alone, but like a gulf doth draw
> What's near it with it; or it is a massy wheel
> Fixed on the summit of the highest mount,
> To whose huge spokes ten thousand lesser things
> Are mortised and adjoined, which when it falls,
> Each small annexment, petty consequence,
> Attends the boist'rous ruin. Never alone
> Did the King sigh, but with a general groan.

Surely it is understandable that the deaths of, say, Lincoln and Kennedy had a vastly greater effect upon America than the deaths of any number of men in private life. Put crudely, they mattered more.

The speeches together afford some justification of the Elizabethan view that tragedy is concerned with violence done to and by people of high rank. The fall of a man in high position evokes deeper woe and wonder than the snuffing out of a nonentity. The latter may evoke pity, but scarcely awe at the terrifying power of destructiveness or at the weakness that is at the heart of power.

Shakespeare does not merely slap the label of king or prince or general on a character and then assume that greatness has been established. His characters speak great language and perform great deeds. (And, no less important, they have the capacity to suffer greatly.) Lear, in the first scene, gives away — almost seems to create — fertile kingdoms:

> Of all these bounds, even from this line to this,
> With shadowy forests, and with champains riched,
> With plenteous rivers, and wide-skirted meads,
> We make thee lady.

Even in injustice, when he banishes his daughter, Cordelia, for speaking the truth as she sees it, he has a kind of terrible grandeur:

> Let it be so, thy truth then be thy dower!
> For, by the sacred radiance of the sun,
> The mysteries of Hecate and the night,
> By all the operation of the orbs
> From whom we do exist and cease to be,
> Here I disclaim all my paternal care,
> Propinquity and property of blood,
> And as a stranger to my heart and me
> Hold thee from this for ever.

Finally, even in his madness — "a sight most pitiful in the meanest wretch, / Past speaking of in a king" — he has grandeur. To Gloucester's "Is't not the king?" he replies:

> Ay, every inch a king.
> When I do stare, see how the subject quakes.
> I pardon that man's life. What was thy cause?
> Adultery?
> Thou shalt not die: die for adultery! No:
> The wren goes to 't, and the small gilded fly
> Does lecher in my sight.
> Let copulation thrive. . . .

We might contrast Lear's noble voice with Edmund's materialistic comment on the way of the world:

> This is the excellent foppery of the world, that when we are sick in fortune, often the surfeits of our own behavior, we make guilty of our disasters the sun, the moon, and stars; as if we were villains on necessity; fools by heavenly compulsion; knaves, thieves, and treachers by spherical predominance; drunkards, liars, and adulterers by an enforced obedience of planetary influence; and all that we are evil in, by a divine thrusting on. An admirable evasion of whoremaster man, to lay his goatish disposition on the charge of a star. . . . Fut! I should have been that I am, had the maidenliest star in the firmament twinkled on my bastardizing.

Lear seems to be displacing *Hamlet* as the play that speaks to our time. *Hamlet* was especially popular with nineteenth-century audiences, who often found in the uncertain prince an image of their own doubts in a world in which belief in a benevolent divine order was collapsing under the influence of scientific materialism and bourgeois aggressiveness. Many audiences in our age find in *Lear* — where "for many miles about / There's scarce a bush" — a play thoroughly in the spirit of Beckett's *Waiting for Godot*, where the scenery consists of a single tree. Moreover, Lear denounces the hypocrisy of the power structure and exposes the powerlessness of the disenfranchised: "Robes and furred gowns hide all. Plate sin with gold, / And the strong lance of justice hurtless breaks; / Arm it in rags, a pygmy's straw does pierce it." And what of the gods? There are several comments about their nature, but perhaps the most memorable reference to the gods is not a mere comment but one followed by an action: learning that Cordelia is in danger, Albany cries out, "The gods defend her!" and immediately his words are mocked by Lear's entrance on the stage, with the dead Cordelia in his arms.

But the interpretation of *King Lear* as a revelation of the emptiness of life fails to consider at least two things. First, there is an affirmation in those passages in which Lear comes, through heart-rending anguish, to see that he was not what he thought he was. Second, this anagnorisis or recognition is several times associated with love or charity, as when (III.IV) Lear invites the Fool to enter the hovel first and then confesses his guilt in having cared too little for humanity. And this care for humanity is seen in Cordelia, who comes — though ineffectually in the long run — to the aid of her father. It is seen, too, in the nameless servant who at the end of III.VII promises to apply medicine to Gloucester's eyeless sockets; it is seen even in the villainous Edmund, who in dying repents and says, "Some good I mean to do, / Despite mine own nature" (V.III), and who thereupon tries, unsuccessfully, to save Cordelia. No one would say that these actions turn *King Lear* into a happy vision, but it is perverse to ignore them and to refuse to see that in this play love humanizes as surely as egoism dehumanizes. If the play dramatizes man's desolation, it also dramatizes the love that, while providing no protection against pain or death, makes man's life different from the life of "a dog, a horse, a rat."

HEDDA GABLER

Henrik Ibsen

Translated by Otto Reinert

Henrik Ibsen (1828–1906) was born in Skien, Norway, of wealthy parents who soon after his birth lost their money. Ibsen worked as a pharmacist's apprentice, but at the age of twenty-two he had written his first play, a promising melodrama entitled *Cataline*. He engaged in theater work in Norway, and then in Denmark and Germany. By 1865 his plays had won him a state pension that enabled him to settle in Rome. After writing romantic, historic, and poetic plays, he turned to realistic drama with *The League of Youth* (1869). Among the major realistic "problem plays" are *A Doll's House* (1879), *Ghosts* (1881), and *An Enemy of the People* (1882). In *The Wild Duck* (1884) he moved toward a more symbolic tragic comedy, and his last plays, written in the nineties, are highly symbolic. *Hedda Gabler* (1890) looks backward to the plays of the eighties rather than forward to the plays of the nineties.

CHARACTERS

JØRGEN TESMAN, *University Research Fellow
    in the History of Civilization*
HEDDA, *his wife*
MISS JULIANE TESMAN, *his aunt*

MRS. ELVSTED
JUDGE BRACK
EILERT LØVBORG
BERTE, *the Tesmans' maid*

Scene: The TESMANS' *villa in a fashionable residential section of the town.*

A note on pronunciation

The approximate Norwegian pronunciation of names likely to be difficult to a speaker of English is suggested below (the syllable in capitals is accented; the unaccented *e* is close to English *e* in *quiet*).

JØRGEN YUR-gen (*g* as in *bargain*)
EILERT LØVBORG AY-lert LUV-borg[1]

JULLE YOOL-le (short *oo*)
BERTE BAIR-te

[1] *Løvborg* means, literally, "leaf-castle" — a fact of possible bearing on the play's symbolism. [Reinert.]

Maggie Smith as Hedda Gabler in the National Theatre Company production directed by Ingmar Bergman, London, 1970. (Photograph: Dominic.)

ACT I

A *spacious, handsome, tastefully furnished room. Dark décor. In the rear, a wide doorway with open portieres. Beyond is a smaller room, furnished in the same style as the front room. A door, right, leads to the front hall. Left, French doors, with portieres drawn aside, through which can be seen a part of a roofed verandah and trees with autumn foliage. Front center, an oval table covered with a cloth. Chairs around it. Front right, a wide, dark, porcelain stove, a high-backed easy chair, a footstool with a pillow, and two ottomans. In the corner far right, a sofa and a small, round table. Front left, a sofa, set out from the wall. Far left, beyond the French doors, an upright piano. On both sides of the doorway, rear center, whatnots with knickknacks. Against the rear wall of the inner room, a sofa, and in front of it a table and two chairs. Above the sofa, a portrait of a handsome, elderly man in general's uniform. Over the table hangs a lamp with milky, white glass. There are several bouquets of flowers, in vases and glasses, in various places in the front room. Others are lying on the tables. Thick carpets on the floors of both rooms. The morning sun is shining through the French doors.*

MISS JULIANE TESMAN, *with hat and parasol, enters right, followed by* BERTE, *who carries a bouquet of flowers wrapped in paper.* MISS TESMAN *is a nice-looking woman of 65, of pleasant mien, neatly but not expensively dressed in a gray suit.* BERTE *is a middle-aged servant girl, of rather plain and countrified appearance.*

MISS TESMAN (*stops inside the door, listens, says in a low voice*): On my word — I don't think they are even up yet!

BERTE (*also softly*): That's what I told you, miss. When you think how late the steamer got in last night. And afterwards! — Goodness! — all the stuff she wanted unpacked before she turned in.

MISS TESMAN: Well — just let them sleep. But fresh morning air — *that* we can give them when they come in here. (*Goes and opens the French doors wide.*)

BERTE (*by the table, lost, still holding the flowers*): Please, miss — I just don't see a bit of space anywhere! I think I'd better put these over here. (*Puts the flowers down on the piano.*)

MISS TESMAN: Well, well, my dear Berte. So you've got yourself a new mistress now. The good Lord knows it was hard for me to let you go.

BERTE (*near tears*): What about me, then, miss! What shall I say? I who have served you and Miss Rina all these blessed years.

MISS TESMAN: We shall just have to make the best of it, Berte. That's all. Jørgen can't do without you, you know. He just can't. You've looked after him ever since he was a little boy.

BERTE: Yes, but miss — I'm ever so worried about leaving Miss Rina. The poor dear lying there all helpless. With that new girl and all! She'll never learn how to make things nice and comfortable for an invalid.

MISS TESMAN: Oh yes, you'll see. I'll teach her. And of course, you know, I'll do most of it myself. So don't you worry yourself about my poor sister, Berte.

BERTE: Yes, but there's another thing, too, miss. I'm scared I won't be able to suit young Mrs. Tesman.

MISS TESMAN: Oh, well. Good heavens. So there is a thing or two — Right at first —

BERTE: For I believe she's ever so particular.

MISS TESMAN: Can you wonder? General Gabler's daughter? Just think of the kind of life she was used to when the General was alive. Do you remember when she rode by with her father? That long black riding habit she wore? And the feather in her hat?

BERTE: Oh, I remember, all right. But I'll be blessed if I ever thought she and the young master would make a pair of it.

MISS TESMAN: Nor did I. By the way, while I think of it, Berte. Jørgen has a new title now. From now on you should call him "the Doctor."

BERTE: Yes, the young mistress said something about that, too, last night. Soon as they were inside the door. Then it's really so, miss?

MISS TESMAN: It certainly is. Just think, Berte — they have made him a doctor abroad. During the trip, you know. I hadn't heard a thing about it till last night on the pier.

BERTE: Well, I daresay he could be anything he put his mind to, *he* could — smart as *he* is. But I must say I'd never thought he'd turn to doctoring people, too.

MISS TESMAN: Oh, that's not the kind of doctor he is. (*Nods significantly.*) And as far as that is concerned, there is no telling but pretty soon you may have to call him something grander yet.

BERTE: You don't say! What might that be, miss?

MISS TESMAN (*smiles*): Wouldn't you like to know! (*Moved.*) Ah yes, indeed — ! If only dear Jochum could see from his grave what has become of his little boy! (*Looking around.*) But look, Berte — what's this for? Why have you taken off all the slip covers?

BERTE: She told me to. Said she can't stand slip covers on chairs.

MISS TESMAN: Do you think they mean to make this their everyday living room, then?

BERTE: It sure sounded that way. Mrs. Tesman did, I mean. For he — the doctor — he didn't say anything.

(JØRGEN TESMAN *enters from the right side of the inner room. He is humming to himself. He carries an open, empty suitcase. He is of medium height, youthful-looking, thirty-three years old; somewhat stoutish. Round, open, cheerful face. Blond hair and beard. He wears glasses and is dressed in a comfortable, rather casual suit.*)

MISS TESMAN: Good morning, good morning, Jørgen!

TESMAN (*in the doorway*): Auntie! Dearest Aunt Julle! (*Comes forward and shakes her hand.*) All the way out here — as early as this! Hm?

MISS TESMAN: Well — I just had to drop in for a moment. To see how you are getting along, you know.

TESMAN: Even though you haven't had a good night's sleep.

MISS TESMAN: Oh, that doesn't matter at all.

TESMAN: But you did get home from the pier all right, I hope. Hm?

MISS TESMAN: Oh yes, I certainly did, thank you. The Judge was kind enough to see me all the way to my door.

TESMAN: We were so sorry we couldn't give you a ride in our carriage. But you saw for yourself — all the boxes Hedda had.

MISS TESMAN: Yes, she certainly brought quite a collection.

BERTE (*to* TESMAN): Should I go and ask Mrs. Tesman if there's anything I can help her with?

TESMAN: No, thank you, Berte — you'd better not. She said she'll ring if she wants you.

BERTE (*going right*): Well, all right.

TESMAN: But, look — you might take this suitcase with you.

BERTE (*takes it*): I'll put it in the attic. (*Exits right.*)

TESMAN: Just think, Auntie — that whole suitcase was brimful of copies of old documents. You wouldn't believe me if I told you all the things I have collected from libraries and archives all over. Quaint old items nobody has known anything about.

MISS TESMAN: Well, no, Jørgen. I'm sure you haven't wasted your time on your honeymoon.

TESMAN: No, I think I may say I have not. But take your hat off, Auntie — for goodness' sake. Here! Let me untie the ribbon for you. Hm?

MISS TESMAN (*while he does so*): Ah, God forgive me, if this isn't just as if you were still at home with us!

TESMAN (*inspecting the hat*): My, what a fine-looking hat you've got yourself!

MISS TESMAN: I bought it for Hedda's sake.

TESMAN: For Hedda's sake? Hm?

MISS TESMAN: So she won't need to feel ashamed of me if we ever go out together.

TESMAN (*patting her cheek*): If you don't think of everything, Auntie! (*Puts the hat down on a chair by the table.*) And now — over here to the sofa — we'll just sit and chat for a while till Hedda comes.

(*They seat themselves. She places her parasol in the corner by the sofa.*)

MISS TESMAN (*takes both his hands in hers and gazes at him*): What a blessing it is to have you back again, Jørgen, big as life! You — Jochum's little boy!

TESMAN: For me, too, Aunt Julle. Seeing

you again. For you have been both father and mother to me.

MISS TESMAN: Ah, yes — don't you think I know you'll always keep a spot in your heart for these two old aunts of yours!

TESMAN: So Aunt Rina isn't any better, hm?

MISS TESMAN: Oh no. We mustn't look for improvement in her case, poor dear. She is lying there just as she has been all these years. Just the same, may the good Lord keep her for me a long time yet! For else I just wouldn't know what to do with myself, Jørgen. Especially now, when I don't have you to look after any more.

TESMAN (*pats her back*): There, there, now!

MISS TESMAN (*changing tone*): And to think that you are a married man, Jørgen! And that you were the one to walk off with Hedda Gabler. The lovely Hedda Gabler. Just think! As many admirers as she had!

TESMAN (*hums a little, smiles complacently*): Yes, I daresay I have quite a few good friends here in town who'd gladly be in my shoes, hm?

MISS TESMAN: And such a long and lovely honeymoon you had! More than five — almost six months!

TESMAN: Well, you know — for me it has been a kind of study tour as well. All the collections I had to go through. And the books I had to read!

MISS TESMAN: Yes, I suppose. (*More confidentially, her voice lowered a little.*) But listen, Jørgen — haven't you got something — something special to tell me?

TESMAN: About the trip?

MISS TESMAN: Yes.

TESMAN: No — I don't know of anything besides what I wrote in my letters. They gave me a doctor's degree down there — but I told you that last night; I'm sure I did.

MISS TESMAN: Well, yes, that sort of thing — What I mean is — don't you have certain — certain — expectations?

TESMAN: Expectations?

MISS TESMAN: Ah for goodness' sake, Jørgen! I am your old Auntie, after all!

TESMAN: Certainly I have expectations.

MISS TESMAN: Well!!

TESMAN: I fully expect to be made a professor one of these days.

MISS TESMAN: Professor — oh yes —

TESMAN: I may even say I am quite certain of it. But dear Aunt Julle — you know this just as well as I do!

MISS TESMAN (*laughing a little*): Of course I do. You're quite right. (*Changing topic.*) But about the trip. It must have cost a great deal of money — hm, Jørgen?

TESMAN: Well, now; you know that large stipend went quite a long way.

MISS TESMAN: I just don't see how you made it do for both of you, though.

TESMAN: No, I suppose that's not so easy to understand, hm?

MISS TESMAN: Particularly with a lady along. For I have always heard that is ever so much more expensive.

TESMAN: Well, yes, naturally. That *is* rather more expensive. But Hedda had to have this trip, Auntie! She really had to. Nothing less would do.

MISS TESMAN: No, I daresay. For a wedding journey is quite the thing these days. But now tell me — have you had a chance to look around here yet?

TESMAN: I certainly have. I have been up and about ever since dawn.

MISS TESMAN: And what do you think of it all?

TESMAN: Delightful! Perfectly delightful! The only thing is I don't see what we are going to do with the two empty rooms between the second sitting room in there and Hedda's bedroom.

MISS TESMAN (*with a chuckle*): Oh my dear Jørgen — you may find them useful enough — when the time comes!

TESMAN: Of course, you're right, Auntie! As my library expands, hm?

MISS TESMAN: Quite so, my dear boy. It was your library I was thinking of.

TESMAN: But I'm really most happy on Hedda's behalf. For you know, before we were engaged she used to say she wouldn't care to live anywhere but in Secretary Falk's house.

MISS TESMAN: Yes, just think — wasn't that a lucky coincidence, that it was up for sale right after you had left?

TESMAN: Yes, Aunt Julle. We've certainly been lucky. Hm?

MISS TESMAN: But it will be expensive, my dear Jørgen. Terribly expensive — all this.

TESMAN (*looks at her, a bit crestfallen*): Yes, I daresay it will, Auntie.

MISS TESMAN: Heavens, yes!

TESMAN: How much, do you think? Roughly. Hm?

MISS TESMAN: No, I couldn't possibly say till all the bills arrive.

TESMAN: Well, anyway, Judge Brack managed to get very reasonable terms for us. He said so himself in a letter to Hedda.

MISS TESMAN: Yes, and I won't have you uneasy on that account, Jørgen. Besides, I have given security for the furniture and the carpets.

TESMAN: Security? You? But dear Aunt Julle — what kind of security could you give?

MISS TESMAN: The annuity.

TESMAN (*jumps up*): What! Your and Aunt Rina's annuity?

MISS TESMAN: Yes. I didn't know what else to do, you see.

TESMAN (*standing before her*): But are you clear out of your mind, Auntie! That annuity — that's all the two of you have to live on!

MISS TESMAN: Oh well, there's nothing to get so excited about, I'm sure. It's all just a matter of form, you know. That's what the Judge said, too. For he was kind enough to arrange the whole thing for me. Just a matter of form — those were his words.

TESMAN: That's all very well. Still —

MISS TESMAN: For now you'll have your own salary, you know. And, goodness — what if we do have a few expenses — Help out a bit right at first — ? That would only be a joy for us —

TESMAN: Oh, Auntie! When will you ever stop making sacrifices for my sake!

MISS TESMAN (*gets up, puts her hands on his shoulders*): But what other happiness do I have in this world than being able to smooth your way a little, my own dear boy? Orphan as you were, with no one to lean on but us? And now the goal is in sight, Jørgen. Things may have looked black at times. But heaven be praised; now you've arrived!

TESMAN: Yes, it's really quite remarkable the way things have worked out.

MISS TESMAN: Yes — and those who were against you — who tried to block your way — now they are tasting defeat. They are down, Jørgen! He, the most dangerous of them all, his fall was the greatest! He made his bed, and now he is lying in it — poor, lost wretch that he is!

TESMAN: Have you had any news about Eilert? Since I went away, I mean?

MISS TESMAN: Just that he is supposed to have published a new book.

TESMAN: What? Eilert Løvborg? Recently? Hm?

MISS TESMAN: That's what they say. But I wonder if there can be much to it. What do you think? Ah — but when *your* new book comes, that will be something quite different, Jørgen! What is it going to be about?

TESMAN: It deals with the domestic industries of Brabant during the Middle Ages.

MISS TESMAN: Just think — being able to write about something like that!

TESMAN: But as far as that is concerned, it may be quite some time before it is ready. I have all these collections to put in order first, you see.

MISS TESMAN: Yes, collecting and putting things in order — you certainly know how to do that. In that you are your father's own son.

TESMAN: Well, I must say I am looking forward to getting started. Particularly now, that I've got my own delightful home to work in.

MISS TESMAN: And most of all now that you have the one your heart desired, dear Jørgen.

TESMAN (*embracing her*): Oh yes, yes, Aunt Jule! Hedda — she is the most wonderful part of it all! (*Looks toward the doorway.*) There — I think she is coming now, hm?

(HEDDA *enters from the left side of the inner room. She is twenty-nine years old. Both features and figure are noble and elegant. Pale, ivory complexion. Steel-gray eyes, expressive of cold, clear calm. Beautiful brown hair, though not particularly ample. She is dressed in a tasteful, rather loose-fitting morning costume.*)

MISS TESMAN (*going toward her*): Good morning, my dear Hedda! A very happy morning to you!

HEDDA (*giving her hand*): Good morning, dear Miss Tesman! So early a call? That is most kind.

MISS TESMAN (*seems slightly embarrassed*): And — has the little lady of the house slept well the first night in her new home?

HEDDA: Passably, thank you.

TESMAN (*laughs*): Passably! You are a good one, Hedda! You were sleeping like a log when I got up.

HEDDA: Fortunately. And then, of course, Miss Tesman, it always takes time to get used to new surroundings. That has to come gradually. (*Looks left.*) Oh dear. The maid has left the verandah doors wide open. There's a veritable flood of sunlight in here.

MISS TESMAN (*toward the doors*): Well, then, we'll just close them.

HEDDA: No, no, not that. Tesman, dear, please pull the curtains. That will give a softer light.

TESMAN (*over by the French doors*): Yes, dear. There, now! Now you have both shade and fresh air, Hedda.

HEDDA: We certainly can use some air in here. Such loads of flowers — but, Miss Tesman, please — won't you be seated?

MISS TESMAN: No thanks. I just wanted to see if everything was all right — and so it is, thank goodness. I had better get back to Rina. I know she is waiting for me, poor thing.

TESMAN: Be sure to give her my love, Auntie. And tell her I'll be around to see her later today.

MISS TESMAN: I'll certainly do that! — Oh my! I almost forgot! (*Searches the pocket of her dress.*) I have something for you, Jørgen. Here.

TESMAN: What's that, Auntie? Hm?

MISS TESMAN (*pulls out a flat parcel wrapped in newspaper and gives it to him*): Here you are, dear.

TESMAN (*opens the parcel*): Well, well, well! So you took care of them for me, Aunt Julle! Hedda! Now, isn't that sweet, hm?

HEDDA (*by the whatnot, right*): If you'd tell me what it is —

TESMAN: My old slippers! You know!

HEDDA: Oh really? I remember you often talked about them on the trip.

TESMAN: Yes, for I missed them so. (*Walks over to her.*) Here — now you can see what they're like, Hedda.

HEDDA (*crosses toward stove*): Thanks. I don't know that I really care.

TESMAN (*following*): Just think — Aunt Rina embroidered these slippers for me. Ill as she was. You can't imagine how many memories they hold for me!

HEDDA (*by the table*): Hardly for me.

MISS TESMAN: That's true, you know, Jørgen.

TESMAN: Yes, but — I just thought that now that she's one of the family —

HEDDA (*interrupting*): I don't think we'll get on with that maid, Tesman.

MISS TESMAN: Not get on with Berte?

TESMAN: Whatever makes you say that, dear? Hm?

HEDDA (*points*): Look — she has left her old hat on the chair over there.

TESMAN (*appalled, drops the slippers*): But Hedda — !

HEDDA: What if somebody were to come and see it!

TESMAN: No, no, Hedda — that's Aunt Julle's hat!

HEDDA: Oh?

MISS TESMAN (*picking up the hat*): Yes, indeed it is. And it isn't old either, my dear young lady.

HEDDA: I really didn't look that closely —

MISS TESMAN (*tying the ribbons*): I want you to know that this is the first time I have had it on my head. On my word it is!

TESMAN: And very handsome it is, too. Really a splendid-looking hat!

MISS TESMAN: Oh, I don't know that it is anything so special, Jørgen. (*Looks around.*) My parasol —? Ah, here it is. (*Picks it up.*) For that is mine, too. (*Mutters.*) Not Berte's.

TESMAN: New hat and new parasol! What do you think of that, Hedda?

HEDDA: Very nice indeed.

TESMAN: Yes, don't you think so? Hm? But, Auntie, take a good look at Hedda before you leave. See how pretty and blooming she looks.

MISS TESMAN: Dear me, Jørgen; that's nothing new. Hedda has been lovely all her days. (*She nods and walks right.*)

TESMAN (*following*): Yes, but have you noticed how full-figured and healthy she looks after the trip? How she has filled out?

HEDDA (*crossing*): Oh — stop it!

MISS TESMAN (*halts, turns around*): Filled out?

TESMAN: Yes, Aunt Julle. You can't see it so well now when she wears that dress. But I, who have the opportunity —

HEDDA (*by the French doors, impatiently*): Oh, you haven't any opportunities at all!

TESMAN: It must be the mountain air in Tyrol.

HEDDA (*curtly interrupting*): I am just as I was when I left.

TESMAN: Yes, so you say. I just don't think you're right. What do you think, Auntie?

MISS TESMAN (*has folded her hands, gazes at HEDDA*): Lovely — lovely — lovely; that is what Hedda is. (*Goes over to her, inclines her head forward with both her hands, and kisses her hair.*) God bless and keep Hedda Tesman. For Jørgen's sake.

HEDDA (*gently freeing herself*): There, there. Now let me go.

MISS TESMAN (*in quiet emotion*): Every single day I'll be over and see you two.

TESMAN: Yes, please do, Auntie. Hm?

MISS TESMAN: Goodbye, goodbye!

(*She leaves through door, right.* TESMAN *sees her out. The door remains ajar.* TESMAN *is heard repeating his greetings for Aunt Rina and his thanks for the slippers. In the meantime,* HEDDA *paces up and down, raises her arms, clenching her fists, as in quiet rage. Opens the curtains by the French doors and stands looking out. In a few moments,* TESMAN *re-enters and closes the door behind him.*)

TESMAN (*picking up the slippers*): What are you looking at, Hedda?

HEDDA (*once again calm and controlled*): Just the leaves. They are so yellow. And withered.

TESMAN (*wrapping the slippers in their paper, putting the parcel down on the table*): Well, you know — we're in September now.

HEDDA (*again restless*): Yes — just think. It's already — September.

TESMAN: Don't you think Aunt Julle acted strange, Hedda? Almost solemn. I wonder why. Hm?

HEDDA: I hardly know her, you see. Isn't she often like that?

TESMAN: Not the way she was today.

HEDDA (*turning away from the French doors*): Do you think she minded that business with the hat?

TESMAN: Oh, I don't think so. Not much. Perhaps a little bit right at the moment —

HEDDA: Well, I'm sorry, but I must say it strikes me as very odd — putting her hat down here in the living room. One just doesn't do that.

TESMAN: Well, you may be sure Aunt Julle won't ever do it again.

HEDDA: Anyway, I'll make it up to her, somehow.

TESMAN: Oh yes, Hedda; if only you would!

HEDDA: When you go over there today, why don't you ask her over for tonight?

TESMAN: I'll certainly do that. And then there is one other thing you could do that she'd appreciate ever so much.

HEDDA: What?

TESMAN: If you could just bring yourself to call her Auntie. For my sake, Hedda, hm?

HEDDA: No, Tesman, no. You really mustn't ask me to do that. I have already told you I can't. I'll try to call her Aunt Juliane. That will have to do.

TESMAN: All right, if you say so. I just thought that now that you're in the family —

HEDDA: Hmmm — I don't know about that — (*She walks toward the doorway.*)

TESMAN (*after a brief pause*): Anything the matter, Hedda? Hm?

HEDDA: I'm just looking at my old piano. It doesn't quite go with the other furniture in here.

TESMAN: As soon as I get my first pay check we'll have it traded in.

HEDDA: No — I don't want to do that. I want to keep it. But let's put it in this inner room and get another one for out here. Whenever it's convenient. I mean.

TESMAN (*a little taken back*): Well — yes — we could do that —

HEDDA (*picks up the bouquet from the piano*): These flowers weren't here last night.

TESMAN: I suppose Aunt Julle brought them for you.

HEDDA (*looking at the flowers*): There's a card here. (*Takes it out and reads.*) "Will be back later." Can you guess who it's from?

TESMAN: No. Who? Hm?

HEDDA: Thea Elvsted.

TESMAN: No, really? Mrs. Elvsted! Miss Rysing that was.

HEDDA: That's right. The one with that irritating head of hair she used to show off with. An old flame of yours, I understand.

TESMAN (*laughs*): Well, now — that didn't last long! Anyway, that was before I knew you, Hedda. Just think — her being in town.

HEDDA: Strange, that she'd call on us. I have hardly seen her since we went to school together.

TESMAN: As far as that goes, I haven't seen her either for — God knows how long. I don't see how she can stand living in that out-of-the-way place. Hm?

HEDDA (*suddenly struck by a thought*): Listen, Tesman — isn't it some place near there that he lives — what's his name — Eilert Løvborg?

TESMAN: Yes, that's right. He is up there, too.

(BERTE *enters right.*)

BERTE: Ma'am, she's here again, that lady who brought those flowers a while back. (*Pointing.*) The flowers you're holding in your hand, ma'am.

HEDDA: Ah, she is? Well, show her in, please.

(BERTE *opens the door for* MRS. ELVSTED *and exits.* MRS. ELVSTED *is of slight build, with a pretty, soft face. Her eyes are light blue, large, round, rather prominent, of a timid and querying expression. Her hair is strikingly light in color, almost whitish, and unusually rich and wavy. She is a couple of years younger than* HEDDA. *She is dressed in a dark visiting dress, tasteful, but not quite in the most recent fashion.*)

HEDDA (*walks toward her. Friendly*): Good morning, my dear Mrs. Elvsted. How very nice to see you again.

MRS. ELVSTED (*nervous, trying not to show it*): Well, yes, it is quite some time since we met.

TESMAN (*shaking hands*): And we, too. Hm?

HEDDA: Thank you for your lovely flowers —

MRS. ELVSTED: Please, don't — I would have come here yesterday afternoon. But I was told you were still traveling —

TESMAN: You've just arrived in town, hm?

MRS. ELVSTED: I got here yesterday, at noon. Oh, I was quite desperate when I learned you weren't home.

HEDDA: Desperate? But why?

TESMAN: But my dear Mrs. Rysing — I mean Mrs. Elvsted —

HEDDA: There is nothing wrong, I hope?

MRS. ELVSTED: Yes there is. And I don't know a single soul other than you that I can turn to here.

HEDDA (*putting the flowers down on the table*): Come — let's sit down here on the sofa.

MRS. ELVSTED: Oh, I'm in no mood to sit!

HEDDA: Of course you are. Come on. (*She pulls* MRS. ELVSTED *over to the sofa and sits down next to her.*)

TESMAN: Well, now, Mrs. — ? Exactly what — ?

HEDDA: Has something — special happened at home?

MRS. ELVSTED: Well, yes — and no. Oh, but I am so afraid you won't understand!

HEDDA: In that case, it seems to me you ought to tell us exactly what has happened, Mrs. Elvsted.

TESMAN: After all, that's why you are here. Hm?

MRS. ELVSTED: Yes, yes, of course. Well, then, maybe you already know — Eilert Løvborg is in town.

HEDDA: Is Løvborg — !

TESMAN: No! You don't say! Just think, Hedda — Løvborg's back!

HEDDA: All right. I can hear.

MRS. ELVSTED: He has been here a week already. Imagine — a whole week! In this dangerous place. Alone! With all that bad company around.

HEDDA: But my dear Mrs. Elvsted — why is he a concern of yours?

MRS. ELVSTED (*with an apprehensive look at her, says quickly*): He tutored the children.

HEDDA: Your children?

MRS. ELVSTED: My husband's. I don't have any.

HEDDA: In other words, your stepchildren.

MRS. ELVSTED: Yes.

TESMAN (*with some hesitation*): But was he — I don't quite know how to put this — was he sufficiently — regular — in his way of life to be thus employed? Hm?

MRS. ELVSTED: For the last two years, there hasn't been a thing to object to in his conduct.

TESMAN: No, really? Just think, Hedda!

HEDDA: I hear.

MRS. ELVSTED: Not the least little bit, I assure you! Not in any respect. And yet — knowing he's here — in the big city — And with all that money, too! I'm scared to death!

TESMAN: But in that case, why didn't he remain with you and your husband? Hm?

MRS. ELVSTED: After his book came out, he was too restless to stay.

TESMAN: Ah yes, that's right. Aunt Julle said he has published a new book.

MRS. ELVSTED: Yes, a big new book, about the course of civilization in general. It came out about two weeks ago. And since it has had such big sales and been discussed so much and made such a big splash —

TESMAN: It has, has it? I suppose this is something he has had lying around from better days?

MRS. ELVSTED: You mean from earlier?

TESMAN: Yes.

MRS. ELVSTED: No; it's all been written since he came to stay with us. During this last year.

TESMAN: Well, now! That's very good news, Hedda! Just think!

MRS. ELVSTED: Yes, if it only would last!

HEDDA: Have you seen him since you came to town?

MRS. ELVSTED: No, not yet. I had a great deal of trouble finding his address. But this morning I finally tracked him down.

HEDDA (*looks searchingly at her*): Isn't it rather odd that your husband — hm —

MRS. ELVSTED (*with a nervous start*): My husband! What about him?

HEDDA: That he sends you to town on such an errand? That he doesn't go and look after his friend himself?

MRS. ELVSTED: Oh, no, no — my husband doesn't have time for things like that. Besides, I have some — some shopping to do, anyway.

HEDDA (*with a slight smile*): Well, in that case, of course —

MRS. ELVSTED (*getting up, restlessly*): And now I beg of you, Mr. Tesman — won't you please receive Eilert Løvborg nicely if he calls on you? And I am sure he will. After all — Such good friends as you two used to be. And then you both do the same kind of work — the same field of study, as far as I know.

TESMAN: We used to, at any rate.

MRS. ELVSTED: Yes. And that's why I implore you to please, please, try to keep an eye on him — you too. You'll do that, Mr. Tesman, won't you? Promise?

TESMAN: With the greatest pleasure, Mrs. Rysing.

HEDDA: Elvsted.

TESMAN: I'll gladly do as much for Eilert as I possibly can. You may certainly count on that.

MRS. ELVSTED: Oh, how good and kind you are! (*Clasps his hands.*) Thank you, thank you, thank you! (*Nervously.*) You see, my husband is so very fond of him.

HEDDA (*getting up*): You ought to write him a note, Tesman. Maybe he won't come without an invitation.

TESMAN: Yes, I suppose that would be the right thing to do, Hedda. Hm?

HEDDA: The sooner the better. Right away, *I* think.

MRS. ELVSTED (*pleadingly*): If only you would!

TESMAN: I'll write this minute. Do you have his address, Mrs. — Mrs. Elvsted?

MRS. ELVSTED: Yes. (*Pulls a slip of paper from her bag and gives it to him.*) Here it is.

TESMAN: Very good. Well, then, if you'll excuse me — (*Looks around.*) By the way — the slippers? Ah, here we are. (*Leaving with the parcel.*)

HEDDA: Be sure you write a nice, warm, friendly letter, Tesman. And a long one, too.

TESMAN: Certainly, certainly.

MRS. ELVSTED: But not a word that it is I who — !

TESMAN: No, that goes without saying, I should think. Hm? (*Goes out right through inner room.*)

HEDDA (*goes over to* MRS. ELVSTED, *smiles, says in a low voice*): There! We just killed two birds with one stone.

MRS. ELVSTED: What do you mean?

HEDDA: Didn't you see I wanted him out of the room?

MRS. ELVSTED: Yes, to write that letter —

HEDDA: And to speak to you alone.

MRS. ELVSTED (*flustered*): About this same thing?

HEDDA: Exactly.

MRS. ELVSTED (*anxious*): But there is nothing more, Mrs. Tesman! Really, there isn't!

HEDDA: Oh yes, there is. There is considerably more. I can see that much. Over here — We are going to have a real, nice, confidential talk, you and I. (*She forces* MRS. ELVSTED *down in the easy chair and seats herself on one of the ottomans.*)

MRS. ELVSTED (*worried, looks at her watch*): But my dear Mrs. Tesman — I had really thought I would be on my way now.

HEDDA: Oh I am sure there is no rush. Now, then. Tell me about yourself. How are things at home?

MRS. ELVSTED: That is just what I don't want to talk about.

HEDDA: But to me — ! After all, we are old schoolmates.

MRS. ELVSTED: But you were a year ahead of me. And I used to be so scared of you!

HEDDA: Scared of me?

MRS. ELVSTED: Terribly. For when we met on the stairs, you always ruffled my hair.

HEDDA: Did I really?

MRS. ELVSTED: Yes. And once you said you were going to burn it off.

HEDDA: Oh, but you know — I wasn't serious!

MRS. ELVSTED: No, but I was such a silly, then. Anyway, afterwards we drifted far apart. Our circles are so very different, you know.

HEDDA: All the more reason for getting close again. Listen. In school we called each other by our first names.

MRS. ELVSTED: Oh I'm sure you're wrong —

HEDDA: I'm sure I'm not! I remember it quite clearly. And now we want to be open with one another, just the way we used to. (*Moves the ottoman closer.*) There, now! (*Kisses her cheek.*) You call me Hedda.

MRS. ELVSTED (*seizes her hands*): Oh you are so good and kind! I'm not used to that.

HEDDA: There, there! And I'll call you my dear Thora, just as in the old days.

MRS. ELVSTED: My name is Thea.

HEDDA: So it is. Of course. I meant Thea. (*Looks at her with compassion.*) So you're not much used to goodness and kindness, Thea? Not in your own home?

MRS. ELVSTED: If I even had a home! But I don't. I never have had one.

HEDDA (*looks at her for a moment*): I thought there might be something like this.

MRS. ELVSTED (*helplessly, looking straight ahead*): Yes — yes — yes —

HEDDA: I ˙ am not sure if I quite remember — Didn't you first come to your husband as his housekeeper?

MRS. ELVSTED: I was really hired as governess. But his wife — his first wife — was ailing already then and practically bedridden. So I had to take charge of the household as well.

HEDDA: But in the end you became his wife.

MRS. ELVSTED (*dully*): So I did.

HEDDA: Let's see. How long ago is that?

MRS. ELVSTED: Since my marriage?

HEDDA: Yes.

MRS. ELVSTED: About five years.

HEDDA: Right. It must be that long.

MRS. ELVSTED: Oh, those five years! Or mostly the last two or three! Oh, Mrs. Tesman — if you could just imagine!

HEDDA (*slaps her hand lightly*): Mrs. Tesman? Shame on you!

MRS. ELVSTED: Oh yes; all right, I'll try. Yes — if you could just — conceive — understand —

HEDDA (*casually*): And Eilert Løvborg has been living near you for some three years or so, hasn't he?

MRS. ELVSTED (*looks at her uncertainly*): Eilert Løvborg? Yes — he has.

HEDDA: Did you know him before? Here in town?

MRS. ELVSTED: Hardly at all. That is, of course I did in a way. I mean, I knew *of* him.

HEDDA: But up there — You saw a good deal of him; did you?

MRS. ELVSTED: Yes, he came over to us every day. He was supposed to tutor the children, you see. For I just couldn't do it all by myself.

HEDDA: Of course not. And your husband — ? I suppose he travels quite a bit.

MRS. ELVSTED: Well, yes, Mrs. Tes — Hedda — as a public magistrate, you know, he very often has to travel all over his district.

HEDDA (*leaning against the armrest on the easy chair*): Thea — poor, sweet Thea — now you have to tell me everything — just as it is.

MRS. ELVSTED: You'd better ask me, then.

HEDDA: How *is* your husband, Thea? I mean — you know — *really*? To be with. What kind of person is he? Is he good to you?

MRS. ELVSTED (*evasively*): I believe he thinks he does everything for the best.

HEDDA: But isn't he altogether too old for you? He is more than twenty years older, isn't he?

MRS. ELVSTED (*with irritation*): Yes, there is that, too. But there isn't just one thing. Every single little thing about him repels me! We don't have a thought in common, he and I. Not a thing in the world!

HEDDA: But isn't he fond of you all the same? I mean in his own way?

MRS. ELVSTED: I don't know. I think I am just useful to him. And I don't use much money. I am inexpensive.

HEDDA: That is foolish of you.

MRS. ELVSTED (*shakes her head*): Can't be changed. Not with him. I don't think he cares for anybody much except himself. Perhaps the children a little.

HEDDA: And Eilert Løvborg, Thea.

MRS. ELVSTED (*looks at her*): Eilert Løvborg? What makes you think that?

HEDDA: Well, it seems to me that when he sends you all the way to town to look after him. (*With an almost imperceptible smile.*) Besides, you said so yourself. To Tesman.

MRS. ELVSTED (*with a nervous twitch*): Did I? I suppose I did. (*With a muted outburst.*) No! I might as well tell you now as later. For it's bound to come out, anyway.

HEDDA: But my dear Thea — ?

MRS. ELVSTED: All right. My husband doesn't know I've gone!

HEDDA: What! He doesn't know?

MRS. ELVSTED: He wasn't even home. He's away again. Oh, I just couldn't take it any longer, Hedda! It had become utterly impossible. All alone as I was.

HEDDA: So what did you do?

MRS. ELVSTED: I packed some of my things. Just the most necessary. Without telling anybody. And left.

HEDDA: Just like that?

MRS. ELVSTED: Yes. And took the next train to town.

HEDDA: But dearest Thea — how did you dare to do a thing like that!

MRS. ELVSTED (rises, walks): What else could I do?

HEDDA: But what do you think your husband will say when you go back?

MRS. ELVSTED (by the table; looks at her): Go back to him?

HEDDA: Yes!

MRS. ELVSTED: I'll never go back.

HEDDA (rises, approaches her slowly): So you have really, seriously — left everything?

MRS. ELVSTED: Yes. It seemed to me there was nothing else I could do.

HEDDA: And quite openly, too.

MRS. ELVSTED: You can't keep a thing like that secret, anyway.

HEDDA: But what do you think people will say, Thea?

MRS. ELVSTED: In God's name, let them say whatever they like. (Sits down on the sofa, dully, tired.) For I have only done what I had to do.

HEDDA (after a brief silence): And what do you plan to do with yourself? What sort of work will you do?

MRS. ELVSTED: I don't know yet. I only know I have to live where Eilert Løvborg is. If I am to live at all.

HEDDA (moves a chair from the table closer to MRS. ELVSTED, sits down, strokes her hands): Thea — tell me. How did this — this friendship between you and Eilert — how did it begin?

MRS. ELVSTED: Oh, it grew little by little. I got some sort of power over him.

HEDDA: Oh?

MRS. ELVSTED: He dropped his old ways. Not because I asked him to. I never dared to do that. But I think he must have noticed how I felt about that kind of life. So he changed.

HEDDA (quickly suppresses a cynical smile): So you have — rehabilitated him, as they say. Haven't you, Thea?

MRS. ELVSTED: At least, that's what he says. On the other hand, he has turned me into a real human being. Taught me to think — and understand — all sorts of things.

HEDDA: Maybe he tutored you, too?

MRS. ELVSTED: No, not tutored exactly. But he talked to me. About so many, many things. And then came that lovely, lovely time when I could share his work with him. He let me help him!

HEDDA: He did?

MRS. ELVSTED: Yes! Whatever he wrote, he wanted us to be together about it.

HEDDA: Just like two good comrades.

MRS. ELVSTED (with animation): Comrades! — that's it! Imagine, Hedda — that's just what he called it, too, Oh, I really ought to feel so happy. But I can't. For you see, I don't know if it will last.

HEDDA: You don't trust him any more than that?

MRS. ELVSTED (heavily): The shadow of a woman stands between Eilert Løvborg and me.

HEDDA (tensely, looks at her): Who?

MRS. ELVSTED: I don't know. Somebody or other from — his past. I don't think he has ever really forgotten her.

HEDDA: What has he told you about it?

MRS. ELVSTED: He has mentioned it only once — just casually.

HEDDA: And what did he say?

MRS. ELVSTED: He said that when they parted she was going to kill him with a gun.

HEDDA (cold, controlled): Oh, nonsense. People don't do that sort of thing here.

MRS. ELVSTED: No, I know. And that is why I think it must be that red-headed singer he used to —

HEDDA: Yes, I suppose so.

MRS. ELVSTED: For I remember people said she carried a loaded gun.

HEDDA: Well, then I'm sure it's she.

MRS. ELVSTED (wringing her hands): Yes, but just think, Hedda — now I hear that she — that singer — that she's here in town again, too! Oh, I'm just desperate — !

HEDDA (with a glance toward the inner room): Shhh! Here's Tesman. (Rises and whispers.) Not a word about all this to anybody, Thea!

MRS. ELVSTED (jumps up): No, no. For God's sake — !

(TESMAN, carrying a letter, enters from the right side of the inner room.)

TESMAN: There now — here's the missive, all ready to go!

HEDDA: Good. But I believe Mrs. Elvsted wants to be on her way. Wait a moment. I'll see you to the garden gate.

TESMAN: Say, Hedda — do you think Berte could take care of this?

HEDDA (*takes the letter*): I'll tell her.

(BERTE *enters right.*)

BERTE: Judge Brack is here and wants to know if you're receiving.

HEDDA: Yes, ask the Judge please to come in. And — here — drop this in a mailbox, will you?

BERTE (*takes the letter*): Yes, ma'am.

(*She opens the door for* JUDGE BRACK *and exits. The* JUDGE *is forty-five years of age. Rather thickset, but well-built and with brisk athletic movements. Roundish face, aristocratic profile. His hair is short, still almost completely black, very neatly dressed. Lively, sparkling eyes. Thick eyebrows and mustache with cut-off points. He is dressed in an elegant suit, a trifle youthful for his age. He wears pince-nez glasses, attached to a string, and lets them drop from time to time.*)

JUDGE BRACK (*hat in hand, salutes*): May one pay one's respects as early as this?

HEDDA: One certainly may.

TESMAN (*shaking his hand*): You are always welcome. (*Introducing.*) Judge Brack — Miss Rysing —

(HEDDA *groans.*)

BRACK (*bowing*): Delighted!

HEDDA (*looks at him, laughs*): How nice it is to see you in daylight, Judge!

BRACK: You find me changed, perhaps?

HEDDA: A bit younger, I think.

BRACK: Much obliged.

TESMAN: But what do you think of Hedda? Hm? Did you ever see her in such bloom? She positively —

HEDDA: Will you please leave me out of this? You had better thank the Judge for all the trouble he has taken.

BRACK: Oh, nonsense. It's been a pleasure.

HEDDA: Yes, you are indeed a faithful soul. But my friend here is dying to be off. Don't leave, Judge. I'll be back in a minute.

(*Mutual goodbyes.* MRS. ELVSTED *and* HEDDA *exit, right.*)

BRACK: Well, now — your wife — is she tolerably satisfied?

TESMAN: Yes, indeed, and we really can't thank you enough. That is, I understand there will have to be some slight changes made here and there. And there are still a few things — just a few trifles — we'll have to get.

BRACK: Oh? Really?

TESMAN: But we certainly don't want to bother you with that. Hedda said she's going to take care of it herself. But do sit down, hm?

BRACK: Thanks. Maybe just for a moment — (*Sits down by the table.*) There's one thing I'd like to talk to you about, my dear Tesman.

TESMAN: Oh? Ah, I see! (*Sits down.*) I suppose it's the serious part of the festivities that's beginning now. Hm?

BRACK: Oh — there's no great rush as far as the money is concerned. Though I must say I wish we could have established ourselves a trifle more economically.

TESMAN: Out of the question, my dear fellow! Remember, it's all for Hedda! You, who know her so well — ! After all, I couldn't put her up like any little middle-class housewife —

BRACK: No, I suppose — That's just it.

TESMAN: Besides — fortunately — it can't be long now before I receive my appointment.

BRACK: Well, you know — things like that have a way of hanging fire.

TESMAN: Perhaps you have heard something? Something definite? Hm?

BRACK: No, nothing certain — (*Interrupting himself.*) But that reminds me. I have some news for you.

TESMAN: Oh?

BRACK: Your old friend Eilert Løvborg is back in town.

TESMAN: I know that already.

BRACK: So? Who told you?

TESMAN: The lady who just left.

BRACK: I see. What did you say her name was again? I didn't quite catch —

TESMAN: Mrs. Elvsted.

BRACK: Ah yès — the Commissioner's wife. Yes, it's up in her part of the country that Løvborg has been staying, too.

TESMAN: And just think. I am so glad to hear it. He is quite respectable again.

BRACK: Yes, so they say.

TESMAN: And he has published a new book, hm?

BRACK: Oh yes.

TESMAN: Which is making quite a stir.

BRACK: Quite an unusual stir.

TESMAN: Just think! Isn't that just wonderful! He — with his remarkable gifts. And I was so sure he'd gone under for good.

BRACK: That seems to have been the general opinion.

TESMAN: What I don't understand, though, is what he is going to do with himself. What sort of living can he make? Hm?

(*During the last remark* HEDDA *re-enters, right.*)

HEDDA (*to* BRACK, *with a scornful little laugh*): Tesman is forever worrying about how people are going to make a living.

TESMAN: Well, you see, we are talking about poor Eilert Løvborg, Hedda.

HEDDA (*with a quick look at him*): You are? (*Sits down in the easy chair by the stove and asks casually.*) What is the matter with him?

TESMAN: Well, you see, I believe he's run through his inheritance a long time ago. And I don't suppose he can write a new book every year. Hm? So I really must ask how he is going to make out.

BRACK: Maybe I could help you answer that.

TESMAN: Yes?

BRACK: Remember, he has relatives with considerable influence.

TESMAN: Ah — unfortunately, those relatives have washed their hands of him long ago.

BRACK: Just the same, they used to call him the hope of the family.

TESMAN: Yes, before! But he has ruined all that.

HEDDA: Who knows? (*With a little smile.*) I hear the Elvsteds have rehabilitated him.

BRACK: And then this book —

TESMAN: Well, I certainly hope they will help him to find something or other. I just wrote him a letter. Hedda, dear, I asked him to come out here tonight.

BRACK: Oh dear, I am sorry. Don't you remember — you're supposed to come to my little stag dinner tonight? You accepted last night on the pier, you know.

HEDDA: Had you forgotten, Tesman?

TESMAN: So I had.

BRACK: Oh well. I'm sure he won't come, so it doesn't really make any difference.

TESMAN: Why is that? Hm?

BRACK (*gets up somewhat hesitantly, rests his hands on the back of the chair*): Dear Tesman — and you, too, Mrs. Tesman — I cannot in good conscience let you remain in ignorance of something, which — which —

TESMAN: Something to do with Eilert?

BRACK: With both you and him.

TESMAN: But my dear Judge, do speak!

BRACK: You must be prepared to find that your appointment will not come through as soon as you hope and expect.

TESMAN (*jumps up, nervously*): Something's happened? Hm?

BRACK: It may conceivably be made contingent upon the result of a competition.

TESMAN: Competition! Just think, Hedda!

HEDDA (*leaning farther back in her chair*): Ah — I see, I see — !

TESMAN: But with whom? Don't tell me with — ?

BRACK: Precisely. With Eilert Løvborg.

TESMAN (*claps his hands together*): No, no! This can't be! It is unthinkable! Quite impossible! Hm?

BRACK: All the same, that's the way it may turn out.

TESMAN: No, but Judge, this would amount to the most incredible callousness toward me! (*Waving his arms.*) For just think — I'm a married man! We married on the strength of these prospects, Hedda and I. Got ourselves deep in debt. Borrowed money from Aunt Julle, too. After all, I had practically been promised the post, you know. Hm?

BRACK: Well, well. I daresay you'll get it in the end. If only after a competition.

HEDDA (*motionless in her chair*): Just think, Tesman. It will be like a kind of contest.

TESMAN: But dearest Hedda, how can you be so unconcerned!

HEDDA (*still without moving*): I'm not at all unconcerned. I'm dying to see who wins.

BRACK: In any case, Mrs. Tesman, I'm glad you know the situation as it is. I mean — before you proceed to make the little additional purchases I understand you threaten us with.

HEDDA: This makes no difference as far as that is concerned.

BRACK: Really? Well, in that case, of course — Goodbye! (*To* TESMAN.) I'll pick you up on my afternoon walk.

TESMAN: What? Oh yes, yes, of course. I'm sorry; I'm just all flustered.

HEDDA (*without getting up, gives her hand*): Goodbye, Judge. Come back soon.

BRACK: Thanks. Goodbye, goodbye.

TESMAN (*sees him to the door*): Goodbye, my dear Judge. You really must excuse me —

(JUDGE BRACK *exits, right.*)

TESMAN (*pacing the floor*): Oh, Hedda, Hedda! One should never venture into fairyland. Hm?

HEDDA (*looks at him, smiles*): Do you do that?

TESMAN: Well, yes — it can't be denied — it was most venturesome of me to rush into marriage and set up a home on the strength of mere prospects.

HEDDA: Well, maybe you're right.

TESMAN: Anyway — we do have our own nice, comfortable home, now. Just think, Hedda — the very home both of us dreamed about. Set our hearts on, I may almost say. Hm?

HEDDA (*rises, slowly, tired*): The agreement was that we were to maintain a certain position — entertain —

TESMAN: Don't I know it! Dearest Hedda — I have been so looking forward to seeing you as hostess in a select circle! Hm? Well, well, well! In the meantime, we'll just have to be content with one another. See Aunt Julle once in a while. Nothing more. And you were meant for such a different kind of life, altogether!

HEDDA: I suppose a footman is completely out of the question.

TESMAN: I'm afraid so. Under the circumstances, you see — we couldn't possibly —

HEDDA: And as for getting my own riding horse —

TESMAN (*aghast*): Riding horse!

HEDDA: I suppose I mustn't even think of that.

TESMAN: Good heavens, no! That goes without saying, I hope!

HEDDA (*walking*): Well — at least I have one thing to amuse myself with in the meantime.

TESMAN (*overjoyed*): Oh thank goodness for that! And what *is* that, Hedda, hm?

HEDDA (*in the doorway, looks at him with suppressed scorn*): My guns — Jørgen!

TESMAN (*in fear*): Your guns!

HEDDA (*with cold eyes*): General Gabler's guns. (*She exits left, through the inner room.*)

TESMAN (*runs up to the doorway, calls after her*): But Hedda! Good gracious! Hedda, dear! Please don't touch those dangerous things! For my sake, Hedda! Hm?

ACT II

The same room at the TESMANS'. *The piano has been moved out and replaced by an elegant little writing desk. A small table has been placed near the sofa, left. Most of the flowers have been removed.* MRS. ELVSTED'S *bouquet is on the big table front center. Afternoon.*

HEDDA, *dressed to receive callers, is alone. She is standing near the open French doors, loading a revolver. Its mate is lying in an open case on the desk.*

HEDDA (*looking down into the garden, calls*): Hello there, Judge! Welcome back!

JUDGE BRACK (*off stage*): Thanks, Mrs. Tesman!

HEDDA (*raises the gun, sights*): I am going to shoot you, Judge Brack!

BRACK (*calls off stage*): No — no — no! Don't point the gun at me like that!

HEDDA: That's what you get for sneaking in the back door! (*Fires.*)

BRACK (*closer*): Are you out of your mind — !

HEDDA: Oh dear — did I hit you?

BRACK (*still off stage*): Stop that nonsense!

HEDDA: Come on in, then.

(JUDGE BRACK, *dressed for dinner, enters, left. He carries a light overcoat over his arm.*)

BRACK: Dammit! Do you still fool around with that thing? What are you shooting at, anyway?

HEDDA: Oh — just firing off into blue air.

BRACK (*gently but firmly taking the gun away from her*): With your permission, Mrs. Tesman. (*Looks at it.*) Ah yes, I remember this gun very well. (*Looks around.*) Where is the case? Ah, here we are. (*Puts the gun in the case and closes it.*) That's enough of that silliness for today.

HEDDA: But in the name of heaven, what do you expect me to do with myself?

BRACK: No callers?

HEDDA (*closing the French doors*): Not a soul. All my close friends are still out of town, it seems.

BRACK: And Tesman is out, too, perhaps?

HEDDA (*by the desk, puts the gun case in a drawer*): Yes. He took off for the aunts' right after lunch. He didn't expect you so early.

BRACK: I should have thought of that. That was stupid of me.

HEDDA (*turns her head, looks at him*): Why stupid?

BRACK: I would have come a little — sooner.

HEDDA (*crossing*): If you had, you wouldn't have found anybody home. For I have been in my room ever since lunch, changing my clothes.

BRACK: And isn't there the tiniest little opening in the door for negotiations?

HEDDA: You forgot to provide one.

BRACK: Another stupidity.

HEDDA: So we'll have to stay in here. And wait. For I don't think Tesman will be back for some time.

BRACK: By all means. I'll be very patient.

(HEDDA *sits on the sofa in the corner.* BRACK *puts his overcoat over the back of the nearest chair and sits down, keeping his hat in his hand. Brief silence. They look at one another.*)

HEDDA: Well?

BRACK (*in the same tone*): Well?

HEDDA: I said it first.

BRACK (*leans forward a little*): All right. Let's have a nice little chat, Mrs. Tesman.

HEDDA (*leans back*): Don't you think it's an eternity since last time we talked! I don't count last night and this morning. That was nothing.

BRACK: You mean — just the two of us?

HEDDA: Mmm. If you like.

BRACK: There hasn't been a day I haven't wished you were back again.

HEDDA: My feelings, exactly.

BRACK: Yours? Really, Mrs. Tesman? And I have been assuming you were having such a wonderful time.

HEDDA: I'd say!

BRACK: All Tesman's letters said so.

HEDDA: Oh yes, he! He's happy just poking through old collections of books. And copying old parchments — or whatever they are.

BRACK (*with a touch of malice*): Well, that's his calling, you know. Partly, anyway.

HEDDA: Yes, so it is. And in that case I suppose — But I! Oh, Judge! You've no idea how bored I've been.

BRACK (*with sympathy*): Really? You're serious?

HEDDA: Surely you can understand that? For a whole half year never to see anyone who knows even a little bit about our circle? And talks our language?

BRACK: Yes, I think I would find that trying, too.

HEDDA: And then the most unbearable thing of all —

BRACK: Well?

HEDDA: — everlastingly to be in the company of the same person —

BRACK (*nods in agreement*): Both early and late — yes. I can imagine — at all possible times —

HEDDA: I said everlastingly.

BRACK: All right. Still, it seems to me that with as excellent a person as our Tesman, it ought to be possible —

HEDDA: My dear Judge — Tesman is a specialist.

BRACK: Granted.

HEDDA: And specialists are not at all entertaining travel companions. Not in the long run, at any rate.

BRACK: Not even — the specialist — one happens to love?

HEDDA: Bah! That nauseating word!

BRACK (*puzzled*): Really, now, Mrs. Tesman — ?

HEDDA (*half laughing, half annoyed*): You ought to try it some time! Listening to talk about the history of civilization, early and late —

BRACK: Everlastingly —

HEDDA: All right. And then this business about the domestic industry in the Middle Ages — ! That's the ghastliest part of it all!

BRACK (*looking searchingly at her*): But in that case — tell me — how am I to explain — ?

HEDDA: That Jørgen Tesman and I made a pair of it, you mean?

BRACK: If you want to put it that way — yes.

HEDDA: Come now. Do you really find that so strange?

BRACK: Both yes and no — Mrs. Tesman.

HEDDA: I had danced myself tired, my dear

Judge. My season was over — (*Gives a slight start.*) No, no — I don't really mean that. Won't think it, either!

BRACK: Nor do you have the slightest reason to, I am sure.

HEDDA: Oh — as far as reasons are concerned — (*Looks at him as if trying to read his mind.*) And, after all, Jørgen Tesman must be said to be a most proper young man in all respects.

BRACK: Both proper and substantial. Most certainly.

HEDDA: And one can't say there is anything exactly comical about him. Do you think there is?

BRACK: Comical? No — o. I wouldn't say that —

HEDDA: All right, then. And he is a most assiduous collector. Nobody can deny that. I think it is perfectly possible he may go quite far, after all.

BRACK (*looks at her rather uncertainly*): I assumed that you, like everybody else, thought he'll in time become an exceptionally eminent man?

HEDDA (*with a weary expression*): Yes, I did. And then, you see — there he was, wanting so desperately to be allowed to provide for me — I don't know why I shouldn't have accepted?

BRACK: No, certainly. From that point of view —

HEDDA: For you know, Judge, that was considerably more than my other admirers were willing to do.

BRACK (*laughs*): Well! Of course I can't answer for all the others. But as far as I am concerned, I have always had a certain degree of — respect for the bonds of matrimony. You know — as a general proposition, Mrs. Tesman.

HEDDA (*lightly*): Well, I never really counted very heavily on you —

BRACK: All I want is a nice, confidential circle, in which I can be of service, both in deed and in counsel. Be allowed to come and go like a true and trusted friend —

HEDDA: You mean, of the master of the house — ?

BRACK (*with a slight bow*): To be perfectly frank — rather of the mistress. But by all means — the master, too, of course. Do you know, that kind of — shall I say, triangular? — relationship can really be a great comfort to all parties involved.

HEDDA: Yes, many were the times I missed a second travel companion. To be twosome in the compartment — brrr!

BRACK: Fortunately, the wedding trip is over.

HEDDA (*shakes her head*): There's a long journey ahead. I've just arrived at a station on the way.

BRACK: Well, at the station one gets out and moves around a bit, Mrs. Tesman.

HEDDA: I never get out.

BRACK: Really?

HEDDA: No. For there's always someone around, who —

BRACK (*laughs*): — looks at one's legs; is that it?

HEDDA: Exactly.

BRACK: Oh well, really, now —

HEDDA (*with a silencing gesture*): I won't have it! Rather stay in my seat — once I'm seated. Twosome and all.

BRACK: I see. But what if a third party were to join the couple?

HEDDA: Well, now — *that* would be something altogether different!

BRACK: A proven, understanding friend —

HEDDA: — entertaining in all sorts of lively ways —

BRACK: — and not at all a specialist!

HEDDA (*with audible breath*): Yes, that would indeed be a comfort.

BRACK (*hearing the front door open, looking at her*): The triangle is complete.

HEDDA (*half aloud*): And the train goes on.

(TESMAN, *in gray walking suit and soft hat, enters, right. He carries a pile of paperbound books under his arm. Others are stuffed in his pockets.*)

TESMAN (*as he walks up to the table in front of the corner sofa*): Puuhh — ! Quite some load to carry, all this — and in this heat, too. (*Puts the books down.*) I am positively perspiring, Hedda. Well, well. So you're here already, my dear Judge. Hm? And Berte didn't tell me.

BRACK (*rises*): I came through the garden.

HEDDA: What are all those books?

TESMAN (*leafing through some of them*): Just some new publications in my special field.

HEDDA: Special field, hm?

BRACK: Ah yes — professional publications, Mrs. Tesman.

(BRACK *and* HEDDA *exchange knowing smiles.*)

HEDDA: Do you still need more books?

TESMAN: Yes, my dear. There is no such thing as having too many books in one's special field. One has to keep up with what is being written and published, you know.

HEDDA: I suppose.

TESMAN (*searching among the books*): And look. Here is Eilert Løvborg's new book, too. (*Offers it to her.*) Want to take a look at it, Hedda? Hm?

HEDDA: No — thanks just the same. Or perhaps later.

TESMAN: I glanced at it on my way home.

BRACK: And what do you think of it? As a specialist yourself?

TESMAN: It is remarkable for its sobriety. He never wrote like that before. (*Gathers up all the books.*) I just want to take these into my study. I am so much looking forward to cutting them open! And then I'll change. (*To* BRACK.) I assume there's no rush to be off, is there?

BRACK: Not at all. We have plenty of time.

TESMAN: In that case, I think I'll indulge myself a little. (*On his way out with the books he halts in the doorway and turns.*) By the way, Hedda — Aunt Julle won't be out to see you tonight, after all.

HEDDA: No? Is it that business with the hat, do you think?

TESMAN: Oh, no — not at all. How can you believe a thing like that about Aunt Julle! Just think! No, it's Aunt Rina. She's feeling very poorly.

HEDDA: Isn't she always?

TESMAN: Yes, but it's especially bad today, poor thing.

HEDDA: Well, in that case I suppose she ought to stay home. I shall have to put up with it; that's all.

TESMAN: And you have no idea how perfectly delighted Aunt Julle was, even so. Because of how splendid you look after the trip, Hedda!

HEDDA (*half aloud, rising*): Oh, these everlasting aunts!

TESMAN: Hm?

HEDDA (*walks over to the French doors*): Nothing.

TESMAN: No? All right. Well, excuse me. (*Exits right, through inner room.*)

BRACK: What is this about a hat?

HEDDA: Oh, something with Miss Tesman this morning. She had put her hat down on the chair over there. (*Looks at him, smiles.*) So I pretended to think it was the maid's.

BRACK (*shakes his head*): But my dear Mrs. Tesman — how could you do a thing like that! And to that excellent old lady, too!

HEDDA (*nervously pacing the floor*): Well, you see — something just takes hold of me at times. And then I can't help myself — (*Throws herself down in the easy chair near the stove.*) Oh I can't explain it even to myself.

BRACK (*behind her chair*): You aren't really happy — that's the trouble.

HEDDA (*staring into space*): I don't know any reason why I should be. Do you?

BRACK: Well, yes — partly because you've got the home you've always wanted.

HEDDA (*looks up at him and laughs*): So you too believe that story about my great wish?

BRACK: You mean, there is nothing to it?

HEDDA: Well, yes; there is *something* to it.

BRACK: Well?

HEDDA: There is this much to it, that last summer I used Tesman to see me home from evening parties.

BRACK: Unfortunately — my route was in quite a different direction.

HEDDA: True. You walked on other roads last summer.

BRACK (*laughs*): Shame on you, Mrs. Tesman! So, all right — you and Tesman — ?

HEDDA: One evening we passed by here. And Tesman, poor thing, was practically turning himself into knots trying to find something to talk about. So I felt sorry for all that erudition —

BRACK (*with a doubting smile*): You did? Hm —

HEDDA: I really did. So, just to help him out of his misery, I happened to say that I'd like to live in this house.

BRACK: Just that?

HEDDA: That was all — *that* evening.

BRACK: But afterwards — ?

HEDDA: Yes, my frivolity had consequences, Judge.

BRACK: Unfortunately — that's often the way with frivolities. It happens to all of us, Mrs. Tesman.

HEDDA: Thanks! So in our common enthusiasm for Mr. Secretary Falk's villa Tesman and I found each other, you see! The result was engagement and wedding and honeymoon abroad and all the rest of it. Well, yes, my dear Judge — I've made my bed — I almost said.

BRACK: But this is priceless! And you didn't really care for the house at all?

HEDDA: Certainly not.

BRACK: Not even now? After all, we've set up quite a comfortable home for you here, haven't we?

HEDDA: Oh — it seems to me I smell lavender and rose sachets in all the rooms. But maybe that's a smell Aunt Julle brought with her.

BRACK (*laughs*): My guess is rather the late lamented Secretary's wife.

HEDDA: It smells of mortality, whoever it is. Like corsages — the next day. (*Clasps her hands behind her neck, leans back, looks at him.*) Judge, you have no idea how dreadfully bored I'll be — out here.

BRACK: But don't you think life may hold some task for you, too, Mrs. Tesman?

HEDDA: A task? With any kind of appeal?

BRACK: Preferably that, of course.

HEDDA: Heaven knows what kind of task that might be. There are times when I wonder if — (*Interrupts herself.*) No; I'm sure that wouldn't work, either.

BRACK: Who knows? Tell me.

HEDDA: It has occurred to me that maybe I could get Tesman to enter politics.

BRACK (*laughs*): Tesman! No, really — I must confess that — politics doesn't strike me as being exactly Tesman's line.

HEDDA: I agree. But suppose I were to prevail on him, all the same?

BRACK: What satisfaction could you possibly find in that? If he can't succeed — why do you want him even to try?

HEDDA: Because I am bored, I tell you! (*After a brief pause.*) So you think it's quite out of the question that Tesman could ever become prime minister?

BRACK: Well, you see, Mrs. Tesman — to do that he'd first of all have to be a fairly wealthy man.

HEDDA (*getting up, impatiently*): Yes! There we are! These shabby circumstances I've married into! (*Crosses the floor.*) That's what makes life so mean. So — so — ridiculous! For that's what it is, you know.

BRACK: Personally I believe something else is to blame.

HEDDA: What?

BRACK: You've never been through anything that's really stirred you.

HEDDA: Something serious, you mean?

BRACK: If you like. But maybe it's coming now.

HEDDA (*with a toss of her head*): You are thinking of that silly old professorship! That's Tesman's business. I refuse to give it a thought.

BRACK: As you wish. But now — to put it in the grand style — now when a solemn challenge of responsibility is being posed? Demands made on you? (*Smiles.*) New demands, Mrs. Tesman.

HEDDA (*angry*): Quiet! You'll never see anything of the kind.

BRACK (*cautiously*): We'll talk about this a year from now — on the outside.

HEDDA (*curtly*): I'm not made for that sort of thing, Judge! No demands for me!

BRACK: But surely you, like most women, are made for a duty, which —

HEDDA (*over by the French doors*): Oh, do be quiet! Often it seems to me there's only one thing in the world that I am made for.

BRACK (*coming close*): And may I ask what that is?

HEDDA (*looking out*): To be bored to death. Now you know. (*Turns, looks toward the inner room, laughs.*) Just as I thought. Here comes the professor.

BRACK (*warningly, in a low voice*): Steady, now, Mrs. Tesman!

(TESMAN, *dressed for a party, carrying his hat and gloves, enters from the right side of the inner room.*)

TESMAN: Hedda, any word yet from Eilert Løvborg that he isn't coming, hm?

HEDDA: No.

TESMAN: In that case, I wouldn't be a bit surprised if we have him here in a few minutes.

BRACK: You really think he'll come?

TESMAN: I am almost certain he will. For I'm sure it's only idle gossip that you told me this morning.

BRACK: Oh?

TESMAN: Anyway, that's what Aunt Julle said. She doesn't for a moment believe he'll stand in my way. Just think!

BRACK: I'm very glad to hear that.

TESMAN (*puts his hat and his gloves down*

on a chair, right): But you must let me wait for him as long as possible.

BRACK: By all means. We have plenty of time. Nobody will arrive at my place before seven — seven-thirty, or so.

TESMAN: And in the meantime we can keep Hedda company. Take our time. Hm?

HEDDA (*carrying* BRACK's *hat and coat over to the sofa in the corner*): And if worst comes to worst, Mr. Løvborg can stay here with me.

BRACK (*trying to take the things away from her*): Let me, Mrs. Tesman — What do you mean — "if worst comes to worst"?

HEDDA: If he doesn't want to go with you and Tesman.

TESMAN (*looks dubiously at her*): But, dearest Hedda — do you think that will quite do? He staying here with you? Hm? Remember, Aunt Julle won't be here.

HEDDA: No, but Mrs. Elvsted will. The three of us will have a cup of tea together.

TESMAN: Oh yes; *that* will be perfectly all right!

BRACK (*with a smile*): And perhaps the wiser course of action for him.

HEDDA: What do you mean?

BRACK: Begging your pardon, Mrs. Tesman — you've often enough looked askance at my little stag dinners. It's been your opinion that only men of the firmest principles ought to attend.

HEDDA: I should think Mr. Løvborg is firm-principled enough now. A reformed sinner —

(BERTE *appears in door, right.*)

BERTE: Ma'am — there's a gentleman here who asks if —

HEDDA: Show him in, please.

TESMAN (*softly*): I'm sure it's he! Just think!

(EILERT LØVBORG *enters, right. He is slim, gaunt. Of* TESMAN's *age, but he looks older and somewhat dissipated. Brown hair and beard. Pale, longish face, reddish spots on the cheekbones. Dressed for visiting in elegant, black, brand-new suit. He carries a silk hat and dark gloves in his hand. He remains near the door, makes a quick bow. He appears a little embarrassed.*)

TESMAN (*goes over to him, shakes his hand*): My dear Eilert — at last we meet again!

EILERT LØVBORG (*subdued voice*): Thanks

for your note, Jørgen! (*Approaching* HEDDA.) Am I allowed to shake your hand, too, Mrs. Tesman?

HEDDA (*accepting his proffered hand*): I am very glad to see you, Mr. Løvborg. (*With a gesture.*) I don't know if you two gentlemen —

LØVBORG (*with a slight bow*): Judge Brack, I believe.

BRACK (*also bowing lightly*): Certainly. Some years ago —

TESMAN (*to* LØVBORG, *both hands on his shoulders*): And now I want you to feel quite at home here, Eilert! Isn't that right, Hedda? For you plan to stay here in town, I understand. Hm?

LØVBORG: Yes, I do.

TESMAN: Perfectly reasonable. Listen — I just got hold of your new book, but I haven't had a chance to read it yet.

LØVBORG: You may save yourself the trouble.

TESMAN: Why do you say that?

LØVBORG: There's not much to it.

TESMAN: Just think — you saying that!

BRACK: Nevertheless, people seem to have very good things to say about it.

LØVBORG: That's exactly why I wrote it — so everybody would like it.

BRACK: Very wise of you.

TESMAN: Yes, but Eilert — !

LØVBORG: For I am trying to rebuild my position. Start all over again.

TESMAN (*with some embarrassment*): Yes, I suppose you are, aren't you? Hm?

LØVBORG (*smiles, puts his hat down, pulls a parcel out of his pocket*): When *this* appears — Jørgen Tesman — this you must read. For this is the real thing. This is me.

TESMAN: Oh really? And what is it?

LØVBORG: The continuation.

TESMAN: Continuation? Of what?

LØVBORG: Of the book.

TESMAN: Of the new book?

LØVBORG: Of course.

TESMAN: But Eilert — you've carried the story all the way up to the present!

LØVBORG: So I have. And this is about the future.

TESMAN: The future! But, heavens — we don't know a thing about the future!

LØVBORG: No, we don't. But there are a couple of things to be said about it all the same. (*Unwraps the parcel.*) Here, let me show you —

TESMAN: But that's not your handwriting.

LØVBORG: I have dictated it. (*Leafs through portions of the manuscript.*) It's in two parts. The first is about the forces that will shape the civilization of the future. And the second (*riffling through more pages*) — about the course which that future civilization will take.

TESMAN: How remarkable! It would never occur to me to write anything like that.

HEDDA (*over by the French doors, her fingers drumming the pane*): Hmm — I dare say —

LØVBORG (*replacing the manuscript in its wrappings and putting it down on the table*): I brought it along, for I thought maybe I'd read parts of it aloud to you this evening.

TESMAN: That's very good of you, Eilert. But this evening — ? (*Looks at* BRACK.) I'm not quite sure how to arrange that —

LØVBORG: Some other time, then. There's no hurry.

BRACK: You see, Mr. Løvborg, there's a little get-together over at my house tonight. Mainly for Tesman, you know —

LØVBORG (*looking for his hat*): In that case, I certainly won't —

BRACK: No, listen. Won't you do me the pleasure to join us?

LØVBORG (*firmly*): No, I won't. But thanks all the same.

BRACK: Oh come on! Why don't you do that? We'll be a small, select circle. And I think I can promise you a fairly lively evening, as Hed — as Mrs. Tesman would say.

LØVBORG: I don't doubt that. Nevertheless —

BRACK: And you may bring your manuscript along and read aloud to Tesman over at my house. I have plenty of room.

TESMAN: Just think, Eilert! Wouldn't that be nice, hm?

HEDDA (*intervening*): But can't you see that Mr. Løvborg doesn't want to? I'm sure he would rather stay here and have supper with me.

LØVBORG (*looks at her*): With you, Mrs. Tesman?

HEDDA: And with Mrs. Elvsted.

LØVBORG: Ah — ! (*Casually.*) I ran into her at noon today.

HEDDA: Oh? Well, she'll be here tonight. So you see your presence is really required, Mr. Løvborg. Otherwise she won't have anybody to see her home.

LØVBORG: True. All right, then, Mrs. Tesman — I'll stay, thank you.

HEDDA: Good. I'll just tell the maid. (*She rings for* BERTE *over by the door, right.*)

(BERTE *appears just off stage.* HEDDA *talks with her in a low voice, points toward the inner room.* BERTE *nods and exits.*)

TESMAN (*while* HEDDA *and* BERTE *are talking, to* LØVBORG): Tell me, Eilert — is it this new subject — about the future — is that what you plan to lecture on?

LØVBORG: Yes.

TESMAN: For the bookseller told me you have announced a lecture series for this fall.

LØVBORG: Yes, I have. I hope you won't mind too much.

TESMAN: Of course not! But —

LØVBORG: For of course I realize it is rather awkward for you.

TESMAN (*unhappily*): Oh well — I certainly can't expect — that just for my sake —

LØVBORG: But I will wait till you receive your appointment.

TESMAN: Wait? But — but — but — you mean you aren't going to compete with me? Hm?

LØVBORG: No. Just triumph over you. In people's opinion.

TESMAN: Oh, for goodness' sake! Then Aunt Julle was right, after all! I knew it all the time. Hedda! Do you hear that! Just think — Eilert Løvborg isn't going to stand in our way after all.

HEDDA (*tersely*): Our? I have nothing to do with this.

(HEDDA *walks into the inner room, where* BERTE *is bringing in a tray with decanters and glasses.* HEDDA *nods her approval and comes forward again.*)

TESMAN (*during the foregoing business*): How about that, Judge? What do you say to this? Hm?

BRACK: I say that moral victory and all that — hm — may be glorious enough and beautiful enough —

TESMAN: Oh, I agree. All the same —

HEDDA (*looks at* TESMAN *with a cold smile*): You look thunderstruck.

TESMAN: Well, I am — pretty much — I really believe —

BRACK: After all, Mrs. Tesman, that was quite a thunderstorm that just passed over.

HEDDA (*points to the inner room*): How about a glass of cold punch, gentlemen?

BRACK (*looks at his watch*): A stirrup cup. Not a bad idea.

TESMAN: Splendid, Hedda. Perfectly splendid. In such a lighthearted mood as I am now —

HEDDA: Please. You, too, Mr. Løvborg.

LØVBORG (*with a gesture of refusal*): No, thanks. Really. Nothing for me.

BRACK: Good heavens, man! Cold punch isn't poison, you know!

LØVBORG: Perhaps not for everybody.

HEDDA: I'll keep Mr. Løvborg company in the meantime.

TESMAN: All right, Hedda. You do that.

(*He and* BRACK *go into the inner room, sit down, drink punch, smoke cigarettes, and engage in lively conversation during the next scene.* EILERT LØVBORG *remains standing near the stove.* HEDDA *walks over to the desk.*)

HEDDA (*her voice a little louder than usual*): I'll show you some pictures, if you like. You see — Tesman and I, we took a trip through Tyrol on our way back.

(*She brings an album over to the table by the sofa. She sits down in the far corner of the sofa.* LØVBORG *approaches, stops, looks at her. He takes a chair and sits down at her left, his back toward the inner room.*)

HEDDA (*opens the album*): Do you see these mountains, Mr. Løvborg? They are the Ortler group. Tesman has written their name below. Here it is: "The Ortler group near Meran."

LØVBORG (*has looked steadily at her all this time. Says slowly*): Hedda — Gabler!

HEDDA (*with a quick glance sideways*): Not that! Shhh!

LØVBORG (*again*): Hedda Gabler!

HEDDA (*looking at the album*): Yes, that used to be my name. When— when we two knew each other.

LØVBORG: And so from now on — for the whole rest of my life — I must get used to never again saying Hedda Gabler.

HEDDA (*still occupied with the album*): Yes, you must. And you might as well start right now. The sooner the better, I think.

LØVBORG (*with indignation*): Hedda Gabler married? And married to — Jørgen Tesman!

HEDDA: Yes — that's the way it goes.

LØVBORG: Oh, Hedda, Hedda — how could you throw yourself away like that!

HEDDA (*with a fierce glance at him*): What's this? I won't have any of that!

LØVBORG: What do you mean?

(TESMAN *enters from the inner room.*)

HEDDA (*hears him coming and remarks casually*): And this here, Mr. Løvborg, this is from somewhere in the Ampezzo valley. Just look at those peaks over there. (*With a kindly look at* TESMAN.) What did you say those peaks were called, dear?

TESMAN: Let me see. Oh, they — they are the Dolomites.

HEDDA: Right. Those are the Dolomites, Mr. Løvborg.

TESMAN: Hedda, I thought I'd just ask you if you don't want me to bring you some punch, after all? For you, anyway? Hm?

HEDDA: Well, yes; thanks. And a couple of cookies, maybe.

TESMAN: No cigarettes?

HEDDA: No.

TESMAN: All right.

(*He returns to the inner room, then turns right.* BRACK *is in there, keeping an eye on* HEDDA *and* LØVBORG *from time to time.*)

LØVBORG (*still in a low voice*): Answer me, Hedda. How could you do a thing like that?

HEDDA (*apparently engrossed in the album*): If you keep on using my first name I won't talk to you.

LØVBORG: Not even when we're alone?

HEDDA: No. You may think it, but you must not say it.

LØVBORG: I see. It offends your love for — Jørgen Tesman.

HEDDA (*glances at him, smiles*): Love? That's a good one!

LØVBORG: Not love, then.

HEDDA: But no infidelities, either! I won't have it.

LØVBORG: Hedda — answer me just one thing —

HEDDA: Shhh!

(TESMAN *enters with a tray from the inner room.*)

TESMAN: Here! Here are the goodies. (*Puts the tray down.*)

HEDDA: Why don't you get Berte to do it?

TESMAN (*pouring punch*): Because I think it's so much fun waiting on you, Hedda.

HEDDA: But you've filled both glasses. And Mr. Løvborg didn't want any —

TESMAN: I know, but Mrs. Elvsted will soon be here, won't she?

HEDDA: That's right. So she will.

TESMAN: Had you forgotten about her? Hm?

HEDDA: We've been so busy looking at this. (*Shows him a picture.*) Remember that little village?

TESMAN: That's the one just below the Brenner Pass, isn't it? We spent the night there —

HEDDA: — and ran into that lively crowd of summer guests.

TESMAN: Right! Just think — if we only could have had you with us, Eilert! Oh well.

(*Returns to the inner room, sits down, and resumes his conversation with* BRACK.)

LØVBORG: Just tell me this, Hedda —

HEDDA: What?

LØVBORG: Wasn't there love in your feelings for me, either? Not a touch — not a shimmer of love? Wasn't there?

HEDDA: I wonder. To me, we seemed to be simply two good comrades. Two close friends. (*Smiles.*) You, particularly, were very frank.

LØVBORG: You wanted it that way.

HEDDA: And yet — when I look back upon it now, there was something beautiful, something thrilling, something brave, I think, about the secret frankness — that comradeship that not a single soul so much as suspected.

LØVBORG: Yes, wasn't there, Hedda? Wasn't there? When I called on your father in the afternoons — And the General sat by the window with his newspapers — his back turned —

HEDDA: And we two in the sofa in the corner —

LØVBORG: — always with the same illustrated magazine —

HEDDA: — for want of an album, yes —

LØVBORG: Yes, Hedda — and then when I confessed to you — ! Told you all about myself, things the others didn't know. Sat and told you about my orgies by day and night. Dissipation day in and day out! Oh, Hedda — what sort of power in you was it that forced me to tell you things like that?

HEDDA: You think there was some power in me?

LØVBORG: How else can I explain it? And all those veiled questions you asked —

HEDDA: — which you understood so perfectly well —

LØVBORG: That you could ask such questions! With such complete frankness!

HEDDA: *Veiled*, if you please.

LØVBORG: But frankly all the same. All about — that!

HEDDA: And to think that you answered, Mr. Løvborg!

LØVBORG: Yes, that's just what I can't understand — now, afterwards. But tell me, Hedda; wasn't love at the bottom of our whole relationship? Didn't you feel some kind of urge to — purify me — when I came to you in confession? Wasn't that it?

HEDDA: No, not quite.

LØVBORG: Then what made you do it?

HEDDA: Do you find it so very strange that a young girl — when she can do so, without anyone knowing —

LØVBORG: Yes — ?

HEDDA: — that she wants to take a peek into a world which —

LØVBORG: — which — ?

HEDDA: — she is not supposed to know anything about?

LØVBORG: So that was it!

HEDDA: That, too. That, too — I think —

LØVBORG: Companionship in the lust for life. But why couldn't *that* at least have continued?

HEDDA: That was your own fault.

LØVBORG: You were the one who broke off.

HEDDA: Yes, when reality threatened to enter our relationship. Shame on you, Eilert Løvborg! How could you want to do a thing like that to your frank and trusting comrade!

LØVBORG (*clenching his hands*): Oh, why didn't you do it! Why didn't you shoot me down, as you said you would!

HEDDA: Because I'm scared of scandal.

LØVBORG: Yes, Hedda. You are really a coward.

HEDDA: A terrible coward. (*Changing her tone.*) But that was your good luck, wasn't it? And now the Elvsteds have healed your broken heart very nicely.

LØVBORG: I know what Thea has told you.

HEDDA: Perhaps you have told her about us?

LØVBORG: Not a word. She is too stupid to understand.

HEDDA: Stupid?

LØVBORG: In things like that.

HEDDA: And I'm a coward. (*Leans forward, without looking in his eyes, whispers.*) But now I am going to confess something to you.

LØVBORG (*tense*): What?

HEDDA: That I didn't dare to shoot —

LØVBORG: Yes — ?

HEDDA: — that was not the worst of my cowardice that night.

LØVBORG (*looks at her a moment, understands, whispers passionately*): Oh, Hedda! Hedda Gabler! Now I begin to see what was behind the companionship! You and I! So it *was* your lust for life — !

HEDDA (*in a low voice, with an angry glance*): Take care! Don't you believe it!

(*Darkness is falling. The door, right, is opened, and* BERTE *enters.*)

HEDDA (*closing the album, calls out, smiling*): At last! So there you are, dearest Thea! Come in!

(MRS. ELVSTED *enters. She is dressed for a party.* BERTE *exits, closing the door behind her.*)

HEDDA (*on the sofa, reaching out for* MRS. ELVSTED): Sweetest Thea, you have no idea how I've waited for you.

(*In passing,* MRS. ELVSTED *exchanges quick greetings with* TESMAN *and* BRACK *in the inner room. She walks up to the table and shakes* HEDDA's *hand.* EILERT LØVBORG *rises. He and* MRS. ELVSTED *greet one another with a silent nod.*)

MRS. ELVSTED: Shouldn't I go in and say hello to your husband?

HEDDA: No, never mind that. Leave them alone. They're soon leaving, anyway.

MRS. ELVSTED: Leaving?

HEDDA: They're going out to drink.

MRS. ELVSTED (*quickly, to* LØVBORG): Not you?

LØVBORG: No.

HEDDA: Mr. Løvborg stays here with us.

MRS. ELVSTED (*pulls up a chair, is about to sit down next to* LØVBORG): Oh, how wonderful it is to be here!

HEDDA: Oh no, little Thea. Not that. Not there. Over here by me, please. *I* want to be in the middle.

MRS. ELVSTED: Just as you like. (*She walks in front of the table and seats herself on the sofa, on* HEDDA's *right.* LØVBORG *sits down again on his chair.*)

LØVBORG (*after a brief pause, to* HEDDA): Isn't she lovely to look at?

HEDDA (*gently stroking her hair*): Just to look at?

LØVBORG: Yes. For you see — she and I — we are real comrades. We have absolute faith in one another. And we can talk together in full freedom.

HEDDA: Unveiled, Mr. Løvborg?

LØVBORG: Well —

MRS. ELVSTED (*in a low voice, clinging to* HEDDA): Oh, I am so happy, Hedda! For just think — he also says I have inspired him!

HEDDA (*looks at her with a smile*): No, really! He says that?

LØVBORG: And she has such courage, Mrs. Tesman! Such courage of action.

MRS. ELVSTED: Oh, my God — courage — ! I!

LØVBORG: Infinite courage — when it concerns the comrade.

HEDDA: Yes, courage — if one only had that.

LØVBORG: What then?

HEDDA: Then maybe life would be tolerable, after all. (*Changing her tone.*) But now, dearest Thea, you want a glass of nice, cold punch.

MRS. ELVSTED: No, thanks. I never drink things like that.

HEDDA: Then what about you, Mr. Løvborg?

LØVBORG: Thanks. Nothing for me, either.

MRS. ELVSTED: No, nothing for him, either.

HEDDA (*looks firmly at him*): If I say so?

LØVBORG: Makes no difference.

HEDDA (*laughs*): Oh dear! So I have no power over you at all. Is that it?

LØVBORG: Not in that respect.

HEDDA: Seriously, though; I really think you should. For your own sake.

MRS. ELVSTED: No, but Hedda — !

LØVBORG: Why so?

HEDDA: Or rather for people's sake.

LØVBORG: Oh?

HEDDA: For else they might think you don't really trust yourself — That you lack self-confidence —

MRS. ELVSTED (*softly*): Don't, Hedda!

LØVBORG: People may think whatever they like for all I care — for the time being.

MRS. ELVSTED (*happy*): Exactly!

HEDDA: I could easily tell from watching Judge Brack just now.

LØVBORG: Tell what?

HEDDA: He smiled so contemptuously when you didn't dare to join them in there.

LØVBORG: Didn't I dare to! It's just that I'd much rather stay here and talk with you!

MRS. ELVSTED: But that's only natural, Hedda.

HEDDA: The Judge had no way of knowing that. And I also noticed he smiled and looked at Tesman when you didn't dare to go to his silly old party.

LØVBORG: Didn't dare! Are you saying I didn't dare?

HEDDA: *I* am not. But that's how Judge Brack understood it.

LØVBORG: Let him.

HEDDA: So you're not going?

LØVBORG: I'm staying here with you and Thea.

MRS. ELVSTED: Of course, he is, Hedda!

HEDDA (*smiles, nods approvingly*): That's what I call firm foundations. Principled forever; that's the way a man ought to be! (*Turning to* MRS. ELVSTED, *stroking her cheek.*) What did I tell you this morning — when you came here, quite beside yourself — ?

LØVBORG (*puzzled*): Beside herself?

MRS. ELVSTED (*in terror*): Hedda — Hedda — don't!

HEDDA: Now do you see? There was no need at all for that mortal fear of yours — (*Interrupting herself.*) There, now! Now we can all three relax and enjoy ourselves.

LØVBORG (*startled*): What's all this, Mrs. Tesman?

MRS. ELVSTED: Oh, God, Hedda — what are you saying? What are you doing?

HEDDA: Please be quiet. That horrible Judge is looking at you.

LØVBORG: In mortal fear? So that's it. For my sake.

MRS. ELVSTED (*softly, wailing*): Oh, Hedda — if you only knew how utterly miserable you have made me!

LØVBORG (*stares at her for a moment. His face is distorted*): So that was the comrade's happy confidence in me!

MRS. ELVSTED: Oh, my dearest friend — listen to me first — !

LØVBORG (*picks up one of the glasses of punch, raises it, says hoarsely*): Here's to you, Thea! (*Empties the glass, puts it down, picks up the other one.*)

MRS. ELVSTED (*softly*): Hedda, Hedda — why did you want to do this?

HEDDA: Want to! I! Are you mad?

LØVBORG: And here's to you, too, Mrs. Tesman! Thanks for telling me the truth. Long live the truth! (*He drains the glass and is about to fill it again.*)

HEDDA (*restrains him*): That's enough for now. Remember you are going to a party.

MRS. ELVSTED: No, no, no!

HEDDA: Shhh! They are looking at you.

LØVBORG (*puts his glass down*): Listen, Thea — tell me the truth —

MRS. ELVSTED: I will, I will!

LØVBORG: Did your husband know you were coming after me?

MRS. ELVSTED (*wringing her hands*): Oh, Hedda — do you hear what he's asking?

LØVBORG: Did the two of you agree that you were to come here and look after me? Maybe it was his idea, even? Did he send you? Ah, I know what it was — he missed me in the office, didn't he? Or was it at the card table?

MRS. ELVSTED (*softly, in agony*): Oh, Løvborg, Løvborg!

LØVBORG (*grabs a glass and is about to fill it*): Here's to the old Commissioner, too!

HEDDA (*stops him*): No more now. You're supposed to read aloud for Tesman tonight — remember?

LØVBORG (*calm again, puts the glass down*): This was silly of me, Thea. I'm sorry. Taking it this way. Please, don't be angry with me. You'll see — both you and all those others — that even if I have been down — ! With your help, Thea — dear comrade.

MRS. ELVSTED (*beaming*): Oh, thank God — !

(*In the meantime,* BRACK *has looked at his watch. He and* TESMAN *get up and come forward.*)

BRACK (*picking up his coat and hat*): Well, Mrs. Tesman; our time is up.

HEDDA: I suppose it is.

LØVBORG (*rising*): Mine, too, Judge.

MRS. ELVSTED (*softly, pleadingly*): Oh, Løvborg — don't do it!

HEDDA (*pinches her arm*): They can hear you!

MRS. ELVSTED (*with a soft exclamation*): Ouch!

LØVBORG (*to* BRACK): You were good enough to ask me —

BRACK: So you're coming, after all?

LØVBORG: If I may.

BRACK: I'm delighted.

LØVBORG (*picks up his manuscript and says*

to TESMAN): For there are a couple of things here I'd like to show you before I send it off.

TESMAN: Just think! Isn't that nice! But — dearest Hedda — ? In that case, how are you going to get Mrs. Elvsted home? Hm?

HEDDA: We'll manage somehow.

LØVBORG (*looking at the two women*): Mrs. Elvsted? I'll be back to pick her up, of course. (*Coming closer.*) About ten o'clock, Mrs. Tesman? Is that convenient?

HEDDA: Certainly. That will be fine.

TESMAN: Then everything is nice and settled. But don't expect me that early, Hedda.

HEDDA: You just stay as long as — as long as you want to, dear.

MRS. ELVSTED (*in secret fear*): I'll be waiting for you here, then, Mr. Løvborg.

LØVBORG (*hat in hand*): Of course, Mrs. Elvsted.

BRACK: All aboard the pleasure train, gentlemen! I hope we'll have a lively evening — as a certain fair lady would say.

HEDDA: Ah — if only the fair lady could be present. Invisibly.

BRACK: Why invisibly?

HEDDA: To listen to some of your unadulterated liveliness, Judge.

BRACK (*laughs*): I shouldn't advise the fair lady to do that!

TESMAN (*also laughing*): You're a good one, Hedda! Just think!

BRACK: Well — good night, ladies!

LØVBORG (*with a bow*): Till about ten, then.

(BRACK, LØVBORG, *and* TESMAN *go out, right. At the same time* BERTE *enters from the inner room with a lighted lamp, which she places on the table, front center. She goes out the same way.*)

MRS. ELVSTED (*has risen and paces restlessly up and down*): Hedda, Hedda — how do you think all this will end?

HEDDA: At ten o'clock he'll be here. I see him already. With vine leaves in his hair. Flushed and confident.

MRS. ELVSTED: I only hope you're right.

HEDDA: For then, you see, he'll have mastered himself. And be a free man for all the days of his life.

MRS. ELVSTED: Dear God — how I hope you are right! That he'll come back like that.

HEDDA: That is the way he will come. No other way. (*She rises and goes closer to* MRS. ELVSTED.) You may doubt as long as you like. I believe in him. And now we'll see —

MRS. ELVSTED: There is something behind all this, Hedda. Some hidden purpose.

HEDDA: Yes, there is! For once in my life I want to have power over a human destiny.

MRS. ELVSTED: But don't you already?

HEDDA: I don't and I never have.

MRS. ELVSTED: But your husband — ?

HEDDA: You think that's worth the trouble? Oh, if you knew how poor I am! And you got to be so rich! (*Embraces her passionately.*) I think I'll have to burn your hair off, after all!

MRS. ELVSTED: Let me go! Let me go! You scare me, Hedda!

BERTE (*in the doorway*): Supper is served, ma'am.

HEDDA: Good. We're coming.

MRS. ELVSTED: No, no, no! I'd rather go home by myself! Right now!

HEDDA: Nonsense! You'll have your cup of tea first, you little silly. And then — at ten o'clock — Eilert Løvborg comes — with vine leaves in his hair! (*She almost pulls* MRS. ELVSTED *toward the doorway.*)

ACT III

The same room at the TESMANS'. *The doorway and the French windows both have their portieres closed. The lamp, turned half down, is still on the table. The stove is open. Some dying embers can be seen.* MRS. ELVSTED, *wrapped in a big shawl, is in the easy chair near the stove, her feet on a footstool.* HEDDA, *also dressed, is lying on the sofa, covered by a blanket.*

MRS. ELVSTED (*after a while suddenly sits up, listens anxiously; then she wearily sinks back in her chair, whimpers softly*): Oh my God, my God — not yet!

(BERTE *enters cautiously, right, carrying a letter.*)

MRS. ELVSTED (*turns and whispers tensely*): Well — has anybody been here?

BERTE (*in a low voice*): Yes. Just now there was a girl with this letter.

MRS. ELVSTED (*quickly, reaches for it*): A letter! Give it to me.

BERTE: No, ma'am. It's for the Doctor.

MRS. ELVSTED: I see.

BERTE: Miss Tesman's maid brought it. I'll leave it here on the table.

MRS. ELVSTED: All right.

BERTE (*puts the letter down*): I'd better put out the lamp. It just reeks.

MRS. ELVSTED: Yes, do that. It must be daylight soon, anyway.

BERTE (*putting out the lamp*): It's light already, ma'am.

MRS. ELVSTED: Light already! And still not back!

BERTE: No, so help us. Not that I didn't expect as much —

MRS. ELVSTED: You did?

BERTE: Yes, when I saw a certain character was back in town. Taking them off with him. We sure heard enough about him in the old days!

MRS. ELVSTED: Not so loud. You are waking up Mrs. Tesman.

BERTE (*looks toward the sofa, sighs*): God forbid — ! Let her sleep, poor thing. Do you want me to get the fire going again?

MRS. ELVSTED: Not on my account, thank you.

BERTE: All right. (*Exits quietly, right.*)

HEDDA (*awakened by the closing door*): What's that?

MRS. ELVSTED: Just the maid.

HEDDA (*looks around*): Why in here — ? Oh, I remember! (*Sits up, rubs her eyes, stretches.*) What time is it, Thea?

MRS. ELVSTED (*looks at her watch*): Past seven.

HEDDA: When did Tesman get home?

MRS. ELVSTED: He didn't.

HEDDA: Not home yet!

MRS. ELVSTED (*getting up*): Nobody's come.

HEDDA: And we waited till four!

MRS. ELVSTED (*wringing her hands*): And how we waited!

HEDDA (*her hand covering a yawn*): We — ll. We could have saved ourselves that trouble.

MRS. ELVSTED: Did you get any sleep at all?

HEDDA: Yes, I slept pretty well, I think. Didn't you?

MRS. ELVSTED: Not a wink. I just couldn't, Hedda! It was just impossible.

HEDDA (*rises, walks over to her*): Well, now! There's nothing to worry about, for heaven's sake. I know exactly what's happened.

MRS. ELVSTED: Then tell me please. Where do you think they are?

HEDDA: Well, first of all, I'm sure they were terribly late leaving the Judge's —

MRS. ELVSTED: Dear, yes. I'm sure you're right. Still —

HEDDA: — and so Tesman didn't want to wake us up in the middle of the night. (*Laughs.*) Maybe he didn't want us to see him, either — after a party like that.

MRS. ELVSTED: But where do you think he has gone?

HEDDA: To the aunts', of course. His old room is still there, all ready for him.

MRS. ELVSTED: No, he can't be there. Just a few minutes ago there came a letter for him from Miss Tesman. It's over there.

HEDDA: Oh? (*Looks at the envelope.*) So it is — Auntie Julle herself. In that case, I suppose he's still at Brack's. And there's Eilert Løvborg, too — reading aloud, with vine leaves in his hair.

MRS. ELVSTED: Oh Hedda — you're only saying things you don't believe yourself.

HEDDA: My, what a little imbecile you really are, Thea!

MRS. ELVSTED: Yes, I suppose I am.

HEDDA: And you look dead tired, too.

MRS. ELVSTED: I *am* dead tired.

HEDDA: Why don't you do as I say. Go into my room and lie down.

MRS. ELVSTED: No, no — I wouldn't be able to go to sleep, anyway.

HEDDA: Of course, you would.

MRS. ELVSTED: And your husband is bound to be home any minute now. And I have to know right away.

HEDDA: I'll let you know as soon as he gets here.

MRS. ELVSTED: You promise me that, Hedda?

HEDDA: I do. You just go to sleep.

MRS. ELVSTED: Thanks. At least I'll try. (*Exits through inner room.*)

(HEDDA *goes to the French doors, opens the portieres. The room is now in full daylight. She picks up a little hand mirror from the desk, looks at herself, smooths her hair. Walks over to door, right, rings the bell for the maid.* BERTE *presently appears.*)

BERTE: You want something, ma'am?

HEDDA: Yes. You'll have to start the fire again. I'm cold.

BERTE: Yes, ma'am! I'll get it warm in no time. (*Rakes the embers together and puts in another piece of wood. Then she suddenly listens.*) There's the doorbell, ma'am.

HEDDA: All right. See who it is. I'll take care of the stove myself.

BERTE: You'll have a nice blaze going in a minute. (*Exits right.*)

(HEDDA *kneels on the footstool and puts in more pieces of wood. Presently* TESMAN *enters, right. He looks tired and somber. He tiptoes toward the doorway and is about to disappear between the portieres.*)

HEDDA (*by the stove, without looking up*): Good morning.

TESMAN (*turning*): Hedda! (*Comes closer.*) For heaven's sake — you up already! Hm?

HEDDA: Yes, I got up very early this morning.

TESMAN: And I was sure you'd still be sound asleep! Just think!

HEDDA: Not so loud. Mrs. Elvsted is asleep in my room.

TESMAN: Mrs. Elvsted stayed here all night?

HEDDA: Yes. Nobody came for her, you know.

TESMAN: No, I suppose —

HEDDA (*closes the stove, rises*): Well, did you have a good time at the Judge's?

TESMAN: Were you worried about me? Hm?

HEDDA: I'd never dream of worrying about you. I asked if you had a good time.

TESMAN: Yes, indeed. Nice for a change anyway. But I think I liked it best early in the evening. For then Eilert read to me. Just think — we were more than an hour early! And Brack, of course, had things to see to. So Eilert read.

HEDDA (*sits down at the right side of the table*): So? Tell me all about it.

TESMAN (*sits down on an ottoman near the stove*): Oh Hedda, you'll never believe what a book that will be! It must be just the most remarkable thing ever written! Just think!

HEDDA: Yes, but I don't really care about that —

TESMAN: I must tell you, Hedda — I have a confession to make. As he was reading — something ugly came over me —

HEDDA: Ugly?

TESMAN: I sat there envying Eilert for being able to write like that! Just think, Hedda!

HEDDA: All right. I'm thinking!

TESMAN: And yet, with all his gifts — he's incorrigible, after all.

HEDDA: I suppose you mean he has more courage for life than the rest of you?

TESMAN: No, no — I don't mean that. I mean that he's incapable of exercising moderation in his pleasures.

HEDDA: What happened — in the end?

TESMAN: Well — I would call it bacchanal, Hedda.

HEDDA: Did he have vine leaves in his hair?

TESMAN: Vine leaves? No, I didn't notice any vine leaves. But he gave a long, muddled speech in honor of the woman who had inspired him in his work. Those were his words.

HEDDA: Did he mention her name?

TESMAN: No, he didn't. But I'm sure it must be Mrs. Elvsted. You just wait and see if I'm not right!

HEDDA: And where did you and he part company?

TESMAN: On the way back to town. We left — the last of us did — at the same time. And Brack came along, too, to get some fresh air. Then we decided we'd better see Eilert home. You see, he had had altogether too much to drink!

HEDDA: I can imagine.

TESMAN: But then the strangest thing of all happened, Hedda! Or maybe I should say the saddest. I'm almost ashamed — on Eilert's behalf — even talking about it.

HEDDA: Well — ?

TESMAN: You see, on the way back I happened to be behind the others a little. Just for a minute or two — you know —

HEDDA: All right, all right — !

TESMAN: And when I hurried to catch up with them, can you guess what I found by the roadside? Hm?

HEDDA: How can I possibly — ?

TESMAN: You mustn't tell this to a living soul, Hedda! Do you hear! Promise me that, for Eilert's sake. (*Pulls a parcel out of his coat pocket.*) Just think — I found this!

HEDDA: Isn't that what he had with him here yesterday?

TESMAN: Yes! It's his whole, precious, irreplaceable manuscript! And he had dropped it — just like that! Without even noticing! Just think, Hedda! Isn't that awfully sad?

HEDDA: But why didn't you give it back to him?

TESMAN: In the condition he was in! Dear — I just didn't dare to.

HEDDA: And you didn't tell any of the others that you had found it, either?

TESMAN: Of course not. I didn't want to, for Eilert's sake — don't you see?

HEDDA: So nobody knows that you have Eilert Løvborg's papers?

TESMAN: Nobody. And nobody must know, either.

HEDDA: And what did you and he talk about afterwards?

TESMAN: I didn't have a chance to talk to him at all after that. For when we came into town, he and a couple of the others simply vanished. Just think!

HEDDA: Oh? I expect they took him home.

TESMAN: I suppose that must be it. And Brack took off on his own, too.

HEDDA: And what have you been doing with yourself since then?

TESMAN: Well, you see, I and some of the others went home with one of the younger fellows and had a cup of early morning coffee. Or night coffee maybe, rather. Hm? And now, after I've rested a bit and poor Eilert's had some sleep, I'll take this back to him.

HEDDA (reaches for the parcel): No — don't do that! Not right away, I mean. Let me look at it first.

TESMAN: Dearest Hedda — honestly, I just don't dare to.

HEDDA: Don't you dare to?

TESMAN: No, for I'm sure you realize how utterly desperate he'll be when he wakes up and finds that the manuscript is gone. For he hasn't a copy, you know. He said so himself.

HEDDA (looks searchingly at him): But can't a thing like that be written over again?

TESMAN: Hardly. I really don't think so. For, you see — the inspiration —

HEDDA: Yes, I daresay that's the main thing. (Casually.) By the way, here's a letter for you.

TESMAN: Imagine!

HEDDA (gives it to him): It came early this morning.

TESMAN: It's from Aunt Julle, Hedda! I wonder what it can be. (Puts the manuscript down on the other ottoman, opens the letter, skims the content, jumps up.) Oh Hedda! She says here that poor Aunt Rina is dying!

HEDDA: You know we had to expect that.

TESMAN: And if I want to see her again I had better hurry. I'll rush over right away.

HEDDA (suppressing a smile): You'll rush?

TESMAN: Dearest Hedda of mine — if only you could bring yourself to come along! Hm?

HEDDA (rises, weary, with an air of refusal): No, no. You mustn't ask me that. I don't want to look at death and disease. I don't want anything to do with ugliness.

TESMAN: Well, all right — (Rushing around.) My hat? My coat? Oh — out here in the hall. I just hope I won't be too late, Hedda. Hm?

HEDDA: Oh I'm sure that if you rush —

(BERTE appears in the door, right.)

BERTE: Judge Brack is here and wants to know if he may see you.

TESMAN: At this hour! No, no. I can't possibly see him now!

HEDDA: But I can. (To BERTE.) Tell the Judge please to come in.

(BERTE exits.)

HEDDA (with a quick whisper): Tesman! The package! (She grabs it from the ottoman.)

TESMAN: Yes! Give it to me!

HEDDA: No, no. I'll hide it for you till later.

(She walks over to the desk and sticks the parcel in among the books on the shelf. In his hurry TESMAN is having difficulties getting his gloves on. JUDGE BRACK enters, right.)

HEDDA (nods to him): If you aren't an early bird —

BRACK: Yes, don't you think so? (To TESMAN.) You're going out, too?

TESMAN: Yes, I must go and see the aunts. Just think, the invalid — she's dying!

BRACK: Oh, I'm terribly sorry! In that case, don't let me keep you. At such a moment —

TESMAN: Yes, I really must run. Goodbye, goodbye! (Hurries out, right.)

HEDDA (approaching BRACK): It appears that things were quite lively last night over at your house.

BRACK: Indeed, Mrs. Tesman — I didn't get to bed at all.

HEDDA: You didn't either?

BRACK: As you see. But tell me — what has Tesman told you about the night's adventures?

HEDDA: Just some tiresome story about having coffee with somebody someplace —

BRACK: I believe I know all about that coffee. Eilert Løvborg wasn't one of them, was he?

HEDDA: No, they had taken him home first.

BRACK: Tesman, too?

HEDDA: No. Some of the others, he said.

BRACK (*smiles*): Jørgen Tesman is really an ingenuous soul, you know.

HEDDA: He certainly is. But why do you say that? Is there something more to all this?

BRACK: Yes, there is.

HEDDA: Well! In that case, why don't we make ourselves comfortable, Judge. You'll tell your story better, too.

(*She sits down at the left side of the table,* BRACK *near her at the adjacent side.*)

HEDDA: All right?

BRACK: For reasons of my own I wanted to keep track of my guests' movements last night. Or, rather — some of my guests.

HEDDA: Eilert Løvborg was one of them, perhaps?

BRACK: As a matter of fact — he was.

HEDDA: Now you are really making me curious.

BRACK: Do you know where he and a couple of the others spent the rest of the night, Mrs. Tesman?

HEDDA: No — tell me. If it can be told.

BRACK: Oh, certainly. They turned up at an exceptionally gay early morning gathering.

HEDDA: Of the lively kind?

BRACK: Of the liveliest.

HEDDA: A little more about this, Judge.

BRACK: Løvborg had been invited beforehand. I knew about that. But he had declined. He is a reformed character, you know.

HEDDA: As of his stay with the Elvsteds — yes. But he went after all?

BRACK: Well, yes, you see, Mrs. Tesman — unfortunately, the spirit moved him over at my house last evening.

HEDDA: Yes, I understand he became inspired.

BRACK: Quite violently inspired. And that, I gather, must have changed his mind. You know, we men don't always have as much integrity as we ought to have.

HEDDA: Oh, I'm sure you're an exception, Judge Brack. But about Løvborg — ?

BRACK: To make a long story short — he ended up at Miss Diana's establishment.

HEDDA: Miss Diana's?

BRACK: She was the hostess at this gathering — a select circle of intimate friends, male and female.

HEDDA: Is she a redhead, by any chance?

BRACK: That's correct.

HEDDA: And a singer — of sorts?

BRACK: Yes — that, too. And a mighty huntress — of men, Mrs. Tesman. You seem to have heard of her. Eilert Løvborg used to be one of her most devoted protectors in his more affluent days.

HEDDA: And how did it all end?

BRACK: Not in a very friendly fashion, apparently. It seems that after the tenderest reception Miss Diana resorted to brute force —

HEDDA: Against Løvborg?

BRACK: Yes. He accused her or her women friends of having stolen something of his. Said his wallet was gone. And other things, too. In brief, he's supposed to have started a pretty wicked row.

HEDDA: And — ?

BRACK: Well — there was a general free-for-all — men and women both. Fortunately, the police stepped in —

HEDDA: The police — !

BRACK: Yes. But I'm afraid this will be an expensive escapade for Eilert Løvborg, crazy fool that he is.

HEDDA: Well!

BRACK: It appears that he made quite violent objection — struck an officer in the car and tore his coat. So they had to take him along.

HEDDA: How do you know all this?

BRACK: From the police.

HEDDA (*staring straight ahead*): So that's how it was. No vine leaves in his hair.

BRACK: Vine leaves, Mrs. Tesman?

HEDDA (*changing her tone*): But tell me, Judge Brack — why did you keep such a close watch on Eilert Løvborg?

BRACK: Well — for one thing, it is obviously of some concern to me if he testifies that he came straight from my party.

HEDDA: So you think there will be an investigation?

BRACK: Naturally. But I suppose that doesn't really matter too much. However, as a friend of the house I considered it my duty to give you and Tesman a full account of his nighttime exploits.

HEDDA: Yes, but why?

BRACK: Because I very strongly suspect that he intends to use you as a kind of screen.

HEDDA: Really! Why do you think that?

BRACK: Oh, come now, Mrs. Tesman! We can use our eyes, can't we? This Mrs. Elvsted — she isn't leaving town right away you know.

HEDDA: Well, even if there should be something going on between those two, I'd think there would be plenty of other places they could meet.

BRACK: But no home. After last night, every respectable house will once again be closed to Eilert Løvborg.

HEDDA: And so should mine, you mean?

BRACK: Yes. I admit I would find it more than embarrassing if the gentleman were to become a daily guest here, Mrs. Tesman. If he, as an outsider — a highly dispensable outsider — if he were to intrude himself —

HEDDA: — into the triangle?

BRACK: Precisely. It would amount to home-lessness for me.

HEDDA (smiling): Sole cock-o'-the-walk — so, that's your goal, is it, Judge?

BRACK (nods slowly, lowers his voice): Yes. That is my goal. And for that I will fight with every means at my disposal.

HEDDA (her smile fading): You're really a dangerous person, you know — when you come right down to it.

BRACK: You think so?

HEDDA: Yes. I am beginning to think so now. And I must say I am exceedingly glad you don't have any kind of hold on me.

BRACK (with a noncommittal laugh): Well, well, Mrs. Tesman! Maybe there is something to what you are saying, at that. Who knows what I might do if I did.

HEDDA: Really, now, Judge Brack! Are you threatening me?

BRACK (rising): — Nonsense! For the triangle, you see — is best maintained on a voluntary basis.

HEDDA: My sentiments, exactly.

BRACK: Well, I have said what I came to say. And now I should get back to town. Goodbye, Mrs. Tesman! (Walks toward the French doors.)

HEDDA (rises): You're going through the garden?

BRACK: Yes. For me that's a short cut.

HEDDA: Yes, and then it's a back way.

BRACK: Quite true. I have nothing against back ways. There are times when they are most intriguing.

HEDDA: You mean when real ammunition is used?

BRACK (in the doorway, laughs back at her): Oh good heavens! I don't suppose one shoots one's tame roosters!

HEDDA (laughs also): No — not if one has only one — !

(They nod to each other, both still laughing. He leaves. She closes the door behind him. For a few moments she remains by the door, quite serious now, looking into the garden. Then she walks over to the doorway and opens the portieres wide enough to look into the inner room. Goes to the desk, pulls LØVBORG's manuscript from the bookshelf and is about to read it when BERTE's voice, very loud, is heard from the hall, right. HEDDA turns around, listens. She hurriedly puts the manuscript into the drawer of the desk and puts the key down on its top. EILERT LØVBORG, wearing his coat and with his hat in his hand, flings open the door, right. He looks somewhat confused and excited.)

LØVBORG (turned toward the invisible BERTE in the hall): — And I say I must! You can't stop me! (He closes the door, turns, sees HEDDA, immediately controls himself, greets her.)

HEDDA (by the desk): Well, well, Mr. Løvborg — aren't you a trifle late coming for Thea?

LØVBORG: Or a trifle early for calling on you. I apologize.

HEDDA: How do you know she is still here?

LØVBORG: The people she is staying with told me she's been gone all night.

HEDDA (walks over to the table): Did they seem — strange — when they said it?

LØVBORG (puzzled): Strange?

HEDDA: I mean, did they seem to find it a little — unusual?

LØVBORG (suddenly understands): Ah, I see what you mean! Of course! I'm dragging her down with me. No, as a matter of fact, I didn't notice anything. I suppose Tesman isn't up yet?

HEDDA: I — I don't think so —

LØVBORG: When did he get home?

HEDDA: Very late.

LØVBORG: Did he tell you anything?

HEDDA: Yes, he said you'd all had quite a time over at Brack's.

LØVBORG: Just that?

HEDDA: I think so. But I was so awfully sleepy —

(MRS. ELVSTED enters through portieres in the rear.)

MRS ELVSTED (toward him): Oh, Løvborg! At last!

LØVBORG: Yes, at last. And too late.

MRS. ELVSTED (*in fear*): What is too late?

LØVBORG: Everything is too late now. It's all over with me.

MRS. ELVSTED: Oh no, no! Don't say things like that!

LØVBORG: You'll say the same yourself when you hear —

MRS. ELVSTED: I don't want to hear — !

HEDDA: Maybe you'd rather talk with her alone? I'll leave.

LØVBORG: No stay — you, too. I beg you to.

MRS. ELVSTED: But I don't want to listen, do you hear?

LØVBORG: It isn't last night I want to talk about.

MRS. ELVSTED: What about, then?

LØVBORG: We'll have to part, Thea.

MRS. ELVSTED: Part!

HEDDA (*involuntarily*): I knew it!

LØVBORG: For I don't need you any more.

MRS. ELVSTED: And you can stand there and tell me a thing like that! Don't need me! Why can't I help you the way I did before? Aren't we going to keep on working together?

LØVBORG: I don't intend to work any more.

MRS. ELVSTED (*desperately*): What am I going to do with my life, then?

LØVBORG: You'll have to try to live your life as if you'd never known me.

MRS. ELVSTED: But I can't do that!

LØVBORG: Try, Thea. Go back home.

MRS. ELVSTED (*agitated*): Never again! Where you are I want to be! And you can't chase me away just like that. I want to stay right here! Be with you when the book appears.

HEDDA (*in a tense whisper*): Ah — yes — the book!

LØVBORG (*looks at her*): My book — and Thea's. For that's what it is.

MRS. ELVSTED: That's what I feel, too. And that's why I have the right to be with you when it comes out. I want to see all the honor and all the fame you'll get. And the joy — I want to share the joy, too.

LØVBORG: Thea, our book is never going to come out.

HEDDA: Ah!

MRS. ELVSTED: It won't!

LØVBORG: *Can't* ever appear.

MRS. ELVSTED (*with fearful suspicion*): Løvborg, what have you done with the manuscript?

HEDDA (*watching him tensely*): Yes — what about the manuscript?

MRS. ELVSTED: Where is it?

LØVBORG: Oh Thea — please, don't ask me about that!

MRS. ELVSTED: Yes, yes — I want to be told! I have the right to know — right now!

LØVBORG: All right. I've torn it to pieces.

MRS. ELVSTED (*screams*): Oh, no! No!

HEDDA (*involuntarily*): But that's not — !

LØVBORG (*looks at her*): Not true, you think?

HEDDA (*composing herself*): Well, of course, if you say so. You should know. It just sounds so — so unbelievable.

LØVBORG: All the same, it's true.

MRS. ELVSTED (*hands clenched*): Oh God — Oh God, Hedda. He has torn his own work to pieces!

LØVBORG: I have torn my whole life to pieces, so why not my life's work as well?

MRS. ELVSTED: And that's what you did last night?

LØVBORG: Yes, I tell you! In a thousand pieces. And scattered them in the fjord. Far out — where the water is clean and salty. Let them drift there, with wind and current. Then they'll sink. Deep, deep down. Like me, Thea.

MRS. ELVSTED: Do you know, Løvborg — this thing you've done to the book — all the rest of my life I'll think of it as killing a little child.

LØVBORG: You are right. It is like murdering a child.

MRS. ELVSTED: But then, how could you? For the child was mine, too!

HEDDA (*almost soundlessly*): The child —

MRS. ELVSTED (*with a deep sigh*): So it's all over. I'll go now, Hedda.

HEDDA: But you aren't leaving town?

MRS. ELVSTED: Oh, I don't know myself what I'll do. There's only darkness before me. (*Exits, right.*)

HEDDA (*waits for a moment*): Aren't you going to see her home, Mr. Løvborg?

LØVBORG: I? Through the streets? Letting people see her with me?

HEDDA: Of course, I don't know what else may have happened last night. But is it really so absolutely irreparable — ?

LØVBORG: Last night is not the end of it. That I know. And yet, I don't really care for that kind of life any more. Not again. She has broken all the courage for life and all the defiance that was in me.

HEDDA (*staring ahead*): So that sweet little goose has had her hand in a human destiny. (*Looks at him.*) But that you could be so heartless, even so!

LØVBORG: Don't tell me I was heartless!

HEDDA: To ruin everything that's filled her soul for such a long time! You don't call that heartless!

LØVBORG: Hedda — to you I can tell the truth.

HEDDA: The truth?

LØVBORG: But first promise me — give me your word you'll never let Thea know what I'm going to tell you now.

HEDDA: You have it.

LØVBORG: All right. It isn't true, what I just told her.

HEDDA: About the manuscript?

LØVBORG: Yes. I have not torn it up. Not thrown it in the sea, either.

HEDDA: But then — where is it?

LØVBORG: I've destroyed it just the same. Really, I have, Hedda!

HEDDA: I don't understand.

LØVBORG: Thea said that what I had done seemed to her like murdering a child.

HEDDA: Yes — she did.

LØVBORG: But killing a child, that's not the worst thing a father can do to it.

HEDDA: No?

LØVBORG: No. And the worst is what I don't want Thea to know.

HEDDA: What *is* the worst?

LØVBORG: Hedda — suppose a man, say, early in the morning, after a stupid, drunken night — suppose he comes home to his child's mother and says: Listen, I've been in such and such a place. I've been here — and I've been there. And I had our child with me. In all those places. And the child is lost. Gone. Vanished. I'll be damned if I know where it is. Who's got hold of it —

HEDDA: Yes — but when all is said and done — it is only a book, you know.

LØVBORG: Thea's pure soul was in that book.

HEDDA: I realize that.

LØVBORG: Then you surely also realize that she and I can have no future together.

HEDDA: Where do you go from here?

LØVBORG: Nowhere. Just finish everything off. The sooner the better.

HEDDA (*a step closer*): Listen — Eilert Løvborg — Couldn't you make sure it's done beautifully?

LØVBORG: Beautifully? (*Smiles.*) With vine leaves in the hair, as you used to say.

HEDDA: Oh no. I don't believe in vine leaves any more. But still beautifully! For once. Goodbye. Go now. And don't come back.

LØVBORG: Goodbye, Mrs. Tesman. Give my regards to Jørgen Tesman. (*He is about to leave.*)

HEDDA: Wait! I want to give you something — a remembrance. (*Goes to the desk, opens the drawer, takes out the gun case. Returns to* LØVBORG *with one of the revolvers.*)

LØVBORG: The gun? That's the remembrance?

HEDDA (*nods slowly*): Do you recognize it? It was pointed at you once.

LØVBORG: You should have used it then.

HEDDA: Take it! *You* use it.

LØVBORG (*pockets the gun*): Thanks!

HEDDA: And beautifully, Eilert Løvborg! That's all I ask!

LØVBORG: Goodbye, Hedda Gabler. (*Exits, right.*)

(HEDDA *listens by the door for a moment. Then she crosses to the desk, takes out the manuscript, glances inside the cover, pulls some of the pages halfway out and looks at them. Carries the whole manuscript over to the chair by the stove. She sits down with the parcel in her lap. After a moment she opens the stove and then the manuscript.*)

HEDDA (*throws a bundle of sheets into the fire, whispers*): Now I'm burning your child, Thea. You — curlyhead! (*Throws more sheets in.*) Your and Eilert Løvborg's child. (*Throws all the rest of the manuscript into the stove.*) I am burning — I am burning your child.

ACT IV

The same rooms at the TESMANS'. *Evening. The front room is dark. The inner room is lighted by the ceiling lamp over the table. Portieres cover the French doors.*

HEDDA, *in black, is walking up and down in the dark of the front room. She goes into the inner room, turning left in the doorway. She is heard playing a few bars on the piano. She reappears and comes forward again.* BERTE *enters from the right side of the inner room. She carries a lighted lamp, which she puts down on the table in front of the corner sofa. Her eyes show signs of weeping; she wears black ribbons on her uniform. She exits quietly, right.* HEDDA *goes over to the French windows, looks between the portieres into the dark. Presently* MISS TESMAN, *in mourning, with hat and veil, enters, right.* HEDDA *walks over to meet her, gives her her hand.*

MISS TESMAN: Yes, my dearest Hedda — herc you see me in my garb of grief. For now at last my poor sister has fought her fight to the end.

HEDDA: I already know — as you see. Tesman sent word.

MISS TESMAN: Yes, he promised he'd do that. But I thought that to you, Hedda — here in the house of life — I really ought to bring you the tidings of death myself.

HEDDA: That is very kind of you.

MISS TESMAN: Ah, but Rina shouldn't have died just now. There should be no mourning in Hedda's house at this time.

HEDDA (*changing the topic*): I understand she had a very quiet end.

MISS TESMAN: Oh so beautiful, so peaceful! She left us so quietly! And then the unspeakable happiness of seeing Jørgen one more time! To say goodbye to him to her heart's content! Isn't he back yet?

HEDDA: No. He wrote I mustn't expect him back very soon. But do sit down.

MISS TESMAN: No — no, thanks, my dear, blessed Hedda. Not that I wouldn't like to. But I don't have much time. I must go back and prepare her as best I can. I want her to look right pretty when she goes into her grave.

HEDDA: Is there anything I can help you with?

MISS TESMAN: I won't have you as much as think of it! That's not for Hedda Tesman to lend a hand to. Or lend thoughts to either. Not now, of all times!

HEDDA: Oh — thoughts! We can't always control our thoughts —

MISS TESMAN (*still preoccupied*): Ah yes — such is life. At home we're making a shroud for Rina. And here, too, there'll be sewing to do soon, I expect. But of quite a different kind, thank God!

(TESMAN *enters, right.*)

HEDDA: Finally!

TESMAN: You here, Aunt Julle? With Hedda? Just think!

MISS TESMAN: I am just about to leave, Jørgen dear. Well — did you do all the things you promised me you'd do?

TESMAN: No, I'm afraid I forgot half of them, Auntie. I'd better run in again tomorrow. I'm all confused today. I can't seem to keep my thoughts together.

MISS TESMAN: But dearest Jørgen — you mustn't take it this way!

TESMAN: Oh, I mustn't? How do you mean?

MISS TESMAN: You ought to be joyful in the midst of your sorrow. Glad for what's happened. The way I am.

TESMAN: Oh yes, of course. You're thinking of Aunt Rina.

HEDDA: You're going to feel lonely now, Miss Tesman.

MISS TESMAN: The first few days, yes. But I hope that won't last long. Dear Rina's little parlor won't be empty for long, if I can help it!

TESMAN: Oh? And who do you want to move in there? Hm?

MISS TESMAN: Ah — it's not very hard to find some poor soul who needs nursing and comfort.

HEDDA: And you really want to take on such a burden all over again?

MISS TESMAN: Heavens! God forgive you, child — burden? It has not been a burden to me.

HEDDA: Still — a stranger, who —

MISS TESMAN: Oh, it's easy to make friends with sick people. And I need somebody to live for, too. Well, the Lord be praised, maybe soon there'll be a thing or two an old aunt can turn her hand to here.

HEDDA: Oh, never mind us —

TESMAN: Yes, just think — how lovely it would be for the three of us, if only —

HEDDA: If only — ?

TESMAN (*uneasy*): Oh, nothing. I daresay it will all work out. Let's hope it will, hm?

MISS TESMAN: Well, well. I can see that you two have something to talk about. (*With a smile.*) And perhaps Hedda has something to tell you, Jørgen! Goodbye! I'm going home to Rina, now. (*Turns round in the door.*) Dear, dear — how strange to think — Now Rina is both with me and with Jochum!

TESMAN: Yes, just think, Aunt Julle! Hm?

(MISS TESMAN *exits, right.*)

HEDDA (*coldly scrutinizing* TESMAN): I wouldn't be at all surprised if you aren't more affected by this death than she is.

TESMAN: Oh, it isn't just Aunt Rina's death, Hedda. It's Eilert I worry about.

HEDDA (*quickly*): Any news about him?

TESMAN: I went over to his room this afternoon to tell him the manuscript is safe.

HEDDA: Well? And didn't you see him?

TESMAN: No. He wasn't home. But I ran into Mrs. Elvsted and she told me he'd been here early this morning.

HEDDA: Yes, right after you'd left.

TESMAN: And he said he'd torn up the manuscript? Did he really say that?

HEDDA: Yes. So he claimed.

TESMAN: But dear God — in that case he really must have been out of his mind! So I assume you didn't give it to him either, hm, Hedda?

HEDDA: No. He didn't get it.

TESMAN: But you told him we had it, of course?

HEDDA: No. (*Quickly.*) Did you tell Mrs. Elvsted?

TESMAN: No, I didn't want to. But you ought to have told him, Hedda. Just think — what if he does something rash — something to hurt himself! Give me the manuscript, Hedda! I want to rush down to him with it right this minute. Where is it?

HEDDA (*cold motionless, one arm resting on the chair*): I haven't got it any more.

TESMAN: You haven't got it! What do you mean by that?

HEDDA: I burned it — the whole thing.

TESMAN (*jumps up*): Burned it! Burned Eilert's book!

HEDDA: Don't shout. The maid might hear you.

TESMAN: Burned it? But good God — no, no, no — ! This can't be — !

HEDDA: It is, all the same.

TESMAN: But do you realize what you've done, Hedda? It's illegal! Willful destruction of lost property! You just ask Judge Brack! He'll tell you!

HEDDA: You'd better not talk about this to anyone — the Judge or anybody else.

TESMAN: But how could you do a thing like that! I never heard anything like it! What came over you? What can possibly have been going on in your head? Answer me! Hm?

HEDDA (*suppresses an almost imperceptible smile*): I did it for your sake, Jørgen.

TESMAN: For my sake!

HEDDA: When you came back this morning and told me he had read aloud to you —

TESMAN: Yes, yes! What then?

HEDDA: You admitted you were jealous of him for having written such a book.

TESMAN: But good gracious — ! I didn't mean it as seriously as all that!

HEDDA: All the same. I couldn't stand the thought that somebody else was to overshadow you.

TESMAN (*in an outburst of mingled doubt and joy*): Hedda — oh Hedda! Is it true what you're saying. But — but — but — I never knew you loved me like that! Just think!

HEDDA: In that case, I might as well tell you — that — just at this time — (*Breaks off, vehemently.*) No, no! You can ask Aunt Julle. She'll tell you.

TESMAN: I almost think I know what you mean, Hedda! (*Claps his hands.*) For goodness' sake! Can that really be so! Hm?

HEDDA: Don't shout so! The maid can hear you.

TESMAN (*laughing with exuberant joy*): The maid! Well, if you don't take the prize, Hedda! The maid — but that's Berte! I'm going to tell Berte myself this very minute!

HEDDA (*her hands clenched in despair*): Oh I'll die — I'll die, in all this!

TESMAN: In what, Hedda? Hm?

HEDDA (*cold and composed*): In all this — ludicrousness, Jørgen.

TESMAN: Ludicrous? That I'm so happy? Still — maybe I oughtn't to tell Berte, after all.

HEDDA: Oh, go ahead. What difference does it make?

TESMAN: No, not yet. But on my word — Aunt Julle must be told. And that you've started to call me "Jørgen," too! Just think! She'll be ever so happy — Aunt Julle will!

HEDDA: Even when you tell her that I have burned Eilert Løvborg's papers?

TESMAN: No, oh no! That's true! That about the manuscript — nobody must know about that. But to think that you'd burn for me, Hedda — I certainly want to tell *that* to Aunt Julle! I wonder now — is that sort of thing usual with young wives, hm?

HEDDA: Why don't you ask Aunt Julle about that, too?

TESMAN: I shall — I certainly shall, when I get the chance. (*Looks uneasy and disturbed again.*) But the manuscript! Good God — I don't dare to think what this is going to do to poor Eilert!

(MRS. ELVSTED, *dressed as on her first visit wearing hat and coat, enters, right.*)

MRS. ELVSTED (*gives a hurried greeting, is obviously upset*): Oh Hedda, you must forgive me for coming here again!

HEDDA: What has happened, Thea?

TESMAN: Something to do with Eilert Løvborg again? Hm?

MRS. ELVSTED: Yes, yes — I'm so terribly afraid something's happened to him.

HEDDA (*seizing her arm*): Ah — you think so?

TESMAN: Oh dear — why do you think that, Mrs. Elvsted?

MRS. ELVSTED: I heard them talking about him in the boarding house, just as I came in. And people are saying the most incredible things about him today.

TESMAN: Yes, imagine! I heard that, too! And I can testify that he went straight home to bed! Just think!

HEDDA: And what did they say in the boarding house?

MRS. ELVSTED: Oh, I didn't find out anything. Either they didn't know any details or — They all became silent when they saw me. And I didn't dare to ask.

TESMAN (*pacing the floor uneasily*): We'll just have to hope — to hope that you heard wrong, Mrs. Elvsted!

MRS. ELVSTED: No, no. I'm sure it was he they were talking about. And somebody said something about the hospital or —

TESMAN: The hospital — !

HEDDA: Surely, that can't be so!

MRS. ELVSTED: I got so terribly frightened! So I went up to his room and asked for him there.

HEDDA: Could you bring yourself to do that, Thea?

MRS. ELVSTED: What else could I do? For I felt I just couldn't stand the uncertainty any longer.

TESMAN: But I suppose you didn't find him in, either, did you? Hm?

MRS. ELVSTED: No. And the people there didn't know anything about him. He hadn't been home since yesterday afternoon, they said.

TESMAN: Yesterday! Just think! How could they say that!

MRS. ELVSTED: I don't know what else to

think — something bad must have happened to him!

TESMAN: Hedda, dear — ? What if I were to walk downtown and ask around for him — ?

HEDDA: No, no — don't you go and get mixed up in all this.

(JUDGE BRACK, *hat in hand, enters through the door, right, which* BERTE *opens and closes for him. He looks serious and greets the others in silence.*)

TESMAN: So here you are, Judge, hm?

BRACK: Yes. I had to see you this evening.

TESMAN: I can see you have got Aunt Julle's message.

BRACK: That, too — yes.

TESMAN: Isn't it sad, though?

BRACK: Well, my dear Tesman — that depends on how you look at it.

TESMAN (*looks at him uncertainly*): Has something else happened?

BRACK: Yes.

HEDDA (*tense*): Something sad, Judge Brack?

BRACK: That, too, depends on how you look at it, Mrs. Tesman.

MRS. ELVSTED (*bursting out*): Oh, I'm sure it has something to do with Eilert Løvborg!

BRACK (*looks at her for a moment*): Why do you think that, Mrs. Elvsted? Maybe you already know something — ?

MRS. ELVSTED (*confused*): No, no; not at all. It's just —

TESMAN: For heaven's sake, Brack, out with it!

BRACK (*shrugging his shoulders*): Well — unfortunately, Eilert Løvborg's in the hospital. Dying.

MRS. ELVSTED (*screams*): Oh God, oh God!

TESMAN: In the hospital! And dying!

HEDDA (*without thinking*): So soon — !

MRS. ELVSTED (*wailing*): And we didn't even part as friends, Hedda!

HEDDA (*whispers*): Thea, Thea — for heaven's sake — !

MRS. ELVSTED (*paying no attention to her*): I want to see him! I want to see him alive!

BRACK: Won't do you any good, Mrs. Elvsted. Nobody can see him.

MRS. ELVSTED: Then tell me what's happened to him! What?

TESMAN: For, surely, he hasn't himself — !

HEDDA: I'm sure he has.

TESMAN: Hedda! How can you — !

BRACK (*observing her all this time*): I am sorry to say that your guess is absolutely correct, Mrs. Tesman.

MRS. ELVSTED: Oh, how awful!

TESMAN: Did it himself! Just think!

HEDDA: Shot himself!

BRACK: Right again, Mrs. Tesman.

MRS. ELVSTED (*trying to pull herself together*): When did this happen, Judge?

BRACK: This afternoon. Between three and four.

TESMAN: But dear me — where can he have done a thing like that? Hm?

BRACK (*a little uncertain*): Where? Well — I suppose in his room. I don't really know —

MRS. ELVSTED: No, it can't have been there. For I was up there sometime between six and seven.

BRACK: Well, then, some other place. I really can't say. All I know is that he was found. He had shot himself — in the chest.

MRS. ELVSTED: Oh, how horrible to think! That he was to end like that!

HEDDA (*to* BRACK): In the chest?

BRACK: Yes — as I just told you.

HEDDA: Not the temple?

BRACK: In the chest, Mrs. Tesman.

HEDDA: Well, well — the chest is a good place, too.

BRACK: How is that, Mrs. Tesman?

HEDDA: (*turning him aside*): Oh — nothing.

TESMAN: And you say the wound is fatal? Hm?

BRACK: No doubt about it — absolutely fatal. He's probably dead already.

MRS. ELVSTED: Yes, yes! I feel you're right! It's over! It's all over! Oh, Hedda!

TESMAN: But tell me — how do *you* know all this?

BRACK (*tersely*): A man on the force told me. One I had some business with.

HEDDA (*loudly*): At last a deed!

TESMAN (*appalled*): Oh dear — what are you saying, Hedda!

HEDDA: I am saying there is beauty in this.

BRACK: Well, now — Mrs. Tesman —

TESMAN: Beauty — ! Just think!

MRS. ELVSTED: Oh, Hedda — how can you talk about beauty in a thing like this!

HEDDA: Eilert Løvborg has settled his account with himself. He has had the courage to do — what had to be done.

MRS. ELVSTED: But you mustn't believe it

happened that way! He did it when he was not himself!

TESMAN: In despair! That's how!

HEDDA: He did not. I am certain of that.

MRS. ELVSTED: Yes he did! He was not himself! That's the way he tore up the book, too!

BRACK (*puzzled*): The book? You mean the manuscript? Has he torn it up?

MRS. ELVSTED: Yes, last night.

TESMAN (*whispers*): Oh, Hedda — we'll never get clear of all this!

BRACK: That is strange.

TESMAN (*walking the floor*): To think that this was to be the end of Eilert! Not to leave behind him anything that would have preserved his name —

MRS. ELVSTED: Oh, if only it could be put together again!

TESMAN: Yes, if only it could. I don't know what I wouldn't give —

MRS. ELVSTED: Maybe it can, Mr. Tesman.

TESMAN: What do you mean?

MRS. ELVSTED (*searching her dress pocket*): Look. I have kept these little slips he dictated from.

HEDDA (*a step closer*): Ah — !

TESMAN: You've kept them, Mrs. Elvsted? Hm?

MRS. ELVSTED: Yes. Here they are. I took them with me when I left. And I've had them in my pocket ever since —

TESMAN: Please, let me see —

MRS. ELVSTED (*gives him a pile of small paper slips*): But it's such a mess. Without any kind of system or order — !

TESMAN: But just think if we could make sense out of them, all the same! Perhaps if we helped each other —

MRS. ELVSTED: Oh yes! Let's try, anyway!

TESMAN: It will work! It *has* to work! I'll stake my whole life on this!

HEDDA: You, Jørgen? Your life?

TESMAN: Yes, or at any rate all the time I can set aside. My own collections can wait. Hedda, you understand — don't you? Hm? This is something I owe Eilert's memory.

HEDDA: Maybe so.

TESMAN: And now, my dear Mrs. Elvsted, we want to get to work. Good heavens, there's no point brooding over what's happened. Hm? We'll just have to acquire sufficient peace of mind to —

MRS. ELVSTED: All right, Mr. Tesman. I'll try to do my best.

TESMAN: Very well, then. Come over here. Let's look at these slips right away. Where can we sit? Here? No, it's better in the other room. If you'll excuse us, Judge! Come along, Mrs. Elvsted.

MRS. ELVSTED: Oh dear God — if only it were possible — !

(TESMAN and MRS. ELVSTED go into the inner room. She takes off her hat and coat. Both sit down at the table under the hanging lamp and absorb themselves in the slips. HEDDA walks over toward the stove and sits down in the easy chair. After a while, BRACK walks over to her.)

HEDDA (in a low voice): Ah, Judge — what a liberation there is in this thing with Eilert Løvborg!

BRACK: Liberation, Mrs. Tesman? Well, yes, for him perhaps one may say there was liberation of a kind —

HEDDA: I mean for me. There is liberation in knowing that there is such a thing in the world as an act of free courage. Something which becomes beautiful by its very nature.

BRACK (smiles): Well — dear Mrs. Tesman —

HEDDA: Oh I know what you're going to say! For you see — you really are a kind of specialist, too!

BRACK (looks at her fixedly): Eilert Løvborg has meant more to you than perhaps you're willing to admit, even to yourself. Or am I wrong?

HEDDA: I won't answer such questions. All I know is that Eilert Løvborg had the courage to live his own life. And then now — this — magnificence! The beauty of it! Having the strength and the will to get up and leave life's feast — so early —

BRACK: Believe me, Mrs. Tesman, this pains me, but I see it is necessary that I destroy a pretty illusion —

HEDDA: An illusion?

BRACK: Which could not have been maintained for very long, anyway.

HEDDA: And what is that?

BRACK: He didn't shoot himself — of his own free will.

HEDDA: Not of his own — !

BRACK: No. To tell the truth, the circumstances of Eilert Løvborg's death aren't exactly what I said they were.

HEDDA (tense): You've held something back? What?

BRACK: For the sake of poor Mrs. Elvsted I used a few euphemisms.

HEDDA: What?

BRACK: First — he is already dead.

HEDDA: In the hospital.

BRACK: Yes. And without regaining consciousness.

HEDDA: What else haven't you told?

BRACK: That fact that it didn't happen in his room.

HEDDA: Well, does that really make much difference?

BRACK: Some. You see — Eilert Løvborg was found shot in Miss Diana's bedroom.

HEDDA (is about to jump up, but sinks back): That's impossible, Judge Brack! He can't have been there again today!

BRACK: He was there this afternoon. He came to claim something he said they had taken from him. Spoke some gibberish about a lost child —

HEDDA: So that's why — !

BRACK: I thought maybe he meant his manuscript. But now I hear he has destroyed that himself. So I suppose it must have been something else.

HEDDA: I suppose. So it was there — so they found him there?

BRACK: Yes. With a fired gun in his pocket. Mortally wounded.

HEDDA: Yes — in the chest.

BRACK: No — in the guts.

HEDDA (looks at him with an expression of disgust): That, too! What is this curse that turns everything I touch into something ludicrous and low!

BRACK: There is something else, Mrs. Tesman. Something I'd call — nasty.

HEDDA: And what is that.

BRACK: The gun they found —

HEDDA (breathless): What about it?

BRACK: He must have stolen it.

HEDDA (jumps up): Stolen! That's not true! He didn't!

BRACK: Anything else is impossible. He must have stolen it. — Shhh!

(TESMAN and MRS. ELVSTED have risen from the table and come forward into the front room.)

TESMAN (*with papers in both hands*): D'you know, Hedda — you can hardly see in there with that lamp! Just think!

HEDDA: I am thinking.

TESMAN: I wonder if you'd let us use your desk, hm?

HEDDA: Certainly, if you like. (*Adds quickly.*) Wait a minute, though! Let me clear it off a bit first.

TESMAN: Ah, there's no need for that, Hedda. There's plenty of room.

HEDDA: No, no. I want to straighten it up. I'll carry all this in here. I'll put it on top of the piano for the time being.

(*She has pulled an object, covered by note paper, out of the bookcase. She puts several other sheets of paper on top of it and carries the whole pile into the left part of the inner room.* TESMAN *puts the papers down on the desk and moves the lamp from the corner table over to the desk. He and* MRS. ELVSTED *sit down and resume their work.* HEDDA *returns.*)

HEDDA (*behind* MRS. ELVSTED's *chair, softly ruffling her hair*): Well, little Thea — how is Eilert Løvborg's memorial coming along?

MRS. ELVSTED (*looks up at her, discouraged*): Oh God — I'm sure it's going to be terribly hard to make anything out of all this.

TESMAN: But we have to. We just don't have a choice. And putting other people's papers in order — that's just the thing for me.

(HEDDA *walks over to the stove and sits down on one of the ottomans.* BRACK *stands over her, leaning on the easy chair.*)

HEDDA (*whispers*): What were you saying about the gun?

BRACK (*also softly*): That he must have stolen it.

HEDDA: Why, necessarily?

BRACK: Because any other explanation ought to be out of the question, Mrs. Tesman.

HEDDA: Oh?

BRACK (*looks at her for a moment*): Eilert Løvborg was here this morning, of course. Isn't that so?

HEDDA: Yes.

BRACK: Were you alone with him?

HEDDA: Yes, for a while.

BRACK: You didn't leave the room while he was here?

HEDDA: No.

BRACK: Think. Not at all? Not even for a moment?

HEDDA: Well — maybe just for a moment — out in the hall.

BRACK: And where was the gun case?

HEDDA: In the —

BRACK: Mrs. Tesman?

HEDDA: On the desk.

BRACK: Have you looked to see if both guns are still there?

HEDDA: No.

BRACK: You needn't bother. I saw the gun they found on Løvborg, and I knew it immediately. From yesterday — and from earlier occasions, too.

HEDDA: Perhaps you have it?

BRACK: No, the police do.

HEDDA: What are the police going to do with it?

BRACK: Try to find the owner.

HEDDA: Do you think they will?

BRACK (*leans over her, whispers*): No, Hedda Gabler — not as long as I keep quiet.

HEDDA (*with a hunted look*): And if you don't?

BRACK (*shrugs his shoulders*): Of course, there's always the chance that the gun was stolen.

HEDDA (*firmly*): Rather die!

BRACK (*smiles*): People *say* things like that. They don't *do* them.

HEDDA (*without answering*): And if the gun was not stolen — and if they find the owner — then what happens?

BRACK: Well, Hedda — then comes the scandal!

HEDDA: The scandal!

BRACK: Yes — the scandal. That you are so afraid of. You will of course be required to testify. Both you and Miss Diana. Obviously, she'll have to explain how the whole thing happened. Whether it was accidental or homicide. Did he try to pull the gun out of his pocket to threaten her? And did it fire accidentally? Or did she grab the gun away from him, shoot him, and put it back in his pocket? She might just possibly have done that. She's a pretty tough girl — Miss Diana.

HEDDA: But this whole disgusting mess has nothing to do with me.

BRACK: Quite so. But you'll have to answer the question: Why did you give Eilert Løvborg the gun? And what inferences will be drawn from the fact that you did?

HEDDA (*lowers her head*): That's true. I hadn't thought of that.

BRACK: Well — luckily, there's nothing to worry about as long as I don't say anything.

HEDDA (*looks up at him*): So then I'm in your power, Judge. From now on you can do anything you like with me.

BRACK (*in an even softer whisper*): Dearest Hedda — believe me, I'll not misuse my position.

HEDDA: In your power, all the same. Dependent on your will. Servant to your demands. Not free. Not free! (*Rises suddenly.*) No — I can't stand that thought! Never!

BRACK (*looks at her, half mockingly*): Most people submit to the inevitable.

HEDDA (*returning his glance*): Perhaps. (*Walks over to the desk. Suppresses a smile and mimics* TESMAN's *way of speaking.*) Well? Do you think you can do it, Jørgen? Hm?

TESMAN: Lord knows, Hedda. Anyway, I can already see it will take months.

HEDDA (*still mimicking*): Just think! (*Runs her hands lightly through* MRS. ELVSTED's *hair.*) Doesn't this seem strange to you, Thea? Sitting here with Tesman — just the way you used to with Eilert Løvborg.

MRS. ELVSTED: Oh dear — if only I could inspire your husband, too!

HEDDA: Oh, I'm sure that will come — in time.

TESMAN: Well, yes — do you know, Hedda? I really think I begin to feel something of the kind. But why don't you go and talk to the Judge again.

HEDDA: Isn't there anything you two can use me for?

TESMAN: No, not a thing, dear. (*Turns around.*) From now on, you must be good enough to keep Hedda company, my dear Judge!

BRACK (*glancing at* HEDDA): I'll be only too delighted.

HEDDA: Thank you. But I'm tired tonight. I think I'll go and lie down for a while.

TESMAN: Yes, you do that, dear; why don't you? Hm?

(HEDDA *goes into the inner room, closes the portieres behind her. Brief pause. Suddenly, she is heard playing a frenzied dance tune on the piano.*)

MRS. ELVSTED (*jumps up*): Oh God! What's that!

TESMAN (*running to the doorway*): But dearest Hedda — you mustn't play dance music tonight, for goodness' sake! Think of Aunt Rina! And Eilert, too!

HEDDA (*peeks in from between the portieres*): And Aunt Julle. And everybody. I'll be quiet. (*She pulls the portieres shut again.*)

TESMAN (*back at the desk*): I don't think it's good for her to see us at such a melancholy task. I'll tell you what, Mrs. Elvsted. You move in with Aunt Julle, and then I'll come over in the evenings. Then we can sit and work over there. Hm?

MRS. ELVSTED: Maybe that would be better —

HEDDA (*from inner room*): I hear every word you're saying, Tesman. And how am I going to spend my evenings?

TESMAN (*busy with the papers*): Oh, I'm sure Judge Brack will be good enough to come out and see you, anyway.

BRACK (*in the easy chair, calls out gaily*): Every single night, as far as I'm concerned, Mrs. Tesman! I'm sure we're going to have a lovely time, you and I!

HEDDA (*loud and clear*): Yes, don't you think that would be nice, Judge Brack? You — sole cock-o'-the-walk —

(*A shot is heard from the inner room,* TESMAN, MRS. ELVSTED, *and* JUDGE BRACK *all jump up.*)

TESMAN: There she is, fooling with those guns again.

(*He pulls the portieres apart and runs inside.* MRS. ELVSTED *also.* HEDDA, *lifeless, is lying on the sofa. Cries and confusion,* BERTE, *flustered, enters, right.*)

TESMAN (*shouts to* BRACK): She's shot herself! In the temple! Just think!

BRACK (*half stunned in the easy chair*): But, merciful God — ! One just doesn't *do* that!

Before he was forty Ibsen had written two masterpieces of poetic drama, *Brand* (1866) and *Peer Gynt* (1867). But a few years later he came to feel, along with many others, that the future of dramatic literature was not in poetic language, but in language that closely resembled ordinary speech.* He devoted his subsequent efforts to prose drama, and we find him, in his letters, occasionally prophesying that poetic drama has no future, and warning his translators to avoid all expressions that depart from "everyday speech." In the 1870's and 1880's he wrote the so-called "problem plays" (including *A Doll's House, Ghosts,* and *An Enemy of the People*) that for the next seventy-five years made his name familiar to the English-speaking world. A problem play, or "play of ideas," or *pièce à thèse,* is concerned with some troublesome social institution, its author hoping to arouse the audience to do something about the problem (for example, to modify the divorce laws, to extend the ballot, to alter the tax structure). The more successful the play, the more it insures its own demise, for when the social institutions have been altered and the problem has been solved, the play has no relevance to experience; it is merely a thing of historical importance, a museum curio. The violent reviews that *Ghosts* and some of Ibsen's other plays engendered are evidence that more was at stake than aesthetic matters; discussions of the plays inevitably became discussions of divorce, venereal disease, incest, etc. Almost a century has passed, and readers have found that Ibsen has something more to offer than thoughts on how to improve society.

In December 1890, a few weeks after he finished *Hedda Gabler,* Ibsen made the point that "it was not really my intention to deal in this play with so-called problems. What I principally wanted to do was to depict human beings, human emotions, and human destinies, upon a groundwork of certain of the social conditions and principles of the present day." We get some idea of what Ibsen meant by "the social conditions and principles of the present day" from another jotting he made while he was getting the play into shape: "Tesman represents propriety. Hedda represents *ennui.* Mrs. R. [i.e., Mrs. Elvsted] modern nervousness and hysteria. Brack the representative of bourgeois society." This early summary does not, of course, correspond exactly to the finished play, but it gives us some idea of the direction Ibsen was taking. "Propriety," "*ennui,*" "nervousness and hysteria," and even "bourgeois society" are not problems that can be solved by legislation or by any other form of tinkering. The play, after all, is not about a society that foolishly restrains energetic women from putting their energy to use — though it is in part about the

* Prose, and indeed prose clearly imitative of speech, had, of course, been occasionally used much earlier, even during the Renaissance, but prose tragedy with its middle-class figures was for a long while a poor relation of poetic tragedy. With the increasing power of the middle class and the rise of science (which not only helped to enlarge the middle class but also helped to popularize the view that all matter is equally interesting and presumably equally fit for literature), the days of "heroic" tragedy were numbered. Probably Darwin's *Origin of Species* (1859) was the *coup de grâce;* one could hardly take a very high view of creatures that had survived because accidental variations made them more suited to their environment than other creatures.

social conventions (especially aristocratic pride) that Hedda cannot abandon. The other jottings show even more clearly that Ibsen was concerned with unchanging experiences rather than with transitory problems. Here are two of them:

> They aren't all created to be mothers.
> The daemon in Hedda is that she wants to influence another human being, but once that has happened, she despises him.

Hedda wishes to influence someone, to shape a human destiny. Her own destiny, like everyone else's, has been partly shaped by the circumstances of her birth. She is the daughter of an aristocrat, General Gabler (in a letter Ibsen called attention to the fact that the play is entitled *Hedda Gabler*, and not, despite her marriage to Jørgen Tesman, *Hedda Tesman*). Her aristocratic background has given her leisure but no direction, energy but no channel for it, and we see her becoming increasingly desperate. Having married rashly, she now feels her identity is threatened. The point is obvious, but it is worth quoting Ibsen's own description, from a letter: "Jørgen Tesman, his old aunts, and the faithful servant Berte together form a picture of complete unity. They think alike, they share the same memories and have the same outlook on life. To Hedda they appear like a strange and hostile power, aimed at her very being." Tesman is a bore, scarcely worth shaping, and the aunt and the maid are no challenge. Yet this family group frightens Hedda because (she thinks) it would lessen her identity if it absorbed her. Her distress at the thought of having a child is a further indication that although she yearns to shape a human destiny, she does not want to become involved in any sort of relationship in which she herself may be shaped; that is, she evades responsibilities. Presumably when she rejected Eilert Løvborg's overtures, she did so not only because she feared scandal, but also because she feared the relationship itself. Now she seeks to fulfill herself by controlling Løvborg's life to the point that he will be a Dionysian figure who will kill himself "beautifully." Hedda apparently has in mind something of the romantic view of Greek tragedy that Ibsen himself had held twenty-five years earlier, when he rhapsodized over a statue of "the Tragic Muse," with its "laurel-crowned head with something supernaturally exuberant and bacchantic about it."

In Ibsen's world, as everywhere, people impinge upon each other and relationships are necessarily established. Miss Tesman's life, for example, is intertwined with the invalid Aunt Rina's, and when Rina dies, a replacement must be found: "Ah — it's not very hard to find some poor soul who needs nursing and comfort." To Hedda's question, "And you really want to take on such a burden all over again?" Miss Tesman replies, "Heavens! God forgive you, child — burden? It has not been a burden to me." Similarly, Mrs. Elvsted and Løvborg require each other, and are shaped by each other as they shape each other, and Tesman is at his best when he is bringing to completion someone else's work. The play is built on a groundwork of "social conditions and principles" of nineteenth-century Norwegian life, but these conditions themselves, as

Ibsen presents them, are rooted in elementary facts of life and are not out-moded institutions that needlessly create problems. (In *Peer Gynt* Ibsen had earlier represented this matter of interrelationships with a brilliant image. Peer wishes "to be himself," but he finds he has no individuality when apart from others. He peels an onion, to get at the core, and finds that after all layers — or relationships — are removed, there is nothing left.) Hedda seeks power divorced from responsibility, which means that finally her power must be directed against herself. The attempt to have Løvborg do some "beautiful" deed in defiance of society fails because she cannot have full power over Løvborg unless she gives something of herself to him. When Løvborg is dead, and Tesman and Mrs. Elvsted are occupied with each other, and Hedda is at Judge Brack's mercy, Hedda releases her energy against herself, killing herself "beautifully." Judge Brack's final comment, "One just doesn't *do* that!" is the sort of scandalized remark that Hedda had feared all her life, the voice of society, a society that does not know the depths of Hedda's anguish, a society that holds itself together by dull virtues, petty vices, and all sorts of dodges. But society does help men to survive, and to reject it is to annihilate oneself.

DEATH OF A SALESMAN

Certain private conversations in two acts and a requiem

Arthur Miller

Arthur Miller was born in New York in 1915. In 1938 he graduated from the University of Michigan, where he won several prizes for drama. Six years later he had his first Broadway production, *The Man Who Had All the Luck*, but the play was unlucky and closed after four days. By the time of his first commercial success, *All My Sons* (1947), he had already written eight or nine plays. In 1949 he won a Pulitzer prize with *Death of a Salesman* and achieved an international reputation. Among his other works are an adaptation (1950) of Ibsen's *Enemy of the People* and a play about the Salem witch trials, *The Crucible* (1953), both containing political implications, and *The Misfits* (1961, a screen-play), *After the Fall* (1964), and *Incident at Vichy* (1965).

The action takes place in WILLY LOMAN's *house and yard and in various places he visits in the New York and Boston of today.*

Throughout the play, in the stage directions, left and right mean stage left and stage right.

Design for Act I of *Death of a Salesman*. Painting by Jo Mielziner. (Photograph: Peter A. Juley & Sons.)

ACT I

A melody is heard, played upon a flute. It is small and fine, telling of grass and trees and the horizon. The curtain rises.

Before us is the Salesman's house. We are aware of towering, angular shapes behind it, surrounding it on all sides. Only the blue light of the sky falls upon the house and forestage; the surrounding area shows an angry glow of orange. As more light appears, we see a solid vault of apartment houses around the small, fragile-seeming home. An air of the dream clings to the place, a dream rising out of reality. The kitchen at center seems actual enough, for there is a kitchen table with three chairs, and a refrigerator. But no other fixtures are seen. At the back of the kitchen there is a draped entrance, which leads to the living-room. To the right of the kitchen, on a level raised two feet, is a bedroom furnished only with a brass bedstead and a straight chair. On a shelf over the bed a silver athletic trophy stands. A window opens onto the apartment house at the side.

Behind the kitchen, on a level raised six and a half feet, is the boys' bedroom, at present barely visible. Two beds are dimly seen, and at the back of the room a dormer window. (This bedroom is above the unseen living-room.) At the left a stairway curves up to it from the kitchen.

The entire setting is wholly or, in some places, partially transparent. The roof-line of the house is one-dimensional; under and

Death of a Salesman by Arthur Miller. Copyright 1949 by Arthur Miller. All rights reserved. Reprinted by permission of The Viking Press, Inc.

over it we see the apartment buildings. Before the house lies an apron, curving beyond the forestage into the orchestra. This forward area serves as the back yard as well as the locale of all WILLY's imaginings and of his city scenes. Whenever the action is in the present the actors observe the imaginary wall-lines, entering the house only through its door at the left. But in the scenes of the past these boundaries are broken, and characters enter or leave a room by stepping "through" a wall onto the forestage.

From the right, WILLY LOMAN, the Salesman, enters, carrying two large sample cases. The flute plays on. He hears but is not aware of it. He is past sixty years of age, dressed quietly. Even as he crosses the stage to the doorway of the house, his exhaustion is apparent. He unlocks the door, comes into the kitchen, and thankfully lets his burden down, feeling the soreness of his palms. A word-sigh escapes his lips — it might be "Oh, boy, oh, boy." He closes the door, then carries his cases out into the living-room, through the draped kitchen doorway.

LINDA, his wife, has stirred in her bed at the right. She gets out and puts on a robe, listening. Most often jovial, she has developed an iron repression of her exceptions to WILLY's behavior — she more than loves him, she admires him, as though his mercurial nature, his temper, his massive dreams and little cruelties, served her only as sharp reminders of the turbulent longings within him, longings which she shares but lacks the temperament to utter and follow to their end.

LINDA (hearing WILLY outside the bedroom, calls with some trepidation): Willy!

WILLY: It's all right. I came back.

LINDA: Why? What happened? (Slight pause.) Did something happen, Willy?

WILLY: No, nothing happened.

LINDA: You didn't smash the car, did you?

WILLY (with casual irritation): I said nothing happened. Didn't you hear me?

LINDA: Don't you feel well?

WILLY: I am tired to the death. (The flute

has faded away. He sits on the bed beside her, a little numb.) I couldn't make it. I just couldn't make it, Linda.

LINDA (*very carefully, delicately*): Where were you all day? You look terrible.

WILLY: I got as far as a little above Yonkers. I stopped for a cup of coffee. Maybe it was the coffee.

LINDA: What?

WILLY (*after a pause*): I suddenly couldn't drive any more. The car kept going off onto the shoulder, y'know?

LINDA (*helpfully*): Oh. Maybe it was the steering again. I don't think Angelo knows the Studebaker.

WILLY: No, it's me, it's me. Suddenly I realize I'm goin' sixty miles an hour and I don't remember the last five minutes. I'm — I can't seem to — keep my mind to it.

LINDA: Maybe it's your glasses. You never went for your new glasses.

WILLY: No, I see everything. I came back ten miles an hour. It took me nearly four hours from Yonkers.

LINDA (*resigned*): Well, you'll just have to take a rest, Willy, you can't continue this way.

WILLY: I just got back from Florida.

LINDA: But you didn't rest your mind. Your mind is overactive, and the mind is what counts, dear.

WILLY: I'll start out in the morning. Maybe I'll feel better in the morning. (*She is taking off his shoes.*) These goddam arch supports are killing me.

LINDA: Take an aspirin. Should I get you an aspirin? It'll soothe you.

WILLY (*with wonder*): I was driving along, you understand? And I was fine. I was even observing the scenery. You can imagine, me looking at scenery, on the road every week of my life. But it's so beautiful up there, Linda, the trees are so thick, and the sun is warm. I opened the windshield and just let the warm air bathe over me. And then all of a sudden I'm goin' off the road! I'm tellin' ya, I absolutely forgot I was driving. If I'd've gone the other way over the white line I might've killed somebody. So I went on again — and five minutes later I'm dreamin' again, and I nearly — (*He presses two fingers against his eyes.*) I have such thoughts, I have such strange thoughts.

LINDA: Willy, dear. Talk to them again.

There's no reason why you can't work in New York.

WILLY: They don't need me in New York. I'm the New England man. I'm vital in New England.

LINDA: But you're sixty years old. They can't expect you to keep traveling every week.

WILLY: I'll have to send a wire to Portland. I'm supposed to see Brown and Morrison tomorrow morning at ten o'clock to show the line. Goddammit, I could sell them! (*He starts putting on his jacket.*)

LINDA (*taking the jacket from him*): Why don't you go down to the place tomorrow and tell Howard you've simply got to work in New York? You're too accommodating, dear.

WILLY: If old man Wagner was alive I'd a been in charge of New York now! That man was a prince, he was a masterful man. But that boy of his, that Howard, he don't appreciate. When I went north the first time, the Wagner Company didn't know where New England was!

LINDA: Why don't you tell those things to Howard, dear?

WILLY (*encouraged*): I will, I definitely will. Is there any cheese?

LINDA: I'll make you a sandwich.

WILLY: No, go to sleep. I'll take some milk. I'll be up right away. The boys in?

LINDA: They're sleeping. Happy took Biff on a date tonight.

WILLY (*interested*): That so?

LINDA: It was so nice to see them shaving together, one behind the other, in the bathroom. And going out together. You notice? The whole house smells of shaving lotion.

WILLY: Figure it out. Work a lifetime to pay off a house. You finally own it, and there's nobody to live in it.

LINDA: Well, dear, life is a casting off. It's always that way.

WILLY: No, no, some people — some people accomplish something. Did Biff say anything after I went this morning?

LINDA: You shouldn't have criticized him, Willy, especially after he just got off the train. You mustn't lose your temper with him.

WILLY: When the hell did I lose my temper? I simply asked him if he was making any money. Is that a criticism?

LINDA: But, dear, how could he make any money?

WILLY (*worried and angered*): There's such an undercurrent in him. He became a moody man. Did he apologize when I left this morning?

LINDA: He was crestfallen, Willy. You know how he admires you. I think if he finds himself, then you'll both be happier and not fight any more.

WILLY: How can he find himself on a farm? Is that a life? A farmhand? In the beginning, when he was young, I thought, well, a young man, it's good for him to tramp around, take a lot of different jobs. But it's more than ten years now and he has yet to make thirty-five dollars a week!

LINDA: He's finding himself, Willy.

WILLY: Not finding yourself at the age of thirty-four is a disgrace!

LINDA: Shh!

WILLY: The trouble is he's lazy, goddammit!

LINDA: Willy, please!

WILLY: Biff is a lazy bum!

LINDA: They're sleeping. Get something to eat. Go on down.

WILLY: Why did he come home? I would like to know what brought him home.

LINDA: I don't know. I think he's still lost, Willy. I think he's very lost.

WILLY: Biff Loman is lost. In the greatest country in the world a young man with such — personal attractiveness, gets lost. And such a hard worker. There's one thing about Biff — he's not lazy.

LINDA: Never.

WILLY (*with pity and resolve*): I'll see him in the morning; I'll have a nice talk with him. I'll get him a job selling. He could be big in no time. My God! Remember how they used to follow him around in high school? When he smiled at one of them their faces lit up. When he walked down the street ... (*He loses himself in reminiscences.*)

LINDA (*trying to bring him out of it*): Willy, dear, I got a new kind of American-type cheese today. It's whipped.

WILLY: Why do you get American when I like Swiss?

LINDA: I just thought you'd like a change —

WILLY: I don't want a change! I want Swiss cheese. Why am I always being contradicted?

LINDA (*with a covering laugh*): I thought it would be a surprise.

WILLY: Why don't you open a window in here, for God's sake?

LINDA (*with infinite patience*): They're all open, dear.

WILLY: The way they boxed us in here. Bricks and windows, windows and bricks.

LINDA: We should've bought the land next door.

WILLY: The street is lined with cars. There's not a breath of fresh air in the neighborhood. The grass don't grow any more, you can't raise a carrot in the back yard. They should've had a law against apartment houses. Remember those two beautiful elm trees out there? When I and Biff hung the swing between them?

LINDA: Yeah, like being a million miles from the city.

WILLY: They should've arrested the builder for cutting those down. They massacred the neighborhood. (*Lost.*) More and more I think of those days, Linda. This time of year it was lilac and wisteria. And then the peonies would come out, and the daffodils. What fragrance in this room!

LINDA: Well, after all, people had to move somewhere.

WILLY: No, there's more people now.

LINDA: I don't think there's more people. I think —

WILLY: There's more people! That's what's ruining this country! Population is getting out of control. The competition is maddening! Smell the stink from that apartment house! And another one on the other side ... How can they whip cheese?

(*On* WILLY's *last line,* BIFF *and* HAPPY *raise themselves up in their beds, listening.*)

LINDA: Go down, try it. And be quiet.

WILLY (*turning to* LINDA, *guiltily*): You're not worried about me, are you, sweetheart?

BIFF: What's the matter?

HAPPY: Listen!

LINDA: You've got too much on the ball to worry about.

WILLY: You're my foundation and my support, Linda.

LINDA: Just try to relax, dear. You make mountains out of molehills.

WILLY: I won't fight with him any more. If he wants to go back to Texas, let him go.

LINDA: He'll find his way.

WILLY: Sure. Certain men just don't get started till later in life. Like Thomas Edison, I think. Or B. F. Goodrich. One of them was deaf. (*He starts for the bedroom doorway.*) I'll put my money on Biff.

LINDA: And Willy — if it's warm Sunday we'll drive in the country. And we'll open the windshield, and take lunch.

WILLY: No, the windshields don't open on the new cars.

LINDA: But you opened it today.

WILLY: Me? I didn't. (*He stops.*) Now isn't that peculiar! Isn't that a remarkable — (*He breaks off in amazement and fright as the flute is heard distantly.*)

LINDA: What, darling?

WILLY: That is the most remarkable thing.

LINDA: What, dear?

WILLY: I was thinking of the Chevvy. (*Slight pause.*) Nineteen twenty-eight . . . when I had that red Chevvy — (*Breaks off.*) That funny? I coulda sworn I was driving that Chevvy today.

LINDA: Well, that's nothing. Something must've reminded you.

WILLY: Remarkable. Ts. Remember those days? The way Biff used to simonize that car? The dealer refused to believe there was eighty thousand miles on it. (*He shakes his head.*) Heh! (*To Linda.*) Close your eyes, I'll be right up. (*He walks out of the bedroom.*)

HAPPY (*to BIFF*): Jesus, maybe he smashed up the car again!

LINDA (*calling after WILLY*): Be careful on the stairs, dear! The cheese is on the middle shelf! (*She turns, goes over to the bed, takes his jacket, and goes out of the bedroom.*)

(*Light has risen on the boys' room. Unseen, WILLY is heard talking to himself, "Eighty thousand miles," and a little laugh. BIFF gets out of bed, comes downstage a bit, and stands attentively. BIFF is two years older than his brother HAPPY, well built, but in these days bears a worn air and seems less self-assured. He has succeeded less, and his dreams are stronger and less acceptable than HAPPY's. HAPPY is tall, powerfully made. Sexuality is like a visible color on him, or a scent that many women have discovered. He, like his brother, is lost, but in a different way, for he has never allowed himself to turn his face toward defeat and is thus more confused and hard-skinned, although seemingly more content.*)

HAPPY (*getting out of bed*): He's going to get his license taken away if he keeps that up.

I'm getting nervous about him, y'know, Biff?

BIFF: His eyes are going.

HAPPY: No, I've driven with him. He sees all right. He just doesn't keep his mind on it. I drove into the city with him last week. He stops at a green light and then it turns red and he goes. (*He laughs.*)

BIFF: Maybe he's color-blind.

HAPPY: Pop? Why he's got the finest eye for color in the business. You know that.

BIFF (*sitting down on his bed*): I'm going to sleep.

HAPPY: You're not still sour on Dad, are you, Biff?

BIFF: He's all right, I guess.

WILLY (*underneath them, in the living-room*): Yes, sir, eighty thousand miles — eighty-two thousand!

BIFF: You smoking?

HAPPY (*holding out a pack of cigarettes*): Want one?

BIFF (*taking a cigarette*): I can never sleep when I smell it.

WILLY: What a simonizing job, heh!

HAPPY (*with deep sentiment*): Funny, Biff. y'know? Us sleeping in here again? The old beds. (*He pats his bed affectionately.*) All the talk that went across those two beds, huh? Our whole lives.

BIFF: Yeah. Lotta dreams and plans.

HAPPY (*with a deep and masculine laugh*): About five hundred women would like to know what was said in this room.

(*They share a soft laugh.*)

BIFF: Remember that big Betsy something — what the hell was her name — over on Bushwick Avenue?

HAPPY (*combing his hair*): With the collie dog!

BIFF: That's the one. I got you in there, remember?

HAPPY: Yeah, that was my first time — I think. Boy, there was a pig! (*They laugh, almost crudely.*) You taught me everything I know about women. Don't forget that.

BIFF: I bet you forgot how bashful you used to be. Especially with girls.

HAPPY: Oh, I still am, Biff.

BIFF: Oh, go on.

HAPPY: I just control it, that's all. I think I got less bashful and you got more so. What happened, Biff? Where's the old humor, the old confidence? (*He shakes BIFF's knee. BIFF*

gets up and moves restlessly about the room.)
What's the matter?

BIFF: Why does Dad mock me all the time?

HAPPY: He's not mocking you, he —

BIFF: Everything I say there's a twist of
mockery on his face. I can't get near him.

HAPPY: He just wants you to make good,
that's all. I wanted to talk to you about Dad
for a long time, Biff. Something's — happening
to him. He — talks to himself.

BIFF: I noticed that this morning. But he
always mumbled.

HAPPY: But not so noticeable. It got so
embarrassing I sent him to Florida. And you
know something? Most of the time he's talking to you.

BIFF: What's he say about me?

HAPPY: I can't make it out.

BIFF: What's he say about me?

HAPPY: I think the fact that you're not
settled, that you're still kind of up in the
air . . .

BIFF: There's one or two other things
depressing him, Happy.

HAPPY: What do you mean?

BIFF: Never mind. Just don't lay it all to me.

HAPPY: But I think if you just got started
— I mean — is there any future for you out
there?

BIFF: I tell ya, Hap, I don't know what the
future is. I don't know — what I'm supposed
to want.

HAPPY: What do you mean?

BIFF: Well, I spent six or seven years after
high school trying to work myself up. Shipping
clerk, salesman, business of one kind or another.
And it's a measly manner of existence. To get
on that subway on the hot mornings in summer. To devote your whole life to keeping
stock, or making phone calls, or selling or
buying. To suffer fifty weeks of the year for
the sake of a two-week vacation, when all you
really desire is to be outdoors, with your shirt
off. And always to have to get ahead of the
next fella. And still — that's how you build a
future.

HAPPY: Well, you really enjoy it on a farm?
Are you content out there?

BIFF (*with rising agitation*): Hap, I've had
twenty or thirty different kinds of jobs since I
left home before the war, and it always turns
out the same. I just realized it lately. In
Nebraska when I herded cattle, and the Da-

kotas, and Arizona, and now in Texas. It's why
I came home now, I guess, because I realized
it. This farm I work on, it's spring there now,
see? And they've got about fifteen new colts.
There's nothing more inspiring or — beautiful
than the sight of a mare and a new colt. And
it's cool there now, see? Texas is cool now, and
it's spring. And whenever spring comes to
where I am, I suddenly get the feeling, my
God, I'm not gettin' anywhere! What the hell
am I doing, playing around with horses, twenty-
eight dollars a week! I'm thirty-four years
old, I oughta be makin' my future. That's
when I come running home. And now, I get
here, and I don't know what to do with
myself. (*After a pause.*) I've always made a
point of not wasting my life, and everytime I
come back here I know that all I've done is to
waste my life.

HAPPY: You're a poet, you know that, Biff?
You're a — you're an idealist!

BIFF: No, I'm mixed up very bad. Maybe I
oughta get married. Maybe I oughta get stuck
into something. Maybe that's my trouble. I'm
like a boy. I'm not married, I'm not in
business, I just — I'm like a boy. Are you
content, Hap? You're a success, aren't you?
Are you content?

HAPPY: Hell, no!

BIFF: Why? You're making money, aren't
you?

HAPPY (*moving about with energy, ex-
pressiveness*): All I can do now is wait for the
merchandise manager to die. And suppose I
get to be merchandise manager? He's a good
friend of mine, and he just built a terrific
estate on Long Island. And he lived there
about two months and sold it, and now he's
building another one. He can't enjoy it once
it's finished. And I know that's just what I
would do. I don't know what the hell I'm
workin' for. Sometimes I sit in my apartment — all alone. And I think of the rent I'm
paying. And it's crazy. But then, it's what
I always wanted. My own apartment, a car,
and plenty of women. And still, goddammit,
I'm lonely.

BIFF (*with enthusiasm*): Listen, why don't
you come out West with me?

HAPPY: You and I, heh?

BIFF: Sure, maybe we could buy a ranch.
Raise cattle, use our muscles. Men built like
we are should be working out in the open.

HAPPY (*avidly*): The Loman Brothers, heh?

BIFF (*with vast affection*): Sure, we'd be known all over the counties!

HAPPY (*enthralled*): That's what I dream about, Biff. Sometimes I want to just rip my clothes off in the middle of the store and outbox that goddam merchandise manager. I mean I can outbox, outrun, and outlift anybody in that store, and I have to take orders from those common, petty sons-of-bitches till I can't stand it any more.

BIFF: I'm tellin' you, kid, if you were with me I'd be happy out there.

HAPPY (*enthused*): See, Biff, everybody around me is so false that I'm constantly lowering my ideals . . .

BIFF: Baby, together we'd stand up for one another, we'd have someone to trust.

HAPPY: If I were around you —

BIFF: Hap, the trouble is we weren't brought up to grub for money. I don't know how to do it.

HAPPY: Neither can I!

BIFF: Then let's go!

HAPPY: The only thing is — what can you make out there?

BIFF: But look at your friend. Builds an estate and then hasn't the peace of mind to live in it.

HAPPY: Yeah, but when he walks into the store the waves part in front of him. That's fifty-two thousand dollars a year coming through the revolving door, and I got more in my pinky finger than he's got in his head.

BIFF: Yeah, but you just said —

HAPPY: I gotta show some of those pompous, self-important executives over there that Hap Loman can make the grade. I want to walk into the store the way he walks in. Then I'll go with you, Biff. We'll be together yet, I swear. But take those two we had tonight. Now weren't they gorgeous creatures?

BIFF: Yeah, yeah, most gorgeous I've had in years.

HAPPY: I get that any time I want, Biff. Whenever I feel disgusted. The only trouble is, it gets like bowling or something. I just keep knockin' them over and it doesn't mean anything. You still run around a lot?

BIFF: Naa. I'd like to find a girl — steady, somebody with substance.

HAPPY: That's what I long for.

BIFF: Go on! You'd never come home.

HAPPY: I would! Somebody with character, with resistance! Like Mom, y'know? You're gonna call me a bastard when I tell you this. That girl Charlotte I was with tonight is engaged to be married in five weeks. (*He tries on his new hat.*)

BIFF: No kiddin'!

HAPPY: Sure, the guy's in line for the vice-presidency of the store. I don't know what gets into me, maybe I just have an overdeveloped sense of competition or something, but I went and ruined her, and furthermore I can't get rid of her. And he's the third executive I've done that to. Isn't that a crummy characteristic? And to top it all, I go to their weddings! (*Indignantly, but laughing.*) Like I'm not supposed to take bribes. Manufacturers offer me a hundred-dollar bill now and then to throw an order their way. You know how honest I am, but it's like this girl, see. I hate myself for it. Because I don't want the girl, and, still, I take it and — I love it!

BIFF: Let's go to sleep.

HAPPY: I guess we didn't settle anything, heh?

BIFF: I just got one idea that I think I'm going to try.

HAPPY: What's that?

BIFF: Remember Bill Oliver?

HAPPY: Sure, Oliver is very big now. You want to work for him again?

BIFF: No, but when I quit he said something to me. He put his arm on my shoulder, and he said, "Biff, if you ever need anything, come to me."

HAPPY: I remember that. That sounds good.

BIFF: I think I'll go to see him. If I could get ten thousand or even seven or eight thousand dollars I could buy a beautiful ranch.

HAPPY: I bet he'd back you. 'Cause he thought highly of you, Biff. I mean, they all do. You're well liked, Biff. That's why I say to come back here, and we both have the apartment. And I'm tellin' you, Biff, any babe you want . . .

BIFF: No, with a ranch I could do the work I like and still be something. I just wonder though. I wonder if Oliver still thinks I stole that carton of basketballs.

HAPPY: Oh, he probably forgot that long ago. It's almost ten years. You're too sensitive. Anyway, he didn't really fire you.

BIFF: Well, I think he was going to. I think that's why I quit. I was never sure whether he knew or not. I know he thought the world of me, though. I was the only one he'd let lock up the place.

WILLY (*below*): You gonna wash the engine, Biff?

HAPPY: Shh!

(BIFF *looks at* HAPPY, *who is gazing down, listening.* WILLY *is mumbling in the parlor.*)

HAPPY: You hear that?

(*They listen.* WILLY *laughs warmly.*)

BIFF (*growing angry*): Doesn't he know Mom can hear that?

WILLY: Don't get your sweater dirty, Biff!

(*A look of pain crosses* BIFF's *face.*)

HAPPY: Isn't that terrible? Don't leave again, will you? You'll find a job here. You gotta stick around. I don't know what to do about him, it's getting embarrassing.

WILLY: What a simonizing job!

BIFF: Mom's hearing that!

WILLY: No kiddin', Biff, you got a date? Wonderful!

HAPPY: Go on to sleep. But talk to him in the morning, will you?

BIFF (*reluctantly getting into bed*): With her in the house. Brother!

HAPPY (*getting into bed*): I wish you'd have a good talk with him.

(*The light on their room begins to fade.*)

BIFF (*to himself in bed*): That selfish, stupid . . .

HAPPY: Sh . . . Sleep, Biff.

(*Their light is out. Well before they have finished speaking,* WILLY's *form is dimly seen below in the darkened kitchen. He opens the refrigerator, searches in there, and takes out a bottle of milk. The apartment houses are fading out, and the entire house and surroundings become covered with leaves. Music insinuates itself as the leaves appear.*)

WILLY: Just wanna be careful with those girls, Biff, that's all. Don't make any promises. No promises of any kind. Because a girl, y'know, they always believe what you tell 'em, and you're very young, Biff, you're too young to be talking seriously to girls.

(*Light rises on the kitchen.* WILLY, *talking, shuts the refrigerator door and comes downstage to the kitchen table. He pours milk into a glass. He is totally immersed in himself, smiling faintly.*)

WILLY: Too young entirely, Biff. You want to watch your schooling first. Then when you're all set, there'll be plenty of girls for a boy like you. (*He smiles broadly at a kitchen chair.*) That so? The girls pay for you? (*He laughs.*) Boy, you must really be makin' a hit.

(WILLY *is gradually addressing — physically — a point offstage, speaking through the wall of the kitchen, and his voice has been rising in volume to that of a normal conversation.*)

WILLY: I been wondering why you polish the car so careful. Ha! Don't leave the hubcaps, boys. Get the chamois to the hubcaps. Happy, use newspaper on the windows, it's the easiest thing. Show him how to do it, Biff! You see, Happy? Pad it up, use it like a pad. That's it, that's it, good work. You're doin' all right, Hap. (*He pauses, then nods in approbation for a few seconds, then looks upward.*) Biff, first thing we gotta do when we get time is clip that big branch over the house. Afraid it's gonna fall in a storm and hit the roof. Tell you what. We get a rope and sling her around, and then we climb up there with a couple of saws and take her down. Soon as you finish the car, boys, I wanna see ya. I got a surprise for you, boys.

BIFF (*offstage*): Whatta ya got, Dad?

WILLY: No, you finish first. Never leave a job till you're finished — remember that. (*Looking toward the "big trees."*) Biff, up in Albany I saw a beautiful hammock. I think I'll buy it next trip, and we'll hang it right between those two elms. Wouldn't that be something? Just swingin' there under those branches. Boy, that would be . . .

(YOUNG BIFF *and* YOUNG HAPPY *appear from the direction* WILLY *was addressing.* HAPPY *carries rags and a pail of water.* BIFF, *wearing a sweater with a block "S," carries a football.*)

BIFF (*pointing in the direction of the car offstage*): How's that, Pop, professional?

WILLY: Terrific. Terrific job, boys. Good work, Biff.

HAPPY: Where's the surprise, Pop?

WILLY: In the back seat of the car.

HAPPY: Boy! (*He runs off.*)

BIFF: What is it, Dad? Tell me, what'd you buy?

WILLY (*laughing, cuffs him*): Never mind, something I want you to have.

BIFF (*turns and starts off*): What is it, Hap?

HAPPY (*offstage*): It's a punching bag!

BIFF: Oh, Pop!

WILLY: It's got Gene Tunney's signature on it!

(HAPPY *runs onstage with a punching bag.*)

BIFF: Gee, how'd you know we wanted a punching bag?

WILLY: Well, it's the finest thing for the timing.

HAPPY (*lies down on his back and pedals with his feet*): I'm losing weight, you notice, Pop?

WILLY (*to* HAPPY): Jumping rope is good too.

BIFF: Did you see the new football I got?

WILLY (*examining the ball*): Where'd you get a new ball?

BIFF: The coach told me to practice my passing.

WILLY: That so? And he gave you the ball, heh?

BIFF: Well, I borrowed it from the locker room. (*He laughs confidentially.*)

WILLY (*laughing with him at the theft*): I want you to return that.

HAPPY: I told you he wouldn't like it!

BIFF (*angrily*): Well, I'm bringing it back!

WILLY (*stopping the incipient argument, to* HAPPY): Sure, he's gotta practice with a regulation ball, doesn't he? (*To* BIFF.) Coach'll probably congratulate you on your initiative!

BIFF: Oh, he keeps congratulating my initiative all the time, Pop.

WILLY: That's because he likes you. If somebody else took that ball there'd be an uproar. So what's the report, boys, what's the report?

BIFF: Where'd you go this time, Dad? Gee we were lonesome for you.

WILLY (*pleased, puts an arm around each boy and they come down to the apron*): Lonesome, heh?

BIFF: Missed you every minute.

WILLY: Don't say? Tell you a secret, boys.

Don't breathe it to a soul. Someday I'll have my own business, and I'll never have to leave home any more.

HAPPY: Like Uncle Charley, heh?

WILLY: Bigger than Uncle Charley! Because Charley is not — liked. He's liked, but he's not — well liked.

BIFF: Where'd you go this time, Dad?

WILLY: Well, I got on the road, and I went north to Providence. Met the Mayor.

BIFF: The Mayor of Providence!

WILLY: He was sitting in the hotel lobby.

BIFF: What'd he say?

WILLY: He said, "Morning!" And I said, "You got a fine city here, Mayor." And then he had coffee with me. And then I went to Waterbury. Waterbury is a fine city. Big clock city, the famous Waterbury clock. Sold a nice bill there. And then Boston — Boston is the cradle of the Revolution. A fine city. And a couple of other towns in Mass., and on to Portland and Bangor and straight home!

BIFF: Gee, I'd love to go with you sometime, Dad.

WILLY: Soon as summer comes.

HAPPY: Promise?

WILLY: You and Hap and I, and I'll show you all the towns. America is full of beautiful towns and fine, upstanding people. And they know me, boys, they know me up and down New England. The finest people. And when I bring you fellas up, there'll be open sesame for all of us, 'cause one thing, boys: I have friends. I can park my car in any street in New England, and the cops protect it like their own. This summer, heh?

BIFF AND HAPPY (*together*): Yeah! You bet!

WILLY: We'll take our bathing suits.

HAPPY: We'll carry your bags, Pop!

WILLY: Oh, won't that be something! Me comin' into the Boston stores with you boys carryin' my bags. What a sensation!

(BIFF *is prancing around, practicing passing the ball.*)

WILLY: You nervous, Biff, about the game?

BIFF: Not if you're gonna be there.

WILLY: What do they say about you in school, now that they made you captain?

HAPPY: There's a crowd of girls behind him everytime the classes change.

BIFF (*taking* WILLY'S *hand*): This Saturday, Pop, this Saturday — just for you, I'm going to break through for a touchdown.

HAPPY: You're supposed to pass.

BIFF: I'm takin' one play for Pop. You watch me, Pop, and when I take off my helmet, that means I'm breakin' out. Then you watch me crash through that line!

WILLY (*kisses* BIFF): Oh, wait'll I tell this in Boston!

(BERNARD *enters in knickers. He is younger than* BIFF, *earnest and loyal, a worried boy.*)

BERNARD: Biff, where are you? You're supposed to study with me today.

WILLY: Hey, looka Bernard. What're you lookin' so anemic about, Bernard?

BERNARD: He's gotta study, Uncle Willy. He's got Regents next week.

HAPPY (*tauntingly, spinning* BERNARD *around*): Let's box, Bernard!

BERNARD: Biff! (*He gets away from* HAPPY.) Listen, Biff, I heard Mr. Birnbaum say that if you don't start studyin' math he's gonna flunk you, and you won't graduate. I heard him!

WILLY: You better study with him, Biff. Go ahead now.

BERNARD: I heard him!

BIFF: Oh, Pop, you didn't see my sneakers! (*He holds up a foot for* WILLY *to look at.*)

WILLY: Hey, that's a beautiful job of printing!

BERNARD (*wiping his glasses*): Just because he printed University of Virginia on his sneakers doesn't mean they've got to graduate him, Uncle Willy!

WILLY (*angrily*): What're you talking about? With scholarships to three universities they're gonna flunk him?

BERNARD: But I heard Mr. Birnbaum say —

WILLY: Don't be a pest, Bernard! (*To his boys.*) What an anemic!

BERNARD: Okay, I'm waiting for you in my house, Biff.

(*Bernard goes off.* THE LOMANS *laugh.*)

WILLY: Bernard is not well liked, is he?

BIFF: He's liked, but he's not well liked.

HAPPY: That's right, Pop.

WILLY: That's just what I mean. Bernard can get the best marks in school, y'understand, but when he gets out in the business world, y'understand, you are going to be five times ahead of him. That's why I thank Almighty God you're both built like Adonises. Because the man who makes an appearance in the business world, the man who creates personal interest, is the man who gets ahead. Be liked and you will never want. You take me, for instance. I never have to wait in line to see a buyer. "Willy Loman is here!" That's all they have to know, and I go right through.

BIFF: Did you knock them dead, Pop?

WILLY: Knocked 'em cold in Providence, slaughtered 'em in Boston.

HAPPY (*on his back, pedaling again*): I'm losing weight, you notice, Pop?

(LINDA *enters, as of old, a ribbon in her hair, carrying a basket of washing.*)

LINDA (*with youthful energy*): Hello, dear!

WILLY: Sweetheart!

LINDA: How'd the Chevvy run?

WILLY: Chevrolet, Linda, is the greatest car ever built. (*To the boys.*) Since when do you let your mother carry wash up the stairs?

BIFF: Grab hold there, boy!

HAPPY: Where to, Mom?

LINDA: Hang them up on the line. And you better go down to your friends, Biff. The cellar is full of boys. They don't know what to do with themselves.

BIFF: Ah, when Pop comes home they can wait!

WILLY (*laughs appreciatively*): You better go down and tell them what to do, Biff.

BIFF: I think I'll have them sweep out the furnace room.

WILLY: Good work, Biff.

BIFF (*goes through wall-line of kitchen to doorway at back and calls down*): Fellas! Everybody sweep out the furnace room! I'll be right down!

VOICES: All right! Okay, Biff.

BIFF: George and Sam and Frank, come out back! We're hangin' up the wash! Come on, Hap, on the double! (*He and* HAPPY *carry out the basket.*)

LINDA: The way they obey him!

WILLY: Well, that's training, the training. I'm tellin' you, I was sellin' thousands and thousands, but I had to come home.

LINDA: Oh, the whole block'll be at that game. Did you sell anything?

WILLY: I did five hundred gross in Providence and seven hundred gross in Boston.

LINDA: No! Wait a minute, I've got a pencil. (*She pulls pencil and paper out of her apron pocket.*) That makes your commission . . . Two hundred — my God! Two hundred and twelve dollars!

WILLY: Well, I didn't figure it yet, but . . .

LINDA: How much did you do?

WILLY: Well, I — I did — about a hundred and eighty gross in Providence. Well, no — it came to — roughly two hundred gross on the whole trip.

LINDA (*without hesitation*): Two hundred gross. That's . . . (*She figures.*)

WILLY: The trouble was that three of the stores were half closed for inventory in Boston. Otherwise I woulda broke records.

LINDA: Well, it makes seventy dollars and some pennies. That's very good.

WILLY: What do we owe?

LINDA: Well, on the first there's sixteen dollars on the refrigerator —

WILLY: Why sixteen?

LINDA: Well, the fan belt broke, so it was a dollar eighty.

WILLY: But it's brand new.

LINDA: Well, the man said that's the way it is. Till they work themselves in, y'know.

(*They move through the wall-line into the kitchen.*)

WILLY: I hope we didn't get stuck on that machine.

LINDA: They got the biggest ads of any of them!

WILLY: I know, it's a fine machine. What else?

LINDA: Well, there's nine-sixty for the washing machine. And for the vacuum cleaner there's three and a half due on the fifteenth. Then the roof, you got twenty-one dollars remaining.

WILLY: It don't leak, does it?

LINDA: No, they did a wonderful job. Then you owe Frank for the carburetor.

WILLY: I'm not going to pay that man! That goddam Chevrolet, they ought to prohibit the manufacture of that car!

LINDA: Well, you owe him three and a half. And odds and ends, comes to around a hundred and twenty dollars by the fifteenth.

WILLY: A hundred and twenty dollars! My God, if business don't pick up I don't know what I'm gonna do!

LINDA: Well, next week you'll do better.

WILLY: Oh, I'll knock 'em dead next week. I'll go to Hartford. I'm very well liked in Hartford. You know, the trouble is, Linda, people don't seem to take to me.

(*They move onto the forestage.*)

LINDA: Oh, don't be foolish.

WILLY: I know it when I walk in. They seem to laugh at me.

LINDA: Why? Why would they laugh at you? Don't talk that way, Willy.

(WILLY *moves to the edge of the stage.* LINDA *goes into the kitchen and starts to darn stockings.*)

WILLY: I don't know the reason for it, but they just pass me by. I'm not noticed.

LINDA: But you're doing wonderful, dear. You're making seventy to a hundred dollars a week.

WILLY: But I gotta be at it ten, twelve hours a day. Other men — I don't know — they do it easier. I don't know why — I can't stop myself — I talk too much. A man oughta come in with a few words. One thing about Charley. He's a man of few words, and they respect him.

LINDA: You don't talk too much, you're just lively.

WILLY (*smiling*): Well, I figure, what the hell, life is short, a couple of jokes. (*To himself.*) I joke too much! (*The smile goes.*)

LINDA: Why? You're —

WILLY: I'm fat. I'm very — foolish to look at, Linda. I didn't tell you, but Christmas time I happened to be calling on F. H. Stewarts, and a salesman I know, as I was going in to see the buyer I heard him say something about — walrus. And I — I cracked him right across the face. I won't take that. I simply will not take that. But they do laugh at me. I know that.

LINDA: Darling . . .

WILLY: I gotta overcome it. I know I gotta overcome it. I'm not dressing to advantage, maybe.

LINDA: Willy, darling, you're the handsomest man in the world —

WILLY: Oh, no, Linda.

LINDA: To me you are. (*Slight pause.*) The handsomest.

(*From the darkness is heard the laughter of a woman.* WILLY *doesn't turn to it, but it continues through* LINDA's *lines.*)

LINDA: And the boys, Willy. Few men are idolized by their children the way you are.

(*Music is heard as behind a scrim, to the left of the house,* THE WOMAN, *dimly seen, is dressing.*)

WILLY (*with great feeling*): You're the best there is, Linda, you're a pal, you know that? On the road — on the road I want to grab you sometimes and just kiss the life outa you.

(*The laughter is loud now, and he moves into a brightening area at the left, where* THE WOMAN *has come from behind the scrim and is standing, putting on her hat, looking into a "mirror" and laughing.*)

WILLY: 'Cause I get so lonely — especially when business is bad and there's nobody to talk to. I get the feeling that I'll never sell anything again, that I won't make a living for you, or a business, a business for the boys. (*He talks through* THE WOMAN'S *subsiding laughter;* THE WOMAN *primps at the "mirror."*) There's so much I want to make for —

THE WOMAN: Me? You didn't make me, Willy. I picked you.

WILLY (*pleased*): You picked me?

THE WOMAN (*who is quite proper-looking,* WILLY'S *age*): I did. I've been sitting at that desk watching all the salesmen go by, day in, day out. But you've got such a sense of humor, and we do have such a good time together, don't we?

WILLY: Sure, sure. (*He takes her in his arms.*) Why do you have to go now?

THE WOMAN: It's two o'clock . . .

WILLY: No, come on in! (*He pulls her.*)

THE WOMAN: . . . my sisters'll be scandalized. When'll you be back?

WILLY: Oh, two weeks about. Will you come up again?

THE WOMAN: Sure thing. You do make me laugh. It's good for me. (*She squeezes his arm, kisses him.*) And I think you're a wonderful man.

WILLY: You picked me, heh?

THE WOMAN: Sure. Because you're so sweet. And such a kidder.

WILLY: Well, I'll see you next time I'm in Boston.

THE WOMAN: I'll put you right through to the buyers.

WILLY (*slapping her bottom*): Right. Well, bottoms up!

THE WOMAN (*slaps him gently and laughs*): You just kill me, Willy. (*He suddenly grabs her and kisses her roughly.*) You kill me. And thanks for the stockings. I love a lot of stockings. Well, good night.

WILLY: Good night. And keep your pores open!

THE WOMAN: Oh, Willy!

(THE WOMAN *bursts out laughing, and* LINDA'S *laughter blends in.* THE WOMAN *disappears into the dark. Now the area at the kitchen table brightens.* LINDA *is sitting where she was at the kitchen table, but now is mending a pair of her silk stockings.*)

LINDA: You are, Willy. The handsomest man. You've got no reason to feel that —

WILLY (*coming out of* THE WOMAN'S *dimming area and going over to* LINDA): I'll make it all up to you, Linda, I'll —

LINDA: There's nothing to make up, dear. You're doing fine, better than —

WILLY (*noticing her mending*): What's that?

LINDA: Just mending my stockings. They're so expensive —

WILLY (*angrily, taking them from her*): I won't have you mending stockings in this house! Now throw them out!

(LINDA *puts the stockings in her pocket.*)

BERNARD (*entering on the run*): Where is he? If he doesn't study!

WILLY (*moving to the forestage, with great agitation*): You'll give him the answers!

BERNARD: I do, but I can't on a Regents! That's a state exam! They're liable to arrest me!

WILLY: Where is he? I'll whip him, I'll whip him!

LINDA: And he'd better give back that football, Willy, it's not nice.

WILLY: Biff! Where is he? Why is he taking everything?

LINDA: He's too rough with the girls, Willy. All the mothers are afraid of him!

WILLY: I'll whip him!

BERNARD: He's driving the car without a license!

(THE WOMAN'S *laugh is heard.*)

WILLY: Shut up!

LINDA: All the mothers —

WILLY: Shut up!

BERNARD (*backing quietly away and out*): Mr. Birnbaum says he's stuck up.

WILLY: Get outa here!

BERNARD: If he doesn't buckle down he'll flunk math! (*He goes off.*)

LINDA: He's right, Willy, you've gotta —

WILLY (*exploding at her*): There's nothing the matter with him! You want him to be a worm like Bernard? He's got spirit, personality . . .

(*As he speaks,* LINDA, *almost in tears, exits into the living-room.* WILLY *is alone in the kitchen, wilting and staring. The leaves are gone. It is night again, and the apartment houses look down from behind.*)

WILLY: Loaded with it. Loaded! What is he stealing? He's giving it back, isn't he? Why is he stealing? What did I tell him? I never in my life told him anything but decent things.

(HAPPY *in pajamas has come down the stairs;* WILLY *suddenly becomes aware of* HAPPY's *presence.*)

HAPPY: Let's go now, come on.

WILLY (*sitting down at the kitchen table*): Huh! Why did she have to wax the floors herself? Everytime she waxes the floors she keels over. She knows that!

HAPPY: Shh! Take it easy. What brought you back tonight?

WILLY: I got an awful scare. Nearly hit a kid in Yonkers. God! Why didn't I go to Alaska with my brother Ben that time! Ben! That man was a genius, that man was success incarnate! What a mistake! He begged me to go.

HAPPY: Well, there's no use in —

WILLY: You guys! There was a man started with the clothes on his back and ended up with diamond mines!

HAPPY: Boy, someday I'd like to know how he did it.

WILLY: What's the mystery? The man knew what he wanted and went out and got it! Walked into a jungle, and comes out, the age of twenty-one, and he's rich! The world is an oyster, but you don't crack it open on a mattress!

HAPPY: Pop, I told you I'm gonna retire you for life.

WILLY: You'll retire me for life on seventy goddam dollars a week? And your women and your car and your apartment, and you'll retire me for life! Christ's sake, I couldn't get past Yonkers today! Where are you guys, where are you? The woods are burning! I can't drive a car!

(CHARLEY *has appeared in the doorway. He is a large man, slow of speech, laconic, immovable. In all he says, despite what he says, there is pity, and, now, trepidation. He has a robe over pajamas, slippers on his feet. He enters the kitchen.*)

CHARLEY: Everything all right?

HAPPY: Yeah, Charley, everything's . . .

WILLY: What's the matter?

CHARLEY: I heard some noise. I thought something happened. Can't we do something about the walls? You sneeze in here, and in my house hats blow off.

HAPPY: Let's go to bed, Dad. Come on.

(CHARLEY *signals to* HAPPY *to go.*)

WILLY: You go ahead, I'm not tired at the moment.

HAPPY (*to* WILLY): Take it easy, huh? (*He exits.*)

WILLY: What're you doin' up?

CHARLEY (*sitting down at the kitchen table opposite* WILLY): Couldn't sleep good. I had a heartburn.

WILLY: Well, you don't know how to eat.

CHARLEY: I eat with my mouth.

WILLY: No, you're ignorant. You gotta know about vitamins and things like that.

CHARLEY: Come on, let's shoot. Tire you out a little.

WILLY (*hesitantly*): All right. You got cards?

CHARLEY (*taking a deck from his pocket*): Yeah, I got them. Someplace. What is it with those vitamins?

WILLY (*dealing*): They build up your bones. Chemistry.

CHARLEY: Yeah, but there's no bones in a heartburn.

WILLY: What are you talkin' about? Do you know the first thing about it?

CHARLEY: Don't get insulted.

WILLY: Don't talk about something you don't know anything about.

(*They are playing. Pause.*)

CHARLEY: What're you doin' home?

WILLY: A little trouble with the car.

CHARLEY: Oh. (*Pause.*) I'd like to take a trip to California.

WILLY: Don't say.

CHARLEY: You want a job?

WILLY: I got a job, I told you that. (*After a slight pause.*) What the hell are you offering me a job for?

CHARLEY: Don't get insulted.

WILLY: Don't insult me.

CHARLEY: I don't see no sense in it. You don't have to go on this way.

WILLY: I got a good job. (*Slight pause.*) What do you keep comin' in here for?

CHARLEY: You want me to go?

WILLY (*after a pause, withering*): I can't understand it. He's going back to Texas again. What the hell is that?

CHARLEY: Let him go.

WILLY: I got nothin' to give him, Charley, I'm clean, I'm clean.

CHARLEY: He won't starve. None a them starve. Forget about him.

WILLY: Then what have I got to remember?

CHARLEY: You take it too hard. To hell with it. When a deposit bottle is broken you don't get your nickel back.

WILLY: That's easy enough for you to say.

CHARLEY: That ain't easy for me to say.

WILLY: Did you see the ceiling I put up in the living-room?

CHARLEY: Yeah, that's a piece of work. To put up a ceiling is a mystery to me. How do you do it?

WILLY: What's the difference?

CHARLEY: Well, talk about it.

WILLY: You gonna put up a ceiling?

CHARLEY: How could I put up a ceiling?

WILLY: Then what the hell are you bothering me for?

CHARLEY: You're insulted again.

WILLY: A man who can't handle tools is not a man. You're disgusting.

CHARLEY: Don't call me disgusting, Willy.

(UNCLE BEN, *carrying a valise and an umbrella, enters the forestage from around the right corner of the house. He is a stolid man, in his sixties, with a mustache and an authoritative air. He is utterly certain of his destiny, and there is an aura of far places about him. He enters exactly as* WILLY *speaks.*)

WILLY: I'm getting awfully tired, Ben.

(BEN's *music is heard.* BEN *looks around at everything.*)

CHARLEY: Good, keep playing; you'll sleep better. Did you call me Ben?

(BEN *looks at his watch.*)

WILLY: That's funny. For a second there you reminded me of my brother Ben.

BEN: I only have a few minutes. (*He strolls, inspecting the place.* WILLY *and* CHARLEY *continue playing.*)

CHARLEY: You never heard from him again, heh? Since that time?

WILLY: Didn't Linda tell you? Couple of weeks ago we got a letter from his wife in Africa. He died.

CHARLEY: That so.

BEN (*chuckling*): So this is Brooklyn, eh?

CHARLEY: Maybe you're in for some of his money.

WILLY: Naa, he had seven sons. There's just one opportunity I had with that man . . .

BEN: I must make a train, William. There are several properties I'm looking at in Alaska.

WILLY: Sure, sure! If I'd gone with him to Alaska that time, everything would've been totally different.

CHARLEY: Go on, you'd froze to death up there.

WILLY: What're you talking about?

BEN: Opportunity is tremendous in Alaska, William. Surprised you're not up there.

WILLY: Sure, tremendous.

CHARLEY: Heh?

WILLY: There was the only man I ever met who knew the answers.

CHARLEY: Who?

BEN: How are you all?

WILLY (*taking a pot, smiling*): Fine, fine.

CHARLEY: Pretty sharp tonight.

BEN: Is Mother living with you?

WILLY: No, she died a long time ago.

CHARLEY: Who?

BEN: That's too bad. Fine specimen of a lady, Mother.

WILLY (*to* CHARLEY): Heh?

BEN: I'd hoped to see the old girl.

CHARLEY: Who died?

BEN: Heard anything from Father, have you?

WILLY (*unnerved*): What do you mean, who died?

CHARLEY (*taking a pot*): What're you talkin' about?

BEN (*looking at his watch*): William, it's half-past eight!

WILLY (*as though to dispel his confusion he*

angrily stops CHARLEY's *hand*): That's my build!

CHARLEY: I put the ace —

WILLY: If you don't know how to play the game I'm not gonna throw my money away on you!

CHARLEY (*rising*): It was my ace, for God's sake!

WILLY: I'm through, I'm through!

BEN: When did Mother die?

WILLY: Long ago. Since the beginning you never knew how to play cards.

CHARLEY (*picks up the cards and goes to the door*): All right! Next time I'll bring a deck with five aces.

WILLY: I don't play that kind of game!

CHARLEY (*turning to him*): You ought to be ashamed of yourself!

WILLY: Yeah?

CHARLEY: Yeah! (*He goes out.*)

WILLY (*slamming the door after him*): Ignoramus!

BEN (*as* WILLY *comes toward him through the wall-line of the kitchen*): So you're William.

WILLY (*shaking* BEN's *hand*): Ben! I've been waiting for you so long! What's the answer? How did you do it?

BEN: Oh, there's a story in that.

(LINDA *enters the forestage, as of old, carrying the wash basket.*)

LINDA: Is this Ben?

BEN (*gallantly*): How do you do, my dear.

LINDA: Where've you been all these years? Willy's always wondered why you —

WILLY (*pulling* BEN *away from her impatiently*): Where is Dad? Didn't you follow him? How did you get started?

BEN: Well, I don't know how much you remember.

WILLY: Well, I was just a baby, of course, only three or four years old —

BEN: Three years and eleven months.

WILLY: What a memory, Ben!

BEN: I have many enterprises, William, and I have never kept books.

WILLY: I remember I was sitting under the wagon in — was it Nebraska?

BEN: It was South Dakota, and I gave you a bunch of wild flowers.

WILLY: I remember you walking away down some open road.

BEN (*laughing*): I was going to find Father in Alaska.

WILLY: Where is he?

BEN: At that age I had a very faulty view of geography, William. I discovered after a few days that I was heading due south, so instead of Alaska, I ended up in Africa.

LINDA: Africa!

WILLY: The Gold Coast!

BEN: Principally diamond mines.

LINDA: Diamond mines!

BEN: Yes, my dear. But I've only a few minutes —

WILLY: No! Boys! Boys! (YOUNG BIFF *and* HAPPY *appear.*) Listen to this. This is your Uncle Ben, a great man! Tell my boys, Ben!

BEN: Why, boys, when I was seventeen I walked into the jungle, and when I was twenty-one I walked out. (*He laughs.*) And by God I was rich.

WILLY (*to the boys*): You see what I been talking about? The greatest things can happen!

BEN (*glancing at his watch*): I have an appointment in Ketchikan Tuesday week.

WILLY: No, Ben! Please tell about Dad. I want my boys to hear. I want them to know the kind of stock they spring from. All I remember is a man with a big beard, and I was in Mamma's lap, sitting around a fire, and some kind of high music.

BEN: His flute. He played the flute.

WILLY: Sure, the flute, that's right!

(*New music is heard, a high, rollicking tune.*)

BEN: Father was a very great and a very wild-hearted man. We would start in Boston, and he'd toss the whole family into the wagon, and then he'd drive the team right across the country; through Ohio, and Indiana, Michigan, Illinois, and all the Western states. And we'd stop in the towns and sell the flutes that he'd made on the way. Great inventor, Father. With one gadget he made more in a week than a man like you could make in a lifetime.

WILLY: That's just the way I'm bringing them up, Ben — rugged, well liked, all-around.

BEN: Yeah? (*To* BIFF.) Hit that, boy — hard as you can. (*He pounds his stomach.*)

BIFF: Oh, no, sir!

BEN (*taking boxing stance*): Come on, get to me! (*He laughs.*)

WILLY: Go to it, Biff! Go ahead, show him!

BIFF: Okay! (*He cocks his fists and starts in.*)

LINDA (*to* WILLY): Why must he fight, dear?

BEN (*sparring with* BIFF): Good boy! Good boy!

WILLY: How's that, Ben, heh?

HAPPY: Give him the left, Biff!

LINDA: Why are you fighting?

BEN: Good boy! (*Suddenly comes in, trips* BIFF, *and stands over him, the point of his umbrella poised over* BIFF's *eye.*)

LINDA: Look out, Biff!

BIFF: Gee!

BEN (*patting* BIFF's *knee*): Never fight fair with a stranger, boy. You'll never get out of the jungle that way. (*Taking* LINDA's *hand and bowing.*) It was an honor and a pleasure to meet you, Linda.

LINDA (*withdrawing her hand coldly, frightened*): Have a nice — trip.

BEN (*to* WILLY): And good luck with your — what do you do?

WILLY: Selling.

BEN: Yes. Well . : . (*He raises his hand in farewell to all.*)

WILLY: No, Ben, I don't want you to think . . . (*He takes* BEN's *arm to show him.*) It's Brooklyn, I know, but we hunt too.

BEN: Really, now.

WILLY: Oh, sure, there's snakes and rabbits and — that's why I moved out here. Why, Biff can fell any one of these trees in no time! Boys! Go right over to where they're building the apartment house and get some sand. We're gonna rebuild the entire front stoop right now! Watch this, Ben!

BIFF: Yes, sir! On the double, Hap!

HAPPY (*as he and* BIFF *run off*): I lost weight, Pop, you notice?

(CHARLEY *enters in knickers, even before the boys are gone.*)

CHARLEY: Listen, if they steal any more from that building the watchman'll put the cops on them!

LINDA (*to* WILLY): Don't let Biff . . .

(BEN *laughs lustily.*)

WILLY: You shoulda seen the lumber they brought home last week. At least a dozen six-by-tens worth all kinds a money.

CHARLEY: Listen, if that watchman —

WILLY: I gave them hell, understand. But I got a couple of fearless characters there.

CHARLEY: Willy, the jails are full of fearless characters.

BEN (*clapping* WILLY *on the back, with a laugh at* CHARLEY): And the stock exchange, friend!

WILLY (*joining in* BEN's *laughter*): Where are the rest of your pants?

CHARLEY: My wife bought them.

WILLY: Now all you need is a golf club and you can go upstairs and go to sleep. (*To* BEN.) Great athlete! Between him and his son Bernard they can't hammer a nail!

BERNARD (*rushing in*): The watchman's chasing Biff!

WILLY (*angrily*): Shut up! He's not stealing anything!

LINDA (*alarmed, hurrying off left*): Where is he? Biff, dear! (*She exits.*)

WILLY (*moving toward the left, away from* BEN): There's nothing wrong. What's the matter with you?

BEN: Nervy boy. Good!

WILLY (*laughing*): Oh, nerves of iron, that Biff!

CHARLEY: Don't know what it is. My New England man comes back and he's bleedin', they murdered him up there.

WILLY: It's contacts, Charley, I got important contacts!

CHARLEY (*sarcastically*): Glad to hear it, Willy. Come in later, we'll shoot a little casino. I'll take some of your Portland money. (*He laughs at* WILLY *and exists.*)

WILLY (*turning to* BEN): Business is bad, it's murderous. But not for me, of course.

BEN: I'll stop by on my way back to Africa.

WILLY (*longingly*): Can't you stay a few days? You're just what I need, Ben, because I — I have a fine position here, but I — well, Dad left when I was such a baby and I never had a chance to talk to him and I still feel — kind of temporary about myself.

BEN: I'll be late for my train.

(*They are at opposite ends of the stage.*)

WILLY: Ben, my boys — can't we talk? They'd go into the jaws of hell for me, see, but I —

BEN: William, you're being first-rate with your boys. Outstanding, manly chaps!

WILLY (*hanging on to his words*): Oh, Ben, that's good to hear! Because sometimes I'm afraid that I'm not teaching them the right kind of — Ben, how should I teach them?

BEN (*giving great weight to each word, and with a certain vicious audacity*): William, when I walked into the jungle, I was seventeen. When I walked out I was twenty-one. And, by God, I was rich! (*He goes off into darkness around the right corner of the house.*)

WILLY: . . . was rich! That's just the spirit I want to imbue them with! To walk into a jungle! I was right! I was right! I was right!

(BEN *is gone, but* WILLY *is still speaking to him as* LINDA, *in nightgown and robe, enters the kitchen, glances around for* WILLY, *then goes to the door of the house, looks out and sees him. Comes down to his left. He looks at her.*)

LINDA: Willy, dear? Willy?

WILLY: I was right!

LINDA: Did you have some cheese? (*He can't answer.*) It's very late, darling. Come to bed, heh?

WILLY (*looking straight up*): Gotta break your neck to see a star in this yard.

LINDA: You coming in?

WILLY: Whatever happened to that diamond watch fob? Remember? When Ben came from Africa that time? Didn't he give me a watch fob with a diamond in it?

LINDA: You pawned it, dear. Twelve, thirteen years ago. For Biff's radio correspondence course.

WILLY: Gee, that was a beautiful thing. I'll take a walk.

LINDA: But you're in your slippers.

WILLY (*starting to go around the house at the left*): I was right! I was! (*Half to* LINDA, *as he goes, shaking his head.*) What a man! There was a man worth talking to. I was right!

LINDA (*calling after* WILLY): But in your slippers, Willy!

(WILLY *is almost gone when* BIFF, *in his pajamas, comes down the stairs and enters the kitchen.*)

BIFF: What is he doing out there?

LINDA: Sh!

BIFF: God Almighty, Mom, how long has he been doing this?

LINDA: Don't, he'll hear you.

BIFF: What the hell is the matter with him?

LINDA: It'll pass by morning.

BIFF: Shouldn't we do anything?

LINDA: Oh, my dear, you should do a lot of things, but there's nothing to do, so go to sleep.

(HAPPY *comes down the stairs and sits on the steps.*)

HAPPY: I never heard him so loud, Mom.

LINDA: Well, come around more often; you'll hear him. (*She sits down at the table and mends the lining of* WILLY's *jacket.*)

BIFF: Why didn't you ever write me about this, Mom?

LINDA: How would I write to you? For over three months you had no address.

BIFF: I was on the move. But you know I thought of you all the time. You know that, don't you, pal?

LINDA: I know, dear, I know. But he likes to have a letter. Just to know that there's still a possibility for better things.

BIFF: He's not like this all the time, is he?

LINDA: It's when you come home he's always the worst.

BIFF: When I come home?

LINDA: When you write you're coming, he's all smiles, and talks about the future, and — he's just wonderful. And then the closer you seem to come, the more shaky he gets, and then, by the time you get here, he's arguing, and he seems angry at you. I think it's just that maybe he can't bring himself to — to open up to you. Why are you so hateful to each other? Why is that?

BIFF (*evasively*): I'm not hateful, Mom.

LINDA: But you no sooner come in the door than you're fighting!

BIFF: I don't know why. I mean to change. I'm tryin', Mom, you understand?

LINDA: Are you home to stay now?

BIFF: I don't know. I want to look around, see what's doin'.

LINDA: Biff, you can't look around all your life, can you?

BIFF: I just can't take hold, Mom. I can't take hold of some kind of a life.

LINDA: Biff, a man is not a bird, to come and go with the springtime.

BIFF: Your hair . . . (*He touches her hair.*) Your hair got so gray.

LINDA: Oh, it's been gray since you were in high school. I just stopped dyeing it, that's all.

BIFF: Dye it again, will ya? I don't want my pal looking old. (*He smiles.*)

LINDA: You're such a boy! You think you can go away for a year and . . . You've got to get it into your head now that one day you'll knock on this door and there'll be strange people here —

BIFF: What are you talking about? You're not even sixty, Mom.

LINDA: But what about your father?

BIFF (lamely): Well, I meant him too.

HAPPY: He admires Pop.

LINDA: Biff, dear, if you don't have any feeling for him, then you can't have any feeling for me.

BIFF: Sure I can, Mom.

LINDA: No. You can't just come to see me, because I love him. (With a threat, but only a threat, of tears.) He's the dearest man in the world to me, and I won't have anyone making him feel unwanted and low and blue. You've got to make up your mind now, darling, there's no leeway any more. Either he's your father and you pay him that respect, or else you're not to come here. I know he's not easy to get along with — nobody knows that better than me — but . . .

WILLY (from the left, with a laugh): Hey, hey, Biffo!

BIFF (starting to go out after WILLY): What the hell is the matter with him? (HAPPY stops him.)

LINDA: Don't — don't go near him!

BIFF: Stop making excuses for him! He always, always wiped the floor with you. Never had an ounce of respect for you.

HAPPY: He's always had respect for —

BIFF: What the hell do you know about it?

HAPPY (surlily): Just don't call him crazy!

BIFF: He's got no character — Charley wouldn't do this. Not in his own house — spewing out that vomit from his mind.

HAPPY: Charley never had to cope with what he's got to.

BIFF: People are worse off than Willy Loman. Believe me, I've seen them!

LINDA: Then make Charley your father, Biff. You can't do that, can you? I don't say he's a great man. Willy Loman never made a lot of money. His name was never in the paper. He's not the finest character that ever lived. But he's a human being, and a terrible thing is happening to him. So attention must be paid. He's not to be allowed to fall into his grave like an old dog. Attention, attention must be finally paid to such a person. You called him crazy —

BIFF: I didn't mean —

LINDA: No, a lot of people think he's lost his — balance. But you don't have to be very smart to know what his trouble is. The man is exhausted.

HAPPY: Sure!

LINDA: A small man can be just as exhausted as a great man. He works for a company thirty-six years this March, opens up unheard-of territories to their trademark, and now in his old age they take his salary away.

HAPPY (indignantly): I didn't know that, Mom.

LINDA: You never asked, my dear! Now that you get your spending money someplace else you don't trouble your mind with him.

HAPPY: But I gave you money last —

LINDA: Christmas time, fifty dollars! To fix the hot water it cost ninety-seven fifty! For five weeks he's been on straight commission, like a beginner, an unknown!

BIFF: Those ungrateful bastards!

LINDA: Are they any worse than his sons? When he brought them business, when he was young, they were glad to see him. But now his old friends, the old buyers that loved him so and always found some order to hand him in a pinch — they're all dead, retired. He used to be able to make six, seven calls a day in Boston. Now he takes his valises out of the car and puts them back and takes them out again and he's exhausted. Instead of walking he talks now. He drives seven hundred miles, and when he gets there no one knows him any more, no one welcomes him. And what goes through a man's mind, driving seven hundred miles home without having earned a cent? Why shouldn't he talk to himself? Why? When he has to go to Charley and borrow fifty dollars a week and pretend to me that it's his pay? How long can that go on? How long? You see what I'm sitting here and waiting for? And you tell me he has no character? The man who never worked a day but for your benefit? When does he get the medal for that? Is this his reward — to turn around at the age of sixty-three and find his sons, who he loved better than his life, one a philandering bum —

HAPPY: Mom!

LINDA: That's all you are, my baby! (To BIFF.) And you! What happened to the love you had for him? You were such pals! How you used to talk to him on the phone every night! How lonely he was till he could come home to you!

BIFF: All right, Mom. I'll live here in my room, and I'll get a job. I'll keep away from him, that's all.

LINDA: No, Biff. You can't stay here and fight all the time.

BIFF: He threw me out of this house, remember that.

LINDA: Why did he do that? I never knew why.

BIFF: Because I know he's a fake and he doesn't like anybody around who knows!

LINDA: Why a fake? In what way? What do you mean?

BIFF: Just don't lay it all at my feet. It's between me and him — that's all I have to say. I'll chip in from now on. He'll settle for half my pay check. He'll be all right. I'm going to bed. (*He starts for the stairs.*)

LINDA: He won't be all right.

BIFF (*turning on the stairs, furiously*): I hate this city and I'll stay here. Now what do you want?

LINDA: He's dying, Biff.

(HAPPY *turns quickly to her, shocked.*)

BIFF (*after a pause*): Why is he dying?

LINDA: He's been trying to kill himself.

BIFF (*with great horror*): How?

LINDA: I live from day to day.

BIFF: What're you talking about?

LINDA: Remember I wrote you that he smashed up the car again? In February?

BIFF: Well?

LINDA: The insurance inspector came. He said that they have evidence. That all these accidents in the last year — weren't — weren't — accidents.

HAPPY: How can they tell that? That's a lie.

LINDA: It seems there's a woman ... (*She takes a breath as —*)

{ BIFF (*sharply but contained*): What woman?
{ LINDA (*simultaneously*): . . . and this woman ...

LINDA: What?

BIFF: Nothing. Go ahead.

LINDA: What did you say?

BIFF: Nothing. I just said what woman?

HAPPY: What about her?

LINDA: Well, it seems she was walking down the road and saw his car. She says that he wasn't driving fast at all, and that he didn't

skid. She says he came to that little bridge, and then deliberately smashed into the railing, and it was only the shallowness of the water that saved him.

BIFF: Oh, no, he probably just fell asleep again.

LINDA: I don't think he fell asleep.

BIFF: Why not?

LINDA: Last month ... (*With great difficulty.*) Oh, boys, it's so hard to say a thing like this! He's just a big stupid man to you, but I tell you there's more good in him than in many other people. (*She chokes, wipes her eyes.*) I was looking for a fuse. The lights blew out, and I went down the cellar. And behind the fuse box — it happened to fall out — was a length of rubber pipe — just short.

HAPPY: No kidding?

LINDA: There's a little attachment on the end of it. I knew right away. And sure enough, on the bottom of the water heater there's a new little nipple on the gas pipe.

HAPPY (*angrily*): That — jerk.

BIFF: Did you have it taken off?

LINDA: I'm — I'm ashamed to. How can I mention it to him? Every day I go down and take away that little rubber pipe. But, when he comes home, I put it back where it was. How can I insult him that way? I don't know what to do. I live from day to day, boys. I tell you, I know every thought in his mind. It sounds so old-fashioned and silly, but I tell you he put his whole life into you and you've turned your backs on him. (*She is bent over in the chair, weeping, her face in her hands.*) Biff, I swear to God! Biff, his life is in your hands!

HAPPY (*to* BIFF): How do you like that damned fool!

BIFF (*kissing her*): All right, pal, all right. It's all settled now. I've been remiss. I know that, Mom. But now I'll stay, and I swear to you, I'll apply myself. (*Kneeling in front of her, in a fever of self-reproach.*) It's just — you see, Mom, I don't fit in business. Not that I won't try. I'll try, and I'll make good.

HAPPY: Sure you will. The trouble with you in business was you never tried to please people.

BIFF: I know, I —

HAPPY: Like when you worked for Harrison's. Bob Harrison said you were tops, and then you go and do some damn fool thing like whistling whole songs in the elevator like a comedian.

BIFF (*against* HAPPY): So what? I like to whistle sometimes.

HAPPY: You don't raise a guy to a responsible job who whistles in the elevator!

LINDA: Well, don't argue about it now.

HAPPY: Like when you'd go off and swim in the middle of the day instead of taking the line around.

BIFF (*his resentment rising*): Well, don't you run off? You take off sometimes, don't you? On a nice summer day?

HAPPY: Yeah, but I cover myself!

LINDA: Boys!

HAPPY: If I'm going to take a fade the boss can call any number where I'm supposed to be and they'll swear to him that I just left. I'll tell you something that I hate to say, Biff, but in the business world some of them think you're crazy.

BIFF (*angered*): Screw the business world!

HAPPY: All right, screw it! Great, but cover yourself!

LINDA: Hap, Hap!

BIFF: I don't care what they think! They've laughed at Dad for years, and you know why? Because we don't belong in this nut-house of a city! We should be mixing cement on some open plain, or — or carpenters. A carpenter is allowed to whistle!

(WILLY *walks in from the entrance of the house, at left.*)

WILLY: Even your grandfather was better than a carpenter. (*Pause. They watch him.*) You never grew up. Bernard does not whistle in the elevator, I assure you.

BIFF (*as though to laugh* WILLY *out of it*): Yeah, but you do, Pop.

WILLY: I never in my life whistled in an elevator! And who in the business world thinks I'm crazy?

BIFF: I didn't mean it like that, Pop. Now don't make a whole thing out of it, will ya?

WILLY: Go back to the West! Be a carpenter, a cowboy, enjoy yourself!

LINDA: Willy, he was just saying —

WILLY: I heard what he said!

HAPPY (*trying to quiet* WILLY): Hey, Pop, come on now . . .

WILLY (*continuing over* HAPPY's *line*): They laugh at me, heh? Go to Filene's, go to the Hub, go to Slattery's, Boston. Call out the name Willy Loman and see what happens! Big shot!

BIFF: All right, Pop.

WILLY: Big!

BIFF: All right!

WILLY: Why do you always insult me?

BIFF: I didn't say a word. (*To* LINDA.) Did I say a word?

LINDA: He didn't say anything, Willy.

WILLY (*going to the doorway of the living-room*): All right, good night, good night.

LINDA: Willy, dear, he just decided . . .

WILLY (*to* BIFF): If you get tired hanging around tomorrow, paint the ceiling I put up in the living-room.

BIFF: I'm leaving early tomorrow.

HAPPY: He's going to see Bill Oliver, Pop.

WILLY (*interestedly*): Oliver? For what?

BIFF (*with reserve, but trying, trying*): He always said he'd stake me. I'd like to go into business, so maybe I can take him up on it.

LINDA: Isn't that wonderful?

WILLY: Don't interrupt. What's wonderful about it? There's fifty men in the City of New York who'd stake him. (*To* BIFF.) Sporting goods?

BIFF: I guess so. I know something about it and —

WILLY: He knows something about it! You know sporting goods better than Spalding, for God's sake! How much is he giving you?

BIFF: I don't know, I didn't even see him yet, but —

WILLY: Then what're you talkin' about?

BIFF (*getting angry*): Well, all I said was I'm gonna see him, that's all!

WILLY (*turning away*): Ah, you're counting your chickens again.

BIFF (*starting left for the stairs*): Oh, Jesus, I'm going to sleep!

WILLY (*calling after him*): Don't curse in this house!

BIFF (*turning*): Since when did you get so clean?

HAPPY (*trying to stop them*): Wait a . . .

WILLY: Don't use that language to me! I won't have it!

HAPPY (*grabbing* BIFF, *shouts*): Wait a minute! I got an idea. I got a feasible idea. Come here, Biff, let's talk this over now, let's talk some sense here. When I was down in Florida last time, I thought of a great idea to sell sporting goods. It just came back to me. You and I, Biff — we have a line, the Loman Line. We train a couple of weeks, and put on a couple of exhibitions, see?

WILLY: That's an idea!

HAPPY: Wait! We form two basketball teams, see? Two water-polo teams. We play each other. It's a million dollars' worth of publicity. Two brothers, see? The Loman Brothers. Displays in the Royal Palms — all the hotels. And banners over the ring and the basketball court: "Loman Brothers." Baby, we could sell sporting goods!

WILLY: That is a one-million-dollar idea!

LINDA: Marvelous!

BIFF: I'm in great shape as far as that's concerned.

HAPPY: And the beauty of it is, Biff, it wouldn't be like a business. We'd be out playin' ball again . . .

BIFF (enthused): Yeah, that's . . .

WILLY: Million-dollar . . .

HAPPY: And you wouldn't get fed up with it, Biff. It'd be the family again. There'd be the old honor, and comradeship, and if you wanted to go off for a swim or somethin' — well, you'd do it! Without some smart cooky gettin' up ahead of you!

WILLY: Lick the world! You guys together could absolutely lick the civilized world.

BIFF: I'll see Oliver tomorrow. Hap, if we could work that out . . .

LINDA: Maybe things are beginning to —

WILLY (wildly enthused, to LINDA): Stop interrupting! (To BIFF.) But don't wear sport jacket and slacks when you see Oliver.

BIFF: No, I'll —

WILLY: A business suit, and talk as little as possible, and don't crack any jokes.

BIFF: He did like me. Always liked me.

LINDA: He loved you!

WILLY (to LINDA): Will you stop! (To BIFF.) Walk in very serious. You are not applying for a boy's job. Money is to pass. Be quiet, fine, and serious. Everybody likes a kidder, but nobody lends him money.

HAPPY: I'll try to get some myself, Biff. I'm sure I can.

WILLY: I see great things for you kids, I think your troubles are over. But remember, start big and you'll end big. Ask for fifteen. How much you gonna ask for?

BIFF: Gee, I don't know —

WILLY: And don't say "Gee." "Gee" is a boy's word. A man walking in for fifteen thousand dollars does not say "Gee!"

BIFF: Ten, I think, would be top though.

WILLY: Don't be so modest. You always started too low. Walk in with a big laugh. Don't look worried. Start off with a couple of your good stories to lighten things up. It's not what you say, it's how you say it — because personality always wins the day.

LINDA: Oliver always thought the highest of him —

WILLY: Will you let me talk?

BIFF: Don't yell at her, Pop, will ya?

WILLY (angrily): I was talking, wasn't I?

BIFF: I don't like you yelling at her all the time, and I'm tellin' you, that's all.

WILLY: What're you, takin' over this house?

LINDA: Willy —

WILLY (turning on her): Don't take his side all the time, goddammit!

BIFF (furiously): Stop yelling at her!

WILLY (suddenly pulling on his cheek, beaten down, guilt ridden): Give my best to Bill Oliver — he may remember me. (He exits through the living-room doorway.)

LINDA (her voice subdued): What'd you have to start that for? (BIFF turns away.) You see how sweet he was as soon as you talked hopefully? (She goes over to BIFF.) Come up and say good night to him. Don't let him go to bed that way.

HAPPY: Come on, Biff, let's buck him up.

LINDA: Please, dear. Just say good night. It takes so little to make him happy. Come. (She goes through the living-room doorway, calling upstairs from within the living-room.) Your pajamas are hanging in the bathroom, Willy!

HAPPY (looking toward where LINDA went out): What a woman! They broke the mold when they made her. You know that, Biff?

BIFF: He's off salary. My God, working on commission!

HAPPY: Well, let's face it: he's no hot-shot selling man. Except that sometimes, you have to admit, he's a sweet personality.

BIFF (deciding): Lend me ten bucks, will ya? I want to buy some new ties.

HAPPY: I'll take you to a place I know. Beautiful stuff. Wear one of my striped shirts tomorrow.

BIFF: She got gray. Mom got awful old. Gee, I'm gonna go in to Oliver tomorrow and knock him for a —

HAPPY: Come on up. Tell that to Dad. Let's give him a whirl. Come on.

BIFF (steamed up): You know, with ten thousand bucks, boy!

HAPPY (as they go into the living-room): That's the talk, Biff, that's the first time I've heard the old confidence out of you! (From within the living-room, fading off.) You're gonna live with me, kid, and any babe you want just say the word . . . (*The last lines are hardly heard. They are mounting the stairs to their parents' bedroom.*)

LINDA (*entering her bedroom and addressing* WILLY, *who is in the bathroom. She is straightening the bed for him*): Can you do anything about the shower? It drips.

WILLY (*from the bathroom*): All of a sudden everything falls to pieces! Goddam plumbing, oughta be sued, those people. I hardly finished putting it in and the thing . . . (*His words rumble off.*)

LINDA: I'm just wondering if Oliver will remember him. You think he might?

WILLY (*coming out of the bathroom in his pajamas*): Remember him? What's the matter with you, you crazy? If he'd've stayed with Oliver he'd be on top by now! Wait'll Oliver gets a look at him. You don't know the average caliber any more. The average young man today — (*he is getting into bed*) — is got a caliber of zero. Greatest thing in the world for him was to bum around.

(BIFF *and* HAPPY *enter the bedroom. Slight pause.*)

WILLY (*stops short, looking at* BIFF): Glad to hear it, boy.

HAPPY: He wanted to say good night to you, sport.

WILLY (*to* BIFF): Yeah. Knock him dead, boy. What'd you want to tell me?

BIFF: Just take it easy, Pop. Good night. (*He turns to go.*)

WILLY (*unable to resist*): And if anything falls off the desk while you're talking to him — like a package or something — don't you pick it up. They have office boys for that.

LINDA: I'll make a big breakfast —

WILLY: Will you let me finish? (*To* BIFF.) Tell him you were in the business in the West. Not farm work.

BIFF: All right, Dad.

LINDA: I think everything —

WILLY (*going right through her speech*): And don't undersell yourself. No less than fifteen thousand dollars.

BIFF (*unable to bear him*): Okay. Good night, Mom. (*He starts moving.*)

WILLY: Because you got a greatness in you, Biff, remember that. You got all kinds a greatness . . . (*He lies back, exhausted.* BIFF *walks out.*)

LINDA (*calling after* BIFF): Sleep well, darling!

HAPPY: I'm gonna get married, Mom. I wanted to tell you.

LINDA: Go to sleep, dear.

HAPPY (*going*): I just wanted to tell you.

WILLY: Keep up the good work. (HAPPY *exits.*) God . . . remember that Ebbets Field game? The championship of the city?

LINDA: Just rest. Should I sing to you?

WILLY: Yeah. Sing to me. (LINDA *hums a soft lullaby.*) When that team came out — he was the tallest, remember?

LINDA: Oh, yes. And in gold.

(BIFF *enters the darkened kitchen, takes a cigarette, and leaves the house. He comes downstage into a golden pool of light. He smokes, staring at the night.*)

WILLY: Like a young god. Hercules — something like that. And the sun, the sun all around him. Remember how he waved to me? Right up from the field, with the representatives of three colleges standing by? And the buyers I brought, and the cheers when he came out — Loman, Loman, Loman! God Almighty, he'll be great yet. A star like that, magnificent, can never really fade away!

(*The light on* WILLY *is fading. The gas heater begins to glow through the kitchen wall, near the stairs, a blue flame beneath red coils.*)

LINDA (*timidly*): Willy dear, what has he got against you?

WILLY: I'm so tired. Don't talk any more.

(BIFF *slowly returns to the kitchen. He stops, stares toward the heater.*)

LINDA: Will you ask Howard to let you work in New York?

WILLY: First thing in the morning. Everything'll be all right.

(BIFF *reaches behind the heater and draws out a length of rubber tubing. He is horrified and turns his head toward* WILLY'S *room, still dimly lit, from which the strains of* LINDA'S *desperate but monotonous humming rise.*)

WILLY (*staring through the window into the*

moonlight): Gee, look at the moon moving between the buildings!

(BIFF *wraps the tubing around his hand and quickly goes up the stairs.*)

CURTAIN

ACT II

Music is heard, gay and bright. The curtain rises as the music fades away. WILLY, *in shirt sleeves, is sitting at the kitchen table, sipping coffee, his hat in his lap.* LINDA *is filling his cup when she can.*

WILLY: Wonderful coffee. Meal in itself.

LINDA: Can I make you some eggs?

WILLY: No. Take a breath.

LINDA: You look so rested, dear.

WILLY: I slept like a dead one. First time in months. Imagine, sleeping till ten on a Tuesday morning. Boys left nice and early, heh?

LINDA: They were out of here by eight o'clock.

WILLY: Good work!

LINDA: It was so thrilling to see them leaving together. I can't get over the shaving lotion in this house!

WILLY (*smiling*): Mmm —

LINDA: Biff was very changed this morning. His whole attitude seemed to be hopeful. He couldn't wait to get downtown to see Oliver.

WILLY: He's heading for a change. There's no question, there simply are certain men that take longer to get — solidified. How did he dress?

LINDA: His blue suit. He's so handsome in that suit. He could be a — anything in that suit!

(WILLY *gets up from the table.* LINDA *holds his jacket for him.*)

WILLY: There's no question, no question at all. Gee, on the way home tonight I'd like to buy some seeds.

LINDA (*laughing*): That'd be wonderful. But not enough sun gets back there. Nothing'll grow any more.

WILLY: You wait, kid, before it's all over we're gonna get a little place out in the country, and I'll raise some vegetables, a couple of chickens . . .

LINDA: You'll do it yet, dear.

(WILLY *walks out of his jacket.* LINDA *follows him.*)

WILLY: And they'll get married, and come for a weekend. I'd build a little guest house. 'Cause I got so many fine tools, all I'd need would be a little lumber and some peace of mind.

LINDA (*joyfully*): I sewed the lining . . .

WILLY: I could build two guest houses, so they'd both come. Did he decide how much he's going to ask Oliver for?

LINDA (*getting him into the jacket*): He didn't mention it, but I imagine ten or fifteen thousand. You going to talk to Howard today?

WILLY: Yeah. I'll put it to him straight and simple. He'll just have to take me off the road.

LINDA: And Willy, don't forget to ask for a little advance, because we've got the insurance premium. It's the grace period now.

WILLY: That's a hundred . . . ?

LINDA: A hundred and eight, sixty-eight. Because we're a little short again.

WILLY: Why are we short?

LINDA: Well, you had the motor job on the car . . .

WILLY: That goddam Studebaker!

LINDA: And you got one more payment on the refrigerator . . .

WILLY: But it just broke again!

LINDA: Well, it's old, dear.

WILLY: I told you we should've bought a well-advertised machine. Charley bought a General Electric and it's twenty years old and it's still good, that son-of-a-bitch.

LINDA: But, Willy —

WILLY: Whoever heard of a Hastings refrigerator? Once in my life I would like to own something outright before it's broken! I'm always in a race with the junkyard! I just finished paying for the car and it's on its last legs. The refrigerator consumes belts like a goddam maniac. They time those things. They time them so when you finally paid for them, they're used up.

LINDA (*buttoning up his jacket as he unbuttons it*): All told, about two hundred dollars would carry us, dear. But that includes the last payment on the mortgage. After this payment, Willy, the house belongs to us.

WILLY: It's twenty-five years!

LINDA: Biff was nine years old when we bought it.

WILLY: Well, that's a great thing. To weather a twenty-five year mortgage is —

LINDA: It's an accomplishment.

WILLY: All the cement, the lumber, the reconstruction I put in this house! There ain't a crack to be found in it any more.

LINDA: Well, it served its purpose.

WILLY: What purpose? Some stranger'll come along, move in, and that's that. If only Biff would take this house, and raise a family ... (*He starts to go.*) Good-by, I'm late.

LINDA (*suddenly remembering*): Oh, I forgot! You're supposed to meet them for dinner.

WILLY: Me?

LINDA: At Frank's Chop House on Forty-eighth near Sixth Avenue.

WILLY: Is that so! How about you?

LINDA: No, just the three of you. They're gonna blow you to a big meal!

WILLY: Don't say! Who thought of that?

LINDA: Biff came to me this morning, Willy, and he said, "Tell Dad, we want to blow him to a big meal." Be there six o'clock. You and your two boys are going to have dinner.

WILLY: Gee whiz! That's really somethin'. I'm gonna knock Howard for a loop, kid. I'll get an advance, and I'll come home with a New York job. Goddammit, now I'm gonna do it!

LINDA: Oh, that's the spirit, Willy!

WILLY: I will never get behind a wheel the rest of my life!

LINDA: It's changing, Willy, I can feel it changing!

WILLY: Beyond a question. G'by, I'm late. (*He starts to go again.*)

LINDA (*calling after him as she runs to the kitchen table for a handkerchief*): You got your glasses?

WILLY (*feels for them, then comes back in*): Yeah, yeah, got my glasses.

LINDA (*giving him the handkerchief*): And a handkerchief.

WILLY: Yeah, handkerchief.

LINDA: And your saccharine?

WILLY: Yeah, my saccharine.

LINDA: Be careful on the subway stairs.

(*She kisses him, and a silk stocking is seen hanging from her hand.* WILLY *notices it.*)

WILLY: Will you stop mending stockings? At least while I'm in the house. It gets me nervous. I can't tell you. Please.

(LINDA *hides the stocking in her hand as she follows* WILLY *across the forestage in front of the house.*)

LINDA: Remember, Frank's Chop House.

WILLY (*passing the apron*): Maybe beets would grow out there.

LINDA (*laughing*): But you tried so many times.

WILLY: Yeah. Well, don't work hard today. (*He disappears around the right corner of the house.*)

LINDA: Be careful!

(*As* WILLY *vanishes,* LINDA *waves to him. Suddenly the phone rings. She runs across the stage and into the kitchen and lifts it.*)

LINDA: Hello? Oh, Biff! I'm so glad you called, I just ... Yes, sure, I just told him. Yes, he'll be there for dinner at six o'clock, I didn't forget. Listen, I was just dying to tell you. You know that little rubber pipe I told you about? That he connected to the gas heater? I finally decided to go down the cellar this morning and take it away and destroy it. But it's gone! Imagine? He took it away himself, it isn't there! (*She listens.*) When? Oh, then you took it. Oh — nothing, it's just that I'd hoped he'd taken it away himself. Oh, I'm not worried, darling, because this morning he left in such high spirits, it was like the old days! I'm not afraid any more. Did Mr. Oliver see you? ... Well, you wait there then. And make a nice impression on him, darling. Just don't perspire too much before you see him. And have a nice time with Dad. He may have big news too! ... That's right, a New York job. And be sweet to him tonight, dear. Be loving to him. Because he's only a little boat looking for a harbor. (*She is trembling with sorrow and joy.*) Oh, that's wonderful, Biff, you'll save his life. Thanks, darling. Just put your arm around him when he comes into the restaurant. Give him a smile. That's the boy ... Good-by, dear. ... You got your comb? ... That's fine. Good-by, Biff dear.

(*In the middle of her speech,* HOWARD WAGNER, *thirty-six, wheels on a small typewriter table on which is a wire-recording machine and proceeds to plug it in. This is on the left forestage. Light slowly fades on* LINDA *as it rises on* HOWARD. HOWARD *is intent on threading the machine and only glances over his shoulder as* WILLY *appears.*)

WILLY: Pst! Pst!

HOWARD: Hello, Willy, come in.

WILLY: Like to have a little talk with you, Howard.

HOWARD: Sorry to keep you waiting. I'll be with you in a minute.

WILLY: What's that, Howard?

HOWARD: Didn't you ever see one of these? Wire recorder.

WILLY: Oh. Can we talk a minute?

HOWARD: Records things. Just got delivery yesterday. Been driving me crazy, the most terrific machine I ever saw in my life. I was up all night with it.

WILLY: What do you do with it?

HOWARD: I bought it for dictation, but you can do anything with it. Listen to this. I had it home last night. Listen to what I picked up. The first one is my daughter. Get this. (*He flicks the switch and "Roll out the Barrel" is heard being whistled.*) Listen to that kid whistle.

WILLY: That is lifelike, isn't it?

HOWARD: Seven years old. Get that tone.

WILLY: Ts, ts. Like to ask a little favor if you . . .

(*The whistling breaks off, and the voice of* HOWARD'S DAUGHTER *is heard.*)

HIS DAUGHTER: "Now you, Daddy."

HOWARD: She's crazy for me! (*Again the same song is whistled.*) That's me! Ha! (*He winks.*)

WILLY: You're very good!

(*The whistling breaks off again. The machine runs silent for a moment.*)

HOWARD: Sh! Get this now, this is my son.

HIS SON: "The capital of Alabama is Montgomery; the capital of Arizona is Phoenix; the capital of Arkansas is Little Rock; the capital of California is Sacramento . . ." (*And on, and on.*)

HOWARD (*holding up five fingers*): Five years old, Willy!

WILLY: He'll make an announcer some day!

HIS SON (*continuing*): "The capital . . ."

HOWARD: Get that — alphabetical order! (*The machine breaks off suddenly.*) Wait a minute. The maid kicked the plug out.

WILLY: It certainly is a —

HOWARD: Sh, for God's sake!

HIS SON: "It's nine o'clock, Bulova watch time. So I have to go to sleep."

WILLY: That really is —

HOWARD: Wait a minute! The next is my wife.

(*They wait.*)

HOWARD'S VOICE: "Go on, say something." (*Pause.*) "Well, you gonna talk?"

HIS WIFE: "I can't think of anything."

HOWARD'S VOICE: "Well, talk — it's turning."

HIS WIFE (*shyly, beaten*): "Hello." (*Silence.*) "Oh, Howard, I can't talk into this . . ."

HOWARD (*snapping the machine off*): That was my wife.

WILLY: That is a wonderful machine. Can we —

HOWARD: I tell you, Willy, I'm gonna take my camera, and my bandsaw, and all my hobbies, and out they go. This is the most fascinating relaxation I ever found.

WILLY: I think I'll get one myself.

HOWARD: Sure, they're only a hundred and a half. You can't do without it. Supposing you wanna hear Jack Benny, see? But you can't be at home at that hour. So you tell the maid to turn the radio on when Jack Benny comes on, and this automatically goes on with the radio . . .

WILLY: And when you come home you . . .

HOWARD: You can come home twelve o'clock, one o'clock, any time you like, and you get yourself a Coke and sit yourself down, throw the switch, and there's Jack Benny's program in the middle of the night!

WILLY: I'm definitely going to get one. Because lots of time I'm on the road, and I think to myself, what I must be missing on the radio!

HOWARD: Don't you have a radio in the car?

WILLY: Well, yeah, but who ever thinks of turning it on?

HOWARD: Say, aren't you supposed to be in Boston?

WILLY: That's what I want to talk to you about, Howard. You got a minute? (*He draws a chair in from the wing.*)

HOWARD: What happened? What're you doing here?

WILLY: Well . . .

HOWARD: You didn't crack up again, did you?

WILLY: Oh, no. No . . .

HOWARD: Geez, you had me worried there for a minute. What's the trouble?

WILLY: Well, tell you the truth, Howard. I've come to the decision that I'd rather not travel any more.

HOWARD: Not travel! Well, what'll you do?

WILLY: Remember, Christmas time, when you had the party here? You said you'd try to think of some spot for me here in town.

HOWARD: With us?

WILLY: Well, sure.

HOWARD: Oh, yeah, yeah. I remember. Well, I couldn't think of anything for you, Willy.

WILLY: I tell ya, Howard. The kids are all grown up, y'know. I don't need much any more. If I could take home — well, sixty-five dollars a week, I could swing it.

HOWARD: Yeah, but Willy, see I —

WILLY: I tell ya why, Howard. Speaking frankly and between the two of us, y'know — I'm just a little tired.

HOWARD: Oh, I could understand that, Willy. But you're a road man, Willy, and we do a road business. We've only got a half-dozen salesmen on the floor here.

WILLY: God knows, Howard, I never asked a favor of any man. But I was with the firm when your father used to carry you in here in his arms.

HOWARD: I know that, Willy, but —

WILLY: Your father came to me the day you were born and asked me what I thought of the name of Howard, may he rest in peace.

HOWARD: I appreciate that, Willy, but there just is no spot here for you. If I had a spot I'd slam you right in, but I just don't have a single solitary spot.

(*He looks for his lighter.* WILLY *has picked it up and gives it to him. Pause.*)

WILLY (*with increasing anger*): Howard, all I need to set my table is fifty dollars a week.

HOWARD: But where am I going to put you, kid?

WILLY: Look, it isn't a question of whether I can sell merchandise, is it?

HOWARD: No, but it's a business, kid, and everybody's gotta pull his own weight.

WILLY (*desperately*): Just let me tell you a story, Howard —

HOWARD: 'Cause you gotta admit, business is business.

WILLY (*angrily*): Business is definitely business, but just listen for a minute. You don't understand this. When I was a boy — eighteen, nineteen — I was already on the road. And there was a question in my mind as to whether selling had a future for me. Because in those days I had a yearning to go to Alaska. See, there were three gold strikes in one month in Alaska, and I felt like going out. Just for the ride, you might say.

HOWARD (*barely interested*): Don't say.

WILLY: Oh, yeah, my father lived many years in Alaska. He was an adventurous man. We've got quite a little streak of self-reliance in our family. I thought I'd go out with my older brother and try to locate him, and maybe settle in the North with the old man. And I was almost decided to go, when I met a salesman in the Parker House. His name was Dave Singleman. And he was eighty-four years old, and he'd drummed merchandise in thirty-one states. And old Dave, he'd go up to his room, y'understand, put on his green velvet slippers — I'll never forget — and pick up his phone and call the buyers, and without ever leaving his room, at the age of eighty-four, he made his living. And when I saw that, I realized that selling was the greatest career a man could want. 'Cause what could be more satisfying than to be able to go, at the age of eighty-four, into twenty or thirty different cities, and pick up a phone, and be remembered and loved and helped by so many different people? Do you know? when he died — and by the way he died the death of a salesman, in his green velvet slippers in the smoker of the New York, New Haven and Hartford, going into Boston — when he died, hundreds of salesmen and buyers were at his funeral. Things were sad on a lotta trains for months after that. (*He stands up.* HOWARD *has not looked at him.*) In those days there was personality in it, Howard. There was respect, and comradeship, and gratitude in it. Today, it's all cut and dried, and there's no chance for bringing friendship to bear — or personality. You see what I mean? They don't know me any more.

HOWARD (*moving away, to the right*): That's just the thing, Willy.

WILLY: If I had forty dollars a week — that's all I'd need. Forty dollars, Howard.

HOWARD: Kid, I can't take blood from a stone, I —

WILLY (*desperation is on him now*): Howard, the year Al Smith was nominated, your father came to me and —

HOWARD (*starting to go off*): I've got to see some people, kid.

WILLY (*stopping him*): I'm talking about your father! There were promises made across this desk! You mustn't tell me you've got people to see — I put thirty-four years into this firm, Howard, and now I can't pay my insurance! You can't eat the orange and throw the peel away — a man is not a piece of fruit! (*After a pause.*) Now pay attention. Your father — in 1928 I had a big year. I averaged a hundred and seventy dollars a week in commissions.

HOWARD (*impatiently*): Now, Willy, you never averaged —

WILLY (*banging his hand on the desk*): I averaged a hundred and seventy dollars a week in the year of 1928! And your father came to me — or rather, I was in the office here — it was right over this desk — and he put his hand on my shoulder —

HOWARD (*getting up*): You'll have to excuse me, Willy, I gotta see some people. Pull yourself together. (*Going out.*) I'll be back in a little while.

(*On* HOWARD's *exit, the light on his chair grows very bright and strange.*)

WILLY: Pull myself together! What the hell did I say to him? My God, I was yelling at him! How could I! (WILLY *breaks off, staring at the light, which occupies the chair, animating it. He approaches this chair, standing across the desk from it.*) Frank, Frank, don't you remember what you told me that time? How you put your hand on my shoulder, and Frank . . . (*He leans on the desk and as he speaks the dead man's name he accidentally switches on the recorder, and instantly —*)

HOWARD'S SON: ". . . of New York is Albany. The capital of Ohio is Cincinnati, the capital of Rhode Island is . . ." (*The recitation continues.*)

WILLY (*leaping away with fright, shouting*): Ha! Howard! Howard! Howard!

HOWARD (*rushing in*): What happened?

WILLY (*pointing at the machine, which continues nasally, childishly, with the capital cities*): Shut it off! Shut it off!

HOWARD (*pulling the plug out*): Look, Willy . . .

WILLY (*pressing his hands to his eyes*): I gotta get myself some coffee. I'll get some coffee . . .

(WILLY *starts to walk out.* HOWARD *stops him.*)

HOWARD (*rolling up the cord*): Willy, look . . .

WILLY: I'll go to Boston.

HOWARD: Willy, you can't go to Boston for us.

WILLY: Why can't I go?

HOWARD: I don't want you to represent us. I've been meaning to tell you for a long time now.

WILLY: Howard, are you firing me?

HOWARD: I think you need a good long rest, Willy.

WILLY: Howard —

HOWARD: And when you feel better, come back, and we'll see if we can work something out.

WILLY: But I gotta earn money, Howard. I'm in no position to —

HOWARD: Where are your sons? Why don't your sons give you a hand?

WILLY: They're working on a very big deal.

HOWARD: This is no time for false pride, Willy. You go to your sons and you tell them that you're tired. You've got two great boys, haven't you?

WILLY: Oh, no question, no question, but in the meantime . . .

HOWARD: Then that's that, heh?

WILLY: All right, I'll go to Boston tomorrow.

HOWARD: No, no.

WILLY: I can't throw myself on my sons. I'm not a cripple!

HOWARD: Look, kid, I'm busy this morning.

WILLY (*grasping* HOWARD's *arm*): Howard, you've got to let me go to Boston!

HOWARD (*hard, keeping himself under control*): I've got a line of people to see this morning. Sit down, take five minutes, and pull yourself together, and then go home, will ya? I need the office, Willy. (*He starts to go, turns, remembering the recorder, starts to push off the table holding the recorder.*) Oh, yeah. Whenever you can this week, stop by and drop off the samples. You'll feel better, Willy, and then come back and we'll talk. Pull yourself together, kid, there's people outside.

(HOWARD *exits, pushing the table off left.* WILLY *stares into space, exhausted. Now the music is heard —* BEN's *music — first distantly, then closer, closer. As* WILLY *speaks,* BEN *enters from the right. He carries valise and umbrella.*)

WILLY: Oh, Ben, how did you do it? What

is the answer? Did you wind up the Alaska deal already?

BEN: Doesn't take much time if you know what you're doing. Just a short business trip. Boarding ship in an hour. Wanted to say good-by.

WILLY: Ben, I've got to talk to you.

BEN (*glancing at his watch*): Haven't the time, William.

WILLY (*crossing the apron to* BEN): Ben, nothing's working out. I don't know what to do.

BEN: Now, look here, William. I've bought timberland in Alaska and I need a man to look after things for me.

WILLY: God, timberland! Me and my boys in those grand outdoors!

BEN: You've a new continent at your doorstep, William. Get out of these cities, they're full of talk and time payments and courts of law. Screw on your fists and you can fight for a fortune up there.

WILLY: Yes, yes! Linda, Linda!

(LINDA *enters as of old, with the wash.*)

LINDA: Oh, you're back?

BEN: I haven't much time.

WILLY: No, wait! Linda, he's got a proposition for me in Alaska.

LINDA: But you've got — (*To* BEN.) He's got a beautiful job here.

WILLY: But in Alaska, kid, I could —

LINDA: You're doing well enough, Willy!

BEN (*to* LINDA): Enough for what, my dear?

LINDA (*frightened of* BEN *and angry at him*): Don't say those things to him! Enough to be happy right here, right now. (*To* WILLY, *while* BEN *laughs.*) Why must everybody conquer the world? You're well liked, and the boys love you, and someday — (*to* BEN) — why, old man Wagner told him just the other day that if he keeps it up he'll be a member of the firm, didn't he, Willy?

WILLY: Sure, sure. I am building something with this firm, Ben, and if a man is building something he must be on the right track, mustn't he?

BEN: What are you building? Lay your hand on it. Where is it?

WILLY (*hesitantly*): That's true, Linda, there's nothing.

LINDA: Why? (*To* BEN.) There's a man eighty-four years old —

WILLY: That's right, Ben, that's right. When I look at that man I say, what is there to worry about?

BEN: Bah!

WILLY: It's true, Ben. All he has to do is go into any city, pick up the phone, and he's making his living and you know why?

BEN (*picking up his valise*): I've got to go.

WILLY (*holding* BEN *back*): Look at this boy!

(BIFF, *in his high school sweater, enters carrying suitcase.* HAPPY *carries* BIFF's *shoulder guards, gold helmet, and football pants.*)

WILLY: Without a penny to his name, three great universities are begging for him, and from there the sky's the limit, because it's not what you do, Ben. It's who you know and the smile on your face! It's contacts, Ben, contacts! The whole wealth of Alaska passes over the lunch table at the Commodore Hotel, and that's the wonder, the wonder of this country, that a man can end with diamonds here on the basis of being liked! (*He turns to* BIFF.) And that's why when you get out on that field today it's important. Because thousands of people will be rooting for you and loving you. (*To* BEN, *who has again begun to leave.*) And Ben! when he walks into a business office his name will sound out like a bell and all the doors will open to him! I've seen it, Ben, I've seen it a thousand times! You can't feel it with your hand like timber, but it's there!

BEN: Good-by, William.

WILLY: Ben, am I right? Don't you think I'm right? I value your advice.

BEN: There's a new continent at your doorstep, William. You could walk out rich. Rich! (*He is gone.*)

WILLY: We'll do it here, Ben! You hear me? We're gonna do it here!

(YOUNG BERNARD *rushes in. The gay music of the boys is heard.*)

BERNARD: Oh, gee, I was afraid you left already!

WILLY: Why? What time is it?

BERNARD: It's half-past one!

WILLY: Well, come on, everybody! Ebbets Field next stop! Where's the pennants? (*He rushes through the wall-line of the kitchen and out into the living-room.*)

LINDA (*to* BIFF): Did you pack fresh underwear?

BIFF (*who has been limbering up*): I want to go!

BERNARD: Biff, I'm carrying your helmet, ain't I?

HAPPY: No, I'm carrying the helmet.

BERNARD: Oh, Biff, you promised me.

HAPPY: I'm carrying the helmet.

BERNARD: How am I going to get in the locker room?

LINDA: Let him carry the shoulder guards. (*She puts her coat and hat on in the kitchen.*)

BERNARD: Can I, Biff? 'Cause I told everybody I'm going to be in the locker room.

HAPPY: In Ebbets Field it's the clubhouse.

BERNARD: I meant the clubhouse. Biff!

HAPPY: Biff!

BIFF (*grandly, after a slight pause*): Let him carry the shoulder guards.

HAPPY (*as he gives* BERNARD *the shoulder guards*): Stay close to us now.

(WILLY *rushes in with the pennants.*)

WILLY (*handing them out*): Everybody wave when Biff comes out on the field. (HAPPY *and* BERNARD *run off.*) You set now, boy?

(*The music has died away.*)

BIFF: Ready to go, Pop. Every muscle is ready.

WILLY (*at the edge of the apron*): You realize what this means?

BIFF: That's right, Pop.

WILLY (*feeling* BIFF'*s muscles*): You're comin' home this afternoon captain of the All-Scholastic Championship Team of the City of New York.

BIFF: I got it, Pop. And remember, pal, when I take off my helmet, that touchdown is for you.

WILLY: Let's go! (*He is starting out, with his arm around* BIFF, *when* CHARLEY *enters, as of old, in knickers.*) I got no room for you, Charley.

CHARLEY: Room? For what?

WILLY: In the car.

CHARLEY: You goin' for a ride? I wanted to shoot some casino.

WILLY (*furiously*): Casino! (*Incredulously.*) Don't you realize what today is?

LINDA: Oh, he knows, Willy. He's just kidding you.

WILLY: That's nothing to kid about!

CHARLEY: No, Linda, what's goin' on?

LINDA: He's playing in Ebbets Field.

CHARLEY: Baseball in this weather?

WILLY: Don't talk to him. Come on, come on! (*He is pushing them out.*)

CHARLEY: Wait a minute, didn't you hear the news?

WILLY: What?

CHARLEY: Don't you listen to the radio? Ebbets Field just blew up.

WILLY: You go to hell! (CHARLEY *laughs. Pushing them out.*) Come on, come on! We're late.

CHARLEY (*as they go*): Knock a homer, Biff, knock a homer!

WILLY (*the last to leave, turning to* CHARLEY): I don't think that was funny, Charley. This is the greatest day of his life.

CHARLEY: Willy, when are you going to grow up?

WILLY: Yeah, heh? When this game is over, Charley, you'll be laughing out of the other side of your face. They'll be calling him another Red Grange. Twenty-five thousand a year.

CHARLEY (*kidding*): Is that so?

WILLY: Yeah, that's so.

CHARLEY: Well, then, I'm sorry, Willy. But tell me something.

WILLY: What?

CHARLEY: Who is Red Grange?

WILLY: Put up your hands. Goddam you, put up your hands!

(CHARLEY, *chuckling, shakes his head and walks away, around the left corner of the stage.* WILLY *follows him. The music rises to a mocking frenzy.*)

WILLY: Who the hell do you think you are, better than everybody else? You don't know everything, you big, ignorant, stupid . . . Put up your hands!

(*Light rises, on the right side of the forestage, on a small table in the reception room of* CHARLEY'*s office. Traffic sounds are heard.* BERNARD, *now mature, sits whistling to himself. A pair of tennis rackets and an overnight bag are on the floor beside him.*)

WILLY (*offstage*): What are you walking away for? Don't walk away! If you're going to say something say it to my face! I know you laugh at me behind my back. You'll laugh out of the other side of your goddam face after this game. Touchdown! Touchdown! Eighty thousand people! Touchdown! Right between the goal posts.

(BERNARD *is a quiet, earnest, but self-assured young man.* WILLY's *voice is coming from right upstage now.* BERNARD *lowers his feet off the table and listens.* JENNY, *his father's secretary, enters.*)

JENNY (*distressed*): Say, Bernard, will you go out in the hall?

BERNARD: What is that noise? Who is it?

JENNY: Mr. Loman. He just got off the elevator.

BERNARD (*getting up*): Who's he arguing with?

JENNY: Nobody. There's nobody with him. I can't deal with him any more, and your father gets all upset everytime he comes. I've got a lot of typing to do, and your father's waiting to sign it. Will you see him?

WILLY (*entering*): Touchdown! Touch — (*He sees* JENNY.) Jenny, Jenny, good to see you. How're ya? Workin'? Or still honest?

JENNY: Fine. How've you been feeling?

WILLY: Not much any more, Jenny. Ha, ha! (*He is surprised to see the rackets.*)

BERNARD: Hello, Uncle Willy.

WILLY (*almost shocked*): Bernard! Well, look who's here! (*He comes quickly, guiltily, to* BERNARD *and warmly shakes his hand.*)

BERNARD: How are you? Good to see you.

WILLY: What are you doing here?

BERNARD: Oh, just stopped by to see Pop. Get off my feet till my train leaves. I'm going to Washington in a few minutes.

WILLY: Is he in?

BERNARD: Yes, he's in his office with the accountant. Sit down.

WILLY (*sitting down*): What're you going to do in Washington?

BERNARD: Oh, just a case I've got there, Willy.

WILLY: That so? (*Indicating the rackets.*) You going to play tennis there?

BERNARD: I'm staying with a friend who's got a court.

WILLY: Don't say. His own tennis court. Must be fine people, I bet.

BERNARD: They are, very nice. Dad tells me Biff's in town.

WILLY (*with a big smile*): Yeah, Biff's in. Working on a very big deal, Bernard.

BERNARD: What's Biff doing?

WILLY: Well, he's been doing very big things in the West. But he decided to establish himself here. Very big. We're having dinner. Did I hear your wife had a boy?

BERNARD: That's right. Our second.

WILLY: Two boys! What do you know!

BERNARD: What kind of a deal has Biff got?

WILLY: Well, Bill Oliver — very big sporting-goods man — he wants Biff very badly. Called him in from the West. Long distance, carte blanche, special deliveries. Your friends have their own private tennis court?

BERNARD: You still with the old firm, Willy?

WILLY (*after a pause*): I'm — I'm overjoyed to see how you made the grade, Bernard, overjoyed. It's an encouraging thing to see a young man really — really — Looks very good for Biff — very — (*He breaks off, then.*) Bernard — (*He is so full of emotion, he breaks off again.*)

BERNARD: What is it, Willy?

WILLY (*small and alone*): What — what's the secret?

BERNARD: What secret?

WILLY: How — how did you? Why didn't he ever catch on?

BERNARD: I wouldn't know that, Willy.

WILLY (*confidentially, desperately*): You were his friend, his boyhood friend. There's something I don't understand about it. His life ended after that Ebbets Field game. From the age of seventeen nothing good ever happened to him.

BERNARD: He never trained himself for anything.

WILLY: But he did, he did. After high school he took so many correspondence courses. Radio mechanics; television; God knows what, and never made the slightest mark.

BERNARD (*taking off his glasses*): Willy, do you want to talk candidly?

WILLY (*rising, faces* BERNARD): I regard you as a very brilliant man, Bernard. I value your advice.

BERNARD: Oh, the hell with the advice, Willy. I couldn't advise you. There's just one thing I've always wanted to ask you. When he was supposed to graduate, and the math teacher flunked him —

WILLY: Oh, that son-of-a-bitch ruined his life.

BERNARD: Yeah, but, Willy, all he had to do was go to summer school and make up that subject.

WILLY: That's right, that's right.

BERNARD: Did you tell him not to go to summer school?

WILLY: Me? I begged him to go. I ordered him to go!

BERNARD: Then why wouldn't he go?

WILLY: Why? Why! Bernard, that question has been trailing me like a ghost for the last fifteen years. He flunked the subject, and laid down and died like a hammer hit him!

BERNARD: Take it easy, kid.

WILLY: Let me talk to you — I got nobody to talk to. Bernard, Bernard, was it my fault? Y'see? It keeps going around in my mind, maybe I did something to him. I got nothing to give him.

BERNARD: Don't take it so hard.

WILLY: Why did he lay down? What is the story there? You were his friend!

BERNARD: Willy, I remember, it was June, and our grades came out. And he'd flunked math.

WILLY: That son-of-a-bitch!

BERNARD: No, it wasn't right then. Biff just got very angry, I remember, and he was ready to enroll in summer school.

WILLY (surprised): He was?

BERNARD: He wasn't beaten by it at all. But then, Willy, he disappeared from the block for almost a month. And I got the idea that he'd gone up to New England to see you. Did he have a talk with you then?

(WILLY stares in silence.)

BERNARD: Willy?

WILLY (with a strong edge of resentment in his voice): Yeah, he came to Boston. What about it?

BERNARD: Well, just that when he came back — I'll never forget this, it always mystifies me. Because I'd thought so well of Biff, even though he'd always taken advantage of me. I loved him, Willy, y'know? And he came back after that month and took his sneakers — remember those sneakers with "University of Virginia" printed on them? He was so proud of those, wore them every day. And he took them down in the cellar, and burned them up in the furnace. We had a fist fight. It lasted at least half an hour. Just the two of us, punching each other down the cellar, and crying right through it. I've often thought of how strange it was that I knew he'd given up his life. What happened in Boston, Willy?

(WILLY looks at him as at an intruder.)

BERNARD: I just bring it up because you asked me.

WILLY (angrily): Nothing. What do you mean, "What happened?" What's that got to do with anything?

BERNARD: Well, don't get sore.

WILLY: What are you trying to do, blame it on me? If a boy lays down is that my fault?

BERNARD: Now, Willy, don't get —

WILLY: Well, don't — don't talk to me that way! What does that mean, "What happened?"

(CHARLEY enters. He is in his vest, and he carries a bottle of bourbon.)

CHARLEY: Hey, you're going to miss that train. (He waves the bottle.)

BERNARD: Yeah, I'm going. (He takes the bottle.) Thanks, Pop. (He picks up his rackets and bag.) Good-by, Willy, and don't worry about it. You know, "If at first you don't succeed . . ."

WILLY: Yes, I believe in that.

BERNARD: But sometimes, Willy, it's better for a man just to walk away.

WILLY: Walk away?

BERNARD: That's right.

WILLY: But if you can't walk away?

BERNARD (after a slight pause): I guess that's when it's tough. (Extending his hand.) Good-by, Willy.

WILLY (shaking BERNARD's hand): Good-by, boy.

CHARLEY (an arm on BERNARD's shoulder): How do you like this kid? Gonna argue a case in front of the Supreme Court.

BERNARD (protesting): Pop!

WILLY (genuinely shocked, pained, and happy): No! The Supreme Court!

BERNARD: I gotta run. 'By, Dad!

CHARLEY: Knock 'em dead, Bernard!

(BERNARD goes off.)

WILLY (as CHARLEY takes out his wallet): The Supreme Court! And he didn't even mention it!

CHARLEY (*counting out money on the desk*): He don't have to — he's gonna do it.

WILLY: And you never told him what to do, did you? You never took any interest in him.

CHARLEY: My salvation is that I never took any interest in anything. There's some money — fifty dollars. I got an accountant inside.

WILLY: Charley, look . . . (*With difficulty.*) I got my insurance to pay. If you can manage it — I need a hundred and ten dollars.

(CHARLEY *doesn't reply for a moment; merely stops moving.*)

WILLY: I'd draw it from my bank but Linda would know, and I . . .

CHARLEY: Sit down, Willy.

WILLY (*moving toward the chair*): I'm keeping an account of everything, remember. I'll pay every penny back. (*He sits.*)

CHARLEY: Now listen to me, Willy.

WILLY: I want you to know I appreciate . . .

CHARLEY (*sitting down on the table*): Willy, what're you doin'? What the hell is goin' on in your head?

WILLY: Why? I'm simply . . .

CHARLEY: I offered you a job. You can make fifty dollars a week. And I won't send you on the road.

WILLY: I've got a job.

CHARLEY: Without pay? What kind of a job is a job without pay? (*He rises.*) Now, look, kid, enough is enough. I'm no genius but I know when I'm being insulted.

WILLY: Insulted!

CHARLEY: Why don't you want to work for me?

WILLY: What's the matter with you? I've got a job.

CHARLEY: Then what're you walkin' in here every week for?

WILLY (*getting up*): Well, if you don't want me to walk in here —

CHARLEY: I am offering you a job.

WILLY: I don't want your goddam job!

CHARLEY: When the hell are you going to grow up?

WILLY (*furiously*): You big ignoramus, if you say that to me again I'll rap you one! I don't care how big you are! (*He's ready to fight.*)

(*Pause.*)

CHARLEY (*kindly, going to him*): How much do you need, Willy?

WILLY: Charley, I'm strapped. I'm strapped. I don't know what to do. I was just fired.

CHARLEY: Howard fired you?

WILLY: That snotnose. Imagine that? I named him. I named him Howard.

CHARLEY: Willy, when're you gonna realize that them things don't mean anything? You named him Howard, but you can't sell that. The only thing you got in this world is what you can sell. And the funny thing is that you're a salesman, and you don't know that.

WILLY: I've always tried to think otherwise, I guess. I always felt that if a man was impressive, and well liked, that nothing —

CHARLEY: Why must everybody like you? Who liked J. P. Morgan? Was he impressive? In a Turkish bath he'd look like a butcher. But with his pockets on he was very well liked. Now listen, Willy, I know you don't like me, and nobody can say I'm in love with you, but I'll give you a job because — just for the hell of it, put it that way. Now what do you say?

WILLY: I — I just can't work for you, Charley.

CHARLEY: What're you, jealous of me?

WILLY: I can't work for you, that's all, don't ask me why.

CHARLEY (*angered, takes out more bills*): You been jealous of me all your life, you damned fool! Here, pay your insurance. (*He puts the money in* WILLY's *hand.*)

WILLY: I'm keeping strict accounts.

CHARLEY: I've got some work to do. Take care of yourself. And pay your insurance.

WILLY (*moving to the right*): Funny, y'know? After all the highways, and the trains, and the appointments, and the years, you end up worth more dead than alive.

CHARLEY: Willy, nobody's worth nothin' dead. (*After a slight pause.*) Did you hear what I said?

(WILLY *stands still, dreaming.*)

CHARLEY: Willy!

WILLY: Apologize to Bernard for me when you see him. I didn't mean to argue with him. He's a fine boy. They're all fine boys, and they'll end up big — all of them. Someday they'll all play tennis together. Wish me luck, Charley. He saw Bill Oliver today.

CHARLEY: Good luck.

WILLY (*on the verge of tears*): Charley, you're the only friend I got. Isn't that a remarkable thing? (*He goes out.*)

CHARLEY: Jesus!

(CHARLEY *stares after him a moment and follows. All light blacks out. Suddenly raucous music is heard, and a red glow rises behind the screen at right.* STANLEY, *a young waiter, appears, carrying a table, followed by* HAPPY, *who is carrying two chairs.*)

STANLEY (*putting the table down*): That's all right, Mr. Loman, I can handle it myself. (*He turns and takes the chairs from* HAPPY *and places them at the table.*)

HAPPY (*glancing around*): Oh, this is better.

STANLEY: Sure, in the front there you're in the middle of all kinds a noise. Whenever you got a party, Mr. Loman, you just tell me and I'll put you back here. Y'know, there's a lotta people they don't like it private, because when they go out they like to see a lotta action around them because they're sick and tired to stay in the house by theirself. But I know you, you ain't from Hackensack. You know what I mean?

HAPPY (*sitting down*): So how's it coming, Stanley?

STANLEY: Ah, it's a dog's life. I only wish during the war they'd a took me in the Army. I coulda been dead by now.

HAPPY: My brother's back, Stanley.

STANLEY: Oh, he come back, heh? From the Far West.

HAPPY: Yeah, big cattle man, my brother, so treat him right. And my father's coming too.

STANLEY: Oh, your father too!

HAPPY: You got a couple of nice lobsters?

STANLEY: Hundred per cent, big.

HAPPY: I want them with the claws.

STANLEY: Don't worry, I don't give you no mice. (HAPPY *laughs.*) How about some wine? It'll put a head on the meal.

HAPPY: No. You remember, Stanley, that recipe I brought you from overseas? With the champagne in it?

STANLEY: Oh, yeah, sure. I still got it tacked up yet in the kitchen. But that'll have to cost a buck apiece anyways.

HAPPY: That's all right.

STANLEY: What'd you, hit a number or somethin'?

HAPPY: No, it's a little celebration. My brother is — I think he pulled off a big deal today. I think we're going into business together.

STANLEY: Great! That's the best for you. Because a family business, you know what I mean? — that's the best.

HAPPY: That's what I think.

STANLEY: 'Cause what's the difference? Somebody steals? It's in the family. Know what I mean? (*Sotto voce.*) Like this bartender here. The boss is goin' crazy what kinda leak he's got in the cash register. You put it in but it don't come out.

HAPPY (*raising his head*): Sh!

STANLEY: What?

HAPPY: You notice I wasn't lookin' right or left, was I?

STANLEY: No.

HAPPY: And my eyes are closed.

STANLEY: So what's the — ?

HAPPY: Strudel's comin'.

STANLEY (*catching on, looks around*): Ah, no, there's no —

(*He breaks off as a furred, lavishly dressed* GIRL *enters and sits at the next table. Both follow her with their eyes.*)

STANLEY: Geez, how'd ya know?

HAPPY: I got radar or something. (*Staring directly at her profile.*) Oooooooo . . . Stanley.

STANLEY: I think that's for you, Mr. Loman.

HAPPY: Look at that mouth. Oh, God. And the binoculars.

STANLEY: Geez, you got a life, Mr. Loman.

HAPPY: Wait on her.

STANLEY (*going to* THE GIRL's *table*): Would you like a menu, ma'am?

GIRL: I'm expecting someone, but I'd like a —

HAPPY: Why don't you bring her — excuse me, miss, do you mind? I sell champagne, and I'd like you to try my brand. Bring her a champagne, Stanley.

GIRL: That's awfully nice of you.

HAPPY: Don't mention it. It's all company money. (*He laughs.*)

GIRL: That's a charming product to be selling, isn't it?

HAPPY: Oh, gets to be like everything else. Selling is selling, y'know.

GIRL: I suppose.

HAPPY: You don't happen to sell, do you?

GIRL: No, I don't sell.

HAPPY: Would you object to a compliment from a stranger? You ought to be on a magazine cover.

GIRL (*looking at him a little archly*): I have been.

(STANLEY *comes in with a glass of champagne.*)

HAPPY: What'd I say before, Stanley? You see? She's a cover girl.

STANLEY: Oh, I could see, I could see.

HAPPY (*to* THE GIRL): What magazine?

GIRL: Oh, a lot of them. (*She takes the drink.*) Thank you.

HAPPY: You know what they say in France, don't you? "Champagne is the drink of the complexion" — Hya, Biff!

(BIFF *has entered and sits with* HAPPY.)

BIFF: Hello, kid. Sorry I'm late.

HAPPY: I just got here. Uh, Miss — ?

GIRL: Forsythe.

HAPPY: Miss Forsythe, this is my brother.

BIFF: Is Dad here?

HAPPY: His name is Biff. You might've heard of him. Great football player.

GIRL: Really? What team?

HAPPY: Are you familiar with football?

GIRL: No, I'm afraid I'm not.

HAPPY: Biff is quarterback with the New York Giants.

GIRL: Well, that is nice, isn't it? (*She drinks.*)

HAPPY: Good health.

GIRL: I'm happy to meet you.

HAPPY: That's my name. Hap. It's really Harold, but at West Point they called me Happy.

GIRL (*now really impressed*): Oh, I see. How do you do? (*She turns her profile.*)

BIFF: Isn't Dad coming?

HAPPY: You want her?

BIFF: Oh, I could never make that.

HAPPY: I remember the time that idea would never come into your head. Where's the old confidence, Biff?

BIFF: I just saw Oliver —

HAPPY: Wait a minute. I've got to see that old confidence again. Do you want her? She's on call.

BIFF: Oh, no. (*He turns to look at* THE GIRL.)

HAPPY: I'm telling you. Watch this. (*Turning to* THE GIRL.) Honey? (*She turns to him.*) Are you busy?

GIRL: Well, I am . . . but I could make a phone call.

HAPPY: Do that, will you, honey? And see if you can get a friend. We'll be here for a while. Biff is one of the greatest football players in the country.

GIRL (*standing up*): Well, I'm certainly happy to meet you.

HAPPY: Come back soon.

GIRL: I'll try.

HAPPY: Don't try, honey, try hard.

(THE GIRL *exits.* STANLEY *follows, shaking his head in bewildered admiration.*)

HAPPY: Isn't that a shame now? A beautiful girl like that? That's why I can't get married. There's not a good woman in a thousand. New York is loaded with them, kid!

BIFF: Hap, look —

HAPPY: I told you she was on call!

BIFF (*strangely unnerved*): Cut it out, will ya? I want to say something to you.

HAPPY: Did you see Oliver?

BIFF: I saw him all right. Now look, I want to tell Dad a couple of things and I want you to help me.

HAPPY: What? Is he going to back you?

BIFF: Are you crazy? You're out of your goddam head, you know that?

HAPPY: Why? What happened?

BIFF (*breathlessly*): I did a terrible thing today, Hap. It's been the strangest day I ever went through. I'm all numb, I swear.

HAPPY: You mean he wouldn't see you?

BIFF: Well, I waited six hours for him, see? All day. Kept sending my name in. Even tried to date his secretary so she'd get me to him, but no soap.

HAPPY: Because you're not showin' the old confidence, Biff. He remembered you, didn't he?

BIFF (*stopping* HAPPY *with a gesture*): Finally, about five o'clock, he comes out. Didn't remember who I was or anything. I felt like such an idiot, Hap.

HAPPY: Did you tell him my Florida idea?

BIFF: He walked away. I saw him for one minute. I got so mad I could've torn the walls down! How the hell did I ever get the idea I was a salesman there? I even believed myself that I'd been a salesman for him! And then he gave me one look and — I realized what a ridiculous lie my whole life has been! We've been talking in a dream for fifteen years. I was a shipping clerk.

HAPPY: What'd you do?

BIFF (*with great tension and wonder*): Well, he left, see. And the secretary went out. I was all alone in the waiting-room. I don't know what came over me, Hap. The next thing I know I'm in his office — paneled walls, everything. I can't explain it. I — Hap, I took his fountain pen.

HAPPY: Geez, did he catch you?

BIFF: I ran out. I ran down all eleven flights. I ran and ran and ran.

HAPPY: That was an awful dumb — what'd you do that for?

BIFF (agonized): I don't know, I just — wanted to take something, I don't know. You gotta help me, Hap, I'm gonna tell Pop.

HAPPY: You crazy? What for?

BIFF: Hap, he's got to understand that I'm not the man somebody lends that kind of money to. He thinks I've been spiting him all these years and it's eating him up.

HAPPY: That's just it. You tell him something nice.

BIFF: I can't.

HAPPY: Say you got a lunch date with Oliver tomorrow.

BIFF: So what do I do tomorrow?

HAPPY: You leave the house tomorrow and come back at night and say Oliver is thinking it over. And he thinks it over for a couple of weeks, and gradually it fades away and nobody's the worse.

BIFF: But it'll go on forever!

HAPPY: Dad is never so happy as when he's looking forward to something!

(WILLY enters.)

HAPPY: Hello, scout!

WILLY: Gee, I haven't been here in years!

(STANLEY has followed WILLY in and sets a chair for him. STANLEY starts off but HAPPY stops him.)

HAPPY: Stanley!

(STANLEY stands by, waiting for an order.)

BIFF (going to WILLY with guilt, as to an invalid): Sit down, Pop. You want a drink?

WILLY: Sure, I don't mind.

BIFF: Let's get a load on.

WILLY: You look worried.

BIFF: N-no. (To STANLEY.) Scotch all around. Make it doubles.

STANLEY: Doubles, right. (He goes.)

WILLY: You had a couple already, didn't you?

BIFF: Just a couple, yeah.

WILLY: Well, what happened, boy?

(Nodding affirmatively, with a smile.) Everything go all right?

BIFF (takes a breath, then reaches out and grasps WILLY's hand): Pal... (He is smiling bravely, and WILLY is smiling too.) I had an experience today.

HAPPY: Terrific, Pop.

WILLY: That so? What happened?

BIFF (high, slightly alcoholic, above the earth): I'm going to tell you everything from first to last. It's been a strange day. (Silence. He looks around, composes himself as best he can, but his breath keeps breaking the rhythm of his voice.) I had to wait quite a while for him, and —

WILLY: Oliver?

BIFF: Yeah, Oliver. All day, as a matter of cold fact. And a lot of — instances — facts, Pop, facts about my life came back to me. Who was it, Pop? Who ever said I was a salesman with Oliver?

WILLY: Well, you were.

BIFF: No, Dad, I was a shipping clerk.

WILLY: But you were practically —

BIFF (with determination): Dad, I don't know who said it first, but I was never a salesman for Bill Oliver.

WILLY: What're you talking about?

BIFF: Let's hold on to the facts tonight, Pop. We're not going to get anywhere bullin' around. I was a shipping clerk.

WILLY (angrily): All right, now listen to me —

BIFF: Why don't you let me finish?

WILLY: I'm not interested in stories about the past or any crap of that kind because the woods are burning, boys, you understand? There's a big blaze going on all around. I was fired today.

BIFF (shocked): How could you be?

WILLY: I was fired, and I'm looking for a little good news to tell your mother, because the woman has waited and the woman has suffered. The gist of it is that I haven't got a story left in my head, Biff. So don't give me a lecture about facts and aspects. I am not interested. Now what've you got to say to me?

(STANLEY enters with three drinks. They wait until he leaves.)

WILLY: Did you see Oliver?

BIFF: Jesus, Dad!

WILLY: You mean you didn't go up there?

HAPPY: Sure he went up there.

BIFF: I did. I — saw him. How could they fire you?

WILLY (*on the edge of his chair*): What kind of a welcome did he give you?

BIFF: He won't even let you work on commission?

WILLY: I'm out! (*Driving.*) So tell me, he gave you a warm welcome?

HAPPY: Sure, Pop, sure!

BIFF (*driven*): Well, it was kind of —

WILLY: I was wondering if he'd remember you. (*To* HAPPY.) Imagine, man doesn't see him for ten, twelve years and gives him that kind of a welcome!

HAPPY: Damn right!

BIFF (*trying to return to the offensive*): Pop, look —

WILLY: You know why he remembered you, don't you? Because you impressed him in those days.

BIFF: Let's talk quietly and get this down to the facts, huh?

WILLY (*as though* BIFF *had been interrupting*): Well, what happened? It's great news, Biff. Did he take you into his office or'd you talk in the waiting-room?

BIFF: Well, he came in, see, and —

WILLY (*with a big smile*): What'd he say? Betcha he threw his arm around you.

BIFF: Well, he kinda —

WILLY: He's a fine man. (*To* HAPPY.) Very hard man to see, y'know.

HAPPY (*agreeing*): Oh, I know.

WILLY (*to* BIFF): Is that where you had the drinks?

BIFF: Yeah, he gave me a couple of — no, no!

HAPPY (*cutting in*): He told him my Florida idea.

WILLY: Don't interrupt. (*To* BIFF.) How'd he react to the Florida idea?

BIFF: Dad, will you give me a minute to explain?

WILLY: I've been waiting for you to explain since I sat down here! What happened? He took you into his office and what?

BIFF: Well — I talked. And — and he listened, see.

WILLY: Famous for the way he listens, y'know. What was his answer?

BIFF: His answer was — (*He breaks off, suddenly angry.*) Dad, you're not letting me tell you what I want to tell you!

WILLY (*accusing, angered*): You didn't see him, did you?

BIFF: I did see him!

WILLY: What'd you insult him or something? You insulted him, didn't you?

BIFF: Listen, will you let me out of it, will you just let me out of it!

HAPPY: What the hell!

WILLY: Tell me what happened!

BIFF (*to* HAPPY): I can't talk to him!

(*A single trumpet note jars the ear. The light of green leaves stains the house, which holds the air of night and a dream.* YOUNG BERNARD *enters and knocks on the door of the house.*)

YOUNG BERNARD (*frantically*): Mrs. Loman, Mrs. Loman!

HAPPY: Tell him what happened!

BIFF (*to* HAPPY): Shut up and leave me alone!

WILLY: No, no! You had to go and flunk math!

BIFF: What math? What're you talking about?

YOUNG BERNARD: Mrs. Loman, Mrs. Loman!

(LINDA *appears in the house, as of old.*)

WILLY (*wildly*): Math, math, math!

BIFF: Take it easy, Pop!

YOUNG BERNARD: Mrs. Loman!

WILLY (*furiously*): If you hadn't flunked you'd've been set by now!

BIFF: Now, look, I'm gonna tell you what happened, and you're going to listen to me.

YOUNG BERNARD: Mrs. Loman!

BIFF: I waited six hours —

HAPPY: What the hell are you saying?

BIFF: I kept sending in my name but he wouldn't see me. So finally he ... (*He continues unheard as light fades low on the restaurant.*)

YOUNG BERNARD: Biff flunked math!

LINDA: No!

YOUNG BERNARD: Birnbaum flunked him! They won't graduate him!

LINDA: But they have to. He's gotta go to the university. Where is he? Biff! Biff!

YOUNG BERNARD: No, he left. He went to Grand Central.

LINDA: Grand — You mean he went to Boston!

YOUNG BERNARD: Is Uncle Willy in Boston?

LINDA: Oh, maybe Willy can talk to the teacher. Oh, the poor, poor boy!

(*Light on house area snaps out.*)

BIFF (*at the table, now audible, holding up a gold fountain pen*): . . . so I'm washed up with Oliver, you understand? Are you listening to me?

WILLY (*at a loss*): Yeah, sure. If you hadn't flunked —

BIFF: Flunked what? What're you talking about?

WILLY: Don't blame everything on me! I didn't flunk math — you did! What pen?

HAPPY: That was awful dumb, Biff, a pen like that is worth —

WILLY (*seeing the pen for the first time*): You took Oliver's pen?

BIFF (*weakening*): Dad, I just explained it to you.

WILLY: You stole Bill Oliver's fountain pen!

BIFF: I didn't exactly steal it! That's just what I've been explaining to you!

HAPPY: He had it in his hand and just then Oliver walked in, so he got nervous and stuck it in his pocket!

WILLY: My God, Biff!

BIFF: I never intended to do it, Dad!

OPERATOR'S VOICE: Standish Arms, good evening!

WILLY (*shouting*): I'm not in my room!

BIFF (*frightened*): Dad, what's the matter? (*He and* HAPPY *stand up.*)

OPERATOR: Ringing Mr. Loman for you!

WILLY: I'm not there, stop it!

BIFF (*horrified, gets down on one knee before* WILLY): Dad, I'll make good, I'll make good. (WILLY *tries to get to his feet.* BIFF *holds him down.*) Sit down now.

WILLY: No, you're no good, you're no good for anything.

BIFF: I am, Dad, I'll find something else, you understand? Now don't worry about anything. (*He holds up* WILLY's *face.*) Talk to me, Dad.

OPERATOR: Mr. Loman does not answer. Shall I page him?

WILLY (*attempting to stand, as though to rush and silence the* OPERATOR): No, no, no!

HAPPY: He'll strike something, Pop.

WILLY: No, no . . .

BIFF (*desperately, standing over* WILLY): Pop, listen! Listen to me! I'm telling you

something good. Oliver talked to his partner about the Florida idea. You listening? He — he talked to his partner, and he came to me . . . I'm going to be all right, you hear? Dad, listen to me, he said it was just a question of the amount!

WILLY: Then you . . . got it?

HAPPY: He's gonna be terrific, Pop!

WILLY (*trying to stand*): Then you got it, haven't you? You got it! You got it!

BIFF (*agonized, holds* WILLY *down*): No, no. Look, Pop. I'm supposed to have lunch with them tomorrow. I'm just telling you this so you'll know that I can still make an impression, Pop. And I'll make good somewhere, but I can't go tomorrow, see?

WILLY: Why not? You simply —

BIFF: But the pen, Pop!

WILLY: You give it to him and tell him it was an oversight!

HAPPY: Sure, have lunch tomorrow!

BIFF: I can't say that —

WILLY: You were doing a crossword puzzle and accidentally used his pen!

BIFF: Listen, kid, I took those balls years ago, now I walk in with his fountain pen? That clinches it, don't you see? I can't face him like that! I'll try elsewhere.

PAGE'S VOICE: Paging Mr. Loman!

WILLY: Don't you want to be anything?

BIFF: Pop, how can I go back?

WILLY: You don't want to be anything, is that what's behind it?

BIFF (*now angry at* WILLY *for not crediting his sympathy*): Don't take it that way! You think it was easy walking into that office after what I'd done to him? A team of horses couldn't have dragged me back to Bill Oliver!

WILLY: Then why'd you go?

BIFF: Why did I go? Why did I go! Look at you! Look at what's become of you!

(*Off left,* THE WOMAN *laughs.*)

WILLY: Biff, you're going to go to that lunch tomorrow, or —

BIFF: I can't go. I've got no appointment!

HAPPY: Biff, for . . . !

WILLY: Are you spiting me?

BIFF: Don't take it that way! Goddammit!

WILLY (*strikes* BIFF *and falters away from the table*): You rotten little louse! Are you spiting me?

THE WOMAN: Someone's at the door, Willy!

BIFF: I'm no good, can't you see what I am?

HAPPY (*separating them*): Hey, you're in a restaurant! Now cut it out, both of you! (THE GIRLS *enter.*) Hello, girls, sit down.

(THE WOMAN *laughs, off left.*)

MISS FORSYTHE: I guess we might as well. This is Letta.

THE WOMAN: Willy, are you going to wake up?

BIFF (*ignoring* WILLY): How're ya, miss, sit down. What do you drink?

MISS FORSYTHE: Letta might not be able to stay long.

LETTA: I gotta get up very early tomorrow. I got jury duty. I'm so excited! Were you fellows ever on a jury?

BIFF: No, but I been in front of them! (THE GIRLS *laugh.*) This is my father.

LETTA: Isn't he cute? Sit down with us, Pop.

HAPPY: Sit him down, Biff!

BIFF (*going to him*): Come on, slugger, drink us under the table. To hell with it! Come on, sit down, pal.

(*On* BIFF's *last insistence,* WILLY *is about to sit.*)

THE WOMAN (*now urgently*): Willy, are you going to answer the door!

(THE WOMAN's *call pulls* WILLY *back. He starts right, befuddled.*)

BIFF: Hey, where are you going?

WILLY: Open the door.

BIFF: The door?

WILLY: The washroom ... the door ... where's the door?

BIFF (*leading* WILLY *to the left*): Just go straight down.

(WILLY *moves left.*)

THE WOMAN: Willy, Willy, are you going to get up, get up, get up, get up?

(WILLY *exits left.*)

LETTA: I think it's sweet you bring your daddy along.

MISS FORSYTHE: Oh, he isn't really your father!

BIFF (*at left, turning to her resentfully*): Miss Forsythe, you've just seen a prince walk by. A fine, troubled prince. A hard-working, unappreciated prince. A pal, you understand? A good companion. Always for his boys.

LETTA: That's so sweet.

HAPPY: Well, girls, what's the program? We're wasting time. Come on, Biff. Gather round. Where would you like to go?

BIFF: Why don't you do something for him?

HAPPY: Me!

BIFF: Don't you give a damn for him, Hap?

HAPPY: What're you talking about? I'm the one who —

BIFF: I sense it, you don't give a good goddam about him. (*He takes the rolled-up hose from his pocket and puts it on the table in front of* HAPPY.) Look what I found in the cellar, for Christ's sake. How can you bear to let it go on?

HAPPY: Me? Who goes away? Who runs off and —

BIFF: Yeah, but he doesn't mean anything to you. You could help him — I can't! Don't you understand what I'm talking about? He's going to kill himself, don't you know that?

HAPPY: Don't I know it! Me!

BIFF: Hap, help him! Jesus ... help him ... Help me, help me, I can't bear to look at his face! (*Ready to weep, he hurries out, up right.*)

HAPPY (*starting after him*): Where are you going?

MISS FORSYTHE: What's he so mad about?

HAPPY: Come on, girls, we'll catch up with him.

MISS FORSYTHE (*as* HAPPY *pushes her out*): Say, I don't like that temper of his!

HAPPY: He's just a little overstrung, he'll be all right!

WILLY (*off left, as* THE WOMAN *laughs*): Don't answer! Don't answer!

LETTA: Don't you want to tell your father —

HAPPY: No, that's not my father. He's just a guy. Come on, we'll catch Biff, and, honey, we're going to paint this town! Stanley, where's the check! Hey, Stanley!

(*They exit.* STANLEY *looks toward left.*)

STANLEY (*calling to* HAPPY *indignantly*): Mr. Loman! Mr. Loman!

(STANLEY *picks up a chair and follows them off. Knocking is heard off left.* THE WOMAN *enters, laughing.* WILLY *follows her. She is in a black slip; he is buttoning his shirt. Raw, sensuous music accompanies their speech.*)

WILLY: Will you stop laughing? Will you stop?

THE WOMAN: Aren't you going to answer the door? He'll wake the whole hotel.

WILLY: I'm not expecting anybody.

THE WOMAN: Whyn't you have another drink, honey, and stop being so damn self-centered?

WILLY: I'm so lonely.

THE WOMAN: You know you ruined me, Willy? From now on, whenever you come to the office, I'll see that you go right through to the buyers. No waiting at my desk any more, Willy. You ruined me.

WILLY: That's nice of you to say that.

THE WOMAN: Gee, you are self-centered! Why so sad? You are the saddest self-centerdest soul I ever did see-saw. (*She laughs. He kisses her.*) Come on inside, drummer boy. It's silly to be dressing in the middle of the night. (*As knocking is heard.*) Aren't you going to answer the door?

WILLY: They're knocking on the wrong door.

THE WOMAN: But I felt the knocking. And he heard us talking in here. Maybe the hotel's on fire!

WILLY (*his terror rising*): It's a mistake.

THE WOMAN: Then tell him to go away!

WILLY: There's nobody there.

THE WOMAN: It's getting on my nerves, Willy. There's somebody standing out there and it's getting on my nerves!

WILLY (*pushing her away from him*): All right, stay in the bathroom here, and don't come out. I think there's a law in Massachusetts about it, so don't come out. It may be that new room clerk. He looked very mean. So don't come out. It's a mistake, there's no fire.

(*The knocking is heard again. He takes a few steps away from her, and she vanishes into the wing. The light follows him, and now he is facing* YOUNG BIFF, *who carries a suitcase.* BIFF *steps toward him. The music is gone.*)

BIFF: Why didn't you answer?

WILLY: Biff! What are you doing in Boston?

BIFF: Why didn't you answer? I've been knocking for five minutes, I called you on the phone —

WILLY: I just heard you. I was in the bathroom and had the door shut. Did anything happen home?

BIFF: Dad — I let you down.

WILLY: What do you mean?

BIFF: Dad . . .

WILLY: Biffo, what's this about? (*Putting his arm around* BIFF.) Come on, let's go downstairs and get you a malted.

BIFF: Dad, I flunked math.

WILLY: Not for the term?

BIFF: The term. I haven't got enough credits to graduate.

WILLY: You mean to say Bernard wouldn't give you the answers?

BIFF: He did, he tried, but I only got a sixty-one.

WILLY: And they wouldn't give you four points?

BIFF: Birnbaum refused absolutely. I begged him, Pop, but he won't give me those points. You gotta talk to him before they close the school. Because if he saw the kind of man you are, and you just talked to him in your way, I'm sure he'd come through for me. The class came right before practice, see, and I didn't go enough. Would you talk to him? He'd like you, Pop. You know the way you could talk.

WILLY: You're on. We'll drive right back.

BIFF: Oh, Dad, good work! I'm sure he'll change it for you!

WILLY: Go downstairs and tell the clerk I'm checkin' out. Go right down.

BIFF: Yes, sir! See, the reason he hates me, Pop — one day he was late for class so I got up at the blackboard and imitated him. I crossed my eyes and talked with a lithp.

WILLY (*laughing*): You did? The kids like it?

BIFF: They nearly died laughing!

WILLY: Yeah? What'd you do?

BIFF: The thquare root of thixthy twee is . . . (WILLY *bursts out laughing;* BIFF *joins him.*) And in the middle of it he walked in!

(WILLY *laughs and* THE WOMAN *joins in offstage.*)

WILLY (*without hesitation*): Hurry downstairs and —

BIFF: Somebody in there?

WILLY: No, that was next door.

(THE WOMAN *laughs offstage.*)

BIFF: Somebody got in your bathroom!

WILLY: No, it's the next room, there's a party —

THE WOMAN (*enters, laughing. She lisps*

this): Can I come in? There's something in the bathtub, Willy, and it's moving!

(WILLY *looks at* BIFF, *who is staring open-mouthed and horrified at* THE WOMAN.)

WILLY: Ah — you better go back to your room. They must be finished painting by now. They're painting her room so I let her take a shower here. Go back, go back . . . (*He pushes her.*)

THE WOMAN (*resisting*): But I've got to get dressed, Willy, I can't —

WILLY: Get out of here! Go back, go back . . . (*Suddenly striving for the ordinary.*) This is Miss Francis, Biff, she's a buyer. They're painting her room. Go back, Miss Francis, go back . . .

THE WOMAN: But my clothes, I can't go out naked in the hall!

WILLY (*pushing her offstage*): Get outa here! Go back, go back!

(BIFF *slowly sits down on his suitcase as the argument continues offstage.*)

THE WOMAN: Where's my stockings? You promised me stockings, Willy!

WILLY: I have no stockings here!

THE WOMAN: You had two boxes of size nine sheers for me, and I want them!

WILLY: Here, for God's sake, will you get outa here!

THE WOMAN (*enters holding a box of stockings*): I just hope there's nobody in the hall. That's all I hope. (*To* BIFF.) Are you football or baseball?

BIFF: Football.

THE WOMAN (*angry, humiliated*): That's me too. G'night. (*She snatches her clothes from* WILLY, *and walks out.*)

WILLY (*after a pause*): Well, better get going. I want to get to the school first thing in the morning. Get my suits out of the closet. I'll get my valise. (BIFF *doesn't move.*) What's the matter? (BIFF *remains motionless, tears falling.*) She's a buyer. Buys for J. H. Simmons. She lives down the hall — they're painting. You don't imagine — (*He breaks off. After a pause.*) Now listen, pal, she's just a buyer. She sees merchandise in her room and they have to keep it looking just so . . . (*Pause. Assuming command.*) All right, get my suits. (BIFF *doesn't move.*) Now stop crying and do as I say. I gave you an order. Biff, I gave you an order! Is that what you do when I give you

an order? How dare you cry! (*Putting his arm around* BIFF.) Now look, Biff, when you grow up you'll understand about these things. You mustn't — you mustn't overemphasize a thing like this. I'll see Birnbaum first thing in the morning.

BIFF: Never mind.

WILLY (*getting down beside* BIFF): Never mind! He's going to give you those points. I'll see to it.

BIFF: He wouldn't listen to you.

WILLY: He certainly will listen to me. You need those points for the U. of Virginia.

BIFF: I'm not going there.

WILLY: Heh? If I can't get him to change that mark you'll make it up in summer school. You've got all summer to —

BIFF (*his weeping breaking from him*): Dad . . .

WILLY (*infected by it*): Oh, my boy . . .

BIFF: Dad . . .

WILLY: She's nothing to me, Biff. I was lonely, I was terribly lonely.

BIFF: You — you gave her Mama's stockings! (*His tears break through and he rises to go.*)

WILLY (*grabbing for* BIFF): I gave you an order!

BIFF: Don't touch me, you — liar!

WILLY: Apologize for that!

BIFF: You fake! You phony little fake! You fake! (*Overcome, he turns quickly and weeping fully goes out with his suitcase.* WILLY *is left on the floor on his knees.*)

WILLY: I gave you an order! Biff, come back here or I'll beat you! Come back here! I'll whip you!

(STANLEY *comes quickly in from the right and stands in front of* WILLY.)

WILLY (*shouts at* STANLEY): I gave you an order . . .

STANLEY: Hey, let's pick it up, pick it up, Mr. Loman. (*He helps* WILLY *to his feet.*) Your boys left with the chippies. They said they'll see you home.

(A *second waiter watches some distance away.*)

WILLY: But we were supposed to have dinner together.

(*Music is heard,* WILLY'S *theme.*)

STANLEY: Can you make it?

WILLY: I'll — sure, I can make it. (*Suddenly*

concerned about his clothes.) Do I — I look all right?

STANLEY: Sure, you look all right. (*He flicks a speck off* WILLY'S *lapel.*)

WILLY: Here — here's a dollar.

STANLEY: Oh, your son paid me. It's all right.

WILLY (*putting it in* STANLEY'S *hand*): No, take it. You're a good boy.

STANLEY: Oh, no, you don't have to . . .

WILLY: Here — here's some more, I don't need it any more. (*After a slight pause.*) Tell me — is there a seed store in the neighborhood?

STANLEY: Seeds? You mean like to plant?

(*As* WILLY *turns,* STANLEY *slips the money back into his jacket pocket.*)

WILLY: Yes. Carrots, peas . . .

STANLEY: Well, there's hardware stores on Sixth Avenue, but it may be too late now.

WILLY (*anxiously*): Oh, I'd better hurry. I've got to get some seeds. (*He starts off to the right.*) I've got to get some seeds, right away. Nothing's planted. I don't have a thing in the ground.

(WILLY *hurries out as the light goes down.* STANLEY *moves over to the right after him, watches him off. The other waiter has been staring at* WILLY.)

STANLEY (*to the waiter*): Well, whatta you looking at?

(*The waiter picks up the chairs and moves off right.* STANLEY *takes the table and follows him. The light fades on this area. There is a long pause, the sound of the flute coming over. The light gradually rises on the kitchen, which is empty.* HAPPY *appears at the door of the house, followed by* BIFF. HAPPY *is carrying a large bunch of long-stemmed roses. He enters the kitchen, looks around for* LINDA. *Not seeing her, he turns to* BIFF, *who is just outside the house door, and makes a gesture with his hands, indicating "Not here, I guess." He looks into the living-room and freezes. Inside,* LINDA, *unseen, is seated,* WILLY's *coat on her lap. She rises ominously and quietly and moves toward* HAPPY, *who backs up into the kitchen, afraid.*)

HAPPY: Hey, what're you doing up? (LINDA *says nothing but moves toward him impla-*

cably.) Where's Pop? (*He keeps backing to the right, and now* LINDA *is in full view in the doorway to the living-room.*) Is he sleeping?

LINDA: Where were you?

HAPPY (*trying to laugh it off*): We met two girls, Mom, very fine types. Here, we brought you some flowers. (*Offering them to her.*) Put them in your room, Ma.

(*She knocks them to the floor at* BIFF's *feet. He has now come inside and closed the door behind him. She stares at* BIFF, *silent.*)

HAPPY: Now what'd you do that for? Mom, I want you to have some flowers —

LINDA (*cutting* HAPPY *off, violently to* BIFF): Don't you care whether he lives or dies?

HAPPY (*going to the stairs*): Come upstairs, Biff.

BIFF (*with a flare of disgust, to* HAPPY): Go away from me! (*To* LINDA.) What do you mean, lives or dies? Nobody's dying around here, pal.

LINDA: Get out of my sight! Get out of here!

BIFF: I wanna see the boss.

LINDA: You're not going near him!

BIFF: Where is he? (*He moves into the living-room and* LINDA *follows.*)

LINDA (*shouting after* BIFF): You invite him for dinner. He looks forward to it all day — (BIFF *appears in his parents' bedroom, looks around, and exits*) — and then you desert him there. There's no stranger you'd do that to!

HAPPY: Why? He had a swell time with us. Listen, when I — (LINDA *comes back into the kitchen*) — desert him I hope I don't outlive the day!

LINDA: Get out of here!

HAPPY: Now look, Mom . . .

LINDA: Did you have to go to women tonight? You and your lousy rotten whores!

(BIFF *re-enters the kitchen.*)

HAPPY: Mom, all we did was follow Biff around trying to cheer him up! (*To* BIFF.) Boy, what a night you gave me!

LINDA: Get out of here, both of you, and don't come back! I don't want you tormenting him any more. Go on now, get your things together! (*To* BIFF.) You can sleep in his apartment. (*She starts to pick up the flowers and stops herself.*) Pick up this stuff, I'm not your maid any more. Pick it up, you bum, you!

(HAPPY *turns his back to her in refusal.* BIFF *slowly moves over and gets down on his knees, picking up the flowers.*)

LINDA: You're a pair of animals! Not one, not another living soul would have had the cruelty to walk out on that man in a restaurant!

BIFF (*not looking at her*): Is that what he said?

LINDA: He didn't have to say anything. He was so humiliated he nearly limped when he came in.

HAPPY: But, Mom, he had a great time with us —

BIFF (*cutting him off violently*): Shut up!

(*Without another word,* HAPPY *goes upstairs.*)

LINDA: You! You didn't even go in to see if he was all right!

BIFF (*still on the floor in front of* LINDA, *the flowers in his hand; with self-loathing*): No. Didn't. Didn't do a damned thing. How do you like that, heh? Left him babbling in a toilet.

LINDA: You louse. You . . .

BIFF: Now you hit it on the nose! (*He gets up, throws the flowers in the wastebasket.*) The scum of the earth, and you're looking at him!

LINDA: Get out of here!

BIFF: I gotta talk to the boss, Mom. Where is he?

LINDA: You're not going near him. Get out of this house!

BIFF (*with absolute assurance, determination*): No. We're gonna have an abrupt conversation, him and me.

LINDA: You're not talking to him!

(*Hammering is heard from outside the house, off right.* BIFF *turns toward the noise.*)

LINDA (*suddenly pleading*): Will you please leave him alone?

BIFF: What's he doing out there?

LINDA: He's planting the garden!

BIFF (*quietly*): Now? Oh, my God!

(BIFF *moves outside,* LINDA *following. The light dies down on them and comes up on the center of the apron as* WILLY *walks into*

it. *He is carrying a flashlight, a hoe, and a handful of seed packets. He raps the top of the hoe sharply to fix it firmly, and then moves to the left, measuring off the distance with his foot. He holds the flashlight to look at the seed packets, reading off the instructions. He is in the blue of night.*)

WILLY: Carrots . . . quarter-inch apart. Rows . . . one-foot rows. (*He measures it off.*) One foot. (*He puts down a package and measures off.*) Beets. (*He puts down another package and measures again.*) Lettuce. (*He reads the package, puts it down.*) One foot — (*He breaks off as* BEN *appears at the right and moves slowly down to him.*) What a proposition, ts, ts. Terrific, terrific. 'Cause she's suffered, Ben, the woman has suffered. You understand me? A man can't go out the way he came in, Ben, a man has got to add up to something. You can't, you can't — (BEN *moves toward him as though to interrupt.*) You gotta consider, now. Don't answer so quick. Remember, it's a guaranteed twenty-thousand-dollar proposition. Now look, Ben, I want you to go through the ins and outs of this thing with me. I've got nobody to talk to, Ben, and the woman has suffered, you hear me?

BEN (*standing still, considering*): What's the proposition?

WILLY: It's twenty thousand dollars on the barrelhead. Guaranteed, gilt-edged, you understand?

BEN: You don't want to make a fool of yourself. They might not honor the policy.

WILLY: How can they dare refuse? Didn't I work like a coolie to meet every premium on the nose? And now they don't pay off? Impossible!

BEN: It's called a cowardly thing, William.

WILLY: Why? Does it take more guts to stand here the rest of my life ringing up a zero?

BEN (*yielding*): That's a point, William. (*He moves, thinking, turns.*) And twenty thousand — that *is* something one can feel with the hand, it is there.

WILLY (*now assured, with rising power*): Oh, Ben, that's the whole beauty of it! I see it like a diamond, shining in the dark, hard and rough, that I can pick up and touch in my hand. Not like — like an appointment! This would not be another damned-fool appointment, Ben, and it changes all the aspects.

Because he thinks I'm nothing, see, and so he spites me. But the funeral — (*Straightening up.*) Ben, that funeral will be massive! They'll come from Maine, Massachusetts, Vermont, New Hampshire! All the old-timers with the strange license plates — that boy will be thunder-struck, Ben, because he never realized — I am known! Rhode Island, New York, New Jersey — I am known, Ben, and he'll see it with his eyes once and for all. He'll see what I am, Ben! He's in for a shock, that boy!

BEN (*coming down to the edge of the garden*): He'll call you a coward.

WILLY (*suddenly fearful*): No, that would be terrible.

BEN: Yes. And a damned fool.

WILLY: No, no, he mustn't, I won't have that! (*He is broken and desperate.*)

BEN: He'll hate you, William.

(*The gay music of the boys is heard.*)

WILLY: Oh, Ben, how do we get back to all the great times? Used to be so full of light, and comradeship, the sleigh-riding in winter, and the ruddiness on his cheeks. And always some kind of good news coming up, always something nice coming up ahead. And never even let me carry the valises in the house, and simonizing, simonizing that little red car! Why, why can't I give him something and not have him hate me?

BEN: Let me think about it. (*He glances at his watch.*) I still have a little time. Remarkable proposition, but you've got to be sure you're not making a fool of yourself.

(BEN *drifts off upstage and goes out of sight.* BIFF *comes down from the left.*)

WILLY (*suddenly conscious of* BIFF, *turns and looks up at him, then begins picking up the packages of seeds in confusion*): Where the hell is that seed? (*Indignantly.*) You can't see nothing out here! They boxed in the whole goddam neighborhood!

BIFF: There are people all around here. Don't you realize that?

WILLY: I'm busy. Don't bother me.

BIFF (*taking the hoe from* WILLY): I'm saying good-by to you, Pop. (WILLY *looks at him, silent, unable to move.*) I'm not coming back any more.

WILLY: You're not going to see Oliver tomorrow?

BIFF: I've got no appointment, Dad.

WILLY: He put his arm around you, and you've got no appointment?

BIFF: Pop, get this now, will you? Everytime I've left it's been a fight that sent me out of here. Today I realized something about myself and I tried to explain it to you and I — I think I'm just not smart enough to make any sense out of it for you. To hell with whose fault it is or anything like that. (*He takes* WILLY's *arm.*) Let's just wrap it up, heh? Come on in, we'll tell Mom. (*He gently tries to pull* WILLY *to left.*)

WILLY (*frozen, immobile, with guilt in his voice*): No, I don't want to see her.

BIFF: Come on! (*He pulls again, and* WILLY *tries to pull away.*)

WILLY (*highly nervous*): No, no, I don't want to see her.

BIFF (*tries to look into* WILLY's *face, as if to find the answer there*): Why don't you want to see her?

WILLY (*more harshly now*): Don't bother me, will you?

BIFF: What do you mean, you don't want to see her? You don't want them calling you yellow, do you? This isn't your fault; it's me, I'm a bum. Now come inside! (WILLY *strains to get away.*) Did you hear what I said to you?

(WILLY *pulls away and quickly goes by himself into the house.* BIFF *follows.*)

LINDA (*to* WILLY): Did you plant, dear?

BIFF (*at the door, to* LINDA): All right, we had it out. I'm going and I'm not writing any more.

LINDA (*going to* WILLY *in the kitchen*): I think that's the best way, dear. 'Cause there's no use drawing it out, you'll just never get along.

(WILLY *doesn't respond.*)

BIFF: People ask where I am and what I'm doing, you don't know, and you don't care. That way it'll be off your mind and you can start brightening up again. All right? That clears it, doesn't it? (WILLY *is silent, and* BIFF *goes to him.*) You gonna wish me luck, scout? (*He extends his hand.*) What do you say?

LINDA: Shake his hand, Willy.

WILLY (*turning to her, seething with hurt*): There's no necessity to mention the pen at all, y'know.

BIFF (*gently*): I've got no appointment, Dad.

WILLY (*erupting fiercely*): He put his arm around . . . ?

BIFF: Dad, you're never going to see what I am, so what's the use of arguing? If I strike oil I'll send you a check. Meantime forget I'm alive.

WILLY (*to* LINDA): Spite, see?

BIFF: Shake hands, Dad.

WILLY: Not my hand.

BIFF: I was hoping not to go this way.

WILLY: Well, this is the way you're going. Good-by.

(BIFF *looks at him a moment, then turns sharply and goes to the stairs.*)

WILLY (*stops him with*): May you rot in hell if you leave this house!

BIFF (*turning*): Exactly what is it that you want from me?

WILLY: I want you to know, on the train, in the mountains, in the valleys, wherever you go, that you cut down your life for spite!

BIFF: No, no.

WILLY: Spite, spite, is the word of your undoing! And when you're down and out, remember what did it. When you're rotting somewhere beside the railroad tracks, remember, and don't you dare blame it on me!

BIFF: I'm not blaming it on you!

WILLY: I won't take the rap for this, you hear?

(HAPPY *comes down the stairs and stands on the bottom step, watching.*)

BIFF: That's just what I'm telling you!

WILLY (*sinking into a chair at the table, with full accusation*): You're trying to put a knife in me — don't think I don't know what you're doing!

BIFF: All right, phony! Then let's lay it on the line. (*He whips the rubber tube out of his pocket and puts it on the table.*)

HAPPY: You crazy —

LINDA: Biff! (*She moves to grab the hose, but* BIFF *holds it down with his hand.*)

BIFF: Leave it there! Don't move it!

WILLY (*not looking at it*): What is that?

BIFF: You know goddam well what that is.

WILLY (*caged, wanting to escape*): I never saw that.

BIFF: You saw it. The mice didn't bring it into the cellar! What is this supposed to do, make a hero out of you? This supposed to make me sorry for you?

WILLY: Never heard of it.

BIFF: There'll be no pity for you, you hear it? No pity!

WILLY (*to* LINDA): You hear the spite!

BIFF: No, you're going to hear the truth — what you are and what I am!

LINDA: Stop it!

WILLY: Spite!

HAPPY (*coming down toward* BIFF): You cut it now!

BIFF (*to* HAPPY): The man don't know who we are! The man is gonna know! (*To* WILLY.) We never told the truth for ten minutes in this house!

HAPPY: We always told the truth!

BIFF (*turning on him*): You big blow, are you the assistant buyer? You're one of the two assistants to the assistant, aren't you?

HAPPY: Well, I'm practically —

BIFF: You're practically full of it! We all are! And I'm through with it. (*To* WILLY.) Now hear this, Willy, this is me.

WILLY: I know you!

BIFF: You know why I had no address for three months? I stole a suit in Kansas City and I was in jail. (*To* LINDA, *who is sobbing.*) Stop crying. I'm through with it.

(LINDA *turns away from them, her hands covering her face.*)

WILLY: I suppose that's my fault!

BIFF: I stole myself out of every good job since high school!

WILLY: And whose fault is that?

BIFF: And I never got anywhere because you blew me so full of hot air I could never stand taking orders from anybody! That's whose fault it is!

WILLY: I hear that!

LINDA: Don't, Biff!

BIFF: It's goddam time you heard that! I had to be boss big shot in two weeks, and I'm through with it!

WILLY: Then hang yourself! For spite, hang yourself!

BIFF: No! Nobody's hanging himself, Willy! I ran down eleven flights with a pen in my hand today. And suddenly I stopped, you hear me? And in the middle of that office building, do you hear this? I stopped in the middle of that building and I saw — the sky. I saw the things that I love in this world. The work and the food and time to sit and smoke. And I looked at the pen and said to myself, what the hell am I grabbing this for? Why am I trying to become what I don't want to be? What am I doing in an office, making a contemptuous, begging fool of myself, when all I want is out there, waiting for me the minute I say I know who I am! Why can't I say that, Willy? (*He tries to make* WILLY *face him, but* WILLY *pulls away and moves to the left.*)

WILLY (*with hatred, threateningly*): The door of your life is wide open!

BIFF: Pop! I'm a dime a dozen, and so are you!

WILLY (*turning on him now in an uncontrolled outburst*): I am not a dime a dozen! I am Willy Loman, and you are Biff Loman!

(BIFF *starts for* WILLY, *but is blocked by* HAPPY. *In his fury,* BIFF *seems on the verge of attacking his father.*)

BIFF: I am not a leader of men, Willy, and neither are you. You were never anything but a hard-working drummer who landed in the ash can like all the rest of them! I'm one dollar an hour, Willy! I tried seven states and couldn't raise it. A buck an hour! Do you gather my meaning? I'm not bringing home any prizes any more, and you're going to stop waiting for me to bring them home!

WILLY (*directly to* BIFF): You vengeful, spiteful mut!

(BIFF *breaks from* HAPPY. WILLY, *in fright, starts up the stairs.* BIFF *grabs him.*)

BIFF (*at the peak of his fury*): Pop, I'm nothing! I'm nothing, Pop. Can't you understand that? There's no spite in it any more. I'm just what I am, that's all.

(BIFF's *fury has spent itself, and he breaks down, sobbing, holding on to* WILLY, *who dumbly fumbles for* BIFF's *face.*)

WILLY (*astonished*): What're you doing? What're you doing? (*To* LINDA.) Why is he crying?

BIFF (*crying, broken*): Will you let me go, for Christ's sake? Will you take that phony dream and burn it before something happens? (*Struggling to contain himself, he pulls away and moves to the stairs.*) I'll go in the morning. Put him — put him to bed. (*Exhausted,* BIFF *moves up the stairs to his room.*)

WILLY (*after a long pause, astonished, ele-* vated): Isn't that — isn't that remarkable? Biff — he likes me!

LINDA: He loves you, Willy!

HAPPY (*deeply moved*): Always did, Pop.

WILLY: Oh, Biff! (*Staring wildly.*) He cried! Cried to me. (*He is choking with his love, and now cries out his promise.*) That boy — that boy is going to be magnificent!

(BEN *appears in the light just outside the kitchen.*)

BEN: Yes, outstanding, with twenty thousand behind him.

LINDA (*sensing the racing of his mind, fearfully, carefully*): Now come to bed, Willy. It's all settled now.

WILLY (*finding it difficult not to rush out of the house*): Yes, we'll sleep. Come on. Go to sleep, Hap.

BEN: And it does take a great kind of a man to crack the jungle.

(*In accents of dread,* BEN's *idyllic music starts up.*)

HAPPY (*his arm around* LINDA): I'm getting married, Pop, don't forget it. I'm changing everything. I'm gonna run that department before the year is up. You'll see, Mom. (*He kisses her.*)

BEN: The jungle is dark but full of diamonds, Willy.

(WILLY *turns, moves, listening to* BEN.)

LINDA: Be good. You're both good boys, just act that way, that's all.

HAPPY: 'Night, Pop. (*He goes upstairs.*)

LINDA (*to* WILLY): Come, dear.

BEN (*with greater force*): One must go in to fetch a diamond out.

WILLY (*to* LINDA, *as he moves slowly along the edge of the kitchen, toward the door*): I just want to get settled down, Linda. Let me sit alone for a little.

LINDA (*almost uttering her fear*): I want you upstairs.

WILLY (*taking her in his arms*): In a few minutes, Linda. I couldn't sleep right now. Go on, you look awful tired. (*He kisses her.*)

BEN: Not like an appointment at all. A diamond is rough and hard to the touch.

WILLY: Go on now. I'll be right up.

LINDA: I think this is the only way, Willy.

WILLY: Sure, it's the best thing.

BEN: Best thing!

WILLY: The only way. Everything is gonna be — go on, kid, get to bed. You look so tired.

LINDA: Come right up.

WILLY: Two minutes.

(LINDA *goes into the living-room, then reappears in her bedroom.* WILLY *moves just outside the kitchen door.*)

WILLY: Loves me. (*Wonderingly.*) Always loved me. Isn't that a remarkable thing? Ben, he'll worship me for it!

BEN (*with promise*): It's dark there, but full of diamonds.

WILLY: Can you imagine that magnificence with twenty thousand dollars in his pocket?

LINDA (*calling from her room*): Willy! Come up!

WILLY (*calling into the kitchen*): Yes! Yes. Coming! It's very smart, you realize that, don't you, sweetheart? Even Ben sees it. I gotta go, baby. 'By! 'By! (*Going over to* BEN, *almost dancing.*) Imagine? When the mail comes he'll be ahead of Bernard again!

BEN: A perfect proposition all around.

WILLY: Did you see how he cried to me? Oh, if I could kiss him, Ben!

BEN: Time, William, time!

WILLY: Oh, Ben, I always knew one way or another we were gonna make it, Biff and I!

BEN (*looking at his watch*): The boat. We'll be late. (*He moves slowly off into the darkness.*)

WILLY (*elegiacally, turning to the house*): Now when you kick off, boy, I want a seventy-yard boot, and get right down the field under the ball, and when you hit, hit low and hit hard, because it's important, boy. (*He swings around and faces the audience.*) There's all kinds of important people in the stands, and the first thing you know ... (*Suddenly realizing he is alone.*) Ben! Ben, where do I ...? (*He makes a sudden movement of search.*) Ben, how do I ...?

LINDA (*calling*): Willy, you coming up?

WILLY (*uttering a gasp of fear, whirling about as if to quiet her*): Sh! (*He turns around as if to find his way; sounds, faces, voices, seem to be swarming in upon him and he flicks at them, crying*) Sh! Sh! (*Suddenly music, faint and high, stops him. It rises in intensity, almost to an unbearable scream. He goes up and down on his toes, and rushes off around the house.*) Shhh!

LINDA: Willy?

(*There is no answer.* LINDA *waits.* BIFF *gets up off his bed. He is still in his clothes.* HAPPY *sits up.* BIFF *stands listening.*)

LINDA (*with real fear*): Willy, answer me! Willy!

(*There is the sound of a car starting and moving away at full speed.*)

LINDA: No!

BIFF (*rushing down the stairs*): Pop!

(*As the car speeds off, the music crashes down in a frenzy of sound, which becomes the soft pulsation of a single cello string.* BIFF *slowly returns to his bedroom. He and* HAPPY *gravely don their jackets.* LINDA *slowly walks out of her room. The music has developed into a dead march. The leaves of day are appearing over everything.* CHARLEY *and* BERNARD, *somberly dressed, appear and knock on the kitchen door.* BIFF *and* HAPPY *slowly descend the stairs to the kitchen as* CHARLEY *and* BERNARD *enter. All stop a moment when* LINDA, *in clothes of mourning, bearing a little bunch of roses, comes through the draped doorway into the kitchen. She goes to* CHARLEY *and takes his arm. Now all move toward the audience, through the wall-line of the kitchen. At the limit of the apron,* LINDA *lays down the flowers, kneels, and sits back on her heels. All stare down at the grave.*)

REQUIEM

CHARLEY: It's getting dark, Linda.

(LINDA *doesn't react. She stares at the grave.*)

BIFF: How about it, Mom? Better get some rest, heh? They'll be closing the gate soon.

(LINDA *makes no move. Pause.*)

HAPPY (*deeply angered*): He had no right to do that. There was no necessity for it. We would've helped him.

CHARLEY (*grunting*): Hmmm.

BIFF: Come along, Mom.

LINDA: Why didn't anybody come?

CHARLEY: It was a very nice funeral.

LINDA: But where are all the people he knew? Maybe they blame him.

CHARLEY: Naa. It's a rough world, Linda. They wouldn't blame him.

LINDA: I can't understand it. At this time especially. First time in thirty-five years we were just about free and clear. He only needed a little salary. He was even finished with the dentist.

CHARLEY: No man only needs a little salary.

LINDA: I can't understand it.

BIFF: There were a lot of nice days. When he'd come home from a trip; or on Sundays, making the stoop; finishing the cellar; putting on the new porch; when he built the extra bathroom; and put up the garage. You know something, Charley, there's more of him in that front stoop than in all the sales he ever made.

CHARLEY: Yeah. He was a happy man with a batch of cement.

LINDA: He was so wonderful with his hands.

BIFF: He had the wrong dreams. All, all, wrong.

HAPPY (*almost ready to fight* BIFF): Don't say that!

BIFF: He never knew who he was.

CHARLEY (*stopping* HAPPY's *movement and reply. To* BIFF): Nobody dast blame this man. You don't understand: Willy was a salesman. And for a salesman, there is no rock bottom to the life. He don't put a bolt to a nut, he don't tell you the law or give you medicine. He's a man way out there in the blue, riding on a smile and a shoeshine. And when they start not smiling back — that's an earthquake. And then you get yourself a couple of spots on your hat, and you're finished. Nobody dast blame this man. A salesman is got to dream, boy. It comes with the territory.

BIFF: Charley, the man didn't know who he was.

HAPPY (*infuriated*): Don't say that!

BIFF: Why don't you come with me, Happy?

HAPPY: I'm not licked that easily. I'm staying right in this city, and I'm gonna beat this racket! (*He looks at* BIFF, *his chin set.*) The Loman Brothers!

BIFF: I know who I am, kid.

HAPPY: All right, boy. I'm gonna show you and everybody else that Willy Loman did not die in vain. He had a good dream. It's the only dream you can have — to come out number-one man. He fought it out here, and this is where I'm gonna win it for him.

BIFF (*with a hopeless glance at* HAPPY, *bends toward his mother*): Let's go, Mom.

LINDA: I'll be with you in a minute. Go on, Charley. (*He hesitates.*) I want to, just for a minute. I never had a chance to say good-by.

(CHARLEY *moves away, followed by* HAPPY. BIFF *remains a slight distance up and left of* LINDA. *She sits there, summoning herself. The flute begins, not far away, playing behind her speech.*)

LINDA: Forgive me, dear. I can't cry. I don't know what it is, but I can't cry. I don't understand it. Why did you ever do that? Help me, Willy, I can't cry. It seems to me that you're just on another trip. I keep expecting you. Willy, dear, I can't cry. Why did you do it? I search and search and I search, and I can't understand it, Willy. I made the last payment on the house today. Today, dear. And there'll be nobody home. (*A sob rises in her throat.*) We're free and clear. (*Sobbing more fully, released.*) We're free. (BIFF *comes slowly toward her.*) We're free . . . We're free . . .

(BIFF *lifts her to her feet and moves out up right with her in his arms.* LINDA *sobs quietly.* BERNARD *and* CHARLEY *come together and follow them, followed by* HAPPY. *Only the music of the flute is left on the darkening stage as over the house the hard towers of the apartment buildings rise into sharp focus, and —*)

THE CURTAIN FALLS

For the ancient Greeks, at least for Aristotle, *pathos* was the destructive or painful act common in tragedy; but in English "pathos" refers to an element in art or life that evokes tenderness or sympathetic pity. Modern English critical usage distinguishes between tragic figures and pathetic figures by recognizing some element either of strength or of regeneration in the former that is not in the latter. The tragic protagonist perhaps acts so that he brings his destruction upon himself, or if his destruction comes from outside, he resists it, and in either case he comes to at least a partial understanding of the causes of his suffering. The pathetic figure, however, is largely passive, an unknowing and unresisting innocent. In such a view Macbeth is tragic, Duncan pathetic; Lear is tragic, Cordelia pathetic; Othello is tragic, Desdemona pathetic; Hamlet is tragic (the situation is not of his making, but he does what he can to alter it), Ophelia pathetic. (Note, by the way, that of the four pathetic figures named, the first is old and the remaining three are women. Pathos is more likely to be evoked by persons assumed to be relatively defenseless than by the able-bodied.)

The guardians of critical terminology, then, have tended to insist that "tragedy" be reserved for a play showing action that leads to suffering which in turn leads to knowledge. They get very annoyed when a newspaper describes as a tragedy the death of a promising high school football player in an automobile accident, and they insist that such a death is pathetic not tragic; it is unexpected, premature, and deeply regrettable, but it does not give us a sense of man's greatness achieved through understanding the sufferings that a sufferer has at least in some degree chosen. Probably critics hoard the term "tragedy" because it is also a word of praise: to call a play a comedy or a problem play is not to imply anything about its merits, but to call a play a tragedy is tantamount to calling it an important or even a great play. In most of the best-known Greek tragedies the protagonist either does some terrible deed, or resists mightily. But Greek drama has its pathetic figures too, figures who do not so much act as suffer. Euripides' *The Trojan Women* is perhaps the greatest example of a play which does not allow its heroes to choose and to act but only to undergo, to be in agony. When we think of pathetic figures in Greek drama, however, we probably think chiefly of the choruses, groups of rather commonplace persons who do not perform a tragic deed but who suffer in sympathy with the tragic hero, who lament the hardness of the times, and who draw the spectators into the range of the hero's suffering.

That the spectators were not themselves heroic figures seems to have been assumed by the Greeks and by the Elizabethans; at least there are usually these lesser choral figures, nameless citizens, who interpret the action and call attention to the fact that even highly placed great heroes are not exempt from pain: indeed, high place and strenuous activity invite pain: the lofty pine tree, or the mariner who ventures far from the coast, is more likely to meet destruction than the lowly shrub or the fair-weather sailor. For Greeks of the fifth century B.C., and for Elizabethans, high place was not a mere matter of rank, but of worth. In both ages, it was of course known that a king may be unkingly, but it was assumed that kingship required a special nature — though that nature was not always forthcoming. Put it this way: tragedy deals with kings not because they are men with a certain title (though of course the title does give them special power), but because they are men with a certain nature. This nature is an extraordinary capacity for action and for feeling; when they make an error its consequences are enormous, and they themselves feel it as lesser people would not. When Oedipus is polluted, all of Thebes feels it. Arthur Miller is somewhat misleading when he argues (p. 306) that because Oedipus has given his name to a complex that the common man may have, the common man is therefore "as apt a subject for tragedy." It is not Oedipus' "complex" but his unique importance that is the issue in the play. Moreover, even if one argues that a man of no public importance may suffer as much as a man of public importance (and surely no one doubts this), one may be faced with the fact that the unimportant man by his ordinariness is not particularly good material for drama, and we are here concerned with drama rather than with life. In *Death of a Salesman* Willy Loman's wife says, rightly, "A small man can be just as exhausted as a great man." Yes, but is his exhaustion itself interesting, and do his activities (and this includes the words he utters) before his exhaustion have interesting dramatic possibilities? Isn't there a colorlessness that may weaken the play, an impoverishment of what John Milton called "gorgeous tragedy"?

Inevitably the rise of the bourgeoisie brought about the rise of bourgeois drama, and in the eighteenth century we get a fair number of tragedies with prologues that insist that characters like ourselves deserve our *pity*:

> No fustian hero rages here tonight,
> No armies fall, to fix a tyrant's right.
> From lower life we draw our scene's distress:
> — Let not your equals move your pity less.
> George Lillo, *Fatal Curiosity* (1733)

Note the deflation of older tragedy, the implication that its heroes were "fustian" (bombastic, pretentious) rather than genuinely heroic persons of deep feelings and high aspirations. Or, to put it differently, older tragedy in the bourgeois view dealt with persons of high rank, but rank (in this view) is not significant; therefore one may as well show persons of middle rank with whom the middle-class audience may readily identify. At the same time, the dismissal of heroic activities ("no fustian hero *rages*," "no armies *fall*") and the substitution of "distress" indicates that we are well on the road to The Hero As Victim.

And we have kept on that road. As early as the sixteenth century Copernicus had shown that man and his planet were not the center of the universe, but the thought did not distress the bulk of men until much later. In 1859 Darwin published *The Origin of Species*, arguing that man was not a special creation but a creature that had evolved because "accidental variations" had aided him in the struggle for survival. At about the same time, Marx (who wished to dedicate *Capital* to Darwin) argued that economic forces guided men's lives. Early in the twentieth century Freud seemed to argue that men are conditioned by infantile experiences and are enslaved by the dark forces of the id. All in all, by the time of the Depression of the 1930's, it was difficult to have much confidence in man's ability to shape his destiny. The human condition was a sorry one; man was an insignificant lust-ridden, soulless creature in a terrifying materialistic universe. He was no Oedipus whose moral pollution infected a great city, no Brutus whose deed might bring civil war to Rome. He was really not much of anything, except perhaps to a few who immediately depended upon him.

Arthur Miller accurately noted (*Theatre Arts*, October, 1953) that American drama "has been a steady year by year documentation of the frustration of man," and it is evident that Miller has set out to restore a sense of importance if not greatness to the individual. In "Tragedy and the Common Man," published in the same year that *Death of a Salesman* was produced and evidently a defense of the play, he argues on behalf of the common man as a tragic figure and he insists that tragedy and pathos are very different: "Pathos truly is the mode of the pessimist.... The plays we revere, century after century, are the tragedies. In them, and in them alone, lies the belief — optimistic, if you will — in the perfectibility of man." Elsewhere (*Harper's*, August 1958) he has said that pathos is an oversimplification and therefore is the "counterfeit of meaning." Curiously, however, many spectators and readers find that by Miller's own terms Willy Loman fails to be a tragic figure; he seems to them pathetic rather than tragic, a victim rather than a man who acts and who wins our esteem. True, he is partly the victim of his own actions (although he could have chosen to be a carpenter, he chose to live by the bourgeois code that values a white collar), but he seems in larger part to be a victim of the system itself, a system of ruthless competition that has no place for the man who can no longer produce. (Here is an echo of the social-realist drama of the 'thirties.) Willy had believed in this system; and although his son Biff comes to the realization that Willy "had the wrong dreams," Willy himself seems not to achieve this insight. Of course he knows that he is out of a job, that the system does not value him any longer, but he still seems not to question the values he had subscribed to. Even in the last minutes of the play, when he is planning his suicide in order to provide money for his family — really for Biff — he says such things as "Can you imagine his magnificence with twenty thousand dollars in his pocket?" and "When the mail comes he'll be ahead of Bernard again." In the preface to his *Collected Plays* Miller comments on the "exultation" with which Willy faces the end, but it is questionable whether an audience shares it. Many people find that despite the gulf in rank, they can share King Lear's feelings more easily than Willy's.

Perhaps, however, tradition has been too arbitrary in its use of the word "tragedy." Perhaps we should be as liberal as the ancient Greeks were, who did not withhold it from any play that was serious and dignified.

DUTCHMAN

LeRoi Jones (Imamu Amiri Baraka)

LeRoi Jones (born in 1934), who has taken the name Imamu Amiri Baraka, was born in Newark, N.J., attended Rutgers, and graduated from Howard University. After his graduation he served for three years in the United States Air Force, and then did graduate work at the New School for Social Research and at Columbia. In addition to writing plays, poems, stories, essays, and a book on black music, he founded the Black Arts Repertory Theatre/School. *Dutchman*, produced off Broadway in 1964, was made into a film in 1967. During the Newark riots of 1967, Jones was arrested and charged with illegal possession of weapons. He was convicted in 1968 and was sentenced to two and one-half to three years in jail but he appealed and his appeal was upheld. He continues to be active as a writer and an educator in Newark.

CHARACTERS

CLAY, *twenty-year-old Negro*
LULA, *thirty-year-old white woman*
RIDERS OF COACH, *white and black*
YOUNG NEGRO
CONDUCTOR

In the flying underbelly of the city. Steaming hot, and summer on top, outside. Underground. The subway heaped in modern myth.

Opening scene is a man sitting in a subway seat, holding a magazine but looking vacantly just above its wilting pages. Occasionally he looks blankly toward the window on his right. Dim lights and darkness whistling by against the glass. (Or paste the lights, as admitted props, right on the subway windows. Have them move, even dim and flicker. But give the sense of speed. Also stations, whether the train is stopped or the glitter and activity of these stations merely flashes by the windows.)

The man is sitting alone. That is, only his seat is visible, though the rest of the car is outfitted as a complete subway car. But only his seat is shown. There might be, for a time, as the play begins, a loud scream of the actual train. And it can recur throughout the play, or continue on a lower key once the dialogue starts.

The train slows after a time, pulling to a brief stop at one of the stations. The man looks idly up, until he sees a woman's face staring at him through the window; when it realizes that the man has noticed the face, it begins very premeditatedly to smile. The man smiles too, for a moment, without a trace of self-consciousness. Almost an instinctive though undesirable response. Then a kind of awkwardness or embarrassment sets in, and the man makes to look away, is further embarrassed, so he brings back his eyes to where the face was, but by now the train is moving again, and the face would seem to be left behind by the way the man turns his head to look back through the other windows at the slowly fading platform. He smiles then; more comfortably confident, hoping perhaps that his memory of this brief encounter will be pleasant. And then he is idle again.

SCENE I

Train roars. Lights flash outside the windows.

LULA enters from the rear of the car in bright, skimpy summer clothes and sandals. She carries a net bag full of paper books, fruit, and other anonymous articles. She is wearing sunglasses, which she pushes up on her forehead from time to time. LULA is a tall, slender, beautiful woman with long red hair hanging straight down her back, wearing only loud lipstick in somebody's good taste. She is eating an apple, very daintily. Coming down the car toward CLAY.

She stops beside CLAY's seat and hangs languidly from the strap, still managing to eat the apple. It is apparent that she is going to sit in the seat next to CLAY, and that she is only waiting for him to notice her before she sits.

CLAY sits as before, looking just beyond his magazine, now and again pulling the magazine slowly back and forth in front of his face in a hopeless effort to fan himself. Then he sees the woman hanging there beside him and he looks up into her face, smiling quizzically.

LULA: Hello.
CLAY: Uh, hi're you?
LULA: I'm going to sit down. . . . O.K.?

CLAY: Sure.
LULA (*swings down onto the seat, pushing her legs straight out as if she is very weary*): Ooooof! Too much weight.
CLAY: Ha, doesn't look like much to me. (*Leaning back against the window, a little surprised and maybe stiff.*)
LULA: It's so anyway.

(*And she moves her toes in the sandals, then pulls her right leg up on the left knee, better to inspect the bottoms of the sandals and the back of her heel. She appears for a second not to notice that CLAY is sitting next to her or that she has spoken to him just a second before. CLAY looks at the magazine, then out the black window. As he does this, she turns very quickly toward him.*)

Weren't you staring at me through the window?
CLAY (*wheeling around and very much stiffened*): What?
LULA: Weren't you staring at me through the window? At the last stop?
CLAY: Staring at you? What do you mean?
LULA: Don't you know what staring means?
CLAY: I saw you through the window . . . if that's what it means. I don't know if I was staring. Seems to me you were staring through the window at me.
LULA: I was. But only after I'd turned around and saw you staring through that

window down in the vicinity of my ass and legs.

CLAY: Really?

LULA: Really. I guess you were just taking those idle potshots. Nothing else to do. Run your mind over people's flesh.

CLAY: Oh boy. Wow, now I admit I was looking in your direction. But the rest of that weight is yours.

LULA: I suppose.

CLAY: Staring through train windows is weird business. Much weirder than staring very scdately at abstract asses.

LULA: That's why I came looking through the window ... so you'd have more than that to go on. I even smiled at you.

CLAY: That's right.

LULA: I even got into this train, going some other way than mine. Walked down the aisle ... searching you out.

CLAY: Really? That's pretty funny.

LULA: That's pretty funny. . . . God, you're dull.

CLAY: Well, I'm sorry, lady, but I really wasn't prepared for party talk.

LULA: No, you're not. What are you prepared for? (*Wrapping the apple core in a Kleenex and dropping it on the floor.*)

CLAY (*takes her conversation as pure sex talk. He turns to confront her squarely with this idea*): I'm prepared for anything. How about you?

LULA (*laughing loudly and cutting it off abruptly*): What do you think you're doing?

CLAY: What?

LULA: You think I want to pick you up, get you to take me somewhere and screw me, huh?

CLAY: Is that the way I look?

LULA: You look like you been trying to grow a beard. That's exactly what you look like. You look like you live in New Jersey with your parents and are trying to grow a beard. That's what. You look like you've been reading Chinese poetry and drinking lukewarm sugarless tea. (*Laughs, uncrossing and recrossing her legs.*) You look like death eating a soda cracker.

CLAY (*cocking his head from one side to the other, embarrassed and trying to make some comeback, but also intrigued by what the woman is saying ... even the sharp city coarseness of her voice, which is still a kind of gentle sidewalk throb*): Really? I look like all that?

LULA: Not all of it. (*She feints a seriousness to cover an actual somber tone.*) I lie a lot. (*Smiling.*) It helps me control the world.

CLAY (*relieved and laughing louder than the humor*): Yeah, I bet.

LULA: But it's true, most of it, right? Jersey? Your bumpy neck?

CLAY: How'd you know all that? Huh? Really, I mean about Jersey ... and even the beard. I met you before? You know Warren Enright?

LULA: You tried to make it with your sister when you were ten.

(CLAY *leans back hard against the back of the seat, his eyes opening now, still trying to look amused.*)

But I succeeded a few weeks ago. (*She starts to laugh again.*)

CLAY: What're you talking about? Warren tell you that? You're a friend of Georgia's?

LULA: I told you I lie. I don't know your sister. I don't know Warren Enright.

CLAY: You mean you're just picking these things out of the air?

LULA: Is Warren Enright a tall skinny black boy with a phony English accent?

CLAY: I figured you knew him.

LULA: But I don't. I just figured you would know somebody like that. (*Laughs.*)

CLAY: Yeah, yeah.

LULA: You're probably on your way to his house now.

CLAY: That's right.

LULA (*putting her hand on* CLAY's *closest knee, drawing it from the knee up to the thigh's hinge, then removing it, watching his face very closely, and continuing to laugh, perhaps more gently than before*): Dull, dull, dull. I bet you think I'm exciting.

CLAY: You're O.K.

LULA: Am I exciting you now?

CLAY: Right. That's not what's supposed to happen?

LULA: How do I know? (*She returns her hand, without moving it, then takes it away and plunges it in her bag to draw out an apple.*) You want this?

CLAY: Sure.

LULA (*she gets one out of the bag for herself*): Eating apples together is always the first step. Or walking up uninhabited Seventh Avenue in the twenties on weekends. (*Bites and giggles, glancing at* CLAY *and speaking in loose sing-song.*) Can get you involved . . . boy! Get us involved. Um-huh. (*Mock seriousness.*) Would you like to get involved with me, Mister Man?

CLAY (*trying to be as flippant as* LULA, *whacking happily at the apple*): Sure. Why not? A beautiful woman like you. Huh, I'd be a fool not to.

LULA: And I bet you're sure you know what you're talking about. (*Taking him a little roughly by the wrist, so he cannot eat the apple, then shaking the wrist.*) I bet you're sure of almost everything anybody ever asked you about . . . right? (*Shakes his wrist harder.*) Right?

CLAY: Yeah, right. . . . Wow, you're pretty strong, you know? Whatta you, a lady wrestler or something?

LULA: What's wrong with lady wrestlers? And don't answer because you never knew any. Huh. (*Cynically.*) That's for sure. They don't have any lady wrestlers in that part of Jersey. That's for sure.

CLAY: Hey, you still haven't told me how you know so much about me.

LULA: I told you I didn't know anything about *you* . . . you're a well-known type.

CLAY: Really?

LULA: Or at least I know the type very well. And your skinny English friend too.

CLAY: Anonymously?

LULA (*settles back in seat, single-mindedly finishing her apple and humming snatches of rhythm and blues song*): What?

CLAY: Without knowing us specifically?

LULA: Oh boy. (*Looking quickly at* CLAY.) What a face. You know, you could be a handsome man.

CLAY: I can't argue with you.

LULA (*vague, off-center response*): What?

CLAY (*raising his voice, thinking the train noise has drowned part of his sentence*): I can't argue with you.

LULA: My hair is turning gray. A gray hair for each year and type I've come through.

CLAY: Why do you want to sound so old?

LULA: But it's always gentle when it starts. (*Attention drifting.*) Hugged against tenements, day or night.

CLAY: What?

LULA (*refocusing*): Hey, why don't you take me to that party you're going to?

CLAY: You must be a friend of Warren's to know about the party.

LULA: Wouldn't you like to take me to the party? (*Imitates clinging vine.*) Oh, come on, ask me to your party.

CLAY: Of course I'll ask you to come with me to the party. And I'll bet you're a friend of Warren's.

LULA: Why not be a friend of Warren's? Why not? (*Taking his arm.*) Have you asked me yet?

CLAY: How can I ask you when I don't know your name?

LULA: Are you talking to my name?

CLAY: What is it, a secret?

LULA: I'm Lena the Hyena.

CLAY: The famous woman poet?

LULA: Poetess! The same!

CLAY: Well, you know so much about me . . . what's my name?

LULA: Morris the Hyena.

CLAY: The famous woman poet?

LULA: The same. (*Laughing and going into her bag.*) You want another apple?

CLAY: Can't make it, lady. I only have to keep one doctor away a day.

LULA: I bet your name is . . . something like . . . uh, Gerald or Walter. Huh?

CLAY: God, no.

LULA: Lloyd, Norman? One of those hopeless colored names creeping out of New Jersey. Leonard? Gag. . . .

CLAY: Like Warren?

LULA: Definitely. Just exactly like Warren. Or Everett.

CLAY: Gag. . . .

LULA: Well, for sure, it's not Willie.

CLAY: It's Clay.

LULA: Clay? Really? Clay what?

CLAY: Take your pick. Jackson, Johnson, or Williams.

LULA: Oh, really? Good for you. But it's got to be Williams. You're too pretentious to be a Jackson or Johnson.

CLAY: Thass right.

LULA: But Clay's O.K.

CLAY: So's Lena.

LULA: It's Lula.

CLAY: Oh?

LULA: Lula the Hyena.

CLAY: Very good.

LULA (*starts laughing again*): Now you say to me, "Lula, Lula, why don't you go to this party with me tonight?" It's your turn, and let those be your lines.

CLAY: Lula, why don't you go to this party with me tonight, huh?

LULA: Say my name twice before you ask, and no huh's.

CLAY: Lula, Lula, why don't you go to this party with me tonight?

LULA: I'd like to go, Clay, but how can you ask me to go when you barely know me?

CLAY: That is strange, isn't it?

LULA: What kind of reaction is that? You're supposed to say, "Aw, come on, we'll get to know each other better at the party."

CLAY: That's pretty corny.

LULA: What are you into anyway? (*Looking at him half sullenly but still amused.*) What thing are you playing at, Mister? Mister Clay Williams? (*Grabs his thigh, up near the crotch.*) What are *you* thinking about?

CLAY: Watch it now, you're gonna excite me for real.

LULA (*taking her hand away and throwing her apple core through the window*): I bet. (*She slumps in the seat and is heavily silent.*)

CLAY: I thought you knew everything about me? What happened?

(LULA *looks at him, then looks slowly away, then over where the other aisle would be. Noise of the train. She reaches in her bag and pulls out one of the paper books. She puts it on her leg and thumbs the pages listlessly.* CLAY *cocks his head to see the title of the book. Noise of the train.* LULA *flips pages and her eyes drift. Both remain silent.*)

Are you going to the party with me, Lula?

LULA (*bored and not even looking*): I don't even know you.

CLAY: You said you know my type.

LULA (*strangely irritated*): Don't get smart with me, Buster. I know you like the palm of my hand.

CLAY: The one you eat the apples with?

LULA: Yeh. And the one I open doors late Saturday evening with. That's my door. Up at the top of the stairs. Five flights. Above a lot of Italians and lying Americans. And scrape carrots with. Also . . . (*looks at him*) the same hand I unbutton my dress with, or let my skirt fall down. Same hand. Lover.

CLAY: Are you angry about anything? Did I say something wrong?

LULA: Everything you say is wrong. (*Mock smile.*) That's what makes you so attractive. Ha. In that funnybook jacket with all the buttons. (*More animate, taking hold of his jacket.*) What've you got that jacket and tie on in all this heat for? And why're you wearing a jacket and tie like that? Did your people ever burn witches or start revolutions over the price of tea? Boy, those narrow-shoulder clothes come from a tradition you ought to feel oppressed by. A three-button suit. What right do you have to be wearing a three-button suit and striped tie? Your grandfather was a slave, he didn't go to Harvard.

CLAY: My grandfather was a night watchman.

LULA: And you went to a colored college where everybody thought they were Averell Harriman.

CLAY: All except me.

LULA: And who did you think you were? Who do you think you are now?

CLAY (*laughs as if to make light of the whole trend of the conversation*): Well, in college I thought I was Baudelaire. But I've slowed down since.

LULA: I bet you never once thought you were a black nigger.

(*Mock serious, then she howls with laughter.* CLAY *is stunned but after initial reaction, he quickly tries to appreciate the humor.* LULA *almost shrieks.*)

A black Baudelaire.

CLAY: That's right.

LULA: Boy, are you corny. I take back what I said before. Everything you say is not wrong. It's perfect. You should be on television.

CLAY: You act like you're on television already.

LULA: That's because I'm an actress.

CLAY: I thought so.

LULA: Well, you're wrong. I'm no actress. I told you I always lie. I'm nothing, honey, and don't you ever forget it. (*Lighter.*) Although my mother was a Communist. The only person in my family ever to amount to anything.

CLAY: My mother was a Republican.

LULA: And your father voted for the man rather than the party.

CLAY: Right!

LULA: Yea for him. Yea, yea for him.

CLAY: Yea!

LULA: And yea for America where he is free to vote for the mediocrity of his choice! Yea!

CLAY: Yea!

LULA: And yea for both your parents who even though they differ about so crucial a matter as the body politic still forged a union of love and sacrifice that was destined to flower at the birth of the noble Clay . . . what's your middle name?

CLAY: Clay.

LULA: A union of love and sacrifice that was destined to flower at the birth of the noble Clay Clay Williams. Yea! And most of all yea yea for you, Clay Clay. The Black Baudelaire! Yes! (*And with knifelike cynicism.*) My Christ. My Christ.

CLAY: Thank you, ma'am.

LULA: May the people accept you as a ghost of the future. And love you, that you might not kill them when you can.

CLAY: What?

LULA: You're a murderer, Clay, and you know it. (*Her voice darkening with significance.*) You know goddamn well what I mean.

CLAY: I do?

LULA: So we'll pretend the air is light and full of perfume.

CLAY (*sniffing at her blouse*): It is.

LULA: And we'll pretend the people cannot see you. That is, the citizens. And that you are free of your own history. And I am free of my history. We'll pretend that we are both anonymous beauties smashing along through the city's entrails. (*She yells as loud as she can.*) GROOVE!

BLACK

SCENE II

Scene is the same as before, though now there are other seats visible in the car. And throughout the scene other people get on the subway. There are maybe one or two seated in the car as the scene opens, though neither CLAY nor LULA notices them. CLAY's tie is open. LULA is hugging his arm.

CLAY: The party!

LULA: I know it'll be something good. You can come in with me, looking casual and significant. I'll be strange, haughty, and silent, and walk with long slow strides.

CLAY: Right.

LULA: When you get drunk, pat me once, very lovingly on the flanks, and I'll look at you cryptically, licking my lips.

CLAY: It sounds like something we can do.

LULA: You'll go around talking to young men about your mind, and to old men about your plans. If you meet a very close friend who is also with someone like me, we can stand together, sipping our drinks and exchanging codes of lust. The atmosphere will be slithering in love and half-love and very open moral decision.

CLAY: Great. Great.

LULA: And everyone will pretend they don't know your name, and then . . . (*she pauses heavily*) later, when they have to, they'll claim a friendship that denies your sterling character.

CLAY (*kissing her neck and fingers*): And then what?

LULA: Then? Well, then we'll go down the street, late night, eating apples and winding very deliberately toward my house.

CLAY: Deliberately?

LULA: I mean, we'll look in all the shopwindows, and make fun of the queers. Maybe we'll meet a Jewish Buddhist and flatten his conceits over some very pretentious coffee.

CLAY: In honor of whose God?

LULA: Mine.

CLAY: Who is . . . ?

LULA: Me . . . and you?

CLAY: A corporate Godhead.

LULA: Exactly. Exactly. (*Notices one of the other people entering.*)

CLAY: Go on with the chronicle. Then what happens to us?

LULA (*a mild depression, but she still makes her description triumphant and increasingly direct*): To my house, of course.

CLAY: Of course.

LULA: And up the narrow steps of the tenement.

CLAY: You live in a tenement?

LULA: Wouldn't live anywhere else. Reminds me specifically of my novel form of insanity.

CLAY: Up the tenement stairs.

LULA: And with my apple-eating hand I push open the door and lead you, my tender big-eyed prey, into my . . . God, what can I call it . . . into my hovel.

CLAY: Then what happens?

LULA: After the dancing and games, after the long drinks and long walks, the real fun begins.

CLAY: Ah, the real fun. (*Embarrassed, in spite of himself.*) Which is . . . ?

LULA (*laughs at him*): Real fun in the dark house. Hah! Real fun in the dark house, high up above the street and the ignorant cowboys. I lead you in, holding your wet hand gently in my hand . . .

CLAY: Which is not wet?

LULA: Which is dry as ashes.

CLAY: And cold?

LULA: Don't think you'll get out of your responsibility that way. It's not cold at all. You Fascist! Into my dark living room. Where we'll sit and talk endlessly, endlessly.

CLAY: About what?

LULA: About what? About your manhood, what do you think? What do you think we've been talking about all this time?

CLAY: Well, I didn't know it was that. That's for sure. Every other thing in the world but that. (*Notices another person entering, looks quickly, almost involuntarily up and down the car, seeing the other people in the car.*) Hey, I didn't even notice when those people got on.

LULA: Yeah, I know.

CLAY: Man, this subway is slow.

LULA: Yeah, I know.

CLAY: Well, go on. We were talking about my manhood.

LULA: We still are. All the time.

CLAY: We were in your living room.

LULA: My dark living room. Talking endlessly.

CLAY: About my manhood.

LULA: I'll make you a map of it. Just as soon as we get to my house.

CLAY: Well, that's great.

LULA: One of the things we do while we talk. And screw.

CLAY (*trying to make his smile broader and less shaky*): We finally got there.

LULA: And you'll call my rooms black as a grave. You'll say, "This place is like Juliet's tomb."

CLAY (*laughs*): I might.

LULA: I know. You've probably said it before.

CLAY: And is that all? The whole grand tour?

LULA: Not all. You'll say to me very close to my face, many, many times, you'll say, even whisper, that you love me.

CLAY: Maybe I will.

LULA: And you'll be lying.

CLAY: I wouldn't lie about something like that.

LULA: Hah. It's the only kind of thing you will lie about. Especially if you think it'll keep me alive.

CLAY: Keep you alive? I don't understand.

LULA (*bursting out laughing, but too shrilly*): Don't understand? Well, don't look at me. It's the path I take, that's all. Where both feet take me when I set them down. One in front of the other.

CLAY: Morbid. Morbid. You sure you're not an actress? All that self-aggrandizement.

LULA: Well, I told you I wasn't an actress . . . but I also told you I lie all the time. Draw your own conclusions.

CLAY: Morbid. Morbid. You sure you're not an actress? All scribed? There's no more?

LULA: I've told you all I know. Or almost all.

CLAY: There's no funny parts?

LULA: I thought it was all funny.

CLAY: But you mean peculiar, not ha-ha.

LULA: You don't know what I mean.

CLAY: Well, tell me the almost part then. You said almost all. What else? I want the whole story.

LULA (*searching aimlessly through her bag. She begins to talk breathlessly, with a light and silly tone*): All stories are whole stories. All of 'em. Our whole story . . . nothing but change. How could things go on like that forever? Huh? (*Slaps him on the shoulder, begins finding things in her bag, taking them out and throwing them over her shoulder into the aisle.*) Except I do go on as I do. Apples and long walks with deathless intelligent lovers. But you mix it up. Look out the window, all the time. Turning pages. Change change change. Till, shit, I don't know you. Wouldn't, for that matter. You're too serious. I bet you're even too serious to be psychoanalyzed. Like all those Jewish poets from Yonkers, who leave their mothers looking for other mothers, or others' mothers, on whose baggy tits they lay their fumbling heads. Their poems are always funny, and all about sex.

CLAY: They sound great. Like movies.

LULA: But you change. (*Blankly.*) And things work on you till you hate them.

(*More people come into the train. They come closer to the couple, some of them not sitting, but swinging drearily on the straps, staring at the two with uncertain interest.*)

CLAY: Wow. All these people, so suddenly. They must all come from the same place.

LULA: Right. That they do.

CLAY: Oh? You know about them too?

LULA: Oh yeah. About them more than I know about you. Do they frighten you?

CLAY: Frighten me? Why should they frighten me?

LULA: 'Cause you're an escaped nigger.

CLAY: Yeah?

LULA: 'Cause you crawled through the wire and made tracks to my side.

CLAY: Wire?

LULA: Don't they have wire around plantations?

CLAY: You must be Jewish. All you can think about is wire. Plantations didn't have any wire. Plantations were big open white-washed places like heaven, and everybody on 'em was grooved to be there. Just strummin' and hummin' all day.

LULA: Yes, yes.

CLAY: And that's how the blues was born.

LULA: Yes, yes. And that's how the blues was born. (*Begins to make up a song that becomes quickly hysterical. As she sings she rises from her seat, still throwing things out of her bag into the aisle, beginning a rhythmical shudder and twistlike wiggle, which she continues up and down the aisle, bumping into many of the standing people and tripping over the feet of those sitting. Each time she runs into a person she lets out a very vicious piece of profanity, wiggling and stepping all the time.*) And that's how the blues was born. Yes. Yes. Son of a bitch, get out of the way. Yes. Quack. Yes. Yes. And that's how the blues was born. Ten little niggers sitting on a limb, but none of them ever looked like him. (*Points to* CLAY, *returns toward the seat, with her hands extended for him to rise and dance with her.*) And that's how blues was born. Yes. Come on, Clay. Let's do the nasty. Rub bellies. Rub bellies.

CLAY (*waves his hands to refuse. He is embarrassed, but determined to get a kick out of the proceedings*): Hey, what was in those apples? Mirror, mirror on the wall, who's the fairest one of all? Snow White, baby, and don't you forget it.

LULA (*grabbing for his hands, which he draws away*): Come on, Clay. Let's rub bellies on the train. The nasty. The nasty. Do the gritty grind, like your ol' rag-head mammy. Grind till you lose your mind. Shake it, shake it, shake it, shake it! OOOOweeee! Come on, Clay. Let's do the choochoo train shuffle, the navel scratcher.

CLAY: Hey, you coming on like the lady who smoked up her grass skirt.

LULA (*becoming annoyed that he will not dance, and becoming more animated as if to embarrass him still further*): Come on, Clay ... let's do the thing. Uhh! Uhh! Clay! Clay! You middle-class black bastard. Forget your social-working mother for a few seconds and let's knock stomachs. Clay, you liver-lipped white man. You would-be Christian. You ain't no nigger, you're just a dirty white man. Get up, Clay. Dance with me, Clay.

CLAY: Lula! Sit down, now. Be cool.

LULA (*mocking him, in wild dance*): Be cool. Be cool. That's all you know ... shaking that wildroot cream-oil on your knotty head, jackets buttoning up to your chin, so full of white man's words. Christ. God. Get up and scream at these people. Like scream meaningless shit in these hopeless faces. (*She screams at people in train, still dancing.*) Red trains cough Jewish underwear for keeps! Expanding smells of silence. Gravy snot whistling like sea birds. Clay. Clay, you got to break out. Don't sit there dying the way they want you to die. Get up.

CLAY: Oh, sit the fuck down. (*He moves to restrain her.*) Sit down, goddamn it.

LULA (*twisting out of his reach*): Screw yourself, Uncle Tom. Thomas Woolly-Head. (*Begins to dance a kind of jig, mocking* CLAY *with loud forced humor.*) There is Uncle Tom ... I mean, Uncle Thomas Woolly-Head. With old white matted mane. He hobbles on his wooden cane. Old Tom. Old Tom. Let the white man hump his ol' mama, and he jes' shuffle off in the woods and hide his gentle gray head. Ol' Thomas Woolly-Head.

(*Some of the other riders are laughing now. A drunk gets up and joins* LULA *in her dance, singing, as best he can, her "song."* CLAY *gets up out of his seat and visibly scans the faces of the other riders.*)

CLAY: Lula! Lula!

(*She is dancing and turning, still shouting as loud as she can. The drunk too is shouting, and waving his hands wildly.*)

Lula ... you dumb bitch. Why don't you stop it? (*He rushes half stumbling from his seat, and grabs one of her flailing arms.*)

LULA: Let me go! You black son of a bitch. (*She struggles against him.*) Let me go! Help!

(CLAY *is dragging her toward her seat, and the drunk seeks to interfere. He grabs* CLAY *around the shoulders and begins wrestling with him.* CLAY *clubs the drunk to the floor without releasing* LULA, *who is still screaming.* CLAY *finally gets her to the seat and throws her into it.*)

CLAY: Now you shut the hell up. (*Grabbing her shoulders.*) Just shut up. You don't know what you're talking about. You don't know anything. So just keep your stupid mouth closed.

LULA: You're afraid of white people. And your father was. Uncle Tom Big Lip!

CLAY (*slaps her as hard as he can, across the mouth.* LULA's *head bangs against the back of the seat. When she raises it again,* CLAY *slaps her again*): Now shut up and let me talk.

(*He turns toward the other riders, some of whom are sitting on the edge of their seats. The drunk is on one knee, rubbing his head, and singing softly the same song. He shuts up too when he sees* CLAY *watching him. The others go back to newspapers or stare out the windows.*)

Shit, you don't have any sense, Lula, nor feelings either. I could murder you now. Such a tiny ugly throat. I could squeeze it flat, and watch you turn blue, on a humble. For dull kicks. And all these weak-faced ofays squatting around here, staring over their papers at me. Murder them too. Even if they expected it. That man there ... (*Points to well-dressed man.*) I could rip that *Times* right out of his hand, as skinny and middle-classed as I am, I could rip that paper out of his hand and just as easily rip out his throat. It takes no great effort. For what? To kill you soft idiots? You don't understand anything but luxury.

LULA: You fool!

CLAY (*pushing her against the seat*): I'm not telling you again, Tallulah Bankhead! Luxury. In your face and your fingers. You telling me what I ought to do. (*Sudden scream frightening the whole coach.*) Well, don't! Don't you tell me anything! If I'm a middle-class fake white man ... let me be. And let me be in the way I want. (*Through his teeth.*) I'll rip your lousy breasts off! Let me be who I feel

like being. Uncle Tom. Thomas. Whoever. It's none of your business. You don't know anything except what's there for you to see. An act. Lies. Device. Not the pure heart, the pumping black heart. You don't ever know that. And I sit here, in this buttoned-up suit, to keep myself from cutting all your throats. I mean wantonly. You great liberated whore! You fuck some black man, and right away you're an expert on black people. What a lotta shit that is. The only thing you know is that you come if he bangs you hard enough. And that's all. The belly rub? You wanted to do the belly rub? Shit, you don't even know how. You don't know how. That ol' dipty-dip shit you do, rolling your ass like an elephant. That's not my kind of belly rub. Belly rub is not Queens. Belly rub is dark places, with big hats and overcoats held up with one arm. Belly rub hates you. Old bald-headed four-eyed ofays popping their fingers ... and don't know yet what they're doing. They say, "I love Bessie Smith." And don't even understand that Bessie Smith is saying, "Kiss my ass, kiss my black unruly ass." Before love, suffering, desire, anything you can explain, she's saying, and very plainly, "Kiss my black ass." And if you don't know that, it's you that's doing the kissing.

Charlie Parker? Charlie Parker. All the hip white boys scream for Bird. And Bird saying, "Up your ass, feeble-minded ofay! Up your ass." And they sit there talking about the tortured genius of Charlie Parker. Bird would've played not a note of music if he just walked up to East Sixty-seventh Street and killed the first ten white people he saw. Not a note! And I'm the great would-be poet. Yes. That's right! Poet. Some kind of bastard literature ... all it needs is a simple knife thrust. Just let me bleed you, you loud whore, and one poem vanished. A whole people of neurotics, struggling to keep from being sane. And the only thing that would cure the neurosis would be your murder. Simple as that. I mean if I murdered you, then other white people would begin to understand me. You understand? No. I guess not. If Bessie Smith had killed some white people she wouldn't have needed that music. She could have talked very straight and plain about the world. No metaphors. No grunts. No wiggles in the dark of her soul. Just straight two and two are four. Money. Power. Luxury. Like that. All of them. Crazy niggers turning their backs on sanity.

When all it needs is that simple act. Murder. Just murder! Would make us all sane.

(*Suddenly weary.*) Ahhh. Shit. But who needs it? I'd rather be a fool. Insane. Safe with my words, and no deaths, and clean, hard thoughts, urging me to new conquests. My people's madness. Hah! That's a laugh. My people. They don't need me to claim them. They got legs and arms of their own. Personal insanities. Mirrors. They don't need all those words. They don't need any defense. But listen, though, one more thing. And you tell this to your father, who's probably the kind of man who needs to know at once. So he can plan ahead. Tell him not to preach so much rationalism and cold logic to these niggers. Let them alone. Let them sing curses at you in code and see your filth as simple lack of style. Don't make the mistake, through some irresponsible surge of Christian charity, of talking too much about the advantages of Western rationalism, or the great intellectual legacy of the white man, or maybe they'll begin to listen. And then, maybe one day, you'll find they actually do understand exactly what you are talking about, all these fantasy people. All these blues people. And on that day, as sure as shit, when you really believe you can "accept" them into your fold, as half-white trusties late of the subject peoples. With no more blues, except the very old ones, and not a watermelon in sight, the great missionary heart will have triumphed, and all of those ex-coons will be stand-up Western men, with eyes for clean hard useful lives, sober, pious and sane, and they'll murder you. They'll murder you, and have very rational explanations. Very much like your own. They'll cut your throats, and drag you out to the edge of your cities so the flesh can fall away from your bones, in sanitary isolation.

LULA (*her voice takes on a different, more businesslike quality*): I've heard enough.

CLAY (*reaching for his books*): I bet you have. I guess I better collect my stuff and get off this train. Looks like we won't be acting out that little pageant you outlined before.

LULA: No. We won't. You're right about that, at least. (*She turns to look quickly around the rest of the car.*) All right!

(*The others respond.*)

CLAY (*bending across the girl to retrieve his belongings*): Sorry, baby, I don't think we could make it.

(*As he is bending over her, the girl brings up a small knife and plunges it into* CLAY's *chest. Twice. He slumps across her knees, his mouth working stupidly.*)

LULA: Sorry is right. (*Turning to the others in the car who have already gotten up from their seats.*) Sorry is the rightest thing you've said. Get this man off me! Hurry, now!

(*The others come and drag* CLAY's *body down the aisle.*)

Open the door and throw his body out.

(*They throw him off.*)

And all of you get off at the next stop.

(LULA *busies herself straightening her things. Getting everything in order. She takes out a notebook and makes a quick scribbling note. Drops it in her bag. The train apparently stops and all the others get off, leaving her alone in the coach.*

Very soon a young Negro of about twenty comes into the coach, with a couple of books under his arm. He sits a few seats in back of LULA. *When he is seated she turns and gives him a long slow look. He looks up from his book and drops the book on his lap. Then an old Negro conductor comes into the car, doing a sort of restrained soft shoe, and half mumbling the words of some song. He looks at the young man, briefly, with a quick greeting.*)

CONDUCTOR: Hey, brother!
YOUNG MAN: Hey.

(*The conductor continues down the aisle with his little dance and the mumbled song.* LULA *turns to stare at him and follows his movements down the aisle. The conductor tips his hat when he reaches her seat, and continues out the car.*)

CURTAIN

Near the end of the nineteenth century, Joseph Conrad wrote:

My task which I am trying to achieve is, by the power of the written word, to make you hear, to make you feel — it is, before all, to make you see. That — and no more, and it is everything.

To make an audience see has been the aim of many writers, but LeRoi Jones argues, in several essays in a collection entitled *Home*, that the black writer, such as Jones, who by his very status as outsider may be equipped to see American society with special clarity, will inevitably be opposed by the white Establishment, which regularly demands that writers see only what glorifies the Establishment. Not surprisingly, Jones has been harassed by public officials who claim that his revolutionary vision is a threat to public morality.

Jones admits the charge. Several quotations from "The Revolutionary Theatre" (included in *Home*) will give the gist of his position:

The Revolutionary Theatre should force change; it should be change. ... The Revolutionary Theatre must EXPOSE! Show up the insides of these humans, look into black skulls. White men will cower before this theatre because it hates them. Because they themselves have been trained to hate.

The Revolutionary Theatre must take dreams and give them a reality. ... It must be food for all those who need food, and daring propaganda for the beauty of the Human Mind. It is a political theatre, a weapon to help in the slaughter of these dim-witted fatbellied white guys who somehow believe that the rest of the world is here for them to slobber on.

Our theatre will show victims so that their brothers in the audience will be better able to understand that they are the brothers of victims, and that they themeslves are victims if they are blood brothers.*

Finally, here is a passage from the short essay that concludes *Home*:

The Black Artist's role in America is to aid in the destruction of America as he knows it. His role is to report and reflect so precisely the nature of the society, that other men will be moved by the exactness of his rendering and, if they are black men, grow strong through this moving, having seen their own strength, and weakness; and if they are white men, tremble, curse, and go mad, because they will be drenched with the filth of their evil.

Jones thus assumes that art is enormously potent, and in so doing he takes his place in a tradition that can be traced back to Chekhov (who said that he wrote his plays in order to make people see that their lives were dreary and to make them create a better life for themselves), back to Shakespeare (whose Hamlet had heard that "guilty creatures sitting at a play" may see their own image on the stage and may be moved to "proclaim" their malefactions), and finally back to Plato, who in the fourth century B.C. argued that the tragic

* The four extracts on this page and the one on page 246 are reprinted from LeRoi Jones's *Home*, pages 210–11, 211–12, 213, 251, and 188, by permission of The Sterling Lord Agency, Inc. Copyright © 1961, 1962, 1963, 1964, 1965, 1966 by LeRoi Jones.

dramatists should be barred from the ideal commonwealth precisely because they have the power to stir up pity and terror in men and thus to obscure men's rational faculty. For Plato the emotional effect of dramatic art is harmful. People ought not to be stirred by such emotions. (If this seems hopelessly old fashioned, one can reflect that probably some such thinking plays a part in our own prohibition of such entertainments as bull fighting and public executions.) Aristotle apparently tried to reply to Plato by arguing that the playwrights arouse pity and terror for the sake of moral well-being. There is a good deal of uncertainty about the meaning of Aristotle's remarks on the catharsis of pity and terror, but perhaps he meant that spectators were educated by being shown on the stage the proper objects of these emotions, or perhaps he meant that these emotions are expended harmlessly in the theater and thus the spectators are healthier when they leave the theater — rather as a boxing match or a prize fight may drain off the aggressions of the spectators who otherwise might expend their aggression outside of the stadium. In any case, the doctrine of catharsis, though much disputed, tends to be seen as counter-revolutionary; it stimulates the passions in order to diminish them, making spectators more willing to accept the affairs of the daily world.

Acceptance of the daily world is intolerable to Jones, for whom psychic health depends not on calm acceptance but on drastically changed social conditions. So Jones shows us an intolerable society, and in *Dutchman* he does this not by abstract preaching (though his essays are full of such preaching) but by vividly setting forth on the stage characters engaged in a human relationship. Jones has denied that Clay and Lula are symbols: they are, he says, real people in a real world. At the same time, however, he admits that these characters are not only individuals but are recognizable human types:

> Lula, for all her alleged insanity, just barely reflects the insanity of this hideous place. And Clay is a young boy trying desperately to become a man. *Dutchman* is about the difficulty of becoming a man in America. It is very difficult, to be sure, if you are black, but I think it is now much harder to become one if you're white. In fact, you will find very few white American males with the slightest knowledge of what manhood involves. They are too busy running the world, or running from it.

Let us begin with Lula. Jones presents her in such a way that we see her, we know her, and he does this as a dramatist must, by endowing the character with gestures and with language that ring true. Early in the play we see her as a vivid rendition of a fairly common type, someone whose precise kind of vulgarity is especially revealed in pretentiousness. She says that Clay was staring "in the vicinity of my ass" (not "at my ass"), and before she tosses her apple core onto the floor of the subway car she wraps it in a Kleenex. Through such bits of dialogue and such gestures a very real human being is rendered visible to us — but our perception of her reality is partly indebted to our recognition of her as a type. Moreover, she is not just one of millions of people whose special sort of coarseness reveals itself in ludicrous attempts at being genteel: she is also a *femme fatale,* a woman who seeks out victims, an Eve tempting Adam with her apple — specifically, the white woman who, surrounded by a myth of purity, lures black men to their destruction. Early in her conversation with Clay, Lula admits that she sought him out, and that she often lies because "it helps me to control the world." We can say that Lula — while never ceasing to be a specific woman who encounters a specific man on the subway — at least in part stands for, or, perhaps better, embodies the white society that Jones sees as enslaving all blacks.

And what of Clay, the black man? Jones said that "Clay is a young boy trying desperately to become a man." Just because Jones said so in an essay does not make it true in the play, but when we return to the play we can see ample evidence. Lula immediately sees Clay's effort to mature: "You look like you live in New Jersey with your parents and are trying to grow a beard." Again the specific details embody a type. She knows him well because he is, as she says, "a well-known type," and she later calls to Clay's attention that they have all the while been talking (however indirectly) about his manhood. The kind of man Clay wants to be is clear to Lula and to us, from his clothing:

> Boy, those narrow-shoulder clothes come from a tradition you ought to feel oppressed by. A three-button suit. What right do you have to be wearing a three-button suit and striped tie? Your grandfather was a slave, he didn't go to Harvard.

Clay is, Lula says, a "middle-class black bastard. . . . You ain't no nigger, you're just a dirty white man." Clay half knows that he is trying to surrender his black identity, and he also knows that he embodies the slave's murderous impulses toward his white oppressor. But Clay's bourgeois aspirations enslave him, and rather than achieve manhood by murdering his oppressor (so Jones seems to see it) Clay makes the mistake of thinking that murder can be avoided. "I sit here, in this buttoned-up suit, to keep myself from cutting your throats." Clay, self-imprisoned in the white man's clothes, thinks he is achieving manhood but he is ensuring his own destruction. The white oppressor, having none of Clay's illusions, knows that in white America the whites must murder the blacks (deprive them of "manhood") or the whites will be murdered by the blacks.

This commentary has become increasingly abstract, and a reader does well to remember that the play is about individuals as well as about ideas. But ideas are not antithetical to individuals and to realities, and the individuals and the realistic details that fill the play are endowed with metaphoric implications that insistently point beyond themselves. The very first line of the first stage direction is metaphoric: the play is set "in the flying underbelly of the city." The subway is the belly, the guts, of the city, invisible to the eye that dwells on the surface but real and teeming, like the passions that churn within an individual and like the political, social, and economic structures that, though invisible to many, dominate men's lives. The stage direction also tells that from time to time there is "a loud scream" of a train. Such screams are not only bits of realism, representations of trains; the title forces us, on reflection, toward a symbolic reading.

There is no Dutchman in the play; in fact the word is never used within the play. But, in conjunction with the description of the locale — "the *flying* underbelly of the city . . . the subway heaped in modern *myth*" — is it fanciful to see the endlessly shuttling subway as a modern version of the ship of the mythical flying Dutchman, who was condemned to sail the stormy seas until redeemed by the love of a pure woman? Both Lula and Clay are condemned to restlessness; Clay thinks he can find peace in the white man's world but he finds only the loss of identity; Lula's fate is that she is condemned to go on riding the subway, murdering one black after another.

EQUUS

Peter Shaffer

Peter Shaffer (b. 1926) is an Englishman who, after studying at Cambridge University, worked for three years in the United States. He returned to England, where he wrote his first play, *Five Finger Exercise* (produced in New York in 1959). Among his other plays are *The Royal Hunt of the Sun* (1964), *Black Comedy* (1965), and of course *Equus* (1973), which when produced in New York won the Tony Award for the best play of the year.

CHARACTERS

MARTIN DYSART, *a psychiatrist*   DORA STRANG, *his mother*   HARRY DALTON, *a stable owner*
ALAN STRANG   HESTHER SALOMON, *a magistrate*   A YOUNG HORSEMAN
FRANK STRANG, *his father*   JILL MASON   A NURSE

SIX ACTORS — *including the* YOUNG HORSEMAN, *who also plays* NUGGET — *appear as* HORSES.

THE HORSES: The actors wear track-suits of chestnut velvet. On their feet are light strutted hooves, about four inches high, set on metal horse-shoes. On their hands are gloves of the same colour. On their heads are tough masks made of alternating bands of silver wire and leather: their eyes are outlined by leather blinkers. The actors' own heads are seen beneath them: no attempt should be made to conceal them.

Any literalism which could suggest the cosy familiarity of a domestic animal — or worse, a pantomime horse — should be avoided. The actors should never crouch on all fours, or even bend forward. They must always — except on the one occasion where NUGGET is ridden — stand upright, as if the body of the horse extended invisibly behind them. Animal effect must be created entirely mimetically, through the use of legs, knees, neck, face, and the turn of the head which can move the mask above it through all the gestures of equine wariness and pride. Great care must also be taken that the masks are put on before the audience with very precise timing — the actors watching each other, so that the masking has an exact and ceremonial effect.

THE CHORUS: References are made in the text to the Equus Noise. I have in mind a choric effect, made by all the actors sitting round upstage, and composed of humming, thumping, and stamping — though never of neighing or whinnying. This Noise heralds or illustrates the presence of Equus the God.

Peter Firth as Alan in the New York production of *Equus*, directed by John Dexter, 1974. (Photograph: Van Williams.)

A Note on the Play — One weekend over two years ago, I was driving with a friend through bleak countryside. We passed a stable. Suddenly he was reminded by it of an alarming crime which he had heard about recently at a dinner party in London. He knew only one horrible detail, and his complete mention of it could barely have lasted a minute — but it was enough to arouse in me an intense fascination.

The act had been committed several years before by a highly disturbed young man. It had deeply shocked a local bench of magistrates. It lacked, finally, any coherent explanation.

A few months later my friend died. I could not verify what he had said, or ask him to expand it. He had given me no name, no place, and no time. I don't think he knew them. All I possessed was his report of a dreadful event, and the feeling it engendered in me. I knew very strongly that I wanted to interpret it in some entirely personal way. I had to create a mental world in which the deed could be made comprehensible.

Every person and incident in *Equus* is of my own invention, save the crime itself: and even that I modified to accord with what I feel to be acceptable theatrical proportion. I am grateful now that I have never received confirmed details of the real story, since my concern has been more and more with a different kind of exploration.

I have been lucky, in doing final work on the play, to have enjoyed the advice and expert comment of a distinguished child psychiatrist. Through him I have tried to keep things real in a more naturalistic sense. I have also come to perceive that psychiatrists are an immensely varied breed, professing immensely varied methods and techniques. MARTIN DYSART is simply one doctor in one hospital. I must take responsibility for him, as I do for his patient.

The Set — A square of wood set on a circle of wood.

The square resembles a railed boxing ring. The rail, also of wood, encloses three sides. It is perforated on each side by an opening. Under the rail are a few vertical slats, as if in a fence. On the downstage side there is no rail. The whole square is set on ball bearings, so that by slight pressure from actors standing round it on the circle, it can be made to turn round smoothly by hand.

On the square are set three little plain benches, also of wood. They are placed parallel with the rail, against the slats, but can be moved out by the actors to stand at right angles to·them.

Set into the floor of the square, and flush with it, is a thin metal pole, about a yard high. This can be raised out of the floor, to stand upright. It acts as a support for the actor playing NUGGET, when he is ridden.

In the area outside the circle stand benches. Two downstage left and right, are curved to accord with the circle. The left one is used by DYSART as a listening and observing post when he is out of the square, and also by ALAN as his hospital bed. The right one is used by ALAN's parents, who sit side by side on it. (Viewpoint is from the main body of the audience.)

Further benches stand upstage, and accommodate the other actors. All the cast of *Equus* sits on stage the entire evening. They get up to perform their scenes, and return when they are done to their places around the set. They are witnesses, assistants — and especially a CHORUS.

Upstage, forming a backdrop to the whole, are tiers of seats in the fashion of a dissecting theatre, formed into two railed-off blocks, pierced by a central tunnel. In these blocks sit members of the audience. During the play, DYSART addresses them directly from time to time, as he addresses the main body of the theatre. No other actor ever refers to them.

To left and right, downstage, stand two ladders on which are suspended horse masks.

The colour of all benches is olive green.

Above the stage hangs a battery of lights, set in a huge metal ring. Light cues, in this version, will be only of the most general description.

The main action of the play takes place in Rokeby Psychiatric Hospital in Southern England.

The time is the present.

The play is divided into numbered scenes, indicating a change of time or locale or mood. The action, however, is continuous.

ACT 1

SCENE 1

Darkness.
Silence.
Dim light up on the square. In a spotlight stands ALAN STRANG, *a lean boy of seventeen, in sweater and jeans. In front of him, the horse* NUGGET. ALAN's *pose represents a contour of great tenderness: his head is pressed against the shoulder of the horse, his hands stretching up to fondle its head.*

The horse in turn nuzzles his neck.
The flame of a cigarette lighter jumps in the dark. Lights come up slowly on the circle. On the left bench, downstage, MARTIN DYSART, *smoking. A man in his mid-forties.*

DYSART: With one particular horse, called Nugget, he embraces. The animal digs its sweaty brow into his cheek, and they stand in the dark for an hour — like a necking couple. And of all nonsensical things — I keep thinking about the *horse!* Not the boy: the horse, and what it may be trying to do. I keep seeing that huge head kissing him with its chained mouth. Nudging through the metal some desire absolutely irrelevant to filling its belly or propagating its own kind. What desire could that be? Not to stay a horse any longer? Not to remain reined up for ever in those particular genetic strings? Is it possible, at certain moments we cannot imagine, a horse can add its sufferings together — the non-stop jerks and jabs that are its daily life — and turn them into grief? What use is grief to a horse?

(ALAN *leads* NUGGET *out of the square and they disappear together up the tunnel, the horse's hooves scraping delicately on the wood.*

DYSART *rises, and addresses both the large audience in the theatre and the smaller one on stage.*)

You see, I'm lost. What use, I should be asking, are questions like these to an overworked psychiatrist in a provincial hospital? They're worse than useless: they are, in fact, subversive.

(*He enters the square. The light grows brighter.*)

The thing is, I'm desperate. You see, I'm wearing that horse's head myself. That's the feeling. All reined up in old language and old assumptions, straining to jump clean-hoofed on to a whole new track of being I only suspect is there. I can't see it, because my educated, average head is being held at the wrong angle. I can't jump because the bit forbids it, and my own basic force — my horsepower, if you like — is too little. The only thing I know for sure is this: a horse's head is finally unknowable to me. Yet I handle children's heads — which I must presume to be more complicated, at least in the area of my chief concern. . . . In a way, it has nothing to do with this boy. The doubts have been there for years, piling up steadily in this dreary place. It's only the extremity of this case that's made them active. I know that. The *extremity* is the point! All the same, whatever the reason, they are now, these doubts, not just vaguely worrying — but intolerable . . . I'm sorry. I'm not making much sense. Let me start properly: in order. It began one Monday last month, with Hesther's visit.

SCENE 2

The light gets warmer.
He sits. NURSE *enters the square.*

NURSE: Mrs. Salomon to see you, Doctor.
DYSART: Show her in, please.

(NURSE *leaves and crosses to where* HESTHER *sits.*)

Some days I blame Hesther. She brought him to see me. But of course that's nonsense. What is he but a last straw? a last symbol? If it hadn't been him, it would have been the next patient, or the next. At least, I suppose so.

(HESTHER *enters the square: a woman in her mid-forties.*)

HESTHER: Hallo, Martin.

(DYSART *rises and kisses her on the cheek.*)

DYSART: Madam Chairman! Welcome to the torture chamber!
HESTHER: It's good of you to see me right away.
DYSART: You're a welcome relief. Take a couch.
HESTHER: It's been a day?
DYSART: No — just a fifteen year old schizophrenic, and a girl of eight thrashed into catatonia by her father. Normal, really . . . You're in a state.
HESTHER: Martin, this is the most shocking case I ever tried.
DYSART: So you said on the phone.
HESTHER: I mean it. My bench wanted to send the boy to prison. For life, if they could manage it. It took me two hours solid arguing to get him sent to you instead.
DYSART: Me?
HESTHER: I mean, to hospital.
DYSART: Now look, Hesther. Before you say anything else, I can take no more patients at the moment. I can't even cope with the ones I have.
HESTHER: You must.
DYSART: Why?
HESTHER: Because most people are going to be disgusted by the whole thing. Including doctors.
DYSART: May I remind you I share this room with two highly competent psychiatrists?
HESTHER: Bennett and Thoroughgood. They'll be as shocked as the public.
DYSART: That's an absolutely unwarrantable statement.
HESTHER: Oh, they'll be cool and exact. And underneath they'll be revolted, and immovably English. Just like my bench.
DYSART: Well, what am I? Polynesian?
HESTHER: You know exactly what I mean! . . . (*Pause.*) Please, Martin. It's vital. You're this boy's only chance.
DYSART: Why? What's he done? Dosed some little girl's Pepsi with Spanish Fly? What could possibly throw your bench into two-hour convulsions?
HESTHER: He blinded six horses with a metal spike.

(*A long pause.*)

DYSART: Blinded?
HESTHER: Yes.
DYSART: All at once, or over a period?
HESTHER: All on the same night.
DYSART: Where?
HESTHER: In a riding stable near Winchester. He worked there at weekends.
DYSART: How old?
HESTHER: Seventeen.
DYSART: What did he say in Court?
HESTHER: Nothing. He just sang.
DYSART: Sang?
HESTHER: Any time anyone asked him anything.

(*Pause.*)

Please take him, Martin. It's the last favour I'll ever ask you.
DYSART: No, it's not.
HESTHER: No, it's not — and he's probably abominable. All I know is, he needs you badly. Because there really is nobody within a hundred miles of your desk who can handle him. And perhaps understand what this is about. Also . . . .
DYSART: What?
HESTHER: There's something very special about him.
DYSART: In what way?
HESTHER: Vibrations.
DYSART: You and your vibrations.
HESTHER: They're quite startling. You'll see.
DYSART: When does he get here?
HESTHER: Tomorrow morning. Luckily there was a bed in Neville Ward. I know this is an awful imposition, Martin. Frankly I didn't know what else to do.

(*Pause.*)

DYSART: Can you come in and see me on Friday?
HESTHER: Bless you!
DYSART: If you come after work I can give you a drink. Will 6:30 be all right?
HESTHER: You're a dear. You really are.
DYSART: Famous for it.
HESTHER: Goodbye.
DYSART: By the way, what's his name?
HESTHER: Alan Strang.

(*She leaves and returns to her seat.*)

DYSART (*to audience*): What did I expect of him? Very little, I promise you. One more

dented little face. One more adolescent freak. The usual unusual. One great thing about being in the adjustment business: you're never short of customers.

(NURSE *comes down the tunnel, followed by* ALAN. *She enters the square.*)

NURSE: Alan Strang, Doctor.

(*The boy comes in.*)

DYSART: Hallo. My name's Martin Dysart. I'm pleased to meet you.

(*He puts out his hand.* ALAN *does not respond in any way.*)

That'll be all, Nurse, thank you.

SCENE 3

NURSE *goes out and back to her place.*
DYSART *sits, opening a file.*

So: did you have a good journey? I hope they gave you lunch at least. Not that there's much to choose between a British Rail meal and one here.

(ALAN *stands staring at him.*)

DYSART: Won't you sit down?

(*Pause. He does not.* DYSART *consults his file.*)

Is this your full name? Alan Strang?

(*Silence.*)

And you're seventeen. Is that right? Seventeen? . . . Well?
ALAN (*singing low*):
    Double your pleasure,
    Double your fun
    With Doublemint, Doublemint
    Doublemint gum.
DYSART (*unperturbed*): Now, let's see. You work in an electrical shop during the week. You live with your parents, and your father's a printer. What sort of things does he print?
ALAN (*singing louder*):
    Double your pleasure
    Double your fun
    With Doublemint, Doublemint
    Doublemint gum.
DYSART: I mean does he do leaflets and calendars? Things like that?

(*The boy approaches him, hostile.*)

ALAN (*singing*):
Try the taste of Martini
The most beautiful drink in the world.
It's the right one —
The bright one —
That's Martini!

DYSART: I wish you'd sit down, if you're going to sing. Don't you think you'd be more comfortable?

(*Pause.*)

ALAN (*singing*):
There's only one T in Typhoo!
In packets and in teabags too.
Any way you make it, you'll find it's true:
There's only one T in Typhoo!

DYSART (*appreciatively*): Now that's a good song. I like it better than the other two. Can I hear that one again?

(ALAN *starts away from him, and sits on the upstage bench.*)

ALAN (*singing*):
Double your pleasure
Double your fun
With Doublemint, Doublemint
Doublemint gum.

DYSART (*smiling*): You know I was wrong. I really do think that one's better. It's got such a catchy tune. Please do that one again.

(*Silence. The boy glares at him.*)

I'm going to put you in a private bedroom for a little while. There are one or two available, and they're rather more pleasant than being in a ward. Will you please come and see me tomorrow? . . . (*He rises.*) By the way, which parent is it who won't allow you to watch television? Mother or father? Or is it both? (*Calling out of the door.*) Nurse!

(ALAN *stares at him.* NURSE *comes in.*)

NURSE: Yes, Doctor?
DYSART: Take Strang here to Number Three, will you? He's moving in there for a while.
NURSE: Very good, Doctor.
DYSART (*to* ALAN): You'll like that room. It's nice.

(*The boy sits staring at* DYSART.
DYSART *returns the stare.*)

NURSE: Come along, young man. This way. . . . I said this way, please.

(*Reluctantly* ALAN *rises and goes to* NURSE, *passing dangerously close to* DYSART, *and out through the left door.* DYSART *looks after him, fascinated.*)

SCENE 4

NURSE *and patient move on to the circle, and walk downstage to the bench where the doctor first sat, which is to serve also as* ALAN's *bed.*

NURSE: Well now: isn't this nice? You're lucky to be in here, you know, rather than the ward. That ward's a noisy old place.
ALAN (*singing*):
Let's go where you wanna go — Texaco!
NURSE (*contemplating him*): I hope you're not going to make a nuisance of yourself. You'll have a much better time of it here, you know, if you behave yourself.
ALAN: Fuck off.
NURSE (*tight*): That's the bell there. The lav's down the corridor.

(*She leaves him, and goes back to her place.* ALAN *lies down.*)

SCENE 5

DYSART *stands in the middle of the square and addresses the audience. He is agitated.*

DYSART: That night, I had this very explicit dream. In it I'm a chief priest in Homeric Greece. I'm wearing a wide gold mask, all noble and bearded, like the so-called Mask of Agamemnon found at Mycenae. I'm standing by a thick round stone and holding a sharp knife. In fact, I'm officiating at some immensely important ritual sacrifice, on which depends the fate of the crops or of a military expedition. The sacrifice is a herd of children: about five hundred boys and girls. I can see them stretching away in a long queue, right across the plain of Argos. I know it's Argos because of the red soil. On either side of me stand two assistant priests, wearing masks as well: lumpy, pop-eyed masks, such as also were found at Mycenae. They are enormously strong, these other priests, and absolutely tireless. As each child steps forward, they grab it from behind and throw it over the stone. Then with a surgical skill which amazes even me, I fit in the knife and slice elegantly down to the navel, just like a seamstress following a pattern. I part the flaps, sever the inner tubes, yank them out and throw them hot and steaming on to the floor. The other two then study the pattern they make, as if they were reading hieroglyphics. It's obvious to me that I'm tops as chief priest. It's this unique talent for carving that has got me where I am. The only thing is, unknown to them, I've started to feel distinctly nauseous. And with each victim, it's getting worse. My face is going green behind the mask. Of course, I redouble my efforts to look professional – cutting and snipping for all I'm worth: mainly because I know that if ever those two assistants so much as glimpse my distress – and the implied doubt that this repetitive and smelly work is doing any social good at all – I will be the next across the stone. And then, of course – the damn mask begins to slip. The priests both turn and look at it – it slips some more – they see the green sweat running down my face – their gold pop-eyes suddenly fill up with blood – they tear the knife out of my hand . . . and I wake up.

SCENE 6

HESTHER *enters the square. Light grows warmer.*

HESTHER: That's the most indulgent thing I ever heard.

DYSART: You think?

HESTHER: Please don't be ridiculous. You've done the most superb work with children. You must know that.

DYSART: Yes, but do the children?

HESTHER: Really!

DYSART: I'm sorry.

HESTHER: So you should be.

DYSART: I don't know why you listen. It's just professional menopause. Everyone gets it sooner or later. Except you.

HESTHER: Oh, of course. I feel totally fit to be a magistrate all the time.

DYSART: No, you don't – but then that's you feeling unworthy to fill a job. I feel the job is unworthy to fill me.

HESTHER: Do you seriously?

DYSART: More and more. I'd like to spend the next ten years wandering very slowly around the *real* Greece. . . . Anyway, all this dream nonsense is your fault.

HESTHER: Mine?

DYSART: It's that lad of yours who started it off. Do you know it's his face I saw on every victim across the stone?

HESTHER: Strang?

DYSART: He has the strangest stare I ever met.

HESTHER: Yes.

DYSART: It's exactly like being accused. Violently accused. But what of? . . . Treating him is going to be unsettling. Especially in my present state. His singing was direct enough. His speech is more so.

HESTHER (*surprised*): He's talking to you, then?

DYSART: Oh yes. It took him two more days of commercials, and then he snapped. Just like that – I suspect it has something to do with his nightmares.

(NURSE *walks briskly round the circle, a blanket over her arm, a clipboard of notes in her hand.*)

HESTHER: He has nightmares?

DYSART: Bad ones.

NURSE: We had to give him a sedative or two, Doctor. Last night it was exactly the same.

DYSART (*to* NURSE): What does he do? Call out?

NURSE (*to desk*): A lot of screaming, Doctor.

DYSART (*to* NURSE): Screaming?

NURSE: One word in particular.

DYSART (*to* NURSE): You mean a special word?

NURSE: Over and over again. (*Consulting clipboard.*) It sounds like "Ek."

HESTHER: Ek?

NURSE: Yes, Doctor. Ek. . . . "Ek!" he goes. "Ek!"

HESTHER: How weird.

NURSE: When I woke him up he clung to me like he was going to break my arm.

(*She stops at* ALAN's *bed. He is sitting up. She puts the blanket over him, and returns to her place.*)

DYSART: And then he burst in – just like that – without knocking or anything. Fortunately, I didn't have a patient with me.

ALAN (*jumping up*): *Dad!*

HESTHER: What?

DYSART: The answer to a question I'd asked him two days before. Spat out with the same anger as he sang the commercials.

HESTHER: Dad what?

ALAN: Who hates telly.

(*He lies downstage on the circle, as if watching television.*)

HESTHER: You mean his dad forbids him to watch?

DYSART: Yes.

ALAN: It's a dangerous drug.

HESTHER: Oh, really!

(FRANK *stands up and enters the scene downstage. A man in his fifties.*)

FRANK (*to* ALAN): It may not look like that, but that's what it is. Absolutely fatal mentally, if you receive my meaning.

(DORA *follows him on. She is also middle-aged.*)

DORA: That's a little extreme, dear, isn't it?

FRANK: You sit in front of that thing long enough, you'll become stupid for life — like most of the population. (*To* ALAN.) The thing is, it's a *swiz*. It seems to be offering you something, but actually it's taking something away. Your intelligence and your concentration, every minute you watch it. That's a true swiz, do you see?

(*Seated on the floor,* ALAN *shrugs.*)

I don't want to sound like a spoilsport, old chum — but there really is no substitute for reading. What's the matter: don't you like it?

ALAN: It's all right.

FRANK: I know you think it's none of my beeswax, but it really is you know . . . Actually, it's a disgrace when you come to think of it. You the son of a printer, and never opening a book! If all the world was like you, I'd be out of a job, if you receive my meaning!

DORA: All the same, times change, Frank.

FRANK (*reasonably*): They change if you let them change, Dora. Please return that set in the morning.

ALAN (*crying out*): No!

DORA: Frank! No!

FRANK: I'm sorry, Dora, but I'm not having that thing in the house a moment longer. I told you I didn't want it to begin with.

DORA: But, dear, everyone watches television these days!

FRANK: Yes, and what do they watch? Mindless violence! Mindless jokes! Every five minutes some laughing idiot selling you something you don't want, just to bolster up the economic system. (*To* ALAN.) I'm sorry, old chum.

(*He leaves the scene and sits again in his place.*)

HESTHER: He's a Communist, then?

DYSART: Old-type Socialist, I'd say. Relentlessly self-improving.

HESTHER: They're *both* older than you'd expect.

DYSART: So I gather.

DORA (*looking after* FRANK): Really, dear, you are very extreme!

(*She leaves the scene too, and again sits beside her husband.*)

HESTHER: She's an ex-school teacher, isn't she?

DYSART: Yes. The boy's proud of that. We got on to it this afternoon.

ALAN (*belligerently, standing up*): She knows more than you.

(HESTHER *crosses and sits by* DYSART. *During the following, the boy walks round the circle, speaking to* DYSART *but not looking at him.* DYSART *replies in the same manner.*)

DYSART (*to* ALAN): Does she?

ALAN: I bet I do too. I bet I know more history than you.

DYSART (*to* ALAN): Well, I bet you don't.

ALAN: All right: who was the Hammer of the Scots?

DYSART (*to* ALAN): I don't know: who?

ALAN: King Edward the First. Who never smiled again?

DYSART (*to* ALAN): I don't know: who?

ALAN: You don't know anything, do you? It was Henry the First. I know all the Kings.

DYSART (*to* ALAN): And who's your favourite?

ALAN: John.

DYSART (*to* ALAN) Why?

ALAN: Because he put out the eyes of that smarty little —

(*Pause.*)

(*Sensing he has said something wrong.*) Well, he didn't really. He was prevented, because the gaoler was merciful!

HESTHER: Oh dear.

ALAN: *He was prevented!*

DYSART: Something odder was to follow.

ALAN: Who said "Religion is the opium of the people"?

HESTHER: Good Lord!

(ALAN *giggles.*)

DYSART: The odd thing was, he said it with a sort of guilty snigger. The sentence is obviously associated with some kind of tension.

HESTHER: What did you say?

DYSART: I gave him the right answer. (*To* ALAN.) Karl Marx.

ALAN: No.

DYSART (*to* ALAN): Then who?

ALAN: Mind your own beeswax.

DYSART: It's probably his dad. He may say it to provoke his wife.

HESTHER: And you mean she's religious?

DYSART: She could be. I tried to discover — none too successfully.

ALAN: Mind your own beeswax!

(ALAN *goes back to bed and lies down in the dark.*)

DYSART: However, I shall find out on Sunday.

HESTHER: What do you mean?

DYSART (*getting up*): I want to have a look at his home, so I invited myself over.

HESTHER: Did you?

DYSART: If there's any tension over religion, it should be evident on a Sabbath evening! I'll let you know.

(*He kisses her cheek and they part, both leaving the square.* HESTHER *sits in her place again;* DYSART *walks round the circle, and greets* DORA *who stands waiting for him downstage.*)

SCENE 7

DYSART (*shaking hands*): Mrs. Strang.

DORA: Mr. Strang's still at the Press, I'm afraid. He should be home in a minute.

DYSART: He works Sundays as well?

DORA: Oh, yes. He doesn't set much store by Sundays.

DYSART: Perhaps you and I could have a little talk before he comes in.

DORA: Certainly. Won't you come into the living room?

(*She leads the way into the square. She is very nervous.*)

Please. . . .

(*She motions him to sit, then holds her hands tightly together.*)

DYSART: Mrs. Strang, have you any idea how this thing could have occurred?

DORA: I can't imagine, Doctor. It's all so unbelievable! . . . Alan's always been such a gentle boy. He loves animals! Especially horses.

DYSART: Especially?

DORA: Yes. He even has a photograph of one up in his bedroom. A beautiful white one, looking over a gate. His father gave it to him a few years ago, off a calendar he'd printed — and he's never taken it down . . . And when he was seven or eight, I used to have to read him the same book over and over, all *about* a horse.

DYSART: Really?

DORA: Yes: it was called Prince, and no one could ride him.

(ALAN *calls from his bed, not looking at his mother.*)

ALAN (*excited, younger voice*): Why not? . . . Why not? . . . Say it! In his voice!

DORA: He loved the idea of animals talking.

DYSART: Did he?

ALAN: *Say it! Say it! . . . Use his voice!*

DORA ("*proud*" *voice*): "Because I am faithful!"

(ALAN *giggles.*)

"My name is Prince, and I'm a Prince among horses! Only my young Master can ride me! Anyone else — I'll *throw off!*"

(ALAN *giggles louder.*)

And then I remember I used to tell him a funny thing about falling off horses. Did you know that when Christian cavalry first appeared in the New World, the pagans thought horse and rider was one person?

DYSART: Really?

ALAN (*sitting up, amazed*): One person?

DORA: Actually they thought it must be a god.

ALAN: *A god!*

DORA: It was only when one rider fell off, they realized the truth.

DYSART: That's fascinating. I never heard that before. . . . Can you remember anything else like that you may have told him about horses?

DORA: Well, not really. They're in the Bible, of course. "He saith among the trumpets, Ha, ha."

DYSART: Ha, ha?

DORA: The Book of Job. Such a noble passage. *You* know — (*Quoting.*) "Hast thou given the horse strength?"

ALAN (*responding*): "Hast thou clothed his neck with thunder?"

DORA (*to* ALAN): "The glory of his nostrils is terrible!"

ALAN: "He swallows the ground with fierceness and rage!"

DORA: "He saith among the trumpets —"

ALAN (*trumpeting*): "Ha! Ha!"

DORA (*to* DYSART): Isn't that splendid?

DYSART: It certainly is.

ALAN (*trumpeting*): Ha! Ha!

DORA: And then, of course, we saw an awful lot of Westerns on the television. He couldn't have enough of those.

DYSART: But surely you don't have a set, do you? I understood Mr. Strang doesn't approve.

DORA (*conspiratorially*): He doesn't . . . I used to let him slip off in the afternoons to a friend next door.

DYSART (*smiling*): You mean without his father's knowledge?

DORA: What the eye does not see, the heart does not grieve over, does it? Anyway, Westerns are harmless enough, surely?

(FRANK *stands up and enters the square.* ALAN *lies back under the blanket.*)

(*To* FRANK.) Oh, hallo dear. This is Dr. Dysart.

FRANK (*shaking hands*): How d'you do?

DYSART: How d'you do?

DORA: I was just telling the Doctor, Alan's always adored horses.

FRANK (*tight*): We assumed he did.

DORA: You know he did, dear. Look how he liked that photograph you gave him.

FRANK (*startled*): What about it?

DORA: Nothing dear. Just that he pestered

you to have it as soon as he saw it. Do you remember? (*To* DYSART.) We've always been a horsey family. At least my side of it has. My grandfather used to ride every morning on the downs behind Brighton, all dressed up in bowler hat and jodhpurs! He used to look splendid. Indulging in equitation, he called it.

(FRANK *moves away from them and sits wearily.*)

ALAN (*trying the word*): Equitation. . . .

DORA: I remember I told him how that came from *equus*, the Latin word for horse. Alan was fascinated by that word, I know. I suppose because he'd never come across one with two U's together before.

ALAN (*savouring it*): Equus!

DORA: I always wanted the boy to ride himself. He'd have so enjoyed it.

DYSART: But surely he did?

DORA: No.

DYSART: Never?

DORA: He didn't care for it. He was most definite about not wanting to.

DYSART: But he must have had to at the stables? I mean, it would be part of the job.

DORA: You'd have thought so, but no. He absolutely wouldn't, would he, dear?

FRANK (*dryly*): It seems he was perfectly happy raking out manure.

DYSART: Did he ever give a reason for this?

DORA: No. I must say we both thought it most peculiar, but he wouldn't discuss it. I mean, you'd have thought he'd be longing to get out in the air after being cooped up all week in that dreadful shop. Electrical and kitchenware! Isn't *that* an environment for a sensitive boy, Doctor? . . .

FRANK: Dear, have you offered the doctor a cup of tea?

DORA: Oh dear, no, I haven't . . . And you must be dying for one.

DYSART: That would be nice.

DORA: Of course it would. . . . Excuse me . . .

(*She goes out — but lingers on the circle, eavesdropping near the right door.* ALAN *stretches out under his blanket and sleeps.* FRANK *gets up.*)

FRANK: My wife has romantic ideas, if you receive my meaning.

DYSART: About her family?

FRANK: She thinks she married beneath her. I daresay she did. I don't understand these things myself.

DYSART: Mr. Strang, I'm fascinated by the fact that Alan wouldn't ride.

FRANK: Yes, well that's him. He's always been a weird lad, I have to be honest. Can you imagine spending your weekends like that — just cleaning out stalls — with all the things that he could have been doing in the way of Further Education?

DYSART: Except he's hardly a scholar.

FRANK: How do we know? He's never really tried. His mother indulged him. She doesn't care if he can hardly write his own name, and she a school teacher that was. Just as long as he's happy, she says . . .

(DORA *wrings her hands in anguish.*
FRANK *sits again.*)

DYSART: Would you say she was closer to him than you are?

FRANK: They've always been thick as thieves. I can't say I entirely approve — especially when I hear her whispering that Bible to him hour after hour, up there in his room.

DYSART: Your wife is religious?

FRANK: Some might say excessively so. Mind you that's her business. But when it comes to dosing it down the boy's throat — well, frankly, he's my son as well as hers. She doesn't see that. Of course, that's the funny thing about religious people. They always think their susceptibilities are more important than non-religious.

DYSART: And you're non-religious, I take it?

FRANK: I'm an atheist, and I don't mind admitting it. If you want my opinion, it's the Bible that's responsible for all this.

DYSART: Why?

FRANK: Well, look at it yourself. A boy spends night after night having this stuff read into him: an innocent man tortured to death — thorns driven into his head — nails into his hands — a spear jammed through his ribs. It can mark anyone for life, that kind of thing. I'm not joking. The boy was absolutely fascinated by all that. He was always mooning over religious pictures. I mean real kinky ones, if you receive my meaning. I had to put a stop to it once or twice! . . . (*Pause.*) Bloody religion — it's our only real problem in this house, but it's insuperable: I don't mind admitting it.

(*Unable to stand any more,* DORA *comes in again.*)

DORA (*pleasantly*): You must excuse my husband, Doctor. This one subject is something of an obsession with him, isn't it, dear? You must admit.

FRANK: Call it what you like. All that stuff to me is just bad sex.

DORA: And what has that got to do with Alan?

FRANK: Everything! . . . (*Seriously.*) Everything, Dora!

DORA: I don't understand. What are you saying?

(*He turns away from her.*)

DYSART (*calmingly*): Mr. Strang, exactly how informed do you judge your son to *be* about sex?

FRANK (*tight*): I don't know.

DYSART: You didn't actually instruct him yourself?

FRANK: Not in so many words, no.

DYSART: Did *you*, Mrs. Strang?

DORA: Well, I spoke a little, yes. I had to. I've been a teacher, Doctor, and I know what happens if you don't. They find out through magazines and dirty books.

DYSART: What sort of thing did you tell him? I'm sorry if this is embarrassing.

DORA: I told him the biological facts. But I also told him what I believed. That sex is not *just* a biological matter, but spiritual as well. That if God willed, he would fall in love one day. That his task was to prepare himself for the most important happening of his life. And after that, if he was lucky, he might come to know a higher love still . . . I simply . . . don't understand. . . . *Alan!* . . .

(*She breaks down in sobs.*
Her husband gets up and goes to her.)

FRANK (*embarrassed*): There now. There now, Dora. Come on!

DORA (*with sudden desperation*): All right — laugh! Laugh, as usual!

FRANK (*kindly*): No one's laughing, Dora.

(*She glares at him. He puts his arms round her shoulders.*)

No one's laughing, are they, Doctor?

(*Tenderly, he leads his wife out of the square, and they resume their places on the bench.*
Lights grow much dimmer.)

SCENE 8

A strange noise begins. ALAN *begins to murmur from his bed. He is having a bad nightmare, moving his hands and body as if frantically straining to tug something back.* DYSART *leaves the square as the boy's cries increase.*

ALAN: Ek! . . . Ek! . . . Ek! . . .

(*Cries of* Ek! *on tape fill the theatre, from all around.*
DYSART *reaches the foot of* ALAN's *bed as the boy gives a terrible cry —*)

EK!

(*—and wakes up. The sounds snap off.* ALAN *and the* DOCTOR *stare at each other. Then abruptly* DYSART *leaves the area and re-enters the square.*)

SCENE 9

Lights grow brighter.
DYSART *sits on his bench, left, and opens his file.* ALAN *gets out of bed, leaves his blanket, and comes in. He looks truculent.*

DYSART: Hallo. How are you this morning?

(ALAN *stares at him.*)

Come on: sit down.

(ALAN *crosses the stage and sits on the bench, opposite.*)

Sorry if I gave you a start last night. I was collecting some papers from my office, and I thought I'd look in on you. Do you dream often?

ALAN: Do *you?*

DYSART: It's my job to ask the questions. Yours to answer them.

ALAN: Says who?

DYSART: Says me. Do you dream often?

ALAN: Do *you?*

DYSART: Look — Alan.

ALAN: I'll answer if you answer. In turns.

(*Pause.*)

DYSART: Very well. Only we have to speak the truth.

ALAN (*mocking*): Very well.

DYSART: So. Do you dream often?

ALAN: Yes. Do you?

DYSART: Yes. Do you have a special dream?

ALAN: No. Do you?

DYSART: Yes. What was your dream about last night?

ALAN: Can't remember. What's yours about?

DYSART: I said the truth.

ALAN: That is the truth. What's yours about? The special one.

DYSART: Carving up children.

(ALAN *smiles.*)

My turn!

ALAN: What?

DYSART: What is your first memory of a horse?

ALAN: What d'you mean?

DYSART: The first time one entered your life, in any way.

ALAN: Can't remember.

DYSART: Are you sure?

ALAN: Yes.

DYSART: You have no recollection of the first time you noticed a horse?

ALAN: I told you. Now it's my turn. Are you married?

DYSART (*controlling himself*): I am.

ALAN: Is she a doctor too?

DYSART: It's my turn.

ALAN: Yes, well what?

DYSART: What is Ek?

(*Pause.*)

You shouted it out last night in your sleep. I thought you might like to talk about it.

ALAN (*singing*):
    Double your pleasure,
    Double your fun!

DYSART: Come on, now. You can do better than that.

ALAN (*singing louder*):
    With Doublemint, Doublemint
    Doublemint gum!

DYSART: All right. Good morning.

ALAN: What d'you mean?

DYSART: We're finished for today.

ALAN: But I've only had ten minutes.

DYSART: Too bad.

(He picks up a file and studies it.
ALAN *lingers.)*

Didn't you hear me? I said, Good morning.
ALAN: That's not fair!
DYSART: No?
ALAN *(savagely)*: The Government pays you twenty quid an hour to see me. I know. I heard downstairs.
DYSART: Well, go back there and hear some more.
ALAN: *That's not fair!*

(He springs up, clenching his fists in a sudden violent rage.)

You're a — you're a — You're a swiz! . . . Bloody swiz! . . . Fucking swiz!
DYSART: Do I have to call Nurse?
ALAN: She puts a finger on me, I'll bash her!
DYSART: She'll bash you much harder, I can assure you. Now go away.

(He reads his file. ALAN *stays where he is, emptily clenching his hands. He turns away.*
A pause.
A faint hum starts from the CHORUS.*)*

ALAN *(suddenly)*: On a beach. . . .

SCENE 10

He steps out of the square, upstage, and begins to walk round the circle. Warm light glows on it.

DYSART: What?
ALAN: Where I saw a horse, Swizzy.

(Lazily he kicks at the sand, and throws stones at the sea.)

DYSART: How old were you?
ALAN: How should I know? . . . Six.
DYSART: Well, go on. What were you doing there?
ALAN: Digging.

(He throws himself on the ground, downstage centre of the circle, and starts scuffing with his hands.)

DYSART: A sandcastle?
ALAN: Well, what else?
DYSART *(warningly)*: And?
ALAN: Suddenly I heard this noise. Coming up behind me.

(A young HORSEMAN *issues in slow motion out of the tunnel. He carries a riding crop with which he is urging on his invisible horse, down the right side of the circle. The hum increases.)*

DYSART: What noise?
ALAN: Hooves. Splashing.
DYSART: Splashing?
ALAN: The tide was out and he was galloping.
DYSART: Who was?
ALAN: This fellow. Like a college chap. He was on a big horse — urging him on. I thought he hadn't seen me. I called out: Hey!

(The HORSEMAN *goes into natural time, charging fast round the downstage corner of the square straight at* ALAN.*)*

and they just swerved in time!
HORSEMAN *(reining back)*: Whoa! . . . Whoa there! *Whoa!* . . . Sorry! I didn't see you! . . . Did I scare you?
ALAN: No!
HORSEMAN *(looking down on him)*: That's a terrific castle!
ALAN: What's his name?
HORSEMAN: Trojan. You can stroke him, if you like. He won't mind.

(Shyly ALAN *stretches up on tip-toe, and pats an invisible shoulder.)*

(Amused.) You can hardly reach down there. Would you like to come up?

*(ALAN *nods, eyes wide.)*

All right. Come round this side. You always mount a horse from the left. I'll give you a lift. O.K.?

*(ALAN *goes round on the other side.)*

Here we go, now. Just do nothing. Upsadaisy!

*(ALAN *sets his foot on the* HORSEMAN'S *thigh, and is lifted by him up on to his shoulders.*
The hum from the CHORUS *becomes exultant. Then stops.)*

All right?

*(ALAN *nods.)*

Good. Now all you do is hold onto his mane.

(*He holds up the crop, and* ALAN *grips on to it.*)

Tight now. And grip with your knees. All right? All set? . . . Come on, then, Trojan. Let's go!

(*The* HORSEMAN *walks slowly upstage round the circle, with* ALAN'S *legs tight round his neck.*)

DYSART: How was it? Was it wonderful?

(ALAN *rides in silence.*)

Can't you remember?
HORSEMAN: Do you want to go faster?
ALAN: Yes!
HORSEMAN: O.K. All you have to do is say "Come on, Trojan — bear me away!" . . . Say it, then!
ALAN: Bear me away!

(*The* HORSEMAN *starts to run with* ALAN *round the circle.*)

DYSART: You went fast?
ALAN: Yes!
DYSART: Weren't you frightened?
ALAN: No!
HORSEMAN: Come on now, Trojan! Bear us away! Hold on! Come on now! . . .

(*He runs faster.* ALAN *begins to laugh. Then suddenly, as they reach again the right downstage corner,* FRANK *and* DORA *stand up in alarm.*)

DORA: Alan!
FRANK: Alan!
DORA: Alan, stop!

(FRANK *runs round after them.* DORA *follows behind.*)

FRANK: Hey, you! You! . . .
HORSEMAN: Whoa, boy! . . . Whoa! . . .

(*He reins the horse round, and wheels to face the parents. This all goes fast.*)

FRANK: What do you imagine you are doing?
HORSEMAN (*ironic*): "Imagine"?
FRANK: What is my son doing up there?
HORSEMAN: Water-skiing!

(DORA *joins them, breathless.*)

DORA: Is he all right, Frank? . . . He's not hurt?
FRANK: Don't you think you should ask permission before doing a stupid thing like that?
HORSEMAN: What's stupid?
ALAN: It's lovely, dad!
DORA: Alan, come down here!
HORSEMAN: The boy's perfectly safe. Please don't be hysterical.
FRANK: Don't you be la-di-da with me, young man! Come down here, Alan. You heard what your mother said.
ALAN: No.
FRANK: Come down at once. Right this moment.
ALAN: No . . . NO!
FRANK (*in a fury*): I said — this moment!

(*He pulls* ALAN *from the* HORSEMAN'S *shoulders. The boy shrieks, and falls to the ground.*)

HORSEMAN: Watch it!
DORA: Frank!

(*She runs to her son, and kneels. The* HORSEMAN *skitters.*)

HORSEMAN: Are you mad? D'you want to terrify the horse?
DORA: He's grazed his knee. Frank — the boy's hurt!
ALAN: I'm not! I'm *not!*
FRANK: What's your name?
HORSEMAN: Jesse James.
DORA: Frank, he's bleeding!
FRANK: I intend to report you to the police for endangering the lives of children.
HORSEMAN: Go right ahead!
DORA: Can you stand, dear?
ALAN: Oh, *stop* it! . . .
FRANK: You're a public menace, d'you know that? How dare you pick up children and put them on dangerous animals.
HORSEMAN: Dangerous?
FRANK: Of course dangerous. Look at his eyes. They're rolling.
HORSEMAN: So are yours!
FRANK: In my opinion that is a dangerous animal. In my considered opinion you are both dangers to the safety of this beach.
HORSEMAN: And in my opinion, you're a stupid fart!
DORA: Frank, leave it!
FRANK: What did you say?

DORA: It's not important, Frank — really!

FRANK: *What did you say?*

HORSEMAN: Oh bugger off! Sorry, chum! Come on, Trojan!

(*He urges his horse straight at them, then wheels it and gallops off round the right side of the circle and away up the tunnel, out of sight. The parents cry out, as they are covered with sand and water. Frank runs after him, and round the left side of the circle, with his wife following after.*)

ALAN: Splash, splash, splash! All three of us got covered with water! Dad got absolutely soaked!

FRANK (*shouting after the* HORSEMAN): Hooligan! Filthy hooligan!

ALAN: I wanted to laugh!

FRANK: Upper class riff-raff! That's all they are, people who go riding! That's what they *want* — trample on ordinary people!

DORA: Don't be absurd, Frank.

FRANK: It's why they do it. It's why they bloody do it!

DORA (*amused*): Look at you. You're covered!

FRANK: Not as much as you. There's sand all over your hair!

(*She starts to laugh.*)

(*Shouting.*) Hooligan! Bloody hooligan!

(*She starts to laugh more. He tries to brush the sand out of her hair.*)

What are you laughing at? It's not funny. It's not funny at all, Dora!

(*She goes off, right, still laughing.* ALAN *edges into the square, still on the ground.*)

It's just not funny! . . .

(FRANK *returns to his place on the beach, sulky. Abrupt silence.*)

ALAN: And that's all I remember.

DYSART: And a lot, too. Thank you. . . . You know, I've never been on a horse in my life.

ALAN (*not looking at him*): Nor me.

DYSART: You mean, after that?

ALAN: Yes.

DYSART: But you must have done at the stables?

ALAN: No.

DYSART: Never?

ALAN: No.

DYSART: How come?

ALAN: I didn't care to.

DYSART: Did it have anything to do with falling off like that, all those years ago?

ALAN (*tight*): I just didn't care to, that's all.

DYSART: Do you think of that scene often?

ALAN: I suppose.

DYSART: Why, do you think?

ALAN: 'Cos it's funny.

DYSART: Is that all?

ALAN: What else? My turn. . . . I told you a secret: now you tell me one.

DYSART: All right. I have patients who've got things to tell me, only they're ashamed to say them to my face. What do you think I do about that?

ALAN: What?

DYSART: I give them this little tape recorder.

(*He takes a small tape recorder and microphone from his pocket.*)

They go off to another room, and send me the tape through Nurse. They don't have to listen to it with me.

ALAN: That's stupid.

DYSART: All you do is press this button, and speak into this. It's very simple. Anyway, your time's up for today. I'll see you tomorrow.

ALAN (*getting up*): Maybe.

DYSART: Maybe?

ALAN: If I feel like it.

(*He is about to go out. Then suddenly he returns to* DYSART *and takes the machine from him.*)

It's stupid.

(*He leaves the square and goes back to his bed.*)

SCENE 11

DORA (*calling out*): Doctor!

(DORA *re-enters and comes straight on to the square from the right. She wears an overcoat, and is nervously carrying a shopping bag.*)

DYSART: That same evening, his mother appeared.

DORA: Hallo, Doctor.

DYSART: Mrs. Strang!

DORA: I've been shopping in the neighbour-hood. I thought I might just look in.

DYSART: Did you want to see Alan?

DORA (*uncomfortably*): No, no . . . Not just at the moment. Actually, it's more you I wanted to see.

DYSART: Yes?

DORA: You see, there's something Mr. Strang and I thought you ought to know. We dis-cussed it, and it might just be important.

DYSART: Well, come and sit down.

DORA: I can't stay more than a moment. I'm late as it is. Mr. Strang will be wanting his dinner.

DYSART: Ah. (*Encouragingly.*) So, what was it you wanted to tell me?

(*She sits on the upstage bench.*)

DORA: Well, do you remember that photo-graph I mentioned to you. The one Mr. Strang gave Alan to decorate his bedroom a few years ago?

DYSART: Yes. A horse looking over a gate, wasn't it?

DORA: That's right. Well, actually, it took the place of another kind of picture alto-gether.

DYSART: What kind?

DORA: It was a reproduction of Our Lord on his way to Calvary. Alan found it in Reeds Art Shop, and fell absolutely in love with it. He insisted on buying it with his pocket money, and hanging it at the foot of his bed where he could see it last thing at night. My husband was very displeased.

DYSART: Because it was religious?

DORA: In all fairness I must admit it was a little extreme. The Christ was loaded down with chains, and the centurions were really laying on the stripes. It certainly would not have been my choice, but I don't believe in interfering too much with children, so I said nothing.

DYSART: But Mr. Strang did?

DORA: He stood it for a while, but one day we had one of our tiffs about religion, and he went straight upstairs, tore it off the boy's wall and threw it in the dustbin. Alan went quite hysterical. He cried for days without stopping — and he was not a crier, you know.

DYSART: But he recovered when he was given the photograph of the horse in its place?

DORA: He certainly seemed to. At least, he

hung it in exactly the same position, and we had no more of that awful weeping.

DYSART: Thank you, Mrs. Strang. That *is* interesting . . . Exactly how long ago was that? Can you remember?

DORA: It must be five years ago, Doctor. Alan would have been about twelve. How is he, by the way?

DYSART: Bearing up.

(*She rises.*)

DORA: Please give him my love.

DYSART: You can see him any time you want, you know.

DORA: Perhaps if I could come one after-noon without Mr. Strang. He and Alan don't exactly get on at the moment, as you can imagine.

DYSART: Whatever you decide, Mrs. Strang . . . Oh, one thing.

DORA: Yes?

DYSART: Could you describe that photo-graph of the horse in a little more detail for me? I presume it's still in his bedroom?

DORA: Oh, yes. It's a most remarkable pic-ture, really. You very rarely see a horse taken from that angle — absolutely head on. That's what makes it so interesting.

DYSART: Why? What does it look like?

DORA: Well, it's most extraordinary. It comes out all eyes.

DYSART: Staring straight at you?

DORA: Yes, that's right . . .

(*An uncomfortable pause.*)

I'll come and see him one day very soon, Doctor. Goodbye.

(*She leaves, and resumes her place by her husband.*)

DYSART (*to audience*): It was then — that moment — I felt real alarm. What was it? The shadow of a giant head across my desk? . . . At any rate, the feeling got worse with the stable-owner's visit.

Scene 12

DALTON *comes in to the square: heavy-set: mid-fifties.*

DALTON: Dr. Dysart?

DYSART: Mr. Dalton. It's very good of you to come.

DALTON: It is, actually. In my opinion the boy should be in prison. Not in a hospital at the tax-payers' expense.

DYSART: Please sit down.

(DALTON *sits.*)

This must have been a terrible experience for you.

DALTON: Terrible? I don't think I'll ever get over it. Jill's had a nervous breakdown.

DYSART: Jill?

DALTON: The girl who worked for me. Of course, she feels responsible in a way. Being the one who introduced him in the first place.

DYSART: He was introduced to the stable by a girl?

DALTON: Jill Mason, He met her somewhere, and asked for a job. She told him to come and see me. I wish to Christ she never had.

DYSART: But when he first appeared he didn't seem in any way peculiar?

DALTON: No, he was bloody good. He'd spend hours with the horses cleaning and grooming them, way over the call of duty. I thought he was a real find.

DYSART: Apparently, during the whole time he worked for you, he never actually rode.

DALTON: That's true.

DYSART: Wasn't that peculiar?

DALTON: Very . . . *If* he didn't.

DYSART: What do you mean?

(DALTON *rises.*)

DALTON: Because on and off, that whole year, I had the feeling the horses were being taken out at night.

DYSART: At night?

DALTON: There were just odd things I noticed. I mean too often one or other of them would be sweaty first thing in the morning, when it wasn't sick. Very sweaty, too. And its stall wouldn't be near as mucky as it should be if it had been in all night. I never paid it much mind at the time. It was only when I realised I'd been hiring a loony, I came to wonder if he hadn't been riding all the time, behind our backs.

DYSART: But wouldn't you have noticed if things had been disturbed?

DALTON: Nothing ever was. Still, he's a neat worker. That wouldn't prove anything.

DYSART: Aren't the stables locked at night?

DALTON: Yes.

DYSART: And someone sleeps on the premises?

DALTON: Me and my son.

DYSART: Two people?

DALTON: I'm sorry, Doctor. It's obviously just my fancy. I tell you, this thing has shaken me so bad, I'm liable to believe anything. If there's nothing else, I'll be going.

DYSART: Look: even if you were right, why should anyone do that? Why would any boy prefer to ride by himself at night, when he could go off with others during the day.

DALTON: Are you asking me? He's a loony, isn't he?

(DALTON *leaves the square and sits again in his place.* DYSART *watches him go.*)

ALAN: It was *sexy*.

DYSART: His tape arrived that evening.

SCENE 13

ALAN *is sitting on his bed holding the tape-recorder.* NURSE *approaches briskly, takes the machine from him — gives it to* DYSART *in the square — and leaves again, resuming her seat.* DYSART *switches on the tape.*

ALAN: That's what you want to know, isn't it? All right: it was. I'm talking about the beach. That time when I was a kid. What I told you about. . . .

(*Pause. He is in great emotional difficulty.* DYSART *sits on the left bench listening, file in hand.* ALAN *rises and stands directly behind him, but on the circle, as if recording the ensuing speech. He never, of course, looks directly at the* DOCTOR.)

I was pushed forward on the horse. There was sweat on my legs from his neck. The fellow held me tight, and let me turn the horse which way I wanted. All that power going any way you wanted . . . His sides were all warm, and the smell . . . Then suddenly I was on the ground, where Dad pulled me. I could have bashed him . . .

(*Pause.*)

Something else. When the horse first appeared, I looked up into his mouth. It was huge. There was this chain in it. The fellow pulled it, and cream dripped out. I said "Does it hurt?" And he said — the horse said — said —

(He stops, in anguish. DYSART *makes a note in his file.)*

(Desperately.) It was always the same, after that. Every time I heard one clop by, I had to run and see. Up a country lane or anywhere. They sort of pulled me. I couldn't take my eyes off them. Just to watch their skins. The way their necks twist, and sweat shines in the folds . . . *(Pause.)* I can't remember when it started. Mum reading to me about Prince who no one could ride, except one boy. Or the white horse in Revelations. "He that sat upon him was called Faithful and True. His eyes were as flames of fire, and he had a name written that no man knew but himself" . . . Words like reins. Stirrup. Flanks . . . "Dashing his spurs against his charger's flanks!" . . . Even the words made me feel — . . . Years, I never told anyone. Mum wouldn't understand. She likes "Equitation." Bowler hats and jodhpurs! "My grandfather dressed for the horse," she says. What does that mean? The horse isn't dressed. It's the most naked thing you ever saw! More than a dog or a cat or anything. Even the most broken down old nag has got its *life!* To put a bowler on it is *filthy!* . . . Putting them through their paces! Bloody gymkhanas! . . . No one understands! . . . Except cowboys. They do. I wish I was a cowboy. They're free. They just swing up and then it's miles of grass . . . I bet all cowboys are *orphans!* . . . I bet they are!

NURSE: Mr. Strang to see you, Doctor.

DYSART *(in surprise)*: Mr. Strang? Show him up, please.

ALAN: No one ever says to cowboys "Receive my meaning"! They wouldn't dare. Or "God" all the time. *(Mimicking his mother.)* "God sees you, Alan. God's got eyes everywhere — "

(He stops abruptly.)

I'm not doing any more! . . . I hate this! . . . You can whistle for anymore. I've had it!

(He returns angrily to his bed, throwing the blanket over him.
DYSART *switches off the tape.)*

SCENE 14

FRANK STRANG *comes into the square, his hat in his hand. He is nervous and embarrassed.*

DYSART *(welcoming)*: Hallo, Mr. Strang.

FRANK: I was passing. I hope it's not too late.

DYSART: Of course not. I'm delighted to see you.

FRANK: My wife doesn't know I'm here. I'd be grateful to you if you didn't enlighten her, if you receive my meaning.

DYSART: Everything that happens in this room is confidential, Mr. Strang.

FRANK: I hope so . . . I hope so . . .

DYSART *(gently)*: Do you have something to tell me?

FRANK: As a matter of fact I have. Yes.

DYSART: Your wife told me about the photograph.

FRANK: I know, it's not that! It's *about* that, but it's — worse. . . . I wanted to tell you the other night, but I couldn't in front of Dora. Maybe I should have. It might show her where all that stuff leads to, she drills into the boy behind my back.

DYSART: What kind of thing is it?

FRANK: Something I witnessed.

DYSART: Where?

FRANK: At home. About eighteen months ago.

DYSART: Go on.

FRANK: It was late. I'd gone upstairs to fetch something. The boy had been in bed hours, or so I thought.

DYSART: Go on.

FRANK: As I came along the passage I saw the door of his bedroom was ajar. I'm sure he didn't know it was. From inside I heard the sound of this chanting.

DYSART: Chanting?

FRANK: Like the Bible. One of those lists his mother's always reading to him.

DYSART: What kind of list?

FRANK: Those Begats. So-and-so begat, you know. Genealogy.

DYSART: Can you remember what Alan's list sounded like?

FRANK: Well, the *sort* of thing. I stood there absolutely astonished. The first word I heard was . . .

ALAN *(rising and chanting)*: Prince!

DYSART: Prince?

FRANK: Prince begat Prance. That sort of nonsense.

(ALAN moves slowly to the center of the circle, downstage.)

ALAN: And Prance begat Prankus! And Prankus begat Flankus!

FRANK: I looked through the door, and he was standing in the moonlight in his pyjamas, right in front of that big photograph.

DYSART: The horse with the huge eyes?

FRANK: Right.

ALAN: Flankus begat Spankus. And Spankus begat Spunkus the Great, who lived three score years!

FRANK: It was all like that. I can't remember the exact names, of course. Then suddenly he knelt down.

DYSART: In front of the photograph?

FRANK: Yes. Right there at the foot of his bed.

ALAN (*kneeling*): And Legwus begat Neckwus. And Neckwus begat Fleckwus, the King of Spit. And Fleckwus spoke out of his chinkle-chankle!

(*He bows himself to the ground.*)

DYSART: What?

FRANK: I'm sure that was the word. I've never forgotten it. Chinkle-chankle.

(ALAN *raises his head and extends his hands up in glory.*)

ALAN: And he said "Behold — I give you Equus, my only begotten son!"

DYSART: Equus?

FRANK: Yes. No doubt of that. He repeated that word several times. "Equus my only begotten son."

ALAN (*reverently*): Ek . . . wus!

DYSART (*suddenly understanding: almost "aside"*): Ek . . . Ek . . .

FRANK (*embarrassed*): And then . . .

DYSART: Yes: what?

FRANK: He took a piece of string out of his pocket. Made up into a noose. And put it in his mouth.

(ALAN *bridles himself with invisible string, and pulls it back.*)

And then with his other hand he picked up a coat hanger. A wooden coat hanger, and — and —

DYSART: Began to beat himself?

(ALAN, *in mime, begins to thrash himself, increasing the strokes in speed and viciousness.*)
(*Pause.*)

FRANK: You see why I couldn't tell his mother. . . . Religion. Religion's at the bottom of all this!

DYSART: What did you do?

FRANK: Nothing. I coughed — and went back downstairs.

(*The boy starts guiltily — tears the string from his mouth — and scrambles back to bed.*)

DYSART: Did you ever speak to him about it later? Even obliquely?

FRANK (*unhappily*): I can't speak of things like that, Doctor. It's not in my nature.

DYSART (*kindly*): No. I see that.

FRANK: But I thought you ought to know. So I came.

DYSART (*warmly*): Yes. I'm very grateful to you. Thank you.

(*Pause.*)

FRANK: Well, that's it. . . .

DYSART: Is there anything else?

FRANK (*even more embarrassed*): There is actually. One thing.

DYSART: What's that?

FRANK: On the night that he did it — that awful thing in the stable —

DYSART: Yes?

FRANK: That very night, he was out with a girl.

DYSART: How d'you know that?

FRANK: I just know.

DYSART (*puzzled*): Did he tell you?

FRANK: I can't say any more.

DYSART: I don't quite understand.

FRANK: Everything said in here is confidential, you said.

DYSART: Absolutely.

FRANK: Then ask him. Ask him about taking a girl out, that very night he did it. . . . (*Abruptly.*) Goodbye, Doctor.

(*He goes.* DYSART *looks after him.* FRANK *resumes his seat.*)

SCENE 15

ALAN *gets up and enters the square.*

DYSART: Alan! Come in. Sit down. (*Pleasantly.*) What did you do last night?

ALAN: Watched telly.

DYSART: Any good?

ALAN: All right.

DYSART: Thanks for the tape. It was excellent.

ALAN: I'm not making any more.

DYSART: One thing I didn't quite understand. You began to say something about the horse on the beach talking to you.

ALAN: That's stupid. Horses don't talk.

DYSART: So I believe.

ALAN: I don't know what you mean.

DYSART: Never mind. Tell me something else. Who introduced you to the stable to begin with?

(*Pause.*)

ALAN: Someone I met.

DYSART: Where?

ALAN: Bryson's.

DYSART: The shop where you worked?

ALAN: Yes.

DYSART: That's a funny place for you to be. Whose idea was that?

ALAN: Dad.

DYSART: I'd have thought he'd have wanted you to work with him.

ALAN: I haven't the aptitude. And printing's a failing trade. If you receive my meaning.

DYSART (*amused*): I see . . . What did your mother think?

ALAN: Shops are common.

DYSART: And you?

ALAN: I loved it.

DYSART: Really?

ALAN (*sarcastic*): Why not? You get to spend every minute with electrical things. It's fun.

(NURSE, DALTON *and the actors playing horses call out to him as* CUSTOMERS, *seated where they are. Their voices are aggressive and demanding. There is a constant background mumbling, made up of trade names, out of which can clearly be distinguished the italicized words, which are shouted out.*)

CUSTOMER: *Philco!*

ALAN (*to* DYSART): Of course it might just drive you off your chump.

CUSTOMER: I want to buy a hot-plate. I'm told the *Philco* is a good make!

ALAN: I think it is, madam.

CUSTOMER: *Remington* ladies' shavers?

ALAN: I'm not sure, madam.

CUSTOMER: *Robex* tableware?

CUSTOMER: *Croydex?*

CUSTOMER: *Volex?*

CUSTOMER: *Pifco* automatic toothbrushes?

ALAN: I'll find out, sir.

CUSTOMER: *Beautiflor!*

CUSTOMER: *Windowlene!*

CUSTOMER: I want a *Philco* transistor radio!

CUSTOMER: This isn't a *Remington!* I wanted a *Remington!*

ALAN: Sorry.

CUSTOMER: Are you a dealer for *Hoover?*

ALAN: Sorry.

CUSTOMER: I wanted the heat retaining *Pifco!*

ALAN: *Sorry!*

(JILL *comes into the square; a girl in her early twenties, pretty and middle class. She wears a sweater and jeans. The mumbling stops.*)

JILL: Hallo.

ALAN: Hallo.

JILL: Have you any blades for a clipping machine?

ALAN: Clipping?

JILL: To clip horses.

(*Pause. He stares at her, open-mouthed.*)

What's the matter?

ALAN: You work at Dalton's stables. I've seen you.

(*During the following, he mimes putting away a pile of boxes on a shelf in the shop.*)

JILL: I've seen you too, haven't I? You're the boy who's always staring into the yard around lunch-time.

ALAN: Me?

JILL: You're there most days.

ALAN: Not me.

JILL (*amused*): Of course it's you. Mr. Dalton was only saying the other day: "Who's that boy keeps staring in at the door?" Are you looking for a job or something?

ALAN (*eagerly*): Is there one?

JILL: I don't know.

ALAN: I can only do weekends.

JILL: That's when most people ride. We can always use extra hands. It'd mainly be mucking out.

ALAN: I don't mind.

JILL: Can you ride?

ALAN: No . . . No . . . I don't want to.

(*She looks at him curiously.*)

Please.

JILL: Come up on Saturday. I'll introduce you to Mr. Dalton.

(*She leaves the square.*)

DYSART: When was this? About a year ago?
ALAN: I suppose.
DYSART: And she did?
ALAN: Yes.

(*Briskly he moves the three benches to form three stalls in the stable.*)

SCENE 16

Rich light falls on the square.
An exultant humming from the CHORUS.
Tramping is heard. Three actors playing horses rise from their places. Together they unhook three horse masks from the ladders to left and right, put them on with rigid timing, and walk with swaying horse-motion into the square. Their metal hooves stamp on the wood. Their masks turn and toss high above their heads — as they will do sporadically throughout all horse scenes — making the steel gleam in the light.
For a moment they seem to converge on the boy as he stands in the middle of the stable, but then they swiftly turn and take up positions as if tethered by the head, with their invisible rumps towards him, one by each bench. ALAN *is sunk in this glowing world of horses. Lost in wonder, he starts almost involuntarily to kneel on the floor in reverence — but is sharply interrupted by the cheery voice of* DALTON, *coming into the stable, followed by* JILL. *The boy straightens up guiltily.*

DALTON: First thing to learn is drill. Learn it and keep to it. I want this place neat, dry and clean at all times. After you've mucked out, Jill will show you some grooming. What we call strapping a horse.
JILL: I think Trooper's got a stone.
DALTON: Yes? Let's see.

(*He crosses to the horse by the left bench, who is balancing one hoof on its tip. He picks up the hoof.*)

You're right. (*To* ALAN.) See this? This V here. It's what's called a frog. Sort of shock-absorber. Once you pierce that, it take ages to

heal — so you want to watch for it. You clean it out with this. What we call a hoof-pick.

(*He takes from his pocket an invisible pick.*)

Mind how you go with it. It's very sharp. Use it like this.

(*He quickly takes the stone out.*)

See?

(ALAN *nods, fascinated.*)

You'll soon get the hang of it. Jill will look after you. What she doesn't know about stables, isn't worth knowing.
JILL (*pleased*): Oh yes, I'm sure!
DALTON (*handing* ALAN *the pick*): Careful how you go with that. The main rule is: anything you don't know — ask. Never pretend you know something when you don't. (*Smiling.*) Actually, the main rule is: enjoy yourself. All right?
ALAN: Yes, sir.
DALTON: Good lad. See you later.

(*He nods to them cheerfully, and leaves the square.* ALAN *clearly puts the invisible hoof-pick on the rail, downstage left.*)

JILL: All right, let's start on some grooming. Why don't we begin with him? He looks as if he needs it.

(*They approach* NUGGET, *who is standing to the right. She pats him.* ALAN *sits and watches her.*)

This is Nugget. He's my favorite. He's as gentle as a baby, aren't you? But terribly fast if you want him to be.

(*During the following, she mimes both the actions and the objects, which she picks up from the right bench.*)

Now this is the dandy, and we start with that. Then you move on to the body brush. This is the most important, and you use it with this curry-comb. Now you always groom the same way: from the ears downward. Don't be afraid to do it hard. The harder you do it, the more the horse loves it. Push it right through the coat: like this.

(*The boy watches in fascination as she brushes the invisible body of* NUGGET, *scraping the dirt and hair off on to the invisible curry-comb. Now and then the horse mask moves very slightly in pleasure.*)

Down towards the tail and right through the coat. See how he loves it? I'm giving you a lovely massage, boy, aren't I? . . . You try.

(*She hands him the brush. Gingerly he rises and approaches* NUGGET. *Embarrassed and excited, he copies her movements, inexpertly.*)

Keep it nice and easy. Never rush. Down towards the tail and right through the coat. That's it. Again. Down towards the tail and right through the coat. . . . Very good. Now you keep that up for fifteen minutes and then do old Trooper. Will you?

(ALAN *nods.*)

You've got a feel for it. I can tell. It's going to be nice teaching you. See you later.

(*She leaves the square and resumes her place.* ALAN *is left alone with the horses.*
They all stamp. He approaches NUGGET *again, and touches the horse's shoulder. The mask turns sharply in his direction. The boy pauses, then moves his hand gently over the outline of the neck and back. The mask is re-assured. It stares ahead unmoving. Then* ALAN *lifts his palm to his face and smells it deeply, closing his eyes.*
DYSART *rises from his bench, and begins to walk slowly upstage round the circle.*)

DYSART: Was that good? Touching them.

(ALAN *gives a faint groan.*)

ALAN: Mmm.
DYSART: It must have been marvelous, being near them at last . . . Stroking them . . . Making them fresh and glossy . . . Tell me . . .

(*Silence.* ALAN *begins to brush* NUGGET.)

How about the girl? Did you like her?
ALAN (*tight*): All right.
DYSART: Just all right?

(ALAN *changes his position, moving round* NUGGET's *rump so that his back is to the audience. He brushes harder.* DYSART *comes downstage around the circle, and finally back to his bench.*)

Was she friendly?

ALAN: Yes.
DYSART: Or stand-offish?
ALAN: Yes.
DYSART: Well which?
ALAN: What?
DYSART: Which was she?

(ALAN *brushes harder.*)

Did you take her out? Come on now: tell me. Did you have a date with her?
ALAN: What?
DYSART (*sitting*): Tell me if you did.

(*The boy suddenly explodes in one of his rages.*)

ALAN (*yelling*): TELL ME!

(*All the masks toss at the noise.*)

DYSART: What?
ALAN: *Tell me, tell me, tell me, tell me!*

(ALAN *storms out of the square, and downstage to where* DYSART *sits. He is raging. During the ensuing, the horses leave by all three openings.*)

On and on, sitting there! Nosey Parker! That's all you are! Bloody Nosey Parker! Just like Dad. On and on and bloody on! Tell me, tell me . . . Answer this. Answer that. Never stop! —

(*He marches round the circle and back into the square.* DYSART *rises and enters it from the other side.*)

Scene 17

Lights brighten.

DYSART: I'm sorry.

(ALAN *slams about what is now the office again, replacing the benches to their usual position.*)

ALAN: All right, it's my turn now. You tell me! Answer me!
DYSART: We're not playing that game now.
ALAN: We're playing what I say.
DYSART: All right. What do you want to know?

(*He sits.*)

ALAN: Do *you* have dates?
DYSART: I told you. I'm married.

(ALAN *approaches him, very hostile.*)

ALAN: I know. Her name's Margaret. She's a dentist! You see, I found out! What made you go with her? Did you use to bite her hands when she did you in the chair?

(*The boy sits next to him, close.*)

DYSART: That's not very funny.
ALAN: Do you have girls behind her back?
DYSART: No.
ALAN: Then what? Do you fuck her?
DYSART: That's enough now.

(*He rises and moves away.*)

ALAN: Come on, tell me! Tell me, tell me!
DYSART: I said that's enough now.

(ALAN *rises too and walks around him.*)

I bet you don't. I bet you never touch her. Come on, tell me. You've got no kids, have you? Is that because you don't fuck?
DYSART (*sharp*): Go to your room. Go on: quick march.

(*Pause.* ALAN *moves away from him, insolently takes up a packet of* DYSART'S *cigarettes from the bench, and extracts one.*)

Give me those cigarettes.

(*The boy puts one in his mouth.*)

(*Exploding.*) Alan, *give them to me!*

(*Reluctantly* ALAN *shoves the cigarette back in the packet, turns and hands it to him.*)

Now go!

(ALAN *bolts out of the square, and back to his bed.* DYSART, *unnerved, addresses the audience.*)

Brilliant! Absolutely brilliant! The boy's on the run, so he gets defensive. What am I, then? . . . Wicked little bastard — he knew exactly what questions to try. He'd actually marched himself round the hospital, making enquiries about my wife. Wicked and — of course, perceptive. Ever since I made that crack about carving up children, he's been aware of me in an absolutely specific way. Of course, there's nothing novel in that. Advanced neurotics can

be dazzling at that game. They aim unswervingly at your area of maximum vulnerability. . . . Which I suppose is as good a way as any of describing Margaret.

(*He sits.* HESTHER *enters the square. Light grows warmer.*)

SCENE 18

HESTHER: Now stop it.
DYSART: Do I embarrass you?
HESTHER: I suspect you're about to.

(*Pause.*)

DYSART: My wife doesn't understand me, Your Honour.
HESTHER: Do you understand her?
DYSART: No. Obviously I never did.
HESTHER: I'm sorry. I've never liked to ask but I've always imagined you weren't exactly compatible.

(*She moves to sit opposite.*)

DYSART: We were. It actually worked for a bit. I mean for both of us. We worked for each other, she actually for me through a kind of briskness. A clear, red-headed, inaccessible briskness which kept me keyed up for months. Mind you, if you're kinky for Northern Hygienic, as I am, you can't find anything much more compelling than a Scottish Lady Dentist.
HESTHER: It's *you* who are wicked, you know!
DYSART: Not at all: She got exactly the same from me. Antiseptic proficiency. I was like that in those days. We suited each other admirably. I see us in our wedding photo: Doctor and Doctor Mac Brisk. We were brisk in our wooing, brisk in our wedding, brisk in our disappointment. We turned from each other briskly into our separate surgeries: and now there's damn all.
HESTHER: You have no children, have you?
DYSART: No, we didn't go in for them. Instead, she sits beside our salmon-pink, glazed brick fireplace, and knits things for orphans in a home she helps with. And I sit opposite, turning the pages of art books on Ancient Greece. Occasionally, I still trail a faint scent of my enthusiasm across her path. I pass her a picture of the sacred acrobats of Crete leaping through the horns of running bulls — and she'll say: "Och, Martin, what an *absurred* thing to be doing! The Highland Games, now there's

norrmal sport!" Or she'll observe, just after
I've told her a story from the Iliad: "You
know, when you come to think of it, Agamemnon and that lot were nothing but a bunch of
ruffians from the Gorbals, only with fancy
names!" (*He rises.*) You get the picture. She's
turned into a Shrink. The familiar domestic
monster. Margaret Dysart: the Shrink's Shrink.

HESTHER: That's cruel, Martin.

DYSART: Yes. Do you know what it's like for
two people to live in the same house as if they
were in different parts of the world? Mentally,
she's always in some drizzly kirk of her own
inheriting: and I'm in some Doric temple —
clouds tearing through pillars — eagles bearing
prophecies out of the sky. She finds all that
repulsive. All my wife has ever taken from the
Mediterranean — from that whole vast intuitive
culture — are four bottles of Chianti to make
into lamps, and two china condiment donkeys
labelled Sally and Peppy.

(*Pause.*)

(*More intimately.*) I wish there was one person in my life I could show. One instinctive,
absolutely unbrisk person I could take to
Greece, and stand in front of certain shrines
and sacred streams and say "Look! Life is only
comprehensible through a thousand local
Gods." And not just the old dead ones with
names like Zeus — no, but living Geniuses of
Place and Person! And not just Greece but
modern England! Spirits of certain trees, certain curves of brick wall, certain chip shops, if
you like, and slate roofs — just as of certain
frowns in people and slouches . . . I'd say to
them — "Worship as many as you can see —
and more will appear!" . . . If I had a son, I
bet you he'd come out exactly like his mother.
Utterly worshipless. Would you like a drink?

HESTHER: No, thanks. Actually, I've got to
be going. As usual . . .

DYSART: Really?

HESTHER: Really. I've got an Everest of
papers to get through before bed.

DYSART: You never stop, do you?

HESTHER: Do you?

DYSART: This boy, with his stare. He's trying
to save himself through me.

HESTHER: I'd say so.

DYSART: What am I trying to do to him?

HESTHER: Restore him, surely?

DYSART: To what?

HESTHER: A normal life.

DYSART: Normal?

HESTHER: It still means something.

DYSART: Does it?

HESTHER: Of course.

DYSART: You mean a normal boy has one
head: a normal head has two ears?

HESTHER: You know I don't.

DYSART: Then what else?

HESTHER (*lightly*): Oh, stop it.

DYSART: No, what? You tell me.

HESTHER (*rising: smiling*): I won't be put
on the stand like this, Martin. You're really
disgraceful! . . . (*Pause.*) You know what I
mean by a normal smile in a child's eyes, and
one that isn't — even if I can't exactly define
it. Don't you?

DYSART: Yes.

HESTHER: Then we have a duty to that,
surely? Both of us.

DYSART: Touché. . . . I'll talk to you.

HESTHER: Dismissed?

DYSART: You said you had to go.

HESTHER: I do. . . . (*She kisses his cheek.*)
Thank you for what you're doing. . . . You're
going through a rotten patch at the moment.
I'm sorry . . . I suppose one of the few things
one can do is simply hold on to priorities.

DYSART: Like what?

HESTHER: Oh — children before grown-ups.
Things like that.

(*He contemplates her.*)

DYSART: You're really quite splendid.

HESTHER: Famous for it. Goodnight.

(*She leaves him.*)

DYSART (*to himself — or to the audience*):
Normal! . . . Normal!

SCENE 19

ALAN *rises and enters the square. He is
subdued.*

DYSART: Good afternoon.

ALAN: Afternoon.

DYSART: I'm sorry about our row yesterday.

ALAN: It was stupid.

DYSART: It was.

ALAN: What I said, I mean.

DYSART: How are you sleeping?

(ALAN *shrugs.*)

You're not feeling well, are you?

ALAN: All right.

DYSART: Would you like to play a game? It could make you feel better.

ALAN: What kind?

DYSART: It's called *Blink*. You have to fix your eyes on something: say, that little stain over there on the wall — and I tap this pen on the desk. The first time I tap it, you close your eyes. The next time you open them. And so on. Close, open, close, open, till I say Stop.

ALAN: How can that make you feel better?

DYSART: It relaxes you. You'll feel as though you're talking to me in your sleep.

ALAN: It's stupid.

DYSART: You don't have to do it, if you don't want to.

ALAN: I didn't say I didn't want to.

DYSART: Well?

ALAN: I don't mind.

DYSART: Good. Sit down and start watching that stain. Put your hands by your sides, and open the fingers wide.

(*He opens the left bench and* ALAN *sits on the end of it.*)

The thing is to feel comfortable, and relax absolutely. . . . Are you looking at the stain?

ALAN: Yes.

DYSART: Right. Now try and keep your mind as blank as possible.

ALAN: That's not difficult.

DYSART: Ssh. Stop talking . . . On the first tap, close. On the second, open. Are you ready?

(ALAN *nods.* DYSART *taps his pen on the wooden rail.* ALAN *shuts his eyes.* DYSART *taps again.* ALAN *opens them. The taps are evenly spaced. After four of them the sound cuts out, and is replaced by a louder, metallic sound, on tape.* DYSART *talks through this, to the audience — the light changes to cold — while the boy sits in front of him, staring at the wall, opening and shutting his eyes.*)

The Normal is the good smile in a child's eyes — all right. It is also the dead stare in a million adults. It both sustains and kills — like a God. It is the Ordinary made beautiful: it is also the Average made lethal. The Normal is the indispensable, murderous God of Health, and I am his Priest. My tools are very delicate. My compassion is honest. I have honestly assisted children in this room. I have talked away terrors and relieved many agonies. But also — beyond question — I have cut from them parts of individuality repugnant to this God, in both his aspects. Parts sacred to rarer and more wonderful Gods. And at what length . . . Sacrifices to Zeus took at the most surely, sixty seconds each. Sacrifices to the Normal can take as long as sixty months.

(*The natural sound of the pencil resumes. Light changes back.*)

(*To* ALAN.) Now your eyes are feeling heavy. You want to sleep, don't you? You want a long, deep sleep. Have it. Your head is heavy. Very heavy. Your shoulders are heavy. Sleep.

(*The pencil stops.* ALAN's *eyes remain shut and his head has sunk on his chest.*)

Can you hear me?

ALAN: Mmm.

DYSART: You can speak normally. Say Yes, if you can.

ALAN: Yes.

DYSART: Good boy. Now raise your head, and open your eyes.

(*He does so.*)

Now, Alan, you're going to answer questions I'm going to ask you. Do you understand?

ALAN: Yes.

DYSART: And when you wake up, you are going to remember everything you tell me. All right?

ALAN: Yes.

DYSART: Good. Now I want you to think back in time. You are on that beach you told me about. The tide has gone out, and you're making sandcastles. Above you, staring down at you, is that great horse's head, and the cream dropping from it. Can you see that?

ALAN: Yes.

DYSART: You ask him a question. "Does the chain hurt?"

ALAN: Yes.

DYSART: Do you ask him aloud?

ALAN: No.

DYSART: And what does the horse say back?

ALAN: "Yes."

DYSART: Then what do you say?

ALAN: "I'll take it out for you."

DYSART: And he says?

ALAN: "It never comes out. They have me in chains."

DYSART: Like Jesus?

ALAN: Yes!

DYSART: Only his name isn't Jesus, is it?

ALAN: No.

DYSART: What is it?

ALAN: No one knows but him and me.

DYSART: You can tell me, Alan. Name him.

ALAN: Equus.

DYSART: Thank you. Does he live in all horses or just some?

ALAN: All.

DYSART: Good boy. Now: you leave the beach. You're in your bedroom at home. You're twelve years old. You're in front of the picture. You're looking at Equus from the foot of your bed. Would you like to kneel down?

ALAN: Yes.

DYSART (encouragingly): Go on, then.

(ALAN kneels.)

Now tell me. Why is Equus in chains?

ALAN: For the sins of the world.

DYSART: What does he say to you?

ALAN: "I see you." "I will save you."

DYSART: How?

ALAN: "Bear you away. Two shall be one."

DYSART: Horse and rider shall be one beast?

ALAN: One person!

DYSART: Go on.

ALAN: "And my chinkle-chankle shall be in thy hand."

DYSART: Chinkle-chankle? That's his mouth chain?

ALAN: Yes.

DYSART: Good. You can get up . . . Come on.

(ALAN rises.)

Now: think of the stable. What is the stable? His Temple? His Holy of Holies?

ALAN: Yes.

DYSART: Where you wash him? Where you tend him, and brush him with many brushes?

ALAN: Yes.

DYSART: And there he spoke to you, didn't he? He looked at you with his gentle eyes, and spake unto you?

ALAN: Yes.

DYSART: What did he say? "Ride me? Mount me, and ride me forth at night?"

ALAN: Yes.

DYSART: And you obeyed?

ALAN: Yes.

DYSART: How did you learn? By watching others?

ALAN: Yes.

DYSART: It must have been difficult. You bounced about?

ALAN: Yes.

DYSART: But he showed you, didn't he? Equus showed you the way.

ALAN: No!

DYSART: He didn't?

ALAN: He showed me nothing! He's a mean bugger! Ride — or fall! That's Straw Law.

DYSART: Straw Law?

ALAN: He was born in the straw, and this is his law.

DYSART: But you managed? You mastered him?

ALAN: Had to!

DYSART: And then you rode in secret?

ALAN: Yes.

DYSART: How often?

ALAN: Every three weeks. More, people would notice.

DYSART: On a particular horse?

ALAN: No.

DYSART: How did you get into the stable?

ALAN: Stole a key. Had it copied at Bryson's.

DYSART: Clever boy.

(ALAN smiles.)

Then you'd slip out of the house?

ALAN: Midnight! On the stroke!

DYSART: How far's the stable?

ALAN: Two miles.

(Pause.)

DYSART: Let's do it! Let's go riding! . . . Now!

(He stands up, and pushes in his bench.)

You are there now, in front of the stable door.

(ALAN turns upstage.)

That key's in your hand. Go and open it.

SCENE 20

ALAN moves upstage, and mimes opening the door.
Soft light on the circle.
Humming from the CHORUS: the Equus noise.

The horse-actors enter, raise high their masks, and put them on all together. They stand around the circle — NUGGET in the mouth of the tunnel.

DYSART: Quietly as possible. Dalton may still be awake. Sssh . . . Quietly . . . Good. Now go in.

(ALAN steps secretly out of the square through the central opening on to the circle, now glowing with a warm light. He looks about him. The horses stamp uneasily: their masks turn towards him.)

You are on the inside now. All the horses are staring at you. Can you see them?

ALAN (*excited*): Yes!

DYSART: Which one are you going to take?

ALAN: Nugget.

(ALAN reaches up and mimes leading NUGGET carefully round the circle downstage with a rope, past all the horses on the right.)

DYSART: What colour is Nugget?

ALAN: Chestnut.

(The horse picks his way with care. ALAN halts him at the corner of the square.)

DYSART: What do you do, first thing?

ALAN: Put on his sandals.

DYSART: Sandals?

(He kneels, downstage centre.)

ALAN: Sandals of majesty! . . . Made of sack.

(He picks up the invisible sandals, and kisses them devoutly.)

Tie them round his hooves.

(He taps NUGGET's right leg: the horse raises it and the boy mimes tying the sack round it.)

DYSART: All four hooves?

ALAN: Yes.

DYSART: Then?

ALAN: Chinkle-chankle.

(He mimes picking up the bridle and bit.)

He doesn't like it so late, but he takes it for my sake. He bends for me. He stretches forth his neck to it.

(NUGGET bends his head down. ALAN first ritually puts the bit into his own mouth, then crosses, and transfers it into NUGGET's. He reaches up and buckles on the bridle. Then he leads him by the invisible reins, across the front of the stage and up round the left side of the circle. NUGGET follows obediently.)

ALAN: Buckle and lead out.

DYSART: No saddle?

ALAN: Never.

DYSART: Go on.

ALAN: Walk down the path behind. He's quiet. Always is, this bit. Meek and mild legs. At least till the field. Then there's trouble.

(The horse jerks back. The mask tosses.)

DYSART: What kind?

ALAN: Won't go in.

DYSART: Why not?

ALAN: It's his place of Ha Ha.

DYSART: What?

ALAN: Ha Ha.

DYSART: Make him go into it.

ALAN (*whispering fiercely*): Come on! . . . Come on! . . .

(He drags the horse into the square as DYSART steps out of it.)

SCENE 21

NUGGET *comes to a halt staring diagonally down what is now the field. The Equus noise dies away. The boy looks about him.*

DYSART (*from the circle*): Is it a big field?

ALAN: Huge!

DYSART: What's it like?

ALAN: Full of mist. Nettles on your feet.

(He mimes taking off his shoes — and the sting.)

Ah!

DYSART (*going back to his bench*): You take your shoes off?

ALAN: Everything.

DYSART: All your clothes?

ALAN: Yes.

(He mimes undressing completely in front of the horse. When he is finished and obviously quite naked, he throws out his arms

and shows himself fully to his God, bowing his head before NUGGET.)

DYSART: Where do you leave them?
ALAN: Tree hole near the gate. No one could find them.

(*He walks upstage and crouches by the bench, stuffing the invisible clothes beneath it.* DYSART *sits again on the left bench, downstage beyond the circle.*)

DYSART: How does it feel now?
ALAN (*holds himself*): Burns.
DYSART: Burns?
ALAN: The mist!
DYSART: Go on. Now what?
ALAN: The Manbit.

(*He reaches again under the bench and draws out an invisible stick.*)

DYSART: Manbit?
ALAN: The stick for my mouth.
DYSART: Your mouth?
ALAN: To bite on.
DYSART: Why? What for?
ALAN: So's it won't happen too quick.
DYSART: Is it always the same stick?
ALAN: Course. Sacred stick. Keep it in the hole. The Ark of the Manbit.
DYSART: And now what? . . . What do you do now?

(*Pause. He rises and approaches* NUGGET.)

ALAN: Touch him!
DYSART: Where?
ALAN (*in wonder*): All over. Everywhere. Belly. Ribs. His ribs are of ivory. Of great value! . . . His flank is cool. His nostrils open for me. His eyes shine. They can see in the dark . . . *Eyes!* —

(*Suddenly he dashes in distress to the farthest corner of the square.*)

DYSART: Go on! . . . Then?

(*Pause.*)

ALAN: Give sugar.
DYSART: A lump of sugar?

(ALAN *returns to* NUGGET.)

ALAN: His Last Supper.
DYSART: Last before what?
ALAN: Ha Ha.

(*He kneels before the horse, palms upward and joined together.*)

DYSART: Do you say anything when you give it to him?
ALAN (*offering it*): Take my sins. Eat them for my sake . . . He always does.

(NUGGET *bows the mask into* ALAN's *palm, then takes a step back to eat.*)

And then he's ready.
DYSART: You can get up on him now?
ALAN: Yes!
DYSART: Do it, then. Mount him.

(ALAN, *lying before* NUGGET, *stretches out on the square. He grasps the top of the thin metal pole embedded in the wood. He whispers his God's name ceremonially.*)

ALAN: Equus! . . . Equus! . . . Equus!

(*He pulls the pole upright. The actor playing* NUGGET *leans forward and grabs it. At the same instant all the other horses lean forward around the circle, each placing a gloved hand on the rail.* ALAN *rises and walks right back to the upstage corner, left.*)

Take me!

(*He runs and jumps high on to* NUGGET's *back.*)

(*crying out*) Ah!
DYSART: What is it?
ALAN: Hurts!
DYSART: Hurts?
ALAN: Knives in his skin! Little knives — all inside my legs.

(NUGGET *mimes restiveness.*)

ALAN: Stay, Equus. No one said Go! . . . That's it. He's good. Equus the Godslave, Faithful and True. Into my hands he commends himself — naked in his chinkle-chankle. (*He punches.*) Stop it! . . . He wants to go so badly.
DYSART: Go, then. Leave me behind. Ride away now, Alan. Now! . . . Now you are alone with Equus.

(ALAN *stiffens his body.*)

ALAN: (*ritually*) Equus — son of Fleckwus — son of Neckwus — *Walk.*

(*A hum from the* CHORUS.
Very slowly the horses standing on the circle begin to turn the square by gently pushing the wooden rail. ALAN *and his mount start to revolve. The effect, immediately, is of a statue being slowly turned round on a plinth. During the ride however the speed increases, and the light decreases until it is only a fierce spotlight on horse and rider, with the overspill glinting on the other masks leaning in towards them.*)

Here we go. The King rides out on Equus, mightiest of horses. Only I can ride him. He lets me turn him this way and that. His neck comes out of my body. It lifts in the dark. Equus, my Godslave! . . . Now the King commands you. Tonight, we ride against them all.
    DYSART: Who's all?
    ALAN: My foes and His.
    DYSART: Who are your foes?
    ALAN: The Hosts of Hoover. The Hosts of Philco. The Hosts of Pifco. The House of Remington and all its tribe!
    DYSART: Who are His foes?
    ALAN: The Hosts of Jodhpur. The Hosts of Bowler and Gymkhana. All those who show him off for their vanity. Tie rosettes on his head for their vanity! Come on, Equus. Let's get them! . . . *Trot!*

(*The speed of the turning square increases.*)

Stead-y! Stead-y! Stead-y! Stead-y! Cowboys are watching! Take off their stetsons. They know who we are. They're admiring us! Bowing low unto us! Come on now — show them! *Canter!* . . . CANTER!

(*He whips* NUGGET.)

And Equus the Mighty rose against All!
His enemies scatter, his enemies fall!
TURN!
Trample them, trample them,
Trample them, trample them,
TURN!
TURN!!
TURN!!!

(*The Equus noise increases in volume.*)

(*Shouting.*) WEE! . . . WAA! . . . WON-
DERFUL! . . .
I'm stiff! Stiff in the wind!

My mane, stiff in the wind!
My flanks! *My* hooves!
Mane on my legs, on my flanks, like whips!
Raw!
Raw!
I'm raw! Raw!
Feel me on you! *On* you! *On* you! *On* you!
I want to be *in* you!
I want to BE you forever and ever! —
Equus, I love you!
Now! —
Bear me away!
Make us One Person!

(*He rides Equus frantically.*)

One Person! One Person! One Person! One Person!

(*He rises up on the horse's back, and calls like a trumpet.*)

Ha-HA! . . . Ha-HA! . . . Ha HA!

(*The trumpet turns to great cries.*)

HA-HA! HA-HA! HA-HA! HA-HA! HA! . . .
HA! . . . HAAAAA!

(*He twists like a flame.*
Silence.
The turning square comes to a stop in the same position it occupied at the opening of the Act.
Slowly the boy drops off the horse's back on to the ground.
He lowers his head and kisses NUGGET'*s hoof.*
Finally he flings back his head and cries up to him:)

AMEN!

(NUGGET *snorts, once.*)

BLACKOUT

ACT 2

SCENE 22

Darkness.
Lights come slowly up on ALAN *kneeling in the night at the hooves of* NUGGET. *Slowly he gets up, climbing lovingly up the body of the horse until he can stand and kiss it.*
DYSART *sits on the downstage bench where he began Act 1.*

DYSART: With one particular horse, called Nugget, he embraces. He showed me how he stands with it afterwards in the night, one hand on its chest, one on its neck, like a frozen tango dancer, inhaling its cold sweet breath. "Have you noticed," he said, "about horses: how they'll stand one hoof on its end, like those girls in the ballet?"

(ALAN *leads* NUGGET *out of the square.* DYSART *rises. The horse walks away up the tunnel and disappears. The boy comes downstage and sits on the bench* DYSART *has vacated.* DYSART *crosses downstage and moves slowly up round the circle, until he reaches the central entrance to the square.*)

Now he's gone off to rest, leaving me alone with Equus. I can hear the creature's voice. It's calling me out of the black cave of the Pysche. I shove in my dim little torch, and there he stands — waiting for me. He raises his matted head. He opens his great square teeth, and says — (*Mocking.*) "Why? . . . Why Me? . . . Why — ultimately — Me? . . . Do you really imagine you can account for Me? Totally, infallibly, inevitably account for Me? . . . Poor Doctor Dysart!"

(*He enters the square.*)

Of course I've stared at such images before. Or been stared at by them, whichever way you look at it. And weirdly often now with me the feeling is that *they* are staring at *us* — that in some quite palpable way they precede us. Meaningless, but unsettling . . . In either case, this one is the most alarming yet. It asks questions I've avoided all my professional life. (*Pause.*) A child is born into a world of phenomena all equal in their power to enslave. It sniffs — it sucks — it strokes its eyes over the whole uncountable range. Suddenly one strikes. Why? Moments snap together like magnets, forging a chain of shackles. Why? I can trace them. I can even, with time, pull them apart again. But why at the start they were ever magnetized at all — just those particular moments of experience and no others — I don't know. *And nor does anyone else.* Yet *if* I don't know — if I can never know that — then what am I doing here? I don't mean clinically doing or socially doing — I mean *fundamentally*! These questions, these Whys, are fundamental — yet they have no place in a consulting room. So then, do I? . . . This is the feeling more and more with me — No Place. Displacement. . . . "Account for me," says staring Equus. "First account for Me! . . ." I fancy this is more than menopause.

(NURSE *rushes in.*)

NURSE: Doctor! . . . Doctor! There's a terrible scene with the Strang boy. His mother came to visit him, and I gave her the tray to take in. He threw it at her. She's saying the most dreadful things.

(ALAN *springs up, down left.* DORA *springs up, down right. They face each other across the bottom end of the stage. It is observable that at the start of this Act* FRANK *is not sitting beside his wife on their bench. It is hopefully not observable that he is placed among the audience upstage, in the gloom, by the central tunnel.*)

DORA: Don't you dare! *Don't you dare!*
DYSART: Is she still there?
NURSE: Yes!

(*He quickly leaves the square, followed by the* NURSE. DORA *moves towards her son.*)

DORA: Don't you look at me like that! I'm not a doctor, you know, who'll take anything. Don't you dare give me that stare, young man!

(*She slaps his face.* DYSART *joins them.*)

DYSART: Mrs. Strang!
DORA: I know your stares. They don't work on me!
DYSART (*to her*): Leave this room.
DORA: What did you say?
DYSART: I tell you to leave here at once.

(DORA *hesitates. Then:*)

DORA: Goodbye, Alan.

(*She walks past her son, and round into the square.* DYSART *follows her. Both are very upset.* ALAN *returns to his bench and* NURSE *to her place.*)

SCENE 23

Lights up on the square.

DYSART: I must ask you never to come here again.

DORA: Do you think I want to? Do you think I want to?

DYSART: Mrs. Strang, what on earth has got into you? Can't you see the boy is highly distressed?

DORA (*ironic*): Really?

DYSART: Of course! He's at a most delicate stage of treatment. He's totally exposed. Ashamed. Everything you can imagine!

DORA (*exploding*): *And me? What about me? . . . What do you think I am? . . .* I'm a parent, of course — so it doesn't count. That's a dirty word in here, isn't it, "parent"?

DYSART: You know that's not true.

DORA: Oh, I know. I know, all right! I've heard it all my life. It's *our* fault. Whatever happens, *we* did it. Alan's just a little victim. He's really done nothing at all! (*Savagely.*) What do you have to do in this world to get any sympathy — blind animals?

DYSART: Sit down, Mrs. Strang.

DORA (*ignoring him: more and more urgently*): Look, Doctor: you don't have to live with this. Alan is one patient to you: one out of many. He's my son. I lie awake every night thinking about it. Frank lies there beside me. I can hear him. Neither of us sleeps all night. You come to us and say Who forbids television? who does what behind whose back? — as if we're criminals. Let me tell you something. We're not criminals. We've done nothing wrong. We loved Alan. We gave him the best love we could. All right, we quarrel sometimes — all parents quarrel — we always make it up. My husband is a good man. He's an upright man, religion or no religion. He cares for his home, for the world, and for his boy. Alan had love and care and treats, and as much fun as any boy in the world. I know about loveless homes: I was a teacher. Our home wasn't loveless. I know about privacy too — not invading a child's privacy. All right, Frank may be at fault there — he digs into him too much — but nothing in excess. He's not a bully. . . . (*Gravely.*) No, doctor. Whatever's happened has happened *because of Alan*. Alan is himself. Every soul is itself. If you added up everything we ever did to him, from his first day on earth to this, you wouldn't find why he did this terrible thing — because that's *him*: not just all of our things added up. Do you understand what I'm saying? I want you to understand, because I lie awake and awake thinking it out, and I want you to know that I deny it

absolutely what he's doing now, staring at me, attacking me for what *he's* done, for what *he* is! (*Pause: calmer.*) You've got your words, and I've got mine. You call it a complex, I suppose. But if you knew God, Doctor, you would know about the Devil. You'd know the Devil isn't made by what mummy says and daddy says. The Devil's *there*. It's an old-fashioned word, but a true thing . . . I'll go. What I did in there was inexcusable. I only know he was my little Alan, and then the Devil came.

(*She leaves the square, and resumes her place.* DYSART *watches her go, then leaves himself by the opposite entrance, and approaches* ALAN.)

SCENE 24

Seated on his bench, the boy glares at him.

DYSART: I thought you liked your mother.

(*Silence.*)

She doesn't know anything, you know. I haven't told her what you told me. You do know that, don't you?

ALAN: It was lies anyway.

DYSART: What?

ALAN: You and your pencil. Just a con trick, that's all.

DYSART: What do you mean?

ALAN: Made me say a lot of lies.

DYSART: Did it? . . . Like what?

ALAN: All of it. Everything I said. Lot of lies.

(*Pause.*)

DYSART: I see.

ALAN: You ought to be locked up. Your bloody tricks.

DYSART: I thought you liked tricks.

ALAN: It'll be the drug next. I know.

(DYSART *turns, sharply.*)

DYSART: What drug?

ALAN: I've heard. I'm not ignorant. I know what you get up to in here. Shove needles in people, pump them full of truth drug, so they can't help saying things. That's next, isn't it?

(*Pause.*)

DYSART: Alan, do you know why you're here?

ALAN: So you can give me truth drugs.

(*He glares at him.*
DYSART *leaves abruptly, and returns to the square.*)

SCENE 25

HESTHER *comes in simultaneously from the other side.*

DYSART (*agitated*): He actually thinks they exist! And of course he wants one.
HESTHER: It doesn't sound like that to me.
DYSART: Of course he does. Why mention them otherwise? He wants a way to speak. To finally tell me what happened in that stable. Tape's too isolated, and hypnosis is a trick. At least that's the pretence.
HESTHER: Does he still say that today?
DYSART: I haven't seen him. I cancelled his appointment this morning, and let him stew in his own anxiety. Now I am almost tempted to play a real trick on him.
HESTHER (*sitting*): Like what?
DYSART: The old placebo.
HESTHER: You mean a harmless pill?
DYSART: Full of *alleged* Truth Drug. Probably an aspirin.
HESTHER: But he'd deny it afterwards. Same thing all over.
DYSART: No. Because he's ready to abreact.
HESTHER: Abreact?
DYSART: Live it all again. He won't be able to deny it after that, because he'll have shown me. Not just told me – but acted it out in front of me.
HESTHER: Can you get him to do that?
DYSART: I think so. He's nearly done it already. Under all that glowering, he trusts me. Do you realise that?
HESTHER (*warmly*): I'm sure he does.
DYSART: Poor bloody fool.
HESTHER: Don't start that again.

(*Pause.*)

DYSART (*quietly*): Can you think of anything worse one can do to anybody than take away their worship?
HESTHER: Worship?
DYSART: Yes, that word again!
HESTHER: Aren't you being a little extreme?
DYSART: Extremity's the point.
HESTHER: Worship isn't destructive, Martin. I know that.

DYSART: I don't. I only know it's the core of his life. What else has he got? Think about him. He can hardly read. He knows no physics or engineering to make the world real for him. No paintings to show him how others have enjoyed it. No music except television jingles. No history except tales from a desperate mother. No friends. Not one kid to give him a joke, or make him know himself more moderately. He's a modern citizen for whom society doesn't exist. He lives *one hour* every three weeks – howling in a mist. And after the service kneels to a slave who stands over him obviously and unthrowably his master. With my body I thee worship! . . . Many men have less vital with their wives.

(*Pause.*)

HESTHER: All the same, they don't usually blind their wives, do they?
DYSART: Oh, come on!
HESTHER: Well, do they?
DYSART (*sarcastically*): You mean he's dangerous? A violent, dangerous madman who's going to run round the country doing it again and again?
HESTHER: I mean he's in pain, Martin. He's been in pain for most of his life. That much, at least, you *know*.
DYSART: Possibly.
HESTHER: *Possibly? !* . . . That cut-off little figure you just described must have been in pain for years.
DYSART (*doggedly*): Possibly.
HESTHER: And you can take it away.
DYSART: Still – possibly.
HESTHER: Then that's enough. That simply has to be enough for you, surely?
DYSART: No!
HESTHER: Why not?
DYSART: Because it's his.
HESTHER: I don't understand.
DYSART: His pain. His own. He made it.

(*Pause.*)

(*Earnestly.*) Look . . . to go through life and call it yours – *your life* – you first have to get your own pain. Pain that's unique to you. You can't just dip into the common bin and say "That's enough!" . . . He's done that. All right, he's sick. He's full of misery and fear. He was dangerous, and could be again, though I doubt it. But that boy has known a passion more ferocious than I have felt in any second of my life. And let me tell you something: I envy it.

HESTHER: You can't.

DYSART (*vehemently*): Don't you see? That's the Accusation! That's what his stare has been saying to me all the time. "*At least I galloped! When did you?*" . . . (*Simply.*) I'm jealous, Hester. Jealous of Alan Strang.

HESTHER: That's absurd.

DYSART: Is it? . . . I go on about my wife. That smug woman by the fire. Have you thought of the fellow on the other side of it? The finicky, critical husband looking through his art books on mythical Greece. What worship has *he* ever known? Real worship! Without worship you shrink, it's as brutal as that . . . I shrank my *own* life. No one can do it for you. I settled for being pallid and provincial, out of my own eternal timidity. The old story of bluster, and do bugger-all . . . I imply that we can't have children: but actually, it's only me. I had myself tested behind her back. The lowest sperm count you could find. And I never told her. That's all I need – her sympathy mixed with resentment . . . I tell everyone Margaret's the puritan, I'm the pagan. Some pagan! Such wild returns I make to the womb of civilization. Three weeks a year in the Peleponnese, every bed booked in advance, every meal paid for by vouchers, cautious jaunts in hired Fiats, suitcase crammed with Kao-Pectate! Such a fantastic surrender to the primitive. And I use that word endlessly: "primitive." "Oh, the primitive world," I say. "What instinctual truths were lost with it!" And while I sit there, baiting a poor unimaginative woman with the word, that freaky boy tries to conjure the reality! I sit looking at pages of centaurs trampling the soil of Argos – and outside my window he is trying to *become* one, in a Hampshire field! . . . I watch that woman knitting, night after night – a woman I haven't *kissed* in six years – and he stands in the dark for an hour, sucking the sweat off his God's hairy cheek! (*Pause.*) Then in the morning, I put away my books on the cultural shelf, close up the kodachrome snaps of Mount Olympus, touch my reproduction statue of Dionysus for luck – and go off to hospital to treat him for insanity. Do you see?

HESTHER: The boy's in pain, Martin. That's all I see. In the end . . . I'm sorry.

(*He looks at her.* ALAN *gets up from his bench and stealthily places an envelope in the left-hand entrance of the square, then goes back and sits with his back to the audience, as if watching television.* HESTHER *rises.*)

HESTHER: That stare of his. Have you thought it might not be accusing you at all?

DYSART: What then?

HESTHER: Claiming you.

DYSART: For what?

HESTHER (*mischievously*): A new God.

(*Pause.*)

DYSART: Too conventional, for him. Finding a religion in Psychiatry is really for very ordinary patients.

(*She laughs.*)

HESTHER: Maybe he just wants a new Dad. Or is that too conventional too? . . . Since you're questioning your profession anyway, perhaps you ought to try it and see.

DYSART (*amused*): I'll talk to you.

HESTHER: Goodbye.

(*She smiles, and leaves him.*)

SCENE 26

DYSART *becomes aware of the letter lying on the floor. He picks it up, opens and reads it.*

ALAN (*speaking stiffly, as* DYSART *reads*): "It is all true, what I said after you tapped the pencil. I'm sorry if I said different. Post Scriptum: I know why I'm in here."

(*Pause.*)

DYSART (*calling, joyfully*): Nurse!

(NURSE *comes in.*)

NURSE: Yes, Doctor?

DYSART (*trying to conceal his pleasure*): Good evening!

NURSE: You're in late tonight.

DYSART: Yes! . . . Tell me, is the Strang boy in bed yet?

NURSE: Oh, no, Doctor. He's bound to be upstairs looking at television. He always watches to the last possible moment. He doesn't like going to his room at all.

DYSART: You mean he's still having nightmares?

NURSE: He had a bad one last night.

DYSART: Would you ask him to come down here, please?

NURSE (*faint surprise*): Now?

DYSART: I'd like a word with him.

NURSE (*puzzled*): Very good, Doctor.

DYSART: If he's not back in his room by lights out, tell Night Nurse not to worry. I'll see he gets back to bed all right. And would you phone my home and tell my wife I may be in late?

NURSE: Yes, Doctor.

DYSART: Ask him to come straight away, please.

(NURSE *goes to the bench, taps* ALAN *on the shoulder, whispers her message in his ear, and returns to her place.* ALAN *stands up and pauses for a second — then steps into the square.*)

SCENE 27

He stands in the doorway, depressed.

DYSART: Hallo.

ALAN: Hallo.

DYSART: I got your letter. Thank you. (*Pause.*) Also the Post Scriptum.

ALAN (*defensively*): That's the right word. My mum told me. It's Latin for "After-writing."

DYSART: How are you feeling?

ALAN: All right.

DYSART: I'm sorry I didn't see you today.

ALAN: You were fed up with me.

DYSART: Yes. (*Pause.*) Can I make it up to you now?

ALAN: What d'you mean?

DYSART: I thought we'd have a session.

ALAN (*startled*): Now?

DYSART: Yes! At dead of night! . . . Better than going to sleep, isn't it?

(*The boy flinches.*)

Alan — look. Everything I say has a trick or a catch. Everything I do is a trick or a catch. That's all I know to do. But they work — and you know that. Trust me.

(*Pause.*)

ALAN: You got another trick, then?

DYSART: Yes.

ALAN: A truth drug?

DYSART: If you like.

ALAN: What's it do?

DYSART: Make it easier for you to talk.

ALAN: Like you can't help yourself?

DYSART: That's right. Like you have to speak the truth at all costs. And all of it.

(*Pause.*)

ALAN (*slyly*): Comes in a needle, doesn't it?

DYSART: No.

ALAN: Where is it?

DYSART (*indicating his pocket*): In here.

ALAN: Let's see.

(DYSART *solemnly takes a bottle of pills out of his pocket.*)

DYSART: There.

ALAN (*suspicious*): That really it?

DYSART: It is . . . Do you want to try it?

ALAN: No.

DYSART: I think you do.

ALAN: I don't. Not at all.

DYSART: Afterwards you'd sleep. You'd have no bad dreams all night. Probably many nights, from then on . . .

(*Pause.*)

ALAN: How long's it take to work?

DYSART: It's instant. Like coffee.

ALAN (*half believing*): It isn't!

DYSART: I promise you . . . Well?

ALAN: Can I have a fag?

DYSART: Pill first. Do you want some water?

ALAN: No.

(DYSART *shakes one out on to his palm.* ALAN *hesitates for a second — then takes it and swallows it.*)

DYSART: Then you can chase it down with this. Sit down.

(*He offers him a cigarette, and lights it for him.*)

ALAN (*nervous*): What happens now?

DYSART: We wait for it to work.

ALAN: What'll I feel first?

DYSART: Nothing much. After a minute, about a hundred green snakes should come out of that cupboard singing the Hallelujah Chorus.

ALAN (*annoyed*): I'm serious!

DYSART (*earnestly*): You'll feel nothing.

Nothing's going to happen now but what you want to happen. You're not going to say anything to me but what you want to say. Just relax. Lie back and finish your fag.

(ALAN *stares at him. Then accepts the situation, and lies back.*)

DYSART: Good boy.
ALAN: I bet this room's heard some funny things.
DYSART: It certainly has.
ALAN: I like it.
DYSART: This room?
ALAN: Don't you?
DYSART: Well, there's not much to like, is there?
ALAN: How long am I going to be in here?
DYSART: It's hard to say. I quite see you want to leave.
ALAN: No.
DYSART: You don't?
ALAN: Where would I go?
DYSART: Home. . . .

(*The boy looks at him.* DYSART *crosses and sits on the rail upstage, his feet on the bench. A pause.*)

Actually, I'd like to leave this room and never see it again in my life.
ALAN (*surprise*): Why?
DYSART: I've been in it too long.
ALAN: Where would you go?
DYSART: Somewhere.
ALAN: Secret?
DYSART: Yes. There's a sea – a great sea – I love . . . It's where the Gods used to go to bathe.
ALAN: What Gods?
DYSART: The old ones. Before they died.
ALAN: Gods don't die.
DYSART: Yes, they do.

(*Pause.*)

There's a village I spent one night in, where I'd like to live. It's all white.
ALAN: How would you Nosey Parker, though? You wouldn't have a room for it any more.
DYSART: I wouldn't mind. I don't actually enjoy being a Nosey Parker, you know.
ALAN: Then why do it?
DYSART: Because you're unhappy.
ALAN: So are you.

(DYSART *looks at him sharply.* ALAN *sits up in alarm.*)

Oooh, I didn't mean that!
DYSART: Didn't you?
ALAN: Here – is that how it works? Things just slip out, not feeling anything?
DYSART: That's right.
ALAN: But it's so quick!
DYSART: I told you: it's instant.
ALAN (*delighted*): It's wicked, isn't it? I mean, you can say anything under it.
DYSART: Yes.
ALAN: Ask me a question.
DYSART: Tell me about Jill.

(*Pause. The boy turns away.*)

ALAN: There's nothing to tell.
DYSART: Nothing?
ALAN: No.
DYSART: Well, for example – is she pretty? You've never described her.
ALAN: She's all right.
DYSART: What colour hair?
ALAN: Dunno.
DYSART: Is it long or short?
ALAN: Dunno.
DYSART (*lightly*): You must know that.
ALAN: I don't remember. *I don't!*

(DYSART *rises and comes down to him. He takes the cigarette out of his hand.*)

DYSART (*firmly*): Lie back . . . Now listen. You have to do this. And now. You are going to tell me everything that happened with this girl. And not just *tell* me – *show* me. Act it out, if you like – even more than you did when I tapped the pencil. I want you to feel free to do absolutely anything in this room. The pill will help you. I will help you. . . . Now, where does she live?

(*A long pause.*)

ALAN (*tight*): Near the stables. About a mile.

(DYSART *steps down out of the square as* JILL *enters it. He sits again on the downstage bench.*)

SCENE 28

The light grows warmer.

JILL: It's called The China Pantry.

(She comes down and sits casually on the rail. Her manner is open and lightly provocative. During these scenes ALAN acts directly with her, and never looks over at DYSART when he replies to him.)

When Daddy disappeared, she was left without a bean. She had to earn her own living. I must say she did jolly well, considering she was never trained in business.

DYSART: What do you mean, "disappeared"?

ALAN *(to DYSART)*: He ran off. No one ever saw him again.

JILL: Just left a note on her dressing table saying "Sorry. I've had it." Just like that. She never got over it. It turned her right off men. All my dates have to be sort of secret. I mean, she knows about them, but I can't ever bring anyone back home. She's so rude to them.

ALAN *(to DYSART)*: She was always looking.

DYSART: At you?

ALAN *(to DYSART)*: Saying stupid things.

(She jumps off the bench.)

JILL: You've got super eyes.

ALAN *(to DYSART)*: Anyway, *she* was the one who had them.

(She sits next to him. Embarrassed, the boy tries to move away as far as he can.)

JILL: There was an article in the paper last week saying what points about boys fascinate girls. They said Number One is bottoms. I think it's eyes every time. . . . They fascinate you too, don't they?

ALAN: Me?

JILL *(sly)*: Or is it only horses' eyes?

ALAN *(startled)*: What d'you mean?

JILL: I saw you staring into Nugget's eyes yesterday for ages. I spied on you through the door!

ALAN *(hotly)*: There must have been something in it!

JILL: You're a real Man of Mystery, aren't you?

ALAN *(to DYSART)*: Sometimes, it was like she knew.

DYSART: Did you ever hint?

ALAN *(to DYSART)*: Course not!

JILL: I love horses' eyes. The way you can see yourself in them. D'you find them sexy?

ALAN *(outraged)*: What? !

JILL: Horses.

ALAN: Don't be daft!

(He springs up, and away from her.)

JILL: Girls do. I mean, they go through a period when they pat them and kiss them a lot. I know *I* did. I suppose it's just a substitute, really.

ALAN *(to DYSART)*: That kind of thing, all the time. Until one night . . .

DYSART: Yes? What?

ALAN *(to DYSART: defensively)*: She did it! Not me. It was her idea, the whole thing! . . . She got me into it!

DYSART: What are you saying? "One night": go on from there.

(A pause.)

ALAN *(to DYSART)*: Saturday night. We were just closing up.

JILL: How would you like to take me out?

ALAN: What?

JILL *(coolly)*: How would you like to take me out tonight?

ALAN: I've got to go home.

JILL: What for?

(He tries to escape upstage.)

ALAN: They expect me.

JILL: Ring up and say you're going out.

ALAN: I can't.

JILL: Why?

ALAN: They expect me.

JILL: Look. Either we go out together and have some fun, or you go back to your boring home, *as usual*, and I go back to mine. That's the situation, isn't it?

ALAN: Well . . . where would we go?

JILL: The pictures! There's a skinflick over in Winchester! I've never seen one, have you?

ALAN: No.

JILL: Wouldn't you like to? I would. All those heavy Swedes, panting at each other! . . . What d'you say?

ALAN *(grinning)*: Yeh! . . .

JILL: Good! . . .

(He turns away.)

DYSART: Go on, please.

(He steps off the square.)

ALAN *(to DYSART)*: I'm tired now!

DYSART: Come on now. You can't stop there.

(*He storms round the circle to* DYSART, *and faces him directly.*)

ALAN: I'm *tired!* I want to go to bed!
DYSART (*sharply*): Well, you can't. I want to hear about the film.
ALAN (*hostile*): Hear what? . . . *What?*
. . . It was bloody awful!

(*The actors playing horses come swiftly on to the square, dressed in sports coats or raincoats. They move the benches to be parallel with the audience, and sit on them — staring out front.*)

DYSART: Why?
ALAN: Nosey Parker!
DYSART: *Why?*
ALAN: *Because!* . . . Well — we went into the Cinema!

SCENE 29

A burst of Rock music, instantly fading down. Lights darken.
ALAN *re-enters the square.* JILL *rises and together they grope their way to the downstage bench, as if in a dark auditorium.*

ALAN (*to* DYSART): The whole place was full of men. Jill was the only girl.

(*They push by a patron seated at the end, and sit side by side, staring up at the invisible screen, located above the heads of the main audience. A spotlight hits the boy's face.*)

We sat down and the film came on. It was daft. Nothing happened for ages. There was this girl Brita, who was sixteen. She went to stay in this house, where there was an older boy. He kept giving her looks, but she ignored him completely. In the end she took a shower. She went into the bathroom and took off all her clothes. The lot. Very slowly. . . . What she didn't know was the boy was looking through the door all the time. . . . (*He starts to become excited.*) It was fantastic! The water fell on her breasts, bouncing down her. . . .

(FRANK *steps into the square furtively from the back, hat in hand, and stands looking about for a place.*)

DYSART: Was that the first time you'd seen a girl naked?

ALAN (*to* DYSART): Yes! You couldn't see everything, though. . . . (*Looking about him.*) All round me they were all looking. All the men — staring up like they were in church. Like they were a sort of congregation. And then — (*He sees his father.*) Ah!

(*At the same instant* FRANK *sees him.*)

FRANK: Alan!
ALAN: God!
JILL: What is it?
ALAN: *Dad!*
JILL: *Where?*
ALAN: At the back! *He saw me!*
JILL: You sure?
ALAN: Yes!
FRANK (*calling*): Alan!
ALAN: Oh God!

(*He tries to hide his face in the girl's shoulder. His father comes down the aisle towards him.*)

FRANK: Alan! You can hear me! Don't pretend!
PATRONS: Sssssh!
FRANK (*approaching the row of seats*): Do I have to come and fetch you out? . . . Do I? . . .

(*Cries of "Sssh!" and "Shut up!"*)

Do I, Alan?
ALAN (*through gritted teeth*): Oh, fuck!

(*He gets up as the noise increases.* JILL *gets up too and follows him.*)

DYSART: You went?
ALAN (*to* DYSART): What else could I do? He kept shouting. Everyone was saying Shut up!

(*They go out, right, through the group of* PATRONS — *who rise protesting as they pass, quickly replace the benches and leave the square.*
DYSART *enters it.*)

SCENE 30

Light brightens from the cinema, but remains cold: streets at night.
The three walk round the circle downstage in a line: FRANK *leading, wearing his hat. He halts in the middle of the left rail, and*

stands staring straight ahead of him, rigid with embarrassment.
ALAN *is very agitated.*

ALAN (*to* DYSART): We went into the street, all three of us. It was weird. We just stood there by the bus stop — like we were three people in a queue, and we didn't know each other. Dad was all white and sweaty. He didn't look at us at all. It must have gone on for about five minutes. I tried to speak. I said — (*To his father.*) I — I — I've never been there before. Honest . . . Never . . . (*To* DYSART.) He didn't seem to hear. Jill tried.
JILL: It's true. Mr. Strang. It wasn't Alan's idea to go there. It was mine.
ALAN (*to* DYSART): He just went on staring, straight ahead. It was awful.
JILL: I'm not shocked by films like that. I think they're just silly.
ALAN (*to* DYSART): The bus wouldn't come. We just stood and stood. . . . Then suddenly he spoke.

(FRANK *takes off his hat.*)

FRANK (*stiffly*): I'd like you to know something. Both of you. I came here tonight to see the Manager. He asked me to call on him for business purposes. I happen to be a printer, Miss. A picture house needs posters. That's entirely why I'm here. To discuss posters. While I was waiting I happened to glance in, that's all. I can only say I'm going to complain to the council. I had no idea they showed films like this. I'm certainly going to refuse my services.
JILL (*kindly*): Yes, of course.
FRANK: So long as that's understood.
ALAN (*to* DYSART): Then the bus came along.
FRANK: Come along now, Alan.

(*He moves away downstage.*)

ALAN: No.
FRANK (*turning*): No fuss, please. Say Goodnight to the young lady.
ALAN (*timid but firm*): No. I'm stopping here . . . I've got to see her home . . . It's proper.

(*Pause.*)

FRANK (*as dignified as possible*): Very well. I'll see you when you choose to return. Very well then . . . Yes . . .

(*He walks back to his original seat, next to his wife. He stares across the square at his son — who stares back at him. Then, slowly, he sits.*)

ALAN (*to* DYSART): And he got in, and we didn't. He sat down and looked at me through the glass. And I saw . . .
DYSART (*soft*): What?
ALAN (*to* DYSART): His face. It was scared.
DYSART: Of you?
ALAN (*to* DYSART): It was terrible. We had to walk home. Four miles. I got the shakes.
DYSART: You were scared too?
ALAN (*to* DYSART): It was like a hole had been drilled in my tummy. A hole — right here. And the air was getting in!

(*He starts to walk upstage, round the circle.*)

SCENE 31

The girl stays still.

JILL (*aware of other people looking*): Alan . . .
ALAN (*to* DYSART): People kept turning round in the street to look.
JILL: Alan!
ALAN (*to* DYSART): I kept seeing him, just as he drove off. Scared of me. . . . And me scared of *him.* . . . I kept thinking — all those airs he put on! . . . "Receive my meaning. Improve your mind!" . . . All those nights he said he'd be in late. "Keep my supper hot, Dora!" "Your poor father: he works so hard!" . . . Bugger! Old bugger! . . . Filthy old bugger!

(*He stops, clenching his fists.*)

JILL: Hey! Wait for me!

(*She runs after him. He waits.*)

What are you thinking about?
ALAN: Nothing.
JILL: Mind my own beeswax?

(*She laughs.*)

ALAN (*to* DYSART): And suddenly she began to laugh.
JILL: I'm sorry. But it's pretty funny, when you think of it.
ALAN (*bewildered*): What?

JILL: Catching him like that! I mean, it's terrible — but it's very funny.

ALAN: Yeh!

(*He turns from her.*)

JILL: No, wait! . . . I'm sorry. I know you're upset. But it's not the end of the world, is it? I mean, what was he doing? Only what we were. Watching a silly film. It's a case of like father like son, I'd say! . . . I mean, when that girl was taking a shower, you were pretty interested, weren't you?

(*He turns round and looks at her.*)

We keep saying old people are square. Then when they suddenly aren't — we don't like it!

DYSART: What did you think about that?

ALAN (*to* DYSART): I don't know. I kept looking at all the people in the street. They were mostly men coming out of pubs. I suddenly thought — *they all do it! All of them!* . . . They're not just Dads — they're people with pricks! . . . And Dad — he's just not Dad either. He's a man with a prick too. You know, I'd never thought about it.

(*Pause.*)

We went into the country.

(*He walks again.* JILL *follows. They turn the corner and come downstage, right.*)

We kept walking. I just thought about Dad, and how he was nothing special — just a poor old sod on his own.

(*He stops.*)

(*To* JILL: *realising it.*) Poor old sod!

JILL: That's right!

ALAN (*grappling with it*): I mean, what else has he got? . . . He's got mum, of course, but well — she — she — she ——

JILL: She doesn't give him anything?

ALAN: That's right. I bet you . . . She doesn't give him anything. That's right . . . That's really right! . . . She likes Ladies and Gentlemen. Do you understand what I mean?

JILL (*mischievously*): Ladies and gentlemen aren't naked?

ALAN: That's right! Never! . . . *Never!* That would be disgusting! She'd have to put bowler hats on them! . . . Jodhpurs!

(JILL *laughs.*)

DYSART: Was that the first time you ever thought anything like that about your mother? . . . I mean, that she was unfair to your dad?

ALAN (*to* DYSART): Absolutely!

DYSART: How did you feel?

ALAN (*to* DYSART): Sorry. I mean for him. Poor old sod, that's what I felt — he's just like me! He hates ladies and gents just like me! Posh things — and la-di-da. He goes off by himself at night, and does his own secret thing which no one'll know about, just like me! There's no difference — he's just the same as me — just the same! —

(*He stops in distress, then bolts back a little upstage.*)

Christ!

DYSART (*sternly*): Go on.

ALAN (*to* DYSART): I can't.

DYSART: Of course you can. You're doing wonderfully.

ALAN (*to* DYSART): No, please. *Don't make me!*

DYSART (*firm*): Don't think: just answer. You were happy at that second, weren't you? When you realised about your dad. How lots of people have secrets, not just you?

ALAN (*to* DYSART): Yes.

DYSART: You felt sort of free, didn't you? I mean, free to do anything?

ALAN (*to* DYSART, *looking at* JILL): Yes!

DYSART: What was she doing?

ALAN (*to* DYSART): Holding my hand.

DYSART: And that was good?

ALAN (*to* DYSART): Oh, yes!

DYSART: Remember what you thought. *As if it's happening to you now. This very moment* . . . What's in your head?

ALAN (*to* DYSART): Her eyes. *She's* the one with eyes! . . . I keep looking at them, because I really want —

DYSART: To look at her breasts?

ALAN (*to* DYSART): Yes.

DYSART: Like in the film.

ALAN (*to* DYSART): Yes . . . Then she starts to scratch my hand.

JILL: You're really very nice, you know that?

ALAN (*to* DYSART): Moving her nails on the back. Her face so warm. Her eyes.

DYSART: You want her very much?

ALAN (*to* DYSART): Yes . . .

JILL: I love your eyes.

(*She kisses him.*)

(*Whispering.*) Let's go!
ALAN: Where?
JILL: I know a place. It's right near here.
ALAN: Where?
JILL: Surprise! . . . Come on!

(*She darts away round the circle, across the stage and up the left side.*)

Come *on!*
ALAN (*to* DYSART): She runs ahead. I follow. And then — and then — !

(*He halts.*)

DYSART: What?
ALAN (*to* DYSART): I see what she means.
DYSART: What? . . . Where are you? . . . Where has she taken you?
ALAN (*to* JILL): *The Stables?*
JILL: Of course!

SCENE 32

CHORUS *makes a warning hum.*
The horse-actors enter, and ceremonially put on their masks — first raising them high above their heads. NUGGET *stands in the central tunnel.*

ALAN (*recoiling*): No!
JILL: Where else? They're perfect!
ALAN: No!

(*He turns his head from her.*)

JILL: Or do you want to go home now and face your dad?
ALAN: No!
JILL: Then come on!

(*He edges nervously past the horse standing at the left, which turns its neck and even moves a challenging step after him.*)

ALAN: Why not your place?
JILL: I can't. Mother doesn't like me bringing back boys. I told you. . . . Anyway, the Barn's better.
ALAN: No!
JILL: All that straw. It's cosy.
ALAN: No.
JILL: *Why not?*
ALAN: Them!
JILL: Dalton will be in bed . . . What's the matter? . . . Don't you want to?

ALAN (*aching to*): Yes!
JILL: So?
ALAN (*desperate*): Them! . . . Them! . . .
JILL: *Who?*
ALAN (*low*): Horses.
JILL: *Horses?* . . . You're really dotty, aren't you? . . . What do you mean?

(*He starts shaking.*)

Oh, you're freezing . . . Let's get under the straw. You'll be warm there.
ALAN (*pulling away*): No!
JILL: What on earth's the matter with you? . . .

(*Silence. He won't look at her.*)

Look, if the sight of horses offends you, my lord, we can just shut the door. You won't have to see them. All right?
DYSART: What door is that? In the barn?
ALAN (*to* DYSART): Yes.
DYSART: So what do you do? You go in?
ALAN (*to* DYSART): Yes.

SCENE 33

A rich light falls.
Furtively ALAN *enters the square from the top end, and* JILL *follows. The horses on the circle retire out of sight on either side.* NUGGET *retreats up the tunnel and stands where he can just be glimpsed in the dimness.*

DYSART: Into the Temple? The Holy of Holies?
ALAN (*to* DYSART: *desperate*): What else can I do? . . . I can't say! I can't tell her. . . . (*To* JILL.) Shut it tight.
JILL: All right . . . You're crazy!
ALAN: Lock it.
JILL: Lock?
ALAN: Yes.
JILL: It's just an old door. What's the matter with you? They're in their boxes. They can't get out . . . Are you all right?
ALAN: Why?
JILL: You look weird.
ALAN: *Lock it!*
JILL: Ssssh! D'you want to wake up Dalton? . . . Stay there, idiot.

(*She mimes locking a heavy door, upstage.*)

DYSART: Describe the barn, please.

ALAN (*walking round it: to* DYSART): Large room. Straw everywhere. Some tools . . . (*as if picking it up off the rail where he left it in Act 1*) A hoof pick! . . .

(*He "drops" it hastily, and dashes away from the spot.*)

DYSART: *Go on.*

ALAN (*to* DYSART): At the end this big door. Behind it —

DYSART: Horses.

ALAN (*to* DYSART): Yes.

DYSART: How many?

ALAN (*to* DYSART): Six.

DYSART: Jill closes the door so you can't see them?

ALAN (*to* DYSART): Yes.

DYSART: And then? . . . What happens now? . . . Come on, Alan. Show me.

JILL: See, it's all shut. There's just us . . . Let's sit down. Come on.

(*They sit together on the same bench, left.*)

Hallo.

ALAN (*quickly*): Hallo.

(*She kisses him lightly. He responds. Suddenly a faint trampling of hooves, off-stage, makes him jump up.*)

JILL: What is it?

(*He turns his head upstage, listening.*)

Relax. There's no one there. Come here.

(*She touches his hand. He turns to her again.*)

You're very gentle. I love that . . .

ALAN: So are you . . . I mean . . .

(*He kisses her spontaneously. The hooves trample again, harder. He breaks away from her abruptly towards the upstage corner.*)

JILL (*rising*): What is it?

ALAN: Nothing!

(*She moves towards him. He turns and moves past her. He is clearly distressed. She contemplates him for a moment.*)

JILL (*gently*): Take your sweater off.

ALAN: What?

JILL: I will, if you will.

(*He stares at her. A pause.*

She lifts her sweater over head: he watches — then unzips his. They each remove their shoes, their socks, and their jeans. Then they look at each other diagonally across the square, in which the light is gently increasing.)

ALAN: You're . . . You're very . . .

JILL: So are you. . . . (*Pause.*) Come here.

(*He goes to her. She comes to him. They meet in the middle, and hold each other, and embrace.*)

ALAN (*to* DYSART): She put her mouth in mine. It was lovely! *Oh, it was lovely!*

(*They burst into giggles. He lays her gently on the floor in the centre of the square, and bends over her eagerly. Suddenly the noise of Equus fills the place. Hooves smash on wood. Alan straightens up, rigid. He stares straight ahead of him over the prone body of the girl.*)

DYSART: Yes, what happened then, Alan?

ALAN (*to* DYSART: *brutally*): I put it in her!

DYSART: Yes?

ALAN (*to* DYSART): I put it in her.

DYSART: You did?

ALAN (*to* DYSART): Yes!

DYSART: Was it easy?

ALAN (*to* DYSART): Yes.

DYSART: Describe it.

ALAN (*to* DYSART): I told you.

DYSART: More exactly.

ALAN (*to* DYSART): I put it in her!

DYSART: Did you?

ALAN (*to* DYSART): All the way!

DYSART: Did you, Alan?

ALAN (*to* DYSART): All the way. I shoved it. I put it in her all the way.

DYSART: Did you?

ALAN (*to* DYSART): Yes!

DYSART: Did you?

ALAN (*to* DYSART): Yes! . . . Yes!

DYSART: Give me the TRUTH! . . . Did you? . . . Honestly?

ALAN (*to* DYSART): Fuck off!

(*He collapses, lying upstage on his face.* JILL *lies on her back motionless, her head downstage, her arms extended behind her. A pause.*)

DYSART (*gently*): What was it? You

couldn't? Though you wanted to very much?

ALAN (*to* DYSART): I couldn't . . . see her.

DYSART: What do you mean?

ALAN (*to* DYSART): Only Him. Every time I kissed her — *He* was in the way.

DYSART: Who?

(ALAN *turns on his back.*)

ALAN (*to* DYSART): You *know* who! . . . When I touched her, I felt *Him*. Under me . . . His side, waiting for my hand . . . His flanks . . . I refused him. I looked. I looked right at her . . . and I couldn't do it. When I shut my eyes, I saw him at once. The streaks on his belly . . . (*With more desperation.*) I couldn't feel *her* flesh at all! I wanted the foam off his neck. His sweaty hide. Not flesh. *Hide! Horse-hide!* . . . Then I couldn't even kiss her.

(JILL *sits up.*)

JILL: What is it?

ALAN (*dodging her hand*): No!

(*He scrambles up and crouches in the corner against the rails, like a little beast in a cage.*)

JILL: Alan!

ALAN: Stop it!

(JILL *gets up.*)

JILL: It's all right . . . It's all right . . . Don't worry about it. It often happens — honest. . . . There's nothing wrong. I don't mind, you know . . . I don't at all.

(*He dashes past her downstage.*)

Alan, look at me . . . Alan? . . . Alan!

(*He collapses again by the rail.*)

ALAN: Get out! . . .

JILL: What?

ALAN (*soft*): Out!

JILL: There's nothing wrong: believe me! It's very common.

ALAN: *Get* out!

(*He snatches up the invisible pick.*)

GET OUT!

JILL: Put that down!

ALAN: Leave me alone!

JILL: Put that down, Alan. It's very dangerous. Go on, please — drop it.

(*He "drops" it, and turns from her.*)

ALAN: You ever tell anyone. Just you tell . . .

JILL: Who do you think I am? . . . I'm your friend — Alan . . .

(*She goes towards him.*)

Listen: you don't have to do anything. Try to realize that. Nothing at all. Why don't we just lie here together in the straw. And talk.

ALAN (*low*): Please . . .

JILL: Just talk.

ALAN: *Please!*

JILL: All right, I'm going . . . Let me put my clothes on first.

(*She dresses, hastily.*)

ALAN: You tell anyone! . . . Just tell and see. . . .

JILL: *Oh, stop it!* . . . I wish you could believe me. It's not in the least important.

(*Pause.*)

Anyway, I won't say anything. You know that. You know I won't. . . .

(*Pause. He stands with his back to her.*)

Goodnight, then, Alan. . . . I wish — I really wish —

(*He turns on her, hissing. His face is distorted — possessed. In horrified alarm she turns — fumbles the door open — leaves the barn — shuts the door hard behind her, and dashes up the tunnel out of sight, past the barely visible figure of* NUGGET.)

SCENE 34

ALAN *stands alone, and naked.*
A *faint humming and drumming. The boy looks about him in growing terror.*

DYSART: What?

ALAN (*to* DYSART): He was there. Through the door. The door was shut, but he was there! . . . He'd seen everything. I could hear him. He was laughing.

DYSART: Laughing?

ALAN (*to* DYSART): Mocking! . . . *Mocking!* . . .

(*Standing downstage he stares up towards the*

tunnel. *A great silence weighs on the square.*)

(*To the silence: terrified.*) Friend . . . Equus the Kind . . . The Merciful! . . . *Forgive me!* . . .

(*Silence.*)

It wasn't me. Not really me. Me! . . . Forgive me! . . . Take me back again! Please! . . . PLEASE!

(*He kneels on the downstage lip of the square, still facing the door, huddling in fear.*)

I'll never do it again. I swear . . . I swear! . . .

(*Silence.*)

(*In a moan.*) Please! ! ! . . .
    DYSART: And He? What does He say?
    ALAN (*to* DYSART: *whispering*): "Mine! . . . You're mine! . . . I am yours and you are mine!" . . . Then I see his eyes. They are rolling!

(NUGGET *begins to advance slowly, with relentless hooves, down the central tunnel.*)

"I see you. I see you. Always! Everywhere! Forever!"
    DYSART: Kiss anyone and I will see?
    ALAN (*to* DYSART): Yes!
    DYSART: Lie with anyone and I will see?
    ALAN (*to* DYSART): Yes!
    DYSART: And you will fail! Forever and ever you will *fail!* You will see ME — and you will FAIL!

(*The boy turns round, hugging himself in pain. From the sides two more horses converge with* NUGGET *on the rails. Their hooves stamp angrily. The Equus noise is heard more terribly.*)

The Lord thy God is a Jealous God. He sees you. He sees you forever and ever, Alan. He sees you! . . . *He sees you!*
    ALAN (*in terror*): Eyes! . . . White eyes — never closed! Eyes like flames — coming — coming! . . . God seest! God seest! . . . NO! . . .

(*Pause. He steadies himself. The stage begins to blacken.*)

(*Quieter.*) No more. No more, Equus.

(*He gets up. He goes to the bench. He takes up the invisible pick. He moves slowly upstage towards* NUGGET, *concealing the weapon behind his naked back, in the growing darkness. He stretches out his hand and fondles* NUGGET's *mask.*)

(*Gently.*) Equus . . . Noble Equus . . . Faithful and True . . . Godslave . . . Thou — God — Seest — NOTHING!

(*He stabs out* NUGGET's *eyes. The horse stamps in agony. A great screaming begins to fill the theatre, growing ever louder.* ALAN *dashes at the other two horses and blinds them too, stabbing over the rails. Their metal hooves join in the stamping.*
Relentlessly, as this happens, three more horses appear in cones of light: not naturalistic animals like the first three, but dreadful creatures out of nightmare. Their eyes flare — their nostrils flare — their mouths flare. They are archetypal images — judging, punishing, pitiless. They do not halt at the rail, but invade the square. As they trample at him, the boy leaps desperately at them, jumping high and naked in the dark, slashing at their heads with arms upraised.
The screams increase. The other horses follow into the square. The whole place is filled with cannoning, blinded horses — and the boy dodging among them, avoiding their slashing hooves as best he can. Finally they plunge off into darkness and away out of sight. The noise dies abruptly, and all we hear is ALAN *yelling in hysteria as he collapses on the ground — stabbing at his own eyes with the invisible pick.*)

    ALAN: Find me! . . . Find me! . . . Find me! . . . KILL ME! . . . KILL ME! . . .

SCENE 35

The light changes quickly back to brightness. DYSART *enters swiftly, hurls a blanket on the left bench, and rushes over to* ALAN. *The boy is having convulsions on the floor.* DYSART *grabs his hands, forces them from his eyes, scoops him up in his arms and carries him over to the bench.* ALAN *hurls his arms round* DYSART *and clings to him, gasping and kicking his legs in dreadful frenzy.*

DYSART *lays him down and presses his head back on the bench. He keeps talking — urgently talking — soothing the agony as he can.*

DYSART: Here . . . Here . . . Ssssh . . . Ssssh . . . Calm now . . . Lie back. *Just lie back!* Now breathe in deep. Very deep. In . . . Out . . . In . . . Out . . . That's it. . . . In. Out . . . In . . . Out . . .

(*The boy's breath is drawn into his body with a harsh rasping sound, which slowly grows less.* DYSART *puts the blanket over him.*)

Keep it going . . . That's a good boy . . . Very good boy . . . It's all over now, Alan. It's all over. He'll go away now. You'll never see him again, I promise. You'll have no more bad dreams. No more awful nights. Think of that! . . . You are going to be well. I'm going to make you well, I promise you. . . . You'll be here for a while, but I'll be here too, so it won't be so bad. Just trust me . . .

(*He stands upright. The boy lies still.*)

Sleep now. Have a good long sleep. You've earned it. . . . Sleep. Just sleep. . . . I'm going to make you well.

(*He steps backwards into the centre of the square. The light brightens some more. A pause.*)

DYSART: I'm lying to you, Alan. He won't really go that easily. Just clop away from you like a nice old nag. Oh, no! When Equus leaves — if he leaves at all — it will be with your intestines in his teeth. And I don't stock replacements. . . . If you knew anything, you'd get up this minute and run from me fast as you could.

(HESTHER *speaks from her place.*)

HESTHER: The boy's in pain, Martin.
DYSART: Yes.
HESTHER: And you can take it away.
DYSART: Yes.
HESTHER: Then that has to be enough for you, surely? . . . In the end!
DYSART (*crying out*): *All right! I'll take it away!* He'll be delivered from madness. *What then?* He'll feel himself acceptable! *What then?* Do you think feelings like his can be simply re-attached, like plasters? Stuck on to other objects we select? *Look at him!* . . . My desire might be to make this boy an ardent husband — a caring citizen — a worshipper of abstract and unifying God. My achievement, however, is more likely to make a ghost! . . . Let me tell you exactly what I'm going to do to him!

(*He steps out of the square and walks round the upstage end of it, storming at the audience.*)

I'll heal the rash on his body. I'll erase the welts cut into his mind by flying manes. When that's done, I'll set him on a nice mini-scooter and send him puttering off into the Normal world where animals are treated *properly*: made extinct, or put into servitude, or tethered all their lives in dim light, just to feed it! I'll give him the good Normal world where we're tethered beside them — blinking our nights away in a nonstop drench of cathode-ray over our shrivelling heads! I'll take away his Field of Ha Ha, and give him Normal places for his ecstasy — multi-lane highways driven through the guts of cities, extinguishing Place altogether, *even the idea of Place!* He'll trot on his metal pony tamely through the concrete evening — and one thing I promise you: he will never touch hide again! With any luck his private parts will come to feel as plastic to him as the products of the factory to which he will almost certainly be sent. Who knows? He may even come to find sex funny. Smirky funny. Bit of grunt funny. Trampled and furtive and entirely in control. Hopefully, he'll feel nothing at his fork but Approved Flesh. I *doubt, however, with much passion!* . . . Passion, you see, can be destroyed by a doctor. It cannot be created.

(*He addresses* ALAN *directly, in farewell.*)

You won't gallop any more, Alan. Horses will be quite safe. You'll save your pennies every week, till you can change that scooter in for a car, and put the odd fifty P on the gee-gees, quite forgetting that they were ever anything more to you than bearers of little profits and little losses. You will, however, be without pain. More or less completely without pain.

(*Pause.*

He speaks directly to the theatre, standing by the motionless body of ALAN STRANG, *under the blanket.*)

And now for me it never stops: that voice of Equus out of the cave — "Why Me? . . . Why Me? . . . Account for Me!" . . . All right — I surrender! I say it . . . In an ultimate sense I cannot know what I do in this place — yet I do ultimate things. Essentially I cannot know what I do — yet I do essential things. Irreversible, terminal things. I stand in the dark with a pick in my hand, striking at heads!

(*He moves away from* ALAN, *back to the downstage bench, and finally sits.*)

I need — more desperately than my children need me — a way of seeing in the dark. What way is this? . . . *What dark is this?* . . . I cannot call it ordained of God: I can't get that far. I will however pay it so much homage. There is now, in my mouth, this sharp chain. And it never comes out.

(*A long pause.*
DYSART *sits staring.*)

BLACKOUT

The first play in this group of tragedies, and the most ancient, is Sophocles' *Oedipus the King* (about 430 B.C.). It is a commonplace of dramatic criticism that *Oedipus* is a sort of detective story in which the detective, Oedipus, searches for the criminal and discovers that he himself is the object of his search. Part of the greatness of the play surely resides in the fact that Oedipus, in his relentless search for the truth, strips away all comforting illusions, pursuing his quest even when it becomes evident that he himself may be the culprit. Oedipus' triumph, and, in part, ours as we watch him, is that he is determined to know the truth at whatever cost.

In some ways, Peter Shaffer's *Equus*, too, is a sort of detective story. We are told at the start of the play that Alan Strang has blinded six horses. As the play progresses, we learn, through the psychiatrist's careful analytic or detective work, why Alan blinded the horses. The analyst uses the devices of a detective: for example, he invites himself to the boy's home to see what he can learn, and he does so on a Sunday: "If there's any tension over religion, it should be evident on a Sabbath evening." And bit by bit the full story of the crime is revealed. In Scene 6 we are told that Alan screams something that sounds like "Ek," but not until Scene 14 is this puzzle explained, when Alan's father mentions that he heard the boy say, "Equus my only begotten son." Similarly, we first hear about Jill, very casually, in Scene 12, but not until much later do we understand the part she played in Alan's life.

The stage-set itself — "tiers of seats in the fashion of a dissecting theatre" surrounding the place of action — contributes to this sense that we are watching a detective find his way, like a surgeon, to the hidden disease or crime. Two other implications of the set are also significant: the tiers surround a square that "resembles a railed boxing ring," and it is here that the two chief characters, Alan Strang and Dr. Martin Dysart, slug it out; the set perhaps also suggests a sort of courtroom, with Alan as both the witness and the criminal at the bar. The whole set, the square embraced by tiers on which spectators sit, is itself a sort of entire theater with actors and audience, but those of us who are spectators in the auditorium are linked to the action by means of our fellow spectators who, like the audience in a Greek amphitheater, sit in the tiers. We are onlookers, but insofar as we are aware of the spectators in the tiers we are looking at people like ourselves, and all of us are looking at a boy who had "always been such a gentle boy," and who had seemed, to the owner of the stable, an ideal stable-hand. We are watching, then, the uncovering of the deepest feelings that reside in what seems — or had seemed — to be a fairly ordinary boy.

But of course Alan is not a fairly ordinary boy; he had only seemed to be one. Although it is risky enough even for experts to try to psychoanalyze real people, and it is usually foolish to try to psychoanalyze characters in a play, it seems fairly clear that Alan is schizoid. That is, he has markedly withdrawn from reality. As the play progresses, we come to see that Alan, like the classic schizophrenic — at least as understood by R. D. Laing in *The Politics of Experience* (1967) — allows his outer self to live in the normal world (Alan lives a humdrum life at home and in the electrical supply store) but preserves an inner self that is radically contemptuous of the normal world and that sometimes suddenly shows itself in some violent, unsocial action. The inner life of such a person is more "real" than the outer, daily bodily life, and so Alan can insist to his god Equus, after the abortive sexual episode with Jill, "It wasn't me. Not really me." This is not mere weaseling; for the schizophrenic, there is a sharp separation between the real, inner "me" and the body that goes through a daily hateful routine.

In his prefatory material Shaffer tells us that the play had its origins in a real occurrence, but it is clear, too, that the play is also indebted to a Freudian interpretation of reality, and it may not be a coincidence that horses figure in one of Freud's most interesting analyses, the case of Little Hans: Hans feared that he would be bitten by a horse, and it seems fairly clear that the horse symbolized Hans's father, a potential castrator. We can compare Hans's father to Alan's father, Frank Strang, who deprives his child of various pleasures and who, when he pulled the child Alan off a horse, caused the boy to fall. This is not, of course, to suggest that the play is a dramatization of the case of Little Hans, or of any specific case, for Shaffer tells us that although he began with a real episode he had recently heard of, he freely changed it as he worked on his play. For Alan, the horse is not (as it was for Hans) simply frightening: it is, among other things, an escape from the father and the dull world he represents ("Come on, Trojan — bear me away"). "All that power going any way you wanted," and "Then suddenly I was on the ground where Dad pulled me. I could have bashed him." Moreover, the horse is the god Alan worships. This worship is filled with echoes from the Bible, especially with suggestions of Christ. Equus, "born in the straw," is "in chains" for "the sins of the world"; when Alan takes Nugget out of the stable, he gives the horse a lump of sugar which is "His last supper"; when the horse eats the sugar he takes upon himself Alan's "sins," and Alan says, "Into my hands he commends himself," echoing Jesus' words in Luke 23:46, "Father, into thy hands I commend my spirit." And Alan, fascinated by Nugget's eyes, believes Nugget sees everything, because Alan's mother had said, "God sees you, Alan. God's got eyes everywhere."

It is interesting to note that in the early drafts of the play both parents were religiously obsessed, but Shaffer reduced the mother's obsession and eliminated the father's, lest the audience find the boy too obvious or neat a case. As we shall see, the boy is not supposed to be understood as the sick manifestation of sick parents. The play seeks to be much more than a dramatization of schizoid behavior, and that is why it concerns us. It claims, finally, not to present one strange case but to offer a vision of life. (Similarly, if Sophocles' *Oedipus the King* were merely a dramatization of a man who killed his father and married his mother — if it were simply a dramatization of a curious episode rooted in the Oedipus complex — rather than a dramatization of what can be taken as a story of a hero, it would scarcely be of interest to more than a few psychiatrists.)

Any comments of what a play is "about" must, of course, be imprecise, for a play consists of thousands of details that inevitably make any summary and brief interpretation a distortion. Still, we can say that the play dramatizes not a curious case history but the tragic conflict between the world of passion and mystery and the world of numbness and sociability. We have seen glimpses of some such conflict in other tragedies: Oedipus' passionate desire to find out the truth about his origins, versus Iocasta's sensible suggestion that it is best to let sleeping dogs lie; or King Lear's madness on the heath ("I abjure all roofs"), versus his wicked daughters' seemingly reasonable view that old men should not try to hang on to the power they cannot effectively wield. The paradox in this play is that Dysart, the apparently rational psychiatrist who is charged with restoring Alan to the normal world, envies Alan's irrationality. It is Dysart's fate to be married to a dentist, a thoroughly sensible Scottish woman who cannot share his interest in the world of ancient art and ritual:

> I pass her a picture of the sacred acrobats of Crete leaping through the horns of running bulls — and she'll say: "Och, Martin, what an *absurred* thing to be doing! The Highland Games, now there's a *norrmal sport!*" Or she'll observe, just after I've told her a story from the Iliad: "You know, when you come to think of it, Agamemnon and that lot were nothing but a bunch of ruffians from the Gorbals, only with fancy names!" You get the picture. She's turned into a Shrink.

But what of Dysart himself? Is he an Alan who has somehow bridged the gulf and managed to live a socially useful life? First of all, as he knows, he has none of Alan's passion. His trips to Greece are not "wild returns . . . to the womb of civilization":

> Three weeks a year in the Peleponnese, every bed booked in advance, every meal paid for by vouchers, cautious jaunts in hired Fiats, suitcase crammed with Kao-Pectate! Such a fantastic surrender to the primitive. And I use that word endlessly: "primitive." "Oh, the primitive world," I say. "What instinctual truths were lost with it!" . . . I sit looking at pages of centaurs trampling the soil of Argos — and outside my window he is trying to *become one*, in a Hampshire field!

Dysart's awareness of his own lack of deep feeling and of separation from mystery makes him envy Alan, particularly Alan's pain. "His pain. His own. He made it." It is a curious fact that as we look at the sufferings of tragic characters — Oedipus insisting on an agonizing search for the truth that culminates when he blinds himself, Lear rejecting the shelter of a daughter's roof in preference to a stormy heath — we feel that these sufferings are, in a way, their most precious possession. Lesser people are numbed by sufferings, but by taking on sufferings tragic heroes somehow fulfill themselves. They choose their way of life, and all that it entails. With Melville's Ahab they say, "Oh, now I feel my topmost greatness in my topmost grief." Some such awareness causes Dysart to say, "That boy has known a passion more ferocious than I have felt in any second of my life. And let me tell you something: I envy it." He has been critical of his way, and he goes on to dissect his own failure:

> The finicky, critical husband looking through his art books on mythical Greece. What worship has *he* ever known? Real worship! Without worship you shrink, it's as brutal as that . . . I shrank my own life.

If Alan's tragedy is that he has chosen a life radically different from the normal world's, and he must suffer for it, Dysart's is that he chose the normal world, and he suffers — though less intensely — from the knowledge that he has made the wrong choice. Even at the start of the play we heard suggestions to this effect. Dysart tells us that he is

> all reined up in old language and old assumptions, straining to jump clean-hoofed on to a whole new track of being I only suspect is there. I can't see it, because my educated, average head is being held at the wrong angle. I can't jump because the bit forbids it, and my own basic force — my horsepower, if you like — is too little. The only thing I know for sure is this: a horse's head is finally unknowable to me. Yet I handle children's heads — which I must presume to be more complicated, at least in the area of my chief concern. . . . In a way, it has nothing to do with this boy. The doubts have been there for years, piling up steadily in this dreary place. It's only the extremity of this case that's made them active. I know that. The *extremity* is the point.

Tragic heroes thrive on "extremity," situations in which all of the normal responses, all of the world's good sense, prove to be inadequate, or at least are found to be inadequate by the passionate individual who cannot let well enough alone, who cannot go along with the way of the world. We can think of Oedipus' determination to learn of his parentage, or Lear's determination to do more than merely subsist. As Arthur Miller puts it on page 306, the tragic hero "is ready to lay down his life, if need be, to secure one thing — his sense of personal dignity."

Dysart clearly sees himself as one who does go the way of the world, as one who is unwilling, or unable, to lay down his life in order to achieve his personal dignity. His job is to make people normal, to make healthy the sick, but he has come to feel that he is the "priest" of the "murderous God of Health." On the first night after he meets Alan he dreams that he sacrifices children to the "normal," but he cannot bring himself to sacrifice himself to his new insight. On the other hand, Alan, superficially a most unlikely tragic hero, rides with the god Equus against the world of the normal, against "The Hosts of Hoover. The Hosts of Philco. . . . The House of Remington and all its tribe." It is Dysart's job to reconcile Alan to the normal world that Dysart scorns and yet participates in. It is, in short, Dysart's sickening job to deprive Alan of the worship of Equus. "Can you think of anything worse one can do to anybody than to take away their worship?" Or to take away the pain by which a worshipper knows he has preserved himself from the deadly claims of a normal, socialized world? Dysart may be able to cure Alan of his worship of Equus, but only at the cost of robbing Alan of his most precious possession. "If you knew anything, you'd get up this minute and run from me as fast as you could. . . . My desire might be to make this boy an ardent husband — a caring citizen — a worshipper of abstract and unifying God. My achievement, however, is more likely to make a ghost." If we have read *Oedipus* and *Lear*, we are familiar with a vision that shows greatness finding itself in a painful sacrifice of self. And this sacrifice somehow purifies or strengthens the society that survives it. In *Equus*, Shaffer suggests that the sacrifice of the deeply feeling hero brings not new strength or health to society but only death, or death in life, for it represents only the triumph of the normal.

The normal, reasonable, social world has always been opposed to the world of tragic heroes and tragic poets. Plato, in *The Republic*, in a passage called "The Myth of Er," tells how the tragic king Agamemnon chose to be reincarnated as an eagle, thereby implying that the passionate, tragic figure is at heart really less than a human being, not more than one. And in the same book Plato bans the tragic poets from his ideal city because they feed the passions instead of starving them as rational men wish. *The Republic* is no less great a vision of man than any tragic play, but it is a very different vision, and — like a tragic play — it cannot tell the whole truth.

A few words must be said about the nudity in Scene 33 because it has provoked much comment. Surely, however, one thing it does not provoke is any erotic feeling. It is not strictly necessary, since in an earlier scene Alan simply mimes taking off his clothes, but it is entirely justifiable theatrically. In a way, it is foreshadowed in Scene 23, when Dysart explains to Alan's mother that the boy is "at a most delicate stage of treatment! He's totally exposed." And so in Scene 33, when Alan, reliving the sexual episode with Jill, collapses under the stress of his betrayal and failure, it is not only literally appropriate but also symbolically appropriate for him to be utterly naked, utterly vulnerable. Of course Shakespeare was content, when Lear tears at his clothes, to keep Lear minimally attired, and O'Neill similarly did not strip the Emperor Jones of every shred of clothing. But, as Brecht says (see p. 573), much tragic drama is a sort of striptease in which an individual's "innermost being is . . . driven into the open," and Shaffer has only made explicit and theatrical what is implicit. If the device has a fault, it is not that it is obscene but that it may embarrass an audience.

The Poetics

Aristotle

Translated by L. J. Potts

It is no exaggeration to say that the history of tragic criticism is a series of footnotes to Aristotle. In a fragmentary treatise usually called the *Poetics*, Aristotle (384–322 B.C.) raises almost all the points that have subsequently been argued, such as the nature of the hero, the emotional effect on the spectator, the coherence of the plot. Whether or not he gave the right answers, it has seemed for more than two thousand years that he asked the right questions.

[ART IS IMITATION]

Let us talk of the art of poetry as a whole, and its different species with the particular force of each of them; how the fables must be put together if the poetry is to be well formed; also what are its elements and their different qualities; and all other matters pertaining to the subject.

To begin in the proper order, at the beginning. The making of epics and of tragedies, and also comedy, and the art of the dithyramb, and most flute and lyre art, all have this in common, that they are imitations. But they differ from one another in three respects: the different kinds of medium in which they imitate, the different objects they imitate, and the different manner in which they imitate (when it does differ).... When the imitators imitate the doings of people, the people in the imitation must be either high or low; the characters almost always follow this line exclusively, for all men differ in character according to their degree of goodness or badness. They must therefore be either above our norm, or below it, or normal; as, in painting, Polygnōtus depicted superior, Pauson inferior, and Dionysius normal, types. It is clear that each variant of imitation

Reprinted from *Aristotle on the Art of Fiction* by L. J. Potts by permission of Cambridge University Press. © 1953 by Cambridge University Press.

that I have mentioned will have these differences, and as the object imitated varies in this way so the works will differ. Even in the ballet, and in flute and lyre music, these dissimilarities can occur; and in the art that uses prose, or verse without music.... This is the difference that marks tragedy out from comedy; comedy is inclined to imitate persons below the level of our world, tragedy persons above it.

[ORIGINS OF POETRY]

There seem to be two causes that gave rise to poetry in general, and they are natural. The impulse to imitate is inherent in man from his childhood; he is distinguished among the animals by being the most imitative of them, and he takes the first steps of his education by imitating. Everyone's enjoyment of imitation is also inborn. What happens with works of art demonstrates this: though a thing itself is disagreeable to look at, we enjoy contemplating the most accurate representations of it — for instance, figures of the most despicable animals, or of human corpses. The reason for this lies in another fact: learning is a great pleasure, not only to philosophers but likewise to everyone else, however limited his gift for it may be. He enjoys looking at these representations, because in the act of studying them he is learning — identifying the object by an inference (for instance, recognizing who is the original of a portrait); since, if he happens not to have already seen the object depicted, it will not be the imitation as such that is giving him pleasure, but the finish of the workmanship, or the colouring, or some such other cause.

And just as imitation is natural to us, so also are music and rhythm (metres, clearly, are constituent parts of rhythms). Thus, from spontaneous beginnings, mankind developed poetry by a series of mostly minute changes out of these improvisations.

[THE ELEMENTS OF TRAGEDY]

Let us now discuss tragedy, having first picked up from what has been said the definition of its essence that has so far emerged. Tragedy, then, is an imitation of an action of high importance, complete and of some amplitude; in language enhanced by distinct and varying beauties; acted not narrated; by means of pity and fear effecting its purgation of these emotions. By the beauties enhancing the language I mean rhythm and melody; by "distinct and varying" I mean that some are produced by metre alone, and others at another time by melody.

Now since the imitating is done by actors, it would follow of necessity that one element in a tragedy must be the *Mise en scène*. Others are Melody and Language, for these are the media in which the imitating is done. By Language, I mean the component parts of the verse, whereas Melody has an entirely sensuous effect. Again, since the object imitated is an action, and doings are done by persons, whose individuality will be determined by their Character and their Thought (for these are the factors we have in mind when we define the quality of their doings), it follows that there are two natural causes of these doings, Thought and Character; and these causes determine the good or ill fortune of everyone. But the Fable is the imitation of the action; and by the Fable I mean the whole structure of the incidents. By Character I mean the factor that enables us to define the particular quality of the people involved in the doings; and Thought is shown in everything they say when they are demonstrating a fact or disclosing an opinion. There are therefore necessarily six elements in every tragedy, which give it its quality; and they are the Fable, Character, Language, Thought, the *Mise en scène*, and Melody. Two of these are the media in which the imitating is done, one is the manner of imitation, and three are its objects; there is no other element besides these. Numerous poets have turned these essential components to account; all of them are always present — the *Mise en scene*, Character, the Fable, Language, Melody, and Thought.

The chief of these is the plotting of the incidents; for tragedy is an imitation not of men but of doings, life, happiness; unhappiness is located in doings, and our end is a certain kind of doing, not a personal quality; it is their characters that give men their quality, but their doings that make them happy or the opposite. So it is not the purpose of the actors to imitate character, but they include character as a factor in the doings. Thus it is the incidents (that is to say the Fable) that are the end for which tragedy exists; and the end is more important than anything else. Also, without an action there could not be a tragedy, but without Character there could. (In fact, the tragedies of most of the moderns are non-moral, and there are many non-moral poets of all periods; this also applies to the paintings of Zeuxis, if he is compared with Polygnōtus, for whereas Polygnōtus is a good portrayer of character the painting of Zeuxis leaves it out.) Again, if any one strings together moral speeches with the language and thought well worked out, he will be doing what is the business of tragedy; but it will be done much better by a tragedy that handles these elements more weakly, but has a fable with the incidents connected by a plot. Further, the chief means by which tragedy moves us, Irony of events and Disclosure, are elements in the Fable. A pointer in the same direction is that beginners in the art of poetry are able to get the language and characterization right before they can plot their incidents, and so were almost all the earliest poets.

So the source and as it were soul of tragedy is the Fable; and Character comes next. For, to instance a parallel from the art of painting, the most beautiful colours splashed on anyhow would not be as pleasing as a recognizable picture in black and white. Tragedy is an imitation of an action, and it is chiefly for this reason that it imitates the persons involved.

Third comes Thought: that is, the ability to say what circumstances allow and what is appropriate to them. It is the part played by social morality and rhetoric in making the dialogue: the old poets made their characters talk like men of the world, whereas our contemporaries make them talk like public speakers. Character

is what shows a man's disposition — the kind
of things he chooses or rejects when his choice is
not obvious. Accordingly those speeches where
the speaker shows no preferences or aversions
whatever are non-moral. Thought, on the other
hand, is shown in demonstrating a matter of
fact or disclosing a significant opinion.

Fourth comes the Language. By Language I
mean, as has already been said, words used se-
mantically. It has the same force in verse as in
prose.

Of the remaining elements, Melody is the
chief of the enhancing beauties. The *Mise en
scène* can excite emotion, but it is the crudest
element and least akin to the art of poetry; for
the force of tragedy exists even without stage
and actors; besides, the fitting out of a *Mise en
scène* belongs more to the wardrobe-master's
art than to the poet's.

[THE TRAGIC FABLE]

So much for analysis. Now let us discuss in
what sort of way the incidents should be plotted, since that is the first and chief consideration in tragedy. Our data are that tragedy is an
imitation of a whole and complete action of
some amplitude (a thing can be whole and yet
quite lacking in amplitude). Now a whole is
that which has a beginning, a middle, and an
end. A beginning is that which does not itself
necessarily follow anything else, but which leads
naturally to another event or development; an
end is the opposite, that which itself naturally
(either of necessity or most commonly) follows
something else, but nothing else comes after it;
and a middle is that which itself follows something else and is followed by another thing. So,
well-plotted fables must not begin or end casually, but must follow the pattern here described.

But, besides this, a picture, or any other com-
posite object, if it is to be beautiful, must not
only have its parts properly arranged, but be of
an appropriate size; for beauty depends on size
and structure. Accordingly, a minute picture
cannot be beautiful (for when our vision has almost lost its sense of time it becomes confused); nor can an immense one (for we cannot
take it all in together, and so our vision loses its
unity and wholeness) — imagine a picture a
thousand miles long! So, just as there is a
proper size for bodies and pictures (a size that
can be well surveyed), there is also a proper amplitude for fables (what can be kept well in
one's mind). The length of the performance on

the stage has nothing to do with art; if a hundred tragedies had to be produced, the length
of the production would be settled by the clock,
as the story goes that another kind of performance once was. But as to amplitude, the invariable rule dictated by the nature of the action is
the fuller the more beautiful so long as the outline remains clear; and for a simple rule of size,
the number of happenings that will make a
chain of probability (or necessity) to change a
given situation from misfortune to good fortune
or from good fortune to misfortune is the minimum.

[UNITY]

Unity in a fable does not mean, as some
think, that it has one man for its subject. To
any one man many things happen — an infinite
number — and some of them do not make any
sort of unity; and in the same way one man has
many doings which cannot be made into a unit
of action.... Accordingly, just as in the other
imitative arts the object of each imitation is a
unit, so, since the fable is an imitation of an action, that action must be a complete unit, and
the events of which it is made up must be so
plotted that if any of these elements is moved
or removed the whole is altered and upset. For
when a thing can be included or not included
without making any noticeable difference, that
thing is no part of the whole.

[PROBABILITY]

From what has been said it is also clear that
it is not the poet's business to tell what has happened, but the kind of things that would happen
— what is possible according to probability
or necessity. The difference between the his-
torian and the poet is not the difference between writing in verse or prose; the work of
Herodotus could be put into verse, and it would
be just as much a history in verse as it is in
prose. The difference is that the one tells what
has happened, and the other kind of things
that would happen. It follows therefore that
poetry is more philosophical and of higher value
than history; for poetry unifies more, whereas
history aggregates. To unify is to make a man of
a certain description say or do the things that
suit him, probably or necessarily, in the circumstances (this is the point of the descriptive
proper names in poetry); what Alcibiades did or
what happened to him is an aggregation. In
comedy this has now become clear. They first

plot the fable on a base of probabilities, and then find imaginary names for the people — unlike the lampooners, whose work was an aggregation of personalities. But in tragedy they keep to the names of real people. This is because possibility depends on conviction; if a thing has not happened we are not yet convinced that it is possible, but if it has happened it is clearly possible, for it would not have happened if it were impossible. Even tragedies, however, sometimes have all their persons fictitious except for one or two known names; and sometimes they have not a single known name, as in the *Anthos* of Agathon, in which both the events and the names are equally fictitious, without in the least reducing the delight it gives. It is not, therefore, requisite at all costs to keep to the traditional fables from which our tragedies draw their subject-matter. It would be absurd to insist on that, since even the known legends are known only to a few, and yet the delight is shared by every one. . . .

[SIMPLE AND COMPLEX FABLES]

The action imitated must contain incidents that evoke fear and pity, besides being a complete action; but this effect is accentuated when these incidents occur logically as well as unexpectedly, which will be more sensational than if they happen arbitrarily, by chance. Even when events are accidental the sensation is greater if they appear to have a purpose, as when the statue of Mitys at Argos killed the man who had caused his death, by falling on him at a public entertainment. Such things appear not to have happened blindly. Inevitably, therefore, plots of this sort are finer.

Some fables are simple, others complex: for the obvious reason that the original actions imitated by the fables are the one or the other. By a simple action I mean one that leads to the catastrophe in the way we have laid down, directly and singly, without Irony of events or Disclosure.

An action is complex when the catastrophe involves Disclosure, or Irony, or both. But these complications should develop out of the very structure of the fable, so that they fit what has gone before, either necessarily or probably. To happen after something is by no means the same as to happen because of it.

[IRONY]

Irony is a reversal in the course of events, of the kind specified, and, as I say, in accordance with probability or necessity. Thus in the *Oedipus* the arrival of the messenger, which was expected to cheer Oedipus up by releasing him from his fear about his mother, did the opposite by showing him who he was; and in the *Lynceus* [Abas], who was awaiting sentence of death, was acquitted, whereas his prosecutor Dănaüs was killed, and all this arose out of what had happened previously.

A Disclosure, as the term indicates, is a change from ignorance to knowledge; if the people are marked out for good fortune it leads to affection, if for misfortune, to enmity. Disclosure produces its finest effect when it is connected with Irony, as the disclosure in the *Oedipus* is. There are indeed other sorts of Disclosure: the process I have described can even apply to inanimate objects of no significance, and mistakes about what a man has done or not done can be cleared up. But the sort I have specified is more a part of the fable and of the action than any other sort; for this coupling of Irony and Disclosure will carry with it pity or fear, which we have assumed to be the nature of the doings tragedy imitates; and further, such doings will constitute good or ill fortune. Assuming then that it is a disclosure of the identity of persons, it may be of one person only, to the other, when the former knows who the latter is; or sometimes both have to be disclosed — for instance, the sending of the letter led Orestes to the discovery of Iphigeneia, and there had to be another disclosure to make him known to her.

This then is the subject-matter of two elements in the Fable, Irony and Disclosure. A third element is the Crisis of feeling. Irony and Disclosure have been defined; the Crisis of feeling is a harmful or painful experience, such as deaths in public, violent pain, physical injuries, and everything of that sort.

[THE TRAGIC PATTERN]

Following the proper order, the next subject to discuss after this would be: What one should aim at and beware of in plotting fables; that is to say, What will produce the tragic effect. Since, then, tragedy, to be at its finest, requires a complex, not a simple, structure, and its structure should also imitate fearful and pitiful events (for that is the peculiarity of this sort of imitation), it is clear: first, that decent people must not be shown passing from good fortune to misfortune (for that is not fearful or pitiful but disgusting); again, vicious people must not be shown passing from misfortune to good fortune (for that is the most untragic situation possible — it has none of the requisites, it is neither humane, nor pitiful, nor fearful); nor again should an utterly evil man fall from good fortune into misfortune (for though a plot of that kind would be humane, it would not induce pity or fear — pity is induced by undeserved misfortune, and fear by the misfortunes of normal people, so that this situation will be neither pitiful nor fearful). So we are left with the man between these extremes: that is to say, the kind of man who neither is distinguished for excellence and virtue, nor comes to grief on account of baseness and vice, but on account of some error; a man of great reputation and prosperity, like Oedipus and Thyestes and conspicuous people of such families as theirs. So, to be well informed, a fable must be single rather than (as some say) double — there must be no change from misfortune to good fortune, but only the opposite, from good fortune to misfortune; the cause must not be vice, but a great error; and the man must be either of the type specified or better, rather than worse. This is borne out by the practice of poets; at first they picked a fable at random and made an inventory of its contents, but now the finest tragedies are plotted, and concern a few families — for example, the tragedies about Alcmeon, Oedipus, Orestes, Mĕlĕager, Thyestes, Tēlĕphus, and any others whose lives were attended by terrible experiences or doings.

This is the plot that will produce the technically finest tragedy. Those critics are therefore wrong who censure Euripides on this very ground — because he does this in his tragedies, and many of them end in misfortune; for it is, as I have said, the right thing to do. This is clearly demonstrated on the stage in the competitions, where such plays, if they succeed, are the most tragic, and Euripides, even if he is inefficient in every other respect, still shows himself the most tragic of our poets. The next best plot, which is said by some people to be the best, is the tragedy with a double plot, like the *Odyssey*, ending in one way for the better people and in the opposite way for the worse. But it is the weakness of theatrical performances that gives priority to this kind; when poets write what the audience would like to happen, they are in leading strings. This is not the pleasure proper to tragedy, but rather to comedy, where the greatest enemies in the fable, say Orestes and Aegisthus, make friends and go off at the end, and nobody is killed by anybody.

[THE TRAGIC EMOTIONS]

The pity and fear can be brought about by the *Mise en scène;* but they can also come from the mere plotting of the incidents, which is preferable, and better poetry. For, without seeing anything, the fable ought to have been so plotted that if one heard the bare facts, the chain of circumstances would make one shudder and pity. That would happen to anyone who heard the fable of the *Oedipus.* To produce this effect by the *Mise en scène* is less artistic and puts one at the mercy of the technician; and those who use it not to frighten but merely to startle have lost touch with tragedy altogether. We should not try to get all sorts of pleasure from tragedy, but the particular tragic pleasure. And clearly, since this pleasure coming from pity and fear has to be produced by imitation, it is by his handling of the incidents that the poet must create it.

Let us, then, take next the kind of circumstances that seem terrible or lamentable. Now, doings of that kind must be between friends, or enemies, or neither. If an enemy injures an enemy, there is no pity either beforehand or at the time, except on account of the bare fact; nor is there if they are neutral; but when sufferings are engendered among the affections — for example, if murder is done or planned, or some similar outrage is committed, by brother on brother, or son on father, or mother on son, or son on mother — that is the thing to aim at.

Though it is not permissible to ruin the traditional fables — I mean, such as the killing of Clytemnestra by Orestes, or Erīphyle by Alcmeon — the poet should use his own invention to refine on what has been handed down to him. Let me explain more clearly what I mean by "refine." The action may take place, as the old poets used to make it, with the knowledge and understanding of the participants; this was how Euripides made Medea kill her children. Or they may do it, but in ignorance of the horror of the deed, and then afterwards discover the tie of affection, like the Oedipus of Sophocles; his act was outside the play, but there are examples where it is inside the tragedy itself — Alcmeon in the play by Astydāmas, or Tēlĕgōnus in *The Wounded Odysseus.* Besides these, there is a third possibility: when a man is about to do some fatal act in ignorance, but is enlightened before he does it. These are the only possible alternatives. One must either act or not act, and either know or not know. Of these alternatives, to know, and to be about to act, and then not to act, is thoroughly bad — it is disgusting without being tragic, for there is no emotional crisis; accordingly poets only rarely create such situations, as in the *Antigone*, when Haemon fails to kill Creon. Next in order is to act; and if the deed is done in ignorance and its nature is disclosed afterwards, so much the better — there is no bad taste in it, and the revelation is overpowering. But the last is best; I mean, like Měrŏpe in the *Cresphontes*, intending to kill her son, but recognizing him and not killing him; and the brother and sister in the *Iphigeneia*; and in the *Helle*, the son recognizing his mother just as he was going to betray her. — This is the reason for what was mentioned earlier: that the subject-matter of our tragedies is drawn from a few families. In their search for matter they discovered this recipe in the fables, not by cunning but by luck. So they are driven to have recourse to those families where such emotional crises have occurred. . . .

[CHARACTER]

And in the characterization, as in the plot-ting of the incidents, the aim should always be either necessity or probability: so that they say or do such things as it is necessary or probable that they would, being what they are; and that for this to follow that is either necessary or probable. . . . As for extravagant incidents, there should be none in the story, or if there are they should be kept outside the tragedy, as is the one in the *Oedipus* of Sophocles.

Since tragedy is an imitation of people above the normal, we must be like good portrait-painters, who follow the original model closely, but refine on it; in the same way the poet, in imitating people whose character is choleric or phlegmatic, and so forth, must keep them as they are and at the same time make them attractive. So Homer made Achilles noble, as well as a pattern of obstinacy. . . .

[CHORUS]

Treat the chorus as though it were one of the actors; it should be an organic part of the play and reinforce it, not as it is in Euripides, but as in Sophocles. In their successors the songs belong no more to the fable than to that of any other tragedy. This has led to the insertion of borrowed lyrics, an innovation for which Agathon was responsible.

Tragedy and the Common Man

Arthur Miller

Arthur Miller's "Tragedy and the Common Man" was written while his *Death of a Salesman* was running on Broadway. Implicitly a defense of his play, the essay's assertions about the nature of the tragic hero have implications for other plays about middle-class figures and even for earlier tragedies with heroes of high rank.

In this age few tragedies are written. It has often been held that the lack is due to a paucity of heroes among us, or else that modern man has had the blood drawn out of his organs of belief by the skepticism of science, and the heroic attack on life cannot feed on an attitude of reserve and circumspection. For one reason or another, we are often held to be below tragedy — or tragedy above us. The inevitable conclusion is, of course, that the tragic mode is archaic, fit only for the very highly placed, the kings or the kingly, and where this admission is not made in so many words it is most often implied.

I believe that the common man is as apt a subject for tragedy in its highest sense as kings were. On the face of it this ought to be obvious in the light of modern psychiatry, which bases its analysis upon classific formulations, such as the Oedipus and Orestes complexes, for instance, which were enacted by royal beings, but which apply to everyone in similar emotional situations.

More simply, when the question of tragedy in art is not at issue, we never hesitate to attribute to the well-placed and the exalted the very same mental processes as the lowly. And finally, if the exaltation of tragic action were truly a property of the high-bred character alone, it is inconceivable that the mass of mankind should

cherish tragedy above all other forms, let alone be capable of understanding it.

As a general rule, to which there may be exceptions unknown to me, I think the tragic feeling is evoked in us when we are in the presence of a character who is ready to lay down his life, if need be, to secure one thing — his sense of personal dignity. From Orestes to Hamlet, Medea to Macbeth, the underlying struggle is that of the individual attempting to gain his "rightful" position in his society.

Sometimes he is one who has been displaced from it, sometimes one who seeks to attain it for the first time, but the fateful wound from which the inevitable events spiral is the wound of indignity, and its dominant force is indignation. Tragedy, then, is the consequence of a man's total compulsion to evaluate himself justly.

In the sense of having been initiated by the hero himself, the tale always reveals what has been called his "tragic flaw," a failing that is not peculiar to grand or elevated characters. Nor is it necessarily a weakness. The flaw, or crack in the character, is really nothing — and need be nothing — but his inherent unwillingness to remain passive in the face of what he conceives to be a challenge to his dignity, his image of his rightful status. Only the passive, only those who accept their lot without active retaliation, are "flawless." Most of us are in that category.

But there are among us today, as there always have been, those who act against the scheme of things that degrades them, and in the process of action, everything we have accepted out of fear or insensitivity or ignorance is shaken before us and examined, and from this total onslaught by an individual against the seemingly stable cosmos surrounding us — from this total examination of the "unchangeable" environment — comes the terror and the fear that is classically associated with tragedy.

More important, from this total questioning of what has been previously unquestioned, we learn. And such a process is not beyond the common man. In revolutions around the world, these past thirty years, he has demonstrated again and again this inner dynamic of all tragedy.

Insistence upon the rank of the tragic hero, or the so-called nobility of his character, is really but a clinging to the outward forms of tragedy. If rank or nobility of character was indispensable, then it would follow that the problems of those with rank were the particular problems of tragedy. But surely the right of one monarch to capture the domain from another no longer raises our passions, nor are our concepts of justice what they were to the mind of an Elizabethan king.

The quality in such plays that does shake us, however, derives from the underlying fear of being displaced, the disaster inherent in being torn away from our chosen image of what and who we are in this world. Among us today this fear is as strong, and perhaps stronger, than it ever was. In fact, it is the common man who knows this fear best.

Now, if it is true that tragedy is the consequence of a man's total compulsion to evaluate himself justly, his destruction in the attempt posits a wrong or an evil in his environment. And this is precisely the morality of tragedy and its lesson. The discovery of the moral law, which is what the enlightenment of tragedy consists of, is not the discovery of some abstract or metaphysical quantity.

The tragic right is a condition of life, a condition in which the human personality is able to flower and realize itself. The wrong is the condition which suppresses man, perverts the flowing out of his love and creative instinct. Tragedy enlightens — and it must, in that it points the heroic finger at the enemy of man's freedom. The thrust for freedom is the quality in tragedy which exalts. The revolutionary questioning of the stable environment is what terrifies. In no way is the common man debarred from such thoughts or such actions.

Seen in this light, our lack of tragedy may be partially accounted for by the turn which modern literature has taken toward the purely psychiatric view of life, or the purely sociological. If all our miseries, our indignities, are born and bred within our minds, then all action, let alone the heroic action, is obviously impossible.

And if society alone is responsible for the cramping of our lives, then the protagonist must needs be so pure and faultless as to force us to deny his validity as a character. From neither of these views can tragedy derive, simply because neither represents a balanced concept of life. Above all else, tragedy requires the finest appreciation by the writer of cause and effect.

No tragedy can therefore come about when its author fears to question absolutely everything, when he regards any institution, habit or custom as being either everlasting, immutable or inevitable. In the tragic view the need of man to wholly realize himself is the only fixed star, and whatever it is that hedges his nature and lowers it is ripe for attack and examination. Which is not to say that tragedy must preach revolution.

The Greeks could probe the very heavenly origin of their ways and return to confirm the rightness of laws. And Job could face God in anger, demanding his right, and end in submission. But for a moment everything is in suspension, nothing is accepted, and in this stretching and tearing apart of the cosmos, in the very action of so doing, the character gains "size," the tragic stature which is spuriously attached to the royal or the high born in our minds. The commonest of men may take on that stature to the extent of his willingness to throw all he has into the contest, the battle to secure his rightful place in his world.

There is a misconception of tragedy with which I have been struck in review after review, and in many conversations with writers and readers alike. It is the idea that tragedy is of necessity allied to pessimism. Even the dictionary says nothing more about the word than that it means a story with a sad or unhappy ending. This impression is so firmly fixed that I almost hesitate to claim that in truth tragedy implies more optimism in its author than does comedy, and that its final result ought to be the reinforcement of the onlooker's brightest opinions of the human animal.

For, if it is true to say that in essence the tragic hero is intent upon claiming his whole due as a personality, and if this struggle must be total and without reservation, then it automatically demonstrates the indestructible will of man to achieve his humanity.

The possibility of victory must be there in tragedy. Where pathos rules, where pathos is finally derived, a character has fought a battle he could not possibly have won. The pathetic is achieved when the protagonist is, by virtue of his witlessness, his insensitivity, or the very air he gives off, incapable of grappling with a much superior force.

Pathos truly is the mode for the pessimist.

But tragedy requires a nicer balance between what is possible and what is impossible. And it is curious, although edifying, that the plays we revere, century after century, are the tragedies. In them, and in them alone, lies the belief — optimistic, if you will — in the perfectibility of man.

It is time, I think, that we who are without kings, took up this bright thread of our history and followed it to the only place it can possibly lead in our time — the heart and spirit of the average man.

COMEDY

LYSISTRATA

Aristophanes

English version by Dudley Fitts

Nothing of much interest is known about Aristophanes (c. 450 B.C.–c. 385 B.C.). An Athenian, he competed for about forty years in the annual festivals of comic drama to which three playwrights each contributed one play. His first play was produced in 427 B.C., his last extant play in 388 B.C., but he is known to have written two comedies after this date. Of the forty or so plays he wrote, eleven survive. *Lysistrata* (accent on the second syllable) was produced in 411 B.C.

PERSONS REPRESENTED

LYSISTRATA
KALONIKE
MYRRHINE
LAMPITO
CHORUS
COMMISSIONER
KINESIAS
SPARTAN HERALD
SPARTAN AMBASSADOR
A SENTRY

Until the *éxodos*, the CHORUS is divided into two hemichori: the first, of Old Men; the second, of Old Women. Each of these has its KORYPHAIOS [i.e., leader]. In the *éxodos*, the hemichori return as Athenians and Spartans.

The supernumeraries include the BABY SON of Kinesias; STRATYL-LIS, a member of the hemichorus of Old Women; various individual speakers, both Spartan and Athenian.

Scene: Athens. First, a public square; later, beneath the walls of the Akropolis; later, a courtyard within the Akropolis.

Patrick Hines in the Phoenix Theater production of *Lysistrata* in New York, 1959. (Photograph: Joseph Abeles Studio.)

PROLOGUE

[*Athens; a public square; early morning;* LYSISTRATA *alone.*]

LYSISTRATA:
If someone had invited them to a festival —
of Bacchos, say; or to Pan's shrine, or to
    Aphrodite's°[1]
over at Kolias —, you couldn't get through
    the streets,
what with the drums and the dancing. But
    now,
not a woman in sight!
                 Except — oh, yes!

5

[*Enter* KALONIKE.]

Here's one of my neighbors, at last. Good
morning, Kalonike.
    KALONIKE: Good morning, Lysistrata.
                              Darling,
don't frown so! You'll ruin your face!
    LYSISTRATA: Never mind my face.
Kalonike,
the way we women behave! Really, I don't

10   blame the men
for what they say about us.
    KALONIKE: No; I imagine they're right.
    LYSISTRATA:
For example: I call a meeting
to think out a most important matter — and
    what happens?
The women all stay in bed!
    KALONIKE: Oh, they'll be along.
It's hard to get away, you know: a husband, a

15   cook,

Lysistrata by Aristophanes: New English Version by Dudley Fitts, copyright 1954 by Harcourt Brace Jovanovich, Inc. and reprinted with their permission. *Caution:* All rights, including professional, amateur, motion picture, recitation, lecturing, public reading, radio broadcasting, and television are strictly reserved. Inquiries on all rights should be addressed to Harcourt Brace Jovanovich, Inc., 757 Third Avenue, New York, N.Y. 10017.

[1] The degree sign (°) indicates a footnote, which is keyed to the text by the line number. Text references are printed in **boldface** type; the annotation follows in lightface type.

2 **Bacchos, Pan, Aphrodite:** The first two are gods associated with wine; Aphrodite is the goddess of love.

a child . . . Home life can be *so* demanding!
    LYSISTRATA:
What I have in mind is even more demanding.
    KALONIKE:
Tell me: what is it?
    LYSISTRATA: It's big.
    KALONIKE: Goodness! *How* big?
    LYSISTRATA:
Big enough for all of us.
    KALONIKE: But we're not all here!
    LYSISTRATA:
We would be, if *that's* what was up!
                      No, Kalonike, 20
this is something I've been turning over for
    nights,
long sleepless nights.
    KALONIKE: It must be getting worn down, then,
if you've spent so much time on it.
    LYSISTRATA: Worn down or not,
it comes to this: Only we women can save
    Greece!
    KALONIKE:
Only we women? Poor Greece!
    LYSISTRATA: Just the same, 25
it's up to us. First, we must liquidate
the Peloponnesians —
    KALONIKE: Fun, fun!
    LYSISTRATA: — and then the Boiotians.°
    KALONIKE:
Oh! But not those heavenly eels!
    LYSISTRATA: You needn't worry.
I'm not talking about eels. — But here's the
    point:
If we can get the women from those places — 30
all those Boiotians and Peloponnesians —
to join us women here, why, we can save
all Greece!
    KALONIKE: But dearest Lysistrata!
How can women do a thing so austere, so
political? We belong at home. Our only
    armor's 35
our perfumes, our saffron dresses and
our pretty little shoes!
    LYSISTRATA: Exactly. Those
transparent dresses, the saffron, the

27 **Boiotia:** A country north of Attika, noted for the crudity of its inhabitants and the excellence of its seafood.

perfume, those pretty shoes —

KALONIKE: Oh?

LYSISTRATA: Not a single man would lift
his spear —

KALONIKE:

40   I'll send my dress to the dyer's tomorrow!

LYSISTRATA:
— or grab a shield —

KALONIKE: The sweetest little negligée —

LYSISTRATA:
— or haul out his sword.

KALONIKE: I know where I can buy
the dreamiest sandals!

LYSISTRATA:
          Well, so you see. Now, shouldn't
the women have come?

KALONIKE: Come? They should have *flown!*

LYSISTRATA:
Athenians are always late.

45   But imagine!
There's no one here from the South Shore, or
    from Salamis.

KALONIKE:
Things are hard over in Salamis, I swear.
They have to get going at dawn.

LYSISTRATA: And nobody from Acharnai.
I thought they'd be here hours ago.

KALONIKE: Well, you'll get

50 that awful Theagenes woman: she'll be
a sheet or so in the wind.

                But look!
Someone at last! Can you see who they are?

[*Enter* MYRRHINE *and other women.*]

LYSISTRATA:
They're from Anagyros.

KALONIKE: They certainly are.
You'd know them anywhere, by the scent.

MYRRHINE:
Sorry to be late, Lysistrata.

55   Oh come,
don't scowl so. Say something!

LYSISTRATA: My dear Myrrhine,
what is there to say? After all,
you've been pretty casual about the whole
    thing.

MYRRHINE: Couldn't find
my girdle in the dark, that's all.

              But what *is*
"the whole thing"?

60   KALONIKE: No, we've got to wait
for those Boiotians and Peloponnesians.

LYSISTRATA:
That's more like it. — But, look!

Here's Lampito!

[*Enter* LAMPITO *with women from Sparta.*]

LYSISTRATA: Darling Lampito,
how pretty you are today! What a nice color!
Goodness, you look as though you could
    strangle a bull!   65

LAMPITO:
Ah think Ah could! It's the work-out
in the gym every day; and, of co'se that dance
    of ahs
where y' kick yo' own tail.

KALONIKE: What an adorable figure!

LAMPITO:
Lawdy, when y' touch me lahk that,
Ah feel lahk a heifer at the altar!

LYSISTRATA: And this young lady?   70
Where is she from?

LAMPITO: Boiotia. Social-Register type.

LYSISTRATA:
Ah. "Boiotia of the fertile plain."

KALONIKE: And if you look,
you'll find the fertile plain has just been
    mowed.

LYSISTRATA:
And this lady?

LAMPITO: Hagh, wahd, handsome. She
    comes from Korinth.

KALONIKE:
High and wide's the word for it.

LAMPITO: Which one of you   75
called this heah meeting, and why?

LYSISTRATA: I did.

LAMPITO: Well, then, tell us:
What's up?

MYRRHINE: Yes, darling, what *is* on your
    mind, after all?

LYSISTRATA:
I'll tell you. — But first, one little question.

MYRRHINE: Well?

LYSISTRATA:
It's your husbands. Fathers of your children.
    Doesn't it bother you
that they're always off with the Army? I'll
    stake my life,   80
not one of you has a man in the house this
    minute!

KALONIKE:
Mine's been in Thrace the last five months,
    keeping an eye
on that General.

MYRRHINE: Mine's been in Pylos for seven.

LAMPITO: And mahn,
whenever he gets a *dis*charge, he goes raht back

85 with that li'l ole shield of his, and enlists again!
LYSISTRATA:
And not the ghost of a lover to be found!
From the very day the war began —
                              those Milesians!
I could skin them alive!
                    — I've not seen so much, even,
as one of those leather consolation prizes. —
But there! What's important is: If I've found
90   a way
to end the war, are you with me?
MYRRHINE: I should *say* so!
Even if I have to pawn my best dress and
drink up the proceeds.
KALONIKE: Me, too! Even if they split me
right up the middle, like a flounder.
LAMPITO: Ah'm shorely with you.
95 Ah'd crawl up Taygetos° on mah knees
if that'd bring peace.
LYSISTRATA: All right, then; here it is:
Women! Sisters!
If we really want our men to make peace,
we must be ready to give up —
MYRRHINE: Give up what?
Quick, tell us!
LYSISTRATA:
          But *will* you?
100   MYRRHINE: We will, even if it kills us.
LYSISTRATA:
Then we must give up going to bed with our
      men.
[*Long silence.*]
Oh? So now you're sorry? Won't look at me?
Doubtful? Pale? All teary-eyed?
                    But come: be frank with me.
Will you do it, or not? Well? Will you do it?
MYRRHINE: I couldn't. No.
Let the war go on.
105   KALONIKE: Nor I. Let the war go on.
LYSISTRATA:
You, you little flounder,
ready to be split up the middle?
KALONIKE: Lysistrata, no!
I'd walk through fire for you — you *know* I
      would! — but don't
ask us to give up *that*! Why, there's nothing
      like it!
LYSISTRATA:
And you?
BOIOTIAN:
110   No. I must say *I'd* rather walk through fire.

95 **Taygetos**: A mountain range.

LYSISTRATA:
What an utterly perverted sex we women are!
No wonder poets write tragedies about us.
There's only one thing we can think of.
                    But you from Sparta:
if you stand by me, we may win yet! Will you?
It means so much!
LAMPITO: Ah sweah, it means *too* much! 115
By the Two Goddesses, it does! Asking a girl
to sleep — Heaven knows how long! — in a
      great big bed
with nobody there but herself! But Ah'll stay
      with you!
Peace comes first!
LYSISTRATA: Spoken like a true Spartan!
KALONIKE:
But if —
      oh dear!
          — if we give up what you tell us to,   120
will there *be* any peace?
LYSISTRATA:
               Why, mercy, of course there will!
We'll just sit snug in our very thinnest gowns,
perfumed and powdered from top to bottom,
      and those men
simply won't stand still! And when we say No,
they'll go out of their minds! And there's your
      peace.   125
You can take my word for it.
LAMPITO: Ah seem to remember
that Colonel Menelaos threw his sword away
when he saw Helen's breast all bare.
KALONIKE: But, goodness me!
What if they just get up and leave us?
LYSISTRATA: In that case
we'll have to fall back on ourselves, I suppose.   130
But they won't.
KALONIKE:
          I must say that's not much help. But
what if they drag us into the bedroom?
LYSISTRATA: Hang on to the door.
KALONIKE:
What if they slap us?
LYSISTRATA: If they do, you'd better give in.
But be sulky about it. Do I have to teach you
      how?
You know there's no fun for men when they
      have to force you.   135
There are millions of ways of getting them to
      see reason.
Don't you worry: a man
doesn't like it unless the girl co-operates.
KALONIKE:
I suppose so. Oh, all right. We'll go along.

LAMPITO:
Ah imagine us Spahtans can arrange a peace.
140   But you
Athenians! Why, you're just war-mongerers!
LYSISTRATA: Leave that to me.
I know how to make them listen.
LAMPITO: Ah don't see how.
After all, they've got their boats; and there's
    lots of money
piled up in the Akropolis.°
LYSISTRATA: The Akropolis? Darling,
145 we're taking over the Akropolis today!
That's the older women's job. All the rest of us
are going to the Citadel to sacrifice — you
    understand me?
And once there, we're in for good!
LAMPITO: Whee! Up the rebels!
Ah can see you're a good strate*egist*.
LYSISTRATA: Well, then, Lampito,
150 what we have to do now is take a solemn oath.
LAMPITO:
Say it. We'll sweah.
LYSISTRATA: This is it.
— But where's our Inner Guard?
                — Look, Guard: you see this shield?
Put it down here. Now bring me the victim's
    entrails.
KALONIKE:
But the oath?
LYSISTRATA:
        You remember how in Aischylos' *Seven*
they killed a sheep and swore on a shield?
155   Well, then?
KALONIKE:
But I don't see how you can swear for peace
    on a shield.
LYSISTRATA:
What else do you suggest?
KALONIKE: Why not a white horse?
We could swear by that.
LYSISTRATA:
        And where will you get a white horse?
KALONIKE:
I never thought of that. *What* can we do?
LYSISTRATA: I have it!
Let's set this big black wine-bowl on the
160   ground
and pour in a gallon or so of Thasian, and
    swear

144 **Akropolis:** At the beginning of the war,
Perikles stored emergency funds in the Akropolis,
the citadel sacred to Athene.

not to add one drop of water.
LAMPITO: Ah lahk *that* oath!
LYSISTRATA:
Bring the bowl and the wine-jug.
KALONIKE: Oh, what a simply *huge* one!
LYSISTRATA:
Set it down. Girls, place your hands on the
    gift-offering.

O Goddess of Persuasion! And thou, O
    Loving-cup: 165
Look upon this our sacrifice, and
be gracious!

KALONIKE:
See the blood spill out. How red and pretty
    it is!
LAMPITO:
And Ah must say it smells good.
MYRRHINE: Let me swear first!
KALONIKE:
No, by Aphrodite, we'll match for it!   170
LYSISTRATA:
Lampito: all of you women: come, touch the
    bowl,
and repeat after me — remember, this is an
    oath — :
I WILL HAVE NOTHING TO DO WITH
    MY HUSBAND OR MY LOVER
KALONIKE:
*I will have nothing to do with my husband or
    my lover*
LYSISTRATA:
THOUGH HE COME TO ME IN PITI-
    ABLE CONDITION   175
KALONIKE:
Though he come to me in pitiable condition
(Oh Lysistrata! This is killing me!)
LYSISTRATA:
IN MY HOUSE I WILL BE UNTOUCH-
    ABLE
KALONIKE:
In my house I will be untouchable
LYSISTRATA:
IN MY THINNEST SAFFRON SILK   180
KALONIKE:
In my thinnest saffron silk
LYSISTRATA:
AND MAKE HIM LONG FOR ME.
KALONIKE:
And make him long for me.
LYSISTRATA:
I WILL NOT GIVE MYSELF
KALONIKE:
I will not give myself   185

LYSISTRATA:
AND IF HE CONSTRAINS ME
KALONIKE:
And if he constrains me
LYSISTRATA:
I WILL BE COLD AS ICE AND NEVER
MOVE
KALONIKE:
I will be cold as ice and never move
LYSISTRATA:
190   I WILL NOT LIFT MY SLIPPERS
TOWARD THE CEILING
KALONIKE:
I will not lift my slippers toward the ceiling
LYSISTRATA:
OR CROUCH ON ALL FOURS LIKE THE
LIONESS IN THE CARVING
KALONIKE:
*Or crouch on all fours like the lioness in the
carving*
LYSISTRATA:
AND IF I KEEP THIS OATH LET ME
DRINK FROM THIS BOWL
KALONIKE:
And if I keep this oath let me drink from this
195   *bowl*
LYSISTRATA:
IF NOT, LET MY OWN BOWL BE
FILLED WITH WATER.
KALONIKE:
If not, let my own bowl be filled with water.
LYSISTRATA:
You have all sworn?
MYRRHINE: We have.
LYSISTRATA: Then thus
I sacrifice the victim.

[*Drinks largely.*]

KALONIKE: Save some for us!
200   Here's to you, darling, and to you, and to you!
[*Loud cries off-stage.*]
LAMPITO:
What's all *that* whoozy-goozy?
LYSISTRATA: Just what I told you.
The older women have taken the Akropolis.
Now you, Lampito,
rush back to Sparta. We'll take care of things
here. Leave
these girls here for hostages.
205   The rest of you,
up to the Citadel: and mind you push in the
bolts.
KALONIKE:
But the men? Won't they be after us?

LYSISTRATA: Just you leave
the men to me. There's not fire enough in the
world,
or threats either, to make me open these doors
except on my own terms.
KALONIKE: I hope not, by Aphrodite!   210
After all,
we've got a reputation for bitchiness to live
up to.
[*Exeunt.*]

PARODOS:
CHORAL EPISODE

[*The hillside just under the Akropolis. Enter*
CHORUS OF OLD MEN *with burning torches
and braziers; much puffing and coughing.*]

KORYPHAIOS⁽ᵐᵃⁿ⁾:
Forward march, Drakes, old friend: never you
mind
that damn big log banging hell down on your
back.
CHORUS⁽ᵐᵉⁿ⁾:

[STROPHE 1]
There's this to be said for longevity:
You see things you thought that you'd never
see.
    Look, Strymodoros, who would have thought
it?   5
    We've caught it —
                the New Femininity!
The wives of our bosom, our board, our bed —
Now, by the gods, they've gone ahead
And taken the Citadel (Heaven knows why!),
Profanèd the sacred statuar-y,   10
              And barred the doors,
              The subversive whores!
KORYPHAIOS⁽ᵐ⁾:
Shake a leg there, Philurgos, man: the
Akropolis or bust!
Put the kindling around here. We'll build one
almighty big
bonfire for the whole bunch of bitches, every
last one;   15
and the first we fry will be old Lykon's woman.
CHORUS⁽ᵐ⁾:

[ANTISTROPHE 1]
They're not going to give me the old horse-
laugh!
No, by Demeter, they won't pull this off!
    Think of Kleomenes: even he

Didn't go free
20   till he brought me his stuff.
A good man he was, all stinking and shaggy,
Bare as an eel except for the bag he
Covered his rear with. God, what a mess!
Never a bath in six years, I'd guess.
25   Pure Sparta, man!
               He also ran.

KORYPHAIOS(m):
That was a siege, friends! Seventeen ranks
     strong
we slept at the Gate. And shall we not do as
     much
against these women, whom God and
     Euripides hate?
If we don't, I'll turn in my medals from
30   Marathon.

CHORUS(m):
                  [STROPHE 2]
Onward and upward! A little push,
     And we're there.
Ouch, my shoulders! I could wish
     For a pair
35 Of good strong oxen. Keep your eye
     On the fire there, it mustn't die.
           Akh! Akh!
     The smoke would make a cadaver cough!

Holy Herakles, a hot spark   [ANTISTROPHE 2]
40   Bit my eye!
Damn this hellfire, damn this work!
     So say I.
Onward and upward just the same.
(Laches, remember the Goddess: for shame!)
45   Akh! Akh!
     The smoke would make a cadaver cough!

KORYPHAIOS(m):
At last (and let us give suitable thanks to God
for his infinite mercies) I have managed to
     bring
my personal flame to the common goal. It
     breathes, it lives.
Now, gentlemen, let us consider. Shall we
50   insert
the torch, say, into the brazier, and thus
     extract
a kindling brand? And shall we then, do you
     think,
push on to the gate like valiant sheep? On the
     whole, yes.
But I would have you consider this, too: if
     they —
55 I refer to the women — should refuse to open,
what then? Do we set the doors afire

and smoke them out? At ease, men. Meditate.
Akh, the smoke! Woof! What we really need
is the loan of a general or two from the Samos
     Command.
At least we've got this lumber off our backs.   60
That's something. And now let's look to our
     fire.

O Pot, brave Brazier, touch my torch with
     flame!
Victory, Goddess, I invoke thy name!
Strike down these paradigms of female pride,
And we shall hang our trophies up inside.   65

[Enter CHORUS OF OLD WOMEN on the walls
of the Akropolis, carrying jars of water.]

KORYPHAIOS(woman):
Smoke, girls, smoke! There's smoke all over
     the place!
Probably fire, too. Hurry, girls! Fire! Fire!

CHORUS(women):
     Nikodike, run!   [STROPHE 1]
     Or Kalyke's done
     To a turn, and poor Kritylla's   70
     Smoked like a ham.
               Damn
These old men! Are we too late?
I nearly died down at the place
Where we fill our jars:
     Slaves pushing and jostling —   75
     Such a hustling
I never saw in all my days.

But here's water at last. [ANTISTROPHE 1]
Haste, sisters, haste!
Slosh it on them, slosh it down,   80
The silly old wrecks!
           Sex
Almighty! What they want's
A hot bath? Good. Send one down.
Athena of Athens town,
     Trito-born!° Helm of Gold!   85
     Cripple the old
Firemen! Help us help them drown!

[The OLD MEN capture a woman,
STRATYLLIS.]

STRATYLLIS:
Let me go! Let me go!
KORYPHAIOS(w):   You walking corpses,

85 **Trito-born:** i.e., Athene, said to be born near
Lake Tritonis, in Libya.

have you no shame?
KORYPHAIOS^(m):
                                  I wouldn't have believed it!
90 An army of women in the Akropolis!
KORYPHAIOS^(w):
So we scare you, do we? Grandpa, you've seen
only our pickets yet!
KORYPHAIOS^(m): Hey, Phaidrias!
Help me with the necks of these jabbering
    hens!
KORYPHAIOS^(w):
Down with your pots, girls! We'll need both
    hands
if these antiques attack us.
95 KORYPHAIOS^(m): Want your face kicked in?
KORYPHAIOS^(w):
Want your balls chewed off?
KORYPHAIOS^(m): Look out! I've got a stick!
KORYPHAIOS^(w):
You lay a half-inch of your stick on Stratyllis,
and you'll never stick again!
KORYPHAIOS^(m):
Fall apart!
KORYPHAIOS^(w):
        I'll spit up your guts!
KORYPHAIOS^(m):   Euripides!° Master!
How well you knew women!
100 KORYPHAIOS^(w): Listen to him, Rhodippe,
up with the pots!
KORYPHAIOS^(m):
                Demolition of God,
what good are your pots?
KORYPHAIOS^(w):
                You refugee from the tomb,
what good is your fire?
KORYPHAIOS^(m):
                Good enough to make a pyre
to barbecue you!
KORYPHAIOS^(w):
                We'll squizzle your kindling!
KORYPHAIOS^(m):
You think so?
KORYPHAIOS^(w):
105   Yah! Just hang around a while!
KORYPHAIOS^(m):
Want a touch of my torch?
KORYPHAIOS^(w):   It needs a good soaping.
KORYPHAIOS^(m):
How about you?
KORYPHAIOS^(w):
                Soap for a senile bridegroom!

99 **Euripides:** A tragic dramatist.

KORYPHAIOS^(m):
Senile? Hold your trap!
KORYPHAIOS^(w):   Just *you* try to hold it!
KORYPHAIOS^(m):
The yammer of women!
KORYPHAIOS^(w):   Oh is that so?
You're not in the jury room now, you know.   110
KORYPHAIOS^(m):
Gentlemen, I beg you, burn off that woman's
    hair!
KORYPHAIOS^(w):
Let it come down!

[*They empty their pots on the men.*]

KORYPHAIOS^(m):
What a way to drown!
KORYPHAIOS^(w):   Hot, hey?
KORYPHAIOS^(m):   Say,
enough!
KORYPHAIOS^(w):
        Dandruff
needs watering. I'll make you   115
nice and fresh.
KORYPHAIOS^(m):
            For God's sake, you,
hold off!

SCENE I

[*Enter a* COMMISSIONER *accompanied by
four constables.*]

COMMISSIONER:
These degenerate women! What a racket of
    little drums,
what a yapping for Adonis on every house-top!
It's like the time in the Assembly when I was
    listening
to a speech — out of order, as usual — by that
    fool
Demostratos,° all about troops for Sicily,°   5
that kind of nonsense —
                    and there was his wife
trotting around in circles howling
Alas for Adonis!° —
                    and Demostratos insisting

5 **Demostratos:** Athenian orator and jingoist
politician; **Sicily:** A reference to the Sicilian Expedition (416 B.C.), in which Athens was
decisively defeated.
8 **Adonis:** Fertility god.

we must draft every last Zakynthian that can
    walk —
10 and his wife up there on the roof,
drunk as an owl, yowling
Oh weep for Adonis! —
            and that damned ox Demostratos
mooing away through the rumpus. That's what
    we get
for putting up with this wretched woman-
    business!
    KORYPHAIOS^(m):
Sir, you haven't heard the half of it. They
15   laughed at us!
Insulted us! They took pitchers of water
and nearly drowned us! We're still wringing
    out our clothes,
for all the world like unhousebroken brats.
    COMMISSIONER:
Serves you right, by Poseidon!
20 Whose fault is it if these women-folk of ours
get out of hand? We coddle them,
we teach them to be wasteful and loose. You'll
    see a husband
go into a jeweler's. "Look," he'll say,
"jeweler," he'll say, "you remember that gold
    choker
you made for my wife? Well, she went to a
25   dance last night
and broke the clasp. Now, I've got to go to
    Salamis,
and can't be bothered. Run over to my house
    tonight,
will you, and see if you can put it together for
    her."
Or another one
goes to a cobbler — a good strong workman,
30   too,
with an awl that was never meant for child's
    play. "Here,"
he'll tell him, "one of my wife's shoes is
    pinching
her little toe. Could you come up about noon
and stretch it out for her?"
                    Well, what do you expect?
35 Look at me, for example, I'm a Public Officer,
and it's one of my duties to pay off the sailors.
And where's the money? Up there in the
    Akropolis!
And those blasted women slam the door in my
    face!
But what are we waiting for?
                    — Look here, constable,
40   stop sniffing around for a tavern, and get us

some crowbars. We'll force their gates! As a
    matter of fact,
I'll do a little forcing myself.

[*Enter* LYSISTRATA, *above, with* MYRRHINE,
KALONIKE, *and the* BOIOTIAN.]

    LYSISTRATA: No need of forcing.
Here I am, of my own accord. And all this talk
about locked doors — ! We don't need locked
    doors,
but just the least bit of common sense.   45
    COMMISSIONER:
Is that so, ma'am!
                    — Where's my constable?
                              — Constable,
arrest that woman, and tie her hands behind
    her.
    LYSISTRATA:
If he touches me, I swear by Artemis
there'll be one scamp dropped from the public
    pay-roll tomorrow!
    COMMISSIONER:
Well, constable? You're not afraid, I suppose?
    Grab her,   50
two of you, around the middle!
    KALONIKE: No, by Pandrosos!
Lay a hand on her, and I'll jump on you so
    hard
your guts will come out the back door!
    COMMISSIONER: That's what *you* think!
Where's the sergeant? — Here, you: tie up that
    trollop first,
the one with the pretty talk!
    MYRRHINE: By the Moon-Goddess, 55
just try! They'll have to scoop you up with a
    spoon!
    COMMISSIONER:
Another one!
            Officer, seize that woman!
                              I swear
I'll put an end to this riot!
    BOIOTIAN: By the Taurian,
one inch closer, you'll be one screaming bald-
    head!
    COMMISSIONER:
Lord, what a mess! And my constables seem
    ineffective.   60
But — women get the best of us? By God, no!
                              — Skythians!
Close ranks and forward march!
    LYSISTRATA: "Forward," indeed!
By the Two Goddesses, what's the sense in
    that?

They're up against four companies of women
armed from top to bottom.

65   COMMISSIONER: Forward, my Skythians!
      LYSISTRATA:
Forward, yourselves, dear comrades!
You grainlettucebeanseedmarket girls!
You garlicandonionbreadbakery girls!
Give it to 'em! Knock 'em down! Scratch 'em!
Tell 'em what you think of 'em!

[*General mêlée; the Skythians yield.*]

70   — Ah, that's enough!
Sound a retreat: good soldiers don't rob the
      dead.
      COMMISSIONER:
A nice day *this* has been for the police!
      LYSISTRATA:
Well, there you are. — Did you really think we
      women
would be driven like slaves? Maybe now you'll
      admit
that a woman knows something about spirit.
75   COMMISSIONER: Spirit enough,
especially spirits in bottles! Dear Lord Apollo!
      KORYPHAIOS(m):
Your Honor, there's no use talking to them.
      Words
mean nothing whatever to wild animals like
      these.
Think of the sousing they gave us! and the
      water
80   was not, I believe, of the purest.
      KORYPHAIOS(w):
You shouldn't have come after us. And if you
      try it again,
you'll be one eye short! — Although, as a
      matter of fact,
what I like best is just to stay at home and
      read,
like a sweet little bride: never hurting a soul,
      no,
never going out. But if you *must* shake hor-
85   nets' nests,
look out for the hornets.
      CHORUS(m):
                              [STROPHE 1]
Of all the beasts that God hath wrought
    What monster's worse than woman?
Who shall encompass with his thought
90   Their guile unending? No man.

They've seized the Heights, the Rock, the
    Shrine —
But to what end? I wot not.

Sure there's some clue to their design!
    Have you the key? I thought not.
      KORYPHAIOS(m):
We might question them, I suppose. But I
      warn you, sir,   95
don't believe anything you hear! It would be
      un-Athenian
not to get to the bottom of this plot.
      COMMISSIONER: Very well.
My first question is this: Why, so help you
      God,
did you bar the gates of the Akropolis?
      LYSISTRATA: Why?
To keep the money, of course. No money, no
      war.   100
      COMMISSIONER:
You think that money's the cause of war?
      LYSISTRATA: I do.
Money brought about that Peisandros°
      business
and all the other attacks on the State. Well
      and good!
They'll not get another cent here!
      COMMISSIONER: And what will you do?
      LYSISTRATA:
What a question! From now on, we intend   105
to control the Treasury.
      COMMISSIONER: Control the Treasury!
      LYSISTRATA:
Why not? Does that seem strange? After all,
we control our household budgets.
      COMMISSIONER: But that's different!
      LYSISTRATA:
"Different"? What do you mean?
      COMMISSIONER: I mean simply this:
it's the Treasury that pays for National
      Defense.   110
      LYSISTRATA:
Unnecessary. We propose to abolish war.
      COMMISSIONER:
Good God. — And National Security?
      LYSISTRATA: Leave that to us.
      COMMISSIONER:
You?
      LYSISTRATA:
    Us.
      COMMISSIONER:
      We're done for, then!
      LYSISTRATA: Never mind.
We women will save you in spite of yourselves.

102 **Peisandros**: A plotter against the Athenian
democracy.

COMMISSIONER: What nonsense!
LYSISTRATA:

15 If you like. But you must accept it, like it or
        not.
COMMISSIONER:
Why, this is downright subversion!
LYSISTRATA: Maybe it is.
But we're going to save you, Judge.
COMMISSIONER: I don't *want* to be saved.
LYSISTRATA:
Tut. The death-wish. All the more reason.
COMMISSIONER: But the idea
of women bothering themselves about peace
        and war!
LYSISTRATA:
Will you listen to me?
20 COMMISSIONER: Yes. But be brief, or I'll —
LYSISTRATA:
This is no time for stupid threats.
COMMISSIONER: By the gods,
I can't stand any more!
AN OLD WOMAN: Can't stand? Well, well.
COMMISSIONER:
That's enough out of you, you old buzzard!
Now, Lysistrata: tell me what you're thinking.
LYSISTRATA:
Glad to.
        Ever since this war began
We women have been watching you men,
        agreeing with you,
keeping our thoughts to ourselves. That
        doesn't mean
we were happy: we weren't, for we saw how
        things were going;
but we'd listen to you at dinner
arguing this way and that.
30   — Oh you, and your big
Top Secrets! —
        And then we'd grin like little patriots
(though goodness knows we didn't feel like
        grinning) and ask you:
"Dear, did the Armistice come up in Assembly
        today?"
And you'd say, "None of your business! Pipe
        down!," you'd say.
And so we would.
35 AN OLD WOMAN: *I* wouldn't have, by God!
COMMISSIONER:
You'd have taken a beating, then!
                              — Go on.

LYSISTRATA:
Well, we'd be quiet. But then, you know, all
        at once

you men would think up something worse
        than ever.
Even *I* could see it was fatal. And, "Darling,"
        I'd say,
"have you gone completely mad?" And my
        husband would look at me   140
and say, "Wife, you've got your weaving to
        attend to.
Mind your tongue, if you don't want a slap.
        'War's
a man's affair!' "°
COMMISSIONER:
                    Good words, and well pronounced.
LYSISTRATA:
You're a fool if you think so.
                              It was hard enough
to put up with all this banquet-hall strategy.   145
But then we'd hear you out in the public
        square:
"Nobody left for the draft-quota here in
        Athens?"
you'd say; and, "No," someone else would say,
        "not a man!"
And so we women decided to rescue Greece.
You might as well listen to us now: you'll
        have to, later.   150
COMMISSIONER:
You rescue Greece? Absurd.
LYSISTRATA: You're the absurd one.
COMMISSIONER:
You expect me to take orders from a woman?
                                    I'd die first!
LYSISTRATA:
Heavens, if that's what's bothering you, take
        my veil,
here, and wrap it around your poor head.
KALONIKE: Yes,
and you can have my market-basket, too.   155
Go home, tighten your girdle, do the washing,
        mind
your beans! "War's
a woman's affair!"
KORYPHAIOS(w):
                    Ground pitchers! Close ranks!
CHORUS(w):
                                        [ANTISTROPHE]
    This is a dance that I know well,
        My knees shall never yield.   160
    Wobble and creak I may, but still
        I'll keep the well-fought field.

143 **War's a man's affair:** Quoted from Homer's
Iliad, VI, 492, Hector to his wife Andromache.

Valor and grace march on before,
Love prods us from behind.
165   Our slogan is EXCELSIOR,
Our watchword SAVE MANKIND.
KORYPHAIOS^(w):
Women, remember your grandmothers! Remember
that little old mother of yours, what a stinger
she was!
On, on, never slacken. There's a strong wind
astern!
LYSISTRATA:
170   O Eros of delight! O Aphrodite! Kyprian!
If ever desire has drenched our breasts or
dreamed
in our thighs, let it work so now on the men
of Hellas
that they shall tail us through the land, slaves,
slaves
to Woman, Breaker of Armies!
COMMISSIONER: And if we do?
LYSISTRATA:
Well, for one thing, we shan't have to watch
175   you
going to market, a spear in one hand, and
heaven knows
what in the other.
KALONIKE: Nicely said, by Aphrodite!
LYSISTRATA:
As things stand now, you're neither men nor
women.
Armor clanking with kitchen pans and pots —
180   you sound like a pack of Korybantes!
COMMISSIONER:
A man must do what a man must do.
LYSISTRATA: So I'm told.
But to see a General, complete with Gorgon-
shield,
jingling along the dock to buy a couple of
herrings!
KALONIKE:
I saw a Captain the other day — lovely fellow
he was,
nice curly hair — sitting on his horse; and —
185   can you believe it? —
he'd just bought some soup, and was pouring
it into his helmet!
And there was a soldier from Thrace
swishing his lance like something out of
Euripides,
and the poor fruit-store woman got so scared
that she ran away and let him have his figs
190   free!

COMMISSIONER:
All this is beside the point.
Will you be so kind
as to tell me how you mean to save Greece?
LYSISTRATA: Of course.
Nothing could be simpler.
COMMISSIONER: I assure you, I'm all ears.
LYSISTRATA:
Do you know anything about weaving?
Say the yarn gets tangled: we thread it   195
this way and that through the skein, up and
down,
until it's free. And it's like that with war.
We'll send our envoys
up and down, this way and that, all over Greece,
until it's finished.
COMMISSIONER: Yarn? Thread? Skein?   200
Are you out of your mind? I tell you,
war is a serious business.
LYSISTRATA: So serious
that I'd like to go on talking about weaving.
COMMISSIONER:
All right. Go ahead.
LYSISTRATA: The first thing we have to do
is to wash our yarn, get the dirt out of it.   205
You see? Isn't there too much dirt here in
Athens?
You must wash those men away.
Then our spoiled wool —
that's like your job-hunters, out for a life
of no work and big pay. Back to the basket,
citizens or not, allies or not,   210
or friendly immigrants.
And your colonies?
Hanks of wool lost in various places. Pull them
together, weave them into one great whole,
and our voters are clothed for ever.
COMMISSIONER: It would take a woman
to reduce state questions to a matter of carding
and weaving.   215
LYSISTRATA:
You fool! Who were the mothers whose sons
sailed off
to fight for Athens in Sicily?
COMMISSIONER: Enough!
I beg you, do not call back those memories.
LYSISTRATA: And then,
instead of the love that every woman needs,
we have only our single beds, where we can
dream   220
of our husbands off with the Army.
Bad enough for wives!
But what about our girls, getting older every
day,

and older, and no kisses?
COMMISSIONER: Men get older, too.
LYSISTRATA:
Not in the same sense.
                    A soldier's discharged,
and he may be bald and toothless, yet he'll
225   find
a pretty young thing to go to bed with.
                          But a woman!
Her beauty is gone with the first grey hair.
She can spend her time
consulting the oracles and the fortune-tellers,
230   but they'll never send her a husband.
COMMISSIONER:
Still, if a man can rise to the occasion —
LYSISTRATA:
Rise? Rise, yourself!

[*Furiously.*]

Go invest in a coffin!
                    You've money enough.
                          I'll bake you
a cake for the Underworld.
                    And here's your funeral
wreath!

[*She pours water upon him.*]

MYRRHINE:
    And here's another!

[*More water.*]

KALONIKE:
235   And here's
my contribution!

[*More water.*]

LYSISTRATA: What are you waiting for?
All aboard Styx Ferry!
                    Charon's° calling for you!
It's sailing-time: don't disrupt the schedule!
COMMISSIONER:
The insolence of women! And to me!
240   No, by God, I'll go back to town and show
the rest of the Commission what might hap-
    pen to them.
                          [*Exit* COMMISSIONER.]
LYSISTRATA:
Really, I suppose we should have laid out his
    corpse
on the doorstep, in the usual way.
                          But never mind.

237 **Charon:** God who ferried the souls of the
newly dead across the Styx to Hades.

We'll give him the rites of the dead tomorrow
    morning.
            [*Exit* LYSISTRATA *with* MYRRHINE *and*
                                    KALONIKE.]

PARABASIS: CHORAL
EPISODE

KORYPHAIOS[(m)]:
                                    [ODE 1]
Sons of Liberty, awake! The day of glory is at
    hand.
CHORUS[(m)]:
I smell tyranny afoot, I smell it rising from
    the land.
I scent a trace of Hippias,° I sniff upon the
    breeze
A dismal Spartan hogo that suggests King
    Kleisthenes.°
Strip, strip for action, brothers!   5
Our wives, aunts, sisters, mothers
Have sold us out: the streets are full of godless
    female rages.
Shall we stand by and let our women confis-
    cate our wages?
KORYPHAIOS[(m)]:
                              [EPIRRHEMA 1]
Gentlemen, it's a disgrace to Athens, a disgrace
to all that Athens stands for, if we allow these
    grandmas   10
to jabber about spears and shields and making
    friends
with the Spartans. What's a Spartan? Give me
    a wild wolf
any day. No. They want the Tyranny back, I
    suppose.
Are we going to take that? No. Let us look like
the innocent serpent, but be the flower under
    it,   15
as the poet sings. And just to begin with,
I propose to poke a number of teeth
down the gullet of that harridan over there.
KORYPHAIOS[(w)]:
                                  [ANTODE 1]
Oh, is that so? When you get home, your own
    mammá won't know you!
CHORUS[(w)]:
Who do you think we are, you senile bravos?
    Well, I'll show you.   20

3 **Hippias:** An Athenian tyrant (d. 490 B.C.).
4 **Kleisthenes:** An ambisexual Athenian.

I bore the sacred vessels in my eighth year,
    and at ten
I was pounding out the barley for Athena
    Goddess; then
    They made me Little Bear
    At the Braunonian Fair;
I'd held the Holy Basket by the time I was of
25   age,
The Blessed Dry Figs had adorned my plump
    décolletage.

KORYPHAIOS^(w):

[ANTEPIRRHEMA 1]

A "disgrace to Athens," am I, just at the
    moment
I'm giving Athens the best advice she ever had?
Don't I pay taxes to the State? Yes, I pay
    them
30 in baby boys. And what do you contribute,
you impotent horrors? Nothing but waste: all
our Treasury,° dating back to the Persian
    Wars,
gone! rifled! And not a penny out of your
    pockets!
Well, then? Can you cough up an answer to
    that?
Look out for your own gullet, or you'll get a
35   crack
from this old brogan that'll make your teeth
    see stars!

CHORUS^(m):

    Oh insolence!   [ODE 2]
    Am I unmanned?
    Incontinence!
40   Shall my scarred hand
    Strike never a blow
    To curb this flow-
    ing female curse?

    Leipsydrion!°
45   Shall I betray
    The laurels won
    On that great day?
    Come, shake a leg,
    Shed old age, beg
50   The years reverse!

KORYPHAIOS^(m):

[EPIRRHEMA 2]

Give them an inch, and we're done for! We'll
    have them
launching boats next and planning naval
    strategy,
sailing down on us like so many Artemisias.
Or maybe they have ideas about the cavalry.
That's fair enough, women are certainly good   55
in the saddle. Just look at Mikon's paintings,
all those Amazons wrestling with all those
    men!
On the whole, a straitjacket's their best uni-
    form.

CHORUS^(w):

    Tangle with me,   [ANTODE 2]
    And you'll get cramps.   60
    Ferocity
    's no use now, Gramps!
    By the Two,
    I'll get through
    To you wrecks yet!   65

    I'll scramble your eggs,
    I'll burn your beans,
    With my two legs.
    You'll see such scenes
    As never yet   70
    Your two eyes met.
    A curse? You bet!

KORYPHAIOS^(w):

[ANTEPIRRHEMA 2]

If Lampito stands by me, and that delicious
    Theban girl,
Ismenia — what good are *you?* You and your
    seven
Resolutions! Resolutions? Rationing Boiotian
    eels   75
and making our girls go without them at
    Hekate's Feast!
That was statesmanship! And we'll have to put
    up with it
and all the rest of your decrepit legislation
until some patriot — God give him strength! —
grabs you by the neck and kicks you off the
    Rock.   80

32 **Treasury:** Money originally contributed by
Athens and her allies, intended to finance an ex-
tension of the sea-war against Persia. Since the
failure of the Sicilian Expedition, the contributions
of the allies had fallen off; and the fund itself was
now being raided by Athenian politicians.
    44 **Leipsydrion:** A place where patriots had
gallantly fought.

SCENE II

[*Re-enter* LYSISTRATA *and her lieutenants.*]

KORYPHAIOS^(w) [*Tragic tone*]:
Great Queen, fair Architect of our emprise,

Why lookst thou on us with foreboding eyes?
LYSISTRATA:
The behavior of these idiotic women!
There's something about the female tempera-
    ment
that I can't bear!
        KORYPHAIOS⁽ᵂ⁾:
5   What in the world do you mean?
LYSISTRATA:
Exactly what I say.
        KORYPHAIOS⁽ᵂ⁾:
                What dreadful thing has happened?
Come, tell us: we're all your friends.
        LYSISTRATA: It isn't easy
to say it; yet, God knows, we can't hush it up.
        KORYPHAIOS⁽ᵂ⁾:
Well, then? Out with it!
        LYSISTRATA: To put it bluntly,
we're dying to get laid.
10   KORYPHAIOS⁽ᵂ⁾:   Almighty God!
        LYSISTRATA:
Why bring God into it? — No, it's just as I
    say.
I can't manage them any longer: they've gone
    man-crazy,
they're all trying to get out.
                        Why, look:
one of them was sneaking out the back door
15 over there by Pan's cave; another
was sliding down the walls with rope and
    tackle;
another was climbing aboard a sparrow, ready
    to take off
for the nearest brothel — I dragged *her* back
    by the hair!
They're all finding some reason to leave.
                        Look there!
There goes another one.
20   — Just a minute, you!
Where are you off to so fast?
        FIRST WOMAN: I've got to get home.
I've a lot of Milesian wool, and the worms are
    spoiling it.
        LYSISTRATA:
Oh bother you and your worms! Get back in-
    side!
        FIRST WOMAN:
I'll be back right away, I swear I will.
25 I just want to get it stretched out on my bed.
        LYSISTRATA:
You'll do no such thing. You'll stay right here.
        FIRST WOMAN: And my wool?
You want it ruined?
        LYSISTRATA: Yes, for all I care.

        SECOND WOMAN:
Oh dear! My lovely new flax from Amorgos —
I left it at home, all uncarded!
        LYSISTRATA: Another one!
And all she wants is someone to card her flax.   30
Get back in there!
        SECOND WOMAN:
                But I swear by the Moon-Goddess,
the minute I get it done, I'll be back!
        LYSISTRATA: I say No.
If you, why not all the other women as well?
        THIRD WOMAN:
O Lady Eileithyia!° Radiant goddess! Thou
intercessor for women in childbirth! Stay, I
    pray thee,   35
oh stay this parturition. Shall I pollute
a sacred spot?
        LYSISTRATA:
                And what's the matter with *you?*
        THIRD WOMAN:
I'm having a baby — any minute now.
        LYSISTRATA:
But you weren't pregnant yesterday.
        THIRD WOMAN: Well, I am today.
Let me go home for a midwife, Lysistrata: 40
there's not much time.
        LYSISTRATA: I never heard such nonsense.
What's that bulging under your cloak?
        THIRD WOMAN: A little baby boy.
        LYSISTRATA:
It certainly isn't. But it's something hollow,
like a basin or — Why, it's the helmet of
    Athena!
And you said you were having a baby.
        THIRD WOMAN: Well, I am! So there!   45
        LYSISTRATA:
Then why the helmet?
        THIRD WOMAN: I was afraid that my pains
might begin here in the Akropolis; and I
    wanted
to drop my chick into it, just as the dear
    doves do.
        LYSISTRATA:
Lies! Evasions! — But at least one thing's clear:
you can't leave the place before your puri-
    fication.   50
        THIRD WOMAN:
But I can't stay here in the Akropolis! Last
    night I dreamed
of the Snake.
        FIRST WOMAN:
And those horrible owls, the noise they make!

34 **Eileithyia:** Goddess of childbirth.

I can't get a bit of sleep; I'm just about dead.
LYSISTRATA:
You useless girls, that's enough: Let's have no
     more lying.
Of course you want your men. But don't you
55   imagine
that they want you just as much? I'll give you
     my word,
their nights must be pretty hard.
                                        Just stick it out!
A little patience, that's all, and our battle's
     won.
I have heard an Oracle. Should you like to
     hear it?
FIRST WOMAN:
An Oracle? Yes, tell us!
60   LYSISTRATA: Here is what it says:
WHEN   SWALLOWS   SHALL   THE
     HOOPOE SHUN
     AND SPURN HIS HOT DESIRE,
ZEUS WILL PERFECT WHAT THEY'VE
     BEGUN
     AND SET THE LOWER HIGHER.
FIRST WOMAN:
65   Does that mean we'll be on top?
LYSISTRATA:
BUT IF THE SWALLOWS SHALL FALL
     OUT
     AND TAKE THE HOOPOE'S BAIT,
A CURSE MUST MARK THEIR HOUR
     OF DOUBT,
     INFAMY SEAL THEIR FATE.
THIRD WOMAN:
I swear, *that* Oracle's all too clear.
70   FIRST WOMAN: Oh the dear gods!
LYSISTRATA:
Let's not be downhearted, girls. Back to our
     places!
The god has spoken. How can we possibly
     fail him?
[*Exit* LYSISTRATA *with the dissident women.*]

CHORAL EPISODE

CHORUS(m):
                                        [STROPHE]
I know a little story that I learned way back
     in school
Goes like this:
Once upon a time there was a young man —
     and no fool —
Named Melanion; and his

One aversi-on was marriage. He loathed the
     very thought.   5
So he ran off to the hills, and in a special grot
Raised a dog, and spent his days
Hunting rabbits. And it says
That he never never never did come home.
It might be called a refuge *from* the womb.   10
All right,
          all right,
                    all right!
We're as bright as young Melanion, and we
     hate the very sight
Of you women!
A MAN:
How about a kiss, old lady?
A WOMAN:
Here's an onion for your eye!   15
A MAN:
A kick in the guts, then?
A WOMAN:
Try, old bristle-tail, just try!
A MAN:
Yet they say Myronides
On hands and knees
Looked just as shaggy fore and aft as I!   20
CHORUS(w):   [ANTISTROPHE]
Well, *I* know a little story, and it's just as
     good as yours.
Goes like this:
Once there was a man named Timon — a
     rough diamond, of course,
And that whiskery face of his
Looked like murder in the shrubbery. By God,
     he was a son   25
Of the Furies, let me tell you! And what did
     he do but run
From the world and all its ways,
Cursing mankind! And it says
That his choicest execrations as of then
Were leveled almost wholly at *old* men.   30
All right,
          all right,
                    all right!
But there's one thing about Timon: he could
     always stand the sight
Of us women.
A WOMAN:
How about a crack in the jaw, Pop?
A MAN:
I can take it, Ma — no fear!   35
A WOMAN:
How about a kick in the face?
A MAN:
You'd reveal your old caboose?

A WOMAN:
What I'd show,
I'll have you know,
40 Is an instrument you're too far gone to use.

SCENE III

[*Re-enter* LYSISTRATA.]

LYSISTRATA:
Oh, quick, girls, quick! Come here!
  A WOMAN: What is it?
LYSISTRATA: A man.
A man simply bulging with love.
        O Kyprian Queen,°
O Paphian, O Kythereian! Hear us and aid us!
  A WOMAN:
Where is this enemy?
LYSISTRATA:
      Over there, by Demeter's shrine.
  A WOMAN:
5 Damned if he isn't. But who *is* he?
  MYRRHINE: My husband.
Kinesias.
  LYSISTRATA:
    Oh then, get busy! Tease him! Under-
mine him!
Wreck him! Give him everything – kissing,
  tickling, nudging,
whatever you generally torture him with – :
  give him everything
except what we swore on the wine we would
  not give.
  MYRRHINE:
Trust me.
  LYSISTRATA:
10   I do. But I'll help you get him started.
The rest of you women, stay back.

[*Enter* KINESIAS.]

  KINESIAS: Oh God! Oh my God!
I'm stiff from lack of exercise. All I can do to
  stand up.
  LYSISTRATA:
Halt! Who are you, approaching our lines?
  KINESIAS: Me? I.
  LYSISTRATA:
A man?
  KINESIAS:
    You have eyes, haven't you?
  LYSISTRATA: Go away.

2 **Kyprian Queen:** Aphrodite, goddess of love.

KINESIAS:
Who says so?
  LYSISTRATA:
      Officer of the Day.
  KINESIAS: Officer, I beg you, 15
by all the gods at once, bring Myrrhine out.
  LYSISTRATA:
Myrrhine? And who, my good sir, are you?
  KINESIAS:
Kinesias. Last name's Pennison. Her husband.
  LYSISTRATA:
Oh, of course. I beg your pardon. We're glad
  to see you.
We've heard so much about you. Dearest
  Myrrhine 20
is always talking about Kinesias – never nibbles
  an egg
or an apple without saying
"Here's to Kinesias!"
  KINESIAS: Do you really mean it?
  LYSISTRATA: I do.
When we're discussing men, she always says
"Well, after all, there's nobody like Kinesias!" 25
  KINESIAS:
Good God. – Well, then, please send her
  down here.
  LYSISTRATA:
And what do *I* get out of it?
  KINESIAS: A standing promise.
  LYSISTRATA:
I'll take it up with her.

        [*Exit* LYSISTRATA.]
  KINESIAS: But be quick about it!
Lord, what's life without a wife? Can't eat.
  Can't sleep.
Every time I go home, the place is so
  empty, so 30
insufferably sad. Love's killing me, Oh,
hurry!

[*Enter* MANES, *a slave, with* KINESIAS' *baby;
the voice of* MYRRHINE *is heard off-stage.*]

MYRRHINE:
  But of course I love him! Adore him –
  But no,
he hates love. No. I won't go down.

[*Enter* MYRRHINE, *above.*]

  KINESIAS: Myrrhine!
Darlingest Myrrhinette! Come down quick!
  MYRRHINE:
Certainly not.
  KINESIAS: Not? But why, Myrrhine? 35

MYRRHINE:
Why? You don't need me.
KINESIAS:
Need you? My God, *look* at me!
MYRRHINE:
So long!

[*Turns to go.*]

KINESIAS:
Myrrhine, Myrrhine, Myrrhine!
If not for my sake, for our child!

[*Pinches* BABY.]

— All right, you: pipe up!
BABY:
Mummie! Mummie! Mummie!
KINESIAS: You hear that?
40 Pitiful, I call it. Six days now
with never a bath; no food; enough to break
    your heart!
MYRRHINE:
My darlingest child! What a father *you*
    acquired!
KINESIAS:
At least come down for his sake.
MYRRHINE: I suppose I must.
Oh, this mother business!

[*Exit.*]

KINESIAS: How pretty she is! And younger!
The harder she treats me, the more bothered
    I get.

[MYRRHINE *enters, below.*]

45 MYRRHINE:
Dearest child,
you're as sweet as your father's horrid. Give me
    a kiss.
KINESIAS:
Now don't you see how wrong it was to get
    involved
in this scheming League of women? It's bad
for us both.
MYRRHINE:
Keep your hands to yourself!
KINESIAS: But our house
going to rack and ruin?
MYRRHINE: *I* don't care.
50 KINESIAS: And your knitting
all torn to pieces by the chickens? Don't you
    care?
MYRRHINE:
Not at all.
KINESIAS:
And our debt to Aphrodite?

Oh, *won't* you come back?
MYRRHINE:
No. — At least, not until you men
make a treaty and stop this war.
KINESIAS: Why, I suppose
that might be arranged.
MYRRHINE: Oh? Well, I suppose   55
I might come down then. But meanwhile,
I've sworn not to.
KINESIAS:
Don't worry. — Now let's have fun.
MYRRHINE:
No! Stop it! I said no!
— Although, of course,
I *do* love you.
KINESIAS:
I know you do. Darling Myrrhine:
come, shall we?
MYRRHINE: Are you out of your mind? In
    front of the child?   60
KINESIAS:
Take him home, Manes.

[*Exit* MANES *with* BABY.]
There. He's gone.
Come on!
There's nothing to stop us now.
MYRRHINE: You devil! But where?
KINESIAS:
In Pan's cave. What could be snugger than
    that?
MYRRHINE:
But my purification before I go back to the
    Citadel?
KINESIAS:
Wash in the Klepsydra.°
MYRRHINE: And my oath?
KINESIAS: Leave the oath to me.   65
After all, I'm the man.
MYRRHINE: Well . . . if you say so.
I'll go find a bed.
KINESIAS:
Oh, bother a bed! The ground's good enough
    for me.
MYRRHINE:
No. You're a bad man, but you deserve some-
    thing better than dirt.

[*Exit* MYRRHINE.]
KINESIAS:
What a love she is! And how thoughtful!

65 **Klepsydra:** A sacred spring beneath the walls
of the Akropolis. Kinesias' suggestion has overtones
of blasphemy.

[*Re-enter* MYRRHINE.]

MYRRHINE: Here's your bed.
Now let me get my clothes off.
70   But, good horrors!
We haven't a mattress.
   KINESIAS: Oh, forget the mattress!
   MYRRHINE: No.
Just lying on blankets? Too sordid.
   KINESIAS: Give me a kiss.
   MYRRHINE:
Just a second.
                              [*Exit* MYRRHINE.]
   KINESIAS: I swear, I'll explode!

[*Re-enter* MYRRHINE.]

MYRRHINE: Here's your mattress.
I'll just take my dress off.
                              But look —
where's our pillow?
   KINESIAS: I don't *need* a pillow!
75   MYRRHINE: Well, *I* do.
                              [*Exit* MYRRHINE.]

   KINESIAS:
I don't suppose even Herakles
would stand for this!

[*Re-enter* MYRRHINE.]

MYRRHINE: There we are. Ups-a-daisy!
   KINESIAS:
So we are. Well, come to bed.
   MYRRHINE: But I wonder:
is everything ready now?
   KINESIAS:
                    I can swear to that. Come, darling!
   MYRRHINE:
Just getting out of my girdle.
80   But remember, now,
what you promised about the treaty.
   KINESIAS: Yes, yes, yes!
   MYRRHINE:
But no coverlet!
   KINESIAS: Damn it, I'll be
your coverlet!
   MYRRHINE:
                    Be right back.
                              [*Exit* MYRRHINE.]
   KINESIAS: This girl and her coverlets
will be the death of me.

[*Re-enter* MYRRHINE.]

MYRRHINE: Here we are. Up you go!

   KINESIAS:
Up? I've been up for ages.
   MYRRHINE: Some perfume?   85
   KINESIAS:
No, by Apollo!
   MYRRHINE: Yes, by Aphrodite!
I don't care whether you want it or not.
                              [*Exit* MYRRHINE.]
   KINESIAS:
For love's sake, hurry!

[*Re-enter* MYRRHINE.]

MYRRHINE:
Here, in your hand. Rub it right in.
   KINESIAS: Never cared for perfume.
And this is particularly strong. Still, here goes.   90
   MYRRHINE:
What a nitwit I am! I brought you the
          Rhodian bottle.
   KINESIAS:
Forget it.
   MYRRHINE:
                    No trouble at all. You just wait here.
                              [*Exit* MYRRHINE.]
   KINESIAS:
God damn the man who invented perfume!

[*Re-enter* MYRRHINE.]

MYRRHINE:
At last! The right bottle!
   KINESIAS: I've got the rightest
bottle of all, and it's right here waiting for you.   95
Darling, forget everything else. Do come to
          bed.
   MYRRHINE:
Just let me get my shoes off.
                              — And, by the way,
you'll vote for the treaty?
   KINESIAS: I'll think about it.
                    [MYRRHINE *runs away.*]
There! That's done it! The damned woman,
she gets me all bothered, she half kills me,   100
and off she runs! What'll I do? Where
can I get laid?
                    — And you, little prodding pal,
who's going to take care of *you?* No, you and I
had better get down to old Foxdog's Nursing
          Clinic.
   CHORUS[(m)]:
Alas for the woes of man, alas   105
          Specifically for you.
She's brought you to a pretty pass:
          What are you going to do?

Split, heart! Sag, flesh! Proud spirit, crack!
110   Myrrhine's got you on your back.
        KINESIAS:
The agony, the protraction!
        KORYPHAIOS(m):   Friend,
What woman's worth a damn?
They bitch us all, world without end.
        KINESIAS:
Yet they're so damned sweet, man!
        KORYPHAIOS(m):
115   Calamitous, that's what I say.
You should have learned that much today.
        CHORUS(m):
O blessed Zeus, roll womankind.
    Up into one great ball;
Blast them aloft on a high wind,
120   And once there, let them fall.
Down, down they'll come, the pretty dears,
And split themselves on our thick spears.
                            [Exit KINESIAS.]

SCENE IV

[Enter a SPARTAN HERALD.]

HERALD:
Gentlemen, Ah beg you will be so kind
as to direct me to the Central Committee.
Ah have a communication.

[Re-enter COMMISSIONER.]

    COMMISSIONER: Are you a man,
or a fertility symbol?
    HERALD:
                Ah refuse to answer that question!
Ah'm a certified herald from Spahta, and Ah've
5   come
to talk about an ahmistice.
    COMMISSIONER: Then why
that spear under your cloak?
    HERALD: Ah have no speah!
    COMMISSIONER:
You don't walk naturally, with your tunic
poked out so. You have a tumor, maybe,
or a hernia?
    HERALD: You lost yo' mahnd, man?
10   COMMISSIONER: Well,
something's up, I can see that. And I don't
    like it.
    HERALD:
Colonel, Ah resent this.
    COMMISSIONER: So I see. But what *is* it?
    HERALD: A staff

with a message from Spahta.
    COMMISSIONER:
                Oh. I know about those staffs.
Well, then, man, speak out: How are things
    in Sparta?
    HERALD:
Hahd, Colonel, hahd! We're at a standstill.   15
Cain't seem to think of anything but women.
    COMMISSIONER:
How curious! Tell me, do you Spartans think
that maybe Pan's to blame?
    HERALD:
Pan? No. Lampito and her little naked friends.
They won't let a man come nigh them.   20
    COMMISSIONER:
How are you handling it?
    HERALD: Losing our mahnds,
if y' want to know, and walking around
    hunched over
lahk men carrying candles in a gale.
The women have swohn they'll have nothing
    to do with us
until we get a treaty.
    COMMISSIONER: Yes. I know.   25
It's a general uprising, sir, in all parts of
    Greece.
But as for the answer —
                Sir: go back to Sparta
and have them send us your Armistice
    Commission.
I'll arrange things in Athens.
                        And I may say
that my standing is good enough to make them
    listen.   30
    HERALD:
A man after mah own haht! Seh, Ah thank
    you.
                            [Exit HERALD.]

CHORAL EPISODE

CHORUS(m):
                                [STROPHE]
    Oh these women! Where will you find
    A slavering beast that's more unkind?
        Where a hotter fire?
    Give me a panther, any day.
    He's not so merciless as they,   5
        And panthers don't conspire.
CHORUS(w):
                                [ANTISTROPHE]
    We may be hard, you silly old ass,

But who brought you to this stupid pass?
You're the ones to blame.
10 Fighting with us, your oldest friends,
Simply to serve your selfish ends —
Really, you have no shame!
KORYPHAIOS^(m):
No, I'm through with women for ever.
KORYPHAIOS^(w):   If you say so.
Still, you might put some clothes on. You look
too absurd
standing around naked. Come, get into this
15   cloak.
KORYPHAIOS^(m):
Thank you; you're right. I merely took it off
because I was in such a temper.
KORYPHAIOS^(w):   That's much better.
Now you resemble a man again.
                        Why have you been so horrid?
And look: there's some sort of insect in your
eye.
Shall I take it out?
KORYPHAIOS^(m):
20   An insect, is it? So that's
what's been bothering me. Lord, yes: take it
out!
KORYPHAIOS^(w):
You might be more polite.
                        — But, heavens!
What an enormous mosquito!
KORYPHAIOS^(m):   You've saved my life.
That mosquito was drilling an artesian well
in my left eye.
KORYPHAIOS^(w):
25   Let me wipe
those tears away. — And now: one little kiss?
KORYPHAIOS^(m):
No, no kisses.
KORYPHAIOS^(w):
                        You're so difficult.
KORYPHAIOS^(m):
You impossible women! How you do get
around us!
The poet was right: Can't live with you, or
without you.
30 But let's be friends.
And to celebrate, you might join us in an Ode.
CHORUS^(m and w):
                Let it never be said   [STROPHE 1]
                That my tongue is malicious:
                Both by word and by deed
I would set an example that's noble and
35   gracious.
                We've had sorrow and care
                Till we're sick of the tune.

Is there anyone here
Who would like a small loan?
                My purse is crammed,   40
                As you'll soon find;
And you needn't pay me back if the Peace gets
signed.

I've invited to lunch   [STROPHE 2]
Some Karystian rips —
An esurient bunch,   45
But I've ordered a menu to water their lips.
                I can still make soup
                And slaughter a pig.
                You're all coming, I hope?
                But a bath first, I beg!   50
                Walk right up
                As though you owned the place,
And you'll get the front door slammed to in
your face.

SCENE V

[*Enter* SPARTAN AMBASSADOR, *with en-
tourage.*]

KORYPHAIOS^(m):
The Commission has arrived from Sparta.
                        How oddly
they're walking!
                        Gentlemen, welcome to Athens!
How is life in Lakonia?
AMBASSADOR: Need we discuss that?
Simply use your eyes.
CHORUS^(m):   The poor man's right:
                        W*hat* a sight!
AMBASSADOR: Words fail me.   5
But come, gentlemen, call in your Commis-
sioners,
and let's get down to a Peace.
CHORAGOS^(m):
                        The state we're in! Can't bear
a stitch below the waist. It's a kind of pelvic
paralysis.
COMMISSIONER:
                Won't somebody call Lysistrata? —
                Gentlemen,
we're no better off than you.
AMBASSADOR: So I see.   10
A SPARTAN:
Seh, do y'all feel a certain strain
early in the morning?

AN ATHENIAN:
                    I do, sir. It's worse than a strain.
A few more days, and there's nothing for us
    but Kleisthenes,
that broken blossom.
    CHORAGOS[m]:
                    But you'd better get dressed again.
You know these people going around Athens
15   with chisels,
looking for statues of Hermes.°
    ATHENIAN: Sir, you are right.
    SPARTAN:
He certainly is! Ah'll put mah own clothes
    back on.

[*Enter* ATHENIAN COMMISSIONERS.]

    COMMISSIONER:
Gentlemen from Sparta, welcome. This is a
    sorry business.
    SPARTAN [*To one of his own group*]:
Colonel, we got dressed just in time. Ah sweah,
if they'd seen us the way we were, there'd have
20   been a new wah
between the states.
    COMMISSIONER:
Shall we call the meeting to order?
                    Now, Lakonians,
what's your proposal?
    AMBASSADOR:
                    We propose to consider peace.
    COMMISSIONER:
Good. That's on our minds, too.
                    — Summon Lysistrata.
We'll never get anywhere without her.
25   AMBASSADOR: Lysistrata?
Summon Lysis-*any*body! Only, summon!
    KORYPHAIOS[m]:   No need to summon:
here she is, herself.

[*Enter* LYSISTRATA.]

    COMMISSIONER: Lysistrata! Lion of women!
This is your hour to be
hard and yielding, outspoken and shy, austere
    and
30   gentle. You see here
the best brains of Hellas (confused, I admit,
by your devious charming) met as one man

---

16 **statues of Hermes:** The statues were the
Hermai, stone posts set up in various parts of
Athens. Just before the sailing of the Sicilian
Expedition, a group of anonymous vandals
mutilated these statues with chisels. This was con-
sidered an unhappy augury.

---

to turn the future over to you.
    LYSISTRATA: That's fair enough,
unless you men take it into your heads
to turn to each other instead of to us. But I'd
    know   35
soon enough if you did.
                    — Where is Reconciliation?
Go, some of you: bring her here.
                    [*Exeunt two women.*]
                    And now, women,
lead the Spartan delegates to me: not roughly
or insultingly, as our men handle them, but
    gently,
politely, as ladies should. Take them by the
    hand,   40
or by anything else if they won't give you their
    hands.

[*The* SPARTANS *are escorted over.*]

There. — The Athenians next, by any con-
    venient handle.

[*The* ATHENIANS *are escorted.*]

Stand there, please. — Now, all of you, listen
    to me.

[*During the following speech the two
women re-enter, carrying an enormous statue
of a naked girl; this is* RECONCILIATION.]

I'm only a woman, I know; but I've a mind,
and, I think, not a bad one: I owe it to my
    father   45
and to listening to the local politicians.
So much for that.
                    Now, gentlemen,
since I have you here, I intend to give you a
    scolding.
We are all Greeks.
Must I remind you of Thermopylai,° of
    Olympia,   50
of Delphoi? names deep in all our hearts?
Are they not a common heritage?
                    Yet you men
go raiding through the country from both
    sides,
Greek killing Greek, storming down Greek
    cities —
and all the time the Barbarian across the sea   55

---

50 **Thermopylai:** A narrow pass where, in 480
B.C., an army of 300 Spartans held out for three
days against a vastly superior Persian force.

is waiting for his chance!
                    — That's my first point.
AN ATHENIAN:
Lord! I can hardly contain myself.
    LYSISTRATA: As for you Spartans:
Was it so long ago that Perikleides°
came here to beg our help? I can see him still,
his grey face, his sombre gown. And what did
60   he want?
An army from Athens. All Messene
was hot at your heels, and the sea-god splitting
        your land.
Well, Kimon and his men,
four thousand strong, marched out and saved
        all Sparta.
And what thanks do we get? You come back
65   to murder us.
AN ATHENIAN:
They're aggressors, Lysistrata!
A SPARTAN: Ah admit it.
When Ah look at those laigs, Ah sweah Ah'll
        aggress mahself!
LYSISTRATA:
And you, Athenians: do you think you're
        blameless?
Remember that bad time when we were
        helpless,
70 and an army came from Sparta,
and that was the end of the Thessalian
        menace,
the end of Hippias and his allies.
                        And that was Sparta,
and only Sparta; but for Sparta, we'd be
cringing slaves today, not free Athenians.

[*From this point, the male responses are less
to* LYSISTRATA *than to the statue.*]

A SPARTAN:
A well shaped speech.
75   AN ATHENIAN: Certainly it has its points.
    LYSISTRATA:
Why are we fighting each other? With all this
        history
of favors given and taken, what stands in the
        way
of making peace?
    AMBASSADOR: Spahta is ready, ma'am,
so long as we get that place back.
    LYSISTRATA: What place, man?

58 **Perikleides:** A Spartan ambassador to Athens,
who successfully urged Athenians to aid Sparta in
putting down a rebellion.

AMBASSADOR:
Ah refer to Pylos.
    COMMISSIONER:
                Not a chance, by God!   80
LYSISTRATA:
Give it to them, friend.
    COMMISSIONER:
    But — what shall we have to bargain with?
LYSISTRATA:
Demand something in exchange.
    COMMISSIONER: Good idea. — Well, then:
Cockeville first, and the Happy Hills, and the
        country
between the Legs of Megara.
    AMBASSADOR: Mah government objects.
LYSISTRATA:
Over-ruled. Why fuss about a pair of legs?   85

[*General assent. The statue is removed.*]

AN ATHENIAN:
I want to get out of these clothes and start
        my plowing.
A SPARTAN:
Ah'll fertilize mahn first, by the Heavenly
        Twins!
LYSISTRATA:
And so you shall,
once you've made peace. If you are serious,
go, both of you, and talk with your allies.   90
    COMMISSIONER:
Too much talk already. No, we'll stand
        together.
we've only one end in view. All that we
        want
is our women; and I speak for our allies.
    AMBASSADOR:
Mah government concurs.
    AN ATHENIAN: So does Karystos.
    LYSISTRATA:
Good. — But before you come inside   95
to join your wives at supper, you must perform
the usual lustration. Then we'll open
our baskets for you, and all that we have is
        yours.
But you must promise upright good behavior
from this day on. Then each man home with
        his woman!   100
    AN ATHENIAN:
Let's get it over with.
    A SPARTAN: Lead on. Ah follow.
    AN ATHENIAN:
Quick as a cat can wink!
                [*Exeunt all but the* CHORUSES.]

CHORUS^(w).:

                    Embroideries and   [ANTISTROPHE 1]
                    Twinkling ornaments and
105   Pretty dresses — I hand
Them all over to you, and with never a qualm.
                    They'll be nice for your daughters
                          On festival days
                    When the girls bring the Goddess
110   The ritual prize.
                                Come in, one and all:
                                Take what you will.
I've nothing here so tightly corked that you
          can't make it spill.

                                             [ANTISTROPHE 2]
                    You may search my house,
115   But you'll not find
                    The least thing of use,
Unless your two eyes are keener than mine.
                    Your numberless brats
                    Are half starved? and your slaves?
120   Courage, grandpa! I've lots
                    Of grain left, and big loaves.
                          I'll fill your guts,
                          I'll go the whole hog;
But if you come too close to me, remember:
          'ware the dog!

                                             [Exeunt CHORUSES.]

EXODOS

[A DRUNKEN CITIZEN enters, approaches the
gate, and is halted by a sentry.]

CITIZEN:
Open. The. Door.
     SENTRY: Now, friend, just shove along!
— So you want to sit down. If it weren't such
          an old joke,
I'd tickle your tail with this torch. Just the
          sort of gag
this audience appreciates.
     CITIZEN: I. Stay. Right. Here.
     SENTRY:
Get away from there, or I'll scalp you! The
5   gentlemen from Sparta
are just coming back from dinner.
     [Exit CITIZEN; the general company re-
     enters; the two CHORUSES now represent
     SPARTANS and ATHENIANS.]
     A SPARTAN: Ah must say,
Ah never tasted better grub.
     AN ATHENIAN: And those Lakonians!

They're gentlemen, by the Lord! Just goes to
          show,
a drink to the wise is sufficient.
     COMMISSIONER: And why not?
A sober man's an ass.   10
Men of Athens, mark my words: the only
          efficient
Ambassador's a drunk Ambassador. Is that
          clear?
Look: we go to Sparta,
and when we get there we're dead sober. The
          result?
Everyone cackling at everyone else. They make
          speeches;   15
and even if we understand, we get it all wrong
when we file our reports in Athens. But
          today — !
Everybody's happy. Couldn't tell the difference
between *Drink to Me Only* and
The Star-Spangled Athens.
                                        What's a few lies,   20
washed down in good strong drink?

[*Re-enter the* DRUNKEN CITIZEN.]

     SENTRY: God almighty,
he's back again!
     CITIZEN: I. Resume. My. Place.
     A SPARTAN [*To an* ATHENIAN]:
Ah beg yo', seh,
take yo' instrument in yo' hand and play
          for us.
Ah'm told   25
yo' understand the intricacies of the floot?
Ah'd lahk to execute a song and dance
in honor of Athens,
                         and, of cohse, of Spahta.
     CITIZEN:
Toot. On. Your. Flute.

[*The following song is a solo — an aria —
accompanied by the flute. The* CHORUS OF
SPARTANS *begins a slow dance.*]

A SPARTAN:
O Memory,   30
Let the Muse speak once more
In my young voice. Sing glory.
Sing Artemision's shore,
Where Athens fluttered the Persians. *Alalai,*
Sing glory, that great   35
Victory! Sing also
Our Leonidas and his men,
Those wild boars, sweat and blood
Down in a red drench. Then, then

40 The barbarians broke, though they had stood
Numberless as the sands before!

O Artemis,°
Virgin Goddess, whose darts
Flash in our forests: approve
45 This pact of peace and join our hearts,
From this day on, in love.
Huntress, descend!

LYSISTRATA:
All that will come in time.
                                    But now, Lakonians,
take home your wives. Athenians, take yours.
Each man be kind to his woman; and you,
50   women,
be equally kind. Never again, pray God,
shall we lose our way in such madness.

KORYPHAIOS (Athenian):   And now
let's dance our joy.

[*From this point the dance becomes general.*]

CHORUS (Athenian):
Dance, you Graces
                                    Artemis, dance
Dance, Phoibos,° Lord of dancing
                                                    Dance,
55 In a scurry of Maenads, Lord Dionysos°
                                    Dance, Zeus Thunderer
                        Dance, Lady Hera°
Queen of the sky
                        Dance, dance, all you gods

42 **Artemis:** Goddess of virginity, of the hunt,
and of childbirth.
55 **Phoibos:** God of the sun.
56 **Maenads, Lord Dionysos:** The maenads were
ecstatic women in the train of Dionysos, god of
wine.
57 **Hera:** Wife of Zeus.

Dance witness everlasting of our pact
Evohí Evohé   60
Dance for the dearest
                                    the Bringer of Peace
Deathless Aphrodite!

COMMISSIONER:
Now let us have another song from Sparta.

CHORUS (Spartan):
     From Taygetos, from Taygetos,
          Lakonian Muse, come down.   65
     Sing to the Lord Apollo
          Who rules Amyklai Town.

     Sing Athena of the House of Brass!°
     Sing Leda's Twins,° that chivalry
          Resplendent on the shore   70
     Of our Eurotas; sing the girls
          That dance along before:

     Sparkling in dust their gleaming feet,
          Their hair a Bacchant fire,
     And Leda's daughter, thyrsos° raised,   75
          Leads their triumphant choir.

CHORUSES (S and A):
Evohé!
     Evohaí!
          Evohé!
                    We pass
          Dancing
                    dancing
                         to greet
Athena of the House of Brass.

68 **Athena of the House of Brass:** A temple
standing on the Akropolis of Sparta.
69 **Leda's Twins:** Leda, raped by Zeus, bore
quadruplets: two daughters, Helen and Klytaimne-
stra, and two sons, Kastor and Polydeukes.
75 **thyrsos:** A staff twined with ivy, carried by
Dionysos and his followers.

Of the hundreds of ancient Greek comedies that were written, only
eleven by Aristophanes and four by Menander (c. 342 B.C.–299 B.C.) are extant, and three of Menander's four survive only in long fragments. Aristophanes seems to have written about forty plays, Menander more than twice
as many. Hundreds of other men wrote comedies in ancient Greece, but they
are mere names, or names attached to brief fragments. This means that when
we talk about Greek comedy we are really talking about a fraction of Aristophanes' work, and an even smaller fraction of Menander's.

Greek comedy is customarily divided into three kinds: Old Comedy
(486 B.C., when comedy was first given official recognition at the festival

called the City Dionysia, to 404 B.C., the end of the Peloponnesian War, when Athens was humbled and freedom of speech was curtailed); Middle Comedy (404 B.C. to 336 B.C., the accession of Alexander, when Athens was no longer free); and New Comedy (336 B.C. to c. 250 B.C., the approximate date of the last fragments). Of Old Comedy, there are Aristophanes' plays; of Middle Comedy, there is *Plutus*, one of Aristophanes' last plays; of New Comedy, there are Menander's fragments and his recently discovered *Dyskolos* (*The Disagreeable Man*).

Old Comedy is a curious combination of obscenity, farce, political allegory, satire, and lyricism. Puns, literary allusions, phallic jokes, political jibes, etc. periodically give way to joyful song; Aristophanes seems to have been something of a combination of Joyce, Swift, and Shelley. Other comparisons may be helpful. Perhaps we can say that in their loosely connected episodes and in their rapid shifts from lyricism and fantasy to mockery the plays are something like a Marx Brothers movie (Harpo's musical episodes juxtaposed with Groucho's irreverent wisecracks and outrageous ogling), though the plays are more explicitly political; and they are something like the rock musical, *Hair*, which combined lyricism and politics with sex.

Normally Aristophanes' plays have the following structure:

1. *Prologos*, prologue or exposition. Someone has a bright idea, and sets it forth either in monologue or dialogue. In *Lysistrata*, the prologue consists of lines 1–212, in which Lysistrata persuades the women to refrain from sex with their husbands and thus compel their husbands to give up the war.

2. *Parodos*, entrance of the chorus. The twenty-four or so members of the chorus express their opinion of the idea. (The *koryphaios* or leader of the chorus perhaps sang some lines by himself.) *Lysistrata* is somewhat unusual in having two half-choruses or *hemichori*, one of Old Men and another of Old Women, each with its own leader. Probably each half-chorus had twelve members.

3. *Epeisodion*, episode or scene. In the first scene of *Lysistrata* the women defeat the Commissioner. (A scene in this position, that is, before the *parabasis*, is sometimes called the *agon* or debate.)

4. *Parabasis*, usually an elaborate composition in which the leader of the chorus ordinarily sheds his dramatic character and addresses the audience on the poet's behalf, the other actors having briefly retired. The *parabasis* in *Lysistrata* is unusual; it is much shorter than those in Aristophanes' earlier plays, and the chorus does not speak directly for the playwright.

5. *Epeisodia*, episodes or scenes, sometimes briefly separated by choral songs. These episodes have to do with the working out of the original bright idea. In *Lysistrata* the first scene of this group (labeled Scene II because we have already had one scene before the *parabasis*) shows the women seeking to desert the cause, the second shows Myrrhine — loyal to the idea — tormenting her husband Kinesias, the third shows the Athenian Commissioner discomfited by an erection, and the fourth shows the Spartan ambassadors similarly discomfited.

6. *Exodos* or final scene, customarily of reconciliation and rejoicing. There is often talk of a wedding and a feast. In this play a Spartan sings in praise not only of Sparta but also of Athens, and the chorus praises the deities worshipped in both states.

Perhaps all Old Comedy was rather like this, but it should be remembered that even Aristophanes' eleven plays do not all follow the pattern exactly. *Lysistrata*, for example, is unusual in having two hemichori and in having the chorus retain its identity during the parabasis. But *Lysistrata* (the accent is on the second syllable, and the name in effect means "Disbander-of-the-Army") is typical in its political concern, in its fantasy, in its bawdry, and in its revelry. It touches on serious, destructive themes, but it is joyous and extravagant, ending with a newly unified society. These points require some explanation.

First, Aristophanes' political concern. *Lysistrata* is the last of Aristophanes' three plays opposing the Peloponnesian War (the earlier two are *Acharnians* and *Peace*). This drawn-out war (431–404 B.C.), named for a peninsula forming the southern part of Greece, was fought between Athens (with some allies) and a confederacy headed by Sparta. Though enemies at the time of the play, in 478 B.C. Athens and Sparta and other communities had become allied in order to defeat a common enemy, the Persians, but once the Persian threat was destroyed, Athens deprived most of its allies of their autonomy and, in effect, Athens ruled an empire. Moreover, Athens tried to extend its empire. The war ultimately cost Athens its overseas empire and its leadership on the mainland. In 413 B.C. Athens had suffered an especially disastrous naval defeat; it had made something of a recovery by the time of *Lysistrata* (performed 411 B.C.), but the cost in manpower and money was enormous. Yet Athens persisted in its dream of conquest and of colonizing. To counter this fantastic idea Aristophanes holds up another fantastic idea: the women will end the war by a sex strike. Actually, this is not one fantastic idea but two, for the idea of a sex strike is not more fantastic (for Athenians of the fifth century B.C.) than the idea of women playing a role — not to speak of a decisive role — in national affairs. Lysistrata, reporting her husband's view, is reporting the view of every Athenian: "War's a man's affair." (He was quoting from Homer's *Iliad*, so the point was beyond dispute.) And so there is something wild in her suggestion that the women can save the Greek cities (her hope goes beyond Athens, to Sparta and the other combatants), and in her comparison of the state to a ball of tangled yarn:

> COMMISSIONER:
> All this is beside the point.
>   Will you be so kind
> as to tell me how you mean to save Greece?
>   LYSISTRATA:
>   Of course.
> Nothing could be simpler.

COMMISSIONER:
> I assure you, I'm all ears.

LYSISTRATA:
Do you know anything about weaving?
Say the yarn gets tangled: we thread it
this way and that through the skein, up and down,
until it's free. And it's like that with war.
We'll send our envoys
up and down, this way and that, all over Greece,
until it's finished.

COMMISSIONER:
> Yarn? Thread? Skein?

Are you out of your mind? I tell you,
war is a serious business.

LYSISTRATA:
> So serious

that I'd like to go on talking about weaving.

COMMISSIONER:
All right. Go ahead.

LYSISTRATA:
> The first thing we have to do

is to wash our yarn, get the dirt out of it.
You see? Isn't there too much dirt here in Athens?
You must wash those men away.
> Then our spoiled wool —

that's like your job-hunters, out for a life
of no work and big pay. Back to the basket,
citizens or not, allies or not,
or friendly immigrants.
> And your colonies?

Hanks of wool lost in various places. Pull them
together, weave them into one great whole,
and our voters are clothed for ever.

To the Commissioner, this is utterly fantastic:

COMMISSIONER:
> It would take a woman

to reduce state questions to a matter of carding and weaving.

Such is the male view, and so these fantastic women, in order to exert influence, must resort to another fantastic idea, the sex strike, and here we encounter Aristophanes' famous bawdry. In fact the play's reputation for bawdry is grossly exaggerated. Until recently, when pornography was hard to get, *Lysistrata* — because it was literature — provided one of the few available texts that talked of erections and of female delight in sex, and Aubrey Beardsley's illustrations (1896) doubtless helped to establish the book's reputation as a sexual stimulus. But it is really pretty tame stuff compared to what is now readily available, and the play, for all its sexual jokes, is not really about sex but about peace, harmony, union. Union between husbands and wives, between all in Athens, and between Athens and the other Greek-speaking communities. Almost the last lines of the play are:

> But now, Lakonians,
> take home your wives. Athenians, take yours.
> Each man be kind to his woman; and you, women,
> be equally kind. Never again, pray God,
> shall we lose our way in such madness.

Sex, of course, has brought about this union, for only when Athenian and Spartan men are both afflicted by the power of sex, and thus share a single overriding concern, are they able to compromise on the less important political differences that have divided them. And so, as we think about the play, the heroine is, finally, not so much the fantastic Lysistrata (she is also very much a male Athenian's idea of a woman: "To put it bluntly," she says, "we're dying to get laid"); the real heroine of the play is a rather shadowy figure, a statue of a nude female called Reconciliation, because reconciliation, not sex, is really what the play is about.

During the years of the Vietnam War, one often saw a bumper-sticker, "Make love, not war." The two activities are not mutually incompatible, but we get the idea; Aristophanes, some twenty-five centuries earlier, got the idea too. He saw in sexual union a symbol of a power so great that it subdues even conquest-mad armies. One might say that sex in this play deflects men from divisive self-assertiveness and (may we say?) brings them to their senses. Restored to their senses, they can perceive the mutual good.

One final point: the whole play, of course, not only is utterly improbable but also is utterly impossible: the women complain that they are sex-starved because the men are away at the war, but we soon find that the women will remedy this situation by withholding sex from the men — who, we thought, were away at the war. How can one withhold sex from men who are supposedly not present? But Old Comedy never worried about such consistency.

A few words should be said about Middle Comedy and New Comedy. Middle Comedy is a convenient label to apply to the lost plays that must have marked the transition from Old Comedy to New Comedy, that is, to the surviving work of Menander. In New Comedy, written when Athens' political greatness was gone, and when political invective was impossible, the chorus has dwindled to musicians and dancers who perform intermittently, characters tend to be types (the young lover, the crabby old father, etc.), and the plot is regularly a young man's wooing of a maid. Fortune seems unfair and unpredictable, but in the end the virtuous are rewarded. The personal satire and obscenity of Old Comedy are gone, and in their place is a respectably conducted tale showing how, after humorous difficulties, the young man achieves his goal. The plot steadily moves toward the happy ending, which is far more integral than the more or less elusive allegoric (or metaphoric) union at the end of Lysistrata. It was New Comedy that influenced Rome (which could scarcely have imitated the political satire of Old Comedy), and through Rome modern Europe. Shakespeare, for example, whose comedies have been described as obstacle races to the altar, was a descendant of Menander though he knew nothing of Menander's work first-hand.

A MIDSUMMER NIGHT'S DREAM

William Shakespeare

Edited by Wolfgang Clemen

William Shakespeare (1564–1616) was born in Stratford, England, of middle-class parents. Nothing of interest is known about his early years, but by 1590 he was acting and writing plays in London. He early worked in all three Elizabethan dramatic genres — tragedy, comedy, and history. *Romeo and Juliet*, for example, was written about 1595, the year of *Richard II*, and in the following year he wrote A *Midsummer Night's Dream*. Other major comedies are *The Merchant of Venice* (1596–1597), *As You Like It* (1599–1600), and *Twelfth Night* (1599–1600). His last major works, *The Winter's Tale* (1610–1611) and *The Tempest* (1611), are usually called "romances"; these plays have happy endings but they seem more meditative and less joyful than the earlier comedies.

[*DRAMATIS PERSONAE*

THESEUS, *Duke of Athens*
EGEUS, *father to Hermia*
LYSANDER
DEMETRIUS } *in love with Hermia*
PHILOSTRATE, *Master of the Revels to Theseus*
PETER QUINCE, *a carpenter;* PROLOGUE *in the play*
SNUG, *a joiner;* LION *in the play*
NICK BOTTOM, *a weaver;* PYRAMUS *in the play*
FRANCIS FLUTE, *a bellows mender;* THISBY *in the play*
TOM SNOUT, *a tinker;* WALL *in the play*
ROBIN STARVELING, *a tailor;* MOONSHINE *in the play*
HIPPOLYTA, *Queen of the Amazons, betrothed to Theseus*

HERMIA, *daughter to Egeus, in love with Lysander*
HELENA, *in love with Demetrius*
OBERON, *King of the Fairies*
TITANIA, *Queen of the Fairies*
PUCK, *or Robin Goodfellow*
PEASEBLOSSOM
COBWEB
MOTH } *fairies*
MUSTARDSEED
Other FAIRIES *attending their King and Queen*
ATTENDANTS *on Theseus and Hippolyta*

Scene: Athens, and a wood near it]

A scene from the Royal Shakespeare Theatre production of A *Midsummer Night's Dream*, directed by Peter Brook, 1970. (Photograph: David Farrell.)

[ACT I]

[SCENE I. *The palace of* THESEUS.]

Enter THESEUS, HIPPOLYTA, [PHILOSTRATE,]
with others.

THESEUS.
Now, fair Hippolyta, our nuptial hour
Draws on apace. Four happy days bring in
Another moon; but, O, methinks, how slow
This old moon wanes! She lingers°1 my
    desires,
5 Like to a stepdame, or a dowager,
Long withering out a young man's revenue.°
    HIPPOLYTA:
Four days will quickly steep themselves in
    night,
Four nights will quickly dream away the time;
And then the moon, like to a silver bow
10 New-bent in heaven, shall behold the night
Of our solemnities.
    THESEUS: Go, Philostrate,
Stir up the Athenian youth to merriments,
Awake the pert° and nimble spirit of mirth,
Turn melancholy forth to funerals;
15 The pale companion° is not for our pomp.°
                [*Exit* PHILOSTRATE.]
Hippolyta, I wooed thee with my sword,°
And won thy love, doing thee injuries;
But I will wed thee in another key,
With pomp, with triumph, and with reveling.

(*Enter* EGEUS *and his daughter* HERMIA, *and*
LYSANDER, *and* DEMETRIUS.)

    EGEUS:
20 Happy be Theseus, our renownèd Duke!
    THESEUS:
Thanks, good Egeus.° What's the news with
    thee?

From *A Midsummer Night's Dream* by William
Shakespeare, edited by Wolfgang Clemens. Copyright © 1963 Wolfgang Clemens. Copyright © by
Sylvan Barnet. Reprinted by arrangement with The
New American Library, Inc., New York, New York.
  1 The degree sign (°) indicates a footnote,
which is keyed to the text by line number. Text
references are printed in **bold face** type; the annotation follows in roman type.

I.i. 4 **lingers** makes to linger, delays 6 **Long withering out a young man's revenue** diminishing the
young man's money (because she must be supported
by him) 13 **pert** lively 15 **companion** fellow
(contemptuous) 15 **pomp** festive procession 16
I wooed thee with my sword (Theseus had captured Hippolyta when he conquered the Amazons)
21 **Egeus** (pronounced "E-gé-us")

    EGEUS:
Full of vexation come I, with complaint
Against my child, my daughter Hermia.
Stand forth, Demetrius. My noble lord,
This man hath my consent to marry her.   25
Stand forth, Lysander. And, my gracious Duke
This man hath bewitched the bosom of my
    child.
Thou, thou, Lysander, thou hast given her
    rhymes,
And interchanged love tokens with my child.
Thou hast by moonlight at her window sung,   30
With feigning voice, verses of feigning love,
And stol'n the impression of her fantasy°
With bracelets of thy hair, rings, gauds,
    conceits,
Knacks,° trifles, nosegays, sweetmeats, messengers
Of strong prevailment in unhardened youth.   35
With cunning hast thou filched my daughter's
    heart,
Turned her obedience, which is due to me,
To stubborn harshness. And, my gracious
    Duke,
Be it so she will not here before your Grace
Consent to marry with Demetrius,   40
I beg the ancient privilege of Athens:
As she is mine, I may dispose of her,
Which shall be either to this gentleman
Or to her death, according to our law
Immediately° provided in that case.   45
    THESEUS:
What say you, Hermia? Be advised, fair maid.
To you your father should be as a god,
One that composed your beauties; yea, and one
To whom you are but as a form in wax
By him imprinted and within his power   50
To leave the figure or disfigure it.
Demetrius is a worthy gentleman.
    HERMIA:
So is Lysander.
    THESEUS: In himself he is;
But in this kind, wanting your father's voice,°   55
The other must be held the worthier.

32 **stol'n the impression of her fantasy** fraudulently
impressed your image upon her imagination 33–
34 **gauds, conceits, Knacks** trinkets, cleverly devised tokens, knickknacks 45 **Immediately** expressly
54 **But in . . . father's voice** but in this particular respect, lacking your father's approval

HERMIA:
I would my father looked but with my eyes.
THESEUS:
Rather your eyes must with his judgment look.
HERMIA:
I do entreat your Grace to pardon me.
I know not by what power I am made bold,
60   Nor how it may concern my modesty,
In such a presence here to plead my thoughts;
But I beseech your Grace that I may know
The worst that may befall me in this case,
If I refuse to wed Demetrius.
THESEUS:
65   Either to die the death, or to abjure
Forever the society of men.
Therefore, fair Hermia, question your desires;
Know of° your youth, examine well your blood,°
Whether, if you yield not to your father's choice,
70   You can endure the livery of a nun,
For aye to be in shady cloister mewed,°
To live a barren sister all your life,
Chanting faint hymns to the cold fruitless moon.°
Thrice-blessèd they that master so their blood,
75   To undergo such maiden pilgrimage;
But earthlier happy is the rose distilled,°
Than that which, withering on the virgin thorn,
Grows, lives, and dies in single blessedness.
HERMIA:
So will I grow, so live, so die, my lord,
80   Ere I will yield my virgin patent° up
Unto his lordship, whose unwished yoke
My soul consents not to give sovereignty.
THESEUS:
Take time to pause; and, by the next new moon —
The sealing day betwixt my love and me,
85   For everlasting bond of fellowship —
Upon that day either prepare to die
For disobedience to your father's will,
Or else to wed Demetrius, as he would,
Or on Diana's altar to protest
90   For aye austerity and single life.
DEMETRIUS:
Relent, sweet Hermia: and, Lysander, yield
Thy crazèd title° to my certain right.

LYSANDER:
You have her father's love, Demetrius;
Let me have Hermia's: do you marry him.
EGEUS:
Scornful Lysander! True, he hath my love,   95
And what is mine my love shall render him.
And she is mine, and all my right of her
I do estate unto° Demetrius.
LYSANDER:
I am, my lord, as well derived as he,
As well possessed,° my love is more than his;   100
My fortunes every way as fairly ranked
(If not with vantage°) as Demetrius';
And, which is more than all these boasts can be,
I am beloved of beauteous Hermia.
Why should not I then prosecute my right?   105
Demetrius, I'll avouch it to his head,°
Made love to Nedar's daughter, Helena,
And won her soul; and she, sweet lady, dotes,
Devoutly dotes, dotes in idolatry,
Upon this spotted° and inconstant man.   110
THESEUS:
I must confess that I have heard so much,
And with Demetrius thought to have spoken thereof;
But, being overfull of self-affairs,
My mind did lose it. But, Demetrius, come;
And come, Egeus. You shall go with me;   115
I have some private schooling for you both.
For you, fair Hermia, look you arm yourself
To fit your fancies to your father's will;
Or else the law of Athens yields you up —
Which by no means we may extenuate —   120
To death, or to a vow of single life.
Come, my Hippolyta. What cheer, my love?
Demetrius and Egeus, go along.
I must employ you in some business
Against° our nuptial, and confer with you   125
Of something nearly° that concerns yourselves.
EGEUS:
With duty and desire we follow you
        (Exeunt [all but LYSANDER and HERMIA].)
LYSANDER:
How now, my love! Why is your cheek so pale?
How chance° the roses there do fade so fast?
HERMIA:
Belike° for want of rain, which I could well   130

68 **Know of** ascertain from   68 **blood** passions   71 **mewed** caged   73 **moon** i.e., Diana, goddess of chastity   76 **distilled** made into perfumes   80 **patent** privilege   92 **crazèd title** flawed claim   98 **estate unto** settle upon   100 **As well possessed** as rich   102 **If not with vantage** if not better   106 **to his head** in his teeth   110 **spotted** i.e., morally stained   125 **Against** in preparation for   126 **nearly** closely   129 **How chance** how does it come that   130 **Belike** perhaps

Beteem° them from the tempest of my eyes.
LYSANDER:
Ay me! For aught that I could ever read,
Could ever hear by tale or history,
The course of true love never did run smooth;
135 But, either it was different in blood —
HERMIA:
O cross! Too high to be enthralled to low!
LYSANDER:
Or else misgraffèd° in respect of years —
HERMIA:
O spite! Too old to be engaged to young!
LYSANDER:
Or else it stood upon the choice of friends —
HERMIA:
140 O hell! To choose love by another's eyes!
LYSANDER:
Or, if there were a sympathy in choice,
War, death, or sickness did lay siege to it,
Making it momentany° as a sound,
Swift as a shadow, short as any dream,
145 Brief as the lightning in the collied° night,
That, in a spleen,° unfolds both heaven and
earth,
And ere a man hath power to say "Behold!"
The jaws of darkness do devour it up:
So quick bright things come to confusion.
HERMIA:
150 If then true lovers have been ever crossed,
It stands as an edict in destiny:
Then let us teach our trial patience,°
Because it is a customary cross,
As due to love as thoughts and dreams and
sighs,
155 Wishes and tears, poor Fancy's° followers.
LYSANDER:
A good persuasion.° Therefore, hear me,
Hermia.
I have a widow aunt, a dowager
Of great revenue, and she hath no child.
From Athens is her house remote seven
leagues,
160 And she respects me as her only son.
There, gentle Hermia, may I marry thee,
And to that place the sharp Athenian law
Cannot pursue us. If thou lovest me, then,
Steal forth thy father's house tomorrow night;

And in the wood, a league without the town,   165
Where I did meet thee once with Helena,
To do observance to a morn of May,
There will I stay for thee.
HERMIA: My good Lysander!
I swear to thee, by Cupid's strongest bow,
By his best arrow with the golden head,°   170
By the simplicity of Venus' doves,
By that which knitteth souls and prospers
loves,
And by that fire which burned the Carthage
queen,°
When the false Troyan under sail was seen,
By all the vows that ever men have broke,   175
In number more than ever women spoke,
In that same place thou hast appointed me,
Tomorrow truly will I meet with thee.
LYSANDER:
Keep promise, love. Look, here comes Helena.

(*Enter* HELENA.)

HERMIA:
God speed fair Helena! Whither away?   180
HELENA:
Call you me fair? That fair again unsay.
Demetrius loves your fair.° O happy fair!
Your eyes are lodestars,° and your tongue's
sweet air°
More tunable than lark to shepherd's ear,
When wheat is green, when hawthorn buds
appear.   185
Sickness is catching. O, were favor° so,
Yours would I catch, fair Hermia, ere I go;
My ear should catch your voice, my eye your
eye,
My tongue should catch your tongue's sweet
melody.
Were the world mine, Demetrius being
bated,°   190
The rest I'd give to be to you translated.°
O, teach me how you look, and with what art
You sway the motion of Demetrius' heart!
HERMIA:
I frown upon him, yet he loves me still.
HELENA:
O that your frowns would teach my smiles
such skill!   195

131 **Beteem** bring forth 137 **misgraffèd** ill matched, misgrafted   143 **momentany** momentary, passing   145 **collied** blackened   146 **spleen** flash   152 **teach our trial patience** i.e., teach ourselves to be patient   155 **Fancy's** Love's   156 **persuasion** principle

170 **arrow with the golden head** (Cupid's gold-headed arrows caused love, the leaden ones dislike)   173 **Carthage queen** Dido (who burned herself on a funeral pyre when the Trojan Aeneas left her)   182 **fair** beauty   183 **lodestars** guiding stars   183 **air** music   186 **favor** looks   190 **bated** excepted   191 **translated** transformed

HERMIA:
I give him curses, yet he gives me love.

HELENA:
O that my prayers could such affection move!

HERMIA:
The more I hate, the more he follows me.

HELENA:
The more I love, the more he hateth me.

HERMIA:
200 His folly, Helena, is no fault of mine.

HELENA:
None, but your beauty: would that fault were mine!

HERMIA:
Take comfort. He no more shall see my face;
Lysander and myself will fly this place.
Before the time I did Lysander see,
205 Seemed Athens as a paradise to me.
O, then, what graces in my love do dwell,
That he hath turned a heaven unto a hell!

LYSANDER:
Helen, to you our minds we will unfold.
Tomorrow night, when Phoebe° doth behold
210 Her silver visage in the wat'ry glass,
Decking with liquid pearl the bladed grass,
A time that lovers' flights doth still° conceal,
Through Athens' gates have we devised to steal.

HERMIA:
And in the wood, where often you and I
215 Upon faint primrose beds were wont to lie,
Emptying our bosoms of their counsel sweet,
There my Lysander and myself shall meet,
And thence from Athens turn away our eyes,
To seek new friends and stranger companies.°
220 Farewell, sweet playfellow. Pray thou for us;
And good luck grant thee thy Demetrius!
Keep word, Lysander. We must starve our sight
From lovers' food till tomorrow deep midnight.

LYSANDER:
I will, my Hermia.   (Exit HERMIA.)
Helena, adieu.
225 As you on him, Demetrius dote on you!
(Exit LYSANDER.)

HELENA:
How happy some o'er other some° can be!
Through Athens I am thought as fair as she.

But what of that? Demetrius thinks not so;
He will not know what all but he do know.
And as he errs, doting on Hermia's eyes,   230
So I, admiring of his qualities.
Things base and vile, holding no quantity,°
Love can transpose to form and dignity.
Love looks not with the eyes, but with the mind,
And therefore is winged Cupid painted blind.   235
Nor hath Love's mind of any judgment taste;
Wings, and no eyes, figure° unheedy haste:
And therefore is Love said to be a child,
Because in choice he is so oft beguiled.
As waggish boys in game themselves forswear,   240
So the boy Love is perjured everywhere.
For ere Demetrius looked on Hermia's eyne,°
He hailed down oaths that he was only mine;
And when this hail some heat from Hermia felt,
So he dissolved, and show'rs of oaths did melt.   245
I will go tell him of fair Hermia's flight.
Then to the wood will he tomorrow night
Pursue her; and for this intelligence°
If I have thanks, it is a dear expense:°
But herein mean I to enrich my pain,   250
To have his sight thither and back again.
(Exit.)

[SCENE II. QUINCE's house.]

Enter QUINCE *the Carpenter, and* SNUG *the
Joiner, and* BOTTOM *the Weaver, and* FLUTE
the Bellows Mender, and SNOUT *the Tinker,
and* STARVELING *the Tailor.*°

QUINCE: Is all our company here?
BOTTOM: You were best to call them generally,° man by man, according to the scrip.
QUINCE: Here is the scroll of every man's name, which is thought fit, through all Athens,   5
to play in our interlude° before the Duke and the Duchess, on his wedding day at night.

209 **Phoebe** the moon 212 **still** always 219 **stranger companies** the company of strangers 226 **some o'er other some** some in comparison with others

232 **holding no quantity** having no proportion (therefore unattractive) 237 **figure** symbolize 242 **eyne** eyes 248 **intelligence** piece of news 249 **dear expense** (1) expense gladly incurred (2) heavy cost (in Demetrius' opinion) I.ii.s.d. (the names of the clowns suggest their trades. *Bottom* skein on which the yarn is wound; *Quince* quines, blocks of wood used for building; *Snug* close-fitting; *Flute* suggesting fluted bellows [for church organs]; *Snout* spout of a kettle; *Starveling* an allusion to the proverbial thinness of tailors) 3 **generally** (Bottom means "individually") 6 **interlude** dramatic entertainment

BOTTOM: First, good Peter Quince, say what the play treats on; then read the names of the
10 actors; and so grow to a point.

QUINCE: Marry,° our play is, "The most lamentable comedy, and most cruel death of Pyramus and Thisby."

BOTTOM: A very good piece of work, I assure you, and a merry. Now, good Peter
15 Quince, call forth your actors by the scroll. Masters, spread yourselves.

QUINCE: Answer as I call you. Nick Bottom, the weaver.

20 BOTTOM: Ready. Name what part I am for, and proceed.

QUINCE: You, Nick Bottom, are set down for Pyramus.

BOTTOM: What is Pyramus? A lover, or a
25 tyrant?

QUINCE: A lover that kills himself, most gallant, for love.

BOTTOM: That will ask some tears in the true performing of it: if I do it, let the audi-
30 ence look to their eyes. I will move storms, I will condole° in some measure. To the rest: yet my chief humor° is for a tyrant. I could play Ercles° rarely, or a part to tear a cat in, to make all split.

35
    The raging rocks
    And shivering shocks
    Shall break the locks
        Of prison gates;
    And Phibbus' car°
40 Shall shine from far,
    And make and mar
        The foolish Fates.

This was lofty! Now name the rest of the players. This is Ercles' vein, a tyrant's vein. A
45 lover is more condoling.

QUINCE: Francis Flute, the bellows mender.

FLUTE: Here, Peter Quince.

QUINCE: Flute, you must take Thisby on you.

50 FLUTE: What is Thisby? A wand'ring knight?

QUINCE: It is the lady that Pyramus must love.

FLUTE: Nay, faith, let not me play a woman. I have a beard coming.   55

QUINCE: That's all one.° You shall play it in a mask, and you may speak as small° as you will.

BOTTOM: An° I may hide my face, let me play Thisby too, I'll speak in a monstrous   60 little voice, "Thisne, Thisne!" "Ah Pyramus, my lover dear! Thy Thisby dear, and lady dear!"

QUINCE: No, no; you must play Pyramus: and, Flute, you Thisby.   65

BOTTOM: Well, proceed.

QUINCE: Robin Starveling, the tailor.

STARVELING: Here, Peter Quince.

QUINCE: Robin Starveling, you must play Thisby's mother. Tom Snout, the tinker.   70

SNOUT: Here, Peter Quince.

QUINCE: You, Pyramus' father: myself, Thisby's father: Snug, the joiner; you, the lion's part. And I hope here is a play fitted.

SNUG: Have you the lion's part written?   75 Pray you, if it be, give it me, for I am slow of study.

QUINCE: You may do it extempore, for it is nothing but roaring.

BOTTOM: Let me play the lion too. I will   80 roar that° I will do any man's heart good to hear me. I will roar, that I will make the Duke say, "Let him roar again, let him roar again."

QUINCE: An you should do it too terribly, you would fright the Duchess and the ladies,   85 that they would shriek; and that were enough to hang us all.

ALL: That would hang us, every mother's son.

BOTTOM: I grant you, friends, if you should   90 fright the ladies out of their wits, they would have no more discretion but to hang us: but I will aggravate° my voice so that I will roar you as gently as any sucking dove; I will roar you an 'twere° any nightingale.   95

QUINCE: You can play no part but Pyramus; for Pyramus is a sweet-faced man; a proper° man as one shall see in a summer's day; a most lovely, gentlemanlike man: therefore you must needs play Pyramus.   100

BOTTOM: Well, I will undertake it. What beard were I best to play it in?

---

11 **Marry** (an interjection, originally an oath, "By the Virgin Mary")   31 **condole** lament   32 **humor** disposition   33 **Ercles** Hercules (a part notorious for ranting)   39 **Phibbus' car** (mispronunciation for "Phoebus' car," or chariot, i.e., the sun)

56 **That's all one** it makes no difference   57 **small** softly   59 **An** if   81 **that** so that   93 **aggravate** (Bottom means "moderate")   95 **an 'twere** as if it were   97 **proper** handsome

QUINCE: Why, what you will.

BOTTOM: I will discharge it in either your
105 straw-color beard, your orange-tawny beard,
your purple-in-grain° beard, or your French-
crown-color° beard, your perfit° yellow.

QUINCE: Some of your French crowns° have
no hair at all, and then you will play bare-
110 faced.° But, masters, here are your parts; and
I am to entreat you, request you, and desire
you, to con° them by tomorrow night; and
meet me in the palace wood, a mile without
the town, by moonlight. There will we re-
115 hearse, for if we meet in the city, we shall be
dogged with company, and our devices°
known. In the meantime I will draw a bill of
properties,° such as our play wants. I pray you,
fail me not.
120 BOTTOM: We will meet; and there we may
rehearse most obscenely° and courageously.
Take pains; be perfit: adieu.

QUINCE: At the Duke's Oak we meet.

BOTTOM: Enough; hold or cut bowstrings.°

(*Exeunt.*)

[ACT II

SCENE I.   *A wood near Athens.*]

Enter a FAIRY *at one door, and* ROBIN GOOD-
FELLOW [PUCK] *at another.*

PUCK:

How now, spirit! Whither wander you?

FAIRY:

Over hill, over dale,
  Thorough bush, thorough brier,
Over park, over pale,°
  Thorough flood, thorough fire,
5 I do wander everywhere,
Swifter than the moon's sphere;°
And I serve the Fairy Queen,

To dew her orbs° upon the green.
The cowslips tall her pensioners° be: 10
In their gold coats spots you see;
Those be rubies, fairy favors,°
In those freckles live their savors.°
I must go seek some dewdrops here,
And hang a pearl in every cowslip's ear.   15
Farewell, thou lob° of spirits; I'll be gone.
Our Queen and all her elves come here anon.

PUCK:

The King doth keep his revels here tonight.
Take heed the Queen come not within his
  sight.
For Oberon is passing fell and wrath,°   20
Because that she as her attendant hath
A lovely boy, stolen from an Indian king;
She never had so sweet a changeling.°
And jealous Oberon would have the child
Knight of his train, to trace° the forests wild.   25
But she perforce withholds the lovèd boy,
Crowns him with flowers, and makes him all
  her joy.
And now they never meet in grove or green,
By fountain clear, or spangled starlight sheen,°
But they do square,° that all their elves for
  fear   30
Creep into acorn cups and hide them there.

FAIRY:

Either I mistake your shape and making quite,
Or else you are that shrewd and knavish sprite
Called Robin Goodfellow. Are not you he
That frights the maidens of the villagery,°   35
Skim milk, and sometimes labor in the quern,°
And bootless° make the breathless housewife
  churn,
And sometime make the drink to bear no
  barm,°
Mislead night wanderers, laughing at their
  harm?
Those that Hobgoblin call you, and sweet
  Puck,   40

106 **purple-in-grain** dyed with a fast purple   106–
107 **French-crown-color** color of French gold coin
107 **perfit** perfect   108 **crowns** (1) gold coins (2)
heads bald from the French disease (syphilis)   109–
110 **barefaced** (1) bald (2) brazen   112 **con**
study   116 **devices** plans   117–118 **bill of properties** list of stage furnishings   121 **obscenely** (Bottom means "seemly")   124 **hold or cut bowstrings**
i.e., keep your word or give it up (?)
II.i.4 **pale** enclosed land, park   7 **moon's sphere**
(according to the Ptolemaic system the moon was
fixed in a hollow sphere that surrounded and re-
volved about the earth)

9 **orbs** fairy rings, i.e., circles of darker grass   10
pensioners bodyguards (referring to Elizabeth I's
bodyguard of fifty splendid young noblemen)   12
favors gifts   13 **savors** perfumes   16 **lob** lubber,
clumsy fellow   20 **passing fell and wrath** very
fierce and angry   23 **changeling** (usually a child
left behind by fairies in exchange for one stolen,
but here applied to the stolen child)   25 **trace**
traverse   29 **starlight sheen** brightly shining starlight   30 **square** clash, quarrel   35 **villagery** villag-
ers   36 **quern** hand mill for grinding grain   37
bootless in vain   38 **barm** yeast, froth

You do their work, and they shall have good
      luck.
Are not you he?
   PUCK: Thou speakest aright;
I am that merry wanderer of the night.
I jest to Oberon, and make him smile,
45 When I a fat and bean-fed horse beguile,
Neighing in likeness of a filly foal:
And sometime lurk I in a gossip's° bowl,
In very likeness of a roasted crab;°
And when she drinks, against her lips I bob
50 And on her withered dewlap° pour the ale.
The wisest aunt, telling the saddest° tale,
Sometime for three-foot stool mistaketh me;
Then slip I from her bum, down topples she,
And "tailor"° cries, and falls into a cough;
55 And then the whole quire° hold their hips
      and laugh,
And waxen° in their mirth, and neeze,° and
      swear
A merrier hour was never wasted° there.
But, room, fairy! Here comes Oberon.
   FAIRY:
And here my mistress. Would that he were
      gone!

(*Enter* [OBERON,] *the King of Fairies, at one
door, with his train; and* [TITANIA,] *the
Queen, at another, with hers.*)

   OBERON:
60 Ill met by moonlight, proud Titania.
   TITANIA:
What, jealous Oberon! Fairy, skip hence.
I have forsworn his bed and company.
   OBERON:
Tarry, rash wanton;° am not I thy lord?
   TITANIA:
Then I must be thy lady: but I know
65 When thou hast stolen away from fairy land
And in the shape of Corin° sat all day,
Playing on pipes of corn,° and versing love
To amorous Phillida. Why art thou here,
Come from the farthest steep of India?

But that, forsooth, the bouncing° Amazon,   70
Your buskined° mistress and your warrior love,
To Theseus must be wedded, and you come
To give their bed joy and prosperity.
   OBERON:
How canst thou thus for shame, Titania,
Glance at my credit with Hippolyta,   75
Knowing I know thy love to Theseus?
Didst not thou lead him through the glimmer-
      ing night
From Perigenia, whom he ravishèd?
And make him with fair Aegles break his faith,
With Ariadne and Antiopa?°   80
   TITANIA:
These are the forgeries of jealousy:
And never, since the middle summer's spring,°
Met we on hill, in dale, forest, or mead,
By pavèd° fountain or by rushy brook,
Or in the beachèd margent° of the sea,   85
To dance our ringlets to the whistling wind,
But with thy brawls thou hast disturbed our
      sport.
Therefore the winds, piping to us in vain,
As in revenge, have sucked up from the sea
Contagious° fogs; which, falling in the land,   90
Hath every pelting° river made so proud,
That they have overborne their continents.°
The ox hath therefore stretched his yoke in
      vain,
The plowman lost his sweat, and the green
      corn°
Hath rotted ere his youth attained a beard;   95
The fold stands empty in the drownèd field,
And crows are fatted with the murrion flock;°
The nine men's morris° is filled up with mud;
And the quaint mazes° in the wanton green,°
For lack of tread, are undistinguishable.   100
The human mortals want their winter here;
No night is now with hymn or carol blest.

47 **gossip's** old woman's   48 **crab** crab apple   50
dewlap fold of skin on the throat   51 **saddest** most
serious   54 **tailor** (suggesting the posture of a tailor
squatting; or a term of abuse: Middle English *tail-
lard*, "thief")   55 **quire** company, choir   56 **waxen**
increase   56 **neeze** sneeze   57 **wasted** passed   63
rash wanton hasty willful creature   66 **Corin** (like
Phillida, line 68, a traditional name for a lover in
pastoral poetry)   67 **pipes of corn** musical instruments made of grain stalks

70 **bouncing** swaggering   71 **buskined** wearing a
hunter's boot (buskin)   78–80 **Perigenia, Aegles,
Ariadne, Antiopa** (girls Theseus loved and deserted)
82 **middle summer's spring** beginning of midsummer
84 **pavèd** i.e., with pebbly bottom   85 **margent**
margin, shore   90 **contagious** generating pestilence
91 **pelting** petty   92 **continents** containers (i.e.,
banks)   94 **corn** grain   97 **murrion flock** flock
dead of cattle disease (murrain)   98 **nine men's
morris** square cut in the turf (for a game in which
each player has nine counters or "men")   99
quaint mazes intricate meandering paths on the
grass (kept fresh by running along them)   99
wanton green grass growing without check

Therefore the moon, the governess of floods,
Pale in her anger, washes all the air,
105 That rheumatic diseases do abound.
And thorough this distemperature° we see
The seasons alter: hoary-headed frosts
Fall in the fresh lap of the crimson rose,
And on old Hiems'° thin and icy crown
110 An odorous chaplet° of sweet summer buds
Is, as in mockery, set. The spring, the summer,
The childing° autumn, angry winter, change
Their wonted liveries;° and the mazèd° world,
By their increase, now knows not which is
    which.
115 And this same progeny of evils comes
From our debate,° from our dissension;
We are their parents and original.
    OBERON:
Do you amend it, then; it lies in you:
Why should Titania cross her Oberon?
120 I do but beg a little changeling boy,
To be my henchman.°
    TITANIA: Set your heart at rest.
The fairy land buys not° the child of me.
His mother was a vot'ress° of my order,
And, in the spicèd Indian air, by night,
125 Full often hath she gossiped by my side,
And sat with me on Neptune's yellow sands,
Marking th' embarkèd traders on the flood;
When we have laughed to see the sails
    conceive
And grow big-bellied with the wanton wind;
Which she, with pretty and with swimming
130   gait
Following — her womb then rich with my
    young squire —
Would imitate, and sail upon the land,
To fetch me trifles, and return again,
As from a voyage, rich with merchandise.
135 But she, being mortal, of that boy did die;
And for her sake do I rear up her boy,
And for her sake I will not part with him.
    OBERON:
How long within this wood intend you stay?
    TITANIA:
Perchance till after Theseus' wedding day.
140 If you will patiently dance in our round,°

And see our moonlight revels, go with us.
If not, shun me, and I will spare° your haunts.
    OBERON:
Give me that boy, and I will go with thee.
    TITANIA:
Not for thy fairy kingdom. Fairies, away!
We shall chide downright, if I longer stay.   145
    (*Exeunt* [TITANIA *with her train*].)
    OBERON:
Well, go thy way. Thou shalt not from this
    grove
Till I torment thee for this injury.
My gentle Puck, come hither. Thou remem-
    b'rest
Since° once I sat upon a promontory,
And heard a mermaid, on a dolphin's back,   150
Uttering such dulcet and harmonious breath,
That the rude sea grew civil° at her song,
And certain stars shot madly from their
    spheres,
To hear the sea maid's music.
    PUCK: I remember.
    OBERON:
That very time I saw, but thou couldst not,   155
Flying between the cold moon and the earth,
Cupid all armed. A certain aim he took
At a fair vestal° thronèd by the west,
And loosed his love shaft smartly from his
    bow,
As it should° pierce a hundred thousand
    hearts.   160
But I might° see young Cupid's fiery shaft
Quenched in the chaste beams of the wat'ry
    moon,
And the imperial vot'ress passèd on,
In maiden meditation, fancy-free.°
Yet marked I where the bolt of Cupid fell.   165
It fell upon a little western flower,
Before milk-white, now purple with love's
    wound,
And maidens call it love-in-idleness.°
Fetch me that flow'r; the herb I showed thee
    once:
The juice of it on sleeping eyelids laid   170
Will make or man or woman° madly dote

106 **distemperature** disturbance in nature   109 **old Hiems'** the winter's   110 **chaplet** wreath   112 **childing** breeding, fruitful   113 **wonted liveries** accustomed apparel   113 **mazèd** bewildered   116 **debate** quarrel   121 **henchman** page   122 **The fairy land buys not** i.e., even your whole domain could not buy   123 **vot'ress** woman who has taken a vow   140 **round** circular dance

142 **spare** keep away from   149 **Since** when   152 **civil** well behaved   158 **vestal** virgin (possibly an allusion to Elizabeth, the Virgin Queen)   160 **As it should** as if it would   161 **might** could   164 **fancy-free** free from the power of love   168 **love-in-idleness** pansy   171 **or man or woman** either man or woman

Upon the next live creature that it sees.
Fetch me this herb, and be thou here again
Ere the leviathan° can swim a league.
    PUCK:
175 I'll put a girdle round about the earth
In forty minutes.   [*Exit.*]
    OBERON: Having once this juice,
I'll watch Titania when she is asleep,
And drop the liquor of it in her eyes.
The next thing then she waking looks upon,
180 Be it on lion, bear, or wolf, or bull,
On meddling monkey, or on busy° ape,
She shall pursue it with the soul of love.
And ere I take this charm from off her sight,
As I can take it with another herb,
185 I'll make her render up her page to me.
But who comes here? I am invisible,
And I will overhear their conference.

    (*Enter* DEMETRIUS, HELENA *following him.*)

    DEMETRIUS:
I love thee not, therefore pursue me not.
Where is Lysander and fair Hermia?
190 The one I'll slay, the other slayeth me.
Thou told'st me they were stol'n unto this
    wood;
And here am I, and wood° within this wood,
Because I cannot meet my Hermia.
Hence, get thee gone, and follow me no more!
    HELENA:
195 You draw me, you hardhearted adamant;°
But yet you draw not iron, for my heart
Is true as steel. Leave you your power to draw,
And I shall have no power to follow you.
    DEMETRIUS:
Do I entice you? Do I speak you fair?°
200 Or, rather, do I not in plainest truth
Tell you, I do not nor I cannot love you?
    HELENA:
And even for that do I love you the more.
I am your spaniel; and, Demetrius,
The more you beat me, I will fawn on you.
Use me but as your spaniel, spurn me, strike
205   me,
Neglect me, lose me; only give me leave,
Unworthy as I am, to follow you.
What worser place can I beg in your love —
And yet a place of high respect with me —

174 **leviathan** sea monster, whale 181 **busy**
meddlesome 192 **wood** out of my mind (with perhaps an additional pun on "wooed") 195 **adamant** (1) very hard gem (2) loadstone, magnet
199 **speak you fair** speak kindly to you

Than to be used as you use your dog?   210
    DEMETRIUS:
Tempt not too much the hatred of my spirit,
For I am sick when I do look on thee.
    HELENA:
And I am sick when I look not on you.
    DEMETRIUS:
You do impeach° your modesty too much,
To leave the city, and commit yourself   215
Into the hands of one that loves you not,
To trust the opportunity of night
And the ill counsel of a desert° place
With the rich worth of your virginity.
    HELENA:
Your virtue is my privilege.° For that   220
It is not night when I do see your face,
Therefore I think I am not in the night;
Nor doth this wood lack worlds of company,
For you in my respect° are all the world.
Then how can it be said I am alone   225
When all the world is here to look on me?
    DEMETRIUS:
I'll run from thee and hide me in the brakes,°
And leave thee to the mercy of wild beasts.
    HELENA:
The wildest hath not such a heart as you.
Run when you will, the story shall be changed: 230
Apollo flies, and Daphne° holds the chase;
The dove pursues the griffin;° the mild hind°
Makes speed to catch the tiger; bootless speed,
When cowardice pursues, and valor flies.
    DEMETRIUS:
I will not stay° thy questions. Let me go!   235
Or, if thou follow me, do not believe
But I shall do thee mischief in the wood.
    HELENA:
Ay, in the temple, in the town, the field,
You do me mischief. Fie, Demetrius!
Your wrongs do set a scandal on my sex.   240
We cannot fight for love, as men may do;
We should be wooed, and were not made to
    woo.
                [*Exit* DEMETRIUS.]
I'll follow thee, and make a heaven of hell,
To die upon° the hand I love so well. [*Exit.*]

214 **impeach** expose to reproach 218 **desert** deserted, uninhabited 220 **Your virtue is my privilege** your inherent power is my warrant 224 **in my
respect** in my opinion 227 **brakes** thickets 231
Daphne a nymph who fled from Apollo (at her
prayer she was changed into a laurel tree) 232
griffin fabulous monster with an eagle's head and a
lion's body 232 **hind** doe 235 **stay** wait for 244
To die upon dying by

OBERON:

Fare thee well, nymph: ere he do leave this
245   grove,
Thou shalt fly him, and he shall seek thy love.

(*Enter* PUCK.)

Hast thou the flower there? Welcome,
    wanderer.
    PUCK:
Ay, there it is.
    OBERON: I pray thee, give it me.
I know a bank where the wild thyme blows,
250 Where oxlips and the nodding violet grows,
Quite overcanopied with luscious woodbine,
With sweet musk roses, and with eglantine.
There sleeps Titania sometime of the night,
Lulled in these flowers with dances and delight;
And there the snake throws° her enameled
255   skin,
Weed° wide enough to wrap a fairy in.
And with the juice of this I'll streak her eyes,
And make her full of hateful fantasies.
Take thou some of it, and seek through this
    grove.
260 A sweet Athenian lady is in love
With a disdainful youth. Anoint his eyes;
But do it when the next thing he espies
May be the lady. Thou shalt know the man
By the Athenian garments he hath on.
265 Effect it with some care that he may prove
More fond on her° than she upon her love:
And look thou meet me ere the first cock crow.
    PUCK:
Fear not, my lord, your servant shall do so.
                    (*Exeunt.*)

[SCENE II. *Another part of the wood.*]

Enter TITANIA, *Queen of Fairies, with her
train.*

    TITANIA:
Come, now a roundel° and a fairy song;
Then, for the third part of a minute, hence;
Some to kill cankers in the musk-rose buds,
Some war with reremice° for their leathern
    wings
To make my small elves coats, and some keep
5   back

The clamorous owl, that nightly hoots and
    wonders
At our quaint° spirits. Sing me now asleep.
Then to your offices, and let me rest.

(FAIRIES *sing.*)

1ST FAIRY:
You spotted snakes with double tongue,
    Thorny hedgehogs, be not seen;   10
Newts and blindworms,° do no wrong,
    Come not near our Fairy Queen.

CHORUS:
    Philomele,° with melody
Sing in our sweet lullaby;
Lulla, lulla, lullaby, lulla, lulla, lullaby: 15
    Never harm
    Nor spell nor charm,
Come our lovely lady nigh;
So, good night, with lullaby.

1ST FAIRY:
Weaving spiders, come not here;   20
    Hence, you long-legged spinners, hence!
Beetles black, approach not near;
    Worm nor snail, do no offense.

CHORUS:
    Philomele, with melody, &c.

2ND FAIRY:
Hence, away! Now all is well.   25
One aloof stand sentinel.
            [*Exeunt* FAIRIES. TITANIA *sleeps.*]

(*Enter* OBERON [*and squeezes the flower on*
TITANIA'*s eyelids*].)

OBERON:
What thou seest when thou dost wake,
Do it for thy truelove take;
Love and languish for his sake.
Be it ounce,° or cat, or bear,   30
Pard,° or boar with bristled hair,
In thy eye that shall appear
When thou wak'st, it is thy dear.
Wake when some vile thing is near.   [*Exit.*]

(*Enter* LYSANDER *and* HERMIA.)
    LYSANDER:
Fair love, you faint with wand'ring in the
    wood;   35
And to speak troth,° I have forgot our way.

255 **throws** casts off   256 **Weed** garment   266
fond on her foolishly in love with her
II.ii.1 **roundel** dance in a ring   4 **reremice** bats

7 **quaint** dainty   11 **blindworms** small snakes   13
Philomele nightingale   30 **ounce** lynx   31 **Pard**
leopard   36 **troth** truth

We'll rest us, Hermia, if you think it good,
And tarry for the comfort of the day.
HERMIA:
Be't so, Lysander. Find you out a bed;
40 For I upon this bank will rest my head.
LYSANDER:
One turf shall serve as pillow for us both,
One heart, one bed, two bosoms, and one
  troth.
HERMIA:
Nay, good Lysander. For my sake, my dear,
Lie further off yet, do not lie so near.
LYSANDER:
45 O, take the sense,° sweet, of my innocence!
Love takes the meaning° in love's conference.
I mean, that my heart unto yours is knit,
So that but one heart we can make of it:
Two bosoms interchainèd with an oath;
50 So then two bosoms and a single troth.°
Then by your side no bed-room me deny,
For lying so, Hermia, I do not lie.°
HERMIA:
Lysander riddles very prettily.
Now much beshrew° my manners and my
  pride,
55 If Hermia meant to say Lysander lied.
But, gentle friend, for love and courtesy
Lie further off, in human modesty.
Such separation as may well be said
Becomes a virtuous bachelor and a maid,
So far be distant; and, good night, sweet
60 friend.
Thy love ne'er alter till thy sweet life end!
LYSANDER:
Amen, amen, to that fair prayer, say I,
And then end life when I end loyalty!
Here is my bed. Sleep give thee all his rest!
HERMIA:
With half that wish the wisher's eyes be
65 pressed!   [They sleep.]
(Enter PUCK.)
PUCK:
  Through the forest have I gone,
  But Athenian found I none,
  On whose eyes I might approve°
  This flower's force in stirring love.

Night and silence. — Who is here?   70
Weeds° of Athens he doth wear:
This is he, my master said,
Despisèd the Athenian maid;
And here the maiden, sleeping sound,
On the dank and dirty ground.   75
Pretty soul! She durst not lie
Near this lack-love, this kill-courtesy.
Churl,° upon thy eyes I throw
All the power this charm doth owe.°
When thou wak'st, let love forbid   80
Sleep his seat on thy eyelid.
So awake when I am gone,
  For I must now to Oberon.   (Exit.)

(Enter DEMETRIUS and HELENA, running.)

HELENA:
Stay, though thou kill me, sweet Demetrius.
DEMETRIUS:
I charge thee, hence, and do not haunt me
  thus.   85
HELENA:
O, wilt thou darkling° leave me? Do not so.
DEMETRIUS:
Stay, on thy peril! I alone will go.   [Exit.]
HELENA:
O, I am out of breath in this fond° chase!
The more my prayer, the lesser is my grace.
Happy is Hermia, wheresoe'er she lies,   90
For she hath blessèd and attractive eyes.
How came her eyes so bright? Not with salt
  tears.
If so, my eyes are oft'ner washed than hers.
No, no, I am as ugly as a bear,
For beasts that meet me run away for fear. 95
Therefore no marvel though Demetrius
Do, as a monster, fly my presence thus.
What wicked and dissembling glass of mine
Made me compare with Hermia's sphery
  eyne?°
But who is here? Lysander! On the ground! 100
Dead? Or asleep? I see no blood, no wound.
Lysander, if you live, good sir, awake.
LYSANDER [awaking]:
And run through fire I will for thy sweet sake.
Transparent° Helena! Nature shows art,
That through thy bosom makes me see thy
  heart.   105
Where is Demetrius? O, how fit a word

45 take the sense understand the true meaning 46 Love takes the meaning lovers understand the true meaning of what they say to each other 50 troth faithful love 52 lie be untrue 54 beshrew curse (but commonly, as here, in a light sense) 68 approve try

71 Weeds garments 78 Churl boorish fellow 79 owe possess 86 darkling in the dark 88 fond (1) doting (2) foolish 99 sphery eyne starry eyes 104 Transparent bright

Is that vile name to perish on my sword!
HELENA:
Do not say so, Lysander, say not so.
What though he love your Hermia? Lord,
    what though?
110 Yet Hermia still loves you. Then be content.
LYSANDER:
Content with Hermia! No; I do repent
The tedious minutes I with her have spent.
Not Hermia but Helena I love:
Who will not change a raven for a dove?
115 The will° of man is by his reason swayed
And reason says you are the worthier maid.
Things growing are not ripe until their season:
So I, being young, till now ripe not° to reason.
And touching now the point of human skill,°
120 Reason becomes the marshal to my will,
And leads me to your eyes, where I o'erlook
Love's stories, written in love's richest book.
HELENA:
Wherefore was I to this keen mockery born?
When at your hands did I deserve this scorn?
125 Is't not enough, is't not enough, young man,
That I did never, no, nor never can,
Deserve a sweet look from Demetrius' eye,
But you must flout° my insufficiency?
Good troth,° you do me wrong, good sooth,
    you do,
130 In such disdainful manner me to woo.
But fare you well. Perforce I must confess
I thought you lord of more true gentleness.°
O, that a lady, of one man refused,
Should of another therefore be abused!
                                        (Exit.)
LYSANDER:
135 She sees not Hermia. Hermia, sleep thou there,
And never mayst thou come Lysander near!
For as a surfeit of the sweetest things
The deepest loathing to the stomach brings,
Or as the heresies that men do leave
140 Are hated most of those they did deceive,
So thou, my surfeit and my heresy,
Of all be hated, but the most of me!
And, all my powers, address° your love and
    might
To honor Helen and to be her knight!
                                        (Exit.)

HERMIA [awaking]:
Help me, Lysander, help me! Do thy best   145
To pluck this crawling serpent from my breast!
Ay me, for pity! What a dream was here!
Lysander, look how I do quake with fear.
Methought a serpent eat° my heart away,
And you sat smiling at his cruel prey.°   150
Lysander! What, removed? Lysander! Lord!
What, out of hearing? Gone? No sound, no
    word?
Alack, where are you? Speak, an if° you hear;
Speak, of° all loves! I swoon almost with fear.
No? Then I well perceive you are not nigh.   155
Either death or you I'll find immediately.
                                        (Exit.)

[ACT III

SCENE I. *The wood.* TITANIA *lying asleep.*]

Enter the clowns: [QUINCE, SNUG, BOTTOM,
FLUTE, SNOUT, *and* STARVELING].

BOTTOM: Are we all met?
QUINCE: Pat,° pat; and here's a marvail's°
convenient place for our rehearsal. This green
plot shall be our stage, this hawthorn brake°
our tiring house,° and we will do it in action   5
as we will do it before the Duke.
BOTTOM: Peter Quince?
QUINCE: What sayest thou, bully° Bottom?
BOTTOM: There are things in this comedy of
Pyramus and Thisby that will never please.   10
First, Pyramus must draw a sword to kill himself; which the ladies cannot abide. How
answer you that?
SNOUT: By'r lakin,° a parlous° fear.
STARVELING: I believe we must leave the   15
killing out, when all is done.
BOTTOM: Not a whit. I have a device to
make all well. Write me a prologue, and let
the prologue seem to say, we will do no
harm with our swords, and that Pyramus is   20
not killed indeed; and, for the more better
assurance, tell them that I Pyramus am not
Pyramus, but Bottom the weaver. This will
put them out of fear.

115 **will** desire 118 **ripe not** have not ripened
119 **touching now . . . human skill** now reaching
the fulness of human reason 128 **flout** jeer at
129 **Good troth** indeed (an expletive, like "good
sooth") 132 **gentleness** noble character 143
address apply

149 **eat** ate (pronounced "et") 150 **prey** act of
preying 153 **an if** if 154 **of** for the sake of
III.i.2 **Pat** exactly, on the dot 2 **marvail's** (Quince
means "marvelous") 4 **brake** thicket 5 **tiring
house** attiring house, dressing room 8 **bully** good
fellow 14 **By'r lakin** by our lady (ladykin = little
lady) 14 **parlous** perilous, terrible

25 QUINCE: Well, we will have such a prologue, and it shall be written in eight and six.°

BOTTOM: No, make it two more; let it be written in eight and eight.

SNOUT: Will not the ladies be afeared of the 30 lion?

STARVELING: I fear it, I promise you.

BOTTOM: Masters, you ought to consider with yourselves. To bring in — God shield us! — a lion among ladies, is a most dreadful thing.
35 For there is not a more fearful wild fowl than your lion living; and we ought to look to't.

SNOUT: Therefore another prologue must tell he is not a lion.

BOTTOM: Nay, you must name his name,
40 and half his face must be seen through the lion's neck, and he himself must speak through, saying thus, or to the same defect — "Ladies"— or, "Fair ladies — I would wish you" —or, "I would request you" — or, "I would en-
45 treat you — not to fear, not to tremble: my life for yours. If you think I come hither as a lion, it were pity of my life.° No, I am no such thing. I am a man as other men are." And there indeed let him name his name, and tell
50 them plainly, he is Snug the joiner.

QUINCE: Well, it shall be so. But there is two hard things; that is, to bring the moonlight into a chamber; for, you know, Pyramus and Thisby meet by moonlight.
55 SNOUT: Doth the moon shine that night we play our play?

BOTTOM: A calendar, a calendar! Look in the almanac; find out moonshine, find out moonshine.
60 QUINCE: Yes, it doth shine that night.

BOTTOM: Why, then may you leave a casement of the great chamber window, where we play, open, and the moon may shine in at the casement.
65 QUINCE: Ay; or else one must come in with a bush of thorns° and a lantern, and say he comes to disfigure,° or to present, the person of Moonshine. Then, there is another thing: we must have a wall in the great chamber; for
70 Pyramus and Thisby, says the story, did talk through the chink of a wall.

SNOUT: You can never bring in a wall. What say you, Bottom?

BOTTOM: Some man or other must present Wall: and let him have some plaster, or some 75 loam, or some roughcast° about him, to signify Wall; and let him hold his fingers thus, and through that cranny shall Pyramus and Thisby whisper.

QUINCE: If that may be, then all is well. 80 Come, sit down, every mother's son, and rehearse your parts. Pyramus, you begin. When you have spoken your speech, enter into that brake; and so everyone according to his cue.

(*Enter Robin* [PUCK].)

PUCK:
What hempen homespuns° have we swag-
g'ring here, 85
So near the cradle of the Fairy Queen?
What, a play toward!° I'll be an auditor;
An actor too perhaps, if I see cause.

QUINCE: Speak, Pyramus. Thisby, stand forth. 90

PYRAMUS [BOTTOM]:
Thisby, the flowers of odious savors sweet —

QUINCE: Odors, odors.

PYRAMUS:
— odors savors sweet:
So hath thy breath, my dearest Thisby dear.
But hark, a voice! Stay thou but here awhile, 95
And by and by° I will to thee appear.

(*Exit.*)

PUCK:
A stranger Pyramus than e'er played here!

[*Exit.*]

THISBY [FLUTE]: Must I speak now?

QUINCE: Ay, marry, must you. For you must understand he goes but to see a noise that he 100 heard, and is to come again.

THISBY:
Most radiant Pyramus, most lily-white of hue,
Of color like the red rose on triumphant
brier,
Most brisky juvenal,° and eke° most lovely Jew,
As true as truest horse, that yet would never
tire, 105
I'll meet thee, Pyramus, at Ninny's° tomb.

76 **roughcast** lime mixed with gravel to plaster outside walls   85 **hempen homespuns** coarse fellows (clad in homespun cloth of hemp)   87 **toward in** preparation   96 **by and by** shortly   104 **juvenal** youth   104 **eke** also   106 **Ninny's** (blunder for "Ninus"; Ninus was the legendary founder of Nineveh)

26 **in eight and six** in alternate lines of eight and six syllables (ballad stanza)   47 **pity of my life** a bad thing for me   66 **bush of thorns** (legend held that the man in the moon had been placed there for gathering firewood on Sunday)   67 **disfigure** (Bottom means "figure," "represent")

QUINCE: "Ninus' tomb," man. Why, you must not speak that yet. That you answer to Pyramus. You speak all your part at once, cues
110 and all. Pyramus enter. Your cue is past; it is "never tire."

THISBY:
O — as true as truest horse, that yet would never tire.

[Re-enter PUCK, and BOTTOM with an ass's head.]

PYRAMUS:
If I were fair, Thisby, I were only thine.

QUINCE: O monstrous! O strange! We are
115 haunted. Pray, masters! Fly, masters! Help!
[Exeunt all the clowns but BOTTOM.]

PUCK:
I'll follow you, I'll lead you about a round,°
    Through bog, through bush, through brake, through brier.
Sometime a horse I'll be, sometime a hound,
    A hog, a headless bear, sometime a fire;
And neigh, and bark, and grunt, and roar, and
120   burn,
Like horse, hound, hog, bear, fire, at every
    turn.   (Exit.)
BOTTOM: Why do they run away? This is a knavery of them to make me afeard.

(Enter SNOUT.)

SNOUT: O Bottom, thou art changed! What
125 do I see on thee?

BOTTOM: What do you see? You see an ass head of your own, do you?   [Exit SNOUT.]

(Enter QUINCE.)

QUINCE: Bless thee, Bottom! Bless thee! Thou art translated.°   (Exit.)
130 BOTTOM: I see their knavery. This is to make an ass of me; to fright me, if they could. But I will not stir from this place, do what they can. I will walk up and down here, and will sing, that they shall hear I am not afraid.   [Sings.]
135   The woosel° cock so black of hue,
        With orange-tawny bill,
    The throstle with his note so true,
        The wren with little quill° —
TITANIA [awaking]:
What angel wakes me from my flow'ry bed?

BOTTOM [sings]:
    The finch, the sparrow, and the lark,   140
        The plain-song cuckoo° gray,
    Whose note full many a man doth mark,
        And dares not answer nay —
for, indeed, who would set his wit° to so foolish a bird? Who would give a bird the lie,°   145
though he cry "cuckoo" never so?°

TITANIA:
I pray thee, gentle mortal, sing again:
Mine ear is much enamored of thy note;
So is mine eye enthrallèd to thy shape;
And thy fair virtue's force perforce doth move me   150
On the first view to say, to swear, I love thee.

BOTTOM: Methinks, mistress, you should have little reason for that. And yet, to say the truth, reason and love keep little company together nowadays; the more the pity, that   155
some honest neighbors will not make them friends. Nay, I can gleek° upon occasion.

TITANIA:
Thou art as wise as thou art beautiful.

BOTTOM: Not so, neither; but if I had wit enough to get out of this wood, I have enough   160
to serve mine own turn.

TITANIA:
Out of this wood do not desire to go.
Thou shalt remain here, whether thou wilt or no.
I am a spirit of no common rate.°
The summer still doth tend° upon my state;   165
And I do love thee. Therefore, go with me.
I'll give thee fairies to attend on thee,
And they shall fetch thee jewels from the deep,
And sing, while thou on pressèd flowers dost sleep:
And I will purge thy mortal grossness so,   170
That thou shalt like an airy spirit go.
Peaseblossom! Cobweb! Moth!° And Mustard-seed!

(Enter four Fairies [PEASEBLOSSOM, COB-WEB, MOTH, and MUSTARDSEED].)

116 about a round roundabout   129 translated transformed   135 woosel ouzel, blackbird   138 quill (literally, "reed pipe"; here, "piping voice")

141 the plain-song cuckoo the cuckoo, who sings a simple song   144 set his wit use his intelligence to answer   145 give a bird the lie contradict a bird (the cuckoo's song supposedly tells a man he is a cuckold)   146 never so ever so often   157 gleek make a satirical jest   164 rate rank   165 still doth tend always waits upon   172 Moth (pronounced "mote," and probably a speck rather than an insect is denoted)

PEASEBLOSSOM:
Ready.
COBWEB:
    And I.
MOTH: And I.
MUSTARDSEED: And I.
ALL: Where shall we go.
TITANIA:
Be kind and courteous to this gentleman;
175 Hop in his walks, and gambol in his eyes;
Feed him with apricocks and dewberries,°
With purple grapes, green figs, and mulberries;
The honey bags steal from the humblebees,°
And for night tapers crop their waxen thighs,
180 And light them at the fiery glowworm's eyes,
To have my love to bed and to arise;
And pluck the wings from painted butterflies,
To fan the moonbeams from his sleeping eyes.
Nod to him, elves, and do him courtesies.
PEASEBLOSSOM:
Hail, mortal!
COBWEB: Hail!
MOTH: Hail!
185 MUSTARDSEED: Hail!
BOTTOM: I cry your worships mercy,°
heartily: I beseech your worship's name.
COBWEB:
Cobweb.
BOTTOM: I shall desire you of more acquain-
190 tance,° good Master Cobweb: if I cut my
finger,° I shall make bold with you. Your
name, honest gentleman?
PEASEBLOSSOM:
Peaseblossom.
BOTTOM: I pray you, commend me to
195 Mistress Squash,° your mother, and to Master
Peascod, your father. Good Master Pease-
blossom. I shall desire you of more acquaintance too. Your name, I beseech you, sir?
MUSTARDSEED:
Mustardseed.
200 BOTTOM: Good Master Mustardseed, I know
your patience well. That same cowardly, giant-
like ox-beef hath devoured° many a gentleman
of your house. I promise you your kindred hath

made my eyes water ere now. I desire you of
more acquaintance, good Master Mustardseed.   205
TITANIA:
Come, wait upon him; lead him to my bower.
    The moon methinks looks with a wat'ry eye;
And when she weeps, weeps every little flower,
    Lamenting some enforcèd° chastity.
    Tie up my lover's tongue, bring him silently.   210
    (Exit [TITANIA with BOTTOM and FAIRIES].)

[SCENE II. Another part of the wood.]

Enter [OBERON,] King of Fairies, and Robin
Goodfellow [PUCK].

OBERON:
I wonder if Titania be awaked;
Then, what it was that next came in her eye,
Which she must dote on in extremity.°
Here comes my messenger. How now, mad
    spirit!
What night-rule° now about this haunted
    grove?   5
PUCK:
My mistress with a monster is in love.
Near to her close° and consecrated bower,
While she was in her dull and sleeping hour,
A crew of patches,° rude mechanicals,°
That work for bread upon Athenian stalls,   10
Were met together to rehearse a play,
Intended for great Theseus' nuptial day.
The shallowest thickskin of that barren sort,°
Who Pyramus presented in their sport,
Forsook his scene, and entered in a brake.   15
When I did him at this advantage take,
An ass's nole° I fixèd on his head.
Anon° his Thisby must be answerèd,
And forth my mimic comes. When they him
    spy,
As wild geese that the creeping fowler eye,   20
Or russet-pated choughs, many in sort,°
Rising and cawing at the gun's report,
Sever themselves and madly sweep the sky,
So, at his sight, away his fellows fly;
And, at our stamp, here o'er and o'er one falls; 25
He murder cries, and help from Athens calls.

176 **apricocks and dewberries** apricots and black-
berries 178 **humblebees** bumblebees 186 **I cry
your worships mercy** I beg pardon of your honors
189–190 **I shall desire you of more acquaintance**
I shall want to be better acquainted with you
190–191 **if I cut my finger** (cobweb was used for
stanching blood) 195 **Squash** unripe pea pod
202 **devoured** (because beef is often eaten with
mustard)

209 **enforcèd** violated
III.ii.3 **in extremity** to the extreme 5 **night-rule**
happenings during the night 7 **close** private,
secret 9 **patches** fools, clowns 9 **rude mechanicals** uneducated workingmen 13 **barren sort** stupid
group 17 **nole** "noodle," head 18 **Anon** presently
21 **russet-pated . . . in sort** gray-headed jackdaws,
many in a flock

Their sense thus weak, lost with their fears
    thus strong,
Made senseless things begin to do them wrong;
For briers and thorns at their apparel snatch;
Some sleeves, some hats, from yielders all
30   things catch.
I led them on in this distracted fear,
And left sweet Pyramus translated there:
When in that moment, so it came to pass,
Titania waked, and straightway loved an ass.
    OBERON:
35 This falls out better than I could devise.
But hast thou yet latched° the Athenian's eyes
With the love juice, as I did bid thee do?
    PUCK:
I took him sleeping — that is finished too —
And the Athenian woman by his side;
That, when he waked, of force° she must be
40   eyed.

(*Enter* DEMETRIUS *and* HERMIA.)

    OBERON:
Stand close:° this is the same Athenian.
    PUCK:
This is the woman, but not this the man.
    DEMETRIUS:
O, why rebuke you him that loves you so?
Lay breath so bitter on your bitter foe.
    HERMIA:
45 Now I but chide; but I should use thee worse,
For thou, I fear, hast given me cause to curse.
If thou hast slain Lysander in his sleep,
Being o'er shoes in blood, plunge in the deep,
And kill me too.
50 The sun was not so true unto the day
As he to me. Would he have stolen away
From sleeping Hermia? I'll believe as soon
This whole° earth may be bored, and that the
    moon
May through the center creep, and so displease
55 Her brother's° noontide with th' Antipodes.
It cannot be but thou hast murd'red him.
So should a murderer look, so dead,° so grim.
    DEMETRIUS:
So should the murdered look; and so should I,
Pierced through the heart with your stern
    cruelty.
60 Yet you, the murderer, look as bright, as clear,

As yonder Venus in her glimmering sphere.
    HERMIA:
What's this to my Lysander? Where is he?
Ah, good Demetrius, wilt thou give him me?
    DEMETRIUS:
I had rather give his carcass to my hounds.
    HERMIA:
Out, dog! Out, cur! Thou driv'st me past the
    bounds   65
Of maiden's patience. Hast thou slain him,
    then?
Henceforth be never numb'red among men!
O, once tell true! Tell true, even for my sake!
Durst thou have looked upon him being
    awake?
And hast thou killed him sleeping? O brave
    touch!°   70
Could not a worm, an adder, do so much?
An adder did it; for with doubler tongue
Than thine, thou serpent, never adder stung.
    DEMETRIUS:
You spend your passion on a misprised mood:°
I am not guilty of Lysander's blood;   75
Nor is he dead, for aught that I can tell.
    HERMIA:
I pray thee, tell me then that he is well.
    DEMETRIUS:
An if I could, what should I get therefore?°
    HERMIA:
A privilege, never to see me more.
And from thy hated presence part I so.   80
See me no more, whether he be dead or no.
                        (*Exit.*)
    DEMETRIUS:
There is no following her in this fierce vein.
Here therefore for a while I will remain.
So sorrow's heaviness doth heavier grow
For debt that bankrout sleep doth sorrow
    owe;°   85
Which now in some slight measure it will pay,
If for his tender° here I make some stay.

           (*Lie down [and sleep].*)

    OBERON:
What hast thou done? Thou hast mistaken
    quite,
And laid the love juice on some truelove's
    sight.
Of thy misprision° must perforce ensue   90

---

36 **latched** fastened (or possibly "moistened")   40
of force by necessity   41 **close** concealed   53
whole solid   55 **Her brother's** i.e., the sun's   57
dead deadly pale   70 **brave touch** splendid exploit (ironic)   74 **misprised mood** mistaken anger   78 **therefore** in return   85 **For debt . . . sorrow owe** because of the debt that bankrupt sleep owes to sorrow   87 **tender** offer   90 **misprision** mistake

Some true love turned, and not a false turned
    true.
PUCK:
Then fate o'errules, that, one man holding
    troth,
A million fail, confounding oath on oath.°
OBERON:
About the wood go swifter than the wind,
95 And Helena of Athens look thou find.
All fancy-sick° she is and pale of cheer,°
With sighs of love, that costs the fresh blood
    dear:
By some illusion see thou bring her here.
I'll charm his eyes against she do appear.°
PUCK:
100 I go, I go; look how I go,
Swifter than arrow from the Tartar's bow.
                                    [*Exit.*]
OBERON:
        Flower of this purple dye,
        Hit with Cupid's archery,
        Sink in apple of his eye.
105   When his love he doth espy,
        Let her shine as gloriously
        As the Venus of the sky.
        When thou wak'st, if she be by,
        Beg of her for remedy.

(*Enter* PUCK.)

PUCK:
110   Captain of our fairy band,
        Helena is here at hand;
        And the youth, mistook by me,
        Pleading for a lover's fee.
        Shall we their fond pageant° see?
115   Lord, what fools these mortals be!
OBERON:
        Stand aside. The noise they make
        Will cause Demetrius to awake.
PUCK:
        Then will two at once woo one;
        That must needs be sport alone;°
120   And those things do best please me
        That befall prepost'rously.

(*Enter* LYSANDER *and* HELENA.)

LYSANDER:

Why should you think that I should woo in
    scorn?
Scorn and derision never come in tears:
Look, when I vow, I weep; and vows so born,
    In their nativity all truth appears.   125
How can these things in me seem scorn to you,
Bearing the badge of faith,° to prove them
    true?
HELENA:
You do advance° your cunning more and
    more.
When truth kills truth, O devilish-holy fray!
These vows are Hermia's: will you give her
    o'er?   130
    Weigh oath with oath, and you will nothing
    weigh.
Your vows to her and me, put in two scales,
Will even weigh; and both as light as tales.
LYSANDER:
I had no judgment when to her I swore.
HELENA:
Nor none, in my mind, now you give her o'er.   135
LYSANDER:
Demetrius loves her, and he loves not you.
DEMETRIUS [*awaking*]:
O Helen, goddess, nymph, perfect, divine!
To what, my love, shall I compare thine eyne?
Crystal is muddy. O, how ripe in show°
Thy lips, those kissing cherries, tempting grow!   140
That pure congealèd white, high Taurus'°
    snow,
Fanned with the eastern wind, turns to a crow
When thou hold'st up thy hand: O, let me
    kiss
This princess of pure white, this seal of bliss!
HELENA:
O spite! O hell! I see you all are bent   145
To set against me for your merriment:
If you were civil° and knew courtesy,
You would not do me thus much injury.
Can you not hate me, as I know you do,
But you must join in souls to mock me too?   150
If you were men, as men you are in show,
You would not use a gentle° lady so;
To vow, and swear, and superpraise my parts,°
When I am sure you hate me with your hearts.
You both are rivals, and love Hermia;   155

---

93 **confounding oath on oath** breaking oath after
oath 96 **fancy-sick** love-sick 96 **cheer** face 99
against she do appear in preparation for her appearance 114 **fond pageant** foolish exhibition 119
alone unique, supreme

127 **badge of faith** (Lysander means his tears)
128 **advance** exhibit, display 139 **show** appearance
141 **Taurus'** of the Taurus Mountains (in Turkey)
147 **civil** civilized 152 **gentle** well-born 153 **parts**
qualities

And now both rivals to mock Helena:
A trim° exploit, a manly enterprise,
To conjure tears up in a poor maid's eyes
With your derision! None of noble sort
160 Would so offend a virgin, and extort°
A poor soul's patience, all to make you sport.
    LYSANDER:
You are unkind, Demetrius. Be not so;
For you love Hermia; this you know I know.
And here, with all good will, with all my heart,
165 In Hermia's love I yield you up my part;
And yours of Helena to me bequeath,
Whom I do love, and will do till my death.
    HELENA:
Never did mockers waste more idle° breath.
    DEMETRIUS:
Lysander, keep thy Hermia; I will none.
170 If e'er I loved her, all that love is gone.
My heart to her but as guestwise sojourned,
And now to Helen is it home returned,
There to remain.
    LYSANDER: Helen, it is not so.
    DEMETRIUS:
Disparage not the faith thou dost not know,
175 Lest, to thy peril, thou aby it dear.°
Look, where thy love comes; yonder is thy
    dear.

    (*Enter* HERMIA.)

    HERMIA:
Dark night, that from the eye his° function
    takes,
The ear more quick of apprehension makes;
Wherein it doth impair the seeing sense,
180 It pays the hearing double recompense.
Thou art not by mine eye, Lysander, found;
Mine ear, I thank it, brought me to thy sound.
But why unkindly didst thou leave me so?
    LYSANDER:
Why should he stay, whom love doth press to
    go?
    HERMIA:
185 What love could press Lysander from my side?
    LYSANDER:
Lysander's love, that would not let him bide,
Fair Helena, who more engilds the night
Than all yon fiery oes° and eyes of light.
Why seek'st thou me? Could not this make
    thee know,

The hate I bare thee made me leave thee so?   190
    HERMIA:
You speak not as you think: it cannot be.
    HELENA:
Lo, she is one of this confederacy!
Now I perceive they have conjoined all three
To fashion this false sport, in spite of me.
Injurious° Hermia! Most ungrateful maid!   195
Have you conspired, have you with these con-
    trived
To bait° me with this foul derision?
Is all the counsel that we two have shared,
The sister's vows, the hours that we have
    spent,
When we have chid the hasty-footed time   200
For parting us — O, is all forgot?
All school days friendship, childhood inno-
    cence?
We, Hermia, like two artificial° gods,
Have with our needles created both one flower,
Both on one sampler,° sitting on one cushion,   205
Both warbling of one song, both in one key;
As if our hands, our sides, voices, and minds,
Had been incorporate.° So we grew together,
Like to a double cherry, seeming parted,
But yet an union in partition;   210
Two lovely berries molded on one stem;
So, with two seeming bodies, but one heart;
Two of the first, like coats in heraldry,
Due but to one, and crownèd with one crest.°
And will you rent° our ancient love asunder,   215
To join with men in scorning your poor
    friend?
It is not friendly, 'tis not maidenly.
Our sex, as well as I, may chide you for it,
Though I alone do feel the injury.
    HERMIA:
I am amazèd at your passionate words.   220
I scorn you not. It seems that you scorn me.
    HELENA:
Have you not set Lysander, as in scorn,
To follow me and praise my eyes and face?
And made your other love, Demetrius
(Who even but now did spurn me with his
    foot),   225

---

157 **trim** splendid (ironical)   160 **extort** wear out by torturing   168 **idle** vain, futile   175 **aby it dear** pay dearly for it   177 **his** its (the eye's)   188 **oes** orbs

195 **Injurious** insulting   196–197 **contrived To bait** plotted to assail   203 **artificial** skilled in art   205 **sampler** work of embroidery   208 **incorporate** one body   213–214 **Two of . . . one crest** (Helena apparently envisages a shield on which the coat of arms appears twice but which has a single crest; Helena and Hermia have two bodies but a single heart)   215 **rent** rend, tear

To call me goddess, nymph, divine and rare,
Precious, celestial? Wherefore speaks he this
To her he hates? And wherefore doth
 Lysander
Deny your love,° so rich within his soul,
230 And tender me (forsooth) affection,
But by your setting on, by your consent?
What though I be not so in grace° as you,
So hung upon with love, so fortunate,
But miserable most, to love unloved?
235 This you should pity rather than despise.
 HERMIA:
I understand not what you mean by this.
 HELENA:
Ay, do! Persever,° counterfeit sad° looks,
Make mouths° upon me when I turn my back;
Wink each at other; hold the sweet jest up.
240 This sport, well carried, shall be chronicled.
If you have any pity, grace, or manners,
You would not make me such an argument.°
But fare ye well. 'Tis partly my own fault,
Which death or absence soon shall remedy.
 LYSANDER:
245 Stay, gentle Helena; hear my excuse:
My love, my life, my soul, fair Helena!
 HELENA:
O excellent!
 HERMIA:
             Sweet, do not scorn her so.
 DEMETRIUS:
If she cannot entreat,° I can compel.
 LYSANDER:
Thou canst compel no more than she entreat.
Thy threats have no more strength than her
250   weak prayers.
Helen, I love thee; by my life, I do!
I swear by that which I will lose for thee,
To prove him false that says I love thee not.
 DEMETRIUS:
I say I love thee more than he can do.
 LYSANDER:
255 If thou say so, withdraw and prove it too.
 DEMETRIUS:
Quick, come!
 HERMIA: Lysander, whereto tends all this?
 LYSANDER:
Away, you Ethiope!°
 DEMETRIUS: No, no; he'll

Seem to break loose; take on as° you would
 follow,
But yet come not: you are a tame man, go!
 LYSANDER:
Hang off, thou cat, thou burr! Vile thing, let
 loose,   260
Or I will shake thee from me like a serpent!
 HERMIA:
Why are you grown so rude! What change is
 this,
Sweet love?
 LYSANDER:
            Thy love! Out, tawny Tartar, out!
Out, loathèd med'cine! O hated potion, hence!
 HERMIA:
Do you not jest?
 HELENA: Yes, sooth;° and so do you.   265
 LYSANDER:
Demetrius, I will keep my word° with thee.
 DEMETRIUS:
I would I had your bond, for I perceive
A weak bond holds you. I'll not trust your
 word.
 LYSANDER:
What, should I hurt her, strike her, kill her
 dead?
Although I hate her, I'll not harm her so.   270
 HERMIA:
What, can you do me greater harm than hate?
Hate me! Wherefore? O me! What news, my
 love!
Am not I Hermia? Are not you Lysander?
I am as fair now as I was erewhile.°
Since night° you loved me; yet since night you
 left me.   275
Why, then you left me — O, the gods forbid! —
In earnest, shall I say?
 LYSANDER: Ay, by my life!
And never did desire to see thee more.
Therefore be out of hope, of question, of
 doubt;
Be certain, nothing truer. 'Tis no jest   280
That I do hate thee, and love Helena.
 HERMIA:
O me! You juggler! You canker blossom!°
You thief of love! What, have you come by
 night

229 **your love** his love for you 232 **in grace** in favor 237 **persever** persevere (but accented **on** second syllable) 237 **sad** grave 238 **Make mouths** make mocking faces 242 **argument** subject (of scorn) 248 **entreat** prevail by entreating 257 **Ethiope** blackamoor (brunette)

258 **take on as** make a fuss as if 265 **sooth** truly 266 **my word** my promise to fight with you 274 **erewhile** a little while ago 275 **Since night** since the beginning of this night 282 **canker blossom** dog rose (or possibly worm that cankers the blossom)

And stol'n my love's heart from him?
HELENA: Fine, i' faith!
285 Have you no modesty, no maiden shame,
No touch of bashfulness? What, will you tear
Impatient answers from my gentle tongue?
Fie, fie! You counterfeit, you puppet, you!
HERMIA:
Puppet? Why so? Ay, that way goes the game.
290 Now I perceive that she hath made compare°
Between our statures; she hath urged her
    height,
And with her personage, her tall personage,
Her height, forsooth, she hath prevailed with
    him.
And are you grown so high in his esteem,
295 Because I am so dwarfish and so low?
How low am I, thou painted maypole? Speak!
How low am I? I am not yet so low
But that my nails can reach unto thine eyes.
HELENA:
I pray you, though you mock me, gentlemen,
300 Let her not hurt me, I was never curst;°
I have no gift at all in shrewishness;
I am a right maid° for my cowardice.
Let her not strike me. You perhaps may think,
Because she is something lower than myself,
That I can match her.
305 HERMIA: Lower! Hark, again!
HELENA:
Good Hermia, do not be so bitter with me.
I evermore did love you, Hermia,
Did ever keep your counsels, never wronged
    you;
Save that, in love unto Demetrius,
310 I told him of your stealth unto this wood.
He followed you; for love I followed him.
But he hath chid me hence, and threatened
    me
To strike me, spurn me, nay, to kill me too.
And now, so you will let me quiet go,
315 To Athens will I bear my folly back,
And follow you no further. Let me go.
You see how simple and how fond° I am.
HERMIA:
Why, get you gone. Who is't that hinders
    you?
HELENA:
A foolish heart, that I leave here behind.
HERMIA:
What, with Lysander?

HELENA: With Demetrius.   320
LYSANDER:
Be not afraid. She shall not harm thee,
    Helena.
DEMETRIUS:
No, sir, she shall not, though you take her
    part.
HELENA:
O, when she's angry, she is keen and shrewd!°
She was a vixen when she went to school;
And though she be but little, she is fierce.   325
HERMIA:
"Little" again! Nothing but "low" and
    "little"!
Why will you suffer her to flout me thus?
Let me come to her.
LYSANDER: Get you gone, you dwarf;
You minimus,° of hind'ring knotgrass° made;
You bead, you acorn!
DEMETRIUS: You are too officious   330
In her behalf that scorns your services.
Let her alone. Speak not of Helena;
Take not her part; for, if thou dost intend°
Never so little show of love to her,
Thou shalt aby° it.
LYSANDER: Now she holds me not.   335
Now follow, if thou dar'st, to try whose right,
Of thine or mine, is most in Helena.
DEMETRIUS:
Follow! Nay, I'll go with thee, cheek by jowl.
           [Exeunt LYSANDER and DEMETRIUS.]
HERMIA:
You, mistress, all this coil is 'long of you:°
Nay, go not back.
HELENA: I will not trust you, I,   340
Nor longer stay in your curst company.
Your hands than mine are quicker for a fray,
My legs are longer though, to run away.
HERMIA:
I am amazed,° and know not what to say.
           Exeunt [HELENA and HERMIA].
OBERON:
This is thy negligence. Still thou mistak'st,   345
Or else committ'st thy knaveries willfully.
PUCK:
Believe me, king of shadows, I mistook.
Did not you tell me I should know the man

323 **keen and shrewd** sharp-tongued and shrewish
329 **minimus** smallest thing   329 **knotgrass** (a
weed that allegedly stunted one's growth)   333
intend give sign, direct (or possibly "pretend")
335 **aby** pay for   339 **all this coil is 'long of you**
all this turmoil is brought about by you   344
amazed in confusion

290 **compare** comparison   300 **curst** quarrelsome
302 **right maid** true young woman   317 **fond** foolish

By the Athenian garments he had on?
350 And so far blameless proves my enterprise,
That I have 'nointed an Athenian's eyes;
And so far am I glad it so did sort,°
As this their jangling I esteem a sport.
   OBERON:
Thou see'st these lovers seek a place to fight.
355 Hie therefore, Robin, overcast the night.
The starry welkin° cover thou anon
With drooping fog, as black as Acheron;°
And lead these testy° rivals so astray,
As° one come not within another's way.
360 Like to Lysander sometime frame thy tongue,
Then stir Demetrius up with bitter wrong;°
And sometime rail thou like Demetrius.
And from each other look thou lead them thus,
Till o'er their brows death-counterfeiting sleep
365 With leaden legs and batty° wings doth creep.
Then crush this herb into Lysander's eye,
Whose liquor hath this virtuous° property,
To take from thence all error with his might,
And make his eyeballs roll with wonted sight.
370 When they next wake, all this derision°
Shall seem a dream and fruitless vision,
And back to Athens shall the lovers wend,
With league whose date° till death shall never end.
Whiles I in this affair do thee employ,
375 I'll to my queen and beg her Indian boy;
And then I will her charmèd eye release
From monster's view, and all things shall be peace.
   PUCK:
My fairy lord, this must be done with haste,
For night's swift dragons cut the clouds full fast,
380 And yonder shines Aurora's harbinger;°
At whose approach, ghosts, wand'ring here and there,
Troop home to churchyards: damnèd spirits all,
That in crossways and floods have burial,
Already to their wormy beds are gone.
For fear lest day should look their shames
385   upon,

They willfully themselves exile from light,
And must for aye consort with black-browed night.
   OBERON:
But we are spirits of another sort.
I with the Morning's love° have oft made sport;
And, like a forester, the groves may tread, 390
Even till the eastern gate, all fiery-red,
Opening on Neptune with fair blessèd beams,
Turns into yellow gold his salt green streams.
But, notwithstanding, haste; make no delay.
We may effect this business yet ere day. 395
                      [*Exit.*]
   PUCK:
Up and down, up and down,
I will lead them up and down:
I am feared in field and town:
Goblin,° lead them up and down.
Here comes one. 400

(*Enter* LYSANDER.)

LYSANDER:
Where art thou, proud Demetrius? Speak thou now.
   PUCK:
Here, villain; drawn° and ready. Where art thou?
   LYSANDER:
I will be with thee straight.
   PUCK: Follow me, then,
To plainer° ground.
                   [*Exit* LYSANDER.]

(*Enter* DEMETRIUS.)

DEMETRIUS: Lysander! Speak again!
Thou runaway, thou coward, art thou fled? 405
Speak! In some bush? Where dost thou hide thy head?
   PUCK:
Thou coward, art thou bragging to the stars,
Telling the bushes that thou look'st for wars,
And wilt not come? Come, recreant! Come, thou child!
I'll whip thee with a rod. He is defiled 410
That draws a sword on thee.
   DEMETRIUS: Yea, art thou there?

---

352 **sort** turn out   356 **welkin** sky   357 **Acheron** one of the rivers of the underworld   358 **testy** excited, angry   359 **As** that   361 **wrong** insult   365 **batty** bat-like   367 **virtuous** potent   370 **derision** i.e., ludicrous delusion   373 **With league whose date** in union whose term   380 **Aurora's harbinger** dawn's herald (i.e., the morning star)

389 **the Morning's love** Aurora (or possibly her lover Cephalus)   399 **Goblin** Hobgoblin (one of Puck's names)   402 **drawn** with drawn sword   404 **plainer** more level

PUCK:
Follow my voice. We'll try no manhood° here.
                                    (*Exeunt.*)

[*Enter* LYSANDER.]

LYSANDER:
He goes before me and still dares me on:
When I come where he calls, then he is gone.
415 The villain is much lighter-heeled than I.
I followed fast, but faster he did fly,
That fallen am I in dark uneven way,
And here will rest me. [*Lies down.*] Come,
     thou gentle day!
For if but once thou show me thy gray light,
420 I'll find Demetrius, and revenge this spite.
                                    [*Sleeps.*]

([*Enter*] *Robin* [PUCK] *and* DEMETRIUS.)

PUCK:
Ho, ho, ho! Coward, why com'st thou not?
DEMETRIUS:
Abide me,° if thou dar'st; for well I wot°
Thou runn'st before me, shifting every place,
And dar'st not stand, nor look me in the face.
Where art thou now?
425 PUCK: Come hither. I am here.
DEMETRIUS:
Nay, then, thou mock'st me. Thou shalt buy
     this dear,°
If ever I thy face by daylight see.
Now, go thy way. Faintness constraineth me
To measure out my length on this cold bed.
430 By day's approach look to be visited.°
                            [*Lies down and sleeps.*]

(*Enter* HELENA.)

HELENA:
O weary night, O long and tedious night,
Abate° thy hours! Shine comforts from the
     east,
That I may back to Athens by daylight,
From these that my poor company detest:
And sleep, that sometimes shuts up sorrow's
435   eye,
Steal me awhile from mine own company.
                                    (*Sleep.*)

PUCK:
    Yet but three? Come one more.

412 **try no manhood** have no test of valor 422
Abide me wait for me 422 **wot** know 426 **buy
this dear** pay dearly for this 430 **look to be visited**
be sure to be sought out 432 **Abate** make shorter

Two of both kinds makes up four.
  Here she comes, curst° and sad:
  Cupid is a knavish lad,   440
  Thus to make poor females mad.

[*Enter* HERMIA.]

HERMIA:
Never so weary, never so in woe;
  Bedabbled with the dew and torn with
     briers,
I can no further crawl, no further go;
  My legs can keep no pace with my desires.   445
Here will I rest me till the break of day.
Heavens shield Lysander, if they mean a fray!
                          [*Lies down and sleeps.*]
PUCK:
    On the ground
    Sleep sound:
    I'll apply   450
    To your eye,
  Gentle lover, remedy.

[*Squeezing the juice on* LYSANDER'S *eye.*]

    When thou wak'st,
    Thou tak'st
    True delight   455
    In the sight
  Of thy former lady's eye:
  And the country proverb known,
  That every man should take his own,
  In your waking shall be shown.   460
    Jack shall have Jill;
    Nought shall go ill;
  The man shall have his mare again, and all
     shall be well.
                                    [*Exit.*]

[ACT IV

SCENE I. *The wood.* LYSANDER, DEMETRIUS,
    HELENA, *and* HERMIA, *lying asleep.*]

Enter [TITANIA,] *Queen of Fairies, and* [BOT-
TOM *the*] *Clown, and* FAIRIES; *and* [OBERON,]
the King, behind them.

TITANIA:
Come, sit thee down upon this flow'ry bed,
  While I thy amiable cheeks do coy,°

439 **curst** cross
IV.i.2 **While I . . . do coy** while I caress your
lovely cheeks

And stick musk roses in thy sleek smooth head,
And kiss thy fair large ears, my gentle joy.
5   BOTTOM: Where's Peaseblossom?
PEASEBLOSSOM:
Ready.
BOTTOM: Scratch my head, Peaseblossom.
Where's Mounsieur Cobweb?
COBWEB:
Ready.
10   BOTTOM: Mounsieur Cobweb, good mounsieur, get you your weapons in your hand, and
kill me a red-hipped humblebee on the top of
a thistle; and, good mounsieur, bring me the
honey bag. Do not fret yourself too much in
15   the action, mounsieur; and, good mounsieur,
have a care the honey bag break not; I would
be loath to have you overflown with a honey
bag, signior. Where's Mounsieur Mustardseed?
MUSTARDSEED:
Ready.
20   BOTTOM: Give me your neaf,° Mounsieur
Mustardseed. Pray you, leave your curtsy,°
good mounsieur.
MUSTARDSEED:
What's your will?
BOTTOM: Nothing, good mounsieur, but to
25   help Cavalery° Cobweb to scratch. I must to
the barber's, mounsieur; for methinks I am
marvail's° hairy about the face; and I am such
a tender ass, if my hair do but tickle me, I
must scratch.
TITANIA:
What, wilt thou hear some music, my sweet
30   love?
BOTTOM: I have a reasonable good ear in
music. Let's have the tongs and the bones.°
TITANIA:
Or say, sweet love, what thou desirest to eat.
BOTTOM: Truly, a peck of provender. I
35   could munch your good dry oats. Methinks I
have a great desire to a bottle° of hay. Good
hay, sweet hay, hath no fellow.°
TITANIA:
I have a venturous fairy that shall seek
The squirrel's hoard, and fetch thee new nuts.
40   BOTTOM: I had rather have a handful or two

of dried peas. But, I pray you, let none of your
people stir me: I have an exposition of° sleep
come upon me.
TITANIA:
Sleep thou, and I will wind thee in my arms.
Fairies, be gone, and be all ways° away.   45
[Exeunt FAIRIES.]
So doth the woodbine the sweet honeysuckle
Gently entwist; the female ivy° so
Enrings the barky fingers of the elm.
O, how I love thee! How I dote on thee!
[They sleep.]

(Enter Robin Goodfellow [PUCK].)

OBERON [advancing]:
Welcome, Good Robin. See'st thou this sweet
sight?   50
Her dotage now I do begin to pity:
For, meeting her of late behind the wood,
Seeking sweet favors° for this hateful fool,
I did upbraid her, and fall out with her.
For she his hairy temples then had rounded   55
With coronet of fresh and fragrant flowers;
And that same dew, which sometime° on the
buds
Was wont° to swell, like round and orient°
pearls,
Stood now within the pretty flouriets'° eyes,
Like tears, that did their own disgrace bewail. 60
When I had at my pleasure taunted her,
And she in mild terms begged my patience,
I then did ask of her her changeling child;
Which straight she gave me, and her fairy sent
To bear him to my bower in fairy land.   65
And now I have the boy, I will undo
This hateful imperfection of her eyes:
And, gentle Puck, take this transformèd scalp
From off the head of this Athenian swain,
That, he awaking when the other° do,   70
May all to Athens back again repair,
And think no more of this night's accidents,°
But as the fierce vexation of a dream.
But first I will release the Fairy Queen.
Be as thou wast wont to be;   75
See as thou wast wont to see.
Dian's bud o'er Cupid's flower
Hath such force and blessèd power.

20 neaf fist, hand   21 leave your curtsy i.e., stop
bowing, leave your hat on (a curtsy was any gesture
of respect)   25 Cavalery i.e., Cavalier   27 marvail's (Bottom means "marvelous")   32 the tongs
and the bones rustic music, made by tongs struck
with metal and by bone clappers held between the
fingers   36 bottle bundle   37 fellow equal

42 exposition of (Bottom means "disposition for")
45 all ways in every direction   47 female ivy
(called female because it clings to the elm and is
supported by it)   53 favors love tokens (probably
flowers)   57 sometime formerly   58 Was wont
used to   58 orient lustrous   59 flouriets' flowerets'
70 other others   72 accidents happenings

Now, my Titania, wake you, my sweet Queen.
TITANIA:
80 My Oberon, what visions have I seen!
Methought I was enamored of an ass.
OBERON:
There lies your love.
TITANIA: How came these things to pass?
O, how mine eyes do loathe his visage now!
OBERON:
Silence awhile. Robin, take off this head.
85 Titania, music call; and strike more dead
Than common sleep of all these five the sense.
TITANIA:
Music, ho, music! Such as charmeth sleep!
PUCK:
Now, when thou wak'st, with thine own fool's
    eyes peep.
OBERON:
Sound, music! [*Music.*] Come, my Queen, take
    hands with me,
And rock the ground whereon these sleepers
90   be. [*Dance.*]
Now thou and I are new in amity,
And will tomorrow midnight solemnly°
Dance in Duke Theseus' house triumphantly,°
And bless it to all fair prosperity.
95 There shall the pairs of faithful lovers be
Wedded, with Theseus, all in jollity.
PUCK:
    Fairy King, attend, and mark:
    I do hear the morning lark.
OBERON:
    Then, my Queen, in silence sad,°
100   Trip we after night's shade.
    We the globe can compass soon,
    Swifter than the wand'ring moon.
TITANIA:
    Come, my lord; and in our flight,
    Tell me how it came this night,
105   That I sleeping here was found
    With these mortals on the ground.
                    (*Exeunt.*)

(*Wind horn. Enter* THESEUS, *and all his
train;* [HIPPOLYTA, EGEUS].)

THESEUS:
Go, one of you, find out the forester,
For now our observation° is performed;
And since we have the vaward° of the day,

My love shall hear the music of my hounds.   110
Uncouple in the western valley; let them go.
Dispatch, I say, and find the forester.
                [*Exit an* ATTENDANT.]
We will, fair Queen, up to the mountain's top,
And mark the musical confusion
Of hounds and echo in conjunction.   115
HIPPOLYTA:
I was with Hercules and Cadmus once,
When in a wood of Crete they bayed° the
    bear
With hounds of Sparta. Never did I hear
Such gallant chiding; for, besides the groves,
The skies, the fountains, every region near   120
Seemed all one mutual cry. I never heard
So musical a discord, such sweet thunder.
THESEUS:
My hounds are bred out of the Spartan kind,
So flewed, so sanded;° and their heads are
    hung
With ears that sweep away the morning dew;   125
Crook-kneed, and dew-lapped like Thessalian
    bulls;
Slow in pursuit, but matched in mouth like
    bells,
Each under each.° A cry° more tunable
Was never holloed to, nor cheered with horn,
In Crete, in Sparta, nor in Thessaly.   130
Judge when you hear. But, soft!° What
    nymphs are these?
EGEUS:
My lord, this is my daughter here asleep;
And this, Lysander; this Demetrius is;
This Helena, old Nedar's Helena:
I wonder of their being here together.   135
THESEUS:
No doubt they rose up early to observe
The rite of May; and, hearing our intent,
Came here in grace of our solemnity.°
But speak, Egeus. Is not this the day
That Hermia should give answer of her choice?   140
EGEUS:
It is, my lord.
THESEUS:
Go, bid the huntsmen wake them with their
    horns.

---

92 **solemnly** ceremoniously   93 **triumphantly** in
festive procession   99 **sad** serious, solemn   108
observation observance, i.e., of the rite of May (cf.
I.i.167)   109 **vaward** vanguard, i.e., morning

117 **bayed** brought to bay   124 **So flewed, so
sanded** i.e., like Spartan hounds, with hanging
cheeks and of sandy color   128 **Each under each**
of different tone (like the chime of bells)   128
cry pack of hounds   131 **soft** stop   138 **in grace
of our solemnity** in honor of our festival

(*Shout within. They all start up. Wind horns.*)

Good morrow, friends. Saint Valentine is past:
Begin these wood birds but to couple now?°
  LYSANDER:
Pardon, my lord.
145 THESEUS: I pray you all, stand up.
I know you two are rival enemies.
How comes this gentle concord in the world,
That hatred is so far from jealousy,°
To sleep by hate, and fear no enmity?
  LYSANDER:
150 My lord, I shall reply amazedly,°
Half sleep, half waking: but as yet, I swear,
I cannot truly say how I came here.
But, as I think — for truly would I speak,
And now I do bethink me, so it is —
155 I came with Hermia hither. Our intent
Was to be gone from Athens, where we might,
Without° the peril of the Athenian law —
  EGEUS:
Enough, enough, my lord; you have enough.
I beg the law, the law, upon his head.
They would have stol'n away; they would,
160   Demetrius,
Thereby to have defeated° you and me,
You of your wife and me of my consent,
Of my consent that she should be your wife.
  DEMETRIUS:
My lord, fair Helen told me of their stealth,°
165 Of this their purpose hither to this wood,
And I in fury hither followed them,
Fair Helena in fancy° following me.
But, my good lord, I wot not by what power —
But by some power it is — my love to Hermia,
170 Melted as the snow, seems to me now
As the remembrance of an idle gaud,°
Which in my childhood I did dote upon;
And all the faith, the virtue° of my heart,
The object and the pleasure of mine eye,
175 Is only Helena. To her, my lord,
Was I betrothed ere I saw Hermia:
But, like a sickness,° did I loathe this food;
But, as in health, come to my natural taste,
Now I do wish it, love it, long for it,

144 **Begin these . . . couple now** (it was supposed that birds began to mate on February 14, St. Valentine's Day) 148 **jealousy** suspicion 150 **amazedly** confusedly 157 **Without** outside of 161 **defeated** deprived by fraud 164 **stealth** stealthy flight 167 **in fancy** in love, doting 171 **idle gaud** worthless trinket 173 **virtue** power 177 **like a sickness** like one who is sick

And will for evermore be true to it.   180
  THESEUS:
Fair lovers, you are fortunately met.
Of this discourse we more will hear anon.
Egeus, I will overbear your will,
For in the temple, by and by,° with us
These couples shall eternally be knit;   185
And, for the morning now is something worn,°
Our purposed hunting shall be set aside.
Away with us to Athens! Three and three,
We'll hold a feast in great solemnity.
Come, Hippolyta.   190
  [*Exeunt* THESEUS, HIPPOLYTA, EGEUS,
  and train.]
  DEMETRIUS:
These things seem small and undistinguishable,
Like far-off mountains turnèd into clouds.
  HERMIA:
Methinks I see these things with parted eye,°
When everything seems double.
  HELENA: So methinks:
And I have found Demetrius like a jewel,   195
Mine own, and not mine own.
  DEMETRIUS: Are you sure
That we are awake? It seems to me
That yet we sleep, we dream. Do not you think
The Duke was here, and bid us follow him?
  HERMIA:
Yea, and my father.
  HELENA: And Hippolyta.   200
  LYSANDER:
And he did bid us follow to the temple.
  DEMETRIUS:
Why, then, we are awake. Let's follow him,
And by the way let us recount our dreams.
  [*Exeunt.*]
BOTTOM [*awaking*]: When my cue comes,
call me, and I will answer. My next is, "Most   205
fair Pyramus." Heigh-ho! Peter Quince? Flute,
the bellows mender? Snout, the tinker? Starveling? God's my life,° stol'n hence, and left me
asleep? I have had a most rare vision. I have
had a dream, past the wit of man to say what   210
dream it was. Man is but an ass, if he go
about° to expound this dream. Methought I
was — there is no man can tell what. Methought I was — and methought I had — but
man is but a patched° fool if he will offer to   215

184 **by and by** shortly 186 **something worn** somewhat spent 193 **with parted eye** i.e., with the eyes out of focus 208 **God's my life** an oath (possibly from "God bless my life") 211–212 **go about** endeavor 215 **patched** (referring to the patchwork dress of jesters)

say what methought I had. The eye of man hath not heard, the ear of man hath not seen, man's hand is not able to taste, his tongue to conceive, nor his heart to report, what my
220 dream was. I will get Peter Quince to write a ballet° of this dream. It shall be called "Bottom's Dream," because it hath no bottom; and I will sing it in the latter end of a play, before the Duke. Peradventure to make it the
225 more gracious, I shall sing it at her death.°

[*Exit.*]

[SCENE II. *Athens.* QUINCE'*s house.*]

Enter QUINCE, FLUTE,° *Thisby and the rabble* [SNOUT, STARVELING].

QUINCE: Have you sent to Bottom's house? Is he come home yet?
STARVELING: He cannot be heard of. Out of doubt he is transported.°
5 FLUTE: If he come not, then the play is marred. It goes not forward, doth it?
QUINCE: It is not possible. You have not a man in all Athens able to discharge° Pyramus but he.
10 FLUTE: No, he hath simply the best wit of any handicraft man in Athens.
QUINCE: Yea, and the best person too; and he is a very paramour for a sweet voice.
FLUTE: You must say "paragon." A para-
15 mour is, God bless us, a thing of nought.°

(*Enter* SNUG *the Joiner.*)

SNUG: Masters, the Duke is coming from the temple, and there is two or three lords and ladies more married. If our sport had gone forward, we had all been made men.°
20 FLUTE: O sweet bully Bottom! Thus hath he lost sixpence a day° during his life. He could not have scaped sixpence a day. An the Duke had not given him sixpence a day for playing Pyramus, I'll be hanged. He would
25 have deserved it. Sixpence a day in Pyramus, or nothing.

(*Enter* BOTTOM.)

BOTTOM: Where are these lads? Where are these hearts?
QUINCE: Bottom! O most courageous° day! O most happy hour! 30
BOTTOM: Masters, I am to discourse wonders: but ask me not what; for if I tell you, I am not true Athenian. I will tell you everything, right as it fell out.
QUINCE: Let us hear, sweet Bottom. 35
BOTTOM: Not a word of me.° All that I will tell you is, that the Duke hath dined. Get your apparel together, good strings to your beards, new ribbons to your pumps; meet presently° at the palace; every man look o'er his part; for 40 the short and the long is, our play is preferred.° In any case, let Thisby have clean linen; and let not him that plays the lion pare his nails, for they shall hang out for the lion's claws. And, most dear actors, eat no onions nor 45 garlic, for we are to utter sweet breath,° and I do not doubt but to hear them say it is a sweet comedy. No more words. Away! Go, away!

[*Exeunt.*]

[ACT V

SCENE I. *Athens. The palace of* THESEUS.]

Enter THESEUS, HIPPOLYTA, *and* PHILOSTRATE, [LORDS, *and* ATTENDANTS].

HIPPOLYTA:
'Tis strange, my Theseus, that these lovers speak of.
THESEUS:
More strange than true. I never may believe
These antique° fables, nor these fairy toys.°
Lovers and madmen have such seething brains,
Such shaping fantasies,° that apprehend 5
More than cool reason ever comprehends.
The lunatic, the lover and the poet
Are of imagination all compact.°
One sees more devils than vast hell can hold,
That is the madman. The lover, all as frantic, 10
Sees Helen's beauty in a brow of Egypt.°

221 **ballet** ballad   225 **her death** i.e., Thisby's death in the play
IV.ii.s.d. **Flute** (Shakespeare seems to have forgotten that Flute and Thisby are the same person)
4 **transported** carried off (by the fairies)   8 **discharge** play   15 **a thing of nought** a wicked thing
19 **made men** men whose fortunes are made   21 **sixpence a day** (a pension)

29 **courageous** brave, splendid   36 **of me** from me
39 **presently** immediately   41–42 **preferred** put forward, recommended   46 **breath** (1) exhalation (2) words
V.i.3 **antique** (1) ancient (2) grotesque (antic)
3 **fairy toys** trifles about fairies   5 **fantasies** imagination   8 **compact** composed   11 **brow of Egypt** face of a gypsy

The poet's eye, in a fine frenzy rolling,
Doth glance from heaven to earth, from earth
    to heaven;
And as imagination bodies forth
15 The forms of things unknown, the poet's pen
Turns them to shapes, and gives to airy
    nothing
A local habitation and a name.
Such tricks hath strong imagination,
That, if it would but apprehend some joy,
20 It comprehends some bringer of that joy;°
Or in the night, imagining some fear,°
How easy is a bush supposed a bear!
    HIPPOLYTA:
But all the story of the night told over,
And all their minds transfigured so together,
25 More witnesseth than fancy's images,
And grows to something of great constancy;°
But, howsoever, strange and admirable.°

(*Enter Lovers:* LYSANDER, DEMETRIUS,
HERMIA *and* HELENA.)

    THESEUS:
Here come the lovers, full of joy and mirth.
Joy, gentle friends! Joy and fresh days of love
Accompany your hearts!
30   LYSANDER: More than to us
Wait in your royal walks, your board, your bed!
    THESEUS:
Come now, what masques,° what dances
    shall we have,
To wear away this long age of three hours
Between our aftersupper° and bedtime?
35 Where is our usual manager of mirth?
What revels are in hand? Is there no play,
To ease the anguish of a torturing hour?
Call Philostrate.
    PHILOSTRATE: Here, mighty Theseus.
    THESEUS:
Say, what abridgment° have you for this
    evening?
What masque? What music? How shall we
40   beguile
The lazy time, if not with some delight?

20 **It comprehends . . . that joy** it includes an
imagined bringer of the joy   21 **fear** object of fear
26 **constancy** consistency (and reality)   27 **admirable** wonderful   32 **masques** courtly entertainments
with masked dancers   34 **aftersupper** refreshment
served after early supper   39 **abridgment** entertainment (to abridge or shorten the time)

    PHILOSTRATE:
There is a brief° how many sports are ripe:°
Make choice of which your Highness will see
    first. [*Giving a paper.*]
    THESEUS:
"The battle with the Centaurs, to be sung
By an Athenian eunuch to the harp."   45
We'll none of that. That have I told my love,
In glory of my kinsman Hercules.
"The riot of the tipsy Bacchanals,
Tearing the Thracian singer° in their rage."
That is an old device;° and it was played   50
When I from Thebes came last a conqueror.
"The thrice three Muses mourning for the
    death
Of Learning, late deceased in beggary."
That is some satire, keen and critical,
Not sorting with° a nuptial ceremony.   55
"A tedious brief scene of young Pyramus
And his love Thisby; very tragical mirth."
Merry and tragical? Tedious and brief?
That is, hot ice and wondrous strange snow.
How shall we find the concord of this discord? 60
    PHILOSTRATE:
A play there is, my lord, some ten words long,
Which is as brief as I have known a play;
But by ten words, my lord, it is too long,
Which makes it tedious. For in all the play
There is not one word apt, one player fitted. 65
And tragical, my noble lord, it is,
For Pyramus therein doth kill himself.
Which, when I saw rehearsed, I must confess,
Made mine eyes water; but more merry tears
The passion° of loud laughter never shed.   70
    THESEUS:
What are they that do play it?
    PHILOSTRATE:
Hard-handed men, that work in Athens here,
Which never labored in their minds till now;
And now have toiled their unbreathed°
    memories
With this same play, against° your nuptial.   75
    THESEUS:
And we will hear it.
    PHILOSTRATE: No, my noble lord;
It is not for you. I have heard it over,
And it is nothing, nothing in the world;
Unless you can find sport in their intents,

42 **brief** written list   42 **ripe** ready to be presented
49 **Thracian singer** Orpheus   50 **device** show   55
sorting with suited to   70 **passion** strong emotion
74 **unbreathed** unexercised   75 **against** in preparation for

Extremely stretched and conned with cruel
80   pain,
To do you service.
    THESEUS: I will hear that play;
For never anything can be amiss,
When simpleness and duty tender it.
Go, bring them in: and take your places,
    ladies.   [*Exit* PHILOSTRATE.]
    HIPPOLYTA:
85 I love not to see wretchedness o'ercharged,°
And duty in his service perishing.
    THESEUS:
Why, gentle sweet, you shall see no such
    thing.
    HIPPOLYTA:
He says they can do nothing in this kind.°
    THESEUS:
The kinder we, to give them thanks for
    nothing.
90 Our sport shall be to take what they mistake:
And what poor duty cannot do, noble respect
Takes it in might,° not merit.
Where I have come, great clerks° have
    purposèd
To greet me with premeditated welcomes;
95 Where I have seen them shiver and look pale,
Make periods in the midst of sentences,
Throttle their practiced accent in their fears,
And, in conclusion, dumbly have broke off,
Not paying me a welcome. Trust me, sweet,
100 Out of this silence yet I picked a welcome;
And in the modesty of fearful duty
I read as much as from the rattling tongue
Of saucy and audacious eloquence.
Love, therefore, and tongue-tied simplicity
105 In least speak most, to my capacity.°

    [*Enter* PHILOSTRATE.]

    PHILOSTRATE:
So please your Grace, the Prologue is ad-
    dressed.°
    THESEUS:
Let him approach.   [*Flourish trumpets.*]

    (*Enter the* PROLOGUE [QUINCE].)

    PROLOGUE:
If we offend, it is with our good will.

85 **wretchedness o'ercharged** lowly people overbur-
dened 88 **in this kind** in this kind of thing (i.e.,
acting) 92 **Takes it in might** considers the ability
and the effort made 93 **clerks** scholars 105 **to my
capacity** according to my understanding 106 **addressed** ready

That you should think, we come not to
    offend,
But with good will. To show our simple skill,   110
    That is the true beginning of our end.°
Consider, then, we come but in despite.
    We do not come, as minding to content
    you,
Our true intent is. All for your delight,
    We are not here. That you should here
    repent you,   115
The actors are at hand; and, by their show,°
You shall know all, that you are like to know.
    THESEUS: This fellow doth not stand upon
points.°
    LYSANDER: He hath rid his prologue like a   120
rough colt; he knows not the stop.° A good
moral, my lord: it is not enough to speak, but
to speak true.
    HIPPOLYTA: Indeed he hath played on this
prologue like a child on a recorder;° a sound,   125
but not in government.°
    THESEUS: His speech was like a tangled
chain; nothing impaired, but all disordered.
Who is next?

    (*Enter* PYRAMUS *and* THISBY *and* WALL *and*
    MOONSHINE *and* LION [*as in dumbshow*].)

    PROLOGUE:
Gentles, perchance you wonder at this show;   130
    But wonder on, till truth make all things
    plain.
This man is Pyramus, if you would know;
    This beauteous lady Thisby is certain.
This man, with lime and roughcast, doth
    present
    Wall, that vile Wall which did these lovers
    sunder;   135
And through Wall's chink, poor souls, they are
    content
    To whisper. At the which let no man
    wonder.
This man, with lantern, dog, and bush of
    thorn,
    Presenteth Moonshine; for, if you will know,

111 **end** aim 116 **show** (probably referring to a
kind of pantomime — "dumb show" — that was to
follow, in which the action of the play was acted
without words while the Prologue gave his account)
119 **stand upon points** (1) care about punctuation
(2) worry about niceties 121 **stop** (1) technical
term for the checking of a horse (2) mark of punctuation 125 **recorder** flutelike instrument 126
government control

140 By moonshine did these lovers think no scorn
         To meet at Ninus' tomb, there, there to woo.
     This grisly beast, which Lion hight° by name,
     The trusty Thisby, coming first by night,
     Did scare away, or rather did affright;
145 And, as she fled, her mantle she did fall,°
         Which Lion vile with bloody mouth did
             stain.
     Anon comes Pyramus, sweet youth and tall,°
     And finds his trusty Thisby's mantle slain:
     Whereat, with blade, with bloody blameful
         blade,
     He bravely broached° his boiling bloody
150   breast;
     And Thisby, tarrying in mulberry shade,
         His dagger drew, and died. For all the rest,
     Let Lion, Moonshine, Wall, and lovers twain
         At large° discourse, while here they do
             remain.
155   THESEUS: I wonder if the lion be to speak.
     DEMETRIUS: No wonder, my lord. One lion
     may, when many asses do.
             (*Exit* LION, THISBY *and* MOONSHINE.)
     WALL:
     In this same interlude it doth befall
     That I, one Snout by name, present a wall;
160 And such a wall, as I would have you think,
     That had in it a crannied hole or chink,
     Through which the lovers, Pyramus and
         Thisby,
     Did whisper often very secretly.
     This loam, this roughcast, and this stone, doth
         show
165 That I am that same wall; the truth is so;
     And this the cranny is, right and sinister,°
     Through which the fearful lovers are to
         whisper.
         THESEUS: Would you desire lime and hair to
     speak better?
170   DEMETRIUS: It is the wittiest partition° that
     ever I heard discourse, my lord.
         THESEUS: Pyramus draws near the wall.
     Silence!
     PYRAMUS:
     O grim-looked night! O night with hue so
         black!
175 O night, which ever art when day is not!

O night, O night! Alack, alack, alack,
     I fear my Thisby's promise is forgot!
And thou, O wall, O sweet, O lovely wall,
That stand'st between her father's ground and
     mine!
Thou wall, O wall, O sweet and lovely wall,   180
Show me thy chink, to blink through with
     mine eyne!
[*Wall holds up his fingers.*]
Thanks, courteous wall. Jove shield thee well
     for this!
But what see I? No Thisby do I see.
O wicked wall, through whom I see no bliss!
Cursed be thy stones for thus deceiving me!   185
     THESEUS: The wall, methinks, being sen-
sible,° should curse again.°
     PYRAMUS: No, in truth, sir, he should not.
"Deceiving me" is Thisby's cue. She is to enter
now, and I am to spy her through the wall.   190
You shall see it will fall pat° as I told you.
Yonder she comes.

         (*Enter* THISBY.)

THISBY:
O wall, full often hast thou heard my moans,
     For parting my fair Pyramus and me!
My cherry lips have often kissed thy stones,   195
     Thy stones with lime and hair knit up in
         thee.
PYRAMUS:
I see a voice: now will I to the chink,
To spy an I can hear my Thisby's face.
Thisby!
THISBY:
My love thou art, my love I think.   200
PYRAMUS:
Think what thou wilt, I am thy lover's grace;°
And, like Limander,° am I trusty still.
THISBY:
And I like Helen,° till the Fates me kill.
PYRAMUS:
Not Shafalus to Procrus° was so true.
THISBY:
As Shafalus to Procrus, I to you.   205
PYRAMUS:
O kiss me through the hole of this vile wall!

142 **hight** is called 145 **fall** let fall 147 **tall** brave
150 **bravely broached** gallantly stabbed 154 **At
large** at length 166 **right and sinister** i.e., running
right and left, horizontal 170 **wittiest partition**
most intelligent wall (with a pun on "partition," a
section of a book or of an oration)

186–187 **sensible** conscious 187 **again** in return
191 **pat** exactly 201 **thy lover's grace** thy gracious
lover 202 **Limander** (Bottom means Leander, but
blends him with Alexander) 203 **Helen** (Hero,
beloved of Leander, is probably meant) 204
Shafalus to Procrus (Cephalus and Procris are
meant, legendary lovers)

THISBY:

I kiss the wall's hole, not your lips at all.

PYRAMUS:

Wilt thou at Ninny's tomb meet me straightway?

THISBY:

'Tide life, 'tide death,° I come without delay.
                    [*Exeunt* PYRAMUS *and* THISBY.]

WALL:

210 Thus have I, Wall, my part dischargèd so;
And, being done, this wall away doth go.
                    [*Exit.*]

THESEUS: Now is the moon used° between
the two neighbors.

DEMETRIUS: No remedy, my lord, when
215 walls are so willful to hear without warning.°

HIPPOLYTA: This is the silliest stuff that
ever I heard.

THESEUS: The best in this kind° are but
shadows; and the worst are no worse, if im-
220 agination amend them.

HIPPOLYTA: It must be your imagination
then, and not theirs.

THESEUS: If we imagine no worse of them
than they of themselves, they may pass for ex-
225 cellent men. Here come two noble beasts in,
a man and a lion.

(*Enter* LION *and* MOONSHINE.)

LION:

You, ladies, you, whose gentle hearts do fear
The smallest monstrous mouse that creeps on
    floor,
May now perchance both quake and tremble
    here,
230 When lion rough in wildest rage doth roar.
Then know that I, as Snug the joiner, am
A lion fell,° nor else no lion's dam;
For, if I should as lion come in strife
Into this place, 'twere pity on my life.°
235 THESEUS: A very gentle° beast, and of a
good conscience.

DEMETRIUS: The very best at a beast, my
lord, that e'er I saw.

LYSANDER: This lion is a very fox for his
valor.   240

THESEUS: True; and a goose for his discretion.

DEMETRIUS: Not so, my lord; for his valor
cannot carry° his discretion, and the fox car-
ries the goose.   245

THESEUS: His discretion, I am sure, cannot
carry his valor; for the goose carries not the
fox. It is well. Leave it to his discretion, and
let us listen to the moon.

MOONSHINE:

This lanthorn° doth the hornèd moon pre-
    sent —   250

DEMETRIUS: He should have worn the horns
on his head.°

THESEUS: He is no crescent, and his horns
are invisible within the circumference.

MOONSHINE:

This lanthorn doth the hornèd moon present;   255
Myself the man i' th' moon do seem to be.

THESEUS: This is the greatest error of all the
rest. The man should be put into the lanthorn.
How is it else the man i' th' moon?

DEMETRIUS: He dares not come there for   260
the candle; for, you see, it is already in snuff.°

HIPPOLYTA: I am aweary of this moon.
Would he would change!

THESEUS: It appears, by his small light of discretion, that he is in the wane; but yet, in   265
courtesy, in all reason, we must stay the time.

LYSANDER: Proceed, Moon.

MOONSHINE: All that I have to say is to tell
you that the lanthorn is the moon; I, the man
i' th' moon; this thorn bush, my thorn bush;   270
and this dog, my dog.

DEMETRIUS: Why, all these should be in the
lanthorn; for all these are in the moon. But,
silence! Here comes Thisby.

(*Enter* THISBY.)

THISBY:

This is old Ninny's tomb. Where is my love?   275

LION: Oh — [*The* LION *roars.* THISBY *runs
off.*]

---

209 **'Tide life, 'tide death** come (betide) life or
death   211 **moon used** (the quartos read thus, the
Folio reads *morall downe.* Among suggested emen-
dations are "mural down," and "moon to see")
214–215 **when walls . . . without warning** i.e.,
when walls are so eager to listen without warning
the parents (?)   218 **in this kind** of this sort, i.e.,
plays (or players?)   232 **lion fell** fierce lion (perhaps with a pun on *fell* = "skin")   234 **pity on
my life** a dangerous thing for me   235 **gentle**
gentlemanly, courteous

244 **carry** carry away   249 **lanthorn** (so spelled,
and perhaps pronounced "lant-horn," because lan-
terns were commonly made of horn)   251–252
horns on his head (cuckolds were said to have
horns)   261 **in snuff** (1) in need of snuffing (2)
resentful

DEMETRIUS: Well roared, Lion.

THESEUS: Well run, Thisby.

HIPPOLYTA: Well shone, Moon. Truly, the
280 moon shines with a good grace.

[*The* LION *shakes* THISBY's *mantle, and exit.*]

THESEUS: Well moused,° Lion.

DEMETRIUS: And then came Pyramus.

LYSANDER: And so the lion vanished.

(*Enter* PYRAMUS.)

PYRAMUS:

Sweet Moon, I thank thee for thy sunny
          beams;
285 I thank thee, Moon, for shining now so bright;
For, by thy gracious, golden, glittering gleams,
          I trust to take of truest Thisby sight.
                But stay, O spite!°
                But mark, poor knight,
290   What dreadful dole° is here!
                Eyes, do you see?
                How can it be?
          O dainty duck! O dear!
                Thy mantle good,
295   What, stained with blood!
          Approach, ye Furies fell!°
                O Fates, come, come,
                Cut thread and thrum;°
          Quail,° crush, conclude, and quell!°
300 THESEUS: This passion, and the death of a
dear friend, would go near to make a man look
sad.

HIPPOLYTA: Beshrew° my heart, but I pity
the man.

PYRAMUS:

305 O wherefore, Nature, didst thou lions frame?
     Since lion vile hath here deflow'red my
          dear:
Which is — no, no — which was the fairest
          dame
     That lived, that loved, that liked, that
          looked with cheer.°
                Come, tears, confound;
310   Out, sword, and wound
          The pap of Pyramus;
                Ay, that left pap,
                Where heart doth hop.
                          [*Stabs himself.*]

Thus die I, thus, thus, thus.
     Now am I dead,   315
     Now am I fled;
My soul is in the sky.
     Tongue, lose thy light;
     Moon, take thy flight.
                          [*Exit* MOONSHINE.]
     Now die, die, die, die, die.   [*Dies.*]   320

DEMETRIUS: No die, but an ace,° for him;
for he is but one.

LYSANDER: Less than an ace, man; for he is
dead, he is nothing.

THESEUS: With the help of a surgeon he   325
might yet recover, and yet prove an ass.

HIPPOLYTA: How chance° Moonshine is
gone before Thisby comes back and finds her
lover?

THESEUS: She will find him by starlight.   330
Here she comes; and her passion° ends the
play.

[*Enter* THISBY.]

HIPPOLYTA: Methinks she should not use a
long one for such a Pyramus. I hope she will
be brief.   335

DEMETRIUS: A mote will turn the balance,
which Pyramus, which Thisby, is the better;
he for a man, God warr'nt us; she for a
woman, God bless us!

LYSANDER: She hath spied him already with 340
those sweet eyes.

DEMETRIUS: And thus she means,° videlicet:

THISBY:

     Asleep, my love?
          What, dead, my dove?
     O Pyramus, arise!   345
          Speak, speak. Quite dumb?
          Dead, dead? A tomb
     Must cover thy sweet eyes.
          These lily lips,
          This cherry nose,   350
     These yellow cowslip cheeks,
          Are gone, are gone.
          Lovers, make moan.
     His eyes were green as leeks.
          O Sisters Three,°   355
          Come, come to me,
     With hands as pale as milk;
          Lay them in gore,

281 **moused** shaken (like a mouse)   288 **spite**
vexation   290 **dole** sorrowful thing   296 **fell** fierce
298 **thread and thrum** i.e., everything (*thrum* =
the end of the warp thread)   299 **Quail** destroy
299 **quell** kill   303 **Beshrew** curse (but a mild
word)   308 **cheer** countenance

321 **No die, but an ace** not a die (singular of
"dice"), but a one-spot on a die   327 **How chance**
how does it come that   331 **passion** passionate
speech   342 **means** laments   355 **Sisters Three**
i.e., the three Fates

Since you have shore°
With shears his thread of silk.
Tongue, not a word.
Come, trusty sword,
Come, blade, my breast imbrue!°
                              [*Stabs herself.*]
And, farewell, friends.
Thus Thisby ends.
Adieu, adieu, adieu.   [*Dies.*]

THESEUS: Moonshine and Lion are left to bury the dead.

DEMETRIUS: Ay, and Wall too.

BOTTOM [*starting up*]: No, I assure you; the wall is down that parted their fathers. Will it please you to see the epilogue, or to hear a Bergomask dance° between two of our company?

THESEUS: No epilogue, I pray you; for your play needs no excuse. Never excuse, for when the players are all dead, there need none to be blamed. Marry, if he that writ it had played Pyramus and hanged himself in Thisby's garter, it would have been a fine tragedy: and so it is, truly; and very notably discharged. But, come, your Bergomask. Let your epilogue alone.

[*A dance.*]

The iron tongue of midnight hath told° twelve.
Lovers, to bed; 'tis almost fairy time.
I fear we shall outsleep the coming morn,
As much as we this night have overwatched.
This palpable-gross° play hath well beguiled
The heavy gait of night. Sweet friends, to bed.
A fortnight hold we this solemnity,
In nightly revels and new jollity.   (*Exeunt.*)

(*Enter* PUCK [*with a broom*].)

PUCK:
Now the hungry lion roars,
And the wolf behowls the moon;
Whilst the heavy plowman snores,
All with weary task fordone.°
Now the wasted° brands do glow,
Whilst the screech owl, screeching loud,
Puts the wretch that lies in woe
In remembrance of a shroud.

Now it is the time of night,   400
That the graves, all gaping wide,
Every one lets forth his sprite,
In the churchway paths to glide:
And we fairies, that do run
By the triple Hecate's team,°   405
From the presence of the sun,
Following darkness like a dream,
Now are frolic.° Not a mouse
Shall disturb this hallowed house:
I am sent, with broom, before,   410
To sweep the dust behind the door.°

(*Enter King and Queen of Fairies with all their train.*)

OBERON:
Through the house give glimmering light,
By the dead and drowsy fire:
Every elf and fairy sprite
Hop as light as bird from brier;   415
And this ditty, after me,
Sing, and dance it trippingly.

TITANIA:
First, rehearse your song by rote,
To each word a warbling note:
Hand in hand, with fairy grace,   420
Will we sing, and bless this place.

[*Song and dance.*]

OBERON:
Now, until the break of day,
Through this house each fairy stray.
To the best bride-bed will we,
Which by us shall blessèd be;   425
And the issue there create°
Ever shall be fortunate.
So shall all the couples three
Ever true in loving be;
And the blots of Nature's hand   430
Shall not in their issue stand.
Never mole, harelip, nor scar.
Nor mark prodigious,° such as are
Despisèd in nativity.
Shall upon their children be.   435

359 **shore** shorn 363 **imbrue** stain with blood 373 **Bergomask dance** rustic dance 384 **told** counted, tolled 388 **palpable-gross** obviously grotesque 395 **fordone** worn out 396 **wasted** used-up

405 **triple Hecate's team** i.e., because she had three names: Phoebe in Heaven, Diana on Earth, Hecate in Hades. (Like her chariot — drawn by black horses or dragons — the elves were abroad only at night; but III.ii.388–391 says differently) 408 **frolic** frolicsome 411 **behind the door** i.e., from behind the door (Puck traditionally helped with household chores) 426 **create** created 433 **mark prodigious** ominous birthmark

With this field-dew consecrate,
Every fairy take his gait,°
And each several° chamber bless,
Through this palace, with sweet peace,
440 And the owner of it blest
Ever shall in safety rest.
Trip away; make no stay;
Meet me all by break of day.

            Exeunt [all but PUCK].

PUCK:
If we shadows have offended,
445 Think but this, and all is mended:
That you have but slumb'red here,
While these visions did appear.
And this weak and idle° theme,

No more yielding but° a dream,
Gentles, do not reprehend: 450
If you pardon, we will mend.
And, as I am an honest Puck,
If we have unearnèd luck
Now to scape the serpent's tongue,°
We will make amends ere long;   455
Else the Puck a liar call:
So, good night unto you all.
Give me your hands,° if we be friends,
And Robin shall restore amends.°   [*Exit.*]

FINIS

449 **No more yielding but** yielding no more than
454 **to scape the serpent's tongue** i.e., to escape
hisses from the audience   458 **Give me your hands**
applaud   459 **restore amends** make amends

437 **take his gait** proceed   438 **several** individual
448 **idle** foolish

      Speaking broadly, there are in the Renaissance two comic traditions, which may be called "critical comedy" (or "bitter comedy") and "romantic comedy" (or "sweet comedy"). The former claims, in Hamlet's words, that the "purpose of playing . . . is to hold, as 'twere, the mirror up to nature; to show virtue her own feature, scorn her own image, and the very age and body of the time his form and pressure." Because it aims to hold a mirror up to the audience, its dramatis personae are usually urban citizens — jealous husbands, foolish merchants, and the like. These are ultimately punished, at times merely by exposure, at times by imprisonment or fines or some such thing. The second kind of comedy, romantic comedy, seeks less to correct than to delight with scenes of pleasant behavior. It does not hold a mirror to the audience; rather, it leads the audience into an elegant dream world where charming gentlefolk live in a timeless existence. Thomas Heywood, a playwright contemporary with Shakespeare, briefly set forth the characteristics of both traditions in *An Apology for Actors* (1612). A comedy, he said,

> is pleasantly contrived with merry accidents, and intermixed with apt and witty jests. . . . And what then is the subject of this harmless mirth? Either in the shape of a clown to show others their slovenly behavior, that they may reform that simplicity in themselves, which others make their sport, . . . or to refresh such weary spirits as are tired with labors or study, to moderate the cares and heaviness of the mind, that they may return to their trades and faculties with more zeal and earnestness, after some small soft and pleasant retirement.

      When we think of *A Midsummer Night's Dream,* we think not of critical comedy that seeks to reform "slovenly behavior" but of romantic comedy that offers "harmless mirth," "sport," and the refreshing of "such weary spirits as are tired with labors or study." Yet even *A Midsummer Night's Dream* has its touches of critical comedy, its elements that, in Heywood's words, "may reform" by holding up a mirror to unsocial behavior. There is some satire — a little satire of the crabby father, Egeus, and rather more of the young lovers and of the well-meaning rustics who bumblingly stage a play in an effort to please their duke (and to win pensions), but mostly the play is pervaded by genial spirits and a humane vision that make it moral without moralizing. The first book on Shakespeare's morality, Elizabeth Griffith's *The Morality of Shakespeare's Dramas* (1775), rather impatiently dismissed *A Midsummer Night's Dream:* "I shall not trouble my readers with the Fable of this piece, as I can see no general moral that can be deducted from the Argument."

For one thing, all of the people — including the fairies — in *A Midsummer Night's Dream* are basically decent creatures. Egeus is at first irascible, but at the end of the play we hear no more of his insistence that his daughter marry the young man of his choice; Theseus had engaged in youthful indiscretions, but that was long ago and in another country, and now he is the very model of a benevolent ruler; the fairy king and queen bicker, but at the end they are reconciled and they bless the bridal beds of the newlyweds. The rustics, though inept actors and sometimes too impressed by their own theatrical abilities, are men of good intentions. And if in the last act the young aristocratic lovers are a little too confident of their superiority to the rustic actors, we nevertheless feel that they are fundamentally decent; after all, their comments on the performance are more or less in tune with our own.

If *A Midsummer Night's Dream*, then, employs satire only sparingly, what does it do, and what is it about? Perhaps we can get somewhere near to an answer by briefly looking at some of the interrelationships of the stories that make up the intricate plot. There is the story of Theseus and Hippolyta, who will be married in four days; the story of the four young lovers; the story of Bottom and his fellow craftsmen, who are rehearsing a play; and the story of the quarreling fairies. All these stories are related, and eventually come together: the lovers marry on the same day as Theseus and Hippolyta; the craftsmen perform their play at the wedding; the fairies come to witness the wedding and bless it. One of the play's themes, of course, is love, as shown in the contrasts between the stately love of Theseus and Hippolyta, the changeable romantic love of the four young Athenians, the love of Pyramus and Thisby in the play that the craftsmen are rehearsing, the quarrel between the fairy king and queen, and even Titania's infatuation with Bottom. All these stories play against one another, sometimes very subtly, and sometimes explicitly, as when Lysander, having shifted his affection from Hermia to Helena, says, "Reason says you are the worthier maid" (II.ii. 116), and Bottom in the next scene accepts Titania's love, saying, "Reason and love keep little company together nowadays" (III.i.154–55). The nature of reason is also implicitly discussed in the play, in the numerous references to "fantasy" and "fancy," or imagination. There is scarcely a scene that does not touch on the matter of the power of the imagination. In the opening scene, for example, Egeus says that Lysander has corrupted Hermia's fantasy (I.i.32), and Duke Theseus tells Hermia that she must perceive her suitors as her father perceives them. The most famous of these references is Theseus' speech on "the lunatic, the lover, and the poet" (V.1.7). In addition to setting the time and place, the images help to define the nature of fantasy: there is an emphasis on night and moonlight during the period of confusion, and then references to the "morning lark," "day," and so on, when Theseus (the spokesman for reason) enters the woods and the lovers are properly paired (IV.i.98 ff.). The last scene reintroduces night, and the lovers have moved from the dark wood back to the civilized world of Athens, and the night will bring them to bed. The plot of A Midsummer Night's Dream, then, juxtaposes speech against speech, image against image, and scene against scene, telling not simply a story but a story that "grows to something of great constancy, . . . strange and admirable."

Le Misantrope.

THE MISANTHROPE

Molière

English version by Richard Wilbur

Jean Baptiste Poquelin (1622–1673), who took the name Molière, was born into a prosperous middle-class family. For a while he studied law and philosophy, but by 1643 he was acting. He became the head of a theatrical company which had its initial difficulties and later, thanks largely to Molière's comedies, its great successes. In 1662 he married Armande Béjart. The marriage apparently was unhappy, but the capricious and flirtatious Armande proved to be an accomplished actress. Molière continued to act, with great success in comedy, until his death. In one of those improbable things that happen in real life but that are too strange for art, Molière died of a hemorrhage that he suffered while playing the title role in his comedy *The Hypochondriac*. The early plays are highly farcical; among the later and greater plays are *The Highbrow Ladies* (1659), *Tartuffe* (1664), *Don Juan* (1665), *The Misanthrope* (1666), and *The Miser* (1668).

CHARACTERS

ALCESTE, *in love with Célimène*
PHILINTE, *Alceste's friend*
ORONTE, *in love with Célimène*
CÉLIMÈNE, *Alceste's beloved*
ÉLIANTE, *Célimène's cousin*
ARSINOÉ, *a friend of Célimène's*
ACASTE ⎫
CLITANDRE ⎭ *Marquesses*
BASQUE, *Célimène's servant*
A GUARD *of the Marshalsea*
DUBOIS, *Alceste's valet*

The Scene throughout is in Célimène's house at Paris.

Frontispiece of *Le Misanthrope, Comedie,* Paris, Jean Ribov, 1662. (Photograph: Courtesy of The Houghton Library, Harvard University.)

ACT I

SCENE I. [PHILINTE, ALCESTE.]

PHILINTE:
Now, what's got into you?
    ALCESTE (*seated*):   Kindly leave me alone.
    PHILINTE:
Come, come, what is it? This lugubrious
    tone . . .
    ALCESTE:
Leave me, I said; you spoil my solitude.
    PHILINTE:
Oh, listen to me, now, and don't be rude.
    ALCESTE:
I choose to be rude, Sir, and to be hard of
5   hearing.
    PHILINTE:
These ugly moods of yours are not endearing;
Friends though we are, I really must insist . . .
    ALCESTE (*abruptly rising*):
Friends? Friends, you say? Well, cross me off
    your list.

I've been your friend till now, as you well
    know;
But after what I saw a moment ago   10
I tell you flatly that our ways must part.
I wish no place in a dishonest heart.
    PHILINTE:
Why, what have I done, Alceste? Is this quite
    just?
    ALCESTE:
My God, you ought to die of self-disgust.
I call your conduct inexcusable, Sir,   15
And every man of honor will concur.
I see you almost hug a man to death,
Exclaim for joy until you're out of breath,
And supplement these loving demonstrations
With endless offers, vows, and protestations;   20
Then when I ask you "Who was that?" I find
That you can barely bring his name to mind!
Once the man's back is turned, you cease to
    love him,
And speak with absolute indifference of him!
By God, I say it's base and scandalous   25
To falsify the heart's affections thus;
If I caught myself behaving in such a way,
I'd hang myself for shame, without delay.
    PHILINTE:
It hardly seems a hanging matter to me;
I hope that you will take it graciously   30
If I extend myself a slight reprieve,
And live a little longer, by your leave.
    ALCESTE:
How dare you joke about a crime so grave?
    PHILINTE:
What crime? How else are people to behave?
    ALCESTE:
I'd have them be sincere, and never part   35
With any word that isn't from the heart.
    PHILINTE:
When someone greets us with a show of
    pleasure,
It's but polite to give him equal measure,
Return his love the best that we know how,
And trade him offer for offer, vow for vow.   40
    ALCESTE:
No, no, this formula you'd have me follow,
However fashionable, is false and hollow,
And I despise the frenzied operations
Of all these barterers of protestations,
These lavishers of meaningless embraces,   45
These utterers of obliging commonplaces,

Who court and flatter everyone on earth
And praise the fool no less than the man of
    worth.
Should you rejoice that someone fondles you,
50 Offers his love and service, swears to be true,
And fills your ears with praises of your name,
When to the first damned fop he'll say the
    same?
No, no: no self-respecting heart would dream
Of prizing so promiscuous an esteem;
55 However high the praise, there's nothing worse
Than sharing honors with the universe.
Esteem is founded on comparison:
To honor all men is to honor none.
Since you embrace this indiscriminate vice,
60 Your friendship comes at far too cheap a price:
I spurn the easy tribute of a heart
Which will not set the worthy man apart:
I choose, Sir, to be chosen; and in fine,
The friend of mankind is no friend of mine.

    PHILINTE:
65 But in polite society, custom decrees
That we show certain outward courtesies. . . .

    ALCESTE:
Ah, no! we should condemn with all our force
Such false and artificial intercourse.
Let men behave like men; let them display
70 Their inmost hearts in everything they say;
Let the heart speak, and let our sentiments
Not mask themselves in silly compliments.

    PHILINTE:
In certain cases it would be uncouth
And most absurd to speak the naked truth;
75 With all respect for your exalted notions,
It's often best to veil one's true emotions.
Wouldn't the social fabric come undone
If we were wholly frank with everyone?
Suppose you met with someone you couldn't
    bear;
80 Would you inform him of it then and there?

    ALCESTE:
Yes.

    PHILINTE:
    Then you'd tell old Emilie it's pathetic
The way she daubs her features with cosmetic
And plays the gay coquette at sixty-four?

    ALCESTE:
I would.

    PHILINTE:
    And you'd call Dorilas a bore,
85 And tell him every ear at court is lame
From hearing him brag about his noble name?

    ALCESTE:
Precisely.

    PHILINTE:
    Ah, you're joking.

    ALCESTE: *Au contraire:*
In this regard there's none I'd choose to spare.
All are corrupt; there's nothing to be seen
In court or town but aggravates my spleen.   90
I fall into deep gloom and melancholy
When I survey the scene of human folly,
Finding on every hand base flattery,
Injustice, fraud, self-interest, treachery. . . .
Ah, it's too much; mankind has grown so base,   95
I mean to break with the whole human race.

    PHILINTE:
This philosophic rage is a bit extreme;
You've no idea how comical you seem;
Indeed, we're like those brothers in the play
Called *School for Husbands,* one of whom was
    prey . . .   100

    ALCESTE:
Enough, now! None of your stupid similes.

    PHILINTE:
Then let's have no more tirades, if you please.
The world won't change, whatever you say or
    do;
And since plain speaking means so much to
    you,
I'll tell you plainly that by being frank   105
You've earned the reputation of a crank,
And that you're thought ridiculous when you
    rage
And rant against the manners of the age.

    ALCESTE:
So much the better; just what I wish to hear.
No news could be more grateful to my ear.   110
All men are so detestable in my eyes,
I should be sorry if they thought me wise.

    PHILINTE:
Your hatred's very sweeping, is it not?

    ALCESTE:
Quite right: I hate the whole degraded lot.

    PHILINTE:
Must all poor human creatures be embraced,   115
Without distinction, by your vast distaste?
Even in these bad times, there are surely a
    few . . .

    ALCESTE:
No, I include all men in one dim view:
Some men I hate for being rogues: the others
I hate because they treat the rogues like
    brothers,   120
And, lacking a virtuous scorn for what is vile,
Receive the villain with a complaisant smile.
Notice how tolerant people choose to be
Toward that bold rascal who's at law with me.

125 His social polish can't conceal his nature;
One sees at once that he's a treacherous
    creature;
No one could possibly be taken in
By those soft speeches and that sugary grin.
The whole world knows the shady means by
    which
130 The low-brow's grown so powerful and rich,
And risen to a rank so bright and high
That virtue can but blush, and merit sigh.
Whenever his name comes up in conversation,
None will defend his wretched reputation;
Call him knave, liar, scoundrel, and all the
135   rest,
Each head will nod, and no one will protest.
And yet his smirk is seen in every house,
He's greeted everywhere with smiles and bows,
And when there's any honor that can be got
140 By pulling strings, he'll get it, like as not.
My God! It chills my heart to see the ways
Men come to terms with evil nowadays;
Sometimes, I swear, I'm moved to flee and
    find
Some desert land unfouled by humankind.
    PHILINTE:
145 Come, let's forget the follies of the times
And pardon mankind for its petty crimes;
Let's have an end of rantings and of railings,
And show some leniency toward human fail-
    ings.
This world requires a pliant rectitude;
150 Too stern a virtue makes one stiff and rude;
Good sense views all extremes with detesta-
    tion,
And bids us to be noble in moderation.
The rigid virtues of the ancient days
Are not for us; they jar with all our ways
155 And ask of us too lofty a perfection.
Wise men accept their times without objec-
    tion,
And there's no greater folly, if you ask me,
Than trying to reform society.
Like you, I see each day a hundred and one
160 Unhandsome deeds that might be better done,
But still, for all the faults that meet my view,
I'm never known to storm and rave like you.
I take men as they are, or let them be,
And teach my soul to bear their frailty;
And whether in court or town, whatever the
165   scene,
My phlegm's as philosophic as your spleen.
    ALCESTE:
This phlegm which you so eloquently com-
    mend,

Does nothing ever rile it up, my friend?
Suppose some man you trust should treacher-
    ously
Conspire to rob you of your property,   170
And do his best to wreck your reputation?
Wouldn't you feel a certain indignation?
    PHILINTE:
Why, no. These faults of which you so com-
    plain
Are part of human nature, I maintain,
And it's no more a matter for disgust   175
That men are knavish, selfish and unjust,
Than that the vulture dines upon the dead,
And wolves are furious, and apes ill-bred.
    ALCESTE:
Shall I see myself betrayed, robbed, torn to
    bits,
And not . . . Oh, let's be still and rest our wits.   180
Enough of reasoning, now. I've had my fill.
    PHILINTE:
Indeed, you would do well, Sir, to be still.
Rage less at your opponent, and give some
    thought
To how you'll win this lawsuit that he's
    brought.
    ALCESTE:
I assure you I'll do nothing of the sort.   185
    PHILINTE:
Then who will plead your case before the
    court?
    ALCESTE:
Reason and right and justice will plead for me.
    PHILINTE:
Oh, Lord. What judges do you plan to see?
    ALCESTE:
Why, none. The justice of my cause is clear.
    PHILINTE:
Of course, man; but there's politics to fear. . . .   190
    ALCESTE:
No, I refuse to lift a hand. That's flat.
I'm either right, or wrong.
    PHILINTE: Don't count on that.
    ALCESTE:
No, I'll do nothing.
    PHILINTE: Your enemy's influence
Is great, you know . . .
    ALCESTE: That makes no difference.
    PHILINTE:
It will; you'll see.
    ALCESTE: Must honor bow to guile?   195
If so, I shall be proud to lose the trial.
    PHILINTE:
Oh, really . . .
    ALCESTE: I'll discover by this case

Whether or not men are sufficiently base
And impudent and villainous and perverse
200 To do me wrong before the universe.
    PHILINTE:
What a man!
    ALCESTE:
              Oh, I could wish, whatever the cost,
Just for the beauty of it, that my trial were
    lost.
    PHILINTE:
If people heard you talking so, Alceste,
They'd split their sides. Your name would be a
    jest.
    ALCESTE:
So much the worse for jesters.
205   PHILINTE: May I enquire
Whether this rectitude you so admire,
And these hard virtues you're enamored of
Are qualities of the lady whom you love?
It much surprises me that you, who seem
210 To view mankind with furious disesteem,
Have yet found something to enchant your
    eyes
Amidst a species which you so despise.
And what is more amazing, I'm afraid,
Is the most curious choice your heart has
    made.
215 The honest Éliante is fond of you,
Arsinoé, the prude, admires you too;
And yet your spirit's been perversely led
To choose the flighty Célimène instead,
Whose brittle malice and coquettish ways
220 So typify the manners of our days.
How is it that the traits you most abhor
Are bearable in this lady you adore?
Are you so blind with love that you can't find
    them?
Or do you contrive, in her case, not to mind
    them?
    ALCESTE:
225 My love for that young widow's not the kind
That can't perceive defects; no, I'm not blind.
I see her faults, despite my ardent love,
And all I see I fervently reprove.
And yet I'm weak; for all her falsity,
230 That woman knows the art of pleasing me,
And though I never cease complaining of her,
I swear I cannot manage not to love her.
Her charm outweighs her faults; I can but aim
To cleanse her spirit in my love's pure flame.
    PHILINTE:
235 That's no small task; I wish you all success.
You think then that she loves you?
    ALCESTE: Heavens, yes!

I wouldn't love her did she not love me.
    PHILINTE:
Well, if her taste for you is plain to see,
Why do these rivals cause you such despair?
    ALCESTE:
True love, Sir, is possessive, and cannot bear   240
To share with all the world. I'm here today
To tell her she must send that mob away.
    PHILINTE:
If I were you, and had your choice to make,
Éliante, her cousin, would be the one I'd
    take;
That honest heart, which cares for you alone,   245
Would harmonize far better with your own.
    ALCESTE:
True, true: each day my reason tells me so;
But reason doesn't rule in love, you know.
    PHILINTE:
I fear some bitter sorrow is in store;
This love . . .

SCENE II. [ORONTE, ALCESTE, PHILINTE.]

ORONTE (*to* ALCESTE):
          The servants told me at the door
That Éliante and Célimène were out,
But when I heard, dear Sir, that you were
    about,
I came to say, without exaggeration,
That I hold you in the vastest admiration,   5
And that it's always been my dearest desire
To be the friend of one I so admire.
I hope to see my love of merit requited,
And you and I in friendship's bond united.
I'm sure you won't refuse — if I may be
    frank —   10
A friend of my devotedness — and rank.

(*During this speech of* ORONTE'S ALCESTE *is
abstracted, and seems unaware that he is
being spoken to. He only breaks off his
reverie when* ORONTE *says*:)

It was for you, if you please, that my words
    were intended.
    ALCESTE:
For me, Sir?
    ORONTE:
          Yes, for you. You're not offended?
    ALCESTE:
By no means. But this much surprises me. . . .
The honor comes most unexpectedly. . . .   15
    ORONTE:
My high regard should not astonish you;
The whole world feels the same. It is your due.

ALCESTE:
Sir . . .

ORONTE:
Why, in all the State there isn't one
Can match your merits; they shine, Sir, like
the sun.

ALCESTE:
Sir . . .

ORONTE:
20   You are higher in my estimation
Than all that's most illustrious in the nation.

ALCESTE:
Sir . . .

ORONTE:
If I lie, may heaven strike me dead!
To show you that I mean what I have said,
Permit me, Sir, to embrace you most sincerely,
And swear that I will prize our friendship
25   dearly.
Give me your hand. And now, Sir, if you
choose,
We'll make our vows.

ALCESTE: Sir . . .

ORONTE: What! You refuse?

ALCESTE:
Sir, it's a very great honor you extend:
But friendship is a sacred thing, my friend;
30   It would be profanation to bestow
The name of friend on one you hardly know.
All parts are better played when well-rehearsed;
Let's put off friendship, and get acquainted
first.
We may discover it would be unwise
35   To try to make our natures harmonize.

ORONTE:
By heaven! You're sagacious to the core;
This speech has made me admire you even
more.
Let time, then, bring us closer day by day;
Meanwhile, I shall be yours in every way.
40   If, for example, there should be anything
You wish at court, I'll mention it to the King.
I have his ear, of course; it's quite well known
That I am much in favor with the throne.
In short, I am your servant. And now, dear
friend,
45   Since you have such fine judgment, I intend
To please you, if I can, with a small sonnet
I wrote not long ago. Please comment on it,
And tell me whether I ought to publish it.

ALCESTE:
You must excuse me, Sir; I'm hardly fit
To judge such matters.

ORONTE: Why not?

ALCESTE: I am, I fear,   50
Inclined to be unfashionably sincere.

ORONTE:
Just what I ask; I'd take no satisfaction
In anything but your sincere reaction.
I beg you not to dream of being kind.

ALCESTE:
Since you desire it, Sir, I'll speak my mind.   55

ORONTE:
Sonnet. It's a sonnet. . . . Hope . . . The poem's
addressed
To a lady who wakened hopes within my
breast.
Hope . . . this is not the pompous sort of thing,
Just modest little verses, with a tender ring.

ALCESTE:
Well, we shall see.

ORONTE: Hope . . . I'm anxious to hear   60
Whether the style seems properly smooth and
clear,
And whether the choice of words is good or
bad.

ALCESTE:
We'll see, we'll see.

ORONTE: Perhaps I ought to add
That it took me only a quarter-hour to write it.

ALCESTE:
The time's irrelevant, Sir: kindly recite it.   65

ORONTE (reading):
Hope comforts us awhile, 'tis true,
Lulling our cares with careless laughter,
And yet such joy is full of rue,
My Phyllis, if nothing follows after.

PHILINTE:
I'm charmed by this already; the style's delightful.   70

ALCESTE (sotto voce, to PHILINTE):
How can you say that? Why, the thing is
frightful.

ORONTE:
Your fair face smiled on me awhile,
But was it kindness so to enchant me?
'Twould have been fairer not to smile,
If hope was all you meant to grant me.   75

PHILINTE:
What a clever thought! How handsomely you
phrase it!

ALCESTE (sotto voce, to PHILINTE):
You know the thing is trash. How dare you
praise it?

ORONTE:
If it's to be my passion's fate
Thus everlastingly to wait,
Then death will come to set me free: 80

For death is fairer than the fair;
Phyllis, to hope is to despair
When one must hope eternally.

PHILINTE:
The close is exquisite — full of feeling and
    grace.

ALCESTE (*sotto voce, aside*):
Oh, blast the close; you'd better close your
85 face
Before you send your lying soul to hell.

PHILINTE:
I can't remember a poem I've liked so well.

ALCESTE (*sotto voce, aside*):
Good Lord!

ORONTE (*to* PHILINTE):
            I fear you're flattering me a bit.

PHILINTE:
Oh, no!

ALCESTE (*sotto voce, aside*):
            What else d'you call it, you hypocrite?

ORONTE (*to* ALCESTE):
But you, Sir, keep your promise now: don't
90   shrink
From telling me sincerely what you think.

ALCESTE:
Sir, these are delicate matters; we all desire
To be told that we've the true poetic fire.
But once, to one whose name I shall not
    mention,
95 I said, regarding some verse of his invention,
That gentlemen should rigorously control
That itch to write which often afflicts the soul;
That one should curb the heady inclination
To publicize one's little avocation;
100 And that in showing off one's works of art
One often plays a very clownish part.

ORONTE:
Are you suggesting in a devious way
That I ought not . . .

ALCESTE: Oh, that I do not say.
Further, I told him that no fault is worse
105 Than that of writing frigid, lifeless verse,
And that the merest whisper of such a shame
Suffices to destroy a man's good name.

ORONTE:
D'you mean to say my sonnet's dull and trite?

ALCESTE:
I don't say that. But I went on to cite
110 Numerous cases of once-respected men
Who came to grief by taking up the pen.

ORONTE:
And am I like them? Do I write so poorly?

ALCESTE:
I don't say that. But I told this person, "Surely

You're under no necessity to compose;
Why you should wish to publish, heaven
    knows.   115
There's no excuse for printing tedious rot
Unless one writes for bread, as you do not.
Resist temptation, then, I beg of you;
Conceal your pastimes from the public view;
And don't give up, on any provocation,   120
Your present high and courtly reputation,
To purchase at a greedy printer's shop
The name of silly author and scribbling fop."
These were the points I tried to make him see.

ORONTE:
I sense that they are also aimed at me;   125
But now — about my sonnet — I'd like to be
    told . . .

ALCESTE:
Frankly, that sonnet should be pigeonholed.
You've chosen the worst models to imitate.
The style's unnatural. Let me illustrate:
For example, *Your fair face smiled on me*
    awhile,   130
Followed by, *'Twould have been fairer not to*
    smile!
Or this: *such joy is full of rue;*
Or this: *For death is fairer than the fair;*
Or, *Phyllis, to hope is to despair*
    When one must hope eternally.   135
This artificial style, that's all the fashion,
Has neither taste, nor honesty, nor passion;
It's nothing but a sort of wordy play,
And nature never spoke in such a way.
What, in this shallow age, is not debased?   140
Our fathers, though less refined, had better
    taste;
I'd barter all that men admire today
For one old love song I shall try to say:
    If the King had given me for my own
    Paris, his citadel,   145
    And I for that must leave alone
    Her whom I love so well,
    I'd say then to the Crown,
    Take back your glittering town;
    My darling is more fair, I swear,   150
    My darling is more fair.
The rhyme's not rich, the style is rough and
    old,
But don't you see that it's the purest gold
Beside the tinsel nonsense now preferred,
And that there's passion in its every word?   155
    If the King had given me for my own
    Paris, his citadel,
    And I for that must leave alone
    Her whom I love so well,

160 *I'd say then to the Crown,*
Take back your glittering town;
My darling is more fair, I swear,
My darling is more fair.
There speaks a loving heart. (*To* PHILINTE.)
You're laughing, eh?
165 Laugh on, my precious wit. Whatever you say,
I hold that song's worth all the bibelots
That people hail today with ah's and oh's.
ORONTE:
And I maintain my sonnet's very good.
ALCESTE:
It's not at all surprising that you should.
You have your reasons; permit me to have
170   mine
For thinking that you cannot write a line.
ORONTE:
Others have praised my sonnet to the skies.
ALCESTE:
I lack their art of telling pleasant lies.
ORONTE:
You seem to think you've got no end of wit.
ALCESTE:
175 To praise your verse, I'd need still more of it.
ORONTE:
I'm not in need of your approval, Sir.
ALCESTE:
That's good; you couldn't have it if you were.
ORONTE:
Come now, I'll lend you the subject of my
    sonnet;
I'd like to see you try to improve upon it.
ALCESTE:
I might, by chance, write something just as
180   shoddy;
But then I wouldn't show it to everybody.
ORONTE:
You're most opinionated and conceited.
ALCESTE:
Go find your flatterers, and be better treated.
ORONTE:
Look here, my little fellow, pray watch your
    tone.
ALCESTE:
My great big fellow, you'd better watch your
185   own.
PHILINTE (*stepping between them*):
Oh, please, please, gentlemen! This will never
    do.
ORONTE:
The fault is mine, and I leave the field to you.
I am your servant, Sir, in every way.
ALCESTE:
And I, Sir, am your most abject valet.

SCENE III. [PHILINTE, ALCESTE.]

PHILINTE:
Well, as you see, sincerity in excess
Can get you into a very pretty mess;
Oronte was hungry for appreciation. . . .
ALCESTE:
Don't speak to me.
PHILINTE: What?
ALCESTE: No more conversation.
PHILINTE:
Really, now . . .
ALCESTE: Leave me alone.
PHILINTE: If I . . .
ALCESTE: Out of my sight!   5
PHILINTE:
But what . . .
ALCESTE: I won't listen.
PHILINTE: But . . .
ALCESTE: Silence!
PHILINTE: Now, is it polite . . .
ALCESTE:
By heaven, I've had enough. Don't follow me.
PHILINTE:
Ah, you're just joking. I'll keep you company.

ACT II

SCENE I. [ALCESTE, CÉLIMÈNE.]

ALCESTE:
Shall I speak plainly, Madam? I confess
Your conduct gives me infinite distress,
And my resentment's grown too hot to
    smother.
Soon, I foresee, we'll break with one another.
If I said otherwise, I should deceive you;   5
Sooner or later, I shall be forced to leave you,
And if I swore that we shall never part,
I should misread the omens of my heart.
CÉLIMÈNE:
You kindly saw me home, it would appear,
So as to pour invectives in my ear.   10
ALCESTE:
I've no desire to quarrel. But I deplore
Your inability to shut the door
On all these suitors who beset you so.
There's what annoys me, if you care to know.
CÉLIMÈNE:
Is it my fault that all these men pursue me?   15
Am I to blame if they're attracted to me?
And when they gently beg an audience,

Ought I to take a stick and drive them hence?
ALCESTE:
Madam, there's no necessity for a stick;
20 A less responsive heart would do the trick.
Of your attractiveness I don't complain;
But those your charms attract, you then detain
By a most melting and receptive manner,
And so enlist their hearts beneath your banner.
25 It's the agreeable hopes which you excite
That keep these lovers round you day and
      night;
Were they less liberally smiled upon,
That sighing troop would very soon be gone.
But tell me, Madam, why it is that lately
30 This man Clitandre interests you so greatly?
Because of what high merits do you deem
Him worthy of the honor of your esteem?
Is it that your admiring glances linger
On the splendidly long nail of his little finger?
35 Or do you share the general deep respect
For the blond wig he chooses to affect?
Are you in love with his embroidered hose?
Do you adore his ribbons and his bows?
Or is it that this paragon bewitches
Your tasteful eye with his vast German
40   breeches?
Perhaps his giggle, or his falsetto voice,
Makes him the latest gallant of your choice?
CÉLIMÈNE:
You're much mistaken to resent him so.
Why I put up with him you surely know:
45 My lawsuit's very shortly to be tried,
And I must have his influence on my side.
ALCESTE:
Then lose your lawsuit, Madam, or let it drop;
Don't torture me by humoring such a fop.
CÉLIMÈNE:
You're jealous of the whole world, Sir.
ALCESTE: That's true,
50 Since the whole world is well-received by you.
CÉLIMÈNE:
That my good nature is so unconfined
Should serve to pacify your jealous mind;
Were I to smile on one, and scorn the rest,
Then you might have some cause to be
      distressed.
ALCESTE:
55 Well, if I mustn't be jealous, tell me, then,
Just how I'm better treated than other men.
CÉLIMÈNE:
You know you have my love. Will that not
      do?
ALCESTE:
What proof have I that what you say is true?

CÉLIMÈNE:
I would expect, Sir, that my having said it
Might give the statement a sufficient credit.   60
ALCESTE:
But how can I be sure that you don't tell
The selfsame thing to other men as well?
CÉLIMÈNE:
What a gallant speech! How flattering to me!
What a sweet creature you make me out to be!
Well then, to save you from the pangs of
      doubt,   65
All that I've said I hereby cancel out;
Now, none but yourself shall make a monkey
      of you:
Are you content?
ALCESTE:
            Why, why am I doomed to love you?
I swear that I shall bless the blissful hour
When this poor heart's no longer in your
      power!   70
I make no secret of it: I've done my best
To exorcise this passion from my breast;
But thus far all in vain; it will not go;
It's for my sins that I must love you so.
CÉLIMÈNE:
Your love for me is matchless, Sir; that's clear.   75
ALCESTE:
Indeed, in all the world it has no peer;
Words can't describe the nature of my passion,
And no man ever loved in such a fashion.
CÉLIMÈNE:
Yes, it's a brand-new fashion, I agree:
You show your love by castigating me,   80
And all your speeches are enraged and rude.
I've never been so furiously wooed.
ALCESTE:
Yet you could calm that fury, if you chose.
Come, shall we bring our quarrels to a close?
Let's speak with open hearts, then, and
      begin . . .   85

SCENE II. [CÉLIMÈNE, ALCESTE, BASQUE.]

CÉLIMÈNE:
What is it?
BASQUE: Acaste is here.
CÉLIMÈNE: Well, send him in.

SCENE III. [CÉLIMÈNE, ALCESTE.]

ALCESTE:
What! Shall we never be alone at all?
You're always ready to receive a call,
And you can't bear, for ten ticks of the clock,

Not to keep open house for all who knock.
CÉLIMÈNE:
5 I couldn't refuse him: he'd be most put out.
ALCESTE:
Surely that's not worth worrying about.
CÉLIMÈNE:
Acaste would never forgive me if he guessed
That I consider him a dreadful pest.
ALCESTE:
If he's a pest, why bother with him then?
CÉLIMÈNE:
10 Heavens! One can't antagonize such men;
Why, they're the chartered gossips of the court,
And have a say in things of every sort.
One must receive them, and be full of charm;
They're no great help, but they can do you
      harm,
15 And though your influence be ever so great,
They're hardly the best people to alienate.
ALCESTE:
I see, dear lady, that you could make a case
For putting up with the whole human race;
These friendships that you calculate so
      nicely . . .

SCENE IV. [ALCESTE, CÉLIMÈNE, BASQUE.]

BASQUE:
Madam, Clitandre is here as well.
ALCESTE: Precisely.
CÉLIMÈNE:
Where are you going?
ALCESTE: Elsewhere.
CÉLIMÈNE: Stay.
ALCESTE: No, no.
CÉLIMÈNE:
Stay, Sir.
ALCESTE:
      I can't.
CÉLIMÈNE: I wish it.
ALCESTE: No, I must go.
I beg you, Madam, not to press the matter;
5 You know I have no taste for idle chatter.
CÉLIMÈNE:
Stay. I command you.
ALCESTE: No, I cannot stay.
CÉLIMÈNE:
Very well; you have my leave to go away.

SCENE V. [ÉLIANTE, PHILINTE, ACASTE,
CLITANDRE, ALCESTE, CÉLIMÈNE, BASQUE.]

ÉLIANTE (to CÉLIMÈNE):
The Marquesses have kindly come to call.
Were they announced?

CÉLIMÈNE:
                Yes. Basque, bring chairs for all.

(BASQUE provides the chairs, and exits.)

(To ALCESTE.) You haven't gone?
ALCESTE: No; and I shan't depart
Till you decide who's foremost in your heart.
CÉLIMÈNE:
Oh, hush.
ALCESTE:
            It's time to choose; take them, or me. 5
CÉLIMÈNE:
You're mad.
ALCESTE:
            I'm not, as you shall shortly see.
CÉLIMÈNE:
Oh?
ALCESTE:
    You'll decide.
CÉLIMÈNE: You're joking now, dear friend.
ALCESTE:
No, no; you'll choose; my patience is at an
      end.
CLITANDRE:
Madam, I come from court, where poor
      Cléonte
Behaved like a perfect fool, as is his wont.   10
Has he no friend to counsel him, I wonder,
And teach him less unerringly to blunder?
CÉLIMÈNE:
It's true, the man's a most accomplished
      dunce;
His gauche behavior charms the eye at once;
And every time one sees him, on my word,   15
His manner's grown a trifle more absurd.
ACASTE:
Speaking of dunces, I've just now conversed
With old Damon, who's one of the very worst;
I stood a lifetime in the broiling sun
Before his dreary monologue was done.   20
CÉLIMÈNE:
Oh, he's a wondrous talker, and has the power
To tell you nothing hour after hour:
If, by mistake, he ever came to the point,
The shock would put his jawbone out of
      joint.
ÉLIANTE (to PHILINTE):
The conversation takes its usual turn,   25
And all our dear friends' ears will shortly burn.
CLITANDRE:
Timante's a character, Madam.
CÉLIMÈNE: Isn't he, though?
A man of mystery from top to toe,
Who moves about in a romantic mist
On secret missions which do not exist.   30

His talk is full of eyebrows and grimaces;
How tired one gets of his momentous faces;
He's always whispering something confidential
Which turns out to be quite inconsequential;
35 Nothing's too slight for him to mystify;
He even whispers when he says "good-by."

ACASTE:
Tell us about Géralde.

CÉLIMÈNE: That tiresome ass.
He mixes only with the titled class,
And fawns on dukes and princes, and is bored
40 With anyone who's not at least a lord.
The man's obsessed with rank, and his discourses
Are all of hounds and carriages and horses;
He uses Christian names with all the great,
And the word Milord, with him, is out of date.

CLITANDRE:
45 He's very taken with Bélise, I hear.

CÉLIMÈNE:
She is the dreariest company, poor dear.
Whenever she comes to call, I grope about
To find some topic which will draw her out,
But, owing to her dry and faint replies,
50 The conversation wilts, and droops, and dies.
In vain one hopes to animate her face
By mentioning the ultimate commonplace;
But sun or shower, even hail or frost
Are matters she can instantly exhaust.
55 Meanwhile her visit, painful though it is,
Drags on and on through mute eternities,
And though you ask the time, and yawn, and yawn,
She sits there like a stone and won't be gone.

ACASTE:
Now for Adraste.

CÉLIMÈNE: Oh, that conceited elf
60 Has a gigantic passion for himself;
He rails against the court, and cannot bear it
That none will recognize his hidden merit;
All honors given to others give offense
To his imaginary excellence.

CLITANDRE:
65 What about young Cléon? His house, they say,
Is full of the best society, night and day.

CÉLIMÈNE:
His cook has made him popular, not he:
It's Cléon's table that people come to see.

ÉLIANTE:
He gives a splendid dinner, you must admit.

CÉLIMÈNE:
70 But must he serve himself along with it?
For my taste, he's a most insipid dish
Whose presence sours the wine and spoils the fish.

PHILINTE:
Damis, his uncle, is admired no end.
What's your opinion, Madam?

CÉLIMÈNE: Why, he's my friend.

PHILINTE:
He seems a decent fellow, and rather clever.   75

CÉLIMÈNE:
He works too hard at cleverness, however.
I hate to see him sweat and struggle so
To fill his conversation with bons mots.
Since he's decided to become a wit
His taste's so pure that nothing pleases it;   80
He scolds at all the latest books and plays,
Thinking that wit must never stoop to praise,
That finding fault's a sign of intellect,
That all appreciation is abject,
And that by damning everything in sight   85
One shows oneself in a distinguished light.
He's scornful even of our conversations:
Their trivial nature sorely tries his patience;
He folds his arms, and stands above the battle,
And listens sadly to our childish prattle.   90

ACASTE:
Wonderful, Madam! You've hit him off precisely.

CLITANDRE:
No one can sketch a character so nicely.

ALCESTE:
How bravely, Sirs, you cut and thrust at all
These absent fools, till one by one they fall:
But let one come in sight, and you'll at once   95
Embrace the man you lately called a dunce,
Telling him in a tone sincere and fervent
How proud you are to be his humble servant.

CLITANDRE:
Why pick on us? *Madame's* been speaking, Sir.
And you should quarrel, if you must, with her.   100

ALCESTE:
No, no, by God, the fault is yours, because
You lead her on with laughter and applause,
And make her think that she's the more delightful
The more her talk is scandalous and spiteful.
Oh, she would stoop to malice far, far less   105
If no such claque approved her cleverness.
It's flatterers like you whose foolish praise
Nourishes all the vices of these days.

PHILINTE:
But why protest when someone ridicules
Those you'd condemn, yourself, as knaves or fools?   110

CÉLIMÈNE:
Why, Sir? Because he loves to make a fuss.
You don't expect him to agree with us,

When there's an opportunity to express
His heaven-sent spirit of contrariness?
115 What other people think, he can't abide;
Whatever they say, he's on the other side;
He lives in deadly terror of agreeing;
'Twould make him seem an ordinary being.
Indeed, he's so in love with contradiction,
He'll turn against his most profound convic-
120   tion
And with a furious eloquence deplore it,
If only someone else is speaking for it.
    ALCESTE:
Go on, dear lady, mock me as you please;
You have your audience in ecstasies.
    PHILINTE:
125 But what she says is true: you have a way
Of bridling at whatever people say;
Whether they praise or blame, your angry
    spirit
Is equally unsatisfied to hear it.
    ALCESTE:
Men, Sir, are always wrong, and that's the
    reason
130 That righteous anger's never out of season;
All that I hear in all their conversation
Is flattering praise or reckless condemnation.
    CÉLIMÈNE:
But . . .
    ALCESTE:
        No, no, Madam, I am forced to state
That you have pleasures which I deprecate,
And that these others, here, are much to
135   blame
For nourishing the faults which are your
    shame.
    CLITANDRE:
I shan't defend myself, Sir; but I vow
I'd thought this lady faultless until now.
    ACASTE:
I see her charms and graces, which are many;
140 But as for faults, I've never noticed any.
    ALCESTE:
I see them, Sir; and rather than ignore them,
I strenuously criticize her for them.
The more one loves, the more one should
    object
To every blemish, every least defect.
145 Were I this lady, I would soon get rid
Of lovers who approved of all I did,
And by their slack indulgence and applause
Endorsed my follies and excused my flaws.
    CÉLIMÈNE:
If all hearts beat according to your measure,
The dawn of love would be the end of plea-
150   sure;

And love would find its perfect consummation
In ecstasies of rage and reprobation.
    ÉLIANTE:
Love, as a rule, affects men otherwise,
And lovers rarely love to criticize.
They see their lady as a charming blur,   155
And find all things commendable in her.
If she has any blemish, fault, or shame,
They will redeem it by a pleasing name.
The pale-faced lady's lily-white, perforce;
The swarthy one's a sweet brunette, of course; 160
The spindly lady has a slender grace;
The fat one has a most majestic pace;
The plain one, with her dress in disarray,
They classify as *beauté négligée*;
The hulking one's a goddess in their eyes,   165
The dwarf, a concentrate of Paradise;
The haughty lady has a noble mind;
The mean one's witty, and the dull one's
    kind;
The chatterbox has liveliness and verve,
The mute one has a virtuous reserve.   170
So lovers manage, in their passion's cause,
To love their ladies even for their flaws.
    ALCESTE:
But I still say . . .
    CÉLIMÈNE: I think it would be nice
To stroll around the gallery once or twice.
What! You're not going, Sirs?
    CLITANDRE *and* ACASTE: No, Madam, no.   175
    ALCESTE:
You seem to be in terror lest they go.
Do what you will, Sirs; leave, or linger on,
But I shan't go till after you are gone.
    ACASTE:
I'm free to linger, unless I should perceive
Madame is tired, and wishes me to leave.   180
    CLITANDRE:
And as for me, I needn't go today
Until the hour of the King's *coucher*.
    CÉLIMÈNE (*to* ALCESTE):
You're joking, surely?
    ALCESTE: Not in the least; we'll see
Whether you'd rather part with them, or me.

    SCENE VI. [ALCESTE, CÉLIMÈNE, ÉLIANTE,
    ACASTE, PHILINTE, CLITANDRE, BASQUE.]

    BASQUE (*to* ALCESTE):
Sir, there's a fellow here who bids me state
That he must see you, and that it can't wait.
    ALCESTE:
Tell him that I have no such pressing affairs.

BASQUE:
It's a long tailcoat that this fellow wears,
With gold all over.
CÉLIMÈNE (*to* ALCESTE):
5   You'd best go down and see.
Or — have him enter.

SCENE VII. [ALCESTE, CÉLIMÈNE, ÉLIANTE,
ACASTE, PHILINTE, CLITANDRE, GUARD.]

ALCESTE (*confronting the* GUARD):
                    Well, what do you want with me?
Come in, Sir.
GUARD: I've a word, Sir, for your ear.
ALCESTE:
Speak it aloud, Sir; I shall strive to hear.
GUARD:
The Marshals have instructed me to say
5   You must report to them without delay.
ALCESTE:
Who? Me, Sir?
GUARD: Yes, Sir; you.
ALCESTE: But what do they want?
PHILINTE (*to* ALCESTE):
To scotch your silly quarrel with Oronte.
CÉLIMÈNE (*to* PHILINTE):
What quarrel?
PHILINTE: Oronte and he have fallen out
Over some verse he spoke his mind about;
10   The Marshals wish to arbitrate the matter.
ALCESTE:
Never shall I equivocate or flatter!
PHILINTE:
You'd best obey their summons; come, let's go.
ALCESTE:
How can they mend our quarrel, I'd like to
       know?
Am I to make a cowardly retraction,
15   And praise those jingles to his satisfaction?
I'll not recant; I've judged that sonnet rightly.
It's bad.
PHILINTE:
             But you might say so more politely. . . .
ALCESTE:
I'll not back down; his verses make me sick.
PHILINTE:
If only you could be more politic!
But come, let's go.
20   ALCESTE: I'll go, but I won't unsay
A single word.
PHILINTE: Well, let's be on our way.
ALCESTE:
Till I am ordered by my lord the King
To praise that poem, I shall say the thing

Is scandalous, by God, and that the poet
Ought to be hanged for having the nerve to
       show it.   25

(*To* CLITANDRE *and* ACASTE, *who are laughing.*)

By heaven, Sirs, I really didn't know
That I was being humorous.
CÉLIMÈNE: Go, Sir, go;
Settle your business.
ALCESTE: I shall, and when I'm through,
I shall return to settle things with you.

ACT III

SCENE I. [CLITANDRE, ACASTE.]

CLITANDRE:
Dear Marquess, how contented you appear;
All things delight you, nothing mars your
       cheer.
Can you, in perfect honesty, declare
That you've a right to be so debonair?
ACASTE:
By Jove, when I survey myself, I find   5
No cause whatever for distress of mind.
I'm young and rich; I can in modesty
Lay claim to an exalted pedigree;
And owing to my name and my condition
I shall not want for honors and position.   10
Then as to courage, that most precious trait,
I seem to have it, as was proved of late
Upon the field of honor, where my bearing,
They say, was very cool and rather daring.
I've wit, of course; and taste in such perfection 15
That I can judge without the least reflection,
And at the theater, which is my delight,
Can make or break a play on opening night,
And lead the crowd in hisses or bravos,
And generally be known as one who knows.   20
I'm clever, handsome, gracefully polite;
My waist is small, my teeth are strong and
       white;
As for my dress, the world's astonished eyes
Assure me that I bear away the prize.
I find myself in favor everywhere,   25
Honored by men, and worshiped by the fair;
And since these things are so, it seems to me
I'm justified in my complacency.
CLITANDRE:
Well, if so many ladies hold you dear,
Why do you press a hopeless courtship here?   30

ACASTE:
Hopeless, you say? I'm not the sort of fool
That likes his ladies difficult and cool.
Men who are awkward, shy, and peasantish
May pine for heartless beauties, if they wish,
35 Grovel before them, bear their cruelties,
Woo them with tears and sighs and bended
        knees,
And hope by dogged faithfulness to gain
What their poor merits never could obtain.
For men like me, however, it makes no sense
40 To love on trust, and foot the whole expense.
Whatever any lady's merits be,
I think, thank God, that I'm as choice as she;
That if my heart is kind enough to burn
For her, she owes me something in return;
45 And that in any proper love affair
The partners must invest an equal share.
        CLITANDRE:
You think, then, that our hostess favors you?
        ACASTE:
I've reason to believe that that is true.
        CLITANDRE:
How did you come to such a mad conclusion?
You're blind, dear fellow. This is sheer delu-
50   sion.
        ACASTE:
All right, then: I'm deluded and I'm blind.
        CLITANDRE:
Whatever put the notion in your mind?
        ACASTE:
Delusion.
        CLITANDRE:
            What persuades you that you're right?
        ACASTE:
I'm blind.
        CLITANDRE:
            But have you any proofs to cite?
        ACASTE:
I tell you I'm deluded.
55   CLITANDRE: Have you, then,
Received some secret pledge from Célimène?
        ACASTE:
Oh, no: she scorns me.
        CLITANDRE: Tell me the truth, I beg.
        ACASTE:
She just can't bear me.
        CLITANDRE: Ah, don't pull my leg.
Tell me what hope she's given you, I pray.
        ACASTE:
60 I'm hopeless, and it's you who win the day.
She hates me thoroughly, and I'm so vexed
I mean to hang myself on Tuesday next.

CLITANDRE:
Dear Marquess, let us have an armistice
And make a treaty. What do you say to this?
If ever one of us can plainly prove   65
That Célimène encourages his love,
The other must abandon hope, and yield,
And leave him in possession of the field.
        ACASTE:
Now, there's a bargain that appeals to me;
With all my heart, dear Marquess, I agree.   70
But hush.

SCENE II. [CÉLIMÈNE, ACASTE, CLITANDRE.]

CÉLIMÈNE:
            Still here?
CLITANDRE: 'Twas love that stayed our feet.
CÉLIMÈNE:
I think I heard a carriage in the street.
Whose is it? D'you know?

SCENE III. [CÉLIMÈNE, ACASTE, CLITANDRE,
                BASQUE.]

BASQUE: Arsinoé is here,
Madame.
        CÉLIMÈNE:
            Arsinoé, you say? Oh, dear.
        BASQUE:
Éliante is entertaining her below.
        CÉLIMÈNE:
What brings the creature here, I'd like to
        know?
        ACASTE:
They say she's dreadfully prudish, but in fact   5
I think her piety . . .
        CÉLIMÈNE: It's all an act.
At heart she's worldly, and her poor success
In snaring men explains her prudishness.
It breaks her heart to see the beaux and
        gallants
Engrossed by other women's charms and tal-
        ents,   10
And so she's always in a jealous rage
Against the faulty standards of the age.
She lets the world believe that she's a prude
To justify her loveless solitude,
And strives to put a brand of moral shame   15
On all the graces that she cannot claim.
But still she'd love a lover; and Alceste
Appears to be the one she'd love the best.

His visits here are poison to her pride;
She seems to think I've lured him from her
20   side;
And everywhere, at court or in the town,
The spiteful, envious woman runs me down.
In short, she's just as stupid as can be,
Vicious and arrogant in the last degree,
25 And . . .

SCENE IV. [ARSINOÉ, CÉLIMÈNE, CLITANDRE, ACASTE.]

CÉLIMÈNE:
     Ah! What happy chance has brought
you here?
I've thought about you ever so much, my dear.
ARSINOÉ:
I've come to tell you something you should
know.
CÉLIMÈNE:
How good of you to think of doing so!

(CLITANDRE *and* ACASTE *go out, laughing.*)

SCENE V. [ARSINOÉ, CÉLIMÈNE.]

ARSINOÉ:
It's just as well those gentlemen didn't tarry.
CÉLIMÈNE:
Shall we sit down?
ARSINOÉ   That won't be necessary.
Madam, the flame of friendship ought to burn
Brightest in matters of the most concern,
And as there's nothing which concerns us
5   more
Than honor, I have hastened to your door
To bring you, as your friend, some informa-
   tion
About the status of your reputation.
I visited, last night, some virtuous folk,
And, quite by chance, it was of you they
10   spoke;
There was, I fear, no tendency to praise
Your light behavior and your dashing ways.
The quantity of gentlemen you see
And your by now notorious coquetry
15 Were both so vehemently criticized
By everyone, that I was much surprised.
Of course, I needn't tell you where I stood;
I came to your defense as best I could,
Assured them you were harmless, and declared
20 Your soul was absolutely unimpaired.

But there are some things, you must realize,
One can't excuse, however hard one tries,
And I was forced at last into conceding
That your behavior, Madam, is misleading,
That it makes a bad impression, giving rise   25
To ugly gossip and obscene surmise,
And that if you were more *overtly* good,
You wouldn't be so much misunderstood.
Not that I think you've been unchaste — no!
   no!
The saints preserve me from a thought so low!   30
But mere good conscience never did suffice:
One must avoid the outward show of vice.
Madam, you're too intelligent, I'm sure,
To think my motives anything but pure
In offering you this counsel — which I do   35
Out of a zealous interest in you.
CÉLIMÈNE:
Madam, I haven't taken you amiss;
I'm very much obliged to you for this;
And I'll at once discharge the obligation
By telling you about *your* reputation.   40
You've been so friendly as to let me know
What certain people say of me, and so
I mean to follow your benign example
By offering you a somewhat similar sample.
The other day, I went to an affair   45
And found some most distinguished people
   there
Discussing piety, both false and true.
The conversation soon came round to you.
Alas! Your prudery and bustling zeal
Appeared to have a very slight appeal.   50
Your affectation of a grave demeanor,
Your endless talk of virtue and of honor,
The aptitude of your suspicious mind
For finding sin where there is none to find,
Your towering self-esteem, that pitying face   55
With which you contemplate the human race,
Your sermonizings and your sharp aspersions
On people's pure and innocent diversions —
All these were mentioned, Madam, and, in fact,
Were roundly and concertedly attacked.   60
"What good," they said, "are all these outward
   shows,
When everything belies her pious pose?
She prays incessantly; but then, they say,
She beats her maids and cheats them of their
   pay;
She shows her zeal in every holy place,   65
But still she's vain enough to paint her face;
She holds that naked statues are immoral,
But with a naked *man* she'd have no quarrel."

Of course, I said to everybody there
70 That they were being viciously unfair;
But still they were disposed to criticize you,
And all agreed that someone should advise you
To leave the morals of the world alone,
And worry rather more about your own.
They felt that one's self-knowledge should be
75   great
Before one thinks of setting others straight;
That one should learn the art of living well
Before one threatens other men with hell,
And that the Church is best equipped, no
   doubt,
80 To guide our souls and root our vices out.
Madam, you're too intelligent, I'm sure,
To think my motives anything but pure
In offering you this counsel — which I do
Out of a zealous interest in you.
      ARSINOÉ:
85 I dared not hope for gratitude, but I
Did not expect so acid a reply;
I judge, since you've been so extremely tart,
That my good counsel pierced you to the
   heart.
      CÉLIMÈNE:
Far from it, Madam. Indeed, it seems to me
90 We ought to trade advice more frequently.
One's vision of oneself is so defective
That it would be an excellent corrective.
If you are willing, Madam, let's arrange
Shortly to have another frank exchange
95 In which we'll tell each other, *entre nous*,
What you've heard tell of me, and I of you.
      ARSINOÉ:
Oh, people never censure you, my dear;
It's me they criticize. Or so I hear.
      CÉLIMÈNE:
Madam, I think we either blame or praise
100 According to our taste and length of days.
There is a time of life for coquetry,
And there's a season, too, for prudery.
When all one's charms are gone, it is, I'm
   sure,
Good strategy to be devout and pure:
105 It makes one seem a little less forsaken.
Some day, perhaps, I'll take the road you've
   taken:
Time brings all things. But I have time
   aplenty,
And see no cause to be a prude at twenty.
      ARSINOÉ:
You give your age in such a gloating tone
110 That one would think I was an ancient crone;
We're not so far apart, in sober truth,

That you can mock me with a boast of youth!
Madam, you baffle me. I wish I knew
What moves you to provoke me as you do.
      CÉLIMÈNE:
For my part, Madam, I should like to know   115
Why you abuse me everywhere you go.
Is it my fault, dear lady, that your hand
Is not, alas, in very great demand?
If men admire me, if they pay me court
And daily make me offers of the sort   120
You'd dearly love to have them make to you,
How can I help it? What would you have me
   do?
If what you want is lovers, please feel free
To take as many as you can from me.
      ARSINOÉ:
Oh, come. D'you think the world is losing
   sleep   125
Over the flock of lovers which you keep,
Or that we find it difficult to guess
What price you pay for their devotedness?
Surely you don't expect us to suppose
Mere merit could attract so many beaux?   130
It's not your virtue that they're dazzled by;
Nor is it virtuous love for which they sigh.
You're fooling no one, Madam; the world's not
   blind;
There's many a lady heaven has designed
To call men's noblest, tenderest feelings out,   135
Who has no lovers dogging her about;
From which it's plain that lovers nowadays
Must be acquired in bold and shameless ways,
And only pay one court for such reward
As modesty and virtue can't afford.   140
Then don't be quite so puffed up, if you
   please,
About your tawdry little victories;
Try, if you can, to be a shade less vain,
And treat the world with somewhat less dis-
   dain.
If one were envious of your amours,   145
One soon could have a following like yours;
Lovers are no great trouble to collect
If one prefers them to one's self-respect.
      CÉLIMÈNE:
Collect them then, my dear; I'd love to see
You demonstrate that charming theory;   150
Who knows, you might . . .
      ARSINOÉ: Now, Madam, that will do;
It's time to end this trying interview.
My coach is late in coming to your door,
Or I'd have taken leave of you before.
      CÉLIMÈNE:
Oh, please don't feel that you must rush away;   155

I'd be delighted, Madam, if you'd stay.
However, lest my conversation bore you,
Let me provide some better company for you;
This gentleman, who comes most apropos,
160 Will please you more than I could do, I know.

SCENE VI. [ALCESTE, CÉLIMÈNE, ARSINOÉ.]

CÉLIMÈNE:
Alceste, I have a little note to write
Which simply must go out before tonight;
Please entertain *Madame*; I'm sure that she
Will overlook my incivility.

SCENE VII. [ALCESTE, ARSINOÉ.]

ARSINOÉ:
Well, Sir, our hostess graciously contrives
For us to chat until my coach arrives;
And I shall be forever in her debt
For granting me this little tête-à-tête.
5 We women very rightly give our hearts
To men of noble character and parts,
And your especial merits, dear Alceste,
Have roused the deepest sympathy in my
    breast.
Oh, how I wish they had sufficient sense
10 At court, to recognize your excellence!
They wrong you greatly, Sir. How it must hurt
    you
Never to be rewarded for your virtue!
ALCESTE:
Why, Madam, what cause have I to feel
    aggrieved?
What great and brilliant thing have I
    achieved?
15 What service have I rendered to the King
That I should look to him for anything?
ARSINOÉ:
Not everyone who's honored by the State
Has done great services. A man must wait
Till time and fortune offer him the chance.
20 Your merit, Sir, is obvious at a glance,
And . . .
ALCESTE:
    Ah, forget my merit; I am not neglected.
The court, I think, can hardly be expected
To mine men's souls for merit, and unearth
Our hidden virtues and our secret worth.
ARSINOÉ:
Some virtues, though, are far too bright to
25   hide;
Yours are acknowledged, Sir, on every side.

Indeed, I've heard you warmly praised of late
By persons of considerable weight.
ALCESTE:
This fawning age has praise for everyone,
And all distinctions, Madam, are undone. 30
All things have equal honor nowadays,
And no one should be gratified by praise.
To be admired, one only need exist,
And every lackey's on the honors list.
ARSINOÉ:
I only wish, Sir, that you had your eye 35
On some position at court, however high;
You'd only have to hint at such a notion
For me to set the proper wheels in motion;
I've certain friendships I'd be glad to use
To get you any office you might choose. 40
ALCESTE:
Madam, I fear that any such ambition
Is wholly foreign to my disposition.
The soul God gave me isn't of the sort
That prospers in the weather of a court.
It's all too obvious that I don't possess 45
The virtues necessary for success.
My one great talent is for speaking plain;
I've never learned to flatter or to feign;
And anyone so stupidly sincere
Had best not seek a courtier's career. 50
Outside the court, I know, one must dispense
With honors, privilege, and influence;
But still one gains the right, foregoing these,
Not to be tortured by the wish to please.
One needn't live in dread of snubs and slights, 55
Nor praise the verse that every idiot writes,
Nor humor silly Marquesses, nor bestow
Politic sighs on Madam So-and-So.
ARSINOÉ:
Forget the court, then; let the matter rest.
But I've another cause to be distressed 60
About your present situation, Sir.
It's to your love affair that I refer.
She whom you love, and who pretends to love
    you,
Is, I regret to say, unworthy of you.
ALCESTE:
Why, Madam? Can you seriously intend 65
To make so grave a charge against your friend?
ARSINOÉ:
Alas, I must. I've stood aside too long
And let that lady do you grievous wrong;
But now my debt to conscience shall be paid:
I tell you that your love has been betrayed. 70
ALCESTE:
I thank you, Madam; you're extremely kind.
Such words are soothing to a lover's mind.

ARSINOÉ:

Yes, though she *is* my friend, I say again
You're very much too good for Célimène.
75 She's wantonly misled you from the start.

ALCESTE:

You may be right; who knows another's heart?
But ask yourself if it's the part of charity
To shake my soul with doubts of her sincerity.

ARSINOÉ:

Well, if you'd rather be a dupe than doubt
her,
80 That's your affair. I'll say no more about her.

ALCESTE:

Madam, you know that doubt and vague
suspicion
Are painful to a man in my position;
It's most unkind to worry me this way
Unless you've some real proof of what you say.

ARSINOÉ:

85 Sir, say no more: all doubts shall be removed,
And all that I've been saying shall be proved.
You've only to escort me home, and there
We'll look into the heart of this affair.
I've ocular evidence which will persuade you
Beyond a doubt, that Célimène's betrayed
90 you.
Then, if you're saddened by that revelation,
Perhaps I can provide some consolation.

ACT IV

Scene i. [ÉLIANTE, philinte.]

PHILINTE:

Madam, he acted like a stubborn child;
I thought they never would be reconciled;
In vain we reasoned, threatened, and appealed;
He stood his ground and simply would not
yield.
5 The Marshals, I feel sure, have never heard
An argument so splendidly absurd.
"No, gentlemen," said he, "I'll not retract.
His verse is bad: extremely bad, in fact.
Surely it does the man no harm to know it.
10 Does it disgrace him, not to be a poet?
A gentleman may be respected still,
Whether he writes a sonnet well or ill.
That I dislike his verse should not offend him;
In all that touches honor, I commend him;
15 He's noble, brave, and virtuous — but I fear
He can't in truth be called a sonneteer.

I'll gladly praise his wardrobe; I'll endorse
His dancing, or the way he sits a horse;
But, gentlemen, I cannot praise his rhyme.
In fact, it ought to be a capital crime 20
For anyone so sadly unendowed
To write a sonnet, and read the thing aloud."
At length he fell into a gentler mood
And, striking a concessive attitude,
He paid Oronte the following courtesies: 25
"Sir, I regret that I'm so hard to please,
And I'm profoundly sorry that your lyric
Failed to provoke me to a panegyric."
After these curious words, the two embraced,
And then the hearing was adjourned — in
haste. 30

ÉLIANTE:

His conduct has been very singular lately;
Still, I confess that I respect him greatly.
The honesty in which he takes such pride
Has — to my mind — it's noble, heroic side.
In this false age, such candor seems outra-
geous; 35
But I could wish that it were more contagious.

PHILINTE:

What most intrigues me in our friend Alceste
Is the grand passion that rages in his breast.
The sullen humors he's compounded of
Should not, I think, dispose his heart to love; 40
But since they do, it puzzles me still more
That he should choose your cousin to adore.

ÉLIANTE:

It does, indeed, belie the theory
That love is born of gentle sympathy,
And that the tender passion must be based 45
On sweet accords of temper and of taste.

PHILINTE:

Does she return his love, do you suppose?

ÉLIANTE:

Ah, that's a difficult question, Sir. Who knows?
How can we judge the truth of her devotion?
Her heart's a stranger to its own emotion. 50
Sometimes it thinks it loves, when no love's
there;
At other times it loves quite unaware.

PHILINTE:

I rather think Alceste is in for more
Distress and sorrow than he's bargained for;
Were he of my mind, Madam, his affection 55
Would turn in quite a different direction,
And we would see him more responsive to
The kind regard which he receives from you.

ÉLIANTE:

Sir, I believe in frankness, and I'm inclined,

60   In matters of the heart, to speak my mind.
I don't oppose his love for her; indeed,
I hope with all my heart that he'll succeed,
And were it in my power, I'd rejoice
In giving him the lady of his choice.
65   But if, as happens frequently enough
In love affairs, he meets with a rebuff —
If Célimène should grant some rival's suit —
I'd gladly play the role of substitute;
Nor would his tender speeches please me less
Because they'd once been made without suc-
70   cess.
    PHILINTE:
Well, Madam, as for me, I don't oppose
Your hopes in this affair; and heaven knows
That in my conversations with the man
I plead your cause as often as I can.
75   But if those two should marry, and so remove
All chance that he will offer you his love,
Then I'll declare my own, and hope to see
Your gracious favor pass from him to me.
In short, should you be cheated of Alceste,
80   I'd be most happy to be second best.
    ÉLIANTE:
Philinte, you're teasing.
    PHILINTE: Ah, Madam, never fear;
No words of mine were ever so sincere,
And I shall live in fretful expectation
Till I can make a fuller declaration.

SCENE II. [ALCESTE, ÉLIANTE, PHILINTE.]

    ALCESTE:
Avenge me, Madam! I must have satisfaction,
Or this great wrong will drive me to distrac-
  tion!
    ÉLIANTE:
Why, what's the matter? What's upset you so?
    ALCESTE:
Madam, I've had a mortal, mortal blow.
5   If Chaos repossessed the universe,
I swear I'd not be shaken any worse.
I'm ruined....I can say no more....My
  soul ...
    ÉLIANTE:
Do try, Sir, to regain your self-control.
    ALCESTE:
Just heaven! Why were so much beauty and
  grace
10   Bestowed on one so vicious and so base?
    ÉLIANTE:
Once more, Sir, tell us. . . .
    ALCESTE: My world has gone to wrack;

I'm — I'm betrayed; she's stabbed me in the
  back:
Yes, Célimène (who would have thought it of
  her?)
Is false to me, and has another lover.
    ÉLIANTE:
Are you quite certain? Can you prove these
  things?   15
    PHILINTE:
Lovers are prey to wild imaginings
And jealous fancies. No doubt there's some
  mistake. . . .
    ALCESTE:
Mind your own business, Sir, for heaven's sake.
(To ÉLIANTE.) Madam, I have the proof that
  you demand
Here in my pocket, penned by her own hand. 20
Yes, all the shameful evidence one could want
Lies in this letter written to Oronte —
Oronte! whom I felt sure she couldn't love,
And hardly bothered to be jealous of.
    PHILINTE:
Still, in a letter, appearances may deceive; 25
This may not be so bad as you believe.
    ALCESTE:
Once more I beg you, Sir, to let me be;
Tend to your own affairs; leave mine to me.
    ÉLIANTE:
Compose yourself; this anguish that you
  feel . . .
    ALCESTE:
Is something, Madam, you alone can heal. 30
My outraged heart, beside itself with grief,
Appeals to you for comfort and relief.
Avenge me on your cousin, whose unjust
And faithless nature has deceived my trust;
Avenge a crime your pure soul must detest. 35
    ÉLIANTE:
But how, Sir?
    ALCESTE:
           Madam, this heart within my breast
Is yours; pray take it; redeem my heart from
  her,
And so avenge me on my torturer.
Let her be punished by the fond emotion,
The ardent love, the bottomless devotion, 40
The faithful worship which this heart of mine
Will offer up to yours as to a shrine.
    ÉLIANTE:
You have my sympathy, Sir, in all you suffer;
Nor do I scorn the noble heart you offer;
But I suspect you'll soon be mollified, 45
And this desire for vengeance will subside.

When some belovèd hand has done us wrong
We thirst for retribution — but not for long;
However dark the deed that she's committed,
50 A lovely culprit's very soon acquitted.
Nothing's so stormy as an injured lover,
And yet no storm so quickly passes over.
ALCESTE:
No, Madam, no — this is no lovers' spat;
I'll not forgive her; it's gone too far for that;
55 My mind's made up; I'll kill myself before
I waste my hopes upon her any more.
Ah, here she is. My wrath intensifies.
I shall confront her with her tricks and lies,
And crush her utterly, and bring you then
60 A heart no longer slave to Célimène.

SCENE III. [CÉLIMÈNE, ALCESTE.]

ALCESTE (aside):
Sweet heaven, help me to control my passion.
CÉLIMÈNE (aside):
Oh, Lord. (To ALCESTE.) Why stand there
    staring in that fashion?
And what d'you mean by those dramatic sighs,
And that malignant glitter in your eyes?
ALCESTE:
I mean that sins which cause the blood to
5   freeze
Look innocent beside your treacheries;
That nothing Hell's or Heaven's wrath could
    do
Ever produced so bad a thing as you.
CÉLIMÈNE:
Your compliments were always sweet and
    pretty.
ALCESTE:
10 Madam, it's not the moment to be witty.
No, blush and hang your head; you've ample
    reason,
Since I've the fullest evidence of your treason.
Ah, this is what my sad heart prophesied;
Now all my anxious fears are verified;
15 My dark suspicion and my gloomy doubt
Divined the truth, and now the truth is out.
For all your trickery, I was not deceived;
It was my bitter stars that I believed.
But don't imagine that you'll go scot-free;
20 You shan't misuse me with impunity.
I know that love's irrational and blind;
I know the heart's not subject to the mind,
And can't be reasoned into beating faster;
I know each soul is free to choose its master;
25 Therefore had you but spoken from the heart,

Rejecting my attention from the start,
I'd have no grievance, or at any rate
I could complain of nothing but my fate.
Ah, but so falsely to encourage me —
That was a treason and a treachery   30
For which you cannot suffer too severely,
And you shall pay for that behavior dearly.
Yes, now I have no pity, not a shred;
My temper's out of hand; I've lost my head;
Shocked by the knowledge of your double-deal-
    ings,   35
My reason can't restrain my savage feelings;
A righteous wrath deprives me of my senses,
And I won't answer for the consequences.
CÉLIMÈNE:
What does this outburst mean? Will you
    please explain?
Have you, by any chance, gone quite insane? 40
ALCESTE:
Yes, yes, I went insane the day I fell
A victim to your black and fatal spell,
Thinking to meet with some sincerity
Among the treacherous charms that beckoned
    me.
CÉLIMÈNE:
Pooh. Of what treachery can you complain? 45
ALCESTE:
How sly you are, how cleverly you feign!
But you'll not victimize me any more.
Look: here's a document you've seen before.
This evidence, which I acquired today,
Leaves you, I think, without a thing to say. 50
CÉLIMÈNE:
Is this what sent you into such a fit?
ALCESTE:
You should be blushing at the sight of it.
CÉLIMÈNE:
Ought I to blush? I truly don't see why.
ALCESTE:
Ah, now you're being bold as well as sly;
Since there's no signature, perhaps you'll
    claim . . .   55
CÉLIMÈNE:
I wrote it, whether or not it bears my name.
ALCESTE:
And you can view with equanimity
This proof of your disloyalty to me!
CÉLIMÈNE:
Oh, don't be so outrageous and extreme.
ALCESTE:
You take this matter lightly, it would seem. 60
Was it no wrong to me, no shame to you,
That you should send Oronte this billet-doux?

CÉLIMÈNE:
Oronte! Who said it was for him?
    ALCESTE: Why, those
Who brought me this example of your prose.
But what's the difference? If you wrote the
65   letter
To someone else, it pleases me no better.
My grievance and your guilt remain the same.
    CÉLIMÈNE:
But need you rage, and need I blush for
    shame,
If this was written to a *woman* friend?
    ALCESTE:
70 Ah! Most ingenious. I'm impressed no end;
And after that incredible evasion
Your guilt is clear. I need no more persuasion.
How dare you try so clumsy a deception?
D'you think I'm wholly wanting in perception?
75 Come, come, let's see how brazenly you'll try
To bolster up so palpable a lie:
Kindly construe this ardent closing section
As nothing more than sisterly affection!
Here, let me read it. Tell me, if you dare to,
That this is for a woman . . .
80   CÉLIMÈNE: I don't care to.
What right have you to badger and berate me,
And so highhandedly interrogate me?
    ALCESTE:
Now, don't be angry; all I ask of you
Is that you justify a phrase or two . . .
    CÉLIMÈNE:
85 No, I shall not. I utterly refuse,
And you may take those phrases as you choose.
    ALCESTE:
Just show me how this letter could be meant
For a woman's eyes, and I shall be content.
    CÉLIMÈNE:
No, no, it's for Oronte; you're perfectly right.
90 I welcome his attentions with delight,
I prize his character and his intellect,
And everything is just as you suspect.
Come, do your worst now; give your rage free
    rein;
But kindly cease to bicker and complain.
    ALCESTE (*aside*):
95 Good God! Could anything be more inhuman?
Was ever a heart so mangled by a woman?
When I complain of how she has betrayed me,
She bridles, and commences to upbraid me!
She tries my tortured patience to the limit;
100 She won't deny her guilt; she glories in it!
And yet my heart's too faint and cowardly
To break these chains of passion, and be free,

To scorn her as it should, and rise above
This unrewarded, mad, and bitter love.
(*To* CÉLIMÈNE.) Ah, traitress, in how confident
    a fashion   105
You take advantage of my helpless passion,
And use my weakness for your faithless charms
To make me once again throw down my arms!
But do at least deny this black transgression;
Take back that mocking and perverse confes-
    sion;   110
Defend this letter and your innocence,
And I, poor fool, will aid in your defense.
Pretend, pretend, that you are just and true,
And I shall make myself believe in you.
    CÉLIMÈNE:
Oh, stop it. Don't be such a jealous dunce, 115
Or I shall leave off loving you at once.
Just why should I *pretend*? What could impel
    me
To stoop so low as that? And kindly tell me
Why, if I loved another, I shouldn't merely
Inform you of it, simply and sincerely!   120
I've told you where you stand, and that admis-
    sion
Should altogether clear me of suspicion;
After so generous a guarantee,
What right have you to harbor doubts of me?
Since women are (from natural reticence) 125
Reluctant to declare their sentiments,
And since the honor of our sex requires
That we conceal our amorous desires,
Ought any man for whom such laws are
    broken
To question what the oracle has spoken? 130
Should he not rather feel an obligation
To trust that most obliging declaration?
Enough, now. Your suspicions quite disgust
    me;
Why should I love a man who doesn't trust
    me?
I cannot understand why I continue,   135
Fool that I am, to take an interest in you.
I ought to choose a man less prone to doubt,
And give you something to be vexed about.
    ALCESTE:
Ah, what a poor enchanted fool I am;
These gentle words, no doubt, were all a sham, 140
But destiny requires me to entrust
My happiness to you, and so I must.
I'll love you to the bitter end, and see
How false and treacherous you dare to be.
    CÉLIMÈNE:
No, you don't really love me as you ought. 145

ALCESTE:
I love you more than can be said or thought;
Indeed, I wish you were in such distress
That I might show my deep devotedness.
Yes, I could wish that you were wretchedly
      poor,
150 Unloved, uncherished, utterly obscure;
That fate had set you down upon the earth
Without possessions, rank, or gentle birth;
Then, by the offer of my heart, I might
Repair the great injustice of your plight;
155 I'd raise you from the dust, and proudly prove
The purity and vastness of my love.
      CÉLIMÈNE:
This is a strange benevolence indeed!
God grant that I may never be in need. . . .
Ah, here's Monsieur Dubois, in quaint dis-
      guise.

      SCENE IV. [CÉLIMÈNE, ALCESTE, DUBOIS.]

      ALCESTE:
Well, why this costume? Why those fright-
      ened eyes?
What ails you?
      DUBOIS:
            Well, Sir, things are most mysterious.
      ALCESTE:
What do you mean?
      DUBOIS: I fear they're very serious.
      ALCESTE:
What?
      DUBOIS:
            Shall I speak more loudly?
      ALCESTE: Yes; speak out.
      DUBOIS:
Isn't there someone here, Sir?
5   ALCESTE: Speak, you lout!
Stop wasting time.
      DUBOIS: Sir, we must slip away.
      ALCESTE:
How's that?
      DUBOIS: We must decamp without delay.
      ALCESTE:
Explain yourself.
      DUBOIS: I tell you we must fly.
      ALCESTE:
What for?
      DUBOIS:
            We mustn't pause to say good-by.
      ALCESTE:
Now what d'you mean by all of this, you
10   clown?

DUBOIS:
I mean, Sir, that we've got to leave this town.
      ALCESTE:
I'll tear you limb from limb and joint from
      joint
If you don't come more quickly to the point.
      DUBOIS:
Well, Sir, today a man in a black suit,
Who wore a black and ugly scowl to boot,   15
Left us a document scrawled in such a hand
As even Satan couldn't understand.
It bears upon your lawsuit, I don't doubt;
But all hell's devils couldn't make it out.
      ALCESTE:
Well, well, go on. What then? I fail to see   20
How this event obliges us to flee.
      DUBOIS:
Well, Sir, an hour later, hardly more,
A gentleman who's often called before
Came looking for you in an anxious way.
Not finding you, he asked me to convey   25
(Knowing I could be trusted with the same)
The following message. . . . Now, what was his
      name?
      ALCESTE:
Forget his name, you idiot. What did he say?
      DUBOIS:
Well, it was one of your friends, Sir, anyway.
He warned you to begone, and he suggested   30
That if you stay, you may well be arrested.
      ALCESTE:
What? Nothing more specific? Think, man,
      think!
      DUBOIS:
No, Sir. He had me bring him pen and ink,
And dashed you off a letter which, I'm sure,
Will render things distinctly less obscure.   35
      ALCESTE:
Well — let me have it!
      CÉLIMÈNE: What is this all about?
      ALCESTE:
God knows; but I have hopes of finding out.
How long am I to wait, you blitherer?
      DUBOIS (after a protracted search for the
      letter):
I must have left it on your table, Sir.
      ALCESTE:
I ought to . . .
      CÉLIMÈNE:
                  No, no, keep your self-control;   40
Go find out what's behind his rigmarole.
      ALCESTE:
It seems that fate, no matter what I do,

Has sworn that I may not converse with you;
But, Madam, pray permit your faithful lover
45 To try once more before the day is over.

ACT V

SCENE I. [ALCESTE, PHILINTE.]

ALCESTE:
No, it's too much. My mind's made up, I tell
 you.
  PHILINTE:
Why should this blow, however hard, compel
 you . . .
  ALCESTE:
No, no, don't waste your breath in argument;
Nothing you say will alter my intent;
5 This age is vile, and I've made up my mind
To have no further commerce with mankind.
Did not truth, honor, decency, and the laws
Oppose my enemy and approve my cause?
My claims were justified in all men's sight;
10 I put my trust in equity and right;
Yet, to my horror and the world's disgrace,
Justice is mocked, and I have lost my case!
A scoundrel whose dishonesty is notorious
Emerges from another lie victorious!
15 Honor and right condone his brazen fraud,
While rectitude and decency applaud!
Before his smirking face, the truth stands
 charmed,
And virtue conquered, and the law disarmed!
His crime is sanctioned by a court decree!
20 And not content with what he's done to me,
The dog now seeks to ruin me by stating
That I composed a book now circulating,
A book so wholly criminal and vicious
That even to speak its title is seditious!
25 Meanwhile Oronte, my rival, lends his credit
To the same libelous tale, and helps to spread
 it!
Oronte! a man of honor and of rank,
With whom I've been entirely fair and frank;
Who sought me out and forced me, willy-nilly,
30 To judge some verse I found extremely silly;
And who, because I properly refused
To flatter him, or see the truth abused,
Abets my enemy in a rotten slander!
There's the reward of honesty and candor!
35 The man will hate me to the end of time
For failing to commend his wretched rhyme!

And not this man alone, but all humanity
Do what they do from interest and vanity;
They prate of honor, truth, and righteousness,
But lie, betray, and swindle nonetheless. 40
Come then: man's villainy is too much to
 bear;
Let's leave this jungle and this jackal's lair.
Yes! treacherous and savage race of men,
You shall not look upon my face again.
  PHILINTE:
Oh, don't rush into exile prematurely; 45
Things aren't as dreadful as you make them,
 surely.
It's rather obvious, since you're still at large,
That people don't believe your enemy's charge.
Indeed, his tale's so patently untrue
That it may do more harm to him than you. 50
  ALCESTE:
Nothing could do that scoundrel any harm:
His frank corruption is his greatest charm,
And, far from hurting him, a further shame
Would only serve to magnify his name.
  PHILINTE:
In any case, his bald prevarication 55
Has done no injury to your reputation,
And you may feel secure in that regard.
As for your lawsuit, it should not be hard
To have the case reopened, and contest
This judgment . . .
  ALCESTE: No, no, let the verdict rest. 60
Whatever cruel penalty it may bring,
I wouldn't have it changed for anything.
It shows the times' injustice with such clarity
That I shall pass it down to our posterity
As a great proof and signal demonstration 65
Of the black wickedness of this generation.
It may cost twenty thousand francs; but I
Shall pay their twenty thousand, and gain
 thereby
The right to storm and rage at human evil,
And send the race of mankind to the devil. 70
  PHILINTE:
Listen to me . . .
  ALCESTE:
    Why? What can you possibly say?
Don't argue, Sir; your labor's thrown away.
Do you propose to offer lame excuses
For men's behavior and the times' abuses?
  PHILINTE:
No, all you say I'll readily concede: 75
This is a low, conniving age indeed;
Nothing but trickery prospers nowadays,
And people ought to mend their shabby ways.

Yes, man's a beastly creature; but must we then
80 Abandon the society of men?
Here in the world, each human frailty
Provides occasion for philosophy,
And that is virtue's noblest exercise;
If honesty shone forth from all men's eyes,
85 If every heart were frank and kind and just.
What could our virtues do but gather dust
(Since their employment is to help us bear
The villainies of men without despair)?
A heart well-armed with virtue can endure. . . .
ALCESTE:
90 Sir, you're a matchless reasoner, to be sure;
Your words are fine and full of cogency;
But don't waste time and eloquence on me.
My reason bids me go, for my own good.
My tongue won't lie and flatter as it should;
God knows what frankness it might next
95   commit,
And what I'd suffer on account of it.
Pray let me wait for Célimène's return
In peace and quiet. I shall shortly learn,
By her response to what I have in view,
100 Whether her love for me is feigned or true.
PHILINTE:
Till then, let's visit Éliante upstairs.
ALCESTE:
No, I am too weighed down with somber cares.
Go to her, do; and leave me with my gloom
Here in the darkened corner of this room.
PHILINTE:
105 Why, that's no sort of company, my friend;
I'll see if Éliante will not descend.

SCENE II. [CÉLIMÈNE, ORONTE, ALCESTE.]

ORONTE:
Yes, Madam, if you wish me to remain
Your true and ardent lover, you must deign
To give me some more positive assurance.
All this suspense is quite beyond endurance.
5 If your heart shares the sweet desires of mine,
Show me as much by some convincing sign;
And here's the sign I urgently suggest:
That you no longer tolerate Alceste,
But sacrifice him to my love, and sever
10 All your relations with the man forever.
CÉLIMÈNE:
Why do you suddenly dislike him so?
You praised him to the skies not long ago.
ORONTE:
Madam, that's not the point. I'm here to find
Which way your tender feelings are inclined.

Choose, if you please, between Alceste and me, 15
And I shall stay or go accordingly.
ALCESTE (emerging from the corner):
Yes, Madam, choose; this gentleman's demand
Is wholly just, and I support his stand.
I too am true and ardent; I too am here
To ask you that you make your feelings clear. 20
No more delays, now; no equivocation;
The time has come to make your declaration.
ORONTE:
Sir, I've no wish in any way to be
An obstacle to your felicity.
ALCESTE:
Sir, I've no wish to share her heart with you; 25
That may sound jealous, but at least it's true.
ORONTE:
If, weighing us, she leans in your direction . . .
ALCESTE:
If she regards you with the least affection . . .
ORONTE:
I swear I'll yield her to you there and then.
ALCESTE:
I swear I'll never see her face again. 30
ORONTE:
Now, Madam, tell us what we've come to hear.
ALCESTE:
Madam, speak openly and have no fear.
ORONTE:
Just say which one is to remain your lover.
ALCESTE:
Just name one name, and it will all be over.
ORONTE:
What! Is it possible that you're undecided? 35
ALCESTE:
What! Can your feelings possibly be divided?
CÉLIMÈNE:
Enough: this inquisition's gone too far:
How utterly unreasonable you are!
Not that I couldn't make the choice with ease;
My heart has no conflicting sympathies; 40
I know full well which one of you I favor,
And you'd not see me hesitate or waver.
But how can you expect me to reveal
So cruelly and bluntly what I feel?
I think it altogether too unpleasant 45
To choose between two men when both are
   present;
One's heart has means more subtle and more
   kind
Of letting its affections be divined,
Nor need one be uncharitably plain
To let a lover know he loves in vain. 50
ORONTE:
No, no, speak plainly; I for one can stand it.
I beg you to be frank.

ALCESTE: And I demand it.
The simple truth is what I wish to know,
And there's no need for softening the blow.
55 You've made an art of pleasing everyone,
But now your days of coquetry are done:
You have no choice now, Madam, but to choose,
For I'll know what to think if you refuse;
I'll take your silence for a clear admission
60 That I'm entitled to my worst suspicion.
ORONTE:
I thank you for this ultimatum, Sir,
And I may say I heartily concur.
CÉLIMÈNE:
Really, this foolishness is very wearing:
Must you be so unjust and overbearing?
65 Haven't I told you why I must demur?
Ah, here's Éliante; I'll put the case to her.

SCENE III. [ÉLIANTE, PHILINTE, CÉLIMÈNE,
ORONTE, ALCESTE.]

CÉLIMÈNE:
Cousin, I'm being persecuted here
By these two persons, who, it would appear,
Will not be satisfied till I confess
Which one I love the more, and which the less,
5 And tell the latter to his face that he
Is henceforth banished from my company.
Tell me, has ever such a thing been done?
ÉLIANTE:
You'd best not turn to me; I'm not the one
To back you in a matter of this kind:
10 I'm all for those who frankly speak their mind.
ORONTE:
Madam, you'll search in vain for a defender.
ALCESTE:
You're beaten, Madam, and may as well sur-
render.
ORONTE:
Speak, speak, you must; and end this awful
strain.
ALCESTE:
Or don't, and your position will be plain.
ORONTE:
15 A single word will close this painful scene.
ALCESTE:
But if you're silent, I'll know what you mean.

SCENE IV. [ARSINOÉ, CÉLIMÈNE, ÉLIANTE,
ALCESTE, PHILINTE, ACASTE, CLITANDRE,
ORONTE.]

ACASTE (to CÉLIMÈNE):
Madam, with all due deference, we two
Have come to pick a little bone with you.

CLITANDRE (to ORONTE and ALCESTE):
I'm glad you're present, Sirs, as you'll soon
learn,
Our business here is also your concern.
ARSINOÉ (to CÉLIMÈNE):
Madam, I visit you so soon again   5
Only because of these two gentlemen,
Who came to me indignant and aggrieved
About a crime too base to be believed.
Knowing your virtue, having such confidence
in it,
I couldn't think you guilty for a minute,   10
In spite of all their telling evidence;
And, rising above our little difference,
I've hastened here in friendship's name to see
You clear yourself of this great calumny.
ACASTE:
Yes, Madam, let us see with what composure   15
You'll manage to respond to this disclosure.
You lately sent Clitandre this tender note.
CLITANDRE:
And this one, for Acaste, you also wrote.
ACASTE (to ORONTE and ALCESTE):
You'll recognize this writing, Sirs, I think;
The lady is so free with pen and ink   20
That you must know it all too well, I fear.
But listen: this is something you should hear.

"How absurd you are to condemn my light-
heartedness in society, and to accuse me of
being happiest in the company of others.   25
Nothing could be more unjust; and if you do
not come to me instantly and beg pardon for
saying such a thing, I shall never forgive you as
long as I live. Our big bumbling friend the
Viscount . . ."   30

What a shame that he's not here.

"Our big bumbling friend the Viscount,
whose name stands first in your complaint, is
hardly a man to my taste; and ever since the
day I watched him spend three-quarters of an   35
hour spitting into a well, so as to make circles
in the water, I have been unable to think
highly of him. As for the little Marquess . . ."

In all modesty, gentlemen, that is I.

"As for the little Marquess, who sat squeez-   40
ing my hand for such a long while yesterday, I
find him in all respects the most trifling
creature alive; and the only things of value
about him are his cape and his sword. As for
the man with the green ribbons . . ."   45

(To ALCESTE.) It's your turn now, Sir.

"As for the man with the green ribbons, he amuses me now and then with his bluntness and his bearish ill-humor; but there are many
50 times indeed when I think him the greatest bore in the world. And as for the sonneteer . . ."

(*To* ORONTE.) Here's your helping.

"And as for the sonneteer, who has taken it
55 into his head to be witty, and insists on being an author in the teeth of opinion, I simply cannot be bothered to listen to him, and his prose wearies me quite as much as his poetry. Be assured that I am not always so well-enter-
60 tained as you suppose; that I long for your company, more than I dare to say, at all these entertainments to which people drag me; and that the presence of those one loves is the true and perfect seasoning to all one's pleasures."

65 CLITANDRE: And now for me.

"Clitandre, whom you mention, and who so pesters me with his saccharine speeches, is the last man on earth for whom I could feel any affection. He is quite mad to suppose that I
70 love him, and so are you, to doubt that you are loved. Do come to your senses; exchange your suppositions for his; and visit me as often as possible, to help me bear the annoyance of his unwelcome attentions."

75 It's sweet character that these letters show,
And what to call it, Madam, you well know.
Enough. We're off to make the world acquainted
With this sublime self-portrait that you've painted.
ACASTE:
Madam, I'll make you no farewell oration;
80 No, you're not worthy of my indignation.
Far choicer hearts than yours, as you'll discover,
Would like this little Marquess for a lover.

SCENE V. [CÉLIMÈNE, ÉLIANTE, ARSINOÉ, ALCESTE, ORONTE, PHILINTE.]

ORONTE:
So! After all those loving letters you wrote,
You turn on me like this, and cut my throat!
And your dissembling, faithless heart, I find,
Has pledged itself by turns to all mankind!
5 How blind I've been! But now I clearly see;
I thank you, Madam, for enlightening me.
My heart is mine once more, and I'm content;

The loss of it shall be your punishment.
(*To* ALCESTE.) Sir, she is yours; I'll seek no more to stand
Between your wishes and this lady's hand.   10

SCENE VI. [CÉLIMÈNE, ÉLIANTE, ARSINOÉ, ALCESTE, PHILINTE.]

ARSINOÉ (*to* CÉLIMÈNE):
Madam, I'm forced to speak. I'm far too stirred
To keep my counsel, after what I've heard.
I'm shocked and staggered by your want of morals.
It's not my way to mix in others' quarrels;
But really, when this fine and noble spirit,   5
This man of honor and surpassing merit,
Laid down the offering of his heart before you,
How *could* you . . .
ALCESTE:
                    Madam, permit me, I implore you,
To represent myself in this debate.
Don't bother, please, to be my advocate.   10
My heart, in any case, could not afford
To give your services their due reward;
And if I chose, for consolation's sake,
Some other lady, 'twould not be you I'd take.
ARSINOÉ:
What makes you think you could, Sir? And how dare you   15
Imply that I've been trying to ensnare you?
If you can for a moment entertain
Such flattering fancies, you're extremely vain.
I'm not so interested as you suppose
In Célimène's discarded gigolos.   20
Get rid of that absurd illusion, do.
Women like me are not for such as you.
Stay with this creature, to whom you're so attached;
I've never seen two people better matched.

SCENE VII. [CÉLIMÈNE, ÉLIANTE, ALCESTE, PHILINTE.]

ALCESTE (*to* CÉLIMÈNE):
Well, I've been still throughout this exposé,
Till everyone but me has said his say.
Come, have I shown sufficient self-restraint?
And may I now . . .
CÉLIMÈNE: Yes, make your just complaint.
Reproach me freely, call me what you will;   5
You've every right to say I've used you ill.
I've wronged you, I confess it; and in my shame

I'll make no effort to escape the blame.
The anger of those others I could despise;
My guilt toward you I sadly recognize.
Your wrath is wholly justified, I fear;
I know how culpable I must appear,
I know all things bespeak my treachery,
And that, in short, you've grounds for hating me.
Do so; I give you leave.

ALCESTE: Ah, traitress — how,
How should I cease to love you, even now?
Though mind and will were passionately bent
On hating you, my heart would not consent.
(*To* ÉLIANTE *and* PHILINTE.) Be witness to my madness, both of you;
See what infatuation drives one to;
But wait; my folly's only just begun,
And I shall prove to you before I'm done
How strange the human heart is, and how far
From rational we sorry creatures are.
(*To* CÉLIMÈNE.) Woman, I'm willing to forget your shame,
And clothe your treacheries in a sweeter name;
I'll call them youthful errors, instead of crimes,
And lay the blame on these corrupting times.
My one condition is that you agree
To share my chosen fate, and fly with me
To that wild, trackless, solitary place
In which I shall forget the human race.
Only by such a course can you atone
For those atrocious letters; by that alone
Can you remove my present horror of you,
And make it possible for me to love you.

CÉLIMÈNE:
What! I renounce the world at my young age,
And die of boredom in some hermitage?

ALCESTE:
Ah, if you really loved me as you ought,
You wouldn't give the world a moment's thought;
Must you have me, and all the world beside?

CÉLIMÈNE:
Alas, at twenty one is terrified
Of solitude. I fear I lack the force
And depth of soul to take so stern a course.
But if my hand in marriage will content you,
Why, there's a plan which I might well consent to,
And . . .

ALCESTE:
            No, I detest you now. I could excuse
Everything else, but since you thus refuse
To love me wholly, as a wife should do,
And see the world in me, as I in you,
Go! I reject your hand, and disenthrall
My heart from your enchantments, once for all.

SCENE VIII. [ÉLIANTE, ALCESTE, PHILINTE.]

ALCESTE (*to* ÉLIANTE):
Madam, your virtuous beauty has no peer;
Of all this world you only are sincere;
I've long esteemed you highly, as you know;
Permit me ever to esteem you so,
And if I do not now request your hand,
Forgive me, Madam, and try to understand.
I feel unworthy of it; I sense that fate
Does not intend me for the married state,
That I should do you wrong by offering you
My shattered heart's unhappy residue,
And that in short . . .

ÉLIANTE: Your argument's well taken:
Nor need you fear that I shall feel forsaken.
Were I to offer him this hand of mine,
Your friend Philinte, I think, would not decline.

PHILINTE:
Ah, Madam, that's my heart's most cherished goal,
For which I'd gladly give my life and soul.

ALCESTE (*to* ÉLIANTE *and* PHILINTE):
May you be true to all you now profess,
And so deserve unending happiness.
Meanwhile, betrayed and wronged in everything,
I'll flee this bitter world where vice is king,
And seek some spot unpeopled and apart
Where I'll be free to have an honest heart.

PHILINTE:
Come, Madam, let's do everything we can
To change the mind of this unhappy man.

The introduction to this volume (pp. 9–10) makes the rather obvious point that in both tragedy and comedy we have characters who are motivated by some ideal, and that (for example) the tragic hero who hunts out the polluted man in Thebes or who kills his wife because he thinks she is unfaithful is neither more nor less impassioned than the comic lover who writes sonnets to his mistress' eyebrow. Whether the passion is noble or comic depends not on its depth, or its persistence, but on its context, and especially on its object.

The passion for honesty that drives Molière's misanthrope, Alceste, is said by the equable Éliante to have "its noble, heroic side," and her view has found wide acceptance among audiences and readers. Alceste is sometimes seen as a tragic figure caught in a comic world, and the play is sometimes said to be a sort of tragic comedy. Alceste demands honesty, and he fulminates against flattery and other forms of insincerity that apparently compose the entire life of the other figures. Surrounded by trimmers and gossips and worse, he alone (if we except the gentle Éliante) seems to hold to a noble ideal. The only other ideal given much prominence is Philinte's, a code of such easy tolerance that it is at times almost indistinguishable from mere passive acceptance of everything.

What case can be made that Alceste is comic, not tragic? A few points suggest themselves. First, this champion of honesty is in love (or thinks he is) with a coquette. What can be more comic than the apostle of plain-dealing being himself in the power of the irrational, especially when this power deposits him at the feet of Célimène, a woman who employs all the devices that in others infuriate him? Second, his demand for honesty is indiscriminate; he is as offended at trivial courtesies as at the law's injustice. Philinte "ought to die of self-disgust" for his "crime" of effusively greeting a casual acquaintance whose name he cannot even recall. So disproportionate is Alceste's passion that when he pops onstage in IV.ii, saying to Éliante, "Avenge me, Madam," he is funny, though the words in themselves are scarcely amusing. It is worth comparing a few other lines in this scene with some roughly similar lines in *Othello*. Alceste (still talking to Éliante about Célimène's letter to a rival suitor) says, "My world has gone to wrack" ("Ah! tout est ruiné!"). When, early in the play, Brabantio had cautioned Othello that Desdemona might deceive him, Othello had said, "My life upon her faith," and, in the middle of the play "Perdition catch my soul / But I do love thee! And when I love thee not, / Chaos is come again." Later, poisoned by Iago's insinuations, he believes Desdemona is faithless, and chaos comes again as he calls her a devil, banishes her from his sight, and finally suffocates her. But Othello is "the noble Moor," whose nobility is demonstrated early in the play by his language and his actions. And Desdemona, "the divine Desdemona," "the grace of heaven," and "the sweetest innocent / That e'er did lift up eye," demonstrates her worth in every line and deed. On the other hand, Alceste, lacking all sense of proportion, is at the outset surly and evidently funny. In the very first scene his tirade against Philinte's "loving demonstrations" offered to one who is almost a stranger evokes Philinte's good-natured

> It hardly seems a hanging matter to me;
> I hope that you will take it graciously
> If I extend myself a slight reprieve,
> And live a little longer, by your leave;

but this droll reply acerbates Alceste:

> How dare you joke about a crime so grave?

Alceste is thus laughably introduced; his passion is comic because it is disproportionate — and also because it leads to no action; Othello is heroically introduced (after an initial scene in which he is slandered), and his passion is tragic because it is frightening and pitiable, especially because it leads him to murder an innocent woman who, as he has said, is the center of his being.

Alceste's remark about joking provides a thread that may be followed usefully. He cannot take a joke. Whenever he is laughed at, he becomes indignant, but indignation (when motivated by a desire to protect the self from criticism) itself evokes further laughter because of the gap between the indignant man's presentation of himself and his real worth. Comedy does not allow people to strike attitudes. The man who protests that his argument *is* valid, dammit, or that he *has* a sense of humor, or that his opponent is a fool, is likely to evoke laughter by his monolithic insistence on his merit. When Philinte laughs at the old poem Alceste quotes, Alceste resorts to bitter irony, and when told that his frankness has made him ridiculous, he irritably replies:

> So much the better; just what I wish to hear.
> No news could be more grateful to my ear.
> All men are so detestable in my eyes.
> I should be sorry if they thought me otherwise.

He hopes that he will lose his lawsuit, just to prove that the world *is* as bad as he thinks it is. (An odd psychological state, resembling Master Ford's in Shakespeare's *Merry Wives of Windsor*, whose "God be praised for my jealousy" reveals the comic figure's infatuation with his abnormality.) And when Alceste is told that his hope that he will lose his lawsuit would reduce all hearers to laughter and would make his name a jest, he ill-humoredly replies, "So much the worse for jesters." When his persistent refusal to praise a trivial poem moves two auditors to laughter, he again employs frigid irony, and concludes the scene ominously:

> By heaven, Sirs, I really didn't know
> That I was being humorous.
> CÉLIMÈNE: Go, Sir; go;
> Settle your business.
>   ALCESTE: I shall, and when I'm through,
> I shall return to settle things with you.

Alceste, unable to laugh at the folly of others, cannot, of course, tolerate laugh-

ter at himself. When Philinte puts into practice the frankness Alceste stormily
advocates, Alceste's response is the indignation we have been commenting on.
A sense of humor (as distinct from derisive laughter) involves the ability to
laugh at what one values, and among the things one values is the self. Children
can laugh at surprises and at the distress of other children, but they cannot
laugh at themselves because they cannot see themselves in perspective, at a
distance, as it were. The mature man can laugh at (for example) mimicry of
himself, but the child or the immature adult will, like Alceste, sulk or fly into a
rage.

In *The Misanthrope* it is entirely possible that Molière is in some degree
mimicking himself. In 1662 Molière at forty married Armande Béjart, a
woman less than half his age. The marriage seems to have been unhappy, apparently because his wife enjoyed attracting the attentions of other men. Some
critics, pressing this point, assume that if the play is autobiographical, Alceste
must be expressing Molière's point of view, and therefore he cannot be a
comic figure. If anything, the autobiographic origin shows only that Molière
had (which no one has doubted) a sense of humor. He could laugh at himself.
Alceste's courtship of Célimène may in some degree represent Molière's unhappy marriage to a flirtatious and unappreciative woman, but the point is that
Molière apparently could stand back and laugh at his own exasperation, which
Alceste cannot do. (Molière subtitled the play "The Atrabilious Man in
Love"; one cannot hear Alceste speaking thus of himself.) Alceste can only,
rather childishly, try to maintain his way, and demand that his special merit be
noted and rewarded:

> However high the praise, there's nothing worse
> Than sharing honors with the universe.
> Esteem is founded on comparison:
> To honor all men is to honor none.
> Since you embrace this indiscriminate vice,
> Your friendship comes at far too cheap a price;
> I spurn the easy tribute of a heart
> Which will not set the worthy man apart:
> I choose, Sir, to be chosen; and in fine,
> The friend of mankind is no friend of mine.

Once or twice, when he confesses that his love for Célimène is irrational, he
seems to have some perspective, but mostly the scenes of Alceste as lover serve
to reveal again and again his consuming egotism. His love is so great, he tells
Célimène, that he wishes she were in some peril so that he could prove his
love by saving her. Célimène aptly replies that Alceste's is "a strange benevolence indeed."

The argument thus far has tried to make the point that Alceste is
funny — funny because (among other things) his anger is indiscriminate and
disproportionate, because he is a sort of philosopher and yet is in love, and
because his *idée fixe*, frankness, when turned against him, exasperates him. But

when we return to Éliante's reference to his "noble, heroic side," and we recall his passion for honesty and his passionate desire to be himself, and when we see the hollowness all about him, the comic figure begins to take on a tragic aspect; and when at the end he departs from the stage unrepentant and bitter, banishing himself from the company of men, we feel that the usual comic plot too has taken on a tragic aspect. But this is hardly to say that Alceste is tragic and *The Misanthrope* a tragedy. One cannot, for example, imagine Alceste committing suicide. He is not an Othello.

MAJOR BARBARA

Bernard Shaw

Bernard Shaw (1856–1950) was born in Dublin of Anglo-Irish stock. His father drank too much, his mother — something of an Ibsenite "new woman" — went to London to make her way as singer and voice teacher. Shaw worked in a Dublin real estate office for a while (he did not attend a college or university), and then followed his mother to London, where he wrote critical reviews, and five novels (1879–1883) before turning playwright. His first play, begun with William Archer (playwright and translator of Ibsen), was abandoned in 1885, and then entirely revised by Shaw into *Widowers' Houses* (1892). He had already shown, in a critical study entitled *The Quintessence of Ibsenism* (1891), that he regarded the stage as a pulpit and soap box; before the nineteenth century was over, he wrote nine more plays, in order (he said) to espouse socialism effectively. *Major Barbara* (1905) is his comic masterpiece, but at least a dozen of his plays have established themselves in the repertoire, including one tragedy, *Saint Joan* (1924).

Undershaft (Brewster Mason) visits Lady Britomart (Elizabeth Spriggs) to meet Sara (Lisa Harrow) and Barbara (Judi Dench) in the Royal Shakespeare Company production of *Major Barbara* directed by Clifford Williams and designed by Ralph Koltai, Aldwych, 1970. (Photograph: Patrick Eagar.)

ACT I

It is after dinner in January 1906, in the library in LADY BRITOMART UNDERSHAFT's *house in Wilton Crescent. A large and comfortable settee is in the middle of the room, upholstered in dark leather. A person sitting on it (it is vacant at present) would have, on his right,* LADY BRITOMART's *writing table, with the lady herself busy at it; a smaller writing table behind him on his left; the door behind him on* LADY BRITOMART's *side; and a window with a window seat directly on his left. Near the window is an armchair.*

LADY BRITOMART *is a woman of fifty or thereabouts, well dressed and yet careless of her dress, well bred and quite reckless of her breeding, well mannered and yet appallingly outspoken and indifferent to the opinion of her interlocutors, amiable and yet peremptory, arbitrary, and high-tempered to the last bearable degree, and withal a very typical managing matron of the upper class, treated as a naughty child until she grew into a scolding mother, and finally settling down with plenty of practical ability and worldly experience, limited in the oddest way with domestic and class limitations, conceiving the universe exactly as if it were a large house in Wilton Crescent, though handling her corner of it very effectively on that assumption, and being quite enlightened and liberal as to the books in the library, the pictures on the walls, and the music in the portfolios, and the articles in the papers.*

Her son, STEPHEN, *comes in. He's a gravely correct young man under 25, taking himself very seriously, but still in some awe of his mother, from childish habit and bachelor shyness rather than from any weakness of character.*

STEPHEN: Whats the matter?

LADY BRITOMART: Presently, Stephen.

(STEPHEN *submissively walks to the settee*

and sits down. He takes up a Liberal weekly called The Speaker.)

LADY BRITOMART: Dont begin to read, Stephen. I shall require all your attention.

STEPHEN: It was only while I was waiting —

LADY BRITOMART: Dont make excuses, Stephen. (*He puts down The Speaker.*) Now! (*She finishes her writing; rises; and comes to the settee.*) I have not kept you waiting very long, I think.

STEPHEN: Not at all, mother.

LADY BRITOMART: Bring me my cushion. (*He takes the cushion from the chair at the desk and arranges it for her as she sits down on the settee.*) Sit down. (*He sits down and fingers his tie nervously.*) Don't fiddle with your tie, Stephen: there is nothing the matter with it.

STEPHEN: I beg your pardon. (*He fiddles with his watch chain instead.*)

LADY BRITOMART: Now are you attending to me, Stephen?

STEPHEN: Of course, mother.

LADY BRITOMART: No: it's not of course. I want something much more than your everyday matter-of-course attention. I am going to speak to you very seriously, Stephen. I wish you would let that chain alone.

STEPHEN (*hastily relinquishing the chain*): Have I done anything to annoy you, mother? If so, it was quite unintentional.

LADY BRITOMART (*astonished*): Nonsense! (*With some remorse.*) My poor boy, did you think I was angry with you?

STEPHEN: What is it, then, mother? You are making me very uneasy.

LADY BRITOMART (*squaring herself at him rather aggressively*): Stephen: may I ask how soon you intend to realize that you are a grown-up man, and that I am only a woman?

STEPHEN (*amazed*): Only a —

LADY BRITOMART: Dont repeat my words, please: it is a most aggravating habit. You must learn to face life seriously, Stephen. I really cannot bear the whole burden of our family affairs any longer. You must advise me: you must assume the responsibility.

STEPHEN: I!

LADY BRITOMART: Yes, you, of course. You

were 24 last June. Youve been at Harrow and Cambridge. Youve been to India and Japan. You must know a lot of things, now; unless you have wasted your time most scandalously. Well, advise me.

STEPHEN (*much perplexed*): You know I have never interfered in the household —

LADY BRITOMART: No: I should think not. I dont want you to order the dinner.

STEPHEN: I mean in our family affairs.

LADY BRITOMART: Well, you must interfere now; for they are getting quite beyond me.

STEPHEN (*troubled*): I have thought sometimes that perhaps I ought; but really, mother, I know so little about them; and what I do know is so painful! it is so impossible to mention some things to you — (*He stops, ashamed.*)

LADY BRITOMART: I suppose you mean your father.

STEPHEN (*almost inaudibly*): Yes.

LADY BRITOMART: My dear: we cant go on all our lives not mentioning him. Of course you were quite right not to open the subject until I asked you to; but you are old enough now to be taken into my confidence, and to help me to deal with him about the girls.

STEPHEN: But the girls are all right. They are engaged.

LADY BRITOMART (*complacently*): Yes: I have made a very good match for Sarah. Charles Lomax will be a millionaire at 35. But that is ten years ahead and in the meantime his trustees cannot under the terms of his father's will allow him more than £800 a year.

STEPHEN: But the will says also that if he increases his income by his own exertions, they may double the increase.

LADY BRITOMART: Charles Lomax's exertions are much more likely to decrease his income than to increase it. Sarah will have to find at least another £800 a year for the next ten years; and even then they will be as poor as church mice. And what about Barbara? I thought Barbara was going to make the most brilliant career of all of you. And what does she do? Joins the Salvation Army; discharges her maid; lives on a pound a week; and walks in one evening with a professor of Greek whom she has picked up in the street, and who pretends to be a Salvationist, and actually plays the big drum for her in public because he has fallen head over ears in love with her.

STEPHEN: I was certainly rather taken aback when I heard they were engaged. Cusins is a very nice fellow, certainly: nobody would ever guess that he was born in Australia; but —

LADY BRITOMART: Oh, Adolphus Cusins will make a very good husband. After all, nobody can say a word against Greek: it stamps a man at once as an educated gentleman. And my family, thank Heaven, is not a pig-headed Tory one. We are Whigs, and believe in liberty. Let snobbish people say what they please: Barbara shall marry, not the man they like, but the man I like.

STEPHEN: Of course I was thinking only of his income. However, he is not likely to be extravagant.

LADY BRITOMART: Dont be too sure of that, Stephen. I know your quiet, simple, refined, poetic people like Adolphus: quite content with the best of everything! They cost more than your extravagant people, who are always as mean as they are second rate. No: Barbara will need at least £2000 a year. You see it means two additional households. Besides, my dear, you must marry soon. I dont approve of the present fashion of philandering bachelors and late marriages; and I am trying to arrange something for you.

STEPHEN: It's very good of you, mother; but perhaps I had better arrange that for myself.

LADY BRITOMART: Nonsense! you are much too young to begin matchmaking: you would be taken in by some pretty little nobody. Of course I dont mean that you are not to be consulted: you know that as well as I do. (STEPHEN *closes his lips and is silent.*) Now dont sulk, Stephen.

STEPHEN: I am not sulking, mother. What has all this got to do with — with — my father?

LADY BRITOMART: My dear Stephen: where is the money to come from? It is easy enough for you and the other children to live on my income as long as we are in the same house; but I cant keep four families in four separate houses. You know how poor my father is: he has barely seven thousand a year now; and really, if he were not the Earl of Stevenage, he would have to give up society. He can do nothing for us. He says, naturally enough, that it is absurd that he should be asked to provide for the children of a man who is rolling in money. You see, Stephen, your father must be fabulously wealthy, because there is always a war going on somewhere.

STEPHEN: You need not remind me of that, mother. I have hardly ever opened a newspaper in my life without seeing our name in it. The Undershaft torpedo! The Undershaft quick firers! The Undershaft ten inch! the Undershaft disappearing rampart gun! the Undershaft submarine! and now the Undershaft aerial battleship! At Harrow they called me the Woolwich Infant. At Cambridge it was the same. A little brute at King's who was always trying to get up revivals, spoilt my Bible — your first birthday present to me — by writing under my name, 'Son and heir to Undershaft and Lazarus, Death and Destruction Dealers: address Christendom and Judea.' But that was not so bad as the way I was kowtowed to everywhere because my father was making millions by selling cannons.

LADY BRITOMART: It is not only the cannons, but the war loans that Lazarus arranges under cover of giving credit for the cannons. You know, Stephen, it's perfectly scandalous. Those two men, Andrew Undershaft and Lazarus, positively have Europe under their thumbs. That is why your father is able to behave as he does. He is above the law. Do you think Bismarck or Gladstone or Disraeli could have openly defied every social and moral obligation all their lives as your father has? They simply wouldnt have dared. I asked Gladstone to take it up. I asked The Times to take it up. I asked the Lord Chamberlain to take it up. But it was just like asking them to declare war on the Sultan. They wouldnt. They said they couldnt touch him. I believe they were afraid.

STEPHEN: What could they do? He does not actually break the law.

LADY BRITOMART: Not break the law! He is always breaking the law. He broke the law when he was born: his parents were not married.

STEPHEN: Mother! Is that true?

LADY BRITOMART: Of course it's true: that was why we separated.

STEPHEN: He married without letting you know this!

LADY BRITOMART (rather taken aback by this inference): Oh no. To do Andrew justice, that was not the sort of thing he did. Besides, you know the Undershaft motto: Unashamed. Everybody knew.

STEPHEN: But you said that was why you separated.

LADY BRITOMART: Yes, because he was not content with being a foundling himself: he wanted to disinherit you for another foundling. That was what I couldnt stand.

STEPHEN (ashamed): Do you mean for — for — for —

LADY BRITOMART: Dont stammer, Stephen. Speak distinctly.

STEPHEN: But this is so frightful to me, mother. To have to speak to you about such things!

LADY BRITOMART: It's not pleasant for me, either, especially if you are still so childish that you must make it worse by a display of embarrassment. It is only in the middle classes, Stephen, that people get into a state of dumb helpless horror when they find that there are wicked people in the world. In our class, we have to decide what is to be done with wicked people; and nothing should disturb our self-possession. Now ask your question properly.

STEPHEN: Mother: have you no consideration for me? For Heaven's sake either treat me as a child, as you always do, and tell me nothing at all; or tell me everything and let me take it as best I can.

LADY BRITOMART: Treat you as a child! What do you mean? It is most unkind and ungrateful of you to say such a thing. You know I have never treated any of you as children. I have always made you my companions and friends, and allowed you perfect freedom to do and say whatever you liked, so long as you liked what I could approve of.

STEPHEN (desperately): I daresay we have been the very imperfect children of a very perfect mother; but I do beg you to let me alone for once, and tell me about this horrible business of my father wanting to set me aside for another son.

LADY BRITOMART (amazed): Another son! I never said anything of the kind. I never dreamt of such a thing. This is what comes of interrupting me.

STEPHEN: But you said —

LADY BRITOMART (cutting him short): Now be a good boy, Stephen, and listen to me patiently. The Undershafts are descended from a foundling in the parish of St Andrew Undershaft in the city. That was long ago, in the reign of James the First. Well this foundling was adopted by an armorer and gun-maker. In the course of time the foundling succeeded to the business; and from some notion of gratitude, or some vow or something, he adopted another foundling, and left the business to him. And that foundling did the same. Ever since that, the cannon business has always been left to an adopted foundling named Andrew Undershaft.

STEPHEN: But did they never marry? Were there no legitimate sons?

LADY BRITOMART: Oh yes: they married just as your father did; and they were rich enough to buy land for their own children and leave them well provided for. But they always adopted and trained some foundling to succeed them in the business; and of course they always quarrelled with their wives furiously over it. Your father was adopted in that way; and he pretends to consider himself bound to keep up the tradition and adopt somebody to leave the business to. Of course I was not going to stand that. There may have been some reason for it when the Undershafts could only marry women in their own class, whose sons were not fit to govern great estates. But there could be no excuse for passing over my son.

STEPHEN (dubiously): I am afraid I should make a poor hand of managing a cannon foundry.

LADY BRITOMART: Nonsense! you could easily get a manager and pay him a salary.

STEPHEN: My father evidently had no great opinion of my capacity.

LADY BRITOMART: Stuff, child! you were only a baby: it had nothing to do with your capacity. Andrew did it on principle, just as he did every perverse and wicked thing on principle. When my father remonstrated, Andrew actually told him to his face that history tells us of only two successful institutions: one the Undershaft firm, and the other the Roman Empire under the Antonines. That was because the Antonine emperors all adopted their successors. Such rubbish! The Stevenages are as good as the Antonines, I hope; and you are a Stevenage. But that was Andrew all over. There you have the man! Always clever and unanswerable when he was defending nonsense and wickedness: always awkward and sullen when he had to behave sensibly and decently!

STEPHEN: Then it was on my account that your home life was broken up, mother. I am sorry.

LADY BRITOMART: Well, dear, there were other differences. I really cannot bear an immoral man. I am not a Pharisee, I hope; and I should not have minded his merely doing wrong things: we are none of us perfect. But your father didnt exactly do wrong things: he said them and thought them: that was what was so dreadful. He really had a sort of religion of wrongness. Just as one doesnt mind men practising immorality so long as they own that they are in the wrong by preaching morality; so I couldn't forgive Andrew for preaching immorality while he practised morality. You would all have grown up without principles, without any knowledge of right and wrong, if he had been in the house. You know, my dear, your father was a very attractive man in some ways. Children did not dislike him; and he took advantage of it to put the wickedest ideas into their heads, and make them quite unmanageable. I did not dislike him myself: very far from it; but nothing can bridge over moral disagreement.

STEPHEN: All this simply bewilders me, mother. People may differ about matters of opinion, or even about religion; but how can they differ about right and wrong? Right is right; and wrong is wrong; and if a man cannot distinguish them properly, he is either a fool or a rascal: thats all.

LADY BRITOMART (touched): Thats my own boy (she pats his cheek)! Your father never could answer that: he used to laugh and get out of it under cover of some affectionate nonsense. And now that you understand the situation, what do you advise me to do?

STEPHEN: Well, what can you do?

LADY BRITOMART: I must get the money somehow.

STEPHEN: We cannot take money from him. I had rather go and live in some cheap place like Bedford Square or even Hampstead than take a farthing of his money.

LADY BRITOMART: But after all, Stephen, our present income comes from Andrew.

STEPHEN (shocked): I never knew that.

LADY BRITOMART: Well, you surely didnt suppose your grandfather had anything to give me. The Stevenages could not do everything for you. We gave you social position. Andrew had to contribute something. He had a very good bargain, I think.

STEPHEN (bitterly): We are utterly dependent on him and his cannons, then?

LADY BRITOMART: Certainly not: the money is settled. But he provided it. So you see it is not a question of taking money from him or not: it is simply a question of how much. I don't want any more for myself.

STEPHEN: Nor do I.

LADY BRITOMART: But Sarah does; and Barbara does. That is, Charles Lomax and Adolphus Cusins will cost them more. So I must put my pride in my pocket and ask for it, I suppose. That is your advice, Stephen, is it not?

STEPHEN: No.

LADY BRITOMART (sharply): Stephen!

STEPHEN: Of course if you are determined —

LADY BRITOMART: I am not determined: I ask your advice; and I am waiting for it. I will not have all the responsibility thrown on my shoulders.

STEPHEN (obstinately): I would die sooner than ask him for another penny.

LADY BRITOMART (resignedly): You mean that I must ask him. Very well, Stephen: it shall be as you wish. You will be glad to know that your grandfather concurs. But he thinks I ought to ask Andrew to come here and see the girls. After all, he must have some natural affection for them.

STEPHEN: Ask him here!!!

LADY BRITOMART: Do not repeat my words, Stephen. Where else can I ask him?

STEPHEN: I never expected you to ask him at all.

LADY BRITOMART: Now dont tease, Stephen. Come! you see that it is necessary that he should pay us a visit, dont you?

STEPHEN (reluctantly): I suppose so, if the girls cannot do without his money.

LADY BRITOMART: Thank you, Stephen: I knew you would give me the right advice when it was properly explained to you. I have asked your father to come this evening. (STEPHEN bounds from his seat.) Dont jump, Stephen: it fidgets me.

STEPHEN (in utter consternation): Do you mean to say that my father is coming here tonight — that he may be here at any moment?

LADY BRITOMART (looking at her watch): I said nine. (He gasps. She rises.) Ring the bell, please. (STEPHEN goes to the smaller writing table; presses a button on it; and sits at it with his elbows on the table and his head in his hands, outwitted and overwhelmed.) It is ten minutes to nine yet; and I have to prepare the girls. I asked Charles Lomax and Adolphus to dinner on purpose that they might be here.

Andrew had better see them in case he should cherish any delusions as to their being capable of supporting their wives. (The butler enters: LADY BRITOMART goes behind the settee to speak to him.) Morrison: go up to the drawing room and tell everybody to come down here at once. (MORRISON withdraws. LADY BRITOMART turns to STEPHEN.) Now remember, Stephen: I shall need all your countenance and authority. (He rises and tries to recover some vestige of these attributes.) Give me a chair, dear. (He pushes a chair forward from the wall to where she stands, near the smaller writing table. She sits down; and he goes to the armchair, into which he throws himself.) I dont know how Barbara will take it. Ever since they made her a major in the Salvation Army she has developed a propensity to have her own way and order people about which quite cows me sometimes. It's not ladylike: I'm sure I dont know where she picked it up. Anyhow, Barbara shant bully me; but still it's just as well that your father should be here before she has time to refuse to meet him or make a fuss. Dont look nervous, Stephen: it will only encourage Barbara to make difficulties. I am nervous enough, goodness knows; but I dont shew it.

(SARAH and BARBARA come in with their respective young men, CHARLES LOMAX and ADOLPHUS CUSINS. SARAH is slender, bored, and mundane. BARBARA is robuster, jollier, much more energetic. SARAH is fashionably dressed: BARBARA is in Salvation Army uniform. LOMAX, a young man about town, is like many other young men about town. He is afflicted with a frivolous sense of humor which plunges him at the most inopportune moments into paroxysms of imperfectly suppressed laughter. CUSINS is a spectacled student, slight, thin haired, and sweet voiced, with a more complex form of LOMAX's complaint. His sense of humor is intellectual and subtle, and is complicated by an appalling temper. The lifelong struggle of a benevolent temperament and a high conscience against impulses of inhuman ridicule and fierce impatience has set up a chronic strain which has visibly wrecked his constitution. He is a most implacable, determined, tenacious, intolerant person who by mere force of character presents himself as — and indeed actually is — considerate, gentle, ex-

planatory, even mild and apologetic, capable possibly of murder, but not of cruelty or coarseness. By the operation of some instinct which is not merciful enough to blind him with the illusions of love, he is obstinately bent on marrying BARBARA. LOMAX *likes* SARAH *and thinks it will be rather a lark to marry her. Consequently he has not attempted to resist* LADY BRITOMART's *arrangements to that end.*

All four look as if they had been having a good deal of fun in the drawing room. The girls enter first, leaving the swains outside. SARAH *comes to the settee.* BARBARA *comes in after her and stops at the door.*)

BARBARA: Are Cholly and Dolly to come in?

LADY BRITOMART (*forcibly*): Barbara: I will not have Charles called Cholly: the vulgarity of it positively makes me ill.

BARBARA: It's all right, mother: Cholly is quite correct nowadays. Are they to come in?

LADY BRITOMART: Yes, if they will behave themselves.

BARBARA (*through the door*): Come in, Dolly; and behave yourself.

(BARBARA *comes to her mother's writing table.* CUSINS *enters smiling, and wanders towards* LADY BRITOMART.)

SARAH (*calling*): Come in, Cholly. (LOMAX *enters, controlling his features very imperfectly, and places himself vaguely between* SARAH *and* BARBARA.)

LADY BRITOMART (*peremptorily*): Sit down, all of you. (*They sit.* CUSINS *crosses to the window and seats himself there.* LOMAX *takes a chair.* BARBARA *sits at the writing table and* SARAH *on the settee.*) I dont in the least know what you are laughing at, Adolphus. I am surprised at you, though I expected nothing better from Charles Lomax.

CUSINS (*in a remarkably gentle voice*): Barbara has been trying to teach me the West Ham Salvation March.

LADY BRITOMART: I see nothing to laugh at in that; nor should you if you are really converted.

CUSINS (*sweetly*): You were not present. It was really funny, I believe.

LOMAX: Ripping.

LADY BRITOMART: Be quiet, Charles. Now listen to me, children. Your father is coming here this evening.

(*General stupefaction.* LOMAX, SARAH, *and* BARBARA *rise:* SARAH *scared, and* BARBARA *amused and expectant.*)

LOMAX (*remonstrating*): Oh I say!

LADY BRITOMART: You are not called on to say anything, Charles.

SARAH: Are you serious, mother?

LADY BRITOMART: Of course I am serious. It is on your account, Sarah, and also on Charles's. (*Silence.* SARAH *sits, with a shrug.* CHARLES *looks painfully unworthy.*) I hope you are not going to object, Barbara.

BARBARA: I! why should I? My father has a soul to be saved like anybody else. He's quite welcome as far as I am concerned. (*She sits on the table, and softly whistles 'Onward, Christian Soldiers.'*)

LOMAX (*still remonstrant*): But really, dont you know! Oh I say!

LADY BRITOMART (*frigidly*): What do you wish to convey, Charles?

LOMAX: Well, you must admit that this is a bit thick.

LADY BRITOMART (*turning with ominous suavity to* CUSINS): Adolphus: you are a professor of Greek. Can you translate Charles Lomax's remarks into reputable English for us?

CUSINS (*cautiously*): If I may say so, Lady Brit, I think Charles has rather happily expressed what we all feel. Homer, speaking of Autolycus, uses the same phrase. πυκινὸν δόμον ἐλθεῖν means a bit thick.

LOMAX (*handsomely*): Not that I mind, you know, if Sarah dont. (*He sits.*)

LADY BRITOMART (*crushingly*): Thank you. Have I your permission, Adolphus, to invite my own husband to my own house?

CUSINS (*gallantly*): You have my unhesitating support in everything you do.

LADY BRITOMART: Tush! Sarah: have you nothing to say?

SARAH: Do you mean that he is coming regularly to live here?

LADY BRITOMART: Certainly not. The spare room is ready for him if he likes to stay for a day or two and see a little more of you; but there are limits.

SARAH: Well, he cant eat us, I suppose. *I* dont mind.

LOMAX (*chuckling*): I wonder how the old man will take it.

LADY BRITOMART: Much as the old woman will, no doubt, Charles.

LOMAX (*abashed*): I didnt mean — at least —

LADY BRITOMART: You didnt think, Charles. You never do; and the result is, you never mean anything. And now please attend to me, children. Your father will be quite a stranger to us.

LOMAX: I suppose he hasnt seen Sarah since she was a little kid.

LADY BRITOMART: Not since she was a little kid, Charles, as you express it with that elegance of diction and refinement of thought that seem never to desert you. Accordingly — er — (*Impatiently.*) Now I have forgotten what I was going to say. That comes of your provoking me to be sarcastic, Charles. Adolphus: will you kindly tell me where I was.

CUSINS (*sweetly*): You were saying that as Mr Undershaft has not seen his children since they were babies, he will form his opinion of the way you have brought them up from their behavior tonight, and that therefore you wish us all to be particularly careful to conduct ourselves well, especially Charles.

LADY BRITOMART (*with emphatic approval*): Precisely.

LOMAX: Look here, Dolly: Lady Brit didnt say that.

LADY BRITOMART (*vehemently*): I did, Charles. Adolphus's recollection is perfectly correct. It is most important that you should be good; and I do beg you for once not to pair off into opposite corners and giggle and whisper while I am speaking to your father.

BARBARA: All right, mother. We'll do you credit. (*She comes off the table, and sits in her chair with ladylike elegance.*)

LADY BRITOMART: Remember, Charles, that Sarah will want to feel proud of you instead of ashamed of you.

LOMAX: Oh I say! theres nothing to be exactly proud of, dont you know.

LADY BRITOMART: Well, try and look as if there was.

(*MORRISON, pale and dismayed, breaks into the room in unconcealed disorder.*)

MORRISON: Might I speak a word to you, my lady?

LADY BRITOMART: Nonsense! Shew him up.

MORRISON: Yes, my lady. (*He goes.*)

LOMAX: Does Morrison know who it is?

LADY BRITOMART: Of course. Morrison has always been with us.

LOMAX: It must be a regular corker for him, dont you know.

LADY BRITOMART: Is this a moment to get on my nerves, Charles, with your outrageous expressions?

LOMAX: But this is something out of the ordinary, really —

MORRISON (*at the door*): The — er — Mr Undershaft. (*He retreats in confusion.*)

(*ANDREW UNDERSHAFT comes in. All rise. LADY BRITOMART meets him in the middle of the room behind the settee.*

ANDREW is, on the surface, a stoutish, easy-going elderly man, with kindly patient manners, and an engaging simplicity of character. But he has a watchful, deliberate, waiting, listening face, and formidable reserves of power, both bodily and mental, in his capacious chest and long head. His gentleness is partly that of a strong man who has learnt by experience that his natural grip hurts ordinary people unless he handles them very carefully, and partly the mellowness of age and success. He is also a little shy in his present very delicate situation.)

LADY BRITOMART: Good evening, Andrew.

UNDERSHAFT: How d'ye do, my dear.

LADY BRITOMART: You look a good deal older.

UNDERSHAFT (*apologetically*): I am somewhat older. (*Taking her hand with a touch of courtship.*) Time has stood still with you.

LADY BRITOMART (*throwing away his hand*): Rubbish! This is your family.

UNDERSHAFT (*surprised*): Is it so large? I am sorry to say my memory is failing very badly in some things. (*He offers his hand with paternal kindness to LOMAX.*)

LOMAX (*jerkily shaking his hand*): Ahdedoo.

UNDERSHAFT: I can see you are my eldest. I am very glad to meet you again, my boy.

LOMAX (*remonstrating*): No, but look here dont you know — (*Overcome.*) Oh I say!

LADY BRITOMART (*recovering from momentary speechlessness*): Andrew: do you mean to say that you dont remember how many children you have?

UNDERSHAFT: Well, I am afraid I —. They have grown so much — er. Am I making any ridiculous mistake? I may as well confess: I recollect only one son. But so many things have happened since, of course — er —

LADY BRITOMART (*decisively*): Andrew: you

are talking nonsense. Of course you have only one son.

UNDERSHAFT: Perhaps you will be good enough to introduce me, my dear.

LADY BRITOMART: That is Charles Lomax, who is engaged to Sarah.

UNDERSHAFT: My dear sir, I beg your pardon.

LOMAX: Notatall. Delighted, I assure you.

LADY BRITOMART: This is Stephen.

UNDERSHAFT (bowing): Happy to make your acquaintance, Mr Stephen. Then (going to CUSINS) you must be my son. (Taking CUSINS' hands in his.) How are you, my young friend? (To LADY BRITOMART.) He is very like you, my love.

CUSINS: You flatter me, Mr Undershaft. My name is Cusins: engaged to Barbara. (Very explicitly.) That is Major Barbara Undershaft, of the Salvation Army. That is Sarah, your second daughter. This is Stephen Undershaft, your son.

UNDERSHAFT: My dear Stephen, I beg your pardon. ·

STEPHEN: Not at all.

UNDERSHAFT: Mr Cusins: I am much indebted to you for explaining so precisely. (Turning to SARAH.) Barbara, my dear —

SARAH (prompting him): Sarah.

UNDERSHAFT: Sarah, of course. (They shake hands. He goes over to BARBARA.) Barbara — I am right this time, I hope?

BARBARA: Quite right. (They shake hands.)

LADY BRITOMART (resuming command): Sit down, all of you. Sit down, Andrew. (She comes forward and sits on the settee. CUSINS also brings his chair forward on her left. BARBARA and STEPHEN resume their seats. LOMAX gives his chair to SARAH and goes for another.)

UNDERSHAFT: Thank you, my love.

LOMAX (conversationally, as he brings a chair forward between the writing table and the settee, and offers it to UNDERSHAFT): Takes you some time to find out exactly where you are, dont it?

UNDERSHAFT (accepting the chair, but remaining standing): That is not what embarrasses me, Mr Lomax. My difficulty is that if I play the part of a father, I shall produce the effect of an intrusive stranger; and if I play the part of a discreet stranger, I may appear a callous father.

LADY BRITOMART: There is no need for you to play any part at all, Andrew. You had much better be sincere and natural.

UNDERSHAFT (submissively): Yes, my dear: I daresay that will be best. (He sits down comfortably.) Well, here I am. Now what can I do for you all?

LADY BRITOMART: You need not do anything, Andrew. You are one of the family. You can sit with us and enjoy yourself.

(A painfully conscious pause. BARBARA makes a face at LOMAX, whose too long suppressed mirth immediately explodes in agonized neighings.)

LADY BRITOMART (outraged): Charles Lomax: if you can behave yourself, behave yourself. If not, leave the room.

LOMAX: I'm awfully sorry, Lady Brit; but really you know, upon my soul! (He sits on the settee between LADY BRITOMART and UNDERSHAFT, quite overcome.)

BARBARA: Why dont you laugh if you want to, Cholly? It's good for your inside.

LADY BRITOMART: Barbara: you have had the education of a lady. Please let your father see that; and dont talk like a street girl.

UNDERSHAFT: Never mind me, my dear. As you know, I am not a gentleman; and I was never educated.

LOMAX (encouragingly): Nobody'd know it, I assure you. You look all right, you know.

CUSINS: Let me advise you to study Greek, Mr Undershaft. Greek scholars are privileged men. Few of them know Greek; and none of them know anything else; but their position is unchallengeable. Other languages are the qualifications of waiters and commercial travellers: Greek is to a man of position what the hallmark is to silver.

BARBARA: Dolly: dont be insincere. Cholly: fetch your concertina and play something for us.

LOMAX (jumps up eagerly, but checks himself to remark doubtfully to UNDERSHAFT): Perhaps that sort of thing isnt in your line, eh?

UNDERSHAFT: I am particularly fond of music.

LOMAX (delighted): Are you? Then I'll get it. (He goes upstairs for the instrument.)

UNDERSHAFT: Do you play, Barbara?

BARBARA: Only the tambourine. But Cholly's teaching me the concertina.

UNDERSHAFT: Is Cholly also a member of the Salvation Army?

BARBARA: No: he says it's bad form to be a dissenter. But I dont despair of Cholly. I made him come yesterday to a meeting at the dock gates, and take the collection in his hat.

UNDERSHAFT (*looks whimsically at his wife*): !!

LADY BRITOMART: It is not my doing, Andrew. Barbara is old enough to take her own way. She has no father to advise her.

BARBARA: Oh yes she has. There are no orphans in the Salvation Army.

UNDERSHAFT: Your father there has a great many children and plenty of experience, eh?

BARBARA (*looking at him with quick interest and nodding*): Just so. How did you come to understand that? (LOMAX *is heard at the door trying the concertina.*)

LADY BRITOMART: Come in, Charles. Play us something at once.

LOMAX: Righto! (*He sits down in his former place, and preludes.*)

UNDERSHAFT: One moment, Mr Lomax. I am rather interested in the Salvation Army. Its motto might be my own: Blood and Fire.

LOMAX (*shocked*): But not your sort of blood and fire, you know.

UNDERSHAFT: My sort of blood cleanses: my sort of fire purifies.

BARBARA: So do ours. Come down tomorrow to my shelter — the West Ham shelter — and see what we're doing. We're going to march to a great meeting in the Assembly Hall at Mile End. Come and see the shelter and then march with us: it will do you a lot of good. Can you play anything?

UNDERSHAFT: In my youth I earned pennies, and even shillings occasionally, in the streets and in public house parlors by my natural talent for stepdancing. Later on, I became a member of the Undershaft orchestral society, and performed passably on the tenor trombone.

LOMAX (*scandalized — putting down the concertina*): Oh I say!

BARBARA: Many a sinner has played himself into heaven on the trombone, thanks to the Army.

LOMAX (*to* BARBARA, *still rather shocked*): Yes; but what about the cannon business, dont you know? (*To* UNDERSHAFT.) Getting into heaven is not exactly in your line, is it?

LADY BRITOMART: Charles!!!

LOMAX: Well; but it stands to reason, dont it? The cannon business may be necessary and all that: we cant get on without cannons; but it isnt right, you know. On the other hand, there may be a certain amount of tosh about the Salvation Army — I belong to the Established Church myself — but still you cant deny that it's religion; and you cant go against religion, can you? At least unless youre downright immoral, dont you know.

UNDERSHAFT: You hardly appreciate my position, Mr Lomax —

LOMAX (*hastily*): I'm not saying anything against you personally —

UNDERSHAFT: Quite so, quite so. But consider for a moment. Here I am, a profiteer in mutilation and murder. I find myself in a specially amiable humor just now because, this morning, down at the foundry, we blew twenty-seven dummy soldiers into fragments with a gun which formerly destroyed only thirteen.

LOMAX (*leniently*): Well, the more destructive war becomes, the sooner it will be abolished, eh?

UNDERSHAFT: Not at all. The more destructive war becomes the more fascinating we find it. No, Mr Lomax: I am obliged to you for making the usual excuse for my trade; but I am not ashamed of it. I am not one of those men who keep their morals and their business in watertight compartments. All the spare money my trade rivals spend on hospitals, cathedrals, and other receptacles for conscience money, I devote to experiments and researches in improved methods of destroying life and property. I have always done so; and I always shall. Therefore your Christmas card moralities of peace on earth and goodwill among men are of no use to me. Your Christianity, which enjoins you to resist not evil, and to turn the other check, would make me a bankrupt. My morality — my religion — must have a place for cannons and torpedoes in it.

STEPHEN (*coldly — almost sullenly*): You speak as if there were half a dozen moralities and religions to choose from, instead of one true morality and one true religion.

UNDERSHAFT: For me there is only one true morality; but it might not fit you, as you do not manufacture aerial battleships. There is only one true morality for every man; but every man has not the same true morality.

LOMAX (*overtaxed*): Would you mind saying that again? I didnt quite follow it.

CUSINS: It's quite simple. As Euripides says, one man's meat is another man's poison morally as well as physically.

UNDERSHAFT: Precisely.

LOMAX: Oh, that! Yes, yes, yes. True. True.

STEPHEN: In other words, some men are honest and some are scoundrels.

BARBARA: Bosh! There are no scoundrels.

UNDERSHAFT: Indeed? Are there any good men?

BARBARA: No. Not one. There are neither good men nor scoundrels: there are just children of one Father; and the sooner they stop calling one another names the better. You neednt talk to me: I know them. Ive had scores of them through my hands: scoundrels, criminals, infidels, philanthropists, missionaries, county councillors, all sorts. Theyre all just the same sort of sinner; and theres the same salvation ready for them all.

UNDERSHAFT: May I ask have you ever saved a maker of cannons?

BARBARA: No. Will you let me try?

UNDERSHAFT: Well, I will make a bargain with you. If I go to see you tomorrow in your Salvation Shelter, will you come the day after to see me in my cannon works?

BARBARA: Take care. It may end in your giving up the cannons for the sake of the Salvation Army.

UNDERSHAFT: Are you sure it will not end in your giving up the Salvation Army for the sake of the cannons?

BARBARA: I will take my chance of that.

UNDERSHAFT: And I will take my chance of the other. (*They shake hands on it.*) Where is your shelter?

BARBARA: In West Ham. At the sign of the cross. Ask anybody in Canning Town. Where are your works?

UNDERSHAFT: In Perivale St Andrews. At the sign of the sword. Ask anybody in Europe.

LOMAX: Hadnt I better play something?

BARBARA: Yes. Give us Onward, Christian Soldiers.

LOMAX: Well, thats rather a strong order to begin with, dont you know. Suppose I sing Thou't passing hence, my brother. It's much the same tune.

BARBARA: It's too melancholy. You get saved, Cholly; and youll pass hence, my brother, without making such a fuss about it.

LADY BRITOMART: Really, Barbara, you go

on as if religion were a pleasant subject. Do have some sense of propriety.

UNDERSHAFT: I do not find it an unpleasant subject, my dear. It is the only one that capable people really care for.

LADY BRITOMART (*looking at her watch*): Well, if you are determined to have it, I insist on having it in a proper and respectable way. Charles: ring for prayers.

(*General amazement.* STEPHEN *rises in dismay.*)

LOMAX (*rising*): Oh I say!

UNDERSHAFT (*rising*): I am afraid I must be going.

LADY BRITOMART: You cannot go now, Andrew: it would be most improper. Sit down. What will the servants think?

UNDERSHAFT: My dear: I have conscientious scruples. May I suggest a compromise? If Barbara will conduct a little service in the drawing room, with Mr Lomax as organist, I will attend it willingly. I will even take part, if a trombone can be procured.

LADY BRITOMART: Dont mock, Andrew.

UNDERSHAFT (*shocked — to* BARBARA): You dont think I am mocking, my love, I hope.

BARBARA: No, of course not; and it wouldnt matter if you were: half the Army came to their first meeting for a lark. (*Rising.*) Come along. (*She throws her arm round her father and sweeps him out, calling to the others from the threshold.*) Come, Dolly. Come, Cholly.

(CUSINS *rises.*)

LADY BRITOMART: I will not be disobeyed by everybody. Adolphus: sit down. (*He does not.*) Charles: you may go. You are not fit for prayers: you cannot keep your countenance.

LOMAX: Oh I say! (*He goes out.*)

LADY BRITOMART (*continuing*): But you, Adolphus, can behave yourself if you choose to. I insist on your staying.

CUSINS: My dear Lady Brit: there are things in the family prayer book that I couldnt bear to hear you say.

LADY BRITOMART: What things, pray?

CUSINS: Well, you would have to say before all the servants that we have done things we ought not to have done, and left undone things we ought to have done, and that there is no health in us. I cannot bear to hear you doing yourself such an injustice, and Barbara such an injustice. As for myself, I flatly deny it: I have done my best. I shouldnt dare to marry Barbara — I couldnt look you in the face — if it were true. So I must go to the drawing room.

LADY BRITOMART (*offended*): Well, go. (*He starts for the door.*) And remember this, Adolphus (*he turns to listen*): I have a very strong suspicion that you went to the Salvation Army to worship Barbara and nothing else. And I quite appreciate the very clever way in which you systematically humbug me. I have found you out. Take care Barbara doesnt. Thats all.

CUSINS (*with unruffled sweetness*): Dont tell on me. (*He steals out.*)

LADY BRITOMART: Sarah: if you want to go, go. Anything's better than to sit there as if you wished you were a thousand miles away.

SARAH (*languidly*): Very well, mamma. (*She goes.*)

(LADY BRITOMART, *with a sudden flounce, gives way to a little gust of tears.*)

STEPHEN (*going to her*): Mother: whats the matter?

LADY BRITOMART (*swishing away her tears with her handkerchief*): Nothing. Foolishness. You can go with him, too, if you like, and leave me with the servants.

STEPHEN: Oh, you mustnt think that, mother. I — I dont like him.

LADY BRITOMART: The others do. That is the injustice of a woman's lot. A woman has to bring up her children; and that means to restrain them, to deny them things they want, to set them tasks, to punish them when they do wrong, to do all the unpleasant things. And then the father, who has nothing to do but pet them and spoil them, comes in when all her work is done and steals their affection from her.

STEPHEN: He has not stolen our affection from you. It is only curiosity.

LADY BRITOMART (*violently*): I wont be consoled, Stephen. There is nothing the matter with me. (*She rises and goes towards the door.*)

STEPHEN: Where are you going, mother?

LADY BRITOMART: To the drawing room, of course. (*She goes out. Onward, Christian Soldiers, on the concertina, with tambourine accompaniment, is heard when the door opens.*) Are you coming, Stephen?

STEPHEN: No. Certainly not. (*She goes. He sits down on the settee, with compressed lips and an expression of strong dislike.*)

ACT II

The yard of the West Ham shelter of the Salvation Army is a cold place on a January morning. The building itself, an old warehouse, is newly whitewashed. Its gabled end projects into the yard in the middle, with a door on the ground floor, and another in the loft above it without any balcony or ladder, but with a pulley rigged over it for hoisting sacks. Those who come from this central gable end into the yard have the gateway leading to the street on their left, with a stone horse-trough just beyond it, and, on the right, a penthouse shielding a table from the weather. There are forms at the table; and on them are seated a man and a woman, both much down on their luck, finishing a meal of bread (one thick slice each, with margarine and golden syrup) and diluted milk.

The man, a workman out of employment, is young, agile, a talker, a poser, sharp enough to be capable of anything in reason except honesty or altruistic considerations of any kind. The woman is a commonplace old bundle of poverty and hard-worn humanity. She looks sixty and probably is forty-five. If they were rich people, gloved and muffed and well wrapped up in furs and overcoats, they would be numbed and miserable; for it is a grindingly cold raw January day; and a glance at the background of grimy warehouses and leaden sky visible over the whitewashed walls of the yard would drive any idle rich person straight to the Mediterranean. But these two, being no more troubled with visions of the Mediterranean than of the moon, and being compelled to keep more of their clothes in the pawnshop, and less on their persons, in winter than in summer, are not depressed by the cold: rather are they stung into vivacity, to which their meal has just now given an almost jolly turn. The man takes a pull at his mug, and then gets up and moves about the yard with his hands deep in his pockets, occasionally breaking into a stepdance.

THE WOMAN: Feel better arter your meal, sir?

THE MAN: No. Call that a meal! Good enough for you, praps; but wot is it to me, an intelligent workin man.

THE WOMAN: Workin man! Wot are you?

THE MAN: Painter.

THE WOMAN (*sceptically*): Yus, I dessay.

THE MAN: Yus, you dessay! I know. Every loafer that cant do nothink calls isself a painter. Well, I'm a real painter: grainer, finisher, thirty-eight bob a week when I can get it.

THE WOMAN: Then why dont you go and get it?

THE MAN: I'll tell you why. Fust: I'm intelligent — fffff! it's rotten cold here (*he dances a step or two*) — yes: intelligent beyond the station o life into which it has pleased the capitalists to call me; and they dont like a man that sees through em. Second, an intelligent bein needs a doo share of appiness; so I drink somethink cruel when I get the chawnce. Third, I stand by my class and do as little as I can so's to leave arf the job for me fellow workers. Fourth, I'm fly enough to know wots inside the law and wots outside it; and inside it I do as the capitalists do: pinch wot I can lay me ands on. In a proper state of society I am sober, industrious and honest: in Rome, so to speak, I do as the Romans do. Wots the consequence? When trade is bad — and it's rotten bad just now — and the employers az to sack arf their men, they generally start on me.

THE WOMAN: Whats your name?

THE MAN: Price. Bronterre O'Brien Price. Usually called Snobby Price, for short.

THE WOMAN: Snobby's a carpenter, aint it? You said you was a painter.

PRICE: Not that kind of snob, but the genteel sort. I'm too uppish, owing to my intelligence, and my father being a Chartist and a reading, thinking man: a stationer, too. I'm none of your common hewers of wood and drawers of water; and dont you forget it. (*He returns to his seat at the table, and takes up his mug.*) Wots your name?

THE WOMAN: Rummy Mitchens, sir.

PRICE (*quaffing the remains of his milk to her*): Your elth, Miss Mitchens.

RUMMY (*correcting him*): Missis Mitchens.

PRICE: Wot! Oh Rummy, Rummy! Respectable married woman, Rummy, gittin rescued by the Salvation Army by pretendin to be a bad un. Same old game!

RUMMY: What am I to do? I cant starve.

Them Salvation lasses is dear good girls; but the better you are, the worse they likes to think you were before they rescued you. Why shouldnt they av a bit o credit, poor loves? theyre worn to rags by their work. And where would they get the money to rescue us if we was to let on we're no worse than other people? You know what ladies and gentlemen are.

PRICE: Thievin swine! Wish I ad their job, Rummy, all the same. Wot does Rummy stand for? Pet name praps?

RUMMY: Short for Romola.

PRICE: For wot!?

RUMMY: Romola. It was out of a new book. Somebody me mother wanted me to grow up like.

PRICE: We're companions in misfortune, Rummy. Both on us got names that nobody cawnt pronounce. Consequently I'm Snobby and youre Rummy because Bill and Sally wasnt good enough for our parents. Such is life!

RUMMY: Who saved you, Mr Price? Was it Major Barbara?

PRICE: No: I come here on my own. I'm going to be Bronterre O'Brien Price, the converted painter. I know wot they like. I'll tell em how I blasphemed and gambled and wopped my poor old mother —

RUMMY (*shocked*): Used you to beat your mother?

PRICE: Not likely. She used to beat me. No matter: you come and listen to the converted painter, and youll hear how she was a pious woman that taught me me prayers at er knee, an how I used to come home drunk and drag her out o bed be er snow white airs, an lam into er with the poker.

RUMMY: Thats whats so unfair to us women. Your confessions is just as big lies as ours: you dont tell what you really done no more than us; but you men can tell your lies right out at the meetins and be made much of for it; while the sort o confessions we az to make az to be wispered to one lady at a time. It ain't right, spite of all their piety.

PRICE: Right! Do you spose the Army'd be allowed if it went and did right? Not much. It combs our air and makes us good little blokes to be robbed and put upon. But I'll play the game as good as any of em. I'll see somebody struck by lightnin, or hear a voice sayin 'Snobby Price: where will you spend eternity?' I'll av a time of it, I tell you.

RUMMY: You wont be let drink, though.

PRICE: I'll take it out in gorspellin, then. I dont want to drink if I can get fun enough any other way.

(JENNY HILL, *a pale, overwrought, pretty Salvation lass of 18, comes in through the yard gate, leading* PETER SHIRLEY, *a half hardened, half worn-out elderly man, weak with hunger.*)

JENNY (*supporting him*): Come! pluck up. I'll get you something to eat. Youll be all right then.

PRICE (*rising and hurrying officiously to take the old man off* JENNY's *hands*): Poor old man! Cheer up, brother: youll find rest and peace and appiness ere. Hurry up with the food, miss: e's fair done. (JENNY *hurries into the shelter.*) Ere, buck up, daddy! she's fetchin y'a thick slice o breadn treacle, an a mug o skyblue. (*He seats him at the corner of the table.*)

RUMMY (*gaily*): Keep up your old art! Never say die!

SHIRLEY: I'm not an old man. I'm only 46. I'm as good as ever I was. The grey patch come in my hair before I was thirty. All it wants is three pennorth o hair dye: am I to be turned on the streets to starve for it? Holy God! Ive worked ten to twelve hours a day since I was thirteen, and paid my way all through; and now am I to be thrown into the gutter and my job given to a young man that can do it no better than me because Ive black hair that goes white at the first change?

PRICE (*cheerfully*): No good jawrin about it. Youre ony a jumped-up, jerked-off, orspit-tle-turned-out incurable of an ole workin man: who cares about you? Eh? Make the thievin swine give you a meal: theyve stole many a one from you. Get a bit o your own back. (JENNY *returns with the usual meal.*) There you are, brother. Awsk a blessin an tuck that into you.

SHIRLEY (*looking at it ravenously but not touching it, and crying like a child*): I never took anything before.

JENNY (*petting him*): Come, come! the Lord sends it to you: he wasnt above taking bread from his friends; and why should you be? Besides, when we find you a job you can pay us for it if you like.

SHIRLEY (*eagerly*): Yes, yes: thats true. I can pay you back: it's only a loan. (*Shivering.*) Oh Lord! oh Lord! (*He turns to the table and attacks the meal ravenously.*)

JENNY: Well, Rummy, are you more comfortable now?

RUMMY: God bless you, lovely! youve fed my body and saved my soul, havnt you? (JENNY, *touched, kisses her.*) Sit down and rest a bit: you must be ready to drop.

JENNY: Ive been going hard since morning. But theres more work than we can do. I mustnt stop.

RUMMY: Try a prayer for just two minutes. Youll work all the better after.

JENNY (*her eyes lighting up*): Oh isnt it wonderful how a few minutes prayer revives you! I was quite lightheaded at twelve o'clock, I was so tired; but Major Barbara just sent me to pray for five minutes; and I was able to go on as if I had only just begun. (*To* PRICE.) Did you have a piece of bread?

PRICE (*with unction*): Yes, miss; but Ive got the piece that I value more; and thats the peace that passeth hall hannerstennin.

RUMMY (*fervently*): Glory Hallelujah!

(BILL WALKER, *a rough customer of about 25, appears at the yard gate and looks malevolently at* JENNY.)

JENNY: That makes me so happy. When you say that, I feel wicked for loitering here. I must get to work again.

(*She is hurrying to the shelter, when the new-comer moves quickly up to the door and intercepts her. His manner is so threatening that she retreats as he comes at her truculently, driving her down the yard.*)

BILL: Aw knaow you. Youre the one that took awy maw girl. Youre the one that set er agen me. Well, I'm gowin to ev er aht. Not that Aw care a carse for er or you: see? Bat Aw'll let er knaow; and Aw'll let you knaow. Aw'm gowing to give her a doin thatll teach er to cat awy from me. Nah in wiv you and tell er to cam aht afore Aw cam in and kick er aht. Tell er Bill Walker wants er. She'll knaow wot thet means; and if she keeps me witin itll be worse. You stop to jawr beck at me; and Aw'll stawt on you: d'ye eah? Theres your wy. In you gow. (*He takes her by the arm and slings her towards the door of the shelter. She falls on her hand and knee.* RUMMY *helps her up again.*)

PRICE (*rising, and venturing irresolutely towards* BILL): Easy there, mate. She aint doin you no arm.

BILL: Oo are you callin mite? (*Standing*

over him threateningly.) Youre gowing to stend ap for er, aw yer? Put ap your ends.

RUMMY (*running indignantly to him to scold him*): Oh, you great brute — (*He instantly swings his left hand back against her face. She screams and reels back to the trough, where she sits down, covering her bruised face with her hands and rocking herself and moaning with pain.*)

JENNY (*going to her*): Oh, God forgive you! How could you strike an old woman like that?

BILL (*seizing her by the hair so violently that she also screams, and tearing her away from the old woman*): You Gawd forgimme again an Aw'll Gawd forgive you one on the jawr thetll stop you pryin for a week. (*Holding her and turning fiercely on* PRICE.) Ev you ennything to sy agen it?

PRICE (*intimidated*): No, matey: she aint anything to do with me.

BILL: Good job for you! Aw'd pat two meals into you and fawt you with one finger arter, you stawwed cur. (*To* JENNY.) Nah are you gowin to fetch aht Mog Ebbijem; or em Aw to knock your fice off you and fetch her meself?

JENNY (*writhing in his grasp*): Oh please someone go in and tell Major Barbara — (*She screams again as he wrenches her head down; and* PRICE *and* RUMMY *flee into the shelter.*)

BILL: You want to gow in and tell your Mijor of me, do you?

JENNY: Oh please dont drag my hair. Let me go.

BILL: Do you or downt you? (*She stifles a scream.*) Yus or nao?

JENNY: God give me strength —

BILL (*striking her with his fist in the face*): Gow an shaow her thet, and tell her if she wants one lawk it to cam and interfere with me. (JENNY, *crying with pain, goes into the shed. He goes to the form and addresses the old man.*) Eah: finish your mess; an git aht o maw wy.

SHIRLEY (*springing up and facing him fiercely, with the mug in his hand*): You take a liberty with me, and I'll smash you over the face with the mug and cut your eye out. Aint you satisfied — young whelps like you — with takin the bread out o the mouths of your elders that have brought you up and slaved for you, but you must come shovin and cheekin and bullyin in here, where the bread o charity is sickenin in our stummicks?

BILL (*contemptuously, but backing a little*):

Wot good are you, you aold palsy mag? Wot good are you?

SHIRLEY: As good as you and better. I'll do a day's work agen you or any fat young soaker of your age. Go and take my job at Horrockses, where I worked for ten year. They want young men there: they cant afford to keep men over forty-five. Theyre very sorry — give you a character and happy to help you to get anything suited to your years — sure a steady man wont be long out of a job. Well, let em try you. Theyll find the differ. What do you know? Not as much as how to beeyave yourself — laying your dirty fist acrost the mouth of a respectable woman!

BILL: Downt provowk me to ly it acrost yours: d'ye eah?

SHIRLEY (*with blighting contempt*): Yes: you like an old man to hit, dont you, when youve finished with the women. I aint seen you hit a young one yet.

BILL (*stung*): You loy, you aold soupkitchener, you. There was a yang menn eah. Did Aw offer to itt him or did Aw not?

SHIRLEY: Was he starvin or was he not? Was he a man or only a crosseyed thief an a loafer? Would you hit my son-in-law's brother?

BILL: Oo's ee?

SHIRLEY: Todger Fairmile o Balls Pond. Him that won £20 off the Japanese wrastler at the music hall by standin out 17 minutes 4 seconds agen him.

BILL (*sullenly*): Aw'm nao music awl wrastler. Ken he box?

SHIRLEY: Yes: an you cant.

BILL: Wot! Aw cawnt, cawnt Aw? Wots thet you sy (*threatening him*)?

SHIRLEY (*not budging an inch*): Will you box Todger Fairmile if I put him on to you? Say the word.

BILL (*subsiding with a slouch*): Aw'll stend ap to enny menn alawy, if he was ten Todger Fairmawls. But Aw dont set ap to be a perfeshnal.

SHIRLEY (*looking down on him with unfathomable disdain*): You box! Slap an old woman with the back o your hand! You hadnt even the sense to hit her where a magistrate couldnt see the mark of it, you silly young lump of conceit and ignorance. Hit a girl in the jaw and ony make her cry! If Todger Fairmile'd done it, she wouldnt a got up inside o ten minutes, no more than you would if he got on to you. Yah! I'd set about you myself if I had a week's feedin in me instead o two months' starvation. (*He turns his back on him and sits down moodily at the table.*)

BILL (*following him and stooping over him to drive the taunt in*): You loy! youve the bread and treacle in you that you cam eah to beg.

SHIRLEY (*bursting into tears*): Oh God! it's true: I'm only an old pauper on the scrap heap. (*Furiously.*) But youll come to it yourself; and then youll know. Youll come to it sooner than a teetotaller like me, fillin yourself with gin at this hour o the mornin!

BILL: Aw'm nao gin drinker, you oald lawr; bat wen Aw want to give my girl a bloomin good awdin Aw lawk to ev a bit o devil in me: see? An eah Aw emm, talkin to a rotten aold blawter like you sted o givin her wot for. (*Working himself into a rage.*) Aw'm gowin in there to fetch her aht. (*He makes vengefully for the shelter door.*)

SHIRLEY: Youre going to the station on a stretcher, more likely; and theyll take the gin and the devil out of you there when they get you inside. You mind what youre about: the major here is the Earl o Stevenage's granddaughter.

BILL (*checked*): Garn!

SHIRLEY: Youll see.

BILL (*his resolution oozing*): Well, Aw aint dan nathin to er.

SHIRLEY: Spose she said you did! who'd believe you?

BILL (*very uneasy, skulking back to the corner of the penthouse*): Gawd! theres no jastice in this cantry. To think wot them people can do! Aw'm as good as er.

SHIRLEY: Tell her so. It's just what a fool like you would do.

(BARBARA, *brisk and businesslike, comes from the shelter with a note book, and addresses herself to* SHIRLEY. BILL, *cowed, sits down in the corner of a form, and turns his back on them.*)

BARBARA: Good morning.

SHIRLEY (*standing up and taking off his hat*): Good morning, miss.

BARBARA: Sit down: make yourself at home. (*He hesitates; but she puts a friendly hand on his shoulder and makes him obey.*) Now then! since youve made friends with us, we want to know all about you. Names and addresses and trades.

SHIRLEY: Peter Shirley. Fitter. Chucked out two months ago because I was too old.

BARBARA (*not at all surprised*): Youd pass still. Why didnt you dye your hair?

SHIRLEY: I did. Me age come out at a coroner's inquest on me daughter.

BARBARA: Steady?

SHIRLEY: Teetotaller. Never out of a job before. Good worker. And sent to the knackers like an old horse!

BARBARA: No matter: if you did your part God will do his.

SHIRLEY (*suddenly stubborn*): My religion's no concern of anybody but myself.

BARBARA (*guessing*): I know. Secularist?

SHIRLEY (*hotly*): Did I offer to deny it?

BARBARA: Why should you? My own father's a Secularist, I think. Our Father — yours and mine — fulfills himself in many ways; and I daresay he knew what he was about when he made a Secularist of you. So buck up, Peter! we can always find a job for a steady man like you. (SHIRLEY, *disarmed and a little bewildered, touches his hat. She turns from him to* BILL.) Whats your name?

BILL (*insolently*): Wots thet to you?

BARBARA (*calmly making a note*): Afraid to give his name. Any trade?

BILL: Oo's afride to give is nime? (*Doggedly, with a sense of heroically defying the House of Lords in the person of Lord Stevenage.*) If you want to bring a chawge agen me, bring it. (*She waits, unruffled.*) Moy nime's Bill Walker.

BARBARA (*as if the name were familiar: trying to remember how*): Bill Walker? (*Recollecting.*) Oh, I know: youre the man that Jenny Hill was praying for inside just now. (*She enters his name in her note book.*)

BILL: Oo's Jenny Ill? And wot call as she to pry for me?

BARBARA: I dont know. Perhaps it was you that cut her lip.

BILL (*defiantly*): Yus, it was me that cat her lip. Aw aint afride o you.

BARBARA: How could you be, since youre not afraid of God? Youre a brave man, Mr Walker. It takes some pluck to do our work here; but none of us dare lift our hand against a girl like that, for fear of her father in heaven.

BILL (*sullenly*): I want nan o your kentin jawr. I spowse you think Aw cam eah to beg from you, like this demmiged lot eah. Not me. Aw downt want your bread and scripe and ketlep. Aw dont blieve in your Gawd, no more than you do yourself.

BARBARA (*sunnily apologetic and ladylike, as*

on a new footing with him): Oh, I beg your pardon for putting your name down, Mr Walker. I didnt understand. I'll strike it out.

BILL (*taking this as a slight, and deeply wounded by it*): Eah! you let maw nime alown. Aint it good enaff to be in your book?

BARBARA (*considering*): Well, you see, theres no use putting down your name unless I can do something for you, is there? Whats your trade?

BILL (*still smarting*): Thets nao concern o yours.

BARBARA: Just so. (*Very businesslike.*) I'll put you down as (*writing*) the man who — struck — poor little Jenny Hill — in the mouth.

BILL (*rising threateningly*): See eah. Awve ed enaff o this.

BARBARA (*quite sunny and fearless*): What did you come to us for?

BILL: Aw cam for maw gel, see? Aw cam to tike her aht o this and to brike er jawr for er.

BARBARA (*complacently*): You see I was right about your trade. (BILL, *on the point of retorting furiously, finds himself, to his great shame and terror, in danger of crying instead. He sits down again suddenly.*) Whats her name?

BILL (*dogged*): Er nime's Mog Ebbijem: thets wot her nime is.

BARBARA: Mog Habbijam! Oh, she's gone to Canning Town, to our barracks there.

BILL (*fortified by his resentment of Mog's perfidy*): Is she? (*Vindictively.*) Then Aw'm gowing to Kennintahn arter her. (*He crosses to the gate; hesitates; finally comes back at* BARBARA.) Are you loyin to me to git shat o me?

BARBARA: I dont want to get shut of you. I want to keep you here and save your soul. Youd better stay: youre going to have a bad time today, Bill.

BILL: Oo's gowing to give it to me? You, preps?

BARBARA: Someone you dont believe in. But youll be glad afterwards.

BILL (*slinking off*): Aw'll gow to Kennintahn to be aht o reach o your tangue. (*Suddenly turning on her with intense malice.*) And if Aw downt fawnd Mog there, Aw'll cam beck and do two years for you, selp me Gawd if Aw downt!

BARBARA (*a shade kindlier, if possible*): It's no use, Bill. She's got another bloke.

BILL: Wot!

BARBARA: One of her own converts. He fell in love with her when he saw her with her soul saved, and her face clean, and her hair washed.

BILL (*surprised*): Wottud she wash it for, the carroty slat? It's red.

BARBARA: It's quite lovely now, because she wears a new look in her eyes with it. It's a pity youre too late. The new bloke has put your nose out of joint, Bill.

BILL: Aw'll put his nowse aht o joint for him. Not that Aw care a carse for er, mawnd thet. But Aw'll teach her to drop me as if Aw was dirt. And Aw'll teach him to meddle with maw judy. Wots iz bleedin nime?

BARBARA: Sergeant Todger Fairmile.

SHIRLEY (*rising with grim joy*): I'll go with him, miss. I want to see them two meet. I'll take him to the infirmary when it's over.

BILL (*to* SHIRLEY, *with undissembled misgiving*): Is thet im you was speakin on?

SHIRLEY: Thats him.

BILL: Im that wrastled in the music awl?

SHIRLEY: The competitions at the National Sportin Club was worth nigh a hundred a year to him. He's gev em up now for religion; so he's a bit fresh for want of the exercise he was accustomed to. He'll be glad to see you. Come along.

BILL: Wots is wight?

SHIRLEY: Thirteen four. (BILL'S *last hope expires.*)

BARBARA: Go and talk to him, Bill. He'll convert you.

SHIRLEY: He'll convert your head into a mashed potato.

BILL (*sullenly*): Aw aint afride of im. Aw aint afride of ennybody. Bat e can lick me. She's dan me. (*He sits down moodily on the edge of the horse trough.*)

SHIRLEY: You aint going. I thought not. (*He resumes his seat.*)

BARBARA (*calling*): Jenny!

JENNY (*appearing at the shelter door with a plaster on the corner of her mouth*): Yes, Major.

BARBARA: Send Rummy Mitchens out to clear away here.

JENNY: I think she's afraid.

BARBARA (*her resemblance to her mother flashing out for a moment*): Nonsense! she must do as she's told.

JENNY (*calling into the shelter*): Rummy: the Major says you must come.

(JENNY *comes to* BARBARA, *purposely keeping on the side next* BILL, *lest he should suppose that she shrank from him or bore malice.*)

BARBARA: Poor little Jenny! Are you tired? (*Looking at the wounded cheek.*) Does it hurt?

JENNY: No: it's all right now. It was nothing.

BARBARA (*critically*): It was as hard as he could hit, I expect. Poor Bill! You dont feel angry with him, do you?

JENNY: Oh no, no, no: indeed I dont, Major, bless his poor heart!

(BARBARA *kisses her; and she runs away merrily into the shelter.* BILL *writhes with an agonizing return of his new and alarming symptoms, but says nothing.* RUMMY MITCH-ENS *comes from the shelter.*)

BARBARA (*going to meet* RUMMY): Now Rummy, bustle. Take in those mugs and plates to be washed; and throw the crumbs about for the birds.

RUMMY *takes the three plates and mugs; but* SHIRLEY *takes back his mug from her, as there is still some milk left in it.*)

RUMMY: There aint any crumbs. This aint a time to waste good bread on birds.

PRICE (*appearing at the shelter door*): Gentleman come to see the shelter, Major. Says he's your father.

BARBARA: All right. Coming. (SNOBBY *goes back into the shelter, followed by* BARBARA.)

RUMMY (*stealing across to* BILL *and addressing him in a subdued voice, but with intense conviction*): I'd av the lor of you, you flat eared pignosed potwalloper, if she'd let me. Youre no gentleman, to hit a lady in the face. (BILL, *with greater things moving in him, takes no notice.*)

SHIRLEY (*following her*): Here! in with you and dont get yourself into more trouble by talking.

RUMMY (*with hauteur*): I aint ad the pleasure o being hintroduced to you, as I can remember. (*She goes into the shelter with the plates.*)

SHIRLEY: Thats the —

BILL (*savagely*): Downt you talk to me, d'ye eah? You lea me alown, or Aw'll do you a mischief. Aw'm not dirt under your feet, ennywy.

SHIRLEY (*calmly*): Dont you be afeerd. You aint such prime company that you need expect to be sought after. (*He is about to go into the shelter when* BARBARA *comes out, with* UNDER-SHAFT *on her right.*)

BARBARA: Oh, there you are, Mr Shirley! (*Between them.*) This is my father: I told you he was a Secularist, didn't I? Perhaps youll be able to comfort one another.

UNDERSHAFT (*startled*): A Secularist! Not the least in the world: on the contrary, a confirmed mystic.

BARBARA: Sorry, I'm sure. By the way, papa, what is your religion? in case I have to introduce you again.

UNDERSHAFT: My religion? Well, my dear, I am a Millionaire. That is my religion.

BARBARA: Then I'm afraid you and Mr Shirley wont be able to comfort one another after all. Youre not a Millionaire, are you, Peter?

SHIRLEY: No; and proud of it.

UNDERSHAFT (*gravely*): Poverty, my friend, is not a thing to be proud of.

SHIRLEY (*angrily*): Who made your millions for you? Me and my like. Whats kep us poor? Keepin you rich. I wouldnt have your conscience, not for all your income.

UNDERSHAFT: I wouldnt have your income, not for all your conscience, Mr Shirley. (*He goes to the penthouse and sits down on a form.*)

BARBARA (*stopping* SHIRLEY *adroitly as he is about to retort*): You wouldnt think he was my father, would you, Peter? Will you go into the shelter and lend the lasses a hand for a while: we're worked off our feet.

SHIRLEY (*bitterly*): Yes: I'm in their debt for a meal, aint I?

BARBARA: Oh, not because youre in their debt, but for love of them, Peter, for love of them. (*He cannot understand, and is rather scandalized.*) There! dont stare at me. In with you; and give that conscience of yours a holiday. (*Bustling him into the shelter.*)

SHIRLEY (*as he goes in*): Ah! it's a pity you never was trained to use your reason, miss. Youd have been a very taking lecturer on Secularism.

(BARBARA *turns to her father.*)

UNDERSHAFT: Never mind me, my dear. Go about your work; and let me watch it for a while.

BARBARA: All right.

UNDERSHAFT: For instance, whats the matter with that outpatient over there?

BARBARA (*looking at* BILL, *whose attitude has never changed, and whose expression of brooding wrath has deepened*): Oh, we shall cure him in no time. Just watch. (*She goes over to* BILL *and waits. He glances up at her and casts his eyes down again, uneasy, but grimmer than ever.*) It would be nice to just stamp on Mog Habbijam's face, wouldnt it, Bill?

BILL (*starting up from the trough in consternation*): It's a loy: Aw never said so. (*She shakes her head.*) Oo taold you wot was in moy mawnd?

BARBARA: Only your new friend.

BILL: Wot new friend?

BARBARA: The devil, Bill. When he gets round people they get miserable, just like you.

BILL (*with a heartbreaking attempt at devil-may-care cheerfulness*): Aw aint miserable. (*He sits down again, and stretches his legs in an attempt to seem indifferent.*)

BARBARA: Well, if youre happy, why dont you look happy, as we do?

BILL (*his legs curling back in spite of him*): Aw'm eppy enaff, Aw tell you. Woy cawnt you lea me alown? Wot ev I dan to you? Aw aint smashed your fice, ev Aw?

BARBARA (*softly: wooing his soul*): It's not me thats getting at you, Bill.

BILL: Oo else is it?

BARBARA: Somebody that doesnt intend you to smash women's faces, I suppose. Somebody or something that wants to make a man of you.

BILL (*blustering*): Mike a menn o me! Aint Aw a menn? eh? Oo sez Aw'm not a menn?

BARBARA: Theres a man in you somewhere, I suppose. But why did he let you hit poor little Jenny Hill? That wasnt very manly of him, was it?

BILL (*tormented*): Ev dan wiv it, Aw tell you. Chack it. Aw'm sick o your Jenny Ill and er silly little fice.

BARBARA: Then why do you keep thinking about it? Why does it keep coming up against you in your mind? Youre not getting converted, are you?

BILL (*with conviction*): Not ME. Not lawkly.

BARBARA: Thats right, Bill. Hold out against it. Put out your strength. Dont lets get you cheap. Todger Fairmile said he wrestled for three nights against his salvation harder than he ever wrestled with the Jap at the music hall. He gave in to the Jap when his arm was going to break. But he didnt give in to his salvation until his heart was going to break. Perhaps youll escape that. You havnt any heart, have you?

BILL: Wot d'ye mean? Woy aint Aw got a awt the sime as ennybody else?

BARBARA: A man with a heart wouldnt have bashed poor little Jenny's face, would he?

BILL (*almost crying*): Ow, will you lea me alown? Ev Aw ever offered to meddle with you, that you cam neggin and provowkin me lawk this? (*He writhes convulsively from his eyes to his toes.*)

BARBARA (*with a steady soothing hand on his arm and a gentle voice that never lets him go*): It's your soul thats hurting you, Bill, and not me. Weve been through it all ourselves. Come with us, Bill. (*He looks wildly round.*) To brave manhood on earth and eternal glory in heaven. (*He is on the point of breaking down.*) Come. (*A drum is heard in the shelter; and* BILL, *with a gasp, escapes from the spell as* BARBARA *turns quickly.* ADOLPHUS *enters from the shelter with a big drum.*) Oh! there you are, Dolly. Let me introduce a new friend of mine, Mr Bill Walker. This is my bloke, Bill: Mr Cusins. (CUSINS *salutes with his drumstick.*)

BILL: Gowin to merry im?

BARBARA: Yes.

BILL (*fervently*): Gawd elp im! Gaw-aw-aw-awd elp im!

BARBARA: Why? Do you think he wont be happy with me?

BILL: Awve aony ed to stend it for a mawnin: e'll ev to stend it for a lawftawm.

CUSINS: That is a frightful reflection, Mr Walker. But I cant tear myself away from her.

BILL: Well, Aw ken. (*To* BARBARA.) Eah! do you knaow where Aw'm gowin to, and wot Aw'm gowin to do?

BARBARA: Yes: youre going to heaven; and youre coming back here before the week's out to tell me so.

BILL: You loy. Aw'm gowin to Kennintahn, to spit in Todger Fairmawl's eye. Aw beshed Jenny Ill's fice; an nar Aw'll git me aown fice beshed and cam beck and shaow it to er. Ee'll itt me ardern Aw itt her. Thatll mike us square. (*To* ADOLPHUS.) Is thet fair or is it not? Youre a genlmn: you oughter knaow.

BARBARA: Two black eyes wont make one white one, Bill.

BILL: Aw didnt awst you. Cawnt you never keep your mahth shat? Oy awst the genlmn.

CUSINS (reflectively): Yes: I think youre right, Mr Walker. Yes: I should do it. It's curious: it's exactly what an ancient Greek would have done.

BARBARA: But what good will it do?

CUSINS: Well, it will give Mr Fairmile some exercise; and it will satisfy Mr Walker's soul.

BILL: Rot! there aint nao sach a thing as a saoul. Ah kin you tell wevver Awve a saoul or not? You never seen it.

BARBARA: Ive seen it hurting you when you went against it.

BILL (with compressed aggravation): If you was maw gel and took the word aht o me mahth lawk thet, Aw'd give you sathink youd feel urtin, Aw would. (To ADOLPHUS.) You tike maw tip, mite. Stop er jawr; or youll doy afoah your tawm (With intense expression.) Wore aht: thets wot youll be: wore aht. (He goes away through the gate.)

CUSINS (looking after him): I wonder!

BARBARA: Dolly! (indignant, in her mother's manner).

CUSINS: Yes, my dear, it's very wearing to be in love with you. If it lasts, I quite think I shall die young.

BARBARA: Should you mind?

CUSINS: Not at all. (He is suddenly softened, and kisses her over the drum, evidently not for the first time, as people cannot kiss over a big drum without practice. UNDERSHAFT coughs.)

BARBARA: It's all right, papa, weve not forgotten you. Dolly: explain the place to papa: I havnt time. (She goes busily into the shelter.)

(UNDERSHAFT and ADOLPHUS now have the yard to themselves. UNDERSHAFT, seated on a form, and still keenly attentive, looks hard at ADOLPHUS. ADOLPHUS looks hard at him.)

UNDERSHAFT: I fancy you guess something of what is in my mind, Mr Cusins. (CUSINS flourishes his drumsticks as if in the act of beating a lively rataplan, but makes no sound.) Exactly so. But suppose Barbara finds you out!

CUSINS: You know, I do not admit that I am imposing on Barbara. I am quite genuinely interested in the views of the Salvation Army. The fact is, I am a sort of collector of religions; and the curious thing is that I find I can believe them all. By the way, have you any religion?

UNDERSHAFT: Yes.

CUSINS: Anything out of the common?

UNDERSHAFT: Only that there are two things necessary to Salvation.

CUSINS (disappointed, but polite): Ah, the Church Catechism. Charles Lomax also belongs to the Established Church.

UNDERSHAFT: The two things are —

CUSINS: Baptism and —

UNDERSHAFT: No. Money and gunpowder.

CUSINS (surprised, but interested): That is the general opinion of our governing classes. The novelty is in hearing any man confess it.

UNDERSHAFT: Just so.

CUSINS: Excuse me: is there any place in your religion for honor, justice, truth, love, mercy and so forth?

UNDERSHAFT: Yes: they are the graces and luxuries of a rich, strong, and safe life.

CUSINS: Suppose one is forced to choose between them and money or gunpowder?

UNDERSHAFT: Choose money and gunpowder; for without enough of both you cannot afford the others.

CUSINS: That is your religion?

UNDERSHAFT: Yes.

(The cadence of this reply makes a full close in the conversation, CUSINS twists his face dubiously and contemplates UNDERSHAFT. UNDERSHAFT contemplates him.)

CUSINS: Barbara wont stand that. You will have to choose between your religion and Barbara.

UNDERSHAFT: So will you, my friend. She will find out that that drum of yours is hollow.

CUSINS: Father Undershaft: you are mistaken: I am a sincere Salvationist. You do not understand the Salvation Army. It is the army of joy, of love, of courage: it has banished the fear and remorse and despair of the old hell-ridden evangelical sects: it marches to fight the devil with trumpet and drum, with music and dancing, with banner and palm, as becomes a sally from heaven by its happy garrison. It picks the waster out of the public house and makes a man of him: it finds a worm wriggling in a back kitchen, and lo! a woman! Men and women of rank too, sons and daughters of the Highest. It takes the poor professor of Greek, the most artificial and self-suppressed of human creatures, from his meal of roots, and lets loose the rhapsodist in him; reveals the true worship of Dionysos to him; sends him down the public street drumming dithyrambs. (*He plays a thundering flourish on the drum.*)

UNDERSHAFT: You will alarm the shelter.

CUSINS: Oh, they are accustomed to these sudden ecstasies. However, if the drum worries you — (*He pockets the drumsticks; unhooks the drum; and stands it on the ground opposite the gateway.*)

UNDERSHAFT: Thank you.

CUSINS: You remember what Euripides says about your money and gunpowder?

UNDERSHAFT: No.

CUSINS (*declaiming*):
One and another
In money and guns may outpass his brother;
And men in their millions float and flow
And seethe with a million hopes as leaven;
And they win their will; or they miss their will;
And their hopes are dead or are pined for still;
    But who'er can know
    As the long days go
That to live is happy, has found his heaven.

My translation: what do you think of it?

UNDERSHAFT: I think, my friend, that if you wish to know, as the long days go, that to live is happy, you must first acquire money enough for a decent life, and power enough to be your own master.

CUSINS: You are damnably discouraging. (*He resumes his declamation.*)
    Is it so hard a thing to see
    That the spirit of God — whate'er it be —
The law that abides and changes not, ages long,
The Eternal and Nature-born: these things be strong?
What else is Wisdom? What of Man's endeavor,
Or God's high grace so lovely and so great?
To stand from fear set free? to breathe and wait?
To hold a hand uplifted over Fate?
And shall not Barbara be loved for ever?

UNDERSHAFT: Euripides mentions Barbara, does he?

CUSINS: It is a fair translation. The word means Loveliness.

UNDERSHAFT: May I ask — as Barbara's father — how much a year she is to be loved for ever on?

CUSINS: As for Barbara's father, that is more your affair than mine. I can feed her by teaching Greek: that is about all.

UNDERSHAFT: Do you consider it a good match for her?

CUSINS (*with polite obstinacy*): Mr Undershaft: I am in many ways a weak, timid, ineffectual person; and my health is far from satisfactory. But whenever I feel that I must have anything, I get it, sooner or later. I feel that way about Barbara. I dont like marriage: I feel intensely afraid of it; and I dont know what I shall do with Barbara or what she will do with me. But I feel that I and nobody else must marry her. Please regard that as settled. — Not that I wish to be artibrary; but why should I waste your time in discussing what is inevitable?

UNDERSHAFT: You mean that you will stick at nothing: not even the conversion of the Salvation Army to the worship of Dionysos.

CUSINS: The business of the Salvation Army is to save, not to wrangle about the name of the pathfinder. Dionysos or another: what does it matter?

UNDERSHAFT (*rising and approaching him*): Professor Cusins: you are a young man after my own heart.

CUSINS: Mr Undershaft: you are, as far as I am able to gather, a most infernal old rascal; but you appeal very strongly to my sense of ironic humor.

(UNDERSHAFT *mutely offers his hand. They shake.*)

UNDERSHAFT (*suddenly concentrating himself*): And now to business.

CUSINS: Pardon me. We are discussing religion. Why go back to such an uninteresting and unimportant subject as business?

UNDERSHAFT: Religion is our business at present, because it is through religion alone that we can win Barbara.

CUSINS: Have you, too, fallen in love with Barbara?

UNDERSHAFT: Yes, with a father's love.

CUSINS: A father's love for a grown-up daughter is the most dangerous of all infatuations. I apologize for mentioning my own pale, coy, mistrustful fancy in the same breath with it.

UNDERSHAFT: Keep to the point. We have to win her; and we are neither of us Methodists.

CUSINS: That doesnt matter. The power Barbara wields here — the power that wields Barbara herself — is not Calvinism, not Presbyterianism, not Methodism —

UNDERSHAFT: Not Greek Paganism either, eh?

CUSINS: I admit that. Barbara is quite original in her religion.

UNDERSHAFT (*triumphantly*): Aha! Barbara Undershaft would be. Her inspiration comes from within herself.

CUSINS: How do you suppose it got there?

UNDERSHAFT (*in towering excitement*): It is the Undershaft inheritance. I shall hand on my torch to my daughter. She shall make my converts and preach my gospel —

CUSINS: What! Money and gunpowder!

UNDERSHAFT: Yes, money and gunpowder. Freedom and power. Command of life and command of death.

CUSINS (*urbanely: trying to bring him down to earth*): This is extremely interesting, Mr Undershaft. Of course you know that you are mad.

UNDERSHAFT (*with redoubled force*): And you?

CUSINS: Oh, mad as a hatter. You are welcome to my secret since I have discovered yours. But I am astonished. Can a madman make cannons?

UNDERSHAFT: Would anyone else than a madman make them? And now (*with surging energy*) question for question. Can a sane man translate Euripides?

CUSINS: No.

UNDERSHAFT (*seizing him by the shoulder*): Can a sane woman make a man of a waster or a woman of a worm?

CUSINS (*reeling before the storm*): Father Colossus — Mammoth Millionaire —

UNDERSHAFT (*pressing him*): Are there two mad people or three in this Salvation shelter today?

CUSINS: You mean Barbara is as mad as we are?

UNDERSHAFT (*pushing him lightly off and resuming his equanimity suddenly and completely*): Pooh, Professor! let us call things by their proper names. I am a millionaire; you are a poet: Barbara is a savior of souls. What have we three to do with the common mob of slaves and idolators? (*He sits down again with a shrug of contempt for the mob.*)

CUSINS: Take care! Barbara is in love with the common people. So am I. Have you never felt the romance of that love?

UNDERSHAFT (*cold and sardonic*): Have you ever been in love with Poverty, like St Francis? Have you ever been in love with Dirt, like St Simeon! Have you ever been in love with disease and suffering, like our nurses and philanthropists? Such passions are not virtues, but the most unnatural of all the vices. This love of the common people may please an earl's granddaughter and a university professor; but I have been a common man and a poor man; and it has no romance for me. Leave it to the poor to pretend that poverty is a blessing: leave it to the coward to make a religion of his cowardice by preaching humility: we know better than that. We three must stand together above the common people: how else can we help their children to climb up beside us? Barbara must belong to us, not to the Salvation Army.

CUSINS: Well, I can only say that if you think you will get her away from the Salvation Army by talking to her as you have been talking to me, you don't know Barbara.

UNDERSHAFT: My friend: I never ask for what I can buy.

CUSINS (*in a white fury*): Do I understand you to imply that you can buy Barbara?

UNDERSHAFT: No; but I can buy the Salvation Army.

CUSINS: Quite impossible.

UNDERSHAFT: You shall see. All religious organizations exist by selling themselves to the rich.

CUSINS: Not the Army. That is the Church of the poor.

UNDERSHAFT: All the more reason for buying it.

CUSINS: I don't think you quite know what the Army does for the poor.

UNDERSHAFT: Oh yes I do. It draws their teeth: that is enough for me as a man of business.

CUSINS: Nonsense! It makes them sober —

UNDERSHAFT: I prefer sober workmen. The profits are larger.

CUSINS: — honest —

UNDERSHAFT: Honest workmen are the most economical.

CUSINS: — attached to their homes —

BILL (*contemptuously*): Not lawkly. Aw'd give her anather as soon as look at er. Let her ev the lawr o me as she threatened! She aint forgiven me: not mach. Wot Aw dan to er is not on me mawnd — wot she (*indicating* BARBARA) mawt call on me conscience — no more than stickin a pig. It's this Christian gime o vours that Aw wownt ev plyed agen me: this bloomin forgivin an neggin an jawrin that mikes a menn thet sore that iz lawf's a burdn to im. Aw wownt ev it, Aw tell you; sao tike your manney and stop thraowin your silly beshed fice hap agen me.

JENNY: Major: may I take a little of it for the Army?

BARBARA: No: the Army is not to be bought. We want your soul, Bill; and we'll take nothing less.

BILL (*bitterly*): Aw knaow. Me an maw few shillins is not good enaff for you. Youre a earl's grendorter, you are. Nathink less than a andered pahnd for you.

UNDERSHAFT: Come Barbara! you could do a great deal of good with a hundred pounds. If you will set this gentleman's mind at ease by taking his pound, I will give the other ninety-nine.

(BILL, *dazed by such opulence, instinctively touches his cap.*)

BARBARA: Oh, youre too extravagant, papa. Bill offers twenty pieces of silver. All you need offer is the other ten. That will make the standard price to buy anybody who's for sale. I'm not; and the Army's not. (*To* BILL.) Youll never have another quiet moment, Bill, until you come round to us. You cant stand out against your salvation.

BILL (*sullenly*): Aw cawnt stend aht agen music awl wrastlers and awful tangued women. Awve offered to py. Aw can do no more. Tike it or leave it. There it is. (*He throws the sovereign on the drum, and sits down on the horse-trough. The coin fascinates* SNOBBY PRICE, *who takes an early opportunity of dropping his cap on it.*)

(MRS BAINES *comes from the shelter. She is dressed as a Salvation Army Commissioner. She is an earnest looking woman of about 40, with a caressing, urgent voice, and an appealing manner.*)

BARBARA: This is my father, Mrs Baines. (UNDERSHAFT *comes from the table, taking his hat off with marked civility*). Try what you can do with him. He wont listen to me, because he remembers what a fool I was when I was a baby. (*She leaves them together and chats with* JENNY.)

MRS BAINES: Have you been shewn over the shelter, Mr Undershaft? You know the work we're doing, of course.

UNDERSHAFT (*very civilly*): The whole nation knows it, Mrs Baines.

MRS BAINES: No, sir: the whole nation does not know it, or we should not be crippled as we are for want of money to carry our work through the length and breadth of the land. Let me tell you that there would have been rioting this winter in London but for us.

UNDERSHAFT: You really think so?

MRS BAINES: I know it. I remember 1886, when you rich gentlemen hardened your hearts against the cry of the poor. They broke the windows of your clubs in Pall Mall.

UNDERSHAFT (*gleaming with approval of their method*): And the Mansion House Fund went up next day from thirty thousand pounds to seventy-nine thousand! I remember quite well.

MRS BAINES: Well, wont you help me to get at the people? They wont break windows then. Come here, Price. Let me shew you to this gentleman. (*Price comes to be inspected.*) Do you remember the window breaking?

PRICE: My ole father thought it was the revolution, maam.

MRS BAINES: Would you break windows now?

PRICE: Oh no, maam. The windows of eaven av bin opened to me. I know now that the rich man is a sinner like myself.

RUMMY (*appearing above at the loft door*): Snobby Price!

SNOBBY: Wot is it?

RUMMY: Your mother's askin for you at the other gate in Cripps's Lane. She's heard about your confession. (*Price turns pale.*)

MRS BAINES: Go, Mr Price; and pray with her.

JENNY: You can go through the shelter, Snobby.

PRICE (*to* MRS BAINES): I couldnt face her now, maam, with all the weight of my sins fresh on me. Tell her she'll find her son at ome, waitin for her in prayer. (*He skulks off through the gate, incidentally stealing the sovereign on his way out by picking up his cap from the drum.*)

MRS BAINES (*with swimming eyes*): You see how we take the anger and the bitterness against you out of their hearts, Mr Undershaft.

UNDERSHAFT: It is certainly most convenient and gratifying to all large employers of labor, Mrs Baines.

MRS BAINES: Barbara: Jenny: I have good news: most wonderful news. (JENNY *runs to her.*) My prayers have been answered. I told you they would, Jenny, didnt I?

JENNY: Yes, yes.

BARBARA (*moving nearer to the drum*): Have we got money enough to keep the shelter open?

MRS BAINES: I hope we shall have enough to keep all the shelters open. Lord Saxmundham has promised us five thousand pounds —

BARBARA: Hooray!

JENNY: Glory!

MRS BAINES: — if —

BARBARA: 'If!' If what?

MRS BAINES: — if five other gentlemen will give a thousand each to make it up to ten thousand.

BARBARA: Who is Lord Saxmundham? I never heard of him.

UNDERSHAFT (*who has pricked up his ears at the peer's name, and is now watching* BARBARA *curiously*): A new creation, my dear. You have heard of Sir Horace Bodger?

BARBARA: Bodger! Do you mean the distiller? Bodger's whiskey!

UNDERSHAFT: That is the man. He is one of the greatest of our public benefactors. He restored the cathedral at Hakington. They made him a baronet for that. He gave half a million to the funds of his party: they made him a baron for that.

SHIRLEY: What will they give him for the five thousand?

UNDERSHAFT: There is nothing left to give him. So the five thousand, I should think, is to save his soul.

MRS BAINES: Heaven grant it may! O Mr Undershaft, you have some very rich friends. Cant you help us towards the other five thousand? We are going to hold a great meeting this afternoon at the Assembly Hall in the Mile End Road. If I could only announce that one gentleman had come forward to support Lord Saxmundham, others would follow. Dont you know somebody? couldnt you? wouldn't you? (*her eyes fill with tears*) oh,

think of those poor people, Mr Undershaft: think of how much it means to them, and how little to a great man like you.

UNDERSHAFT (*sardonically gallant*): Mrs Baines: you are irresistible. I cant disappoint you; and I cant deny myself the satisfaction of making Bodger pay up. You shall have your five thousand pounds.

MRS BAINES: Thank God!

UNDERSHAFT: You dont thank me?

MRS BAINES: Oh sir, dont try to be cynical: dont be ashamed of being a good man. The Lord will bless you abundantly; and our prayers will be like a strong fortification round you all the days of your life. (*With a touch of caution.*) You will let me have the cheque to shew at the meeting, wont you? Jenny: go in and fetch a pen and ink. (JENNY *runs to the shelter door.*)

UNDERSHAFT: Do not disturb Miss Hill: I have a fountain pen (JENNY *halts. He sits at the table and writes the cheque.* CUSINS *rises to make room for him. They all watch him silently.*)

BILL (*cynically, aside to* BARBARA, *his voice and accent horribly debased*): Wot prawce selvytion nah?

BARBARA: Stop. (UNDERSHAFT *stops writing: they all turn to her in surprise.*) Mrs Baines: are you really going to take this money?

MRS BAINES (*astonished*): Why not, dear?

BARBARA: Why not! Do you know what my father is? Have you forgotten that Lord Saxmundham is Bodger the whisky man? Do you remember how we implored the County Council to stop him from writing Bodger's Whisky in letters of fire against the sky; so that the poor drink-ruined creatures on the Embankment could not wake up from their snatches of sleep without being reminded of their deadly thirst by that wicked sky sign? Do you know that the worst thing I have had to fight here is not the devil, but Bodger, Bodger, Bodger, with his whisky, his distilleries, and his tied houses? Are you going to make our shelter another tied house for him, and ask me to keep it?

BILL: Rotten dranken whisky it is too.

MRS BAINES: Dear Barbara: Lord Saxmundham has a soul to be saved like any of us. If heaven has found the way to make a good use of his money, are we to set ourselves up against the answer to our prayers?

BARBARA: I know he has a soul to be saved. Let him come down here; and I'll do my best to help him to his salvation. But he wants to send his cheque down to buy us, and go on being as wicked as ever.

UNDERSHAFT (*with a reasonableness which* CUSINS *alone perceives to be ironical*): My dear Barbara: alcohol is a very necessary article. It heals the sick —

BARBARA: It does nothing of the sort.

UNDERSHAFT: Well, it assists the doctor: that is perhaps a less questionable way of putting it. It makes life bearable to millions of people who could not endure their existence if they were quite sober. It enables Parliament to do things at eleven at night that no sane person would do at eleven in the morning. Is it Bodger's fault that this inestimable gift is deplorably abused by less than one per cent of the poor? (*He turns again to the table; signs the cheque; and crosses it.*)

MRS BAINES: Barbara: will there be less drinking or more if all those poor souls we are saving come tomorrow and find the doors of our shelters shut in their faces? Lord Saxmundham gives us the money to stop drinking — to take his own business from him.

CUSINS (*impishly*): Pure self-sacrifice on Bodger's part, clearly! Bless dear Bodger! (BARBARA *almost breaks down as* ADOLPHUS, *too, fails her.*)

UNDERSHAFT (*tearing the cheque and pocketing the book as he rises and goes past* CUSINS *to* MRS BAINES): I also, Mrs Baines, may claim a little disinterestedness. Think of my business! think of the widows and orphans! the men and lads torn to pieces with shrapnel and poisoned with lyddite! (MRS BAINES *shrinks; but he goes on remorselessly*) the oceans of blood, not one drop of which is shed in a really just cause! the ravaged crops! the peaceful peasants forced, women and men, to till their fields under the fire of opposing armies on pain of starvation! the bad blood of the fierce little cowards at home who egg on others to fight for the gratification of their national vanity! All this makes money for me: I am never richer, never busier than when the papers are full of it. Well, it is your work to preach peace on earth and good will to men. (MRS BAINES's *face lights up again.*) Every convert you make is a vote against war. (*Her lips move in prayer.*) Yet I give you this money to help you to

hasten my own commercial ruin. (*He gives her the cheque.*)

CUSINS (*mounting the form in an ecstasy of mischief*): The millennium will be inaugurated by the unselfishness of Undershaft and Bodger. Oh be joyful! (*He takes the drumsticks from his pocket and flourishes them.*)

MRS BAINES (*taking the cheque*): The longer I live the more proof I see that there is an Infinite Goodness that turns everything to the work of salvation sooner or later. Who would have thought that any good could have come out of war and drink? And yet their profits are brought today to the feet of salvation to do its blessed work. (*She is affected to tears.*)

JENNY (*running to* MRS BAINES *and throwing her arms around her*): Oh dear! how blessed, how glorious it all is!

CUSINS (*in a convulsion of irony*): Let us seize this unspeakable moment. Let us march to the great meeting at once. Excuse me just an instant. (*He rushes into the shelter.* JENNY *takes her tambourine from the drum head.*)

MRS BAINES: Mr Undershaft: have you ever seen a thousand people fall on their knees with one impulse and pray? Come with us to the meeting. Barbara shall tell them that the Army is saved, and saved through you.

CUSINS (*returning impetuously from the shelter with a flag and a trombone, and coming between* MRS BAINES *and* UNDERSHAFT): You shall carry the flag down the first street, Mrs Baines (*he gives her the flag*). Mr Undershaft is a gifted trombonist: he shall intone an Olympian diapason to the West Ham Salvation March. (*Aside to* UNDERSHAFT, *as he forces the trombone on him.*) Blow, Machiavelli, blow.

UNDERSHAFT (*aside to him, as he takes the trombone*): The trumpet in Zion! (CUSINS *rushes to the drum, which he takes up and puts on.* UNDERSHAFT *continues, aloud.*) I will do my best. I could vamp a bass if I knew the tune.

CUSINS: It is a wedding chorus from one of Donizetti's operas; but we have converted it. We convert everything to good here, including Bodger. You remember the chorus. 'For thee immense rejoicing — immenso giubilo — immenso giubilo.' (*With drum obbligato.*) Rum tum ti tum tum, tum tum ti ta —

BARBARA: Dolly: you are breaking my heart.

CUSINS: What is a broken heart more or less here? Dionysos Undershaft has descended. I am possessed.

MRS BAINES: Come, Barbara: I must have my dear Major to carry the flag with me.

JENNY: Yes, yes, Major darling.

CUSINS (*snatches the tambourine out of* JENNY'*s hand and mutely offers it to* BARBARA).

BARBARA (*coming forward a little as she puts the offer behind her with a shudder, whilst* CUSINS *recklessly tosses the tambourine back to* JENNY *and goes to the gate*): I cant come.

JENNY: Not come!

MRS BAINES (*with tears in her eyes*): Barbara: do you think I am wrong to take the money?

BARBARA (*impulsively going to her and kissing her*): No, no: God help you, dear, you must: you are saving the Army. Go; and may you have a great meeting!

JENNY: But arnt you coming?

BARBARA: No. (*She begins taking off the silver S brooch from her collar.*)

MRS BAINES: Barbara: what are you doing?

JENNY: Why are you taking your badge off? You cant be going to leave us, Major.

BARBARA (*quietly*): Father: come here.

UNDERSHAFT (*coming to her*): My dear! (*Seeing that she is going to pin the badge on his collar, he retreats to the penthouse in some alarm.*)

BARBARA (*following him*): Dont be frightened. (*She pins the badge on and steps back towards the table, shewing him to the others.*) There! It's not much for £5000, is it?

MRS BAINES: Barbara: if you wont come and pray with us, promise me you will pray for us.

BARBARA: I cant pray now. Perhaps I shall never pray again.

MRS BAINES: Barbara!

JENNY: Major!

BARBARA (*almost delirious*): I cant bear any more. Quick march!

CUSINS (*calling to the procession in the street outside*): Off we go. Play up, there! Immenso giubilo. (*He gives the time with his drum; and the band strikes up the march, which rapidly becomes more distant as the procession moves briskly away.*)

MRS BAINES: I must go, dear. Youre overworked: you will be all right tomorrow. We'll never lose you. Now Jenny: step out with the old flag. Blood and Fire! (*She marches out through the gate with her flag.*)

JENNY: Glory Hallelujah! (*flourishing her tambourine and marching*).

UNDERSHAFT (*to* CUSINS, *as he marches out past him easing the slide of his trombone*): 'My ducats and my daughter'!

CUSINS (*following him out*): Money and gunpowder!

BARBARA: Drunkenness and Murder! My God: why hast thou forsaken me?

(*She sinks on the form with her face buried in her hands. The march passes away into silence.* BILL WALKER *steals across to her.*)

BILL (*taunting*): Wot prawce selvytion nah?

SHIRLEY: Dont you hit her when she's down.

BILL: She itt me wen aw wiz dahn. Waw shouldnt Aw git a bit o me aown beck?

BARBARA (*raising her head*): I didnt take your money, Bill.

(*She crosses the yard to the gate and turns her back on the two men to hide her face from them.*)

BILL (*sneering after her*): Naow, it warnt enaff for you. (*Turning to the drum, he misses the money.*) Ellow! If you aint took it sammun else ez. Weres it gorn? Bly me if Jenny Ill didnt tike it arter all!

RUMMY (*screaming at him from the loft*): You lie, you dirty blackguard! Snobby Price pinched it off the drum when he took up his cap. I was up here all the time an see im do it.

BILL: Wot! Stowl maw manney! Waw didnt you call thief on him, you silly aold macker you?

RUMMY: To serve you aht for ittin me acrost the fice. It's cost y'pahnd, that az. (*Raising a pæan of squalid triumph.*) I done you. I'm even with you. Uve ad it aht o y — (BILL *snatches up* SHIRLEY'*s mug and hurls it at her. She slams the loft door and vanishes. The mug smashes against the door and falls in fragments.*)

BILL (*beginning to chuckle*): Tell us, aol menn, wot o'clock this mawnin was it wen im as they call Snobby Prawce was sived?

BARBARA (*turning to him more composedly, and with unspoiled sweetness*): About half past twelve, Bill. And he pinched your pound at a quarter to two. I know. Well, you cant afford to lose it. I'll send it to you.

BILL (*his voice and accent suddenly improv-*

ing): Not if Aw wiz to stawve for it. Aw aint to be bought.

SHIRLEY: Aint you? Youd sell yourself to the devil for a pint o beer; only there aint no devil to make the offer.

BILL (*unashamed*): Sao Aw would, mite, and often ev, cheerful. But she cawnt baw me. (*Approaching* BARBARA.) You wanted maw saoul, did you? Well, you aint got it.

BARBARA: I nearly got it, Bill. But weve sold it back to you for ten thousand pounds.

SHIRLEY: And dear at the money!

BARBARA: No, Peter: it was worth more than money.

BILL (*salvationproof*): It's nao good: you cawnt get rahnd me nah. Aw downt blieve in it; and Awve seen tody that Aw was rawt. (*Going.*) Sao long, aol soupkitchener! Ta, ta, Mijor Earl's Grendorter! (*Turning at the gate.*) Wot prawce selvytion nah? Snobby Prawce! Ha! ha!

BARBARA (*offering her hand*): Goodbye, Bill.

BILL (*taken aback, half plucks his cap off; then shoves it on again defiantly*): Git aht. (BARBARA *drops her hand, discouraged. He has a twinge of remorse.*) But thets aw rawt, you knaow. Nathink pasnl. Naow mellice. Sao long, Judy. (*He goes.*)

BARBARA: No malice. So long, Bill.

SHIRLEY (*shaking his head*): You make too much of him, miss, in your innocence.

BARBARA (*going to him*): Peter: I'm like you now. Cleaned out, and lost my job.

SHIRLEY: Youve youth an hope. Thats two better than me.

BARBARA: I'll get you a job, Peter. Thats hope for you: the youth will have to be enough for me. (*She counts her money.*) I have just enough left for two teas at Lockharts, a Rowton doss for you, and my tram and bus home. (*He frowns and rises with offended pride. She takes his arm.*) Dont be proud, Peter: it's sharing between friends. And promise me youll talk to me and not let me cry. (*She draws him towards the gate.*)

SHIRLEY: Well, I'm not accustomed to talk to the like of you —

BARBARA (*urgently*): Yes, yes: you must talk to me. Tell me about Tom Paine's books and Bradlaugh's lectures. Come along.

SHIRLEY: Ah, if you would only read Tom Paine in the proper spirit, miss! (*They go out through the gate together.*)

ACT III

Next day after lunch LADY BRITOMART *is writing in the library in Wilton Crescent.* SARAH *is reading in the armchair near the window.* BARBARA, *in ordinary fashionable dress, pale and brooding, is on the settee.* CHARLES LOMAX *enters. He starts on seeing* BARBARA *fashionably attired and in low spirits.*

LOMAX: Youve left off your uniform!

(BARBARA *says nothing; but an expression of pain passes over her face.*)

LADY BRITOMART (*warning him in low tones to be careful*): Charles!

LOMAX (*much concerned, coming behind the settee and bending sympathetically over* BARBARA): I'm awfully sorry, Barbara. You know I helped you all I could with the concertina and so forth. (*Momentously.*) Still, I have never shut my eyes to the fact that there is a certain amount of tosh about the Salvation Army. Now the claims of the Church of England —

LADY BRITOMART: Thats enough, Charles. Speak of something suited to your mental capacity.

LOMAX: But surely the Church of England is suited to all our capacities.

BARBARA (*pressing his hand*): Thank you for your sympathy, Cholly. Now go and spoon with Sarah.

LOMAX (*dragging a chair from the writing table and seating himself affectionately by* SARAH'S *side*): How is my ownest today?

SARAH: I wish you wouldnt tell Cholly to do things, Barbara. He always comes straight and does them. Cholly: we're going to the works this afternoon.

LOMAX: What works?

SARAH: The cannon works.

LOMAX: What? your governor's shop!

SARAH: Yes.

LOMAX: Oh I say!

(CUSINS *enters in poor condition. He also starts visibly when he sees* BARBARA *without her uniform.*)

BARBARA: I expected you this morning, Dolly. Didnt you guess that?

CUSINS (*sitting down beside her*): I'm sorry. I have only just breakfasted.

SARAH: But weve just finished lunch.

BARBARA: Have you had one of your bad nights?

CUSINS: No: I had rather a good night: in fact, one of the most remarkable nights I have ever passed.

BARBARA: The meeting?

CUSINS: No: after the meeting.

LADY BRITOMART: You should have gone to bed after the meeting. What were you doing?

CUSINS: *Drinking*.

LADY BRITOMART. ⎫ ⎧ Adolphus!
SARAH.   ⎪ ⎪ Dolly!
BARBARA.   ⎬ ⎨ Dolly!
LOMAX.   ⎭ ⎩ Oh I say!

LADY BRITOMART: What were you drinking, may I ask?

CUSINS: A most devilish kind of Spanish burgundy, warranted free from added alcohol: a Temperance burgundy in fact. Its richness in natural alcohol made any addition superfluous.

BARBARA: Are you joking, Dolly?

CUSINS (*patiently*): No. I have been making a night of it with the nominal head of this household: that is all.

LADY BRITOMART: Andrew made you drunk!

CUSINS: No: he only provided the wine. I think it was Dionysos who made me drunk. (*To* BARBARA.) I told you I was possessed.

LADY BRITOMART: Youre not sober yet. Go home to bed at once.

CUSINS: I have never before ventured to reproach you, Lady Brit; but how could you marry the Prince of Darkness?

LADY BRITOMART: It was much more excusable to marry him than to get drunk with him. That is a new accomplishment of Andrew's, by the way. He usent to drink.

CUSINS: He doesnt now. He only sat there and completed the wreck of my moral basis, the rout of my convictions, the purchase of my soul. He cares for you, Barbara. That is what makes him so dangerous to me.

BARBARA: That has nothing to do with it, Dolly. There are larger loves and diviner dreams than the fireside ones. You know that, dont you?

CUSINS: Yes: that is our understanding. I know it. I hold to it. Unless he can win me on that holier ground he may amuse me for a while; but he can get no deeper hold, strong as he is.

BARBARA: Keep to that; and the end will be right. Now tell me what happened at the meeting?

CUSINS: It was an amazing meeting. Mrs Baines almost died of emotion. Jenny Hill simply gibbered with hysteria. The Prince of Darkness played his trombone like a madman: its brazen roarings were like the laughter of the damned. 117 conversions took place then and there. They prayed with the most touching sincerity and gratitude for Bodger, and for the anonymous donor of the £5000. Your father would not let his name be given.

LOMAX: That was rather fine of the old man, you know. Most chaps would have wanted the advertisement.

CUSINS: He said all the charitable institutions would be down on him like kites on a battle-field if he gave his name.

LADY BRITOMART: Thats Andrew all over. He never does a proper thing without giving an improper reason for it.

CUSINS: He convinced me that I have all my life been doing improper things for proper reasons.

LADY BRITOMART: Adolphus: now that Barbara has left the Salvation Army, you had better leave it too. I will not have you playing that drum in the streets.

CUSINS: Your orders are already obeyed, Lady Brit.

BARBARA: Dolly: were you ever really in earnest about it? Would you have joined if you had never seen me?

CUSINS (*disingenuously*): Well — er — well, possibly, as a collector of religious —

LOMAX (*cunningly*): Not as a drummer, though, you know. You are a very clearheaded brainy chap, Dolly; and it must have been apparent to you that there is a certain amount of tosh about —

LADY BRITOMART: Charles: if you must drivel, drivel like a grown-up man and not like a schoolboy.

LOMAX (*out of countenance*): Well, drivel is drivel, dont you know, whatever a man's age.

LADY BRITOMART: In good society in England, Charles, men drivel at all ages by repeating silly formulas with an air of wisdom. Schoolboys make their own formulas out of slang, like you. When they reach your age, and get political private secretaryships and things of that sort, they drop slang and get their formulas out of The Spectator or The Times. You had better confine yourself to The Times. You will find that there is a certain amount of tosh about The Times; but at least its language is reputable.

LOMAX (*overwhelmed*): You are so awfully strong-minded, Lady Brit —

LADY BRITOMART: Rubbish! (MORRISON *comes in.*) What is it?

MORRISON: If you please, my lady, Mr Undershaft has just drove up to the door.

LADY BRITOMART: Well, let him in. (MORRISON *hesitates.*) Whats the matter with you?

MORRISON: Shall I announce him, my lady; or is he at home here, so to speak, my lady?

LADY BRITOMART: Announce him.

MORRISON: Thank you, my lady. You wont mind my asking, I hope. The occasion is in a manner of speaking new to me.

LADY BRITOMART: Quite right. Go and let him in.

MORRISON: Thank you, my lady. (*He withdraws.*)

LADY BRITOMART: Children: go and get ready. (SARAH *and* BARBARA *go upstairs for their out-of-door wraps.*) Charles: go and tell Stephen to come down here in five minutes: you will find him in the drawing room. (CHARLES *goes.*) Adolphus: tell them to send round the carriage in about fifteen minutes. (ADOLPHUS *goes.*)

MORRISON (*at the door*): Mr Undershaft.

(UNDERSHAFT *comes in.* MORRISON *goes out.*)

UNDERSHAFT: Alone! How fortunate!

LADY BRITOMART (*rising*): Dont be sentimental, Andrew. Sit down. (*She sits on the settee: he sits beside her, on her left. She comes to the point before he has time to breathe.*) Sarah must have £800 a year until Charles Lomax comes into his property. Barbara will need more, and need it permanently, because Adolphus hasnt any property.

UNDERSHAFT (*resignedly*): Yes, my dear: I will see to it. Anything else? for yourself, for instance?

LADY BRITOMART: I want to talk to you about Stephen.

UNDERSHAFT (*rather wearily*): Dont, my dear. Stephen doesnt interest me.

LADY BRITOMART: He does interest me. He is our son.

UNDERSHAFT: Do you really think so? He has induced us to bring him into the world; but he chose his parents very incongruously, I think. I see nothing of myself in him, and less of you.

LADY BRITOMART: Andrew: Stephen is an excellent son, and a most steady, capable, highminded young man. You are simply trying to find an excuse for disinheriting him.

UNDERSHAFT: My dear Biddy: the Undershaft tradition disinherits him. It would be dishonest of me to leave the cannon foundry to my son.

LADY BRITOMART: It would be most unnatural and improper of you to leave it to anyone else, Andrew. Do you suppose this wicked and immoral tradition can be kept up for ever? Do you pretend that Stephen could not carry on the foundry just as well as all the other sons of the big business houses?

UNDERSHAFT: Yes: he could learn the office routine without understanding the business, like all the other sons; and the firm would go on by its own momentum until the real Undershaft — probably an Italian or a German — would invent a new method and cut him out.

LADY BRITOMART: There is nothing that any Italian or German could do that Stephen could not do. And Stephen at least has breeding.

UNDERSHAFT: The son of a foundling! Nonsense!

LADY BRITOMART: My son, Andrew! And even you may have good blood in your veins for all you know.

UNDERSHAFT: True. Probably I have. That is another argument in favor of a foundling.

LADY BRITOMART: Andrew: dont be aggravating. And dont be wicked. At present you are both.

UNDERSHAFT: This conversation is part of the Undershaft tradition, Biddy. Every Undershaft's wife has treated him to it ever since the house was founded. It is mere waste of breath. If the tradition be ever broken it will be for an abler man than Stephen.

LADY BRITOMART (*pouting*): Then go away.

UNDERSHAFT (*deprecatory*): Go away!

LADY BRITOMART: Yes: Go away. If you will do nothing for Stephen, you are not wanted here. Go to your foundling, whoever he is; and look after him.

UNDERSHAFT: The fact is, Biddy —

LADY BRITOMART: Dont call me Biddy. I dont call you Andy.

UNDERSHAFT: I will not call my wife Britomart: it is not good sense. Seriously, my love, the Undershaft tradition has landed me in a difficulty. I am getting on in years; and my partner Lazarus has at last made a stand and insisted that the succession must be settled one way or the other; and of course he is quite right. You see, I havent found a fit successor yet.

LADY BRITOMART (obstinately): There is Stephen.

UNDERSHAFT: Thats just it: all the foundlings I can find are exactly like Stephen.

LADY BRITOMART: Andrew!

UNDERSHAFT: I want a man with no relations and no schooling: that is, a man who would be out of the running altogether if he were not a strong man. And I cant find him. Every blessed foundling nowadays is snapped up in his infancy by Barnardo homes, or School Board officers, or Boards of Guardians; and if he shews the least ability he is fastened on by schoolmasters; trained to win scholarships like a racehorse; crammed with second-hand ideas; drilled and disciplined in docility and what they call good taste; and lamed for life so that he is fit for nothing but teaching. If you want to keep the foundry in the family, you had better find an eligible foundling and marry him to Barbara.

LADY BRITOMART: Ah! Barbara! Your pet! You would sacrifice Stephen to Barbara.

UNDERSHAFT: Cheerfully. And you, my dear, would boil Barbara to make soup for Stephen.

LADY BRITOMART: Andrew: this is not a question of our likings and dislikings: it is a question of duty. It is your duty to make Stephen your successor.

UNDERSHAFT: Just as much as it is your duty to submit to your husband. Come, Biddy! these tricks of the governing class are of no use with me. I am one of the governing class myself; and it is waste of time giving tracts to a missionary. I have the power in this matter; and I am not to be humbugged into using it for your purposes.

LADY BRITOMART: Andrew: you can talk my head off; but you cant change wrong into right. And your tie is all on one side. Put it straight.

UNDERSHAFT (disconcerted): It wont stay unless it's pinned (he fumbles at it with childish grimaces) —

(STEPHEN comes in.)

STEPHEN (at the door): I beg your pardon (about to retire).

LADY BRITOMART: No: come in, Stephen. (STEPHEN comes forward to his mother's writing table.)

UNDERSHAFT (not very cordially): Good afternoon.

STEPHEN (coldly): Good afternoon.

UNDERSHAFT (to LADY BRITOMART): He knows all about the tradition, I suppose?

LADY BRITOMART: Yes. (To STEPHEN.) It is what I told you last night, Stephen.

UNDERSHAFT (sulkily): I understand you want to come into the cannon business.

STEPHEN: I go into the trade! Certainly not.

UNDERSHAFT (opening his eyes, greatly eased in mind and manner): Oh! in that case —

LADY BRITOMART: Cannons are not trade, Stephen. They are enterprise.

STEPHEN: I have no intention of becoming a man of business in any sense. I have no capacity for business and no taste for it. I intend to devote myself to politics.

UNDERSHAFT (rising): My dear boy: this is an immense relief to me. And I trust it may prove an equally good thing for the country. I was afraid you would consider yourself disparaged and slighted. (He moves towards STEPHEN as if to shake hands with him.)

LADY BRITOMART (rising and interposing): Stephen: I cannot allow you to throw away an enormous property like this.

STEPHEN (stiffly): Mother: there must be an end of treating me as a child, if you please. (LADY BRITOMART recoils, deeply wounded by his tone.) Until last night I did not take your attitude seriously, because I did not think you meant it seriously. But I find now that you left me in the dark as to matters which you should have explained to me years ago. I am extremely hurt and offended. Any further discussion of my intentions had better take place with my father, as between one man and another.

LADY BRITOMART: Stephen! (She sits down again, her eyes filling with tears.)

UNDERSHAFT (with grave compassion): You see, my dear, it is only the big men who can be treated as children.

STEPHEN: I am sorry, mother, that you have forced me —

UNDERSHAFT (*stopping him*): Yes, yes, yes, yes: thats all right, Stephen. She wont interfere with you any more: your independence is achieved: you have won your latchkey. Dont rub it in; and above all, dont apologize. (*He resumes his seat.*) Now what about your future, as between one man and another — I beg your pardon, Biddy: as between two men and a woman.

LADY BRITOMART (*who has pulled herself together strongly*): I quite understand, Stephen. By all means go your own way if you feel strong enough. (STEPHEN *sits down magisterially in the chair at the writing table with an air of affirming his majority.*)

UNDERSHAFT: It is settled that you do not ask for the succession to the cannon business.

STEPHEN: I hope it is settled that I repudiate the cannon business.

UNDERSHAFT: Come, come! dont be so devilishly sulky: it's boyish. Freedom should be generous. Besides, I owe you a fair start in life in exchange for disinheriting you. You cant become prime minister all at once. Havnt you a turn for something? What about literature, art, and so forth?

STEPHEN: I have nothing of the artist about me, either in faculty or character, thank Heaven!

UNDERSHAFT: A philosopher, perhaps? Eh?

STEPHEN: I make no such ridiculous pretension.

UNDERSHAFT: Just so. Well, there is the army, the navy, the Church, the Bar. The Bar requires some ability. What about the Bar?

STEPHEN: I have not studied law. And I am afraid I have not the necessary push — I believe that is the name barristers give to their vulgarity — for success in pleading.

UNDERSHAFT: Rather a difficult case, Stephen. Hardly anything left but the stage, is there? (STEPHEN *makes an impatient movement.*) Well, come! is there anything you know or care for?

STEPHEN (*rising and looking at him steadily*): I know the difference between right and wrong.

UNDERSHAFT (*hugely tickled*): You dont say so! What! no capacity for business, no knowledge of law, no sympathy with art, no pretension to philosophy; only a simple knowledge of

the secret that has puzzled all the philosophers, baffled all the lawyers, muddled all the men of business, and ruined most of the artists: the secret of right and wrong. Why, man, youre a genius, a master of masters, a god! At twentyfour, too!

STEPHEN (*keeping his temper with difficulty*): You are pleased to be facetious. I pretend to nothing more than any honorable English gentleman claims as his birthright (*he sits down angrily*).

UNDERSHAFT: Oh, thats everybody's birthright. Look at poor little Jenny Hill, the Salvation lassie! she would think you were laughing at her if you asked her to stand up in the street and teach grammar or geography or mathematics or even drawing room dancing; but it never occurs to her to doubt that she can teach morals and religion. You are all alike, you respectable people. You cant tell me the bursting strain of a ten-inch gun, which is a very simple matter; but you all think you can tell me the bursting strain of a man under temptation. You darent handle high explosives; but youre all ready to handle honesty and truth and justice and the whole duty of man, and kill one another at that game. What a country! What a world!

LADY BRITOMART (*uneasily*): What do you think he had better do, Andrew?

UNDERSHAFT: Oh, just what he wants to do. He knows nothing and he thinks he knows everything. That points clearly to a political career. Get him a private secretaryship to someone who can get him an Under Secretaryship; and then leave him alone. He will find his natural and proper place in the end on the Treasury Bench.

STEPHEN (*springing up again*): I am sorry, sir, that you force me to forget the respect due to you as my father. I am an Englishman and I will not hear the Government of my country insulted. (*He thrusts his hands in his pockets, and walks angrily across to the window.*)

UNDERSHAFT (*with a touch of brutality*): The government of your country! I am the government of your country: I, and Lazarus. Do you suppose that you and half a dozen amateurs like you, sitting in a row in that foolish gabble shop, can govern Undershaft and Lazarus? No, my friend: you will do what pays us. You will make war when it suits us, and keep peace when it doesnt. You will find out that trade requires certain measures when we have decided on those measures. When I want anything to keep my dividends up, you will discover that my want is a national need. When other people want something to keep my dividends down, you will call out the police and military. And in return you shall have the support and applause of my newspapers, and the delight of imagining that you are a great statesman. Government of your country! Be off with you, my boy, and play with your caucuses and leading articles and historical parties and great leaders and burning questions and the rest of your toys. *I am going back to my counting-house to pay the piper and call the tune.*

STEPHEN (*actually smiling, and putting his hand on his father's shoulder with indulgent patronage*): Really, my dear father, it is impossible to be angry with you. You dont know how absurd all this sounds to me. You are very properly proud of having been industrious enough to make money; and it is greatly to your credit that you have made so much of it. But it has kept you in circles where you are valued for your money and deferred to for it, instead of in the doubtless very old-fashioned and behind-the-times public school and university where I formed my habits of mind. It is natural for you to think that money governs England; but you must allow me to think I know better.

UNDERSHAFT: And what does govern England, pray?

STEPHEN: Character, father, character.

UNDERSHAFT: Whose character? Yours or mine?

STEPHEN: Neither yours nor mine, father, but the best elements in the English national character.

UNDERSHAFT: Stephen: Ive found your profession for you. Youre a born journalist. I'll start you with a high-toned weekly review. There!

(*Before* STEPHEN *can reply* SARAH, BARBARA, LOMAX, *and* CUSINS *come in ready for walking.* BARBARA *crosses the room to the window and looks out.* CUSINS *drifts amiably to the armchair.* LOMAX *remains near the door, whilst* SARAH *comes to her mother.*

STEPHEN *goes to the smaller writing table and busies himself with his letters.*)

SARAH: Go and get ready, mamma: the carriage is waiting. (LADY BRITOMART *leaves the room.*)

UNDERSHAFT (*to* SARAH): Good day, my dear. Good afternoon, Mr Lomax.

LOMAX (*vaguely*): Ahdedoo.

UNDERSHAFT (*to* CUSINS): Quite well after last night, Euripides, eh?

CUSINS: As well as can be expected.

UNDERSHAFT: Thats right. (*To* BARBARA.) So you are coming to see my death and devastation factory, Barbara?

BARBARA (*at the window*): You came yesterday to see my salvation factory. I promised you a return visit.

LOMAX (*coming forward between* SARAH *and* UNDERSHAFT): Youll find it awfully interesting. Ive been through the Woolwich Arsenal; and it gives you a ripping feeling of security, you know, to think of the lot of beggars we could kill if it came to fighting. (*To* UNDERSHAFT, *with sudden solemnity.*) Still, it must be rather an awful reflection for you, from the religious point of view as it were. Youre getting on, you know, and all that.

SARAH: You dont mind Cholly's imbecility, papa, do you?

LOMAX (*much taken aback*): Oh I say!

UNDERSHAFT: Mr Lomax looks at the matter in a very proper spirit, my dear.

LOMAX: Just so. Thats all I meant, I assure you.

SARAH: Are you coming, Stephen?

STEPHEN: Well, I am rather busy — er — (*Magnanimously.*) Oh well, yes: I'll come. That is, if there is room for me.

UNDERSHAFT: I can take two with me in a little motor I am experimenting with for field use. You wont mind its being rather unfashionable. It's not painted yet; but it's bullet proof.

LOMAX (*appalled at the prospect of confronting Wilton Crescent in an unpainted motor*): Oh I say!

SARAH: The carriage for me, thank you. Barbara doesnt mind what she's seen in.

LOMAX: I say, Dolly, old chap: do you really mind the car being a guy? Because of course if you do I'll go in it. Still —

CUSINS: I prefer it.

LOMAX: Thanks awfully, old man. Come, my ownest. (*He hurries out to secure his seat in the carriage.* SARAH *follows him.*)

CUSINS (*moodily walking across to* LADY BRITOMART'S *writing table*): Why are we two coming to this Works Department of Hell? that is what I ask myself.

BARBARA: I have always thought of it as a sort of pit where lost creatures with blackened faces stirred up smoky fires and were driven and tormented by my father? Is it like that, dad?

UNDERSHAFT (*scandalized*): My dear! It is a spotlessly clean and beautiful hillside town.

CUSINS: With a Methodist chapel? Oh do say theres a Methodist chapel.

UNDERSHAFT: There are two: a Primitive one and a sophisticated one. There is even an Ethical Society; but it is not much patronized, as my men are all strongly religious. In the High Explosives Sheds they object to the presence of Agnostics as unsafe.

CUSINS: And yet they dont object to you!

BARBARA: Do they obey all your orders?

UNDERSHAFT: I never give them any orders. When I speak to one of them it is 'Well, Jones, is the baby doing well? and has Mrs Jones made a good recovery?' 'Nicely, thank you, sir.' And thats all.

CUSINS: But Jones has to be kept in order. How do you maintain discipline among your men?

UNDERSHAFT: I dont. They do. You see, the one thing Jones wont stand is any rebellion from the man under him, or any assertion of social equality between the wife of the man with 4 shillings a week less than himself, and Mrs Jones! Of course they all rebel against me, theoretically. Practically, every man of them keeps the man just below him in his place. I never meddle with them. I never bully them. I dont even bully Lazarus. I say that certain things are to be done; but I dont order anybody to do them. I dont say, mind you, that there is no ordering about and snubbing and even bullying. The men snub the boys and order them about; the carmen snub the sweepers; the artisans snub the unskilled laborers; the foremen drive and bully both the laborers and artisans; the assistant engineers find fault with the foremen; the chief engineers drop on the assistants; the departmental managers worry the chiefs; and the clerks have tall hats and hymnbooks and keep up the social tone by refusing to associate on equal terms with anybody. The result is a colossal profit, which comes to me.

CUSINS (*revolted*): You really are a — well, what I was saying yesterday.

BARBARA: What was he saying yesterday?

UNDERSHAFT: Never mind, my dear. He thinks I have made you unhappy. Have I?

BARBARA: Do you think I can be happy in this vulgar silly dress? I! who have worn the uniform. Do you understand what you have done to me? Yesterday I had a man's soul in my hand. I set him in the way of life with his face to salvation. But when we took your money he turned back to drunkenness and derision. (*With intense conviction.*) I will never forgive you that. If I had a child, and you destroyed its body with your explosives — if you murdered Dolly with your horrible guns — I could forgive you if my forgiveness would open the gates of heaven to you. But to take a human soul from me, and turn it into the soul of a wolf! that is worse than any murder.

UNDERSHAFT: Does my daughter despair so easily? Can you strike a man to the heart and leave no mark on him?

BARBARA (*her face lighting up*): Oh, you are right: he can never be lost now: where was my faith?

CUSINS: Oh, clever clever devil!

BARBARA: You may be a devil; but God speaks through you sometimes. (*She takes her father's hands and kisses them.*) You have given me back my happiness: I feel it deep down now, though my spirit is troubled.

UNDERSHAFT: You have learnt something. That always feels at first as if you had lost something.

BARBARA: Well, take me to the factory of death; and let me learn something more. There must be some truth or other behind all this frightful irony. Come, Dolly. (*She goes out.*)

CUSINS: My guardian angel! (*To* UNDERSHAFT.) Avaunt! (*He follows* BARBARA.)

STEPHEN (*quietly, at the writing table*): You must not mind Cusins, father. He is a very amiable good fellow; but he is a Greek scholar and naturally a little eccentric.

UNDERSHAFT: Ah, quite so. Thank you, Stephen. Thank you. (*He goes out.*)

(STEPHEN *smiles patronizingly; buttons his coat responsibly; and crosses the room to the door.* LADY BRITOMART, *dressed for out-of-doors, opens it before he reaches it. She looks round for others; looks at* STEPHEN; *and turns to go without a word.*)

STEPHEN (*embarrassed*): Mother —

LADY BRITOMART: Dont be apologetic, Stephen. And dont forget that you have outgrown your mother. (*She goes out.*)

(*Perivale St Andrews lies between two Middlesex hills, half climbing the northern one. It is an almost smokeless town of white walls, roofs of narrow green slates or red tiles, tall trees, domes, campaniles, and slender chimney shafts, beautifully situated and beautiful in itself. The best view of it is obtained from the crest of a slope about half a mile to the east, where the high explosives are dealt with. The foundry lies hidden in the depths between, the tops of its chimneys sprouting like huge skittles into the middle distance. Across the crest runs an emplacement of concrete, with a firestep, and a parapet which suggests a fortification, because there is a huge cannon of the obsolete Woolwich Infant pattern peering across it at the town. The cannon is mounted on an experimental gun carriage: possibly the original model of the Undershaft disappearing rampart gun alluded to by* STEPHEN. *The firestep, being a convenient place to sit, is furnished here and there with straw disc cushions; and at one place there is the additional luxury of a fur rug.* BARBARA *is standing on the firestep, looking over the parapet towards the town. On her right is the cannon; on her left the end of a shed raised on piles, with a ladder of three or four steps up to the door, which opens outwards and has a little wooden landing at the threshold, with a fire bucket in the corner of the landing. Several dummy soldiers more or less mutilated, with straw protruding from their gashes, have been shoved out of the way under the landing. A few others are nearly upright against the shed; and one has fallen forward and lies, like a grotesque corpse, on the emplacement. The parapet stops short of the shed, leaving a gap which is the beginning of the path down the hill through the foundry to the town. The rug is on the firestep near this gap. Down on the emplacement behind the cannon is a trolley carrying a huge conical bombshell with a red band painted on it. Further to the right is the door of an office, which, like the sheds, is of the lightest possible construction.* CUSINS *arrives by the path from the town.*)

BARBARA: Well?

CUSINS: Not a ray of hope. Everything perfect! wonderful! real! It only needs a cathedral to be a heavenly city instead of a hellish one.

BARBARA: Have you found out whether they have done anything for old Peter Shirley?

CUSINS: They have found him a job as gatekeeper and timekeeper. He's frightfully miserable. He calls the time-keeping brainwork, and says he isnt used to it; and his gate lodge is so splendid that he's ashamed to use the rooms, and skulks in the scullery.

BARBARA: Poor Peter!

(STEPHEN *arrives from the town. He carries a fieldglass.*)

STEPHEN (*enthusiastically*): Have you two seen the place? Why did you leave us?

CUSINS: I wanted to see everything I was not intended to see; and Barbara wanted to make the men talk.

STEPHEN: Have you found anything discreditable?

CUSINS: No. They call him Dandy Andy and are proud of his being a cunning old rascal; but it's all horribly, frightfully, immorally, unanswerably perfect.

(SARAH *arrives.*)

SARAH: Heavens! what a place! (*She crosses to the trolley.*) Did you see the nursing home!? (*She sits down on the shell.*)

STEPHEN: Did you see the libraries and schools!?

SARAH: Did you see the ball room and the banqueting chamber in the Town Hall!?

STEPHEN: Have you gone into the insurance fund, the pension fund, the building society, the various applications of cooperation!?

(UNDERSHAFT *comes from the office, with a sheaf of telegrams in his hand.*)

UNDERSHAFT: Well, have you seen everything? I'm sorry I was called away. (*Indicating the telegrams.*) Good news from Manchuria.

STEPHEN: Another Japanese victory?

UNDERSHAFT: Oh, I dont know. Which side wins does not concern us here. No: the good news is that the aerial battleship is a tremendous success. At the first trial it has wiped out a fort with three hundred soldiers in it.

CUSINS (*from the platform*): Dummy soldiers?

UNDERSHAFT (*striding across to* STEPHEN *and kicking the prostrate dummy brutally out of his way*): No: the real thing.

(CUSINS *and* BARBARA *exchange glances. Then* CUSINS *sits on the step and buries his face in his hands.* BARBARA *gravely lays her hand on his shoulder. He looks up at her in whimsical desperation.*)

UNDERSHAFT: Well, Stephen, what do you think of the place?

STEPHEN: Oh, magnificent. A perfect triumph of modern industry. Frankly, my dear father, I have been a fool: I had no idea of what it all meant: of the wonderful fore-thought, the power of organization, the administrative capacity, the financial genius, the colossal capital it represents. I have been re-peating to myself as I came through your streets 'Peace hath her victories no less re-nowned than War.' I have only one misgiving about it all.

UNDERSHAFT: Out with it.

STEPHEN: Well, I cannot help thinking that all this provision for every want of your workmen may sap their independence and weaken their sense of responsibility. And greatly as we enjoyed our tea at that splendid restaurant — how they gave us all that luxury and cake and jam and cream for threepence I really cannot imagine! — still you must remem-ber that restaurants break up home life. Look at the continent, for instance! Are you sure so much pampering is really good for the men's characters?

UNDERSHAFT: Well you see, my dear boy, when you are organizing civilization you have to make up your mind whether trouble and anxiety are good things or not. If you decide that they are, then, I take it, you simply dont organize civilization; and there you are, with trouble and anxiety enough to make us all angels! But if you decide the other way, you may as well go through with it. However, Stephen, our characters are safe here. A suffi-cient dose of anxiety is always provided by the fact that we may be blown to smithereens at any moment.

SARAH: By the way, papa, where do you make the explosives?

UNDERSHAFT: In separate little sheds, like that one. When one of them blows up, it costs very little; and only the people quite close to it are killed.

(STEPHEN, *who is quite close to it, looks at it rather scaredly, and moves away quickly to the cannon. At the same moment the door of the shed is thrown abruptly open; and a foreman in overalls and list slippers comes out on the little landing and holds the door for* LOMAX, *who appears in the doorway.*)

LOMAX (*with studied coolness*): My good fellow: you neednt get into a state of nerves. Nothing's going to happen to you; and I suppose it wouldnt be the end of the world if anything did. A little bit of British pluck is what you want, old chap. (*He descends and strolls across to* SARAH.)

UNDERSHAFT (*to the foreman*): Anything wrong, Bilton?

BILTON (*with ironic calm*): Gentleman walked into the high explosives shed and lit a cigaret, sir: thats all.

UNDERSHAFT: Ah, quite so. (*Going over to* LOMAX.) Do you happen to remember what you did with the match?

LOMAX: Oh come! I'm not a fool. I took jolly good care to blow it out before I chucked it away.

BILTON: The top of it was red hot inside, sir.

LOMAX: Well, suppose it was! I didnt chuck it into any of your messes.

UNDERSHAFT: Think no more of it, Mr Lomax. By the way, would you mind lending me your matches.

LOMAX (*offering his box*): Certainly.

UNDERSHAFT: Thanks. (*He pockets the matches.*)

LOMAX (*lecturing to the company gener-ally*): You know, these high explosives dont go off like gunpowder, except when theyre in a gun. When theyre spread loose, you can put a match to them without the least risk: they just burn quietly like a bit of paper. (*Warming to the scientific interest of the subject.*) Did you know that, Undershaft? Have you ever tried?

UNDERSHAFT: Not on a large scale, Mr Lomax. Bilton will give you a sample of gun cotton when you are leaving if you ask him. You can experiment with it at home. (BILTON *looks puzzled.*)

SARAH: Bilton will do nothing of the sort, papa. I suppose it's your business to blow up the Russians and Japs; but you might really stop short of blowing up poor Cholly. (BILTON *gives it up and retires into the shed.*)

LOMAX: My ownest, there is no danger. (*He sits beside her on the shell.*)

(LADY BRITOMART *arrives from the town with a bouquet.*)

LADY BRITOMART (*impetuously*): Andrew: you shouldnt have let me see this place.

UNDERSHAFT: Why, my dear?

LADY BRITOMART: Never mind why: you shouldnt have: thats all. To think of all that (*indicating the town*) being yours! and that you have kept it to yourself all these years!

UNDERSHAFT: It does not belong to me. I belong to it. It is the Undershaft inheritance.

LADY BRITOMART: It is not. Your ridiculous cannons and that noisy banging foundry may be the Undershaft inheritance; but all that plate and linen, all that furniture and those houses and orchards and gardens belong to us. They belong to me: they are not a man's business. I wont give them up. You must be out of your senses to throw them all away; and if you persist in such folly, I will call in a doctor.

UNDERSHAFT (*stooping to smell the bouquet*): Where did you get the flowers, my dear?

LADY BRITOMART: Your men presented them to me in your William Morris Labor Church.

CUSINS: Oh! It needed only that. A Labor Church! (*He mounts the firestep distractedly, and leans with his elbows on the parapet, turning his back to them.*)

LADY BRITOMART: Yes, with Morris's words in mosaic letters ten feet high round the dome. NO MAN IS GOOD ENOUGH TO BE ANOTHER MAN'S MASTER. The cynicism of it!

UNDERSHAFT: It shocked the men at first, I am afraid. But now they take no more notice of it than of the ten commandments in church.

LADY BRITOMART: Andrew: you are trying to put me off the subject of the inheritance by profane jokes. Well, you shant. I dont ask it any longer for Stephen: he has inherited far too much of your perversity to be fit for it. But Barbara has rights as well as Stephen. Why should not Adolphus succeed to the inheritance? I could manage the town for him; and he can look after the cannons, if they are really necessary.

UNDERSHAFT: I should ask nothing better if Adolphus were a foundling. He is exactly the sort of new blood that is wanted in English business. But he's not a foundling; and theres an end of it. (*He makes for the office door.*)

CUSINS (*turning to them*): Not quite. (*They all turn and stare at him.*) I think — Mind! I am not committing myself in any way as to my future course — but I think the foundling difficulty can be got over. (*He jumps down to the emplacement.*)

UNDERSHAFT (*coming back to him*): What do you mean?

CUSINS: Well, I have something to say which is in the nature of a confession.

SARAH:
LADY BRITOMART: } Confession!
BARBARA:
STEPHEN:

LOMAX: Oh I say!

CUSINS: Yes, a confession. Listen, all. Until I met Barbara I thought myself in the main an honorable, truthful man, because I wanted the approval of my conscience more than I wanted anything else. But the moment I saw Barbara, I wanted her far more than the approval of my conscience.

LADY BRITOMART: Adolphus!

CUSINS: It is true. You accused me yourself, Lady Brit, of joining the Army to worship Barbara; and so I did. She bought my soul like a flower at a street corner; but she bought it for herself.

UNDERSHAFT: What! Not for Dionysos or another?

CUSINS: Dionysos and all the others are in herself. I adored what was divine in her, and was therefore a true worshipper. But I was romantic about her too. I thought she was a woman of the people, and that a marriage with a professor of Greek would be far beyond the wildest social ambitions of her rank.

LADY BRITOMART: Adolphus!!

LOMAX: Oh I say!!!

CUSINS: When I learnt the horrible truth —

LADY BRITOMART: What do you mean by the horrible truth, pray?

CUSINS: That she was enormously rich; that her grandfather was an earl; that her father was the Prince of Darkness —

UNDERSHAFT: Chut!

CUSINS: — and that I was only an adventurer trying to catch a rich wife, then I stooped to deceive her about my birth.

BARBARA (*rising*): Dolly!

LADY BRITOMART: Your birth! Now Adolphus, dont dare to make up a wicked story for the sake of these wretched cannons. Remember: I have seen photographs of your parents; and the Agent General for South Western Australia knows them personally and has assured me that they are most respectable married people.

CUSINS: So they are in Australia; but here they are outcasts. Their marriage is legal in Australia, but not in England. My mother is my father's deceased wife's sister; and in this island I am consequently a foundling. (*Sensation.*)

BARBARA: Silly! (*She climbs to the cannon, and leans, listening, in the angle it makes with the parapet.*)

CUSINS: Is the subterfuge good enough, Machiavelli?

UNDERSHAFT (*thoughtfully*): Biddy: this may be a way out of the difficulty.

LADY BRITOMART: Stuff! A man cant make cannons any the better for being his own cousin instead of his proper self. (*She sits down on the rug with a bounce that expresses her downright contempt for their casuistry.*)

UNDERSHAFT (*to* CUSINS): You are an educated man. That is against the tradition.

CUSINS: Once in ten thousand times it happens that the schoolboy is a born master of what they try to teach him. Greek has not destroyed my mind: it has nourished it. Besides, I did not learn it at an English public school.

UNDERSHAFT: Hm! Well, I cannot afford to be too particular: you have cornered the foundling market. Let it pass. You are eligible, Euripides: you are eligible.

BARBARA: Dolly: yesterday morning, when Stephen told us all about the tradition, you became very silent; and you have been strange and excited ever since. Were you thinking of your birth then?

CUSINS: When the finger of Destiny suddenly points at a man in the middle of his breakfast, it makes him thoughtful.

UNDERSHAFT: Aha! You have had your eye on the business, my young friend, have you?

CUSINS: Take care! There is an abyss of moral horror between me and your accursed aerial battleships.

UNDERSHAFT: Never mind the abyss for the present. Let us settle the practical details and leave your final decision open. You know that you will have to change your name. Do you object to that?

CUSINS: Would any man named Adolphus — any man called Dolly! — object to be called something else?

UNDERSHAFT: Good. Now, as to money! I propose to treat you handsomely from the beginning. You shall start at a thousand a year.

CUSINS (*with sudden heat, his spectacles twinkling with mischief*): A thousand! You dare offer a miserable thousand to the son-in-law of a millionaire! No, by Heavens, Machiavelli! you shall not cheat me. You cannot do without me; and I can do without you. I must have two thousand five hundred a year for two years. At the end of that time, if I am a failure, I go. But if I am a success, and stay on, you must give me the other five thousand.

UNDERSHAFT: What other five thousand?

CUSINS: To make the two years up to five thousand a year. The two thousand five hundred is only half pay in case I should turn out a failure. The third year I must have ten per cent on the profits.

UNDERSHAFT (*taken aback*): Ten per cent! Why, man, do you know what my profits are?

CUSINS: Enormous, I hope: otherwise I shall require twenty-five per cent.

UNDERSHAFT: But, Mr Cusins, this is a serious matter of business. You are not bringing any capital into the concern.

CUSINS: What! no capital! Is my mastery of Greek no capital? Is my access to the subtlest thought, the loftiest poetry yet attained by humanity, no capital? My character! my intellect! my life! my career! what Barbara calls my soul! are these no capital? Say another word; and I double my salary.

UNDERSHAFT: Be reasonable —

CUSINS (*peremptorily*): Mr Undershaft: you have my terms. Take them or leave them.

UNDERSHAFT (*recovering himself*): Very well. I note your terms; and I offer you half.

CUSINS (*disgusted*): Half!

UNDERSHAFT (*firmly*): Half.

CUSINS: You call yourself a gentleman; and you offer me half!!

UNDERSHAFT: I do not call myself a gentleman; but I offer you half.

CUSINS: This to your future partner! your successor! your son-in-law!

BARBARA: You are selling your own soul,

Dolly, not mine. Leave me out of the bargain, please.

UNDERSHAFT: Come! I will go a step further for Barbara's sake. I will give you three fifths; but that is my last word.

CUSINS: Done!

LOMAX: Done in the eye! Why, *I* get only eight hundred, you know.

CUSINS: By the way, Mac, I am a classical scholar, not an arithmetical one. Is three fifths more than half or less?

UNDERSHAFT: More, of course.

CUSINS: I would have taken two hundred and fifty. How you can succeed in business when you are willing to pay all that money to a University don who is obviously not worth a junior clerk's wages! — well! What will Lazarus say?

UNDERSHAFT: Lazarus is a gentle romantic Jew who cares for nothing but string quartets and stalls at fashionable theatres. He will be blamed for your rapacity in money matters, poor fellow! as he has hitherto been blamed for mine. You are a shark of the first order, Euripides. So much the better for the firm!

BARBARA: Is the bargain closed, Dolly? Does your soul belong to him now?

CUSINS: No: the price is settled: that is all. The real tug of war is still to come. What about the moral question?

LADY BRITOMART: There is no moral question in the matter at all, Adolphus. You must simply sell cannons and weapons to people whose cause is right and just, and refuse them to foreigners and criminals.

UNDERSHAFT (*determined*): No: None of that. You must keep the true faith of an Armorer, or you dont come in here.

CUSINS: What on earth is the true faith of an Armorer?

UNDERSHAFT: To give arms to all men who offer an honest price for them, without respect of persons or principles: to aristocrat and republican, to Nihilist and Tsar, to Capitalist and Socialist, to Protestant and Catholic, to burglar and policeman, to black man, white man and yellow man, to all sorts and conditions, all nationalities, all faiths, all follies, all causes and all crimes. The first Undershaft wrote up in his shop IF GOD GAVE THE HAND, LET NOT MAN WITHHOLD THE SWORD. The second wrote up ALL HAVE THE RIGHT TO FIGHT: NONE HAVE THE RIGHT TO JUDGE. The third wrote up TO MAN THE WEAPON: TO HEAVEN THE VICTORY. The fourth had no literary turn; so he did not write up anything; but he sold cannons to Napoleon under the nose of George the Third. The fifth wrote up PEACE SHALL NOT PREVAIL SAVE WITH A SWORD IN HER HAND. The sixth, my master, was the best of all. He wrote up NOTHING IS EVER DONE IN THIS WORLD UNTIL MEN ARE PREPARED TO KILL ONE ANOTHER IF IT IS NOT DONE. After that, there was nothing left for the seventh to say. So he wrote up, simply, UNASHAMED.

CUSINS: My good Machiavelli, I shall certainly write something up on the wall; only, as I shall write it in Greek, you wont be able to read it. But as to your Armorer's faith, if I take my neck out of the noose of my own morality I am not going to put it into the noose of yours. I shall sell cannons to whom I please and refuse them to whom I please. So there!

UNDERSHAFT: From the moment when you become Andrew Undershaft, you will never do as you please again. Dont come here lusting for power, young man.

CUSINS: If power were my aim I should not come here for it. You have no power.

UNDERSHAFT: None of my own, certainly.

CUSINS: I have more power than you, more will. You do not drive this place: it drives you. And what drives the place?

UNDERSHAFT (*enigmatically*): A will of which I am a part.

BARBARA (*startled*): Father! Do you know what you are saying; or are you laying a snare for my soul?

CUSINS: Dont listen to his metaphysics, Barbara. The place is driven by the most rascally part of society, the money hunters, the pleasure hunters, the military promotion hunters; and he is their slave.

UNDERSHAFT: Not necessarily. Remember the Armorer's Faith. I will take an order from a good man as cheerfully as from a bad one. If you good people prefer preaching and shirking to buying my weapons and fighting the rascals, dont blame me. I can make cannons: I cannot make courage and conviction. Bah! you tire me, Euripides, with your morality mongering. Ask Barbara: she understands. (*He suddenly reaches up and takes* BARBARA's *hands, looking powerfully into her eyes.*) Tell him, my love, what power really means.

BARBARA (*hypnotized*): Before I joined the

Salvation Army, I was in my own power; and the consequence was that I never knew what to do with myself. When I joined it, I had not time enough for all the things I had to do.

UNDERSHAFT (*approvingly*): Just so. And why was that, do you suppose?

BARBARA: Yesterday I should have said, because I was in the power of God. (*She resumes her self-possession, withdrawing her hands from his with a power equal to his own.*) But you came and shewed me that I was in the power of Bodger and Undershaft. Today I feel — oh! how can I put it into words? Sarah: do you remember the earthquake at Cannes, when we were little children? — how little the surprise of the first shock mattered compared to the dread and horror of waiting for the second? That is how I feel in this place today. I stood on the rock I thought eternal; and without a word of warning it reeled and crumbled under me. I was safe with an infinite wisdom watching me, an army marching to Salvation with me; and in a moment, at a stroke of your pen in a cheque book, I stood alone; and the heavens were empty. That was the first shock of the earthquake: I am waiting for the second.

UNDERSHAFT: Come, come, my daughter! dont make too much of your tinpot tragedy. What do we do here when we spend years of work and thought and thousands of pounds of solid cash on a new gun or an aerial battleship that turns out just a hairsbreadth wrong after all? Scrap it. Scrap it without wasting another hour or another pound on it. Well, you have made for yourself something that you call a morality or a religion or what not. It doesn't fit the facts. Well, scrap it. Scrap it and get one that does fit. That is what is wrong with the world at present. It scraps its obsolete steam engines and dynamos; but it wont scrap its old prejudices and its old moralities and its old religions and its old political constitutions. Whats the result? In machinery it does very well; but in morals and religion and politics it is working at a loss that brings it nearer bankruptcy every year. Dont persist in that folly. If your old religion broke down yesterday, get a newer and a better one for tomorrow.

BARBARA: Oh how gladly I would take a better one to my soul! But you offer me a worse one. (*Turning on him with sudden vehe-*

mence.) Justify yourself: shew me some light through the darkness of this dreadful place, with its beautifully clean workshops, and respectable workmen, and model homes.

UNDERSHAFT: Cleanliness and respectability do not need justification, Barbara: they justify themselves. I see no darkness here, no dreadfulness. In your Salvation shelter I saw poverty, misery, cold and hunger. You gave them bread and treacle and dreams of heaven. I give from thirty shillings a week to twelve thousand a year. They find their own dreams; but I look after the drainage.

BARBARA: And their souls?

UNDERSHAFT: I save their souls just as I saved yours.

BARBARA (*revolted*): You saved my soul! What do you mean?

UNDERSHAFT: I fed you and clothed you and housed you. I took care that you should have money enough to live handsomely — more than enough; so that you could be wasteful, careless, generous. That saved your soul from the seven deadly sins.

BARBARA (*bewildered*): The seven deadly sins!

UNDERSHAFT: Yes, the deadly seven. (*Counting on his fingers.*) Food, clothing, firing, rent, taxes, respectability and children. Nothing can lift those seven millstones from Man's neck but money; and the spirit cannot soar until the millstones are lifted. I lifted them from your spirit. I enabled Barbara to become Major Barbara; and I saved her from the crime of poverty.

CUSINS: Do you call poverty a crime?

UNDERSHAFT: The worst of crimes. All the other crimes are virtues beside it: all the other dishonors are chivalry itself by comparison. Poverty blights whole cities; spreads horrible pestilences; strikes dead the very souls of all who come within sight, sound, or smell of it. What you call crime is nothing: a murder here and a theft there, a blow now and a curse then: what do they matter? they are only the accidents and illnesses of life: there are not fifty genuine professional criminals in London. But there are millions of poor people, abject people, dirty people, ill fed, ill clothed people. They poison us morally and physically: they kill the happiness of society: they force us to do away with our own liberties and to organize unnatural cruelties for fear they should rise against us and drag us down into their abyss. Only fools fear crime: we all fear poverty. Pah! (*turning on* BARBARA) you talk of your half-saved ruffian in West Ham: you accuse me of dragging his soul back to perdition. Well, bring him to me here; and I will drag his soul back again to salvation for you. Not by words and dreams; but by thirtyeight shillings a week, a sound house in a handsome street, and a permanent job. In three weeks he will have a fancy waistcoat; in three months a tall hat and a chapel sitting; before the end of the year he will shake hands with a duchess at a Primrose League meeting, and join the Conservative Party.

BARBARA: And will he be the better for that?

UNDERSHAFT: You know he will. Dont be a hypocrite, Barbara. He will be better fed, better housed, better clothed, better behaved; and his children will be pounds heavier and bigger. That will be better than an American cloth mattress in a shelter, chopping firewood, eating bread and treacle, and being forced to kneel down from time to time to thank heaven for it: knee drill, I think you call it. It is cheap work converting starving men with a Bible in one hand and a slice of bread in the other. I will undertake to convert West Ham to Mahometanism on the same terms. Try your hand on my men: their souls are hungry because their bodies are full.

BARBARA: And leave the east end to starve?

UNDERSHAFT (*his energetic tone dropping into one of bitter and brooding remembrance*): I was an east ender. I moralized and starved until one day I swore that I would be a full-fed free man at all costs; that nothing should stop me except a bullet, neither reason nor morals nor the lives of other men. I said 'Thou shalt starve ere I starve'; and with that word I became free and great. I was a dangerous man until I had my will: now I am a useful, beneficent, kindly person. That is the history of most self-made millionaires, I fancy. When it is the history of every Englishman we shall have an England worth living in.

LADY BRITOMART: Stop making speeches, Andrew. This is not the place for them.

UNDERSHAFT (*punctured*): My dear: I have no other means of conveying my ideas.

LADY BRITOMART: Your ideas are nonsense. You got on because you were selfish and unscrupulous.

UNDERSHAFT: Not at all. I had the strongest scruples about poverty and starvation. Your moralists are quite unscrupulous about both: they make virtues of them. I had rather be a thief than a pauper. I had rather be a murderer than a slave. I dont want to be either; but if you force the alternative on me, then, by Heaven, I'll choose the braver and more moral one. I hate poverty and slavery worse than any other crimes whatsoever. And let me tell you this. Poverty and slavery have stood up for centuries to your sermons and leading articles: they will not stand up to my machine guns. Dont preach at them: dont reason with them. Kill them.

BARBARA: Killing. Is that your remedy for everything?

UNDERSHAFT: It is the final test of conviction, the only lever strong enough to overturn a social system, the only way of saying Must. Let six hundred and seventy fools loose in the streets; and three policemen can scatter them. But huddle them together in a certain house in Westminster; and let them go through certain ceremonies and call themselves certain names until at last they get the courage to kill; and your six hundred and seventy fools become a government. Your pious mob fills up ballot papers and imagines it is governing its masters; but the ballot paper that really governs is the paper that has a bullet wrapped up in it.

CUSINS: That is perhaps why, like most intelligent people, I never vote.

UNDERSHAFT: Vote! Bah! When you vote, you only change the names of the cabinet. When you shoot, you pull down governments, inaugurate new epochs, abolish old orders and set up new. Is that historically true, Mr Learned Man, or is it not?

CUSINS: It is historically true. I loathe having to admit it. I repudiate your sentiments. I abhor your nature. I defy you in every possible way. Still, it is true. But it ought not to be true.

UNDERSHAFT: Ought! ought! ought! ought! ought! Are you going to spend your life saying ought, like the rest of our moralists? Turn your oughts into shalls, man. Come and make explosives with me. Whatever can blow men up can blow society up. The history of the world is the history of those who had courage enough to embrace this truth. Have you the courage to embrace it, Barbara?

LADY BRITOMART: Barbara: I positively forbid you to listen to your father's abominable wickedness. And you, Adolphus, ought to know better than to go about saying that wrong things are true. What does it matter whether they are true if they are wrong?

UNDERSHAFT: What does it matter whether they are wrong if they are true?

LADY BRITOMART (*rising*): Children: come home instantly. Andrew: I am exceedingly sorry I allowed you to call on us. You are wickeder than ever. Come at once.

BARBARA (*shaking her head*): It's no use running away from wicked people, mamma.

LADY BRITOMART: It is every use. It shews your disapprobation of them.

BARBARA: It does not save them.

LADY BRITOMART: I can see that you are going to disobey me. Sarah: are you coming home or are you not?

SARAH: I daresay it's very wicked of papa to make cannons; but I dont think I shall cut him on that account.

LOMAX (*pouring oil on the troubled waters*): The fact is, you know, there is a certain amount of tosh about this notion of wickedness. It doesnt work. You must look at facts. Not that I would say a word in favor of anything wrong; but then, you see, all sorts of chaps are always doing all sorts of things; and we have to fit them in somehow, dont you know. What I mean is that you cant go cutting everybody; and thats about what it comes to. (*Their rapt attention to his eloquence makes him nervous.*) Perhaps I dont make myself clear.

LADY BRITOMART: You are lucidity itself, Charles. Because Andrew is successful and has plenty of money to give to Sarah, you will flatter him and encourage him in his wickedness.

LOMAX (*unruffled*): Well, where the carcase is, there will the eagles be gathered, dont you know. (*To* UNDERSHAFT.) Eh? What?

UNDERSHAFT: Precisely. By the way, may I call you Charles?

LOMAX: Delighted. Cholly is the usual ticket.

UNDERSHAFT (*to* LADY BRITOMART): Biddy —

LADY BRITOMART (*violently*): Dont dare call me Biddy. Charles Lomax: you are a fool. Adolphus Cusins: you are a Jesuit. Stephen: you are a prig. Barbara: you are a lunatic. Andrew: you are a vulgar tradesman. Now you all know my opinion; and my conscience is clear, at all events. (*She sits down with a vehemence that the rug fortunately softens.*)

UNDERSHAFT: My dear: you are the incarnation of morality. (*She snorts.*) Your conscience is clear and your duty done when you have called everybody names. Come, Euripides! It is getting late; and we all want to go home. Make up your mind.

CUSINS: Understand this, you old demon —

LADY BRITOMART: Adolphus!

UNDERSHAFT: Let him alone, Biddy. Proceed, Euripides.

CUSINS: You have me in a horrible dilemma. I want Barbara.

UNDERSHAFT: Like all young men, you greatly exaggerate the difference between one young woman and another.

BARBARA: Quite true, Dolly.

CUSINS: I also want to avoid being a rascal.

UNDERSHAFT (*with biting contempt*): You lust for personal righteousness, for self-approval, for what you call a good conscience, for what Barbara calls salvation, for what I call patronizing people who are not so lucky as yourself.

CUSINS: I do not: all the poet in me recoils from being a good man. But there are things in me that I must reckon with. Pity —

UNDERSHAFT: Pity! The scavenger of misery.

CUSINS: Well, love.

UNDERSHAFT: I know. You love the needy and the outcast: you love the oppressed races, the negro, the Indian ryot, the underdog everywhere. Do you love the Japanese? Do you love the English?

CUSINS: No. Every true Englishman detests the English. We are the wickedest nation on earth; and our success is a moral horror.

UNDERSHAFT: That is what comes of your gospel of love, is it?

CUSINS: May I not love even my father-in-law?

UNDERSHAFT: Who wants your love, man? By what right do you take the liberty of offering it to me? I will have your due heed and respect, or I will kill you. But your love! Damn your impertinence!

CUSINS (*grinning*): I may not be able to control my affections, Mac.

UNDERSHAFT: You are fencing, Euripides. You are weakening: your grip is slipping. Come! try your last weapon. Pity and love have broken in your hand: forgiveness is still left.

CUSINS: No: forgiveness is a beggar's refuge. I am with you there: we must pay our debts.

UNDERSHAFT: Well said. Come! you will suit me. Remember the words of Plato.

CUSINS (*starting*): Plato! You dare quote Plato to me!

UNDERSHAFT: Plato says, my friend, that society cannot be saved until either the Professors of Greek take to making gunpowder, or else the makers of gunpowder become Professors of Greek.

CUSINS: Oh, tempter, cunning tempter!

UNDERSHAFT: Come! choose, man, choose.

CUSINS: But perhaps Barbara will not marry me if I make the wrong choice.

BARBARA: Perhaps not.

CUSINS (*desperately perplexed*): You hear!

BARBARA: Father: do you love nobody?

UNDERSHAFT: I love my best friend.

LADY BRITOMART: And who is that, pray?

UNDERSHAFT: My bravest enemy. That is the man who keeps me up to the mark.

CUSINS: You know, the creature is really a sort of poet in his way. Suppose he is a great man, after all!

UNDERSHAFT: Suppose you stop talking and make up your mind, my young friend.

CUSINS: But you are driving me against my nature. I hate war.

UNDERSHAFT: Hatred is the coward's revenge for being intimidated. Dare you make war on war? Here are the means: my friend Mr Lomax is sitting on them.

LOMAX (*springing up*): Oh I say! You dont mean that this thing is loaded, do you? My ownest: come off it.

SARAH (*sitting placidly on the shell*): If I am to be blown up, the more thoroughly it is done the better. Dont fuss, Cholly.

LOMAX (*to* UNDERSHAFT, *strongly remonstrant*): Your own daughter, you know!

UNDERSHAFT: So I see. (*To* CUSINS.) Well, my friend, may we expect you here at six tomorrow morning?

CUSINS (*firmly*): Not on any account. I will see the whole establishment blown up with its own dynamite before I will get up at five. My hours are healthy, rational hours: eleven to five.

UNDERSHAFT: Come when you please: before a week you will come at six and stay until I turn you out for the sake of your health. (*Calling.*) Bilton! (*He turns to* LADY BRITOMART, *who rises.*) My dear: let us leave these

two young people to themselves for a moment. (BILTON *comes from the shed.*) I am going to take you through the gun cotton shed.

BILTON (*barring the way*): You cant take anything explosive in here, sir.

LADY BRITOMART: What do you mean? Are you alluding to me?

BILTON (*unmoved*): No, maam. Mr Undershaft has the other gentleman's matches in his pocket.

LADY BRITOMART (*abruptly*): Oh! I beg your pardon. (*She goes into the shed.*)

UNDERSHAFT: Quite right, Bilton, quite right: here you are. (*He gives* BILTON *the box of matches.*) Come, Stephen. Come, Charles. Bring Sarah. (*He passes into the shed.*)

(BILTON *opens the box and deliberately drops the matches into the fire-bucket.*)

LOMAX: Oh! I say. (BILTON *stolidly hands him the empty box.*) Infernal nonsense! Pure scientific ignorance! (*He goes in.*)

SARAH: Am I all right, Bilton?

BILTON: Youll have to put on list slippers, miss: thats all. Weve got em inside. (*She goes in.*)

STEPHEN (*very seriously to* CUSINS): Dolly, old fellow, think. Think before you decide. Do you feel that you are a sufficiently practical man? It is a huge undertaking, an enormous responsibility. All this mass of business will be Greek to you.

CUSINS: Oh, I think it will be much less difficult than Greek.

STEPHEN: Well, I just want to say this before I leave you to yourselves. Dont let anything I have said about right and wrong prejudice you against this great chance in life. I have satisfied myself that the business is one of the highest character and a credit to our country. (*Emotionally.*) I am very proud of my father. I — (*Unable to proceed, he presses* CUSINS' *hand and goes hastily into the shed, followed by* BILTON.)

(BARBARA *and* CUSINS, *left alone together, look at one another silently.*)

CUSINS: Barbara: I am going to accept this offer.

BARBARA: I thought you would.

CUSINS: You understand, dont you, that I had to decide without consulting you. If I had thrown the burden of the choice on you, you would sooner or later have despised me for it.

BARBARA: Yes: I did not want you to sell your soul for me any more than for this inheritance.

CUSINS: It is not the sale of my soul that troubles me: I have sold it too often to care about that. I have sold it for a professorship. I have sold it for an income. I have sold it to escape being imprisoned for refusing to pay taxes for hangmen's ropes and unjust wars and things that I abhor. What is all human conduct but the daily and hourly sale of our souls for trifles? What I am now selling it for is neither money nor position nor comfort, but for reality and for power.

BARBARA: You know that you will have no power, and that he has none.

CUSINS: I know. It is not for myself alone. I want to make power for the world.

BARBARA: I want to make power for the world too; but it must be spiritual power.

CUSINS: I think all power is spiritual: these cannons will not go off by themselves. I have tried to make spiritual power by teaching Greek. But the world can never be really touched by a dead language and a dead civilization. The people must have power; and the people cannot have Greek. Now the power that is made here can be wielded by all men.

BARBARA: Power to burn women's houses down and kill their sons and tear their husbands to pieces.

CUSINS: You cannot have power for good without having power for evil too. Even mother's milk nourishes murderers as well as heroes. This power which only tears men's bodies to pieces has never been so horribly abused as the intellectual power, the imaginative power, the poetic, religious power that can enslave men's souls. As a teacher of Greek I gave the intellectual man weapons against the common man. I now want to give the common man weapons against the intellectual man. I love the common people. I want to arm them against the lawyers, the doctors, the priests, the literary men, the professors, the artists, and the politicians, who, once in authority, are more disastrous and tyrannical than all the fools, rascals, and impostors. I want a power simple enough for common men to use, yet strong enough to force the intellectual oligarchy to use its genius for the general good.

BARBARA: Is there no higher power than that (*pointing to the shell*)?

CUSINS: Yes; but that power can destroy the higher powers just as a tiger can destroy a man: therefore Man must master that power first. I admitted this when the Turks and Greeks were last at war. My best pupil went out to fight for Hellas. My parting gift to him was not a copy of Plato's Republic, but a revolver and a hundred Undershaft cartridges. The blood of every Turk he shot — if he shot any — is on my head as well as on Undershaft's. That act committed me to this place for ever. Your father's challenge has beaten me. Dare I make war on war? I must. I will. And now, is it all over between us?

BARBARA (*touched by his evident dread of her answer*): Silly baby Dolly! How could it be!

CUSINS (*overjoyed*): Then you — you — you — Oh for my drum! (*He flourishes imaginary drumsticks.*)

BARBARA (*angered by his levity*): Take care, Dolly, take care. Oh, if only I could get away from you and from father and from it all! if I could have the wings of a dove and fly away to heaven!

CUSINS: And leave me!

BARBARA: Yes, you, and all the other naughty mischievous children of men. But I cant. I was happy in the Salvation Army for a moment. I escaped from the world into a paradise of enthusiasm and prayer and soul saving; but the moment our money ran short, it all came back to Bodger: it was he who saved our people: he, and the Prince of Darkness, my papa. Undershaft and Bodger: their hands stretch everywhere: when we feed a starving fellow creature, it is with their bread, because there is no other bread; when we tend the sick, it is in the hospitals they endow; if we turn from the churches they build, we must kneel on the stones of the streets they pave. As long as that lasts, there is no getting away from them. Turning our backs on Bodger and Undershaft is turning our backs on life.

CUSINS: I thought you were determined to turn your back on the wicked side of life.

BARBARA: There is no wicked side: life is all one. And I never wanted to shirk my share in whatever evil must be endured, whether it be sin or suffering. I wish I could cure you of middle-class ideas, Dolly.

CUSINS (*gasping*): Middle cl — ! A snub! A social snub to me! from the daughter of a foundling!

BARBARA: That is why I have no class, Dolly: I come straight out of the heart of the whole people. If I were middle-class I should turn my back on my father's business; and we should both live in an artistic drawing room, with you reading the reviews in one corner, and I in the other at the piano, playing Schumann: both very superior persons, and neither of us a bit of use. Sooner than that, I would sweep out the guncotton shed, or be one of Bodger's barmaids. Do you know what would have happened if you had refused papa's offer?

CUSINS: I wonder!

BARBARA: I should have given you up and married the man who accepted it. After all, my dear old mother has more sense than any of you. I felt like her when I saw this place — felt that I must have it — that never, never, never could I let it go; only she thought it was the houses and the kitchen ranges and the linen and china, when it was really all the human souls to be saved: not weak souls in starved bodies, sobbing with gratitude for a scrap of bread and treacle, but fullfed, quarrelsome, snobbish, uppish creatures, all standing on their little rights and dignities, and thinking that my father ought to be greatly obliged to them for making so much money for him — and so he ought. That is where salvation is really wanted. My father shall never throw it in my teeth again that my converts were bribed with bread. (*She is transfigured.*) I have got rid of the bribe of bread. I have got rid of the bribe of heaven. Let God's work be done for its own sake: the work he had to create us to do because it cannot be done except by living men and women. When I die, let him be in my debt, not I in his; and let me forgive him as becomes a woman of my rank.

CUSINS: Then the way of life lies through the factory of death?

BARBARA: Yes, through the raising of hell to heaven and of man to God, through the unveiling of an eternal light in the Valley of The Shadow. (*Seizing him with both hands.*)

Oh, did you think my courage would never come back? did you believe that I was a deserter? that I, who have stood in the streets, and taken my people to my heart, and talked of the holiest and greatest things with them, could ever turn back and chatter foolishly to fashionable people about nothing in a drawing room? Never, never, never, never: Major Barbara will die with the colors. Oh! and I have my dear little Dolly boy still; and he has found me my place and my work. Glory Hallelujah! (*She kisses him.*)

CUSINS: My dearest: consider my delicate health. I cannot stand as much happiness as you can.

BARBARA: Yes: it is not easy work being in love with me, is it? But it's good for you. (*She runs to the shed, and calls, childlike.*) Mamma! Mamma! (BILTON *comes out of the shed, followed by* UNDERSHAFT.) I want Mamma.

UNDERSHAFT: She is taking off her list slippers, dear. (*He passes on to* CUSINS.) Well? What does she say?

CUSINS: She has gone right up into the skies.

LADY BRITOMART (*coming from the shed and stopping on the steps, obstructing* SARAH, *who follows with* LOMAX. BARBARA *clutches like a baby at her mother's skirt*): Barbara: when will you learn to be independent and to act and think for yourself? I know as well as possible what that cry of 'Mamma, Mamma,' means. Always running to me!

SARAH (*touching* LADY BRITOMART'*s ribs with her finger tips and imitating a bicycle horn*): Pip! pip!

LADY BRITOMART (*highly indignant*): How dare you say Pip! pip! to me, Sarah? You are both very naughty children. What do you want, Barbara?

BARBARA: I want a house in the village to live in with Dolly. (*Dragging at the skirt.*) Come and tell me which one to take.

UNDERSHAFT (*to* CUSINS): Six o'clock tomorrow morning, Euripides.

THE END

One of the earliest English remarks about comedy, Sir Philip Sidney's written about 1580, runs thus:

> Comedy is an imitation of the common errors of our life, which he representeth in the most ridiculous and scornful sort that may be; so that it is impossible that any beholder can be content to be such a one.

Sidney is indebted to Italian commentators, who in turn are indebted to Roman commentators, and behind them are the Greeks, notably Aristotle. Along the way, of course, there are lots of variations, but the basic ideas may fairly be said to constitute the "classical" theory of comedy:

1. The characters are ignoble
2. Their actions arouse derision (rather than, say, terror or pity)
3. The spectators, if they have resembled the dramatis personae, leave the theater morally improved after seeing the absurdity of such behavior.

The "classical" theory, often stated before Sidney, has since been restated at least as often. Almost every comic dramatist who has commented on his work has offered it as his justification. Shaw, in a preface to his *Complete Plays*, put it thus:

> If I make you laugh at yourself, remember that my business as a classic writer of comedies is "to chasten morals with ridicule"; and if I sometimes make you feel like a fool, remember that I have by the same action cured your folly, just as the dentist cures your toothache by pulling out your tooth. And I never do it without giving you plenty of laughing gas.

To begin with the laughing gas in *Major Barbara*: the first act suggests that the play is a drawing-room comedy, full of aristocratic people bouncing elegant lines off each other. (Lady Brit, of course, affects innocence, but she is accomplished at getting what she wants.) Sample:

> I am not a Pharisee, I hope; and I should not have minded his merely doing wrong things: we are none of us perfect. But your father didnt exactly do wrong things: he said them and thought them: that was what was so dreadful. He really had a sort of religion of wrongness. Just as one doesnt mind men practising immorality so long as they own that they are in the wrong by preaching morality; so I couldnt forgive Andrew for preaching immorality while he practised morality.

Another sample:

> CUSINS: Let me advise you to study Greek, Mr. Undershaft. Greek scholars are privileged men. Few of them know Greek; and none of them know anything else; but their position is unchallengeable. Other languages are the qualifications of waiters and commercial travellers: Greek is to a man of position what the hallmark is to silver.

If Shaw had been content to write a comedy in the classical tradition, he would have contrived a plot which would probably have involved an unsuitable wooer of Barbara, maybe a rich old aristocrat, maybe a parvenu, maybe a fortune hunter, who would finally be unmasked and then displaced by an ap-

propriately young and charming and socially acceptable bridegroom. But Shaw
turned to comedy as a propagandist. He had been deeply impressed by Ibsen's
plays, and he saw in the drama an opportunity to preach his economic ideas to
a wider audience than is normally reached by the pamphleteer. For Shaw, the
heart of Ibsen's plays lies in such a "discussion" as the one in A Doll's House,
where Nora explains to her husband that things are all wrong in their apparently happy marriage. (The interested reader is advised to look at Shaw's The
Quintessence of Ibsenism, especially the next to the last chapter, "The Technical Novelty," which insists that post-Ibsen plays must replace the old formula
of exposition-situation-unraveling with "exposition, situation, and discussion;
and the discussion is the test of the playwright. . . . The serious playwright
recognizes not only the main test of his highest powers, but also the real center
of his play's interest.")

What Shaw does, then, is introduce massive discussions into a comedy
that at first seems to be doing little more than spoofing Lady Brit and holding
her son Stephen up to rather obvious ridicule. Stephen is not merely an ass; he
is made to serve as a sort of straightman for Undershaft, who expounds at
length unconventional ideas about munitions, sin, power, and poverty. These
ideas require discussion because Shaw, unlike most comic writers, is not content with the traditional views. Comic playwrights usually criticize eccentric
behavior, and at least implicitly suggest that there is a reasonable norm,
known to all men of sense, from which fools depart. But because Shaw believed that society's norm is itself foolish, he devotes much of his play to ex-
pounding a new creed. Shaw reverses the old joke about the entire platoon
being out of step except Johnny; for Shaw, the deviant, Johnny, is in step, and
the rest of the platoon is laughably out of step. During the central part of
Major Barbara, then, Undershaft, the eccentric, is for Shaw the least laughable character. Even Barbara, the heroine, is exposed as a fool, though with
great tenderness, and is forced to shed her conventional illusions. So great is
the tenderness that as we see her world collapse, she seems almost a tragic
figure:

> I stood on the rock I thought eternal; and without a word of warning it
> reeled and crumbled under me.

But Undershaft dispels the tragedy, harshly but necessarily, with, "Come,
come, my daughter! dont make too much of your little tinpot tragedy. . . .
Dont persist in that folly. If your old religion broke down yesterday, get a
newer and a better one for tomorrow."

Enough has been said to give some idea of the novelty of Shaw's comic
practice, however conventional his theory. But one should note, too, that in
one important way his practice is conventional: his plays have the stock quack
doctors, pompous statesmen, dragonlike matrons, and young lovers of traditional comedy. And in Major Barbara he even uses the ancient motif of the
foundling who proves to be a suitable husband for the heroine.

Something more, however, must be said of Undershaft. Having allowed Undershaft to triumph over Barbara, Shaw does not stop; very late in the play Undershaft himself is threatened with the loss of *his* illusions when Barbara and Adolphus Cusins will make their presence felt in the munitions factory. The play ends with the usual marriage, joy, and promise of a newly organized society; in its suggestion, however, that this new society is not a return to a sensible world that was lost before the play began (think, for example, of the end of *As You Like It*, where the duke is restored to his realm), but rather is the beginning of a totally new sort of world, it marks a departure from comic practice. Maybe that is why the end of the play has seemed to most audiences the least amusing part.

The Comic Rhythm

Susanne K. Langer

In Boswell's *Life of Doctor Johnson* we hear of a man who intended to be a philosopher but who failed because "cheerfulness was always breaking in." Susanne K. Langer is a philosopher, but she does not see cheerfulness as an enemy. She sees in comedy a dramatization of the basic biological patterns of persistence and growth, "human vitality holding its own in the world amid the surprises of unplanned coincidence."

The pure sense of life is the underlying feeling of comedy, developed in countless different ways. To give a general phenomenon one name is not to make all its manifestations one thing, but only to bring them conceptually under one head. Art does not generalize and classify; art sets forth the individuality of forms which discourse, being essentially general, has to suppress. The sense of life is always new, infinitely complex, therefore infinitely variable in its possible expressions. This sense, or "enjoyment" as Alexander would call it,[1] is the realization in direct feeling of what sets organic nature apart from inorganic: self-preservation, self-restoration, functional tendency, purpose. Life is teleological, the rest of nature is, apparently, mechanical; to maintain the pattern of vitality in a non-living universe is the most elementary instinctual purpose. An organism tends to keep its equilibrium amid the bombardment of aimless forces that beset it, to regain equilibrium when it has been disturbed, and to pursue a sequence of actions dictated by the need of keeping all its interdependent parts constantly renewed, their structure intact. Only organisms have needs; lifeless objects whirl or slide or tumble about, are shattered and scattered, stuck together,

[1] S. Alexander, *Space, Time and Deity.* See Vol. I, p. 12.

piled up, without showing any impulse to return to some pre-eminent condition and function. But living things strive to persist in a particular chemical balance, to maintain a particular temperature, to repeat particular functions, and to develop along particular lines, achieving a growth that seems to be preformed in their earliest, rudimentary, protoplasmic structure.

That is the basic biological pattern which all living things share: the round of conditioned and conditioning organic processes that produces the life rhythm. When this rhythm is disturbed, all activities in the total complex are modified by the break; the organism as a whole is out of balance. But, within a wide range of conditions, it struggles to retrieve its original dynamic form by overcoming and removing the obstacle, or if this proves impossible, it develops a slight variation of its typical form and activity and carries on life with a new balance of functions — in other words, it adapts itself to the situation. A tree, for instance, that is bereft of the sunshine it needs by the encroachment of other trees, tends to grow tall and thin until it can spread its own branches in the light. A fish that has most of its tail bitten off partly overcomes the disturbance of its locomotion patterns by growing new tissue, replacing some of the tail, and partly adapts to its new condition by modifying the normal uses of its fins, swimming effectively without trying to correct the list of its whole body in the water, as it did at first.

But the impulse to survive is not spent only in defense and accommodation; it appears also in the varying power of organisms to seize on opportunities. Consider how chimney swifts, which used to nest in crevasses among rocks, have exploited the products of human architecture, and how unfailingly mice find the warmth and other delights of our kitchens. All creatures live by opportunities, in a world fraught with disasters. That is the biological pattern in most general terms. . . .

Mankind has its rhythm of animal existence, too — the strain of maintaining a vital balance amid the alien and impartial chances of the world, complicated and heightened by passional desires. The pure sense of life springs from that basic rhythm, and varies from the composed well-being of sleep to the intensity of spasm, rage, or ecstasy. But the process of living is incomparably more complex for human beings than for even the highest animals; man's world is, above all, intricate and puzzling. The powers of language and imagination have set it utterly apart from that of other creatures. In human society an individual is not, like a member of a herd or a hive, exposed only to others that visibly or tangibly surround him, but is consciously bound to people who are absent, perhaps far away, at the moment. Even the dead may still play into his life. His awareness of events is far greater than the scope of his physical perceptions. Symbolic construction has made this vastly involved and extended world: and mental adroitness is his chief asset for exploiting it. The pattern of his vital feeling, therefore, reflects his deep emotional relation to those symbolic structures that are his realities, and his instinctual life modified in almost every way by thought — a brainy opportunism in face of an essentially dreadful universe.

This human life-feeling is the essence of comedy. It is at once religious and ribald, knowing and defiant, social and freakishly individual. The illusion of life which the comic poet creates is the oncoming future fraught with dangers and opportunities, that is, with physical or social events occurring by chance and building up the coincidences with which individuals cope according to their lights. This ineluctable future — ineluctable because its countless factors are beyond human knowledge and control — is Fortune. Destiny in the guise of Fortune is the fabric of comedy; it is developed by comic action, which is the upset and recovery of the protagonist's equilibrium, his contest with the world and his triumph by wit, luck, personal power, or even humorous, or ironical, or philosophical acceptance of mischance. Whatever the theme — serious and lyrical as in *The Tempest*, coarse slapstick as in the *Schwänke* of Hans Sachs, or clever and polite social satire — the immediate sense of life is the underlying feeling of comedy, and dictates its rhythmically structured unity, that is to say its organic form.

Comedy is an art form that arises naturally wherever people are gathered to celebrate life, in spring festivals, triumphs, birthdays, weddings, or initiations. For it expresses the elementary strains and resolutions of animate nature, the animal drives that persist even in human nature, the delight man takes in his special mental gifts that make him the lord of creation; it is an image of human vitality holding its own in the world amid the surprises of unplanned coincidence. The most obvious occasions for the performance of comedies are thanks or challenges to fortune. What justifies the term "Comedy" is not that the ancient ritual procession, the Comus, honoring the god of that name, was the source of this great art form — for comedy has arisen in many parts of the world, where the Greek god with his particular worship was unknown — but that the Comus was a fertility rite, and the god it celebrated a fertility god, a symbol of perpetual rebirth, eternal life. . . .

Because comedy abstracts, and reincarnates for our perception, the motion and rhythm of living, it enhances our vital feeling, much as the presentation of space in painting enhances our awareness of visual space. The virtual life on the stage is not diffuse and only half felt, as actual life usually is: virtual life, always moving visibly into the future, is intensified, speeded up, exaggerated; the exhibition of vitality rises to a breaking point, to mirth and laughter. We laugh in the theater at small incidents and drolleries which would hardly rate a chuckle offstage. It is not for such psychological reasons that we go there to be amused, nor are we bound by rules of politeness to hide our hilarity, but these trifles at which we laugh are really funnier *where they occur* than they would be elsewhere; they are employed in the play, not merely brought in casually. They occur where the tension of dialogue or other action reaches a high point. As thought breaks into speech — as the wave breaks into form — vitality breaks into humor.

Humor is the brilliance of drama, a sudden heightening of the vital rhythm. A good comedy, therefore, builds up to every laugh; a performance that has been filled up with jokes at the indiscretion of the comedian or of his writer may draw a long series of laughs, yet leave the spectator without any clear impression of a very funny play. The laughs, moreover, are likely to be of a peculiar sameness, almost perfunctory, the formal recognition of a timely "gag."

The amoral character of the comic protagonist goes through the whole range of what may be called the comedy of laughter. Even the most civilized products of this art — plays that George Meredith would honor with the name of "comedy," because they provoke "thoughtful laughter" — do not present moral distinctions and issues, but only the ways of wisdom and of folly. Aristophanes, Menander, Molière — practically the only authors this most exacting of critics admitted as truly comic poets — are not moralists, yet they do not flout or deprecate morality; they have, literally, "no use" for moral principles — that is, they do not use them. Meredith, like practically all his contemporaries, labored under the belief that poetry must teach society lessons, and that comedy was valuable for what it revealed concerning the social order.[2] He tried hard to hold its exposé of foibles and vindication of common sense to an ethical standard, yet in his very efforts to jus-

[2] His well-known little work is called *An Essay on Comedy, and the Uses of the Comic Spirit.* These uses are entirely non-artistic. Praising the virtues of "good sense" (which is whatever has survival value in the eyes of society), he says: "The French have a school of stately comedy to which they can fly for renovation whenever they have fallen away from it; and their having such a school is the main reason why, as John Stuart Mill pointed out, they know men and women more accurately than we do." And a few pages later: "The *Femmes Savantes* is a capital instance of the uses of comedy in teaching the world to understand what ails it. The French had felt the burden of this new nonsense [the fad of academic learning, new after the fad of excessive nicety and precision in speech, that had marked the *Précieuses*]; but they had to see the comedy several times before they were consoled in their suffering by seeing the cause of it exposed."

tify its amoral personages he only admitted their amoral nature, and their simple relish for life, as when he said: "The heroines of comedy are like women of the world, not necessarily heartless from being clear-sighted. . . . Comedy is an exhibition of their battle with men, and that of men with them. . . ."

There it is, in a nutshell: the contest of men and women — the most universal contest, humanized, in fact civilized, yet still the primitive joyful challenge, the self-preservation and self-assertion whose progress is the comic rhythm. . . .

The same impulse that drove people, even in prehistoric times, to enact fertility rites and celebrate all phases of their biological existence, sustains their eternal interest in comedy. It is in the nature of comedy to be erotic, risqué, and sensuous if not sensual, impious, and even wicked. This assures it a spontaneous emotional interest, yet a dangerous one: for it is easy and tempting to command an audience by direct stimulation of feeling and fantasy, not by artistic power. But where the formulation of feeling is really achieved, it probably reflects the whole development of mankind and man's world, for feeling is the intaglio image of reality. The sense of precariousness that is the typical tension of light comedy was undoubtedly developed in the eternal struggle with chance that every farmer knows only too well — with weather, blights, beasts, birds and beetles. The embarrassments, perplexities and mounting panic which characterize that favorite genre, comedy of manners, may still reflect the toils of ritual and taboo that complicated the caveman's existence. Even the element of aggressiveness in comic action serves to develop a fundamental trait of the comic rhythm — the deep cruelty of it, as all life feeds on life. There is no biological truth that feeling does not reflect, and that good comedy, therefore, will not be prone to reveal.

But the fact that the rhythm of comedy is the basic rhythm of life does not mean that biological existence is the "deeper meaning" of all its themes, and that to understand the play is to interpret all the characters as symbols and the story as a parable, a disguised rite of spring or fertility magic, performed four hundred and fifty times on Broadway. The stock characters are probably symbolic both in origin and in appeal. There are such independently symbolic factors, or residues of them, in all the arts,[3] but their value for art lies in the degree to which

[3] E.g., the symbolization of the zodiac in some sacred architecture, of our bodily orientation in the picture plane, or of walking measure, a primitive measure of actual time, in music. But a study of such non-artistic symbolic functions would require a monograph.

their significance can be "swallowed" by the single symbol, the art work. Not the derivation of personages and situations, but of the rhythm of "felt life" that the poet puts upon them, seems to me to be of artistic importance: the essential comic feeling, which is the sentient aspect of organic unity, growth, and self-preservation.

The Rise and Fall of the Custard Pie

Richard Boston

Richard Boston's recent essay on comedy is included here mainly for three reasons: first, it offers a fine modification to the prevailing view (most fully stated by Henri Bergson, and summarized in the introduction to this book) that comic figures usually act mechanically; second, it is one of the very few essays on comic movies that actually gets to some of the sources of their comedy; third, the essay is good reading.

Cinema specialists among my colleagues at the National Institute of Joke Research (a fine body of men, cruelly starved of funds) tell me that Mack Sennett invented what they call "face-pie contact." Ignoring the great weight of their authority, however, I prefer to believe a different, and apparently fallacious, version which has the delightful Mabel Normand enlivening a dull scene with a piece of improvisation that was to have incalculable consequences. In this account the recipient of that first, epoch-making pie was the face of Ben Turpin, and the cream of the jest, so to speak, must have been the moment when the pie was wiped away to reveal the Sartrean strabismus of that comedian's astonished and astonishing eyes.

After that nothing was ever quite the same again. An endless barrage of pies flew across the sets, studios, and screens of the world into the faces of policemen, firemen, bankers, men in top hats, men in bowler hats, tramps, or just anyone who happened to be around. "I figured up once," said Snub Pollard, "I have caught about 14,000 pies in my puss." (He was also hit by 600 automobiles.)

What did people laugh at before the custard pie? "Some hunchbacks, for instance, will excite laughter." Thus Bergson in 1900. "What is there comic about a rubicund nose?" he asks, "And why does one laugh at a Negro?" "A

Reprinted by permission of the author from the *Times Literary Supplement*, June 18, 1971.

man, running along the street, stumbles and falls: the passers-by burst out laughing." I can understand an audience laughing, helplessly, at Chaplin or Buster Keaton impersonating a man falling over, but whenever I have witnessed such a scene in real life it has invariably elicited from bystanders only sympathy and assistance. Perhaps this is one of those changes of taste, like no longer being able to laugh at the torments of Malvolio (though as recently as 1969 Raymond Durgnat was writing " . . . if you slip on a banana-skin, I find that highly comic. . ."). Laughter implies a withdrawal of sympathy from whatever is being laughed at. We laugh at Buster Keaton falling because we know that we needn't worry about his getting hurt, that we can withhold sympathy from him with a clear conscience, and that he will jump up like a rubber ball and start running again.

Those who don't find falling men, red noses, Negroes, and hunchbacks funny may also have certain reservations about the analysis Bergson makes on the assumption that they are. Fortunately these examples are not central to his case. Bergson's axiom — that the attitudes, gestures and movements of the human body are laughable in proportion to the amount they remind us of a machine — at first sight looks like an accurate anticipation of Keaton's style. There *is* something non-human about Keaton. That blank, expressionless face belongs to a statue rather than a living being, and when he walks the stiff, jerky movements of the arms and legs are more like those of a robot than a man. To quote James Agee:

> When he swept a semaphorelike arm to point, you could almost hear the electrical impulse in the signal block. When he ran from a cop his transitions from accelerating walk to easy jogtrot to brisk canter to headlong gallop to flogged-piston sprint — always floating, above this frenzy, the untroubled, untouchable face — were as distinct and as soberly in order as an automatic gearshift.

There is a scene in *The Navigator* which shows Keaton behaving in a completely automatic manner which would have had Bergson doubled up. Keaton puts on a deep-sea-diving suit and goes down on the sea-bed to do some repairs to the ship. Having put up a "Men at work" sign, he fills a bucket, underwater, washes his hands, and then *empties the bucket*.

On the other hand, in refutation of Bergson, the moments when Keaton is at his funniest are precisely those when he *ceases* to be machine-like; when, for example, he escapes from danger in a way that is not only intelligent, resourceful, graceful and unexpected but also totally human. Bergson's evolutionary view that it is witnessing a machine-like failure to adapt that causes laughter is contradicted every time an audience laughs at the marvellous ingenuity with which Keaton faces new and unexpected circumstances.

As in a dream, the world of silent comedy is one in which the normal laws of the universe have been suspended. Inanimate objects take on a life of their own: cars, garden rakes, ladders, wardrobes, folding beds, boats, pianos, planks of wood, hose-pipes, brick walls, and of course custard pies exist only to bring about man's downfall (or pratfall). It is a world in which, not quite in Emerson's sense, "Things are in the saddle and ride mankind." The presence of Keaton, Chaplin, Laurel and Hardy, Harold Lloyd, Ben Turpin, or Fatty Arbuckle ensures that things will fall apart, and neither the centre nor anything else can hold. In the crossfire of flying pies, crashing cars and headlong policemen, mere anarchy is loosed upon the world.

As in a dream, our normal waking feelings are suspended. The most appalling things can happen to screen comedians (or such animated characters as Tom and Jerry) without any sympathy being aroused even in the most tender-hearted. It is here that Chaplin, who moves in and out of reality, tends to leave people rather confused about his work. (Another reason is that opportunities to see his films are so rare.) Chaplin's incomparable gifts as a mime, his agility, his timing, his inventiveness, these are all recognized. What is hard to take is when he asks us at one moment to laugh as he is thrown down a flight of stairs, and at the next to weep when the girl rejects him. Chaplin's work is all flawed by this appeal for sympathy, which is precisely what the audience must withhold from any clown-figure. There are wonderful moments in Chaplin, but they are *only* moments because the comic vision is destroyed the moment we feel sorry for him. We never *pity* Keaton, and this is one reason why Keaton's reputation has gone up in recent years at the expense of Chaplin's. Nor do we pity Max Linder or Jacques Tati. We most certainly never pity Groucho, Harpo, or Chico.

The films of the great clown-comedians are also dream-like in their subversiveness. Everything that is repressed in the waking world is let out to run riot. They are subversive on a straight political level; the preferred targets of the pies are the faces of policemen, fathers-in-law, men in top hats, or any other emblem of authority or representative of capitalism. The bowler hats of Chaplin and Laurel and Hardy are as far as they ever manage to get by way of behaving like ordinary, orderly, respectable, middle-class people. *Duck Soup* was banned in Mussolini's Italy. Jacques Tati, in his early films anyway, is supremely an agent of chaos in the social order. There is a scene in *Les Vacances de Monsieur Hulot* where he is waiting for someone, alone, in an empty room. He starts, if I remember rightly, by straightening the angle of a picture on the wall. In a few minutes, with no assistance but the riding-crop tucked under his arm, he has reduced the room to a shambles.

The uptight Superegoist values of bourgeois respectability are directly confronted by the free libidinous clown in Renoir's *Boudu Sauvé des eaux*. A *clochard*, Boudu, beautifully played by the irresistibly repulsive Michel Simon, jumps in the Seine and is saved from drowning by a book-dealer, who takes the tramp into his own home, feeds him, has him washed and shaved, gives him smart clean clothes and accommodation. This Samaritan-like behaviour is rewarded by Boudu's climbing ape-like over the furniture, spitting on the carpet, wiping his shoes on the bedcovers, and seducing the man's wife. When Boudu is upbraided for this behaviour, he replies unanswerably that he didn't ask to be pulled out of the river. Still, he is a kind fellow at heart and sorry to have upset the book-dealer. He will no longer spit on the carpet. In an unforgettable image we see him take from a book case a precious, leatherbound volume, open it in the middle, spit into it, shut the book and replace it on the shelf.

Renoir's is a gentle vision, which is not how one could describe the Marx Brothers. I have said that one never pities them, and they themselves are pitiless. They attack government (*Duck Soup*), education (*Horse Feathers*), and high society (all the time). There is something pre-human about them. I imagine that *homo australopithecus* walked with something like Groucho's loose-limbed, close-to-the-ground stride; an upright posture has been adopted but options are being kept open on a return to the quadruped in case two legs turn out to be insufficient after all.

And Harpo's dumbness is not simply a physical matter. Rather he seems to have come from an age before the invention of language, a time when people communicated with a range of squeaks and grunts and the other noises that Harpo is able to whistle or hoot. Not that his dumbness in any way inconveniences him. A pair of scissors is all he needs to get the better of whoever he happens to come across, snipping off beards, ties, hat-brims, coat-tails, skirts, or anything else his wild eyes fall upon.

Groucho, by contrast, is all talk, and in his verbal assault on the universe (the refrain of one of his songs is, "Whatever it is, I'm against it") he is as all-conquering as Harpo is physically. It is a typical inversion of waking logic that the only people who ever get the better of fast-talking Groucho are Harpo, who uses no words, and Chico, whose grasp on language is at best tenuous. A good example is the scene in *A Night at the Opera* where Chico and Groucho are negotiating a contract. Whenever one of them objects to a clause it is torn off the top of the piece of paper. Finally there is only one clause left. As Chico makes to tear this up too, Groucho checks him by pointing out that they have to keep that because it's the sanity clause. Chico replies: "You can'ta fool me. Dere ain't no Santy Claus," and tears it up.

Or take the scene in *Duck Soup* where Groucho, as Rufus T. Firefly, President of Freedonia, offers Chico a job in his Cabinet.

GROUCHO: How'd you like a job in the Mint?
CHICO: No . . . ah . . . Haven't you got any other flavour?
GROUCHO: Just for that you don't get the job I was going to offer you.
CHICO: What was it?
GROUCHO: Secretary of War.
CHICO: All right. I take it.
(They shake hands.)

That Laurel and Hardy have the bodies of grown men and happen to wear suits and bowler hats does not for long disguise the fact that they are really babies. Only very small boys could revel for so long in pushing one another into pools of mud. The fact that they so often share a bed signifies not their homosexuality but their pre-sexuality. What could be more infantile than their total delight in destruction, than Laurel's obsession with eating, or his "cry" face, or Hardy's egocentricity?

The Marx Brothers, however, go back further even than infancy. Humour without a sanity clause — their films are often described as "crazy" or "mad" — takes them back into the world of dream, madness and pre-human archetypes. What they are most like is Trickster. Joan Westcott ("The Sculpture and Myths of Eshu-Elegba, the Yoruba Trickster," *Africa* 22, 1962, pages 336–354) describes the Trickster as "a creature of instinct and great energy" one of whose functions is as a "rule-breaker . . . a spanner in the social works," which sounds much like Groucho. Paul Radin, writing of the Winnebago Trickster, describes his primary traits as "his voracious appetite, his wandering and his unbridled sexuality," a fair description of Harpo.

In the Winnebago Trickster myth which was collected by Sam Blowsnake of the Thunderbird clan in 1912 (see Paul Radin, *The Trickster: A Study in American Indian Mythology*), Trickster is able to change sex (cf. female impersonation in music hall and film comedy). His body is an assemblage of semi-autonomous units. His penis, for example, is carried in a box on his shoulder. On one occasion Trickster saw the Chief's daughter swimming on the opposite shore of a lake. He sent his penis swimming across the water to the other side where it lodged firmly in the girl and was only extracted with great difficulty.

Parts of Trickster's body can quarrel with one another. Trickster kills a buffalo with a knife held in his right hand. His left hand grabs the buffalo, and the right hand gets extremely cross. " 'Give that back to me, it's mine! Stop that or I will use my knife on you!' So spoke the right arm." The arms continue to quarrel, eventually fight and the left arm is badly cut.

Compare Trickster's behaviour with that of Harpo. In *Monkey Business* he sits down at the harp, plays a few unsatisfactory notes, looks disapprovingly at his left hand, unscrews it, throws it away, produces his real hand and starts playing properly. In the same film, in the Punch and Judy scene, he gives the illusion of being able to detach a whole leg. In all of his films it is a favourite gag of Harpo's to "give" his knee to other people. He also has a habit of putting his hand into other people's pockets — not always to steal things: often he seems unaware of which leg is his and which is someone else's. Like Trickster, Harpo is apparently able to communicate with animals, and his feeding habits are certainly more animal than human. "He's half goat," Chico explains. Harpo eats buttons, telephones, ties, and cigars with enjoyment.

Groucho too is Trickster-like in his inversions of logic and defiance of social norms. The beginning of the Winnebago Trickster myth is extraordinarily similar to the beginning of *Duck Soup*, but I will have to leave detailed comparison for some other time.

Though the Marx Brothers go furthest, there is something of Trickster to be found in all the great film comedians. But if I am right in thinking that behind them there is something archetypal, and therefore timeless, why is it apparently so difficult to make comedies at this particular time? For the dearth of funny films in recent years is undeniable.

The films of Jacques Tati may point to an answer. His first two films, made with low budgets in black and white, were among the funniest ever made. *Mon Oncle*, more lavish in scale, had hilarious moments but aroused doubts. These were confirmed by the enormously expensive *Playtime* (in which, by a set of curious chances, I myself acted a role) and now by his latest film, *Traffic*, which opened a couple of months ago in Paris.

The way in which the coming of sound ended an era of film comedy is well known. The same has happened again with the coming of wide screens, colour, stereophonic sound, and so on. Everything has become over-explicit, and the old economy, fluency, and ease are gone. Watching Tati at work one can see that he is highly inventive. I am not sure that one would guess this from his recent films. Every gag is painstakingly built up and has every drop squeezed from it as though it was some black-market delicacy in a time of severe food rationing. Compare this with the prodigality of the silent comedies. There are as many gags in five minutes of Keaton as in the whole of *Playtime*. But then people like Keaton, Chaplin, Harold Lloyd, and Laurel and Hardy made as many films in a year as Tati has made in his whole career (Max Linder made something like 400 films in less than ten years).

The prolific rate at which the early comedies were produced gave a freedom to improvise and experiment which is denied the expensive, cumbersome productions of today, when everything has to be done by the script, all carefully planned, and nothing left to the inspiration of the moment. For anything like the freedom of the classic comedies of the beginning of the century you have to look at hastily-produced, low-budget television comedies such as "Monty Python's Flying Circus."

Another reason for Tati's decline may be the subject matter. The rustic pastoral of *Jour de Fête* belongs to a completely different world from the urban industrialism of the three colour films. And there is not yet a comic vocabulary for dealing with this new world. The old images have gone stale or sour. There was quite a good pie fight in the Tony Curtis film *The Great Race*, but it looked more like an exercise in nostalgia than anything else. Keaton could get endless laughter out of situations involving motor-cars speeding, turning over, crashing, or falling apart. It is harder to laugh at Tati's *Traffic*, which is altogether too much like the street outside the cinema. We are too aware of the slaughter on the roads, and of the way traffic is ruining our cities, to find cars funny any longer. In the same way it is now hard to see policemen as the comic figures the Keystone Kops were when we are conscious that the behaviour of the police in Chicago and Paris and other cities has gone so far beyond a joke. When it really is a mad, mad, mad, mad world, and anyone can see that for himself, the comedian is out of business.

At the end of James Sully's *Essay on Laugh-*

ter the author writes gloomily that "the most cheerful of men would perhaps hardly call the present a mirthful moment," and sees "the decline of popular mirth" as "only a part of a larger change, the disappearance of the spirit of play, of a full self-abandonment to the mood of light entertainment. . . . Where is the fun, where is the gaiety, in the football and the cricket matches of today?" If this complaint sounds depressingly familiar, there may be a grain of comfort to be drawn from the fact that Sully's book was published in 1902.

TRAGICOMEDY

THE CHERRY ORCHARD

Anton Chekhov

Translated by Stark Young

Anton Chekhov (1860–1904) received his medical degree from the University of Moscow in 1884, but he had already published some stories. His belief that his medical training assisted him in writing about people caused some people to find him cold, but on the whole the evidence suggests that he was a genial, energetic young man with considerable faith in reason and (as befitted a doctor) in science, and with very little faith in religion and in heroics. His major plays are *The Seagull* (1896), *Uncle Vanya* (1899), *Three Sisters* (1901), and, finally, *The Cherry Orchard* (1903), written during his last illness.

CHARACTERS

RANEVSKAYA, LYUBOFF ANDREEVNA, *a landowner*
ANYA, *her daughter, seventeen years old*
VARYA, *her adopted daughter, twenty-four years old*
GAYEFF, LEONID ANDREEVICH, *brother of Ranevskaya*
LOPAHIN, YERMOLAY ALEXEEVICH, *a merchant*
TROFIMOFF, PYOTR SERGEEVICH, *a student*
SEMYONOFF-PISHTCHIK, BORIS BORISOVICH, *a landowner*
CHARLOTTA IVANOVNA, *a governess*
EPIHODOFF, SEMYON PANTELEEVICH, *a clerk*
DUNYASHA, *a maid*
FIERS, *a valet, an old man of eighty-seven*
YASHA, *a young valet*
A PASSERBY or STRANGER
THE STATIONMASTER
A POST-OFFICE CLERK
VISITORS, SERVANTS

Scene: The action takes place on the estate of L. A. RANEVSKAYA.

Act I of the original production of *The Cherry Orchard* in 1904. (Photograph reproduced from J. L. Styan, *Chekhov in Performance.* Copyright 1971 by Cambridge University Press.)

ACT I

A room that is still called the nursery. One of the doors leads into ANYA's *room. Dawn, the sun will soon be rising. It is May, the cherry trees are in blossom but in the orchard it is cold, with a morning frost. The windows in the room are closed. Enter* DUNYASHA *with a candle and* LOPAHIN *with a book in his hand.*

LOPAHIN: The train got in, thank God! What time is it?

DUNYASHA: It's nearly two. (*Blows out her candle.*) It's already daylight.

LOPAHIN: But how late was the train? Two hours at least. (*Yawning and stretching.*) I'm a fine one, I am, look what a fool thing I did! I drove here on purpose just to meet them at the station, and then all of a sudden I'd overslept myself! Fell asleep in my chair. How provoking! — You could have waked me up.

DUNYASHA: I thought you had gone. (*Listening.*) Listen, I think they are coming now.

LOPAHIN (*listening*): No — No, there's the luggage and one thing and another. (*A pause.*) Lyuboff Andreevna has been living abroad five years. I don't know what she is like now — She is a good woman. An easy-going, simple woman. I remember when I was a boy about fifteen, my father, who is at rest — in those days he ran a shop here in the village — hit me in the face with his fist, my nose was bleeding — We'd come to the yard together for something or other, and he was a little drunk. Lyuboff Andreevna, I can see her now, still so young, so slim, led me to the washbasin here in this very room, in the nursery. "Don't cry," she says, "little peasant, it will be well in time for your wedding" — (*A pause.*) Yes, little peasant — My father was a peasant truly, and here I am in a white waistcoat and yellow shoes. Like a pig rooting in a pastry shop — I've got this rich, lots of money, but if you really stop and think of it, I'm just a peasant — (*Turning the pages of a book.*) Here I was reading a book and didn't get a thing out of it. Reading and went to sleep. (*A pause.*)

DUNYASHA: And all night long the dogs were not asleep, they know their masters are coming.

LOPAHIN: What is it, Dunyasha, you're so —

DUNYASHA: My hands are shaking. I'm going to faint.

LOPAHIN: You're just so delicate, Dunyasha. And all dressed up like a lady, and your hair all done up! Mustn't do that. Must know your place.

(*Enter* EPIHODOFF, *with a bouquet: he wears a jacket and highly polished boots with a loud squeak. As he enters he drops the bouquet.*)

EPIHODOFF (*picking up the bouquet*): Look, the gardener sent these, he says to put them in the dining room. (*Giving the bouquet to* DUNYASHA.)

LOPAHIN: And bring me some kvass.

DUNYASHA: Yes, sir. (*Goes out.*)

EPIHODOFF: There is a morning frost now, three degrees of frost (*sighing*) and the cherries all in bloom. I cannot approve of our climate — I cannot. Our climate can never quite rise to the occasion. Listen, Yermolay Alexeevich, allow me to subtend, I bought myself, day before yesterday, some boots and they, I venture to assure you, squeak so that it is impossible. What could I grease them with?

LOPAHIN: Go on. You annoy me.

EPIHODOFF: Every day some misfortune happens to me. But I don't complain, I am used to it and I even smile.

(DUNYASHA *enters, serves* LOPAHIN *the kvass.*)

EPIHODOFF: I'm going. (*Stumbling over a chair and upsetting it.*) There (*as if triumphant*), there, you see, pardon the expression, a circumstance like that, among others — It is simply quite remarkable. (*Goes out.*)

DUNYASHA: And I must tell you, Yermolay Alexcevich, that Epihodoff has proposed to me.

LOPAHIN: Ah!

DUNYASHA: I don't know really what to — He is a quiet man but sometimes when he starts talking, you can't understand a thing he means. It's all very nice, and full of feeling, but just doesn't make any sense. I sort of like him. He loves me madly. He's a man that's unfortunate, every day there's something or other. They tease him around here, call him twenty-two misfortunes —

LOPAHIN (*cocking his ear*): Listen, I think they are coming —

DUNYASHA: They are coming! But what's the matter with me — I'm cold all over.

LOPAHIN: They're really coming. Let's go meet them. Will she recognize me? It's five years we haven't seen each other.

DUNYASHA (*excitedly*): I'm going to faint this very minute. Ah, I'm going to faint!

(*Two carriages can be heard driving up to the house.* LOPAHIN *and* DUNYASHA *hurry out. The stage is empty. In the adjoining rooms a noise begins.* FIERS *hurries across the stage, leaning on a stick; he has been to meet* LYUBOFF ANDREEVNA, *and wears an old-fashioned livery and a high hat; he mutters something to himself, but you cannot understand a word of it. The noise offstage gets louder and louder. A voice: "Look! Let's go through here —"* LYUBOFF ANDREEVNA, ANYA *and* CHARLOTTA IVANOVNA, *with a little dog on a chain, all of them dressed for traveling,* VARYA, *in a coat and kerchief,* GAYEFF, SEMYONOFF-PISHTCHIK, LOPAHIN, DUNYASHA, *with a bundle and an umbrella,* SERVANTS *with pieces of luggage — all pass through the room.*)

ANYA: Let's go through here. Mama, do you remember what room this is?

LYUBOFF ANDREEVNA (*happily, through her tears*): The nursery!

VARYA: How cold it is, my hands are stiff. (*To* LYUBOFF ANDREEVNA.) Your rooms, the white one and the violet, are just the same as ever, Mama.

LYUBOFF ANDREEVNA: The nursery, my dear beautiful room — I slept here when I was little — (*Crying.*) And now I am like a child — (*Kisses her brother and* VARYA, *then her brother again.*) And Varya is just the same as ever, looks like a nun. And I knew Dunyasha — (*Kisses* DUNYASHA.)

GAYEFF: The train was two hours late. How's that? How's that for good management?

CHARLOTTA (*to* PISHTCHIK): My dog he eats nuts too.

PISHTCHIK (*astonished*): Think of that!

(*Everybody goes out except* ANYA *and* DUNYASHA.)

DUNYASHA: We waited so long — (*Taking off* ANYA's *coat and hat.*)

ANYA: I didn't sleep all four nights on the way. And now I feel so chilly.

DUNYASHA: It was Lent when you left, there was some snow then, there was frost, and now? My darling (*laughing and kissing her*), I waited so long for you, my joy, my life — I'm telling you now, I can't keep from it another minute.

ANYA (*wearily*): There we go again —

DUNYASHA: The clerk Epihodoff, proposed to me after Holy Week.

ANYA: You're always talking about the same thing — (*Arranging her hair.*) I've lost all my hairpins — (*She is tired to the point of staggering.*)

DUNYASHA: I just don't know what to think. He loves me, loves me so!

ANYA (*looks in through her door, tenderly*): My room, my windows, it's just as if I had never been away. I'm home! Tomorrow morning I'll get up, I'll run into the orchard — Oh, if I only could go to sleep! I haven't slept all the way, I was tormented by anxiety.

DUNYASHA: Day before yesterday, Pyotr Sergeevich arrived.

ANYA (*joyfully*): Petya!

DUNYASHA: He's asleep in the bathhouse, he lives there. I am afraid, he says, of being in the way. (*Taking her watch from her pocket and looking at it.*) Somebody ought to wake him up. It's only that Varvara Mikhailovna told us not to. Don't you wake him up, she said.

VARYA (*enter* VARYA *with a bunch of keys at her belt*): Dunyasha, coffee, quick — Mama is asking for coffee.

DUNYASHA: This minute. (*Goes out.*)

VARYA: Well, thank goodness, you've come back. You are home again. (*Caressingly.*) My darling is back! My precious is back!

ANYA: I've had such a time.

VARYA: I can imagine!

ANYA: I left during Holy Week, it was cold then. Charlotta talked all the way and did her tricks. Why did you fasten Charlotta on to me — ?

VARYA: But you couldn't have traveled alone, darling; not at seventeen!

ANYA: We arrived in Paris, it was cold there

and snowing. I speak terrible French. Mama lived on the fifth floor; I went to see her; there were some French people in her room, ladies, an old priest with his prayer book, and the place was full of tobacco smoke — very dreary. Suddenly I began to feel sorry for Mama, so sorry, I drew her to me, held her close and couldn't let her go. Then Mama kept hugging me, crying — yes —

VARYA (*tearfully*): Don't — oh, don't —

ANYA: Her villa near Menton she had already sold, she had nothing left, nothing. And I didn't have a kopeck left. It was all we could do to get here. And Mama doesn't understand! We sit down to dinner at a station and she orders, insists on the most expensive things and gives the waiters rouble tips. Charlotta does the same. Yasha too demands his share; it's simply dreadful. Mama has her butler, Yasha, we've brought him here —

VARYA: I saw the wretch.

ANYA: Well, how are things? Has the interest on the mortgage been paid?

VARYA: How could we?

ANYA: Oh, my God, my God — !

VARYA: In August the estate is to be sold —

ANYA: My God — !

LOPAHIN (*looking in through the door and mooing like a cow*): Moo-o-o — (*Goes away.*)

VARYA (*tearfully*): I'd land him one like that — (*Shaking her fist.*)

ANYA (*embracing* VARYA *gently*): Varya, has he proposed? (VARYA *shakes her head.*) But he loves you — Why don't you have it out with him, what are you waiting for?

VARYA: I don't think anything will come of it for us. He is very busy, he hasn't any time for me — And doesn't notice me. God knows, it's painful for me to see him — Everybody talks about our marriage, everybody congratulates us, and the truth is, there's nothing to it — it's all like a dream — (*In a different tone.*) You have a brooch looks like a bee.

ANYA (*sadly*): Mama bought it. (*Going toward her room, speaking gaily, like a child.*) And in Paris I went up in a balloon!

VARYA: My darling is back! My precious is back! (DUNYASHA *has returned with the coffee pot and is making coffee.* VARYA *is standing by the door.*) Darling, I'm busy all day long with the house and I go around thinking things. If only you could be married to a rich man, I'd be more at peace too, I would go all by myself

to a hermitage — then to Kiev — to Moscow, and I'd keep going like that from one holy place to another — I would go on and on. Heavenly!

ANYA: The birds are singing in the orchard. What time is it now?

VARYA: It must be after two. It's time you were asleep, darling. (*Going into* ANYA's *room.*) Heavenly!

YASHA (YASHA *enters with a lap robe and a traveling bag. Crossing the stage airily*): May I go through here?

DUNYASHA: We'd hardly recognize you, Yasha; you've changed so abroad!

YASHA: Hm — And who are you?

DUNYASHA: When you left here, I was like that — (*Her hand so high from the floor.*) I'm Dunyasha, Fyodor Kozoyedoff's daughter. You don't remember!

YASHA: Hm — You little peach! (*Looking around before he embraces her; she shrieks and drops a saucer;* YASHA *hurries out.*)

VARYA (*at the door, in a vexed tone*): And what's going on here?

DUNYASHA (*tearfully*): I broke a saucer —

VARYA: That's good luck.

ANYA (*emerging from her room*): We ought to tell Mama beforehand: Petya is here —

VARYA: I told them not to wake him up.

ANYA (*pensively*): Six years ago our father died, a month later our brother Grisha was drowned in the river, such a pretty little boy, just seven. Mama couldn't bear it, she went away, went away without ever looking back — (*Shuddering.*) How I understand her, if she only knew I did. (*A pause.*) And Petya Trofimoff was Grisha's tutor, he might remind —

FIERS (*enter* FIERS; *he is in a jacket and white waistcoat. Going to the coffee urn, busy with it*): The mistress will have her breakfast here — (*Putting on white gloves.*) Is the coffee ready? (*To* DUNYASHA, *sternly.*) You! What about the cream?

DUNYASHA: Oh, my God — (*Hurrying out.*)

FIERS (*busy at the coffee urn*): Oh, you good-for-nothing — ! (*Muttering to himself.*) Come back from Paris — And the master used to go to Paris by coach — (*Laughing.*)

VARYA: Fiers, what are you — ?

FIERS: At your service. (*Joyfully.*) My mistress is back! It's what I've been waiting for! Now I'm ready to die — (*Crying for joy.*)

(LYUBOFF ANDREEVNA, GAYEFF *and* SEMYO-
NOFF-PISHTCHIK *enter;* SEMYONOFF-PISHTCHIK
is in a podyovka of fine cloth and sharovary.
GAYEFF *enters; he makes gestures with his
hands and body as if he were playing billiards.*)

LYUBOFF ANDREEVNA: How is it? Let me
remember — Yellow into the corner! Duplicate
in the middle!

GAYEFF: I cut into the corner. Sister, you
and I slept here in this very room once, and
now I am fifty-one years old, strange as that
may seem —

LOPAHIN: Yes, time passes.

GAYEFF: What?

LOPAHIN: Time, I say, passes.

GAYEFF: And it smells like patchouli here.

ANYA: I'm going to bed. Good night, Mama.
(*Kissing her mother.*)

LYUBOFF ANDREEVNA: My sweet little child.
(*Kissing her hands.*) You're glad you are home?
I still can't get myself together.

ANYA: Good-by, Uncle.

GAYEFF (*kissing her face and hands*): God
be with you. How like your mother you are!
(*To his sister.*) Lyuba, at her age you were
exactly like her.

(ANYA *shakes hands with* LOPAHIN *and*
PISHTCHIK, *goes out and closes the door
behind her.*)

LYUBOFF ANDREEVNA: She's very tired.

PISHTCHIK: It is a long trip, I imagine.

VARYA (*to* LOPAHIN *and* PISHTCHIK): Well,
then, sirs? It's going on three o'clock, time for
gentlemen to be going.

LYUBOFF ANDREEVNA (*laughing*): The same
old Varya. (*Drawing her to her and kissing
her.*) There, I'll drink my coffee, then we'll all
go. (FIERS *puts a small cushion under her
feet.*) Thank you, my dear. I am used to
coffee. Drink it day and night. Thank you, my
dear old soul. (*Kissing* FIERS.)

VARYA: I'll go see if all the things have
come. (*Goes out.*)

LYUBOFF ANDREEVNA: Is it really me sitting
here? (*Laughing.*) I'd like to jump around and
wave my arms. (*Covering her face with her
hands.*) But I may be dreaming! God knows I
love my country, love it deeply, I couldn't look
out of the car window, I just kept crying.
(*Tearfully.*) However, I must drink my coffee.

Thank you, Fiers, thank you, my dear old
friend. I'm so glad you're still alive.

FIERS: Day before yesterday.

GAYEFF: He doesn't hear well.

LOPAHIN: And I must leave right now. It's
nearly five o'clock in the morning, for Kharkov. What a nuisance! I wanted to look at
you — talk — You are as beautiful as ever.

PISHTCHIK (*breathing heavily*): Even more
beautiful — In your Paris clothes — It's a feast
for the eyes —

LOPAHIN: Your brother, Leonid Andreevich
here, says I'm a boor, a peasant money grubber, but that's all the same to me, absolutely.
Let him say it. All I wish is you'd trust me as
you used to, and your wonderful, touching eyes
would look at me as they did. Merciful God!
My father was a serf; belonged to your grandfather and your father; but you, your own self,
you did so much for me once that I've
forgotten all that and love you like my own
kin — more than my kin.

LYUBOFF ANDREEVNA: I can't sit still — I
can't. (*Jumping up and walking about in great
excitement.*) I'll never live through this happiness — Laugh at me, I'm silly — My own little
bookcase — ! (*Kissing the bookcase.*) My little
table!

GAYEFF: And in your absence the nurse here
died.

LYUBOFF ANDREEVNA (*sitting down and
drinking coffee*): Yes, may she rest in Heaven!
They wrote me.

GAYEFF: And Anastasy died. Cross-eyed Pe-
trushka left me and lives in town now at the
police officer's. (*Taking out of his pocket a
box of hard candy and sucking a piece.*)

PISHTCHIK: My daughter, Dashenka — sends
you her greetings.

LOPAHIN: I want to tell you something very
pleasant, cheerful. (*Glancing at his watch.*)
I'm going right away. There's no time for
talking. Well, I'll make it two or three words.
As you know, your cherry orchard is to be sold
for your debts; the auction is set for August
twenty-second, but don't you worry, my dear,
you just sleep in peace, there's a way out of it.
Here's my plan. Please listen to me. Your
estate is only thirteen miles from town.
They've run the railroad by it. Now if the
cherry orchard and the land along the river
were cut up into building lots and leased for
summer cottages, you'd have at the very lowest

twenty-five thousand roubles per year income.

GAYEFF: Excuse me, what rot!

LYUBOFF ANDREEVNA: I don't quite understand you, Yermolay Alexeevich.

LOPAHIN: At the very least you will get from the summer residents twenty-five roubles per year for a two-and-a-half acre lot and if you post a notice right off, I'll bet you anything that by autumn you won't have a single patch of land free, everything will be taken. In a word, my congratulations, you are saved. The location is wonderful, the river's so deep. Except, of course, it all needs to be tidied up, cleared — For instance, let's say, tear all the old buildings down and this house, which is no good any more, and cut down the old cherry orchard —

LYUBOFF ANDREEVNA: Cut down? My dear, forgive me, you don't understand at all. If there's one thing in the whole province that's interesting — not to say remarkable — it's our cherry orchard.

LOPAHIN: The only remarkable thing about this cherry orchard is that it's very big. There's a crop of cherries once every two years and even that's hard to get rid of. Nobody buys them.

GAYEFF: This orchard is even mentioned in the encyclopedia.

LOPAHIN (*glancing at his watch*): If we don't cook up something and don't get somewhere, the cherry orchard and the entire estate will be sold at auction on the twenty-second of August. Do get it settled then! I swear there is no other way out. Not a one!

FIERS: There was a time, forty-fifty years ago when the cherries were dried, soaked, pickled, cooked into jam and it used to be —

GAYEFF: Keep quiet, Fiers.

FIERS: And it used to be that the dried cherries were shipped by the wagon-load to Moscow and to Kharkov. And the money there was! And the dried cherries were soft then, juicy, sweet, fragrant — They had a way of treating them then —

LYUBOFF ANDREEVNA: And where is that way now?

FIERS: They have forgotten it. Nobody remembers it.

PISHTCHIK (*to* LYUBOFF ANDREEVNA): What's happening in Paris? How is everything? Did you eat frogs?

LYUBOFF ANDREEVNA: I ate crocodiles.

PISHTCHIK: Think of it — !

LOPAHIN: Up to now in the country there have been only the gentry and the peasants, but now in summer the villa people too are coming in. All the towns, even the least big ones, are surrounded with cottages. In about twenty years very likely the summer resident will multiply enormously. He merely drinks tea on the porch now, but it might well happen that on this two-and-a-half acre lot of his, he'll go in for farming, and then your cherry orchard would be happy, rich, splendid —

GAYEFF (*getting hot*): What rot!

(*Enter* VARYA *and* YASHA.)

VARYA: Here, Mama. Two telegrams for you. (*Choosing a key and opening the old bookcase noisily.*) Here they are.

LYUBOFF ANDREEVNA: From Paris (*Tearing up the telegrams without reading them.*) Paris, that's all over —

GAYEFF: Do you know how old this bookcase is, Lyuba? A week ago I pulled out the bottom drawer and looked, and there the figures were burned on it. The bookcase was made exactly a hundred years ago. How's that? Eh? You might celebrate its jubilee. It's an inanimate object, but all the same, be that as it may, it's a bookcase.

PISHTCHIK (*in astonishment*): A hundred years — ! Think of it — !

GAYEFF: Yes — quite something — (*Shaking the bookcase.*) Dear, honored bookcase! I saluted your existence, which for more than a hundred years has been directed toward the clear ideals of goodness and justice; your silent appeal to fruitful endeavor has not flagged in all the course of a hundred years, sustaining (*tearfully*) through the generations of our family, our courage and our faith in a better future and nurturing in us ideals of goodness and of a social consciousness.

(*A pause.*)

LOPAHIN: Yes.

LYUBOFF ANDREEVNA: You're the same as ever, Lenya.

GAYEFF (*slightly embarrassed*): Carom to the right into the corner pocket! I cut into the side pocket!

LOPAHIN (*glancing at his watch*): Well, it's time for me to go.

YASHA (*handing medicine to* LYUBOFF ANDREEVNA): Perhaps you'll take the pills now —

PISHTCHIK: You should never take medicaments, dear madam — They do neither harm nor good — Hand them here, dearest lady. (*He takes the pillbox, shakes the pills out into his palm, blows on them, puts them in his mouth and washes them down with kvass.*) There! Now!

LYUBOFF ANDREEVNA (*startled*): Why, you've lost your mind!

PISHTCHIK: I took all the pills.

LOPAHIN: Such a glutton!

(*Everyone laughs.*)

FIERS: The gentleman stayed with us during Holy Week, he ate half a bucket of pickles — (*Muttering.*)

LYUBOFF ANDREEVNA: What is he muttering about?

VARYA: He's been muttering like that for three years. We're used to it.

YASHA: In his dotage.

(CHARLOTTA IVANOVNA *in a white dress — she is very thin, her corset laced very tight — with a lorgnette at her belt, crosses the stage.*)

LOPAHIN: Excuse me, Charlotta Ivanovna, I haven't had a chance yet to welcome you. (*Trying to kiss her hand.*)

CHARLOTTA (*drawing her hand away*): If I let you kiss my hand, 'twould be my elbow next, then my shoulder —

LOPAHIN: No luck for me today. (*Everyone laughs.*) Charlotta Ivanovna, show us a trick!

CHARLOTTA: No. I want to go to bed. (*Exit.*)

LOPAHIN: In three weeks we shall see each other. (*Kissing* LYUBOFF ANDREEVNA'S *hand.*) Till then, good-by. It's time. (*To* GAYEFF.) See you then, good-by. It's time. (*To* GAYEFF.) soon. (*Shaking* VARYA'S *hand, then* FIERS' *and* YASHA'S.) I don't feel like going. (*To* LYUBOFF ANDREEVNA.) If you think it over and make up your mind about the summer cottages, let me know and I'll arrange a loan of something like fifty thousand roubles. Think it over seriously.

VARYA (*angrily*): Do go on, anyhow, will you!

LOPAHIN: I'm going, I'm going — (*Exit.*)

GAYEFF: Boor. However, pardon — Varya is going to marry him, it's Varya's little fiancé.

VARYA: Don't talk too much, Uncle.

LYUBOFF ANDREEVNA: Well, Varya, I should be very glad. He's a good man.

PISHTCHIK: A man, one must say truthfully — A most worthy — And my Dashenka — says also that — she says all sorts of things — (*Snoring but immediately waking up.*) Nevertheless, dearest lady, oblige me — With a loan of two hundred and forty roubles — Tomorrow the interest on my mortgage has got to be paid —

VARYA (*startled*): There's not any money, none at all.

LYUBOFF ANDREEVNA: Really, I haven't got anything.

PISHTCHIK: I'll find it, somehow. (*Laughing.*) I never give up hope. There, I think to myself, all is lost, I am ruined and lo and behold — a railroad is put through my land and — they paid me. And then, just watch, something else will turn up — if not today, then tomorrow — Dashenka will win two hundred thousand — She has a ticket.

LYUBOFF ANDREEVNA: We've finished the coffee, now we can go to bed.

FIERS (*brushing* GAYEFF'S *clothes, reprovingly*): You put on the wrong trousers again. What am I going to do with you!

VARYA (*softly*): Anya is asleep. (*Opening the window softly.*) Already the sun's rising — it's not cold. Look, Mama! What beautiful trees! My Lord, what air! The starlings are singing!

GAYEFF (*opening another window*): The orchard is all white. You haven't forgotten, Lyuba? That long lane there runs straight — as a strap stretched out. It glistens on moonlight nights. Do you remember? You haven't forgotten it?

LYUBOFF ANDREEVNA (*looking out of the window on to the orchard*): Oh, my childhood, my innocence! I slept in this nursery and looked out on the orchard from here, every morning happiness awoke with me, it was just as it is now, then, nothing has changed. (*Laughing with joy.*) All, all white! Oh, my orchard! After a dark, rainy autumn and cold winter, you are young again and full of happiness. The heavenly angels have not deserted you — If I only could lift the weight from my breast, from my shoulders, if I could only forget my past!

GAYEFF: Yes, and the orchard will be sold for debt, strange as that may seem.

LYUBOFF ANDREEVNA: Look, our dear mother is walking through the orchard — In a white dress! (*Laughing happily.*) It's she.

GAYEFF: Where?

VARYA: God be with you, Mama!

LYUBOFF ANDREEVNA: There's not anybody, it only seemed so. To the right, as you turn to the summerhouse, a little white tree is leaning there, looks like a woman — (*Enter* TROFI- MOFF, *in a student's uniform, well worn, and glasses.*) What a wonderful orchard! The white masses of blossoms, the sky all blue.

TROFIMOFF: Lyuboff Andreevna! (*She looks around at him.*) I will just greet you and go immediately. (*Kissing her hand warmly.*) I was told to wait until morning, but I hadn't the patience —

(LYUBOFF ANDREEVNA *looks at him puzzled.*)

VARYA (*tearfully*): This is Petya Trofimoff —

TROFIMOFF: Petya Trofimoff, the former tutor of your Grisha — Have I really changed so?

(LYUBOFF ANDREEVNA *embraces him; and crying quietly.*)

GAYEFF (*embarrassed*): There, there, Lyuba.

VARYA (*crying*): I told you, Petya, to wait till tomorrow.

LYUBOFF ANDREEVNA: My Grisha — My boy — Grisha — Son —

VARYA: What can we do, Mama? It's God's will.

TROFIMOFF (*in a low voice, tearfully*): There, there —

LYUBOFF ANDREEVNA (*weeping softly*): My boy was lost, drowned — Why? Why, my friend? (*More quietly.*) Anya is asleep there, and I am talking so loud — Making so much noise — But why, Petya? Why have you lost your looks? Why do you look so much older?

TROFIMOFF: A peasant woman on the train called me a mangy-looking gentleman.

LYUBOFF ANDREEVNA: You were a mere boy then, a charming young student, and now your hair's not very thick any more and you wear glasses. Are you really a student still? (*Going to the door.*)

TROFIMOFF: Very likely I'll be a perennial student.

LYUBOFF ANDREEVNA (*kissing her brother, then* VARYA): Well, go to bed — You've grown older too, Leonid.

PISHTCHIK (*following her*): So that's it, we are going to bed now. Oh, my gout! I'm staying here — I'd like, Lyuboff Andreevna, my soul, tomorrow morning — Two hundred and forty roubles —

GAYEFF: He's still at it.

PISHTCHIK: Two hundred and forty roubles — To pay interest on the mortgage.

LYUBOFF ANDREEVNA: I haven't any money, my dove.

PISHTCHIK: I'll pay it back, my dear — It's a trifling sum —

LYUBOFF ANDREEVNA: Oh, very well, Leonid will give — You give it to him, Leonid.

GAYEFF: Oh, certainly, I'll give it to him. Hold out your pockets.

LYUBOFF ANDREEVNA: What can we do, give it, he needs it — He'll pay it back.

(LYUBOFF ANDREEVNA, TROFIMOFF, PISH- TCHIK *and* FIERS *go out.* GAYEFF, VARYA *and* YASHA *remain.*)

GAYEFF: My sister hasn't yet lost her habit of throwing money away. (*To* YASHA.) Get away, my good fellow, you smell like hens.

YASHA (*with a grin*): And you are just the same as you used to be, Leonid Andreevich.

GAYEFF: What? (*To* VARYA.) What did he say?

VARYA (*to* YASHA): Your mother has come from the village, she's been sitting in the servants' hall every since yesterday, she wants to see you —

YASHA: The devil take her!

VARYA: Ach, shameless creature!

YASHA: A lot I need her! She might have come tomorrow. (*Goes out.*)

VARYA: Mama is just the same as she was, she hasn't changed at all. If she could, she'd give away everything she has.

GAYEFF: Yes — If many remedies are pre- scribed for an illness, you may know the illness is incurable. I keep thinking, I rack my brains, I have many remedies, a great many, and that means, really, I haven't any at all. It would be fine to inherit a fortune from somebody, it would be fine to marry off our Anya to a very rich man, it would be fine to go to Yaroslavl and try our luck with our old aunt, the Countess. Auntie is very, very rich.

VARYA (*crying*): If God would only help us!

GAYEFF: Don't bawl! Auntie is very rich but she doesn't like us. To begin with, Sister married a lawyer, not a nobleman — (ANYA *appears at the door.*) Married not a nobleman and behaved herself, you could say, not very virtuously. She is good, kind, nice, I love her very much, but no matter how much you allow for the extenuating circumstances, you must admit she's a depraved woman. You feel it in her slightest movement.

VARYA (*whispering*): Anya is standing in the door there.

GAYEFF: What? (*A pause.*) It's amazing, something got in my right eye. I am beginning to see poorly. And on Thursday, when I was in the District Court —

(ANYA *enters.*)

VARYA: But why aren't you asleep, Anya?

ANYA: I don't feel like sleeping. I can't.

GAYEFF: My little girl — (*Kissing* ANYA's *face and hands.*) My child — (*Tearfully.*) You are not my niece, you are my angel, you are everything to me. Believe me, believe —

ANYA: I believe you, Uncle. Everybody loves you, respects you — But dear Uncle, you must keep quiet, just keep quiet — What were you saying, just now, about my mother, about your own sister? What did you say that for?

GAYEFF: Yes, yes — (*Putting her hand up over his face.*) Really, it's terrible! My God! Oh, God, save me! And today I made a speech to the bookcase — So silly! And it was only when I finished it that I could see it was silly.

VARYA: It's true, Uncle, you ought to keep quiet. Just keep quiet. That's all.

ANYA: If you kept quiet, you'd have more peace.

GAYEFF: I'll keep quiet. (*Kissing* ANYA's *and* VARYA's *hands.*) I'll keep quiet. Only this, it's about business. On Thursday I was in the District Court; well, a few of us gathered around and a conversation began about this and that, about lots of things; apparently it will be possible to arrange a loan on a promissory note to pay the bank the interest due.

VARYA: If the Lord would only help us!

GAYEFF: Tuesday I shall go and talk it over again. (*To* VARYA.) Don't bawl! (*To* ANYA.) Your mother will talk to Lopahin; of course, he won't refuse her . . . And as soon as you rest up, you will go to Yaroslavl to your great-aunt, the Countess. There, that's how we will move from three directions, and the business is in the bag. We'll pay the interest. I am convinced of that — (*Putting a hard candy in his mouth.*) On my honor I'll swear, by anything you like, that the estate shall not be sold! (*Excitedly.*) By my happiness, I swear! Here's my hand, call me a worthless, dishonorable man, if I allow it to come up for auction! With all my soul I swear it!

ANYA (*a quieter mood returns to her; she is happy*): How good you are, Uncle, how clever! (*Embracing her uncle.*) I feel easy now! I feel easy! I'm happy!

FIERS (FIERS *enters, reproachfully*): Leonid Andreevich, have you no fear of God? When are you going to bed?

GAYEFF: Right away, right away. You may go, Fiers. For this once I'll undress myself. Well, children, beddy bye — More details tomorrow, and now, go to bed. (*Kissing* ANYA *and* VARYA.) I am a man of the eighties — It is a period that's not admired, but I can say, nevertheless, that I've suffered no little for my convictions in the course of my life. It is not for nothing that the peasant loves me. One must know the peasant! One must know from what —

ANYA: Again, Uncle!

VARYA: You, Uncle dear, keep quiet.

FIERS (*angrily*): Leonid Andreevich!

GAYEFF: I'm coming, I'm coming — Go to bed. A double bank into the side pocket! A clean shot — (*Goes out,* FIERS *hobbling after him.*)

ANYA: I feel easy now. I don't feel like going to Yaroslavl; I don't like Great-aunt, but still I feel easy. Thanks to Uncle. (*Sits down.*)

VARYA: I must get to sleep. I'm going. And there was unpleasantness here during your absence. In the old servants' quarters, as you know, live only the old servants: Yephemushka, Polya, Yevstignay, well, and Karp. They began to let every sort of creature spend the night with them — I didn't say anything. But then I hear they've spread the rumor that I'd given orders to feed them nothing but beans. Out of stinginess, you see — And all that from Yevstignay — Very well, I think to myself. If that's the way it is, I think to myself, then you just wait. I call in Yevstignay — (*Yawning.*) He comes — How is it, I say, that you, Yevstignay — You're such a fool — (*Glancing at* ANYA.) Anitchka — (*A pause.*) Asleep! (*Takes* ANYA *by her arm.*) Let's go to bed — Come on! — (*Leading her.*) My little darling fell asleep! Come on — (*They* go. *Far away beyond the orchard a shepherd is playing on a pipe.* TROFIMOFF *walks across the stage and, seeing* VARYA *and* ANYA, *stops.*) Shh — She is asleep — asleep — Let's go, dear.

ANYA (*softly, half dreaming*): I'm so tired — All the bells! — Uncle — dear — And Mama and Uncle — Varya.

VARYA: Come on, my dear, come on. (*They go into* ANYA's *room.*)

TROFIMOFF (*tenderly*): My little sun! My spring!

ACT II

A field. An old chapel, long abandoned, with crooked walls, near it a well, big stones that apparently were once tombstones, and an old bench. A road to the estate of GAYEFF *can be seen. On one side poplars rise, casting their shadows, the cherry orchard begins there. In the distance a row of telegraph poles; and far, far away, faintly traced on the horizon, is a large town, visible only in the clearest weather. The sun will soon be down.* CHARLOTTA, YASHA *and* DUNYASHA *are sitting on the bench;* EPIHODOFF *is standing near and playing the guitar; everyone sits lost in thought.* CHARLOTTA *wears an old peak cap* (fourrage); *she has taken a rifle from off her shoulders and is adjusting the buckle on the strap.*

CHARLOTTA (*pensively*): I have no proper passport, I don't know how old I am — it always seems to me I'm very young. When I was a little girl, my father and mother traveled from fair to fair and gave performances, very good ones. And I did *salto mortale* and different tricks. And when Papa and Mama died, a German lady took me to live with her and began teaching me. Good. I grew up. And became a governess. But where I came from and who I am I don't know — Who my parents were, perhaps they weren't even married — I don't know. (*Taking a cucumber out of her pocket and beginning to eat it.*) I don't know a thing. (*A pause.*) I'd like so much to talk but there's not anybody. I haven't anybody.

EPIHODOFF (*playing the guitar and singing*): "What care I for the noisy world, what care I

for friends and foes." — How pleasant it is to play the mandolin!

DUNYASHA: That's a guitar, not a mandolin. (*Looking into a little mirror and powdering her face.*)

EPIHODOFF: For a madman who is in love this is a mandolin — (*Singing.*) "If only my heart were warm with the fire of requited love."

(YASHA *sings with him.*)

CHARLOTTA: How dreadfully these people sing — Phooey! Like jackals.

DUNYASHA (*to* YASHA): All the same what happiness to have been abroad.

YASHA: Yes, of course. I cannot disagree with you. (*Yawning and then lighting a cigar.*)

EPIHODOFF: That's easily understood. Abroad everything long since attained its complete development.

YASHA: That's obvious.

EPIHODOFF: I am a cultured man. I read all kinds of remarkable books, but the trouble is I cannot discover my own inclinations, whether to live or to shoot myself, but nevertheless, I always carry a revolver on me. Here it is — (*Showing a revolver.*)

CHARLOTTA: That's done. Now I am going. (*Slinging the rifle over her shoulder.*) You are a very clever man, Epihodoff, and a very terrible one; the women must love you madly. Brrrr-r-r-r! (*Going.*) These clever people are all so silly, I haven't anybody to talk with. I'm always alone, alone, I have nobody and — Who I am, why I am, is unknown — (*Goes out without hurrying.*)

EPIHODOFF: Strictly speaking, not touching on other subjects, I must state about myself, in passing, that fate treats me mercilessly, as a storm does a small ship. If, let us suppose, I am mistaken, then why, to mention one instance, do I wake up this morning, look and there on my chest is a spider of terrific size — There, like that. (*Showing the size with both hands.*) And also I take some kvass to drink and in it I find something in the highest degree indecent, such as a cockroach. (*A pause.*) Have you read Buckle? (*A pause.*) I desire to trouble you, Avdotya Feodorovna, with a couple of words.

DUNYASHA: Speak.

EPIHODOFF: I have a desire to speak with you alone — (*Sighing.*)

DUNYASHA (*embarrassed*): Very well — But bring me my cape first — by the cupboard — It's rather damp here —

EPIHODOFF: Very well — I'll fetch it — Now I know what I should do with my revolver — (*Takes the guitar and goes out playing.*)

YASHA: Twenty-two misfortunes! Between us he's a stupid man, it must be said. (*Yawning.*)

DUNYASHA: God forbid he should shoot himself. (*A pause.*) I've grown so uneasy, I'm always fretting. I was only a girl when I was taken into the master's house, and now I've lost the habit of simple living — and here are my hands white, white as a lady's. I've become so delicate, fragile, ladylike, afraid of everything — Frightfully so. And, Yasha, if you deceive me, I don't know what will happen to my nerves.

YASHA (*kissing her*): You little cucumber! Of course every girl must behave properly. What I dislike above everything is for a girl to conduct herself badly.

DUNYASHA: I have come to love you passionately, you are educated, you can discuss anything. (*A pause.*)

YASHA (*yawning*): Yes, sir — To my mind it is like this: If a girl loves someone, it means she is immoral. (*A pause.*) It is pleasant to smoke a cigar in the clear air — (*Listening.*) They are coming here — It is the ladies and gentlemen —

(DUNYASHA *impulsively embraces him.*)

YASHA: Go to the house, as though you had been to bathe in the river, go by this path, otherwise, they might meet you and suspect me of making a rendezvous with you. That I cannot tolerate.

DUNYASHA (*with a little cough*): Your cigar has given me the headache. (*Goes out.*)

(YASHA *remains, sitting near the chapel.* LYUBOFF ANDREEVNA, GAYEFF *and* LOPAHIN *enter.*)

LOPAHIN: We must decide definitely, time doesn't wait. Why, the matter's quite simple. Are you willing to lease your land for summer cottages or are you not? Answer in one word, yes or no? Just one word!

LYUBOFF ANDREEVNA: Who is it smokes those disgusting cigars out here — ? (*Sitting down.*)

GAYEFF: The railroad running so near is a great convenience. (*Sitting down.*) We made a trip to town and lunched there — Yellow in the side pocket! Perhaps I should go in the house first and play one game —

LYUBOFF ANDREEVNA: You'll have time.

LOPAHIN: Just one word! (*Imploringly.*) Do give me your answer!

GAYEFF (*yawning*): What?

LYUBOFF ANDREEVNA (*looking in her purse*): Yesterday there was lots of money in it. Today there's very little. My poor Varya! For the sake of economy she feeds everybody milk soup, and in the kitchen the old people get nothing but beans, and here I spend money — senselessly — (*Dropping her purse and scattering gold coins.*) There they go scattering! (*She is vexed.*)

YASHA: Allow me, I'll pick them up in a second. (*Picking up the coins.*)

LYUBOFF ANDREEVNA: If you will, Yasha. And why did I go in town for lunch — ? Your restaurant with its music is trashy, the tablecloths smell of soap — Why drink so much, Lyonya? Why eat so much? Why talk so much? Today in the restaurant you were talking a lot again, and all of it beside the point. About the seventies, about the decadents. And to whom? Talking to waiters about the decadents!

LOPAHIN: Yes.

GAYEFF (*waving his hand*): I am incorrigible, that's evident — (*To* YASHA, *irritably.*) What is it? — You are forever swirling around in front of us!

YASHA (*laughing*): I cannot hear your voice without laughing.

GAYEFF (*to his sister*): Either I or he —

LYUBOFF ANDREEVNA: Go away, Yasha. Go on —

YASHA (*giving* LYUBOFF ANDREEVNA *her purse*): I am going right away. (*Barely suppressing his laughter.*) This minute. (*Goes out.*)

LOPAHIN: The rich Deriganoff intends to buy your estate. They say he is coming personally to the auction.

LYUBOFF ANDREEVNA: And where did you hear that?

LOPAHIN: In town they are saying it.

GAYEFF: Our Yaroslavl aunt promised to send us something, but when and how much she will send, nobody knows —

LOPAHIN: How much will she send? A hundred thousand? Two hundred?

LYUBOFF ANDREEVNA: Well — maybe ten, fifteen thousand — we'd be thankful for that.

LOPAHIN: Excuse me, but such light-minded people as you are, such odd, unbusinesslike people, I never saw. You are told in plain Russian that your estate is being sold up and you just don't seem to take it in.

LYUBOFF ANDREEVNA: But what are we to do? Tell us what?

LOPAHIN: I tell you every day. Every day I tell you the same thing. Both the cherry orchard and the land have got to be leased for summer cottages, it has to be done right now, quick — The auction is right under your noses. Do understand! Once you finally decide that there are to be summer cottages, you will get all the money you want, and then you'll be saved.

LYUBOFF ANDREEVNA: Summer cottages and summer residents — it is so trivial, excuse me.

GAYEFF: I absolutely agree with you.

LOPAHIN: I'll either burst out crying, or scream, or faint. I can't bear it! You are torturing me! (*To* GAYEFF.) You're a perfect old woman!

GAYEFF: What?

LOPAHIN: A perfect old woman! (*About to go.*)

LYUBOFF ANDREEVNA (*alarmed*): No, don't go, stay, my lamb, I beg you. Perhaps we will think of something!

LOPAHIN: What is there to think about?

LYUBOFF ANDREEVNA: Don't go, I beg you. With you here it is more cheerful anyhow — (*A pause.*) I keep waiting for something, as if the house were about to tumble down on our heads.

GAYEFF (*deep in thought*): Double into the corner pocket — Bank into the side pocket —

LYUBOFF ANDREEVNA: We have sinned so much —

LOPAHIN: What sins have you — ?

GAYEFF (*puts a hard candy into his mouth*): They say I've eaten my fortune up in hard candies — (*Laughing.*)

LYUBOFF ANDREEVNA: Oh, my sins — I've always thrown money around like mad, recklessly, and I married a man who accumulated nothing but debts. My husband died from champagne — he drank fearfully — and to my misfortune I fell in love with another man. I lived with him, and just at that time — it was my first punishment — a blow over the head: right here in the river my boy was drowned and I went abroad — went away for good, never to return, never to see this river again — I shut my eyes, ran away, beside myself, and he after me — mercilessly, brutally. I bought a villa near Menton, because he fell ill there, and for three years I knew no rest day or night, the sick man exhausted me, my soul dried up. And last year when the villa was sold for debts, I went to Paris and there he robbed me of everything, threw me over, took up with another woman; I tried to poison myself — so stupid, so shameful — And suddenly I was seized with longing for Russia, for my own country, for my little girl — (*Wiping away her tears.*) Lord, Lord, have mercy, forgive me my sins! Don't punish me any more! (*Getting a telegram out of her pocket.*) I got this today from Paris, he asks forgiveness, begs me to return — (*Tears up the telegram.*) That sounds like music somewhere. (*Listening.*)

GAYEFF: It is our famous Jewish orchestra. You remember, four violins, a flute and double bass.

LYUBOFF ANDREEVNA: Does it still exist? We ought to get hold of it sometime and give a party.

LOPAHIN (*listening*): Can't hear it — (*Singing softly.*) "And for money the Germans will frenchify a Russian." (*Laughing.*) What a play I saw yesterday at the theatre, very funny!

LYUBOFF ANDREEVNA: And most likely there was nothing funny about it. You shouldn't look at plays, but look oftener at yourselves. How gray all your lives are, what a lot of idle things you say!

LOPAHIN: That's true. It must be said frankly this life of ours is idiotic — (*A pause.*) My father was a peasant, an idiot, he understood nothing, he taught me nothing, he just beat me in his drunken fits and always with a stick. At bottom I am just as big a dolt and idiot as he was. I wasn't taught anything, my handwriting is vile, I write like a pig — I am ashamed for people to see it.

LYUBOFF ANDREEVNA: You ought to get married, my friend.

LOPAHIN: Yes — That's true.

LYUBOFF ANDREEVNA: To our Varya, perhaps. She is a good girl.

LOPAHIN: Yes.

LYUBOFF ANDREEVNA: She comes from simple people, and she works all day long, but the main thing is she loves you. And you, too, have liked her a long time.

LOPAHIN: Why not? I am not against it — She's a good girl. (*A pause.*)

GAYEFF: They are offering me a position in a bank. Six thousand a year — Have you heard that?

LYUBOFF ANDREEVNA: Not you! You stay where you are —

FIERS (FIERS *enters, bringing an overcoat. To* GAYEFF): Pray, Sir, put this on, it's damp.

GAYEFF (*putting on the overcoat*): You're a pest, old man.

FIERS: That's all right — This morning you went off without letting me know. (*Looking him over.*)

LYUBOFF ANDREEVNA: How old you've grown, Fiers!

FIERS: At your service.

LOPAHIN: She says you've grown very old!

FIERS: I've lived a long time. They were planning to marry me off before your papa was born. (*Laughing.*) And at the time the serfs were freed I was already the head footman. I didn't want to be freed then, I stayed with the masters — (*A pause.*) And I remember, everybody was happy, but what they were happy about they didn't know themselves.

LOPAHIN: In the old days it was fine. At least they flogged.

FIERS (*not hearing*): But, of course. The peasants stuck to the masters, the masters stuck to the peasants, and now everything is all smashed up, you can't tell about anything.

GAYEFF: Keep still, Fiers. Tomorrow I must go to town. They have promised to introduce me to a certain general who might make us a loan.

LOPAHIN: Nothing will come of it. And you can rest assured you won't pay the interest.

LYUBOFF ANDREEVNA: He's just raving on. There aren't any such generals.

(TROFIMOFF, ANYA *and* VARYA *enter.*)

GAYEFF: Here they come.

ANYA: There is Mama sitting there.

LYUBOFF ANDREEVNA (*tenderly*): Come, come — My darlings — (*Embracing* ANYA *and* VARYA.) If you only knew how I love you both! Come sit by me — there — like that.

(*Everybody sits down.*)

LOPAHIN: Our perennial student is always strolling with the young ladies.

TROFIMOFF: It's none of your business.

LOPAHIN: He will soon be fifty and he's still a student.

TROFIMOFF: Stop your stupid jokes.

LOPAHIN: But why are you so peevish, you queer duck?

TROFIMOFF: Don't you pester me.

LOPAHIN (*laughing*): Permit me to ask you, what do you make of me?

TROFIMOFF: Yermolay Alexeevich, I make this of you: you are a rich man, you'll soon be a millionaire. Just as it is in the metabolism of nature, a wild beast is needed to eat up everything that comes his way; so you, too, are needed.

(*Everyone laughs.*)

VARYA: Petya, you'd better tell us about the planets.

LYUBOFF ANDREEVNA: No, let's go on with yesterday's conversation.

TROFIMOFF: What was it about?

GAYEFF: About the proud man.

TROFIMOFF: We talked a long time yesterday, but didn't get anywhere. In a proud man, in your sense of the word, there is something mystical. Maybe you are right, from your standpoint, but if we are to discuss it in simple terms, without whimsy, then what pride can there be, is there any sense in it, if man physiologically is poorly constructed, if in the great majority he is crude, unintelligent, profoundly miserable. One must stop admiring oneself. One must only work.

GAYEFF: All the same, you will die.

TROFIMOFF: Who knows? And what does it mean — you will die? Man may have a hundred senses, and when he dies only the five that are known to us may perish, and the remaining ninety-five go on living.

LYUBOFF ANDREEVNA: How clever you are, Petya!

LOPAHIN (*ironically*): Terribly!

TROFIMOFF: Humanity goes forward, perfecting its powers. Everything that's unattainable now will some day become familiar, understandable; it is only that one must work and must help with all one's might those who seek the truth. With us in Russia so far only a very few work. The great majority of the intelligentsia that I know are looking for nothing, doing nothing, and as yet have no capacity for work. They call themselves intelligentsia, are free and easy with the servants, treat the peasants like animals, educate themselves poorly, read nothing seriously, do absolutely nothing; about science they just talk and about art they understand very little. Every one of them is serious, all have stern faces; they all talk of nothing but important things, philosophize, and all the time everybody can see that the workmen eat abominably, sleep without any pillows, thirty or forty to a room, and everywhere there are bedbugs, stench, dampness, moral uncleanness — And apparently with us, all the fine talk is only to divert the attention of ourselves and of others. Show me where we have the day nurseries they are always talking so much about, where are the reading rooms? They only write of these in novels, for the truth is there are not any at all. There is only filth, vulgarity, orientalism — I am afraid of very serious faces and dislike them. I'm afraid of serious conversations. Rather than that let's just keep still.

LOPAHIN: You know I get up before five o'clock in the morning and work from morning till night. Well, I always have money, my own and other people's, on hand, and I see what the people around me are. One has only to start doing something to find out how few honest and decent people there are. At times when I can't go to sleep, I think: Lord, thou gavest us immense forests, unbounded fields and the widest horizons, and living in the midst of them we should indeed be giants —

LYUBOFF ANDREEVNA: You feel the need for giants — They are good only in fairy tales, anywhere else they only frighten us.

(*At the back of the stage* EPIHODOFF *passes by, playing the guitar.*)

LYUBOFF ANDREEVNA (*lost in thought*): Epihodoff is coming —

ANYA (*lost in thought*): Epihodoff is coming.

GAYEFF: The sun has set, ladies and gentlemen.

TROFIMOFF: Yes.

GAYEFF (*not loud and as if he were declaiming*): Oh, Nature, wonderful, you gleam with eternal radiance, beautiful and indifferent, you, whom we call Mother, combine in yourself both life and death, you give life and you take it away.

VARYA (*beseechingly*): Uncle!

ANYA: Uncle, you're doing it again!

TROFIMOFF: You'd better bank the yellow into the side pocket.

GAYEFF: I'll be quiet, quiet.

(*All sit absorbed in their thoughts. There is only the silence.* FIERS *is heard muttering to himself softly. Suddenly a distant sound is heard, as if from the sky, like the sound of a snapped string, dying away, mournful.*)

LYUBOFF ANDREEVNA: What's that?

LOPAHIN: I don't know. Somewhere far off in a mine shaft a bucket fell. But somewhere very far off.

GAYEFF: And it may be some bird — like a heron.

TROFIMOFF: Or an owl —

LYUBOFF ANDREEVNA (*shivering*): It's unpleasant, somehow. (*A pause.*)

FIERS: Before the disaster it was like that. The owl hooted and the samovar hummed without stopping, both.

GAYEFF: Before what disaster?

FIERS: Before the emancipation. (*A pause.*)

LYUBOFF ANDREEVNA: You know, my friends, let's go. Twilight is falling. (*To* ANYA.) You have tears in your eyes — What is it, my dear little girl? (*Embracing her.*)

ANYA: It's just that, Mama. It's nothing.

TROFIMOFF: Somebody is coming.

(*A* STRANGER *appears in a shabby white cap, and an overcoat; he is a little drunk.*)

THE STRANGER: Allow me to ask you, can I go straight through here to the station?

GAYEFF: You can. Go by that road.

THE STRANGER: I am heartily grateful to you. (*Coughing.*) The weather is splendid — (*Declaiming.*) Brother of mine, suffering brother — Go out to the Volga, whose moans — (*To* VARYA.) Mademoiselle, grant a hungry Russian man some thirty kopecks —

(VARYA *is frightened and gives a shriek.*)

LOPAHIN (*angrily*): There's a limit to everything.

LYUBOFF ANDREEVNA (*flustered*): Take this — Here's this for you — (*Searching in her purse.*) No silver — It's all the same, here's a gold piece for you —

THE STRANGER: I am heartily grateful to you. (*Goes out. Laughter.*)

VARYA (*frightened*): I'm going — I'm going — Oh, Mama, you poor little Mama! There's nothing in the house for people to eat, and you gave him a gold piece.

LYUBOFF ANDREEVNA: What is to be done with me, so silly? I shall give you all I have in the house. Yermolay Alexeevich, you will lend me some this once more! —

LOPAHIN: Agreed.

LYUBOFF ANDREEVNA: Let's go, ladies and gentlemen, it's time. And here, Varya, we have definitely made a match for you, I congratulate you.

VARYA (*through her tears*): Mama, that's not something to joke about.

LOPAHIN: Achmelia, get thee to a nunnery.

GAYEFF: And my hands are trembling; it is a long time since I have played billiards.

LOPAHIN: Achmelia, oh nymph, in thine orisons be all my sins remember'd —

LYUBOFF ANDREEVNA: Let's go, my dear friends, it will soon be suppertime.

VARYA: He frightened me. My heart is thumping so!

LOPAHIN: I remind you, ladies and gentlemen: August twenty-second the cherry orchard will be auctioned off. Think about that! — Think! —

(*All go out except* TROFIMOFF *and* ANYA.)

ANYA (*laughing*): My thanks to the stranger, he frightened Varya, now we are alone.

TROFIMOFF: Varya is afraid we might begin to love each other and all day long she won't leave us to ourselves. With her narrow mind she cannot understand that we are above love. To sidestep the petty and illusory, which prevent our being free and happy, that is the aim and meaning of our life. Forward! We march on irresistibly toward the bright star that burns there in the distance. Forward! Do not fall behind, friends!

ANYA (*extending her arms upward*): How well you talk! (*A pause.*) It's wonderful here today!

TROFIMOFF: Yes, the weather is marvelous.

ANYA: What have you done to me, Petya, why don't I love the cherry orchard any longer the way I used to? I loved it so tenderly, it seemed to me there was not a better place on earth than our orchard.

TROFIMOFF: All Russia is our orchard. The earth is immense and beautiful, and on it are many wonderful places. (*A pause.*) Just think, Anya: your grandfather, great-grandfather and all your ancestors were slave owners, in possession of living souls, and can you doubt that from every cherry in the orchard, from every leaf, from every trunk, human beings are looking at you, can it be that you don't hear their voices? To possess living souls, well, that depraved all of you who lived before and who are living now, so that your mother and you, and your uncle no longer notice that you live by debt, at somebody else's expense, at the expense of those very people whom you wouldn't let past your front door — We are at least two hundred years behind the times, we have as yet absolutely nothing, we have no definite attitude toward the past, we only philosophize, complain of our sadness or drink vodka. Why, it is quite clear that to begin to live in the present we must first atone for our past, must be done with it; and we can atone for it only through suffering, only through uncommon, incessant labor. Understand that, Anya.

ANYA: The house we live in ceased to be ours long ago, and I'll go away, I give you my word.

TROFIMOFF: If you have the household keys, throw them in the well and go away. Be free as the wind.

ANYA (*transported*): How well you said that!

TROFIMOFF: Believe me, Anya, believe me! I am not thirty yet, I am young, I am still a student, but I have already borne so much! Every winter I am hungry, sick, anxious, poor as a beggar, and — where has destiny not chased me, where haven't I been! And yet, my soul has always, every minute, day and night, been full of inexplicable premonitions. I have a premonition of happiness, Anya, I see it already —

ANYA (*pensively*): The moon is rising.

(EPIHODOFF *is heard playing on the guitar, always the same sad song. The moon rises. Somewhere near the poplars* VARYA *is looking for* ANYA *and calling: "Anya! Where are you?"*)

TROFIMOFF: Yes, the moon is rising. (*A pause.*) Here is happiness, here it comes, comes always nearer and nearer, I hear its footsteps now. And if we shall not see it, shall not come to know it, what does that matter? Others will see it!

VARYA (off): Anya! Where are you?

TROFIMOFF: Again, that Varya! (Angrily.) It's scandalous!

ANYA: Well, let's go to the river. It's lovely there.

TROFIMOFF: Let's go. (They go out.)

VARYA (off): Anya! Anya!

ACT III

The drawing room, separated by an arch from the ballroom. A chandelier is lighted. A Jewish orchestra is playing — the same that was mentioned in Act II. Evening. In the ballroom they are dancing grand rond. *The voice of* SEMYONOFF-PISHTCHIK: "Promenade à une paire!" *They enter the drawing room; in the first couple are* PISHTCHIK *and* CHARLOTTA IVANOVNA; *in the second,* TROFIMOFF *and* LYUBOFF ANDREEVNA; *in the third,* ANYA *with the* POST-OFFICE CLERK; *in the fourth,* VARYA *with the* STATIONMASTER *et cetera —* VARYA *is crying softly and wipes away her tears while she is dancing.* DUNYASHA *is in the last couple through the drawing room.* PISHTCHIK *shouts: "Grand rond, balancez!" and "Les Cavaliers à genoux et remerciez vos dames!"*

FIERS *in a frock coat goes by with seltzer water on a tray.* PISHTCHIK *and* TROFIMOFF *come into the drawing room.*

PISHTCHIK: I am full-blooded, I have had two strokes already, and dancing is hard for me, but as they say, if you are in a pack of dogs, you may bark and bark, but you must still wag your tail. At that, I have the health of a horse. My dear father — he was a great joker — may he dwell in Heaven — used to talk as if all of our ancient line, the Semyonoff-Pishtchiks, were descended from the very horse that Caligula made a Senator — (Sitting down.) But here's my trouble: I haven't any money. A hungry dog believes in nothing but meat — (Snoring but waking at once.) And the same way with me — I can't talk about anything but money.

TROFIMOFF: Well, to tell you the truth, there is something of a horse about your figure.

PISHTCHIK: Well — a horse is a fine animal — You can sell a horse —

(*The sound of playing billiards comes from the next room.* VARYA *appears under the arch to the ballroom.*)

TROFIMOFF (teasing): Madam Lopahin! Madam Lopahin!

VARYA (angrily): A mangy-looking gentleman!

TROFIMOFF: Yes, I am a mangy-looking gentleman, and proud of it!

VARYA (in bitter thought): Here we have gone and hired musicians and what are we going to pay them with? (Goes out.)

TROFIMOFF (to PISHTCHIK): If the energy you have wasted in the course of your life trying to find money to pay the interest had gone into something else, you could very likely have turned the world upside down before you were done with it.

PISHTCHIK: Nietzsche — the philosopher — the greatest — the most celebrated — a man of tremendous mind — says in his works that one may make counterfeit money.

TROFIMOFF: And have you read Nietzsche?

PISHTCHIK: Well — Dashenka told me. And I'm in such a state now that I could make counterfeit money myself — Day after tomorrow three hundred and ten roubles must be paid — one hundred and thirty I've on hand — (Feeling in his pockets, alarmed.) The money is gone! I have lost the money! (Tearfully.) Where is the money? (Joyfully.) Here it is, inside the lining — I was in quite a sweat —

(LYUBOFF ANDREEVNA *and* CHARLOTTA IVANOVNA *come in.*)

LYUBOFF ANDREEVNA (humming lazginka, a Georgian dance): Why does Leonid take so long? What's he doing in town? (To DUNYASHA.) Dunyasha, offer the musicians some tea —

TROFIMOFF: In all probability the auction did not take place.

LYUBOFF ANDREEVNA: And the musicians came at an unfortunate moment and we planned the ball at an unfortunate moment — Well, it doesn't matter. (Sitting down and singing softly.)

CHARLOTTA (gives PISHTCHIK a deck of cards): Here is a deck of cards for you, think of some one card.

PISHTCHIK: I have thought of one.

CHARLOTTA: Now, shuffle the deck. Very good. Hand it here; oh, my dear Monsieur Pishtchik. *Ein, zwei, drei!* Now look for it, it's in your coat pocket —

PISHTCHIK (*getting a card out of his coat pocket*): The Eight of Spades, that's absolutely right! (*Amazed.*) Fancy that!

CHARLOTTA (*holding a deck of cards in her palm; to* TROFIMOFF): Tell me quick now, which card is on top?

TROFIMOFF: What is it? Well — the Queen of Spades.

CHARLOTTA: Right! (*To* PISHTCHIK.) Well? Which card's on top?

PISHTCHIK: The Ace of Hearts.

CHARLOTTA: Right! (*Strikes the deck against her palm; the deck of cards disappears.*) And what beautiful weather we are having today!

(*A mysterious feminine voice answers her, as if from under the floor: "Oh, yes. The weather is splendid, madame." "You are so nice, you're my ideal —" The voice: "Madame, you too please me greatly."*)

THE STATIONMASTER (*applauding*): Madam Ventriloquist, bravo!

PISHTCHIK (*amazed*): Fancy that! Most charming Charlotta Ivanovna — I am simply in love with you.

CHARLOTTA: In love? (*Shrugging her shoulders.*) Is it possible that you can love? *Guter Mensch aber schlechter Musikant.*

TROFIMOFF (*slapping* PISHTCHIK *on the shoulder*): You horse, you —

CHARLOTTA: I beg your attention, one more trick. (*Taking a lap robe from the chair.*) Here is a very fine lap robe — I want to sell it — (*Shaking it out.*) Wouldn't somebody like to buy it?

PISHTCHIK (*amazed*): Fancy that!

CHARLOTTA: *Ein, zwei, drei!*

(*She quickly raises the lowered robe, behind it stands* ANYA, *who curtseys, runs to her mother, embraces her and runs back into the ballroom amid the general delight.*)

LYUBOFF ANDREEVNA (*applauding*): Bravo, bravo — !

CHARLOTTA: Now again! *Ein, zwei, drei!*

(*Lifting the robe: behind it stands* VARYA, *she bows.*)

PISHTCHIK (*amazed*): Fancy that!

CHARLOTTA: That's all. (*Throwing the robe at* PISHTCHIK, *curtseying and running into the ballroom.*)

PISHTCHIK (*hurrying after her*): You little rascal — What a girl! What a girl! (*Goes out.*)

LYUBOFF ANDREEVNA: And Leonid is not here yet. What he's doing in town so long, I don't understand! Everything is finished there, either the estate is sold by now, or the auction didn't take place. Why keep it from us so long?

VARYA (*trying to comfort her*): Uncle has bought it, I am sure of that.

TROFIMOFF (*mockingly*): Yes.

VARYA: Great-aunt sent him power of attorney to buy it in her name and transfer the debt. She did this for Anya. And I feel certain, God willing, that Uncle will buy it.

LYUBOFF ANDREEVNA: Our Yaroslavl great-aunt has sent fifteen thousand to buy the estate in her name — She doesn't trust us, but that wouldn't be enough to pay the interest even — (*Covering her face with her hands.*) Today my fate will be decided, my fate —

TROFIMOFF (*teasing* VARYA): Madam Lopahin!

VARYA (*angrily*): Perennial student! You have already been expelled from the University twice.

LYUBOFF ANDREEVNA: But why are you angry, Varya? He teases you about Lopahin, what of it? Marry Lopahin if you want to, he is a good man, interesting. If you don't want to, don't marry him; darling, nobody is making you do it.

VARYA: I look at this matter seriously, Mama, one must speak straight out. He's a good man, I like him.

LYUBOFF ANDREEVNA: Then marry him. What there is to wait for I don't understand!

VARYA: But I can't propose to him myself, Mama. It's two years now; everyone has been talking to me about him, everyone talks, and he either remains silent or jokes. I understand. He's getting rich, he's busy with his own affairs, and has no time for me. If there were money, ever so little, even a hundred roubles, I would drop everything, and go far away. I'd go to a nunnery.

TROFIMOFF: How saintly!

VARYA (*to* TROFIMOFF): A student should be intelligent! (*In a low voice, tearfully.*) How homely you have grown, Petya, how old you've got. (*To* LYUBOFF ANDREEVNA, *no longer* crying.) It is just that I can't live without working, Mama. I must be doing something every minute.

YASHA (YASHA *enters. Barely restraining his laughter*): Epihodoff has broken a billiard cue! — (*Goes out.*)

VARYA: But why is Epihodoff here? Who allowed him to play billiards? I don't understand these people — (*Goes out.*)

LYUBOFF ANDREEVNA: Don't tease her, Petya; you can see she has troubles enough without that.

TROFIMOFF: She is just too zealous. Sticking her nose into things that are none of her business. All summer she gave us no peace, neither me nor Anya; she was afraid a romance would spring up between us. What business is that of hers? And besides I haven't shown any signs of it. I am so remote from triviality. We are above love!

LYUBOFF ANDREEVNA: Well, then, I must be beneath love. (*Very anxiously.*) Why isn't Leonid here? Just to tell us whether the estate is sold or not? Calamity seems to me so incredible that I don't know what to think, I'm lost — I could scream this minute — I could do something insane. Save me, Petya. Say something, do say....

TROFIMOFF: Whether the estate is sold today or is not sold — is it not the same? There is no turning back, the path is all grown over. Calm yourself, my dear, all that was over long ago. One mustn't deceive oneself, one must for once at least in one's life look truth straight in the eye.

LYUBOFF ANDREEVNA: What truth? You see where the truth is and where the untruth is, but as for me, it's as if I had lost my sight, I see nothing. You boldly decide all important questions, but tell me, my dear boy, isn't that because you are young and haven't had time yet to suffer through any one of your problems? You look boldly ahead, and isn't that because you don't see and don't expect anything terrible, since life is still hidden from your young eyes? You are braver, more honest, more profound than we are, but stop and think, be magnanimous, have a little mercy on me, just a little. Why, I was born here. My father and mother lived here and my grandfather. I love this house, I can't imagine my life without the cherry orchard and if it is very necessary to sell it, then sell me along with the orchard — (*Embracing* TROFIMOFF *and kissing him on the forehead.*) Why, my son was

drowned here — (*Crying.*) Have mercy on me, good, kind man.

TROFIMOFF: You know I sympathize with you from the bottom of my heart.

LYUBOFF ANDREEVNA: But that should be said differently, differently — (*Taking out her handkerchief; a telegram falls on the floor.*) My heart is heavy today, you can't imagine how heavy. It is too noisy for me here, my soul trembles at every sound, I tremble all over and yet I can't go off to myself, when I am alone the silence frightens me. Don't blame me, Petya — I love you as one of my own. I should gladly have given you Anya's hand, I assure you, only, my dear, you must study and finish your course. You do nothing. Fate simply flings you about from place to place, and that's so strange — Isn't that so? Yes? And you must do something about your beard, to make it grow somehow — (*Laughing.*) You look funny!

TROFIMOFF (*picking up the telegram*): I do not desire to be beautiful.

LYUBOFF ANDREEVNA: This telegram is from Paris. I get one every day. Yesterday and today too. That wild man has fallen ill again, something is wrong again with him — He asks forgiveness, begs me to come, and really I ought to make a trip to Paris and stay awhile near him. Your face looks stern, Petya, but what is there to do, my dear, what am I to do, he is ill, he is alone, unhappy and who will look after him there, who will keep him from doing the wrong thing, who will give him his medicine on time? And what is there to hide or keep still about? I love him, that's plain. I love him, love him — It's a stone about my neck, I'm sinking to the bottom with it, but I love that stone and live without it I cannot. (*Pressing* TROFIMOFF's *hand.*) Don't think harshly of me, Petya, don't say anything to me, don't —

TROFIMOFF (*tearfully*): Forgive my frankness, for God's sake! Why, he picked your bones.

LYUBOFF ANDREEVNA: No, no, no, you must not talk like that. (*Stopping her ears.*)

TROFIMOFF: But he is a scoundrel, only you, you are the only one that doesn't know it. He is a petty scoundrel, a nonentity —

LYUBOFF ANDREEVNA (*angry but controlling herself*): You are twenty-six years old or twenty-seven, but you are still a schoolboy in the second grade!

TROFIMOFF: Very well!

LYUBOFF ANDREEVNA: You should be a man

— at your age you should understand people who love. And you yourself should love someone — you should fall in love! (*Angrily.*) Yes, yes! And there is no purity in you; you are simply smug, a ridiculous crank, a freak —

TROFIMOFF (*horrified*): What is she saying!

LYUBOFF ANDREEVNA: "I am above love!" You are not above love, Petya, you are, as our Fiers would say, just a good-for-nothing. Imagine, at your age, not having a mistress — !

TROFIMOFF (*horrified*): This is terrible! What is she saying! (*Goes quickly into the ballroom, clutching his head.*) This is horrible — I can't bear it, I am going — (*Goes out but immediately returns.*) All is over between us. (*Goes out into the hall.*)

LYUBOFF ANDREEVNA (*shouting after him*): Petya, wait! You funny creature, I was joking! Petya! (*In the hall you hear someone running up the stairs and suddenly falling back down with a crash. You hear* ANYA *and* VARYA *scream but immediately you hear laughter.*) What's that?

ANYA (ANYA *runs in. Laughing*): Petya fell down the stairs! (*Runs out.*)

LYUBOFF ANDREEVNA: What a funny boy that Petya is — ! (*The* STATIONMASTER *stops in the center of the ballroom and begins to recite "The Sinner" by A. Tolstoi. They listen to him but he has recited only a few lines when the strains of a waltz are heard from the hall and the recitation is broken off. They all dance.* TROFIMOFF, ANYA, VARYA *and* LYUBOFF ANDREEVNA *come in from the hall.*) But, Petya — but, dear soul — I beg your forgiveness — Let's go dance. (*She dances with* TROFIMOFF. ANYA *and* VARYA *dance.* FIERS *enters, leaving his stick by the side door.* YASHA *also comes into the drawing room and watches the dancers.*)

YASHA: What is it, Grandpa?

FIERS: I don't feel very well. In the old days there were generals, barons, admirals dancing at our parties, and now we send for the post-office clerk and the stationmaster, and even they are none too anxious to come. Somehow I've grown feeble. The old master, the grandfather, treated everybody with sealing-wax for all sicknesses. I take sealing-wax every day, have done so for twenty-odd years or more; it may be due to that that I'm alive.

YASHA: You are tiresome, Grandpa. (*Yawning.*) Why don't you go off and die?

FIERS: Aw, you — good-for-nothing! — (*Muttering.*)

(TROFIMOFF *and* LYUBOFF ANDREEVNA *dance in the ballroom and then in the drawing room.*)

LYUBOFF ANDREEVNA: *Merci.* I'll sit down awhile — (*Sitting down.*) I'm tired.

ANYA (ANYA *enters. Agitated*): And just now in the kitchen some man was saying that the cherry orchard had been sold today.

LYUBOFF ANDREEVNA: Sold to whom?

ANYA: He didn't say who to. He's gone.

(*Dancing with* TROFIMOFF, *they pass into the ballroom.*)

YASHA: It was some old man babbling there. A stranger.

FIERS: And Leonid Andreevich is still not here, he has not arrived. The overcoat he has on is light, midseason — let's hope he won't catch cold. Ach, these young things!

LYUBOFF ANDREEVNA: I shall die this minute. Go, Yasha, find out who it was sold to.

YASHA: But he's been gone a long time, the old fellow. (*Laughing.*)

LYUBOFF ANDREEVNA (*with some annoyance*): Well, what are you laughing at? What are you so amused at?

YASHA: Epihodoff is just too funny. An empty-headed man. Twenty-two misfortunes!

LYUBOFF ANDREEVNA: Fiers, if the estate is sold, where will you go?

FIERS: Wherever you say, there I'll go.

LYUBOFF ANDREEVNA: Why do you look like that? Aren't you well? You know you ought to go to bed —

FIERS: Yes — (*With a sneer.*) I go to bed and without me who's going to serve, who'll take care of things? I'm the only one in the whole house.

YASHA (*to* LYUBOFF ANDREEVNA): Lyuboff Andreevna, let me ask a favor of you, do be so kind! If you ever go back to Paris, take me with you, please do! It's impossible for me to stay here. (*Looking around him, and speaking in a low voice.*) Why talk about it? You can see for yourself it's an uncivilized country, an immoral people and not only that, there's the boredom of it. The food they give us in that kitchen is abominable and there's that Fiers, too, walking about and muttering all kinds of words that are out of place. Take me with you, be so kind!

PISHTCHIK (*enters*): Allow me to ask you — for a little waltz, most beautiful lady — (LYUBOFF ANDREEVNA *goes with him.*) Charming lady, I must borrow a hundred and eighty roubles from you — will borrow — (*dancing*) a hundred and eighty roubles — (*They pass into the ballroom.*)

YASHA (*singing low*): "Wilt thou know the unrest in my soul!"

(*In the ballroom a figure in a gray top hat and checked trousers waves both hands and jumps about; there are shouts of "Bravo, Charlotta Ivanovna!"*)

DUNYASHA (*stopping to powder her face*): The young lady orders me to dance — there are a lot of gentlemen and very few ladies — but dancing makes my head swim and my heart thump. Fiers Nikolaevich, the post-office clerk said something to me just now that took my breath away.

(*The music plays more softly.*)

FIERS: What did he say to you?
DUNYASHA: You are like a flower, he says.
YASHA (*yawning*): What ignorance — ! (*Goes out.*)
DUNYASHA: Like a flower — I am such a sensitive girl, I love tender words awfully.
FIERS: You'll be getting your head turned.

(EPIHODOFF *enters.*)

EPIHODOFF: Avdotya Feodorovna, you don't want to see me — It's as if I were some sort of insect. (*Sighing.*) Ach, life!
DUNYASHA: What do you want?
EPIHODOFF: Undoubtedly you may be right. (*Sighing.*) But of course, if one considers it from a given point of view, then you, I will allow myself so to express it, forgive my frankness, absolutely led me into a state of mind. I know my fate, every day some misfortune happens to me, but I have long since become accustomed to that, and so I look on my misfortunes with a smile. You gave me your word and, although I —
DUNYASHA: I beg you, we'll talk later on, but leave me now in peace. I'm in a dream now. (*Playing with her fan.*)
EPIHODOFF: I have a something wrong happens every day — I will allow myself so to express it — I just smile, I even laugh.
VARYA (*enters from the ballroom*): You are not gone yet, Semyon? What a really disrespectful man you are! (*To* DUNYASHA.) Get out of here, Dunyasha. (*To* EPIHODOFF.) You either play billiards and break a cue or you walk about the drawing room like a guest.

EPIHODOFF: Allow me to tell you, you cannot make any demands on me.
VARYA: I'm not making any demands on you, I'm talking to you. All you know is to walk from place to place but not do any work. We keep a clerk, but what for, nobody knows.
EPIHODOFF (*offended*): Whether I work, whether I walk, whether I eat, or whether I play billiards are matters to be discussed only by people of understanding and my seniors.
VARYA: You dare to say that to me! (*Flying into a temper.*) You dare? So I don't understand anything? Get out of here! This minute!
EPIHODOFF (*alarmed*): I beg you to express yourself in a delicate manner.
VARYA (*beside herself*): This very minute, get out of here! Get out! (*He goes to the door; she follows him.*) Twenty-two misfortunes! Don't you dare breathe in here! Don't let me set eyes on you! (EPIHODOFF *has gone out, but his voice comes from outside the door: "I shall complain about you."*) Ah, you are coming back? (*Grabbing the stick that* FIERS *put by the door.*) Come on, come — come on, I'll show you — Ah, you are coming? You are coming? Take that then — !

(*She swings the stick, at the very moment when* LOPAHIN *is coming in.*)

LOPAHIN: Most humbly, I thank you.
VARYA (*angrily and ironically*): I beg your pardon!
LOPAHIN: It's nothing at all. I humbly thank you for the pleasant treat.
VARYA: It isn't worth your thanks. (*Moving away, then looking back and asking gently.*) I haven't hurt you?
LOPAHIN: No, it's nothing. There's a great bump coming though.

(*Voices in the ballroom: "Lopahin has come back." "Yermolay Alexeevich!"*)

PISTCHIK (*enters*): See what we see, hear what we hear — ! (*He and* LOPAHIN *kiss one another.*) You smell slightly of cognac, my dear, my good old chap. And we are amusing ourselves here too.
LYUBOFF ANDREEVNA (*enters*): Is that you, Yermolay Alexeevich? Why were you so long? Where is Leonid?
LOPAHIN: Leonid Andreevich got back when I did, he's coming.
LYUBOFF ANDREEVNA (*agitated*): Well, what? Was there an auction? Do speak!
LOPAHIN (*embarrassed, afraid of showing the*

joy he feels): The auction was over by four o'clock — We were late for the train, had to wait till half-past nine. (*Sighing heavily.*) Ugh, my head's swimming a bit!

(GAYEFF *enters; with his right hand he carries his purchases, with his left he wipes away his tears.*)

LYUBOFF ANDREEVNA: Lyona, what? Lyona, eh? (*Impatiently, with tears in her eyes.*) Quick, for God's sake —

GAYEFF (*not answering her, merely waving his hand; to* FIERS, *crying*): Here, take it — There are anchovies, some Kertch herrings — I haven't eaten anything all day — What I have suffered! (*The door into the billiard room is open; you hear the balls clicking and* YASHA'S *voice: "Seven and eighteen!"* GAYEFF'S *expression changes, he is no longer crying.*) I'm terribly tired. You help me change, Fiers. (*Goes to his room through the ballroom,* FIERS *behind him.*)

PISHTCHIK: What happened at the auction? Go on, tell us!

LYUBOFF ANDREEVNA: Is the cherry orchard sold?

LOPAHIN: It's sold.

LYUBOFF ANDREEVNA: Who bought it?

LOPAHIN: I bought it. (*A pause.* LYUBOFF ANDREEVNA *is overcome. She would have fallen had she not been standing near the chair and table.* VARYA *takes the keys from her belt, throws them on the floor in the middle of the drawing room and goes out.*) I bought it. Kindly wait a moment, ladies and gentlemen, everything is muddled up in my head, I can't speak — (*Laughing.*) We arrived at the auction, Deriganoff was already there. Leonid Andreevich had only fifteen thousand and Deriganoff right off bids thirty over and above indebtedness. I see how things are, I match him with forty thousand. He forty-five. I fifty-five. That is to say he raises it by fives, I by tens — So it ended. Over and above the indebtedness, I bid up to ninety thousand, it was knocked down to me. The cherry orchard is mine now. Mine! (*Guffawing.*) My God, Lord, the cherry orchard is mine! Tell me I'm drunk, out of my head, that I'm imagining all this — (*Stamps his feet.*) Don't laugh at me! If only my father and grandfather could rise from their graves and see this whole business, see how their Yermolay, beaten, half-illiterate Yermolay, who used to run around barefoot in winter, how that very Yermolay has bought an estate that nothing in the world can beat. I bought the estate where grandfather and father were slaves, where you wouldn't even let me in the kitchen. I am asleep, it's only some dream of mine, it only seems so to me — That's nothing but the fruit of your imagination, covered with the darkness of the unknown — (*Picking up the keys, with a gentle smile.*) She threw down the keys, wants to show she is not mistress any more — (*Jingling the keys.*) Well, it's all the same. (*The orchestra is heard tuning up.*) Hey, musicians, play, I want to hear you! Come on, everybody, and see how Yermolay Lopahin will swing the ax in the cherry orchard, how the trees will fall to the ground! We are going to build villas and our grandsons and great-grandsons will see a new life here — Music, play! (*The music is playing.* LYUBOFF ANDREEVNA *has sunk into a chair, crying bitterly.* LOPAHIN *reproachfully.*) Why, then, didn't you listen to me? My poor dear, it can't be undone now. (*With tears.*) Oh, if this could all be over soon, if somehow our awkward, unhappy life would be changed!

PISHTCHIK (*taking him by the arm, in a low voice*): She is crying. Come on in the ball-room, let her be by herself — Come on — (*Taking him by the arm and leading him into the ballroom.*)

LOPAHIN: What's the matter? Music, there, play up! (*Sarcastically.*) Everything is to be as I want it! Here comes the new squire, the owner of the cherry orchard. (*Quite accidentally, he bumps into the little table, and very nearly upsets the candelabra.*) I can pay for everything!

(*Goes out with* PISHTCHIK. *There is nobody left either in the ballroom or the drawing room but* LYUBOFF ANDREEVNA, *who sits all huddled up and crying bitterly. The music plays softly.* ANYA *and* TROFIMOFF *enter hurriedly.* ANYA *comes up to her mother and kneels in front of her.* TROFIMOFF *remains at the ballroom door.*)

ANYA: Mama — ! Mama, you are crying? My dear, kind, good Mama, my beautiful, I love you — I bless you. The cherry orchard is sold, it's not ours any more, that's true, true; but don't cry, Mama, you've your life still left you, you've your good, pure heart ahead of you — Come with me, come on, darling, away from here, come on — We will plant a new orchard, finer than this one, you'll see it, you'll understand; and joy, quiet, deep joy will sink into your heart, like the sun at evening, and you'll smile, Mama! Come, darling, come on!

ACT IV

The same setting as in Act I. There are neither curtains on the windows nor are there any pictures on the walls. Only a little furniture remains piled up in one corner as if for sale. A sense of emptiness is felt. Near the outer door, at the rear of the stage, is a pile of suitcases, traveling bags, and so on. The door on the left is open, and through it VARYA's *and* ANYA's *voices are heard.* LOPAHIN *is standing waiting.* YASHA *is holding a tray with glasses of champagne. In the hall* EPIHODOFF *is tying up a box, offstage at the rear there is a hum. It is the peasants who have come to say good-by.* GAYEFF's *voice: "Thanks, brothers, thank you."*

YASHA: The simple folk have come to say good-by. I am of the opinion, Yermolay Alexeevich, that the people are kind enough but don't understand anything.

(The hum subsides. LYUBOFF ANDREEVNA *enters through the hall with* GAYEFF; *she is not crying, but is pale, her face quivers, she is not able to speak.)*

GAYEFF: You gave them your purse, Lyuba. Mustn't do that! Mustn't do that

LYUBOFF ANDREEVNA: I couldn't help it! I couldn't help it!

(Both go out.)

LOPAHIN *(calling through the door after them)*: Please, I humbly beg you! A little glass at parting. I didn't think to bring some from town, and at the station I found just one bottle. Please! *(A pause.)* Well, then, ladies and gentlemen! You don't want it? *(Moving away from the door.)* If I'd known that, I wouldn't have bought it. Well, then I won't drink any either. *(*YASHA *carefully sets the tray down on a chair.)* At least, you have some, Yasha.

YASHA: To those who are departing! Pleasant days to those who stay behind! *(Drinking.)* This champagne is not the real stuff, I can assure you.

LOPAHIN: Eight roubles a bottle. *(A pause.)* It's devilish cold in here.

YASHA: They didn't heat up today, we are leaving anyway. *(Laughing.)*

LOPAHIN: What are you laughing about?

YASHA: For joy.

LOPAHIN: Outside it's October, but it's sunny and still, like summer. Good for building. *(Looking at his watch, then through the door.)* Ladies and gentlemen, bear in mind we have forty-six minutes in all till train time! Which means you have to go to the station in twenty minutes. Hurry up a little.

TROFIMOFF *(in an overcoat, entering from outside)*: Seems to me it is time to go. The carriages are ready. The devil knows where my rubbers are. They've disappeared. *(In the door.)* Anya, my rubbers are not here! I can't find them.

LOPAHIN: And I have to go to Harkoff. I'm going on the same train with you. I'm going to live in Harkoff all winter. I've been dilly-dallying along with you, I'm tired of doing nothing. I can't be without work, look, I don't know what to do with my hands here, see, they are dangling somehow, as if they didn't belong to me.

TROFIMOFF: We are leaving right away, and you'll set about your useful labors again.

LOPAHIN: Here, drink a glass.

TROFIMOFF: I shan't.

LOPAHIN: It's to Moscow now?

TROFIMOFF: Yes. I'll see them off to town, and tomorrow to Moscow.

LOPAHIN: Yes — Maybe the professors are not giving their lectures. I imagine they are waiting till you arrive.

TROFIMOFF: That's none of your business.

LOPAHIN: How many years is it you've been studying at the University?

TROFIMOFF: Think of something newer. This is old and flat. *(Looking for his rubbers.)* You know, perhaps, we shall not see each other again; therefore, permit me to give you one piece of advice at parting! Don't wave your arms! Cure yourself of that habit — of arm waving. And also of building summer cottages, figuring that the summer residents will in time become individual landowners; figuring like that is arm waving too — Just the same, however, I like you. You have delicate soft fingers like an artist, you have a delicate soft heart —

LOPAHIN *(embracing him)*: Good-by, my

dear boy. Thanks for everything. If you need it, take some money from me for the trip.

TROFIMOFF: Why should I? There's no need for it.

LOPAHIN: But you haven't any!

TROFIMOFF: I have. Thank you. I got some for a translation. Here it is in my pocket. (*Anxiously.*) But my rubbers are gone.

VARYA (*from another room*): Take your nasty things! (*Throws a pair of rubbers on to the stage.*)

TROFIMOFF: But what are you angry about, Varya? Hm — Why, these are not my rubbers.

LOPAHIN: In the spring I planted twenty-seven hundred acres of poppies and now I've made forty thousand clear. And when my poppies were in bloom, what a picture it was! So look, as I say, I've made forty thousand, which means I'm offering you a loan because I can afford to. Why turn up your nose? I'm a peasant — I speak straight out.

TROFIMOFF: Your father was a peasant, mine — an apothecary — and from that absolutely nothing follows. (LOPAHIN *takes out his wallet.*) Leave it alone, leave it alone — If you gave me two hundred thousand even, I wouldn't take it. I am a free man. And everything that you all value so highly and dearly, both rich man and beggars, has not the slightest power over me, it's like a mere feather floating in the air. I can get along without you, I can pass you by, I am strong and proud. Humanity is moving toward the loftiest truth, toward the loftiest happiness that is possible on earth and I am in the front ranks.

LOPAHIN: Will you get there?

TROFIMOFF: I'll get there. (*A pause.*) I'll get there, or I'll show the others the way to get there.

(*In the distance is heard the sound of an ax on a tree.*)

LOPAHIN: Well, good-by, my dear boy. It's time to go. We turn up our noses at one another, but life keeps on passing. When I work a long time without stopping, my thoughts are clearer, and it seems as if I, too, know what I exist for, and, brother, how many people are there in Russia who exist, nobody knows for what? Well, all the same, it's not that that keeps things circulating. Leonid Andreevich, they say, has accepted a position — he'll be in a bank, six thousand a year —

the only thing is he won't stay there, he's very lazy —

ANYA (*in the doorway*): Mama begs of you until she's gone, not to cut down the orchard.

TROFIMOFF: Honestly, haven't you enough tact to — (*Goes out through the hall.*)

LOPAHIN: Right away, right away — What people, really! (*Goes out after him.*)

ANYA: Has Fiers been sent to the hospital?

YASHA: I told them to this morning. They must have sent him.

ANYA (*to* EPIHODOFF, *who is passing through the room*): Semyon Panteleevich, please inquire whether or not they have taken Fiers to the hospital.

YASHA (*huffily*): This morning, I told Igor. Why ask ten times over!

EPIHODOFF: The venerable Fiers, according to my conclusive opinion, is not worth mending, he ought to join his forefathers. And I can only envy him. (*Putting a suitcase on a hatbox and crushing it.*) Well, there you are, of course. I knew it. (*Goes out.*)

YASHA (*mockingly*): Twenty-two misfortunes —

VARYA (*on the other side of the door*): Have they taken Fiers to the hospital?

ANYA: They have.

VARYA: Then why didn't they take the letter to the doctor?

ANYA: We must send it on after *them* — (*Goes out.*)

VARYA (*from the next room*): Where is Yasha? Tell him his mother has come, she wants to say good-by to him.

YASHA (*waving his hand*): They merely try my patience.

(DUNYASHA *has been busying herself with the luggage; now when* YASHA *is left alone, she goes up to him.*)

DUNYASHA: If you'd only look at me once, Yasha. You are going away — leaving me — (*Crying and throwing herself on his neck.*)

YASHA: Why are you crying? (*Drinking champagne.*) In six days I'll be in Paris again. Tomorrow we will board the express train and dash off out of sight; somehow, I can't believe it. *Vive la France!* It doesn't suit me here — I can't live here — Can't help that. I've seen enough ignorance — enough for me. (*Drinking champagne.*) Why do you cry? Behave yourself properly, then you won't be crying.

DUNYASHA (*powdering her face, looking into*

a small mirror): Send me a letter from Paris. I loved you, Yasha, you know, loved you so! I am a tender creature, Yasha!

YASHA: They are coming here. (*Bustling about near the suitcases, humming low.*)

(LYUBOFF ANDREEVNA, GAYEFF, ANYA *and* CHARLOTTA IVANOVNA *enter.*)

GAYEFF: We should be going. There is very little time left. (*Looking at* YASHA.) Who is it smells like herring!

LYUBOFF ANDREEVNA: In about ten minutes let's be in the carriage — (*Glancing around the room.*) Good-by, dear house, old Grandfather. Winter will pass, spring will be here, but you won't be here any longer, they'll tear you down. How much these walls have seen! (*Kissing her daughter warmly.*) My treasure, you are beaming, your eyes are dancing like two diamonds. Are you happy? Very?

ANYA: Very! It's the beginning of a new life, Mama!

GAYEFF (*gaily*): Yes, indeed, everything is fine now. Before the sale of the cherry orchard, we all were troubled, distressed, and then when the question was settled definitely, irrevocably, we all calmed down and were even cheerful — I'm a bank official. I am a financier now — Yellow ball into the side pocket, anyway, Lyuba, you look better, no doubt about that.

LYUBOFF ANDREEVNA: Yes. My nerves are better, that's true. (*They hand her her hat and coat.*) I sleep well. Carry out my things, Yasha. It's time. (*To* ANYA.) My little girl, we shall see each other again soon — I am going to Paris, I shall live there on the money your Yaroslavl great-aunt sent for the purchase of the estate — long live Great-aunt! But that money won't last long.

ANYA: Mama, you'll come back soon, soon — Isn't that so? I'll prepare myself, pass the examination at high school, and then I'll work, I will help you. We'll read all sorts of books together. Mama, isn't that so? (*Kissing her mother's hands.*) We'll read in the autumn evenings, read lots of books, and a new, wonderful world will open up before us — (*Daydreaming.*) Mama, do come —

LYUBOFF ANDREEVNA: I'll come, my precious. (*Embracing her daughter.*)

(LOPAHIN *enters with* CHARLOTTA *who is softly humming a song.*)

GAYEFF: Lucky Charlotta: she's singing!

CHARLOTTA (*taking a bundle that looks like a baby wrapped up*): My baby, bye, bye — (*A baby's cry is heard: Ooah, ooah —* ! Hush, my darling, my dear little boy. (*Ooah, ooah —* !) I am so sorry for you! (*Throwing the bundle back.*) Will you please find me a position? I cannot go on like this.

LOPAHIN: We will find something, Charlotta Ivanovna, don't worry.

GAYEFF: Everybody is dropping us, Varya is going away. — All of a sudden we are not needed.

CHARLOTTA: I have no place in town to live. I must go away. (*Humming.*) It's all the same —

(PISHTCHIK *enters.*)

LOPAHIN: The freak of nature — !

PISHTCHIK (*out of breath*): Ugh, let me catch my breath — I'm exhausted — My honored friends — Give me some water —

GAYEFF: After money, I suppose? This humble servant will flee from sin! (*Goes out.*)

PISHTCHIK: It's a long time since I was here — Most beautiful lady — (*To* LOPAHIN.) You here — ? Glad to see you — a man of the greatest intellect — Here — Take it — (*Giving* LOPAHIN *some money.*) Four hundred roubles — That leaves eight hundred and forty I still owe you —

LOPAHIN (*with astonishment, shrugging his shoulders*): I must be dreaming. But where did you get it?

PISHTCHIK: Wait — I'm hot — Most extraordinary event. Some Englishmen came and found on my land some kind of white clay — (*To* LYUBOFF ANDREEVNA.) And four hundred for you — Beautiful lady — Wonderful lady — (*Handing over the money.*) The rest later. (*Taking a drink of water.*) Just now a young man was saying on the train that some great philosopher recommends jumping off roofs — "Jump!" he says, and "therein lies the whole problem." (*With astonishment.*) You don't say! Water!

LOPAHIN: And what Englishmen were they?

PISHTCHIK: I leased them the parcel of land with the clay for twenty-four years — And now, excuse me, I haven't time — I must run along — I'm going to Znoykoff's — To Kardamonoff's — I owe everybody — (*Drinking.*) I wish you well — I'll drop in on Thursday —

LYUBOFF ANDREEVNA: We are moving to

town right away, and tomorrow I'm going abroad —

PISHTCHIK: What? (*Alarmed.*) Why to town? That's why I see furniture — Suitcases — Well, no matter — (*Tearfully.*) No matter — Men of the greatest minds — those Englishmen — No matter — Good luck! God will help you — No matter — Everything in this world comes to an end — (*Kissing* LYUBOFF ANDREEVNA's *hand.*) And should the report reach you that my end has come, think of that well-known horse and say: "There was once on earth a so and so — Semyonoff Pishtchik — The kingdom of Heaven be his." Most remarkable weather — yes — (*Going out greatly disconcerted, but immediately returning and speaking from the door.*) Dashenka sends her greetings! (*Goes out.*)

LYUBOFF ANDREEVNA: And now we can go. I am leaving with two worries. First, that Fiers is sick. (*Glancing at her watch.*) We still have five minutes —

ANYA: Mama, Fiers has already been sent to the hospital. Yasha sent him off this morning.

LYUBOFF ANDREEVNA: My second worry — is Varya. She is used to getting up early and working, and now without any work she is like a fish out of water. She has grown thin, pale and cries all the time, poor thing — (*A pause.*) You know this, Yermolay Alexeevich: I dreamed — of marrying her to you. And there was every sign of your getting married.(*Whispering to* ANYA, *who beckons to* CHARLOTTA; *both go out.*) She loves you, you are fond of her, and I don't know, don't know why it is you seem to avoid each other — I don't understand it!

LOPAHIN: I don't understand it either, I must confess. It's all strange somehow — If there's still time, I am ready right now even — Let's finish it up — and *basta*, but without you I feel I won't propose.

LYUBOFF ANDREEVNA: But that's excellent. Surely it takes only a minute. I'll call her at once.

LOPAHIN: And to fit the occasion there's the champagne. (*Looking at the glasses.*) Empty, somebody has already drunk them. (YASHA *coughs.*) That's what's called lapping it up —

LYUBOFF ANDREEVNA (*vivaciously*): Splendid! We'll go out — Yasha, *allez!* I'll call her — (*Through the door.*) Varya, drop everything and come here. Come on! (*Goes out with* YASHA.)

LOPAHIN (*looking at his watch*): Yes —

(*A pause. Behind the door you hear smothered laughter, whispering, finally* VARYA *enters.*)

VARYA (*looking at the luggage a long time*): That's strange, I just can't find it —

LOPAHIN: What are you looking for?

VARYA: I packed it myself and don't remember where. (*A pause.*)

LOPAHIN: Where do you expect to go now, Varvara Mikhailovna?

VARYA: I? To Regulin's. I agreed to go there to look after the house — As a sort of housekeeper.

LOPAHIN: That's in Yashnevo? It's nigh on to seventy miles. (*A pause.*) And here ends life in this house —

VARYA (*examining the luggage*): But where is it? Either I put it in the trunk, perhaps — Yes, life in this house is ended — it won't be any more—

LOPAHIN: And I am going to Harkoff now — By the next train. I've a lot to do. And I am leaving Epihodoff — on the ground here — I've hired him.

VARYA: Well!

LOPAHIN: Last year at this time it had already been snowing, if you remember, and now it's quiet, it's sunny. It's only that it's cold, about three degrees of frost.

VARYA: I haven't noticed. (*A pause.*) And besides our thermometer is broken — (*A pause. A voice from the yard through the door.*) Yermolay Alexeevich —

LOPAHIN (*as if he had been expecting this call for a long time*): This minute! (*Goes out quickly.*)

(VARYA, *sitting on the floor, putting her head on a bundle of clothes, sobs quietly. The door opens,* LYUBOFF ANDREEVNA *enters cautiously.*)

VARYA (*she is not crying any longer, and has wiped her eyes*): Yes, it's time, Mama. I can get to Regulin's today, if we are just not too late for the train — (*Through the door.*) Anya, put your things on! (ANYA, *then* GAYEFF *and* CHARLOTTA IVANOVNA *enter.* GAYEFF *has on a warm overcoat, with a hood. The servants gather, also the drivers.* EPIHODOFF *busies himself with the luggage.*) Now we can be on our way.

ANYA (*joyfully*): On our way!

GAYEFF: My friends, my dear, kind friends! Leaving this house forever, can I remain silent, can I restrain myself from expressing, as we say, farewell, those feelings that fill now my whole being —

ANYA (*beseechingly*): Uncle!

VARYA: Dear Uncle, don't!

GAYEFF (*dejectedly*): Bank the yellow into the side pocket — I am silent —

(TROFIMOFF *and then* LOPAHIN *enter.*)

TROFIMOFF: Well, ladies and gentlemen, it's time to go!

LOPAHIN: Epihodoff, my coat!

LYUBOFF ANDREEVNA: I'll sit here just a minute more. It's as if I had never seen before what the walls in this house are like, what kind of ceilings, and now I look at them greedily, with such tender love —

GAYEFF: I remember when I was six years old, on Trinity Day, I sat in this window and watched my father going to Church —

LYUBOFF ANDREEVNA: Are all the things taken out?

LOPAHIN: Everything, I think. (*Putting on his overcoat. To* EPIHODOFF.) Epihodoff, you see that everything is in order.

EPIHODOFF (*talking in a hoarse voice*): Don't worry, Yermolay Alexeevich!

LOPAHIN: Why is your voice like that?

EPIHODOFF: Just drank some water, swallowed something.

YASHA (*with contempt*): The ignorance —

LYUBOFF ANDREEVNA: We are going and there won't be a soul left here —

LOPAHIN: Till spring.

VARYA (*she pulls an umbrella out from a bundle, it looks as if she were going to hit someone;* LOPAHIN *pretends to be frightened*): What do you, what do you — I never thought of it.

TROFIMOFF: Ladies and gentlemen, let's get in the carriages — It's time! The train is coming any minute.

VARYA: Petya, here they are, your rubbers, by the suitcase. (*Tearfully.*) And how dirty yours are, how old — !

TROFIMOFF (*putting on the rubbers*): Let's go, ladies and gentlemen!

GAYEFF (*greatly embarrassed, afraid he will cry*): The train — The station — Cross into the side, combination off the white into the corner —

LYUBOFF ANDREEVNA: Let's go!

LOPAHIN: Everybody here? Nobody there? (*Locking the side door on the left.*) Things are stored here, it must be locked up, let's go!

ANYA: Good-by, house! Good-by, the old life!

TROFIMOFF: Long live the new life!

(*Goes out with* ANYA. VARYA *casts a glance around the room and, without hurrying, goes out.* YASHA *and* CHARLOTTA, *with her dog, go out.*)

LOPAHIN: And so, till spring. Out, ladies and gentlemen — Till we meet. (*Goes out.*)

(LYUBOFF ANDREEVNA *and* GAYEFF *are left alone. As if they had been waiting for this, they throw themselves on one another's necks sobbing, but smothering their sobs as if afraid of being heard.*)

GAYEFF (*in despair*): Oh, Sister, Sister —

LYUBOFF ANDREEVNA: Oh, my dear, my lovely, beautiful orchard! My life, my youth, my happiness, good-by!

ANYA (ANYA's *voice, gaily, appealingly*): Mama — !

TROFIMOFF (TROFIMOFF's *voice, gaily, excitedly*): Aaooch!

LYUBOFF ANDREEVNA: For the last time, just to look at the walls, at the window — My dear mother used to love to walk around in this room —

GAYEFF: Oh, Sister, Sister — !

ANYA (ANYA's *voice*): Mama — !

TROFIMOFF (TROFIMOFF's *voice*): Aaooch — !

LYUBOFF ANDREEVNA: We are coming! (*They go out.*)

(*The stage is empty. You hear the keys locking all the doors, then the carriages drive off. It grows quiet. In the silence you hear the dull thud of an ax on a tree, a lonely, mournful sound. Footsteps are heard. From the door on the right* FIERS *appears. He is dressed as usual, in a jacket and a white waistcoat, slippers on his feet. He is sick.*)

FIERS (*going to the door and trying the knob*): Locked. They've gone. (*Sitting down on the sofa.*) They forgot about me — No matter — I'll sit here awhile — And Leonid Andreevich, for sure, didn't put on his fur coat, he went off with his top coat — (*Sighing anxiously.*) And I didn't see to it — The young saplings! (*He mutters something that cannot be understood.*) Life has gone by, as if I hadn't lived at all — (*Lying down.*) I'll lie down awhile — You haven't got any strength, nothing is left, nothing — Ach, you — good-for-nothing — (*He lies still.*)

(*There is a far-off sound as if out of the sky, the sound of a snapped string, dying away, sad. A stillness falls, and there is only the thud of an ax on a tree, far away in the orchard.*)

At the end of *The Cherry Orchard*, the old servant Fiers, forgotten by the family he has long served, wanders onto the stage, locked within the house that is no longer theirs. Is he comic, in his mutterings, in his old maidish frettings about Leonid Andreevich's inadequate coat, and in his implicit realization that although he is concerned about the aristocrats the aristocrats are unconcerned about him? Or is he tragic, dying in isolation? Or neither? The comedy is scarcely uproarious; if there is humor in his realization that his life has been trivial, this humor is surely tinged with melancholy. And the "tragic" reading is also ambiguous: first, the text does not say that he dies; second, if it can be assumed that he dies, the death of an ill eighty-seven-year-old man can scarcely seem untimely; and third, Fiers does not seem particularly concerned about dying.

If this play ends with a death, then, it is not the sort of death that Byron had in mind when he said, "All tragedies are finished by a death, / All comedies are ended by a marriage." We are in the dramatic world that Shaw spoke of when he said that "the curtain no longer comes down on a hero slain or married: it comes down when the audience has seen enough of the life presented to it, . . . and must either leave the theatre or miss its last train." Chekhov insisted that *The Cherry Orchard* was a comedy, but what sort of comedy? In the latter part of the last act there is almost a proposal of marriage, but, typically, it never gets made. For two years everyone has joked about the anticipated marriage between Lopahin and Varya, but when these two are thrust together they are overcome by embarrassment, and the interview is dissipated in small talk. Not that (of course) a comedy must end with a marriage; marriage is only the conventional way of indicating a happy union, or reunion, that symbolizes the triumph of life. But in this play we *begin* with a reunion — the family is reunited in the ancestral home — and we end with a separation, the inhabitants scattering when the home is sold.

Another way of getting at *The Cherry Orchard* is to notice that in this play, although there are innumerable references to Time between the first speech, when Lopahin says "The train got in, thank God! What time is it?" and the last act, where there is much talk about catching the outbound train, Time does not function as it usually functions either in tragedy or in comedy. In tragedy we usually feel, If there had only been more time. . . . For example, in *Romeo and Juliet* Friar Laurence writes a letter to Romeo, explaining that Juliet will take a potion that will put her in a temporary, death-like trance, but the letter is delayed, Romeo mistakenly hears that Juliet is dead, and he kills himself. A few moments after his suicide Juliet revives. Had Friar

Laurence's message arrived on schedule, or had Romeo not been so quick to commit suicide, no great harm would have been done. In *King Lear*, Edmund repents that he has ordered a soldier to kill Cordelia, and a messenger hurries out to change the order, but he is too late.

If in tragedy we usually feel the pressure of time, in comedy there is usually a sense of leisure. Things are difficult now, but in the course of time they will work themselves out. Sooner or later people will realize that the strange goings-on are due to the existence of identical twins; sooner or later the stubborn parents will realize that they cannot forever stand in the way of young lovers; sooner or later the money will turn up and all will be well. In the world of comedy, one is always safe in relying on time. In *The Cherry Orchard*, Lopahin insists, correctly enough, that the family must act *now* if it is to save the orchard: "We must decide definitely, time won't wait." There is ample time to act on Lopahin's suggestion that the orchard be leased for summer houses, and the play covers a period from May to October, but the plan is not acted on because to the aristocrats any sort of selling is unthinkable, and although one Pishtchik is in the course of time miraculously redeemed from financial ruin by some Englishmen who discover and buy "some kind of white clay" on *his* land, time brings Mme. Ranevskaya and her brother Gayeff no such good fortune. So far as the main happenings in the play are concerned, time neither presses nor preserves; it only passes.

During the passage of time in this play, the orchard is lost (tragic?) and the characters reveal themselves to be funny (comic?). The loss of the orchard is itself a happening of an uncertain kind. It stands, partly, for the end of an old way of life. But if that way once included intelligent and gracious aristocrats, it also included slavery, and in any case it now is embodied in the irresponsible heirs we see on the stage, Mme. Ranevskaya and her brother Gayeff, along with their deaf and near-senile servant Fiers. For Gayeff the orchard is important chiefly because it lends prestige, since it is mentioned in the encyclopedia. Mme. Ranevskaya sees more to it. For her it is "all white" and it is "young again and full of happiness"; we are momentarily touched by her vision, but there is yet another way of seeing the orchard: for Trofimoff, a student who envisions a new society as an orchard for all men, the ancestral cherry orchard is haunted by the serfs of the bad old days. Moreover, although the orchard is much talked about, it seems to have decayed to a trivial ornament. Long ago its crop was regularly harvested, pickled, and sold, thus providing food and income, but now "nobody remembers" the pickling formula and nobody buys the crop. There seems to be some truth to Lopahin's assertion that "the only remarkable thing about this cherry orchard is that it's very big," and although one must point out that this remark is made by a despised merchant, Lopahin is neither a fool nor the "money grubber" that Gayeff thinks he is. Lopahin delights in nature put to use. He made "forty thousand clear" from poppies, "And when my poppies were in bloom, what a picture it was!" His enthusiasm for the flowers is undercut for us only a little, if at all, by the fact that they were of use to him and to others.

Lopahin's serious concern, whether for his poppies or for the future of the cherry orchard, contrasts interestingly with Mme. Ranevskaya's and with Gayeff's sporadic passion for the orchard. Mme. Ranevskaya says, "I can't imagine my life without the cherry orchard," and she doubtless means what she says, but that her words have not much relation to reality is indicated by her meaningless addition, "If it is very necessary to sell it, then sell me along with the orchard." After the orchard has been sold, Gayeff confesses, "everything is fine now. Before the sale of the cherry orchard, we all were troubled, distressed, and then when the question was settled definitely, irrevocably, we all calmed down and were even cheerful — I'm a bank official. . . . Lyuba, you look better, no doubt about that." His sister agrees: "Yes. My nerves are better, that's true. . . . I sleep well. Carry out my things, Yasha. It's time." She returns to her lover in Paris, Gayeff goes off to a job in the bank, and though we can imagine that the orchard will continue to be an occasional topic of conversation, we cannot imagine that the loss has in any way changed them. The play ends, but things will go on in the same way; neither a tragic nor a comic action has been completed.

The characters no less than the action are tragicomic. Their longings would touch the heart if only these people did not so quickly digress or engage in little actions that call their depth into doubt. Charlotta laments that she has no proper passport and that her deceased parents may not have been married: "Where I came from and who I am I don't know." And then, having touched on the mighty subject of one's identity, the subject that is the stuff of tragedy in which heroes endure the worst in order to know who they are, she begins to eat a cucumber, and somehow that simple and entirely necessary act diminishes her dignity — though it does not totally dissipate our glimpse of her alienation. In the same scene, when Epihodoff confesses that although he reads "all kinds of remarkable books" he "cannot discover [his] own inclinations," we hear another echo of the tragic hero's quest for self-knowledge, but we also hear an echo from the world of comedy, say of the pedant who guides his life by a textbook. Epihodoff, perhaps like a tragic hero, is particularly concerned with whether to live or to shoot himself, but this racking doubt is diminished by his prompt explanation that since he may someday decide on suicide, he always carries a revolver, which he proceeds to show to his listeners. Almost all of the characters bare their souls, but their slightly addled minds and their hungry bodies expose them to a gentle satirical treatment so that they evoke a curious amused pathos. One can, for example, sympathize with Mme. Ranevskaya's despair — but one cannot forget that she is scatterbrained and that domestic duties and local pieties occupy her mind only occasionally and that her disreputable lover in Paris means as much as the orchard she thinks she cannot live without. And when Gayeff says, "On my honor I'll swear, by anything you like, that the estate shall not be sold," we know that he has very little honor and even less ability to focus on the problem (mostly he takes refuge in thoughts about billiards, and somehow his habit of eating candy does not enhance his status in our eyes) and that the estate will be sold.

Finally, something must be said about the ambiguous treatment of the future. We know, from his correspondence, that Chekhov looked forward to a new and happier society. Russia, like much of the rest of Europe, was ceasing to be an agrarian society, but if the death throes were evident, one could not be so confident about the birth pangs. Something of the presence of two worlds is hinted at in the stage direction at the beginning of the second act, where we see the estate with its orchard, and also "in the distance a row of telegraph poles; and far, far away, faintly traced on the horizon, is a large town." The telegraph poles and the town silently represent the new industrial society, but Trofimoff the student speaks at length of the glorious possibilities of the future, and his speeches were sufficiently close to the bone for the censor to delete two passages sharply critical of the present. But we cannot take Trofimoff's speeches quite at face value. He is a student, but he is almost thirty and still has not received his degree. His speeches in Act II are moving, especially those on the need to work rather than to talk if the future is to be better than the past, but we cannot quite rid ourselves of the suspicion that Trofimoff talks rather than works. Certainly he is contemptuous of the merchant Lopahin, who delights in work. And, worse, Trofimoff frets too much about his overshoes, thinks he is "above love," and is so confounded by Mme. Ranevskaya's remark, "Imagine, at your age, not having a mistress," that he falls down a flight of stairs. None of these personal failings invalidates his noble view of the future; certainly none of them turns this view into a comic pipedream, and yet all of these things, along with a certain nostalgia that we feel for the past, do suffuse even his noblest statements about the future with a delicate irony that puts them, along with the much praised but totally neglected cherry orchard, firmly in the tragicomic world. One understands why Chekhov called the play a comedy, and one understands why Stanislavsky (who directed the first production and played the part of Gayeff) told Chekhov, "It is definitely not a comedy . . . but a tragedy." Perhaps neither of the men fully wanted to see the resonant ambiguities in the play.

SIX CHARACTERS IN SEARCH OF AN AUTHOR

A *Comedy in the Making*

Luigi Pirandello

English version by Edward Storer

Luigi Pirandello (1867–1936) was born in Sicily, the son of the owner of a profitable sulfur mine. Pirandello studied at Rome and then at Bonn, where in 1891 he received a doctorate for a thesis on Sicilian dialect. Back in Rome he wrote poetry, fiction, and literary criticism, and taught Italian at a teachers college. Troubles came thick: his family, and his wife's, suffered financial setbacks, and his wife became intermittently insane. But from 1917 onward he had great success in the theater with many of his forty or so plays. Among the best-known plays are *Right You Are (If You Think You Are)* (1917), *Six Characters in Search of an Author* (1921), and *Henry IV* (1922). In 1934 Pirandello was awarded the Nobel Prize. Curiously, this philosophic skeptic was a supporter of Italian fascism, and he gave his Nobel medal to be melted down for Mussolini's Abyssinian campaign.

CHARACTERS OF THE COMEDY IN THE MAKING

THE FATHER	THE SON	MADAME PACE
THE MOTHER	THE BOY	(THE BOY *and* THE CHILD
THE STEP-DAUGHTER	THE CHILD	*do not speak*)

ACTORS OF THE COMPANY

THE MANAGER	L'INGENUE	MACHINIST
LEADING LADY	JUVENILE LEAD	MANAGER'S SECRETARY
LEADING MAN	OTHER ACTORS AND ACTRESSES	DOOR-KEEPER
SECOND LADY	PROPERTY MAN	SCENE-SHIFTERS
LEAD	PROMPTER	

Daytime. The Stage of a Theatre.
    N. B.   The Comedy is without acts or scenes. The performance is interrupted once, without the curtain being lowered, when the manager and the chief characters withdraw to arrange the scenario. A second interruption of the action takes place when, by mistake, the stage hands let the curtain down.

A scene from *Six Characters in Search of an Author*. (Photograph: The Bettmann Archive.)

503

ACT I

The spectators will find the curtain raised and the stage as it usually is during the day time. It will be half dark, and empty, so that from the beginning the public may have the impression of an impromptu performance.

Prompter's box and a small table and chair for the manager.

Two other small tables and several chairs scattered about as during rehearsals.

The ACTORS *and* ACTRESSES *of the company enter from the back of the stage: first one, then another, then two together; nine or ten in all. They are about to rehearse a Pirandello play: Mixing It Up.[1] Some of the company move off towards their dressing rooms. The* PROMPTER, *who has the "book" under his arm, is waiting for the manager in order to begin the rehearsal.*

The ACTORS *and* ACTRESSES, *some standing, some sitting, chat and smoke. One perhaps reads a paper; another cons his part.*

Finally, the MANAGER *enters and goes to the table prepared for him. His* SECRETARY *brings him his mail, through which he glances. The* PROMPTER *takes his seat, turns on a light, and opens the "book."*

THE MANAGER (*throwing a letter down on the table*): I can't see. (*To* PROPERTY MAN.) Let's have a little light, please!

PROPERTY MAN: Yes sir, yes, at once. (*A light comes down on to the stage.*)

THE MANAGER (*clapping his hands*): Come along! Come along! Second act of "Mixing It Up." (*Sits down.*)

(*The* ACTORS *and* ACTRESSES *go from the front of the stage to the wings, all except the three who are to begin the rehearsal.*)

THE PROMPTER (*reading the "book"*): "Leo Gala's house. A curious room serving as dining-room and study."

[1] i.e. *Il giuoco delle parti.*

THE MANAGER (*to* PROPERTY MAN): Fix up the old red room.

PROPERTY MAN (*noting it down*): Red set, All right!

THE PROMPTER (*continuing to read from the "book"*): "Table already laid and writing desk with books and papers. Book-shelves. Exit rear to Leo's bedroom. Exit left to kitchen. Principal exit to right."

THE MANAGER (*energetically*): Well, you understand: The principal exit over there; here, the kitchen. (*Turning to actor who is to play the part of* SOCRATES.) You make your entrances and exits here. (*To* PROPERTY MAN.) The baize doors at the rear, and curtains.

PROPERTY MAN (*noting it down*): Right!

PROMPTER (*reading as before*): "When the curtain rises, Leo Gala, dressed in cook's cap and apron, is busy beating an egg in a cup. Philip, also dressed as a cook, is beating another egg. Guido Venanzi is seated and listening."

LEADING MAN (*to* MANAGER): Excuse me, but must I absolutely wear a cook's cap?

THE MANAGER (*annoyed*): I imagine so. It says so there anyway. (*Pointing to the "book."*)

LEADING MAN: But it's ridiculous!

THE MANAGER (*jumping up in a rage*): Ridiculous? Ridiculous? Is it my fault if France won't send us any more good comedies, and we are reduced to putting on Pirandello's works, where nobody understands anything, and where the author plays the fool with us all? (*The* ACTORS *grin. The* MANAGER *goes to* LEADING MAN *and shouts.*) Yes sir, you put on the cook's cap and beat eggs. Do you suppose that with all this egg-beating business you are on an ordinary stage? Get that out of your head. You represent the shell of the eggs you are beating! (*Laughter and comments among the* ACTORS.) Silence! and listen to my explanation, please! (*To* LEADING MAN.) "The empty form of reason without the fullness of instinct, which is blind." — You stand for reason, your wife is instinct. It's a mixing up of the parts, according to which you who act your own part become the puppet of yourself. Do you understand?

LEADING MAN: I'm hanged if I do.

THE MANAGER: Neither do I. But let's get on with it. It's sure to be a glorious failure anyway. (*Confidentially.*) But I say, please face three-quarters. Otherwise, what with the abstruseness of the dialogue, and the public that won't be able to hear you, the whole thing will go to hell. Come on! come on!

PROMPTER: Pardon sir, may I get into my box? There's a bit of a draught.

THE MANAGER: Yes, yes, of course!

(*At this point, the* DOOR-KEEPER *has entered from the stage door and advances towards the manager's table, taking off his braided cap. During this manoeuvre, the* SIX CHARACTERS *enter, and stop by the door at back of stage, so that when the* DOOR-KEEPER *is about to announce their coming to the* MANAGER, *they are already on the stage. A tenuous light surrounds them, almost as if irradiated by them — the faint breath of their fantastic reality.*

This light will disappear when they come forward towards the actors. They preserve, however, something of the dream lightness in which they seem almost suspended; but this does not detract from the essential reality of their forms and expressions.

He who is known as THE FATHER *is a man of about 50: hair, reddish in colour, thin at the temples; he is not bald, however; thick moustaches, falling over his still fresh mouth, which often opens in an empty and uncertain smile. He is fattish, pale; with an especially wide forehead. He has blue, oval-shaped eyes, very clear and piercing. Wears light trousers and a dark jacket. He is alternatively mellifluous and violent in his manner.*

THE MOTHER *seems crushed and terrified as if by an intolerable weight of shame and abasement. She is dressed in modest black and wears a thick widow's veil of crêpe. When she lifts this, she reveals a wax-like face. She always keeps her eyes downcast.*

THE STEP-DAUGHTER *is dashing, almost impudent, beautiful. She wears mourning too, but with great elegance. She shows contempt for the timid half-frightened manner of the wretched* BOY [14 *years old, and also dressed in black*]; *on the other hand, she displays a lively tenderness for her little sister, THE* CHILD [*about four*], *who is dressed in white, with a black silk sash at the waist.*

THE SON [22] *is tall, severe in his attitude of contempt for* THE FATHER, *supercilious and indifferent to* THE MOTHER. *He looks as if he had come on the stage against his will.*)

DOOR-KEEPER (*cap in hand*): Excuse me, sir . . .

THE MANAGER (*rudely*): Eh? What is it?

DOOR-KEEPER (*timidly*): These people are asking for you, sir.

THE MANAGER (*furious*): I am rehearsing, and you know perfectly well no one's allowed to come in during rehearsals! (*Turning to the* CHARACTERS.) Who are you, please? What do you want?

THE FATHER (*coming forward a little, followed by the others who seem embarrassed*): As a matter of fact . . . we have come here in search of an author . . .

THE MANAGER (*half angry, half amazed*): An author? What author?

THE FATHER: Any author, sir.

THE MANAGER: But there's no author here. We are not rehearsing a new piece.

THE STEP-DAUGHTER (*vivaciously*): So much the better, so much the better! We can be your new piece.

AN ACTOR (*coming forward from the others*): Oh, do you hear that?

THE FATHER (*to* STEP-DAUGHTER): Yes, but if the author isn't here . . . (*to* MANAGER) unless you would be willing . . .

THE MANAGER: You are trying to be funny.

THE FATHER: No, for Heaven's sake, what are you saying? We bring you a drama, sir.

THE STEP-DAUGHTER: We may be your fortune.

THE MANAGER: Will you oblige me by going away? We haven't time to waste with mad people.

THE FATHER (*mellifluously*): Oh sir, you know well that life is full of infinite absurdities, which, strangely enough, do not even need to appear plausible, since they are true.

THE MANAGER: What the devil is he talking about?

THE FATHER: I say that to reverse the ordinary process may well be considered a madness: that is, to create credible situations, in order that they may appear true. But permit me to observe that if this be madness, it is the sole *raison d'être* of your profession, gentlemen. (*The* ACTORS *look hurt and perplexed.*)

THE MANAGER (*getting up and looking at him*): So our profession seems to you one worthy of madmen then?

THE FATHER: Well, to make seem true that which isn't true . . . without any need . . . for a joke as it were . . . Isn't that your mission, gentlemen: to give life to fantastic characters on the stage?

THE MANAGER (*interpreting the rising anger of the* COMPANY): But I would beg you to believe, my dear sir, that the profession of the comedian is a noble one. If today, as things go, the playwrights give us stupid comedies to play and puppets to represent instead of men, remember we are proud to have given life to immortal works here on these very boards! (*The* ACTORS, *satisfied, applaud their* MANAGER.)

THE FATHER (*interrupting furiously*): Exactly, perfectly, to living beings more alive than those who breathe and wear clothes: beings less real perhaps, but truer! I agree with you entirely. (*The* ACTORS *look at one another in amazement.*)

THE MANAGER: But what do you mean? Before, you said . . .

THE FATHER: No, excuse me, I meant it for you, sir, who were crying out that you had no time to lose with madmen, while no one better than yourself knows that nature uses the instrument of human fantasy in order to pursue her high creative purpose.

THE MANAGER: Very well, — but where does all this take us?

THE FATHER: Nowhere! It is merely to show you that one is born to life in many forms, in many shapes, as tree, or as stone, as water, as butterfly, or as woman. So one may also be born a character in a play.

THE MANAGER (*with feigned comic dismay*): So you and these other friends of yours have been born characters?

THE FATHER: Exactly, and alive as you see! (*MANAGER and ACTORS burst out laughing.*)

THE FATHER (*hurt*): I am sorry you laugh, because we carry in us a drama, as you can guess from this woman here veiled in black.

THE MANAGER (*losing patience at last and almost indignant*): Oh, chuck it! Get away please! Clear out of here! (*To* PROPERTY MAN.) For Heaven's sake, turn them out!

THE FATHER (*resisting*): No, no, look here, we . . .

THE MANAGER (*roaring*): We come here to work, you know.

LEADING ACTOR: One cannot let oneself be made such a fool of.

THE FATHER (*determined, coming forward*): I marvel at your incredulity, gentlemen. Are you not accustomed to see the characters created by an author spring to life in yourselves and face each other? Just because there is no "book" (*pointing to the* PROMPTER'S *box*) which contains us, you refuse to believe . . .

THE STEP-DAUGHTER (*advances towards* MANAGER, *smiling and coquettish*): Believe me, we are really six most interesting characters, sir; side-tracked however.

THE FATHER: Yes, that is the word! (*To* MANAGER *all at once.*) In the sense, that is, that the author who created us alive no longer wished, or was no longer able, materially to put us into a work of art. And this was a real crime, sir; because he who has had the luck to be born a character can laugh even at death. He cannot die. The man, the writer, the instrument of the creation will die, but his creation does not die. And to live for ever, it does not need to have extraordinary gifts or to be able to work wonders. Who was Sancho Panza? Who was Don Abbondio? Yet they live eternally because — live germs as they were — they had the fortune to find a fecundating matrix, a fantasy which could raise and nourish them: make them live for ever!

THE MANAGER: That is quite all right. But what do you want here, all of you?

THE FATHER: We want to live.

THE MANAGER (*ironically*): For Eternity?

THE FATHER: No, sir, only for a moment . . . in you.

AN ACTOR: Just listen to him!

LEADING LADY: They want to live, in us . . . !

JUVENILE LEAD (*pointing to the* STEP-DAUGHTER): I've no objection, as far as that one is concerned!

THE FATHER: Look here! look here! The comedy has to be made. (*To the* MANAGER.) But if you and your actors are willing, we can soon concert it among ourselves.

THE MANAGER (*annoyed*): But what do you want to concert? We don't go in for concerts here. Here we play dramas and comedies!

THE FATHER: Exactly! That is just why we have come to you.

THE MANAGER: And where is the "book"?

THE FATHER: It is in us! (*The* ACTORS *laugh.*) The drama is in us, and we are the drama. We are impatient to play it. Our inner passion drives us on to this.

THE STEP-DAUGHTER (*disdainful, alluring, treacherous, full of impudence*): My passion, sir! Ah, if you only knew! My passion for him! (*Points to the* FATHER *and makes a pretence of embracing him. Then she breaks out into a loud laugh.*)

THE FATHER (*angrily*): Behave yourself! And please don't laugh in that fashion.

THE STEP-DAUGHTER: With your permission, gentlemen, I, who am a two months' orphan, will show you how I can dance and sing. (*Sings and then dances* Prenez garde à Tchou-Tchin-Tchou.)

Les chinois sont un peuple malin,
De Shangaî à Pékin,
Ils ont mis des écriteaux partout:
Prenez garde à Tchou-Tchin-Tchou.

ACTORS AND ACTRESSES: Bravo! Well done! Tip-top!

THE MANAGER: Silence! This isn't a café concert, you know! (*Turning to the* FATHER *in consternation.*) Is she mad?

THE FATHER: Mad? No, she's worse than mad.

THE STEP-DAUGHTER (*to* MANAGER): Worse? Worse? Listen! Stage this drama for us at once! Then you will see that at a certain moment I . . . when this little darling here . . . (*Takes the* CHILD *by the hand and leads her to the* MANAGER.) Isn't she a dear? (*Takes her up and kisses her.*) Darling! Darling! (*Puts her down again and adds feelingly.*) Well, when God suddenly takes this dear little child away from that poor mother there; and this imbecile here (*seizing hold of the* BOY *roughly and pushing him forward*) does the stupidest things, like the fool he is, you will see me run away. Yes, gentlemen, I shall be off. But the moment hasn't arrived yet. After what has taken place between him and me (*indicates the* FATHER *with a horrible wink*) I can't remain any longer in this society, to have to witness the anguish of this mother here for that fool . . . (*Indicates the* SON.) Look at him! Look at him! See how indifferent, how frigid he is, because he is the legitimate son.

He despises me, despises him (*pointing to the* BOY), despises this baby here; because . . . we are bastards. (*Goes to the* MOTHER *and embraces her.*) And he doesn't want to recognize her as his mother — she who is the common mother of us all. He looks down upon her as if she were only the mother of us three bastards. Wretch! (*She says all this very rapidly, excitedly. At the word "bastards" she raises her voice, and almost spits out the final "Wretch!"*)

THE MOTHER (*to the* MANAGER, *in anguish*): In the name of these two little children, I beg you . . . (*She grows faint and is about to fall.*) Oh God!

THE FATHER (*coming forward to support her as do some of the* ACTORS): Quick, a chair, a chair for this poor widow!

THE ACTORS: Is it true? Has she really fainted?

THE MANAGER: Quick, a chair! Here!

(*One of the* ACTORS *brings a chair, the* OTHERS *proffer assistance. The* MOTHER *tries to prevent the* FATHER *from lifting the veil which covers her face.*)

THE FATHER: Look at her! Look at her!

THE MOTHER: No, no; stop it please!

THE FATHER (*raising her veil*): Let them see you!

THE MOTHER (*rising and covering her face with her hands, in desperation*): I beg you, sir, to prevent this man from carrying out his plan which is loathsome to me.

THE MANAGER (*dumbfounded*): I don't understand at all. What is the situation? Is this lady your wife? (*To the* FATHER).

THE FATHER: Yes, gentlemen: my wife!

THE MANAGER: But how can she be a widow if you are alive? (*The* ACTORS *find relief for their astonishment in a loud laugh.*)

THE FATHER: Don't laugh! Don't laugh like that, for Heaven's sake. Her drama lies just here in this: she has had a lover, a man who ought to be here.

THE MOTHER (*with a cry*): No! No!

THE STEP-DAUGHTER: Fortunately for her, he is dead. Two months ago as I said. We are in mourning, as you see.

THE FATHER: He isn't here you see, not because he is dead. He isn't here — look at her a moment and you will understand — because her drama isn't a drama of the love of two men for whom she was incapable of feeling anything except possibly a little gratitude — gratitude not for me but for the other. She isn't a woman, she is a mother, and her drama — powerful sir, I assure you — lies, as a matter of fact, all in these four children she has had by two men.

THE MOTHER: I had them? Have you got the courage to say that I wanted them? (*To the* COMPANY.) It was his doing. It was he who gave me that other man, who forced me to go away with him.

THE STEP-DAUGHTER: It isn't true.

THE MOTHER (*startled*): Not true, isn't it?

THE STEP-DAUGHTER: No, it isn't true, it just isn't true.

THE MOTHER: And what can you know about it?

THE STEP-DAUGHTER: It isn't true. Don't believe it. (*To* MANAGER.) Do you know why she says so? For that fellow there. (*Indicates the* SON.) She tortures herself, destroys herself on account of the neglect of that son there; and she wants him to believe that if she abandoned him when he was only two years old, it was because he (*indicates the* FATHER) made her do so.

THE MOTHER (*vigorously*): He forced me to it, and I call God to witness it. (*To the* MANAGER.) Ask him (*indicates* HUSBAND) if it isn't true. Let him speak. You (*to* DAUGHTER) are not in a position to know anything about it.

THE STEP-DAUGHTER: I know you lived in peace and happiness with my father while he lived. Can you deny it?

THE MOTHER: No, I don't deny it . . .

THE STEP-DAUGHTER: He was always full of affection and kindness for you. (*To the* BOY, *angrily.*) It's true, isn't it? Tell them! Why don't you speak, you little fool?

THE MOTHER: Leave the poor boy alone. Why do you want to make me appear ungrateful, daughter? I don't want to offend your father. I have answered him that I didn't abandon my house and my son through any fault of mine, nor from any wilful passion.

THE FATHER: It is true. It was my doing.

LEADING MAN (*to the* COMPANY): What a spectacle!

LEADING LADY: We are the audience this time.

JUVENILE LEAD: For once, in a way.

THE MANAGER (*beginning to get really interested*): Let's hear them out. Listen!

THE SON: Oh yes, you're going to hear a fine bit now. He will talk to you of the Demon of Experiment.

THE FATHER: You are a cynical imbecile. I've told you so already a hundred times. (*To the* MANAGER.) He tries to make fun of me on account of this expression which I have found to excuse myself with.

THE SON (*with disgust*): Yes, phrases! phrases!

THE FATHER: Phrases! Isn't everyone consoled when faced with a trouble or fact he doesn't understand, by a word, some simple word, which tells us nothing and yet calms us?

THE STEP-DAUGHTER: Even in the case of remorse. In fact, especially then.

THE FATHER: Remorse? No, that isn't true. I've done more than use words to quieten the remorse in me.

THE STEP-DAUGHTER: Yes, there was a bit of money too. Yes, yes, a bit of money. There were the hundred lire he was about to offer me in payment, gentlemen . . . (*Sensation of horror among the* ACTORS.)

THE SON (*to the* STEP-DAUGHTER): This is vile.

THE STEP-DAUGHTER: Vile? There they were in a pale blue envelope on a little mahogany table in the back of Madame Pace's shop. You know Madame Pace — one of those ladies who attract poor girls of good family into their ateliers, under the pretext of their selling *robes et manteaux.*

THE SON: And he thinks he has bought the right to tyrannize over us all with those hundred lire he was going to pay; but which, fortunately — note this, gentlemen — he had no chance of paying.

THE STEP-DAUGHTER: It was a near thing, though, you know! (*Laughs ironically.*)

THE MOTHER (*protesting*): Shame, my daughter, shame!

THE STEP-DAUGHTER: Shame indeed! This is my revenge! I am dying to live that scene . . . The room . . . I see it . . . Here is the window with the mantles exposed, there the divan, the looking-glass, a screen, there in front of the window the little mahogany table with the blue envelope containing one hundred lire. I see it. I see it. I could take hold of it . . . But you, gentlemen, you ought to turn your backs now: I am almost nude, you know. But I don't blush: I leave that to him. (*Indicating* FATHER.)

THE MANAGER: I don't understand this at all.

THE FATHER: Naturally enough. I would ask you, sir, to exercise your authority a little here, and let me speak before you believe all she is trying to blame me with. Let me explain.

THE STEP-DAUGHTER: Ah yes, explain it in your own way.

THE FATHER: But don't you see that the whole trouble lies here. In words, words. Each one of us has within him a whole world of things, each man of us his own special world. And how can we ever come to an understanding if I put in the words I utter the sense and value of things as I see them; while you who listen to me must inevitably translate them according to the conception of things each one of you has within himself. We think we understand each other, but we never really do. Look here! This woman (*indicating the* MOTHER) takes all my pity for her as a specially ferocious form of cruelty.

THE MOTHER: But you drove me away.

THE FATHER: Do you hear her? I drove her away! She believes I really sent her away.

THE MOTHER: You know how to talk, and I don't; but, believe me, sir (*to* MANAGER), after he had married me . . . who knows why? . . . I was a poor insignificant woman . . .

THE FATHER: But, good Heavens! it was just for your humility that I married you. I loved this simplicity in you. (*He stops when he sees she makes signs to contradict him, opens his arms wide in sign of desperation, seeing how hopeless it is to make himself understood.*) You see she denies it. Her mental deafness, believe me, is phenomenal, the limit: (*touches his forehead*) deaf, deaf, mentally deaf! She has plenty of feeling. Oh yes, a good heart for the children; but the brain — deaf, to the point of desperation — !

THE STEP-DAUGHTER: Yes, but ask him how his intelligence has helped us.

THE FATHER: If we could see all the evil that may spring from good, what should we do? (*At this point the* LEADING LADY, *who is biting her lips with rage at seeing the* LEADING MAN *flirting with the* STEP-DAUGHTER, *comes forward and says to the* MANAGER.)

LEADING LADY: Excuse me, but are we going to rehearse today?

MANAGER: Of course, of course; but let's hear them out.

JUVENILE LEAD: This is something quite new.

L'INGENUE: Most interesting!

LEADING LADY: Yes, for the people who like that kind of thing. (*Casts a glance at* LEADING MAN.)

THE MANAGER (*to* FATHER): You must please explain yourself quite clearly. (*Sits down.*)

THE FATHER: Very well then: listen! I had in my service a poor man, a clerk, a secretary of mine, full of devotion, who became friends with her. (*Indicating the* MOTHER.) They understood one another, were kindred souls in fact, without, however, the least suspicion of any evil existing. They were incapable even of thinking of it.

THE STEP-DAUGHTER: So he thought of it — for them!

THE FATHER: That's not true. I meant to do good to them — and to myself, I confess, at the same time. Things had come to the point that I could not say a word to either of them without their making a mute appeal, one to the other, with their eyes. I could see them silently asking each other how I was to be kept in countenance, how I was to be kept quiet. And this, believe me, was just about enough of itself to keep me in a constant rage, to exasperate me beyond measure.

THE MANAGER: And why didn't you send him away then — this secretary of yours?

THE FATHER: Precisely what I did, sir. And then I had to watch this poor woman drifting forlornly about the house like an animal without a master, like an animal one has taken in out of pity.

THE MOTHER: Ah yes . . . !

THE FATHER (*suddenly turning to the* MOTHER): It's true about the son anyway, isn't it?

THE MOTHER: He took my son away from me first of all.

THE FATHER: But not from cruelty. I did it so that he should grow up healthy and strong by living in the country.

THE STEP-DAUGHTER (*pointing to him ironically*): As one can see.

THE FATHER (*quickly*): Is it my fault if he

has grown up like this? I sent him to a wet nurse in the country, a peasant, as *she* did not seem to me strong enough, though she is of humble origin. That was, anyway, the reason I married her. Unpleasant all this may be, but how can it be helped? My mistake possibly, but there we are! All my life I have had these confounded aspirations towards a certain moral sanity. (*At this point the* STEP-DAUGHTER *bursts into a noisy laugh.*) Oh, stop it! Stop it! I can't stand it.

THE MANAGER: Yes, please stop it, for Heaven's sake.

THE STEP-DAUGHTER: But imagine moral sanity from him, if you please — the client of certain ateliers like that of Madame Pace!

THE FATHER: Fool! That is the proof that I am a man! This seeming contradiction, gentlemen, is the strongest proof that I stand here a live man before you. Why, it is just for this very incongruity in my nature that I have had to suffer what I have. I could not live by the side of that woman (*indicating the* MOTHER) any longer; but not so much for the boredom she inspired me with as for the pity I felt for her.

THE MOTHER: And so he turned me out — .

THE FATHER: — well provided for! Yes, I sent her to that man, gentlemen . . . to let her go free of me.

THE MOTHER: And to free himself.

THE FATHER: Yes, I admit it. It was also a liberation for me. But great evil has come of it. I meant well when I did it; and I did it more for her sake than mine. I swear it. (*Crosses his arms on his chest; then turns suddenly to the* MOTHER.) Did I ever lose sight of you until that other man carried you off to another town, like the angry fool he was? And on account of my pure interest in you . . . my pure interest, I repeat, that had no base motive in it . . . I watched with the tenderest concern the new family that grew up around her. She can bear witness to this. (*Points to the* STEP-DAUGHTER.)

THE STEP-DAUGHTER: Oh yes, that's true enough. When I was a kiddie, so so high, you know, with plaits over my shoulders and knickers longer than my skirts, I used to see him waiting outside the school for me to come out. He came to see how I was growing up.

THE FATHER: This is infamous, shameful!

THE STEP-DAUGHTER: No. Why?

THE FATHER: Infamous! infamous! (*Then excitedly to* MANAGER, *explaining.*) After she (*indicating* MOTHER) went away, my house seemed suddenly empty. She was my incubus, but she filled my house. I was like a dazed fly alone in the empty rooms. This boy here (*indicating the* SON) was educated away from home, and when he came back, he seemed to me to be no more mine. With no mother to stand between him and me, he grew up entirely for himself, on his own, apart, with no tie of intellect or affection binding him to me. And then — strange but true — I was driven, by curiosity at first and then by some tender sentiment, towards her family, which had come into being through my will. The thought of her began gradually to fill up the emptiness I felt all around me. I wanted to know if she were happy in living out the simple daily duties of life. I wanted to think of her as fortunate and happy because far away from the complicated torments of my spirit. And so, to have proof of this, I used to watch that child coming out of school.

THE STEP-DAUGHTER: Yes, yes. True. He used to follow me in the street and smiled at me, waved his hand, like this. I would look at him with interest, wondering who he might be. I told my mother, who guessed at once. (*The* MOTHER *agrees with a nod.*) Then she didn't want to send me to school for some days; and when I finally went back, there he was again — looking so ridiculous — with a paper parcel in his hands. He came close to me, caressed me, and drew out a fine straw hat from the parcel, with a bouquet of flowers — all for me!

THE MANAGER: A bit discursive this, you know!

THE SON (*contemptuously*): Literature! Literature!

THE FATHER: Literature indeed! This is life, this is passion!

THE MANAGER: It may be, but it won't act.

THE FATHER: I agree. This is only the part leading up. I don't suggest this should be staged. She (*pointing to the* STEP-DAUGHTER), as you see, is no longer the flapper with plaits down her back — .

THE STEP-DAUGHTER: — and the knickers showing below the skirt!

THE FATHER: The drama is coming now, sir; something new, complex, most interesting.

THE STEP-DAUGHTER: As soon as my father died . . .

THE FATHER: — there was absolute misery for them. They came back here, unknown to me. Through her stupidity! (*Pointing to the* MOTHER.) It is true she can barely write her own name; but she could anyhow have got her daughter to write to me that they were in need . . .

THE MOTHER: And how was I to divine all this sentiment in him?

THE FATHER: That is exactly your mistake, never to have guessed any of my sentiments.

THE MOTHER: After so many years apart, and all that had happened . . .

THE FATHER: Was it my fault if that fellow carried you away? It happened quite suddenly; for after he had obtained some job or other, I could find no trace of them; and so, not unnaturally, my interest in them dwindled. But the drama culminated unforeseen and violent on their return, when I was impelled by my miserable flesh that still lives . . . Ah! what misery, what wretchedness is that of the man who is alone and disdains debasing *liaisons!* Not old enough to do without women, and not young enough to go and look for one without shame. Misery? It's worse than misery; it's a horror; for no woman can any longer give him love; and when a man feels this . . . One ought to do without, you say? Yes, yes, I know. Each of us when he appears before his fellows is clothed in a certain dignity. But every man knows what unconfessable things pass within the secrecy of his own heart. One gives way to the temptation, only to rise from it again, afterwards, with a great eagerness to re-establish one's dignity, as if it were a tombstone to place on the grave of one's shame, and a monument to hide and sign the memory of our weaknesses. Everybody's in the same case. Some folks haven't the courage to say certain things, that's all!

THE STEP-DAUGHTER: All appear to have the courage to do them though.

THE FATHER: Yes, but in secret. Therefore, you want more courage to say these things. Let a man but speak these things out, and folks at once label him a cynic. But it isn't true. He is like all the others, better indeed, because he isn't afraid to reveal with the light of the intelligence the red shame of human bestiality on which most men close their eyes so as not to see it.

Woman — for example, look at her case! She turns tantalizing inviting glances on you.

You seize her. No sooner does she feel herself in your grasp than she closes her eyes. It is the sign of her mission, the sign by which she says to man: "Blind yourself, for I am blind."

THE STEP-DAUGHTER: Sometimes she can close them no more: when she no longer feels the need of hiding her shame to herself, but dry-eyed and dispassionately, sees only that of the man who has blinded himself without love. Oh, all these intellectual complications make me sick, disgust me — all this philosophy that uncovers the beast in man, and then seeks to save him, excuse him . . . I can't stand it, sir. When a man seeks to "simplify" life bestially, throwing aside every relic of humanity, every chaste aspiration, every pure feeling, all sense of ideality, duty, modesty, shame . . . then nothing is more revolting and nauseous than a certain kind of remorse — crocodiles' tears, that's what it is.

THE MANAGER: Let's come to the point. This is only discussion.

THE FATHER: Very good, sir! But a fact is like a sack which won't stand up when it is empty. In order that it may stand up, one has to put into it the reason and sentiment which have caused it to exist. I couldn't possibly know that after the death of that man, they had decided to return here, that they were in misery, and that she (*pointing to the* MOTHER) had gone to work as a modiste, and at a shop of the type of that of Madame Pace.

THE STEP-DAUGHTER: A real high-class modiste, you must know, gentlemen. In appearance, she works for the leaders of the best society: but she arranges matters so that these elegant ladies serve her purpose . . . without prejudice to other ladies who are . . . well . . . only so so.

THE MOTHER: You will believe me, gentlemen, that it never entered my mind that the old hag offered me work because she had her eye on my daughter.

THE STEP-DAUGHTER: Poor mamma! Do you know, sir, what that woman did when I brought her back the work my mother had finished? She would point out to me that I had torn one of my frocks, and she would give it back to my mother to mend. It was I who paid for it, always I; while this poor creature here believed she was sacrificing herself for me and these two children here, sitting up at night sewing Madame Pace's robes.

THE MANAGER: And one day you met there . . .

THE STEP-DAUGHTER: Him, him. Yes sir, an old client. There's a scene for you to play! Superb!

THE FATHER: She, the Mother arrived just then . . .

THE STEP-DAUGHTER (*treacherously*): Almost in time!

THE FATHER (*crying out*): No, in time! in time! Fortunately I recognized her . . . in time. And I took them back home with me to my house. You can imagine now her position and mine; she, as you see her; and I who cannot look her in the face.

THE STEP-DAUGHTER: Absurd! How can I possibly be expected — after that — to be a modest young miss, a fit person to go with his confounded aspirations for "a solid moral sanity"?

THE FATHER: For the drama lies all in this — in the conscience that I have, that each one of us has. We believe this conscience to be a single thing, but it is many-sided. There is one for this person, and another for that. Diverse consciences. So we have this illusion of being one person for all, of having a personality that is unique in all our acts. But it isn't true. We perceive this when, tragically perhaps, in something we do, we are as it were, suspended, caught up in the air on a kind of hook. Then we perceive that all of us was not in that act, and that it would be an atrocious injustice to judge us by that action alone, as if all our existence were summed up in that one deed. Now do you understand the perfidy of this girl? She surprised me in a place, where she ought not to have known me, just as I could not exist for her; and she now seeks to attach to me a reality such as I could never suppose I should have to assume for her in a shameful and fleeting moment of my life. I feel this above all else. And the drama, you will see, acquires a tremendous value from this point. Then there is the position of the others . . . his . . . (*Indicating the* SON.)

THE SON (*shrugging his shoulders scornfully*): Leave me alone! I don't come into this.

THE FATHER: What? You don't come into this?

THE SON: I've got nothing to do with it, and don't want to have; because you know well enough I wasn't made to be mixed up in all this with the rest of you.

THE STEP-DAUGHTER: We are only vulgar folk! He is the fine gentleman. You may have noticed, Mr. Manager, that I fix him now and again with a look of scorn while he lowers his eyes — for he knows the evil he has done me.

THE SON (*scarcely looking at her*): I?

THE STEP-DAUGHTER: You! you! I owe my life on the streets to you. Did you or did you not deny us, with your behaviour, I won't say the intimacy of home, but even that mere hospitality which makes guests feel at their ease? We were intruders who had come to disturb the kingdom of your legitimacy. I should like to have you witness, Mr. Manager, certain scenes between him and me. He says I have tyrannized over everyone. But it was just his behaviour which made me insist on the reason for which I had come into the house, — this reason he calls "vile" — into his house, with my mother who is his mother too. And I came as mistress of the house.

THE SON: It's easy for them to put me always in the wrong. But imagine, gentlemen, the position of a son, whose fate it is to see arrive one day at his home a young woman of impudent bearing, a young woman who inquires for his father, with whom who knows what business she has. This young man has then to witness her return bolder than ever, accompanied by that child there. He is obliged to watch her treat his father in an equivocal and confidential manner. She asks money of him in a way that lets one suppose he must give it her, *must*, do you understand, because he has every obligation to do so.

THE FATHER: But I have, as a matter of fact, this obligation. I owe it to your mother.

THE SON: How should I know? When had I ever seen or heard of her? One day there arrive with her (*indicating* STEP-DAUGHTER) that lad and this baby here. I am told: "This is *your* mother too, you know." I divine from her manner (*indicating* STEP-DAUGHTER *again*) why it is they have come home. I had rather not say what I feel and think about it. I shouldn't even care to confess to myself. No action can therefore be hoped for from me in this affair. Believe me, Mr. Manager, I am an "unrealized" character, dramatically speaking; and I find myself not at all at ease in their company. Leave me out of it, I beg you.

THE FATHER: What? It is just because you are so that . . .

THE SON: How do you know what I am like? When did you ever bother your head about me?

THE FATHER: I admit it. I admit it. But isn't that a situation in itself? This aloofness of yours which is so cruel to me and to your mother, who returns home and sees you almost for the first time grown up, who doesn't recognize you but knows you are her son . . . (*Pointing out the* MOTHER *to the* MANAGER.) See, she's crying!

THE STEP-DAUGHTER (*angrily, stamping her foot*): Like a fool!

THE FATHER (*indicating* STEP-DAUGHTER): She can't stand him you know. (*Then referring again to the* SON.) He says he doesn't come into the affair, whereas he is really the hinge of the whole action. Look at that lad who is always clinging to his mother, frightened and humiliated. It is on account of this fellow here. Possibly his situation is the most painful of all. He feels himself a stranger more than the others. The poor little chap feels mortified, humiliated at being brought into a home out of charity as it were. (*In confidence.*) He is the image of his father. Hardly talks at all. Humble and quiet.

THE MANAGER: Oh, we'll cut him out. You've no notion what a nuisance boys are on the stage . . .

THE FATHER: He disappears soon, you know. And the baby too. She is the first to vanish from the scene. The drama consists finally in this: when that mother re-enters my house, her family born outside of it, and shall we say superimposed on the original, ends with the death of the little girl, the tragedy of the boy and the flight of the elder daughter. It cannot go on, because it is foreign to its surroundings. So after much torment, we three remain: I, the mother, that son. Then, owing to the disappearance of that extraneous family, we too find ourselves strange to one another. We find we are living in an atmosphere of mortal desolation which is the revenge, as he (*indicating* SON) scornfully said of the Demon of Experiment, that unfortunately hides in me. Thus, sir, you see when faith is lacking, it becomes impossible to create certain states of happiness, for we lack the necessary humility. Vaingloriously, we try to substitute ourselves for this faith, creating thus for the rest of the world a reality which we believe after their fashion, while, actually, it doesn't exist. For each one of us has his own reality to be respected before God, even when it is harmful to one's very self.

THE MANAGER: There is something in what you say. I assure you all this interests me very much. I begin to think there's the stuff for a drama in all this, and not a bad drama either.

THE STEP-DAUGHTER (*coming forward*): When you've got a character like me.

THE FATHER (*shutting her up, all excited to learn the decision of the* MANAGER): You be quiet!

THE MANAGER (*reflecting, heedless of interruption*): It's new . . . hem . . . yes . . .

THE FATHER: Absolutely new!

THE MANAGER: You've got a nerve though, I must say, to come here and fling it at me like this . . .

THE FATHER: You will understand, sir, born as we are for the stage . . .

THE MANAGER: Are you amateur actors then?

THE FATHER: No. I say born for the stage, because . . .

THE MANAGER: Oh, nonsense. You're an old hand, you know.

THE FATHER: No sir, no. We act that role for which we have been cast, that role which we are given in life. And in my own case, passion itself, as usually happens, becomes a trifle theatrical when it is exalted.

THE MANAGER: Well, well, that will do. But you see, without an author . . . I could give you the address of an author if you like . . .

THE FATHER: No, no. Look here! You must be the author.

THE MANAGER: I? What are you talking about?

THE FATHER: Yes, you, you! Why not?

THE MANAGER: Because I have never been an author: that's why.

THE FATHER: Then why not turn author now? Everybody does it. You don't want any special qualities. Your task is made much easier by the fact that we are all here alive before you . . .

THE MANAGER: It won't do.

THE FATHER: What? When you see us live our drama . . .

THE MANAGER: Yes, that's all right. But you want someone to write it.

THE FATHER: No, no. Someone to take it down, possibly, while we play it, scene by scene! It will be enough to sketch it out at first, and then try it over.

THE MANAGER: Well . . . I am almost tempted. It's a bit of an idea. One might have a shot at it.

THE FATHER: Of course. You'll see what scenes will come out of it. I can give you one, at once . . .

THE MANAGER: By Jove, it tempts me. I'd like to have a go at it. Let's try it out. Come with me to my office. (*Turning to the* AC-TORS.) You are at liberty for a bit, but don't step out of the theatre for long. In a quarter of an hour, twenty minutes, all back here again! (*To the* FATHER.) We'll see what can be done. Who knows if we don't get something really extraordinary out of it?

THE FATHER: There's no doubt about it. They (*indicating the* CHARACTERS) had better come with us too, hadn't they?

THE MANAGER: Yes, yes. Come on! come on! (*Moves away and then turning to the* AC-TORS.) *Be punctual, please!* (MANAGER *and the* SIX CHARACTERS *cross the stage and go off. The other* ACTORS *remain, looking at one another in astonishment.*)

LEADING MAN: Is he serious? What the devil does he want to do?

JUVENILE LEAD: This is rank madness.

THIRD ACTOR: Does he expect to knock up a drama in five minutes?

JUVENILE LEAD: Like the improvisers!

LEADING LADY: If he thinks I'm going to take part in a joke like this . . .

JUVENILE LEAD: I'm out of it anyway.

FOURTH ACTOR: I should like to know who they are. (*Alludes to* CHARACTERS.)

THIRD ACTOR: What do you suppose? Madmen or rascals!

JUVENILE LEAD: And he takes them seriously!

L'INGENUE: Vanity! He fancies himself as an author now.

LEADING MAN: It's absolutely unheard of. If the stage has come to this . . . well I'm . . .

FIFTH ACTOR: It's rather a joke.

THIRD ACTOR: Well, we'll see what's going to happen next.

(*Thus talking, the* ACTORS *leave the stage; some going out by the little door at the back; others retiring to their dressing-rooms. The curtain remains up. The action of the play is suspended for twenty minutes.*)

ACT II

The stage call-bells ring to warn the company that the play is about to begin again.

The STEP-DAUGHTER *comes out of the* MANAGER's *office along with the* CHILD *and the* BOY. *As she comes out of the office, she cries:* —

Nonsense! nonsense! Do it yourselves! I'm not going to mix myself up in this mess. (*Turning to the* CHILD *and coming quickly with her on to the stage.*) Come on, Rosetta, let's run!

(*The* BOY *follows them slowly, remaining a little behind and seeming perplexed.*)

THE STEP-DAUGHTER (*stops, bends over the* CHILD *and takes the latter's face between her hands*): My little darling! You're frightened, aren't you? You don't know where we are, do you? (*Pretending to reply to a question of the* CHILD.) What is the stage? It's a place, baby, you know, where people play at being serious, a place where they act comedies. We've got to act a comedy now, dead serious, you know; and you're in it also, little one. (*Embraces her, pressing the little head to her breast, and rocking the* CHILD *for a moment.*) Oh darling, darling, what a horrid comedy you've got to play! What a wretched part they've found for you! A garden . . . a fountain . . . look . . . just suppose, kiddie, it's here. Where, you say? Why, right here in the middle. It's all pretence you know. That's the trouble, my pet: it's all make-believe here. It's better to imagine it though, because if they fix it up for you, it'll only be painted cardboard, painted cardboard for the rockery, the water, the plants . . . Ah, but I think a baby like this one would sooner have a make-believe fountain than a real one, so she could play with it. What a joke it'll be for the others! But for you, alas! not quite such a joke: you who are real, baby dear, and really play by a real fountain that is big and green and beautiful, with ever so many bamboos around it that are reflected in the water, and a whole lot of little ducks swimming about . . . No, Rosetta, no, your mother doesn't bother about you on account of that wretch of a son there. I'm in the devil of a temper, and as for that lad . . . (*Seizes* BOY *by the arm to force him to take one of his hands out of his pockets.*) What have you got there? What are you hiding? (*Pulls his hand out of his pocket, looks into it and catches the glint of a revolver.*) Ah! where did you get this? (*The* BOY, *very pale in the face, looks at her, but does not answer*). Idiot! If I'd been in your place, instead of killing myself, I'd have shot one of those two, or both of them: father and son.

(*The* FATHER *enters from the office, all excited from his work. The* MANAGER *follows him.*)

THE FATHER: Come on, come on dear! Come here for a minute! We've arranged everything. It's all fixed up.

THE MANAGER (*also excited*): If you please, young lady, there are one or two points to settle still. Will you come along?

THE STEP-DAUGHTER (*following him towards the office*): Ouff! what's the good, if you've arranged everything.

(*The* FATHER, MANAGER *and* STEP-DAUGHTER *go back into the office again* [*off*] *for a moment. At the same time, the* SON, *followed by the* MOTHER, *comes out.*)

THE SON (*looking at the three entering office*): Oh this is fine, fine! And to think I can't even get away!

(*The* MOTHER *attempts to look at him, but lowers her eyes immediately when he turns away from her. She then sits down. The* BOY *and the* CHILD *approach her. She casts a glance again at the* SON, *and speaks with humble tones, trying to draw him into conversation.*)

THE MOTHER: And isn't my punishment the worst of all? (*Then seeing from the* SON's *manner that he will not bother himself about her.*) My God! Why are you so cruel? Isn't it enough for one person to support all this torment? Must you then insist on others seeing it also?

THE SON (*half to himself, meaning the* MOTHER *to hear, however*): And they want to put it on the stage! If there was at least a reason for it! He thinks he has got at the meaning of it all. Just as if each one of us in every circumstance of life couldn't find his own explanation of it! (*Pauses.*) He complains he was discovered in a place where he ought not to have been seen, in a moment of his life which ought to have remained hidden and kept out of the reach of that convention which he has to maintain for other people. And what about my case? Haven't I had to reveal what no son ought ever to reveal: how father and mother live and are man and wife for themselves quite apart from that idea of father and mother which we give them? When this idea is revealed, our life is then linked at one point only to that man and that woman; and as such it should shame them, shouldn't it?

(*The* MOTHER *hides her face in her hands. From the dressing-rooms and the little door at the back of the stage the* ACTORS *and* STAGE MANAGER *return, followed by the* PROPERTY MAN, *and the* PROMPTER. *At the same moment, the* MANAGER *comes out of his office, accompanied by the* FATHER *and the* STEP-DAUGHTER.)

THE MANAGER: Come on, come on, ladies and gentlemen! Heh! you there, machinist!

MACHINIST: Yes sir?

THE MANAGER: Fix up the white parlor with the floral decorations. Two wings and a drop with a door will do. Hurry up!

(*The* MACHINIST *runs off at once to prepare the scene, and arranges it while the* MANAGER *talks with the* STAGE MANAGER, *the* PROPERTY MAN, *and the* PROMPTER *on matters of detail.*)

THE MANAGER (*to* PROPERTY MAN): Just have a look, and see if there isn't a sofa or divan in the wardrobe . . .

PROPERTY MAN: There's the green one.

THE STEP-DAUGHTER: No no! Green won't do. It was yellow, ornamented with flowers — very large! and most comfortable!

PROPERTY MAN: There isn't one like that.

THE MANAGER: It doesn't matter. Use the one we've got.

THE STEP-DAUGHTER: Doesn't matter? It's most important!

THE MANAGER: We're only trying it now. Please don't interfere. (*To* PROPERTY MAN.) See if we've got a shop window — long and narrowish.

THE STEP-DAUGHTER: And the little table! The little mahogany table for the pale blue envelope!

PROPERTY MAN (*to* MANAGER): There's that little gilt one.

THE MANAGER: That'll do fine.

THE FATHER: A mirror.

THE STEP-DAUGHTER: And the screen! We must have a screen. Otherwise how can I manage?

PROPERTY MAN: That's all right, Miss. We've got any amount of them.

THE MANAGER (*to the* STEP-DAUGHTER): We want some clothes pegs too, don't we?

THE STEP-DAUGHTER: Yes, several, several!

THE MANAGER: See how many we've got and bring them all.

PROPERTY MAN: All right!

(*The* PROPERTY MAN *hurries off to obey his orders. While he is putting the things in their places, the* MANAGER *talks to the* PROMPTER *and then with the* CHARACTERS *and the* ACTORS.)

THE MANAGER (*to* PROMPTER): Take your seat. Look here: this is the outline of the scenes, act by act. (*Hands him some sheets of paper.*) And now I'm going to ask you to do something out of the ordinary.

PROMPTER: Take it down in shorthand?

THE MANAGER (*pleasantly surprised*): Exactly! Can you do shorthand?

PROMPTER: Yes, a little.

THE MANAGER: Good! (*Turning to a* STAGE HAND.) Go and get some paper from my office, plenty, as much as you can find.

(*The* STAGE HAND *goes off, and soon returns with a handful of paper which he gives to the* PROMPTER.)

THE MANAGER (*to* PROMPTER): You follow the scenes as we play them, and try and get the points down, at any rate the most important ones. (*Then addressing the* ACTORS.) Clear the stage, ladies and gentlemen! Come over here (*pointing to the left*) and listen attentively.

LEADING LADY: But, excuse me, we . . .

THE MANAGER (*guessing her thought*): Don't worry! You won't have to improvise.

LEADING MAN: What have we to do then?

THE MANAGER: Nothing. For the moment you just watch and listen. Everybody will get his part written out afterwards. At present we're going to try the thing as best we can. They're going to act now.

THE FATHER (*as if fallen from the clouds into the confusion of the stage*): We? What do you mean, if you please, by a rehearsal?

THE MANAGER: A rehearsal for them. (*Points to the* ACTORS.)

THE FATHER: But since we are the characters . . .

THE MANAGER: All right: "characters" then, if you insist on calling yourselves such. But here, my dear sir, the characters don't act. Here the actors do the acting. The characters are there, in the "book" (*pointing towards* PROMPTER's *box*) — when there is a "book"!

THE FATHER: I won't contradict you; but excuse me, the actors aren't the characters. They want to be, they pretend to be, don't they? Now if these gentlemen here are fortunate enough to have us alive before them . . .

THE MANAGER: Oh this is grand! You want to come before the public yourselves then?

THE FATHER: As we are . . .

THE MANAGER: I can assure you it would be a magnificent spectacle!

LEADING MAN: What's the use of us here anyway then?

THE MANAGER: You're not going to pretend that you can act? It makes me laugh! (*The* ACTORS *laugh.*) There, you see, they are laughing at the notion. But, by the way, I must cast the parts. That won't be difficult. They cast themselves. (*To the* SECOND LADY LEAD.) You play the Mother. (*To the* FATHER.) We must find her a name.

THE FATHER: Amalia, sir.

THE MANAGER: But that is the real name of your wife. We don't want to call her by her real name.

THE FATHER: Why ever not, if it is her name? . . . Still, perhaps, if that lady must . . . (*Makes a slight motion of the hand to indicate the* SECOND LADY LEAD.) I see this woman here (*means the* MOTHER) as Amalia. But do as you like. (*Gets more and more confused.*) I don't know what to say to you. Already, I begin to hear my own words ring false, as if they had another sound . . .

THE MANAGER: Don't you worry about it. It'll be our job to find the right tones. And as for her name, if you want her Amalia, Amalia it shall be; and if you don't like it, we'll find another! For the moment though, we'll call the characters in this way: (*To* JUVENILE LEAD.) You are the Son. (*To the* LEADING

LADY.) You naturally are the Step-Daughter . . .

THE STEP-DAUGHTER (*excitedly*): What? what? I, that woman there? (*Bursts out laughing.*)

THE MANAGER (*angry*): What is there to laugh at?

LEADING LADY (*indignant*): Nobody has ever dared to laugh at me. I insist on being treated with respect; otherwise I go away.

THE STEP-DAUGHTER: No, no, excuse me . . . I am not laughing at you . . .

THE MANAGER (*to* STEP-DAUGHTER): You ought to feel honored to be played by . . .

LEADING LADY (*at once, contemptuously*): "That woman there" . . .

THE STEP-DAUGHTER: But I wasn't speaking of you, you know. I was speaking of myself — whom I can't see at all in you! That is all. I don't know . . . but . . . you . . . aren't in the least like me . . .

THE FATHER: True. Here's the point. Look here, sir, our temperaments, our souls . . .

THE MANAGER: Temperament, soul, be hanged! Do you suppose the spirit of the piece is in you? Nothing of the kind!

THE FATHER: What, haven't we our own temperaments, our own souls?

THE MANAGER: Not at all. Your soul or whatever you like to call it takes shape here. The actors give body and form to it, voice and gesture. And my actors — I may tell you — have given expression to much more lofty material than this little drama of yours, which may or may not hold up on the stage. But if it does, the merit of it, believe me, will be due to my actors.

THE FATHER: I don't dare contradict you, sir; but believe me, it is a terrible suffering for us who are as we are, with these bodies of ours, these features to see . . .

THE MANAGER (*cutting him short and out of patience*): Good heavens! The make-up will remedy all that, man, the make-up . . .

THE FATHER: Maybe. But the voice, the gestures . . .

THE MANAGER: Now, look here! On the stage, you as yourself, cannot exist. The actor here acts you, and that's an end to it!

THE FATHER: I understand. And now I think I see why our author who conceived us as we are, all alive, didn't want to put us on the stage after all. I haven't the least desire to offend your actors. Far from it! But when I think that

I am to be acted by . . . I don't know by whom . . .

LEADING MAN (*on his dignity*): By me, if you've no objection!

THE FATHER (*humbly, mellifluously*): Honored, I assure you, sir. (*Bows.*) Still, I must say that try as this gentleman may, with all his good will and wonderful art, to absorb me into himself . . .

LEADING MAN: Oh chuck it! "Wonderful art!" Withdraw that, please!

THE FATHER: The performance he will give, even doing his best with make-up to look like me . . .

LEADING MAN: It will certainly be a bit difficult! (*The* ACTORS *laugh.*)

THE FATHER: Exactly! It will be difficult to act me as I really am. The effect will be rather — apart from the make-up — according as to how he supposes I am, as he senses me — if he does sense me — and not as I inside of myself feel myself to be. It seems to me then that account should be taken of this by everyone whose duty it may become to criticize us . . .

THE MANAGER: Heavens! The man's starting to think about the critics now! Let them say what they like. It's up to us to put on the play if we can. (*Looking around.*) Come on! come on! Is the stage set? (*To the* ACTORS *and* CHARACTERS.) Stand back — stand back! Let me see, and don't let's lose any more time! (*To the* STEP-DAUGHTER.) Is it all right as it is now?

THE STEP-DAUGHTER: Well, to tell the truth, I don't recognize the scene.

THE MANAGER: My dear lady, you can't possibly suppose that we can construct that shop of Madame Pace piece by piece here? (*To the* FATHER.) You said a white room with flowered wall paper, didn't you?

THE FATHER: Yes.

THE MANAGER: Well then. We've got the furniture right more or less. Bring that little table a bit further forward. (*The* STAGE HANDS *obey the order. To* PROPERTY MAN.) You go and find an envelope, if possible, a pale blue one; and give it to that gentleman. (*Indicates* FATHER.)

PROPERTY MAN: An ordinary envelope?

MANAGER AND FATHER: Yes, yes, an ordinary envelope.

PROPERTY MAN: At once, sir. (*Exit.*)

THE MANAGER: Ready, everyone! First scene

— the Young Lady. (*The* LEADING LADY *comes forward.*) No, no, you must wait. I meant her (*Indicating the* STEP-DAUGHTER.) You just watch —

THE STEP-DAUGHTER (*adding at once*): How I shall play it, how I shall live it! . . .

LEADING LADY (*offended*): I shall live it also, you may be sure, as soon as I begin!

THE MANAGER (*with his hands to his head*): Ladies and gentlemen, if you please! No more useless discussions! Scene I: the Young Lady with Madame Pace: Oh! (*Looks around as if lost.*) And this Madame Pace, where is she?

THE FATHER: She isn't with us, sir.

THE MANAGER: Then what the devil's to be done?

THE FATHER: But she is alive too.

THE MANAGER: Yes, but where is she?

THE FATHER: One minute. Let me speak! (*Turning to the* ACTRESSES.) If these ladies would be so good as to give me their hats for a moment . . .

THE ACTRESSES (*half surprised, half laughing, in chorus*): What?
Why?
Our hats?
What does he say?

THE MANAGER: What are you going to do with the ladies' hats? (*The* ACTORS *laugh.*)

THE FATHER: Oh nothing. I just want to put them on these pegs for a moment. And one of the ladies will be so kind as to take off her mantle . . .

THE ACTORS: Oh, what d'you think of that?
Only the mantle?
He must be mad.

SOME ACTRESSES: But why?
Mantles as well?

THE FATHER: To hang them up here for a moment. Please be so kind, will you?

THE ACTRESSES (*taking off their hats, one or two also their cloaks, and going to hang them on the racks*): After all, why not?
There you are!
This is really funny.
We've got to put them on show.

THE FATHER: Exactly; just like that, on show.

THE MANAGER: May we know why?

THE FATHER: I'll tell you. Who knows if, by arranging the stage for her, she does not come here herself, attracted by the very articles of her trade? (*Inviting the* ACTORS *to look towards the exit at back of stage.*) Look! Look!

(*The door at the back of stage opens and* MADAME PACE *enters and takes a few steps forward. She is a fat, oldish woman with puffy oxygenated hair. She is rouged and powdered, dressed with a comical elegance in black silk. Round her waist is a long silver chain from which hangs a pair of scissors. The* STEP-DAUGHTER *runs over to her at once amid the stupor of the actors.*)

THE STEP-DAUGHTER (*turning towards her*): There she is! There she is!

THE FATHER (*radiant*): It's she! I said so, didn't I? There she is!

THE MANAGER (*conquering his surprise, and then becoming indignant*): What sort of a trick is this?

LEADING MAN (*almost at the same time*): What's going to happen next?

JUVENILE LEAD: Where does *she* come from?

L'INGENUE: They've been holding her in reserve, I guess.

LEADING LADY: A vulgar trick!

THE FATHER (*dominating the protests*): Excuse me, all of you! Why are you so anxious to destroy in the name of a vulgar, commonplace sense of truth, this reality which comes to birth attracted and formed by the magic of the stage itself, which has indeed more right to live here than you, since it is much truer than you — if you don't mind my saying so? Which is the actress among you who is to play Madame Pace? Well, here is Madame Pace herself. And you will allow, I fancy, that the actress who acts her will be less true than this woman here, who is herself in person. You see my daughter recognized her and went over to her at once. Now you're going to witness the scene!

(*But the scene between the* STEP-DAUGHTER *and* MADAME PACE *has already begun despite the protest of the actors and the reply of the* FATHER. *It has begun quietly, naturally, in a manner impossible for the stage. So when the actors, called to attention by the* FATHER, *turn round and see* MADAME PACE, *who has placed one hand under the* STEP-DAUGHTER's *chin to raise her head, they observe her at first with great attention, but hearing her speak in an unintelligible manner their interest begins to wane.*)

THE MANAGER: Well? well?

LEADING MAN: What does she say?

LEADING LADY: One can't hear a word.

JUVENILE LEAD: Louder! Louder please!

THE STEP-DAUGHTER (*leaving* MADAME PACE, *who smiles a Sphinx-like smile, and advancing towards the actors*): Louder? Louder? What are you talking about? These aren't matters which can be shouted at the top of one's voice. If I have spoken them out loud, it was to shame him and have my revenge. (*Indicates* FATHER.) But for Madame it's quite a different matter.

THE MANAGER: Indeed? indeed? But here, you know, people have got to make themselves heard, my dear. Even we who are on the stage can't hear you. What will it be when the public's in the theatre? And anyway, you can very well speak up now among yourselves, since we shan't be present to listen to you as we are now. You've got to pretend to be alone in a room at the back of a shop where no one can hear you.

(*The* STEP-DAUGHTER *coquettishly and with a touch of malice makes a sign of disagreement two or three times with her finger.*)

THE MANAGER: What do you mean by no?

THE STEP-DAUGHTER (*sotto voce, mysteriously*): There's someone who will hear us if she (*indicating* MADAME PACE) speaks out loud.

THE MANAGER (*in consternation*): What? Have you got someone else to spring on us now? (*The* ACTORS *burst out laughing.*)

THE FATHER: No, no sir. She is alluding to me. I've got to be here — there behind that door, in waiting; and Madame Pace knows it. In fact, if you will allow me, I'll go there at once, so I can be quite ready. (*Moves away.*)

THE MANAGER (*stopping him*): No! Wait! wait! We must observe the conventions of the theatre. Before you are ready . . .

THE STEP-DAUGHTER (*interrupting him*): No, get on with it at once! I'm just dying, I tell you, to act this scene. If he's ready, I'm more than ready.

THE MANAGER (*shouting*): But, my dear young lady, first of all, we must have the scene between you and this lady . . . (*Indicates* MADAME PACE.) Do you understand? . . .

THE STEP-DAUGHTER: Good Heavens! She's been telling me what you know already: that mamma's work is badly done again, that the material's ruined; and that if I want her to continue to help us in our misery I must be patient . . .

MADAME PACE (*coming forward with an air of great importance*): Yes indeed, sir, I no wanta take advantage of her, I no wanta be hard . . .

(*Note:* MADAME PACE *is supposed to talk in a jargon half Italian, half English.*)

THE MANAGER (*alarmed*): What? What? She talks like that? (*The* ACTORS *burst out laughing again.*)

THE STEP-DAUGHTER (*also laughing*): Yes yes, that's the way she talks, half English, half Italian! Most comical it is!

MADAME PACE: Itta seem not verra polite gentlemen laugha atta me eef I trya best speaka English.

THE MANAGER: *Diamine!* Of course! Of course! Let her talk like that! Just what we want. Talk just like that, Madame, if you please! The effect will be certain. Exactly what was wanted to put a little comic relief into the crudity of the situation. Of course she talks like that! Magnificent!

THE STEP-DAUGHTER: Magnificent? Certainly! When certain suggestions are made to one in language of that kind, the effect is certain, since it seems almost a joke. One feels inclined to laugh when one hears her talk about an "old signore" "who wanta talka nicely with you." Nice old signore, eh, Madame?

MADAME PACE: Not so old my dear, not so old! And even if you no lika him, he won't make any scandal!

THE MOTHER (*jumping up amid the amazement and consternation of the actors who had not been noticing her. They move to restrain her*): You old devil! You murderess!

THE STEP-DAUGHTER (*running over to calm her* MOTHER): Calm yourself, Mother, calm yourself! Please don't . . .

THE FATHER (*going to her also at the same time*): Calm yourself! Don't get excited! Sit down now!

THE MOTHER: Well then, take that woman away out of my sight!

THE STEP-DAUGHTER (*to* MANAGER): It is impossible for my mother to remain here.

THE FATHER (*to* MANAGER): They can't be here together. And for this reason, you see: that woman there was not with us when we came . . . If they are on together, the whole thing is given away inevitably, as you see.

THE MANAGER: It doesn't matter. This is only a first rough sketch — just to get an idea of the various points of the scene, even confusedly . . . (*Turning to the* MOTHER *and leading her to her chair.*) Come along, my dear lady, sit down now, and let's get on with the scene . . .

(*Meanwhile, the* STEP-DAUGHTER, *coming forward again, turns to* MADAME PACE.)

THE STEP-DAUGHTER: Come on, Madame, come on!

MADAME PACE (*offended*): No, no, *grazie*. I not do anything witha your mother present.

THE STEP-DAUGHTER: Nonsense! Introduce this "old signore" who wants to talk nicely to me. (*Addressing the* COMPANY *imperiously.*) We've got to do this scene one way or another, haven't we? Come on! (*To* MADAME PACE.) You can go!

MADAME PACE: Ah yes! I go'way! I go'way! Certainly! (*Exits furious.*)

THE STEP-DAUGHTER (*to the* FATHER): Now you make your entry. No, you needn't go over here. Come here. Let's suppose you've already come in. Like that, yes! I'm here with bowed head, modest like. Come on! Out with your voice! Say "Good morning, Miss" in that peculiar tone, that special tone . . .

THE MANAGER: Excuse me, but are you the Manager, or am I? (*To the* FATHER, *who looks undecided and perplexed.*) Get on with it, man! Go down there to the back of the stage. You needn't go off. Then come right forward here.

(*The* FATHER *does as he is told, looking troubled and perplexed at first. But as soon as he begins to move, the reality of the action affects him, and he begins to smile and to be more natural. The* ACTORS *watch intently.*)

THE MANAGER (*sotto voce, quickly to the* PROMPTER *in his box*): Ready! ready? Get ready to write now.

THE FATHER (*coming forward and speaking in a different tone*): Good afternoon, Miss!

THE STEP-DAUGHTER (*head bowed down slightly, with restrained disgust*): Good afternoon!

THE FATHER (*looks under her hat which partly covers her face. Perceiving she is very young, he makes an exclamation, partly of surprise, partly of fear lest he compromise himself in a risky adventure*): Ah . . . but . . . ah . . . I say . . . this is not the first time that you have come here, is it?

THE STEP-DAUGHTER (*modestly*): No sir.

THE FATHER: You've been here before, eh? (*Then seeing her nod agreement.*) More than once? (*Waits for her to answer, looks under her hat, smiles, and then says.*) Well then, there's no need to be so shy, is there? May I take off your hat?

THE STEP-DAUGHTER (*anticipating him and with veiled disgust*): No sir . . . I'll do it myself. (*Takes it off quickly.*)

(*The* MOTHER, *who watches the progress of the scene with the* SON *and the other two children who cling to her, is on thorns; and follows with varying expressions of sorrow, indignation, anxiety, and horror the words and actions of the other two. From time to time she hides her face in her hands and sobs.*)

THE MOTHER: Oh, my God, my God!

THE FATHER (*playing his part with a touch of gallantry*): Give it to me! I'll put it down. (*Takes hat from her hands.*) But a dear little head like yours ought to have a smarter hat. Come and help me choose one from the stock, won't you?

L'INGENUE (*interrupting*): I say . . . those are our hats you know.

THE MANAGER (*furious*): Silence! silence! Don't try and be funny, if you please . . . We're playing the scene now, I'd have you notice. (*To the* STEP-DAUGHTER.) Begin again, please!

THE STEP-DAUGHTER (*continuing*): No thank you, sir.

THE FATHER: Oh, come now. Don't talk like that. You must take it. I shall be upset if you don't. There are some lovely little hats here; and then — Madame will be pleased. She expects it, anyway, you know.

THE STEP-DAUGHTER: No, no! I couldn't wear it!

THE FATHER: Oh, you're thinking about what they'd say at home if they saw you come in with a new hat? My dear girl, there's always a way round these little matters, you know.

THE STEP-DAUGHTER (*all keyed up*): No, it's not that. I couldn't wear it because I am . . . as you see . . . you might have noticed . . . (*Showing her black dress.*)

THE FATHER: . . . in mourning! Of course: I beg your pardon: I'm frightfully sorry . . .

THE STEP-DAUGHTER (*forcing herself to conquer her indignation and nausea*): Stop! Stop! It's I who must thank you. There's no need for you to feel mortified or specially sorry. Don't think any more of what I've said. (*Tries to smile.*) I must forget that I am dressed so . . .

THE MANAGER (*interrupting and turning to the* PROMPTER): Stop a minute! Stop! Don't write that down. Cut out that last bit. (*Then to the* FATHER *and* STEP-DAUGHTER.) Fine! it's going fine! (*To the* FATHER *only.*) And now you can go on as we arranged. (*To the* ACTORS.) Pretty good that scene, where he offers her the hat, eh?

THE STEP-DAUGHTER: The best's coming now. Why can't we go on?

THE MANAGER: Have a little patience! (*To the* ACTORS.) Of course, it must be treated rather lightly.

LEADING MAN: Still, with a bit of go in it!

LEADING LADY: Of course! It's easy enough! (*To* LEADING MAN.) Shall you and I try it now?

LEADING MAN: Why, yes! I'll prepare my entrance. (*Exit in order to make his entrance.*)

THE MANAGER (*to* LEADING LADY): See here! The scene between you and Madame Pace is finished. I'll have it written out properly after. You remain here . . . oh, where are you going?

LEADING LADY: One minute. I want to put my hat on again. (*Goes over to hat-rack and puts her hat on her head.*)

THE MANAGER: Good! You stay here with your head bowed down a bit.

THE STEP-DAUGHTER: But she isn't dressed in black.

LEADING LADY: But I shall be, and much more effectively than you.

THE MANAGER (*to* STEP-DAUGHTER): Be quiet please, and watch! You'll be able to learn something. (*Clapping his hands.*) Come on! come on! Entrance, please!

(*The door at rear of stage opens, and the*

LEADING MAN *enters with the lively manner of an old gallant. The rendering of the scene by the* ACTORS *from the very first words is seen to be quite a different thing, though it has not in any way the air of a parody. Naturally, the* STEP-DAUGHTER *and the* FATHER, *not being able to recognize themselves in the* LEADING LADY *and the* LEADING MAN, *who deliver their words in different tones and with a different psychology, express, sometimes with smiles, sometimes with gestures, the impression they receive.*)

LEADING MAN: Good afternoon, Miss . . .

THE FATHER (*at once unable to contain himself*): No! no!

(*The* STEP-DAUGHTER, *noticing the way the* LEADING MAN *enters, bursts out laughing.*)

THE MANAGER (*furious*): Silence! And you please just stop that laughing. If we go on like this, we shall never finish.

THE STEP-DAUGHTER: Forgive me, sir, but it's natural enough. This lady (*indicating* LEADING LADY) stands there still; but if she is supposed to be me, I can assure you that if I heard anyone say "Good afternoon" in that manner and in that tone, I should burst out laughing as I did.

THE FATHER: Yes, yes, the manner, the tone . . .

THE MANAGER: Nonsense! Rubbish! Stand aside and let me see the action.

LEADING MAN: If I've got to represent an old fellow who's coming into a house of an equivocal character . . .

THE MANAGER: Don't listen to them, for Heaven's sake! Do it again! It goes fine. (*Waiting for the* ACTORS *to begin again.*) Well?

LEADING MAN: Good afternoon, Miss.

LEADING LADY: Good afternoon.

LEADING MAN (*imitating the gesture of the* FATHER *when he looked under the hat, and then expressing quite clearly first satisfaction and then fear*): Ah, but . . . I say . . . this is not the first time that you have come here, is it?

THE MANAGER: Good, but not quite so heavily. Like this. (*Acts himself.*) "This isn't the first time that you have come here" . . . (*To* LEADING LADY.) And you say: "No, sir."

LEADING LADY: No, sir.

LEADING MAN: You've been here before, more than once.

THE MANAGER: No, no, stop! Let her nod "yes" first. "You've been here before, eh?" (*The* LEADING LADY *lifts up her head slightly and closes her eyes as though in disgust. Then she inclines her head twice.*)

THE STEP-DAUGHTER (*unable to contain herself*): Oh my God! (*Puts a hand to her mouth to prevent herself from laughing.*)

THE MANAGER (*turning round*): What's the matter?

THE STEP-DAUGHTER: Nothing, nothing!

THE MANAGER (*to* LEADING MAN): Go on!

LEADING MAN: You've been here before, eh? Well then, there's no need to be so shy, is there? May I take off your hat?

(*The* LEADING MAN *says this last speech in such a tone and with such gestures that the* STEP-DAUGHTER, *though she has her hand to her mouth, cannot keep from laughing.*)

LEADING LADY (*indignant*): I'm not going to stop here to be made a fool of by that woman there.

LEADING MAN: Neither am I! I'm through with it!

THE MANAGER (*shouting to* STEP-DAUGHTER): Silence! for once and all, I tell you!

THE STEP-DAUGHTER: Forgive me! forgive me!

THE MANAGER: You haven't any manners: that's what it is! You go too far.

THE FATHER (*endeavouring to intervene*): Yes, it's true, but excuse her . . .

THE MANAGER: Excuse what? It's absolutely disgusting.

THE FATHER: Yes, sir, but believe me, it has such a strange effect when . . .

THE MANAGER: Strange? Why strange? Where is it strange?

THE FATHER: No, sir; I admire your actors — this gentleman here, this lady; but they are certainly not us!

THE MANAGER: I should hope not. Evidently they cannot be you, if they are actors.

THE FATHER: Just so: actors! Both of them act our parts exceedingly well. But, believe me, it produces quite a different effect on us. They want to be us, but they aren't, all the same.

THE MANAGER: What is it then anyway?

THE FATHER: Something that is . . . that is theirs — and no longer ours . . .

THE MANAGER: But naturally, inevitably. I've told you so already.

THE FATHER: Yes, I understand . . . I understand . . .

THE MANAGER: Well then, let's have no more of it! (*Turning to the* ACTORS.) We'll have the rehearsals by ourselves, afterwards, in the ordinary way. I never could stand rehearsing with the author present. He's never satisfied! (*Turning to* FATHER *and* STEP-DAUGHTER.) Come on! Let's get on with it again; and try and see if you can't keep from laughing.

THE STEP-DAUGHTER: Oh, I shan't laugh any more. There's a nice little bit coming for me now: you'll see.

THE MANAGER: Well then: when she says "Don't think any more of what I've said. I must forget, etc.," you (*addressing the* FATHER) come in sharp with "I understand, I understand"; and then you ask her . . .

THE STEP-DAUGHTER (*interrupting*): What?

THE MANAGER: Why she is in mourning.

THE STEP-DAUGHTER: Not at all! See here: when I told him that it was useless for me to be thinking about my wearing mourning, do you know how he answered me? "Ah well," he said, "then let's take off this little frock."

THE MANAGER: Great! Just what we want, to make a riot in the theatre!

THE STEP-DAUGHTER: But it's the truth!

THE MANAGER: What does that matter? Acting is our business here. Truth up to a certain point, but no further.

THE STEP-DAUGHTER: What do you want to do then?

THE MANAGER: You'll see, you'll see! Leave it to me.

THE STEP-DAUGHTER: No sir! What you want to do is to piece together a little romantic sentimental scene out of my disgust, out of all the reasons, each more cruel and viler than the other, why I am what I am. He is to ask me why I'm in mourning; and I'm to answer with tears in my eyes, that it is just two months since papa died. No sir, no! He's got to say to me; as he did say: "Well, let's take off this little dress at once." And I; with my two months' mourning in my heart, went there behind that screen, and with these fingers tingling with shame . . .

THE MANAGER (*running his hands through his hair*): For Heaven's sake! What are you saying?

THE STEP-DAUGHTER (*crying out excitedly*): The truth! The truth!

THE MANAGER: It may be. I don't deny it, and I can understand all your horror; but you must surely see that you can't have this kind of thing on the stage. It won't go.

THE STEP-DAUGHTER: Not possible, eh? Very well! I'm much obliged to you — but I'm off!

THE MANAGER: Now be reasonable! Don't lose your temper!

THE STEP-DAUGHTER: I won't stop here! I won't! I can see you've fixed it all up with him in your office. All this talk about what is possible for the stage . . . I understand! He wants to get at his complicated "cerebral drama," to have his famous remorses and torments acted; but I want to act my part, *my part!*

THE MANAGER (*annoyed, shaking his shoulders*): Ah! Just *your* part! But, if you will pardon me, there are other parts than yours: His (*indicating the* FATHER) and hers (*indicating the* MOTHER)! On the stage you can't have a character becoming too prominent and overshadowing all the others. The thing is to pack them all into a neat little framework and then act what is actable. I am aware of the fact that everyone has his own interior life which he wants very much to put forward. But the difficulty lies in this fact: to set out just so much as is necessary for the stage, taking the other characters into consideration, and at the same time hint at the unrevealed interior life of each. I am willing to admit, my dear young lady, that from your point of view it would be a fine idea if each character could tell the public all his troubles in a nice monologue or a regular one hour lecture. (*Good humoredly.*) You must restrain yourself, my dear, and in your own interest, too; because this fury of yours, this exaggerated disgust you show, may make a bad impression, you know. After you have confessed to me that there were others before him at Madame Pace's and more than once . . .

THE STEP-DAUGHTER (*bowing her head, impressed*): It's true. But remember those others mean him for me all the same.

THE MANAGER (*not understanding*): What? The others? What do you mean?

THE STEP-DAUGHTER: For one who has gone wrong, sir, he who was responsible for the first fault is responsible for all that follow. He is responsible for my faults, was, even before I was born. Look at him, and see if it isn't true!

THE MANAGER: Well, well! And does the weight of so much responsibility seem nothing to you? Give him a chance to act it, to get it over!

THE STEP-DAUGHTER: How? How can he act all his "noble remorses," all his "moral torments," if you want to spare him the horror of being discovered one day — after he had asked her what he did ask her — in the arms of her, that already fallen woman, that child, sir, that child he used to watch come out of school? (*She is moved.*)

(*The* MOTHER *at this point is overcome with emotion, and breaks out into a fit of crying. All are touched. A long pause.*)

THE STEP-DAUGHTER (*as soon as the* MOTHER *becomes a little quieter, adds resolutely and gravely*): At present, we are unknown to the public. Tomorrow, you will act us as you wish, treating us in your own manner. But do you really want to see drama, do you want to see it flash out as it really did?

THE MANAGER: Of course! That's just what I do want, so I can use as much of it as is possible.

THE STEP-DAUGHTER: Well then, ask that Mother there to leave us.

THE MOTHER (*changing her low plaint into a sharp cry*): No! No! Don't permit it, sir, don't permit it!

THE MANAGER: But it's only to try it.

THE MOTHER: I can't bear it. I can't.

THE MANAGER: But since it has happened already . . . I don't understand!

THE MOTHER: It's taking place now. It happens all the time. My torment isn't a pretended one. I live and feel every minute of my torture. Those two children there — have you heard them speak? They can't speak any more. They cling to me to keep up my torment actual and vivid for me. But for themselves, they do not exist, they aren't any more. And she (*indicating the* STEP-DAUGHTER) has run away, she has left me, and is lost. If I now see her here before me, it is only to renew for me the tortures I have suffered for her too.

THE FATHER: The eternal moment! She (*indicating the* STEP-DAUGHTER) is here to catch me, fix me, and hold me eternally in the stocks for that one fleeting and shameful moment of my life. She can't give it up! And you sir, cannot either fairly spare me it.

THE MANAGER: I never said I didn't want to act it. It will form, as a matter of fact, the nucleus of the whole first act right up to her surprise. (*Indicates the* MOTHER.)

THE FATHER: Just so! This is my punishment: the passion in all of us that must culminate in her final cry.

THE STEP-DAUGHTER: I can hear it still in my ears. It's driven me mad, that cry! — You can put me on as you like; it doesn't matter. Fully dressed, if you like — provided I have at least the arm bare; because, standing like this (*she goes close to the* FATHER *and leans her head on his breast*) with my head so, and my arms round his neck, I saw a vein pulsing in my arm here; and then, as if that live vein had awakened disgust in me, I closed my eyes like this, and let my head sink on his breast. (*Turning to the* MOTHER.) Cry out mother! Cry out! (*Buries head in* FATHER's *breast, and with her shoulders raised as if to prevent her hearing the cry, adds in tones of intense emotion.*) Cry out as you did then!

THE MOTHER (*coming forward to separate them*): No! My daughter, my daughter! (*And after having pulled her away from him.*) You brute! you brute! She is my daughter! Don't you see she's my daughter?

THE MANAGER (*walking backwards towards footlights*): Fine! fine! Damned good! And then, of course — curtain!

THE FATHER (*going towards him excitedly*): Yes, of course, because that's the way it really happened.

THE MANAGER (*convinced and pleased*): Oh, yes, no doubt about it. Curtain here, curtain!

(*At the reiterated cry of the* MANAGER, *the* MACHINIST *lets the curtain down, leaving the* MANAGER *and the* FATHER *in front of it before the footlights.*)

THE MANAGER: The darned idiot! I said "curtain" to show the act should end there, and he goes and lets it down in earnest. (*To the* FATHER, *while he pulls the curtain back to go on to the stage again.*) Yes, yes, it's all right. Effect certain! That's the right ending. I'll guarantee the first act at any rate.

ACT III

When the curtain goes up again, it is seen that the stage hands have shifted the bit of scenery used in the last part, and have rigged up instead at the back of the stage a drop, with some trees, and one or two wings. A portion of a fountain basin is visible. The MOTHER *is sitting on the right with the two children by her side. The* SON *is on the same side, but away from the others. He seems bored, angry, and full of shame. The* FATHER *and the* STEP-DAUGHTER *are also seated towards the right front. On the other side (left) are the* ACTORS, *much in the positions they occupied before the curtain was lowered. Only the* MANAGER *is standing up in the middle of the stage, with his hand closed over his mouth in the act of meditating.*

THE MANAGER (*shaking his shoulders after a brief pause*): Ah yes: the second act! Leave it to me, leave it all to me as we arranged, and you'll see! It'll go fine!

THE STEP-DAUGHTER: Our entry into his house (*indicates* FATHER) in spite of him . . . (*Indicates the* SON.)

THE MANAGER (*out of patience*): Leave it to me, I tell you!

THE STEP-DAUGHTER: Do let it be clear, at any rate, that it is in spite of my wishes.

THE MOTHER (*from her corner, shaking her head*): For all the good that's come of it . . .

THE STEP-DAUGHTER (*turning towards her quickly*): It doesn't matter. The more harm done us, the more remorse for him.

THE MANAGER (*impatiently*): I understand! Good Heavens! I understand! I'm taking it into account.

THE MOTHER (*supplicatingly*): I beg you, sir, to let it appear quite plain that for conscience' sake I did try in every way . . .

THE STEP-DAUGHTER (*interrupting indignantly and continuing for the* MOTHER): . . . to pacify me, to dissuade me from spiting him. (*To* MANAGER.) Do as she wants: satisfy her, because it is true! I enjoy it immensely. Anyhow, as you can see, the meeker she is, the more she tries to get at his heart, the more distant and aloof does he become.

THE MANAGER: Are we going to begin this second act or not?

THE STEP-DAUGHTER: I'm not going to talk

any more now. But I must tell you this: you can't have the whole action take place in the garden, as you suggest. It isn't possible!

THE MANAGER: Why not?

THE STEP-DAUGHTER: Because he (*indicates the* SON *again*) is always shut up alone in his room. And then there's all the part of that poor dazed-looking boy there which takes place indoors.

THE MANAGER: Maybe! On the other hand, you will understand — we can't change scenes three or four times in one act.

THE LEADING MAN: They used to once.

THE MANAGER: Yes, when the public was up to the level of that child there.

THE LEADING LADY: It makes the illusion easier.

THE FATHER (*irritated*): The illusion! For Heaven's sake, don't say illusion. Please don't use that word, which is particularly painful for us.

THE MANAGER (*astounded*): And why, if you please?

THE FATHER: It's painful, cruel, really cruel; and you ought to understand that.

THE MANAGER: But why? What ought we to say then? The illusion, I tell you, sir, which we've got to create for the audience . . .

THE LEADING MAN: With our acting.

THE MANAGER: The illusion of a reality.

THE FATHER: I understand; but you, perhaps, do not understand us. Forgive me! You see . . . here for you and your actors, the thing is only — and rightly so . . . a kind of game . . .

THE LEADING LADY (*interrupting indignantly*): A game! We're not children here, if you please! We are serious actors.

THE FATHER: I don't deny it. What I mean is the game, or play, of your art, which has to give, as the gentleman says, a perfect illusion of reality.

THE MANAGER: Precisely — !

THE FATHER: Now, if you consider the fact that we (*indicates himself and the other five* CHARACTERS), as we are, have no other reality outside of this illusion . . .

THE MANAGER (*astonished, looking at his* ACTORS, *who are also amazed*): And what does that mean?

THE FATHER (*after watching them for a moment with a wan smile*): As I say, sir, that which is a game of art for you is our sole reality. (*Brief pause. He goes a step or two nearer the* MANAGER *and adds.*) But not only for us, you know, by the way. Just you think it over well. (*Looks him in the eyes.*) Can you tell me who you are?

THE MANAGER (*perplexed, half smiling*): What? Who am I? I am myself.

THE FATHER: And if I were to tell you that this isn't true, because you and I . . . ?

THE MANAGER: I should say you were mad — ! (*The* ACTORS *laugh.*)

THE FATHER: You're quite right to laugh: because we are all making believe here. (*To* MANAGER.) And you can therefore object that it's only for a joke that the gentleman there (*indicates the* LEADING MAN), who naturally is himself, has to be me, who am on the contrary myself — this thing you see here. You see I've caught you in a trap! (*The* ACTORS *laugh.*)

THE MANAGER (*annoyed*): But we've had all this over once before. Do you want to begin again?

THE FATHER: No, no! That wasn't my meaning! In fact, I should like to request you to abandon this game of art (*looking at the* LEADING LADY *as if anticipating her*) which you are accustomed to play here with your actors, and to ask you seriously once again: who are you?

THE MANAGER (*astonished and irritated, turning to his* ACTORS): If this fellow here hasn't got a nerve! A man who calls himself a character comes and asks me who I am!

THE FATHER (*with dignity, but not offended*): A character, sir, may always ask a man who he is. Because a character has really a life of his own, marked with his especial characteristics; for which reason he is always "somebody." But a man — I'm not speaking of you now — may very well be "nobody."

THE MANAGER: Yes, but you are asking these questions of me, the boss, the manager! Do you understand?

THE FATHER: But only in order to know if you, as you really are now, see yourself as you once were with all the illusions that were yours then, with all the things both inside and outside of you as they seemed to you — as they were then indeed for you. Well, sir, if you think of all those illusions that mean nothing to you now, of all those things which don't even *seem* to you to exist any more, while once they *were* for you, don't you feel that — I won't say these boards — but the very earth under your feet is sinking away from you when you reflect that in the same way this *you* as you feel it today — all this present reality of yours — is fated to seem a mere illusion to you tomorrow?

THE MANAGER (*without having understood much, but astonished by the specious argument*): Well, well! And where does all this take us anyway?

THE FATHER: Oh, nowhere! It's only to show you that if we (*indicating the* CHARACTERS) have no other reality beyond the illusion, you too must not count overmuch on your reality as you feel it today, since, like that of yesterday, it may prove an illusion for you tomorrow.

THE MANAGER (*determining to make fun of him*): Ah, excellent! Then you'll be saying next that you, with this comedy of yours that you brought here to act, are truer and more real than I am.

THE FATHER (*with the greatest seriousness*). But of course; without doubt!

THE MANAGER: Ah, really?

THE FATHER: Why, I thought you'd understand that from the beginning.

THE MANAGER: More real than I?

THE FATHER: If your reality can change from one day to another . . .

THE MANAGER: But everyone knows it can change. It is always changing, the same as anyone else's.

THE FATHER (*with a cry*): No, sir, not ours! Look here! That is the very difference! Our reality doesn't change: it can't change! It can't be other than what it is, because it is already fixed for ever. It's terrible. Ours is an immutable reality which should make you shudder when you approach us if you are really conscious of the fact that your reality is a mere transitory and fleeting illusion, taking this form today and that tomorrow, according to the conditions, according to your will, your sentiments, which in turn are controlled by an intellect that shows them to you today in one manner and tomorrow . . . who knows how? . . . Illusions of reality represented in this fatuous comedy of life that never ends, nor can ever end! Because if tomorrow it were to end . . . then why, all would be finished.

THE MANAGER: Oh for God's sake, will you *at least* finish with this philosophizing and let us try and shape this comedy which you yourself have brought me here? You argue and philosophize a bit too much, my dear sir. You know you seem to me almost, almost . . . (*Stops and looks him over from head to foot.*) Ah, by the way, I think you introduced yourself to me as a — what shall . . . we say — a "character," created by an author who did not afterward care to make a drama of his own creations.

THE FATHER: It is the simple truth, sir.

THE MANAGER: Nonsense! Cut that out, please! None of us believes it, because it isn't a thing, as you must recognize yourself, which one can believe seriously. If you want to know, it seems to me you are trying to imitate the manner of a certain author whom I heartily detest — I warn you — although I have unfortunately bound myself to put on one of his works. As a matter of fact, I was just starting to rehearse it, when you arrived. (*Turning to the* ACTORS.) And this is what we've gained — out of the frying-pan into the fire!

THE FATHER: I don't know to what author you may be alluding, but believe me I feel what I think; and I seem to be philosophizing only for those who do not think what they feel, because they blind themselves with their own sentiment. I know that for many people this self-blinding seems much more "human"; but the contrary is really true. For man never reasons so much and becomes so introspective as when he suffers; since he is anxious to get at the cause of his sufferings, to learn who has produced them, and whether it is just or unjust that he should have to bear them. On the other hand, when he is happy, he takes his happiness as it comes and doesn't analyze it, just as if happiness were his right. The animals suffer without reasoning about their sufferings. But take the case of a man who suffers and begins to reason about it. Oh no! it can't be allowed! Let him suffer like an animal, and then — ah yet, he is "human"!

THE MANAGER: Look here! Look here! You're off again, philosophizing worse than ever.

THE FATHER: Because I suffer, sir! I'm not philosophizing: I'm crying aloud the reason of my sufferings.

THE MANAGER (*makes brusque movement as he is taken with a new idea*): I should like to know if anyone has ever heard of a character who gets right out of his part and perorates and speechifies as you do. Have you ever heard of a case? I haven't.

THE FATHER: You have never met such a

case, sir, because authors, as a rule, hide the labour of their creations. When the characters are really alive before their author, the latter does nothing but follow them in their action, in their words, in the situations which they suggest to him; and he has to will them the way they will themselves — for there's trouble if he doesn't. When a character is born, he acquires at once such an independence, even of his own author, that he can be imagined by everybody even in many other situations where the author never dreamed of placing him; and so he acquires for himself a meaning which the author never thought of giving him.

THE MANAGER: Yes, yes, I know this.

THE FATHER: What is there then to marvel at in us? Imagine such a misfortune for characters as I have described to you: to be born of an author's fantasy, and be denied life by him; and then answer me if these characters left alive, and yet without life, weren't right in doing what they did do and are doing now, after they have attempted everything in their power to persuade him to give them their stage life. We've all tried him in turn, I, she (*indicating the* STEP-DAUGHTER) *and she* (*indicating the* MOTHER).

THE STEP-DAUGHTER: It's true. I too have sought to tempt him, many, many times, when he has been sitting at his writing table, feeling a bit melancholy, at the twilight hour. He would sit in his armchair too lazy to switch on the light, and all the shadows that crept into his room were full of our presence coming to tempt him. (*As if she saw herself still there by the writing table, and was annoyed by the presence of the* ACTORS.) Oh, if you would only go away, go away and leave us alone — mother here with that son of hers — I with that child — that boy there always alone — and then I with him (*just hints at the* FATHER) — and then I alone, alone . . . in those shadows! (*Makes a sudden movement as if in the vision she has of herself illuminating those shadows she wanted to seize hold of herself.*) Ah! my life! my life! Oh, what scenes we proposed to him — and I tempted him more than any of the others!

THE FATHER: Maybe. But perhaps it was your fault that he refused to give us life: because you were too insistent, too troublesome.

THE STEP-DAUGHTER: Nonsense! Didn't he make me so himself? (*Goes close to the* MANAGER *to tell him as if in confidence.*) In my opinion he abandoned us in a fit of depression, of disgust for the ordinary theatre as the public knows it and likes it.

THE SON: Exactly what it was, sir; exactly that!

THE FATHER: Not at all! Don't believe it for a minute. Listen to me! You'll be doing quite right to modify, as you suggest, the excesses both of this girl here, who wants to do too much, and of this young man, who won't do anything at all.

THE SON: No, nothing!

THE MANAGER: You too get over the mark occasionally, my dear sir, if I may say so.

THE FATHER: I? When? Where?

THE MANAGER: Always! Continuously! Then there's this insistence of yours in trying to make us believe you are a character. And then too, you must really argue and philosophize less, you know, much less.

THE FATHER: Well, if you want to take away from me the possibility of representing the torment of my spirit which never gives me peace, you will be suppressing me: that's all. Every true man, sir, who is a little above the level of the beasts and plants does not live for the sake of living, without knowing how to live; but he lives so as to give a meaning and a value of his own to life. For me this is *everything.* I cannot give up this, just to represent a mere fact as she (*indicating the* STEP-DAUGHTER) wants. It's all very well for her, since her "vendetta" lies in the "fact." I'm not going to do it. It destroys my *raison d'être.*

THE MANAGER: Your *raison d'être!* Oh, we're going ahead fine! First she starts off, and then you jump in. At this rate, we'll never finish.

THE FATHER: Now, don't be offended! Have it your own way — provided, however, that within the limits of the parts you assign us each one's sacrifice isn't too great.

THE MANAGER: You've got to understand that you can't go on arguing at your own pleasure. Drama is action, sir, action and not confounded philosophy.

THE FATHER: All right. I'll do just as much arguing and philosophizing as everybody does when he is considering his own torments.

THE MANAGER: If the drama permits! But for Heaven's sake, man, let's get along and come to the scene.

THE STEP-DAUGHTER: It seems to me we've got too much action with our coming into his house. (*Indicating* FATHER.) You said, before, you couldn't change the scene every five minutes.

THE MANAGER: Of course not. What we've got to do is to combine and group up all the facts in one simultaneous, close-knit action. We can't have it as you want, with your little brother wandering like a ghost from room to room, hiding behind doors and meditating a project which — what did you say it did to him?

THE STEP-DAUGHTER: Consumes him, sir, wastes him away!

THE MANAGER: Well, it may be. And then at the same time, you want the little girl there to be playing in the garden . . . one in the house, and the other in the garden: isn't that it?

THE STEP-DAUGHTER: Yes, in the sun, in the sun! That is my only pleasure: to see her happy and careless in the garden after the misery and squalor of the horrible room where we all four slept together. And I had to sleep with her — I, do you understand? — with my vile contaminated body next to hers; with her folding me fast in her loving little arms. In the garden, whenever she spied me, she would run to take me by the hand. She didn't care for the big flowers, only the little ones; and she loved to show me them and pet me.

THE MANAGER: Well then, we'll have it in the garden. Everything shall happen in the garden; and we'll group the other scenes there. (*Calls a* STAGE HAND.) Here, a back-cloth with trees and something to do as a fountain basin. (*Turning round to look at the back of the stage.*) Ah, you've fixed it up. Good! (*To* STEP-DAUGHTER.) This is just to give an idea, of course. The Boy, instead of hiding behind the doors, will wander about here in the garden, hiding behind the trees. But it's going to be rather difficult to find a child to do that scene with you where she shows you the flowers. (*Turning to the* BOY.) Come forward a little, will you please? Let's try it now! Come along! come along! (*Then seeing him come shyly forward, full of fear and looking lost.*) It's a nice business, this lad here. What's the matter with him? We'll have to give him a word or two to say. (*Goes close to him, puts a hand on his shoulders, and leads him behind one of the trees.*) Come on! come on! Let me see you a little! Hide here . . . yes, like that. Try and show your head just a little as if you

were looking for someone . . . (*Goes back to observe the effect, when the* BOY *at once goes through the action.*) Excellent! fine! (*Turning to* STEP-DAUGHTER.) Suppose the little girl there were to surprise him as he looks round, and run over to him, so we could give him a word or two to say?

THE STEP-DAUGHTER: It's useless to hope he will speak, as long as that fellow there is here . . . (*Indicates the* SON.) You must send him away first.

THE SON (*jumping up*): Delighted! Delighted! I don't ask for anything better. (*Begins to move away.*)

THE MANAGER (*at once stopping him*): No! No! Where are you going? Wait a bit!

(*The* MOTHER *gets up alarmed and terrified at the thought that he is really about to go away. Instinctively she lifts her arms to prevent him, without, however, leaving her seat.*)

THE SON (*to* MANAGER *who stops him*): I've got nothing to do with this affair. Let me go please! Let me go!

THE MANAGER: What do you mean by saying you've got nothing to do with this?

THE STEP-DAUGHTER (*calmly, with irony*): Don't bother to stop him: he won't go away.

THE FATHER: He has to act the terrible scene in the garden with his mother.

THE SON (*suddenly resolute and with dignity*): I shall act nothing at all. I've said so from the very beginning. (*To the* MANAGER.) Let me go!

THE STEP-DAUGHTER (*going over to the* MANAGER): Allow me? (*Puts down the* MANAGER'S *arm which is restraining the* SON.) Well, go away then, if you want to! (*The* SON *looks at her with contempt and hatred. She laughs and says.*) You see, he can't, he can't go away! He is obliged to stay here, indissolubly bound to the chain. If I, who fly off when that happens which has to happen, because I can't bear him — if I am still here and support that face and expression of his, you can well imagine that he is unable to move. He has to remain here, has to stop with that nice father of his, and that mother whose only son he is. (*Turning to the* MOTHER.) Come on, mother, come along! (*Turning to* MANAGER *to indicate her.*) You see, she was getting up to keep him back. (*To the* MOTHER, *beckoning her with her hand.*) Come on! come on! (*Then to*

MANAGER.) You can imagine how little she wants to show these actors of yours what she really feels; but so eager is she to get near him that . . . There, you see? She is willing to act her part. (*And in fact, the* MOTHER *approaches him; and as soon as the* STEP-DAUGHTER *has finished speaking, opens her arms to signify that she consents.*)

THE SON (*suddenly*): No! no! If I can't go away, then I'll stop here; but I repeat: I act nothing!

THE FATHER (*to* MANAGER *excitedly*): You can force him, sir.

THE SON: Nobody can force me.

THE FATHER: I can.

THE STEP-DAUGHTER: Wait a minute, wait . . . First of all, the baby has to go to the fountain . . . (*Runs to take the* CHILD *and leads her to the fountain.*)

THE MANAGER: Yes, yes of course; that's it. Both at the same time.

(*The second* LADY LEAD *and the* JUVENILE LEAD *at this point separate themselves from the group of* ACTORS. *One watches the* MOTHER *attentively; the other moves about studying the movements and manner of the* SON *whom he will have to act.*)

THE SON (*to* MANAGER): What do you mean by both at the same time? It isn't right. There was no scene between me and her. (*Indicates the* MOTHER.) Ask her how it was!

THE MOTHER: Yes, it's true. I had come into his room . . .

THE SON: Into my room, do you understand? Nothing to do with the garden.

THE MANAGER: It doesn't matter. Haven't I told you we've got to group the action?

THE SON (*observing the* JUVENILE LEAD *studying him*): What do you want?

THE JUVENILE LEAD: Nothing! I was just looking at you.

THE SON (*turning towards the second* LADY LEAD): Ah! she's at it too: to re-act her part! (*Indicating the* MOTHER.)

THE MANAGER: Exactly! And it seems to me that you ought to be grateful to them for their interest.

THE SON: Yes, but haven't you yet perceived that it isn't possible to live in front of a mirror which not only freezes us with the image of ourselves, but throws our likeness back at us with a horrible grimace?

THE FATHER: That is true, absolutely true. You must see that.

THE MANAGER (*to second* LADY LEAD *and* JUVENILE LEAD): He's right! Move away from them!

THE SON: Do as you like. I'm out of this!

THE MANAGER: Be quiet, you, will you? And let me hear your mother! (*To* MOTHER.) You were saying you had entered . . .

THE MOTHER: Yes, into his room, because I couldn't stand it any longer. I went to empty my heart to him of all the anguish that tortures me . . . But as soon as he saw me come in . . .

THE SON: Nothing happened! There was no scene. I went away, that's all! I don't care for scenes!

THE MOTHER: It's true, true. That's how it was.

THE MANAGER: Well now, we've got to do this bit between you and him. It's indispensable.

THE MOTHER: I'm ready . . . when you are ready. If you could only find a chance for me to tell him what I feel here in my heart.

THE FATHER (*going to* SON *in a great rage*): You'll do this for your mother, for your mother, do you understand?

THE SON (*quite determined*): I do nothing!

THE FATHER (*taking hold of him and shaking him*): For God's sake, do as I tell you! Don't you hear your mother asking you for a favor? Haven't you even got the guts to be a son?

THE SON (*taking hold of the* FATHER): No! No! And for God's sake stop it, or else . . . (*General agitation. The* MOTHER, *frightened, tries to separate them.*)

THE MOTHER (*pleading*): Please! please!

THE FATHER (*not leaving hold of the* SON): You've got to obey, do you hear?

THE SON (*almost crying from rage*): What does it mean, this madness you've got? (*They separate.*) Have you no decency, that you insist on showing everyone our shame? I won't do it! I won't! And I stand for the will of our author in this. He didn't want to put us on the stage, after all!

THE MANAGER: Man alive! You came here . . .

THE SON (*indicating* FATHER): He did! I didn't!

THE MANAGER: Aren't you here now?

THE SON: It was his wish, and he dragged us

along with him. He's told you not only the things that did happen, but also things that have never happened at all.

THE MANAGER: Well, tell me then what did happen. You went out of your room without saying a word?

THE SON: Without a word, so as to avoid a scene!

THE MANAGER: And then what did you do?

THE SON: Nothing . . . walking in the garden . . . (*Hesitates for a moment with expression of gloom.*)

THE MANAGER (*coming closer to him, interested by his extraordinary reserve*): Well, well . . . walking in the garden . . .

THE SON (*exasperated*): Why on earth do you insist? It's horrible! (*The* MOTHER *trembles, sobs, and looks towards the fountain.*)

THE MANAGER (*slowly observing the glance and turning towards the* SON *with increasing apprehension*): The baby?

THE SON: There in the fountain . . .

THE FATHER (*pointing with tender pity to the* MOTHER): She was following him at the moment . . .

THE MANAGER (*to the* SON *anxiously*): And then you . . .

THE SON: I ran over to her; I was jumping in to drag her out when I saw something that froze my blood . . . the boy standing stock still, with eyes like a madman's, watching his little drowned sister, in the fountain! (*The* STEP-DAUGHTER *bends over the fountain to hide the* CHILD. *She sobs.*) Then . . . (*A revolver shot rings out behind the trees where the* BOY *is hidden.*)

THE MOTHER (*with a cry of terror runs over in that direction together with several of the* ACTORS *amid general confusion*): My son! My son!(*Then amid the cries and exclamations one hears her voice.*) Help! Help!

THE MANAGER (*pushing the* ACTORS *aside while they lift up the* BOY *and carry him off*): Is he really wounded?

SOME ACTORS: He's dead! dead!

OTHER ACTORS: No, no, it's only make believe, it's only pretence!

THE FATHER (*with a terrible cry*): Pretence? Reality, sir, reality!

THE MANAGER: Pretence? Reality? To hell with it all! Never in my life has such a thing happened to me. I've lost a whole day over these people, a whole day!

CURTAIN.

In an essay on *Six Characters in Search of an Author*, published several years after the play, Pirandello wryly noted that he had the "misfortune" to be a philosophical writer. Such a writer, he explained, is not content to present characters and stories for the pleasure of presenting them, but is moved by a "profound spiritual need." Something should be said, then, of Pirandello's philosophy, which can be found not only in the plays and in his essay on *Six Characters*, but also in an essay of 1908 entitled "Umorismo" ("Humor"). Reality is fluid, and beyond the grasp of reason. But man *has* reason, and he cannot tolerate a fluid, irrational world, so he sets up reasonable — but false — categories. He creates laws, codes of ethics, religions, and other "communal lies," but in certain dreadful moments he may become aware that these creations are distortions of reality.

In *Six Characters*, take as an example this speech by the Father:

Each of us when he appears before his fellows is clothed in a certain dignity. But every man knows what unconfessable things pass within the secrecy of his own heart. One gives way to the temptation, only to rise from it again, afterwards, with a great eagerness to re-establish one's dignity, as if it were a tombstone to place on the grave of one's shame, and a monument to hide and sign the memory of our weaknesses. Everybody's in the same case. Some folks haven't the courage to say certain things, that's all!

Now, such an attack on the apparent dignity of man is not unprecedented. *King Lear*, for example, offers an even more terrifying indictment of man's hypocrisy, penetrating the fair outside to the "mischief" that breeds about the heart. But Lear's remarks are the remarks of an overwrought speaker, and though we cannot dismiss his insights, we do not take them as the whole truth. Lear forces on us the awareness of the vast discrepancy between appearance and reality, but (1) we do not doubt that there *is* a reality, and (2) the play itself offers evidence that reality is not exactly what the tragic hero, at the height of his agony, perceives it to be. We remember, for example, Cordelia in *King Lear*, and we know that goodness and love are not mere illusions.

Pirandello went beyond suggesting that dignity is an illusion; he suggested that the idea of any sort of coherent personality is an illusion, and that all experience is illusory. Men have, of course, for centuries touched on the idea that what we call reality may be only illusion. One thinks, for example, of Plato, and of Shakespeare's numerous references to the world as a stage. Near the end of *Macbeth*, for example, the protagonist says:

> Life's but a walking shadow, a poor player
> That struts and frets his hour upon the stage
> And then is heard no more. It is a tale
> Told by an idiot, full of sound and fury
> Signifying nothing.

But such a passage is the remark of a particular character, not of Shakespeare. It is not Shakespeare but Macbeth who — finding that he cannot enjoy the crown for which he has given up his humanity and his soul — says that life signifies nothing. To the viewer of *Macbeth*, the significance is fairly clear: the violence that Macbeth does to others he unknowingly does also to himself, and this man who acts as though the lives of others have no significance comes to find his own life lacking any. In short, though Macbeth finds no significance in life, the play clearly implies one. Or take the end of *A Midsummer Night's Dream*, when Puck, in the epilogue, says:

> If we shadows have offended,
> Think but this, and all is mended:
> That you have but slumb'red here,
> While these visions did appear.
> And this weak and idle theme,
> No more yielding but a dream.

Shakespeare is graciously suggesting that his "weak and idle" play yields no more than a dream — but, first, we recognize these words for the modest untruth that they are, and, second, we know that the play itself refutes them, since in this play the several dreams in fact are not "weak and idle" (that is, foolish) but accurate indications of what happens. Macbeth and Puck, then, are not Shakespeare's spokesmen — but Pirandello's Father in *Six Characters* is indeed Pirandello's spokesman when he explains to the superficial Manager that the Manager's "reality is a mere transitory and fleeting illusion, taking this form today and that tomorrow, according to the conditions, according to your will, your sentiments, which in turn are controlled by an intellect that shows them to you today in one manner and tomorrow . . . who knows how?" After all, the Father explains, each day we see things differently; we dismiss as illusions what we earlier took for reality, and we will later dismiss as illusions what we at this moment take for reality:

> Well, sir, if you think of all those illusions that mean nothing to you now, of all those things which don't even *seem* to you to exist any more, while once they *were* for you, don't you feel that — I won't say these boards — but the very earth under your feet is sinking away from you when you reflect that in the same way this *you* as you feel it today — all this present reality of yours — is fated to seem a mere illusion to you tomorrow?

In effect Pirandello is saying that both external reality and personality are fluid, incoherent, elusive, and, for all practical purposes, unreal.

This extreme relativism had been introduced earlier in the play, especially in the Father's speech on conscience, which rejects the concept of personality, of a dominant ego:

> We believe this conscience to be a single thing, but it is many-sided. There is one for this person, and another for that. Diverse consciences. So we have this illusion of being one person for all, of having a personality that is unique in all our acts. But it isn't true. We perceive this when, tragically perhaps, in something we do, we are as it were, suspended, caught up in the air on a kind of hook. Then we perceive that all of us was not in that act, and that it would be an atrocious injustice to judge us by that action alone, as if all our existence were summed up in that one deed.

And the Father is not Pirandello's only spokesman. For example, the churlish Son scoffs at the Father but makes a similar point: "He [the Father] thinks he has got at the meaning of it all. Just as if each one of us in every circumstance of life couldn't find his own explanation of it!"

We have said that Pirandello suggested it was his "misfortune" to be a philosophical writer, and we have tried to sketch the philosophy underlying the play. But *Six Characters* is a play rather than a philosophic treatise, and we should not neglect Pirandello's vivid characterizations and his energetic conflicts. He memorably embodies in his play his vision of characters struggling to express themselves and to achieve reality even though they have no faith in reality. When the Manager impatiently explains to the Father, "Drama is action, sir, action and not confounded philosophy," Pirandello is making a little joke at the expense of those who are impatient with ideas in drama, but he has throughout taken care to embody his philosophy in the theatrical action of a tragicomedy. The serious concerns of the characters seem absurd to the Actors, and the Actors' efforts to impersonate the Characters seem ludicrous to the Characters. The tragic aspects of the play are obvious — for example, the drowning of the little Child, the suicide of the Boy, the emotional paralysis of the Son. Some of the comic aspects are equally obvious — especially the satire on the theater, and the occasional deflation of the Father (he has "aspirations towards a certain moral sanity," but he visits a brothel). But the struggle of the deeply-feeling Characters against the shallow Actors can only be characterized as tragicomic. That the chief spokesman for the Characters, the Father, argues against the concept of personality yet desperately seeks to achieve a full reality in a play to be performed by Actors whom he regards as less real than himself, is perhaps the tragicomic paradox at the heart of the play.

THE GOOD WOMAN OF SETZUAN

Bertolt Brecht

Translated by Eric Bentley

Bertolt Brecht (1898–1956) was born in Germany of middle-class parents, attended public schools and then entered the University of Munich to study medicine, but after one year was drafted for military service in World War I and served as a medical orderly for about a year. At the end of the war he returned to a shattered Germany, and during most of the twenties he seems to have been more or less an anarchist; in any case, his earliest poems and plays (e.g., *The Threepenny Opera*, 1928) cannot be called Communist, though around 1928 he seems to have become a believer in Communism. With the rise of Hitler, Brecht left Germany (1933), spending most of the years 1933 to 1939 in Denmark, 1940 in Finland, and 1941 to 1948 in the United States. Most of his best-known plays (including *The Good Woman of Setzuan*, 1938–1941) were written during his fifteen years of exile. His return in 1948 to Germany — to East Berlin — was somewhat equivocal, for he obtained Austrian citizenship (1950) and arranged for the copyright to his work to be held by a publisher in West Berlin. He died suddenly, of a thrombosis, in 1956.

CHARACTERS

WONG, *a water seller*
THREE GODS
SHEN TE, *a prostitute, later a shopkeeper*
MRS. SHIN, *former owner of Shen Te's shop*
A FAMILY OF EIGHT (*husband, wife, brother, sister-in-law, grandfather, nephew, niece, boy*)
AN UNEMPLOYED MAN
A CARPENTER
MRS. MI TZU, *Shen Te's landlady*

YANG SUN, *an unemployed pilot, later a factory manager*
AN OLD WHORE
A POLICEMAN
AN OLD MAN
AN OLD WOMAN, *his wife*
MR. SHU FU, *a barber*
MRS. YANG, *mother of Yang Sun*
GENTLEMEN, VOICES, CHILDREN (*three*), *etc.*

The Württemburgische Staatstheater production of *The Good Woman of Setzuan*, directed by Peter Palitzsch, set by Gerd Richter, Stuttgart, 1965. (Photograph: Werner Schloske.)

PROLOGUE

At the gates of the half-Westernized city of Setzuan. Evening. WONG *the water seller introduces himself to the audience.*

WONG: I sell water here in the city of Setzuan. It isn't easy. When water is scarce, I have long distances to go in search of it, and when it is plentiful, I have no income. But in our part of the world there is nothing unusual about poverty. Many people think only the gods can save the situation. And I hear from a cattle merchant — who travels a lot — that some of the highest gods are on their way here at this very moment. Informed sources have it that heaven is quite disturbed at all the complaining. I've been coming out here to the city gates for three days now to bid these gods welcome. I want to be the first to greet them. What about those fellows over there? No, no, they *work*. And that one there has ink on his fingers, he's no god, he must be a clerk from the cement factory. *Those* two are another story. They look as though they'd like to beat you. But gods don't need to beat you, do they?

(THREE GODS *appear.*)

What about those three? Old-fashioned clothes — dust on their feet — they *must* be gods! (*He throws himself at their feet.*) Do with me what you will, illustrious ones!

FIRST GOD (*with an ear trumpet*): Ah! (*He is pleased.*) So we were expected?

WONG (*giving them water*): Oh, yes. And I *knew* you'd come.

FIRST GOD: We need somewhere to stay the night. You know of a place?

WONG: The whole town is at your service, illustrious ones! What sort of a place would you like?

(*The* GODS *eye each other.*)

FIRST GOD: Just try the first house you come to, my son.

Bertolt Brecht, *The Good Woman of Setzuan,* © 1956, 1961 by Eric Bentley. Epilogue © 1965 by Eric Bentley. Originally published in *Parables for the Theatre: Two Plays by Bertolt Brecht,* translated by Eric Bentley. University of Minnesota Press, Minneapolis. © 1948 by Eric Bentley.

WONG: That would be Mr. Fo's place.
FIRST GOD: Mr. Fo.
WONG: One moment! (*He knocks at the first house.*)
VOICE FROM MR. FO'S: No!

(WONG *returns a little nervously.*)

WONG: It's too bad. Mr. Fo isn't in. And his servants don't dare do a thing without his consent. He'll have a fit when he finds out who they turned away, won't he?
FIRST GOD (*smiling*): He will, won't he?
WONG: One moment! The next house is Mr. Cheng's. Won't he be thrilled!
FIRST GOD: Mr. Cheng.

(WONG *knocks.*)

VOICE FROM MR. CHENG'S: Keep your gods. We have our own troubles!
WONG (*back with the* GODS): Mr. Cheng is very sorry, but he has a houseful of relations. I think some of them are a bad lot, and naturally, he wouldn't like you to see them.
THIRD GOD: Are we so terrible?
WONG: Well, only with bad people, of course. Everyone knows the province of Kwan is always having floods.
SECOND GOD: Really? How's that?
WONG: Why, because they're so irreligious.
SECOND GOD: Rubbish. It's because they neglected the dam.
FIRST GOD (*to* SECOND): Sh! (*To* WONG.) You're still in hopes, aren't you, my son?
WONG: Certainly. All Setzuan is competing for the honor! What happened up to now is pure coincidence. I'll be back. (*He walks away, but then stands undecided.*)
SECOND GOD: What did I tell you?
THIRD GOD: It *could* be pure coincidence.
SECOND GOD: The same coincidence in Shun, Kwan, and Setzuan? People just aren't religious any more, let's face the fact. Our mission has failed!
FIRST GOD: Oh come, we might run into a good person any minute.
THIRD GOD: How did the resolution read? (*Unrolling a scroll and reading from it.*) "The world can stay as it is if enough people are found (*at the word "found" he unrolls it a little more*) living lives worthy of human beings." Good people, that is. Well, what about this

water seller himself? *He's* good, or I'm very much mistaken.

SECOND GOD: You're very much mistaken. When he gave us a drink, I had the impression there was something odd about the cup. Well, look! (*He shows the cup to the* FIRST GOD.)

FIRST GOD: A false bottom!

SECOND GOD: The man is a swindler.

FIRST GOD: Very well, count *him* out. That's one man among millions. And as a matter of fact, we only need one on *our* side. These atheists are saying, "The world must be changed because no one can *be* good and *stay* good." No one, eh? I say: let us find one — just one — and we have those fellows where we want them!

THIRD GOD (*to* WONG): Water seller, is it so hard to find a place to stay?

WONG: Nothing could be easier. It's just me. I don't go about it right.

THIRD GOD: Really?

(*He returns to the others. A* GENTLEMAN *passes by.*)

WONG: Oh dear, they're catching on. (*He accosts the* GENTLEMAN.) Excuse the intrusion, dear sir, but three gods have just turned up. Three of the very highest. They need a place for the night. Seize this rare opportunity — to have real gods as your guests!

GENTLEMAN (*laughing*): A new way of finding free rooms for a gang of crooks. (*Exit* GENTLEMAN.)

WONG (*shouting at him*): Godless rascal! Have you no religion, gentleman of Setzuan? (*Pause.*) Patience, illustrious ones! (*Pause.*) There's only one person left. Shen Te, the prostitute. She *can't* say no. (*Calls up to a window.*) Shen Te!

(SHEN TE *opens the shutters and looks out.*)

WONG: Shen Te, it's Wong. They're here, and nobody wants them. Will you take them?

SHEN TE: Oh, no, Wong, I'm expecting a gentleman.

WONG: Can't you forget about him for tonight?

SHEN TE: The rent has to be paid by tomorrow or I'll be out on the street.

WONG: This is no time for calculation, Shen Te.

SHEN TE: Stomachs rumble even on the Emperor's birthday, Wong.

WONG: Setzuan is one big dung hill!

SHEN TE: Oh, very well! I'll hide till my gen-

tleman has come and gone. Then I'll take them. (*She disappears.*)

WONG: They mustn't see her gentleman or they'll know what she is.

FIRST GOD (*who hasn't heard any of this*): I think it's hopeless.

(*They approach* WONG.)

WONG (*jumping, as he finds them behind him*): A room has been found, illustrious ones! (*He wipes sweat off his brow.*)

SECOND GOD: Oh, good.

THIRD GOD: Let's see it.

WONG (*nervously*): Just a minute. It has to be tidied up a bit.

THIRD GOD: Then we'll sit down here and wait.

WONG (*still more nervous*): No, no! (*Holding himself back.*) Too much traffic, you know.

THIRD GOD (*with a smile*): Of course, if you *want* us to move.

(*They retire a little. They sit on a doorstep.* WONG *sits on the ground.*)

WONG (*after a deep breath*): You'll be staying with a single girl — the finest human being in Setzuan!

THIRD GOD: That's nice.

WONG (*to the audience*): They gave me such a look when I picked up my cup just now.

THIRD GOD: You're worn out, Wong.

WONG: A little, maybe.

FIRST GOD: Do people here have a hard time of it?

WONG: The good ones do.

FIRST GOD: What about yourself?

WONG: You mean I'm not good. That's true. And I don't have an easy time either!

(*During this dialogue, a* GENTLEMAN *has turned up in front of* SHEN TE's *house, and has whistled several times. Each time* WONG *has given a start.*)

THIRD GOD (*to* WONG, *softly*): Psst! I think he's gone now.

WONG (*confused and surprised*): Ye-e-es.

(*The* GENTLEMAN *has left now, and* SHEN TE *has come down to the street.*)

SHEN TE (*softly*): Wong!

(*Getting no answer, she goes off down the street.* WONG *arrives just too late, forgetting his carrying pole.*)

WONG (*softly*): Shen Te! Shen Te! (*To him-*

self.) So she's gone off to earn the rent. Oh dear, I can't go to the gods *again* with no room to offer them. Having failed in the service of the gods, I shall run to my den in the sewer pipe down by the river and hide from their sight!

(*He rushes off.* SHEN TE *returns, looking for him, but finding the* GODS. *She stops in confusion.*)

SHEN TE: You are the illustrious ones? My name is Shen Te. It would please me very much if my simple room could be of use to you.

THIRD GOD: Where is the water seller, Miss . . . Shen Te?

SHEN TE: I missed him, somehow.

FIRST GOD: Oh, he probably thought you weren't coming, and was afraid of telling us.

THIRD GOD (*picking up the carrying pole*): We'll leave this with you. He'll be needing it.

(*Led by* SHEN TE, *they go into the house. It grows dark, then light. Dawn. Again escorted by* SHEN TE, *who leads them through the half-light with a little lamp, the* GODS *take their leave.*)

FIRST GOD: Thank you, thank you, dear Shen Te, for your elegant hospitality! We shall not forget! And give our thanks to the water seller — he showed us a good human being.

SHEN TE: Oh, I'm not good. Let me tell you something: when Wong asked me to put you up, I hesitated.

FIRST GOD: It's all right to hesitate if you then go ahead! And in giving us that room you did much more than you knew. You proved that good people still exist, a point that has been disputed of late — even in heaven. Farewell!

SECOND GOD: Farewell!

THIRD GOD: Farewell!

SHEN TE: Stop, illustrious ones! I'm not sure you're right. I'd like to be good, it's true, but there's the rent to pay. And that's not all: I sell myself for a living. Even so I can't make ends meet, there's too much competition. I'd like to honor my father and mother and speak nothing but the truth and not covet my neighbor's house. I should love to stay with one man. But how? How is it done? Even breaking a few of your commandments, I can hardly manage.

FIRST GOD (*clearing his throat*): These thoughts are but, um, the misgivings of an unusually good woman!

THIRD GOD: Good-bye, Shen Te! Give our regards to the water seller!

SECOND GOD: And above all: be good! Farewell!

FIRST GOD: Farewell!

THIRD GOD: Farewell!

(*They start to wave good-bye.*)

SHEN TE: But everything is so expensive, I don't feel sure I can do it!

SECOND GOD: That's not in our sphere. We never meddle with economics.

THIRD GOD: One moment. (*They stop.*) Isn't it true she might do better if she had more money?

SECOND GOD: Come, come! How could we ever account for it Up Above?

FIRST GOD: Oh, there are ways. (*They put their heads together and confer in dumb show. To* SHEN TE, *with embarrassment.*) As you say you can't pay your rent, well, um, we're not paupers, so of course we *insist* on paying for our room. (*Awkwardly thrusting money into her hand.*) There! (*Quickly.*) But don't tell anyone! The incident is open to misinterpretation.

SECOND GOD: It certainly is!

FIRST GOD (*defensively*): But there's no law against it! It was never decreed that a god mustn't pay hotel bills!

(*The* GODS *leave.*)

I

A small tobacco shop. The shop is not as yet completely furnished and hasn't started doing business.

SHEN TE (*to the audience*): It's three days now since the gods left. When they said they wanted to pay for the room, I looked down at my hand, and there was more than a thousand silver dollars! I bought a tobacco shop with the money, and moved in yesterday. I don't own the building, of course, but I can pay the rent, and I hope to do a lot of good here. Beginning with Mrs. Shin, who's just coming across the square with her pot. She had the shop before me, and yesterday she dropped in to ask for rice for her children. (*Enter* MRS. SHIN. *Both women bow.*) How do you do, Mrs. Shin.

MRS. SHIN: How do you do, Miss Shen Te. You like your new home?

SHEN TE: Indeed, yes. Did your children have a good night?

MRS. SHIN: In that hovel? The youngest is coughing already.

SHEN TE: Oh, dear!

MRS. SHIN: You're going to learn a thing or two in these slums.

SHEN TE: Slums? That's not what you said when you sold me the shop!

MRS. SHIN: Now don't start nagging! Robbing me and my innocent children of their home and then calling it a slum! That's the limit! (*She weeps.*)

SHEN TE (*tactfully*): I'll get your rice.

MRS. SHIN: And a little cash while you're at it.

SHEN TE: I'm afraid I haven't sold anything yet.

MRS. SHIN (*screeching*): I've got to have it. Strip the clothes from my back and then cut my throat, will you? I know what I'll do: I'll dump my children on your doorstep! (*She snatches the pot out of* SHEN TE's *hands.*)

SHEN TE: Please don't be angry. You'll spill the rice.

(*Enter an elderly* HUSBAND *and* WIFE *with their shabbily dressed* NEPHEW.)

WIFE: Shen Te, dear! You've come into money, they tell me. And we haven't a roof over our heads. A tobacco shop. We had one too. But it's gone. Could we spend the night here, do you think?

NEPHEW (*appraising the shop*): Not bad!

WIFE: He's our nephew. We're inseparable!

MRS. SHIN: And who are these . . . ladies and gentlemen?

SHEN TE: They put me up when I first came in from the country. (*To the audience.*) Of course, when my small purse was empty, they put me out on the street, and they may be afraid I'll do the same to them. (*To the newcomers, kindly.*) Come in, and welcome, though I've only one little room for you — it's behind the shop.

HUSBAND: That'll do. Don't worry.

WIFE (*bringing* SHEN TE *some tea*): We'll stay over here, so we won't be in your way. Did you make it a tobacco shop in memory of your first real home? We can certainly give you a hint or two! That's one reason we came.

MRS. SHIN (*to* SHEN TE): Very nice! As long as you have a few customers too!

HUSBAND: Sh! A customer!

(*Enter an* UNEMPLOYED MAN, *in rags.*)

UNEMPLOYED MAN: Excuse me. I'm unemployed.

(MRS. SHIN *laughs.*)

SHEN TE: Can I help you?

UNEMPLOYED MAN: Have you any damaged cigarettes? I thought there might be some damage when you're unpacking.

WIFE: What nerve, begging for tobacco! (*Rhetorically.*) Why don't they ask for bread?

UNEMPLOYED MAN: Bread is expensive. One cigarette butt and I'll be a new man.

SHEN TE (*giving him cigarettes*): That's very important — to be a new man. You'll be my first customer and bring me luck.

(*The* UNEMPLOYED MAN *quickly lights a cigarette, inhales, and goes off, coughing.*)

WIFE: Was that right, Shen Te, dear?

MRS. SHIN: If this is the opening of a shop, you can hold the closing at the end of the week.

HUSBAND: I bet he had money on him.

SHEN TE: Oh, no, he said he hadn't!

NEPHEW: How d'you know he wasn't lying?

SHEN TE (*angrily*): How do you know he was?

WIFE (*wagging her head*): You're too good, Shen Te, dear. If you're going to keep this shop, you'll have to learn to say no.

HUSBAND: Tell them the place isn't yours to dispose of. Belongs to . . . some relative who insists on all accounts being strictly in order . . .

MRS. SHIN: That's right! What do you think you are — a philanthropist?

SHEN TE (*laughing*): Very well, suppose I ask you for my rice back, Mrs. Shin?

WIFE (*combatively, at* MRS. SHIN): So that's her rice?

(*Enter the* CARPENTER, *a small man.*)

MRS. SHIN (*who, at the sight of him, starts to hurry away*): See you tomorrow, Miss Shen Te! (*Exit* MRS. SHIN.)

CARPENTER: Mrs. Shin, it's you I want!

WIFE (*to* SHEN TE): Has she some claim on you?

SHEN TE: She's hungry. That's a claim.

CARPENTER: Are you the new tenant? And filling up the shelves already? Well, they're not yours till they're paid for, ma'am. I'm the carpenter, so I should know.

SHEN TE: I took the shop "furnishings included."

CARPENTER: You're in league with that Mrs. Shin, of course. All right. I demand my hundred silver dollars.

SHEN TE: I'm afraid I haven't got a hundred silver dollars.

CARPENTER: Then you'll find it. Or I'll have you arrested.

WIFE (*whispering to* SHEN TE): That relative: make it a cousin.

SHEN TE: Can't it wait till next month?

CARPENTER: No!

SHEN TE: Be a little patient, Mr. Carpenter, I can't settle all claims at once.

CARPENTER: Who's patient with me? (*He grabs a shelf from the wall.*) Pay up — or I take the shelves back!

WIFE: Shen Te! Dear! Why don't you let your ... cousin settle this affair? (*To* CARPENTER.) Put your claim in writing. Shen Te's cousin will see you get paid.

CARPENTER (*derisively*): Cousin, eh?

HUSBAND: Cousin, yes.

CARPENTER: I know these cousins!

NEPHEW: Don't be silly. He's a personal friend of mine.

HUSBAND: What a man! Sharp as a razor!

CARPENTER: All right. I'll put my claim in writing. (*Puts shelf on floor, sits on it, writes out bill.*)

WIFE (*to* SHEN TE): He'd tear the dress off your back to get his shelves. Never recognize a claim. That's my motto.

SHEN TE: He's done a job, and wants something in return. It's shameful that I can't give it to him. What will the gods say?

HUSBAND: You did your bit when you took *us* in.

(*Enter the* BROTHER, *limping, and the* SISTER-IN-LAW, *pregnant.*)

BROTHER (*to* HUSBAND *and* WIFE): So this is where you're hiding out! There's family feeling for you! Leaving us on the corner!

WIFE (*embarrassed, to* SHEN TE): It's my brother and his wife. (*To them.*) Now stop grumbling, and sit quietly in that corner. (*To* SHEN TE.) It can't be helped. She's in her fifth month.

SHEN TE: Oh yes. Welcome!

WIFE (*to the couple*): Say thank you. (*They mutter something.*) The cups are there. (*To* SHEN TE.) Lucky you bought this shop when you did!

SHEN TE (*laughing and bringing tea*): Lucky indeed!

(*Enter* MRS. MI TZU, *the landlady.*)

MRS. MI TZU: Miss Shen Te? I am Mrs. Mi Tzu, your landlady. I hope our relationship will be a happy one. I like to think I give my tenants modern, personalized service. Here is your lease. (*To the others, as* SHEN TE *reads the lease.*) There's nothing like the opening of a little shop, is there? A moment of true beauty! (*She is looking around.*) Not very much on the shelves, of course. But everything in the gods' good time! Where are your references, Miss Shen Te?

SHEN TE: Do I *have* to have references?

MRS. MI TZU: After all, I haven't a notion who you are!

HUSBAND: Oh, *we'd* be glad to vouch for Miss Shen Te! We'd go through fire for her!

MRS. MI TZU: And who may *you* be?

HUSBAND (*stammering*): Ma Fu, tobacco dealer.

MRS. MI TZU: Where is your shop, Mr. ... Ma Fu?

HUSBAND: Well, um, I haven't got a shop — I've just sold it.

MRS. MI TZU: I see. (*To* SHEN TE.) Is there no one else that knows you?

WIFE (*whispering to* SHEN TE): Your cousin! Your cousin!

MRS. MI TZU: This is a respectable house, Miss Shen Te. I never sign a lease without certain assurances.

SHEN TE (*slowly, her eyes downcast*): I have ... a cousin.

MRS. MI TZU: On the square? Let's go over and see him. What does he do?

SHEN TE (*as before*): He lives ... in another city.

WIFE (*prompting*): Didn't you say he was in Shung?

SHEN TE: That's right. Shung.

HUSBAND (*prompting*): I had his name on the tip of my tongue. Mr. ...

SHEN TE (*with an effort*): Mr. ... Shui ... Ta.

HUSBAND: That's it! Tall, skinny fellow!

SHEN TE: Shui Ta!

NEPHEW (*to* CARPENTER): *You* were in touch with him, weren't you? About the shelves?

CARPENTER (*surlily*): Give him this bill. (*He hands it over.*) I'll be back in the morning. (*Exit* CARPENTER.)

NEPHEW (*calling after him, but with his eyes on* MRS. MI TZU): Don't worry! Mr. Shui Ta pays on the nail!

MRS. MI TZU (*looking closely at* SHEN TE): I'll be happy to make his acquaintance, Miss Shen Te. (*Exit* MRS. MI TZU.)

(*Pause.*)

WIFE: By tomorrow morning she'll know more about you than you do yourself.

SISTER-IN-LAW (*to* NEPHEW): This thing isn't built to last.

(*Enter* GRANDFATHER.)

WIFE: It's Grandfather! (*To* SHEN TE.) Such a good old soul!

(*The* BOY *enters.*)

BOY (*over his shoulder*): Here they are!

WIFE: And the boy, how he's grown! But he always could eat enough for ten.

(*Enter the* NIECE.)

WIFE (*to* SHEN TE): Our little niece from the country. There are more of us now than in your time. The less we had, the more there were of us; the more there were of us, the less we had. Give me the key. We must protect ourselves from unwanted guests. (*She takes the key and locks the door.*) Just make yourself at home. I'll light the little lamp.

NEPHEW (*a big joke*): I hope her cousin doesn't drop in tonight! The strict Mr. Shui Ta!

(SISTER-IN-LAW *laughs.*)

BROTHER (*reaching for a cigarette*): One cigarette more or less . . .

HUSBAND: One cigarette more or less.

(*They pile into the cigarettes. The* BROTHER *hands a jug of wine round.*)

NEPHEW: Mr. Shui Ta'll pay for it!

GRANDFATHER (*gravely, to* SHEN TE): How do you do?

(SHEN TE, *a little taken aback by the belatedness of the greeting, bows. She has the carpenter's bill in one hand, the landlady's lease in the other.*)

WIFE: How about a bit of a song? To keep Shen Te's spirits up?

NEPHEW: Good idea. Grandfather: you start!

SONG OF THE SMOKE

GRANDFATHER:
I used to think (before old age beset me)
   That brains could fill the pantry of the poor.
But where did all my cerebration get me?
   I'm just as hungry as I was before.
     So what's the use?
      See the smoke float free
     Into ever colder coldness!
      It's the same with me.

HUSBAND:
The straight and narrow path leads to disaster
   And so the crooked path I tried to tread.
That got me to disaster even faster.
   (They say we shall be happy when we're dead.)
     So what's the use?
      See the smoke float free
     Into ever colder coldness!
      It's the same with me.

NIECE:
You older people, full of expectation,
   At any moment now you'll walk the plank!
The future's for the younger generation!
   Yes, even if that future is a blank.
     So what's the use?
      See the smoke float free
     Into ever colder coldness!
      It's the same with me.

NEPHEW (*to the* BROTHER): Where'd you get that wine?

SISTER-IN-LAW (*answering for the* BROTHER): He pawned the sack of tobacco.

HUSBAND (*stepping in*): What? That tobacco was all we had to fall back on! You pig!

BROTHER: You'd call a man a pig because your wife was frigid! Did you refuse to drink it?

(*They fight. The shelves fall over.*)

SHEN TE (*imploringly*): Oh don't! Don't break everything! Take it, take it, take it all, but don't destroy a gift from the gods!

WIFE (*disparagingly*): This shop isn't big enough. I should never have mentioned it to Uncle and the others. When *they* arrive, it's going to be disgustingly overcrowded.

SISTER-IN-LAW: And did you hear our gracious hostess? She cools off quick!

(*Voices outside. Knocking at the door.*)

UNCLE'S VOICE: Open the door!

WIFE: Uncle! Is that you, Uncle?

UNCLE'S VOICE: Certainly, it's me. Auntie says to tell you she'll have the children here in ten minutes.

WIFE (*to* SHEN TE): I'll have to let him in.

SHEN TE (*who scarcely hears her*):
The little lifeboat is swiftly sent down
Too many men too greedily
Hold on to it as they drown.

I A

WONG'S *den in a sewer pipe.*

WONG (*crouching there*): All quiet! It's four days now since I left the city. The gods passed this way on the second day. I heard their steps on the bridge over there. They must be a long way off by this time, so I'm safe. (*Breathing a sigh of relief, he curls up and goes to sleep. In his dream the pipe becomes transparent, and the* GODS *appear. Raising an arm, as if in self-defense.*) I know, I know, illustrious ones! I found no one to give you a room — not in all Setzuan! There, it's out. Please continue on your way!

FIRST GOD (*mildly*): But you did find someone. Someone who took us in for the night, watched over us in our sleep, and in the early morning lighted us down to the street with a lamp.

WONG: It was . . . Shen Te that took you in?

THIRD GOD: Who else?

WONG: And I ran away! "She isn't coming," I thought, "she just can't afford it."

GODS (*singing*):
O you feeble, well-intentioned, and yet feeble chap
Where there's need the fellow thinks there is no goodness!
When there's danger he thinks courage starts to ebb away!
Some people only see the seamy side!
What hasty judgment! What premature desperation!

WONG: I'm *very* ashamed, illustrious ones.

FIRST GOD: Do us a favor, water seller. Go back to Setzuan. Find Shen Te, and give us a report on her. We hear that she's come into a little money. Show interest in her goodness — for no one can be good for long if goodness is not in demand. Meanwhile we shall continue the search, and find other good people. After which, the idle chatter about the impossibility of goodness will stop!

(*The* GODS *vanish.*)

II

A knocking.

WIFE: Shen Te! Someone at the door. Where is she anyway?

NEPHEW: She must be getting the breakfast. Mr. Shui Ta will pay for it.

(*The* WIFE *laughs and shuffles to the door. Enter* MR. SHUI TA *and the* CARPENTER.)

WIFE: Who is it?

SHUI TA: I am Miss Shen Te's cousin.

WIFE: What?

SHUI TA: My name is Shui Ta.

WIFE: Her cousin?

NEPHEW: Her cousin?

NIECE: But that was a joke. She hasn't got a cousin.

HUSBAND: So early in the morning?

BROTHER: What's all the noise?

SISTER-IN-LAW: This fellow says he's her cousin.

BROTHER: Tell him to prove it.

NEPHEW: Right. If you're Shen Te's cousin, prove it by getting the breakfast.

SHUI TA (*whose regime begins as he puts out the lamp to save oil; loudly, to all present, asleep or awake*): Would you all please get dressed! Customers will be coming! I wish to open my shop!

HUSBAND: *Your* shop? Doesn't it belong to our good friend Shen Te?

(SHUI TA *shakes his head.*)

SISTER-IN-LAW: So we've been cheated. Where *is* the little liar?

SHUI TA: Miss Shen Te has been delayed. She wishes me to tell you there will be nothing she can do — now I am here.

WIFE (*bowled over*): I thought she was good!

NEPHEW: Do you have to believe *him*?

HUSBAND: I don't.

NEPHEW: Then do something.

HUSBAND: Certainly! I'll send out a search

party at once. You, you, you, and you, go out and look for Shen Te. (*As the* GRANDFATHER *rises and makes for the door.*) Not you, Grandfather, you and I will hold the fort.

SHUI TA: You won't find Miss Shen Te. She has suspended her hospitable activity for an unlimited period. There are too many of you. She asked me to say: this is a tobacco shop, not a gold mine.

HUSBAND: Shen Te never said a thing like that. Boy, food! There's a bakery on the corner. Stuff your shirt full when they're not looking!

SISTER-IN-LAW: Don't overlook the raspberry tarts.

HUSBAND: And don't let the policeman see you.

(*The* BOY *leaves.*)

SHUI TA: Don't you depend on this shop now? Then why give it a bad name by stealing from the bakery?

NEPHEW: Don't listen to him. Let's find Shen Te. She'll give him a piece of her mind.

SISTER-IN-LAW: Don't forget to leave us some breakfast.

(BROTHER, SISTER-IN-LAW, *and* NEPHEW *leave.*)

SHUI TA (*to the* CARPENTER): You see, Mr. Carpenter, nothing has changed since the poet, eleven hundred years ago, penned these lines:

A governor was asked what was needed
To save the freezing people in the city.
He replied:
"A blanket ten thousand feet long
to cover the city and all its suburbs."

(*He starts to tidy up the shop.*)

CARPENTER: Your cousin owes me money. I've got witnesses. For the shelves.

SHUI TA: Yes, I have your bill. (*He takes it out of his pocket.*) Isn't a hundred silver dollars rather a lot?

CARPENTER: No deductions! I have a wife and children.

SHUI TA: How many children?

CARPENTER: Three.

SHUI TA: I'll make you an offer. Twenty silver dollars.

(*The* HUSBAND *laughs.*)

CARPENTER: You're crazy. Those shelves are real walnut.

SHUI TA: Very well. Take them away.

CARPENTER: What?

SHUI TA: They cost too much. Please take them away.

WIFE: Not bad! (*And she, too, is laughing.*)

CARPENTER (*a little bewildered*): Call Shen Te, someone! (*To* SHUI TA.) She's *good!*

SHUI TA: Certainly. She's ruined.

CARPENTER (*provoked into taking some of the shelves*): All right, you can keep your tobacco on the floor.

SHUI TA (*to the* HUSBAND): Help him with the shelves.

HUSBAND (*grins and carries one shelf over to the door where the* CARPENTER *now is*): Good-bye, shelves!

CARPENTER (*to the* HUSBAND): You dog! You want my family to starve?

SHUI TA: I repeat my offer. I have no desire to keep my tobacco on the floor. Twenty silver dollars.

CARPENTER (*with desperate aggressiveness*): One hundred!

(SHUI TA *shows indifference, looks through the window. The* HUSBAND *picks up several shelves.*)

CARPENTER (*to* HUSBAND): You needn't smash them against the doorpost, you idiot! (*To* SHUI TA.) These shelves were made to measure. They're no use anywhere else!

SHUI TA: Precisely.

(*The* WIFE *squeals with pleasure.*)

CARPENTER (*giving up, sullenly*): Take the shelves. Pay what you want to pay.

SHUI TA (*smoothly*): Twenty silver dollars.

(*He places two large coins on the table. The* CARPENTER *picks them up.*)

HUSBAND (*brings the shelves back in*): And quite enough too!

CARPENTER (*slinking off*): Quite enough to get drunk on.

HUSBAND (*happily*): Well, we got rid of *him!*

WIFE (*weeping with fun, gives a rendition of the dialogue just spoken*): "Real walnut," says he. "Very well, take them away," says his lordship. "I have three children," says he. "Twenty silver dollars," says his lordship. "They're no use anywhere else," says he. "Pre-cisely," said his lordship! (*She dissolves into shrieks of merriment.*)

SHUI TA: And now: go!

HUSBAND: What's that?

SHUI TA: You're thieves, parasites. I'm giving you this chance. Go!

HUSBAND (*summoning all his ancestral dignity*): That sort deserves no answer. Besides, one should never shout on an empty stomach.

WIFE: Where's that boy?

SHUI TA: Exactly. The boy. I want no stolen goods in this shop. (*Very loudly.*) I strongly advise you to leave! (*But they remain seated, noses in the air. Quietly.*) As you wish. (SHUI TA *goes to the door. A* POLICEMAN *appears.* SHUI TA *bows.*) I am addressing the officer in charge of this precinct?

POLICEMAN: That's right, Mr., um, what was the name, sir?

SHUI TA: Mr. Shui Ta.

POLICEMAN: Yes, of course, sir.

(*They exchange a smile.*)

SHUI TA: Nice weather we're having.

POLICEMAN: A little on the warm side, sir.

SHUI TA: Oh, a little on the warm side.

HUSBAND (*whispering to the* WIFE): If he keeps it up till the boy's back, we're done for. (*Tries to signal* SHUI TA.)

SHUI TA (*ignoring the signal*): Weather, of course, is one thing indoors, another out on the dusty street!

POLICEMAN: Oh, quite another, sir!

WIFE (*to the* HUSBAND): It's all right as long as he's standing in the doorway — the boy will see him.

SHUI TA: Step inside for a moment! It's quite cool indoors. My cousin and I have just opened the place. And we attach the greatest importance to being on good terms with the, um, authorities.

POLICEMAN (*entering*): Thank you, Mr. Shui Ta. It *is* cool!

HUSBAND (*whispering to the* WIFE): And now the boy *won't* see him.

SHUI TA (*showing* HUSBAND *and* WIFE *to the* POLICEMAN): Visitors, I think my cousin knows them. They were just leaving.

HUSBAND (*defeated*): Ye-e-es, we were . . . just leaving.

SHUI TA: I'll tell my cousin you couldn't wait.

(*Noise from the street. Shouts of "Stop, Thief!"*)

POLICEMAN: What's that?

(*The* BOY *is in the doorway with cakes and buns and rolls spilling out of his shirt. The* WIFE *signals desperately to him to leave. He gets the idea.*)

POLICEMAN: No, you don't! (*He grabs the* BOY *by the collar.*) Where's all this from?

BOY (*vaguely pointing*): Down the street.

POLICEMAN (*grimly*): So that's it. (*Prepares to arrest the* BOY.)

WIFE (*stepping in*): And *we* knew nothing about it. (*To the* BOY.) Nasty little thief!

POLICEMAN (*dryly*): Can you clarify the situation, Mr. Shui Ta?

(SHUI TA *is silent.*)

POLICEMAN (*who understands silence*): Aha. You're all coming with me — to the station.

SHUI TA: I can hardly say how sorry I am that my establishment . . .

WIFE: Oh, he saw the boy leave not ten minutes ago!

SHUI TA: And to conceal the theft asked a policeman in?

POLICEMAN: Don't listen to her, Mr. Shui Ta, I'll be happy to relieve you of their presence one and all! (*To all three.*) Out! (*He drives them before him.*)

GRANDFATHER (*leaving last, gravely*): Good morning!

POLICEMAN: Good morning!

(SHUI TA, *left alone, continues to tidy up.* MRS. MI TZU *breezes in.*)

MRS. MI TZU: You're her cousin, are you? Then have the goodness to explain what all this means — police dragging people from a respectable house! By what right does your Miss Shen Te turn my property into a house of assignation? — Well, as you see, I know all!

SHUI TA: Yes. My cousin has the worst possible reputation: that of being poor.

MRS. MI TZU: No sentimental rubbish, Mr. Shui Ta. Your cousin was a common . . .

SHUI TA: Pauper. Let's use the uglier word.

MRS. MI TZU: I'm speaking of her conduct, not her earnings. But there must have *been* earnings, or how did she buy all this? Several elderly gentlemen took care of it, I suppose. I repeat: this is a respectable house! I have tenants who prefer not to live under the same roof with such a person.

SHUI TA (*quietly*): How much do you want?

MRS. MI TZU (*he is ahead of her now*): I beg your pardon.

SHUI TA: To reassure yourself. To reassure your tenants. How much will it cost?

MRS. MI TZU: You're a cool customer.

SHUI TA (*picking up the lease*): The rent is high. (*He reads on.*) I assume it's payable by the month?

MRS. MI TZU: Not in her case.

SHUI TA (*looking up*): What?

MRS. MI TZU: Six months' rent payable in advance. Two hundred silver dollars.

SHUI TA: Six . . . ! Sheer usury! And where am I to find it?

MRS. MI TZU: You should have thought of that before.

SHUI TA: Have you no heart, Mrs. Mi Tzu? It's true Shen Te acted foolishly, being kind to all those people, but she'll improve with time. I'll see to it she does. She'll work her fingers to the bone to pay her rent, and all the time be as quiet as a mouse, as humble as a fly.

MRS. MI TZU: Her social background . . .

SHUI TA: Out of the depths! She came out of the depths! And before she'll go back there, she'll work, sacrifice, shrink from nothing. . . . Such a tenant is worth her weight in gold, Mrs. Mi Tzu.

MRS. MI TZU: It's silver we were talking about, Mr. Shui Ta. Two hundred silver dollars or . . .

(*Enter the* POLICEMAN.)

POLICEMAN: Am I intruding, Mr. Shui Ta?

MRS. MI TZU: This tobacco shop is well known to the police, I see.

POLICEMAN: Mr. Shui Ta has done us a service, Mrs. Mi Tzu. I am here to present our official felicitations!

MRS. MI TZU: That means less then nothing to me, sir. Mr. Shui Ta, all I can say is: I hope your cousin will find my terms acceptable. Good day, gentlemen. (*Exit.*)

SHUI TA: Good day, ma'am.

(*Pause.*)

POLICEMAN: Mrs. Mi Tzu a bit of a stumbling block, sir?

SHUI TA: She wants six months' rent in advance.

POLICEMAN: And you haven't got it, eh? (SHUI TA *is silent.*) But surely you can get it, sir? A man like you?

SHUI TA: What about a woman like Shen Te?

POLICEMAN: You're not staying, sir?

SHUI TA: No, and I won't be back. Do you smoke?

POLICEMAN (*taking two cigars, and placing them both in his pocket*): Thank you, sir — I see your point. Miss Te — let's mince no words — Miss Shen Te lived by selling herself. "What else could she have done?" you ask. "How else was she to pay the rent?" True. But the fact remains, Mr. Shui Ta, it is not respectable. Why not? A very deep question. But, in the first place, love — love isn't bought and sold like cigars, Mr. Shui Ta. In the second place, it isn't respectable to go waltzing off with someone that's paying his way, so to speak — it must be for love! Thirdly and lastly, as the proverb has it: not for a handful of rice but for love! (*Pause. He is thinking hard.*) "Well," you may say, "and what good is all this wisdom if the milk's already spilt?" Miss Shen Te is what she is. Is *where* she is. We have to face the fact that if she doesn't get hold of six months' rent pronto, she'll be back on the streets. The question then as I see it — everything in this world is a matter of opinion — the question as I see it is: *how* is she to get hold of this rent? How? Mr. Shui Ta: I don't know. (*Pause.*) I take that back, sir. It's just come to me. A husband. We must find her a husband!

(*Enter a little* OLD WOMAN.)

OLD WOMAN: A good cheap cigar for my husband, we'll have been married forty years tomorrow and we're having a little celebration.

SHUI TA: Forty years? And you still want to celebrate?

OLD WOMAN: As much as we can afford to. We have the carpet shop across the square. We'll be good neighbors, I hope?

SHUI TA: I hope so too.

POLICEMAN (*who keeps making discoveries*): Mr. Shui Ta, you know what we need? We need capital. And how do we acquire capital? We get married.

SHUI TA (*to* OLD WOMAN): I'm afraid I've been pestering this gentleman with my personal worries.

POLICEMAN (*lyrically*): We can't pay six months' rent, so what do we do? We marry money.

SHUI TA: That might not be easy.

POLICEMAN: Oh, I don't know. She's a good match. Has a nice, growing business. (*To the* OLD WOMAN.) What do you think?

OLD WOMAN (*undecided*): Well —

POLICEMAN: Should she put an ad in the paper?

OLD WOMAN (*not eager to commit herself*): Well, if *she* agrees —

POLICEMAN: I'll write it for her. *You* lend us a hand, and *we* write an ad for you! (*He chuckles away to himself, takes out his notebook, wets the stump of a pencil between his lips, and writes away.*)

SHUI TA (*slowly*): Not a bad idea.

POLICEMAN: "What . . . *respectable* . . . man . . . with small capital . . . widower . . . not excluded . . . desires . . . marriage . . . into flourishing . . . tobacco shop?" And now let's add: "Am . . . pretty . . ." No! . . . "Prepossessing appearance."

SHUI TA: If you don't think that's an exaggeration?

OLD WOMAN: Oh, not a bit. I've seen her.

(*The* POLICEMAN *tears the page out of his notebook, and hands it over to* SHUI TA.)

SHUI TA (*with horror in his voice*): How much luck we need to keep our heads above water! How many ideas! How many friends! (*To the* POLICEMAN.) Thank you, sir, I think I see my way clear.

III

Evening in the municipal park. Noise of a plane overhead. YANG SUN, *a young man in rags, is following the plane with his eyes: one can tell that the machine is describing a curve above the park.* YANG SUN *then takes a rope out of his pocket, looking anxiously about him as he does so. He moves toward a large willow. Enter two prostitutes, one the* OLD WHORE, *the other the* NIECE *whom we have already met.*

NIECE: Hello. Coming with me?

YANG SUN (*taken aback*): If you'd like to buy me a dinner.

OLD WHORE: Buy you a dinner! (*To the* NIECE.) Oh, we know him — it's the unemployed pilot. Waste no time on him!

NIECE: But he's the only man left in the park. And it's going to rain.

OLD WHORE: Oh, how do you know?

(*And they pass by.* YANG SUN *again looks about him, again takes his rope, and this time throws it round a branch of the willow tree. Again he is interrupted. It is the two prostitutes returning — and in such a hurry they don't notice him.*)

NIECE: It's going to pour!

(*Enter* SHEN TE.)

OLD WHORE: There's that *gorgon* Shen Te! That *drove* your family out into the cold!

NIECE: It wasn't her. It was that cousin of hers. She offered to pay for the cakes. I've nothing against her.

OLD WHORE: I have, though. (*So that* SHEN TE *can hear.*) Now where could the little lady be off to? She may be rich now but that won't stop her snatching our young men, will it?

SHEN TE: I'm going to the tearoom by the pond.

NIECE: Is it true what they say? You're marrying a widower — with three children?

SHEN TE: Yes. I'm just going to see him.

YANG SUN (*his patience at breaking point*): Move on there! This is a park, not a whorehouse!

OLD WHORE: Shut your mouth!

(*But the two prostitutes leave.*)

YANG SUN: Even in the farthest corner of the park, even when it's raining, you can't get rid of them! (*He spits.*)

SHEN TE (*overhearing this*): And what right have you to scold them? (*But at this point she sees the rope.*) Oh!

YANG SUN: Well, what are you staring at?

SHEN TE: That rope. What is it for?

YANG SUN: Think! Think! I haven't a penny. Even if I had, I wouldn't spend it on you. I'd buy a drink of water.

(*The rain starts.*)

SHEN TE (*still looking at the rope*): What is the rope for? You mustn't!

YANG SUN: What's it to you? Clear out!

SHEN TE (*irrelevantly*): It's raining.

YANG SUN: Well, don't try to come under this tree.

SHEN TE: Oh, no. (*She stays in the rain.*)

YANG SUN: Now go away. (*Pause.*) For one thing, I don't like your looks, you're bowlegged.

SHEN TE (*indignantly*): That's not true!

YANG SUN: Well, don't show 'em to me. Look, it's raining. You better come under this tree.

(*Slowly, she takes shelter under the tree.*)

SHEN TE: Why did you want to do it?

YANG SUN: You really want to know? (*Pause.*) To get rid of you! (*Pause.*) You know what a flyer is?

SHEN TE: Oh yes, I've met a lot of pilots. At the tearoom.

YANG SUN: You call *them* flyers? Think they know what a machine is? Just 'cause they have leather helmets? They gave the airfield director a bribe, that's the way *those* fellows got up in the air! Try one of them out sometime. "Go up to two thousand feet," tell them, "then let it fall, then pick it up again with a flick of the wrist at the last moment." Know what he'll say to that? "It's not in my contract." Then again, there's the landing problem. It's like landing on your own backside. It's no different, planes are human. Those fools don't understand. (*Pause.*) And I'm the biggest fool for reading the book on flying in the Peking school and skipping the page where it says: "We've got enough flyers and we don't need you." I'm a mail pilot with no mail. You understand that?

SHEN TE (*shyly*): Yes. I do.

YANG SUN: No, you don't. You'd never understand that.

SHEN TE: When we were little we had a crane with a broken wing. He made friends with us and was very good-natured about our jokes. He would strut along behind us and call out to stop us going too fast for him. But every spring and autumn when the cranes flew over the villages in great swarms, he got quite restless. (*Pause.*) I understand that. (*She bursts out crying.*)

YANG SUN: Don't!

SHEN TE (*quieting down*): No.

YANG SUN: It's bad for the complexion.

SHEN TE (*sniffing*): I've stopped.

(*She dries her tears on her big sleeve. Leaning against the tree, but not looking at her, he reaches for her face.*)

YANG SUN: You can't even wipe your own face. (*He is wiping it for her with his handkerchief. Pause.*)

SHEN TE (*still sobbing*): I don't know *anything*!

YANG SUN: You interrupted me! What for?

SHEN TE: It's such a rainy day. You only wanted to do . . . *that* because it's such a rainy day. (*To the audience.*)

In our country
The evenings should never be somber
High bridges over rivers
The gray hour between night and morning
And the long, long winter:
Such things are dangerous
For, with all the misery,
A very little is enough
And men throw away an unbearable life.

(*Pause.*)

YANG SUN: Talk about yourself for a change.

SHEN TE: What about me? I have a shop.

YANG SUN (*incredulous*): You have a shop, have you? Never thought of walking the streets?

SHEN TE: I did walk the streets. Now I have a shop.

YANG SUN (*ironically*): A gift of the gods, I suppose!

SHEN TE: How did you know?

YANG SUN (*even more ironical*): One fine evening the gods turned up saying: here's some money!

SHEN TE (*quickly*): One fine morning.

YANG SUN (*fed up*): This isn't much of an entertainment.

(*Pause.*)

SHEN TE: I can play the zither a little. (*Pause.*) And I can mimic men. (*Pause.*) I got the shop, so the first thing I did was to give my zither away. I can be as stupid as a fish now, I said to myself, and it won't matter.

I'm rich now, I said
I walk alone, I sleep alone
For a whole year, I said
I'll have nothing to do with a man.

YANG SUN: And now you're marrying one! The one at the tearoom by the pond?

(SHEN TE *is silent.*)

YANG SUN: What do you know about love?

SHEN TE: Everything.

YANG SUN: Nothing. (*Pause.*) Or d'you just mean you enjoyed it?

SHEN TE: No.

YANG SUN (*again without turning to look at her, he strokes her cheek with his hand*): You like that?

SHEN TE: Yes.

YANG SUN (*breaking off*): You're easily satisfied, I must say. (*Pause.*) What a town!

SHEN TE: You have no friends?

YANG SUN (*defensively*): Yes, I have! (*Change of tone.*) But they don't want to hear I'm still unemployed. "What?" they ask. "Is there still water in the sea?" You have friends?

SHEN TE (*hesitating*): Just a . . . cousin.

YANG SUN: Watch him carefully.

SHEN TE: He only came once. Then he went away. He won't be back. (YANG SUN *is looking away.*) But to be without hope, they say, is to be without goodness!

(*Pause.*)

YANG SUN: Go on talking. A voice is a voice.

SHEN TE: Once, when I was a little girl, I fell, with a load of brushwood. An old man picked me up. He gave me a penny too. Isn't it funny how people who don't have very much like to give some of it away? They must like to show what they can do, and how could they show it better than by being kind? Being wicked is just like being clumsy. When we sing a song, or build a machine, or plant some rice, we're being kind. You're kind.

YANG SUN: You make it sound easy.

SHEN TE: Oh, no. (*Little pause.*) Oh! A drop of rain!

YANG SUN: Where'd you feel it?

SHEN TE: Between the eyes.

YANG SUN: Near the right eye? Or the left?

SHEN TE: Near the left eye.

YANG SUN: Oh, good. (*He is getting sleepy.*) So you're through with men, eh?

SHEN TE (*with a smile*): But I'm not bowlegged.

YANG SUN: Perhaps not.

SHEN TE: Definitely not.

(*Pause.*)

YANG SUN (*leaning wearily against the willow*): I haven't had a drop to drink all day, I haven't eaten anything for *two* days. I couldn't love you if I tried.

(*Pause.*)

SHEN TE: I like it in the rain.

(*Enter* WONG *the water seller, singing.*)

THE SONG OF THE WATER SELLER IN THE RAIN

"Buy my water," I am yelling
And my fury restraining
For no water I'm selling
'Cause it's raining, 'cause it's raining!
    I keep yelling: "Buy my water!"
    But no one's buying
    Athirst and dying
    And drinking and paying!
    Buy water!
    Buy water, you dogs!

Nice to dream of lovely weather!
Think of all the consternation
Were there no precipitation
Half a dozen years together!
    Can't you hear them shrieking: "Water!"
    Pretending they adore me?
    They all would go down on their knees before me!
    Down on your knees!
    Go down on your knees, you dogs!

What are lawns and hedges thinking?
What are fields and forests saying?
"At the cloud's breast we are drinking!
And we've no idea who's paying!"
    I keep yelling: "Buy my water!"
    But no one's buying
    Athirst and dying
    And drinking and paying!
    Buy water!
    Buy water, you dogs!

(*The rain has stopped now.* SHEN TE *sees* WONG *and runs toward him.*)

SHEN TE: Wong! You're back! Your carrying pole's at the shop.

WONG: Oh, thank you, Shen Te. And how is life treating *you*?

SHEN TE: I've just met a brave and clever man. And I want to buy him a cup of your water.

WONG (*bitterly*): Throw back your head and open your mouth and you'll have all the water you need —

SHEN TE (*tenderly*):
I want *your* water, Wong
The water that has tired you so
The water that you carried all this way
The water that is hard to sell because
    it's been raining.

I need it for the young man over there — he's a flyer!

A flyer is a bold man:
Braving the storms
In company with the clouds
He crosses the heavens
And brings to friends in faraway lands
The friendly mail!

(*She pays* WONG, *and runs over to* YANG SUN *with the cup. But* YANG SUN *is fast asleep.*)

SHEN TE (*calling to* WONG, *with a laugh*): He's fallen asleep! Despair and rain and I have worn him out!

IIIa

WONG's *den. The sewer pipe is transparent, and the* GODS *again appear to* WONG *in a dream.*

WONG (*radiant*): I've seen her, illustrious ones! And she hasn't changed!

FIRST GOD: That's good to hear.

WONG: She loves someone.

FIRST GOD: Let's hope the experience gives her the strength to stay good!

WONG: It does. She's doing good deeds all the time.

FIRST GOD: Ah? What sort? What sort of good deeds, Wong?

WONG: Well, she has a kind word for everybody.

FIRST GOD (*eagerly*): And then?

WONG: Hardly anyone leaves her shop without tobacco in his pocket — even if he can't pay for it.

FIRST GOD: Not bad at all. Next?

WONG: She's putting up a family of eight.

FIRST GOD (*gleefully, to the* SECOND GOD): Eight! (*To* WONG.) And that's not all, of course!

WONG: She bought a cup of water from me even though it was raining.

FIRST GOD: Yes, yes, yes, all these smaller good deeds!

WONG: Even they run into money. A little tobacco shop doesn't make so much.

FIRST GOD (*sententiously*): A prudent gardener works miracles on the smallest plot.

WONG: She hands out rice every morning. That eats up half her earnings.

FIRST GOD (*a little disappointed*): Well, as a beginning . . .

WONG: They call her the Angel of the Slums — whatever the carpenter may say!

FIRST GOD: What's this? A carpenter speaks ill of her?

WONG: Oh, he only says her shelves weren't paid for in full.

SECOND GOD (*who has a bad cold and can't pronounce his n's and m's*): What's this? Not paying a carpenter? Why was that?

WONG: I suppose she didn't have the money.

SECOND GOD (*severely*): One pays what one owes, that's in our book of rules! First the letter of the law, then the spirit.

WONG: But it wasn't Shen Te, illustrious ones, it was her cousin. She called *him* in to help.

SECOND GOD: Then her cousin must never darken her threshold again!

WONG: Very well, illustrious ones! But in fairness to Shen Te, let me say that her cousin is a businessman.

FIRST GOD: Perhaps we should inquire what is customary? I find business quite unintelligible. But everybody's doing it. Business! Did the Seven Good Kings do business? Did Kung the Just sell fish?

SECOND GOD: In any case, such a thing must not occur again!

(*The* GODS *start to leave.*)

THIRD GOD: Forgive us for taking this tone with you, Wong, we haven't been getting enough sleep. The rich recommend us to the poor, and the poor tell us they haven't enough room.

SECOND GOD: Feeble, feeble, the best of them!

FIRST GOD: No great deeds! No heroic daring!

THIRD GOD: On such a *small* scale!

SECOND GOD: Sincere, yes, but what is actually *achieved*?

(*One can no longer hear them.*)

WONG (*calling after them*): I've thought of something, illustrious ones: Perhaps you shouldn't ask — too — much — all — at — once!

IV

The square in front of SHEN TE's *tobacco shop. Besides* SHEN TE's *place, two other shops are seen: the carpet shop and a barber's. Morning. Outside* SHEN TE's *the* GRANDFATHER, *the* SISTER-IN-LAW, *the* UNEMPLOYED MAN, *and* MRS. SHIN *stand waiting.*

SISTER-IN-LAW: She's been out all night again.

MRS. SHIN: No sooner did we get rid of that crazy cousin of hers than Shen Te herself starts carrying on! Maybe she does give us an ounce of rice now and then, but can you depend on her? Can you depend on her?

(Loud voices from the barber's.)

VOICE OF SHU FU: What are you doing in my shop? Get out — at once!

VOICE OF WONG: But sir. They all let me sell . . .

*(*WONG *comes staggering out of the barber's shop pursued by* MR. SHU FU, *the barber, a fat man carrying a heavy curling iron.)*

SHU FU: Get out, I said! Pestering my customers with your slimy old water! Get out! Take your cup!

(He holds out the cup. WONG *reaches out for it.* MR. SHU FU *strikes his hand with the curling iron, which is hot.* WONG *howls.)*

SHU FU: You had it coming, my man!

(Puffing, he returns to his shop. The UNEMPLOYED MAN *picks up the cup and gives it to* WONG.*)*

UNEMPLOYED MAN: You can report that to the police.

WONG: My hand! It's smashed up!

UNEMPLOYED MAN: Any bones broken?

WONG: I can't move my fingers.

UNEMPLOYED MAN: Sit down. I'll put some water on it.

*(*WONG *sits.)*

MRS. SHIN: The water won't cost you anything.

SISTER-IN-LAW: You might have got a bandage from Miss Shen Te till she took to staying out all night. It's a scandal.

MRS. SHIN *(despondently)*: If you ask me, she's forgotten we ever existed!

(Enter SHEN TE *down the street, with a dish of rice.)*

SHEN TE *(to the audience)*: How wonderful to see Setzuan in the early morning! I always used to stay in bed with my dirty blanket over my head afraid to wake up. This morning I saw the newspapers being delivered by little boys, the streets being washed by strong men, and fresh vegetables coming in from the country on ox carts. It's a long walk from where Yang Sun lives, but I feel lighter at every step. They say you walk on air when you're in love, but it's even better walking on the rough earth, on the hard cement. In the early morning, the old city looks like a great heap of rubbish! Nice, though, with all its little lights. And the sky, so pink, so transparent, before the dust comes and muddies it! What a lot you miss if you never see your city rising from its slumbers like an honest old craftsman pumping his lungs full of air and reaching for his tools, as the poet says! *(Cheerfully, to her waiting guests.)* Good morning, everyone, here's your rice! *(Distributing the rice, she comes upon* WONG.*)* Good morning, Wong, I'm quite lightheaded today. On my way over, I looked at myself in all the shop windows. I'd love to be beautiful.

(She slips into the carpet shop. MR. SHU FU *has just emerged from his shop.)*

SHU FU *(to the audience)*: It surprises me how beautiful Miss Shen Te is looking today! I never gave her a passing thought before. But now I've been gazing upon her comely form for exactly three minutes! I begin to suspect I am in love with her. She is overpoweringly attractive! *(Crossly, to* WONG.*)* Be off with you, rascal!

(He returns to his shop. SHEN TE *comes back out of the carpet shop with the* OLD MAN, *its proprietor, and his wife — whom we have already met — the* OLD WOMAN. SHEN TE *is wearing a shawl. The* OLD MAN *is holding up a looking glass for her.)*

OLD WOMAN: Isn't it lovely? We'll give you a reduction because there's a little hole in it.

SHEN TE *(looking at another shawl on the* OLD WOMAN's *arm)*: The other one's nice too.

OLD WOMAN *(smiling)*: Too bad there's no hole in that!

SHEN TE: That's right. My shop doesn't make very much.

OLD WOMAN: And your good deeds eat it all up! Be more careful, my dear. . . .

SHEN TE (*trying on the shawl with the hole*): Just now, I'm lightheaded! Does the color suit me?

OLD WOMAN: You'd better ask a man.

SHEN TE (*to the* OLD MAN): Does the color suit me?

OLD MAN: You'd better ask your young friend.

SHEN TE: I'd like to have your opinion.

OLD MAN: It suits you very well. But wear it this way: the dull side out.

(SHEN TE *pays up.*)

OLD WOMAN: If you decide you don't like it, you can exchange it. (*She pulls* SHEN TE *to one side.*) Has he got money?

SHEN TE (*with a laugh*): Yang Sun? Oh, no.

OLD WOMAN: Then how're you going to pay your rent?

SHEN TE: I'd forgotten about that.

OLD WOMAN: And next Monday is the first of the month! Miss Shen Te, I've got something to say to you. After we (*indicating her husband*) got to know you, we had our doubts about that marriage ad. We thought it would be better if you'd let *us* help you. Out of our savings. We reckon we could lend you two hundred silver dollars. We don't need anything in writing — you could pledge us your tobacco stock.

SHEN TE: You're prepared to lend money to a person like me?

OLD WOMAN: It's folks like you that need it. We'd think twice about lending anything to your cousin.

OLD MAN (*coming up*): All settled, my dear?

SHEN TE: I wish the gods could have heard what your wife was just saying, Mr. Ma. They're looking for good people who're happy — and helping me makes you happy because you know it was love that got me into difficulties!

(*The* OLD COUPLE *smile knowingly at each other.*)

OLD MAN: And here's the money, Miss Shen Te.

(*He hands her an envelope.* SHEN TE *takes it. She bows. They bow back. They return to their shop.*)

SHEN TE (*holding up her envelope*): Look, Wong, here's six months' rent! Don't you believe in miracles now? And how do you like my new shawl?

WONG: For the young fellow I saw you with in the park?

(SHEN TE *nods.*)

MRS. SHIN: Never mind all that. It's time you took a look at his hand!

SHEN TE: Have you hurt your hand?

MRS. SHIN: That barber smashed it with his hot curling iron. Right in front of our eyes.

SHEN TE (*shocked at herself*): And I never noticed! We must get you to a doctor this minute or who knows what will happen?

UNEMPLOYED MAN: It's not a doctor he should see, it's a judge. He can ask for compensation. The barber's filthy rich.

WONG: You think I have a chance?

MRS. SHIN (*with relish*): If it's really good and smashed. But is it?

WONG: I think so. It's very swollen. Could I get a pension?

MRS. SHIN: You'd need a witness.

WONG: Well, you all saw it. You could all testify.

(*He looks round. The* UNEMPLOYED MAN, *the* GRANDFATHER, *and the* SISTER-IN-LAW *are all sitting against the wall of the shop eating rice. Their concentration on eating is complete.*

SHEN TE (*to* MRS. SHIN): You saw it yourself.

MRS. SHIN: I want nothing to do with the police. It's against my principles.

SHEN TE (*to* SISTER-IN-LAW): What about you?

SISTER-IN-LAW: Me? I wasn't looking.

SHEN TE (*to the* GRANDFATHER, *coaxingly*): Grandfather, *you'll* testify, won't you?

SISTER-IN-LAW: And a lot of good that will do. He's simple-minded.

SHEN TE (*to the* UNEMPLOYED MAN): You seem to be the only witness left.

UNEMPLOYED MAN: My testimony would only hurt him. I've been picked up twice for begging.

SHEN TE:
Your brother is assaulted, and you shut your
    eyes?
He is hit, cries out in pain, and you are silent?
The beast prowls, chooses and seizes his victim,
    and you say:

"Because we showed no displeasure, he has spared us."

If no one present will be a witness, I will. I'll say *I* saw it.

MRS. SHIN (*solemnly*): The name for that is perjury.

WONG: I don't know if I can accept that. Though maybe I'll have to. (*Looking at his hand.*) Is it swollen enough, do you think? The swelling's not going down?

UNEMPLOYED MAN: No, no, the swelling's holding up well.

WONG: Yes. It's *more* swollen if anything. Maybe my wrist is broken after all. I'd better see a judge at once.

(*Holding his hand very carefully, and fixing his eyes on it, he runs off.* MRS. SHIN *goes quickly into the barber's shop.*)

UNEMPLOYED MAN (*seeing her*): She is getting on the right side of Mr. Shu Fu.

SISTER-IN-LAW: You and I can't change the world, Shen Te.

SHEN TE: Go away! Go away all of you!

(*The* UNEMPLOYED MAN, *the* SISTER-IN-LAW, *and the* GRANDFATHER *stalk off, eating and sulking.*

To the audience.)

They've stopped answering
They stay put
They do as they're told
They don't care
Nothing can make them look up
But the smell of food.

(*Enter* MRS. YANG, YANG SUN's *mother, out of breath.*)

MRS. YANG: Miss Shen Te. My son has told me everything. I am Mrs. Yang, Sun's mother. Just think. He's got an offer. Of a job as a pilot. A letter has just come. From the director of the airfield in Peking!

SHEN TE: So he can fly again? Isn't that wonderful!

MRS. YANG (*less breathlessly all the time*): They won't give him the job for nothing. They want five hundred silver dollars.

SHEN TE: We can't let money stand in his way, Mrs. Yang!

MRS. YANG: If only you could help him out!

SHEN TE: I have the shop. I can try! (*She embraces* MRS. YANG.) I happen to have two hundred with me now. Take it. (*She gives her the old couple's money.*) It was a loan but they said I could repay it with my tobacco stock.

MRS. YANG: And they were calling Sun the Dead Pilot of Setzuan! A friend in need!

SHEN TE: We must find another three hundred.

MRS. YANG: How?

SHEN TE: Let me think. (*Slowly.*) I know someone who can help. I didn't want to call on his services again, he's hard and cunning. But a flyer must fly. And I'll make this the last time.

(*Distant sound of a plane.*)

MRS. YANG: If the man you mentioned can do it. . . . Oh, look, there's the morning mail plane, heading for Peking!

SHEN TE: The pilot can see us, let's wave!

(*They wave. The noise of the engine is louder.*)

MRS. YANG: You know that pilot up there?

SHEN TE: Wave, Mrs. Yang! I know the pilot who will be up there. He gave up hope. But he'll do it now. One man to raise himself above the misery, above us all. (*To the audience.*)

Yang Sun, my lover:
Braving the storms
In company with the clouds
Crossing the heavens
And bringing to friends in faraway lands
The friendly mail!

IVA

In front of the inner curtain. Enter SHEN TE, *carrying* SHUI TA's *mask. She sings.*

THE SONG OF DEFENSELESSNESS

In our country
A useful man needs luck
Only if he finds strong backers
Can he prove himself useful.
The good can't defend themselves and
Even the gods are defenseless.

Oh, why don't the gods have their own ammunition
And launch against badness their own expedition
Enthroning the good and preventing sedition

And bringing the world to a peaceful condition?

Oh, why don't the gods do the buying and selling
Injustice forbidding, starvation dispelling
Give bread to each city and joy to each dwelling?
Oh, why don't the gods do the buying and selling?

(*She puts on* SHUI TA's *mask and sings in his voice.*)

You can only help one of your luckless brothers
By trampling down a dozen others.

Why is it the gods do not feel indignation
And come down in fury to end exploitation
Defeat all defeat and forbid desperation
Refusing to tolerate such toleration?

Why is it?

V

SHEN TE's *tobacco shop. Behind the counter,* MR. SHUI TA, *reading the paper.* MRS. SHIN *is cleaning up. She talks and he takes no notice.*

MRS. SHIN: And when certain rumors get about, what *happens* to a little place like this? It goes to pot. *I* know. So, if you want my advice, Mr. Shui Ta, find out just what has been going on between Miss Shen Te and that Yang Sun from Yellow Street. And remember: a certain interest in Miss Shen Te has been expressed by the barber next door, a man with twelve houses and only one wife, who, for that matter, is likely to drop off at any time. A certain interest has been expressed. He was even inquiring about her means and, if *that* doesn't prove a man is getting serious, what would? (*Still getting no response, she leaves with her bucket.*)

YANG SUN's VOICE: Is that Miss Shen Te's tobacco shop?

MRS. SHIN's VOICE: Yes, it is, but it's Mr. Shui Ta who's here today.

(SHUI TA *runs to the mirror with the short, light steps of* SHEN TE, *and is just about to start primping, when he realizes his mistake, and turns away, with a short laugh. Enter*

YANG SUN. MRS. SHIN *enters behind him and slips into the back room to eavesdrop.*)

YANG SUN: I am Yang Sun. (SHUI TA *bows.*) Is Shen Te in?

SHUI TA: No.

YANG SUN: I guess you know our relationship? (*He is inspecting the stock.*) Quite a place! And I thought she was just talking big. I'll be flying again, all right. (*He takes a cigar, solicits and receives a light from* SHUI TA.) You think we can squeeze the other three hundred out of the tobacco stock?

SHUI TA: May I ask if it is your intention to sell at once?

YANG SUN: It was decent of her to come out with the two hundred but they aren't much use with the other three hundred still missing.

SHUI TA: Shen Te was overhasty promising so much. She might have to sell the shop itself to raise it. Haste, they say, is the wind that blows the house down.

YANG SUN: Oh, she isn't a girl to keep a man waiting. For one thing or the other, if you take my meaning.

SHUI TA: I take your meaning.

YANG SUN (*leering*): Uh, huh.

SHUI TA: Would you explain what the five hundred silver dollars are for?

YANG SUN: Want to sound me out? Very well. The director of the Peking airfield is a friend of mine from flying school. I give him five hundred: he gets me the job.

SHUI TA: The price is high.

YANG SUN: Not as these things go. He'll have to fire one of the present pilots — for negligence. Only the man he has in mind isn't negligent. Not easy, you understand. You needn't mention that part of it to Shen Te.

SHUI TA (*looking intently at* YANG SUN): Mr. Yang Sun, you are asking my cousin to give up her possessions, leave her friends, and place her entire fate in your hands. I presume you intend to marry her?

YANG SUN: I'd be prepared to.

(*Slight pause.*)

SHUI TA: Those two hundred silver dollars would pay the rent here for six months. If you were Shen Te wouldn't you be tempted to continue in business?

YANG SUN: What? Can you imagine Yang Sun the flyer behind a counter? (*In an oily voice.*) "A strong cigar or a mild one, worthy sir?" Not in this century!

SHUI TA: My cousin wishes to follow the promptings of her heart, and, from her own point of view, she may even have what is called the right to love. Accordingly, she has commissioned me to help you to this post. There is nothing here that I am not empowered to turn immediately into cash. Mrs. Mi Tzu, the landlady, will advise me about the sale.

(*Enter* MRS. MI TZU.)

MRS. MI TZU: Good morning, Mr. Shui Ta, you wish to see me about the rent? As you know it falls due the day after tomorrow.

SHUI TA: Circumstances have changed, Mrs. Mi Tzu: my cousin is getting married. Her future husband here, Mr. Yang Sun, will be taking her to Peking. I am interested in selling the tobacco stock.

MRS. MI TZU: How much are you asking, Mr. Shui Ta?

YANG SUN: Three hundred sil —

SHUI TA: Five hundred silver dollars.

MRS. MI TZU: How much did she pay for it, Mr. Shui Ta?

SHUI TA: A thousand. And very little has been sold.

MRS. MI TZU: She was robbed. But I'll make you a special offer if you'll promise to be out by the day after tomorrow. Three hundred silver dollars.

YANG SUN (*shrugging*): Take it, man, take it.

SHUI TA: It is not enough.

YANG SUN: Why not? Why not? Certainly, it's enough.

SHUI TA: Five hundred silver dollars.

YANG SUN: But why? We only need three!

SHUI TA (*to* MRS. MI TZU): Excuse me. (*Takes* YANG SUN *on one side.*) The tobacco stock is pledged to the old couple who gave my cousin the two hundred.

YANG SUN: Is it in writing?

SHUI TA: No.

YANG SUN (*to* MRS. MI TZU): Three hundred will do.

MRS. MI TZU: Of course, I need an assurance that Miss Shen Te is not in debt.

YANG SUN: Mr. Shui Ta?

SHUI TA: She is not in debt.

YANG SUN: When can you let us have the money?

MRS. MI TZU: The day after tomorrow. And remember: I'm doing this because I have a soft spot in my heart for young lovers! (*Exit.*)

YANG SUN (*calling after her*): Boxes, jars and sacks — three hundred for the lot and the pain's over! (*To* SHUI TA.) Where else can we raise money by the day after tomorrow?

SHUI TA: Nowhere. Haven't you enough for the trip and the first few weeks?

YANG SUN: Oh, certainly.

SHUI TA: How much, exactly.

YANG SUN: Oh, I'll dig it up, even if I have to steal it.

SHUI TA: I see.

YANG SUN: Well, don't fall off the roof. I'll get to Peking somehow.

SHUI TA: Two people can't travel for nothing.

YANG SUN (*not giving* SHUI TA *a chance to answer*): I'm leaving *her* behind. No millstones round *my* neck!

SHUI TA: Oh.

YANG SUN: Don't look at me like that!

SHUI TA: How precisely is my cousin to live?

YANG SUN: Oh, you'll think of something.

SHUI TA: A small request, Mr. Yang Sun. Leave the two hundred silver dollars here until you can show me two tickets for Peking.

YANG SUN: You learn to mind your own business, Mr. Shui Ta.

SHUI TA: I'm afraid Miss Shen Te may not wish to sell the shop when she discovers that . . .

YANG SUN: You don't know women. She'll want to. Even then.

SHUI TA (*a slight outburst*): She is a human being, sir! And not devoid of common sense!

YANG SUN: Shen Te is a woman: she *is* devoid of common sense. I only have to lay my hand on her shoulder, and church bells ring.

SHUI TA (*with difficulty*): Mr. Yang Sun!

YANG SUN: Mr. Shui Whatever-it-is!

SHUI TA: My cousin is devoted to you . . . because . . .

YANG SUN: Because I have my hands on her breasts. Give me a cigar. (*He takes one for himself, stuffs a few more in his pocket, then changes his mind and takes the whole box.*) Tell her I'll marry her, then bring me the three hundred. Or let her bring it. One or the other. (*Exit.*)

MRS. SHIN (*sticking her head out of the back room*): Well, he has your cousin under his thumb, and doesn't care if all Yellow Street knows it!

SHUI TA (*crying out*): I've lost my shop! And he doesn't love me! (*He runs berserk through the room, repeating these lines incoherently.*

Then stops suddenly, and addresses MRS. SHIN.) Mrs. Shin, you grew up in the gutter, like me. Are we lacking in hardness? I doubt it. If you steal a penny from me, I'll take you by the throat till you spit it out! You'd do the same to me. The times are bad, this city is hell, but we're like ants, we keep coming, up and up the walls, however smooth! Till bad luck comes. Being in love, for instance. One weakness is enough, and love is the deadliest.

MRS. SHIN (*emerging from the back room*): You should have a little talk with Mr. Shu Fu, the barber. He's a real gentleman and just the thing for your cousin. (*She runs off.*)

SHUI TA:
A caress becomes a stranglehold
A sigh of love turns to a cry of fear
Why are there vultures circling in the air?
A girl is going to meet her lover.

(SHUI TA *sits down and* MR. SHU FU *enters with* MRS. SHIN.)

SHUI TA: Mr. Shu Fu?
SHU FU: Mr. Shui Ta.

(*They both bow.*)

SHUI TA: I am told that you have expressed a certain interest in my cousin Shen Te. Let me set aside all propriety and confess: she is at this moment in grave danger.
SHU FU: Oh, dear!
SHUI TA: She has lost her shop, Mr. Shu Fu.
SHU FU: The charm of Miss Shen Te, Mr. Shui Ta, derives from the goodness, not of her shop, but of her heart. Men call her the Angel of the Slums.
SHUI TA: Yet her goodness has cost her two hundred silver dollars in a single day: we must put a stop to it.
SHU FU: Permit me to differ, Mr. Shui Ta. Let us, rather, open wide the gates to such goodness! Every morning, with pleasure tinged by affection, I watch her charitable ministrations. For they are hungry, and she giveth them to eat! Four of them, to be precise. Why only four? I ask. Why not four hundred? I hear she has been seeking shelter for the homeless. What about my humble cabins behind the cattle run? They are at her disposal. And so forth. And so on. Mr. Shui Ta, do you think Miss Shen Te could be persuaded to listen to certain ideas of mine? Ideas like these?
SHUI TA: Mr. Shu Fu, she would be honored.

(*Enter* WONG *and the* POLICEMAN. MR. SHU FU *turns abruptly away and studies the shelves.*)

WONG: Is Miss Shen Te here?
SHUI TA: No.
WONG: I am Wong the water seller. You are Mr. Shui Ta?
SHUI TA: I am.
WONG: I am a friend of Shen Te's.
SHUI TA: An intimate friend, I hear.
WONG (*to the* POLICEMAN): You see? (*To* SHUI TA.) It's because of my hand.
POLICEMAN: He hurt his hand, sir, that's a fact.
SHUI TA (*quickly*): You need a sling, I see. (*He takes a shawl from the back room, and throws it to* WONG.)
WONG: But that's her new shawl!
SHUI TA: She has no more use for it.
WONG: But she bought it to please someone!
SHUI TA: It happens to be no longer necessary.
WONG (*making the sling*): She is my only witness.
POLICEMAN: Mr. Shui Ta, your cousin is supposed to have seen the barber hit the water seller with a curling iron.
SHUI TA: I'm afraid my cousin was not present at the time.
WONG: But she was, sir! Just ask her! Isn't she in?
SHUI TA (*gravely*): Mr. Wong, my cousin has her own troubles. You wouldn't wish her to add to them by committing perjury?
WONG: But it was she that told me to go to the judge!
SHUI TA: Was the judge supposed to heal your hand?

(MR. SHU FU *turns quickly around.* SHUI TA *bows to* SHU FU, *and vice versa.*)

WONG (*taking the sling off, and putting it back*): I see how it is.
POLICEMAN: Well, I'll be on my way. (*To* WONG.) And you be careful. If Mr. Shu Fu wasn't a man who tempers justice with mercy, as the saying is, you'd be in jail for libel. Be off with you!

(*Exit* WONG, *followed by* POLICEMAN.)

SHUI TA: Profound apologies, Mr. Shu Fu.
SHU FU: Not at all, Mr. Shui Ta. (*Pointing to the shawl.*) The episode is over?

SHUI TA: It may take her time to recover. There are some fresh wounds.

SHU FU: We shall be discreet. Delicate. A short vacation could be arranged. . . .

SHUI TA: First of course, you and she would have to talk things over.

SHU FU: At a small supper in a small, but high-class, restaurant.

SHUI TA: I'll go and find her. (*Exit into back room.*)

MRS. SHIN (*sticking her head in again*): Time for congratulations, Mr. Shu Fu?

SHU FU: Ah, Mrs. Shin! Please inform Miss Shen Te's guests they may take shelter in the cabins behind the cattle run!

(MRS. SHIN *nods, grinning.*)

SHU FU (*to the audience*): Well? What do you think of me, ladies and gentlemen? What could a man do more? Could he be less selfish? More farsighted? A small supper in a small but . . . Does that bring rather vulgar and clumsy thoughts into your mind? Ts, ts, ts. Nothing of the sort will occur. She won't even be touched. Not even accidentally while passing the salt. An exchange of ideas only. Over the flowers on the table — white chrysanthemums, by the way (*he writes down a note of this*) — yes, over the white chrysanthemums, two young souls will . . . shall I say "find each other"? We shall NOT exploit the misfortune of others. Understanding? Yes. An offer of assistance? Certainly. But quietly. Almost inaudibly. Perhaps with a single glance. A glance that could also — also mean more.

MRS. SHIN (*coming forward*): Everything under control, Mr. Shu Fu?

SHU FU: Oh, Mrs. Shin, what do you know about this worthless rascal Yang Sun?

MRS. SHIN: Why, he's the most worthless rascal . . .

SHU FU: Is he really? You're sure? (*As she opens her mouth.*) From now on, he doesn't exist! Can't be found anywhere!

(*Enter* YANG SUN.)

YANG SUN: What's been going on here?

MRS. SHIN: Shall I call Mr. Shui Ta, Mr. Shu Fu? He wouldn't want strangers in here!

SHU FU: Mr. Shui Ta is in conference with Miss Shen Te. Not to be disturbed.

YANG SUN: Shen Te here? I didn't see her come in. What kind of conference?

SHU FU (*not letting him enter the back room*): Patience, dear sir! And if by chance I have an inkling who you are, pray take note that Miss Shen Te and I are about to announce our engagement.

YANG SUN: What?

MRS. SHIN: You didn't expect that, did you?

(YANG SUN *is trying to push past the barber into the back room when* SHEN TE *comes out.*)

SHU FU: My dear Shen Te, ten thousand apologies! Perhaps you . . .

YANG SUN: What is it, Shen Te? Have you gone crazy?

SHEN TE (*breathless*): My cousin and Mr. Shu Fu have come to an understanding. They wish me to hear Mr. Shu Fu's plans for helping the poor.

YANG SUN: Your cousin wants to part us.

SHEN TE: Yes.

YANG SUN: And you've agreed to it?

SHEN TE: Yes.

YANG SUN: They told you I was bad. (SHEN TE *is silent.*) And suppose I am. Does that make me need you less? I'm low, Shen Te, I have no money, I don't do the right thing but at least I put up a fight! (*He is near her now, and speaks in an undertone.*) Have you no eyes? Look at him. Have you forgotten already?

SHEN TE: No.

YANG SUN: How it was raining?

SHEN TE: No.

YANG SUN: How you cut me down from the willow tree? Bought me water? Promised me money to fly with?

SHEN TE (*shakily*): Yang Sun, what do you want?

YANG SUN: I want you to come with me.

SHEN TE (*in a small voice*): Forgive me, Mr. Shu Fu, I want to go with Mr. Yang Sun.

YANG SUN: We're lovers you know. Give me the key to the shop. (SHEN TE *takes the key from around her neck.* YANG SUN *puts it on the counter. To* MRS. SHIN.) Leave it under the mat when you're through. Let's go, Shen Te.

SHU FU: But this is rape! Mr. Shui Ta!!

YANG SUN (*to* SHEN TE): Tell him not to shout.

SHEN TE: Please don't shout for my cousin, Mr. Shu Fu. He doesn't agree with me, I know, but he's wrong.

(*To the audience.*)

I want to go with the man I love
I don't want to count the cost
I don't want to consider if it's wise
I don't want to know if he loves me
I want to go with the man I love.

YANG SUN: That's the spirit.

(*And the couple leave.*)

Vₐ

In front of the inner curtain. SHEN TE *in her wedding clothes, on the way to her wedding.*

SHEN TE: Something terrible has happened. As I left the shop with Yang Sun, I found the old carpet dealer's wife waiting on the street, trembling all over. She told me her husband had taken to his bed sick with all the worry and excitement over the two hundred silver dollars they lent me. She said it would be best if I gave it back now. Of course, I had to say I would. She said she couldn't quite trust my cousin Shui Ta or even my fiancé Yang Sun. There were tears in her eyes. With my emotions in an uproar, I threw myself into Yang Sun's arms, I couldn't resist him. The things he'd said to Shui Ta had taught Shen Te nothing. Sinking into his arms, I said to myself:

To let no one perish, not even oneself
To fill everyone with happiness, even oneself
Is so good

How could I have forgotten those two old people? Yang Sun swept me away like a small hurricane. But he's not a bad man, and he loves me. He'd rather work in the cement factory than owe his flying to a crime. Though, of course, flying *is* a great passion with Sun. Now, on the way to my wedding, I waver between fear and joy.

VI

The "private dining room" on the upper floor of a cheap restaurant in a poor section of town. With SHEN TE: *the* GRANDFATHER, *the* SISTER-IN-LAW, *the* NIECE, MRS. SHIN, *the* UNEMPLOYED MAN. *In a corner, alone, a* PRIEST. *A* WAITER *pouring wine. Downstage,* YANG SUN *talking to his* MOTHER. *He wears a dinner jacket.*

YANG SUN: Bad news, Mamma. She came right out and told me she can't sell the shop for me. Some idiot is bringing a claim because he lent her the two hundred she gave you.

MRS. YANG: What did you say? Of course, you can't marry her now.

YANG SUN: It's no use saying anything to *her*. I've sent for her cousin, Mr. Shui Ta. He said there was nothing in writing.

MRS. YANG: Good idea. I'll go and look for him. Keep an eye on things.

(*Exit* MRS. YANG. SHEN TE *has been pouring wine.*)

SHEN TE (*to the audience, pitcher in hand*): I wasn't mistaken in him. He's bearing up well. Though it must have been an awful blow — giving up flying. I do love him so. (*Calling across the room to him.*) Sun, you haven't drunk a toast with the bride!

YANG SUN: What do we drink to?

SHEN TE: Why, to the future!

YANG SUN: When the bridegroom's dinner jacket won't be a hired one!

SHEN TE: But when the bride's dress will still get rained on sometimes!

YANG SUN: To everything we ever wished for!

SHEN TE: May all our dreams come true!

(*They drink.*)

YANG SUN (*with loud conviviality*): And now, friends, before the wedding gets under way, I have to ask the bride a few questions. I've no idea what kind of wife she'll make, and it worries me. (*Wheeling on* SHEN TE.) For example. Can you make five cups of tea with three tea leaves?

SHEN TE: No.

YANG SUN: So I won't be getting very much tea. Can you sleep on a straw mattress the size of that book? (*He points to the large volume the* PRIEST *is reading.*)

SHEN TE: The two of us?

YANG SUN: The one of you.

SHEN TE: In that case, no.

YANG SUN: What a wife! I'm shocked!

(*While the audience is laughing, his* MOTHER *returns. With a shrug of her shoulders, she tells* YANG SUN *the expected guest hasn't arrived. The* PRIEST *shuts the book with a bang, and makes for the door.*)

MRS. YANG: Where are *you* off to? It's only a matter of minutes.

PRIEST (*watch in hand*): Time goes on, Mrs. Yang, and I've another wedding to attend to. Also a funeral.

MRS. YANG (*irately*): D'you think we planned it this way? I was hoping to manage with one pitcher of wine, and we've run through two already. (*Points to empty pitcher. Loudly.*) My dear Shen Te, I don't know where your cousin can be keeping himself!

SHEN TE: My cousin?!

MRS. YANG: Certainly. I'm old-fashioned enough to think such a close relative should attend the wedding.

SHEN TE: Oh, Sun, is it the three hundred silver dollars?

YANG SUN (*not looking her in the eye*): Are you deaf? Mother says she's old-fashioned. And I say I'm considerate. We'll wait another fifteen minutes.

HUSBAND: Another fifteen minutes.

MRS. YANG (*addressing the company*): Now you all know, don't you, that my son is getting a job as a mail pilot?

SISTER-IN-LAW: In Peking, too, isn't it?

MRS. YANG: In Peking, too! The two of us are moving to Peking!

SHEN TE: Sun, tell your mother Peking is out of the question now.

YANG SUN: Your cousin'll tell her. If he agrees. I don't agree.

SHEN TE (*amazed, and dismayed*): Sun!

YANG SUN: I hate this godforsaken Setzuan. What people! Know what they look like when I half close my eyes? Horses! Whinnying, fretting, stamping, screwing their necks up! (*Loudly.*) And what is it the thunder says? They are su-per-flu-ous! (*He hammers out the syllables.*) They've run their last race! They can go trample themselves to death! (*Pause.*) I've got to get out of here.

SHEN TE: But I've promised the money to the old couple.

YANG SUN: And since you always do the wrong thing, it's lucky your cousin's coming. Have another drink.

SHEN TE (*quietly*): My cousin can't be coming.

YANG SUN: How d'you mean?

SHEN TE: My cousin can't be where I am.

YANG SUN: Quite a conundrum!

SHEN TE (*desperately*): Sun, I'm the one that loves you. Not my cousin. He was thinking of the job in Peking when he promised you the old couple's money —

YANG SUN: Right. And that's why he's bringing the three hundred silver dollars. Here — to my wedding.

SHEN TE: He is not bringing the three hundred silver dollars.

YANG SUN: Huh? What makes you think that?

SHEN TE (*looking into his eyes*): He says you only bought one ticket to Peking.

(*Short pause.*)

YANG SUN: That was yesterday. (*He pulls two tickets part way out of his inside pocket, making her look under his coat.*) Two tickets. I don't want Mother to know. She'll get left behind. I sold her furniture to buy these tickets, so you see . . .

SHEN TE: But what's to become of the old couple?

YANG SUN: What's to become of me? Have another drink. Or do you believe in moderation? If I drink, I fly again. And if you drink, you may learn to understand me.

SHEN TE: You want to fly. But I can't help you.

YANG SUN: "Here's a plane, my darling — but it's only got one wing!"

(*The* WAITER *enters.*)

WAITER: Mrs. Yang!

MRS. YANG: Yes?

WAITER: Another pitcher of wine, ma'am?

MRS. YANG: We have enough, thanks. Drinking makes me sweat.

WAITER: Would you mind paying, ma'am?

MRS. YANG (*to everyone*): Just be patient a few moments longer, everyone, Mr. Shui Ta is on his way over! (*To the* WAITER.) Don't be a spoilsport.

WAITER: I can't let you leave till you've paid your bill, ma'am.

MRS. YANG: But they know me here!

WAITER: That's just it.

PRIEST (*ponderously getting up*): I humbly take my leave. (*And he does.*)

MRS. YANG (*to the others, desperately*): Stay where you are, everybody! The priest says he'll be back in two minutes!

YANG SUN: It's no good, Mamma. Ladies and gentlemen, Mr. Shui Ta still hasn't arrived and the priest has gone home. We won't detain you any longer.

(*They are leaving now.*)

GRANDFATHER (*in the doorway, having for-*

gotten to put his glass down): To the bride!
(He drinks, puts down the glass, and follows the others.)

(Pause.)

SHEN TE: Shall I go too?

YANG SUN: You? Aren't you the bride? Isn't this your wedding? *(He drags her across the room, tearing her wedding dress.)* If we can wait, you can wait. Mother calls me her falcon. She wants to see me in the clouds. But I think it may be St. Nevercome's Day before she'll go to the door and see my plane thunder by. *(Pause. He pretends the guests are still present.)* Why such a lull in the conversation, ladies and gentlemen? Don't you like it here? The ceremony is only slightly postponed — because an important guest is expected at any moment. Also because the bride doesn't know what love is. While we're waiting, the bridegroom will sing a little song. *(He does so.)*

THE SONG OF
ST. NEVERCOME'S DAY

On a certain day, as is generally known,
  One and all will be shouting: Hooray, hooray!
For the beggar maid's son has a solid-gold
  throne
  And the day is St. Nevercome's Day
On St. Nevercome's, Nevercome's, Never-
  come's Day
  He'll sit on his solid-gold throne

Oh, hooray, hooray! That day goodness will
  pay!
That day badness will cost you your head!
And merit and money will smile and be funny
  While exchanging salt and bread
On St. Nevercome's, Nevercome's, Never-
  come's Day
  While exchanging salt and bread

And the grass, oh, the grass will look down at
  the sky
And the pebbles will roll up the stream
And all men will be good without batting an
  eye
  They will make of our earth a dream
On St. Nevercome's, Nevercome's, Never-
  come's Day
  They will make of our earth a dream

And as for me, that's the day I shall be
  A flyer and one of the best
Unemployed man, you will have work to do
  Washerwoman, you'll get your rest

On St. Nevercome's, Nevercome's, Nevercome's Day
Washerwoman, you'll get your rest

MRS. YANG: It looks like he's not coming.

(The three of them sit looking at the door.)

VIA

WONG's *den. The sewer pipe is again transparent and again the* GODS *appear to* WONG *in a dream.*

WONG: I'm so glad you've come, illustrious ones. It's Shen Te. She's in great trouble from following the rule about loving thy neighbor. Perhaps she's *too* good for this world!

FIRST GOD: Nonsense! You are eaten up by lice and doubts!

WONG: Forgive me, illustrious one, I only meant you might deign to intervene.

FIRST GOD: Out of the question! My colleague here intervened in some squabble or other only yesterday. *(He points to the* THIRD GOD *who has a black eye.)* The results are before us!

WONG: She had to call on her cousin again. But not even he could help. I'm afraid the shop is done for.

THIRD GOD *(a little concerned)*: Perhaps we should help after all?

FIRST GOD: The gods help those that help themselves.

WONG: What if we *can't* help ourselves, illustrious ones?

(Slight pause.)

SECOND GOD: Try, anyway! Suffering ennobles!

FIRST GOD: Our faith in Shen Te is unshaken!

THIRD GOD: We certainly haven't found any *other* good people. You can see where we spend our nights from the straw on our clothes.

WONG: You might help her find her way by —

FIRST GOD: The good man finds his own way here below!

SECOND GOD: The good woman too.

FIRST GOD: The heavier the burden, the greater her strength!

THIRD GOD: We're only onlookers, you know.

FIRST GOD: And everything will be all right in the end, O ye of little faith!

(*They are gradually disappearing through these last lines.*)

VII

The yard behind SHEN TE's *shop. A few articles of furniture on a cart.* SHEN TE *and* MRS. SHIN *are taking the washing off the line.*

MRS. SHIN: If you ask me, you should fight tooth and nail to keep the shop.

SHEN TE: How can I? I have to sell the tobacco to pay back the two hundred silver dollars today.

MRS. SHIN: No husband, no tobacco, no house and home! What are you going to live on?

SHEN TE: I can work. I can sort tobacco.

MRS. SHIN: Hey, look, Mr. Shui Ta's trousers! He must have left here stark naked!

SHEN TE: Oh, he may have another pair, Mrs. Shin.

MRS. SHIN: But if he's gone for good as you say, why has he left his pants behind?

SHEN TE: Maybe he's thrown them away.

MRS. SHIN: Can I take them?

SHEN TE: Oh, no.

(*Enter* MR. SHU FU, *running.*)

SHU FU: Not a word! Total silence! I know all. You have sacrificed your own love and happiness so as not to hurt a dear old couple who had put their trust in you! Not in vain does this district — for all its malevolent tongues — call you the Angel of the Slums! That young man couldn't rise to your level, so you left him. And now, when I see you closing up the little shop, that veritable haven of rest for the multitude, well, I cannot, I cannot let it pass. Morning after morning I have stood watching in the doorway not unmoved — while you graciously handed out rice to the wretched. Is that never to happen again? Is the good woman of Setzuan to disappear? If only you would allow *me* to assist you! Now don't say anything! No assurances, no exclamations of gratitude! (*He has taken out his checkbook.*) Here! A blank check. (*He places it on the cart.*) Just my signature. Fill it out as you wish. Any sum in the world. I herewith retire from the scene, quietly, unob-

trusively, making no claims, on tiptoe, full of veneration, absolutely selflessly . . . (*He has gone.*)

MRS. SHIN: Well! You're saved. There's always some idiot of a man. . . . Now hurry! Put down a thousand silver dollars and let me fly to the bank before he comes to his senses.

SHEN TE: I can pay you for the washing without any check.

MRS. SHIN: What? You're not going to cash it just because you might have to marry him? Are you crazy? Men like him *want* to be led by the nose! Are you still thinking of that flyer? All Yellow Street knows how he treated you!

SHEN TE:
When I heard his cunning laugh, I was afraid
But when I saw the holes in his shoes, I loved him dearly.

MRS. SHIN: Defending that good-for-nothing after all that's happened!

SHEN TE (*staggering as she holds some of the washing*): Oh!

MRS. SHIN (*taking the washing from her, dryly*): So you feel dizzy when you stretch and bend? There couldn't be a little visitor on the way? If that's it, you can forget Mr. Shu Fu's blank check: it wasn't meant for a christening present!

(*She goes to the back with a basket.* SHEN TE's *eyes follow* MRS. SHIN *for a moment. Then she looks down at her own body, feels her stomach, and a great joy comes into her eyes.*)

SHEN TE: O joy! A new human being is on the way. The world awaits him. In the cities the people say: he's got to be reckoned with, this new human being! (*She imagines a little boy to be present, and introduces him to the audience.*) This is my son, the well-known flyer!

Say: Welcome
To the conqueror of unknown mountains and unreachable regions
Who brings us our mail across the impassable deserts!

(*She leads him up and down by the hand.*)

Take a look at the world, my son. That's a tree. Tree, yes. Say: "Hello, tree!" And bow. Like this. (*She bows.*) Now you know each other. And, look, here comes the water seller. He's a friend, give him your hand. A cup of fresh water for my little son, please. Yes, it *is* a warm

day. (*Handing the cup.*) Oh dear, a policeman, we'll have to make a circle round *him.*
Perhaps we can pick a few cherries over there in
the rich Mr. Pung's garden. But we mustn't be
seen. You want cherries? Just like children with
fathers. No, no, you can't go straight at them
like that. Don't pull. We must learn to be reasonable. Well, have it your own way. (*She has
let him make for the cherries.*) Can you reach?
Where to put them? Your mouth is the best
place. (*She tries one herself.*) Mmm, they're
good. But the policeman, we must run! (*They
run.*) Yes, back to the street. Calm now, so no
one will notice us. (*Walking the street with her
child, she sings.*)

Once a plum — 'twas in Japan —
Made a conquest of a man
But the man's turn soon did come
For he gobbled up the plum

(*Enter* WONG, *with a* CHILD *by the hand. He
coughs.*)

SHEN TE: Wong!

WONG: It's about the carpenter, Shen Te.
He's lost his shop, and he's been drinking. His
children are on the streets. This is one. Can you
help?

SHEN TE (*to the* CHILD): Come here, little
man. (*Takes him down to the footlights. To
the audience.*)

You there! A man is asking you for shelter!
A man of tomorrow says: what about today?
His friend the conqueror, whom you know,
Is his advocate!

(*To* WONG.) He can live in Mr. Shu Fu's cabins. I may have to go there myself. I'm going
to have a baby. That's a secret — don't tell
Yang Sun — we'd only be in his way. Can you
find the carpenter for me?

WONG: I knew you'd think of something.
(*To the* CHILD.) Good-bye, son, I'm going for
your father.

SHEN TE: What about your hand, Wong? I
wanted to help, but my cousin . . .

WONG: Oh, I can get along with one hand,
don't worry. (*He shows how he can handle his
pole with his left hand alone.*)

SHEN TE: But your right hand! Look, take
this cart, sell everything that's on it, and go to
the doctor with the money . . .

WONG: She's still good. But first I'll bring the
carpenter. I'll pick up the cart when I get back.
(*Exit* WONG.)

SHEN TE (*to the* CHILD): Sit down over here,
son, till your father comes.

(*The* CHILD *sits cross-legged on the ground.
Enter the* HUSBAND *and* WIFE, *each dragging
a large, full sack.*)

WIFE (*furtively*): You're alone, Shen Te,
dear?

(SHEN TE *nods. The* WIFE *beckons to the*
NEPHEW *off-stage. He comes on with another
sack.*)

WIFE: Your cousin's away? (SHEN TE *nods.*)
He's not coming back?

SHEN TE: No. I'm giving up the shop.

WIFE: That's why we're here. We want to
know if we can leave these things in your new
home. Will you do us this favor?

SHEN TE: Why, yes, I'd be glad to.

HUSBAND (*cryptically*): And if anyone asks
about them, say they're yours.

SHEN TE: Would anyone ask?

WIFE (*with a glance back at her husband*):
Oh, someone might. The police, for instance.
They don't seem to like us. Where can we put
it?

SHEN TE: Well, I'd rather not get in any
more trouble . . .

WIFE: Listen to her! The good woman of
Setzuan!

(SHEN TE *is silent.*)

HUSBAND: There's enough tobacco in those
sacks to give us a new start in life. We could
have our own tobacco factory!

SHEN TE (*slowly*): You'll have to put them
in the back room.

(*The sacks are taken off-stage, while the*
CHILD *is alone. Shyly glancing about him, he
goes to the garbage can, starts playing with
the contents, and eating some of the scraps.
The others return.*)

WIFE: We're counting on you, Shen Te!

SHEN TE: Yes. (*She sees the* CHILD *and is
shocked.*)

HUSBAND: We'll see you in Mr. Shu Fu's
cabins.

NEPHEW: The day after tomorrow.

SHEN TE: Yes. Now, go. Go! I'm not feeling
well.

(*Exeunt all three, virtually pushed off.*)

He is eating the refuse in the garbage can!
Only look at his little gray mouth!

(*Pause. Music.*)

As this is the world *my* son will enter
I will study to defend him.
To be good to you, my son,
I shall be a tigress to all others
If I have to.
And I shall have to.

(*She starts to go.*)

One more time, then. I hope really the last.

(*Exit* SHEN TE *taking* SHUI TA's *trousers.*
MRS. SHIN *enters and watches her with
marked interest. Enter the* SISTER-IN-LAW
and the GRANDFATHER.)

SISTER-IN-LAW: So it's true, the shop has
closed down. And the furniture's in the back
yard. It's the end of the road!

MRS. SHIN (*pompously*): The fruit of high living, selfishness, and sensuality! Down the primrose path to Mr. Shu Fu's cabins — with you!

SISTER-IN-LAW: Cabins? Rat holes! He gave
them to us because his soap supplies only went
moldy there!

(*Enter the* UNEMPLOYED MAN.)

UNEMPLOYED MAN: Shen Te is moving?

SISTER-IN-LAW: Yes. She was sneaking away.

MRS. SHIN: She's ashamed of herself, and no
wonder!

UNEMPLOYED MAN: Tell her to call Mr. Shui
Ta or she's done for this time!

SISTER-IN-LAW: Tell her to call Mr. Shui Ta
or *we're* done for this time.

(*Enter* WONG *and* CARPENTER, *the latter
with a* CHILD *on each hand.*)

CARPENTER: So we'll have a roof over our
heads for a change!

MRS. SHIN: Roof? Whose roof?

CARPENTER: Mr. Shu Fu's cabins. And we
have little Feng to thank for it. (FENG, *we find,
is the name of the* CHILD *already there; his* FA-
THER *now takes him. To the other two.*) Bow
to your little brother, you two!

(*The* CARPENTER *and the two new arrivals
bow to* FENG. *Enter* SHUI TA.)

UNEMPLOYED MAN: Sst! Mr. Shui Ta!

(*Pause.*)

SHUI TA: And what is this crowd here for,
may I ask?

WONG: How do you do, Mr. Shui Ta. This is
the carpenter. Miss Shen Te promised him
space in Mr. Shu Fu's cabins.

SHUI TA: That will not be possible.

CARPENTER: We can't go there after all?

SHUI TA: All the space is needed for other
purposes.

SISTER-IN-LAW: You mean we have to get
out? But we've got nowhere to go.

SHUI TA: Miss Shen Te finds it possible to
provide employment. If the proposition interests you, you may stay in the cabins.

SISTER-IN-LAW (*with distaste*): You mean
work? Work for Miss Shen Te?

SHUI TA: Making tobacco, yes. There are
three bales here already. Would you like to get
them?

SISTER-IN-LAW (*trying to bluster*): We have
our own tobacco! We were in the tobacco business before you were born!

SHUI TA (*to the* CARPENTER *and the* UNEM-
PLOYED MAN): You *don't* have your own tobacco. What about you?

(*The* CARPENTER *and the* UNEMPLOYED
MAN *get the point, and go for the sacks.
Enter* MRS. MI TZU.)

MRS. MI TZU: Mr. Shui Ta? I've brought
you your three hundred silver dollars.

SHUI TA: I'll sign your lease instead. I've decided not to sell.

MRS. MI TZU: What? You don't need the
money for that flyer?

SHUI TA: No.

MRS. MI TZU: And you can pay six months'
rent?

SHUI TA (*takes the barber's blank check from
the cart and fills it out*): Here is a check for ten
thousand silver dollars. On Mr. Shu Fu's account. Look! (*He shows her the signature on
the check.*) Your six months' rent will be in
your hands by seven this evening. And now, if
you'll excuse me.

MRS. MI TZU: So it's Mr. Shu Fu now. The
flyer has been given his walking papers. These
modern girls! In my day they'd have said she
was flighty. That poor, deserted Mr. Yang Sun!

(*Exit* MRS. MI TZU. *The* CARPENTER *and
the* UNEMPLOYED MAN *drag the three sacks
back on the stage.*)

CARPENTER (*to* SHUI TA): I don't know why I'm doing this for you.

SHUI TA: Perhaps your children want to eat, Mr. Carpenter.

SISTER-IN-LAW (*catching sight of the sacks*): Was my brother-in-law here?

MRS. SHIN: Yes, he was.

SISTER-IN-LAW: I thought as much. I know those sacks! That's our tobacco!

SHUI TA: Really? I thought it came from my back room! Shall we consult the police on the point?

SISTER-IN-LAW (*defeated*): No.

SHUI TA: Perhaps you will show me the way to Mr. Shu Fu's cabins?

(*Taking* FENG *by the hand,* SHUI TA *goes off, followed by the* CARPENTER *and his two older children, the* SISTER-IN-LAW, *the* GRANDFATHER, *and the* UNEMPLOYED MAN. *Each of the last three drags a sack. Enter* OLD MAN *and* OLD WOMAN.)

MRS. SHIN: A pair of pants — missing from the clothesline one minute — and next minute on the honorable backside of Mr. Shui Ta.

OLD WOMAN: We thought Miss Shen Te was here.

MRS. SHIN (*preoccupied*): Well, she's not.

OLD MAN: There was something she was going to give us.

WONG: She was going to help me too. (*Looking at his hand.*) It'll be too late soon. But she'll be back. This cousin has never stayed long.

MRS. SHIN (*approaching a conclusion*): No, he hasn't, has he?

VIIA

The Sewer Pipe: WONG *asleep. In his dream, he tells the* GODS *his fears. The* GODS *seem tired from all their travels. They stop for a moment and look over their shoulders at the water seller.*

WONG: Illustrious ones. I've been having a bad dream. Our beloved Shen Te was in great distress in the rushes down by the river — the spot where the bodies of suicides are washed up. She kept staggering and holding her head down as if she was carrying something and it was dragging her down into the mud. When I

called out to her, she said she had to take your Book of Rules to the other side, and not get it wet, or the ink would all come off. You had talked to her about the virtues, you know, the time she gave you shelter in Setzuan.

THIRD GOD: Well, but what do you suggest, my dear Wong?

WONG: Maybe a little relaxation of the rules, Benevolent One, in view of the bad times.

THIRD GOD: As for instance?

WONG: Well, um, good will, for instance, might do instead of love?

THIRD GOD: I'm afraid that would create new problems.

WONG: Or, instead of justice, good sportsmanship?

THIRD GOD: That would only mean more work.

WONG: Instead of honor, outward propriety?

THIRD GOD: Still more work! No, no! The rules will have to stand, my dear Wong!

(*Wearily shaking their heads, all three journey on.*)

VIII

SHUI TA's *tobacco factory in* SHU FU's *cabins. Huddled together behind bars, several families, mostly women and children. Among these people the* SISTER-IN-LAW, *the* GRANDFATHER, *the* CARPENTER, *and his* THREE CHILDREN. *Enter* MRS. YANG *followed by* YANG SUN.

MRS. YANG (*to the audience*): There's something I just *have* to tell you: strength and widom are wonderful things. The strong and wise Mr. Shui Ta has transformed my son from a dissipated good-for-nothing into a model citizen. As you may have heard, Mr. Shui Ta opened a small tobacco factory near the cattle runs. It flourished. Three months ago — I shall never forget it — I asked for an appointment, and Mr. Shui Ta agreed to see us — me and my son. I can see him now as he came through the door to meet us. . . .

(*Enter* SHUI TA *from a door.*)

SHUI TA: What can I do for you, Mrs. Yang?

MRS. Yang: This morning the police came to the house. We find you've brought an action for breach of promise of marriage. In the name of Shen Te. You also claim that Sun came by two hundred silver dollars by improper means.

SHUI TA: That is correct.

MRS. YANG: Mr. Shui Ta, the money's all gone. When the Peking job didn't materialize, he ran through it all in three days. I know he's a good-for-nothing. He sold my furniture. He was moving to Peking without me. Miss Shen Te thought highly of him at one time.

SHUI TA: What do *you* say, Mr. Yang Sun?

YANG SUN: The money's gone.

SHUI TA (*to* MRS. YANG): Mrs. Yang, in consideration of my cousin's incomprehensible weakness for your son, I am prepared to give him another chance. He can have a job — here. The two hundred silver dollars will be taken out of his wages.

YANG SUN: So it's the factory or jail?

SHUI TA: Take your choice.

YANG SUN: May I speak with Shen Te?

SHUI TA: You may not.

(*Pause.*)

YANG SUN (*sullenly*): Show me where to go.

MRS. YANG: Mr. Shui Ta, you are kindness itself: the gods will reward you! (*To* YANG SUN.) And honest work will make a man of you, my boy. (YANG SUN *follows* SHUI TA *into the factory.* MRS. YANG *comes down again to the footlights.*) Actually, honest work didn't agree with him — at first. And he got no opportunity to distinguish himself till — in the third week — when the wages were being paid . . .

(SHUI TA *has a bag of money. Standing next to his foreman — the former* UNEMPLOYED MAN — *he counts out the wages. It is* YANG SUN's *turn.*)

UNEMPLOYED MAN (*reading*): Carpenter, six silver dollars. Yang Sun, six silver dollars.

YANG SUN (*quietly*): Excuse me, sir. I don't think it can be more than five. May I see? (*He takes the foreman's list.*) It says six working days. But that's a mistake, sir. I took a day off for court business. And I won't take what I haven't earned, however miserable the pay is!

UNEMPLOYED MAN: Yang Sun. Five silver dollars. (*To* SHUI TA.) A rare case, Mr. Shui Ta!

SHUI TA: How is it the book says six when it should say five?

UNEMPLOYED MAN: I must've made a mistake, Mr. Shui Ta. (*With a look at* YANG SUN.) It won't happen again.

SHUI TA (*taking* YANG SUN *aside*): You don't hold back, do you? You give your all to the firm. You're even honest. Do the foreman's mistakes always favor the workers?

YANG SUN: He does have . . . friends.

SHUI TA: Thank you. May I offer you any little recompense?

YANG SUN: Give me a trial period of one week, and I'll prove my intelligence is worth more to you than my strength.

MRS. YANG (*still down at the footlights*): Fighting words, fighting words! That evening, I said to Sun: "If you're a flyer, then fly, my falcon! Rise in the world!" And he got to be foreman. Yes, in Mr. Shui Ta's tobacco factory, he worked real miracles.

(*We see* YANG SUN *with his legs apart standing behind the workers who are handing along a basket of raw tobacco above their heads.*)

YANG SUN: Faster! Faster! You, there, d'you think you can just stand around, now you're not foreman any more? It'll be your job to lead us in song. Sing!

(UNEMPLOYED MAN *starts singing. The others join in the refrain.*)

SONG OF THE EIGHTH ELEPHANT

Chang had seven elephants — all much the
    same —
But then there was Little Brother
The seven, they were wild, Little Brother, he
    was tame
    And to guard them Chang chose Little
    Brother
        Run faster!
        Mr. Chang has a forest park
        Which must be cleared before tonight
        And already it's growing dark!

When the seven elephants cleared that forest
    park
Mr. Chang rode high on Little Brother
While the seven toiled and moiled till dark
    On his big behind sat Little Brother
        Dig faster!
        Mr. Chang has a forest park
        Which must be cleared before tonight
        And already it's growing dark!

And the seven elephants worked many an hour
    Till none of them could work another
Old Chang, he looked sour, on the seven he did
    glower

But gave a pound of rice to Little Brother
   What was that?
   Mr. Chang has a forest park
   Which must be cleared before tonight
   And already it's growing dark!

And the seven elephants hadn't any tusks
   The one that had the tusks was Little
    Brother!
Seven are no match for one, if the one has a
   gun!
   How old Chang did laugh at Little
    Brother!
     Keep on digging!
    Mr. Chang has a forest park
    Which must be cleared before tonight
    And already it's growing dark!

(*Smoking a cigar,* SHUI TA *strolls by.* YANG SUN, *laughing, has joined in the refrain of the third stanza and speeded up the tempo of the last stanza by clapping his hands.*)

MRS. YANG: And that's why I say: strength and wisdom are wonderful things. It took the strong and wise Mr. Shui Ta to bring out the best in Yang Sun. A real superior man is like a bell. If you ring it, it rings, and if you don't, it don't, as the saying is.

IX

SHEN TE's *shop, now an office with club chairs and fine carpets. It is raining.* SHUI TA, *now fat, is just dismissing the* OLD MAN *and* OLD WOMAN. MRS. SHIN, *in obviously new clothes, looks on, smirking.*

SHUI TA: No! I can NOT tell you when we expect her back.
OLD WOMAN: The two hundred silver dollars came today. In an envelope. There was no letter, but it must be from Shen Te. We want to write and thank her. May we have her address?
SHUI TA: I'm afraid I haven't got it.
OLD MAN (*pulling* OLD WOMAN's *sleeve*): Let's be going.
OLD WOMAN: She's got to come back some time!

(*They move off, uncertainly, worried.* SHUI TA *bows.*)

MRS. SHIN: They lost the carpet shop be-cause they couldn't pay their taxes. The money arrived too late.
SHUI TA: They could have come to me.
MRS. SHIN: People don't like coming to you.
SHUI TA (*sits suddenly, one hand to his head*): I'm dizzy.
MRS. SHIN: After all, you *are* in your seventh month. But old Mrs. Shin will be there in your hour of trial! (*She cackles feebly.*)
SHUI TA (*in a stifled voice*): Can I count on that?
MRS. SHIN: We all have our price, and mine won't be too high for the great Mr. Shui Ta! (*She opens* SHUI TA's *collar.*)
SHUI TA: It's for the child's sake. All of this.
MRS. SHIN: "All for the child," of course.
SHUI TA: I'm so fat. People must notice.
MRS. SHIN: Oh no, they think it's 'cause you're rich.
SHUI TA (*more feelingly*): What will happen to the child?
MRS. SHIN: You ask that nine times a day. Why, it'll have the best that money can buy!
SHUI TA: He must never see Shui Ta.
MRS. SHIN: Oh, no. Always Shen Te.
SHUI TA: What about the neighbors? There are rumors, aren't there?
MRS. SHIN: As long as Mr. Shu Fu doesn't find out, there's nothing to worry about. Drink this.

(*Enter* YANG SUN *in a smart business suit, and carrying a businessman's briefcase.* SHUI TA *is more or less in* MRS. SHIN's *arms.*)

YANG SUN (*surprised*): I guess I'm in the way.
SHUI TA (*ignoring this, rises with an effort*): Till tomorrow, Mrs. Shin.

(MRS. SHIN *leaves with a smile, putting her new gloves on.*)

YANG SUN: Gloves now! She couldn't be fleecing you? And since when did *you* have a private life? (*Taking a paper from the briefcase.*) You haven't been at your desk lately, and things are getting out of hand. The police want to close us down. They say that at the most they can only permit twice the lawful number of workers.
SHUI TA (*evasively*): The cabins are quite good enough.
YANG SUN: For the workers maybe, not for the tobacco. They're too damp. We must take over some of Mrs. Mi Tzu's buildings.
SHUI TA: Her price is double what I can pay.

YANG SUN: Not unconditionally. If she has me to stroke her knees she'll come down.

SHUI TA: I'll never agree to that.

YANG SUN: What's wrong? Is it the rain? You get so irritable whenever it rains.

SHUI TA: Never! I will never . . .

YANG SUN: Mrs. Mi Tzu'll be here in five minutes. *You* fix it. And Shu Fu will be with her. . . . What's all that noise?

(*During the above dialogue,* WONG *is heard off-stage, calling: "The good Shen Te, where is she? Which of you has seen Shen Te, good people? Where is Shen Te?" A knock. Enter* WONG.)

WONG: Mr. Shui Ta, I've come to ask when Miss Shen Te will be back, it's six months now. . . . There are rumors. People say something's happened to her.

SHUI TA: I'm busy. Come back next week.

WONG (*excited*): In the morning there was always rice on her doorstep — for the needy. It's been there again lately!

SHUI TA: And what do people conclude from this?

WONG: That Shen Te is still in Setzuan! She's been . . . (*He breaks off.*)

SHUI TA: She's been what? Mr. Wong, if you're Shen Te's friend, talk a little less about her, that's my advice to you.

WONG: I don't want your advice! Before she disappeared, Miss Shen Te told me something very important — she's pregnant!

YANG SUN: What? What was that?

SHUI TA (*quickly*): The man is lying.

WONG: A good woman isn't so easily forgotten, Mr. Shui Ta.

(*He leaves.* SHUI TA *goes quickly into the back room.*)

YANG SUN (*to the audience*): Shen Te pregnant? So that's why. Her cousin sent her away, so I wouldn't get wind of it. I have a son, a Yang appears on the scene, and what happens? Mother and child vanish into thin air! That scoundrel, that unspeakable . . . (*The sound of sobbing is heard from the back room.*) What was that? Someone sobbing? Who was it? Mr. Shui Ta the Tobacco King doesn't weep his heart out. And where does the rice come from that's on the doorstep in the morning? (SHUI TA *returns. He goes to the door and looks out into the rain.*) Where is she?

SHUI TA: Sh! It's nine o'clock. But the rain's so heavy, you can't hear a thing.

YANG SUN: What do you want to hear?

SHUI TA: The mail plane.

YANG SUN: What?!

SHUI TA: I've been told *you* wanted to fly at one time. Is that all forgotten?

YANG SUN: Flying mail is night work. I prefer the daytime. And the firm is very dear to me — after all it belongs to my ex-fiancée, even if she's not around. And she's not, is she?

SHUI TA: What do you mean by that?

YANG SUN: Oh, well, let's say I haven't altogether — lost interest.

SHUI TA: My cousin might like to know that.

YANG SUN: I might not be indifferent — if I found she was being kept under lock and key.

SHUI TA: By whom?

YANG SUN: By you.

SHUI TA: What could you do about it?

YANG SUN: I could submit for discussion — my position in the firm.

SHUI TA: You are now my manager. In return for a more . . . appropriate position, you might agree to drop the inquiry into your ex-fiancée's whereabouts?

YANG SUN: I might.

SHUI TA: What position *would* be more appropriate?

YANG SUN: The one at the top.

SHUI TA: My own? (*Silence.*) And if I preferred to throw you out on your neck?

YANG SUN: I'd come back on my feet. With suitable escort.

SHUI TA: The police?

YANG SUN: The police.

SHUI TA: And when the police found no one?

YANG SUN: I might ask them not to overlook the back room. (*Ending the pretense.*) In short, Mr. Shui Ta, my interest in this young woman has not been officially terminated. I should like to see more of her. (*Into* SHUI TA's *face.*) Besides, she's pregnant and needs a friend. (*He moves to the door.*) I shall talk about it with the water seller.

(*Exit.* SHUI TA *is rigid for a moment, then he quickly goes into the back room. He returns with* SHEN TE's *belongings: underwear, etc. He takes a long look at the shawl of the previous scene. He then wraps the things in a bundle, which, upon hearing a noise, he hides under the table. Enter* MRS. MI TZU *and* MR. SHU FU. *They put away their umbrellas and galoshes.*)

MRS. MI TZU: I thought your manager was here, Mr. Shui Ta. He combines charm with that famous treatise "The Defense of Poesy and Humanism."

THE ACADEMICIAN: I beg your pardon, but my book concerns itself with twentieth century humanism. (*To* THE FRIEND.) What about composition? What grade did I get in composition?

THE FRIEND: Nine hundred. You have nine hundred points.

THE ACADEMICIAN: That's perfect. My average must be all the way up.

THE FRIEND: Unfortunately not. They're marking on the basis of two thousand. The passing grade is one thousand.

THE ACADEMICIAN: They must have changed the regulations.

THE WIFE: They didn't change them just for you. You have a frightful persecution complex.

THE ACADEMICIAN: I tell you they changed them.

THE FRIEND: They went back to the old ones, back to the time of Napoleon.

THE ACADEMICIAN: Utterly outmoded. Besides, when did they make those changes? It isn't legal. I'm chairman of the Baccalaureate Commission of the Ministry of Public Education. They didn't consult me, and they cannot make any changes without my approval. I'm going to expose them. I'm going to bring government charges against them.

THE WIFE: Darling, you don't know what you're doing. You're in your dotage. Don't you recall handing in your resignation just before taking the examination so that no one could doubt the complete objectivity of the board of examiners?

THE ACADEMICIAN: I'll take it back.

THE WIFE: You should never have taken that test. I warned you. After all, it's not as if you needed it. But you have to collect all the honors, don't you? You're never satisfied. What did you need this diploma for? Now all is lost. You have your Doctorate, your Master's, your high school diploma, your elementary school certificate, and even the first part of the baccalaureate.

THE ACADEMICIAN: There was a gap.

THE WIFE: No one suspected it.

THE ACADEMICIAN: But I knew it. Others might have found out. I went to the office of the Registrar and asked for a transcript of my record. They said to me: "Certainly Professor, Mr. President, Your Excellency. . . ." Then they looked up my file, and the Chief Registrar came

back looking embarrassed, most embarrassed indeed. He said: "There's something peculiar, very peculiar. You have your Master's, certainly, but it's no longer valid." I asked him why, of course. He answered: "There's a gap behind your Master's. I don't know how it happened. You must have registered and been accepted at the University without having passed the second part of the baccalaureate examination."

THE FRIEND: And then?

THE WIFE: Your Master's degree is no longer valid?

THE ACADEMICIAN: No, not quite. It's suspended. "The duplicate you are asking for will be delivered to you upon completion of the baccalaureate. Of course you will pass the examination with no trouble." That's what I was told, so you see now that I had to take it.

THE FRIEND: Your husband, dear friend, wanted to fill the gap. He's a conscientious person.

THE WIFE: It's clear you don't know him as I do. That's not it at all. He wants fame, honors. He never has enough. What does one diploma more or less matter? No one notices them anyway, but he sneaks in at night, on tiptoe, into the living room, just to look at them, and count them.

THE ACADEMICIAN: What else can I do when I have insomnia?

THE FRIEND: The questions asked at the baccalaureate are usually known in advance. You were admirably situated to get this particular information. You could also have sent in a replacement to take the test for you. One of your students, perhaps. Or if you wanted to take the test without people realizing that you already knew the questions, you could have sent your maid to the black market, where one can buy them.

THE ACADEMICIAN: I don't understand how I could have failed in my composition. I filled three sheets of paper. I treated the subject fully, taking into account the historical background. I interpreted the situation accurately . . . at least plausibly. I didn't deserve a bad grade.

THE FRIEND: Do you recall the subject?

THE ACADEMICIAN: Hum . . . let's see. . . .

THE FRIEND: He doesn't even remember what he discussed.

THE ACADEMICIAN: I do . . . wait . . . hum.

THE FRIEND: The subject to be treated was the following: "Discuss the influence of Renaissance painters on novelists of the Third Republic." I have here a photostatic copy of your examination paper. Here is what you wrote.

THE ACADEMICIAN (*grabbing the photostat and reading*): "The trial of Benjamin: After Benjamin was tried and acquitted, the assessors holding a different opinion from that of the President murdered him, and condemned Benjamin to the suspension of his civic rights, imposing on him a fine of nine hundred francs. . . ."

THE FRIEND: That's where the nine hundred points come from.

THE ACADEMICIAN: "Benjamin appealed his case . . . Benjamin appealed his case. . . ." I can't make out the rest. I've always had bad handwriting. I ought to have taken a typewriter along with me.

THE WIFE: Horrible handwriting, scribbling and crossing out; ink spots didn't help you much.

THE ACADEMICIAN (*goes on with his reading after having retrieved the text his wife had pulled out of his hand*): "Benjamin appealed his case. Flanked by policemen dressed in zouave uniforms . . . in zouave uniforms. . . ." It's getting dark. I can't see the rest. . . . I don't have my glasses.

THE WIFE: What you've written has nothing to do with the subject.

THE FRIEND: Your wife's quite right, friend. It has nothing to do with the subject.

THE ACADEMICIAN: Yes, it has. Indirectly.

THE FRIEND: Not even indirectly.

THE ACADEMICIAN: Perhaps I chose the second question.

THE FRIEND: There was only one.

THE ACADEMICIAN: Even if there was only that one, I treated another quite adequately. I went to the end of the story. I stressed the important points, explaining the motivations of the characters, highlighting their behavior. I explained the mystery, making it plain and clear. There was even a conclusion at the end. I can't make out the rest. (*To* THE FRIEND.) Can you read it?

THE FRIEND: It's illegible. I don't have my glasses either.

THE WIFE (*taking the text*): It's illegible and I have excellent eyes. You pretended to write. Mere scribbling.

THE ACADEMICIAN: That's not true. I've even provided a conclusion. It's clearly marked here in heavy print: "Conclusion or sanction . . . Conclusion or sanction. . . ." They can't get away with it. I'll have this examination rendered null and void.

THE WIFE: Since you treated the wrong subject, and treated it badly, setting down only titles, and writing nothing in between, the mark you received is justified. You'd lose your case.

THE FRIEND: You'd most certainly lose. Drop it. Take a vacation.

THE ACADEMICIAN: You're always on the side of the Others.

THE WIFE: After all, these professors know what they're doing. They haven't been granted their rank for nothing. They passed examinations, received serious training. They know the rules of composition.

THE ACADEMICIAN: Who was on the board of examiners?

THE FRIEND: For Mathematics, a movie star. For Greek, one of the Beatles. For Latin, the champion of the automobile race, and many others.

THE ACADEMICIAN: But these people aren't any more qualified than I am. And for composition?

THE FRIEND: A woman, a secretary in the editorial division of the review *Yesterday, the Day Before Yesterday, and Today.*

THE ACADEMICIAN: Now I know. This wretch gave me a poor grade out of spite because I never joined her political party. It's an act of vengeance. But I have ways and means of rendering the examination null and void. I'm going to call the President.

THE WIFE: Don't! You'll make yourself look even more ridiculous. (*To* THE FRIEND.) Please try to restrain him. He listens to you more than to me. (THE FRIEND *shrugs his shoulders, unable to cope with the situation.* THE WIFE *turns to her husband, who has just lifted the receiver off the hook.*) Don't call!

THE ACADEMICIAN (*on the telephone*): Hello, John? It is I . . . What? . . . What did you say? . . . But, listen, my dear friend . . . but, listen to me . . . Hello! Hello! (*Puts down the receiver.*)

THE FRIEND: What did he say?

THE ACADEMICIAN: He said . . . He said . . . , "I don't want to talk to you. My mummy won't let me make friends with boys at the bottom of the class." Then he hung up on me.

THE WIFE: You should have expected it. All is lost. How could you do this to me? How could you do this to me?

THE ACADEMICIAN: Think of it! I lectured at the Sorbonne, at Oxford, at American universities. Ten thousand theses have been written on my work; hundreds of critics have analyzed it. I hold an *honoris causa* doctorate from Amsterdam as well as a secret university Chair with the Duchy of Luxembourg. I received the Nobel Prize three times. The King of Sweden himself was amazed by my erudition. A doctorate *honoris causa, honoris causa . . .* and I failed the baccalaureate examination!

THE WIFE: Everyone will laugh at us!

(THE ACADEMICIAN *takes off his sword and breaks it on his knee.*)

THE FRIEND (*picking up the two pieces*): I wish to preserve these in memory of our ancient glory.

(THE ACADEMICIAN *meanwhile in a fit of rage is tearing down his decorations, throwing them on the floor, and stepping on them.*)

THE WIFE (*trying to salvage the remains*): Don't do this! Don't! That's all we've got left.

CURTAIN

In *Notes and Counter Notes* Ionesco argues that "realism" is deceptive; what we see on the realistic stage is the world as "reason" sees it, but reason is a sort of systemized thinking — a highly selective vision — that is utterly unable to grasp the fluid, elusive reality. Take, the idea of "character." Reason has told us that there is such a thing as character, but what is character? Is there really a coherent self that can be understood by the scientific mind? Polonius says to Laertes, "This above all, to thine own self be true," but what *is* one's own self? Hamlet certainly does not know. He is eager to avenge his father, but he berates himself for not acting, and he wonders if he is a coward or villain rather than a loving son. The idea that a man has a character, a more or less coherent nature which we can understand through our reason, then, is itself perhaps a simplification of reality. Like Pirandello (see p. 530), Ionesco argues that reason cannot comprehend reality; it is merely an illusory device by which man simplifies an absurd world in order to make it bearable. But illusions are the traditional material of comic dramatists, and so reason — and the ridiculous behavior that it engenders — is one of Ionesco's chief subjects.

Fantasy is the weapon with which Ionesco seeks to bludgeon his audience out of its reason-induced illusions and into an awareness of the strangeness of the world. "The authentic nature of things, the truth," he has written "can only be revealed to us through fantasy." His characters at first provoke us to say, "People are not at all like that," and his situations (he scarcely has plots) are wildly improbable — as reason understands improbability. But his gross exaggerations — for example, farcical characters who speak idiotic clichés — serve, first, to make us see that people do indeed speak idiotic clichés, and second, to make us see that they do so because they are terrified of the anguish that would encompass them if they did not fend it off with neat verbal formulas. Without such formulas as "travel broadens us," "we learn from our mistakes," "children develop a sense of responsibility by having a dog," we can hardly stand life; certainly we would have serious doubts about why we bother to cope with foreign money, we would be driven to distraction by our mistakes, and we would kick the dog out. In short, things exist but cannot be justified; existence is absurd (the argument runs) and we hide this terrifying truth from ourselves by imposing on existence a vast mechanism of institutions, including language and traditions, which (though really only a sort of systematic madness) gives us the illusion that there is a meaningful pattern in life.

In *The Gap* a professor cannot tolerate a gap in his career because a gap means that the pattern is not complete, and if the pattern is not complete there may not really be a pattern at all. We have all agreed that college degrees mean something, or are important, and we have agreed that professors are learned men with degrees. Therefore, a man who holds a doctorate *must* have been awarded a baccalaureate earlier; anything else is unthinkable, for it calls the system into doubt, and we are horribly uncomfortable without the system. We *are* our degrees — and our car and our clothes and our children. If a degree is missing, a part of the person is missing, and the person himself becomes unsure of his identity. Not surprisingly Ionesco's professor has a habit of keeping his eye on his framed diplomas: "He sneaks in at night, on tiptoe, into the living room, just to look at them, and count them." The professor is farcical, of course, but the zany reduction of a man to a puppet-like figure gets across the point that we persistently relate the self to externals. The farcical characters thus are not merely farcical or sub-human, for they convey a sense of deep — and real — unhappiness. Ionesco's plays are filled with people who desperately depend on things: chairs in *The Chairs*, coffee cups in *Victims of Duty*, furniture in *The New Tenant* (note too in *The Gap* that the description of the furniture on the set is an embodiment of the protagonist's conception of himself), and eggs in *The Future Is in Eggs*.

The venerable doctor's failure to pass an undergraduate examination is not just a joke about the stupidity of professors; it is also a violent comment on the tissue of conventions that we have invented in order to allow us to have a sense of identity in an irrational world. At the end of the play, when the discredited professor begins to destroy his decorations, his wife salvages the remnants and states quite clearly the dependence of her identity on things: "Don't do this! Don't. That's all we've got left."

We all fail our examination (compare Dr. Borg in *Wild Strawberries*) because we all fend off a frightening irrational reality by taking comfort in simplifications. Ionesco forces us to examine ourselves. The stage direction at the end of *Jack* says, "All this must produce in the audience a feeling of embarrassment, awareness and shame." We are not allowed merely to laugh at the folly of others; we are forced at the same time to look into our own guilt. Is Ionesco's vision comic or tragic? The automatic behavior and the automatic language are traditional comic materials, but the anguish — farcical but felt — has affinities with tragedy. Ionesco himself has often said that for him the comic is tragic. He has even taken Bergson's famous description of the comic as the mechanical encrusted on the living (see the introduction to this book, p. 9) and found tragic implications in it:

At the start, you have "a little of something mechanical encrusted on the living." It's comic. But if the mechanical gets bigger and bigger and the living shrinks and shrinks, things become stifling and then tragic, because we get the impression that the world is slipping from our mental grasp. . . . The sorcerer's apprentice must have had this same anguished feeling of the world escaping his grasp. Perhaps it's also the image of what could happen in the near future. We are, now, no longer masters of the extraordinary machines we set in motion. Our planet could go up in smoke . . . so they tell us.*

Both comedy and tragedy customarily have showed man at the end of his rope, but the attitude that the audience was to take toward tragic desperation was very different from the attitude it was to take toward comic desperation. In our time, however, the distinction has become blurred, partly because, as Thoreau said more than a hundred years ago, most of us live lives of quiet desperation. We can scarcely see ourselves as heroes, but we don't quite see ourselves as mere fools either.

*From *Conversations with Eugène Ionesco* by Claude Bonnefoy, p. 108. Translated by Jan Dawson. Holt, Rinehart and Winston, 1970. Reprinted by permission of the publisher.

THE EFFECT OF GAMMA RAYS ON MAN-IN-THE-MOON MARIGOLDS

Paul Zindel

Paul Zindel (born in 1936) has lived most of his life in New York. He has said that the depiction of the mother in *Marigolds*, written when he was twenty-five, is indebted to his own mother, and that the play as a whole owes something to his experience as a high school teacher of chemistry. Zindel has also written several books for children and two other plays. *Marigolds*, produced in 1970, won the Pulitzer Prize for Drama.

CHARACTERS

TILLIE, *The Girl*
"In front of my eyes, one part of the world was becoming another. Atoms exploding ...atom after atom breaking down into something new ... It would go on for millions of years . . ."

BEATRICE, *The Mother*
"This long street, with all the doors of the houses shut and everything crowded next to each other ... And then I start getting afraid that the vegetables are going to spoil ... and that nobody's going to buy anything . . ."

RUTH, *The Other Daughter*
"Well, they say I came out of my room ... and I started down the stairs, step by step ...and I heard the choking and banging on the bed . . ."

NANNY
. . .

JANICE VICKERY
. . .

The Setting: A room of wood which was once a vegetable store — and a point of debarkation for a horse-drawn wagon to bring its wares to a small town.

But the store is gone, and a widow of confusion has placed her touch on everything. A door to NANNY's *room leads off from this main room, and in front of the door hang faded curtains which allow ventilation in the summer. There is a hallway and a telephone. A heavy wood staircase leads to a landing with a balustrade, two doors, and a short hall.* BEATRICE *sleeps in one room;* TILLIE *and* RUTH *share the other.*

Objects which respectable people usually hide in closets are scattered about the main room: newspapers, magazines, dishes; empty

Sada Thompson as Beatrice, Amy Levitt as Ruth, and, in back, Pamela Payton-Wright as Tillie in the original production directed by Melvin Bernhardt, New York, 1970. (Photograph: Bert Andrews.)

bottles; clothes; suitcases; last week's sheets. Such carelessness is the type which is so perfected it must have evolved from hereditary processes; but in all fairness to the occupants, it can be pointed out that after twilight, when shadows and weak bulbs work their magic, the room becomes interesting.

On a table near the front left of the room is a small wire cage designed to hold a rabbit. Near this are several school books, notebook papers, and other weapons of high school children. A kitchen area, boasting a hot plate, has been carved near the bottom of the staircase, and the window, which was formerly the front of the vegetable store, is now mostly covered with old newspapers so that passers-by cannot see in. A bit of the clear glass remains at the top — but drab, lifeless drapes line the sides of the window.

ACT I

The lights go down slowly as music creeps in — a theme for lost children, the near misbegotten.

From the blackness TILLIE's VOICE *speaks against the music.*

TILLIE'S VOICE: He told me to look at my hand, for a part of it came from a star that exploded too long ago to imagine. This part of me was formed from a tongue of fire that screamed through the heavens until there was our sun. And this part of me — this tiny part of me — was on the sun when it itself exploded and whirled in a great storm until the planets came to be.

(Lights start in.)

And this small part of me was then a whisper of the earth. When there was life, perhaps this part of me got lost in a fern that was crushed and covered until it was coal. And then it was a diamond millions of years later — it must have been a diamond as beautiful as the star from which it had first come.

TILLIE (*taking over from recorded voice*): Or perhaps this part of me became lost in a terrible beast, or became part of a huge bird that flew above the primeval swamps.

And he said this thing was so small — this part of me was so small it couldn't be seen — but it was there from the beginning of the world.

And he called this bit of me an atom. And when he wrote the word, I fell in love with it.

Atom.

Atom.

What a beautiful word.

(*The phone rings.*)

BEATRICE (*off stage*): Will you get that please?

(*The phone rings again before* BEATRICE *appears in her bathrobe from the kitchen.*)

No help! Never any help!

(*She answers the phone.*)

Hello? Yes it is. Who is this? . . . I hope there hasn't been any trouble at school . . . Oh, she's always been like that. She hardly says a word around here, either. I always say some people were born to speak and others born to listen . . .

You know I've been meaning to call you to thank you for that lovely rabbit you gave Matilda. She and I just adore it and it's gotten so big . . .

Well, it certainly was thoughtful. Mr. Goodman, I don't mean to change the subject but aren't you that delightful young man Tillie said hello to a couple of months back at the A & P? You were by the lobster tank and I was near the frozen foods? That delightful and handsome young man? . . . Why, I would very much indeed use the expression *handsome*. Yes, and . . .

Well, I encourage her at every opportunity at home. Did she say I didn't? Both my daughters have their own desks and I put 75-watt bulbs right near them . . . Yes . . . Yes . . . I think those tests are very much overrated, anyway, Mr. Goodman . . . Well, believe me she's nothing like that around this house . . .

Now I don't want you to think I don't appreciate what you're trying to do, Mr. Goodman, but I'm afraid it's simply useless. I've tried just everything, but she isn't a pretty girl — I mean, let's be frank about it — she's going to have her problems. Are you married, Mr. Goodman? Oh, that's too bad. I don't know what's the matter with women today letting a handsome young man like you get away . . .

Well, some days she just doesn't feel like going to school. You just said how bright she is, and I'm really afraid to put too much of a strain on her after what happened to her sister. You know, too much strain is the worst thing in this modern world, Mr. Goodman, and I can't afford to have another convulsive on my hands, now can I? But don't you worry about Matilda. There will be some place for her in this world. And, like I said, some were born to speak and

others just to listen . . . and do call again, Mr. Goodman. It's been a true pleasure speaking with you. Goodbye.

(BEATRICE *hangs up the phone and advances into the main room. The lights come up.*)

Matilda, that wasn't very nice of you to tell them I was forcibly detaining you from school. Why, the way that Mr. Goodman spoke, he must think I'm running a concentration camp. Do you have any idea how embarrassing it is to be accused of running a concentration camp for your own children?

Well, it isn't embarrassing at all.

That school of yours is forty years behind the times anyway, and believe me you learn more around here than that ugly Mr. Goodman can teach you!

You know, I really feel sorry for him. I never saw a man with a more effeminate face in my life. When I saw you talking to him by the lobster tank I said to myself, "Good Lord, for a science teacher my poor girl has got herself a Hebrew hermaphrodite." Of course, he's not as bad as Miss Hanley. The idea of letting her teach girl's gym is staggering.

And you have to place me in the embarrassing position of giving them a reason to call me at eight-thirty in the morning, no less.

TILLIE: I didn't say anything.

BEATRICE: What do you tell them when they want to know why you stay home once in a while?

TILLIE: I tell them I'm sick.

BEATRICE: Oh, you're sick all right, the exact nature of the illness not fully realized, but you're sick all right. Any daughter that would turn her mother in as the administrator of a concentration camp has got to be suffering from something very peculiar.

TILLIE: Can I go in today, Mother?

BEATRICE: You'll go in, all right.

TILLIE: Mr. Goodman said he was going to do an experiment —

BEATRICE: Why — he looks like the kind that would do his experimenting after sundown.

TILLIE: On radioactivity —

BEATRICE: On radioactivity? That's all that high school needs!

TILLIE: He's going to bring in the cloud chamber —

BEATRICE: Why, what an outstanding event. If you had warned me yesterday I would've gotten all dressed to kill and gone with you today. I love seeing cloud chambers being brought in.

TILLIE: You can actually see —

BEATRICE: You're giving me a headache.

TILLIE: Please?

BEATRICE: No, my dear, the fortress of knowledge is not going to be blessed with your presence today. I have a good number of exciting duties for you to take care of, not the least of which is rabbit droppings.

TILLIE: Oh, Mother, please . . . I'll do it after school.

BEATRICE: If we wait a minute longer this house is going to ferment. I found rabbit droppings in my bedroom even.

TILLIE: I could do it after Mr. Goodman's class. I'll say I'm ill and ask for a sick pass.

BEATRICE: Do you want me to chloroform that thing right this minute?

TILLIE: No!

BEATRICE: Then shut up.

(RUTH *comes to the top of the stairs. She is dressed for school, and though her clothes are simple she gives the impression of being slightly strange. Her hair isn't quite combed, her sweater doesn't quite fit, etc.*)

RUTH: Do you have Devil's Kiss down there?

BEATRICE: It's in the bathroom cabinet.

(RUTH *comes downstairs and goes to the bathroom door, located under the stairs. She flings it open and rummages in the cabinet.*)

RUTH: There's so much junk in here it's driving me crazy.

BEATRICE: Maybe it's in my purse . . . If you don't hurry up you'll be late for school.

RUTH: Well, I couldn't very well go in without Devil's Kiss, now could I?

BEATRICE: Doesn't anyone go to school these days without that all over their lips?

RUTH (*finding the lipstick*): Nobody I know, except Tillie, that is. And if she had a little lipstick on I'll bet they wouldn't have laughed at her so much yesterday.

BEATRICE: Why were they laughing?

RUTH: The assembly. Didn't she tell you about the assembly?

BEATRICE: Ruth, you didn't tell me she was in an assembly.

RUTH: Well, I just thought of it right now. How could I tell you anything until I think of it — did you ever stop to consider that? Some crummy science assembly.

BEATRICE (*to* TILLIE): What is she talking about?

RUTH: I thought she'd tell the whole world. Imagine, right in front of the assembly, with everybody laughing at her.

BEATRICE: Will you be quiet, Ruth? *Why were they laughing at you?*

TILLIE: I don't know.

RUTH: You don't know? My heavens, she was a sight. She had that old jumper on — the faded one with that low collar — and a raggy slip that showed all over and her hair looked like she was struck by lightning.

BEATRICE: You're exaggerating . . .

RUTH: She was cranking this model of something —

TILLIE: The atom.

RUTH: This model of the atom . . . you know, it had this crank and a long tower so that when you turned it these little colored balls went spinning around like crazy. And there was Tillie, cranking away, looking weird as a coot . . . that old jumper with the raggy slip and the lightning hair . . . cranking away while some boy with glasses was reading this stupid speech . . . and everybody burst into laughter until the teachers yelled at them. And all day long, the kids kept coming up to me saying, "Is that really your sister? How can you bear it?" And you know, Chris Burns says to me — "She looks like the one that went to the looney doctors." I could have kissed him there and then.

BEATRICE (*taking a backscratcher*): Matilda, if you can't get yourself dressed properly before going to school you're never going to go again. I don't like the idea of everybody laughing at you, because when they laugh at you they're laughing at me. And I don't want you cranking any more . . . atoms.

RUTH (*putting the lipstick back in* BEATRICE's *bag*): You're almost out of Devil's Kiss.

BEATRICE: If you didn't put so much on it would last longer.

RUTH: Who was that calling?

BEATRICE: Matilda turned me in to the Gestapo.

RUTH: Can I earn a cigarette this morning?

BEATRICE: Why not?

(BEATRICE *offers her the backscratcher along with a cigarette.*)

RUTH: Was it Mr. Goodman?

BEATRICE: Who?

RUTH (*lighting the cigarette*): The call this morning. Was it Mr. Goodman?

BEATRICE: Yes.

RUTH (*using the backscratcher on BEATRICE, who squirms with ecstasy*): I figured it would be.

BEATRICE: A little higher, please.

RUTH: There?

BEATRICE: Yes, *there* . . . Why did you figure it would be Mr. Goodman?

RUTH: Well, he called me out of sewing class yesterday — I remember because my blouse wasn't all buttoned — and he wanted to know why Tillie's out of school so much.

BEATRICE: Lower. A little lower . . . And what did you tell him?

RUTH: I wish you'd go back to Kools. I liked Kools better.

TILLIE (*gravely concerned*): What did you tell him?

RUTH: I told him you were ill, and he wanted to know what kind, so I told him you had leprosy.

TILLIE: You didn't!

RUTH: You should have seen his face. He was so cute. And I told him you had ringworm and gangrene.

BEATRICE: What did he say?

RUTH: And I told him you had what Mother's last patient had . . . whatchamacallit?

BEATRICE: Psoriasis?

RUTH: Yeah. Something like that.

TILLIE: Tell me you didn't, Ruth!

RUTH: O.K. I didn't . . . But I really did.

BEATRICE: He knew you were joking.

RUTH: And then I told him to go look up the *history* and then he'd find out. Whenever they go look up the history then they don't bother me anymore 'cause they think I'm crazy.

BEATRICE: Ruth —

RUTH: And I told him the disease you had was fatal and that there wasn't much hope for you.

BEATRICE: What kind of *history* is it?

RUTH: Just a little folder with the story of our lives in it, that's all.

BEATRICE: How did you ever see it?

RUTH: I read the whole thing last term when Miss Hanley dragged me into the record room because I didn't want to climb the ropes in gym and I told her my skull was growing.

BEATRICE: A little *lower*, please.

RUTH: Lower! Higher! I wish you'd make up your mind. If you'd switch back to Kools it might be worth it, but ugh! these are awful. You know, I really did think my skull was growing. Either that or a tumor. So she dragged me out of gym class, and she thought I couldn't read upside down while she was sitting opposite me with the history. But I could.

BEATRICE: What does it say?

RUTH: Oh, it says you're divorced and that I went crazy . . . and my father took a heart attack at Star Lake . . . and now you're a widow —

BEATRICE (*referring to the backscratching*): That's it! Hold it right there! Aaah!

RUTH: And it says that I exaggerate and tell stories and that I'm afraid of death and have nightmares . . . and all that stuff.

BEATRICE: And what else does it say?

RUTH: I can't remember everything you know. Remember this, remember that . . . remember this, that . . .

(*Go to dark. Music in.*)

TILLIE'S VOICE: Today I saw it. Behind the glass a white cloud began to form. He placed a small piece of metal in the center of the chamber and we waited until I saw the first one — a trace of smoke that came from nowhere and then disappeared. And then another . . . and another, until I knew it was coming from the metal. They looked like water-sprays from a park fountain, and they went on and on for as long as I watched.

And he told me the fountain of smoke would come forth for a long time, and if I had wanted to, I could have stayed there all my life and it would never have ended — that fountain, so close I could have touched it. In front of my eyes, one part of the world was becoming another. Atoms exploding, flinging off tiny bullets that caused the fountain, atom after atom breaking down into something new. And no one could stop the fountain. It would go on for millions of years — on and on, this fountain from eternity.

(*By the end of this speech, the lights are in to show TILLIE preparing boxes of dirt in which to plant seeds. The rabbit is in the cage near her, and BEATRICE is reading a newspaper on the other side of the room. She is sipping coffee from a huge coffee cup.*)

BEATRICE: I thought we had everything, but

leave it to you to think of the one thing we're
missing . . .

(*She reads from the newspaper.*)

Twenty-two acres in Prince's Bay. Small pond.
$6,000 . . . That's cheap. I'd take a look at it if
I had any money . . .

What kind of seeds are they?

TILLIE: Marigolds. *They've been exposed to
cobalt-60.*

BEATRICE: If there's one thing I've always
wanted, it's been a living room planted with
marigolds that have been exposed to cobalt-60.
While you're at it, why don't you throw in a to-
mato patch in the bathroom?

TILLIE: Just let me keep them here for a
week or so until they get started and then I'll
transplant them to the backyard.

BEATRICE (*reading again*): Four-family
house. Six and a half and six and a half over five
and five. Eight garages. I could really do something with that. A nursing home . . .

Don't think I'm not kicking myself that I
didn't finish that real estate course. I should
have finished beauty school, too . . .

God, what I could do with eight garages . . .

(*There is a sound from beyond the curtained
doorway.* BEATRICE *gestures in that direction.*)

You know, I'm thinking of getting rid of *that*
and making this place into something.

TILLIE: Yes.

BEATRICE: I've been thinking about a tea
shop. Have you noticed there aren't many of
them around anymore?

TILLIE: Yes.

BEATRICE: And this is just the type of
neighborhood where a good tea shop could
make a go of it. We'd have a good cheesecake.
You've got to have a good cheesecake . . .

(*She calculates.*)

Eight times ten — well, eight times eight, if
they're falling down — that's sixty-four dollars a
month from the garages alone . . . I swear
money makes money.

(*There is a rustling at the curtains. Two thin
and wrinkled hands push the curtains apart
slowly and then the ancient face of* NANNY
*appears. She negotiates her way through the
curtains. She is utterly wrinkled and dried,
perhaps a century old. Time has left her with*

*a whisper of a smile — a smile from a soul
half-departed. If one looked closely, great
cataracts could be seen on each eye, and it is
certain that all that can pierce her soundless
prison are mere shadows from the outside
world. She pervades the room with age.*

NANNY *supports herself by a four-legged
tubular frame which she pushes along in
front of her with a shuffling motion that reminds one of a ticking clock. Inch by inch
she advances into the room.* TILLIE *and* BEA-
TRICE *continue speaking, knowing that it
will be minutes before she is close enough
to know they are there.*)

BEATRICE: What is cobalt-60?

TILLIE: It's something that causes . . .
changes in seeds. Oh, Mother — he set the
cloud chamber up just for me and he told me
about radioactivity and half-life and he got
the seeds for me.

BEATRICE (*her attention still on the newspaper*): What does half-life mean?

(NANNY *is well into the room as* TILLIE *replies.*)

TILLIE (*reciting from memory*): The half-life
of Polonium-210 is one hundred and forty days.

The half-life of Radium-226 is one thousand
five hundred and ninety years.

The half-life of Uranium-238 is four and
one-half billion years.

BEATRICE (*putting away her newspaper*):
Do you know you're giving me a headache?

(*Then, in a loud, horribly saccharine voice,
she speaks to* NANNY *as if she were addressing
a deaf year-old child.*)

LOOK WHO'S THERE! IT'S NANNY!
NANNY CAME ALL THE WAY OUT
HERE BY HERSELF!

I'm going to need a cigarette for this.

NANNY! YOU COME SIT DOWN AND
WE'LL BE RIGHT WITH HER!

You know, sometimes I've got to laugh. I've
got *this* on my hands and all you're worried
about is planting marigolds.

I'VE GOT HOTSY WATER FOR YOU,
NANNY. WOULD YOU LIKE SOME
HOTSY WATER AND HONEY?

(NANNY *has seated herself at a table, smiling
but oblivious to her environment.*)

I've never seen it to fail. Every time I decide to

have a cup of coffee I see that face at the curtains. I wonder what she'd do . . .

(*She holds pot of boiling water.*)

. . . if I just poured this right over her head. I'll bet she wouldn't even notice it.
NANNY'S GOING TO GET JUST WHAT SHE NEEDS!

(*She fills a cup for her and places a honey jar near her.*)

You know if someone told me when I was young that I'd end up feeding honey to a zombie, I'd tell them they were crazy.
SOMETHING WRONG, NANNY? OH, DID I FORGET NANNY'S SPOON? MERCY! MERCY! I FORGOT NANNY'S SPOON!

(*She gets a spoon and stands behind* NANNY.)

I'll give you a spoon, Nanny, I'll give you a spoon.

(*She makes a motion behind* NANNY's *back as if she's going to smack her on the head with the spoon.*)

Matilda! Watch me give Nanny her spoon.
A SPOON FOR NANNY!

(*It manages to be slightly funny and* TILLIE *yields to a laugh, along with her mother.*)

Fifty dollars a week. Fifty dollars. I look at you, Nanny, and I wonder if it's worth it. I think I'd be better off driving a cab.
TAKE HONEY, NANNY. HONEY WITH HOTSY WATER!

You should have seen her daughter bring her here last week . . . I could have used you that day . . . She came in pretending she was Miss Career Woman of the Year. She said she was in real estate and *such a busy little woman,* such a busy little woman — she just couldn't give all the love and care and affection her little momsy needed anymore . . .

(*Then, with a great smile, she speaks right into* NANNY's *uncomprehending face.*)

Nanny's quite a little cross to bear, now aren't you, Nanny dear? But you're a little better than Mr. Mayo was — with the tumor on his brain — or Miss Marion Minto with her cancer, or Mr. Brougham . . . what was his first name?
TILLIE: Alexander.

BEATRICE: Mr. Alexander Brougham with the worms in his legs.
WHY, NANNY'S QUITE SOME LITTLE GIRL, AREN'T YOU, NANNY? A GIRL DRINKING HER HOTSY AND HONEY! . . .
Cobalt-60. Ha! You take me for a fool, don't you?
TILLIE: No, Mother.
BEATRICE: Science, science, science! Don't they teach our misfits anything anymore? Anything decent and meaningful and sensitive? Do you know what I'd be now if it wasn't for this mud pool I got sucked into? I'd probably be a dancer. Miss Betty Frank, The Best Dancer of the Class of 19 . . . something. One minute I'm the best dancer in school — smart as a whip — the head of the whole crowd! And the next minute . . .
One mistake. That's how it starts. Marry the wrong man and before you know it he's got you tied down with two stones around your neck for the rest of your life.
When I was in that lousy high school I was one of the most respected kids you ever saw.
I used to wonder why people always said, "Why, just yesterday . . . why, just yesterday . . . why, just yesterday."
Before I knew what happened I lost my dancing legs and got varicose legs. Beautiful varicose legs. Do you know, everything I ever thought I'd be has exploded!
NANNY, YOU HURRY UP WITH THAT HONEY!
Exploded! You know, I almost forgot about everything I was supposed to be . . .
NANNY'S ALMOST FINISHED. ISN'T THAT WONDERFUL?
She's almost finished, all right.
NANNY'S DAUGHTER IS COMING TO SEE YOU SOON. WILL THAT MAKE NANNY HAPPY?
The day Miss Career Woman of the Year comes to visit again I think I'll drop dead. Nobody's too busy for anything they want to do, don't you tell me. What kind of an idiot do people take me for?
NANNY, YOU'RE SPILLING YOUR HOTSY! JESUS CHRIST!
You know, I ought to kick you right out and open that tea shop tomorrow.
Oh, it's coming. I can feel it. And the first thing I'll do is get rid of that rabbit.
TILLIE (*hardly listening*): Yes, Mother.

BEATRICE: You think I'm kidding?
TILLIE: No, I don't.
BEATRICE: You bet I'm not!

(*She rummages through some drawers in a chest.*)

I was going to do this a month ago.

(*She holds up a small bottle.*)

Here it is. Here's a new word for you.

(*She reads.*)

Trichloro . . . methane. Do you know what this is, Matilda? Well, it's chloroform!

(*She puts the bottle away.*)

I'm saving it for that Angora manure machine of yours. Speaking of manure machines, IS NANNY READY TO GO MAKE DUTY?

(*She starts helping* NANNY *out of the chair and props her up with the tubular frame.*)

NANNY IS ALWAYS READY FOR DUTY, AREN'T. YOU NANNY? BECAUSE NANNY'S A GOODY-GOODY GIRL AND GOODY-GOODY GIRLS ALWAYS GET GOODY-GOODY THINGS. GOD LOOKS OUT FOR GOODY-GOODY GIRLS AND GIVES THEM HOTSY AND HONEY — RIGHT, NANNY?

(BEATRICE *sits down in the hall and watches* NANNY *make her way toward the bathroom. There is a pause as the woman's shuffling continues.*
    The lights go low on TILLIE, NANNY *becomes a silhouette, and the light remains on* BEATRICE. *She starts to read the paper again, but the shuffling gets on her nerves and she flings the paper down.*)

Half-life! If you want to know what a half-life is, just ask me. You're looking at the original half-life!
    I got stuck with one daughter with half a mind; another one who's half a test tube; half a husband — a house half full of rabbit crap — and half a corpse!
    That's what I call a half-life, Matilda! Me and cobalt-60! Two of the biggest half-*lifes* you ever saw!

(*The set goes to dark.*
    After a few seconds, the sound of someone dialing a phone can be heard. As the spot comes up on her, we see BEATRICE *holding the phone and struggling to get a cigarette.*)

BEATRICE (*on the phone*): Hello — Mr. Goodman, please . . . How would I know if he's got a class? . . . Hello, Mr. Goodman? Are you Mr. Goodman? . . . Oh, I beg your pardon, Miss Torgersen . . . Yes, I'll wait.

(*She lights her cigarette.*)

Couldn't you find him, Miss Torgersen? . . . Oh! Excuse me, Mr. Goodman. How are you? . . . I'll bet you'll never guess who this is — it's Mrs. Hunsdorfer — remember the frozen foods?

(*She laughs.*)

You know, Ruth told me she's your new secretary and I certainly think that's a delight. You were paying so much attention to Matilda that I'll bet Ruth just got jealous. She does things like that, you know. I hope she works hard for you, although I can't imagine what kind of work Ruth could be doing in that great big science office. She's a terrible snoop . . .

(*She takes a puff.*)

Your attendance? Isn't that charming. And the *cut* cards! Imagine. You trust her with . . . why, I didn't know she could type *at all* . . . imagine. Well . . . I'll . . . Of course, *too* much work isn't good for anyone, either. No wonder she's failing everything. I mean, I never knew a girl who failed everything regardless of what they were suffering from. I suppose I should say *recovering* from . . .
    Well, it's about the seeds you gave Matilda . . . Well, she's had them in the house for a week now and they're starting to grow. Now, she told me they had been subjected to radioactivity, and I hear such terrible things about radioactivity that I automatically associate radioactivity with sterility, and it positively horrifies me to have those seeds right here in my living room. Couldn't she just grow plain marigolds like everyone else?

(*She takes a puff.*)

Oh . . .

(*Another big puff, forming a mushroom cloud.*)

It does sound like an interesting project, but . . .

(*The biggest puff yet.*)

No, I must admit that at this very moment I don't know what a *mutation* is . . .

(*She laughs uncomfortably.*)

Mr. Goodman . . . Mr. Goodman! I don't want you to think I'm not interested, but please spare me definitions over the phone. I'll go to the library next week and pick me out some little book on science and then I'll know all about mutations . . . No, you didn't insult me, but I just want you to know that I'm not *stupid* . . .

I just thought prevention was better than a tragedy, Mr. Goodman. I mean, Matilda has enough problems to worry about without *sterility* . . .

Well, I was just concerned, but you've put my poor mother's heart at ease. You know, really, our schools need more exciting young men like you, I really mean that. Really. Oh, I do. Goodbye, Mr. Goodman.

(*By the end of her talk on the phone, her face is left in a spotlight, and then the stage goes black. The music theme comes in, in a minor key, softly at first, but accentuated by increasingly loud pulses which transmute into thunder crashes.*
    There is a scream heard from upstairs and we see the set in night shadows.
    TILLIE *tears open her bedroom door and rushes into* BEATRICE'*s room.* RUTH *screams again.*)

TILLIE: Mother! She's going to have one!

(RUTH *appears on the landing and releases another scream which breaks off into gasps. She starts down the stairs and stops halfway to scream again. There is another tremendous thunder crash as* BEATRICE *comes out of her room, puts on the hall light, and catches the hysterical girl on the stairs.*)

BEATRICE (*shouting*): Stop it! Stop it, Ruth!
TILLIE (*at the top of the stairs*): She's going!
BEATRICE: Ruth! Stop it!
TILLIE: She's going to go!
BEATRICE (*Yelling at* TILLIE): Shut up and get back in your room!

(RUTH *screams.*)

You're not going to let yourself go, do you hear me, Ruth? You're not going to go!
RUTH: He's after me!

(*She screams, lightning and thunder crash follow.*)

BEATRICE: You were dreaming, do you hear me? Nobody's after you! Nobody!
TILLIE: I saw her eyes start to go back —
BEATRICE (*to* TILLIE): Get back in your room!

(*She helps* RUTH *down the rest of the stairs.*)

There, now, nobody's after you. Nice and easy. Breathe deeply . . . Did the big bad man come after my little girl?

(*She sits* RUTH *down and then puts both hands up to her own face and pulls her features into a comic mask.* RUTH *begins to laugh at her.*)

That big bad bogey man?

(*They both laugh heartily.*)

Now that wasn't so bad, was it?
RUTH: It was the dream, with Mr. Mayo again.
BEATRICE: Oh. Well, we'll just get you a little hot milk and —

(*A tremendous thunder crash throws the set into shadows.*)

Why, the electricity's gone off. Do you remember what happened to those candles?
RUTH: What candles?
BEATRICE: The little white ones from my birthday cake last year.
RUTH: Tillie melted them down for school a long time ago.
BEATRICE (*searching through drawers*): She had no right doing that.
RUTH: She asked you. She used them to attach a paper straw to a milk bottle with a balloon over it, and it was supposed to tell if it was going to rain.
BEATRICE (*finding a flashlight*): There! It works. I don't want her wasting anything of mine unless she's positive I won't need it. You always need candles.

(*She steers* RUTH *toward the couch as lightning flashes.*)

Why, Ruth — your skin just turned ice cold!

(*She rummages through one of the boxes and grabs a blanket.*)

This will warm you up . . . What's the matter?

RUTH: The flashlight —

BEATRICE: What's wrong with it?

RUTH: It's the same one I used to check on Mr. Mayo with.

BEATRICE: So it is. We don't need it.

RUTH: No, let me keep it.

(*Starting to laugh.*)

Do you want to know how they have it in the history?

BEATRICE: No, I don't.

RUTH: Well, they say I came out of my room . . .

(*She flashes the light on her room.*)

. . . And I started down the stairs, step by step . . . and I heard the choking and banging on the bed, and . . .

BEATRICE: I'm going back to bed.

RUTH: No!

BEATRICE: Well, talk about something nice, then.

RUTH: Oh, Mama, tell me about the wagon.

BEATRICE: You change so fast I can't keep up with you.

RUTH: Mama, *please* . . . the story about the wagon.

BEATRICE: I don't know anything about telling stories. Get those great big smart teachers of yours to do that sort of stuff.

RUTH: Tell me about the horses again, and how you stole the wagon.

BEATRICE: Don't get me started on that.

RUTH: Mama, *please* . . .

BEATRICE (*taking out a pack of cigarettes*): Do you want a cigarette?

RUTH (*taking one*): Leave out the part where they shoot the horses, though.

(*They both light up.*)

BEATRICE: Honey, you know the whole story —

RUTH: "Apples! Pears! C*u* . . . cumbers!"

BEATRICE: No. It's "Apples! Pears! C*ucum* . . . bers!"

(*They say it together.*)

"Apples! Pears! C*ucum* . . . bers!"

(*And they laugh.*)

RUTH: How did you get the wagon out without him seeing you?

BEATRICE: That was easy. Every time he got

home for the day he'd make us both some sandwiches — my mama had been dead for years — and he'd take a nap on the old sofa that used to be . . . there!

(*She points to a corner of the room.*)

And while he was sleeping I got the horses hitched up and went riding around the block waving to everyone.

RUTH: Oh, Mama, you didn't!

BEATRICE: Of course I did. I had more nerve than a bear when I was a kid. Let me tell you it takes nerve to sit up on that wagon every day yelling "Apples! . . .

(*Both together.*)

Pears! C*ucum* . . . bers!"

(*They laugh again.*)

RUTH: Did he find out you took the wagon?

BEATRICE: Did he find out? He came running down the street after me and started spanking me right on top of the wagon — not hard — but it was so embarrassing — and I had one of those penny marshmallow ships in the back pocket of my overalls, and it got all squished. And you better believe I never did it again . . .

You would have loved him, Ruth, and gone out with him on the wagon . . . all over Stapleton yelling as loud as you wanted.

RUTH: "Apples! Pears! C*u* . . . cumbers!"

BEATRICE: No!

RUTH: "C*ucum* . . . bers!"

BEATRICE: My father made up for all the other men in this whole world, Ruth. If only you two could have met. He'd only be about seventy now, do you realize that? And I'll bet he'd still be selling vegetables around town. All that fun — and then I don't think I ever knew what really hit me.

RUTH: Don't tell about —

BEATRICE: Don't worry about the horses.

RUTH: What hit you?

BEATRICE: Well it was just me and Papa . . . and your father hanging around. And then Papa got sick . . . and I drove with him up to the sanatorium. And then I came home and there were the horses —

RUTH: Mother!

BEATRICE: And I had the horses . . . taken care of. And then Papa got terribly sick and he begged me to marry so that he'd be sure I'd be taken care of.

(She laughs.)

If he knew how I was taken care of he'd turn over in his grave.

And *nightmares!* Do you want to know the nightmare I used to have?

I never had nightmares over the fights with your father, or the divorce, or his thrombosis — he deserved it — I never had nightmares over any of that.

Let me tell you about my nightmare that used to come back and back:

Well, I'm on Papa's wagon, but it's newer and shinier, and it's being pulled by beautiful white horses, not dirty workhorses — these are like circus horses with long manes and tinsel — and the wagon is blue, shiny blue. And it's full — filled with yellow apples and grapes and green squash.

You're going to laugh when you hear this. I'm wearing a lovely gown with jewels all over it, and my hair is piled up on top of my head with a long feather in it, and the bells are ringing.

Huge bells swinging on a gold braid strung across the back of the wagon, and they're going DONG, DONG . . . DONG, DONG. And I'm yelling "APPLES! PEARS! CUCUM . . . BERS!"

RUTH: That doesn't sound like a nightmare to me.

BEATRICE: And then I turn down our street and all the noise stops. This long street, with all the doors of the houses shut and everything crowded next to each other, and there's not a soul around. And then I start getting afraid that the vegetables are going to spoil . . . and that nobody's going to buy anything, and I feel as though I shouldn't be on the wagon, and I keep trying to call out.

But there isn't a sound. Not a single sound. Then I turn my head and look at the house across the street. I see an upstairs window, and a pair of hands pull the curtains slowly apart. I see the face of my father and my heart stands still . . .

Ruth . . . take the light out of my eyes.

(A long pause.)

RUTH: Is Nanny going to die here?
BEATRICE: No.
RUTH: How can you be sure?
BEATRICE: I can tell.
RUTH: Are you crying?

BEATRICE: What's left for me, Ruth?
RUTH: What, Mama?
BEATRICE: What's left for me?

(The stage goes slowly to dark as the drizzling rain becomes louder and then disappears.

When the lights come up again NANNY *is seated at the kitchen table with a bottle of beer and a glass in front of her.* TILLIE *comes in the front door with a box of large marigold plants and sets them down where they'll be inconspicuous. She gets the rabbit out of its cage, sits down near* NANNY *and gives her a little wave.* BEATRICE *suddenly appears at the top of the stairs and drops a stack of newspapers with a loud thud. She goes back into her room and lets fly another armful of junk.)*

TILLIE: What are you doing?
BEATRICE: A little housecleaning, and you're going to help. You can start by getting rid of that rabbit or I'll suffocate the bastard.

(She takes a drink from a glass of whiskey.)

You don't think I will, do you? You wait and see. Where's Ruth? She's probably running around the schoolyard in her brassiere.

(She comes downstairs.)

TILLIE: Mother, they want me to do something at school.
BEATRICE: NANNY! DID YOU HEAR THAT? THEY WANT HER TO DO SOMETHING AT SCHOOL! ISN'T THAT MOMENTOUS, NANNY?

Well I want you to do something around here. Like get rid of that bunny. I'm being generous! I'll let you give it away. Far away. Give it to Mr. Goodman. I'd chloroform the thing myself, but that crazy sister of yours would throw convulsions for fifty years . . . and I hate a house that vibrates.

And get rid of those sterile marigolds. They stink!

HI, NANNY — HOW ARE YOU, HONEY? HOW WOULD YOU LIKE TO GO ON A LONG TRIP?

You see, everybody, I spent today taking stock of my life and I've come up with zero. I added up all the separate departments and the total reads zero . . .

zero zero zero zero zero zero zero
zero zero zero zero zero

zero zero zero
zero zero
zero

. . . And do you know how you pronounce that, with all your grammatical schoolin' and foolin'? You pronounce it o,o,o,o,O,O,O,O,O, O! o,o,o,o,O,O,O,O,O,O,O,O!

Right, Nanny? RIGHT, NANNY?

So, by the end of the week, you get rid of that cottontail compost heap and we'll get you a job down at the five-and-ten-cent store. And if you don't do so well with the public, we'll fix you up with some kind of machine. Wouldn't that be nice?

(RUTH *enters at a gallop, throwing her books down and babbling a mile a minute.*)

RUTH (*enthusiastically*): Can you believe it? I didn't, until Chris Burns came up and told me about it in Geography, and then Mr. Goodman told me himself during the eighth period in the office when I was eavesdropping. Aren't you so happy you could bust? Tillie? I'm so proud I can't believe it, Mama. Everybody was talking about it and nobody . . . well, it was the first time they all came up screaming about her and I said, "Yes, she's my sister!" I said it, "She's my sister! My sister! My *sister*!" Give me a cigarette.

BEATRICE: Get your hands off my personal property.

RUTH: I'll scratch your back later.

BEATRICE: I don't want you to touch me!

RUTH: Did he call yet? My God, I can't believe it, I just can't!

BEATRICE: Did who call yet?

RUTH: I'm not supposed to tell you, as Mr. Goodman's private secretary, but you're going to get a call from school.

BEATRICE (*to* TILLIE): What is she talking about?

TILLIE: I was in the Science Fair at school.

RUTH: Didn't she tell you yet? Oh, Tillie, how could you? She's fantastic, Mama! She's a finalist in the Science Fair. There were only five of them out of hundreds and hundreds. She won with all those plants over there. They're freaks! Isn't that a scream? Dr. Berg picked her himself. The principal! And I heard Mr. Goodman say she was going to be another Madam Pasteur and he never saw a girl do anything like that before and . . . so I told everybody, "Yes, she's my sister!" Tillie, "You're my sister!" I

said. And Mr. Goodman called the Advance and they're coming to take your picture. Oh, Mama, isn't it crazy? And nobody laughed at her, Mama. She beat out practically everybody and nobody laughed at her. "She's my sister," I said. "She's my sister!"

(*The telephone rings.*)

That must be him! Mama, answer it — I'm afraid.

(*Ring.*)

Answer it before he hangs up!

(*Ring.*)

Mama! He's gonna hang up!

(RUTH *grabs the phone.*)

Hello? . . . Yes . . .

(*Aside to* BEATRICE.)

It's him! . . . Just a minute, please . . .

(*Covering the mouthpiece.*)

He wants to talk to you.
BEATRICE: Who?
RUTH: The *principal*!
BEATRICE: Hang up.
RUTH: I told him you were here! Mama!

(BEATRICE *gets up and shuffles slowly to the phone.*)

BEATRICE (*finally, into the phone*): Yes? . . . I know who you are, Dr. Berg . . . I see . . . Couldn't you get someone else? There's an awfully lot of work that has to be done around here, because she's not as careful with her home duties as she is with man-in-the-moon marigolds . . .

Me? What would you want with me up on the stage? . . . The other mothers can do as they please . . . I would have thought you had enough in your *history* without . . . I'll think about it . . . Goodbye, Dr. Berg . . .

(*Pause, then screaming.*)

I SAID I'D THINK ABOUT IT!

(*She hangs up the phone, turns her face slowly to* RUTH, *then to* TILLIE, *who has her face hidden in shame in the rabbit's fur.*)

RUTH: What did he say?
BEATRICE (*flinging her glass on the floor*):

How could you do this to me? HOW COULD
YOU LET THAT MAN CALL OUR
HOME!

I have no clothes, do you hear me? I'd look
just like you up on the stage, ugly little you!
DO YOU WANT THEM TO LAUGH AT
US? LAUGH AT THE TWO OF US?

RUTH (*disbelievingly*): Mother . . . aren't
you proud of her? Mother . . . it's an *honor*.

(TILLIE *breaks into tears and moves away
from* BEATRICE. *It seems as though she is
crushed, but then she halts and turns to face
her mother.*)

TILLIE (*through tears*): But . . . nobody
laughed at me.

(BEATRICE's *face begins to soften as she
glimpses what she's done to* TILLIE.)

BEATRICE: Oh, my God . . .

(TILLIE *starts toward her.* BEATRICE *opens
her arms to receive her as music starts in and
lights fade. A chord of finality punctuates
the end of Act I.*)

ACT II

About two weeks later.

*The room looks somewhat cheery and
there is excitement in the air. It is early evening and preparations are being made for* TIL-
LIE *to take her project to the final judging of
the Science Fair.*

TILLIE *has been dressed by her mother in
clothes which are clean but too girlish for her
awkwardness. Her hair has been curled, she
sports a large bow, and her dress is a starched
flair.*

RUTH *has dressed herself up as well. She
has put on too much makeup, and her lipstick has been extended beyond the natural
line of her lips. She almost appears to be sinister.*

*A large three-panel screen stands on one of
the tables. THE EFFECT OF GAMMA
RAYS ON MAN-IN-THE-MOON MARI-
GOLDS is printed in large letters running
across the top of the three panels. Below this
on each panel there is a subtopic:* THE PAST;
THE PRESENT; THE FUTURE. *Additional
charts and data appear below the titles.*

RUTH: The only competition you have to
worry about is Janice Vickery. They say she
caught it near Princess Bay Boulevard and it
was still alive when she took the skin off it.

TILLIE (*taking some plants from* RUTH):
Let me do that, please, Ruth.

RUTH: I'm sorry I touched them, really.

TILLIE: Why don't you feed Peter?

RUTH: Because I don't feel like feeding
him . . . Now I feel like feeding him.

(*She gets some lettuce from a bag.*)

I heard that it screamed for three minutes after
she put it in because the water wasn't boiling
yet. How much talent does it take to boil the
skin off a cat and then stick the bones together
again? That's what I want to know. Ugh. I had
a dream about that, too. I figure she did it in
less than a day and she ends up as one of the
top five winners . . . and you spend months
growing atomic flowers.

TILLIE: Don't you think you should finish
getting ready?

RUTH: Finish? This is it!

TILLIE: Are you going to wear that sweater?

RUTH: Look, don't worry about me. I'm not
getting up on any stage, and if I did I wouldn't
be caught dead with a horrible bow like that.

TILLIE: Mother put it —

RUTH: They're going to laugh you off the
stage again like when you cranked that atom in
assembly . . . I didn't mean that . . . The one
they're going to laugh at is Mama.

TILLIE: What?

RUTH: I said the one they're going to laugh
at is Mama . . . Oh, let me take that bow off.

TILLIE: It's all right.

RUTH: Look, just sit still. I don't want everybody making fun of you.

TILLIE: What made you say that about
Mama?

RUTH: Oh, I heard them talking in the Science Office yesterday. Mr. Goodman and Miss
Hanley. She's getting $12.63 to chaperon the
thing tonight.

TILLIE: What were they saying?

RUTH: Miss Hanley was telling Mr. Goodman about Mama . . . when she found out you
were one of the five winners. And he wanted to
know if there was something wrong with Mama

because she sounded crazy over the phone. And Miss Hanley said she *was* crazy and she always has been crazy and she can't wait to see what she looks like after all these years. Miss Hanley said her nickname used to be *Betty the Loon.*

TILLIE (*as* RUTH *combs her hair*): Ruth, you're hurting me.

RUTH: She was just like you and everybody thought she was a big weirdo. There! You look much better!

(*She goes back to the rabbit.*)

Peter, if anybody stuck you in a pot of boiling water I'd kill them, do you know that? . . .

(*Then to* TILLIE.)

What do they call boiling the skin off a cat? I call it murder, that's what I call it. They say it was hit by a car and Janice just scooped it up and before you could say *bingo* it was screaming in a pot of boiling water . . .

Do you know what they're all waiting to see? Mama's feathers! That's what Miss Hanley said. She said Mama blabs as though she was the Queen of England and just as proper as can be, and that her idea of getting dressed up is to put on all the feathers in the world and go as a bird. Always trying to get somewhere, like a great big bird.

TILLIE: Don't tell Mama, please. It doesn't matter.

RUTH: I was up there watching her getting dressed and sure enough, she's got the feathers out.

TILLIE: You didn't tell her what Miss Hanley said?

RUTH: Are you kidding? I just told her I didn't like the feathers and I didn't think she should wear any. But I'll bet she doesn't listen to me.

TILLIE: It doesn't matter.

RUTH: It doesn't matter? Do you think I want to be laughed right out of the school tonight, with Chris Burns there, and all? Laughed right out of the school, with your electric hair and her feathers on that stage, and Miss Hanley splitting her sides?

TILLIE: Promise me you won't say anything.

RUTH: On one condition.

TILLIE: What?

RUTH: Give Peter to me.

TILLIE (*ignoring her*): The taxi will be here any minute and I won't have all this stuff ready. Did you see my speech?

RUTH: I mean it. Give Peter to me.

TILLIE: He belongs to all of us.

RUTH: For me. All for me. What do you care? He doesn't mean anything to you anymore, now that you've got all those crazy plants.

TILLIE: Will you stop?

RUTH: If you don't give him to me I'm going to tell Mama that everybody's waiting to laugh at her.

TILLIE: Where are those typewritten cards?

RUTH: I MEAN IT! Give him to me!

TILLIE: Does he mean that much to you?

RUTH: Yes!

TILLIE: All right.

RUTH (*after a burst of private laughter*): Betty the Loon . . .

(*She laughs again.*)

That's what they used to call her, you know. Betty the Loon!

TILLIE: I don't think that's very nice.

RUTH: First they had Betty the Loon, and now they've got Tillie the Loon . . .

(*To rabbit.*)

You don't have to worry about me turning you in for any old plants . . .

How much does a taxi cost from here to the school?

TILLIE: Not much.

RUTH: I wish she'd give me the money it costs for a taxi — and for all that cardboard and paint and flowerpots and stuff. The only time she ever made a fuss over me was when she drove me nuts.

TILLIE: Tell her to hurry, please.

RUTH: By the way, I went over to see Janice Vickery's pot, that she did you know what in, and I started telling her and her mother about the worms in Mr. Alexander Brougham's legs, and I got thrown out because it was too near dinner time. That Mrs. Vickery kills me. She can't stand worms in somebody else's legs but she lets her daughter cook a cat.

TILLIE (*calling upstairs*): Mother! The taxi will be here any minute.

(BEATRICE *comes to the top of the stairs. Her costume is strange, but not that strange, by any means. She is even a little attractive tonight, and though her words say she is greatly annoyed with having to attend the night's function, her tone and direction show she is very, very proud.*)

BEATRICE: You're lucky I'm coming, without all this rushing me.

TILLIE: Mama, you look beautiful.

BEATRICE: Don't put it on too thick. I said I'd go and I guess there's no way to get out of it. Do you mind telling me how I'm supposed to get up on the stage? Do they call my name or what? And where are you going to be? If you ask me, they should've sent all the parents a mimeographed sheet of instructions. If this is supposed to be such a great event, why don't they do it right?

TILLIE: You just sit on the stage with the other parents before it begins.

BEATRICE: How long is this thing going to last? And remember, I don't care even if you do win the whole damn thing, I'm not making any speech. I can hold my own anywhere, but I hated that school when I went there and I hate it now . . . and the only thing I'd have to say is, what a pack of stupid teachers and vicious children they have. Imagine someone tearing the skin off a cat.

RUTH: She didn't tear it. She boiled it off.

BEATRICE: You just told me upstairs that girl tore the skin off with an orange knife and . . . do you know, sometimes you exasperate me?

(*To* TILLIE.)

If you've got all the plants in this box, I can manage the folding thing. Do you know I've got a headache from doing those titles? And you probably don't even like them.

TILLIE: I like them very much.

BEATRICE: Look, if you don't want me to go tonight, I don't have to. You're about as enthusiastic as a dummy about this whole thing.

TILLIE: I'm sorry.

BEATRICE: And I refuse to let you get nervous. Put that bow back in your hair.

RUTH: I took it out.

BEATRICE: What did you do that for?

RUTH (*taking the rabbit in her arms*): Because it made her look crazy.

BEATRICE: How would you know what's crazy or not? If that sweater of yours was any tighter it'd cut off the circulation in your chest.

(*Fussing over* TILLIE.)

The bow looks very nice in your hair. There's nothing wrong with looking proper, Matilda, and if you don't have enough money to look expensive and perfect, people like you for *trying* to look nice. You know, one day maybe you will be pretty. You'll have some nice features, when that hair revives and you do some tricks with makeup. I hope you didn't crowd the plants too close together. Did you find your speech?

TILLIE: Yes, Mother.

BEATRICE: You know, Matilda, I was wondering about something. Do you think you're really going to win? I mean, not that you won't be the best, but there's so much politics in school. Don't laugh, but if there's anyone who's an expert on that, it's me, and someday I'm going to write a book and blast that school to pieces. If you're just a little bit different in this world, they try to kill you off.

RUTH (*putting on her coat*): Tillie gave Peter to me.

BEATRICE: Oh? Then you inherited the rabbit droppings I found upstairs. What are you doing with your coat on?

RUTH: I'm going out to wait for the taxi.

BEATRICE: Oh, no you're not. You start right in on the rabbit droppings. Or you won't get another cigarette even if you scratch my back with an orange knife.

RUTH: I'm going down to the school with you.

BEATRICE: Oh, no you're not! You're going to keep company with that corpse in there. If she wakes up and starts gagging just slip her a shot of whiskey.

(*The taxi horn blows outside.*)

Quick! Grab the plants, Matilda —I'll get the big thing.

RUTH: I want to go! I promised Chris Burns I'd meet him.

BEATRICE: Can't you understand English?

RUTH: I've got to go!

BEATRICE: Shut up!

RUTH (*almost berserk*): I don't care. I'M GOING ANYWAY!

BEATRICE (*shoving* RUTH *hard*): WHAT DID YOU SAY?

TILLIE: Mother!

(*After a pause, the horn blows again.*)

BEATRICE: Hurry up with that box, Matilda, and tell him to stop blowing the horn. HURRY UP!

(TILLIE *reluctantly exits with the box of plants*.)

I don't know where you ever got the idea you were going tonight. Did you think nobody was going to hold down the fort? . . .

Now you know how I felt all those years you and everybody else was running out whenever they felt like it — because there was always me to watch over the fifty-dollar-a-week corpse. If there's one thing I demand it's respect. I don't ask for anything from you but respect.

RUTH (*pathetically*): Why are you ashamed of me?

BEATRICE: I've been seen with a lot worse than you. I don't even know why I'm going tonight, do you know that? Do you think I give one goddam about the whole thing? . . .

(*She starts to fold the large three-panel screen with the titles:* THE PAST, THE PRESENT, *and* THE FUTURE.)

Do you want to know why I'm going? Do you really want to know why this once somebody else has to stick with that dried prune for a few minutes? Because this is the first time in my life I've ever felt just a little bit proud over something. Isn't that silly? Somewhere in the back of this turtle-sized brain of mine I feel just a little *proud*! Jesus Christ! And you begrudge me even that, you little bastard.

(*The taxi horn blows impatiently*.)

RUTH (*in a hard voice*): Hurry up. They're waiting for you . . . They're *all* waiting for you.

BEATRICE (*carrying the folded screen so that* THE PAST *is face out in bold black letters*): I hope the paint is dry . . . Who's waiting for me?

RUTH: Everybody . . . including Miss Hanley. She's been telling all the teachers . . . about you . . . and they're all waiting.

BEATRICE: You're such a little liar, Ruth, do you know that? When you can't have what you want, you try to ruin it for everybody else.

(*She starts to the door*.)

RUTH: Goodnight, *Betty the Loon*.

(BEATRICE *stops as if she's been stabbed.*
    The taxi horn blows several times as BEATRICE *puts down the folding screen*.)

BEATRICE (*helplessly*): Take this thing.
RUTH: What for?

BEATRICE: Go with Matilda.
RUTH: I don't want to go now.
BEATRICE (*blasting*): GET OUT OF HERE!
RUTH (*after a long pause*): Now Tillie's going to blame it on me that you're not going — and take the rabbit back.

(*The taxi beeps again, as* RUTH *puts her coat on*.)

I can't help it what people call you.

(*She picks up the screen*.)

I'll tell Tillie you'll be down later, all right? . . . Don't answer me. What do I care!

(RUTH *exits.*
    BEATRICE *breaks into tears that shudder her body, and the lights go down slowly on her pathetic form. Music in.*
    Suddenly a bolt of light strikes an area in the right stage — JANICE VICKERY *is standing in the spotlight holding the skeleton of a cat mounted on a small platform. Her face and voice are smug*.)

JANICE: *The Past:* I got the cat from the A.S.P.C.A. immediately after it had been killed by a high-altitude pressure system. That explains why some of the rib bones are missing, because that method sucks the air out of the aminal's lungs and ruptures all cavities. They say it prevents cruelty to animals but I think it's horrible.

(*She laughs*.)

Then I boiled the cat in a sodium hydroxide solution until most of the skin pulled right off, but I had to scrape some of the grizzle off the joints with a knife. You have no idea how difficult it is to get right down to the bones.

(*A little gong sounds*.)

I have to go on to *The Present*, now — but I did want to tell you how long it took me to put the thing together. I mean, as it is now, it's extremely useful for students of anatomy, even with the missing rib bones, and it can be used to show basic anatomical aspects of many, many animals that are in the same family as felines. I suppose that's about the only present uses I can think for it, but it is nice to remember as an accomplishment, and it looks good on college applications to show you did something else in school besides dating.

(*She laughs, and a second gong sounds.*)

The Future: The only future plans I have for Tabby — my little brother asked the A.S.P.C.A. what its name was when he went to pick it up and they said it was called Tabby, but I think they were kidding him —

(*She laughs again.*)

I mean as far as future plans, I'm going to donate it to the science department, of course, and next year, if there's another Science Fair perhaps I'll do the same thing with a dog.

(*A third gong sounds.*)

Thank you very much for your attention, and I hope I win!

(JANICE *and her spotlight disappear as suddenly as they had arrived, and music returns as the lights come up slowly on* BEATRICE.
    She has obviously been drinking and is going through a phone book. Finding her number, she goes to the phone and dials.)

BEATRICE (*into the phone*): I want to talk to the principal, please . . .
    Well, you'll have to get him down off the stage . . .
    It's none of your goddam business who I am! . . .
    Oh, I see . . . Yes. I have a message for him and Mr. Goodman, and you, too . . . And this is for Miss Hanley, too . . .
    Tell them Mrs. Hunsdorfer called to thank them for making her wish she was dead . . . Would you give them that message, please? . . . Thank you very much.

(*She hangs up the phone, pauses, then surveys the room. Her attention fixes on the store window covered with newspapers. The phone rings several times but she ignores it. She goes to the window and proceeds to rip the paper from it. That finished, she turns and surveys the room again. She goes to the kitchen table and rearranges its position. She spies a card table with school supplies and hurls them on the floor. Next, she goes to a bureau and rummages through drawers, finding tablecloths and napkins. She throws cloths on two or three tables and is heading*

toward the kitchen table when the phone rings again. The ringing triggers off something else she wants to do. She empties a cup filled with scraps of paper and finds a telephone number. She lifts the receiver off the ringing phone and hangs up immediately. She lifts the receiver again, checks to make sure there's a dial tone, and then dials the number on the scrap of paper.)

BEATRICE (*into the phone*): Hello. This is Mrs. Hunsdorfer . . . I'm sorry if I frightened you, I wouldn't want you to think Nanny had deceased or anything like that — I can imagine how terrible you'd feel if anything like that ever happened . . . Terrible tragedy that would be, Miss Career Woman of the Year . . .
    Yes, I'll tell you why I'm calling. I want her out of here by tomorrow. I told you when you rolled her in here I was going to try her out for a while and if I didn't like her she was to get the hell out. Well I don't like her, so get her the hell out . . .
    It's like this. I don't like the way she cheats at solitaire. Is that a good enough reason? . . . Fine. And if she's not out of here by noon I'll send her collect in an ambulance, you son of a bitch!

(*She slams down the phone and bursts into laughter. The laughter subsides somewhat as she pours herself another drink. She takes the drink to a chair and as she sits down her foot accidentally hits the rabbit cage. She gives the cage a little kick and then an idea strikes. She gets up and finds a large blue towel which she flings over her shoulder. She gets the bottle of chloroform and approaches the cage. Having reached a decision she picks up the cage and takes it upstairs.*
    Music in and lights fade.
    From the darkness a beam of light falls on TILLIE *in the same way* JANICE VICKERY *had been presented.*)

TILLIE (*deathly afraid, and referring to her cards*): *The Past:* The seeds were exposed to various degrees . . . of gamma rays from radiation sources in Oak Ridge . . .
    Mr. Goodman helped me pay for the seeds . . . their growth was plotted against . . . time.

(*She loses her voice for a moment and then the first gong sounds.*)

The Present: The seeds which received little radiation have grown to plants which are normal in appearance. The seeds which received moderate radiation gave rise to mutations such as double blooms, giant stems, and variegated leaves. The seeds closest to the gamma source were killed or yielded dwarf plants.

(*The second gong rings.*)

The Future: After radiation is better understood, a day will come when the power from exploding atoms will change the whole world we know.

(*With inspiration.*)

Some of the mutations will be good ones — wonderful things beyond our dreams — and I believe, I believe this with all my heart, THE DAY WILL COME WHEN MANKIND WILL THANK GOD FOR THE STRANGE AND BEAUTIFUL ENERGY FROM THE ATOM.

(*Part of her last speech is reverberated electronically. Deep pulses of music are added as the light focuses on* TILLIE's *face.*
Suddenly there is silence, except for RUTH *picking up* TILLIE's *last words.*
The lights come up on the main set, and the room is empty.
RUTH *bursts in the front door. She is carrying the three-panel card and a shopping bag of plants, both of which she drops on the floor.*)

RUTH: MAMA! MAMA! She won! Mama! Where are you? She won!

(*She runs back to the front door and yells to* TILLIE.)

Hurry up! Hurry! Oh, my God, I can't believe it!

(*Then yelling upstairs.*)

Mama! Come on down! Hurry!

(TILLIE *comes in the front door, carrying the rest of her plants, and the large trophy.* RUTH *takes the trophy.*)

Give me that!

(*She starts upstairs.*)

Mama! Wait till you see this!

(BEATRICE *appears at the top of the stairs. She has been drinking a great deal, and clings fast to a bunch of old cheap curtains and other material.*)

Mama! She won . . .

(BEATRICE *continues mechanically on down the stairs.*)

Didn't you hear me? Tillie won the whole thing! . . . Mama? . . . What's the matter with you? What did you rip the paper off the windows for?

(BEATRICE *commences tacking up one of the curtains.*)

TILLIE: Mama? Are you going to open a . . . shop?
RUTH: What's the matter? Can't you even answer?
BEATRICE (*to* TILLIE): Hand me some of those tacks.
RUTH (*screaming*): I SAID SHE WON! ARE YOU DEAF?
BEATRICE: Ruth, if you don't shut up I'm going to have you put away.
RUTH: They ought to put *you* away, BETTY THE LOON!

(*There is a long pause.*)

BEATRICE: The rabbit is in your room. I want you to bury it in the morning.
RUTH: If you did anything . . . I'LL KILL YOU!

(*She runs upstairs.*)

TILLIE: Mother, you didn't kill it, did you?
BEATRICE: Nanny goes tomorrow. First thing tomorrow.

(*There is a cry from upstairs.*)

TILLIE: Ruth? Are you all right?
BEATRICE: I don't know what it's going to be. Maybe a tea shop. Maybe not.

(RUTH *appears in the doorway of her room. She is holding the dead rabbit on the blue towel. As she reaches the top of the stairs, she begins to moan deeply.*)

After school you're going to have regular hours. You'll work in the kitchen, you'll learn how to cook, and you're going to earn your keep, just like in any other business.

(TILLIE *starts slowly up the stairs toward* RUTH.)

TILLIE (*with great fear*): Mama . . . I think she's going to go.

(RUTH *commences to tremble.* TILLIE *speaks softly to her.*)

Don't go . . . don't go . . .

(RUTH's *eyes roll in her head, and the trembling of her body becomes pronounced throbbing. She drops the rabbit with the towel covering it.*)

Help me! Mama! Help me!
BEATRICE: Snap out of it, do you hear me? RUTH, DON'T LET YOURSELF GO!

(*To* TILLIE.)

Help me get her downstairs!

(*By the time the trio reaches the bottom of the stairs,* RUTH *is consumed by a violent convulsion.* BEATRICE *holds her down and pushes* TILLIE *out of the way.*)

BEATRICE (*screaming*): Get the wooden spoon!

(TILLIE *responds as* BEATRICE *gets* RUTH *onto a sofa. The convulsion runs its course of a full minute, then finally subsides.* TILLIE *gets a blanket and covers* RUTH.)

TILLIE: Shall I call the doctor?

(*There is a long pause.*)

Shall I call the doctor?
BEATRICE: No. She'll be all right.
TILLIE: I think we should call him.
BEATRICE: I DIDN'T ASK YOU WHAT YOU THOUGHT! . . . We're going to need every penny to get this place open.

(BEATRICE *spreads a tablecloth on one of the tables and places a pile of old cloth napkins on it. She sits down and lights a cigarette.*)

TILLIE (*picking up the rabbit on the stairs*): I'd better bury him in the backyard.

(*She starts out.*)

BEATRICE: Don't bury the towel.

(TILLIE *stops, sobs audibly, then gets control.*)

TILLIE: I'll do it in the morning.

(*She gently lays the rabbit near the door. She tucks* RUTH *in on the couch and sits a few minutes by her sleeping sister.*

Music starts in softly as BEATRICE *continues folding napkins with her back to the others.*

There is the sound of someone at the curtained doorway, and NANNY *commences negotiating herself into the room. Slowly she advances with the tubular frame — unaware, desiccated, in some other land.*)

BEATRICE (*weakly*): Matilda?
TILLIE: Yes, Mama?
BEATRICE: I hate the world. Do you know that, Matilda?
TILLIE: Yes, Mama.
BEATRICE: I hate the world.

(*The lights have started down, the music makes its presence known, and a spot clings to* TILLIE. *She moves to the staircase and the rest of the set goes to black during the following speech. As she starts up the stairs her recorded voice takes over as in the opening of the play.*)

TILLIE's VOICE: *The Conclusion:* My experiment has shown some of the strange effects radiation can produce . . . and how dangerous it can be if not handled correctly.

Mr. Goodman said I should tell in this conclusion what my future plans are and how this experiment has helped me make them.

For one thing, the effect of gamma rays on man-in-the-moon marigolds has made me curious about the sun and the stars, for the universe itself must be like a world of great atoms — and I want to know more about it.

But most important, I suppose, my experiment has made me feel important — every atom in me, in everybody, has come from the sun — from places beyond our dreams. The atoms of our hands, the atoms of our hearts . . .

(*All sound out.*

TILLIE *speaks the rest live — hopeful, glowing.*)

Atom.
Atom.
What a beautiful word.

THE END

Most plays deal, in one way or another, with families: Oedipus killed his father and married his mother; King Lear disowns one daughter and is tortured by two others; in *As You Like It* brothers are reconciled and young men and women become husbands and wives. To say that most plays deal with families is only, of course, to say that most plays deal with the impact of people on those nearest to them — parents and children, husbands and wives, brothers and sisters, people in love. To this generalization we can add the first paragraph of Tolstoy's *Anna Karenina*: "All happy families resemble one another; every unhappy family is unhappy in its own way." A debatable idea, of course, but one sees what Tolstoy means: when all of the relationships are right, happiness results, but since any one (or more) of the relationships may not be right (the father may be dominant, or weak, or a philanderer; the mother may be a nag, or a mouse, or a nymphomaniac) there are many special kinds of unhappiness.

Many twentieth-century plays about unhappy families are, by virtue of their abundant concern for young children, markedly different from classical plays about families, where such children scarcely exist. Shakespeare, for example, knowing that children should be seen as little as possible and not heard, wrote very few parts for immature children. (Romeo and Juliet are the chief exceptions, and even they are old enough to marry.) By the time adolescents came to be regarded as a fit subject for literature, i.e., for the contemplation of adults, the novel had become the dominant literary form, with its Oliver Twists and Holden Caulfields; but the drama — ever conservative — held back until about the middle of the twentieth century (with the notable exception of Ibsen), keeping traditional themes and plots: in tragedy, the fall of adults, in comedy, the obstacle race to the altar. But around the middle of the twentieth century the drama caught up with modern thinking and, especially in America where children are less likely than in Europe to continue to hold their parents' ideas and to move into their parents' jobs, the drama now at least occasionally is concerned with children, especially with their psychological states and their roles as victims of their elders.

Marigolds, like a number of other American plays, dramatizes a family unit in which an adult (here, the mother) violently impedes the children's achieving of self-fulfillment. The two daughters, Tillie and Ruth, more or less fall into two modern stage types of children, the Sensitive-but-Sane and the Psychotic. The play is fairly typical too in its relative plotlessness (it is basically a-day-in-the-life-of), its cinematic techniques (e.g., a voice against music, fade-outs), and its black comedy (the talk about psoriasis, boiling a cat, Nanny's bowels, and the somewhat entertaining presentation of the destructive demented mother) but it is almost unique in its final rhapsodic vision of a happy atomic world:

> But most important, I suppose, my experiment has made me feel important — every atom in me, in everybody, has come from the sun — from places beyond our dreams. The atoms of our hands, the atoms of our hearts . . .

Atom.
Atom.
What a beautiful word.

There is irony in the fact that Tillie, the girl who has this vision, is daily subjected to assaults by a desperate mother who does all she can to deny the girl's importance, but the speech itself is unironic, and by showing the freedom of Tillie's mind it provides a happy ending to a play that has shown a world of chaos. Somewhat unfashionably, Zindel takes science and the atom not as symbols of man's alienation and death, but as symbols of man's heavenly origin or his link with the sun, and with only a little exaggeration one can say that the play moves from the chaotic living room of the first stage direction, with its litter, through the mother's crazy dreams of an impossible new life as proprietor of a tea shop, to the uncorrupted daughter's joyful vision of a richly exciting world that shares a single life.

Comedy, Tragedy, and Tragicomedy

Cyrus Hoy

Professor Hoy's essay is chiefly not about a particular dramatic form but about a distinctive vision of the disparity between the ideal and the reality. This vision he finds in the profoundest comedies, which he argues are close to tragedies. He further pursues his argument in a book, *The Hyacinth Room*, which includes discussions of playwrights ranging from Euripides to Ionesco.

In one of the later incidents of the *Satyricon* of Petronius, the disreputable poet Eumolpus relates the story of the widow of Ephesus. It is a well-known tale; Jeremy Taylor related it, in his *Holy Dying*, in the mid-seventeenth century; and in our own time, Christopher Fry has made it the subject of a one-act play, *A Phoenix Too Frequent*. Briefly, the story goes like this: A married woman of Ephesus, famed for her virtue, determines, upon the death of her husband, to immure herself in his underground vault and end her life with his, for she finds her loss unendurable. She is accompanied by a devoted maid, and is hailed throughout the city as "the one true and brilliant example of chastity and love." The ladies spend five days in the tomb without food. At this point, the governor of the province orders some robbers to be crucified near the vault where the widow mourns. A soldier is placed on guard, to watch over the crosses, lest anyone take down a body for burial. When, the next night, he sees a light among the tombs, curiosity leads him to discover its source. Finding the lady weeping over the body of the dead man, he correctly surmises her intentions. Bringing his supper into the tomb, he sets about urging the mourner not to persist in useless grief, but she will not be dissuaded. Neither will she accept his offer of food. But the maid is framed of weaker stuff. She partakes of the soldier's food and drink, and thus refreshed,

sets about to assail her mistress's obstinacy ("What will you gain by all this, if you faint away with hunger, if you bury yourself alive, if you breathe out your undoomed soul before Fate calls for it?"). The lady's resolution is broken; she eats; and then, even as she has been persuaded to live, so is she persuaded to love. The soldier is young, handsome, and eloquent; and the maid, again, is helpful, pleading to her mistress to be gracious ("Wilt thou fight love even when love pleases thee?"). So, in Eumolpus's words, the lady and the soldier pass "not only their wedding night together, but the next and a third, of course shutting the door of the vault, so that any friend or stranger who came to the tomb would imagine that this most virtuous lady had breathed her last over her husband's body." But meanwhile, the parents of one of the crucified robbers, noting that the watch is ill-kept, come in the dark and make off with the body of their man. When the soldier discovers the loss, he is distraught; by the laws of Ephesus, his body must be fixed in the place of the stolen corpse. He explains to the lady what has happened, declaring that he will not wait for a court-martial, but will punish his own neglect with his own hand. It is now the lady's turn to urge the arguments against self-slaughter, and in doing so, she shows herself as practical as she was passionate. "Heaven forbid," she cries, "that I should look at the same moment on the dead bodies of two men whom I love. No, I would rather make a dead man useful, than send a live man to death." Whereupon she orders her hus-

Reprinted by permission of the author from the *Virginia Quarterly Review*.

band's body to be taken out of the coffin and fixed up on the empty cross. "The soldier," says Eumolpus in conclusion, "availed himself of this far-seeing woman's device, and the people wondered the next day by what means the dead man had ascended the cross."

The sailors to whom Eumolpus tells this sophisticated tale greet it with a roar of laughter, which is altogether as it should be, for the irony of the reversal on which the story turns derives from the fine display of the incongruity of human intention and human deed which the Ephesian Widow's tergiversations afford; and incongruity is the essence of comedy. The Widow of Ephesus's high-flown intentions end in an all too human surrender, and her tale is but further testimony to the sad truth that, though the spirit be willing, the flesh is weak. Boundless is the will to do good, but the power of performance is sadly limited; the elevated purpose issues but feebly in action; and the generally inadequate standard of human conduct makes a travesty of the ideals that nourish man's illusions about himself and what he can achieve. The discrepancy between the noble intention and the ignoble deed points directly to the most glaring incongruity in the human condition: that which exists between man as he is, and man as he might be, or as he thinks he might be. "Every man," says Conrad in *The Secret Sharer*, "sets up for himself secretly" an "ideal conception of [his] own personality" to which he would be faithful if he could. The extent to which he is able to keep faith with this ideal of self will go far toward determining his personal destiny. But everything must turn, finally, on the nature of the ideal conception. Is it humanly possible to be faithful to it? If so, is it worth the effort? The questions are relevant, because there is always the possibility that the pursuit of the ideal may turn out to be a delusion and a snare. In a world in which man's purposes are infirm, his knowledge imperfect, and his highest endeavors doomed to issue, ultimately, in death, it is safe to say that any effort to keep faith with the ideal is fated to meet with no more than partial success. The spectacle of man seeking, in despite of all the odds, to fulfill an ideal of self, to live up to his own best intentions, may be a deeply moving and ennobling one; but there comes a point at which the pity that we feel for the embattled idealist gives way to amusement at one who steadfastly refuses to recognize the conditions of his all too

human frailty. Tears turn to laughter as the tragic struggle ends in a rather grotesque effort to transcend the limits of mortality. In one sense it is deeply tragic that the Widow of Ephesus is not able to remain faithful to her ideal of virtuous bereavement; and the fact that she is not might be taken as all too symptomatic of the scurvy tricks that life plays on men and women, undermining their most pious intents, thwarting their most earnest desires, making sport generally of their finest gestures in the direction of heroic virtue. This is the great irony of life: that man can envision an ideal of good, can passionately desire to achieve it, and yet fails to live up to it. The failure can occasion either tears or laughter: tears in recognition of the fact that this is the way life is; laughter at the folly of those who fail to recognize that this is the way life is. The protagonists of tragedy and comedy alike are deficient in their knowledge of human limitations, of what they can hope to achieve and what it is the better part of wisdom not to attempt. In a word, they are lacking in self-knowledge. But there is this difference: that while the tragic protagonist's lack of self-knowledge leads to destruction, the comic protagonist's lack of self-knowledge leads instead to a rude awakening in which he is made aware — often cruelly so — of the truth about himself, and is left to live with it — often a fate worse than death. This at least is true of the protagonists of the greatest comedy: plays that probe so deeply into the irony of human fate as to bring them close upon tragedy. By comic protagonists in this sense I have in mind characters such as Jonson's Volpone, Shakespeare's Angelo in *Measure for Measure*, Molière's Alceste in *Le Misanthrope*, Chekhov's Uncle Vanya, Pirandello's Henry IV. Since all these characters are found in plays that are generally regarded as inhabiting the border regions between tragedy and comedy, and since the term "comedy" generally connotes either farce or comedy of manners, it will be best to label such characters "tragicomic," reserving the adjective "comic" for the Widow of Ephesus and her kind.

She is decidedly not tragic. When her noble intentions collapse, and she goes the way of all flesh, we are not moved to pity; we merely shake our heads knowingly. But her failure to fulfill her ideal of virtue, to remain faithful to her particular conception of self, is fraught with tragic potential. This will be clear if we turn to another lady, also possessed of an ideal of virtuous bereavement, and listen as she declares her intention — not, in this case, to immolate herself on her husband's tomb — but never to re-marry upon her husband's death.

> Nor earth to me give food, nor heaven light,
> Sport and repose lock from me day and night,
> To desperation turn my trust and hope,
> An anchor's cheer in prison be my scope,
> Each opposite that blanks the face of joy,
> Meet what I would have well, and it destroy,
> Both here and hence pursue me lasting strife,
> If once a widow ever I be wife.

The speaker here is, of course, the Player Queen in *Hamlet* (III,2,214 ff.), and in the presence of her, we are but one short step from tragedy; for the Player Queen, as everyone knows, is but a thin disguise for the real Queen Gertrude. The Player King responds to his wife's grandiloquence in respectful but guarded tones:

> I do believe you think what now you speak,
> But what we do determine oft we break.
> Purpose is but the slave to memory,
> Of violent birth but poor validity,

and he continues with a succession of epigrammatic couplets, each having reference to the discrepancy between human intention and deed:

> What to ourselves in passion we propose.
> The passion ending, doth the purpose lose.
>
> .   .   .
>
> Our wills and fates do so contrary run,
> That our devices still are overthrown;
> Our thoughts are ours, their ends none of our
>   own. . . .

Gertrude, viewing the scene, declares that "the lady doth protest too much," and her words have the ring of one who knows whereof she speaks. She has heard all this before, having presumably made similar protestations to the dead King Hamlet. Her ideal of self, if she can be truly said ever to have possessed one, has been shattered, and whatever the effect of this on Gertrude herself, it has precipitated the tragedy of her son.

What our argument comes to, then, is this: that in serious drama, comic or tragic, we are confronted with what is, at bottom, a single truth about the human condition. Man is possessed of an ideal of human conduct, but circumstances together with his own inherent failings conspire to make the belief that the ideal can be fulfilled a finally illusory one. But man persists in despite of all the odds, and in his persistence he may appear as nobly enduring, stubbornly unyielding, foolishly blind, or a combination of all three. The more forcibly and apparently these diverse qualities are linked in combination, the more surely sounds the note of tragicomedy.

As an example of the fully developed tragicomic protagonist, there is the figure of the already mentioned Angelo in Shakespeare's *Measure for Measure*. In the context of the play as a whole, Angelo cannot be viewed as the protagonist of *Measure for Measure*; that rôle clearly falls to the Duke Vincentio, and Angelo must be cast in the rôle of antagonist, both to the Duke and to Isabella. But in the context of the drama that goes forth within the soul of Angelo — which is all that I am concerned with here — Angelo, or the part of him which passes in public under this name, is engaged in desperate struggle with his baser self, his private devil. He is well named; and his name gives us the clue to what he aspires to be, which is nothing less than angelic. He would deny his bodily nature, with all that that implies, for in his ideal conception of himself, he sees himself as one beyond the reach of physical desire, as proof against the clamorous demands of human passion. Since the unique quality in the nature of man is precisely his duality, Angelo, in denying the sensual half of his being, is in effect denying his very humanity. In this respect, the comments made about him by the other characters in the play are instructive. The Duke, for instance, makes some penetrating observations on the character of his Deputy in I,3, when he visits the Friar's cell after his supposed departure from Vienna:

> Lord Angelo is precise;
> Stands at a guard with envy; scarce confesses
> That his blood flows; or that his appetite
> Is more to bread than stone: hence shall we
>   see,
> If power change purpose — what our seemers
>   be.
>
> (I,3,50 ff.)

And Lucio, the fantastic, characterizes him in similar terms for the benefit of Isabella in the following scene (I,4) — the only occasion in the play when the usually foul-mouthed courtier and the righteous Duke are in accord:

> Lord Angelo; a man whose blood
> Is very snow-broth; one who never feels
> The wanton stings and motions of the sense;
> But doth rebate and blunt his natural edge
> With profits of the mind, study and fast.
> (I,4,57 ff.)

But the blood, the very seat of life, which Angelo has sought to deny, will assert itself in the end. "Blood, thou art blood," says Angelo in grim if belated acceptance of a truth he has sought long to ignore; and with that, the struggle that has been waged within him ends in the capitulation of his ideal self to his basest instincts. The angel and the devil have fought, and the devil has won. "Let's write 'good Angel' on the devil's horn, / 'Tis now the devil's crest," he says in conclusion (II,4,16–17). In striving to be more than man, he has ended a good deal less. Recognizing this truth, he puts it to use in the course of his temptation of Isabella later in the same scene (II,4,134–5): "Be that you are," he urges her, "That is, a woman; if you be more, you're none." But she will not be corrupted, and Angelo turns from persuasion to threats. If he cannot be an angel, he will be a very demon of the flesh: "I have begun, / And now I give my sensual race the rein," he announces, and then proceeds to state the terms on which Isabella can redeem her brother. His fall is complete, and thereafter he has forfeited any share in the divine — the angelic — nature which man might justly claim. One of the Duke's octosyllabic couplets near the end of III,2 notes with appropriate horror the infamy that is here:

> O, what may man within him hide,
> Though angel on the outward side.

And at the beginning of V,1, when the Duke refers Isabella to Angelo for justice, she calls him by his own name: "O worthy duke, / You bid me seek redemption of the devil." When the truth has been revealed, and he stands forth in his shame, he judges himself with unsparing severity; "immediate sentence . . . and sequent death" is all the grace he begs (V,1,369–70). And he is still craving "death more willingly than mercy" ("'Tis my deserving, and I do entreat it") in the last lines that he speaks in the play (V,1,472–3). By then he is a strangely dignified and absurd figure: dignified for the manner in which he endures his shame, absurd in the willful blindness through which he has brought it on himself. He has been duped on every hand — by the Duke, by Isabella, by Mariana — he who has seemed to be so thoroughly in command both of himself and of events around him. His reputation for "gravity" (in which, as he admits himself in hushed tones on one occasion, he takes pride) falls from him, and he stands exposed: a singularly unsuccessful lecher, and that when he has reached years of discretion, too. Nothing less than the dignity of death could make him an object of tragic pity, and Shakespeare has denied him that, leaving him instead clutching the tatters of his unyielding pride, stubbornly reiterating his request for death as the only proper punishment for his offenses, and having it denied him. He is doomed not to get what he seeks. The incongruity that I have already stated to be of the essence of comedy is grimly apparent here in the incongruous distance that separates Angelo's pride from Angelo's shame — that separates Angelo as he is, and Angelo as he thinks he might have been, and this is surely the principal reason why *Measure for Measure* is one of Shakespeare's grimmest plays.

The grimness is intensified because Angelo's ideal of self-righteous virtue is such a false one: false both because virtue of the thoroughgoing kind that he has sought is beyond human achievement, and because it is not altogether desirable that it should be within human reach. He has shown himself lamentably ignorant in the knowledge of self, which is to say, in the knowledge of what a man is, and to what he can legitimately aspire. He has draped himself in a cloak of self-righteous virtue, and in it he cuts as ill a figure as does Malvolio in his crossgarters and yellow stockings. And the comparison does not end there, for Malvolio is but a shallower Angelo: more vain, and with even less to justify his vanity. Still, if we do not feel for Angelo the tragic pity that we accord a Hamlet or an Othello or a Lear, we do pity him nonetheless. His ideal is at once so right and so wrong: right because it is surely proper for man to aspire to virtue, wrong because it can never be proper for him to aspire to it self-righteously. It is wrong, too, in the sense that it is the wrong ideal for him. Angelo's ideal conception of self is an ascetic ideal, and in his blindness and his pride, he never sees that he is not the ascetic type. He is no more capable of asceticism than the Widow of Ephesus was of sacrificing herself to her husband's memory, or than the Player Queen — to say nothing of Queen Gertrude — was of refraining from a second marriage. He has deceived himself about human limitations generally, and his personal limitations in particular. And the final crushing irony is that the very things Angelo has sought most feverishly to avoid — the sensual, the physical, the passionate — are precisely the objects of his most secret longings. He is in the terrible position of one who is inwardly seeking the very things that his conscious will has pledged itself to avoid.

Angelo's position is terrible, but because he is a single figure, and that not the principal one, in a larger scene, we are not shown the full intensity of its terror. For that, we must turn to Greek tragedy, and to the *Bacchae* of Euripides. In the figure of Pentheus, the Theban king who opposes himself to Dionysus, we have the tragic extreme of the tragicomic Angelo, even as Malvolio is the comic extreme. Malvolio, Angelo, Pentheus: what these three very diverse characters have in common is what comedy, tragicomedy, and tragedy have in common. All three are possessed of an ideal of virtuous conduct which is more or less febrile as they are more or less tragic, but an ideal which nonetheless fails, all along the line, to square with the facts of life. In their virtuous zeal, they are dedicated to imposing their ideal of conduct upon the world that lies within their charge, be this the kingdom of Thebes, the city of Vienna, or the lower domestic regions of the Lady Olivia's house in Illyria; they are determined that, because they are virtuous, there shall be no more cakes and ale. All three are humiliated for their presumption. For Malvolio, the humiliation is an end in itself; for Angelo, it involves the shame of public exposure; for Pentheus, it is the prelude to a terrible death.

In seeking to prevent the introduction of Dionysiac rites into Thebes, Pentheus is by implication seeking to deny the existence of the Dionysiac principle in man, even as he has sought to deny its existence in himself. He would prohibit the women of Thebes from participating in the Bacchic ceremonies on Mount Cithaeron, which he is convinced are only a pretext for gatherings of lecherous men and lewd women, just as Angelo decrees that all

"the houses of resort" in the suburbs of Vienna be pulled down. As guardians of the public morality, there is much to be said for both; the difficulty is that they would impose restrictions on the conduct of human life which mortal flesh is not able to endure. Seeking to realize a perhaps noble but illusory ideal of life, they are in fact enemies of life. Pompey, the part tapster, part bawd of *Measure for Measure*, says that if Angelo would enforce the laws against immorality in Vienna, he must "geld and splay all the youth in the city," which may be a sad comment on human nature, but is nonetheless true. And the case is even clearer in the *Bacchae*, where Pentheus stands forth as the open enemy of Dionysus, the god of earthly fertility. Pentheus, in his pride, like Angelo, would legislate human weakness out of existence; he would deliver mankind from the infirmities of the flesh by fiat; and he must inevitably pay the price of such presumption. The Chorus comments appropriately:

They who in pride pretend
Beyond man's limit, will lose what lay
Close to their hand and sure.
(lines 396–8)

And later in the same ode the Chorus speaks of the happiness of him who is

Watchful to keep aloof both mind and heart
From men whose pride claims more than mortals may.
(lines 427–8)

The task that Pentheus has appointed himself is impossible for any man to accomplish; it is the more so for him, being the kind of man he is. For Pentheus, like Angelo, is fatally drawn to the very pleasures of human life which he seeks most fervently to deny, both in himself and others. Again the final, crushing — here altogether tragic — irony: the Dionysiac principle against which Pentheus has vowed eternal enmity is strong in him, so strong that through its operation the king is lured to his own destruction. There comes the terrible scene in which god and king confront each other. It is the measure of Pentheus's blindness that he fails throughout the play to recognize Dionysus as the god in person (just as he has refused to acknowledge Dionysus's deity), and he persists in mistaking the figure before him as a mere Bacchic priest. Bit by bit, as he and the god converse, Pentheus betrays an all too passionate interest in the details of the Bacchic revels, and the god is quick to seize upon this. Would the king care to view the revels at first hand, he asks; and Pentheus confesses that he would. It can be arranged, says the god, but the king must disguise himself as a bacchanal, lest he be recognized as an interloper. The king, who is by now altogether under the god's sway, consents; and he appears a little later clad in woman's clothes, thyrsus in hand and fawnskin draped about him, ready to go. Thus bedizened, the grave and dignified king is led by the god through the streets of Thebes, en route to Mount Cithaeron. Having been humiliated in the eyes of his people (shades of Malvolio in his cross garters and yellow stockings) he is ready for the slaughter at the hands of the bacchae, with his mother at their head.

The principle of fertility, of life, has asserted itself and triumphed, as it always does. The enemies of life have been vanquished, even as they always are, whether the enemies of life take the form of a Pentheus, an Angelo, or one of the wretched old men — the perpetual enemy of youth and vitality — who would prevent the marriage of the young lovers, and who are eternally appearing in comedy, from Menander through Plautus and Terence to the present. Comedy notoriously ends in marriage, even as tragedy typically ends in death; and the dance with which comedy traditionally closes — even such a sophisticated piece as *The Way of the World* has one — is something of an act of faith, an affirmation that life, in spite of its follies and its miseries, is worthwhile, and worthy to be perpetuated. Comedy implies, then, an acceptance of life, which implies as well an acceptance of man, and to accept man, one must be prepared to forgive all the weakness and the treachery and the downright depravity which, in spite of man's best intentions, he is continually guilty of. To accept and to forgive, one must be, above everything else, clear-sighted about what man is, and what can be properly expected of him. Only then will one refrain from asking the impossible, of himself and of others, and being plunged into the depths of tragic despair when the impossible is not achieved. Comedy is nothing if not hardheadedly realistic about the nature of man and the nature of human life; but it can also be compassionate in its forgiveness and its acceptance of human failings, because it recognizes the existence of these. That is why the burden of com-

edy, again and again, turns on the need for man to undeceive himself about the limitations of humanity, to see life for what it is, and to make the best of it.

For a fine demonstration of this double theme of acceptance and forgiveness in the terms of sheerest comedy, it is tempting to turn to the operatic stage, and da Ponte's libretto for Mozart's *Così fan tutte*. It is an elegant, rather cynical, and yet finally compassionate performance, and it stands squarely in the tradition of great comedy. We are confronted with two pairs of lovers: the sisters Fiordiligi and Dorabella, and their respective gallants, Guglielmo and Ferrando. The gentlemen have a cynical old bachelor friend, Don Alfonso, who assures them that, if their ladies are faithful, it is only because they have not had occasion to be otherwise. The lovers, in the fullness of their simplicity, laugh him to scorn; but then to vindicate their faith and prove the folly of Don Alfonso's suspicions, they agree to put their ladies to the test that he suggests. They announce to the sisters that they have been called to the wars, and bid them a tearful farewell, amid many protestations of eternal devotion and faith on both sides. After the lovers' departure, the sisters are prostrated with grief, Dorabella viewing her condition as especially terrible:

> Relentless infatuation which thrills my very soul and will not cease till I die of grief. What a wretched example of tragic love shall I give the Eumenides if I manage to live through the horrible sound of my own sighs,

she sings. But Don Alfonso promptly goes to work. The sisters have a maid, even as the Widow of Ephesus had, and Don Alfonso bribes this soubrette, named Despina, to introduce two friends into the presence of her mistresses as prospective lovers. The two new suitors are, of course, Guglielmo and Ferrando, disguised as Albanian noblemen. Despina complies, but the sisters are indignant that she should presume so much, and the lovers' proposals are scornfully rejected. They are sent away, but they return shortly, announcing that if the ladies will not be kind, they will not live; whereupon they drink a reportedly poisonous concoction, and fall to the ground. The sisters are distraught; they call a doctor who appears (it is Despina in disguise) and restores the lovers to life. The ladies are impressed at such devotion, but still faithful to their first vows at the conclusion of Act I. But in the second act, their fall is accomplished. First Dorabella gives way to the advances of Guglielmo, then Fiordiligi yields to the suit of Ferrando. When the lovers compare notes, and find that their respective mistresses have proved false, they are plunged into gloom; that "all those tears, promises, and sighs and vows" should be utterly forgotten in so short a time! They are dedicated to vengeance. But Don Alfonso takes them in hand with timely advice: women are weak, they must not be blamed; young, old, pretty or ugly, they all do it. And he makes them repeat with him: "*Così fan tutte!*" Meanwhile, the sisters are prepared to marry their Albanian suitors. The farce is played through to the end, until the lovers throw off their disguises and confront the ladies with their perfidy. The sisters are overcome with shame, and court their punishment in terms worthy of an Angelo: "punish my guilt with death. I see my faults too late. With that sword pierce this unworthy breast," they sing together. All turn on Don Alfonso, who has engineered the deception. He freely admits it, and justifies having done so, thus pointing the moral of the piece:

> I deceived you [addressing the sisters], but it was to undeceive your lovers, who will be wiser in future. Take my advice, join hands, you are betrothed. Kiss and be friends.

To the credit of them all, they have the wit to do just this, and the opera ends with a final chorus that sums up the wisdom which it is the special province of comedy to celebrate, even as it is the common purpose of comedy, tragedy, and tragicomedy to delineate the sundry consequences that follow when that wisdom is lacking:

> Happy the man who accepts life as it really is, and in all its ups and downs takes a reasonable view; who can laugh when others weep and finds peace in the midst of the world's tumult!

Comedy and Tragedy Transposed

Ellen Douglass Leyburn

Surveying mid-twentieth-century drama, Professor Leyburn suggests that absurd comedy has taken over from tragedy the presentation of rather sympathetic characters in extreme situations and that tragedy (e.g., the plays of Arthur Miller and Tennessee Williams), having been drained of grandeur, now tends to present the small, unsympathetic characters traditionally associated with comedy.

The remark of Socrates at the end of the *Symposium* that the genius of tragedy and comedy are the same has usually been taken as a joking paradox meant to round off gaily a night of talking and drinking. Yet its measure of truth has haunted responses to the supreme achievements in drama. The heightening of the tragedy of Lear by the Fool, "who labours to outjest his heart-struck injuries," on the one hand, and the deepening of the comedy of *Le Misanthrope* through the suffering of Alceste, on the other, are enough to make us pause before dismissing the remark of Socrates. Plato's jest, if indeed it be jest, seems nearer to the truth of what we find in postclassical drama than does Aristotle's strict separation of tragedy and comedy.

Nevertheless, we have had the feeling until recently that when we used the terms, we knew at least vaguely what they meant and could be understood by others when we used them to distinguish kinds of drama which were distinct even when they appeared in the same play. The assumption that tragedy is one dramatic mode and comedy another has been the foundation of all the varied and elaborate structures of definition of both genres. And the same assumption persists in the proliferation of analyses of the death of tragedy which have followed Joseph Wood Krutch's lament over the paralysis of tragic power in modern man in his much-quoted chapter called "The Tragic Fallacy," which

appeared as long ago as the Twenties and fits the whole thesis of his book *The Modern Temper*. The very force of Krutch's indictment grows from his knowing so clearly what he thinks the demands of tragedy are and wherein modern drama is deficient. This clarity of conviction about the nature of tragedy is equally marked in more recent treatments of the same theme, such as William Van O'Connor's *Climates of Tragedy*, which appeared during the Second World War, and George Steiner's *The Death of Tragedy*, which has appeared still more recently. The same assurance marks criticism of comedy. However varied their definitions, the critics resemble each other in seeming to know what it is they are defining.

What I should like to suggest is that in modern drama comedy has so far invaded tragedy — and tragedy, comedy — that the terms have lost their old distinctness. Whereas comedy has for centuries displayed man's weakness, this now seems to be the function of tragedy — or of drama which is intended to arouse the emotions commonly called tragic, whatever new name we try to find for the plays of Tennessee Williams or Arthur Miller or John Osborne. Whereas tragedy has in earlier eras looked at man in "boundary situations," it is now the comedies of Beckett and Ionesco which show man in extremity; and the equally terrifying plays of Pinter and Duerrenmatt make use of grotesque comedy to reveal the precariousness of life and the condition of man confronted with pervasive evil. Duerrenmatt's note on *The Visit* ends: "*The Visit of the Old Lady* is a wicked play, yet for this very reason it must not be presented wickedly, but most humanely, with sadness, not with anger, but also with humor, for nothing harms this comedy — which ends tragically — more than brutal seriousness." Tragedy and comedy seem to have shifted not only in perspective and in substance, but also in effect. Our responses are almost the reverse of what used to be the conventional attitudes to tragedy and comedy. We resist tragic identification with the miserable characters of most of our serious drama and look at them with the detachment which has hitherto seemed appropriate to critical comedy. Conversely, the comedies that end tragically compel us into a strange and unwilling empathy rather than into comic judgment: in the seemingly odd characters we recognize our most familiar selves, and in their fantastic plights, the very situations in which we are involved.

The dramatists of the absurd are clearly conscious of this interpenetration of tragedy and comedy and deliberately exploit its disturbing imaginative effect. Ionesco makes the illuminating statement: "Personally, I have never understood the distinctions that are made between the comic and the tragic. Since the comic is the intuition of the absurd, it seems to me more hopeless than the tragic. . . . The comic offers no escape . . . the comical is tragic, and the tragedy of man, derisory." Ionesco's assertion is highly characteristic not just of his own attitude, repeatedly expressed in comments on his plays and manifested in the plays themselves, but also of the mood of much of the drama of the absurd besides his own. The writers of serious plays, on the contrary, seem unaware of the intrusion of comic elements into their pathetic worlds. They solemnly present their small characters and seem to demand for them the large emotional response aroused by tragedy. This unawareness confuses the artistic effect of their plays; but it is in itself an impressive demonstration of the pervasiveness of the interpenetration of tragedy and comedy which marks the drama of our time. The shifts in the nature of both tragedy and comedy reflect the convulsion of society and of man's sense of himself which characterizes the world which the dramatists inhabit.

Arthur Miller and Tennessee Williams are perhaps the most striking examples of contemporary dramatists who consider themselves writers of tragedies and yet have produced plays in which the themes and characters resemble those of earlier critical comedy. There are almost as many contradictions as theories among definitions of tragedy; but two criteria which are consistently used by critics with otherwise extremely diverse theories are that tragedy should have a hero with stature enough to make his suffering significant and that its course of action should produce enlightenment. Neither of these criteria is fulfilled, I think, by the plays of Williams and Miller. The protagonists arouse pity, but little admiration and little of the identification necessary for tragic terror; and in the rhythm of the plays the emphasis is largely on passion rather than on purpose and perception. On the other hand, both dramatists focus their plays on the very kind of human weakness which has hitherto been the subject of critical or realistic comedy. The self-deception of their leading characters is of the sort which earlier dramatists have held up to ridicule. It is the anomaly of a pathetic view of characters formerly seen as objects of satire which makes the difficulty for the traditionalist in responding to such plays according to the authors' intentions. The contradictory feelings which the characters evoke seem to me more important than their sheer inadequacy as tragic heroes so much stressed by Krutch and his followers. The discrepancy between expectation and event for such characters lacks the kind of irony which has been thought of as tragic; and of enlightenment there is little or none. *Death of a Salesman* and *A Streetcar Named Desire*, each the most successful play of its author, well illustrate all of these points.

It was in answer to the criticism of Willy Loman as a tragic hero that Miller wrote "Tragedy and the Common Man" to serve as introduction to a Viking Press edition of *Death of a Salesman*. His contention is that "the common man is as apt a subject for tragedy in its highest sense as kings were," a judgment with which in our day few would quarrel. It is not Willy's low station, but his low intelligence (or if intelligence seems too narrow a word, his lack of sheer force of being) which keeps his woes from affecting us as do those of Orestes, Hamlet, Medea, and Macbeth — the tragic figures of the past whom Miller cites. "Ineffectual" is the word which seems to characterize Willy both as salesman and as father. His constant need of bolstering from both Linda and Charley and his pitiful efforts to win the respect of Biff in order to feed his own self-esteem make it strange for Miller to say in reference to him that "the tragic hero is intent upon claiming his whole due as a personality," though Willy's personality is so small that the comment has a kind of unintentional irony. Even apart from the hallucinated scenes with Ben and the suggestions of actual insanity, Willy's characteristic state is bewilderment. He enters the play puzzled by his fruitless effort to reach his territory, and he leaves it persuading himself that Biff will be "magnificent . . . with twenty thousand dollars in his pocket." The lack of integrity which has made him teach Biff to steal seems to be the result of inability to distinguish truth from falsehood rather than of deliberate dishonesty. Biff, who for all his limitations comes much nearer to self-realization than his father does, tries to open Willy's eyes: "The man don't know who we are! The man is gonna know! (To Willy) We never told the truth for ten minutes in this house! . . . Pop! I'm a dime a dozen, and so are you!" But Biff's tears simply send Willy into a new "phony dream"; and the son's comment at his father's grave is: "Charley, the man didn't know who he was." This hardly fits Miller's conception of tragedy as "a man's total compulsion to evaluate himself justly." Rather, Willy's self-deception, although Miller treats it so as to win compassion, is of exactly the sort which has regularly marked the comic figure. Even his physical defects of fatness and flabbiness which make the salesman laugh at him and call him "walrus" and his loudmouthed over-heartiness of manner identify him with a long line of aging comic butts who have tried to convince an unbelieving world and themselves that they are "well liked." It is worth notice in passing that A View from the Bridge again depicts a man past middle age who has no power to "evaluate himself justly" and that in the later play sexual jealousy over a young girl brings the pathetic protagonist even nearer to one of the stereotypes of comedy.

The counterpart to the amorous old fool in traditional comedy has been the woman who tries to trade upon fading sexual attractiveness; and it is this forumula which Williams transmutes into the heartrending character of Blanche DuBois. Like Willy, she seeks and is given bolstering from the other characters; and Stella, like Linda in Salesman, not only gives the needed compliments but urges the other characters to tell Blanche how pretty her finery is and how fresh and attractive she looks. But Williams is more willing than Miller is to let harsh judgment of his weakling have expression in the play. Willy hears the voice of reality largely through the kindly tones of Charley, who does tell him to grow up, but endures his insults and gives him money under the fiction of weekly loans, whereas Blanche has to listen to the taunts of Stella's husband, whom she regards as "subhuman." Miller depends primarily on Willy's own self-revelation to show the audience the discrepancies between Willy as he is and Willy as he thinks he is. Williams, in contrast, uses the harsh judgment of Stanley not only to add to Blanche's misery, but also to enlighten the audience about her "lies and conceit and tricks." The conflict between the dream and the grim reality is thus accentuated through the hostility of the character who reveals the ugly truth. By giving Blanche a personal antagonist when she is already incapable of coping with her inner plight and has "run for protection . . . from under one leaky roof to another leaky roof — because it was storm — all storm, and [she] was — caught in the center," Williams intensifies her woe and provides the bitter irony of her seeking shelter under the roof of her sharpest critic. At the same time, the audience is made to see her partly through Stanley's eyes. He becomes a kind of satiric chorus within the play, which heightens the anomaly of our being asked to respond with tragic emotions to so wretched a figure as Blanche. But Stanley is far more than simply an interpreter. It is he who, through his cruel disillusioning of Mitch, makes Blanche lose what tenuous hold on reality she has had and brings about her final desolate departure to the mental hospital, still trying to enact the part of the gracious lady, depending on "the kindness of strangers."

Both of these plays are full of irony, even of the irony of fate; but we miss the grandeur which pits the tragic hero against his fate and leads to tragic irony. There is a strong element of the ludicrous which makes the plights of both Willy and Blanche more painful. Fate, in the form of the social order, does seem to have played a cruel joke on the simple-minded and well-meaning Willy Loman in giving him the false goals of success through personality and of getting away with whatever can be filched. In his refusal to be enlightened by Biff, he does seem to go off to his useless suicide as the dupe of a power he cannot combat. Blanche is equally the victim of a hideous practical joke. She is ridiculous in her effort to charm the naïve Mitch with her pretense of innocence. And in her case, the fate which finally tricks her takes the very palpable form of Stanley, though the state to which she has been reduced before the play begins can be called a joke played on her by fate in the form of the social order, just as society has largely represented fate for Willy. But both are too weak to achieve a tragic protest. Since they are simply victims, the irony leaves us uncomfortable at the advantage taken of weakness rather than filled with awe at heroic man confronting mysterious forces within him and without. The ambivalence of the response to both plays comes from the fact that the protagonists are self-deluded enough to seem appropriate objects of mockery; but they are too miserable and too sympathetically viewed by their creators to allow the audience to feel as comic the irony in what happens to them. Consequently, the plays present a seemingly double vision on the part of the playwrights and have a disconcertingly mixed effect.

This kind of apparently unintentional doubleness marks a great number of contemporary plays. It would be easy to link many other soberly treated characters, such as the disagreeable ones of John Osborne or the sentimentalized ones of William Inge, with the traditional figures of critical comedy. The plays of Williams and Miller seem more impressive demonstrations of the penetration of serious drama by comic types only because Williams and Miller seem to make larger tragic claims.

Since the writers of absurd comedy are highly conscious of the doubleness of their plays and use it with full artistic awareness and often with great artistic skill, their plays are much more profoundly disturbing than are those of the humorless writers of serious plays with weak heroes. The contradictions of pain and amusement in the best comedies of the absurd are evoked with clear intention and the most deliberate finesse. Ionesco is the playwright who has been most explicit about his conception of the theatre as the mirror of the contradictions of life: "I try to project on the stage my inner conflict (incomprehensible to myself) telling myself always that, the microcosm being the image of the macrocosm, it can be that this in-

terior world, broken, disarticulated, is in some way the mirror or the symbol of universal contradictions." It is the absurdity, the tragic comedy, of life itself of which these dramatists seek to make their plays the image. The surface effect of most of their plays is comic; but the vision which informs it is largely tragic. Martin Esslin in *The Theatre of the Absurd* quotes Pinter's comment: "The point about tragedy is that it is *no longer* funny." The writers of the "funny" plays of our time are concerned with the same ultimate questions about man's identity and his destiny which in earlier periods have led to the writing of tragedy. One after another of the plays of Beckett and Ionesco, of Pinter and Duerrenmatt, show man in extremity and posing ultimate questions about his very existence: who he is, why he lives, and why he suffers. Yet these plays which reach no comic resolution and raise ultimate rather than temporal questions are clearly comic in the sense of being outrageously funny. The farcical element in the dramaturgy, with its dependence on mime and music-hall slapstick devices, has been much discussed. My concern here is not with the arts the playwrights use to evoke laughter; but with the fact that the plays do evoke it and use it exactly to sharpen the terror. Comedy is an essential part of the situations presented and makes their desperateness more real. The seemingly meaningless repetitions of the dialogue — as skilful a use of language as the most florid passages in heroic drama, the clowning and dependence on farcical gesture, the monopolizing of the stage by objects, bear an organic relation to the absurd situations and are the very means by which the dramatists produce the feeling (to quote Ionesco again) that "in a space without space, all seems to be volatilized, all is *menaced* [my italics] . . . by an imminent, silent engulfment, in I know not what abyss, beyond day and beyond night." The plays as wholes present comic incongruity raised to tragic proportions and effecting in the audience tragic involvement and the tragic feelings of pity and terror. Because of the intense reality of these dramas and because they do raise more fundamental questions, the mixture of feelings they produce is nearer to the old tragic emotion than that of contemporary plays of solely tragic intention. Again, two very familiar plays offer proof of all the points suggested. *Waiting for Godot* and *The Chairs* are both funny and terrible.

The two tramps in Beckett's play are preoccupied with the question which confronts all men and has lately been asked more insistently perhaps than ever before: why live at all? Indeed, their recurrent attempts at suicide make one of the unifying repetitions in the circular motion of the play, if their painfully funny frustrations of action can be called motion. They debate the question of *The Myth of Sisyphus* and seem to stumble upon a measure of Camus's answer. For if they do not decide to live and protest, their very persistence in waiting constitutes a kind of protest. They differ from Camus, of course, in not being sure that Godot will *not* come in spite of their continually baffled hopes. This refusal quite to accept the logic of their own experience is part of what makes us enter into their situation with the kind of identification we accord to tragic characters. It does not require the constant reminders Beckett puts into their mouths that "We are all humanity," to make us recognize ourselves in their already battered state and in the beatings and subjection to physical infirmity within the play. We are drawn to them not just by their clowning and by our amusement at the brisk turns of stichomythia with which they try to amuse themselves. They are irresistibly appealing in their uneasy need of each other, in their very endurance of what we must endure. And we give them the kind of empathy which we withhold from Willy Loman and Blanche DuBois.

The old couple in *The Chairs* ask the still more elementary question of who we are. They show man not just at the limits of his being as man, but beyond identity; and yet in their need to affirm their identity, to leave some message, they too compel us to ally ourselves with them. The frenzy of their attempts to establish connection with the "real" invisible characters and their being crowded apart even from each other by the oppressive multiplication of chairs make vivid their inability to exist even before their suicide in the dank waters that surround their island. Their own progressive loss of the power of articulate speech and the inane babblings of the dumb orator whom they leave as their surrogate are the audible counterpart of the visual image. The laughter which Ionesco evokes by the farcical movement and by the ridiculous echoing "orphan-dworfan" speech, which finally becomes the "Arf . . . arf . . . arf" of helpless barking, makes the tragic effect much deeper than could a direct appeal to the pity and terror in which the search for identity involves us.

The shifting of ground in the realms of tragedy and comedy poses for contemporary critics an awkward problem of terminology. The old phrases like "mixed drama" and "tragicomedy," which sufficed to describe the combination in one play of known and recognizable modes, have little relevance to the strange new genres which seem to be evolving. Furthermore, while the serious plays with weak characters and the comic plays which move us tragically seem to be opposite and complementary parts of the same phenomenon, the dramatic rendering of the dislocation of our times, they are so different in substance and in effect that no one term could conceivably embrace both. The rather cumbersome phrase "Theatre of the Absurd," to which Esslin's book with that title has given wider currency, is useful for the funny plays of tragic import; *The Dark Comedy*, the title of the valuable study by J. L. Styan, which has appeared since this essay was first written, supplies another usable designation; but no new term seems to have been invented for the corresponding and opposite kind of plays which treat ridiculous characters pathetically. As we grope toward nomenclature and definition (a groping perhaps not unrelated to the struggles of Ionesco's characters with language) we come back broodingly to Plato's joke at the end of the *Symposium*: "the chief thing which he remembered was Socrates compelling the other two to acknowledge that the genius of comedy was the same with that of tragedy, and that the true artist in tragedy was an artist in comedy also. To this they were constrained to assent, being drowsy, and not quite following the argument."

THE SCRIPT AND THE STAGE

Peter Arnott

The dramatic author writing his play is engaged in the same one-to-one relationship as the artist with his canvas or the sculptor with his block of stone. He shapes his material as his particular genius dictates, and is responsive only to those imperatives that he decides to set himself. The production of a play, however, is a much more complex process, involving a variety of factors, and a number of professional skills, each of which may influence the way in which the work is finally presented to the public. Theater is community, and the author must resign himself to being merely one, and not necessarily the most important member, of the group.

Of whom does this group consist? In the modern theater, the production of a play normally involves, besides the author, the director and his assistants; the actors; the set and costume designer (who may not be the same person); the lighting designer; and a stage staff responsible for the mechanical execution of the project. Although these elements have always been present, in some degree, in the theater, their relative importance has changed over the centuries, and it is necessary to consider which held first place when the play was originally conceived.

THE AUTHOR

For those accustomed to think of a play primarily as a work of literature, it comes as a shock to learn that, at some of the most productive periods of the theater, the author was by no means the most important figure. In Elizabethan London, for example, the playwright was often no more than a hack, turning out material on demand as the company's needs and the public taste dictated. As well as writing his own material, he was expected to collaborate with others, to be able to work up a scenario suggested by someone else, or to write new scenes to freshen an old play. Once his work had been sold to the company, he had no further financial interest in it, and no artistic control. Several plays which enjoyed a long life in the Elizabethan public playhouse have come down to us as patchwork pieces, continually revised or added to by different hands over the years. For a long time plays, however distinguished, were not considered as literature. It was not until Ben Jonson had the effrontery to publish his dramatic with his non-dramatic works that the playwright's status began to show a change. French playwrights of the seventeenth century were the first who found themselves able to charge substantial sums for their works, and the first, tentative beginnings of the modern system of author's royalties appear at the same time.

THE ACTORS

In the modern commercial theater, actors are normally cast for each new production on an *ad hoc* basis. When the play closes they go their separate ways, and though their paths may sometimes recross, it may well be that

About the author: PETER ARNOTT was born and educated in Great Britain, where he received degrees from the University of Wales and Oxford University. Currently professor of drama and chairman of the Drama Department at Tufts University, he has written numerous books on the theater and on ancient civilizations. Arnott is also an actor, director, and the creator of the Marionette Theater of Peter Arnott, which specializes in performing Greek drama for audiences throughout the continent.

This essay is published here for the first time with permission from the author, Peter Arnott.

they never meet on the stage again. There are, of course, important exceptions to this. The national theaters of various countries — the United States still does not have one — try to retain at least the nucleus of a permanent company for a period of years. In France, once an actor has been admitted to full membership of the Comédie Française, he may remain, if he wishes, for life. Theaters with a particular aim or identity, such as the Stratford, Ontario, Shakespeare Festival, recruit a large company for a number of plays and then stage the works in repertory. What is the exception now, however, was common practice until the present century. For most of the history of the theater, actors formed themselves into companies that worked together for years, so that the members grew to know one another's work intimately. This gave dramatists of earlier periods an advantage that they rarely enjoy today. They were writing for a known group, and could tailor the roles to particular abilities and talents. Shakespeare wrote *Hamlet* and *Othello* with Richard Burbage in mind. Molière's comedies made the best of his company's physical characteristics. Congreve and Sheridan, similarly, knew who was going to play each part before they wrote them. In this kind of company, actors tended to fall into what were called "lines of business": that is, they would specialize in playing the same kind of character, whatever the play. Certain members of the King's Men would always play the fools and clowns. Sheridan had a gallery of comic types around which to build a new work. Dickens, in *Nicholas Nickleby*, gives a delightful description of a nineteenth-century touring company in which the members are identified, not by their names, but by the roles they customarily play on stage: the swaggering hero, the angry old father, the ingenue, and so forth. You will often find, therefore, that this kind of company organization induces certain sorts of dramatic formulae in playwrights. As early as Sophocles, dramatists were returning to the same types of character, and similar kinds of dramatic situation, because they could rely on actors who were able to exploit them powerfully. The modern author usually lacks this resource. He creates his characters out of the blue. It is up to the producing agency, and the casting director, to find actors capable of bringing them to life.

THE DIRECTOR   The director is the most recent member of the producing group, and still one of the most controversial. Throughout the history of the theater, obviously, someone always had to be in charge. In the Greek theater it was usually the playwright. Aeschylus played his own leading parts, and supervised his assistant actors; as well as providing the script, he was his own composer, choreographer, and designer. The medieval theater provided a *maître de jeu*, who had general responsibility for seeing that his actors knew their lines, rehearsed their moves, and stood more or less in the right places. Shakespeare's playhouse had its "bookholder," who combined the functions of prompter and stage manager. In the eighteenth and nineteenth centuries we see the emergence of the actor-manager, a paternalistic figure who played the leading roles himself and imposed some cohesion on the company — sometimes a difficult task, for many actors were individualists, intent on drawing attention to their own performance at the expense of the ensemble effect. In the late nineteenth century the growing complexity of the theater's technical resources, and dissatisfaction with certain haphazard methods of the past, combined to create the need for a master mind who would stand apart from the production, see it as a whole, and harness its various resources to a common end. This figure emerges, in the twentieth century, as the American director, the British producer, or the European *régisseur*, and there are still widely different views as to what his function should be. Some directors have established themselves as autocrats, allowing nothing to happen on the stage that has not evolved from their minds or, at least, won their considered approval. In many cases, it has been possible to identify a given directorial style as easily as a writing style. A production by Tyrone Guthrie, or by Roger Planchon, was unmistakably his, and could be no one else's. Other directors have considered their function to be to allow the actor's initiative to predominate; they merely shape and control his creative imagination, offering suggestions, not directives. As the theater is constantly in a state of flux, so the director's role is still changing. Twenty years ago, the director expected to walk into his first rehearsal with every move of the play blocked out on paper, or at least in his mind. Now, he hopes to come to the same result after long working sessions with his actors, in the course of which a number of different approaches may be tried and discarded. Particular directors and actors may achieve a long and mutually fruitful working relationship over a number of productions, each helping and inspiring the other. The same may happen between directors and playwrights. Elia Kazan has had a long partnership with Tennessee Williams, contributing materially to the final shaping of the plays. Alan Schneider has done the same for Edward Albee.

Designers too represent a fairly recent innovation in theater practice. For most eras of the past, design as we now know it did not exist. The theater provided a conventional background for its actors. Sometimes, as in the Greek and Elizabethan theaters, this was simply the permanent architectural structure of the stage building, with the audience left to imagine the settings suggested by the language of the author. Even when the theater began to develop painted, illusionistic scenery the same stock settings were used for play after play; each playhouse owned a basic collection which could be used, with minimal adaptation, for the entire repertoire. Costumes, similarly, were drawn from stock, with the actors most of the time wearing the same sorts of clothes that they, and the audience, wore for everyday usage. The role of the designer begins to emerge in the early nineteenth century, out of the same dissatisfactions that eventually created the director. There was a growing desire for greater consistency, and greater appropriateness, in the stage picture, coupled with an increased concern for historical accuracy. The first "designed" production is usually said, with some justice, to be Shakespeare's *King John* as presented on the London stage in 1823, with every character dressed in the historical period indicated by the play, and the settings inspired by authentic medieval records. Since then, of course, the designer has developed into far more than a historical researcher, though that kind of

THE DESIGNERS

study may still represent the basis of his design. He is expected, first, to lay out the playing space in a way that will be usable by actors, and at the same time say something about the play's intent; in other words, he must provide a visual metaphor of the play's action. In the same way, the costumes must be related to the dramatic intent, as seen by the director either alone or in combination with the author. Each costume must make a statement about the character who wears it, and be related to the others as part of a unified concept. The stage lighting, usually in different hands, must also contribute to the total effect, illuminating selectively and significantly the crucial moments of the action and suggesting mood and contrast.

All these things have to be kept in mind when taking a play from the printed page and translating it into stage action. As we have stated, many of the above are functions of the modern theater only. Selective stage lighting was impossible before the appearance of gas; seventeenth-century audiences would have been astonished at the suggestion that they should sit in the dark, while only the stage was lit. But even when considering the plays of the past, it is essential to consider what practical facilities were available to the playwright, and how these influenced the form in which he wrote. Plays are rarely written in a vacuum. When they are, they tend not to be good plays. Normally, an author writes with a particular kind of theater in mind, a particular acting style, a particular audience with reasonably predictable responses. The final shape of his play will be determined by all these things.

THE PLAYHOUSE   Particularly important is the shape of the playhouse at any given period, for this largely determines not what the author says, but how he says it. Was it large or small? Spectacular or intimate? Designed to provide elaborate scenic illusion, or working largely through the active complicity of the audience's imagination? Greek plays, for instance, were written for open-air theaters which were enormous by today's standards (see p. 661). They held upwards of 15,000 spectators, and the actor was dwarfed by his environment. In such a theater there was little place for subtle visual effect, or for the intricate physical business that a modern dramatist now writes into his stage directions. As a compensating factor, the acoustics of these theaters, by reason of their bowl-shaped structure, were superb. Audiences could hear every word, even at so great a remove from the action. Thus, by necessity, the dramatist worked largely in terms of language. In Greek plays, characters tell you everything: who and what they are, what they are doing and going to do, what they feel about it all. In the smaller, more intimate modern theater Greek plays often seem unnecessarily wordy because the actors now have other resources. A modern actor may show in a look what his ancient counterpart had to express in a sentence. Directors who revive Greek plays have to keep these problems of transposition in mind.

In the Elizabethan theater, as most scholars now assume, actors worked on a deep thrust stage which could carry them into the center of their audience (see p. 7). Thus, a characteristic feature of the theater building encouraged the use of the stage soliloquy. Also, Elizabethan theaters seem

Greek Theatre of Epidaurus on the Peloponnesus east of Nauplia. (Photograph: Frederick Ayer. Photo Researchers, Inc.)

to have relied very little on illusionistic, representational scenery. They offered, instead, a neutral space defined largely by the words of the actors. Shakespeare's characters tell you where they are, if it matters; if they do not, then the precise location is unimportant. In these circumstances the theater could develop a fast-moving pattern of action in which one scene followed rapidly on the heels of another with no necessity to drop the curtain for a change of setting. Victorian actor-managers, mounting Shakespeare on their own heavily pictorial stages, found this to be a major problem, for their productions stretched out to an inordinate length as one elaborately painted set was replaced by another. Once again, the factors governing the original production have to be taken into account, even if one intends to depart from them.

Let us now trace the progress of a production through its various stages. First, it is the task of the director to consider his interpretation of the play, and how this may be realized in practical terms. He must determine what he thinks the play means, for on this everything else will hang. If the author is living and accessible, the director will almost certainly consult him. This may be a mixed blessing, for the author will usually have his private vision of the play, shaped by his own proximity to it. The director, standing apart from the work, is able to be more objective. Authors are, notoriously, fallible directors of their own work, though a number have refused to recognize this and tried to impose their will on actors and director alike. George Bernard Shaw is a case in point; his plays contain inordinately lengthy stage directions, dictating the appearance of the stage setting, the properties, costumes and movements in such explicit detail that, if followed to the letter, they would leave the director nothing to do.

In the case of a dead, particularly a long-dead, author the director has different problems. He must arrive at the best interpretation that he can, aided only by the second-hand resources of scholarship. This is not to denigrate the scholar. Any intelligent director will read all the editions and commentaries that he can. But it is in the matter of bringing the play to the stage that the practitioner and the scholar conspicuously part company. Scholarship has space and leisure to be expansive. It can discuss alternative explanations, point to ambiguities, and illuminate textual problems with footnotes suggesting various ways in which they may be resolved. A good scholar is more inclined to discuss a range of interpretations than to commit himself to one. The theater, on the other hand, has to be decisive. It offers no footnotes. It cannot ask the spectator to go back and reconsider. In performance, if something is not clear at first hearing, it is not clear at all. Therefore the director, for better or worse, has to commit himself to one interpretation, to one vision of the play; and, inevitably, there will be those who disagree with him. Laurence Olivier prefaced his film of *Hamlet* with the statement that this is a play about a man who could not make up his mind. An immediate response rang out from a segment of the audience: "Wrong!" It is ever thus. The theater, unfortunately, cannot offer a variety of interpretations and ask the audience to choose. It has to settle for one; and what this is will vary with the director and his times. Part of the measure of greatness of a play is the number of different interpretations it can bear without forfeiting its dramatic viability.

The initial decision, once arrived at, carries others in its train. A directorial interpretation involves matters of setting and costume, and these are usually worked out well in advance with the appropriate people. Let us take, as an example, the case of *King Lear*. The same play may assume a number of stage shapes, depending on what the director assumes its meaning and purpose to be. Does he see it, for instance, on the most rudimentary level, as a chronicle play about certain events in remote British history? (Unlikely, perhaps; but it has been done.) The name of Lear, after all, appears in early British records, and a rough date may be assigned to him. In this case we will have a *Lear* dressed in furs and skins, and set again a background of rocks and monoliths. Alternatively, does the director see the play, as some scholars have suggested, as closely related to political events of Shakespeare's own time? Does Lear's division of his kingdom give stage form to the fears of those who looked uneasily into the future of an England whose queen would die unmarried and childless? This gives another line for sets and costumes to take. Does the director envisage the work as having a particular meaning for now, for the present generation? He may therefore decide to stage it in modern dress, against settings evoking the audience's present. As noted above, "modern-dress" Shakespeare was the regular practice before the nineteenth century; it became modish again in the 1920's and 30's, and still occasionally reappears with value today, though perhaps *Lear* is not the ideal play for such treatment. Is it a cosmic drama, located in no particular time and place, but expressive only of man's constant inhumanity to man, and his subservience to forces beyond his control? Sets and costumes may display this too, by choosing forms linked to no specific style or period but creating their own theatrical logic. Thus the stage has shown us all manner of Lears. One has been Ancient British, another Elizabethan. Olivier's production suggested an almost prehistoric world without actually depicting it, a world of towering crags and swirling mists. Gielgud chose a timeless *Lear*, dressed in costumes of stylized shape and set among abstract sculptural forms. Yet another production looked to the future and set the play in a blackened, smouldering landscape, the neo-primitive world that had survived the atomic war.

The director's basic interpretation must also decide the placement and movement of his characters. It is his task to illuminate what he considers to be the underlying pattern of the play through significant action. To this end he will create a subtext, working with his actors to build up a mental background and justification for the lines they speak. In *Lear* again, the play begins with the King's announcement that he proposes to divide his kingdom, and his challenge to his daughters to proclaim their love for him. Why does he do this? Is it simply the datum, the formal beginning to the play, which neither asks nor needs explanation? In this case, the director may stage the

Engraving of Benjamin Wilson's painting of David Garrick (1717–1770) as King Lear,
Act III. (Photograph: Raymond Mander and Joe Mitchenson Theatre Collection.)

John Gielgud as Lear in the Royal Shakespeare Theatre production, Stratford-upon-Avon,
England, 1955. (Photograph: Royal Shakespeare Theatre.)

opening scenes almost as a prologue, quite simply and formally, a bare proclamation. Or is there a more complex human explanation? Olivier saw Lear in this scene as a man on the verge of senility, making his momentous decision almost as a whim; and he worked up to this from his first appearance on stage, having Lear stop as if to address a remark to a soldier, then changing his mind and going on. Why does Cordelia refuse to answer? Is she simply revolted by her sisters' protestations, or is there some other reason? Nahum Tate, the Restoration playwright, was so obsessed by this problem that he postulated a love affair between Cordelia and Edgar dividing her loyalty so that she was unable to answer her father as he wished; and he carried this idea to such lengths that he rewrote the play. So far may interpretation go.

A further example. What relationship exists between Lear and the Fool? Is the latter intended to be the King's conscience? His *alter ego?* A daughter-substitute? Or an objective commentator on his master's folly? Once again, whatever interpretation is decided upon can be emphasized by the relative placing of the characters and their contact, or lack of it. Gloucester is blinded. Is the director concerned with the physical violence of the act, or its symbolic performance? If the former, the deed can be portrayed most graphically on the stage. If the latter, it can be merely suggested, not shown. All these are things which must be worked out by the director with his actors, and they must ultimately agree on the meaning of what is being done. Discrepancies of interpretation show up with painful clarity in performance. An actor may sometimes disagree totally with his director's interpretation. He will usually follow it, none the less. In the long rehearsal process, the interpretation may change. Alec Guinness has recorded that he went through several interpretations of Shakespeare's *Richard II* before he found a view of the character that satisfied him as being logical and self-consistent.

Amid all these interpretations, then, where is the play? The answer must be that it is in none of them, and all of them. The play's values change as the theaters, the actors, and the audiences change. The *Lear* we see is not the *Lear* that Burbage performed, and the Elizabethan playgoers saw, though the text is the same. The Lear of Garrick (1717–1779) was totally different from that of Edmund Kean (1787–1833). In the same way, Lincoln Center bears small resemblance to the Globe Playhouse, Drury Lane, or the Lyceum. Each generation finds a new meaning in the script, illuminating it with contemporary concerns and preoccupations. It is the theater's continual task to bring about a rapprochement between the play and its successive audiences, finding a new frame of reference in which it will be meaningful. The actor, who works in the ephemeral, who sculpts, as has been said, in snow, accepts this as a condition of his art. The text remains, but its illumination changes.

However ornate the director's conception, the commercial theater imposes strict limitations on time and cost. A Broadway production may expect a minimum of three weeks' rehearsal; the cost, regulated by strict union standards for actors and stage crew, may be upwards of $200,000 for a nonmusical play, vastly more for a musical. In university theaters, which have

THE MECHANICS
OF PRODUCTION

The University of Minnesota production of *King Lear* in Minneapolis, 1956. (Photograph: The University of Minnesota Theatre.)

Paul Scofield as Lear in Peter Brook's production by the Royal Shakespeare Company in London, 1962. (Photograph: Angus McBean. Harvard Theatre Collection.)

tended to become more and more the home of the classics, conditions are somewhat happier. Campus productions usually work with five or six weeks of rehearsal time, uninhibited by union hours, and the budget is far smaller when salaries do not have to be paid: perhaps as little as $1,500 for a *King Lear*. Given these differences, rehearsals in both situations tend to follow the same pattern. They will begin with a general reading of the play, during which the director explains his conception; the cast may also see preliminary designs of sets and costumes, so that they know the environment in which they will be working. Early rehearsals are conducted book-in-hand, with normally only the barest indication of a set. The principal acting areas, steps and levels are marked out on the floor with tape. Any furniture that is to hand may be used; a chair may stand in for a throne, a bench for a bed. During this period cuts and changes may still be made, imposed sometimes by such commercial considerations as the length and expense of the performance, sometimes by changes in the director's conception as he absorbs what his actors bring to their parts. Gradually, the actors memorize. It is the director's hope that parts will be learnt as rapidly as possible, as only then can serious work begin. Once they have discarded their scripts, actors can relate to one another and to their surroundings. During the course of rehearsals the other production elements are added. Actors start to work with the actual props, instead of rehearsal equivalents. In a university theater, the setting begins to grow around the actors as they rehearse. Actual steps replace the lines on the floor and walls appear where there was only empty space. In the commercial theater, again because of expense, the company may never know the actual set until the last stages of rehearsal; they do most of their work in an empty hall lit by a single bulb. In either case, the last days are spent in integrating the total production. The full set appears, and actors have to adjust to its intricacies. The full lighting plot is put into action. Sound effects and music are added. The actors are introduced to their costumes, and have to master, very rapidly, the difficulties of wearing them. There is usually one technical rehearsal, during which the actors are subordinated to the other demands of the performance; they usually move from one lighting or scene cue to the next, so that the technical staff may become accustomed to the changes. Finally, full dress rehearsals, run like a full performance, with the director no longer intervening, but confining himself to notes at the end. In the commercial theater, even this may not be the end of the process. Most Broadway productions go through a series of tryouts out-of-town, before paying public audiences. Depending on the reaction, important changes may be made in the production, or even in the script itself. It is not unknown for actors to be handed new material every day. Thus the production is established; it opens; and even then, over a long commercial run, it may change, as new actors replace the original cast or as those who were with the play from the beginning make new discoveries about it and about each other. A script, once it has been published, achieves a certain permanency. A production is always changing, and no two audiences ever see exactly the same dramatic event.

WRITING ABOUT DRAMA

People write about plays in order to clarify and to account for their responses
to works that interest or excite or frustrate them. In order to put words on
paper you will have to take a second and a third look at what is in front of
you and at what is within you. And so writing is a way of learning. The last
word is never said about complex thoughts and feelings, but when we write
we hope to make at least a little progress in the difficult but rewarding job
of talking about our responses. We learn, and then we hope to interest our
reader because we are communicating our responses to something that for
one reason or another is worth talking about.

This communication is, in effect, teaching. You may think that you are
writing for the teacher, but such a belief is a misconception; when you write,
you are the teacher. An essay on a play is an attempt to help someone to see
the play as you see it. If this chapter had to be boiled down to a single
sentence of advice, that sentence would be: Because you are teaching, your
essay should embody those qualities that you value in teachers — probably
intelligence, open-mindedness, and effort; certainly a desire to offer what help
one can.

Analysis is, literally, a separation into parts in order to understand. An
analysis commonly considers one part and the relation of this part to the
whole. For example, it may consider only the functions of the settings in
Hedda Gabler or the Fool in *King Lear* or the music in *Death of a Salesman*.

Analysis, of course, is not a process used only in talking about literature.
It is commonly applied in thinking about almost any complex matter. Jimmy
Connors plays a deadly game of tennis; what makes it so good? How does his
backhand contribute to his game? What does his serve do to the opponent?
Because a play is usually long and complicated, in a paper written for a
college course you probably do not have enough space to analyze all aspects
of the play, and so you will probably choose one aspect and relate it to the
whole. Of course all of the parts are related; a study of one character, for
example, will have to take some account of other characters and of plot and
perhaps even of setting; but, still, an analysis may legitimately devote most
of its space to one part, taking account of other parts only insofar as they
are relevant to the topic.

If a work is fairly long and complex, and you are writing only a few
pages, almost surely you will write an analysis of some part. Unless you have
an enormous amount of time for reflection and revision, you cannot write a
meaningful essay of five hundred or even a thousand words on *Oedipus* or
The Cherry Orchard. You cannot even write on "Character in *Oedipus*" or
"Symbolism in *The Cherry Orchard*." And probably you won't really want
to write on such topics anyway. Probably *one* character or *one* symbol has
caught your interest. Trust your feelings; you are probably on to something
interesting, and it will be best to think about this smaller topic for the relatively few hours that you have. A "smaller" topic need not be dull or trivial;
treated properly, it may illuminate the entire work, or, to change the metaphor, it may serve as a mine shaft that gives entry to the work. "The

Dramatic Function of the Gloucester Subplot in *King Lear*," carefully thought about, will in five hundred or a thousand words tell a reader more (and will have taught its author more) than will "*King Lear* as a Tragedy." Similarly, "Imagery of Blindness in *King Lear*" is a better topic than "Imagery in *King Lear*," and "The Meanings of 'Nature' in *King Lear*" is a better topic than "The Meaning of *King Lear*."

How do you find a topic and how do you turn it into a thesis, that is, a point you want to make? An idea may hit you suddenly; as you are reading you find yourself jotting it in the margin, "Contrast with Hedda's earlier response," or "Note the change of costume," or "too heavy irony," or "ugh." Or an idea may come slowly on rereading. Perhaps you gradually become aware that *Death of a Salesman* is both a tragedy and a social drama (a play that calls attention to a problem in the organization of society), and perhaps you come to feel that Miller's emphasis on social pressures is not entirely consistent with his effort to present Willy Loman as a tragic hero. At this point, then, you have a thesis — an angle — as well as a topic.

FROM TOPIC TO THESIS

Think of it this way: a topic is a subject, and a thesis is a subject with a predicate: "Imagery in *King Lear*." is a topic, but it can be turned into a thesis thus: "Imagery helps to distinguish the characters in *King Lear*." Once you can formulate a thesis, you are well on the way to writing a good paper. But note that the more precise the formulation of the thesis, the better the paper will probably be. After all, "Imagery in *King Lear* is interesting" is a thesis, but such a vague formulation gives you little to go on. Not until you can turn it into something like "Imagery in *King Lear* serves three important purposes" are you anywhere near to being able to draft your essay.

Every literary work affords its own topics for analysis, and every essayist must set forth his own thesis, but a few useful generalizations may be made. You can often find a thesis by asking one of two questions:

1. *What is this doing?* That is, why is this scene in the novel or play? Why is the Fool in *King Lear*? Why the music in *Death of a Salesman*? Why are these lines verse and those lines prose? Why is a certain action reported to us rather than represented on the stage? What is the significance of the parts of the work? (Titles are often highly significant parts of the work: Ibsen's *Hedda Gabler* and Chekhov's *The Cherry Orchard* would be slightly different if they had other titles.)

2. *Why do I have this response?* Why do I find this scene clever, or moving, or puzzling? How did the author make this character funny or dignified or pathetic? How did he communicate the idea that this character is a bore without boring me?

The first of these questions, "What is this doing?" requires that you identify yourself with the author, wondering, for example, whether this opening scene is the best possible for this story. The second question, "Why do I have this response?" requires that you trust your feelings. If you are amused or bored or puzzled or annoyed, assume that these responses are appropriate and follow them up, at least until a rereading of the play provides other responses.

Here is a short essay, written by a student. The student has told us privately that when she began work on the paper she was hoping to write on the irrationality of the fairies in A *Midsummer Night's Dream* as a sort of mirror of the irrationality of the young lovers, but when she searched the play for supporting detail she found, to her surprise, that she had to revise the thesis.

Fairy Mischief and Morality
and A *Midsummer Night's Dream*

A SAMPLE
ANALYSIS

If we read A *Midsummer Night's Dream* casually, or come away from a delightful performance, we may have the vague impression that the fairies are wild, mischievous, willful creatures who perhaps represent the irrational qualities of mankind. But in fact the text lends only a little support to this view. The irrationality of mankind is really represented chiefly by the human beings in the play — we are told in the first scene, for example, that Demetrius used to love Helena, but now loves Hermia — and the fairies are really largely responsible for the happy ending that is finally achieved.

It is, of course, easy to see why we may think of the fairies as wild and mischievous. Titania accuses Oberon of infidelity, and Oberon returns the charge:

> How canst thou thus for shame, Titania,
> Glance at my credit with Hippolyta,
> Knowing I know thy love to Theseus?
>
> (II.i.74–76)[1]

Titania rejects this countercharge, saying "These are the forgeries of jealousy" (II.i.81), but we are not convinced of her innocence. It would be easy to give additional examples of speeches in which the king and queen of fairyland present unflattering pictures of each other, but probably one of the strongest pieces of evidence of their alleged irrationality is the fact that Oberon causes Titania to fall in love with the asinine Bottom. We should not forget, however, that later Oberon will take pity on her: "Her dotage now I do begin to pity" (IV.i.51).

In fact, it is largely through Oberon's sense of pity — this time for the quarreling young lovers in the forest — that the lovers finally are successfully paired off. And we should remember, too, before we claim that the fairies are consistently quarrelsome and mischievous, that at the very end of the play Oberon and Titania join in a song and dance blessing the newlyweds and promising healthy offspring. The fairies are, fundamentally, benevolent spirits.

But what of Robin Goodfellow, the Puck of this play? Is he not mischievous? One of the fairies says Robin is a "shrewd and knavish sprite" (II.i.33) who frightens maids and plays tricks on housewives;

---

[1] All quotations from this play are from the text reprinted in Sylvan Barnet, Morton Berman, and William Burto, *Types of Drama*, 2nd ed. (Boston: Little, Brown, 1977). Further references to the play will be given parenthetically, within the text of the essay.

Robin admits the charge, saying "Thou speakest aright" (II.i.42), and two lines later he says "I jest to Oberon, and make him smile," and then he goes on to describe some of his practical jokes, including his fondness for neighing to tease a horse, and pulling a stool from under an old lady. But this is not quite the whole story. The fact is, despite this speech, that we do *not* see Robin engage in any mischievous pranks. After all, he does not deliberately anoint the eyes of the wrong Athenian lover. Oberon tells Robin that he will recognize the young man by his Athenian clothing, and when Puck encounters a young man in Athenian clothing he anoints the youth's eyes. The fault is really Oberon's, though of course Oberon meant well when he instructed Robin:

> A sweet Athenian lady is in love
> With a disdainful youth. Anoint his eyes;
> But do it when the next thing he espies
> May be the lady.
>
> (II.i.260–263)

So Robin's error is innocent. He is speaking honestly when he says, "Believe me, king of shadows, I mistook" (III.ii.347). Of course he does enjoy the confusion he mistakenly causes, but we can hardly blame him severely for that. After all, we enjoy it too.

The fairies, by their very nature, of course suggest a mysterious, irrational world, but — even though, as we have just seen, Oberon is called the "king of shadows" — they are not to be confused with "ghosts, wand'ring here and there," "damnèd spirits" who "willfully themselves exile from light / And must for aye consort with black-browed night" (III.ii.381–387). Oberon explicitly says, after this speech, "But we are spirits of another sort," and his speech is filled with references not to darkness but to light: "morning," "eastern gate," "blessèd beams." The closer we observe them in the play, then, the closer their behavior is to that of normal, decent human begins. There is plenty of irrationality in the play, but it is found for the most part in the mortals.

Notice that this first-rate essay, written by a student, has a thesis, and develops the thesis effectively. The title gives the reader some idea of what is coming, and the first paragraph pretty clearly sets forth the thesis. The essay next takes up the evidence that might seem to contradict the thesis — Oberon and Titania, and Robin Goodfellow — and it shows that this evidence is not decisive. All the while, then, it is moving forward, substantiating its thesis, especially by using well-chosen quotations. The last paragraph slightly restates the thesis, in light of what the essay has demonstrated.

WRITING A COMPARISON   Something should be said about an essay organized around a comparison or a contrast between, say, two characters — in one play or even in two plays. Probably the student's first thought, after making some jottings, is to discuss one half of the comparison and then go on to the second half. Instructors and textbooks usually condemn such an organization, arguing that the essay breaks into two parts and that the second part involves a good deal of repetition of categories set up in the first part. Usually they recommend that the student organize his thoughts differently, somewhat along these lines:

1. First similarity
   a. first work (or character, or characteristic)
   b. second work
2. Secondary similarity
   a. first work
   b. second work
3. First difference
   a. first work
   b. second work
4. Second difference
   a. first work
   b. second work

and so on, for as many additional differences as seem relevant. For example, if one wishes to compare King Lear with Willy Loman in *Death of a Salesman*, one may organize the material thus:

1. First similarity: each figure's lack of self-knowledge
   a. Lear
   b. Loman
2. Second similarity: the corrupt world surrounding these figures
   a. Lear's evil daughters and their associates
   b. Society's vulgar idea of success, to which Willy subscribes
3. First difference: degree to which the character attains self-knowledge
   a. Lear's recognition
   b. Willy's continuing blindness

Here is another way of organizing a comparison and contrast:

1. First point: lack of self-knowledge
   a. similarities between Lear and Willy
   b. differences between Lear and Willy
2. Second point: the corrupt world
   a. similarities between the worlds in *King Lear* and *Salesman*
   b. differences between the worlds in *King Lear* and *Salesman*
3. Third point: degree of attainment of self-knowledge
   a. similarities between Lear and Willy
   b. differences between Lear and Willy

But a comparison need not employ either of these structures. There is even the danger that an essay employing either of them may not come into focus until the essayist stands back from his seven-layer cake and announces, in his concluding paragraph, that the odd layers taste better. In one's preparatory thinking, one may want to make comparisons in pairs (Faults: Lear and Willy; Social satire: indictment of injustice in *Lear*, and of capitalism in *Salesman*; Children: Lear's daughters, Willy's sons; Comments by other characters . . .), but one must come to some conclusions about what these add up to before writing the final version. This final version should not duplicate the thought processes; rather, it should be organized so as to make the point clearly and effectively. After reflection, one may believe that although there are superficial similarities between Lear and Willy Loman, there are essential differences; then in the finished essay one probably will not wish to obscure the main point by jumping back and forth from play to play, working through a series of similarities and differences. It may be better to discuss King Lear and then to point out that, although Willy Loman resembles him in A, B, and C, Willy in D, E, and F does *not* resemble Lear. Some repetition in the second half of the essay (for example, "Willy Loman never comes to the deep self-knowledge that we see Lear achieve") will serve to bind the two halves into a meaningful whole, making clear the degree of similarity or difference. The point of the essay presumably is not to list pairs of similarities or differences, but to illuminate a work, or works, by making thoughtful comparison. Although in a long essay one cannot postpone until page 30 a discussion of the second half of the comparison, in an essay of, say, less than ten pages nothing is wrong with setting forth one half of the comparison and then, in light of it, the second half. The essay will break into two unrelated parts if the second half makes no use of the first, or if it fails to modify the first half, but not if the second half looks back to the first half and calls attention to differences that the new material reveals. A student ought to learn how to write an essay with interwoven comparisons, but he ought also to know that there is another, simpler and clearer way to write a comparison.

COMMUNICATING JUDGMENTS
Because a critical essay on a play is a judicious attempt to help a reader see what is going on in a work or in a part of a work, the voice of the critic sounds, on first hearing, impartial; but good criticism includes — at least implicitly — evaluation. You can say not only that the setting changes (a neutral expression) but also that "the playwright aptly shifts the setting" or "unconvincingly introduces a new character," or "effectively juxtaposes . . ." These evaluations you support with evidence. You have feelings about the work under discussion, and you reveal them, not by continually saying "I feel" and "this moves me," but by calling attention to the degree of success or failure you perceive. Nothing is wrong with occasionally using "I," and noticeable avoidances of it — passives, "this writer," "we," and the like — suggest an offensive sham modesty; but too much talk of "I" makes a writer sound like an egomaniac.

One final remark on communicating judgments: Write sincerely. Any attempt to neglect your own thoughtful responses and replace them with fabrications designed to please an instructor will surely fail. It is hard enough to find the words that clearly communicate your responses; it is almost impossible to find the words that express your hunch about what your instructor expects your responses to be. George Orwell shrewdly commented on the obvious signs of insincere writing: "When there is a gap between one's real and one's declared aims, one turns as it were instinctively to long words and exhausted idioms, like a cuttlefish squirting out ink."

We have already suggested that you can often find a thesis by asking two questions: What is this doing? and Why do I have this response? In a moment we will suggest many additional questions, but first we want to mention that the editorial apparatus throughout this book is intended to help you to read, enjoy, and discuss drama as fully as possible. When you are sitting down to write about a play, you may want to reread some parts of this apparatus for guidance on your topic, perhaps paying special attention to the glossary's entries on *character, convention, dialogue, diction, foil, irony, motivation, plot, suspense,* and *unity.* You may also want to reread some of the earlier material in the book, especially "The Language of Drama."

Now for additional questions that may help you to find topics and to sharpen them into theses.

PLOT. Are certain developments (for example, Lear's madness) prepared for by foreshadowing? Are certain happenings or situations recurrent? If so, what significance do you attach to them? If there is a subplot, as in *King Lear,* how is it related? What is the function of a particular scene? Why do certain scenes occur when and where they do? Why are certain episodes reported rather than presented on the stage? Are there irrelevant scenes? Does the plot depend on chance? Is the resolution satisfactory?

CHARACTER. What sort of person is So-and-so? (Of course a dramatic character is not likely to be thoroughly realistic in the sense of being a copy of someone we might know, but is the character coherent, perhaps representative of some human type?) How is the character defined? How trustworthy are the characters when they characterize themselves? Others? (Consider what the character says and does, what others say about him and do to him and also consider other characters who more or less resemble the character in question, because the similarities — and the differences — may be significant.) If a character is tragic, does the tragedy proceed from a flaw, from an intellectual error, from the malice of others, from sheer chance, or from some combination of these? If comic, do we laugh with him or at him? Are the characters adequately motivated? Do the characters change as the play goes on, or do we simply know them better at the end? Is the character so meditative that we feel he is engaged less in a dialogue with others than in a dialogue with his own mind? If so, de we feel that this character is in large degree a spokesman for the author, commenting on the world not only of the play but on the outside world too?

In a typical course paper you need not and probably should not take on all aspects of a character. With a play of great complexity — for example one of Shakespeare's major plays — a short essay may do well to take an even smaller topic, such as Lear's use of prose (Why does he sometimes speak in prose, sometimes in verse, and what does it tell us about him?) or Lear's denunciation of sex (Why is the king obsessed with the idea of lechery?). Even here we will not be able merely to hunt through the play looking at Lear's prose or his remarks about sex; we will have to pay some attention to other uses of prose in *King Lear,* or to references to sex in the play, if we are to see the exact nature of the problem we have chosen to isolate.

NONVERBAL LANGUAGE. Words are not, it has been suggested in our discussion of drama (see especially pages 23–25), the only language of drama, and a student will sometimes want to explore matters of staging. What is especially difficult for most of us confronted with only a printed page, is to catch the full dramatic quality of a play — to read the words and also to have a sense of how they will sound in the context of gestures and a setting. We tend to read drama as literature rather than as dramatic literature, or theater. (When the author is Shakespeare or Shaw, we can sometimes justly examine his works as literature, although even here we may find that things that seem flat on the page come alive in the theater.) Consider the setting, for example. Is it symbolic? Drama of the nineteenth and early twentieth centuries (for example, plays of Ibsen and Chekhov) is often thought to be "realistic," but of course even a realistic playwright or stage designer selects his material. A realistic setting can say a great deal, can serve as a symbol. Here is Ibsen on nonverbal devices:

> I can do quite a lot by manipulating the prosaic details of my plays so that they become theatrical metaphors and come to mean more than what they are; I have used costume in this way, lighting, scenery, landscape, weather; I have used trivial everyday things like inky fingers and candles; and I have used living figures as symbols of spiritual forces that act upon the hero. Perhaps these things could be brought into the context of a modern realistic play to help me to portray the modern hero and the tragic conflict which I now understand so well.[1]

In the setting of *Hedda Gabler,* for example, Ibsen uses two suggestive details as more than mere background: early in the play Hedda is distressed by the sunlight that shines through the opened French doors, a detail that we later see helps to reveal her fear of the processes of nature. More evident and more pervasive is her tendency, when she cannot cope with her present situation, to move to the inner room, at the rear of the stage, in which hangs a picture of her late father. And over and over again in Ibsen we find the realistic setting of a nineteenth-century drawing room, with its heavy draperies and its bulky furniture, helping to convey his vision of a bourgeois world that oppresses the individual who struggles to affirm other values.

Contemporary dramatists are often explicit about the symbolic qualities of the setting. Below is an example from Miller's *Death of a Salesman:*

> Before us is the Salesman's house. We are aware of towering, angular shapes behind it, surrounding it on all sides. Only the blue light of the sky falls upon the house and forestage; the surrounding area shows an angry glow of orange. As more light appears, we see a solid vault of apartment houses around the small, fragile-seeming home.

This setting is a symbol that helps to give the play its meaning. Miller's

[1] Quoted by John Northam, "Ibsen's Search for the Hero," in *Ibsen,* ed. Rolf Fjelde (Englewood Cliffs, N.J.: Prentice-Hall, 1965), p. 99.

"solid vault of apartment houses" that menaces the Salesman's house helps us to see the social forces that warp the individual.

If you set out to write an essay on gestures in *King Lear,* you may come to see how rich the play is in such a symbolic gesture as kneeling or stripping off clothing, and it is similarly rich in sound effects — chiefly, of course, the storm, but also sounds of music and of fighting. Similarly, costume (as we point out on p. 24) often reveals rather than conceals. Again, even a realistic playwright such as Ibsen uses costume symbolically, as a close reading of *Hedda Gabler* will show.

STAGING AND PRODUCTION. How would you stage the first scene of a given play? What kinds of costumes should the characters wear (assuming that these are not specified by the playwright)? If you were producing the play, what scenes or speeches might you cut, and why? Prepare a television script for the first scene of a play, indicating what the viewer would see at first (for example, a group of characters talking to each other) and then, bit by bit, what the camera would focus on. (Because the television screen is small, it cannot accommodate a view of the whole stage for more than a few moments; it must focus on a few figures in proximity, or even on the face of a single speaker or on the face of a character listening to a speaker.)

Everyone must work out his own procedures and rituals (John C. Calhoun liked to plough his farm before writing), but the following suggestions may provide some help.

REVIEW: HOW TO WRITE AN EFFECTIVE ESSAY[2]

1. Read the play carefully.

2. Choose a worthwhile and compassable subject, something that interests you and is not so big that your handling of it must be superficial. As you work, shape your topic into a thesis, moving, for example, from "The Character of Willy Loman" to "The Influence of Society on Willy Loman."

3. Reread the play, jotting down notes of all relevant matters. As you read, reflect on your reading and record your reflections. If you have a feeling or an idea, jot it down; don't assume that you will remember it when you get around to writing your essay. The margins of this book are a good place for initial jottings, but many people find that in the long run it is easiest to transfer these notes to 3 × 5 cards, writing on one side only.

4. Sort out your cards into some kind of reasonable divisions, and reject cards irrelevant to your topic. If you have adequately formulated your thesis (let's say, "Arthur Miller suggests that society is largely responsible for Willy Loman's plight, but Miller is not entirely consistent") you ought to be able to work out a tentative organization. As you work you may discover a better way to group your notes. If so, start reorganizing. Speaking generally, it is a good idea to organize your essay from the lesser material to the greater (to avoid anticlimax) or from the simple to the complex (to ensure intelligibility). If, for example, you are discussing the roles of three characters, it may be best to build up to the one of the three that you think

2 This section is adapted from Sylvan Barnet, *A Short Guide to Writing about Literature,* 3rd ed. (Boston: Little, Brown, 1975), pp. 33–36.

the most important. If you are comparing two characters, it may be best to move from the most obvious contrasts to the least obvious. (In your opening paragraph, which will probably be almost the last thing you will write, you should of course give the reader an idea of the scope of the paper, but at this stage you are organizing the material chiefly for yourself and so you need not yet worry about an introductory paragraph.) When you have arranged your notes into a meaningful sequence of packets, you have approximately divided your material into paragraphs.

5. Get it down on paper. Most essayists find it useful to jot down some sort of outline, indicating the main idea of each paragraph and, under each main idea, supporting details that give it substance. An outline — not necessarily anything highly formal with capital and lowercase letters and Roman and Arabic numerals but merely key phrases in some sort of order — will help you to overcome the paralysis called "writer's block" that commonly afflicts professionals as well as students. A page of paper with ideas in some sort of sequence, however rough, ought to encourage you that you do have something to say. And so, despite the temptation to sharpen another pencil or to put a new ribbon into the typewriter, the best thing to do at this point is to sit down and start writing. If you don't feel that you can work from note cards and a rough outline, try another method: get something down on paper, writing freely, sloppily, automatically, or whatever, but allow your ideas about what the work means to you and how it conveys its meaning — rough as your ideas may be — to begin to take visible form. If you are like most people you can't do much precise thinking until you have committed to paper at least a rough sketch of your initial ideas. Later you can push and polish your ideas into shape, perhaps even deleting all of them and starting over, but it's a lot easier to improve your ideas once you see them in front of you than it is to do the job in your head. On paper one word leads to another; in your head one word often blocks another.

Just keep going; you may realize, as you near the end of a sentence, that you no longer believe it. O.K.; be glad that your first idea led you to a better one, and pick up your better one and keep going with it. What you are doing is, in a sense, by trial and error pushing your way not only toward clear expression but toward sharper ideas and richer responses.

6. If there is time, reread the play, looking for additional material that strengthens or weakens your main point; take account of it in your outline or draft.

7. With your outline or draft in front of you, write a more lucid version, checking your notes for fuller details, such as supporting quotations. If, as you work, you find that some of the points in your earlier jottings are no longer relevant, eliminate them; but make sure that the argument flows from one point to the next. As you write, your ideas will doubtless become clearer; some may prove to be poor ideas. (We rarely know exactly what our ideas are until we have them set down on paper. As the little girl said, replying to the suggestion that she should think before she spoke, "How do I know

what I think until I say it?") Not until you have written a draft do you really have a strong sense of how good your essay may be.

8. After a suitable interval, preferably a few days, read the draft with a view toward revising it, not with a view toward congratulating yourself. A revision, after all, is a re-vision, a second (and presumably sharper) view. When you revise, you will be in the company of Picasso, who said that in painting a picture he advanced by a series of destructions. A revision — say, the substitution of a precise word for an imprecise one — is not a matter of prettifying but of thinking. As you read, correct things that disturb you (for example, awkward repetitions that bore, inflated utterances that grate), add supporting detail where the argument is undeveloped (a paragraph of only one or two sentences is usually an undeveloped paragraph), and ruthlessly delete irrelevancies however well written they may be. But remember that a deletion probably requires some adjustment in the preceding and subsequent material. Make sure that the opening paragraph gives the readers some sense of where they will be going, and that between the opening and the closing paragraphs the argument, aided by transitions (such as "furthermore," "on the other hand," "in the next scene"), runs smoothly. The details should be relevant, the organization reasonable, the argument clear. Check all quotations for accuracy. Quotations are evidence, usually intended to support your assertions, and it is not nice to alter the evidence, even unintentionally. If there is time (there almost never is), put the revision aside, reread it in a day or two, and revise it again, especially with a view toward shortening it.

9. Type or write a clean copy, following the principles concerning margins, pagination, footnotes, and so on set forth in the next section of this discussion. If you have borrowed any ideas, be sure to give credit, usually in footnotes, to your sources. Remember that plagiarism is not limited to the unacknowledged borrowing of words; a borrowed idea, even when put into your own words, requires acknowledgment.

10. Proofread and make corrections.

Basic Manuscript Form. Much of what follows is nothing more than common sense.

REMARKS ABOUT MANUSCRIPT FORM

1. Use 8½ × 11 paper of good weight. Keep as lightweight a carbon copy as you wish, or make a photocopy, but hand in a sturdy original.

2. If you typewrite, use a reasonably fresh ribbon, double-space, and type on one side of the page only. If you submit a handwritten copy, use lined paper and write on one side of the page only, in ink, on every other line. Most instructors do *not* want papers to be enclosed in any sort of binder; and most instructors want papers to be stapled in the upper left corner; do not crimp or crease corners and expect them to hold together.

3. Leave an adequate margin — an inch or an inch and a half — at top, bottom, and sides.

4. Number the pages consecutively, using Arabic numerals in the upper right-hand corner.

5. Put your name and class or course number in the upper right-hand corner of the first page. It is a good idea to put your name in the upper right corner of each page so that your essay can be easily reassembled if a page gets separated.

6. Create your own title — one that reflects your topic or thesis. For example, a paper on *Death of a Salesman* should *not* be called "*Death of a Salesman*" but might be called "Two Kinds of Irony in *Death of a Salesman*."

7. Center the title of your essay below the top margin of the first page. Begin the first word of the title with a capital, and capitalize each subsequent word except articles, conjunctions, and prepositions, thus: The Truth of Dreams in *A Midsummer Night's Dream*.

8. Begin the essay an inch or two below the title.

9. Your extensive revisions should have been made in your drafts, but minor last-minute revisions may be made — neatly — on the finished copy. Proofreading may catch some typographical errors, and you may notice some small weaknesses. Additions should be made *above* the line, with a caret (an upside-down **v**) *below* the line at the appropriate place. Indicate deletions by drawing a horizontal line through the word or words you wish to delete. Delete a single letter by drawing a vertical line through it. Use a vertical line, too, to separate words that should not have been run together.

Quotation and Quotation Marks. Excerpts from the plays you are writing about are indispensable. Such quotations not only let the reader know what you are talking about, they present the material you are responding to, thus letting the reader share your responses.

Here are some mechanical matters:

1. Identify the speaker or writer of the quotation, so that the reader is not left with a sense of uncertainty. Usually this identification precedes the quoted material (for example, "Smith says . . .") in accordance with the principle of letting the reader know where he is going, but occasionally it may follow the quotation, especially if it will provide something of a pleasant surprise. For instance, in a discussion of Arthur Miller's *Death of a Salesman*, you might quote a comment that seems to belittle the play and then reveal that Miller himself was the speaker.

2. The quotation must fit grammatically into your sentence. Suppose you want to use Hedda Gabler's line (she is imagining Løvborg's return from the party), "I see him already." Do not say:

Near the end of the second act, when Mrs. Elvsted wonders in what condition Løvborg will return, Hedda says that she "see him already."

This version is better:

Near the end of the second act, when Mrs. Elvsted wonders in what condition Løvborg will return, Hedda says that she sees "him already."

Or, of course, you can say,

Near the end of the second act, when Mrs. Elvsted wonders in what condition Løvborg will return, Hedda says, "I see him already."

3. The quotation must be exact. Any material that you add — even one or two words — must be in square brackets, thus:

When Hedda says that she sees "him [that is, Løvborg] already," she has in mind something very different from what she seems to be saying.

If you wish to omit material from within a quotation, indicate the ellipsis by three spaced periods. If a sentence ends in an omission, add a closed-up period and then three spaced periods to indicate the omission. The following example is based on a quotation from the sentences immediately above this one:

The chapter says that "if you . . . omit material from within a quotation, [you must] indicate the ellipsis. . . . If a sentence ends in an omission, add a closed-up period and then three spaced periods. . . ."

Notice that although material preceded "If you," periods are not needed to indicate the omission because "If you" began a sentence in the original. Customarily, initial and terminal omissions are indicated only when they are part of the sentence you are quoting. Even such omissions need not be indicated when the quoted material is obviously incomplete — when, for instance, it is a word or phrase. Notice, too, that although quotations must be given word for word, the initial capitalization can be adapted, as here where "If" is reduced to "if."

When a line or more of verse is omitted from a passage that is set off, the three spaced periods are printed on a separate line:

> If we shadows have offended,
> Think but this, and all is mended:
> .   .   .
> Give me your hands, if we be friends,
> And Robin shall restore amends.

4. Distinguish between short and long quotations, and treat each appropriately. Short quotations (usually defined as less than three lines of verse or five lines of prose) are enclosed within quotation marks and run into the text (rather than set off, without quotation marks). Examples:

Near the end of *Oedipus Rex* the Chorus reminds the audience that Oedipus "solved the famous riddle," but it does not tell us what the riddle was.

King Lear's first long speech begins authoritatively: "Meantime we shall express our darker purpose. / Give me the map there. Know that we have divided/In three our kingdom."

Notice in the first passage that although four words only are being quoted, quotation marks are used, indicating that these are Sophocles' words, not the essayist's. Notice that in the second example a slash (diagonal line, virgule) is used to indicate the end of a line of verse other than the last line quoted. The slash is, of course, not used if the poetry is set off, indented, and printed as verse, thus:

> King Lear's first long speech begins authoritatively:
>
>> Meantime we shall express our darker purpose.
>> Give me the map there. Know that we have divided
>> In three our kingdom; and 'tis our fast intent
>> To shake all cares and business from our age,
>> Conferring them on younger strengths, while we
>> Unburthened crawl toward death.

Material that is set off (usually three or more lines of verse, five or more lines of prose) is not enclosed within quotation marks. To set it off, triple-space before and after the quotation and single-space the quotation. Poetry should be centered; prose quotations should be flush with both right and left margins. (Note: Some manuals of style call for double-spacing, some for indenting prose quotations; but whichever procedure you adopt, be consistent. Be sparing in your use of long quotations.) Use quotations as evidence, not as padding. Do not bore the reader with material that can be effectively reduced either by paraphrase or by cutting. If you cut, indicate ellipses as explained above under 3.

5. Commas and periods go inside the quotation marks. (Exception: if the quotation is immediately followed by material in parentheses or in square brackets, close the quotation, then give the parenthetic or bracketed material, and then — after the closing parenthesis or bracket, put the comma or period.) Marks of punctuation other than periods and commas (that is, semicolons, colons, and dashes) go outside. Question marks and exclamation points go inside if they are part of the quotation, outside if they are your own.

> Hedda says to Løvborg, "So you're not going?" Can we be confident of Løvborg when he replies "I'm staying here with you and Thea"?

6. Use *single* quotation marks for material contained within a quotation that itself is within quotation marks, thus:

> The editors of *Types of Drama* say, "With Puck we look at the antics in the forest, smile tolerantly, and say with a godlike perspective, 'Lord, what fools these mortals be!' "

7. Use quotation marks around titles of short works, that is, for titles of chapters in books and for essays that might not be published by themselves. Unpublished works, even book-length dissertations, are also enclosed in quotation marks. Use italics (indicated by underlining) for books, that is, for plays, periodicals, and collections of essays.

A Note on Footnotes. You may wish to use a footnote, telling the reader of your paper that the passage you are quoting is found in this book on such-and-such a page. Let us assume that you have already mentioned the author and the title of the play, and have just quoted a passage. At the end of the sentence that includes the quotation, or at the end of the quotation if you are offering it as an independent sentence, following the period type or write the number 1, elevating it slightly above the line. Do not put a period after the digit. Near the bottom of the paper, indent a few spaces and type or write the number 1, elevated and without a period. Then write (giving the appropriate page number):

> [1] Reprinted in Sylvan Barnet, Morton Berman, and William Burto, *Types of Drama*, 2nd ed. (Boston: Little, Brown, 1977), p. 236.

Notice that the abbreviation for *page* is p., not pg.; the abbreviation for *pages* is pp., thus: pp. 236–237. For verse plays, whose lines are numbered, the usual procedure is not to cite a page but to cite act, scene, and line numbers in parentheses after the quotation. Give the act in capital Roman numerals, the scene in small Roman numerals, and the line in Arabic numerals. Periods follow the act and the scene.

> The lunatic, the lover and the poet
> Are of imagination all compact.
> One sees more devils than vast hell can hold,
> That is the madman. The lover, all as frantic,
> Sees Helen's beauty in a brow of Egypt.
>
> (V.i.7–11)[1]

The footnote will then read:

> [1] All quotations from *A Midsummer Night's Dream* are from the text reprinted in Sylvan Barnet, Morton Berman, and William Burto, *Types of Drama*, 2nd ed. (Boston: Little, Brown, 1977).

If you have not mentioned the author or title of the work quoted, you need to give that information in the note, thus:

> [1] William Shakespeare, *A Midsummer Night's Dream*, reprinted in Sylvan Barnet, Morton Berman, and William Burto, *Types of Drama*, 2nd ed. (Boston: Little, Brown, 1977).

If you have mentioned the author, but not the work, the note will go thus:

> [1] *A Midsummer Night's Dream*, reprinted in Sylvan Barnet, Morton Berman, and William Burto, *Types of Drama*, 2nd ed. (Boston: Little, Brown, 1977).

In short, you need not give information in the note that is already given in the main body of the essay.

In order to eliminate writing many footnotes, each one merely citing the page of a quotation, you can say, in the first footnote, after giving the bibliographical information as above, something like this:

All further references to this work will be given parenthetically, within the text of the essay.

Thus, when you quote the next passage from the play, at the end of the sentence — just before the period — you need only insert a pair of parentheses enclosing the page number or the act, scene, and line number. Here is an example:

At this point Lear goes out, saying, "O Fool, I shall go mad" (p. 100).

or

At this point Lear goes out, saying, "O Fool, I shall go mad" (II.iv.287).

Notice that in the sample analysis on pp. 679–680 we used only one footnote, and then cited all of the other quotations parenthetically.

A GLOSSARY
OF DRAMATIC TERMS

Absurd, Theater of the. Drama of such writers as Eugène Ionesco and Samuel Beckett in France and Harold Pinter in England that imitates the absurdity of man's existence. "Everything, as I see it, is an aberration," Ionesco has said. Among the basic themes are man's loneliness in a world without God, man's inability to communicate, man's dehumanization at the hands of mass media, and man's impotence in the face of society and of death. Though the plays are serious, they may contain extravagantly comic scenes in depicting a reality that is absurd, illogical, senseless, a world of futility and meaningless clichés. In Ionesco's *The Chairs* (1951) an elderly couple rush about, filling a room with chairs for nonexistent visitors. Old age is a fact, but an absurdity, too, and old people are incomprehensible. At the end of *The Chairs*, an orator, who is to deliver a solemn talk about the truths of life, turns out to be deaf and dumb and merely makes unintelligible noises and gestures to the invisible crowd. Ionesco summarizes the theme of *The Chairs* (*The New York Times*, June 1, 1958): "I have tried to deal . . . with emptiness, with frustration, with this world, at once fleeting and crushing. The characters I have used are not fully conscious of their spiritual rootlessness, but they feel it instinctively and emotionally." One basis of man's inability to communicate, and one which the "Absurd" dramatists seize upon, is the corruption of language. The absurdity of trying to communicate by means of a debased language is dramatized by Ionesco in *The Bald Soprano* (1948), where the characters speak in clichés. Because the characters are incomprehensible and the happenings illogical and baffling, the spectators cannot simply sit back in ease, but are continually challenged to grasp the play's meaning. Consult M. Esslin, *The Theatre of the Absurd*.

act. A main division in drama or opera. Act divisions probably arose in Roman theory and derive ultimately from the Greek practice of separating episodes in a play by choral interludes, but Greek (and probably Roman) plays were performed without interruption, for the choral interludes were part of the plays themselves. The division of Elizabethan plays into five acts is often the work of editors rather than authors. No play of Shakespeare's was published in his lifetime with divisions into five acts. Today an act division is commonly indicated by lowering the curtain and turning up the houselights. A **scene** is a smaller unit, either: (1) a division with no change of locale or abrupt shift of time, or (2) a division consisting of an actor or a group of actors on the stage; according to the second definition, the departure or entrance of an actor changes the composition of the group and thus produces a new scene. In an entirely different sense, the scene is the locale where a work is set. The first speech in *Romeo and Juliet* informs the audience of the play's locale: "In fair Verona, where we lay our scene. . . ." Often the décor lets the spectator know where the play is set, but during the last hundred years playwrights have tended, for the convenience of readers, to write long stage directions describing the scene. Here is the beginning of the first stage direction in Shaw's *Candida*: "A fine morning in October 1894 in the north east quarter of London, a vast district miles away from the London of Mayfair and St James's, and much less narrow, squalid, fetid and airless in its slums. . . ."

action. (1) The physical movement of an actor, whether he is leaping into Ophelia's grave or speaking softly to himself. That talk is action is easily seen in the Bastard's remark (*King John*, II.i.466): "Zounds! I was never so bethumped with words / Since I first called my brother's father dad." (2) An incident in the plot, an episode. (3) Aristotle's statement that a drama is an "imitation of an action" (*praxis*) has provoked considerable controversy; recently there has been a tendency to regard this action as the motive underlying the outward deeds of the plot. Francis Fergusson says (in *The Human Image in Dramatic Literature*, p. 116), for example, that the action of *Oedipus the King* "is the quest for Laius's slayer, . . . which persists through the changing circumstances of the play." See pp. 3–5.

aesthetic distance, or **psychical distance.** The detachment between the receptor and the work of art. The concept is chiefly associated with Edward Bullough (see the essay in his *Aesthetics*, reprinted in Melvin Rader, *A Modern Book of Aesthetics*). Bullough explains that there must be some sort of psychical "distance" (gap) between our practical self (our personal needs) and the work of art. Thus, an old man who has been treated harshly by his children may be unable to divorce his personal feelings from *King Lear*.

He may be too involved with the piece as life to see it as art. But "distance" does not mean that the receptor is totally detached or objective. Rather, he is detached from his usual personal involvements, and because of this detachment he can look with a new vigorous interest — he can look with a new sort of passion born of his new personality — at the work of art as art. Persons who do not understand the need for distance between themselves and a work, Bullough explains, commonly say that they do not wish to see a tragedy because there is enough suffering in real life. But the more sophisticated spectator at a tragedy realizes that as a picture is distanced by the frame, a play is distanced (the characters may speak verse, they perform behind footlights, and their deeds cohere to make a unified harmonious pattern); the feelings it evokes in him are not the feelings evoked by a roughly similar event in real life. In the theater we feel "rapturous awe" at what in life would be depressing. See also dramatic illusion, empathy, epic drama. Consult Oscar Budel, "Contemporary Theater and Aesthetic Distance," *PMLA*, 76 (1961), 277–291.

agon (Greek: *contest*). A debate in a Greek comedy. See p. 336. In the last few decades the term has been used (e.g., by Francis Fergusson, *The Idea of a Theater*) to designate a scene of conflict in tragedy, such as the agonizing struggle between Oedipus and Teiresias.

agroikos. See character.

alazon. See character.

alienation effect. See epic drama.

allegory. Frequently an allegory is a narrative wherein abstractions (e.g., virtue, fear) are made concrete (Mr. Virtue, Giant Fear), for the purpose of effectively communicating a moral, but in essence an allegory is merely a system of equivalents. Though allegory need not personify abstractions, allegoric drama almost always does. *Everyman* (c. 1500), an allegoric morality play, includes among its dramatis personae Death, Good Deeds, Beauty, and of course, Everyman. But morality plays may also include allegoric castles (standing for strength or chastity), roses (standing for love or virtue), etc. Consult Bernard Spivack, *Shakespeare and the Allegory of Evil.*

anagnorisis, or disclosure, discovery, recognition. For Aristotle the "recognition" or "disclosure" seems to be merely a recognition of who is who, by such tokens as birthmarks, clothes, etc., but the term has been extended to include the tragic hero's recognition of himself and/or the essence of life. Thus Othello, having murdered his faithful wife, learns he was beguiled into thinking her dishonest, and finally recognizes himself as "one not easily jealous, but being wrought / Perplexed in the extreme"; and he exacts justice from himself by suicide. See pp. 6–7.

antagonist. See protagonist.

antecedent action. See plot.

anticlimax. A descent, the lines or happenings being markedly less important or less impressive than their predecessors. In melodrama, a decrease in tension may cause disappointment and loss of interest; in comedy, a sharp descent (the beautiful princess opens her mouth and sounds like a burlesque queen) may get a desirable laugh. On the desirability of a gradual decrease in tension in tragedy (i.e., a "quiet ending"), consult Max Beerbohm, "Last Acts," in *Around Theatres.*

antimasque. See masque.

arena stage. (1) In British usage, a stage with a back wall and with an audience on three sides. (2) In American usage, a playing space surrounded by spectators, theater-in-the-round. Proponents of arena staging (in the American sense) stress the intimacy afforded by having actors in the midst of the audience, but opponents suggest that at least for some plays the intimacy ought not to be very great. (See aesthetic distance.) It has been noted, too, that even in arena staging the audience normally feels set apart from the actors, for the audience is in the dark while the actors are in an illuminated playing area. Critics of arena staging cite the following difficulties: soliloquies, asides, and direct addresses are hard to deliver in such a theater; directors, aware that the back of an actor's head is not very expressive, tend to have the actors gyrate disturbingly and meaninglessly; entrances and exits are cumbersome; little use can be made of elevation and of groupings of actors.

Apollonian. See Dionysus.

arras. See Elizabethan playhouse.

aside. See soliloquy, convention.

bombast. From a word meaning "cotton stuffing"; rant, speech that is too inflated for the occasion. In Marlowe's *Tamburlaine* (c. 1587), Tamburlaine brags thus:

> Our quivering lances, shaking in the air,
> And bullets, like Jove's dreadful thunderbolts,
> Enrolled in flames and fiery smoldering mists,
> Shall threat the gods more than Cyclopian wars:
> And with our sun-bright armor as we march,
> Will chase the stars from Heaven and dim their eyes
> That stand and muse at our admirèd arms.

bomolochos. See character.

bourgeois drama. A serious play with middle-class dramatis personae. There are a few Elizabethan tragedies of middle-class life, but bourgeois drama, with its emphasis on pathos, is more or less an eighteenth-century invention. Bourgeois dramas were written in the eighteenth and nineteenth centuries, apparently in response to the middle class's desire to see itself on the stage; the bourgeois by the eighteenth century regarded himself as a suitable replacement for the nobleman of earlier tragedy. Speaking generally, the characteristics of these plays are: middle-class dramatis personae, virtue in distress, sentimentality, and an unreasonably high moral tone. Eighteenth-century critics, not sure what to do with pathetic plays on middle-class life, used the terms *drame, drame bourgeois, comédie larmoyante* (tearful comedy), *tragédie bourgeoise, bürgerliches Trauerspiel* (bourgeois tragedy) interchangeably. (Note that a *comédie larmoyante* need not end happily, nor a *tragédie bourgeoise* end sadly.) In England, George Lillo's *The London Merchant* (1731), "a tale of private woe. A London 'prentice ruined," depicted an apprentice who murdered his benefactor. Bourgeois drama in the nineteenth century became melodrama in many hands and tragedy in Ibsen's hands. Consult Fred O. Nolte, *Early Middle Class Drama*; and Eric Auerbach, *Mimesis*, Ch. 17. On Ibsen as a bourgeois dramatist, consult Eric Bentley, *The Playwright as Thinker*. See

domestic tragedy, sentimental, and pp. 230–232, 640–641.

box set. See realism.

braggart soldier. See character.

burla. See *commedia dell'arte*.

burlesque. Any imitation which, by distortion, aims to amuse. Its subject matter is sometimes said to be faults rather than vices, and its tone is neither shrill nor savage. Thus, in distinction from satire it can be defined as a comic imitation of a mannerism or a minor fault (either in style or subject matter), contrived to arouse amusement rather than indignation. In the theater, a burlesque may be a play that amusingly criticizes another play by grotesquely imitating aspects of it, as Gay's *The Beggar's Opera* (1728) mimicked serious operas. In England, a burlesque may be a musical extravaganza in which fantasy has almost entirely ousted criticism. In America, burlesque (especially popular in the late nineteenth and first half of the twentieth century) is usually a sort of vaudeville or variety show stressing bawdy humor and sex. The sexual theme is most fully revealed in the striptease, introduced about 1920. Consult V. C. Clinton-Baddeley, *The Burlesque Tradition in the English Theater after 1660*; Gypsy Rose Lee, *The G-String Murders*. See comedy, satire.

catastrophe. See plot.

catharsis. Aristotle and countless followers said that tragedy evokes pity and fear, and that it produces in the spectator a catharsis (purgation, or, some scholars hold, purification) of these emotions: it drains or perhaps refines or modifies these emotions, and thus tragedy is socially useful. (Aristotle's *Poetics* is the subject of much controversy; one cannot with security assert that Aristotle said anything, without a counter-argument being offered. For various views of catharsis, consult F. L. Lucas, *Tragedy*, and Gerald F. Else's monumental *Aristotle's Poetics*.) For Brecht on catharsis, see p. 573.

character. (1) One of the dramatis personae, e.g., King Lear. (2) The personality of such a figure. Characters are sometimes divided into **flat** and **round characters.** The former have only one "side," representing a single trait (e.g., the faithful wife, the genial drunkard); the latter have many traits and are seen, as it were, from all sides, in the round. The behavior of flat characters is thoroughly predictable, that of round characters is sometimes unexpected though credible. A **stock character** is a type that recurs in many works. For example, from Greek comedy to the present there have been numerous braggart soldiers, stubborn fathers, jealous husbands. Northrop Frye finds four chief types of comic figures: (1) the *alazon,* the imposter, boaster, hypocrite; (2) the *eiron* (see irony), the man who deprecates himself and exposes the boaster; (3) the *bomolochos,* the buffoon, or more generally, the man who entertains by his mannerisms and talk; (4) the *agroikos,* the straightman who is the unwitting butt of humor. Each of these types appears in many dresses; the *alazon,* for example, is most commonly the braggart soldier (*miles gloriosus*), but he is also the pedant, the crank, or anyone who is full of ideas that have no relation to reality. (See *commedia dell'arte;* consult Northrop Frye, *Anatomy of Criticism,* pp. 171–176.) Stock characters are not limited to comedy: the proud tragic hero is a stock character, as are, for example, the cruel stepmother and the son who wishes to avenge his father. See also motivation, plot. Consult J. L. Styan, *The Elements of Drama,* Ch. 8.

chorus. In Greek drama, a group of performers who play a role, e.g., Old Men of Corinth. (The chorus leader is the **koryphaios.**) In Aeschylus' *The Suppliants* (c. 490 B.C.), perhaps the earliest extant play, the chorus consists of the heroines, but in most Greek plays the chorus consists of subsidiary figures who comment rather helplessly on what is happening to the important people. Aeschylus reduced the chorus of fifty to twelve; Sophocles increased it to fifteen, where it remained. The Greek chorus, it is often said, is a sort of middle-man between the unusual main figures and the humdrum spectators. Elizabethan dramas occasionally had a chorus of one actor who, not a participant in the story, commented on it. The Chorus (or prologue) in Shakespeare's *Henry* V urges the audience to

Think when we talk of horses that you see them

Printing their proud hoofs i' the receiving earth;
For 'tis your thoughts that now must deck our kings,
Carry them here and there, jumping o'er times,
Turning the accomplishment of many years
Into an hour-glass: for the which supply,
Admit me Chorus to this history:
Who prologue-like your humble patience pray,
Gently to hear, kindly to judge, our play.

A **chorus character,** or *raisonneur,* however, such as Enobarbus in *Antony and Cleopatra,* is a character who participates in the story yet seems to be the author's mouthpiece, intelligently commenting (often with irony) on the actions of the other characters. But Alfred Harbage, in *As They Liked It,* skeptically and aptly calls such a figure "The Unreliable Spokesman." The use of the chorus, in one form or another, continues into our times, for example in T. S. Eliot's *Murder in the Cathedral,* whose "Chorus of Women of Canterbury," like a Greek chorus and like the audience, "are forced to bear witness"; and in Tennessee Williams's *The Glass Menagerie,* whose Tom Wingfield tells the audience he is "the narrator of the play, and also a character in it."

climax. See plot.

closet drama. A play suited only for reading, not for acting. Most nineteenth-century English poetic dramas (e.g., Coleridge's, Shelley's, Tennyson's) fit into this category, although Byron's plays have recently been moving out of the closet. Consult Moody Prior, *The Language of Tragedy.*

comedy. Most broadly, anything amusing — a literary work or a situation — is a comedy. More specifically, comedy is (in Dr. Johnson's words) "such a dramatic representation of human life, as may excite mirth." Dramatic comedies generally depict a movement from unhappiness to happiness, from (for example) young lovers frustrated by their parents to young lovers happily married. The unhappy situation is so presented that it entertains rather than distresses the spectator; it is ridiculous and/or diverting rather than painful.

Comic drama seems related to fertility rituals; it celebrates generation, renewal, variety (laughing away any narrow-minded persons who seek to limit life's abundance), and it celebrates man's triumphs over the chances of life. Irate parents and shipwrecks cannot prevent journeys from ending with lovers meeting. For the kinds of Greek comedy (Old, Middle, and New) see pp. 336–339. For the characters in Greek comedy, see character. Consult C. Hoy, *The Hyacinth Room; Theories of Comedy*, ed. P. Lauter; L. J. Potts, *Comedy*.

comedy of humors. A term sometimes applied to plays — notably those of Ben Jonson — wherein the characters, though somewhat individualized, obviously represent types or moods (the jealous husband, the witless pedant). A humor was a bodily liquid (blood [Latin: *sanguis*], phlegm, yellow bile, black bile) thought to control one's behavior. Allegedly, a proper mixture produced a well adjusted man, but a preponderance of any one humor produced a distorted personality. The old sense of the word survives in the phrase, "He is in a bad humor"; "sanguine," "phlegmatic," and "bilious" are also modern survivals of the old psychology of humors. **Humor characters** are common in **situational comedy**; they are engineered by a clever plot into a situation that displays their absurdity: the man who craves silence is confronted with a talkative woman; the coward is confronted by the braggart.

comedy of manners, comedy of wit. See high comedy.

comic relief. Humorous episodes in tragedy, alleged to alleviate or lighten the tragic effect. Some comic scenes in tragedy, however, not only provide "relief" but enlarge the canvas of tragedy, showing us a fuller picture of life. The clown who brings Cleopatra the poisonous asp sets her tragedy against the daily world. Critics have increasingly noted that the comic scenes (such as the macabre comments of the gravediggers in *Hamlet*) often deepen rather than alleviate the tragic effect. See tragicomedy. Consult A. P. Rossiter, *Angel with Horns*, Ch. 14.

commedia dell'arte. Italian drama, more or less improvised, performed by professionals in Italy and abroad, mostly in the sixteenth century but still alive in the early eighteenth century. In contrast to the classically-inspired written drama (*commedia erudita*) performed by actors who memorized their lines, *com-*

media dell'arte (perhaps best translated as "professional drama") employed sketches of plots (*scenario;* plural: *scenarii*) specifying entrances and exits and the gist of the dialogue; in performance these *scenarii* were fleshed out with stock bits of comic stage business (*lazzi*) or larger pieces of business (*burle*) such as practical jokes. (The singulars are *lazzo* and *burla.*) Thus a *scenario* may call for the *lazzo* of anger, or the *burla* of chasing a fly, and leave it to the actor to work out the swats and the smile when at last he munches the fly. Though these plays are said to have been improvised, the stock characters, stock situations, and stock stage business make them something more — or less — than improvised. The chief characters — most of whom wore masks — are Pantalone, an elderly Venetian merchant wearing a little cap, a red jacket, loose trousers (hence our word "pants"), and slippers: his age, amours, and avarice make him ridiculous; Dottore, a Bolognese doctor wearing a black academic gown: his age and his pedantry make him ridiculous; Capitano, a soldier, ridiculous because a braggart and a coward; several servants called *zanne* (singular: *zanni*, from *Gianni*, "Johnny") including Arlecchino (later Harlequin), who in the sixteenth century wore patches that in the next century were represented by triangles or diamonds; Brighella, a rather cruel and crafty rogue; Pulcinella, noted for his resourcefulness and his disguises; Pedrolino, a naive valet who becomes the melancholy Pagliacci and Pierrot; Colombina, who later becomes Columbine and loves Harlequin. Further, there are usually four lovers, children of the two Old Men. Consult Allardyce Nicoll, *Masks, Mimes and Miracles*, and *The World of Harlequin*; and K. M. Lea, *Italian Popular Comedy*.

complication. See plot.

confidant (feminine: **confidante**). A character in whom a principal character confides, revealing his state of mind and often furthering the exposition. Horatio is Hamlet's confidant; Oenone is Phèdre's. Although Horatio and Oenone are memorable, the confidant is sometimes absurdly vapid; though the French defended the device as more plausible than the soliloquy, the confidant may be more trouble than he is worth. In *The Critic* (1779), Sheridan ridiculed it thus: "Enter Tilburina stark mad in white satin, and her confidante stark mad in white linen."

conflict. See plot.

convention. An unrealistic device that the public agrees to tolerate. Thus, a character in a drama may express his thoughts aloud and not be heard by other characters (the **aside**), or he may speak his thoughts aloud on the empty stage (the **soliloquy**). Italian characters (e.g., Desdemona and Iago) speak English, yet are understood to be speaking Italian. In motion pictures, one image fades out, another fades in, and through this convention the audience knows that there is a shift in time or place. More generally any character-type, any theme, or motif (e.g., the suspected butler) widely used in literature or drama is a convention. Consult Harry Levin, *Refractions*; M. C. Bradbrook, *Themes and Conventions of Elizabethan Tragedy*.

cosmic irony. See irony.

cothurnus. See sock and buskin.

coup de théatre. A surprise, especially a striking turn of events in the plot. Consult Alan R. Thompson, *The Anatomy of Drama*.

crisis. See plot.

Cruelty, Theater of. Antonin Artaud (1896–1948) used the term in 1933 to refer to a drama that, working rather like a plague, would shock man out of the bonds of his "logical" or "civilized" conceptions and would release the suppressed primitive or pre-logical powers within him, such as criminal instincts and erotic obsessions, revealing the "cruelty" or terrible mystery of existence. This drama, relying more on gestures, shapes, music, and light than on words (Artaud was immensely impressed by Balinese drama although he did not understand Indonesian), would bypass mere realism (i.e., psychology) and would make manifest the truly real supernatural, creating in the spectator a "kind of terror" or a purifying delirium. Artaud, a poet, actor, and director, published relatively little, but his metaphysics and his emphasis on an anti-realistic theater in various ways have influenced Sartre, Camus, Beckett, Ionesco, Genet (con-

sult the preface to *The Maids*) and others: language sometimes becomes gibberish, and madness and violence are presented in order to jolt the spectator out of his comfortable false view of man and of the universe – or, in less metaphysical plays, in order to reflect on the stage the cruelty of the modern world. Consult Artaud's *The Theater and Its Double*; several articles in *Tulane Drama Review*, 8 (Winter 1963); and the "Conclusion" in Jacques Guicharnaud and June Beckelman, *Modern French Theatre*.

denouement. See plot.

deus ex machina. Literally, a god out of a machine. (1) In Greek drama a god who descends by a crane-like arrangement and solves a problem in the story, thus allowing the play to end. It was much used by Euripides; Sophocles in his old age borrowed the idea and introduced Heracles at the end of *Philoctetes* to induce the title-character to go to Troy. (2) Any unexpected and improbable device (e.g., an unexpected inheritance from a long-lost uncle in Australia) used to unknot a problem and thus conclude the work.

deuteragonist. See protagonist.

dialogue. The speech exchanged between characters, or, loosely, even the speech of a single character. Dialogue is sometimes contrasted to action, but Elizabeth Bowen aptly says that dialogue is what the characters *do* to each other, and Shaw aptly says that his plays are all talk just as Beethoven's symphonies are all music. **Stichomythia** is a special form of dialogue, wherein two speakers in a verbal duel thrust and parry in alternating lines. Example:

QUEEN:
Hamlet, thou hast thy father much offended.
HAMLET:
Mother, you have my father much offended.
QUEEN:
Come, come, you answer with an idle tongue.
HAMLET:
Go, go, you question with a wicked tongue.

See action, soliloquy. Consult J. L. Styan, *The Elements of Drama*, Chs. 1–2; and Eric Bentley, *The Life of the Drama*.

diction. (1) Choice of words, wording. Dr. Johnson objected to the "knife" ("an instrument used by butchers and cooks," he said) which Lady Macbeth says she will use to murder the King. "Words too familiar, or too remote," Johnson said, "defeat the purpose of a poet." Consult Moody Prior, *The Language of Tragedy.* (2) A performer's manner or style of speaking, including pronunciation and phrasing.

Dionysus. Greek god of wine, the phallus, the surge of growth, and (to join all these) irrational impulse. It is commonly held that Greek tragedy grew from choral celebrations in his honor; in any case, from the sixth century B.C. tragedies were performed in Athens at the **Great** (or **Greater,** or **City**) **Dionysia,** a festival in Dionysus' honor. (The Dionysiac origin is interestingly rejected by H. D. F. Kitto, in *Theatre Survey,* 1 [1960], 3–17.) Friedrich Nietzsche suggested in *The Birth of Tragedy* (1872) that Greek tragedy, usually considered calm and poised, was not the product of quiet minds. If tragedy, Nietzsche said, showed light and beauty (over which the god Apollo presided), it was nevertheless also indebted to Dionysus, who represented the frenzied, buried self-assertions of the mind. That is, Greek tragedy was the product of **Dionysian** ecstatic and violent self-assertion tamed by (or fused with) the **Apollonian** sense of reason, of moderation, and of external order. "Apollonian" is often associated with classicism, and "Dionysian" with romanticism.

direct address. See soliloquy.

disclosure, discovery. See anagnorisis.

disguising. See masque.

domestic tragedy. A serious play showing the misfortunes (especially within the family) of a private citizen rather than of a man of high rank who is involved in events that shake a realm. See bourgeois drama. Consult Henry H. Adams, *English Domestic or Homiletic Tragedy 1575 to 1642.*

double plot. See plot.

drama (from Greek *dran:* to do). (1) A play, a work that tells a story by means of impersonators. (2) The whole body of work written for the theater. (3) A serious but untragic play (see drame). (4) Events con-

taining conflict, tension, surprise ("life is full of drama"; "the first act lacks drama"). See closet drama, comedy, melodrama, tragedy. A play is written by a **dramatist;** the art of writing plays is **dramaturgy.** A person who writes plays is also a **playwright.** (Note that the last syllable is not "-write" but "-wright," denoting a maker, as a shipwright is a maker of ships.) Consult Kenneth T. Rowe, *Write That Play;* Walter Kerr, *How Not to Write a Play;* Bernard Grebanier, *Playwriting.*

drama of ideas. See *pièce à thèse.*

dramatic illusion. The state between delusion (the spectator thinks the world on the stage is real), and full awareness (the spectator never forgets he is looking at scenery and actors). In *A Midsummer Night's Dream,* Bottom fears that delusion will occur unless the audience is carefully warned: "Write me a prologue, and let the prologue seem to say we will do no harm with our swords, and that Pyramus is not killed indeed. And, for the more better assurance, tell them that I Pyramus am not Pyramus, but Bottom the Weaver. This will put them out of fear." See aesthetic distance.
George Henry Lewes (1817–1878) introduced into English dramatic criticism the term *optique du théâtre,* taken from the French actor François René Molé (1734–1802). A spectator must have this "theater view," this understanding of "scenic illusion," if he is to enjoy the theater; if he lacks it, he will complain that Hamlet ought to be speaking Danish (see convention). *Optique du théâtre* requires that we be given not reality but a symbolic representation of it. A stage miser should finger his gold differently from a real miser; a stage character must be heard, even though in real life the character he is playing might speak softly.
Staging that aims at delusion or a high degree of illusion is **representational staging.** Here the stage-characters eat real food on stage, speak with their backs to the audience, etc. (See naturalism, realism.) When David Belasco staged *The Governor's Lady* in 1912, he was representational, placing on the stage an exact duplicate of a particular (Child's) restaurant. On the other hand, **presentational staging** is antirealistic; in Thornton Wilder's *Our Town* (1938), a drugstore counter, for example, consisted of a board across the backs

of two chairs. The staging in musical comedies, ballets, and puppet shows is, of course, presentational. Presentational staging is sometimes called **theatrical staging. Theatricalism,** by its unreality, continually reminds us that we are in the theater, not in the street. On theatricalism, see style. A derogatory way of saying a work is theatrical is to say it is **stagy.**

drame. A solemn but untragic play, especially an eighteenth-century play that, quietly glorifying the bourgeois virtues, preaches and appeals to the audience's emotions. See bourgeois drama. Consult Alan R. Thompson, *The Anatomy of Drama,* which classifies most naturalistic and realistic plays (e.g., Ibsen's and Chekhov's) as *drames.*

eiron. See character.

Elizabethan playhouse. The first permanent structure built in England for plays was The Theatre, built outside the city limits of London in 1576 by James Burbage. It soon had several competitors, but little is known about any of these playhouses. The contract for one, The Fortune (built in 1600), survives; it tells us that the three-storied building was square, 80 feet on the outside, 55 feet on the inside. The stage was 43 feet broad and 27½ feet deep. It has been calculated that about 800 people (the **groundlings**) could stand around the three sides of the stage on the ground that was called the **yard,** and another 1500 could be seated in the three galleries. The other chief pieces of evidence concerning the physical nature of the theater are (1) the "De Witt drawing," which is really a copy of a sketch made by a visitor (c. 1596) to The Swan, and (2) bits of evidence that can be gleaned from the plays themselves, such as "Enter a Fairy at one door, and Robin Goodfellow at another." Conclusions vary and scholarly tempers run high; the following statements are not indisputable. Most theaters were polygonal or round structures (Shakespeare calls the theater a "wooden O") with three galleries; the yard was open to the sky. From one side a raised stage (or open **platform**) jutted into the middle. A sort of wooden canopy (the **heavens,** or the **shadow**) projected over the stage and in some theaters rested on two pillars; these pillars could conveniently serve as a hiding place for an actor supposed to be unseen by the other characters. At the rear of the stage there sometimes was a curtained alcove or booth, which when uncurtained might represent a room or a cave. The curtain is often called an **arras,** and it was probably behind this curtain that Polonius hid, only to be stabbed. At the rear of the stage (flanking the curtained space?) there were perhaps also two or three doors, through which entrances and exits were made. Probably the **tiring house** ("attiring house," i.e., dressing room) was behind the rear of the stage. Above the alcove or booth was an area that could be used for an **upper stage** (for example, in scenes of people standing on a city's walls); flanking the upper stage were windows, one of which may have served Juliet for her misnamed balcony scene. Some scholars argue that in a yet higher place were musicians, and at the very top — called the **top** — was an opening from which an actor could look; in *Henry VI, Part I,* Joan of Arc appears "on the top, thrusting out a torch burning." Most of the acting was done on the main stage (the platform), but the "inner stage," "upper stage," "windows," and "top" must have been useful occasionally (if they existed). The **cellar** (beneath the stage) was used, for example for the voice of the ghost in *Hamlet,* and for Ophelia's grave. Though some scenery was used, the absence of a front curtain precluded many elaborate scenic effects (much, however, could be done by carrying banners) and encouraged continuous action. The stage that was a battlefield could in an instant, by the introduction of a throne, become a room in a palace. Two readable books are A. M. Nagler, *Shakespeare's Stage,* and C. Walter Hodges, *The Globe Restored.* Nagler (Ch. 12) also gives information about a second kind of Elizabethan theater — basically a platform at one end of a hall — that catered to a courtly group. Interesting specialized items on playhouses are in *Shakespeare Survey,* 1 and 12, ed. Allardyce Nicoll.

empathy. The projection of one's feelings into a perceived object. The Germans call it *Einfühlung* — "a feeling into." Vernon Lee, one of the formulators of the idea, claimed that when we say "the mountain rises" we do so not because the mountain rises (it doesn't) but because we have often raised our eyes, head, and total muscular structure to look at mountains or other tall objects. In perceiving a mountain, we merge (unawares) its image with the previously accumulated idea of rising. We are said to empathize with a character if we flinch at a blow directed at him, or if we feel bowed with his grief; if, in short, we *experience* as well as *see* his behavior. Empathy is often distinguished from **sympathy**: we empathize if we feel *with* the character; we sympathize if we feel *for* the character. See aesthetic distance. Consult Vernon Lee's essay in *A Modern Book of Aesthetics*, ed. Melvin Rader; Herbert S. Langfeld, *The Aesthetic Attitude*.

epic drama. Bertolt Brecht (1898–1956) labeled "aristotelian" most drama before his own. He held that it aimed at enthralling the spectators by building up to a climax, thus arousing and then purging their emotions. In contrast, Brecht said, epic drama (he borrowed the phrase from Erwin Piscator) aims at arousing the audience's detached thought; it teaches, keeping the spectators alert by preventing any emotional involvement. The epic drama (probably so-called because it resembles the epic in its abundance of loosely connected scenes and its tendency to deal with a society rather than merely with a few individuals) achieves this estrangement or **alienation effect** (German: *Verfremdungseffekt*) by many means: the epic play (e.g., Brecht's *The Good Woman of Setzuan*, or his *Mother Courage*) commonly consists of a series of loosely connected scenes rather than a tightly organized plot with a climax; the settings are not realistic but merely suggest the locale, and they are often changed in full view of the audience, preventing any entrancing illusion (a night scene may be done on an illuminated stage, again to prevent the audience from emotionally entering into the play); the actor may address the audience directly, sometimes in song, and he aims not at becoming the character but at presenting him, or, to put it differently, at making a comment on him, as we might do when we put aside a cigarette and say, "He said to me, '. . . .'"; loudspeakers, films, and placards may be used, and the whole is something of a lecture-demonstration, aimed not at arousing and then quieting the audience's emotions, but at making things somewhat strange to the audience so that the audience will look sharply and will think. Consult Bertolt Brecht, "A Short Organum,"

in *Playwrights on Playwriting*, ed. Toby Cole; *Brecht on Theatre*, trans. John Willett; R. Gray, *Brecht*; *The Tulane Drama Review*, 6 (Sept. 1961). See pp. 573–575.

epilogue. (1) An appendix (usually a concluding address) to a play; (2) the actor who recites such an appendix (e.g., Puck, at the close of Shakespeare's *A Midsummer Night's Dream*).

exposition. See plot.

expressionism. An anti-naturalistic movement chiefly associated with Germany just after World War I, but which was foreshadowed by Strindberg, notably in his trilogy, *To Damascus* (1898–1904), and in his *A Dream Play* (1902). Expressionism does not seek to present reality dispassionately imitated, but reality passionately felt. Thus, when Mr. Zero shakes his employer (in Elmer Rice's *The Adding Machine* [1923]), the office spins; when he is on trial, the walls of the courtroom veer crazily. Speaking broadly, expressionist plays (in addition to being unrealistic) usually (1) depict types or classes (Rice's Mr. Zero; the Man, the Woman, the Nameless One in Ernst Toller's *Man and Masses* [1921], (2) employ dream sequences, (3) assume that society is responsible for man's troubles. In *The Emperor Jones*, Eugene O'Neill's concentration on a single figure representative of man (Jones) and his use of visions and unrealistic settings illustrate the first two points. Though Arthur Miller's *Death of a Salesman* (1949) is in many ways "realistic," it also is indebted to expressionism, especially in the scenes involving Willy's memories. (Miller originally planned to call the play *The Inside of His Head*.) Note, too, the name of Miller's hero – Loman, i.e., low man. Consult John Willett, *Expressionism*.

falling action. See plot.

farce. A sort of comedy based not on clever language or subtleties of character, but on broadly humorous situations (a man mistakenly enters the ladies' locker room), is lucidly defended by Eric Bentley in his introduction to *"Let's Get a Divorce" and Other Plays*, where he suggests that farce, like dreams, shows "the disguised fulfillment of repressed wishes." Farce is usually filled with surprise, with swift physical action, and with assault. The characters are physically and intellectually insensitive, and characterization is subordinated to plot. See also Bentley's *The Life of the Drama.* **Slapstick** (named for an implement made of two slats which resound when slapped against a posterior) is farce that relies on physical assault. Farce and slapstick are **low comedy,** as is comedy that depends on obscenity.

foil. A character who sets off another, as Laertes and Fortinbras — young men who, like Hamlet, have lost a father — help to set off Hamlet, or as a braggart soldier helps to set off a courageous one.

foreshadowing. See suspense.

Great Dionysia. See Greek theater.

Greek and **Hellenistic theater.** The great age of the Greek drama was the fifth century B.C. The audience sat on wooden benches in tiers on a hillside, looking down at a flat circular dancing-place (the **orchestra**), in the middle of which was an altar to Dionysus; behind the dancing place was a playing-area, which logic (but no concrete evidence) suggests may have been slightly elevated; visible behind the playing-area was the *skene,* a wooden "scene-building" introduced about 458 B.C. that served as a background, as a place for actors to make entrances from and exits to, and as a dressing room. To speak of these elements in a little more detail: the seating-area, which held as many as 16,000 people, was the *theatron* ("seeing-place"); fan-shaped or horseshoe shaped, it swept around the orchestra in a segment a little greater than a semicircle. The chorus, entering by an aisle (*parodos*) at each side of the *theatron,* danced in the orchestra. The front (i.e., the façade) of the *skene* (or perhaps a temporary screen) and sometimes the playing-area in front of it seem to have been called the *proskenion.* Though the *skene's* façade perhaps suggested the front of a palace, there were further efforts at indicating locale: Sophocles is said to have invented scene-painting (a painted cloth or screen in front of the *skene?*), and there are allusions to *periaktoi,* upright prisms bearing a different decoration on each side. Apparently when a

new locality in the same town was to be indicated, the *periaktos* at the right was turned, when an entirely new locality was to be indicated, both *periaktoi* were turned. Other machines were the **eccyclema,** a platform that was rolled out of the *skene* to indicate a scene indoors, and the **mechane,** a crane from which a god could descend or by means of which a character could soar through the air. (See *deus ex machina.*)

Plays were put on chiefly during two holidays, the **Lenaea** (Feast of the Wine-press) in January, and the **Great** (or **Greater,** or **City**) **Dionysia** in March or April. The Lenaea was chiefly associated with comedy, the Great Dionysia with tragedy. At the latter, on each of three mornings a tragic dramatist presented three tragedies and one satyr-play. The expense was born by a **choregus,** a rich citizen ordered by the state to assume the financial burden. See comedy, satyr-play, tragedy.

The **Hellenistic theater** (i.e., theaters of, say, the third and second centuries B.C. erected in towns to which Greek culture had been spread by Alexander's conquests) seems to have been much like the Greek theater, though now the *proskenion* is apparently more highly decorated, having pillars a few feet in front of it and being fitted with painted panels called *pinakes.* And the *skene,* now of stone rather than of wood, may have had projections at the sides (*paraskenia*) and an upper story (*episkenion*). The playing-area on this upper level is the *logeion.* Consult Margarete Bieber, *The History of the Greek and Roman Theater.*

hamartia. This Greek word is variously translated as "tragic flaw" or "error" or "shortcoming" or "weakness," and in many plays it *is* a flaw or even a vice such as *hybris* (also *hubris*) — Greek for overweening pride, arrogance, excessive confidence. But in other plays it is merely a misstep, such as a choice that turns out badly. Indeed, the tragic hero may be undone by his virtue — his courage, for example, when others are not merely prudent but cowardly. See pp. 5–8. On *hamartia* and *hybris* see Richmond Lattimore, *Story Patterns in Greek Tragedy.*

happening. A kind of theatrical activity popular in the early 1960's, named for Allan Kaprow's *18 Happenings in 6 Parts* (1959). Instead of a conventional theater there is simply a place (art gallery, backyard), instead of actors who play roles there are participants, instead of a plot there are discontinuous actions or happenings. Sample: a man asks if Howard Saretta is in the audience; when there is no answer he sits down among the spectators, and someone else gets up, skips rope, washes his face, and then breaks a pair of eyeglasses. Often there is some violence directed against people (participants and audience) and against objects (here, against eyeglasses). Consult *Happenings*, ed. Michael Kirby; Susan Sontag, *Against Interpretation*; and A. Kaprow, *Art News* (May 1961).

Hellenistic theater. See Greek theater.

high comedy. Intellectual rather than physical, it requires the close attention of a sophisticated audience, flourishing (says George Meredith in his *Essay on Comedy* [1877]) in a "society of cultivated men and women . . . wherein ideas are current, and the perceptions quick." Etherege, Wycherley, Congreve, and other playwrights of the decades following the Restoration of Charles II to the throne of England (1660) wrote **Restoration comedy,** high comedy of a particular sort, often called **comedy of manners** or **comedy of wit.** Their plays abound in witty **repartee** (what Dr. Johnson called "gay remarks and unexpected answers"), and often strike modern audiences as cynical. Restoration comedy has no precise terminal date, but can be said to end about 1700, with the development of sentimental comedy, plays of venerable parents and middle-class dutiful sons who love pure young things. Example: Richard Steele's *The Conscious Lovers* (1722). Consult Thomas H. Fujimura, *The Restoration Comedy of Wit*; Louis Kronenberger, *The Thread of Laughter*; Norman N. Holland, *The First Modern Comedies*.

humor character. See comedy of humors.

hubris. See *hamartia.*

hybris. See *hamartia.*

imitation (Greek: *mimesis*). Not a pejorative term in much criticism, for it often implies a "making" or "re-creating" or "re-presenting" of a form in a substance not natural to it. Thus Michelangelo reproduced or imitated the form of Moses, in stone. For Aristotle, tragedy is the imitation (i.e., representation, re-creation) by means of words, gesture, music, and scenery, of an important action.

irony. Irony is of several sorts. **Socratic irony,** named for Socrates, who commonly feigned more ignorance than he possessed, denotes understatement. The *eiron* (see character) is the cunning fellow who plays the underdog. **Dramatic irony,** or **Sophoclean irony,** or **tragic irony** refers to a condition of affairs which is the tragic reverse of what the participants think. Thus, it is ironic that Macbeth kills Duncan, thinking he will achieve happiness; he later finds he loses all that makes life worth living. Oedipus accuses the blind prophet of corruption, but by the end of the play Oedipus learns (as the audience knew at the outset) that he himself is corrupt, that he has been mentally blind (ignorant) and that the prophet has had vision (knowledge). Oedipus meant what he said, but his words have proved to be ironic. (Aristotle's word for reversal is *peripeteia*.) We have dramatic irony, it can be said, when a speech or action is more fully understood by the spectators than by the characters. This sort of irony, based on misunderstanding, or partial knowledge, is common in tragedy, but comedy too has its misunderstandings; comic speeches or actions are ironic if they bring about the opposite of what is intended. More generally, the contrast implied in "irony" need be neither tragic nor comic; it is "ironic" that the strong man is overthrown by the weak man and that the liar unknowingly tells the truth.

irony of fate (a phrase which H. W. Fowler's *Modern English Usage* aptly says is hackneyed), or **cosmic irony,** denotes the view that God, or fate, or some sort of supernatural figure, is amused to manipulate human beings as a puppeteer manipulates his puppets. Thus, by an irony of fate the messenger delivers the prisoner's pardon an instant too late. Consult Garnett G. Sedgewick, *Of Irony*; Alan R. Thompson, *The Dry Mock*.

koryphaios. See chorus.

kothurnus. See sock and buskin.

lazzo. See *commedia dell' arte.*

Lenaea. See Greek theater.

liturgical drama. A play that is part of the church service or liturgy. In the tenth century the churchmen put on a playlet of a few lines as part of the Easter liturgy. The text is based on Mark 16:1–7: clerics dressed as the Three Marys approach the "tomb" of Christ (the altar) and are asked by a cleric, disguised as an angel, whom they seek. When they reply that they seek Christ, he tells them that Christ has risen and shows them the empty "tomb." The performers were all male, and the dialogue (in Latin) was chanted or sung; probably the gestures were stylized.

low comedy. See farce.

masque, mask, disguising. An entertainment (apparently derived from an ancient ritual) in the Renaissance court, wherein noblemen performed a dignified playlet, usually allegorical and mythological. The masque was lavishly produced, but its basic structure was generally simple: the masquers (costumed and masked noble performers) enter, supposedly having come from afar, they dance with the ladies of the court, and then they depart. Because the masquers are of the same rank as the ladies, and because performers and audience join in a dance, the masque is very close to the masked ball, Ben Jonson (1572–1637) popularized what he called the **antimasque** (a grotesque dance of monsters or clowns), performed by professionals representing chaos, who are dispelled by the courtly performers. ("Anti," from "antic," meaning "a grotesque caper" or "a fool," is sometimes written "ante" because the antimasque precedes the masque.) Consult Enid Welsford, *The Court Masque*; E. K. Chambers, *The Mediaeval Stage* and *The Elizabethan Stage*.

melodrama. Originally, in Renaissance Italy, an opera; later, a drama with occasional songs, or with music (*melos* is Greek for "song") expressing a character's thoughts, much as in films today. In the early nineteenth century plays with musical accompaniment became so stereotyped that the word acquired a second (and now dominant) meaning: a play wherein characters clearly virtuous or vicious are pitted against each other in sensational situations filled with suspense, until justice triumphs.

The situations, not the characters, are exciting. The exotic horror (castles with dungeons) dominant in early nineteenth-century melodramas was often replaced later in the century by local horror (the cruel landlord), but whether exotic or local, melodrama is improbable, and virtue — unsullied by any touch of guilt — triumphs over unlikely circumstances. Melodrama is sometimes said to be tragedy with character left out (i.e., it contains serious happenings), but by virtue of its happy ending and its one-sided characters it can better be described as comedy with good-humor left out. Some critics use "melodrama" without any pejorative connotation to describe such serious, often sensational, plays as Emlyn Williams's *Night Must Fall* (1935), Robert Ardrey's *Thunder Rock* (1939), and Arthur Miller's *All My Sons*. Consult Robert B. Heilman, *Tragedy and Melodrama*.

miracle play. A medieval play on a Biblical episode or a saint's life. Consult Arnold Williams, *The Drama of Medieval England*.

morality play. A late medieval development, popular well into the sixteenth century, allegorically dramatizing some aspect of the moral life, including such characters as Everyman, Good Deeds, and Avarice. It usually showed the conflict between good and evil, or the way in which the Christian faces death. Consult Arnold Williams, *The Drama of Medieval England*; Bernard Spivack, *Shakespeare and the Allegory of Evil*.

motivation. Grounds in character and situation that make behavior plausible. Such grounds are not always present, even in great drama: when Othello asks why Iago "hath thus ensnared my soul," Iago replies, "Demand me nothing: what you know, you know." See character. Consult J. I. M. Stewart, *Character and Motive in Shakespeare*.

naturalism. Sometimes defined, like realism, as the portrayal of "a scientifically accurate, detached picture of life, including everything and selecting nothing." The spectator looking through the peephole of the proscenium, as a scientist looks through the eyepiece of a microscope, is to feel he is witnessing life rather than a symbolic representation of life. More commonly, however, "naturalism" alludes neither to a panoramic view nor to the detailed presentation of a narrow **slice of life** (French: *tranche de vie*), but to a particular attitude held by some writers since the middle of the nineteenth century. Though claiming to be dispassionate observers, they were influenced by evolutionary thought, and regarded man not as possessed of a soul and of free will, but as a creature determined by his heredity and environment. The movement in drama can be said to begin with the Goncourt Brothers' unsuccessful *Henriette Maréchal* (1865), but it is usual to say that the opening gun in the battle for naturalism was fired in Émile Zola's dramatization (1873) of his novel, *Thérèse Raquin*. Thérèse and her lover drown her husband, but are then so guilt-ridden that they poison themselves. In his preface Zola urged that the theater be brought "into closer relation with the great movement toward truth and experimental science which has since the last century been on the increase. . . . I have chosen characters who were completely dominated by their nerves and blood." In Paris, André Antoine opened his Théâtre Libre in 1887, devoting it mostly to plays showing the power of instincts and the influence of heredity and environment. These plays were staged as untheatrically as possible; for example, the actors turned their backs to the audience. In Germany, Otto Brahm opened the Freie Bühne in 1889, and in England J. T. Grein opened the Independent Theatre in 1891, both with Ibsen's *Ghosts* (1881), a play showing the destruction of a young man by inherited syphilis. Ibsen's greatness does not allow him to be pinned down by the label "naturalist," but he can be said to be naturalistic (among other things) by virtue of his serious interest in the effects of heredity and environment. Other dramatists who wrote naturalistic plays include August Strindberg (e.g., his *Miss Julie* [1888]) and Gerhart Hauptmann (early in his career, say, through *The Weavers* [1892]), and Eugene O'Neill (again, the early plays such as *The Rope* [1918] and *Diff'rent* [1920]). Note, however, that the major naturalistic writers usually are more than naturalistic; Strindberg's *Miss Julie*, for example, has a preface that talks about the influence of heredity and environment, and it deals with sordid aspects of reality, but it also has symbolic overtones, notably in Julie's and Jean's dreams. Consult Mordecai Gorelik, *New Theatres for Old; TDR: The Drama Review*, 13 (Winter 1968); and (for Strindberg, O'Neill, and the sources of their ideas) Oscar Cargill, *Intellectual America*.

nuntius. See Senecan tragedy.

obligatory scene. See *scène à faire*.

pathos. The quality that evokes pity. The pathetic is often distinguished from the tragic; in the former, the suffering is experienced by the passive and the innocent (especially women and children), while in the latter it is experienced by persons who act, struggle, and are in some measure responsible for their sufferings. Discussing Aeschylus' *The Suppliants*, H. D. F. Kitto says in *Greek Tragedy* (2nd ed.): "The Suppliants are not only pathetic, as the victims of outrage, but also tragic, as the victims of their own misconceptions." See bourgeois drama, and the afterword to Arthur Miller's *Death of a Salesman*, pp. 230–232.

peripeteia (anglicized to **peripety**, meaning **reversal**). The reversal occurs when an action produces the opposite of what was intended or expected, and it is therefore a kind of irony. In *Julius Caesar*, Brutus kills Caesar in order to free Rome from tyranny, but the deed introduces tyranny into Rome. (See irony, plot.)

pièce à thèse. A play with a thesis, a play in which the dramatist argues a point. Commonly the thesis is not about, say, the benevolence of God, but about the merits or defects of some social institution; a play dealing with a social institution may also be called a **problem play** or a **drama of ideas**. Some critics distinguish between the terms, saying that a problem play merely poses a social problem, as Galsworthy does in *Strife* (1909), while a thesis play propounds a solution. Shaw says that "The material of the dramatist is always some conflict of human feeling with circumstances"; when the circumstances are "human institutions" (e.g., divorce laws, penal codes) rather than unchanging facts of life (e.g., death), and the audience is forced to meditate on the value of the institutions, we have a problem play. Shaw's essay, "The Play of Ideas," is in *Shaw on Theatre*, ed. E. J. West. Consult also Walter Kerr, *How Not to Write a Play*, Ch. 5.

pièce bien faite, or **well-made play.** A play, with much suspense and with little depth of characterization, that relies on a cleverly constructed plot, first developing a situation, then building the crisis to a climax, and then resolving the business. The type, which perhaps can be described as melodrama with the fisticuffs left out, is chiefly associated with Victorien Sardou (1831–1908), but Sardou was indebted to Eugène Scribe (1791–1861). Shaw called their plays clockwork mice, and Sardoodledom, but the influence of Sardou on Shaw's hero, Ibsen, is undeniable. See plot, and consult Walter Kerr, *How Not to Write a Play*, Ch. 10; Eric Bentley, "Homage to Scribe," *What Is Theatre?*; C. E. Montague, *Dramatic Values*, pp. 63–74; *Camille and Other Plays*, ed. Stephen S. Stanton.

plot and **character.** The plot is sometimes the "story," the "narrative," but usually it is the happenings *as the author arranges them.* In *Hamlet*, for example, the story involves the poisoning of Hamlet's father, but Shakespeare omits this scene from his plot. Aristotle, in Chapter 6 of the *Poetics*, calls plot "the whole structure of the incidents," and he speaks of plot as the "soul of tragedy," thus making it more important than character. By character he means the personalities of the figures in the story. Menander (a Greek comic dramatist) is said to have told a friend that he had finished a comedy, though he had not yet written a line of dialogue; the anecdote implies that Menander had completed his idea of *what happens* (action) and in *what order* (plot), and he would find it easy then to write the lines of the characters necessary to this plot. The separation, however, between plot and character is misleading, for the two usually interplay. Although it is true that there may be much plot and little character (as in a thriller), in most great plays there is such a fusion between what is done and the personality of the doer that we feel the truth of Henry James's questions: "What is character but the determination of incident? What is incident but the illustration of character?" (See also character.)

Most plots entail a **conflict**, wherein the protagonist is somehow opposed. If he is opposed chiefly by another person rather than by a force such as Fate or God or by an aspect of himself, the opposing figure is the antago-

nist. The German critic, Gustav Freytag, in *Technique of the Drama* (1863), held that a play dramatizes "the rushing forth of will power from the depths of man's soul toward the external world," and "the coming into being of a deed and its consequences on the human soul." The five-act play, he said, commonly arranged such an action into a **pyramidal structure,** consisting of a **rising action,** a **climax,** and a **falling action.** The rising action begins with the **exposition,** in which is given essential information, especially about the **antecedent action** (what has occurred before this piece of action begins). The two gossiping servants who tell each other that after a year away in Paris the young master is coming home today with his new wife are giving the audience the exposition. The exposition in Shakespeare's *The Tempest* is almost ruthlessly direct: Prospero tells his naive daughter "I should inform thee farther," and for about one hundred and fifty lines he proceeds to tell her why she is on an almost uninhabited island. The action rises through a **complication** (the protagonist is opposed) to a high point or **crisis** or **climax** (a moment at which tension is high, and which is a decisive turning point). The falling action goes through a **reversal** (if a tragedy, the protagonist loses power), and then into a **catastrophe,** also called a **denouement** (unknotting) or resolution. (Aristotle's word for the reversal is *peripeteia,* anglicized to **peripety,** and, translated as "irony of events," would in a comedy be a change from bad fortune to good, and the catastrophe would thus be happy.) The denouement frequently involves what Aristotle called an *anagnorisis* (**recognition, disclosure, discovery**). This recognition may be as simple as the identification of a long-lost brother by a birth mark, or it may involve a character's recognition of his own true condition. Shakespeare sometimes used a pyramidal structure, placing his climax neatly in the middle of what seems to us to be the third of five acts. In *Julius Caesar*, Brutus rises in the first half of the play, reaching his height in III.i, with the death of Caesar; but later in this scene he gives Marc Antony permission to speak at Caesar's funeral and thus sets in motion his own fall, which occupies the second half of the play. In *Macbeth*, the protagonist attains his height in III.i. ("Thou hast it now: King"), but he soon perceives that he is going downhill:

> I am in blood
> Stepped in so far that, should I wade no more,
> Returning were as tedious as go o'er.

Some works have a **double plot,** that is, two plots, usually with some sort of relation. For example, the **subplot** or **underplot** (the secondary narrative) might be a grotesque version of the serious main plot. In Shakespeare's *The Tempest*, the main plot and subplot both deal with usurpation. In *King Lear*, the main plot concerns Lear's relation to his daughters, while the parallel subplot concerns Gloucester's relation to his sons. For another aspect of the subplot, see comic relief; consult William Empson, *Some Versions of Pastoral*, Ch. 2. On plotting see *pièce bien faite* and *scène à faire*.

poetic justice. A term coined by Thomas Rymer in 1678, denoting the reward of the virtuous and the punishment of the vicious. Aristotle had said or implied that the tragic hero is undone partly by some sort of personal flaw — i.e., he is at least partly responsible for the suffering he later encounters. (See *hamartia*, and pp. 5–8.) "Poetic justice," with its idea that all characters reap the harvest of their just deserts, is a hardening of Aristotle's suggestion. Consult M. A. Quinlan, *Poetic Justice in the Drama*.

problem play. See *pièce à thèse*.

prologue. (1) A preface or introduction. For the Greeks the *prologos* was the first scene, which gave the exposition. Elizabethan prologues commonly summarize the plot, as the Chorus does in the prologue to *Romeo and Juliet*, but in the English theater of the late seventeenth century, the prologue was almost an independent verse essay spoken before the play began. Consult Autrey N. Wiley, *Rare Prologues and Epilogues 1642–1700*. (2) The actor who speaks a piece of the sort described above.

proscenium stage, or **picture-frame stage.** A playing-area framed in the front, and thus separated from the audience. This frame is the **proscenium arch** or the **proscenium;** the empty space it contains, sometimes filled with a curtain, is the **proscenium opening.** Basically a **proscenium theater** has two rooms, one for the audience and another (with a hole in the mutual wall) for the performers. Such a theater is at least as old as the early seventeenth century, when the Farnese Theater was built in Parma. Consult Allardyce Nicoll, *The Development of the Theatre.*

protagonist. The chief figure in a play. In Greek the word means literally the "first contender," i.e., the chief actor (*protos*: first). The second role was given to the **deuteragonist,** the third to the **tritagonist.** The protagonist is commonly opposed by the **antagonist,** played by the deuteragonist. For the relationship between the protagonist and the antagonist, see plot.

psychical distance. See aesthetic distance.

pyramidal structure. See plot.

raisonneur. See chorus character.

rising action. See plot.

realism. The reproduction of life, especially as it appears to the eye and ear; the illusion of nature. Usually it deals with ordinary men in ordinary situations, moving in scenery that closely imitates reality. In England, T. W. Robertson (1829–1871) insisted, for example, that doorknobs not be painted on the doors but be three-dimensional. Wings and a backcloth (i.e., projecting flats at the sides and a painted cloth at the rear) were increasingly replaced by the box set (a room with the front wall missing, containing real furniture) for interior scenes. Gas lighting, introduced to the stage about 1820, soon became capable of producing effects of sunlight, moonlight, etc. The dialogue, as well as the sets, came closer to what the senses perceive. Realistic plays (in prose, of course) avoided soliloquies, asides, and declamation. The great playwrights of the movement are Ibsen and Chekhov. As Mary McCarthy says of American realistic drama (*On the Contrary*), "realism is a depreciation of the real," for in "its resolve to tell the whole truth" it tends to deflate, to reveal human littleness. (It doesn't believe in exceptional, heroic people; when it treats the upper classes, it usually tends toward satire.) The oppressive box set of realistic plays, Miss McCarthy points out, "is the box or 'coffin' of average middle-class life opened at one end to reveal the corpse within." That realism shades into naturalism is clear; that in Ibsen it shades into symbolism is less obvious but is well demonstrated by John Northam, *Ibsen's Dramatic Method*. A simple example of Ibsen's symbolism: in *Hedda Gabler*, Hedda's hair is "not particularly ample," but Thea's is "unusually rich and wavy," suggesting Hedda's barrenness and Thea's fertility. Consult Mordecai Gorelik, *New Theatres for Old*; A. Nicholas Vardac, *Stage to Screen*, Chs. 4, 9; Ernest B. Watson, *Sheridan to Robertson*. In **selective realism,** some of the scenery (e.g., a window and a door) closely reproduces reality, but some (e.g., a framework *suggesting* a roof) does not.

recognition. See *anagnorisis*.

repartee. See high comedy.

Restoration comedy. See high comedy.

revenge play. See Senecan tragedy.

reversal. See *peripeteia*.

Roman theater. A permanent theater was not built at Rome until the first century B.C. The plays of Plautus (254?–184 B.C.) and Terence (190?–159? B.C.) were performed on temporary stages erected in the Circus Maximus and the Forum during holidays. In the permanent Roman theater, the enormous audience (40,000 or more) sat in a semicircle around a level space that was a vestige of what had been called the "orchestra" ("dancing place") of the Greek theater. Behind this vestige was the stage, running through what would have been the diameter of the circle. The long, slightly elevated stage was backed by a façade (painted to resemble two or three houses) with several doors through which actors made some of their exits and entrances, the others being made at the ends of the stage. Behind the façade was the dressing-room. The Roman theater, unlike the Greek and Hellenistic theaters, was a self-enclosed structure, built on level ground, not against a hillside. Consult Margarete Bieber, *The History of the Greek and Roman Theater*.

satire. A work ridiculing aspects of human behavior and seeking to arouse in the audience contempt for its object. Satirists almost always justify their attacks by claiming that satire is therapeutic. Shaw says, in the preface to his *Complete Plays*, "If I make you laugh at yourself, remember that my business as a classic writer of comedies is to 'chasten morals with ridicule'; and if I sometimes make you feel like a fool, remember that I have by the same action cured your folly." Satire, however, is sometimes distinguished from comedy on the grounds that satire aims to correct by ridiculing, while comedy aims simply to evoke amusement. Among notable satires are the plays of Aristophanes; Gay's *The Beggar's Opera* (1728); Brecht's *The Threepenny Opera* (1928); Kaufman, Ryskind, and Gershwin's *Of Thee I Sing* (1931) — though Kaufman himself has defined satire as "that which closes on Saturday night." See burlesque, comedy. Consult Dane F. Smith, *Plays about the Theatre in England from "The Rehearsal" in 1671 to the Licensing Act in 1737*; Northrop Frye, *Anatomy of Criticism*.

satyr-play. A piece in which there is a chorus of lewd satyrs (creatures half-man, the other half either horse or goat). The Greek tragic playwright of the fifth century B.C. presented three tragedies and a satyr-play for the dramatic festival. Apparently the satyr-play often burlesqued a hero, showing him in a ludicrous situation. Only one complete satyr-play (Euripides' *The Cyclops*) is extant; it travesties the legend of Odysseus' encounter with Polyphemus. Consult Philip W. Harsh, *A Handbook of Classical Drama*.

scene. See act.

scenery. The carpentry and painted cloths (and projected images) used on a stage. Scenery may be used to conceal parts of the stage, to decorate, to imitate or suggest locales, to establish time or to evoke mood. For comments on early scenery, see Greek theater and Elizabethan playhouse. The Elizabethan public theater did not use much scenery. In *Twelfth Night*, when Viola asks "What country, friends, is this?" she is told "This is Illyria, lady" and the audience knows all that carpenters and painters can tell them. But even before Shakespeare's birth, Renaissance Italians had placed buildings, probably of lath and cloth, at the right and left of the stage. Behind the buildings, which were three-dimensional and were embellished with moldings. projected flat pieces cut and painted to look like other buildings at a distance, and behind these flat pieces were yet other flats, still smaller. On the symbolic use of scenery, see pp. 23–24.

scenario. See *commedia dell'arte.*

scène à faire, or (in William Archer's translation of Francisque Sarcey's term) **obligatory scene.** "An obligatory scene [Archer says] is one which the audience (more or less clearly and consciously) foresees and desires, and the absence of which it may with reason resent." For example, a familiar legend may make a scene obligatory, or a dramatist may cause the audience to expect a certain scene. In *Hamlet* the play-within-the-play (III.ɪɪ) has been called such a scene: Hamlet has doubted the ghost, and we must see the ghost's words verified. Consult William Archer, *Play-making.*

selective realism. See realism.

Senecan tragedy. Any of the serious plays by the Roman author Seneca (4 B.C.–65 A.D.), or imitations of them. Of the ten extant Roman tragedies, nine are attributed to Seneca, and these were probably written not for the stage but for private readings. The heroes seem to us to be almost madmen, but perhaps they are to be regarded sympathetically as people overwhelmed by passion. Seneca's influence on the Elizabethan dramatists was considerable; the **revenge play,** with its ghosts and its deranged hero who seeks vengeance, doubtless would have been different had Seneca not existed. Among the signs of Seneca's influence are: ghosts, revenge, deeds of horror (e.g., children stewed and served to their parents), occasional stoical speeches but a predominance of passionate speeches, use of stichomythia (see dialogue), a *nuntius* (messenger) who recites in a heightened style an off-stage happening (e.g., the wounded soldier in *Macbeth,* I.ɪ). But, of course, not every use of any of these characteristics is necessarily attributable to Seneca's influence. And there are differences: e.g., the horrors in Seneca are narrated, but in *King Lear* Gloucester is blinded on the stage. Consult F. L. Lucas, *Seneca and Elizabethan Tragedy;* Madeleine Doran, *Endeavors of Art;*

Willard Farnham, *The Medieval Heritage of Elizabethan Tragedy;* Howard Baker, *Induction to Tragedy,* minimizes Seneca's influence.

sensibility. See sentimental.

sentimental. Generally a pejorative word in criticism, indicating a superabundance of tender emotion, a disproportionate amount of sentiment (feeling). It is sentimental to be intensely distressed because one has stepped on a flower. A character, say Hamlet, may display deep emotions, but they are sentimental only if they are in excess of what the situation warrants. More specifically, "sentimental" writing refers to writing wherein evil is facilely conquered, denied, overlooked, or bathed in a glow of forgiving tenderness. In the eighteenth century the ability to respond emotionally (usually tearfully) to acts of benevolence or malevolence was called **sensibility.** In its **sentimental drama** there is at the expense of reason an emphasis on tearful situations; man's benevolent emotions are overestimated, for he is assumed to be innately good, and villains reform, usually in bursts of repenting tears. There is little wit, the characters are usually of the middle class, and they demonstrate their virtue by weeping at the sight of distress. In his "Comparison between Sentimental and Laughing Comedy" (1772), Oliver Goldsmith attacked sentimental comedy, saying that in it:

> the virtues of private life are exhibited, rather than the vices exposed; and the distresses rather than the faults of mankind make our interest in the piece. . . . Almost all the characters are good, . . . and though they want humor, have abundance of sentiment and feeling. If they happen to have faults or foibles, the spectator is taught, not only to pardon, but to applaud them, in consideration of the goodness of their hearts; so that folly, instead of being ridiculed, is commended, and the comedy aims at touching our passions, without the power of being truly pathetic.

See bourgeois drama. Consult Ernest Bernbaum, *The Drama of Sensibility;* Arthur Sherbo, *English Sentimental Drama.*

slapstick. See farce.

situational comedy. See comedy of humors.

slice of life. See naturalism.

sock and **buskin.** Performers of Latin comedy wore a light slipper or sandal called the *soccus*. The sock is either this piece of footwear or comedy itself. The high boot worn by Greek tragic actors was the *cothurnus* or *kothurnus*. In Hellenistic times it acquired a very thick sole, giving the performer the height appropriate to a great man. In English this footgear (or tragic drama in general) is called the buskin, apparently from Old French *broissequin*, from Middle Dutch *brosekin*, a small leather boot. Consult Margarete Bieber, *The History of the Greek and Roman Theater*.

Socratic irony. See irony.

Sophoclean irony. See irony.

soliloquy. A speech wherein a character utters his thoughts aloud while alone. An **aside** is a speech wherein a character expresses his thoughts in words audible to the spectators but supposedly unheard by the other stage characters present. Both were important conventions in Elizabethan drama and, later, in melodrama, but the late nineteenth century sought so vigorously to present on the stage the illusion of real life that both techniques were banished. They have, however, been revived in the twentieth century, e.g., in Eugene O'Neill's *Strange Interlude*, where the asides represent the characters' thoughts and unspoken desires. In **direct address,** a character turns from the world on the stage and speaks directly to the audience, telling it, for instance, to watch closely. Consult Una Ellis-Fermor. *The Frontiers of Drama*, Ch. 6; George E. Duckworth, *The Nature of Roman Comedy*; Max Beerbohm, "Soliloquies in Drama," *Around Theatres*. The soliloquy, the aside, and direct address are all monologues, but more often a **monologue** is either a long speech delivered by one character, which may be heard but not interrupted by others in his presence, or a performance by a single actor.

sound effect. An imitative noise, usually produced by simple machinery. Though a sound effect may be a mere imitation of nature, it may also be a richly symbolic suggestion. Chekhov's *The Cherry Orchard* (1904) concludes: "There is a far-off sound as if out of the sky, the sound of a snapped string, dying away, sad. A stillness falls, and there is only the thud of an ax on a tree, far away in the orchard." Consult Frank Napier, *Noises Off*.

spectacle. The last of Aristotle's six elements of drama, spectacle denotes what appeals to the eye, e.g., costume and scenery. Greek drama was splendidly costumed and made some use of scenery. Aeschylus especially seems to have contrived moments that caught the eye, such as Agamemnon's entrance in a chariot. The Elizabethan stage, though sparse in scenery, apparently was architecturally impressive, and doubtless military scenes were embellished with waving banners. In the Restoration, spectacle sometimes got the upper hand. Alexander Pope complained:

The play stands still; damn action and discourse,
Back fly the scenes, and enter foot and horse;
Pageants on pageants, in long order drawn,
Peers, heralds, bishops, ermine, gold, and lawn.

In the nineteenth century the development of gas light and then electric light made possible elaborate sunrises and twilights, and at the end of the century (especially in Russia) there was an emphasis on ensemble acting which gave a tableau-effect. Pictorial effects in late-nineteenth-century productions of Shakespeare were often achieved at the cost of Shakespeare's lines. At the very end of the century William Poel rejected spectacle and helped establish a trend to stage Shakespeare in what was thought to be an Elizabethan manner: an uncluttered stage, allowing the action to proceed rapidly. Consult James Laver, *Drama*; A. Nicholas Vardac, *Stage to Screen*, Chs. 3–4.

stage business. Minor physical action — including posture and facial expression — by a performer. Business ranges from headscratching to an addition Henry Irving made to *The Merchant of Venice*, II.vi: in Shakespeare's scene, Jessica and Lorenzo elope and the scene ends quietly; Irving added business in which Shylock entered, and knocked on the door of his empty house while the curtain fell. His successors amplified this business; Shylock entered the house, cried out, and reappeared, etc. Consult Arthur C. Sprague, *Shakespeare and the Actors*.

stichomythia. See dialogue.

stock character. See character.

style. The mode of expression. Newman, talking of the writer's style, called it "a thinking out into language." This idea of "a thinking out" (but not into language) is applicable also to the style of the scene designer, the costume designer, etc. Kenneth Tynan in *Curtains* defines good style as "a happy consonance of manner with matter, of means with end, of tools with job." To **stylize** a play commonly means to present it with a noticeable artful manner rather than to present it realistically, though in fact realism itself is a style. A **stylized production** usually is presentational or anti-illusionistic rather than representational (see dramatic illusion). Consult George R. Kernodle, "Style, Stylization, and Styles of Acting," *Educational Theatre Journal*, 12 (1960), 251–261.

subplot. See plot.

surprise. See suspense.

surrealism. A literary movement, especially vigorous in France in the 1920's and 1930's, that insisted that reality is grasped by the unconscious, the irrational, rather than by the conscious. The best art, it is held, is the dream. Among the forerunners were Alfred Jarry, whose *Ubu Roi* (1896) combined grotesque farce with anti-bourgeois satire, August Strindberg, whose *To Damascus* (three parts, 1898–1904) and *The Dream Play* (1902) had presented dream-like worlds, and Guillaume Apollinaire, whose *Breasts of Tiresias* (1917) was called a *"drame surréaliste"* (the first use of the word) by the author. Perhaps the chief surrealist dramatist is Jean Cocteau, notably in his *Orpheus* (1926), in which a glazier is an angel and a horse dictates prophetic words. Consult Georges E. Lemaître, *From Cubism to Surrealism in French Literature*.

suspense. Uncertainty, often characterized by anxiety. Suspense is usually a curious mixture of pain and pleasure, as Gwendolen, in Oscar Wilde's *The Importance of Being Earnest*, implies: "This suspense is terrible. I hope it will last." Most great art relies more heavily on suspense than on **surprise** (the unexpected). One can rarely sit twice through a play depending on surprise; the surprise gone, the interest is gone. Suspense is usually

achieved in part by **foreshadowing** — hints of what is to come. Dumas *fils* put it this way: "The art of the theater is the art of preparations." Coleridge, who held that Shakespeare gives us not surprise but expectation and then the satisfaction of perfect knowledge, once wrote: "As the feeling with which we startle at a shooting star, compared with that of watching the sunrise at the pre-established moment, such and so low is surprise compared with expectation." Thus, in *Hamlet*, the ghost does not pop up surprisingly, but satisfies the eager expectations that have been aroused by references to "this thing," "this dreaded sight," and "this apparition." Often, in fact, Shakespeare — like the Greek dramatists — used traditional stories; the audience presumably was not surprised by the deaths of Caesar and Brutus, and it enjoyed the suspense of anticipating them. Suspense is thus related to tragic irony. The tragic character moves closer and closer to his doom, and though he may be surprised by it, we are not; we are held by suspense. On surprise, consult David L. Grossvogel, *The Self-Conscious Stage in Modern French Drama* (reprinted in paperback as *Twentieth-Century French Drama*).

symbolism. Derived from Greek *symballein*, "to throw together," which thus suggests the essential quality of symbolism, the drawing together of two worlds; it presents the concrete material world of roses, toads, caves, stars, etc., and through them reveals an otherwise invisible world. As a noun, the original Greek word denoted half of something broken in two, and thus the word suggests not something that stands for something else, but something that is part of a larger unit.

Symbolism is often distinguished from allegory. Where the allegorist commonly invents a world (the author of *Everyman* [c. 1500] invents a figure called Everyman, who seeks aid from figures called Goods, Kindred, etc.) in order to talk about the real world, the symbolist commonly presents the phenomena of what we usually call the real world in order to reveal a "higher," eternal world of which the symbol is a part. The allegorist is free to invent any number of imaginary worlds to talk about the real world, but the symbolist feels that there is only one way by which he can present the "higher" real world he envisions. The everyday world is often considered by symbolists as a concrete but transient version of a more important realm, and the symbolist who presents, say, a rose, is (he might hold) speaking about a rose and also about the eternal beauty of womanhood in the only possible way.

In the second half of the nineteenth century there arose in France the so-called **Symbolist Movement,** but it must be emphasized that symbolism of a sort is probably as old as literature. An author's insistence on some object may cause us to regard it as more than its apparent nature. For example, the forest or greenwood in *As You Like It* suggests a benevolent nature that restores man to his best part. But on the whole Shakespeare's plays do not leave the world of sensible reality. The plays of the Symbolists do. The Symbolic writer presents a world that seems to be a dream world, a world that is not the usual world enriched, but a new world. In his preface to *The Dream Play* (1902), Strindberg says he "has tried to imitate the disconnected but seemingly logical form of the dream. Anything may happen. . . . The characters split, double, multiply, vanish, solidify, blur, clarify." A play is the expression of a "soul-state" (Stéphane Mallarmé's term) rather than an imitation of an external action. See surrealism.

The best naturalists (Ibsen, Chekhov, Strindberg, and Hauptmann) at times wrote symbolic works, but the chief Symbolic dramatists are the French (if we include the Belgian Maurice Maeterlinck) and William Butler Yeats. In Maeterlink's *The Intruder* (1890) a blind old man sees with his soul the approach of Death. In *The Blind* (1890) a group of blind men are lost in a forest; their leader was a priest, but he has died. Maeterlinck occasionally said some of his plays were for marionettes, and though his statement is sometimes held to be a mildly self-deprecating joke, in fact there is much in the plays that belongs to the realm of impassive, otherworldly dolls, not surprising in the work of a writer who said he wished to study "man . . . in the presence of eternity and mystery." Paul Claudel's *Tidings Brought to Mary* (written in 1892, revised in 1899 and 1912) was acted in 1912. Claudel, who said he had gained from Arthur Rimbaud (one of the leading Symbolists) "an almost physical impression of the supernatural," in this play envelops his medieval characters in a divine world, and dramatizes salvation. In Ireland, Yeats, who compared an artistic work to a magic talisman ("it

entangles . . . a part of the Divine essence") wrote verse plays of Irish supernatural creatures and heroes. In *On Baile's Strand* (1903), for instance, Cuchulain, the protagonist, is said to have been sired by a hawk. The bird imagery is insisted on; Cuchulain's associates are chicks and nestlings, and the Fool (who represents Cuchulain on another level) is delighted with feathers. Near the conclusion of the play, Cuchulain rushes out to fight the waves, literally doing what Hamlet spoke metaphorically of doing.

In Russia, Meyerhold in 1906 staged Ibsen's *Hedda Gabler* (1890) as symbolically as possible, turning what had been a naturalistic play into a vision suggestive of another world, something (in the words of a hostile critic) "halfway between metaphysics and ballet." (Consult Nikolai Gorchakov, *The Theater in Soviet Russia.*) For symbolism in the sense of richly suggestive images, consult Alan S. Downer, "The Life of Our Design: the Function of Imagery in the Poetic Drama," *The Hudson Review*, 2 (Summer 1949), 242–260. On the Symbolist Movement, consult William Butler Yeats, *Essays and Introductions*; Arthur Symons, *The Symbolist Movement in Literature*; *Yale French Studies*, No. 9; Eric Bentley, *The Playwright as Thinker*; John Gassner, *Form and Idea in the Modern Theatre*.

theater-in-the-round. See arena stage.

Three Unities. See unity.

total theater. The idea that the theater should not try to imitate realistically an aspect of life but should embody a synthesis of all of the expressive arts, e.g., music, movement, speech, lighting, etc. The expression "total theater" probably is derived from Richard Wagner's *Gesamtkunstwerk*, "united" or "total artwork." Consult *Total Theatre*, ed. E. T. Kirby.

tragedy. For Aristotle, tragedy was a dramatic imitation (representation) of an "action of high importance." A Greek tragedy was serious, but it did not necessarily end unhappily. Aeschylus' *Eumenides*, for example, ends on a note of solemn joy. For us a tragedy is generally a play that faces evil, depicts suffering, and ends with death or (especially in the naturalistic tragedies since the latter part of the nineteenth century) ends with the hero alive but spiritually crushed. Tragedy's essence, Alfred North Whitehead says (*Science and the Modern World*, Ch. 1), resides not in unhappiness but "in the solemnity of the remorseless working of things." H. D. F. Kitto says (*The Greeks*, Ch. 4) that Greek tragedy — and perhaps one might add the great tragedy of other countries — was in part the product of intellectualism and humanism. Intellectualism let the Greeks see that human life must be lived within a great framework of what might be called the will of the gods, or Necessity: "Actions must have their consequences; ill-judged actions must have uncomfortable results." Humanism denied the Greeks an easy view of a heavenly life, and gave them an "almost fierce joy in life, the exultation in human achievement and in human personality." The tragic note, Kitto suggests, is produced by a tension between this unalterable framework and this passionate delight in life. Consult R. Sewall, *The Vision of Tragedy*; T. R. Henn, *The Harvest of Tragedy*; H. J. Muller, *The Spirit of Tragedy*.

tragicomedy. Renaissance critical theorists, embroidering on Aristotle's *Poetics*, assumed that tragedy dealt with noble (important) figures and ended with a death; comedy dealt with trivial (laughable) figures and ended with a celebration. A tragicomedy was some sort of mixture: high characters in a play ending happily, or a mingling of deaths and feasts, or, most often (as in many American films) threats of death which are happily — and unconvincingly — evaded. John Fletcher (1579–1625), who, with his collaborator Francis Beaumont, wrote graceful dramas relying heavily on passionate outbursts and surprising turns of plot, defined a tragicomedy as a play that lacks deaths (and thus is no tragedy) but "brings some near it, which is enough to make it no comedy." One of the speakers in John Dryden's *Essay of Dramatick Poesie* (1668) says: "There is no theater in the world has anything so absurd as the English tragi-comedy; . . . here a course of mirth, there another of sadness and passion, and a third of honor and a duel: thus, in two hours and a half, we run through all the fits of Bedlam." Consult Eugene Waith, *The Pattern of Tragi-Comedy*. On what can roughly be called the bitter or ironic comedy of the nineteenth and twentieth centuries, consult K. S. Guthke, *Modern Tragicomedy*; C. Hoy, *The Hyacinth*

Room; and Eric Bentley, *The Life of the Drama*.

trilogy. A unit of three works. Though Greek tragic dramatists submitted three tragedies at a time, the plays are only a trilogy if they have an internal unity. Aeschylus' *Oresteia* (458 B.C.) is the only extant complete Greek trilogy; Sophocles' three plays on the Oedipus legend — *Antigone* (c. 422 B.C.), *Oedipus the King* (c. 425), and *Oedipus at Colonus* (c. 406) are not properly a trilogy because they were written at widely separated times and do not cohere into a consistent, unified whole. A modern trilogy: O'Neill's *Mourning Becomes Electra* (1931).

tritagonist. See protagonist.

underplot. See plot.

unity. Generally means something like "coherence," "congruence"; in a unified piece the parts work together and jointly contribute to the whole. The subplot of a play may parallel the main plot, or one character may be a foil to another. In any case, unity suggests "completeness" or "pattern" resulting from a controlling intelligence. In the *Poetics*, Aristotle had said that a tragedy should have a unified action, and he had mentioned that most tragedies cover a period of twenty-four hours. Italian critics, making his comments rigid, in the late sixteenth century established the **Three Unities** of Time, Place, and Action: a play (1) must not cover more than twenty-four hours, (2) must be set in one locale only, or, at worst, in various parts of a single city, and (3) must be either entirely tragic or entirely comic, rather than a mixture of (as Sir Philip Sidney said) "hornpipes and funerals." (Consult H. B. Charlton, *Castelvetro's Theory of Poetry*.) Actually, the time covered by Greek tragedies is vague; characters come from distant places in the space of relatively few lines. For example, in *Oedipus the King*, a shepherd, who lives in the "farthest" fields from Corinth, is sent for in line 863 and arrives in line 1108. Nor is unity of place invariable in Greek tragedy; there are violations of it in, for example, Aeschylus' *The Eumenides* and Sophocles' *Ajax*.

well-made play. See *pièce bien faite*.

To the student:

As educational publishers we realize it is our responsibility to try to improve the textbooks we publish. In order to make TYPES OF DRAMA, SECOND EDITION a better book next time, we need to know what you, our ultimate consumer, think of what we've already done. Please help us by filling out this questionnaire and returning it to Little, Brown and Company, College English Developmental Group, 34 Beacon St., Boston, Mass. 02106.

School_____City and State_____

Instructor's Name_____

Please give us your reaction to the selections:

	Keep	Drop	Didn't read	Read in high school
THE EMPEROR JONES	____	____	_____	_____
OEDIPUS THE KING	____	____	_____	_____
THE TRAGEDY OF KING LEAR	____	____	_____	_____
HEDDA GABLER	____	____	_____	_____
DEATH OF A SALESMAN	____	____	_____	_____
DUTCHMAN	____	____	_____	_____
EQUUS	____	____	_____	_____
LYSISTRATA	____	____	_____	_____
A MIDSUMMER NIGHT'S DREAM	____	____	_____	_____
THE MISANTHROPE	____	____	_____	_____
MAJOR BARBARA	____	____	_____	_____
THE CHERRY ORCHARD	____	____	_____	_____
SIX CHARACTERS IN SEARCH OF AN AUTHOR	____	____	_____	_____
WILD STRAWBERRIES	____	____	_____	_____
THE GAP	____	____	_____	_____
THE EFFECT OF GAMMA RAYS ON MAN-IN-THE-MOON MARIGOLDS	____	____	_____	_____

1. Are there any plays or playwrights not included that you would like to see included next time? _____

2. Did you find the general introduction helpful? _____ How might it have been improved? _____

3. Were the headnotes and commentaries for each play useful? _____ Did they tell you too much? _____ Too little? _____

4. Did you read "The Script and the Stage?" _____ Did you find it interesting? _____ How might it be improved? _____

5. Was the section "Writing About Drama" helpful? _____ How might it be improved? _____

6. Did you use the glossary of dramatic terms? _____ How might it be improved? _____

7. Do you like the book's appearance (cover, illustrations, layout)? _____
_____
_____

8. Do you feel your instructor should continue to assign this book? _____ Why, or why not? _____

9. Will you keep this book? _____

10. Please add any comments or suggestions on how we might improve this book. _____
_____
_____
_____

Optional: Your name _____ Date _____
Address _____

May we quote you, either in promotion for this book or in future publishing ventures?

Yes _____ No _____

THANK YOU!